SPEEDWAY PUE

P9-DBO-039

3 5550 43137 9646

Rick Steves®

914.3 STE
Steves, Rick, 1955-
Rick Steves' Germany 2015.

WITHDRAWN

G

SPEEDWAY PUBLIC LIBRARY
SPEEDWAY, INDIANA

3/15

2015

CONTENTS

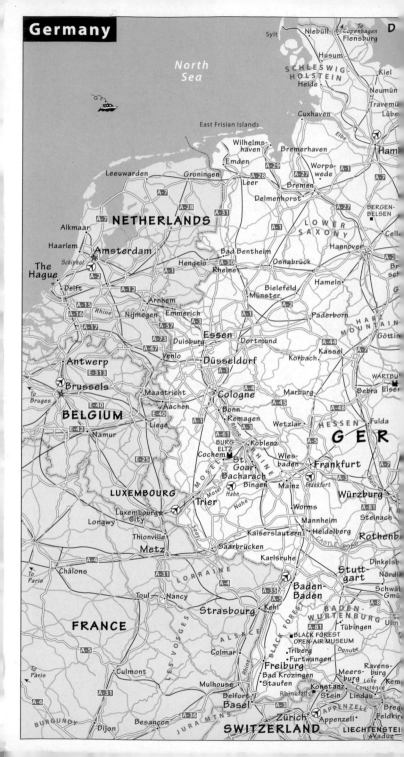

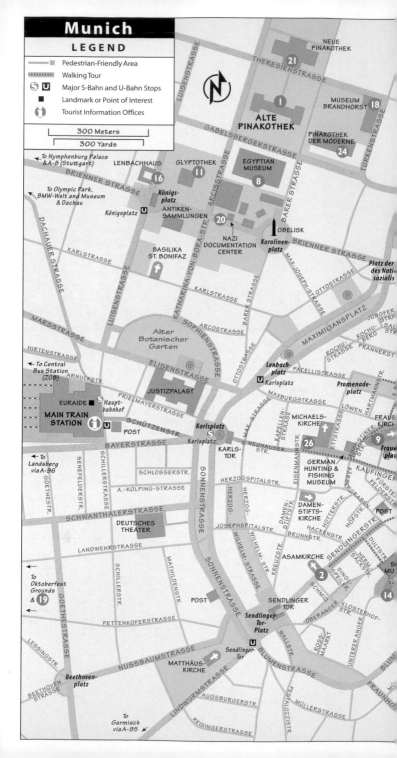

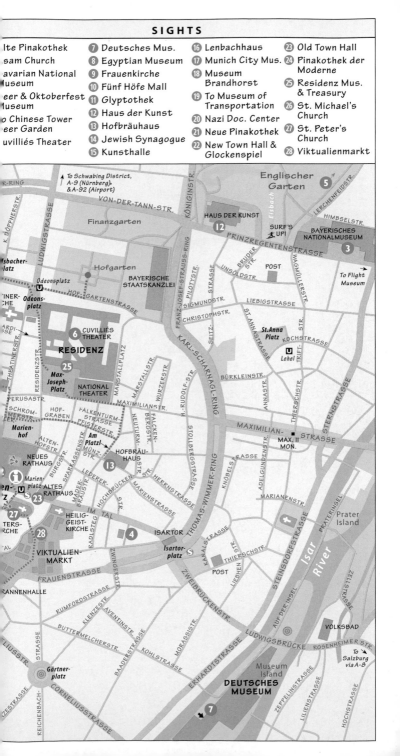

SIGHTS

SIGHTS

1. Alexanderplatz
2. Bebelplatz
3. Berlin Cathedral
4. Berlin Wall Memorial
5. Bode Museum
6. Brandenburg Gate
7. City Hall
8. DDR Museum
9. Europa Center
10. Gemäldegalerie
11. Gendarmenmarkt
12. German Cathedral
13. German History Museum
14. German Resistance Mem.
15. Hackesche Höfe
16. Hauptbahnhof (Main Train Station)
17. Jewish Museum Berlin
18. KaDeWe Department Store
19. Kaiser Wilhelm Memorial Church
20. Käthe Kollwitz Museum
21. The Kennedys Museum
22. Memorial to the Murdered Jews of Europe
23. Museum of Decorative Arts
24. Museum of the Wall at Checkpoint Charlie
25. Musical Instruments Museum
26. Natural History Museum
27. Neue Wache Memorial
28. Neues Museum
29. New National Gallery
30. New Synagogue
31. Old National Gallery
32. Pergamon Museum
33. Philharmonic Concert
34. Potsdamer Platz & Sony Center
35. Reichstag
36. Spree River Cruises
37. Stasi Museum
38. Topography of Terror
39. TV Tower
40. Zoo & Aquarium

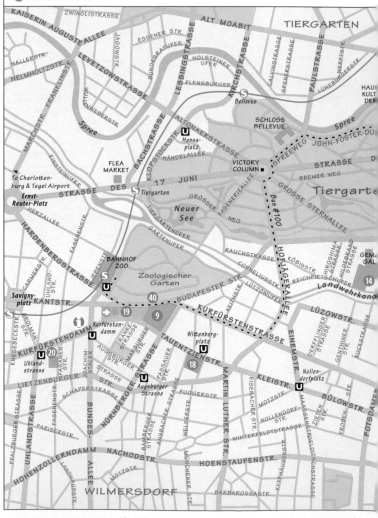

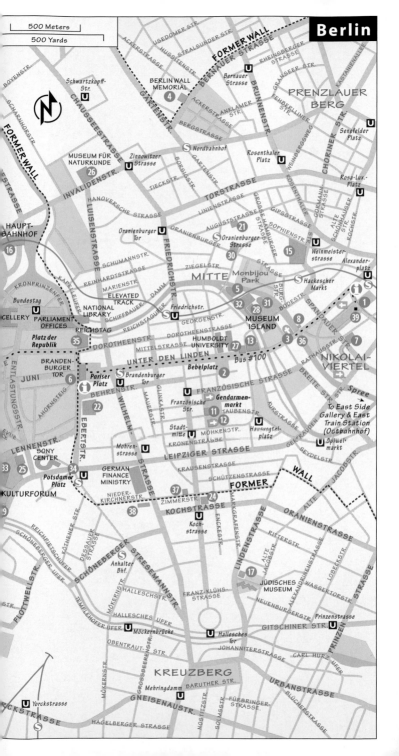

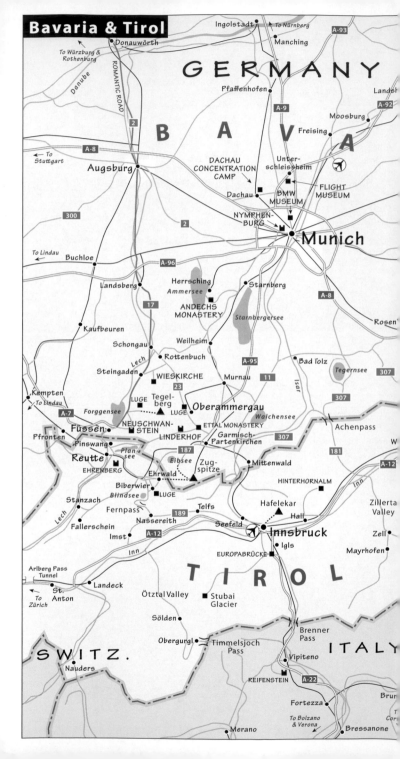

Germany

Deutschland

Germany is blessed with some of
Europe's most high-powered sights.
There's spectacular scenery—the jagged
Alps, flower-filled meadows, rolling hills
of forests and farms, and rivers such as
the raging Rhine and moseying Mosel.
Germany has hundreds of castles, some
ruined and mysterious; others stout,
crenellated, and imposing; and still others
right out of a Disney fairy tale. In this
land of the Protestant Reformation—and
Catholic Counter-Reformation—churches
and cathedrals are another forte.
Austere Lutheran houses of worship
tower silently next to exuberantly
overripe Baroque churches dripping with
curlicues.

Deutschland is energetic, efficient, and organized. It's
Europe's muscleman, both economically and wherever
people line up (Germans have a reputation for pushing
ahead). It's the European Union's most populous country
and biggest economy, with a geographic diversity and cultural richness that draw millions of visitors every year.

Germany's dark side is recalled in eerie Nazi remnants—
stern office buildings, thoughtfully presented "documentation centers," haunting concentration camps—and chilling
reminders of the Cold War, embodied in a few quickly
disappearing sites, such as the scant fragments of the notorious Berlin Wall. And of course there are the cultural clichés,
kept alive more by tradition-loving Germans than by tourist

demand. The country is dotted with idyllic half-timbered villages where you can enjoy strudel at the bakery or sip a stein of beer while men in lederhosen play oompah music. Peruse a wonderland of chocolates, stock up on Hummels and cuckoo clocks, and learn how to polka.

All of these traditions stand at sharp contrast with the "real" Germany of today. Despite its respect for the past, this truly is a 21st-century country. At the forefront of human progress, Germany is a world of high-tech trains, gleaming cities, social efficiency, and world-class museums celebrating many of history's greatest cultural achievements.

Modern Germany bustles. Its cities hold 75 percent of its people, and average earnings are among the highest in the world. Most workers get at least a month of paid vacation, and during the other 11 months, this land that's roughly the size of Montana creates a gross domestic product that's about 20 percent of the United States'. Germany has risen from the ashes of World War II to become the world's fifth-largest industrial power.

People all over the world enjoy the fruits of Germany's labor. Their cars are legendary—BMW, Mercedes-Benz, Volkswagen, Audi, and Porsche. We ride German elevators and trains (ThyssenKrupp and Siemens AG), take German medicines (Bayer), use German cosmetics (Nivea)...and eat German goodies (Haribo's Gummi Bears).

Germany beats out all but two countries in the production of books, Nobel laureates, and professors. In the world of physics, there's Einstein's relativity theory, Planck's

constant, and Heisenberg's uncertainty principle. German inventions range from Gutenberg's printing press to Zeppelin's zeppelins to Röntgen's X-rays to Daimler's and Benz's cars to Geiger's counter. Musically, Germany dominated the scene for more than two centuries—Bach, Beethoven, Brahms, Handel, Pachelbel, Wagner, and more. Germans have a reputation as profound analytical thinkers, sprouting philosophers such as Kant, Hegel, Nietzsche, Marx, and Engels.

Germany is geographically big (at least, relative to other European countries) but closely knit by transportation. Its autobahns—miles and miles of high-quality freeways—are famous (or notorious) for their no-speed-limit system (more fully explained on page 964). Intercity-Express (ICE) trains zip by at up to 200 miles per hour, linking major cities quickly and efficiently.

As a nation, Germany is less than 150 years old ("born" in

Germany Almanac

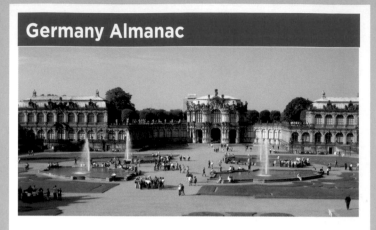

Official Name: Bundesrepublik Deutschland, or simply Deutschland.

Population: Germany's 82 million people (more than three times the population of Texas) are largely of Teutonic extraction (about 90 percent), plus a small but significant minority (2.4 percent) of Turkish descent. A third of Germans are Catholic, and a third are Protestant. About 4 percent are Muslim; the rest are unaffiliated.

Latitude and Longitude: 51°N and 9°E. The latitude is similar to Alberta, Canada.

Area: At 138,000 square miles, Germany is about half the size of Texas. It's bordered by nine countries.

Geography: The terrain gradually rises—from flat land in the north to the rugged Alps in the south, culminating in the 9,700-foot Zugspitze mountain. The climate is temperate.

Biggest Cities: The capital city of Berlin has 3.4 million people, followed by Hamburg's 1.8 million and Munich's 1.5 million.

Economy: With a GDP of $3.2 trillion—similar to America's Midwest states combined—Germany is Europe's largest economy. Still, the GDP per capita is approximately $39,500, or about 25 percent less than America's. Germany's strength is in technology and manufacturing—exporting machinery and other high-quality items that developing countries (including China) want to buy. It's one of the world's most advanced economies, producing steel, cars, chemicals, pharmaceuticals, consumer electronics, and more. Germany also has around 1,300 breweries (Bavaria boasts about half), but much of the

production is consumed domestically. Germany trades almost equally with a half-dozen neighboring countries and the United States.

Since the 1990 reunification, Germany's economy has been burdened by the cost of integrating the former East Germany into the modern West. Germany's expensive social security system gets even costlier as the population ages. Thanks to powerful trade unions, workers get good benefits. Unemployment reached a post-reunification low of just 5 percent in 2014.

Government: In the 2005 elections, Angela Merkel became Germany's first woman chancellor. Her center-right party won a resounding victory in 2013, and the conservative Merkel currently leads a coalition government that is expected to continue her business-friendly policies. Germany's chancellor, similar to a prime minister, is not elected by the people but is the head of the lead party in parliament. The less-powerful president (currently Joachim Gauck) is elected by parliament. The legislative branch includes the Bundestag (currently 631 seats, elected by both direct and proportional representation) and Bundesrat (69 votes by officials of Germany's 16 states).

Flag: Deutschland's flag is composed of three horizontal bands of (from top to bottom) black, red, and gold.

The Average Deutscher: The average German is 45 years old—8 years older than the average American—has 1.4 kids, and will live to be 80. He or she lives in a household with two other people, may either own or rent their house (only about half prefer to own), and watches 3.75 hours of TV a day. The average German drinks a pint of beer every 32 hours—slightly less than the average Irish or Czech.

1871), quite young compared to most of its European neighbors. In medieval times, there were 300 "countries" in what is now Germany, each with its own weights, measures, coinage, king, and lottery. By 1850, the number had dropped to a still formidable 35 countries. Today's Germany is a federation of 16 states, each with its own cultural identity and customs.

Traditionally—and in some ways even today—German culture divides at a sort of North-South Mason-Dixon Line.

Northern Germany was barbarian, is predominantly Protestant, and tackles life aggressively, while southern Germany (Bavaria) was Roman, is largely Catholic, and enjoys a more relaxed

tempo. The romantic American image of Germany is beer-and-pretzel Bavaria (probably because that was "our" sector after the war). This historic North-South division is growing less pronounced as Germany becomes a more mobile society.

Germany's roots run deep. Thoughtful travelers can easily trace the country's history in their sightseeing. Find Germany's Roman roots at the impressive Porta Nigra Gate and Basilica of scenic Trier. When Rome fell, German lands fragmented into hundreds of small feudal kingdoms, each with its own castle—many of which still dot the German countryside today. Magnificent Gothic cathedrals, like the one in Cologne, attest to the faith of medieval people. As Germany's economy recovered, it became an important European hub for trade and transportation. Prosperous cities sprung up along the Romantic Road—today's prime tourist trail.

It was from Germany that a humble monk named

Martin Luther rocked Europe with religious reform, and you'll see monuments, cities, and churches associated with him (especially in Erfurt and Wittenberg—covered in the Lutherland chapter). Meanwhile, German Catholics lavishly decorated their churches (including the glorious Wieskirche) and palaces (in Munich and Würzburg) in the ornate Baroque/Rococo style, giving a glimpse of the heaven that awaited the faithful. Germany became a Europe-wide battleground for Protestants and Catholics in the Thirty Years' War that was duked out in towns such as Rothenburg (which today is besieged by tourists).

In the 1800s, Germany unified politically, and it became a cultural powerhouse. European nobles flocked to Baden-Baden's casino and thermal baths, while composer Richard Wagner spun operatic tales about German folk legends at the castle of Neuschwanstein with his friend "Mad" King Ludwig II.

Germany's prosperity ended in the humiliating defeat of World War I. You can see the rising specter of Hitler and Nazism at the Nürnberg Rally Grounds (where huge propaganda events were staged—now home to an excellent museum documenting the Nazis' rise to power), at Berlin's

Reichstag (whose destruction helped the Nazis take control), and at the concentration camp museums at Dachau and Sachsenhausen (two of many places where the Nazis snuffed out millions of lives). Germany's utter destruction in World War II is evident in the skylines of today's cities. Some, like Munich and Dresden, were rebuilt in a faux-Baroque style, while Frankfurt sprouted skyscrapers.

At war's end, Germany was divided East-West between the victorious Allies, and the Cold War set in (1945-1990). In Berlin, you can see a few surviving stretches of the Wall that divided the country, and the famous Checkpoint Charlie that controlled the East-West flow. Even today, Eastern cities such as Dresden and Leipzig bear the scars and stunted growth of Soviet occupation. Some friction still exists between the residents of the former East Germany ("Ossies" in impolite slang) and those from

West Germany ("Wessies"). More than two decades after reunification, and despite billions of dollars of economic aid, the East lags behind the West, with a higher unemployment rate (about double the West's), lower income, and a few old-timers who miss the Red old days.

Many visitors can't help but associate Germany with its dark Nazi past. But while a small neo-Nazi skinhead element still survives in the back alleys of German society, for the most part the nation has evolved into a surprisingly progressive, almost touchy-feely place. A genuine sense of responsibility for World War II and the Holocaust pervades much of German society. If you visit a concentration camp memorial, you'll likely see several field-trip groups of

German teens visiting there to learn the lessons of the past.

Germany was a founding member of the European Union and continues to lead the way in creating a healthy Europe for the future—with peace, unity, tolerance (e.g., legalized gay marriage), and human rights as its central motivations. It's the world's second-biggest foreign-aid donor, after the US. Even to a skeptical visitor, it's clear that most Germans are trying to make up for the ugliness their ancestors subjected Europe to not so long ago.

How does a country achieve such robust economic and social success, despite losing two world wars? This is a country of "Type A" personalities. Bold, brassy Germans typically aren't shy to speak their minds. Their directness (some might say "bluntness") is refreshing to some, and startling to others. At least you'll know where you stand. People who enjoy trains that run on time are perfectly suited for travel in everything-has-its-place Germany. Those who like to play it fast and loose might find that improvisation has its limits here.

Paradoxically, the ultra-efficient Germans also have a weak spot for Hummel-esque quaintness and a sentimentality for their own history. They love nature. They love to go a-wandering along a mountain path with their hiking sticks, rucksacks, and state-of-the-art outdoor gear. Dramatic cable cars whisk visitors to sweeping cut-glass panoramas. Learn the word *schön*—"beautiful"— because you'll hear it often, from little old ladies and grown men alike as they survey beautiful vistas of their home-land. They're also prone to get misty-eyed when, after a glass or two of white wine, they and their mates start singing a tra-ditional song from their youth. Cutesy traditions are respected and celebrated—especially

in Bavaria, where people wear dirndls and lederhosen on holidays, erect maypoles in spring, host exuberant Christmas markets in winter, and frequent Oktoberfest-type beer halls year-round.

Germans love to travel, throughout their own country and beyond. They're cosmopolitan and outward-looking. Two-thirds speak at least one other language (mostly English), and they enjoy watching TV and movies beamed in from other countries. Watch out—they may know American politics and history better than you do. They're products of high-quality schools that put kids on either fast or slow tracks, depending on ability and desire. To move on to college, they must pass a major SAT-like test. Once there, the university system is top-quality...and tuition, if there is any at all, is only a few hundred dollars a semester.

Germans aren't all work and no play. All Europeans love watching sports—but Germans actually play them. More than six million are registered to play *Fussball* (soccer) every year in the official league. There's a big following for the Bundesliga, the professional soccer league, and the German

national team is always a strong contender for the Euro Cup and World Cup (which they won in 2014) and championship tournaments.

Motorsports are big time, especially Formula One—the European answer to NASCAR—where racing legend Michael Schumacher is one of the world's highest-paid athletes. In the Olympics (winter and summer), Germany is consistently one of the world's top medal-finishers.

Just try to keep up with them on one of their summer luge courses *(Sommerrodelbahn)*, which allow amateur thrill seekers to scream down a mountain at top speed.

As Germany speeds into the future, it's faced with a number of challenges—none bigger than immigration. After World War II, Germany needed cheap blue-collar laborers to help rebuild, and they welcomed many Turkish people as *Gastarbeiter* (guest workers). While many earned money and went home, many others married, had kids, and stayed. Today, more than 8 million immigrants (roughly 10 percent of Germany's population) live within its borders—more than any country except the US and Russia. Of these, almost 3 million are Turks, most of whom are Muslims—not always the easiest fit within a traditionally Christian nation.

Germany today is trying to stay competitive in the global marketplace while maintaining generous social services. It has taken a tough stance on bailing out other EU nations that have been less fiscally responsible. Neo-Nazism is a festering sore, and there's a declining birthrate (one of the world's lowest). And its enormous appetite for energy is increasingly at odds with its love for the environment (the government has strong incentives for sustainable energy in place, and Chancellor Merkel has announced plans to phase out nuclear power by 2022).

After the end of World War II, as the US evolved from an occupying force to a close ally, the two countries gradually built a strong relationship. Today more than 100,000 Americans live in Germany (many of them at US military bases, such as Ramstein

near the Rhine). Americans generally find Germany to be one of Europe's most accessible nations. It's efficient, the people are almost aggressively welcoming, the language barrier is minimal...and the German roots that pervade America's melting pot don't hurt matters, either. (More than 15 percent of Americans have some German ancestry—more than any other background.)

Germany today is reunited, a nation of cutting-edge industry, medieval castles, speedy autobahns, old-time beer halls, modern skyscrapers, and the best wurst. This young country with a long past continues to make history.

INTRODUCTION

This book focuses on Germany's top big-city, small-town, and rural destinations. It gives you all the information and opinions necessary to wring the maximum value out of your limited time and money. If you plan a month or less in Germany and have a normal appetite for information, this book is all you need. If you're a travel-info fiend, this book sorts through all the superlatives and provides a handy rack upon which to hang your supplemental information.

Experiencing Europe's culture, people, and natural wonders economically and hassle-free has been my goal through three decades of traveling, tour guiding, and travel writing. With this new edition, I pass on to you the lessons I've learned, updated for your trip in 2015.

The German destinations covered in this book are balanced to include a comfortable mix of cities and villages, mountaintop hikes and forgotten Roman ruins, sleepy river cruises and sky-high gondola rides. I've also included a taste of neighboring Austria, with side-trips into Tirol and Salzburg. While you'll find the predictable biggies (such as Rhine castles and chunks of the Berlin Wall), I've also mixed in a healthy dose of Back Door intimacy (a soak in a Black Forest mineral spa, a beer with Bavarian monks, and a thrilling mountain luge ride). I've been selective, including only the most exciting sights. For example, of the many castles in the Mosel Valley, I guide you to the best: Burg Eltz.

The best is, of course, only my opinion. But after spending half my adult life exploring and researching Europe, I've developed a sixth sense for what travelers enjoy. The places featured in this book will make anyone want to yodel.

INTRODUCTION

Map Legend

⅃⋮ Viewpoint	✈ Airport	)(Tunnel
↑ Entrance	Ⓣ Taxi Stand	▭▭▭ Pedestrian Zone
❶ Tourist Info	🇹 Tram Stop	- - - - Railway
WC Restroom	Ⓑ Bus Stop	·········· Ferry/Boat Route
⌂ Castle	Ⓜ Metro Stop	⊢——⊣ Tram
✝ Church	Ⓤ U-Bahn	▥▥▥▥ Stairs
▪ Statue/Point of Interest	Ⓢ S-Bahn	· · · · · Walk/Tour Route
▨ Park	Ⓟ Parking	- - - - - Trail
	)(Mtn. Pass	

Use this legend to help you navigate the maps in this book.

ABOUT THIS BOOK

Rick Steves Germany 2015 is your friendly Franconian, your German in a jam, a tour guide in your pocket. This book is organized by destinations. Each is a mini-vacation on its own, filled with exciting sights, strollable neighborhoods, affordable places to stay, and memorable places to eat. In the following chapters, you'll find these sections:

Planning Your Time suggests a schedule for how to best use your limited time.

Orientation includes specifics on public transportation, helpful hints, local tour options, easy-to-read maps, and tourist information.

Sights describes the top attractions and includes their cost and hours.

Self-Guided Walks take you through interesting neighborhoods, with a personal tour guide in hand.

Sleeping describes my favorite hotels, from good-value deals to cushy splurges.

Eating serves up a range of options, from inexpensive eateries to fancy restaurants.

Connections outlines your options for traveling to destinations by train, bus, and plane, and has route tips for drivers.

The **German History** chapter introduces you to some of the key people and events in this nation's complicated past, making your sightseeing that much more meaningful.

Practicalities is a traveler's tool kit, with my best travel tips and advice about money, sightseeing, sleeping, eating, staying connected, and transportation (trains, buses, car rentals, driving, and flights). There's also a list of recommended books and films.

The **appendix** has nuts-and-bolts information, including use-

Key to This Book

Updates

This book is updated every year—but things change. For the latest, visit www.ricksteves.com/update.

Abbreviations and Times

I use the following symbols and abbreviations in this book: Sights are rated:

▲▲▲	**Don't miss**
▲▲	**Try hard to see**
▲	**Worthwhile if you can make it**
No rating	**Worth knowing about**

Tourist information offices are abbreviated as **TI,** and bathrooms are **WC**s. To categorize accommodations, I use a **Sleep Code** (described on page 920).

Like Europe, this book uses the **24-hour clock.** It's the same through 12:00 noon, then keeps going: 13:00, 14:00, and so on. For anything over 12, subtract 12 and add p.m. (14:00 is 2:00 p.m.).

When giving **opening times,** I include both peak season and off-season hours if they differ. So, if a museum is listed as "May-Oct daily 9:00-16:00," it should be open from 9:00 a.m. until 4:00 p.m. from the first day of May until the last day of October (but expect exceptions).

For **transit** or **tour departures,** I first list the frequency, then the duration. So, a train connection listed as "2/hour, 1.5 hours" departs twice each hour, and the journey lasts an hour and a half.

ful phone numbers and websites, a festival list, a climate chart, a handy packing checklist, and German survival phrases.

Browse through this book, choose your favorite destinations, and link them up. Then have a *wunderbar* trip! Traveling like a temporary local, you'll get the absolute most out of every mile, minute, and dollar. As you visit places I know and love, I'm happy that you'll be meeting some of my favorite German people.

Planning

This section will help you get started on planning your trip—with advice on trip costs, when to go, and what you should know before you take off.

TRAVEL SMART

Your trip to Germany is like a complex play—it's easier to follow and to really appreciate on a second viewing. While no one does the same trip twice to gain that advantage, reading this book in its entirety before your trip accomplishes much the same thing.

Design an itinerary that enables you to visit sights at the best possible times. Note festivals and holidays, specifics on sights, and days when sights are closed or most crowded (all covered in this book). To get between destinations smoothly, read the tips in the Practicalities chapter on taking trains and buses, or renting a car and driving. A smart trip is a puzzle—a fun, doable, and worthwhile challenge.

When you're plotting your itinerary, strive for a mix of intense and relaxed stretches. To maximize rootedness, minimize one-night stands. It's worth taking a long drive after dinner (or a train ride with a dinner picnic) to get settled in a town for two nights. Every trip—and every traveler—needs slack time (laundry, picnics, people-watching, and so on). Pace yourself. Assume you will return.

Reread this book as you travel, and visit local tourist information offices (abbreviated as TI in this book). Upon arrival in a new town, lay the groundwork for a smooth departure; get the schedule for the train or bus you'll take when you depart. Drivers can figure out the best route to their next destination.

Update your plans as you travel. You can carry a small mobile device (phone, tablet, laptop) to find out tourist information, learn the latest on sights (special events, tour schedules, etc.), book tickets and tours, make reservations, reconfirm hotels, research transportation connections, and keep in touch with your loved ones. If you don't want to bring a pricey device, you can use guest computers at hotels and make phone calls from landlines.

Enjoy the friendliness of the German people. Connect with the culture. Set up your own quest for the best beer-and-bratwurst, castle, cathedral, or whatever. Slow down and be open to unexpected experiences. Ask questions—most locals are eager to point you in their idea of the right direction. Keep a notepad in your pocket for noting directions, organizing your thoughts, and confirming prices. Wear your money belt, learn the currency, and figure out how to estimate prices in dollars. Those who expect to travel smart, do.

TRIP COSTS

Five components make up your trip costs: airfare, surface transportation, room and board, sightseeing and entertainment, and shopping and miscellany.

Airfare: A basic round-trip flight from the US to Frankfurt can cost, on average, about $1,000-2,000 total, depending on where you fly from and when (cheaper in winter). Consider saving time and money in Europe by flying into one city and out of anoth-

Please Tear Up This Book!

There's no point in hauling around a big chapter on Berlin for a day in Frankfurt. That's why I hope you'll rip this book apart. Before your trip, attack this book with a utility knife to create an army of pocket-sized mini-guidebooks—one for each area you visit.

I love the ritual of trimming down the size of guidebooks I'll be using: Fold the pages back until you break the spine, neatly slice apart the sections you want with a utility knife, then pull them out with the gummy edge intact. If you want, finish each one off with some clear, sturdy packing tape to smooth and reinforce the spine, or use a heavy-duty stapler along the edge to prevent the first and last pages from coming loose.

To make things even easier, I've created a line of laminated covers with slide-on binders. Every evening, you can make a ritual of swapping out today's pages for tomorrow's. (For more on these binders, see www.ricksteves.com.)

While you may be tempted to keep this book intact as a souvenir of your travels, you'll appreciate even more the foot-loose freedom of traveling light.

er; for instance, into Frankfurt and out of Berlin. Overall, Kayak. com is the best place to start searching for flights on a combination of mainstream and budget carriers.

Surface Transportation: For a three-week whirlwind trip of my recommended destinations by public transportation, allow $400 per person. If you'll be renting a car, allow $200 per week, not including tolls, gas, and supplemental insurance. If you'll be keeping the car for three weeks or more, look into leasing, which can save you money on insurance and taxes for trips of this length. Car rentals and leases are cheapest if arranged from the US. Train passes normally must be purchased outside Europe but aren't necessarily your best option—you may save money by simply buying tickets as you go. Don't hesitate to consider flying, as budget airlines can be cheaper than taking the train (check www.skyscanner. com for intra-European flights). For more on public transportation and car rental, see "Transportation" in Practicalities.

Room and Board: You can thrive in Germany in 2015 on $115 a day per person for room and board (more in big cities). This allows $15 for lunch, $25 for dinner, $5 for beer and *Eis* (ice cream), and $70 for lodging (based on two people splitting the cost of a $140 double room that includes breakfast). Students and tightwads can enjoy Germany for as little as $65 a day ($35 for a bed in a hostel, $30 for cheap meals and picnics).

Sightseeing and Entertainment: In big cities, figure about

Germany at a Glance

▲▲▲**Munich** Lively city with a traffic-free center, excellent museums, Baroque palaces, stately churches, rowdy beer halls, convivial beer gardens, and beautiful parks (such as the English Garden)—plus the sobering concentration camp memorial at nearby Dachau.

▲▲▲**Bavaria and Tirol** Pair of Alps-straddling regions (one in Germany, the other in Austria) boasting the fairy-tale castles of Neuschwanstein, Hohenschwangau, and Linderhof; inviting villages such as the handy home base Füssen, Austrian retreat Reutte, and adorable Oberammergau; the towering Zugspitze and its high-altitude lifts; and hiking, luge, and other mountain activities.

▲▲**Salzburg and Berchtesgaden** Austrian musical mecca for fans of Mozart and *The Sound of Music*, offering a dramatic castle, concerts, Baroque churches, and an old town full of winding lanes; plus nearby Berchtesgaden, soaked in alpine scenery and Nazi history.

▲**Baden-Baden and the Black Forest** High-class resort/spa town of Baden-Baden, with decadent bath experiences, a peaceful riverside stroll, and a grand casino; lively university city of Freiburg and cozy village of Staufen; and a thickly forested countryside rife with healthy hikes, folk museums, cute hamlets, and cream cakes.

▲▲**Rothenburg and the Romantic Road** Well-preserved medieval city full of half-timbered buildings and cobbled lanes surrounded by intact and walkable medieval walls; jumping-off point for the "Romantic Road" scenic route through lovely countryside and time-passed towns, including Dinkelsbühl and Nördlingen.

▲**Würzburg** Residenz complex (with a palace, manicured gardens, and dazzling Rococo chapel) and lively wine bars and restaurants.

▲**Frankfurt** Europe's bustling banking center, offering a stunning skyscraper skyline and a look at today's Germany.

▲▲Rhine Valley Mighty river steeped in legend, where story-book villages (including charming home-base towns Bacharach and St. Goar) cluster under imposing castles, such as Rheinfels and Marksburg.

▲▲Mosel Valley Peaceful meandering river lined with tiny wine-loving cobbled towns, such as handy Cochem and quaint Beil-stein, plus my favorite European castle, Burg Eltz.

▲Trier Germany's oldest city, with a lively pedestrian zone and imposing Roman monuments, including the Porta Nigra gate.

▲Cologne Spectacular Gothic cathedral looming above a busy, museum-packed riverside city.

▲▲Nürnberg City with old-fashioned sandstone core and great museums, with reminders of Nazi past thoughtfully presented on the outskirts of town.

▲Lutherland Charming university town of Erfurt, where Martin Luther spent his youth; Wartburg Castle, where he hid out from the pope's goons; and Wittenberg, where he taught, preached, and revolutionized Christianity.

▲Leipzig Formerly derelict "second city" of East Germany, now rejuvenated (if architecturally dull) with excellent Bach and Cold War sights, and a funky nightlife district.

▲▲Dresden Art-filled city offering exquisite museums, Baroque palaces, a delightful riverside promenade, and hard memories of a notorious WWII firebombing.

▲▲▲Berlin Germany's vibrant capital, featuring world-class mu-seums, gleaming modern architecture, and trendy nightlife, along with evocative monuments and memories of the Wall that once divided the city and country.

▲Hamburg Big port city with emigration, World War II, Beatles' history, and Las Vegas-style nightlife.

$10-18 per major sight (Munich's Residenz-$9, Berlin's Museum of the Wall-$17), $5-7 for minor ones, and $25-50 for splurge experiences (such as walking tours, concerts, alpine lifts, and conducting the beer-hall band). An overall average of $30 a day works for most people. Don't skimp here. After all, this category is the driving force behind your trip—you came to sightsee, enjoy, and experience Germany.

Shopping and Miscellany: Figure roughly $3 per postcard (including postage), coffee, beer, and ice-cream cone. Shopping can vary in cost from nearly nothing to a small fortune. Good budget travelers find that this category has little to do with assembling a trip full of lifelong and wonderful memories.

SIGHTSEEING PRIORITIES

Depending on the length of your trip, and taking geographic proximity into account, here are my recommended priorities:

3 days:	Munich, Bavarian castles
5 days, add:	Rhine Valley, Rothenburg
7 days, add:	More of Bavaria and Tirol, side-trip to Salzburg
10 days, add:	Berlin
14 days, add:	Baden-Baden, Black Forest, Dresden
17 days, add:	Nürnberg, Mosel Valley, Trier
21 days, add:	Würzburg, and slow down
More time:	Choose among Frankfurt, Cologne, Hamburg, Leipzig, and the Martin Luther towns (Erfurt and Wittenberg).

This includes nearly everything on the map on page 11. If you don't have time to see it all, prioritize according to your interests. The "Germany at a Glance" sidebar can help you decide where to go (page 6).

WHEN TO GO

The "tourist season" runs roughly from May through September. Summer has its advantages: the best weather, snow-free alpine trails, very long days (light until after 21:00), and the busiest schedule of tourist fun.

Travel during "shoulder season" (April, May, Sept, and early Oct) is easier and can be a bit less expensive. Shoulder-season travelers usually enjoy smaller crowds, decent weather, the full range of sights and tourist fun spots, and the ability to grab a room almost whenever and wherever they like—often at a flexible price. Also, in fall, fun harvest and wine festivals enliven many towns and villages, while forests and vineyards display beautiful fiery colors.

Winter travelers find concert seasons in full swing, with absolutely no crowds, but some accommodations and sights are either closed or run on a limited schedule. Confirm your sightseeing plans

Top Destinations in Germany

HAMBURG

GERMANY

BERLIN

COLOGNE

LUTHERLAND

RHINE VALLEY

LEIPZIG

DRESDEN

MOSEL VALLEY

FRANKFURT

WÜRZBURG

TRIER

NÜRNBERG

ROTHENBURG & ROMANTIC ROAD

BADEN-BADEN & BLACK FOREST

MUNICH

BAVARIA & TIROL

SALZBURG (AUSTRIA) & BERCHTESGADEN

locally, especially when traveling off-season. The weather can be cold and dreary, and nightfall draws the shades on sightseeing well before dinnertime. But dustings of snow turn German towns and landscapes into a wonderland, and December offers the chance to wander through Germany's famous Christmas markets (this tinseled fun often comes with higher hotel prices, but also longer museum hours).

For more information, see the climate chart in the appendix.

KNOW BEFORE YOU GO

Your trip is more likely to go smoothly if you plan ahead. Check this list of things to arrange while you're still at home.

You need a **passport**—but no visa or shots—to travel in Germany. You may be denied entry into certain European countries if

Germany's Best Three-Week Trip by Car

Day	Plan	Sleep in
1	Fly into Frankfurt, pick up car to Rhine	Bacharach
2	Rhine Valley	Bacharach
3	To Mosel Valley	Beilstein or Trier
4	Mosel Valley and/or Trier	Beilstein or Trier
5	To Baden-Baden	Baden-Baden
6	Relax and soak in Baden-Baden	Baden-Baden
7	Drive through the Black Forest	Staufen or Freiburg
8	To Bavaria and Tirol	Füssen or Reutte
9	Bavaria/Tirol and castles	Füssen or Reutte
10	More Bavaria/Tirol, then to Munich	Munich
11	Munich	Munich
12	More Munich, or side-trip to Salzburg	Munich
13	To Dachau, then follow Romantic Road to Rothenburg	Rothenburg
14	Rothenburg	Rothenburg
15	To Würzburg, drop off car*, then train to Nürnberg	Nürnberg or Würzburg
16	Nürnberg	Nürnberg
17	Train to Dresden	Dresden
18	Train to Berlin	Berlin
19	Berlin	Berlin
20	Berlin	Berlin
21	Fly home	

*After Day 15, you're visiting well-connected cities, making a car unnecessary. Drop the car in Würzburg to save several days of car-rental costs and parking fees.

Smaller Towns vs. Bigger Towns: This itinerary (especially the first half) is heavy on half-timbered villages—a German specialty. But for some, a little cuteness goes a long way. Depending on your preference, you can plan your overnights either to maximize or reduce quaintness. For example, for Days 3-4, 7, and 15, you can opt for smaller towns (Beilstein, Staufen, and mid-size Würzburg) or for bigger cities (Trier, Freiburg, and Nürnberg).

With Less Time: This trip can be pared down to two weeks by making the following changes: Skip the Mosel (a sleepier version of the Rhine), and go directly from the Rhine to Baden-Baden. From Baden-Baden, head straight for Füssen/Reutte

instead of overnighting in Staufen/Freiburg. Skip the Salzburg side-trip; choose between Würzburg and Nürnberg, and stay just one night there; and reduce the stay in Berlin to two nights.

With More Time: Berlin and Salzburg are each easily worth another day. Depending on your interests, you could stay a day in Frankfurt (upon arrival) and add another day for the Rhine to visit Cologne from Bacharach. The Martin Luther towns (Erfurt and Wittenberg) and Leipzig fit well between towns to the west and south (Frankfurt, Nürnberg) and those in the north and east (Berlin, Dresden). Hamburg isn't on the way to anything in Germany (it's near Denmark), but it's a worthwhile detour for those interested in its history.

By Train: This itinerary is designed to be done by car, but could be done by train with some modifications: Skip the southern Black Forest and take the train from Baden-Baden to Munich, which works well as a home base for visiting Bavaria and Salzburg. Then take the train or bus to Rothenburg; from there, Würzburg, Nürnberg, and Dresden are all on the way to Berlin. Or, for the best of both worlds, consider using trains to connect major cities, and then renting a car strategically to explore worthwhile countryside regions (such as Bavaria/Tirol).

Rick Steves Audio Europe

If you're bringing a mobile device, be sure to check out **Rick Steves Audio Europe,** where you can download free audio tours and hours of travel interviews (via the Rick Steves Audio Europe app, www.ricksteves.com/audioeurope, Google Play, or iTunes).

My self-guided **audio tours** are user-friendly, easy-to-follow, fun, and informative. For Germany, my audio tours include a tour by boat or train along the Rhine, and neighborhood walks in Munich, Salzburg, and Berlin. Compared to live tours, my audio tours are hard to beat: Nobody will stand you up, the quality is reliable, you can take the tour exactly when you like, and they're free.

Rick Steves Audio Europe also offers a far-reaching library of intriguing **travel interviews** with experts from around the globe. The interviews are organized by destination, including many of the places in this book.

---

your passport is due to expire within three months of your ticketed date of return. Get it renewed if you'll be cutting it close. It can take up to six weeks to get or renew a passport (for more on passports, see www.travel.state.gov). Pack a photocopy of your passport in your luggage in case the original is lost or stolen.

Book rooms well in advance if you'll be traveling during peak season (May-Sept) or any major holidays or festivals, such as Oktoberfest in Munich (see page 976). Try to schedule visits to Frankfurt and Cologne outside of convention season to keep your hotel costs down.

Call your **debit- and credit-card companies** to let them know the countries you'll be visiting, to ask about fees, request your PIN code (it will be mailed to you), and more. See page 913 for details.

Do your homework if you want to buy **travel insurance.** Compare the cost of the insurance to the likelihood of your using it and your potential loss if something goes wrong. Also, check whether your existing insurance (health, homeowners, or renters) covers you and your possessions overseas. For more tips, see www.ricksteves.com/insurance.

Consider buying a **rail pass** after researching your options (see page 952 and www.ricksteves.com/rail for all the specifics) or getting point-to-point tickets through Deutsche Bahn, Germany's train system, at www.bahn.com (you can usually save money by booking more expensive train journeys online; tickets sold three months ahead).

If you're planning on **renting a car** in Germany, note that many German cities—including Munich, Freiburg, Frankfurt,

Cologne, Dresden, and Berlin—require drivers to buy a **special sticker** *(Umweltplakette)* to drive in the city center (see page 964).

To avoid peak-season lines at **Neuschwanstein Castle,** reserve tickets ahead on their website; see page 145 for tips.

For a **Munich BMW factory tour,** sign up by phone a couple of months in advance (see page 92).

To visit the **Reichstag dome in Berlin,** reserve a free entry slot online a week or two in advance (see page 741).

To see **Dresden's Historic Green Vault,** book your tickets online at least a week or two before your visit. Or take your chances and line up early for same-day tickets (see page 693).

Tickets for the music-packed **Salzburg Festival** (late July through August) can go fast. Consider buying tickets ahead if there's a specific event you want to see; for details, see page 243.

If you plan to hire a **local guide,** reserve ahead by email. Popular guides can get booked up.

If you're bringing a **mobile device,** download any apps you might want to use on the road, such as translators, maps, and transit schedules. Check out **Rick Steves Audio Europe,** featuring audio tours of major sights, hours of travel interviews on Germany, and more (see page 12).

Check the **Rick Steves guidebook updates** page for any recent changes to this book (www.ricksteves.com/update).

Because **airline carry-on restrictions** are always changing, visit the Transportation Security Administration's website (www.tsa.gov) for a list of what you can bring on the plane and for the latest security measures (including screening of electronic devices, which you may be asked to power up).

Traveling as a Temporary Local

We travel all the way to Germany to enjoy differences—to become temporary locals. You'll experience frustrations. Certain truths that we find "God-given" or "self-evident," such as ice in drinks, bottomless cups of coffee, and bigger being better, are suddenly not so true. One of the benefits of travel is the eye-opening realization that there are logical, civil, and even better alternatives. A willing-ness to go local ensures that you'll enjoy a full dose of German hospitality.

Europeans generally like Americans. But if there is a negative aspect to the European image of Americans, it's that we are loud,

INTRODUCTION

How Was Your Trip?

Were your travels fun, smooth, and meaningful? If you'd like to share your tips, concerns, and discoveries, please fill out the survey at www.ricksteves.com/feedback. To check out readers' hotel and restaurant reviews—or leave one yourself—visit my travel forum at www.ricksteves.com/travel-forum. I value your feedback. Thanks in advance—it helps a lot.

wasteful, ethnocentric, too informal (which can seem disrespectful), and a bit naive.

While Europeans look bemusedly at some of our Yankee excesses—and worriedly at others—they nearly always afford us individual travelers all the warmth we deserve.

Judging from all the happy feedback I receive from travelers who have used this book, it's safe to assume you'll enjoy a great, affordable vacation—with the finesse of an independent, experienced traveler.

Thanks, and *gute Reise!*

Rick Steves

Back Door Travel Philosophy

From *Rick Steves Europe Through the Back Door*

Travel is intensified living—maximum thrills per minute and one of the last great sources of legal adventure. Travel is freedom. It's recess, and we need it.

Experiencing the real Europe requires catching it by surprise, going casual..."through the Back Door."

Affording travel is a matter of priorities. (Make do with the old car.) You can eat and sleep—simply, safely, and enjoyably—anywhere in Europe for $125 a day plus transportation costs. In many ways, spending more money only builds a thicker wall between you and what you traveled so far to see. Europe is a cultural carnival, and time after time, you'll find that its best acts are free and the best seats are the cheap ones.

A tight budget forces you to travel close to the ground, meeting and communicating with the people. Never sacrifice sleep, nutrition, safety, or cleanliness to save money. Simply enjoy the local-style alternatives to expensive hotels and restaurants.

Connecting with people carbonates your experience. Extroverts have more fun. If your trip is low on magic moments, kick yourself and make things happen. If you don't enjoy a place, maybe you don't know enough about it. Seek the truth. Recognize tourist traps. Give a culture the benefit of your open mind. See things as different, but not better or worse. Any culture has plenty to share.

Of course, travel, like the world, is a series of hills and valleys. Be fanatically positive and militantly optimistic. If something's not to your liking, change your liking.

Travel can make you a happier American, as well as a citizen of the world. Our Earth is home to seven billion equally precious people. It's humbling to travel and find that other people don't have the "American Dream"—they have their own dreams. Europeans like us, but with all due respect, they wouldn't trade passports.

Thoughtful travel engages us with the world. In tough economic times, it reminds us what is truly important. By broadening perspectives, travel teaches new ways to measure quality of life.

Globetrotting destroys ethnocentricity, helping us understand and appreciate other cultures. Rather than fear the diversity on this planet, celebrate it. Among your most prized souvenirs will be the strands of different cultures you choose to knit into your own character. The world is a cultural yarn shop, and Back Door travelers are weaving the ultimate tapestry. Join in!

MUNICH

München

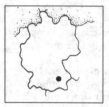

Munich ("München" in German), often called Germany's most livable city, is also one of its most historic, artistic, and entertaining. It's big and growing, with a population of 1.5 million. Until 1871, it was the capital of an independent Bavaria. Its imperial palaces, jewels, and grand boulevards constantly remind visitors that Munich has long been a political and cultural powerhouse. Meanwhile, the concentration camp in nearby Dachau reminds us that eight decades ago, it provided a springboard for Nazism.

Orient yourself in Munich's old center, with its colorful pedestrian zones. Immerse yourself in the city's art and history—crown jewels, Baroque theater, Wittelsbach palaces, great paintings, and beautiful parks. Spend your Munich evenings in a frothy beer hall or outdoor *Biergarten,* prying big pretzels from buxom, no-nonsense beer maids amidst an oompah, bunny-hopping, and belching Bavarian atmosphere.

PLANNING YOUR TIME

Munich is worth two days, including a half-day side-trip to Dachau. But if all you have for Munich is one day, follow the "Munich City Walk" laid out in this chapter (visiting museums along the way), tour one of the royal palaces (the Residenz or Nymphenburg), and drink in the beer-hall culture for your evening's entertainment. With a second day, choose from the following: Tour the Dachau Concentration Camp Memorial, rent a bike to enjoy the English Garden, or—if you're into art—tour your choice of the city's many fine art museums (especially the Alte Pinakothek). With all these blockbuster sights and activities, the city could easily fill three days. And many visitors spend an entire day side-tripping south to "Mad" King Ludwig's Castles (covered in the Bavaria and Tirol chapter). Austria's Salzburg (about 2 hours one-way by direct train) is also within day-tripping distance.

Orientation to Munich

The tourist's Munich is circled by a ring road (site of the old town wall) marked by four old gates: Karlstor (near the main train station—the Hauptbahnhof), Sendlinger Tor, Isartor (near the river), and Odeonsplatz (no surviving gate, near the palace). Marienplatz marks the city's center. A great pedestrian-only zone (Kaufingerstrasse and Neuhauser Strasse) cuts this circle in half, running neatly from the Karlstor and the train station through Marienplatz to the Isartor. Orient yourself along this east-west axis. Ninety percent of the sights and hotels I recommend are within a 20-minute walk of Marienplatz and each other.

Despite its large population, Munich feels small. This big-city elegance is possible because of its determination to be pedestrian- and bike-friendly, and because of a law that no building can be taller than the church spires. Despite ongoing debate about changing this policy, there are still no skyscrapers in downtown Munich.

TOURIST INFORMATION

Munich has two helpful city-run TIs (www.muenchen.de). One is in front of the **main train station** (with your back to the tracks, walk through the central hall, step outside, and turn right; Mon-Sat 9:00-20:00, Sun 10:00-18:00, hotel reservations tel. 089/2339-6500—no info at this number). The other TI is on Munich's main square, **Marienplatz,** below the glockenspiel (Mon-Fri 9:00-19:00, Sat 9:00-16:00, Sun 10:00-14:00).

At either TI, pick up brochures and buy the city map (€0.40, better than the free map in hotel lobbies—especially for anyone using public transit), and confirm your sightseeing plans. Private Munich Ticket offices inside the TIs sell concert and event tickets. The free, twice-monthly magazine *In München* lists all movies and entertainment in town (in German, organized by date). The TI can book you a room (you'll pay about 10 percent here, then pay the rest at the hotel), but you'll get a better value by contacting my recommended hotels directly. If you're interested in a Gray Line tour of the city or to nearby castles, don't buy your ticket at the TI; instead, you can get discounted tickets for these same tours at EurAide (described later). For advice on transport and sightseeing passes, see "Getting Around Munich," later in this section.

The Bavarian Palace Department offers a 14-day ticket (called the *Mehrtagesticket*) that covers admission to Munich's Residenz and Nymphenburg Palace complexes, as well as other castles and

MUNICH

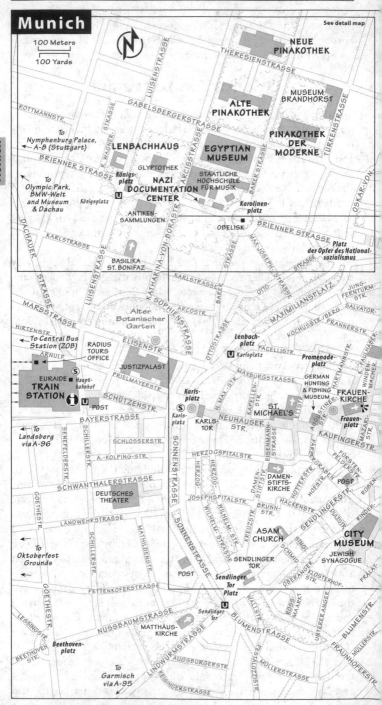

Munich

100 Meters
100 Yards

See detail map

NEUE PINAKOTHEK

THERESIENSTRASSE

MUSEUM BRANDHORST

ALTE PINAKOTHEK

PINAKOTHEK DER MODERNE

ROTTMANNSTR.

GABELSBERGERSTRASSE

LUISENSTRASSE

R. WAGNER STRASSE

ARCISSTRASSE

BAKER STRASSE

TÜRKENSTRASSE

OSKAR-VON-

LENBACHHAUS

EGYPTIAN MUSEUM

GLYPTOTHEK

To Nymphenburg Palace, A-8 (Stuttgart)

BRIENNER STRASSE

Königs-platz

NAZI DOCUMENTATION CENTER

STAATLICHE HOCHSCHULE FÜR MUSIK

To Olympic Park, BMW-Welt and Museum & Dachau

Königsplatz

ANTIKEN-SAMMLUNGEN

Karolinen-platz

OBELISK

BRIENNER STRASSE

Platz der Opfer des National-sozialismus

DACHAUER STRASSE

KARLSTRASSE

KARLSTRASSE

MAX-JOSEPH-STRASSE

BASILIKA ST. BONIFAZ

KATHARINA-VON-BORA-STR.

BAKER STR.

OTTO-STR.

MAXIMILIANSPLATZ

JUNG-FERNTURM-STR.

MARSSTRASSE

K.-SOPHIENSTRASSE

ARCOSTR.

SALVATOR-

HIRTENSTR.

Alter Botanischer Garten

KOCHUSSTR./BERG.

PRANNERSTR.

To Central Bus Station (ZOB)

RADIUS TOURS OFFICE

ELISENSTR.

Lenbach-platz

Karlsplatz

PACELLISTR.

Promenade-platz

THEATINERSTRASSE

WEINSTR.

WINDEN-MACHER.

ARNULF

JUSTIZPALAST

PRIELMAYERSTR.

MAXBURGSTRASSE

GERMAN HUNTING & FISHING MUSEUM

FRAUEN-KIRCHE

EURAIDE TRAIN STATION

Haupt-bahnhof

SCHÜTZENSTR.

POST

Karls-platz

M. MAX-STR.

KAPELLEN-STR.

ST. MICHAEL'S

AUGUSTINER-STR.

Frauen-platz

To Landsberg via A-96

BAYERSTRASSE

Karls-platz

KARLS-TOR

NEUHAUSER STR.

EISENMANN-STRASSE

FÄRBERGRABEN

KAUFINGERSTR.

FÜRSTEN-FELDER STR.

SENEFELDERSTR.

SCHILLERSTR.

SCHLOSSERSTR.

A.-KOLPING-STR.

HERZOGSPITALSTR.

HERZOG-STR.

DAMEN-STIFTS-KIRCHE

HOTTERSTR.

HOFSTR.

POST

ROSEN-

SCHWANTHALERSTRASSE

DEUTSCHES THEATER

JOSEPHSPITALSTR.

HACKENSTR.

SENDLINGERSTR.

DULTSTR.

KINDER-

GOETHESTR.

LANDWEHRSTRASSE

MATHILDENSTR.

BRUNN-STR.

WILHELM-STR.

KREUZSTR.

SINGL-

ASAM CHURCH

SCHMID-

CITY MUSEUM

To Oktoberfest Grounds

SCHILLERSTR.

SONNENSTRASSE

SENDLINGER TOR

JEWISH SYNAGOGUE

KLOSTERHOF-

PRÄLAT-

FETTENKOFERSTRASSE

POST

Sendlinger Tor Platz

OBERANGER

KOSS

UNTERER ANGER

BLUMENSTR.

LESSINGSTR.

NUSSBAUMSTRASSE

Sendlinger Tor

BLUMENSTRASSE

WALLSTR.

FUGGERSTR.

MÜLLERSTR.

BLUMENSTR.

Beethoven-platz

BEETHOVEN STR.

MATTHÄUS-KIRCHE

LINDWURMSTRASSE

AUGSBURGERSTR.

RESINGERSTRASSE

MAARKT

FRAUNHOFERSTR.

To Garmisch via A-95

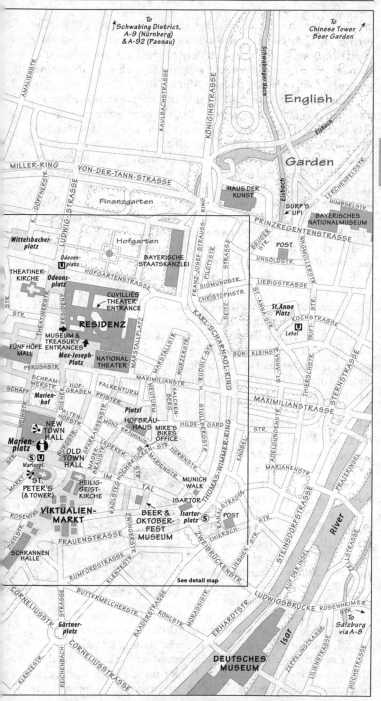

palaces in Bavaria (for a partial list, see page 130; €24, €40 family/partner pass, annual pass also available, not sold at TI—purchase at participating sights, www.schloesser.bayern.de). For avid castle-goers, this is a deal: Two people will save €5 with a family/partner pass even if only visiting the two Munich sights.

EurAide: At counter #1 in the train station's main *Reisezentrum* (travel center, opposite track 21), the hardworking, eager-to-help EurAide desk is a godsend for Eurailers and budget travelers. Alan Wissenberg and his EurAide staff can answer your train-travel and day-trip questions in clear American English. Paid by the German rail company to help you design your train travels, EurAide makes reservations and sells tickets, *couchettes*, and sleepers for the train at the same price you'd pay at the other counters (open May-Oct Mon-Fri 8:30-20:00, Sat 8:30-14:00, closed Sun; off-season Mon-Fri 10:00-19:00, closed Sat-Sun and Jan-Feb). EurAide sells a €0.50 city map and offers a free, information-packed newsletter, *The Inside Track* (described on page 22; also see www.euraide.com). As EurAide helps about 500 visitors per day in the summer, a line can build up; do your homework and have a list of questions ready. Chances are that your questions are already answered in their *Inside Track* newsletter—grab it and scan it first.

EurAide also sells cash-only tickets for Munich Walk city walking tours and Gray Line city bus tours, as well as for Gray Line tours to Neuschwanstein and Linderhof castles (all described later, under "Tours in Munich"). They offer a discount on these tickets to travelers with this book.

ARRIVAL IN MUNICH

By Train: Munich's main train station (München Hauptbahnhof) is a sight in itself—one of those places that can turn a homebody into a carefree vagabond.

Clean, high-tech, pay **public toilets** and **showers** are downstairs near track 26. For a quick rest stop, Burger King's toilets (upstairs, €0.50 donation requested) are open to the public and as pleasant and accessible as its hamburgers.

Check out the bright and modern **food court** opposite track 14. For sandwiches and prepared meals to bring on board, I shop at **Yorma's** (three branches: one by track 26, one at street level next to the TI, and one in the passageway under Bahnhofplatz).

You'll find a city-run **TI** (out front of station and to the right) and **lockers** (opposite track 26). The **k presse + buch** shop (across from track 23) is great for English-language books, newspapers, and magazines. **Radius Tours** (at track 32) rents bikes and organizes tours (see pages 27, 28, and 29).

Up the stairs opposite track 21 are **car-rental agencies** (overlooking track 22), a quiet, non-smoking **waiting room** *(Warteraum)* that's open to anybody (overlooking track 23), and next door (opposite track 24) the **DB Lounge,** which is only for those with a first-class ticket issued by the Deutsche Bahn (German Railway; rail passes don't get you in).

Subway lines, trams, and buses connect the station to the rest of the city (though many of my recommended hotels are within walking distance of the station). If you get lost in the underground maze of subway corridors while you're simply trying to get to the train station, follow the signs for *DB* (Deutsche Bahn) to surface successfully. Watch out for the hallways with blue ticket-stamping machines in the middle—these lead to the subway, where you could be fined if nabbed without a validated ticket.

By Bus: Munich's central bus station (ZOB) is by the Hackerbrücke S-Bahn station (from the train station, it's one S-Bahn stop; www.muenchen-zob.de). The Romantic Road bus leaves from here, as do many buses to Eastern Europe and the Balkans (including the Deutsche Bahn's express buses to Prague and Zagreb).

By Plane: For airport information, see "Munich Connections" at the end of this chapter.

HELPFUL HINTS

Museum Hours: Sights closed on Monday include the Alte Pinakothek, Munich City Museum, Jewish History Museum, Pinakothek der Moderne, Bavarian National Museum, Beer and Oktoberfest Museum, and the BMW Museum. The Neue Pinakothek closes on Tuesday. The art museums are generally open late one night a week. On Sunday, the Pinakotheks and Bavarian National Museum cost just €1 apiece, but you'll pay extra for the usually free audioguides.

Festivals: Oktoberfest lasts around two weeks (Sept 19-Oct 4 in 2015), starting on the third Saturday in September and usually ending on the first Sunday in October (www.oktoberfest. de). The same fairgrounds also host a **Spring Festival** *(Frühlingsfestival,* two weeks in late April-early May, www. fruehlingsfest-muenchen.de) as well as Tollwood, an artsy, multicultural, alternative **Christmas market** (late Nov-Dec, www.tollwood.de).

Internet Access: There's free Wi-Fi on Marienplatz, courtesy of the city (connect to M-WLAN network, then click to accept terms). If you need to use a computer, try the hole-in-the-wall call centers in the blocks surrounding the train station.

Bookstore: The German bookstore **Hugendubel** towers above

Marienplatz with a good selection of English books, comfy nooks for reading, and a view café (Mon-Sat 9:30-20:00, closed Sun, Marienplatz 22, tel. 089/3075-7575).

Need a Toilet? Munich had outdoor urinals until the 1972 Olympics and then decided to beautify the city by doing away with them. What about the people's needs? By law, any place serving beer must admit the public (whether or not they're customers) to use the toilets.

Laundry: A handy self-service **Waschcenter** is a 10-minute walk from the train station (wash-€4-8/load, dry-€1/10 minutes, drop-off service-€12/load; self-service daily 7:00-23:00, drop-off Mon-Sat 10:00-20:00, Sun 11:00-18:00; English instructions, Paul-Heyse-Strasse 21, near intersection with Landwehrstrasse, mobile 0171-734-2094). Theresienwiese is the closest U-Bahn station.

Bikes and Pedestrians: Signs painted on the sidewalk or blue-and-white street signs show which part of the sidewalk is designated for pedestrians and which is for cyclists. The strip of pathway closest to the street is usually reserved for bikes. Pedestrians wandering into the bike path may hear the cheery ding-ding of a cyclist's bell just before being knocked unconscious.

Taxi: Call 089/21610 for a taxi.

Private Driver: Johann Fayoumi is reliable and speaks English (€70/hour, mobile 0174-183-8473, www.firstclasslimousines. de, johannfayoumi@gmail.com).

Car Rental: Several car-rental agencies are located upstairs at the train station, opposite track 21 (open daily, hours vary).

The Inside Track **Train Travelers' Newsletter:** Anyone traveling by train should pick up this wonkish-yet-brilliant quarterly newsletter published by the wonkish-yet-brilliant Alan Wissenberg of EurAide (free, always available at the EurAide counter in the train station—described earlier, under "Tourist Information"). You'll find all the tedious but important details on getting to Neuschwanstein, Dachau, Nymphenburg, and Prague; the ins and outs of supplements and reservations necessary for rail-pass holders; a daily schedule of various tours in Munich; and (of course) plenty of tips on how to take advantage of EurAide's services.

Great City Views: Downtown Munich's best city viewpoints (described in this chapter) are from the towers of St. Peter's Church (stairs only) and New Town Hall (elevator). Normally the Frauenkirche would make the list, but its towers are likely to be closed for renovation during your visit.

What's with Monaco? People walking around with guidebooks to Monaco aren't lost. "Monaco di Baviera" means "Munich" in *Italiano*.

Updates to this Book: For updates to this book, check www. ricksteves.com/update.

GETTING AROUND MUNICH

Much of Munich is walkable. But—given that the city is laced by many trams, buses, and subways—it's worth learning the system and considering getting a day pass. Public transit also makes it super-easy to access sights outside the historic core, such as Dachau or Nymphenburg Palace (see the map on page 24).

By Public Transit

Subways are called U-Bahns and S-Bahns (S-Bahns are actually commuter railways that run underground through the city and are covered by rail passes—but it's smarter to save your limited number of pass days for long-distance trips). These transit lines are numbered (for example, S-3 or U-5). The U-Bahn lines mainly run north-south, while the S-Bahn lines are generally east-west.

Ticket Options: The entire transit system (subway/bus/tram) works on the same tickets.

• A one-zone **regular ticket** *(Einzelfahrkarte)* costs €2.60 and is good for three hours in one direction, including changes and stops. Most every sight I list in Munich (except Dachau) is inside the white/inner zone. For short rides (four stops max, only two of which can be on the subway lines), buy the €1.30 **short-stretch ticket** *(Kurzstrecke)*. The €6 **all-day pass** *(Single-Tageskarte)* for the white/inner zone is a great deal for a single traveler. If you're going to Dachau, buy the *XXL* version of the *Single-Tageskarte*, which also includes the green zone (€8.10); the *Gesamtnetz* version of the pass—a.k.a. the **Airport-City-Day-Ticket**—covers all four zones and gets you to the airport (€11.70).

• **All-day small-group passes** *(Partner-Tageskarte)* are an even better deal—they cover all public transportation for up to five adults (two kids count as one adult, so two adults and six kids can travel with this ticket). A *Partner-Tageskarte* for the white/inner zone costs €11.20. The *XXL* version, which includes Dachau, costs €14.20; and the *Gesamtnetz* version, including the airport, costs €21.30. These partner tickets—while seemingly impossibly cheap—are for real. Read it again and do the arithmetic. Even two people traveling together save money, and for groups, it's a real steal. The only catch is that you've got to stay together.

• For longer stays, consider a **three-day ticket** (€15/person,

MUNICH

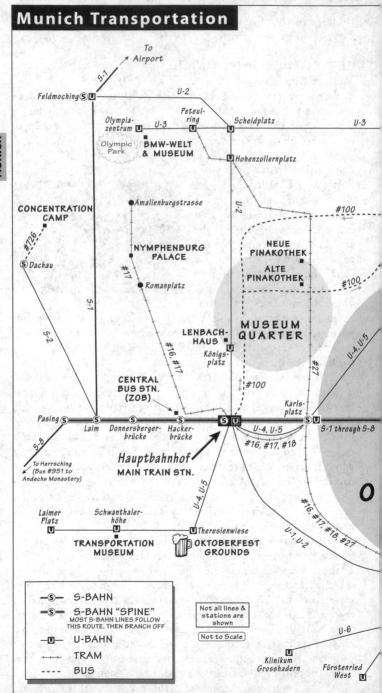

Munich Transportation

To Airport

Feldmoching Ⓢ Ⓤ

S-1

U-2

Olympia-zentrum Ⓤ U-3 Peteul-ring Scheidplatz U-3

Olympic Park

BMW-WELT & MUSEUM

Ⓤ Hohenzollernplatz

CONCENTRATION CAMP

#726

Ⓢ Dachau

● Amalienburgstrasse

U-2

#100

NYMPHENBURG PALACE

NEUE PINAKOTHEK ■

ALTE PINAKOTHEK ■

#100

S-1

#17

● Romanplatz

S-2

LENBACH-HAUS

MUSEUM QUARTER

U-4, U-5

Königs-platz

#16, #17

#27

CENTRAL BUS STN. (ZOB) ■

↑ #100

Karls-platz

Pasing Ⓢ   Ⓢ Laim   Ⓢ Donnersberger-brücke   Ⓢ Hacker-brücke   Ⓢ Ⓤ   Ⓤ Ⓢ

U-4, U-5

S-1 through S-8

S-8

#16, #17, #18

To Herrsching
(Bus #951 to
Andechs Monastery)

Hauptbahnhof
MAIN TRAIN STN.

U-4, U-5

O

Laimer Platz
Ⓤ

Schwanthaler-höhe ■

Ⓤ Theresienwiese

#16, #17, #18, #27

TRANSPORTATION MUSEUM

🍺 **OKTOBERFEST GROUNDS**

U-1, U-2

—Ⓢ— S-BAHN

━Ⓢ━ S-BAHN "SPINE"
MOST S-BAHN LINES FOLLOW
THIS ROUTE, THEN BRANCH OFF

—Ⓤ— U-BAHN

+++ TRAM

---- BUS

Not all lines & stations are shown

Not to Scale

U-6

Ⓤ
Klinikum Grosshadern

Fürstenried West Ⓤ

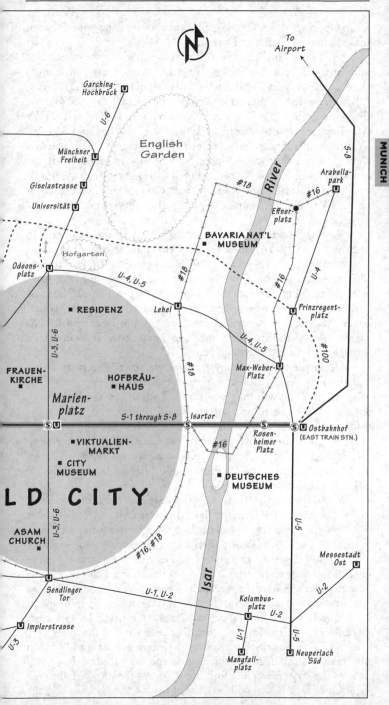

MUNICH

€25.90/partner ticket for the gang, white/inner zone only, does not include transportation to Dachau).

• The **City Tour Card,** which covers public transportation and adds stingy discounts on a few sights and tours, costs a little more than a transit pass (white/inner zone single traveler-€11/1 day, €21/3 days; white/inner zone partner ticket-€18/1 day, €31/3 days; discounts include the Residenz, Nymphenburg Palace, and BMW Museum, plus tours offered by Gray Line, Radius, and Munich Walk; details at www.citytourcard-muenchen.com). The partner tickets are the best value—three adults can save money with just one visit to the BMW Museum on public transit. For single travelers, the card usually isn't worth it. Students, seniors, and readers of this book qualify for many of the same discounts without having to buy the card.

Buying Tickets: Transit tickets are sold at TIs, at booths in the subway, and at any ticket machine that has the MVV logo. Machines take coins and €5 and €10 bills; newer ones take PIN-enabled credit cards, too. Start the transaction by choosing "English," then by pressing "Transit Association-MVV," which displays the array of tickets and passes. There are four concentric zones—white, green, yellow, and orange. Almost everything described in this chapter is within the white/inner zone, except for Dachau (green zone) and the airport (orange zone).

Using the System: Study a transit map (available everywhere, also see map on page 24) and figure out where you need to go and what transit line will take you there. To find the right platform, look for the name of the last station in the direction *(Richtung)* you want to travel. For example, a sign saying *Richtung: Marienplatz* means that that particular subway, bus, or tram is traveling in the direction of Marienplatz. Know where you're going relative to Marienplatz, the Hauptbahnhof, and Ostbahnhof, as these are often referred to as end points.

You must stamp tickets with the date and time prior to using them (for an all-day or multi-day pass, you only have to stamp it the first time you use it; tickets bought at a machine come pre-stamped). For the subway, punch your ticket in the blue machine *before* going down to the platform. For buses and trams, stamp your ticket once on board. Plainclothes ticket-checkers enforce this honor system, rewarding freeloaders with stiff €40 fines. All-day and multi-day passes are valid until 6:00 the following morning.

Handy Lines: Several subway lines, trams, and buses are especially convenient for tourists. All the main S-Bahn lines (S-1 through S-8) run east-west along the main tourist axis between the Hauptbahnhof, Marienplatz, and the Ostbahnhof. For travel within the city center, just find the platform for lines S-1 through S-8. One track *(Gleis)* will be headed east to the Ostbahnhof, the other west to the Hauptbahnhof. Hop on any train going your direction.

The U-3 goes to Olympic Park and the BMW sights, and the S-2 goes to Dachau. Bus #100 is useful for getting to the museum quarter and the English Garden. Tram #17 goes to Nymphenburg Palace.

For more information, visit the transit customer-service center underground at Marienplatz (Mon-Fri 9:00-20:00, Sat 9:00-16:00, closed Sun, go down stairs by Beck's department store), call 0800-344-226-600 (Mon-Fri only), or visit www.mvv-muenchen.de.

MUNICH

By Taxi

Taxis are honest and professional, but expensive (about €12 between the Hauptbahnhof and Marienplatz) and generally unnecessary.

By Bike

Level, compact, and with plenty of bike paths, Munich feels made for those on two wheels. When biking in Munich, follow these simple rules: You must walk your bike through pedestrian zones; you can take your bike on the subway, but not during rush hour (Mon-Fri 6:00-9:00 & 16:00-18:00) and only if you buy a €2.50 bike day pass; and cyclists are expected to follow the rules of the road, just like drivers.

You can **rent bikes** quickly and easily from Radius Tours (in the train station) or Mike's Bike Tours (near the Hofbräuhaus). Each has an extensive selection of bikes; provides helmets, maps, and route advice; and offers bike tours. Radius and Mike's Bike both give a 10 percent discount with this book.

Radius Tours (*Rad* means "bike" in German) is in the train station in front of track 32 (3- to 7-speed city bikes-€3/hour, €14.50/day, €17/24 hours, €28/48 hours, fancier bikes cost more, give credit-card number as deposit, April-Oct daily 8:30-19:00, May-Aug until 20:00; closed Nov-March, tel. 089/543-487-7730, www.radiustours.com).

Mike's Bike Tours is around the corner from the rear entrance to the Hofbräuhaus (€6 plus €2/hour, €16/day, daily mid-April-early Oct 10:00-20:00, shorter hours off-season, open by appointment mid-Nov-Feb, Bräuhausstrasse 10—enter around corner on Hochbrückenstrasse, tel. 089/2554-3987, www.mikesbiketours.com).

Suggested Ride: For a great city ride, consider this day on a bike: Rent from Radius at the train station, and take the bike path out Arnulfstrasse, pedaling out to Nymphenburg Palace. Then head to Olympic Park and the BMW sights, and finish at the English Garden (for the late-afternoon or early-evening scene) before returning to the center. Or go for the Isar River bike ride described on page 94.

Tours in Munich

MUNICH

Here's an overview of your tour options.

Munich's two largest conventional tour companies, Radius Tours and Munich Walk, both run bike tours, walking tours, and day trips to Dachau, Neuschwanstein Castle, and other places. Radius and Munich Walk compete directly with each other, and in my experience, they're comparable. Each company's website explains its ever-growing list of offerings (www.radiustours.com and www.munichwalktours.de). **Radius Tours** has a convenient office and meeting point in the main train station, in front of track 32 (see map on page 108, run by Gaby Holder). **Munich Walk,** run by Ralph Lünstroth, uses Marienplatz as its meeting point. Both offer €2 off some of their tours with this book (described under "Walking Tours," below).

There's also **Gray Line,** which runs sightseeing buses around town and on day trips (tel. 089/5490-7560, www.sightseeing-munich.com), and a couple of bike tour companies. You can buy discounted cash-only tickets for Gray Line and Munich Walk tours at EurAide.

"Free" Tours: You'll encounter brochures advertising "free" walking and biking tours. These tours aren't really free—tipping is expected, and the guides actually have to pay the company for each person who takes the tour—so unless you tip more than they owe the company, they don't make a penny. The tours tend to be light on history, and the guides work hard to promote their company's other tours (which are not free).

WITHIN MUNICH
Walking Tours
Munich Walk offers two daytime tours (€2 Rick Steves discount on each tour): a "City Walk" (€12, daily year-round at 10:45, April-Oct also daily at 14:45, 2.25 hours) and "Hitler's Munich" (€15, daily year-round at 10:15, 2.5 hours, extended €24 five-hour version Mon and Sat only). Their "Beer and Brewery" tour is more mature than your typical hard-partying pub crawl. You visit Paulaner, Munich's oldest brewery, to learn, eat, and drink in the city that made beer famous. The price includes two beers in the brewery;

afterward, the tour ends at the Hofbräuhaus (€25, May-mid-Sept daily at 18:15, fewer tours off-season, 3.5 hours). They also offer a Bavarian food-tasting tour, where you visit the Viktualienmarkt for lunch (€24 includes food). All Munich Walk tours depart from in front of the TI on Marienplatz. You don't need to reserve—just show up.

Radius Tours runs two city walking tours, both with reliably good guides: a daily city tour (likely €14—more if tour includes food tasting, €2 Rick Steves discount, daily at 10:00, 2 hours) and "Birthplace of the Third Reich" (€15, €2 Rick Steves discount, April-mid-Oct daily at 15:00; mid-Oct-March Fri-Tue at 11:30; 2.5 hours). They also offer an educational "Bavarian Beer and Food" tour that includes a visit to the Beer and Oktoberfest Museum (see page 52), samples of four varieties of beer, and regional food (€30, €2 Rick Steves discount; April-mid-Oct Mon-Sat 18:00; 3.5 hours; no tours during Oktoberfest except their Oktoberfest tour— see page 52). All tours depart from the Radius office in front of track 32 at the train station. No need to reserve; just show up.

The **Size Matters Beer Tour,** run by Kenyan-German-American Tim Muutuki, stops at the Augustiner Biergarten, Löwenbräu, and Park Café. Depart from Euro Youth Hotel, near the train station, at Senefelderstrasse 5 (€15 if booked online, readers of this book can get online rate in person by asking for the Rick Steves discount, otherwise €20, daily at 18:45, mobile 0157-7574-8886, www.sizemattersbeertour.de).

Local Guides

A guide can be a great value—especially if you assemble a small group. Six people splitting the cost can make the luxury of a private guide affordable. I've had great days with two good guides: **Georg Reichlmayr** (€165/3 hours, tel. 08131/86800, mobile 0170-341-6384, program explained on his website, www.muenchen-stadtfuehrung.de, info@muenchen-stadtfuehrung.de) and **Monika Hank** (€115/2 hours, €135/3 hours, tel. 089/311-4819, mobile 0172-547-8123, monika.hank@web.de). They've both helped me generously with much of the historical information in this chapter.

Bike Tours

Munich lends itself to bike touring, and four outfits fit the bill. You don't need to reserve for any of these—just show up—but do confirm times in advance online or by phone. Prices include bike rental (you'll pick up your bike after meeting your guide).

Munich Walk offers 3.5-hour bike tours around Munich (€20, €2 Rick Steves discount, June-Oct daily at 10:45, April-May Sat-Sun only at 10:45, no tours Nov-March, depart from Marienplatz TI). Confirm times at www.munichwalktours.de.

Radius Tours has similar 3.5-hour bike tours (€24, €2 Rick

Munich at a Glance

In the Center

▲▲**Marienplatz** Munich's main square, at the heart of a lively pedestrian zone, watched over by New Town Hall (and its glockenspiel show). **Hours:** Always open; glockenspiel jousts daily at 11:00 and 12:00, plus 17:00 May-Oct; New Town Hall tower elevator runs May-Oct daily 10:00-19:00; Nov-April Mon-Fri 10:00-17:00, closed Sat-Sun. See page 34.

▲▲**Viktualienmarkt** Munich's "small-town" open-air market, perfect for a quick snack or meal. **Hours:** Beer garden open Mon-Sat until late, closed Sun. See page 40.

▲▲**Hofbräuhaus** World-famous beer hall, worth a visit even if you're not chugging. **Hours:** Daily 9:00-23:30. See page 52.

▲▲**The Residenz** Elegant family palace of the Wittelsbachs, awash in Bavarian opulence. Complex includes the Residenz Museum (private apartments), Residenz Treasury (housing Wittelsbach family crowns and royal knickknacks), and the impressive, heavily restored Cuvilliés Theater. **Hours:** Museum and treasury—daily April-mid-Oct 9:00-18:00, mid-Oct-March 10:00-17:00; theater—April-mid-Sept Mon-Sat 14:00-18:00, Sun 9:00-18:00; mid-Sept-March Mon-Sat 14:00-17:00, Sun 10:00-17:00. See page 58.

▲▲**Alte Pinakothek** Bavaria's best painting gallery, with a wonderful collection of European masters from the 14th through the 19th century. **Hours:** Wed-Sun 10:00-18:00, Tue 10:00-20:00, closed Mon. See page 71.

▲▲**Egyptian Museum** Easy-to-enjoy collection of ancient Egyptian treasures. **Hours:** Tue-Sun 10:00-18:00, Tue until 20:00, closed Mon. See page 76.

▲**Munich City Museum** The city's history in five floors. **Hours:** Tue-Sun 10:00-18:00, closed Mon. See page 68.

▲**Asam Church** Private church of the Asam brothers, dripping with Baroque. **Hours:** Sat-Thu 9:00-18:00, Fri 13:00-18:00. See page 43.

▲**Neue Pinakothek** The Alte's twin sister, with paintings from 1800 to 1920. **Hours:** Thu-Mon 10:00-18:00, Wed 10:00-20:00, closed Tue. See page 75.

▲**Pinakothek der Moderne** Munich's modern art museum with works by Picasso, Dalí, Miró, Magritte, and Ernst. **Hours:** Tue-Sun 10:00-18:00, Thu until 20:00, closed Mon. See page 76.

▲**English Garden** The largest city park on the Continent, packed with locals, tourists, surfers, and nude sunbathers. (On a bike, I'd rate this ▲▲.) **Hours:** Always open. See page 79.

▲**Deutsches Museum** Germany's version of our Smithsonian Institution, with 10 miles of science and technology exhibits. **Hours:** Daily 9:00-17:00. See page 81.

St. **Peter's Church** Munich's oldest church, packed with relics. **Hours:** Church—long hours daily; spire—Mon-Fri 9:00-18:30, Sat-Sun 10:00-18:30, off-season until 17:30. See page 38.

St. **Michael's Church** Renaissance church housing Baroque decor and a crypt of 40 Wittelsbachs. **Hours:** Church—Tue-Thu and Sat 8:00-19:00, Mon and Fri 10:00-19:00, Sun 7:00-22:15, open longer on summer evenings; crypt—Mon-Fri 9:30-16:30, Sat 9:30-14:30, closed Sun. See page 46.

Frauenkirche Huge, distinctive twin-domed church looming over the city center. **Hours:** Sat-Wed 7:00-19:00, Thu 7:00-20:30, Fri 7:00-18:00. See page 47.

Outside the City Center

▲▲**Nymphenburg Palace** The Wittelsbachs' impressive summer palace, featuring a hunting lodge, coach museum, fine royal porcelain collection, and vast park. **Hours:** Park—daily 6:30-dusk, palace buildings—daily April-mid-Oct 9:00-18:00, mid-Oct-March 10:00-16:00. See page 85.

▲▲**BMW-Welt and Museum** The carmaker's futuristic museum and floating-cloud showroom shows you BMW past, present, and future in some unforgettable architecture. **Hours:** BMW-Welt—building 7:30-24:00, exhibits 9:00-18:00; museum—Tue-Sun 10:00-18:00, closed Mon. See page 92.

▲▲**Dachau Concentration Camp** Notorious Nazi camp on the outskirts of Munich, now a powerful museum and memorial. **Hours:** Daily 9:00-17:00. See page 94.

▲**Museum of Transportation** Deutsches Museum's cross-town annex devoted to travel. **Hours:** Daily 9:00-17:00. See page 83.

▲**Andechs Monastery** Baroque church, hearty food, and Bavaria's best brew, in the nearby countryside. **Hours:** Beer garden daily 10:00-20:00, church open until 19:00. See page 100.

Steves discount, April-mid-Oct only, daily at 10:00). Tours leave from the Radius office at track 32 in the train station (confirm times at www.radiustours.com).

Mike's Bike Tours, in their 21st season, packs four hours of "edutainment" on wheels into their "Classic" bike tour (€25, €3 Rick Steves discount, €19 for backpackers who show hostel receipt, 1-hour break in Chinese Tower beer garden, daily March-mid-Nov at 11:30, mid-April-Aug also at 16:30, meet under tower of Old Town Hall at east end of Marienplatz; more tour options in summer, tel. 089/2554-3987, www.mikesbiketours.com).

Lenny's Bike Tours has a 3.5-hour tour that is pitched toward backpackers and is generally led by young Brits (€15 with request for tips at the end, 1-hour break in Chinese Tower beer garden, starts at fish fountain in Marienplatz, daily mid-April-Aug at 11:30 and 16:00, March-mid-April and Sept-mid-Nov at 12:30, www.discovermunichnow.com).

Hop-on, Hop-off Bus Tour

Gray Line Tours has hop-on, hop-off bus tours that leave from in front of the Karstadt department store at Bahnhofplatz, directly across from the train station. Choose from a basic, one-hour "Express Circle" that heads past the Pinakotheks, Marienplatz, and Karlsplatz (3/hour, 9:40-18:00); or the more extensive "Grand Circle" that lasts 2.5 hours and also includes Nymphenburg Palace and BMW-Welt/Museum (1/hour, 9:40-16:00). If you plan on visiting Nymphenburg and the BMW center, this is a very efficient way to see both—just plan your visits to these sights around the tour schedule (bus generally leaves from Nymphenburg  at :30 past the hour, and from BMW at :45 past). This tour is actually well worthwhile—sitting upstairs on the topless double-decker bus, you'll see lots of things missed by the typical visitor wandering around the center. It complements the information in this book, though the live narration (in German and English) is delivered as stiffly as a tape recording. Just show up and pay the driver (€15 Express tour—valid all day, €20 Grand tour—valid 24 hours, daily in season, tel. 089/5490-7560, www.sightseeing-munich.com). You'll get a €1-2 discount by buying your ticket in advance on their website or (cash only) at EurAide.

BEYOND MUNICH

While you can do all these day trips from Munich on your own by train, going as part of an organized group can be convenient—especially to Neuschwanstein.

"Mad" King Ludwig's Castle at Neuschwanstein

Choose between an escorted tour to Neuschwanstein by train and local bus, or guided private bus tours that include extras such as Linderhof Castle. Though they're a little more expensive, I prefer the bus tours—you're guaranteed a seat (public transport to Neuschwanstein is routinely standing-room only in summer), and you get to see more. All these tours can sell out, especially in summer, so it's wise to buy your ticket a day ahead (for information on visiting the castle on your own, see the next chapter).

Gray Line Tours offers rushed all-day bus tours of Neuschwanstein that also include Ludwig's Linderhof Castle and 30 minutes in Oberammergau (€51, €7 Rick Steves discount if you buy your ticket at EurAide—cash only, two castle admissions-€23 extra, daily all year, www.sightseeing-munich.com). Tours meet at 8:10 and depart at 8:30 from the Karstadt department store (across from the station). While tours are designed to be in both English and German, if groups are large they may split them up and you'll get only English. **Munich Walk** advertises a tour that sounds similar—because they're simply selling tickets for this Gray Line trip.

Bus Bavaria (run by Mike's Bike Tours) offers a similar private bus tour for English-speakers with an outdoor theme—a bike ride and short hike near Neuschwanstein are included (€59, €4 Rick Steves discount, Neuschwanstein admission-€12 extra; June-mid-Aug Mon-Tue and Thu-Sat; less frequent May and mid-Aug-Oktoberfest; daily during Oktoberfest; check web for departure times, meet at Mike's Bike Tours office near Hofbräuhaus, Bräuhausstrasse 10—enter around corner on Hochbrückenstrasse, tel. 089/2554-3987, mobile 0172-852-0660, www.mikesbiketours.com).

Radius Tours runs all-day tours to Neuschwanstein Castle using public transportation. Your guide will escort you onto the train to Füssen and then the bus from there to the castle, give you some general information, and help you into the castle for the standard tour that's included with any admission ticket (€39, €32 with rail pass, €2 Rick Steves discount, castle admission-€12 extra; daily April-Dec at 9:30, back by 19:00; Jan-March tours run Mon, Wed, and Fri-Sun at 9:30; smart to reconfirm times, departs from the Radius office near track 32 in the train station, www.radiustours.com).

Dachau Concentration Camp

The camp is easy to see on your own (see page 94). But if you'd prefer a guided visit, Radius and Munich Walk tours are a great value, considering how good and passionate their guides are—and that you're only paying about €10 for the guiding, once you factor in transportation costs. Allow about five hours total. Both companies charge the same price (€22, includes €8 cost of public transportation, €2 Rick Steves discount). It's smart to reserve the day before, especially for the morning tours. Choose between **Radius** (April-mid-Oct daily at 9:15 and 12:15; mid-Oct-March daily at 10:00) and **Munich Walk** (April-Oct daily at 10:15 and 13:15; Nov-March daily at 10:15).

Nürnberg

Just an hour away by fast train, this makes a great day trip from Munich. Do it on your own using this book (see Nürnberg chapter), or take the **Radius Tours** all-day excursion (see their website for details—www.radiustours.com).

Other Day Tours

Radius Tours also offers all-day trips to Salzburg and the castles at Herrenchiemsee (€44 including train fare, April-Dec daily at 9:15; fewer days off-season; details at www.radiustours.com).

Munich City Walk

Munich is big and modern, with a million and a half citizens, but, with its pedestrian-friendly historic core, it feels a lot like an easygoing Bavarian town. On this self-guided walk, rated ▲▲▲, we'll start in the central square, see its famous glockenspiel, stroll through a thriving open-air market, and visit historic churches with lavish Baroque decor. We'll sample chocolates at a venerable deli and take a spin through the world's most famous beer hall. Allow two or three hours for this walk through a thousand years of Munich's history. Allow extra time if you want to take a break from the walk to tour the museums (details on visiting the sights are given later, under "Sights in Munich").

You can also download this walk as a free Rick Steves audio tour; see page 12.

• *Begin your walk at the heart of the old city, with a stroll through...*

❶ Marienplatz

Riding the escalator out of the subway into sunlit Marienplatz (mah-REE-en-platz, "Mary's Square," rated ▲▲) gives you a fine first look at the glory of Munich: great buildings, outdoor cafés, and people bustling and lingering like the birds and breeze with which they share this square.

The square is both old and new: For a thousand years, it's been the center of Munich. It was the town's marketplace and public forum, standing at a crossroads along the Salt Road, which ran between Salzburg and Augsburg.

Lining one entire side of the square is the impressive facade of the **New Town Hall** (Neues Rathaus), with its soaring 280-foot spire. The structure looks medieval, but it was actually built in the late 1800s (1867-1908). The style is "Neo"-Gothic—pointed arches over the doorways and a roofline bristling with prickly spires. The 40 statues look like medieval saints, but they're from around 1900, depicting more recent Bavarian kings and nobles. This medieval-looking style was all the rage in the 19th century as Germans were rediscovering their historical roots and uniting as a modern nation.

The New Town Hall is famous for its **glockenspiel.** A carillon in the tower chimes a tune while colorful little figurines come

out on the balcony to spin and dance. It happens daily at 11:00 and 12:00 all year (also at 17:00 May-Oct). The *Spiel* of the glockenspiel tells the story of a noble wedding that actually took place on the market square in 1568. You see the wedding procession and the friendly joust of knights on horseback. The duke and his bride watch the action as the groom's Bavarian family (in Bavarian white and blue) joyfully jousts with the bride's French family (in red and white). Below, the barrel-makers—famous for being the first to dance in the streets after a deadly plague lifted—do their popular jig. Finally, the solitary cock crows.

At the very top of the New Town Hall is a statue of a child with outstretched arms, dressed in monk's garb and holding a book in its left hand. This is the **Münchner Kindl,** the symbol of Munich. The town got its name from the people who first settled here: the monks *(Mönchen)*. You'll spot this mini-monk all over town, on everything from the city's coat of arms to souvenir shot glasses to ad campaigns (often holding not a book, but maybe a beer or a smartphone). The city symbol was originally depicted as a grown man, wearing a gold-lined black cloak and red shoes. By the 19th century, artists were representing him as a young boy, then a gender-neutral child, and, more recently, a young girl. These days, a teenage girl dressed as the *Kindl* kicks off the annual Oktoberfest by leading the opening parade on horseback, and then serves as the mascot throughout the festivities.

For great **views** of the city, you can ride an elevator to the top

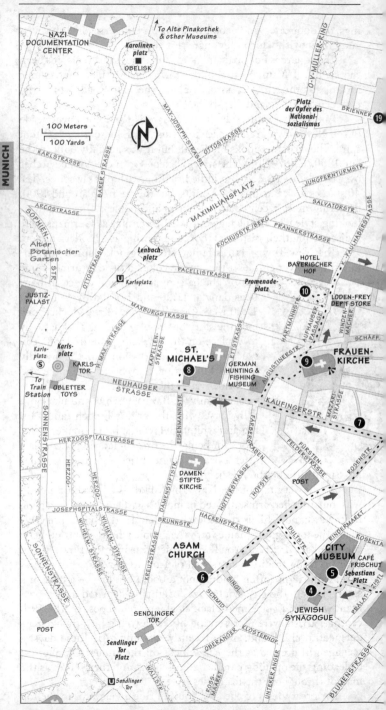

MUNICH

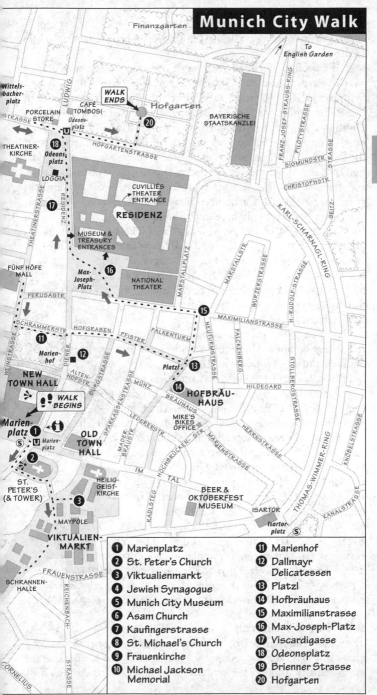

Munich City Walk

1. Marienplatz
2. St. Peter's Church
3. Viktualienmarkt
4. Jewish Synagogue
5. Munich City Museum
6. Asam Church
7. Kaufingerstrasse
8. St. Michael's Church
9. Frauenkirche
10. Michael Jackson Memorial
11. Marienhof
12. Dallmayr Delicatessen
13. Platzl
14. Hofbräuhaus
15. Maximilianstrasse
16. Max-Joseph-Platz
17. Viscardigasse
18. Odeonsplatz
19. Brienner Strasse
20. Hofgarten

of the New Town Hall tower (€2.50, elevator located under glock-enspiel; May-Oct daily 10:00-19:00; Nov-April Mon-Fri 10:00-17:00, closed Sat-Sun).

The **golden statue** at the top of the column in the center of Marienplatz honors the square's namesake, the Virgin Mary. Sculpted in 1590, it was a rallying point in the religious wars of the Reformation. Back then, Munich was a bastion of southern-German Catholicism against the heresies of Martin Luther to the north. Notice how, at the four corners of the statue, cherubs fight the four great biblical enemies of civilization: the dragon of war, the lion of hunger, the rooster-headed monster of plague and disease, and the serpent. The serpent represents heresy—namely, Protestants. Bavaria is still Catholic country, and Protestants weren't allowed to worship openly here until about 1800.

To the right of the New Town Hall, the gray pointy build-ing with the green spires is the **Old Town Hall** (Altes Rathaus). On its adjoining bell tower, find the city seal. It has the Münchner Kindl (symbolizing the first monks), a castle (representing the first fortifications), and a lion (representing the first ruler—Henry the Lion, who built them).

As you look around, keep in mind that the Allies bombed Marienplatz and much of Munich during World War II. Most of the buildings had to be rebuilt; the question was whether to do so in a way that matched their original design or in a modern style. The Old Town Hall looks newer now because it was completely destroyed by bombs and had to be rebuilt after the war. The New Town Hall survived the bombs, and it served as the US military headquarters after the Americans occupied Munich in 1945.

Before moving on, face the New Town Hall one more time and get oriented. Straight ahead is north. To the left is the pedes-trian shopping street called Kaufingerstrasse, which leads to the old gate called Karlstor, and the train station. To the right, the street leads to the Isartor gate and the Deutsches Museum. This east-west axis cuts through the historic core of Munich.

• *Turn around to the right to find Rindermarkt, the street leading from the southeast corner of Marienplatz. Head to St. Peter's Church, just beyond the square, with its steeple poking up above a row of buildings.*

❷ St. Peter's Church

The oldest church in town, St. Peter's stands on the hill where Mu-nich's original monks probably settled—perhaps as far back as the ninth century (though the city marks its official birthday as 1158).

Today's church (from 1368) replaced the original monastery church.

St. Peter's ("Old Peter" to locals) is part of the soul of the city. There's even a popular song about it that goes, "Munich is not Munich without St. Peter's."

Cost and Hours: Church entry free, tower-€2, Mon-Fri 9:00-18:30, Sat-Sun 10:00-18:30, off-season until 17:30, last exit 30 minutes after closing.

Visiting the Church: On the outside of the church, notice the 16th- and 17th-century tombstones plastered onto the wall. Originally, people were buried in the holy ground around the church. But in the Napoleonic age, the cemeteries were dug up and relocated outside the city walls for hygienic and space reasons. They kept a few tombstones here as a reminder.

Step inside. (If there's a Mass in progress, visitors are welcome, but stay in the back. If there's no Mass, feel free to explore.) Typical of so many Bavarian churches, it's whitewashed and light-filled, with highlights in pastel pinks and blues framed by gold curlicue. The ceiling painting opens up to the heavens, where Peter is crucified upside down.

Some photos (on a pillar near the entrance) show how St. Peter's was badly damaged in World War II—the roof caved in, and the altar was damaged. But the beloved church was rebuilt and restored, thanks to donations—half from the Augustiner brewery, the rest from private donors. (The accuracy of the restoration was possible thanks to Nazi catalog photos—see "The History of Munich: Part 2," on page 48.) For decades after World War II, the bells played a popular tune that stopped before the last note, reminding locals that the church still needed money to rebuild.

Explore further. The nave is lined with bronze statues of the apostles, and the altar shows a statue of St. Peter being adored by four Church fathers. The finely crafted, gray iron fences that line the nave were donated after World War II by the local blacksmiths of the national railway. The precious and fragile sandstone Gothic chapel altar (to the left of the main altar) survived the war only because it was buried in sandbags.

Find the second chapel on the left side. Now there's something you don't see every day: a skeleton in a box. As the red Latin inscription says, this is St. Munditia. In the fourth century, she was beheaded by the Romans for her Christian faith. Munich has more relics of saints than any city outside of Rome. That's because it was the Pope's Catholic bastion against the rising tide of Protestantism in northern Europe during the Reformation. In 1675, St. Munditia's remains were given to Munich by the Pope as thanks for the city's devoted service. It was also a vivid reminder to the faithful that those who die for the cause of the Roman Church go directly to heaven without waiting for Judgment Day.

It's a long climb to the top of the **spire** (306 steps, no elevator)—much of it with two-way traffic on a one-lane staircase—but the view is dynamite. Try to be two flights from the top when the bells ring at the top of the hour. Then, when your friends back home ask you about your trip, you'll say, "What?"

• *Just behind and beyond (downhill from) St. Peter's, join the busy commotion of the...*

❸ Viktualienmarkt

The market (rated ▲▲, closed Sun) is a lively world of produce stands and budget eateries. Browse your way through the stalls and pavilions, as you make your way to the market's main landmark, the blue-and-white striped maypole. Early in the morning, you can still feel small-town Munich here. Remember, Munich has been a market town since its earliest days as a stop on the salt-trade crossroads. By the 1400s, the

market bustled, most likely beneath a traditional maypole, just like you see today.

Besides salt, Munich gained a reputation for beer. By the 15th century, more than 30 breweries pumped out the golden liquid, brewed by monks, who were licensed to sell it. They stored their beer in cellars under courtyards kept cool by the shade of bushy chestnut trees—a tradition Munich's breweries still stick to.

The market's centerpiece seems to be its **beer garden.** Its picnic tables are filled with hungry and thirsty locals, all in the shade of the traditional chestnut trees. Shoppers pause here for a late-morning snack of *Weisswurst*—white sausage—served with mustard, a pretzel, and a beer. Here, you can order just half a liter—unlike at other *Biergartens* that only sell by the full liter. This is handy for shoppers who want just a quick sip. As is the tradition at all of the city's beer gardens, a few tables—those without tablecloths—are set aside for patrons who bring their own food; they're welcome here as long as they buy a drink. The Viktualienmarkt is ideal for a light meal (see page 121).

Now make your way to the towering **maypole.** Throughout Bavaria, colorfully ornamented maypoles decorate town squares. Many are painted, like this one, in Bavaria's colors, white and blue. The decorations are festively replaced every year on the first of May.

Traditionally, rival communities try to steal each other's maypole. Locals guard their new pole day and night as May Day approaches. Stolen poles are ransomed only with lots of beer for the clever thieves.

The decorations that line each side of the pole explain which merchants are doing business in the market. Munich's maypole gives prominence (on the bottom level) to a horse-drawn wagon bringing in beer barrels. And you can't have a kegger without coopers—find the merry barrel-makers, the four cute guys dancing. Today, traditional barrel making is enjoying a comeback as top breweries like to have real wooden kegs.

The bottom of the pole celebrates the world's oldest food law. The German Beer Purity Law *(Reinheitsgebot)* of 1516 actually originated here in Bavaria. It stipulated that beer could only consist of three ingredients: barley, hops, and water, with no additives. (Later they realized that a fourth ingredient, yeast, is always present in fermentation.) Why was beer so treasured? Back in the Middle Ages, it was considered liquid food.

From the maypole, take in the bustling scene around you. The market was modernized in the 1800s as the city grew. Old buildings were torn down, replaced with stalls and modern market halls. Now, in the 21st century, it's a wonder such a traditional place survives—especially because it sits on the most expensive real estate in town. But locals love their market, so the city protects these old-time shops, charging them only a small percentage of their gross income, enabling them to carry on. The city also bans most fast-food chains. This keeps the market classy and authentic. Münchners consider the produce here to be top quality, if on the expensive side.

• *At the bottom end of the Viktualienmarkt, spot* **Café Frischhut,** *with its colorful old-time sign hanging out front (at Prälat-Zistl-Strasse 8). This is Munich's favorite place to stop for a fresh* Schmalznudel—*pop in to pick up one of these traditional fried-dough treats (best enjoyed warm with a sprinkling of sugar).*

Across the street, you'll pass the Pschorr beer hall. Continue just past it to a modern glass-and-iron building, the **Schrannenhalle.** *Go inside. This 1800s grain exchange has been recently renovated into a high-end mall of deli shops. Stroll through, making your way to the far end, where chocoholics could detour downstairs into* **Milka Coco World** *for tasty samples (and a good WC).*

When you're ready to move on, exit the Schrannenhalle midway down on the right-hand side. You'll spill out into Sebastiansplatz, a small square lined with healthy eateries (see page 122). Continue through Sebastiansplatz and veer left, where you'll see a cube-shaped building, the...

❹ Jewish Synagogue

This modern synagogue anchors a revitalized Jewish quarter. In the 1930s, about 10,000 Jews lived in Munich, and the main syna-

gogue stood near here. Then, in 1938, Hitler demanded that the synagogue be torn down. By the end of World War II, Munich's Jewish community was gone. But thanks to Germany's acceptance of religious refugees from former Soviet states, the Jewish population has now reached its pre-war size. The new synagogue was built in 2006. There's also a kindergarten and day school, children's playground, fine kosher restaurant (at #18), and bookstore. Standing in the middle of the square, notice the low-key but efficient security.

While the synagogue is shut tight to non-worshippers, its architecture is striking from the outside. Lower stones of travertine evoke the Wailing Wall in Jerusalem, while an upper section represents the tent that held important religious wares during the 40 years of wandering through the desert. The synagogue's door features the first 10 letters of the Hebrew alphabet, symbolizing the Ten Commandments.

The cube-shaped **Jewish History Museum** (behind the cube-shaped synagogue) is stark, windowless, and as inviting as a bomb shelter. While the museum's small permanent collection is disappointing, good temporary exhibits might justify the entry fee (€6, €3 with Munich City Museum ticket, Tue-Sun 10:00-18:00, closed Mon, St.-Jakobs-Platz 16, tel. 089/2339-6096, www.juedisches-museum-muenchen.de).

• *Facing the synagogue, on the same square, is the...*

❺ Munich City Museum (Münchner Stadtmuseum)

The highs and lows of Munich's history are covered in this surprisingly honest municipal museum (rated ▲). It covers the cultural upheavals of the early 1900s, Munich's role as the birthplace of the Nazis, and the city's renaissance during Germany's postwar "economic miracle." There's scant information posted in English, but an included audioguide can fill in the gaps. For more information, see the museum listing on page 68.

• *Continue through the synagogue's square, past the fountain, across the street, and one block further to the pedestrianized Sendlinger Strasse. Down the street 100 yards to the left, the fancy facade (at #62) marks the...*

❻ Asam Church (Asamkirche)

This tiny church (rated ▲) is a slice of heaven on earth—a gooey, drippy Baroque-concentrate masterpiece by Bavaria's top two Rococonuts—the Asam brothers. Just 30 feet wide, it was built in 1740 to fit within this row of homes. Originally, it was a private chapel where these two brother-architects could show off their work (on their own land, next to their home and business headquarters—to the left), but it's now a public place of worship.

MUNICH

Cost and Hours: Free, Sat-Thu 9:00-18:00, Fri 13:00-18:00, tel. 089/2368-7989. The church is small, so visitors are asked not to enter during Mass (held Tue and Thu-Fri 17:00-18:00, Wed 8:30-9:30, and Sun 10:00-11:00).

Visiting the Church: This place of worship served as a promotional brochure to woo clients, and is packed with every architectural trick in the books. Imagine approaching the church not as a worshipper, but as a shopper representing your church's building committee. First stand outside: Hmmm, the look of those foundation stones really packs a punch. And the legs hanging over the portico...nice effect. Those starbursts on the door would be a hit back home, too.

Then step inside: I'll take a set of those over-the-top golden capitals, please. We'd also like to order the gilded garlands draping the church in jubilation, and the twin cupids capping the confessional. And how about some fancy stucco work, too? (Molded-and-painted plaster was clearly an Asam brothers specialty.) Check out the illusion of a dome on the flat ceiling—that'll save us lots of money. The yellow glass above the altar has the effect of the thin-sliced alabaster at St. Peter's in Rome, but it's within our budget! And, tapping the "marble" pilasters to determine that they are just painted fakes, we decide to take that, too. Crammed between two buildings, light inside this narrow church is limited, so there's a big, clear window in the back for maximum illumination—we'll order one to cut back on our electricity bill.

Visiting the Asam Church, you can see why the Asam brothers were so prolific and successful. Speaking of the brothers, there are black-and-white portraits of the two Asams in oval frames flanking the altar. On the way out, say good-bye to the gilded grim reaper in the narthex (left side as we're leaving) as he cuts the thread of life—reminding all who visit of our mortality...and, by the way, that shrouds have no pockets.

• *Leaving the church, look to your right, noticing the Sendlinger Tor at*

The History of Munich: Part 1
Monastic Beginnings to the Age of Kings

Born from Salt (1100-1500)

Munich began in the 12th century, when Henry the Lion (Heinrich der Löwe) muscled in on the lucrative salt trade, burning a rival's bridge over the Isar River and building his own near a monastery of "monks"—München. (The town's coat of arms features the Münchner Kindl, a child in monk's robes; see page 35.) Henry built walls and towers and opened a market, and peasants flocked in from the countryside. Marienplatz was the center of town and the crossroads of the Salzstrasse (Salt Road) from Salzburg to Augsburg. After Henry's death, the town was taken over by an ambitious merchant family, the Wittelsbachs (1240), and became the capital of the region (1255). Munich-born Louis IV (1282-1347) was elected king of Germany and Holy Roman Emperor, temporarily making Munich a major European capital.

By the 1400s, Munich's maypole-studded market bustled with trade. Besides salt, Munich gained a reputation for beer. More than 30 breweries pumped out the golden liquid that lubricated both trade and traders. The Bavarian Beer Purity Law assured quality control. Wealthy townspeople erected the twin-domed Frauenkirche and the Altes Rathaus on Marienplatz, and the Wittelsbachs built a stout castle that would eventually become the cushy Residenz. When the various regions of Bavaria united in 1506, Munich (pop. 14,000) was the natural capital.

Religious Wars, Plagues, Decline (1500-1800)

While Martin Luther and the Protestant Reformation raged in northern Germany, Munich became the ultra-Catholic heart of the Counter-Reformation. The devout citizens poured enormous funds into building the massive St. Michael's Church (1583) as a home for the Jesuits, and into the Residenz (early 1600s) as home of the Wittelsbachs. Both were showpieces of conservative power and the Baroque and Rococo styles.

During the Thirty Years' War, the Catholic city was surrounded by Protestants (1632). The Wittelsbachs surrendered quickly and paid a ransom, sparing the city from pillage, but it was soon hit by the bubonic plague. After that passed, the leaders erected the Virgin's column on Marienplatz to thank God for killing only 7,000 citizens. (Munich's many plagues are also remembered today when the glockenspiel's barrel-makers do their daily dance to ward off the plague.)

The double whammy of invasion and disease left Munich bankrupt and weak, overshadowed by the more powerful Habsburgs of Austria. The Wittelsbachs took their cultural cues from France (Nymphenburg Palace is a mini-Versailles), England (the English Garden), and Italy (the Pitti Palace-inspired Residenz). While the rest of Europe modernized and headed toward democracy, Munich remained conservative and behind the times. The Wittelsbachs gained one new bargaining chip; from 1624 until 1806, one of the seven electors of the Holy Roman Emperor was always a Wittelsbach.

The Kings (1806-1918): Max I, Ludwig I, Max II, Ludwig II, Ludwig III

When Napoleon's army surrounded the city (1800), the Wittelsbachs again surrendered hospitably. Napoleon rewarded the Wittelsbach "duke" with more territory and a royal title: "king." **Maximilian I** (r. 1806-1825; see page 55), a.k.a. Max Joseph, now ruled the Kingdom of Bavaria, a nation bigger than Switzerland, with a constitution and parliament. When Max's popular son Ludwig married (September 1810), it touched off a two-week celebration that became an annual event: Oktoberfest.

As king, **Ludwig I** (r. 1825-1848) set about rebuilding the capital in the Neoclassical style we see today. Medieval walls and ramshackle houses were replaced with grand buildings of columns and arches (including the Residenz and Alte Pinakothek). Connecting these were broad boulevards and plazas for horse carriages and promenading citizens (Ludwigstrasse and Königsplatz). Ludwig established the university and built the first railway line, turning Munich (pop. 90,000) into a major transportation hub, budding industrial city, and fitting capital.

In 1846, the skirt-chasing Ludwig was beguiled by a notorious Irish dancer named Lola Montez. She became his mistress, and he fawned over her in public, scandalizing Munich. The Münchners resented her spending their tax money and dominating their king (supposedly inspiring the phrase "Whatever Lola wants, Lola gets"). In 1848, as Europe was swept by a tide of revolution, the citizens rose up and forced Ludwig to abdicate. His son **Maximilian II** (r. 1848-1864) continued Ludwig's enlightened program of modernizing, while studiously avoiding dancers from Ireland.

In 1864, 18-year-old **Ludwig II** (r. 1864-1886) became king. He invited the composer Richard Wagner to Munich, planning a lavish new opera house to stage Wagner's operas. Munich didn't like the idea, and Ludwig didn't like Munich. For most of his reign, Ludwig avoided the Residenz and Nymphenburg, instead building castles in the Bavarian countryside at the expense of Munich taxpayers. (For more on the king, see page 149.)

In 1871, Bavaria became part of the newly united Germany, and overnight, Berlin overtook Munich as Germany's power center. Turn-of-the-century Munich was culturally rich, giving birth to the abstract art of Wassily Kandinsky, Paul Klee, and the Blue Rider group. But this artistic flourishing didn't last long. World War I devastated Munich. Poor, hungry, disillusioned, unemployed Münchners roamed the streets. Extremists from the left and right battled for power. In 1918, a huge mob marched to the gates of the Residenz and drove the forgettable Ludwig III (r. 1913-1918)— the last Bavarian king—out of the city, ending nearly 700 years of continuous Wittelsbach rule.

For "The History of Munich: Part 2," see page 48.

the end of the street—part of the fortified town wall that circled Munich in the 14th century. Then turn left and walk straight up Sendlinger Strasse. Walk toward the Münchner Kindl, still capping the spire of the New Town Hall in the distance, and then up (pedestrian-only) Rosenstrasse, until you hit Marienplatz and the big, busy...

❼ Kaufingerstrasse

This car-free street leads you through a great shopping district, past cheap department stores, carnivals of street entertainers, and good old-fashioned slicers and dicers. As far back as the 12th century, this was the town's main commercial street. Traders from Salzburg and Augsburg would enter the town through the fortified Karlstor. This street led past the Augustiner beer hall (opposite St. Michael's Church to this day), right to the main square and cathedral.

Up until the 1970s, the street was jammed with car traffic. Then, for the 1972 Olympics, it was turned into one of Europe's first pedestrian zones. At first, shopkeepers were afraid that would ruin business. Now it's Munich's living room. Nearly 9,000 shoppers pass through it each hour. Merchants nearby are begging for their streets to become traffic-free, too. Imagine this street in Hometown, USA.

The 1972 Olympics transformed this part of Munich—the whole area around Marienplatz was pedestrianized and the transit system expanded. Since then, Munich has become one of the globe's greenest cities. Skyscrapers have been banished to the suburbs, and the nearby Frauenkirche is still the tallest building in the center.

• *Stroll a few blocks away from Marienplatz toward the Karlstor, until you arrive at the big church on the right.*

❽ St. Michael's Church

This is one of the first great Renaissance buildings north of the Alps. The ornate facade, with its sloped roofline, was inspired by the Gesù Church in Rome—home of the Jesuit order. Jesuits saw themselves as the intellectual defenders of Catholicism. St. Michael's was built in the late 1500s—at the height of the Protestant Reformation—to serve as the northern outpost of the Jesuits.  Appropriately, the facade features a statue of Michael fighting a Protestant demon.

Cost and Hours: Church entry free, open Tue-Thu and Sat 8:00-19:00, Mon and Fri 10:00-19:00, Sun 7:00-22:15, open longer on summer evenings; crypt-€2, Mon-Fri 9:30-16:30, Sat 9:30-

14:30, closed Sun; frequent concerts—check the schedule outside; tel. 089/231-7060, www.st-michael-muenchen.de.

Visiting the Church: Inside, admire the ornate Baroque interior, topped with a barrel vault, the largest of its day. Stroll up the nave to the ornate pulpit, where Jesuit priests would hammer away at Reformation heresy. The church's acoustics are spectacular, and the choir—famous in Munich—sounds heavenly singing from the organ loft high in the rear.

The **crypt** (*Fürstengruft*, down the stairs by the altar) contains 40 stark, somewhat forlorn tombs of Bavaria's ruling family, the Wittelsbachs. There's the tomb of Wilhelm V, who built this church, and Maximilian I, who saved Munich from Swedish invaders during the Thirty Years' War. Finally, there's Otto, who went insane and was deposed in 1916, virtually bringing the Wittelsbachs' seven-century reign to an end.

The most ornate tomb holds the illustrious Ludwig II, known for his fairy-tale castle at Neuschwanstein. Ludwig didn't care much for Munich. He escaped to the Bavarian countryside where he spent his days building castles, listening to music, and dreaming about knights of old. His excesses earned him the nickname "Mad" King Ludwig. But of all the Wittelsbachs, it's his tomb that's decorated with flowers—placed here by romantics still mad about their "mad" king.

• *Our next stop, the Frauenkirche, is a couple hundred yards away. Backtrack a couple blocks up Kaufingerstrasse to the wild boar statue, which marks the* **German Hunting and Fishing Museum.** *This place has outdoorsy regalia, kid-friendly exhibits, and the infamous* Wolpertinger—*a German "jackalope" created by very creative local taxidermists. At the boar statue, turn left on Augustinerstrasse, which leads to Munich's towering, twin-domed cathedral, the...*

❾ Frauenkirche

These twin onion domes are the symbol of the city. They're unusual in that most Gothic churches have either pointed steeples or square towers. Some say Crusaders, inspired by the Dome of the Rock in Jerusalem, brought home the idea. Or it may be that, due to money problems, the towers weren't completed until Renaissance times, when domes were popular. Whatever the reason, the Frauenkirche's domes may be the inspiration for the characteristic domed church spires that mark villages all over Bavaria.

The History of Munich: Part 2
Troubled 20th Century and Today's Revitalization

This picks up where "Part 1" leaves off (see page 44).

Nazis, World War II, and Munich Bombed (1918-1945)

Germany after World War I was in chaos. In quick succession, the prime minister was gunned down, Communists took power, and the army restored the old government. In the hubbub, one fringe group emerged—the Nazi party, headed by the charismatic war veteran Adolf Hitler.

Hitler—an Austrian who'd settled in Munich—made stirring speeches in Munich's beer halls (including the Hofbräuhaus) and galvanized the city's disaffected. On November 8-9, 1923, the Nazis launched a coup d'état known as the Beer Hall Putsch. They kidnapped the mayor, and Hitler led a mob to overthrow the German government in Berlin. The march got as far as Odeonsplatz before Hitler was arrested and sent to prison in nearby Landsberg. Though the Nazis eventually gained power in Berlin, they remembered their roots, dubbing Munich "Capital of the Movement." The Nazi headquarters stood near today's obelisk on Brienner Strasse, Dachau was chosen as the regime's first concentration camp, and Odeonsplatz was designated as a place where all who passed by were required to perform the Nazi salute.

As World War II drew to a close, it was clear that Munich would be destroyed. Hitler did not allow the evacuation of much of the town's portable art treasures and heritage—a mass emptying of churches and civil buildings would have caused hysteria and been a statement of no confidence in his leadership. While museums were closed (and could be systematically emptied over the war years), public buildings were not. Rather than save the treasures, the Nazis photographed everything.

Munich was indeed pummeled mercilessly by air raids, leveling nearly half the city. What the bombs didn't get was destroyed by 10 years of rain and freezing winters.

Cost and Hours: Free, Sat-Wed 7:00-19:00, Thu 7:00-20:30, Fri 7:00-18:00, tel. 089/290-0820, www.muenchner-dom.de.

Restorations: The church towers are currently closed for maintenance and it's likely they won't be open for climbing in 2015.

Visiting the Church: The church was built in just 22 years, from 1466 to 1488. Note that it's made of brick, not quarried stone—easy to make locally, and cheaper and faster to build with than stone. Construction was partly funded with the sale of indul-

Munich Rebuilds (1945-Present)

After the war, with generous American aid, Münchners set to reconstructing their city. During this time, many German cities established commissions to debate their rebuilding strategy: They could restore the old towns, or bulldoze and go modern. While Frankfurt decided to start from scratch (hence its Manhattan-like feel today), Munich voted—by a close margin—to rebuild its old town.

Münchners took care to preserve the original street plan and re-create the medieval steeples, Neo-Gothic facades, and Neoclassical buildings. They blocked off the city center to cars, built the people-friendly U-Bahn system, and opened up Europe's first pedestrian-only zone (Kaufingerstrasse and Neuhauser Strasse). Only now, 70 years after the last bombs fell, are the restorations—based on those Nazi photographs—finally being wrapped up. And those postwar decisions still shape the city: Buildings cannot exceed the height of the church spires.

The 1972 Olympic Games, featuring a futuristic stadium, a sleek new subway system, and radical-at-the-time pedestrian zones, were to be Munich's postwar statement that it had arrived. However, the Games turned tragic when a Palestinian terrorist group stormed a dormitory and kidnapped (and eventually killed) 11 Israeli athletes. In 1989, when Germany reunited, Berlin once again became the focal point of the country, relegating Munich to the role of sleepy Second-City.

These days, Munich seems to be comfortable just being itself rather than trying to keep up with Berlin. Today's Munich is rich—home to BMW and Siemens, and a producer of software, books, movies, and the latest fashions. It's consistently voted one of Germany's most livable cities—safe, clean, cultured, a university town, built on a human scale, and close to the beauties of nature. Though it's the capital of Bavaria and a major metropolis, Munich's low-key atmosphere has led Germans to dub it *Millionendorf*—the "village of a million people."

gences. It's dedicated to the Virgin—Our Lady *(Frau)*—and has been the city's cathedral since 1821.

Step inside. Just inside the entrance, on the right, are photos showing how much of the church was destroyed during World War II. The towers survived, and the rest was rebuilt essentially from scratch.

Near the entrance is a big, black, ornate, tomb-like monument honoring Ludwig IV the Bavarian (1282-1347), who was elected Holy Roman Emperor—a big deal. The Frauenkirche was built a century later with the express purpose of honoring his memory. His monument was originally situated in front at the high altar, right near Christ. Those Wittelsbachs—always trying to be associated with God. This alliance was instilled in people through the prayers they were forced to recite: "Virgin Mary, mother of our duke, please protect us."

Nearby, a plaque (over the back pew on the left) honors one of Munich's more recent citizens. Joseph Ratzinger was born in Bavaria in 1927, became archbishop of the Frauenkirche (1977-1982), then moved to the Vatican where he later served as Pope Benedict XVI (2005-2013).

Now walk slowly up the main aisle, enjoying stained glass right and left. This glass is obviously modern, having replaced the original glass that was shattered in World War II. Ahead is the high altar, under a huge hanging crucifix. Find the throne—the ceremonial seat of the local bishop. From here, look up to the tops of the columns, and notice the tiny painted portraits. They're the craftsmen from five centuries ago who helped build the church.

Now walk behind the altar to the apse, where there are three tall windows. These still have their original 15th-century glass. To survive the bombs of 1944, each pane had to be lovingly removed and stored safely away.

• *Our next stop is at Promenadeplatz, about 400 yards north of here. Leaving the church, turn right and walk 50 yards, where you'll see a tiny but well-signed passageway called the Aufhauser Passage. Follow it through a modern building, where you emerge at a park called Promenadeplatz. Detour a few steps left into the park, where you'll find a colorful modern memorial.*

⑩ Michael Jackson Memorial

When Michael Jackson was in town, like many VIPs, he'd stay at the Hotel Bayerischer Hof. Fans would gather in the park waiting for him to appear at his window. He'd sometimes oblige (but his infamous baby-dangling incident happened in Berlin, not here). When he died in 2009, devotees created this memorial by taking over a statue of Renaissance composer Orlando di Lasso. They still visit daily, leave a memento, and keep it tidy.

• *Now backtrack and turn left, up Kardinal-Faulhaber-Strasse. The street is lined with former 18th-century mansions that have since become offices and bank buildings. At #11, turn right and enter a modern shopping mall called the* **Fünf Höfe Passage**. *The place tries* *to take your basic shopping mall and give it more class. It's divided into five connecting courtyards (the "fünf Höfe"), spruced up with bubbling fountains, exotic plants, and a hanging garden.*

Emerging on a busy pedestrian street, turn right, and head down the street (noticing the Münchner Kindl again high above), to a big green square: Marienhof.

⓫ Marienhof

This square, tucked behind the New Town Hall, was left as a green island after the 1945 bombings. If you find that the square's all dug up, it's because Munich has finally started building an additional subway tunnel here. With virtually the entire underground system converging on nearby Marienplatz, this new tunnel will provide a huge relief to the city's congested subterranean infrastructure.

MUNICH

On the far side of Marienhof is the most aristocratic grocery store in all of Germany: ⓬ **Dallmayr Delicatessen.** When the king called out for dinner, he called Alois Dallmayr. This place became famous for its exotic and luxurious food items: tropical fruits, seafood, chocolates, fine wines, and coffee (there are meat and cheese counters, too). As you enter, read the black plaque with the royal seal by the door: *Königlich Bayerischer Hof-Lief-erant* ("Deliverer for the King of Bavaria and his Court"). Catering to royal and aristocratic tastes (and budgets), it's still the choice of Munich's old rich. Today,

it's most famous for its sweets, chocolates, and coffee—dispensed from fine hand-painted Nymphenburg porcelain jugs (Mon-Sat 9:30-19:00, closed Sun; Dienerstrasse 13-15, www.dallmayr.com).

• *Leaving Dallmayr, turn right and right again, heading down Hofgra-ben (which becomes Pfisterstrasse). Go three blocks, going gently downhill to Platzl—"small square." (If you get turned around, just ask any local to point you toward the Hofbräuhaus.)*

⓭ Platzl

As you stand here—admiring classic facades in the heart of medieval Munich—recall that everything around you was flattened in World War II. Here on Platzl, the reconstruction happened in stages: From 1945 to 1950, they removed 12 million tons of bricks and replaced roofs to make buildings weather-tight. From 1950 to 1972, they redid the exteriors. From 1972 to 2000, they refurbished the interiors. Today, the rebuilt Platzl sports new—but old-looking—facades.

Officials estimate that hundreds of unexploded bombs still

Oktoberfest

The 1810 marriage reception of King Ludwig I was such a success that it turned into an annual bash. These days, the Oktoberfest lasts just over two weeks (Sept 19-Oct 4 in 2015), starting on the third Saturday in September and usually ending on the first Sunday in October (www.oktoberfest.de).

Oktoberfest is held at the Theresienwiese fairground south of the main train station, in a meadow known as the "Wies'n" (VEE-zen). They set up eight huge tents that can each seat several thousand beer drinkers. The festivities kick off with an opening parade of more than 6,000 participants. Then, for the next two weeks, it's a frenzy of drinking, dancing, music, and food. There's a huge Ferris wheel, and the triple-loop roller coaster must be the wildest on earth (best before the beer-drinking). Total strangers stroll arm-in-arm down rows of picnic tables, while beer maids pull mustard packs from their cleavage. It's a carnival of beer, pretzels, and wurst, drawing visitors from all over the globe. A million gallons of beer later, they roast the last ox.

If you'll be here during the festivities, it's best to reserve a room early, but if you arrive in the morning (except Fri or Sat) and haven't called ahead, the TI can usually help. During the fair, the city functions even better than normal, but is admittedly more expensive and crowded. It's a good time to sightsee, even if beer-hall rowdiness isn't your cup of tea.

lie buried under Munich. As recently as 2012, they found a 550-pound bomb in Schwabing, a neighborhood just north of the old city center. They had to evacuate the neighborhood and detonate the bomb, which created a huge fireball—a stark reminder of Munich's scary past.

Today's Platzl hosts a lively mix of places to eat and drink—pop-culture chains like Starbucks and Hard Rock Café alongside top-end restaurants like the recommended Wirtshaus Ayinger and Schuhbecks (Schuhbecks Eis is a favorite for ice cream; Pfisterstrasse 9-11).

• *At the bottom of the square (#9), you can experience the venerable...*

⓮ Hofbräuhaus

The world's most famous beer hall (rated ▲▲) is a trip. Whether or not you slide your lederhosen on its polished benches, it's a great

Even though the beer tents are enormous, they're often full, especially on weekends—if possible, avoid going on a Friday or Saturday night. If you find yourself inside a tent with nowhere to sit, be bold—find an underused table and ask some potential new friends to scoot (or at least keep your elbows sharp). Even when it's really crowded, you can eventually get a seat with some patience: Stand near a table for a while, and grab it as soon as the group leaves. For some cultural background with your Wies'n visit, consider hiring a local guide (see page 29) or going with a group (Radius Tours, for example, offers a €105 tour that includes two beers, half a chicken, and guaranteed seating, Sun-Fri at 10:00, no tours on Sat, reserve ahead, www.radiustours.com; Size Matters Beer Tour runs one for €95, includes breakfast, lunch, four beers, and reserved seating, www.sizemattersbeer-tour.de).

If you're not visiting while the party's on, don't worry: You can still dance to oompah bands, munch huge pretzels, and show off your stein-hoisting skills any time of year at Munich's classic beer halls, including the venerable Hofbräuhaus (for descriptions of my favorite beer halls, see page 113).

In the city center, check out the humble **Beer and Oktoberfest Museum** (Bier- und Oktoberfestmuseum), which offers a low-tech and underwhelming take on history. Exhibits and artifacts outline the centuries-old quest for the perfect beer (apparently achieved in Munich) and the origins of the city's Oktoberfest celebration. The oldest house in the city center, the museum's home is noteworthy in itself (€4, Tue-Sat 13:00-18:00, closed Sun-Mon, between the Isartor and Viktualienmarkt at Sterneckerstrasse 2, tel. 089/2423-1607, www.bier-und-oktoberfestmuseum.de).

experience just to walk through the place in all its rowdy glory (with its own gift shop).

Cost and Hours: Free to enter, daily 9:00-23:30, live oompah music during lunch and dinner; a 5-minute walk northeast of Marienplatz at Platzl 9, tel. 089/290-136-100, for details on eating at the Hofbräuhaus, see page 113, www.hofbraeuhaus.de.

Visiting the Hofbräuhaus: Before going in, check out the huge arches at the entrance and the crown logo. The original brewery was built here in 1583. As the crown suggests, it was the Wittelsbachs' personal brewery, to make the "court brew" *(Hof Brau)*. In 1880, the brewery moved out, and this 5,000-seat food-and-beer palace was built in its place. After being bombed in World War II, the Hofbräuhaus was one of the first places to be rebuilt (German priorities).

Now, take a deep breath and go on in. Dive headlong into the sudsy Hofbräu mosh pit. Don't be shy. Everyone's drunk anyway. The atmosphere is thick with the sounds of oompah music, played here every night of the year.

You'll see locals stuffed into lederhosen and dirndls, giant gingerbread cookies that sport romantic messages, and kiosks selling postcards of the German (and apparently beer-drinking) ex-pope. Notice the quirky 1950s-style painted ceiling, with Bavarian colors, grapes, chestnuts, and fun "eat, drink, and be merry" themes. You'll see signs on some tables reading *Stammtisch*, meaning they're reserved for regulars, and their racks of old beer steins made of pottery and pewter. Beer halls like the Hofbräuhaus only sell beer by the liter mug, called a *Mass* (mahs). You can get it light *(helles)* or dark *(dunkles)*. A slogan on the ceiling above the band reads, *Durst ist schlimmer als Heimweh*—"Thirst is worse than homesickness."

You can explore upstairs too. Next to the entrance, a staircase leads up, past historic photos and old menus to the big folk-show hall on the top floor. There, at the far end of the hall is a small (free) Hofbräuhaus museum.

• *Leaving the Hofbräuhaus, turn right and walk two blocks, then turn left when you reach the street called...*

⓯ Maximilianstrasse

This broad east-west boulevard, lined with grand buildings and exclusive shops, introduces us to Munich's golden age of the 1800s. In that period, Bavaria was ruled by three important kings: Max Joseph, Ludwig I, and Ludwig II. They transformed Munich from a cluster of medieval lanes to a modern city of spacious squares, Neoclassical monuments, and wide boulevards. At the east end of this boulevard is the palatial home of the Bavarian parliament.

The street was purposely designed for people and for shopping, not military parades. And to this day, Maximilianstrasse is busy with shoppers browsing Munich's most exclusive shops. Many are wealthy visitors from the Middle East, places like Dubai and the United Arab Emirates. These families often come here for medical treatment. And they make a vacation out of it, bringing the whole family and often even their own car and driver. The shopping is great, there's no stress (like they might feel in a more frenetic city, like London), security is excellent, the weather is cool, and they're free of the societal constraints that keep them on the straight and narrow back home. Germans just politely provide the services, happy to make back some of the money that pours eastward every time they pull up to a gas station.

• *Maximilianstrasse leads to a big square—Max-Joseph-Platz.*

⑯ Max-Joseph-Platz

The square is fronted by two big buildings: the National Theater (with its columns) and the Residenz (with its intimidating stone facade).

The **Residenz**, the former "residence" of the royal Wittelsbach family, started as a crude castle (c. 1385). Over the centuries, it evolved into one of Europe's most opulent palaces. The facade takes its cue from Pitti Palace in Florence. Today, you can visit the Residenz for its lavish Rococo interior, its crown jewels, and exquisite Cuvilliés Theater (all described under "Sights in Munich"; see page 67).

MUNICH

The centerpiece of the square is a grand statue of Maximilian I—a.k.a. Max Joseph. In 1806, Max was the city's duke, serving in the long tradition of his Wittelsbach family...until Napoleon invaded and deposed the duke. But then Napoleon—eager to marry into the aristocracy—agreed to reinstate Max, with one condition: that his daughter marry Napoleon's stepson. Max Joseph agreed, and was quickly crowned not duke but king of Bavaria.

Max Joseph and his heirs ruled as constitutional monarchs. Now a king, Max Joseph was popular; he emancipated Protestants

and Jews, revamped the Viktualienmarkt, and graced Munich with grand buildings like the **National Theater.** This Neoclassical building, opened in 1818, celebrated Bavaria's strong culture, deep roots, and legitimacy as a nation; four of Richard Wagner's operas were first performed here. It's now where the Bavarian State Opera and the Bavarian State Orchestra perform. (The Roman numerals MCMLXIII in the frieze mark the year the theater reopened after WWII bombing restoration—1963.)

• *Leave Max-Joseph-Platz opposite where you entered, walking alongside the Residenz on Residenzstrasse for about 100 yards to the next grand square. But before you get to Odeonsplatz, pause at the first corner on the left and look down Viscardigasse at the gold-cobbled swoosh in the pavement.*

⑰ Viscardigasse

The cobbles in Viscardigasse recall one of Munich's most dramatic moments: It was 1923, and Munich was in chaos. World War I had left Germany in shambles. Angry mobs roamed the streets. Out of the fury rose a new and frightening movement—Adolf Hitler and the Nazi Party. On November 9, Hitler launched a coup, later known as the Beer Hall Putsch, to try to topple the German government. It started a few blocks from here in a beer hall (that no longer exists). Hitler and his mob of 2,000 Nazis marched up Residenzstrasse. A block ahead, where Residenzstrasse spills into Odeonsplatz, stood a hundred government police waiting for the Nazi mob. Shots were fired. Hitler was injured, and sixteen Nazis were killed, along with four policemen. The coup was put down, and Hitler was sent to a prison outside Munich. During his nine months there, he wrote down his twisted ideas in his book *Mein Kampf*.

Ten years later, when Hitler finally came to power, he made a memorial at Odeonsplatz to honor the so-called "first martyrs of the Third Reich." Germans were required to raise their arms in a *Sieg Heil* salute as they entered the square. The only way to avoid the indignity of saluting Nazism was to turn left down Viscardigasse instead. That stream of shiny cobbles marks the detour taken by those brave dissenters.

• *But now that Hitler's odious memorial is long gone, you can continue to...*

⑱ Odeonsplatz

This square links Munich's illustrious past with the Munich of today. It was laid out by the Wittelsbach kings in the 1800s. They incorporated the much older (yellow) church that was already on the square, the Theatinerkirche. This church contains about half of the Wittelsbach tombs. The church's twin towers and 230-foot-high dome are classic Italian Baroque, reflecting Munich's strong Catholic bent in the 1600s.

Nearby, overlooking the square from the south, is an arcaded loggia filled with statues. In the 1800s the Wittelsbachs commissioned this Hall of Heroes to honor Bavarian generals. It was modeled after the famous Renaissance loggia in Florence. Odeonsplatz was part of the Wittelsbachs' grand vision of modern urban planning. It was designed to connect the historic core with the expanding metropolis.

At the far end of the square, several wide boulevards lead away from here. First, face west (left) down ⑲ **Brienner Strasse** (watch out for bikes). In the distance, and just out of sight, a black obelisk commemorates the 30,000 Bavarians who marched with Napoleon to Moscow and never returned. Beyond the obelisk is the grand Königsplatz, or "King's Square," with its Neoclassical buildings. Back in the 1930s, Königsplatz was the center of the Nazi party. Remember, Munich was the cradle of Nazism. (For more on the

Nazi sights in Königsplatz, see page 78). Today, the Nazi shadow has largely lifted from that square (only two buildings from that era remain) and Königsplatz is home to Munich's cluster of great art museums. A few miles beyond Königsplatz is the Wittelsbachs' impressive summer home, Nymphenburg Palace.

Now turn your attention 90 degrees to the right. The boulevard heading north from Odeonsplatz is Ludwigstrasse. It stretches a full mile, flanked by an impressive line of uniform 60-foot-tall buildings in the Neo-Gothic style. In the far distance is the city's Triumphal Arch, capped with a figure of Bavaria, a goddess riding a lion-drawn chariot. She's looking out, away from the city, to welcome home returning soldiers. The street is named for the great Wittelsbach builder-king Ludwig I, the grandfather of "Mad" King Ludwig. It was Ludwig I who truly made Munich into a grand capital. ("I won't rest," he famously swore, "until Munich looks like Athens.") The street that bears his name, Ludwigstrasse, was used for big parades and processions, as it leads to that Roman-style arch.

Beyond the arch—and beyond what you can see—lie the suburbs of modern Munich, including the city's modern skyscrapers, Olympic Park, and the famous BMW headquarters.

As you enjoy the busy scene on Odeonsplatz, let's bring Munich's 850-year history up to the present. Munich today, with a population of 1.5 million, is Germany's third-largest city, after Berlin and Hamburg. It's the capital of the independent-minded German state of Bavaria, and proudly waves two flags: the white-and-blue diamonds of Bavaria and the black-and-gold of the city of Munich. Munich is home to more banks and financial firms than any German city besides Frankfurt. It's a center for book publishing and hosts two TV networks. Information technology is big, as well—it's home to electronics giant Siemens and the German branch of Microsoft. And, of course, Munich is home to makers of some of the world's finest cars—BMW (for "Bayerische Motoren Werke"—Bavarian Motor Works). Yes, Munich is a major metropolis, but you'd hardly know it by walking through its pleasant streets and parks.

• *We'll finish our walk in the pleasant Hofgarten. Its formal gate is to your right as you're facing up Ludwigstrasse. Step through the gate and enter the...*

❷⓿ Hofgarten

The elegant "garden of the royal court" is a delight. Built by the Wittelsbachs as their own private backyard to the Residenz palace, it's now open to everyone. Just inside the gate is an arcade decorated with murals commissioned by Ludwig I in the early 1800s. While faded, they still tell the glorious story of Bavaria from 1155 until 1688. The garden's 400-year-old centerpiece is a Renaissance-style temple with great acoustics. (There's often a musician performing here for tips.) It's decorated with the same shell decor as was popular inside the Residenz.

For a good antidote to all the beer halls, try the venerable **Café Tambosi,** with its chairs lined up facing the boulevard as if to watch a parade (see page 122). In the garden beyond the café tables is a gravel *boules* court.

• *With this city walk completed, you've seen the essential Munich. From here, a path leads to a building that houses the government offices of Bavaria, the Bayerischen Staatskanzlei, with an impressive Neoclassical central building flanked by modern glass halls. Look for the war memorial in front, which honors the fallen heroes of World War I, but only the fallen of World War II. Beyond this point is the stern Haus der Kunst (a rare fascist building surviving in Munich) and a happy place where locals surf in the river—the gateway into Munich's sprawling English Garden, described later.*

From the Hofgarten you're within easy reach of Munich's top sights. You could make the quick walk back to tour the museum and treasury at the Residenz; or descend into the U-Bahn from the Odeonsplatz stop for points elsewhere. These—and many other—sights are described in the next section. If you're ready to eat, you have several choices. Café Tambosi, Café Luitpold (best for coffee and cake), and the elegant, recommended Spatenhaus are nearby, and there are more options if you head toward Marienplatz (see "Eating in Munich," later).

Sights in Munich

Most of the top sights in the city center are covered on my self-guided walk. But there's much more to see in this city.

▲▲THE RESIDENZ

For 500 years, this was the palatial "residence" and seat of power of the ruling Wittelsbach family. It began (1385) as a crude castle with a moat around it. The main building was built from 1550 to 1650, and decorated in Rococo style during the 18th century. The final touch (under Ludwig I) was the grand south facade  modeled after Florence's Pitti Palace. In March 1944, Allied air raids left the Residenz in shambles, so much of what we see today is reconstructed—a condition you'll encounter repeatedly throughout your visit to Munich.

Today, the vast Residenz complex is divided into three sections, each with its own admission ticket: The **Residenz Museum** is a long hike through 90 lavishly decorated rooms. The **Residenz Treasury** shows off the Wittelsbach crown jewels. The **Cuvilliés Theater** is an ornate Rococo opera house. You can see the three sights individually or get a combo-ticket to see them all. I consider the museum and treasury to be the essential Residenz visit, with the Cuvilliés Theater as extra credit.

There are entrances on Max-Joseph-Platz and Residenzstrasse, both of which lead to the ticket office, gift shop, and start of the treasury and museum tours. You can see the three sights—treasury, museum, and theater—in any order. I'd start with the Residenz Treasury, because it's small and easy to manage your time. Then visit the sprawling Residenz Museum, where you can wander until you say "Enough." The Cuvilliés Theater doesn't take long to see and is easy to fit in before or after.

If you're torn about which of Munich's top two palaces to visit, the Residenz is more central and has the best interior, while Nymphenburg (described on page 85) has the finest garden, grounds, and outdoor views.

Cost and Hours: Residenz Museum—€7, Residenz Treasury—€7 (both include audioguides), Cuvilliés Theater—€3.50; €11 combo-ticket covers both museum and treasury; €13 version covers all three; treasury and museum open daily April-mid-Oct 9:00-18:00, mid-Oct-March 10:00-17:00, last entry one hour before closing; theater open April-mid-Sept Mon-Sat 14:00-18:00, Sun 9:00-18:00; mid-Sept-March Mon-Sat 14:00-17:00, Sun 10:00-17:00; last entry one hour before closing, no English information provided for theater. The complex is located three blocks north of Marienplatz; tel. 089/290-671, www.residenz-muenchen. de.

Residenz Treasury (Schatzkammer)

The treasury shows off a thousand years of Wittelsbach crowns and knickknacks. You'll see the regalia used in Bavaria's coronation ceremonies; the revered sacred objects that gave the Wittelsbachs divine legitimacy; and miscellaneous wonders that dazzled their European relatives. It's the best treasury in Bavaria, with fine 13th- and 14th-century crowns and delicately carved ivory and glass. Slow down and narrow your focus in order to fully appreciate the tiniest details.

Visiting the Treasury: In **Room 1,** the oldest jewels are 200 years older than Munich itself. The sapphire-studded Crown of Kunigunde (on the left) is associated with the saintly Queen of

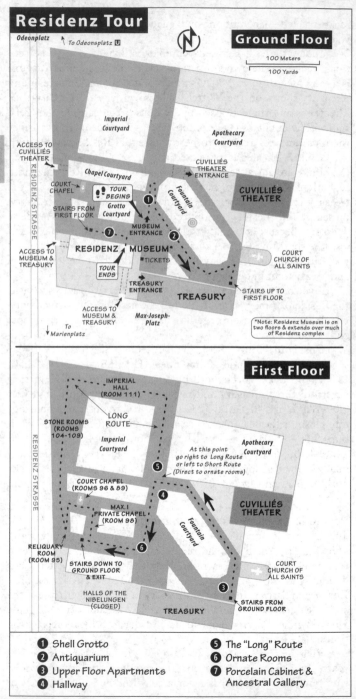

Residenz Tour

Ground Floor

Odeonplatz
To Odeonsplatz Ⓤ

N

100 Meters
100 Yards

Imperial Courtyard

Apothecary Courtyard

ACCESS TO CUVILLIÉS THEATER

RESIDENZ STRASSE

Chapel Courtyard

COURT CHAPEL

TOUR BEGINS

Grotto Courtyard

STAIRS FROM FIRST FLOOR

CUVILLIÉS THEATER ENTRANCE

Fountain Courtyard

CUVILLIÉS THEATER

❶

MUSEUM ENTRANCE

❷

❼

RESIDENZ MUSEUM

ACCESS TO MUSEUM & TREASURY

TICKETS

COURT CHURCH OF ALL SAINTS

TOUR ENDS

TREASURY ENTRANCE

TREASURY

STAIRS UP TO FIRST FLOOR

ACCESS TO MUSEUM & TREASURY

Max-Joseph-Platz

To Marienplatz

*Note: Residenz Museum is on two floors & extends over much of Residenz complex

First Floor

IMPERIAL HALL (ROOM 111)

LONG ROUTE

STONE ROOMS (ROOMS 104-109)

RESIDENZ STRASSE

Imperial Courtyard

Apothecary Courtyard

At this point go right to Long Route or left to Short Route (Direct to ornate rooms)

❺

COURT CHAPEL (ROOMS 96 & 89)

MAX. I PRIVATE CHAPEL (ROOM 98)

❹

Fountain Courtyard

CUVILLIÉS THEATER

RELIQUARY ROOM (ROOM 95)

❻

STAIRS DOWN TO GROUND FLOOR & EXIT

COURT CHURCH OF ALL SAINTS

HALLS OF THE NIBELUNGEN (CLOSED)

TREASURY

❸

STAIRS FROM GROUND FLOOR

❶ Shell Grotto
❷ Antiquarium
❸ Upper Floor Apartments
❹ Hallway
❺ The "Long" Route
❻ Ornate Rooms
❼ Porcelain Cabinet & Ancestral Gallery

Bavaria who was crowned Holy Roman Empress in 1014 by the pope in St. Peter's Basilica in Rome. The pearl-studded prayer book of Charles the Bald (Charlemagne's grandson) allowed the book's owner to claim royal roots dating all the way back to that first Holy Roman Emperor crowned in 800. The spiky Crown of an English Queen (a.k.a. the Palatine Crown, c. 1370) is actually England's oldest crown, brought to Munich by an English princess who married a Wittelsbach duke. The lily-shaped Crown of Henry II (c. 1270-1280) dates from Munich's roots, when the town was emerging as a regional capital.

Along the right side of the room are religious objects such as reliquaries and portable altars. The tiny mobile altar allowed a Carolingian king (from Charlemagne's family of kings) to pack light in 890—and still have a little Mass while on the road. Many of the precious and very old objects in this room came from various prince-bishop collections when they were secularized (and their realms came under the rule of the Bavarian king from Munich) in the Napoleonic Era (c. 1800).

Room 3: Study the reliquary with St. George killing the dragon—sparkling with more than 2,000 precious stones. Get up close (it's OK to walk around the rope posts)...you can almost hear the dragon hissing. A gold-armored St. George, seated atop a ruby-studded ivory horse, tramples an emerald-green dragon. The golden box below contained the supposed relics of St. George, who was the patron saint of the Wittelsbachs.

If you could lift the minuscule visor, you'd see that the carved ivory face of St. George is actually the Wittelsbach Duke Wilhelm V—the great champion of the Catholic Counter-Reformation—slaying the dragon of Protestantism.

Room 4: The incredibly realistic carved ivory crucifixes from 1630 were done by local artist Georg Petel, who was inspired by his friend Peter Paul Rubens' painting (now in the Alte Pinakothek). Look at the flesh of Jesus' wrist pulling around the nails. In the center of the room is the intricate portable altarpiece (1573-74) of Duke Albrecht V, the Wittelsbach ruler who (as we'll see in the Residenz Museum) made a big mark on the Residenz.

Room 5: The freestanding glass case (#245) holds the impressive royal regalia of the 19th-century Wittelsbach kings—the crown, scepter, orb, and sword that were given to the king during the coronation ceremony. (The smaller pearl crown was for the queen.) They date from the early 1800s when Bavaria had been conquered by Napoleon. The Wittelsbachs struck a deal that al-

lowed them to stay in power, under the elevated title of "king" (not just "duke" or "elector" or "prince-arch-bishop"). These objects were made in France by the same craftsmen who created Napoleon's crown. For the next century-plus, Wittelsbach kings (including Ludwig II) received these tokens of power. However, during the coronation ceremony, the crown you see was not actually placed on the king's head. It was brought in on a cushion (as it's displayed) and laid at the new monarch's feet.

Rooms 6-10: The rest of the treasury has objects that are more beautiful than historic. Admire the dinnerware made of rock crystal (Room 6), stone (Room 7), and gold and enamel (Room 8). Room 9 has a silver-gilt-and-marble replica of Trajan's Column. Finally, explore the "Exotica" of Room 10, including a green Olmec figure, knives from Turkey, and a Chinese rhino-horn bowl with a teeny-tiny Neptune inside.

• *From the micro-detail of the treasury, it's time to visit the expansive Residenz Museum. Cross the hall, exchange your treasury audioguide for the museum audioguide, and enter the...*

Residenz Museum (Residenzmuzeum)

Though called a "museum," what's really on display here are the 90 rooms of the Residenz itself: the palace's spectacular banquet and reception halls, and the Wittelsbachs' lavish private apartments. The rooms are decorated with period (but generally not original) furniture: chandeliers, canopied beds, Louis XIV-style chairs, old clocks, tapestries, and dinnerware of porcelain and silver. It's the best place to glimpse the opulent lifestyle of Bavaria's late, great royal family. (Whatever happened to the Wittelsbachs, the longest continuously ruling family in European history? They're still around, but they're no longer royalty, so most of them have real jobs now—you may well have just passed one on the street.)

Self-Guided Tour: The place is big. Follow the museum's prescribed route, using this section to hit the highlights, and supplementing it with the audioguide. Use my maps as a general guide and grab a free museum floor plan to help locate specific room numbers mentioned here. Be flexible. The route can vary, as rooms are occasionally closed off. Despite that, you should see most of the rooms I've described in approximately this order.

• *One of the first "rooms" you encounter (it's actually part of an outdoor courtyard) is the...*

❶ Shell Grotto (Room 6): This artificial grotto is made of

volcanic tuff and covered completely in Bavarian freshwater shells. In its day, it was an exercise in man controlling nature—a celebration of the Renaissance humanism that flourished in the 1550s. Mercury—the pre-Christian god of trade and business—oversees the action. Check out the statue in the courtyard—in the Wittelsbachs' heyday, red wine would have flowed from the mermaid's breasts and dripped from Medusa's severed head.

The grotto courtyard is just one of 10 such courtyards in the complex. Like the rest of the palace, this courtyard and its grotto were destroyed by Allied bombs. After World War II, Germans had no money to contribute to the reconstruction—but they could gather shells. All the shells you see here were donated by small-town Bavarians, as the grotto was rebuilt according to Nazi photos (see "The History of Munich: Part 2" sidebar).

• *Before moving on, note the door marked* OO, *leading to handy WCs. Now continue into the next room, the...*

❷ **Antiquarium** (Room 7): This long, low, arched hall stretches 220 feet end to end. It's the oldest room in the Residenz, built around 1550. The room was, and still is, a festival banquet hall. The ruler presided from the raised dais at the near end (warmed by the fireplace). Two hundred dignitaries can dine here, surrounded by allegories of the goodness of just rule on the ceiling.

The hall is lined with busts of Roman emperors. In the mid-16th century, Europe's royal families (such as the Wittelsbachs) collected and displayed such busts, implying a connection between themselves and the enlightened ancient Roman rulers. There was such huge demand for these classical statues in the courts of Europe that many of the "ancient busts" were fakes cranked out by crooked Romans. Still, a third of the statuary you see here is original.

The small paintings around the room (which survived the WWII bombs because they were painted in arches) show 120 Bavarian villages as they looked in 1550. Even today, when a Bavarian historian wants a record of how his village once looked, he comes here. Notice the town of Dachau in 1550 (in the archway closest to the entrance door).

• *After pausing in the hall, keep going through a few more rooms, then up a stairway to the upper floor. Pause in the **Black Hall** (Room 13) to*

MUNICH

admire the head-spinning trompe l'oeil ceiling, which makes the nearly flat roof appear to be a much grander arched vault. From here, the pre-scribed route winds through a couple dozen rooms surrounding a large courtyard.

❸ **Upper Floor Apartments** (Rooms 14-45): In this series of rooms we get the first glimpse of the Residenz Museum's forte: chandeliered rooms decorated with ceiling paintings, stucco work, tapestries, parquet floors, and period furniture.

Rooms to the left of the Black Hall are the **Electoral Apartments** (Rooms 22-31), the private apartments of the monarch and his consort.

The door from the Black Hall that's opposite the staircase leads to the long **All Saints Corridor** (Room 32), where you may be able to glance into the adjoining All Saints' Chapel. This early-19th-century chapel, commissioned by Ludwig I, was severely damaged in World War II, didn't reopen until 2003, and is still being refurbished.

From the All Saints Corridor you can reach the **Charlotte Chambers/Court-Garden Rooms,** a long row of impressive rooms across the courtyard from the Electoral Apartments, first used to house visiting rulers. Some of them later served as the private rooms of Princess Charlotte, Max Joseph's daughter.

• *Your visit eventually reaches a hallway—*❹ *Room 45—where you have a choice: to the left is the "short" route that heads directly to the stunning Ornate Rooms (described later). But we'll take the "long" route to the right (starting in Room 47) that adds a dozen-plus rooms to your visit.*

❺ **The "Long" Route:** Use your Residenz-issued map to find some of the following highlights on the long route. The large **Imperial Hall** is in Room 111; the **Stone Rooms** (104-109) are so-called for their colorful marble—both real and fake. Then come several small rooms, where the centerpiece painting on the ceiling is just blank black, as no copy of the original survived World War II.

The **Reliquary Room** (Room 95) harbors a collection of gruesome Christian relics (bones, skulls, and even several mummified hands) in ornate golden cases (this and the next two chapels may be under renovation during your visit).

• *A few more steps brings you to the balcony of the...*

Court Chapel (Rooms 96/89). Dedicated to Mary, this late-Renaissance/early-Baroque gem was the site of "Mad" King Ludwig's funeral after his mysterious murder—or suicide—in 1886. (He's buried in St. Michael's Church, described on page 46.) Though Ludwig II was not popular in political circles, he was beloved by his people, and his funeral drew huge crowds. About 75 years earlier, in 1810, his grandfather and namesake (Ludwig I) was married here. After the wedding ceremony, carriages rolled his guests to a rollicking reception, which turned out to be such a hit that it became an annual tradition—Oktoberfest.

A couple rooms ahead is the **Private Chapel of Maximilian I** (Room 98). Duke Maximilian I, the dominant Bavarian figure in the Thirty Years' War, built one of the most precious rooms in the palace. The miniature pipe organ (from about 1600) still works. The room is sumptuous, from the gold leaf and the fancy hinges to the miniature dome and the walls made of stucco marble. (Stucco marble is fake marble—a special mix of stucco, applied and polished. Designers liked it because it was less expensive than real marble and the color could be controlled.) Note the post-Renaissance perspective tricks decorating the walls; they were popular in the 17th century. The case (on the right wall as you enter) supposedly contains skeletons of three babies from the Massacre of the Innocents in Bethlehem (where Herod, in an attempt to murder the baby Jesus, ordered all sons of a certain age killed).

• Whichever route you take—long or short—you'll eventually reach a set of rooms known as the...

❻ Ornate Rooms (Rooms 55-62): As the name implies, these are some of the richest rooms in the palace. The Wittelsbachs were always trying to keep up with the Habsburgs, and this long string of ceremonial rooms—used for official business—was designed to impress. The decor and furniture are Rococo—over-the-top Baroque. The family art collection, now in the Alte Pinakothek, once decorated these walls.

The rooms were designed in the 1730s by François de Cuvilliés. The Belgian-born Cuvilliés first attracted notice as the clever court dwarf for the Bavarian ruler. He was sent to Paris to study art and returned to become the court architect. Besides the Residenz, he went on to also design the Cuvilliés Theater (described later) and the Great Hall and Amalienburg at Nymphenburg Palace. Cuvilliés' style defined Bavarian Rococo, featuring incredibly intricate stucco tracery twisted into unusual shapes. The stucco work frames paintings and mirrors. His assistant in the stucco department was Johann Baptist Zimmerman, who also did the Wieskirche (in southern Bavaria, near Füssen).

Each room is unique. The **Green Gallery** (Room 58)—so-called for its green silk damask wallpaper—was the ballroom. Imagine the parties they had here—aristocrats in powdered wigs, a string quartet playing Baroque tunes, a card game going on, while everyone admired the paintings on the walls or themselves reflected in the mirrors. The **State Bedroom** (Room 60), though furnished with a canopy bed, wasn't an actual bedroom—it was just for show. Rulers invited their subjects to come at morning and evening to stand at the railing and watch their boss ceremonially rise from his slumber to symbolically start and end the working day.

Perhaps the most ornate of these Ornate Rooms is the **Cabinet of Mirrors** (Room 61) and the adjoining **Cabinet of Miniatures** (Room 62) from 1740. (Coral red

was *the* most royal of colors in Germany.) Imagine visiting the duke and having him take you here to ogle miniature copies of the most famous paintings of the day, composed with one-haired brushes. In the Cabinet of Mirrors, notice the fun effect of the mirrors around you—the corner mirrors make things go forever and ever. As you glide through this section of the palace, be sure to appreciate the gilded stucco ceilings above you.

• *After exploring the Ornate Rooms (and the many, many other elaborate rooms here on the upper floor), find the staircase (near Room 65) that heads back downstairs. On the ground floor, you emerge in the long Ancestral Gallery (Room 4). Before walking down it, detour to the right, into Room 5.*

❼ **Porcelain Cabinet** (Room 5) and **Ancestral Gallery** (Room 4): In the 18th century, the royal family bolstered their status with an in-house porcelain works: Nymphenburg porcelain. See how the mirrors enhance the porcelain vases, creating the effect of infinite pedestals. If this inspires you to acquire some pieces of your own, head to the Nymphenburg Porcelain Store at Odeonsplatz (listed under "Shopping in Munich," later).

The Ancestral Gallery (Room 4) was built in the 1740s to display portraits of the Wittelsbachs. All official guests had to

pass through here to meet the duke (and his 100 Wittelsbach relatives). The room's symbolism reinforced the Wittelsbachs' claims to being as powerful as the Habsburgs of Vienna. Standing here, you're essentially surrounded by a scrapbook covering centuries of royal family history.

Midway down the hall, find the family tree labeled (in Latin) "genealogy of an imperial family." The tree is shown being planted by Hercules, to boost their royal street cred. Opposite the tree are two notable portraits: Charlemagne, the first Holy Roman Emperor, and to his right, Louis IV (wearing the same crown), the first Wittelsbach H.R.E., crowned in 1328. For the next 500 years, this lineage was used to substantiate the family's claim to power as they competed with the Habsburgs. (After failing to sort out their differences through strategic weddings, the two families eventually went to war.)

Allied bombs took their toll on this hall. The central ceiling painting has been restored, but since there were no photos documenting the other two ceiling paintings, those spots remain empty. Looking carefully at the walls, you can see how each painting was hastily cut out of its frame. That's because—though most of Munich's museums were closed during World War II to prevent damage—the Residenz remained open to instill confidence in local people. It wasn't until 1944, when bombs were imminent, that the last-minute order was given to hurriedly slice all these portraits out of their frames and hide them away.

Unless you're coming back in 2016, you'll miss the **Halls of the Nibelungen** *(Nibelungensäle)*. The mythological scenes in these halls—currently closed for renovation—were the basis of Wagner's *Der Ring des Nibelungen*. Wagner and "Mad" King Ludwig were friends and spent time hanging out here (c. 1864). The images in this hall could well have inspired Wagner to write his *Ring* and Ludwig to build his "fairy-tale castle," Neuschwanstein.

• *Your Residenz Museum tour is over. The doorway at the end of the hall leads back to the museum entrance. If you're visiting the Cuvilliés Theater, exit the Residenz and head a half-block north on Residenzstrasse to another Residenz entrance. From there, follow signs to the Cuvilliés Theater.*

Cuvilliés Theater

In 1751, this was Germany's ultimate Rococo theater. Mozart conducted here several times. Designed by the same brilliant architect who did the Amalienburg (see page 91), this theater is dazzling enough to send you back to the days of divine monarchs.

Your visit consists of just one small-but-plush theater hall. It's an intimate, horseshoe-shaped performance venue, seating fewer than 400. The four tiers of box seats were for the four classes of society: city burghers on bottom, royalty next up (in the most elaborate seats), and lesser court-iers in the two highest tiers. The ruler occupied the large Royal Box directly opposite the stage (i.e., over the entrance doorway). "Mad" King Ludwig II occasionally bought out the entire theater to watch performances here by himself.

François Cuvilliés' interior is exquisite. Red, white, and gold hues dominate. Most of the decoration is painted wood, even parts that look like marble. Even the proscenium above the stage—seemingly draped with a red-velvet "curtain"—is actually made of carved wood. Also above the stage is an elaborate Wittelsbach coat of arms. The balconies seem to be supported by statues of the four seasons, and are adorned with gold garlands. Cuvilliés achieved the Rococo ideal of giving theater-goers a multimedia experience—uniting the beauty of his creation with the beautiful performance on stage. It's still a working theater.

WWII bombs completely obliterated the old Cuvilliés The-ater, which originally stood at a different location a short distance from here. Fortunately, much of the carved wooden interior had been removed from the walls and stored away for safekeeping. After the war, they built this entirely new building near the ruins of the old theater and paneled it with the original décor. It's so heavily restored, you can almost smell the paint.

NEAR THE RESIDENZ
▲Munich City Museum (Münchner Stadtmuseum)
The museum's permanent exhibit on Munich's history (called "Typically Munich!") is interesting, but it's exhaustive, and there's no posted English information. I'd use the following mini-tour for an overview, then supplement it with the audioguide and English booklet. Skip the parts of the museum that re-quire the more expensive temporary-exhibit ticket.

Cost and Hours: €4, includes good audioguide, €7 includes tempo-rary exhibits, Tue-Sun 10:00-18:00, closed Mon, no crowds, bored but friendly guards, ticket gets you half-price admission to Jewish Museum or Lenbachhaus, St.-Jakobs-Platz 1, tel. 089/2332-2370, www.stadtmuseum-online.de. The humorous Servus Heimat sou-venir shop in the courtyard is worth a stop.

Eating: The museum's Stadt Café is handy for a good meal (listed under "Eating in Munich," later).

Visiting the Museum: Start in the ticketing hall with the wooden model showing Munich today. Find the Frauenkirche, Isar River, New Town Hall, Residenz...and no skyscrapers. The city looks remarkably similar in scale to the model (in the next room) from 1570.

Ground Floor—Medieval: A big gray statue of Henry the Lion introduces us to the city's 12th-century founder. The eight statues of Morris dancers (1480) became a symbol of the vibrant market town (and the tradition continued with the New Town Hall glockenspiel's dancing coopers). On the rest of the ground floor, paintings, armor, and swords capture more medieval ambience.

First Floor—1800s: The "New Munich" was created when the city was expanded beyond the old medieval walls (see the illuminated view of the city from 1761 in the "Canaletto-Blick" opposite the top of the stairs). The city was prosperous, as evidenced by the furniture and paintings on display. In the center of the room, find big paintings ("Effigies") of the century's magnificent kings—Maximilian I, Ludwig I, and Ludwig II (as well as Lola Montez, Ludwig I's most famous mistress).

Second Floor—Munich 1900: As Munich approached its 700th birthday, it was becoming aware of itself as a major capital. The Münchner Kindl logo was born. It was a city of artists (Wagner operas, Lenbach portraits, von Stuck soirées), *Jugendstil* furniture, beer, and a cosmopolitan outlook (see the "emperor panorama," the big barrel-shaped 3-D peep show of African/Asian peoples). But after the destruction of World War I, Munich became a hotbed of discontent. The "revue" room shows the city's clash of ideas: communists, capitalists, Nazis, and the anarchic theater of comedian Karl Valentin and early works by playwright Bertolt Brecht. A nearby display gives some background on Munich's role as the birthplace of Nazism (much more thoroughly covered in the museum's National Socialism wing).

From here, you can detour upstairs to the **third floor puppet theater** to see an extensive collection of marionettes, Punch-and-Judy hand puppets, and paper cutouts of this unique Bavarian art form with a long cabaret tradition.

Back on the second floor, finish with a kaleidoscope of images capturing the contemporary Munich scene—rock music, World Cup triumphs, beer gardens, and other things that are..."typically Munich."

National Socialism Wing: Your permanent-exhibit ticket (and audioguide) includes this small but worthwhile exhibit of photos and uniforms that takes you chronologically through the Nazi years, focused on Munich: the post-WWI struggles, Hitler's 1923 Beer Hall Putsch, his writing of *Mein Kampf*, the mass rallies in Königsplatz and Odeonsplatz, establishment of the Dachau concentration camp, and the destruction rained on Munich in World War II.

MUNICH'S MUSEUM QUARTER (KUNSTAREAL)

This quarter's cluster of blockbuster museums displays art spanning from 3000 B.C. right up to the present (Egyptian Museum, Glyptothek, Alte and Neue Pinakotheks, Lenbachhaus, Moderne Pinakothek, and the Museum Brandhorst). Most people don't come to Munich for the art, but this group makes a case for the city's world-class status. The Alte Pinakothek is the best of the bunch, but modern art is also surprisingly well-represented. Consider spending an afternoon here (and maybe an evening; most of these museums are open late one night of the week).

Getting There: The Glyptothek and Lenbachhaus are right by the Königsplatz stop on the U-2 subway line. The three Pinakothek museums, the Egyptian Museum, and the Brandhorst are a few blocks to the northeast. Handy tram #27 whisks you right to the Pinakothek stop from Karlsplatz (between the train station and Marienplatz). You can also take bus #100 from the train station, or walk 10 minutes from the Theresienstrasse or Königsplatz stops on the U-2 line.

Tickets: A €12 day pass covers the three Pinakotheks, plus the Brandhorst on a single day (or covers five people in one museum at the same time). A €29 combo-ticket covers them all with no time restriction. On Sundays, these museums and the Glyptothek let you in for just a token €1, but charge for the useful audioguides (normally included).

▲▲Alte Pinakothek

Bavaria's best painting gallery (the "Old Art Gallery," pronounced ALL-teh pee-nah-koh-TEHK) shows off a world-class collection

of European masterpieces from the 14th to 19th century, starring the two tumultuous centuries (1450-1650) when Europe went from medieval to modern. See paintings from the Italian Renaissance (Raphael, Leonardo, Botticelli, Titian) and the German Renaissance it inspired (Albrecht Dürer). The Reformation of Martin Luther eventually split Europe into two subcultures—Protestants and Catholics—with their two distinct art styles (exemplified by Rembrandt and Rubens, respectively).

MUNICH

Renovation: In 2015, Rooms I-VI (the majority of our tour) will likely be closed for renovation. However, the major works may be on display elsewhere in the museum—ask when you arrive.

Cost and Hours: €4 during renovation (otherwise €7), €1 on Sun, covered by €12 day pass and €29 combo-ticket, open Wed-Sun 10:00-18:00, Tue 10:00-20:00, closed Mon, last entry 30 minutes before closing, free and excellent audioguide (€4.50 on Sun), no flash photos; U-2: Theresienstrasse, tram #27, or bus #100; Barer Strasse 27, tel. 089/2380-5216, www.pinakothek.de/alte-pinakothek.

➋ **Self-Guided Tour:** All the paintings we'll see are on the upper floor, which is laid out like a barbell. This tour starts at one fat end and works its way through the "handle" to the other end. From the ticket counter, head up the stairway to the left to reach the first rooms.

German Renaissance—Room II: Albrecht Altdorfer's *The Battle of Issus (Schlacht bei Issus)* shows a world at war. Masses of soldiers are swept along in the currents and

tides of a battle completely beyond their control, their confused motion reflected in the swirling sky. We see the battle from a great height, giving us a godlike perspective. Though the painting depicts Alexander the Great's history-changing victory over the Persians (find the Persian king Darius turning and fleeing), it could as easily have been Germany in the 1520s. Christians were fighting Muslims, peasants battled masters, and Catholics and Protestants were squaring off for a century of con-

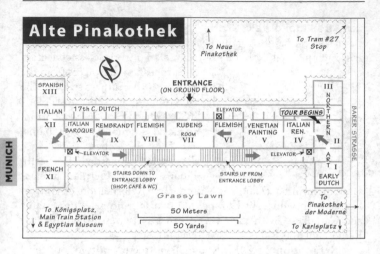

MUNICH

flict. The armies melt into a huge landscape, leaving the impression that the battle goes on forever.

Albrecht Dürer's larger-than-life *Four Apostles* (*Johannes und Petrus* and *Paulus und Marcus*) are saints of a radical new religion: Martin Luther's Protestantism. Just as Luther challenged Church authority, Dürer—a friend of Luther's—strips these saints of any rich clothes, halos, or trappings of power and gives them down-to-earth human features: receding hairlines, wrinkles, and suspicious eyes. The inscription warns German rulers to follow the Bible rather than Catholic Church leaders. The figure of Mark—a Bible in one hand and a sword in the other—is a fitting symbol of the dangerous times.

Dürer's *Self-Portrait in Fur Coat (Selbstbildnis im Pelzrock)* looks like Jesus Christ but is actually 28-year-old Dürer himself (per his inscription: "XXVIII"), gazing out, with his right hand solemnly giving a blessing. This is the ultimate image of humanism: the artist as an instrument of God's continued creation. Get close and enjoy the intricately braided hair, the skin texture, and the fur collar. To the left of the head is Dürer's famous monogram—"A.D." in the form of a pyramid.

Italian Renaissance—Room IV: With the Italian Renaissance—the "rebirth" of interest in the art and learning of ancient Greece and Rome—artists captured the

realism, three-dimensionality, and symmetry found in classical statues. Twenty-one-year-old Leonardo da Vinci's *Virgin and Child (Maria mit dem Kinde)* need no halos—they radiate purity. Mary is a solid pyramid of maternal love, flanked by Renaissance-arch windows that look out on the hazy distance. Baby Jesus reaches out to play innocently with a carnation, the blood-colored symbol of his eventual death.

MUNICH

Raphael's *Holy Family at the Canigiani House (Die hl. Familie aus dem Hause Canigiani)* takes Leonardo's pyramid form and runs with it. Father Joseph forms the peak, with his staff as the strong central axis. Mary and Jesus (on the right) form a pyramid-within-the-pyramid, as do Elizabeth and baby John the Baptist on the left. They all exchange meaningful eye contact, safe within the bounds of the stable family structure.

In Botticelli's *Lamentation over Christ (Die Beweinung Christi)*, the Renaissance "pyramid" implodes, as the weight of the dead Christ drags everyone down, and the tomb grins darkly behind them.

Venetian Painting—Room V: In Titian's *Christ Crowned with Thorns (Die Dornenkrönung)*, a powerfully built Christ sits si-

lently enduring torture by prison guards. The painting is by Venice's greatest Renaissance painter, but there's no symmetry, no pyramid form, and the brushwork is intentionally messy and Impressionistic. By the way, this is the first painting we've seen done on canvas rather than wood, as artists experimented with vegetable oil-based paints.

Rubens and Baroque—Room VII: Europe's religious wars split the Continent in two—Protestants in the northern countries, Catholics in the south. (Germany itself was divided, with Bavaria remaining Catholic.) The Baroque style, popular in Catholic countries, featured large canvases, bright colors, lots of flesh, rippling motion, wild emotions, grand themes...and pudgy winged babies, the sure sign of Baroque. This room holds several canvases by the great Flemish painter Peter Paul Rubens.

In Rubens' 300-square-foot *Great Last Judgment (Das Grosse*

Jüngste Gericht), Christ raises the righteous up to heaven (left side) and damns the sinners to hell (on the right). This swirling cycle of nudes was considered risqué and kept under wraps by the very monks who'd commissioned it.

Rubens and Isabella Brant shows the artist with his first wife, both of them the very picture of health, wealth, and success. They lean together unconsciously, as people in love will do, with their hands clasped in mutual affection. When his first wife died, 53-year-old Rubens found a replacement—16-year-old Hélène Fourment, shown in an adjacent painting (just to the left) in her wedding dress. You may recognize Hélène's face in other Rubens paintings.

The Rape of the Daughters of Leucippus (Der Raub der Töchter des Leukippos) has many of Rubens' most typical elements—fleshy, emotional, rippling motion; bright colors; and a classical subject. The legendary twins Castor and Pollux crash a wedding and steal the brides as their own. The chaos of flailing limbs and rearing horses is all held together in a subtle X-shaped composition. Like the weaving counterpoint in a Baroque fugue, Rubens balances opposites.

Notice that Rubens' canvases were—to a great extent—cranked out by his students and assistants from small "cartoons" the master himself made (displayed in the side room).

Rembrandt and Dutch—Room IX: From Holland, Rembrandt van Rijn's *Six Paintings from the Life of Christ* are a down-

to-earth look at supernatural events. The *Adoration (Die Anbetung der Hirten)* of Baby Jesus takes place in a 17th-century Dutch barn with ordinary folk as models. The canvases are dark brown, lit by strong light. The *Adoration's* light source is the Baby Jesus himself—literally the "light of the world." In the *Deposition (Kreuzabnahme),* the light bounces off Christ's pale body onto his mother Mary, who has fainted in the shadows, showing how his death also hurts her. The drama is underplayed, with subdued emotions. In the *Raising of the Cross (Kreuzaufrichtung),* a man dressed in blue is looking on—a self-portrait of Rembrandt.

▲Neue Pinakothek

The Alte Pinakothek's younger sister is an easy-to-like collection located just across the street, showing paintings from 1800 to 1920. Breeze through a smattering of Romantics on your way to the museum's highlight: some world-class Impressionist paintings, and one of Van Gogh's *Sunflowers*.

Cost and Hours: €7, €1 on Sun, covered by €12 day pass and €29 combo-ticket, open Thu-Mon 10:00-18:00, Wed 10:00-20:00, closed Tue, well-done audioguide is usually free but €4.50 on Sun, classy Café Hunsinger in basement spills into park; U-2: Theresienstrasse, tram #27, or bus #100; Barer Strasse 29 but enter on Theresienstrasse, tel. 089/2380-5195, www.pinakothek.de/neue-pinakothek.

Visiting the Museum: Pick up the audioguide and floor plan, and follow their prescribed route. Along the way, be sure to hit these highlights.

Rooms 1-3: In Room 1, Jacques-Louis David's curly-haired *Comtesse de Sorcy* shows the French noblewoman dressed in the ancient-Greek-style fashions popular during the Revolution. Room 3 features English painters—Turner's stormy seascapes and Gainsborough's contemplative *Mrs. Thomas Hibbert*. Nearby, you'll see other less-famous works by other major European artists.

Rooms 4-18: These rooms—the bulk of the museum—feature colorful, pretty, realistic (and mostly forgettable) paintings by German Romantics. In the remarkable *King Ludwig I in Coronation Robes* (Room 8), the young playboy king is both regal and rakish. (For more on the king, the artist, and their Gallery of Beauties, see page 89.) Caspar David Friedrich (Room 9) is Germany's best-known chronicler of the awe-inspiring power of nature (though these small canvases aren't his best). Carl Spitzweg's tiny *The Poor Poet* (Room 10a) is often reproduced. Room 13 has huge (hard-to-miss) canvases: *The Destruction of Jerusalem by Titus,* and the nationalist-themed *Thusnelda Led in Germanicus' Triumph,* showing a German noblewoman and her son, captured by the Romans, being paraded before the emperor.

Rooms 19-22: In these rooms, you'll find classic examples of all the Impressionist and Post-Impressionist masters: Degas' snapshots of women at work, Monet's sunny landscapes and water lilies, Manet's bourgeois Realism, Cézanne's still lifes, and Gauguin's languid Tahitian ladies. Van Gogh's *Sunflowers* is one of 11 such canvases he did, which he used to decorate his home in Arles when Gauguin came to visit. In the final rooms, see works by Gustav Klimt and Munich's answer to Klimt, Franz von Stuck. The Neue Pinakothek may whet your appetite for even *neuer* art, found nearby at the Lenbachhaus, Pinakothek der Moderne, and the Museum Brandhorst.

MUNICH

▲Pinakothek der Moderne

This museum picks up where the other two Pinakothek's leave off, covering the 20th century. Most of the building houses temporary

exhibits and constantly rotating collections, but there are two (fairly) permanent exhibits, with excellent English descriptions throughout.

Cost and Hours: €10, €1 on Sun, covered by €12 day pass and €29 combo-ticket, open Tue-Sun 10:00-18:00, Thu until 20:00, closed Mon, audioguide is usually free but €4.50 on Sun; U-2: Theresienstrasse, tram #27, or bus #100; Barer Strasse 40, tel. 089/2380-5360, www.pinakothek.de/pinakothek-der-moderne.

Visiting the Museum: The manageably sized Classical Modernism wing covers many of the stars of modern art—Picasso, Dalí, Miró, and so on. The museum's strength is the German contribution. The Expressionists rendered reality in deep colors and bold black outlines. Munich's Blue Rider Group (Kandinsky, Klee, Marc) took it the next step, by abandoning reality altogether and expressing themselves with only color and line. One or two rooms display "degenerate art"—paintings confiscated by the Nazis and eventually rescued by an art lover. Max Beckmann (whose work is usually in Room 9) witnessed the rise of Nazism—and was branded a degenerate—and his symbol-laced works chronicle the cynicism of the time.

The design wing is easy to appreciate. From chairs to bikes to blenders to cars and computers, these are everyday objects that work efficiently but also have a sleek artistic flair.

The striking, white, high-ceilinged building itself is worth a look—it's free to step into the atrium.

▲▲Egyptian Museum
(Staatliches Museum Ägyptischer Kunst)

To enjoy this museum, you don't need a strong interest in ancient Egypt (but you may have one by the time you leave). This new space was custom-made to evoke the feeling of being deep in an ancient tomb, from the wide staircase outside that descends to the narrow entry, to the twisty interior rooms that grow narrower and more catacomb-

like as you progress. The art here is beautifully lit, explained well in English, and accompanied by touch-screen terminals that give more background for the curious. The museum's clever design creates a low-stress visit (just follow the one-way route marked by brass arrows in the floor), and makes up for the fact that the collection lacks a rock-star showpiece (such as Nefertiti, who still holds her head high in Berlin's Neues Museum).

Cost and Hours: €12, €6 on Sun, Tue-Sun 10:00-18:00, Tue until 20:00, closed Mon, included audioguide may be available in English in time for your trip, U-2 or U-8 to Königsplatz or tram #27 to Karolinenplatz or bus #100 to Pinakothek stop, 10-minute walk from main train station, Gabelsbergerstrasse 35, tel. 089/2892-7630, www.smaek.de.

MUNICH

Lenbachhaus

Little ol' Munich blew the art world's mind when a bunch of art-school cronies got fed up with being told how and what to paint, and together as the revolutionary "Blue Rider" *(Blaue Reiter)* group galloped toward a brand new horizon—abstract art. In the Lenbachhaus' series of pleasant galleries you can witness the birth of Modernist non-representational art, with paintings by Kandinsky, Klee, and Marc, then stroll the rest of the building's offerings (including the apartments of painter Franz von Lenbach, whose original villa and studio are now largely enclosed by the modern museum building).

Cost and Hours: €10, includes well-done audioguide, half-price with City Museum ticket, Tue-Sun 10:00-18:00, Tue until 21:00, closed Mon, pricey but good café, tel. 089/2333-2000, www.lenbachhaus.de.

Visiting the Museum: The revolution begins on the second floor, with seemingly innocuous paintings of the cute Bavarian town of Murnau. It was here in 1908 that two Munich couples—Wassily Kandinsky, Alexej Jawlensky, and their artist girlfriends—came for vacation. The four painted together—it's hard to tell their work apart—employing intense colors, thick paint, and bold black outlines. Over the next few years (c. 1911-1914), they'd gather together into a group of Munich-based artists calling themselves the Blue Rider (the origin of the name is debated), which included Paul Klee and Franz Marc. They were all devoted to expressing the spiritual truths they felt within by using intense colors and geometric shapes.

The Blue Rider might have remained a minor offshoot of German Expressionism, but, as the next rooms show, its members went on to greater things, pioneering abstract art. As they focused on the spiritual, they paid less attention to recreating the physical world realistically on canvas and more attention to the colors and lines alone. Kandinsky's "Improvisations"—like a jazz musician improvising a new pattern of notes from a set scale—eventually became the art world's first purely abstract canvases. Soon Kandinsky was teaching at the famous Bauhaus school in Weimar, and his style spread everywhere. Jawlensky and Klee also went on to a simpler and more abstract style. Between the second-floor Blue Rider rooms is one section ("New Objectivity") with German art from the interwar years.

One floor down, in the "Art After 1945" section, you'll see big, empty canvases by the Abstract Expressionists who—like Kandinsky and his Blue Rider contemporaries—tried to "express" deep truths through "abstract" color and line alone. You'll see other recent pieces, most of them provocative. This floor also has a section devoted to several oddball installations by Joseph Beuys. (Is that art, or did the janitor just leave a broom here?) The far wing's stash of 19th-century paintings (on both floors) provides a nice contrast to all the abstract stuff (but skip it if you're also hitting the Neue Pinakothek, which has a better collection of similar works). Finally, across the entry hall from the ticket desk and up one floor, check out portraits of 19th-century notables by the painter who lived and worked here in what is now the museum that bears his name, Franz von Lenbach.

Other Nearby Art Museums

The museum quarter has several more highly regarded museums, but for the typical tourist on a quick visit they probably don't merit a stop. However, if you have a special interest in art, you'll want to know about these two:

The **Museum Brandhorst** covers the end of the 20th century and the beginning of the 21st, with a particular emphasis on Andy Warhol

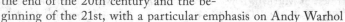

and Cy Twombly. Its collection is contained in a striking building with thousands of colored cylinders lining the outside (closed Mon, www. museum-brandhorst.de). And the **Glyptothek** is an impressive collection of Greek and Roman sculpture started by Ludwig I (closed Mon, www.antike-am-koenigsplatz.mwn.de/glyptothek).

Nazi Documentation Center

Munich was the birthplace of Nazism, and—even after the Nazis took power and moved to Berlin—it remained the official Nazi Party headquarters. It was in Munich that Hitler and other disillusioned World War I veterans gathered to lick their wounds. The Nazi Party was founded here in 1919, and this is where Hitler staged his attempted coup (the Beer Hall Putsch). In nearby Landsberg, he was imprisoned and wrote his *Mein Kampf* manifesto.

As soon as the Nazis took power (in 1933), they opened their first concentration camp, outside Munich in Dachau. Munich was the site of the infamous failed peace pact, the Munich Agreement of 1938, where Britain's prime minister tried to avoid war by appeasing Hitler. Once in power, Hitler officially proclaimed Munich "Capital of the Movement."

Königsplatz was ground central for Nazi activities. (Remember that Hitler fancied himself an artist, and with its world-class museums, art academies, and artists' villas, this square was at the heart of the German art world—thus making it a perfect stage for Hitler's ego; the monumental Neoclassical buildings that surround the square were also right up his alley.) Mass rallies were held on Königsplatz, where they burned forbidden books. Some 50 buildings in the neighborhood housed dozens of Nazi departments and thousands of employees. Most of the Nazi-built architecture is gone now, but at Arcisstrasse 12, once the Führerbau ("Führer building," now used as a music academy), you can still see the window of Hitler's personal office above the entrance porch. And the official Nazi Party headquarters (called the Brown House) was next door, along Brienner Strasse. That structure was destroyed in World War II and has now been replaced by a brand-new building—the Nazi Documentation Center.

The center—housed in a stark, light-filled, cube-shaped building scheduled to open sometime in 2015—documents the rise and fall of Nazism with a focus on Munich's role and the reasons behind it, as this city, like the rest of Germany, is determined to learn from its 20th-century nightmare (check with TI or website for latest information, U-2: Königsplatz, Brienner Strasse 34, tel. 089/233-26142, www.ns-dokumentationszentrum-muenchen.de).

THE ENGLISH GARDEN AND NEARBY
▲English Garden (Englischer Garten)

Munich's "Central Park," the largest urban park on the Continent, was laid out in 1789 by an American. More than 100,000 locals commune with nature here on sunny summer days. The park stretches three miles from the center, past the university and the trendy

> # Green Munich
>
> Although the capital of a very conservative part of Germany, Munich has long been a liberal stronghold. For nearly two decades, the city council has been controlled by a Social Democrat/Green Party coalition. The city policies are pedestrian-friendly—you'll find much of the town center closed to normal traffic, with plenty of bike lanes and green spaces. As you talk softly and hear birds rather than motors, it's easy to forget you're in the center of a big city. On summer Mondays, the peace and quiet make way for "blade Monday"—when streets in the center are closed to cars and as many as 30,000 inline skaters swarm around town in a giant rolling party.

Schwabing quarter. For the best quick visit, take bus #100 or tram #18 to the Nationalmuseum/Haus der Kunst stop. Under the bridge, you may see surfers. Follow the path downstream into the garden. Just beyond the hilltop temple (walk up for a postcard view of the city), you'll find the big Chinese Tower beer garden and other places to enjoy a drink or a meal (described later, under "Eating in Munich"). Afterward, instead of retracing your steps, you can walk (or take bus #54 a couple stops) to the Giselastrasse U-Bahn station and return to town on the U-3 or U-6.

A rewarding respite from the city, the park is especially fun—and worth ▲▲—on a bike under the summer sun and on warm evenings (unfortunately, there are no bike-rental agencies in or near the park; to rent some wheels, see page 27). Caution: While local law requires sun-worshippers to wear clothes on the tram, the park is sprinkled with buck-naked sunbathers—quite a shock to prudish Americans (they're the ones riding their bikes into the river and trees).

Haus der Kunst

Built by Hitler as a temple of Nazi art, this bold and fascist building—a rare surviving example of a purpose-built Nazi structure—is now an impressive shell for various temporary art exhibits. Ironically, the art now displayed in Hitler's "house of art" is the kind that annoyed the Führer most—modern. Its cellar, which served as a nightclub for GIs in 1945, is now the extremely exclusive P-1 nightclub.

Cost and Hours: €5-10 per exhibit, combo-tickets save money if seeing at least two exhibits, daily 10:00-20:00, Thu until 22:00, exhibits usually well-explained in English, at south end of English Garden, tram #18 or bus #100 from station to Nationalmuseum/Haus der Kunst, Prinzregentenstrasse 1, tel. 089/2112-7113, www.hausderkunst.de.

Nearby: Just beyond the Haus der Kunst, where Prinzregentenstrasse crosses the Eisbach canal, you can watch adventure-seekers surfing in the rapids created as the small river tumbles underground.

Bavarian National Museum (Bayerisches Nationalmuseum)

This tired but interesting collection features Tilman Riemenschneider woodcarvings, manger scenes, traditional living rooms, and old Bavarian houses.

Cost and Hours: €5, €1 on Sun, open Tue-Sun 10:00-17:00, Thu until 20:00, closed Mon, tram #18 or bus #100 from station to Nationalmuseum/Haus der Kunst, Prinzregentenstrasse 3, tel. 089/211-2401, www.bayerisches-nationalmuseum.de.

Villa Stuck

Franz von Stuck, Munich's top Art Nouveau artist and fin-desiècle tastemaker, designed this mansion for himself, then lived and worked (and partied) here from 1898 until his death in 1928. Within Munich's cutting-edge art scene, you were nobody until you were invited to an evening here. The rooms' original dark-wood/gold-leaf decor dazzle Jugendstil fans; upstairs in von Stuck's former studio is his "Sin Altar" with a version of his most famous (and perhaps most erotically charged) painting, *The Sin (Die Sünde)*.

Cost and Hours: €4, Tue-Sun 11:00-18:00, closed Mon, Prinzregentenstrasse 60, tel. 089/455-5510, www.villastuck.de. The villa is a short ride across the river from the north end of the city center (tram #16 or bus #100 to Friedensengel/Villa Stuck, or U-4: Prinzregentenplatz).

DEUTSCHES MUSEUM BRANCHES

Germany's answer to our Smithsonian National Air and Space Museum, the Deutsches Museum traces the evolution of science and technology. The main branch of the Deutsches Museum is centrally located. The two other branches—the Museum of Transportation and the Flight Museum—are situated outside the city center, but are worth the effort for enthusiasts. You can pay separately for each museum, or buy one €15 combo-ticket, which covers all three.

▲Deutsches Museum (Main Branch)

Enjoy wandering through rooms of historic airplanes, spaceships, mining, the harnessing of wind and water power, hydraulics, musical instruments, printing, chemistry, computers, astronomy, and nanotechnology...it's the Louvre of technical know-how. That said, the museum feels a bit dated, some exhibits are more wonky than gee-whiz, and not all the displays have English descriptions. Still, there's something here for everyone, from tech geeks to kids to poetry majors.

It's impossible to see everything in one visit. With 11 acres of floor space and 10 miles of exhibits, even those on roller skates will need to be selective. Use my mini-tour to get oriented, then study the floor plan and choose which departments interest you. The museum is designed to be hands-on; if you see a button, push it.

Cost and Hours: €8.50, €15 combo-ticket includes Museum of Transportation and Flight Museum, daily 9:00-17:00, worthwhile €4 English guidebook, no guided tours in English, several small cafés in the museum, tel. 089/21791, www.deutsches-museum.de.

Getting There: Take tram #16 to the Deutsches Museum stop. Alternatively, take the S-Bahn or tram #18 to Isartor, then walk 300 yards over the river, following signs. (The entrance is near the far end of the building.)

Visiting the Museum: After buying your ticket, ask about the day's schedule of demonstrations (for example, electric power or glass-blowing). Pick up a floor plan, then continue past the ticket taker, straight ahead, into a vast high-ceilinged room dominated by a tall-masted ship—Room 10.

Ground Floor: Get oriented. Above you hang early airplanes of the excellent aeronautics exhibit on the first floor (which we'll visit later). Behind you, locate the handy elevator—it's one of the few elevators in this labyrinthine building that goes to all six floors. Now, let's explore.

Room 10's exhibit on **marine navigation** is anchored by the 60-foot sailing ship *Maria*. Take the staircase down, where you can look inside her cut-away hull and imagine life below decks. Before heading back upstairs, find the bisected U1 submarine (past the bottom of the stairs, on the wall farthest from the entrance)—the first German *U-Boot* (undersea boat), dating from 1906.

Back up on the ground floor from Room 10, continue straight ahead to spacious Room 18, filled with airplanes, helicopters, and jets. A staircase at the back spirals around a V-2 rocket—a German invention that terrorized London in World War II and was a forerunner to the US space program. (The top floor at the top of the staircase has a great exhibit on space travel.) There are motors from the American Saturn rockets that went to the moon. On the ground-floor hall, you can step up into the European-built Spacelab capsule that went up on the US Space Shuttle *Columbia* in 1993.

From Room 18, make your way to several new technology exhibits—DNA, nano-technology, robotics—clustered in the far right corner (Rooms 11-16 and 25). Children will enjoy the "Kinderreich" (downstairs in Room 24), the model railway (Room 15), and the exciting twice-daily high-voltage demonstrations

(Room 9) showing the noisy creation of a five-foot bolt of lightning.

First Floor: The **aeronautics** collection occupies virtually the entire floor (Room 33). You'll see early attempts at flight—gliders, hot-air balloons, and a model of the airship pioneered by Germany's Count Zeppelin. The highlight is a Wright Brothers double-decker airplane from 1909—six years after their famous first flight, when they began to manufacture multiple copies of their prototype. By World War I, airplanes were becoming a formidable force. The Fokker tri-plane was made famous by Germany's war ace the Red Baron (Manfred von Richthofen, whose exploits, I've heard, prompted enemies to drop the f-bomb). The exhibit continues into WWII-era Junkers and Messerschmitts and post-war passenger planes.

Second Floor: Gathered together near the main elevator, you'll find a replica of prehistoric **cave paintings** (Room 39), and daily **glass-blowing** demonstrations (Room 40).

Third Floor: The third floor traces the **history of measurement,** including time (from a 16th-century sundial and an 18th-century clock to a scary Black Forest wall clock complete with grim reaper), weights, and geodesy (surveying and mapping). In the computer section (Rooms 52-53), you go from the ancient abacus to a 1956 Univac computer—as big as a room, with a million components, costing a million dollars, and with less computing power than your smartphone.

Floors 4-6: (If you have trouble finding your way to these floors, there's always that main elevator.) The focus here is on **astronomy.** A light-show exhibit (Room 62) traces the evolution of the universe. The recently renovated planetarium (Room 63) requires a €2 extra ticket and the lecture is in German, but it might be worth it if you love the stars. Finally, you emerge on the museum rooftop—the "sundial garden" (Room 64)—with great views. On a clear day, you can see the Alps.

▲Museum of Transportation (Verkehrszentrum)

While it veers a little toward the wonky, this fun museum has enough to interest the casual visitor—and it's heaven for any driving enthusiast. In 2003, the Deutsches Museum celebrated its centennial by opening this annex across town that shows off all aspects of transport, from old big-wheeled bikes to Benz's first car (a three-wheeler from the 1880s) to sleek ICE super-trains (serious train buffs going to Nürnberg will be more excited by the Deutsche Bahn Museum there). The museum asks what our lives would be like without transportation, and the exhibits show how modes of transportation developed from Neolithic "bone" skates (predecessors to today's in-line skates) to 19th-century Lapland skis, to today's snowboards and fast cars. It's housed in three giant hangar-like exhibition halls near the Oktoberfest grounds, a.k.a. Theresienwiese. All the exhibits are in both English and German.

Cost and Hours: €6, €15 combo-ticket includes Deutsches Museum and Flight Museum, daily 9:00-17:00, Theresienhöhe 14a, tel. 089/500-806-123, www.deutsches-museum.de.

Getting There: Take the U-4 or U-5 to Schwanthalerhöhe and follow signs for *Deutsches Museum* from the platform. The museum is just a few steps from the station exit.

Visiting the Museum: True to the Deutsches Museum's interactive spirit, the Museum of Transportation is engaging and well-explained.

Hall I focuses on urban transport, with special attention to Munich. Climb into the original 1927 prototype of a Berliner S-Bahn car, marvel at a cross-section of the intricate and multilayered subway system, learn about the history of the bicycle, and admire the vintage cars—including a deluxe 1930s Mercedes-Benz 370—arrayed into mock traffic jams. Twice a day (10:00-10:30 and 15:30-16:00) they fire up an S-Bahn simulator and let visitors pretend to drive the train.

Hall II gives you a look at the development of long-distance overland travel. The focus here is on trains and bus travel. Don't miss the Maffei S3/6, a.k.a. "The Pride of Bavaria" (in its heyday the fastest steam engine, at nearly 80 miles per hour); climb aboard the clever old postal train car (complete with a mail slot on the side); and check out the 1950s panorama bus that shuttled eager tourists to fashionable destinations such as Italy. If you're here at either 10:30 or 15:00 (or see a tour in progress), be sure to take a ride in the old carriage. The metal track simulates what it would have felt like to travel in the 18th century over different terrain (grass and cobblestones—pretty uncomfortable).

Hall III is all about fun: motorcycles, bicycles, skis, and race cars. Famous prewar models include the Mercedes-Benz SS and the Auto Union Type C "Grand Prix" race car. Other tiny racers—which resemble metal pickles to the uninitiated—include the 1950s Mercedes-Benz 300 SLR and the famous Messerschmitt 200. You'll also find early 18th-century bicycles based on Leonardo da Vinci's drawings. Before the invention of the pedal crank, bikes were just silly-looking scooters for adults.

Flight Museum (Flugwerft Schleissheim)

Fans of all things winged will enjoy the Deutsches Museum's Flight Museum, with more than 50 planes, helicopters, gliders, and an original Europa rocket housed in a historical aerodrome on a former military airfield. Inside the museum, try a helicopter simulator (for an extra charge) and watch antique planes being restored in the glass-walled workshop. The museum is well-done and has English explanations, but probably only those interested in the history of flight will find the trek worthwhile.

Cost and Hours: €6, €15 combo-ticket includes Deutsches Museum and Museum of Transportation, daily 9:00-17:00; tiny café, indoor benches provided for picnicking, other eating options in neighborhood; 20-minute S-Bahn trip from Marienplatz, take S-1 (direction: Freising Flughafen) and get off at Oberschleissheim (trip covered by Munich XXL day pass), then walk 15 minutes following "Museen" signs to Effnerstrasse 18, tel. 089/3157-1410, www.deutsches-museum.de.

Nearby: The impressively grand Schleissheim Palace is just a two-minute walk away. Even if you're too Wittlesbached out to visit the interior, the manicured Baroque gardens just behind the palace make for a lovely post-museum stroll (gardens free and open to the public, www.schloesser-schleissheim.de).

Sights Outside the City Center

▲▲NYMPHENBURG PALACE COMPLEX

For 200 years, this oasis of palaces and gardens was the Wittelsbach rulers' summer vacation home, a getaway from the sniping politics of court life in the city. Their kids could play, picnic, ride horses, and frolic in the ponds and gardens, while the adults played cards, listened to music, and sipped coffee on the veranda. It was at Nymphenburg that a seven-year-old Mozart gave a widely heralded concert, that 60-year-old Ludwig I courted the femme fatale Lola Montez, and that "Mad" King Ludwig II (Ludwig I's grandson) was born and baptized.

Today, Nymphenburg Palace and the surrounding one-square-mile park are a great place for a royal stroll or discreet picnic (see map on page 88). Indoors, you can tour the Bavarian royal family's summer quarters, and visit the Royal Stables Museum (carriages, sleighs, and porcelain). If you have time, check out playful extras such as a hunting lodge (Amalienburg), bathhouse (Badenburg), pagoda (Pagodenburg), and fake ruins (Magdalenenklause). The complex also houses a humble natural history museum and Baroque chapel. Allow at least three hours (including travel time) to see the palace complex at a leisurely pace.

Cost and Hours: Palace-€6; combo-ticket-€11.50 (€8.50 off-

MUNICH

season) covers the palace, Royal Stables Museum, and outlying sights open in summer. All of these sights are open daily April–mid-Oct 9:00-18:00, mid-Oct-March 10:00-16:00—except for Amalienburg and the other small palaces in the park, which are closed mid-Oct-March. The park is open daily 6:30-dusk and free to enter. Tel. 089/179-080, www.schloss-nymphenburg.de.

Getting There: The palace is three miles northwest of central Munich. Take tram #17 (direction: Amalienburgstrasse) from the north side of the train station (or catch it at Karlsplatz). In 15 minutes you reach the Schloss Nymphenburg stop. From the bridge by the tram stop, you'll see the palace—a 10-minute walk away. The palace is a pleasant 30-minute bike ride from the main train station (either follow Arnulfstrasse all the way to Nymphenburg, or turn up Landshuter Allee—at Donersburgerbrücke—then follow Nymphenburger Strasse until you hit the canal that stretches to the palace). Be aware that biking in the palace grounds is not permitted.

Eating: A café serves lunches in the former palm house, behind and to the right of the palace (open year-round). More eating options are near the tram stop, including a bakery with sandwiches.

NYMPHENBURG PALACE

In 1662, after 10 years of trying, the Bavarian ruler Ferdinand Maria and his wife, Henriette Adelaide of Savoy, finally had a son, Max Emanuel. In gratitude for a male heir, Ferdinand gave this land to his Italian wife, who proceeded to build an Italian-style Baroque palace. Their son expanded the palace to today's size. (Today's Wittelsbachs, who still refer to themselves as "princes" or "dukes," live in one wing of the palace.)

The palace interior, while interesting, is much less extensive than Munich's Residenz—you can only visit 16 rooms. The place is stingy on free information; you'll need the serviceable audioguide (€3.50) if you'd like more info than what I've provided below.

> **Self-Guided Tour:** Your visit starts in the **Great Hall** (a.k.a. **Stone Hall**). As the central room of the palace, this light and airy space was the dining hall, site of big Wittelsbach family festivals. One of the grandest and best-preserved Rococo rooms in Bavaria (from about 1760), it sports elaborate stucco work by François de Cuvilliés (of Residenz fame) and a ceiling fresco by Johann Baptist Zimmermann (of Wieskirche fame).

Zimmerman's fresco opens a sunroof to the heavens, where Greek gods cavort. In the sunny center, Apollo drives his chariot to bring the dawn, while bearded Zeus (astride an eagle) and peacock-carrying Juno look on. The rainbow symbolizes the peace brought by the enlightened Wittelsbachs. Around the borders of the painting, notice the fun optical illusions: For example, a painted dog holds a stucco bird in its mouth. The painting's natural setting and joie de vivre reflect the pastoral pleasures enjoyed here at the Wittelsbachs' summer home. At one end of the fresco (away from the windows) lounges a lovely maiden with flowers in her hair: it's Flora, the eponymous nymph who inspired this "nymph's castle"—Nymphenburg.

From here, two wings stretch to the left and right. They're mirror images of one another: antechamber, audience chamber, bedchamber, and private living quarters. Guests would arrive here in the Great Hall for an awe-inspiring first impression, then make

MUNICH

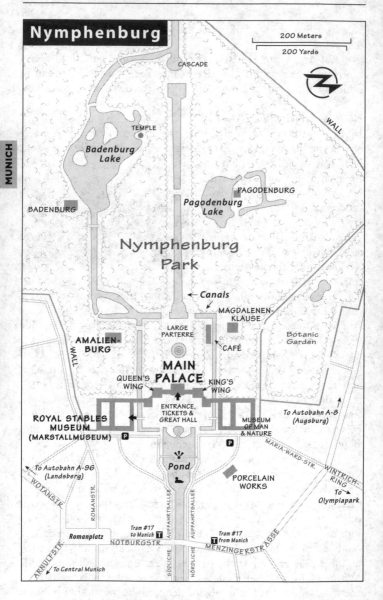

Nymphenburg

200 Meters
200 Yards

CASCADE

WALL

TEMPLE

Badenburg Lake

PAGODENBURG

BADENBURG

Pagodenburg Lake

Nymphenburg Park

← *Canals*

MAGDALENEN-KLAUSE

LARGE PARTERRE

Botanic Garden

AMALIEN-BURG

CAFÉ

WALL

MAIN PALACE

QUEEN'S WING

KING'S WING

ROYAL STABLES MUSEUM (MARSTALLMUSEUM)

ENTRANCE, TICKETS & GREAT HALL

MUSEUM OF MAN & NATURE

To Autobahn A-8 (Augsburg)

P

P

MARIA-WARD-STR.

To Autobahn A-96 (Landsberg)

Pond

PORCELAIN WORKS

WINTRICH-RING

To Olympiapark

WOTANSTR.

ROMANSTR.

Romanplatz

Tram #17 to Munich

SÜDLICHE AUFFAHRTSALLEE

NÖRDLICHE AUFFAHRTSALLEE

NOTBURGSTR.

Tram #17 from Munich

MENZINGERSTRASSE

ARNULFSTR.

To Central Munich

their way through a series of (also-impressive) waiting rooms for their date with the Wittelsbach nobility.

• *The tour continues to the left (as you look out the big windows).*

North Wing (Rooms 2-9): Breeze quickly through this less interesting wing, filled with tapestries and Wittelsbach portraits (including curly-haired Max Emanuel, who built this wing). Pause in the long corridor lined with paintings of various Wittelsbach palaces. The ones of Nymphenburg show the place around 1720, back when there was nothing but countryside between it and downtown (and gondolas plied the canals). Imagine the logistics when the royal family—with their entourage of 200—decided to move out to the summer palace. Find the painting of Fürstenried Palace (in another Munich suburb), and look for the twin onion domes of the Frauenkirche in the distance.

• *Return to the Great Hall and enter the other wing.*

South Wing (Rooms 10-20): Pass through the gold-and-white Room 10 and turn right into the red-walled Audience Chamber. The room calls up the exuberant time of Nymphenburg's founding couple, Ferdinand and Henriette. A portrait on the wall shows them posing together in their rich courtly dress. Another painting depicts them in a Greek myth: Henriette (as the moon-goddess Diana) leads little Max Emanuel by the hand, while Ferdinand (as her mortal lover Endymion) receives the gift of a sword. The ceiling painting (of the earth goddess Cybele) and the inlaid table also date from the time of Nymphenburg's first family.

After admiring the Queen's Bedroom and Chinese lacquer cabinet, head down the long hall to **King Ludwig I's Gallery of Beauties**. The room is decorated top to bottom with portraits of 36 beautiful women (all of them painted by Joseph Stieler between 1827 and 1850). Ludwig I was a consummate girl-watcher. (His rakish coronation portrait—by Stieler—hangs in the Neue Pinakothek.)

Ludwig prided himself on his ability to appreciate beauty regardless of social rank. He enjoyed picking out the prettiest women from the general public and, with one of the most effective pickup lines of all time, inviting them to the palace for a portrait. Who could refuse? The portraits were on public display in the Residenz, and catapulted their subjects to stardom. The women range from commoners to princesses, but notice that they share one physical trait—Ludwig obviously preferred brunettes. The portraits are done in the modest and slightly sentimental Biedermeier style popular in central Europe, as opposed to the more flamboyant Romanticism (so beloved of Ludwig's "mad" grandson) also thriving at that time.

Most of these portraits have rich stories behind them (each of the following are at eye level): Find Helene Sedlmayr, a humble cobbler's daughter who caught Ludwig's eye; she poses in a dress way beyond her budget. Though poor, she was considered Munich's comeliest Fräulein, and she eventually married the king's valet and had 10 children. To the left of Helene, Lady Jane Ellenborough Digby—an elegant English baroness—went through four marriages and numerous affairs, including one with Ludwig (and, much later, with his son Otto, after Otto had become king of Greece).

She was fluent in nine languages, including Arabic, after marrying a Syrian sheik 20 years her junior.

Lola Montez was the king's most notorious mistress, who led him to his downfall (see "The History of Munich, Part 1" on page 44). The portrait shows her the year she met Ludwig (she was 29, he was 60), wearing the black-lace mantilla and red flowers of a Spanish dancer. (And where in the "gallery of beauties" is the portrait of Ludwig's wife, Queen Therese? She's not here...you'll have to duck into the elegant, green Queen's Study to see her portrait.) Near Lola, find Princess Marie of Prussia—Ludwig's daughter-in-law—who once lived in the last rooms we'll visit.

Pass through the blue Audience Room (with elaborate curtain rods and mahogany furniture in the French-inspired Empire style) and into the (other) **Queen's Bedroom**. The room has much the same furniture it had on August 25, 1845, when Princess Marie gave birth to the future King Ludwig II. Little Ludwig (see his bust, next to brother Otto's) was greatly inspired by Nymphenburg—riding horses in summer, taking sleigh rides in winter, reading poetry at Amalienburg. The love of nature and solitude he absorbed at Nymphenburg eventually led Ludwig to abandon Munich for his castles in the remote Bavarian countryside. By the way, note the mirror in this bedroom. Royal births were carefully witnessed, and the mirror allowed for a better view. While Ludwig's birth was well-documented, his death was shrouded in mystery (see page 149).

Palace Grounds

The wooded grounds extend far back beyond the formal gardens and are popular with joggers and walkers (biking is not allowed). Find a bench for a low-profile picnic. The park is laced with canals and small lakes, where court guests once rode on Venetian-style gondolas.

Royal Stables Museum (Marstallmuseum)

These former stables (to the left of the main palace as you approach the complex) are full of gilded coaches that will make you think of Cinderella's journey to the king's ball. Upstairs, a porcelain exhibit shows off some of the famous Nymphenburg finery. If you don't want to visit the main palace, you can buy a €4.50 ticket just for this museum (no audioguide available).

Visiting the Museum: Wandering through the collection, you can trace the evolution of 300 years of coaches—getting lighter and with better suspension as they were harnessed to faster horses. In the big entrance hall is a golden carriage drawn by eight fake white horses. In 1742, it carried Karl Albrecht Wittelsbach to Frankfurt to be crowned Holy Roman Emperor. As emperor, he got eight horses—kings got only six. The event is depicted in a frieze on the museum wall; Karl's carriage is #159.

Other objects bear witness to the good times of the relaxed Nymphenburg lifestyle. You'll see the sleigh of Max Emanuel, decorated with a carved Hercules. The carousel (not always on display) was for the royal kids. It helped them develop dexterity through fun and games.

Next up are things owned by Ludwig II—several sleighs, golden carriages, and (in the glass cases) harnesses. A painting (just around the corner, on the right) shows "Mad" King Ludwig on his sleigh at night. In his later years, Ludwig was a Howard Hughes-type recluse who stayed away from the public eye and only went out at night. (At his nearby Linderhof Palace, he actually had a hydraulic-powered dining table that would rise from the kitchen below, completely set for the meal—so he wouldn't be seen by his servants.) Ludwig's over-the-top coaches were Baroque. But this was 1870. The coaches, like the king, were in the wrong century.

Notice the photos (c. 1865, in the glass case) of Ludwig and the Romantic composer Richard Wagner. Ludwig cried on the day Wagner was married. Hmmm.

Backtrack to the entrance, then pass the courtyard into another hall, this one filled with more practical coaches for everyday use. At the end of the hall, Ludwig II's favorite horse, "Cosa-Rara," is stuffed and mounted.

Head upstairs to a collection of **Nymphenburg porcelain**. You'll see plates and cups painted in various styles, from ancient Greek to Old Masters, Romantic, and Art Nouveau. Historically, royal families such as the Wittelsbachs liked to have their own porcelain factories to make fit-for-a-king plates, vases, and so on. The Nymphenburg Palace porcelain works is still in operation (not open to the public—but the factory store on Odeonsplatz is happy to see you—see "Shopping in Munich," later). Find the large room with copies of 17th-century Old Masters' paintings from the Wittelsbach art collection (now at the Alte Pinakothek). Ludwig I had these paintings copied onto porcelain for safekeeping into the distant future. Take a close look—they're exquisite.

Amalienburg

Three hundred yards from Nymphenburg Palace, hiding in the park (head into the sculpted garden and veer to the left, following signs), you'll find a fine little Rococo hunting lodge which takes just a few minutes to tour. In 1734, Elector Karl Albrecht had it built for his

wife, Maria Amalia. Like the palace's Great Hall, Amalienburg was designed by François de Cuvilliés and decorated by Johann Baptist Zimmermann. It's the most worthwhile of the four small "extra" palaces buried in the park that are included on the combo-ticket. The others are the Pagodenburg, a Chinese-inspired pavilion; Badenburg, an opulent bathing house and banquet hall; and the Magdalenenklause, a mini-palace that looks like a ruin from the outside but has an elaborate altar and woody apartments inside.

Visiting Amalienburg: As you approach, circle to the front and notice the facade. Above the pink-and-white grand entryway, Diana, goddess of the chase, is surrounded by themes of the hunt and flanked by busts of satyrs. The queen would shoot from the perch atop the roof. Behind a wall in the garden, dogs would scare non-flying pheasants. When they jumped up in the air above the wall, the sporting queen—as if shooting skeet—would pick the birds off.

Tourists now enter this tiny getaway through the back door. Doghouses under gun cupboards fill the first room. In the fine yellow-and-silver bedroom, the bed is flanked by portraits of Karl Albrecht and Maria Amalia—decked out in hunting attire. She liked her dogs. The door under the portrait leads to stairs to the rooftop pheasant-shooting perch. The relief on the door's lower panel shows Vulcan forging arrows for amorous cupids.

The mini-Hall of Mirrors is a blue-and-silver commotion of Rococo nymphs designed by Cuvilliés. In the next room, paintings depict court festivities, formal hunting parties, and no-contest kills (where the animal is put at an impossible disadvantage—like shooting fish in a barrel). Finally, the unfinished-feeling kitchen is decorated with Chinese-style drawings on Dutch tile.

OTHER SIGHTS OUTSIDE THE CENTER
▲▲BMW-Welt and Museum
At the headquarters of BMW ("beh-em-VEH" to Germans), Beamer dreamers can visit two space-age buildings to learn more about this brand's storied heritage. The renowned *Autos* and *Motorräder* are beautifully displayed (perhaps even fetishized). This vast complex—built on the site of Munich's first airstrip and home to the BMW factory since 1920—has four components: the headquarters (in the building nicknamed "the Four Cylinders"—not open to the public), the factory (tourable with advance reserva-

tions), the showroom (called BMW-Welt—"BMW World"), and the BMW Museum.

The futuristic, bowl-shaped **BMW Museum** encloses a world of floating walkways linking exhibits highlighting BMW motorcycle and car design and technology through the years. Employing seven themes and great English descriptions, the museum traces the Bavarian Motor Works' history since 1917, when the company began making airplane engines. Motorcycles came next,

MUNICH

followed by the first BMW sedan in 1929. You'll see how design was celebrated here from the start. Exhibits showcase motorsports, roadsters, and luxury cars. Stand on an *E* for English to hear the chief designer talk about his favorite cars in the "treasury." And the 1956 BMW 507 is enough to rev almost anyone's engine.

The **BMW-Welt** building itself—a cloud-shaped, glass-and-steel architectural masterpiece—is reason enough to visit. It's free and filled with exhibits designed to enthuse car lovers so they'll find a way to afford a Beamer. While the adjacent museum reviews the BMW past, BMW-Welt shows you the present and gives you a breathtaking look at the future. With interactive stations, high-powered videos, an inviting cafeteria, and lots of horsepower, this is where customers come to pick up their new Beamers, and where hopeful customers-to-be come to nurture their automotive dreams.

Cost and Hours: The museum costs €9 (Tue-Sun 10:00-18:00, closed Mon, tel. 089/125-016-001, www.bmw-welt.com). BMW-Welt is free and open daily (building open 7:30-24:00, exhibits open 9:00-18:00). English tours are offered of both the museum (€12, 1.5 hours, call ahead for times) and BMW-Welt (€7, daily at 14:00, 80 minutes). Factory tours must be booked at least two months in advance (€8, 2.5 hours, Mon-Fri only, ages 7 and up, book by calling 089/125-016-001, more info at www.bmw-werk-muenchen.de; ask at the BMW-Welt building about cancellations—open spots are released to the public a half-hour before each tour).

Getting There: It's very easy: Ride the U-3 to Olympia-Zentrum; the stop faces the BMW-Welt entry. To reach the museum, walk through BMW-Welt and over the swoopy bridge. This area also makes for a pleasant destination by bike, and is easily reached, and well-signed, from the English Garden.

Olympic Park (Olympiapark München)

Munich's great 1972 Olympic stadium and sports complex is now a lush park. You can get a good look at the center's striking "cob-

web" style of architecture while enjoying the park's picnic potential. In addition, there are several activities on offer at the park, including a tower (Olympiaturm) with a commanding but so-high-it's-boring view from 820 feet and an excellent swimming pool, the Olympia-Schwimmhalle. After the construction of Munich's Allianz Arena for the 2006 World Cup, Olympic Park has been left in the past, and has melted into the neighborhood as simply a fine park and swimming pool.

Cost and Hours: Tower—€5.50, daily 9:00-24:00, tel. 089/30670, www.olympiapark.de. Pool—€4.40, daily 7:00-23:00, tel. 089/2361-5050, www.swm.de. The U-3 runs from Marienplatz directly to the Olympia-Zentrum stop.

▲Isar River Bike Ride

Munich's river, lined by a gorgeous park, leads bikers into the pristine countryside in just a few minutes. From downtown (easy access from the English Garden or Deutsches Museum), follow the riverside bike path south (upstream) along the east (left) bank. You can't get lost. Just stay on the lovely bike path. It crosses the river after a while, passing tempting little *Biergartens* and lots of Bavarians having their brand of fun—including gangs enjoying Munich's famous river-party rafts. Go as far as you like, then retrace your route to get home. The closest bike rental is Mike's Bike Tours, by the Hofbräuhaus (see page 27).

Day Trips from Munich

▲▲DACHAU CONCENTRATION CAMP MEMORIAL (KZ-GEDENKSTÄTTE DACHAU)

Dachau was the first Nazi concentration camp (1933). Today, it's an easily accessible camp for travelers and an effective voice from our recent but grisly past, pleading "Never again." A visit here is a powerful and valuable experience and, when approached thoughtfully, well worth the trouble. Many people come away with more respect for history and the dangers of mixing fear, the promise of jobs, blind patriotism, and an evil government. You'll likely see lots of students here, as all Bavarian schoolchildren are required to visit a concentration camp. It's interesting to think that little more than

Near Munich

MUNICH

a couple of generations ago, people greeted each other with a robust *"Sieg Heil!"* Today, almost no Germans know the lyrics of their national anthem, and German flags are a rarity outside of major soccer matches.

Cost and Hours: Free, daily 9:00-17:00, last entry 30 minutes before closing. Though the museum shuts down at 17:00, the grounds are unofficially open until about 17:30 or 18:00 (as it takes a while for people to walk back to the entrance). The museum discourages parents from bringing children under age 12.

Planning Your Time: Allow yourself about five hours—giving you at least two and a half hours at the camp, plus round-trip travel from central Munich. With limited time you could do the whole trip in as little as three and a half hours by concentrating on the museum and skipping the powerful-but-long walk to the memorials and crematorium.

Getting There: The camp is a 45-minute trip from downtown Munich. Take the S-2 (direction: Petershausen) from any of the central S-Bahn stops in Munich to Dachau (3/hour, 20-minute trip from Hauptbahnhof). Then, at Dachau station, go down the stairs and follow the crowds out to the bus platforms; find the one marked *KZ–Gedenkstätte-Concentration Camp Memorial Sight*. Here, catch bus #726 and ride it seven minutes to the KZ-Gedenkstätte stop (3/hour). Before you leave this bus stop, be sure to note the return times back to the station. To return to Munich, you'll catch the S-2 again at Dachau station (direction: Erding or Markt Schwaben).

The Munich XXL day pass covers the entire trip, both ways (€8.10/person, €14.20/partner ticket for up to 5 adults). If you've already invested in a three-day Munich transport pass (which covers only the white/inner zone), you can save a couple euros by buying and stamping single tickets (€2.60/person each way) to cover the part of the trip that's in the green zone. You can also take a guided tour from Munich (described on page 34).

Drivers follow Dachauer Strasse from downtown Munich to Dachau-Ost, then follow *KZ-Gedenkstätte* signs.

The Town: The town of Dachau—quiet, tree-lined, and residential—is more pleasant than its unfortunate association with the camp on its outskirts, and tries hard to encourage you to visit its old town and castle (www.dachau.de). With 40,000 residents and quick access to downtown Munich, Dachau is now a high-priced and in-demand place to live.

Visitors Center: Coming from the bus stop or parking lot, you'll first see the visitors center, outside the camp wall. It lacks exhibits, but does have a small cafeteria (sandwiches and pasta dishes), a bookstore with English-language books on Holocaust themes, and a WC (more WCs inside the camp). At the information desk, you can rent an audioguide or sign up for a tour.

Tours: The €3.50 **audioguide** covers the grounds and museum; its basic itinerary includes 1.5 hours of information. It gives you a few extras (mainly short reminiscences by two camp survivors and three members of the Allied forces who liberated the camp), but isn't essential, since the camp is fully labeled in English (rental desk closes right at 17:00). Two different **guided walks** in English are offered, starting from the visitors center (€3, daily at 11:00 and 13:00, 2.5 hours; limited to 30 people, so show up early—especially in summer, 13:00 walk fills up first; call or visit website to confirm times, tel. 08131/669-970, www.kz-gedenkstaette-dachau.de).

⊘ **Self-Guided Tour:** From the visitors center, you approach the main compound. You enter, like the inmates did, through the infamous **iron gate** that held the taunting slogan *Arbeit macht frei* ("Work makes you free"). The original sign was stolen in 2014; a replica may be on display. Inside are the four key experiences of the memorial: the museum, the bunker behind the museum, the re-

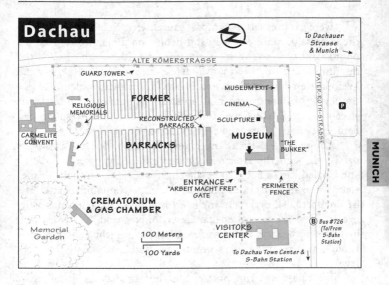

stored barracks, and a pensive walk across the huge but now-empty camp to the memorials and crematorium at the far end.

Enter the museum, housed in a former camp maintenance building. Just inside is a small bookshop that funds a nonprofit

organization (founded by former prisoners) that researches and preserves the camp's history. Here you can pick up a €0.50 information sheet, or buy the excellent 200-page book with a CD (€15) that contains the same text and images that you'll see in the museum.

Check show times for the museum's powerful 22-minute documentary film (English showings generally at 10:00, 11:30, 12:30, 14:00, and 15:00; ages 12 and up only).

The museum is organized chronologically, everything is thoughtfully described in English, and computer touch-screens let you watch early newsreels.

Rooms 1-2—The Camp is Founded: On January 30, 1933, Adolf Hitler took power. Two months later, Dachau opened. It was a "concentration" camp, to gather together and isolate enemies of the state, so they could not infect the rest of society. The camp was built well outside Dachau's residential zone, surrounded by a mile-wide restricted area.

A map of the Nazi camp system shows that Dachau was just one of many such camps. Some were concentration camps (marked with a square, like Dachau). Others (marked with a triangle with a V) were extermination camps—Auschwitz, Sobibor—built with the express purpose of executing people on a mass scale. Nearby, photos and posters chronicle the rise of Hitler in the 1920s: the resentment bred by Germany's defeat in World War I, the weak Weimar Republic, Hitler's solution to Germany's problems (blame the Jews), his failed Beer Hall Putsch, his participation in mainstream politics. No sooner did he take power than he suspended democracy and began squelching all opposition.

Rooms 3-7—Life at the Camp: In 1933, the first prisoners passed through the *Arbeit macht frei* gates. They were classified and labeled with a badge (see the chart) according to their "crime" against the state. Besides political activists (communists and leftist intellectuals), prisoners included homosexuals, Jehovah's Witnesses, Gypsies, so-called career criminals, and Germans who had tried to flee the country. A special badge—the yellow Star of David—was reserved for a group the Nazis particularly loathed, Jews.

The camp was run by the SS, the organization (headed by mastermind Heinrich Himmler) charged with Germany's internal security. Dachau was a training center for future camp managers. Rudolf Höss, who worked at Dachau from 1934 to 1938, went on to become the first commandant of Auschwitz.

Life at Dachau was horrific. It was a work camp, where inmates were expected to pay for their "crimes" with slave labor. It was strictly regimented: a wake-up call at 4:00, an 11-hour workday, roll call at 5:15 and 19:00, lights out at 21:00. The work was hard, whether quarrying or hauling loads or constructing the very buildings you see today. The rations were meager. Rule-breakers were punished severely—all manner of torture took place here. The most common punishment was being forced to stand at attention until you collapsed.

On September 1, 1939, Germany invaded Poland, World War II began, and Dachau's role changed.

Cinema: The 22-minute film, dating from the 1960s, is a sobering, graphic, and sometimes grisly account of the rise of Hitler and the atrocities of the camp (usually shown 5 times/day in English, not recommended for children under 12).

Rooms 8-15—The War Years: Once the war began, conditions at Dachau deteriorated. The original camp had been designed to hold just under 3,000 inmates. In 1937 and 1938, the camp was expanded and the building that now houses the museum was built, as well as barracks intended to hold 6,000 prisoners. With the war, the prisoner population swelled, and the Nazis found other purposes for the camp. It was less a concentration camp for German dissidents and more a dumping ground for foreigners and POWs. It was used as a special prison for 2,000 Catholic priests. From

Dachau, Jewish prisoners were sent east to the gas chambers. Inmates were put to use as slave labor for the German war machine—many were shipped to nearby camps to make armaments. Prisoners were used as human guinea pigs for war-related medical experiments of human tolerance for air pressure, hypothermia, and biological agents like malaria; the photos of these victims may be the most painful to view.

As the Allies closed in on both fronts, Dachau was bursting with more than 30,000 prisoners jammed into its 34 barracks. Disease broke out, and food ran short in the winter of 1944-1945. With coal for the crematorium running low, the corpses of those who died were buried in mass graves outside the camp site. The Allies arrived on April 29. Even so, 2,000 prisoners were so weak or sick that they died soon after. After 12 years of existence, Dachau was finally liberated.

Postscript: About 32,000 people died in Dachau between 1933 and 1945. (By comparison, more than a million were killed at Auschwitz in Poland.) But Dachau remains notorious because it was the Nazis' first camp. Oddly, Dachau actually housed people longer *after* the war than during the war. First, it housed Nazi officials arrested by the Allies, as they awaited trial at Nürnberg for war crimes. From 1948 to 1964, the camp became cheap housing for ethnic Germans expelled from Eastern Europe, complete with a cinema, shops, and so on. The last of the barracks was torn down in 1964, and the museum opened the following year.

• *Consider using the WC before leaving the museum building (there aren't any bathrooms elsewhere within the camp walls). Find the side door, at the end of the exhibition, which leads out to the long, low bunker behind the museum building.*

Bunker: This was a cellblock for prominent "special prisoners," such as failed Hitler assassins, German religious leaders, and politicians who challenged Nazism. Most of the 136 cells are empty, but exhibits in a few of them (near the entrance) profile the inmates and the SS guards who worked at Dachau, and allow you to listen to some inmates' testimonies. Cell #2 was the interrogation room. Cell #9 was a "standing cell"—inmates  were tortured here by being forced to stay on their feet for days at a time.

• *Exit the bunker, and walk around past the* Arbeit macht frei *gate to the big square between the museum and the reconstructed barracks, which was used for roll call. In front of the museum, notice the power-*

ful **memorial** *to the victims created in 1968 by Nandor Glid, a Jewish Holocaust survivor and artist, which includes humanity's vow:* Never Again. *Cross the square to the farther of the two reconstructed...*

Barracks: Take a quick look inside to get an idea of what sleeping and living conditions were like in the camp. There were 34 barracks, each measuring about 10 yards by 100 yards. When the camp was at its fullest, there was only about one square yard of living space per inmate.

• *Now walk between the two reconstructed barracks and down the tree-lined path past the foundations of the other barracks. At the end of the camp, in space that once housed the camp vegetable garden, rabbit farm, and brothel, there are now three places of meditation and worship (Jewish to your right, Catholic straight ahead, and Protestant to your left). Beyond them, just outside the camp, is a Carmelite convent. Turn left toward the corner of the camp and find the small bridge leading to the...*

Camp Crematorium: A memorial garden surrounds the two camp crematorium buildings, which were used to burn the bodies

of prisoners who had died or been killed. The newer, larger concrete crematorium was built to replace the smaller wooden one. One of its rooms is a **gas chamber,** which worked on the same principles as the much larger one at Auschwitz, and was originally disguised as a shower room (the fittings are gone now). It was never put to use at Dachau for mass murder, but some historians suspect that a few people were killed in it experimentally. In the garden near the buildings is a Russian Orthodox shrine.

▲ANDECHS MONASTERY

This monastery crouches quietly with a big smile between two lakes just south of Munich. For a fine Baroque church in a rural Bavarian setting at a monastery that serves hearty cafeteria-quality food—and perhaps the best beer in Germany—consider a short side-trip here. The cafeteria terrace offers first-class views and second-class prices. Don't miss the stroll up to the church, where you can sit peacefully and ponder the striking contrasts a trip through Germany offers.

Cost and Hours: Free, *Biergarten* open daily 10:00-20:00, church open until 19:00, tel. 08152/3760, www.andechs.de.

Getting There: Reaching Andechs from Munich without a car is doable with a little planning. Bus #951 stops at the monastery on its run between Herrsching (at the end of the S-8 subway line) and Starnberg Nord (on the S-6 line). Bus #958 runs to Andechs from Tutzing (also on the S-6 line). Use the online schedules at www.bahn.com or www.mvv-muenchen.de to find a convenient connection (use Kloster Andechs as your destination; trip takes 1-1.5 hours, buy Munich *Gesamtnetz* day pass for €11.70 or pay €21.30 for the partner pass good for up to 5 people). You can also take the S-8 train to Herrsching, then hike, bike, or catch a taxi for the three miles to the monastery.

MORE DAY TRIPS FROM MUNICH

For day trips to many Bavarian destinations, consider traveling by train with the **Bayern-Ticket.** It covers up to five people from Munich to anywhere in Bavaria (plus Salzburg) and back for a very low price (€23 for the first person plus €4 for each additional person, €2 more if bought at counter instead of machine, not valid before 9:00 Mon-Fri, valid only on slower "regional" trains—most of them labeled on schedules as either "RB," "RE," or "IRE," also valid on city transport). The ticket is explained in *The Inside Track* newsletter and sold at EurAide (see page 20).

▲▲▲"Mad" King Ludwig's Castles

The spectacular Neuschwanstein and Linderhof castles each make a great day trip (it's possible to do both in a day, but exhausting). Your easiest option is to take a tour (see "Tours in Munich" on page 28). Without a tour, only Neuschwanstein is easy (2 hours by train to Füssen, then 10-minute bus ride to the castle). Or spend the night in Füssen. For all the details, see the next chapter.

▲▲Nürnberg

A handy but expensive ICE express train zips you to Nürnberg in about an hour (departures several times an hour), making this very historic city a viable day trip from Munich. Cheaper RE trains, covered by the Bayern-Ticket, take a little longer. For information, see the Nürnberg chapter.

▲▲Salzburg

This Austrian city is an easy day trip and offers some exciting sightseeing (hourly trains from Munich get you there in around 2 hours). For details, see the Salzburg chapter.

Berchtesgaden

This resort, near Hitler's Eagle's Nest getaway, is easier as a side-trip from Salzburg (just 12 miles from there). For more, see page 262.

Shopping in Munich

While the whole city is great for shopping, the most glamorous area is around Marienplatz. It's fun to window-shop, even if you have no plans to buy. Here are a few stores and streets to consider.

Bavarian Souvenirs: Servus Heimat's amusing shops are a good source of unusual gifts; the one adjacent to the Munich City Museum is even something of a permanent flea market (City Museum store: Mon-Sat 10:00-19:00, Sun 10:00-18:00, St.-Jakobs-Platz 1, tel. 089/2370-2380; also stores at Im Tal 20—between Marienplatz and the Isartor—and at Brunnstrasse 3—near Asam Church, same hours except closed Sun; www.servusheimat.com).

Books: The big **Hugendubel bookstore** on Marienplatz is your best spot for English-language books; the Hugendubel on Karlsplatz also has some English offerings (and free Wi-Fi).

Dirndls and Lederhosen: For fine-quality (and very expensive) traditional clothing (*Trachten* in German), head to **Loden-Frey Verkaufshaus.** The third floor of this fine department store is dedicated to classic Bavarian wear for men and women (Mon-Sat 10:00-20:00, closed Sun, a block west of Marienplatz at Maffeistrasse 7, tel. 089/210-390, www.loden-frey.com). For less expensive (but still good quality) gear, visit **Angermaier Trachten,** near the Viktualienmarkt (Mon-Fri 10:00-19:00, Sat 9:00-19:00, closed Sun; Rosental 10, tel. 089/2300-0199, www.trachten-angermaier.de).

Toys: Obletter, right on Karlsplatz, has a good selection of wooden toys in its underground level, and a fun section full of puppets (Mon-Sat 9:30-20:00, closed Sun, Karlsplatz 11, tel. 089/5508-9510).

Porcelain: For contemporary and classic dinnerware and figurines, go to Odeonsplatz, where you'll find the **Nymphenburg Porcelain Store** (Mon-Fri 10:00-17:00, closed Sat-Sun, Odeonsplatz 1, tel. 089/282-428, www.nymphenburg.com).

Window Shopping and Malls: Shoppers will want to stroll from Marienplatz down the pedestrianized Weinstrasse (it begins to the left as you face New Town Hall). After a few short blocks, the street name changes to Theatinerstrasse; look for **Fünf Höfe** on your left, a delightful mall filled with Germany's top shops (open Mon-Fri 10:00-19:00, Sat 10:00-18:00, closed Sun). Named for its five courtyards, this is where tradition meets modern. Note how its Swiss architects (who also designed Munich's grand Allianz soccer stadium for the 2006 World Cup) play with light and color. Even if you're not a shopper, wander through the **Kunsthalle** to appreciate the architecture, the elegant window displays, and the sight of Bavarians living very well.

Built by Maximilian II in the 1850s, the nearby **Maximilianstrasse** was designed for shoppers. Today it's home to Munich's most exclusive shops.

Department Stores: Ludwig Beck, an upscale department store at Marienplatz, has been a local institution since 1861. With six floors of expensive designer clothing (plus some music, stationery, and cosmetics), this is the place to go for a €200 pair of jeans. Beck has long been to fabrics what Dallmayr is to fine food—too expensive to actually buy anything in, but fun to browse (Mon-Sat 9:30-20:00, closed Sun). For more reasonable prices near Marienplatz, try **C&A** (considered cheap yet respected; sells only clothing), **Kaufhof** (mid-range; sells everything), and more upmarket **Karstadt**.

Lowbrow Tips: For that beer stein you promised to take home to your uncle, try the shops on the pedestrian zone by St. Michael's Church and the gift shops that surround the Hofbräuhaus. If you're looking for a used cell phone or exotic groceries, the area south of the train station fits the bill.

MUNICH

Nightlife in Munich

Here are a few nightlife alternatives to the beer-and-oompah scene.

MUSIC AND DANCE

Ballet and opera fans can check the schedule at the **Bayerisch Staatsoper,** centrally located right by the Residenz. Because of high demand, book at least a month ahead—seats range from €13 to very pricey (Max-Joseph-Platz 2, tel. 089/2185-1920, www.bayerische. staatsoper.de). The **Hotel Bayerischerhof's** nightclub has live music—major jazz acts plus pop/soul/disco—in a posh, dress-up, expensive setting (Promenadeplatz 2, tel. 089/212-0994, www. bayerischerhof.de). For familiar Broadway-style musicals (though most are performed in German), try the **Deutsches Theatre**, conveniently located near my train-station hotels (Schwanthalerstrasse 13, tel. 089/5523-4120, www.deutsches-theater.de).

PUBS

If you just want to explore an untouristed area known for its nightlife—both gay and straight—get out your map and find **Gärtnerplatz** (a 30-minute walk due south of Marienplatz, bus #52 from Marienplatz, or U-1 or U2 to Fraunhoferstrasse).

Closer to the city center, **Heilig-Geist-Stüberl** ("Holy Ghost

Pub") is a funky, retro little hole-in-the-wall where you are sure to meet locals (the German cousins of those who go to Reno because it's cheaper than Vegas, and who consider karaoke high culture). The interior, a 1980s time warp, makes you feel like you're stepping into an alcoholic cuckoo clock. There's no food—just drink here (Mon-Sat 9:00-22:00, Sun 14:00-22:00, just off the Viktualien-markt at Heiliggeiststrasse 1).

Sleeping in Munich

Unless you hit Munich during a fair, convention, or big holiday, you can sleep reasonably here. Lots of student hotels around the station house anyone who's young at heart for €25, and it's possible to find a fine double with breakfast in a good basic hotel for €90. I've listed accommodations in two neighborhoods: within a few blocks of the central train station (Hauptbahnhof), and in the old center, between Marienplatz and Sendlinger Tor. Many of these places have complicated, slippery pricing schemes. I've listed the normal non-convention, non-festival prices. There are major conventions about 30 nights a year—prices increase from 20 percent to as much as 300 percent during Oktoberfest (Sept 19-Oct 4 in 2015; reserve well in advance). During slow times, you may be able to do better than the rates listed here—always ask. Sunday is very slow and usually comes with a huge discount if you ask.

NEAR THE TRAIN STATION

Good-value hotels cluster in the multicultural area immediately south of the station. To some it's a colorful neighborhood, for others it feels seedy after dark (erotic cinemas and men with moustaches loitering in the shadows), but it's sketchy only for those in search of trouble. Still, hotels in the old center (listed later) might feel more comfortable to some.

$$$ Marc München—polished, modern, and with 80 newly renovated rooms—is a good option if you need a little more luxury than the other listings here. It's just a half-block from the station on a relatively tame street, and has four-star comforts like a nice lobby and classy breakfast spread. The cheaper "superior king" rooms are fine (around Sb-€127-151, Db-€147-221); the more expensive rooms (Sb-€137-197, Db-€167-251) add more cost than value (no triples, 10 percent discount with this book and direct reservation except during events, parking-€10-16/day, air-con, guest computer, cable Internet and Wi-Fi, Senefelderstrasse 12, tel. 089/559-820, www.hotel-marc.de, info@hotel-marc.de).

$$ Hotel Monaco is a delightful and welcoming little hide-away, tucked inside the fifth floor of a giant, nondescript building two blocks from the station. Emerging from the elevator, you're

> # Sleep Code
>
> **Abbreviations**   (€1 = about $1.40, country code: 49)
> **S** = Single, **D** = Double/Twin, **T** = Triple, **Q** = Quad, **b** = bath-
> room, **s** = shower only
> **Price Rankings**
> **$$$** **Higher Priced**—Most rooms €130 or more.
>   **$$** **Moderately Priced**—Most rooms between €90-130.
>   **$** **Lower Priced**—Most rooms €90 or less.
> Unless otherwise noted, credit cards are accepted, English
> is spoken, breakfast is included, Wi-Fi is generally free, and
> there is an elevator but no air-conditioning. Prices change;
> verify the hotel's current rates online or by email. For the best
> prices, always book directly with the hotel.

warmly welcomed by Christine and her staff into a flowery, cherub-filled oasis. It's homey, with 22 clean and fresh rooms, and lots of special touches (S-€59, Sb-€69-89, D-€75, Db-€79-99, Tb-€139, €9/person less without breakfast—but I wouldn't skip it, cash strongly preferred, guest computer, Wi-Fi, Schillerstrasse 9, entrance on Adolf-Kolping-Strasse, tel. 089/545-9940, www.hotel-monaco.de, info@hotel-monaco.de).

$$ Hotel Uhland is a stately mansion that rents 29 delightful rooms in a safe-feeling, genteel residential neighborhood a slightly longer walk from the station than the others in this section (toward the Theresienwiese Oktoberfest grounds). It's been in the Hauzenberger and Reim families for 60 years (Sb-€75-87, small Db-€95, big Db-€105-118, Tb-€125-143, price depends on room size, great family rooms, online deals, Wi-Fi, limited free parking, Uhlandstrasse 1, tel. 089/543-350, www.hotel-uhland.de, info@hotel-uhland.de). From the station, take bus #58 (direction: Silberhornstrasse) to Georg-Hirth-Platz, or walk 15 minutes: Out the station's south exit, cross Bayerstrasse, take Paul-Heyse-Strasse three blocks to Georg-Hirth-Platz, then take a soft right on Uhlandstrasse.

$$ Hotel Belle Blue, three blocks from the station, has 30 comfortable, modern rooms with air-conditioning. And yes, the decor is in shades of blue (Sb-€75-82, Db-€96, book direct for these prices, cable Internet and Wi-Fi, Schillerstrasse 21, tel. 089/550-6260, www.hotel-belleblue.de, info@hotel-belleblue.com, Irmgard).

$$ Hotel Bristol is bright and efficient, with 57 business-like rooms. While walkable from the station, it's actually just across the street from the Sendlinger Tor U-Bahn station, one stop from the train station on the U-1 or U-2 (Sb-€79, Db-€97, guest computer,

Wi-Fi, air-con in lobby, Pettenkoferstrasse 2, tel. 089/5434-8880, www.bristol-munich.de, info@bristol-munich.de).

$$ Hotel Deutsches Theater is a brass-and-marble-filled place with 27 three-star rooms. The back rooms face the courtyard of a neighboring theater—when there's a show, there can be some noise (Sb-€70-80, Db-€90-100, Tb-€120-130, pricier suites, €9/person less without breakfast, Wi-Fi, Landwehrstrasse 18, tel. 089/545-8525, www.hoteldeutschestheater.de, info@hoteldeutschestheater.de).

$$ Hotel Europäischer Hof, across the street from the station, is a huge, impersonal hotel with 150 decent rooms. During cool weather when you can keep the windows shut, the street-facing rooms are an acceptable option. The quieter, courtyard-facing rooms are more expensive and a lesser value, except for a few cheap rooms with shared bath—you'll have to email about these, as they're not listed on the website (streetside Sb-€82, Db-€98; courtyard S-€45-50, D with head-to-toe twin beds-€45-60; 10 percent discount on prevailing rates with this book and direct advance reservation, *or* if you pay cash—no double discounts; no discounts during conventions, major events, and Oktoberfest weekends; check website for current rates, family rooms, guest computer, Wi-Fi, parking-€13.50/day, Bayerstrasse 31, tel. 089/551-510, www.heh.de, info@heh.de).

$ Hotel Royal is one of the best values in the neighborhood (as long as you can look past the strip joints flanking the entry). While a bit institutional, it's clean and plenty comfortable. Most importantly, it's energetically run by Pasha and Christiane. Each of its 40 rooms is fresh and bright (Sb-€54-74, Db-€74-94, Tb-€99-119, Qb-€124-144, lower prices generally Nov-March, book direct for a 10 percent discount off the prevailing price with this book, ask for a room on the quiet side—especially in summer when you'll want the window open, guest computer, Wi-Fi, Schillerstrasse 11a, tel. 089/5998-8160, www.hotel-royal.de, info@hotel-royal.de).

$ Litty's Hotel is a basic hotel with 37 rooms—most of them small, but all of them serviceable—run by Verena and Bernd Litty (S-€52, Ss-€58, Sb-€68, D-€72, Ds-€78, Db-€88, T-€99, Wi-Fi at reception reaches lower floors, near Schillerstrasse at Landwehrstrasse 32c, tel. 089/5434-4211, www.littyshotel.de, info@littyshotel.de).

$ The CVJM (YMCA), open to all ages, rents 85 beds in clean, slightly worn rooms with sinks in the rooms and showers and toilets down the hall. Doubles are head-to-head; triples are like doubles with a bunk over one of the beds (S-€37, D-€64, T-€86, €28/bed in a shared triple, guests over 26 pay €3/person more, cheaper for 3 nights or more and in winter; only €10/night per person more during Oktoberfest—reserve at least 6 months ahead for

Oktoberfest weekdays, a year ahead for Oktoberfest weekends; includes sheets, breakfast, and guest computer, but no lockers; cheap Wi-Fi by reception, Landwehrstrasse 13, tel. 089/552-1410, www.cvjm-muenchen.org/hotel, hotel@cvjm-muenchen.org).

"Hostel Row" on Senefelderstrasse, a Block from the Station

All three of the following hostels are casual and well-run, with friendly and creative management, and all cater expertly to the needs of young beer-drinking backpackers enjoying Munich on a shoestring. With 900 cheap dorm beds, this is a spirited street. There's no curfew, and each place has a lively bar that rages until the wee hours, along with staff who speak English as the primary language. All have 24-hour receptions, guest computer, Wi-Fi, laundry facilities, lockers, and included linens; none has a kitchen, but each offers a buffet breakfast for €4-5. Sleep cheap in big dorms, or spend a little more for a two-, three-, or four-bed room. Prices vary with demand, and can range a little higher than the rates listed here in summer, quite a bit higher for Oktoberfest, and quite a bit lower in the off-season, when you might find a dorm bed for €12.

$ **Wombat's Hostel,** perhaps the most hip and colorful, rents cheap doubles and dorm beds with lockers. The rooms and dorms are fresh, modern, and contain bathrooms; and there's a relaxing and peaceful winter garden (300 beds, bunk in 8- and 10-bed dorms-€21-26, bunk in 4- and 6-bed dorms-€24-29, Db-€80, Senefelderstrasse 1, tel. 089/5998-9180, www.wombats-hostels.eu, office@wombats-munich.de).

$ **Euro Youth Hotel** fills a rare pre-WWII building (200 beds, bunk in 10- to 12-bed dorms-€22-26, bunk in 3- to 5-bed dorms-€23-30; S-€50, D-€77, Db-€90-94, breakfast included for private rooms; Senefelderstrasse 5, tel. 089/5990-8811, www.euro-youth-hotel.de, info@euro-youth-hotel.de, run by Alfio and Andy).

$ **Jaeger's Hostel** rounds out this trio, with 300 cheap beds and all the fun and efficiency you'd hope for in a hostel—plus the only air-conditioning on the street. If you're not looking to party, this is your hostel—it seems to be the quietest (bunk in 40-bed dorm-€19-22, bunk in 8- or 10-bed dorm-€22-27, bunk in 4- or 6-bed dorm-€26-29, hotel-quality Sb-€59, Db-€78, breakfast-€5, towel-€1/day if staying in dorm, Senefelderstrasse 3, tel. 089/555-281, www.jaegershostel.de, office@jaegershostel.de).

IN THE OLD CENTER

A few good deals remain in the area south of Marienplatz, going toward the Sendlinger Tor. This neighborhood feels more genteel

MUNICH

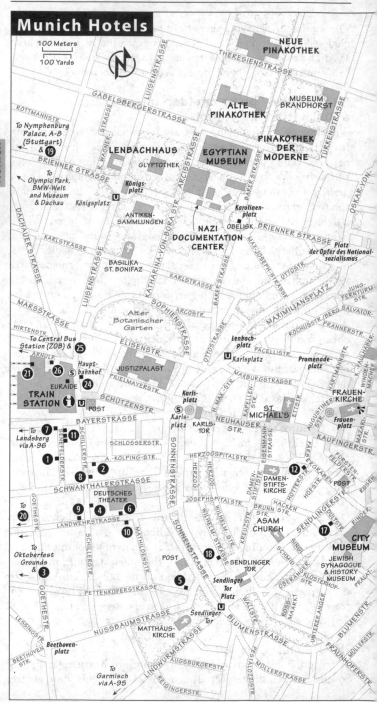

Munich Hotels

100 Meters
100 Yards

NEUE PINAKOTHEK

THERESIENSTRASSE

ALTE PINAKOTHEK

MUSEUM BRANDHORST

GABELSBERGERSTRASSE

LUISENSTRASSE

ROTTMANNSTR

To Nymphenburg Palace, A-8 (Stuttgart) & 19

LENBACHHAUS

GLYPTOTHEK

EGYPTIAN MUSEUM

PINAKOTHEK DER MODERNE

BRIENNER STRASSE

Königs-platz

OSKAR-VON-

To Olympic Park, BMW-Welt and Museum & Dachau

Königsplatz

K. WAGNER STRASSE

KATHARINA-VON-BORA-STR

ARCISSTRASSE

BARER STRASSE

TÜRKENSTRASSE

ANTIKEN-SAMMLUNGEN

Karolinen-platz

OBELISK

BRIENNER STRASSE

DACHAUER STRASSE

KARLSTRASSE

LUISENSTRASSE

BASILIKA ST. BONIFAZ

NAZI DOCUMENTATION CENTER

MAX-JOSEPH-STRASSE

OTTOSTR.

Platz der Opfer des National-sozialismus

KARLSTRASSE

KARLSTRASSE

SOPHIENSTRASSE

ARCOSTR.

BARER STRASSE

MAXIMILIANSPLATZ

JUNG-FERNTURM-STR.

MARSSTRASSE

Alter Botanischer Garten

ELISENSTR.

OTTOSTRASSE

Lenbach-platz

ROCHUSSTR./BERG SALVATOR-

PRANNERST

HIRTENSTR

To Central Bus Station (ZOB) & 25

ARNULF

21   26   Haupt-bahnhof   S   24

EURAIDE

TRAIN STATION

ELISENSTR.

JUSTIZPALAST

PRIELMAYERSTR.

Karls-platz

Karlsplatz

PACELLISTR.

Promenade-platz

MAXBURGSTR.

Karls-platz

PACELLISTR.

HARTMANNSTR.

K. FAULHABER-

WINDEN-MACHER

FRAUEN-KIRCHE

POST

SCHÜTZENSTR.

S   Karls-platz

KARLS-TOR

ST. MICHAEL'S

AUGUSTINER-STR.

ETTST.R

Frauen-platz

MAZARI-STR.

BAYERSTRASSE

SENEFELDERSTR.

SCHILLERSTR.

NEUHAUSER-STR.

KAPELLEN-STR.

H. MAX-STR.

EISENMANN-STR.

KAUFINGERSTR.

FÜRST EN-FELDERSTR.

To Landsberg via A-96   7   11

SCHLOSSERSTR.

A.-KOLPING-STR.

HERZOGSPITALSTR.

FÄRBERGRABEN

HOFSTR.

POST

ROSEN

1   8   2

SONNENSTRASSE

HERZOG-STR.

DAMEN-STIFTS-KIRCHE

12

ETTSTR

SENDLINGERSTR.

DULTSTR.

SCHWANTHALERSTRASSE

DEUTSCHES THEATER

JOSEPHSPITALSTR.

WILHELM-STR.

HACKEN-STR.

SINGL

17

RINDER-

To 20

9   4   6

LANDWEHRSTRASSE

10

MATHILDENSTR.

BRUNN-STR.

KREUZSTR.

ASAM CHURCH

SCHMID

CITY MUSEUM

To Oktoberfest Grounds & 3

SCHILLERSTR.

POST

18

SENDLINGER TOR

OBERANGER

SCHMID

KLOSTERHOF

JEWISH SYNAGOGUE & HISTORY MUSEUM

PRÄLAT-

5

Sendlinger Tor Platz

RUSS-MARKT

ROSENTAL

GOETHESTR.

PETTENKOFERSTRASSE

U   Sendlinger Tor

WALLST.

BLUMENSTRASSE

UNTERER-ANGER

BLUMENSTR.

LESSINGSTR.

NUSSBAUMSTRASSE

Matthäus-Kirche

LINDWURMSTRASSE

AUGSBURGERSTR.

FESTALOZZISTR.

MÜLLERSTR.

FRAUNHOFERSTR.

BEETHOVEN-STR.

Beethoven-platz

MÖLLERSTRASSE

PESTALOZZISTR.

To Garmisch via A-95

REISINGERSTR.

MUNICH

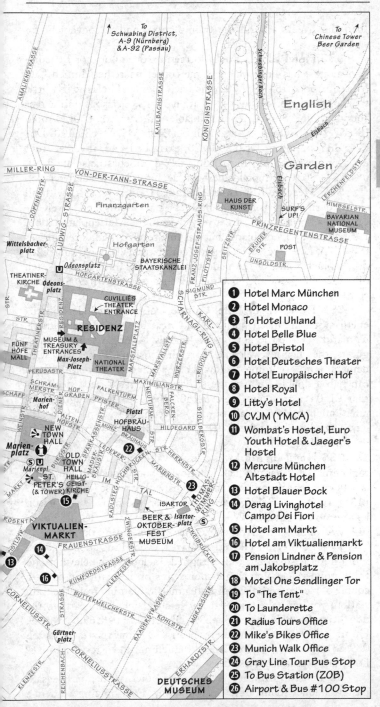

① Hotel Marc München
② Hotel Monaco
③ To Hotel Uhland
④ Hotel Belle Blue
⑤ Hotel Bristol
⑥ Hotel Deutsches Theater
⑦ Hotel Europäischer Hof
⑧ Hotel Royal
⑨ Litty's Hotel
⑩ CVJM (YMCA)
⑪ Wombat's Hostel, Euro Youth Hotel & Jaeger's Hostel
⑫ Mercure München Altstadt Hotel
⑬ Hotel Blauer Bock
⑭ Derag Livinghotel Campo Dei Fiori
⑮ Hotel am Markt
⑯ Hotel am Viktualienmarkt
⑰ Pension Lindner & Pension am Jakobsplatz
⑱ Motel One Sendlinger Tor
⑲ To "The Tent"
⑳ To Launderette
㉑ Radius Tours Office
㉒ Mike's Bikes Office
㉓ Munich Walk Office
㉔ Gray Line Tour Bus Stop
㉕ To Bus Station (ZOB)
㉖ Airport & Bus #100 Stop

than the streets around the train station, and is convenient for sightseeing.

$$$ Hotel Blauer Bock, formerly a dormitory for Benedictine monks, has been on the same corner near the Munich City Museum since 1841. Its 70 remodeled rooms are classy, if a little spartan for the price, but the location is great. Various online discounts (senior, Sunday, nonrefundable) can save you €10-20/room (S-€57-77, Sb-€89-109, premium Sb-€125-145, D-€80-100, Db-€145-165, premium Db-€200-220, extra bed-€40, iPads at front desk for guest use, Wi-Fi, parking-€22/day, Sebastiansplatz 9, tel. 089/231-780, www.hotelblauerbock.de, info@hotelblauerbock.de).

$$$ Mercure München Altstadt Hotel is reliable, with all the modern comforts in its 75 business-class rooms, and is well-located on a boring, quiet street very close to the Marienplatz action. It's a chain, and a bit bland, but has fine services and decent prices (Sb-€134, Db-€176, air-con, guest computer, Wi-Fi, parking-€20/day, a block south of the pedestrian zone at Hotterstrasse 4, tel. 089/232-590, www.mercure-muenchen-altstadt.de, h3709@accor.com).

$$$ Derag Livinghotel Campo Dei Fiori's 83 sleek kitchenette suites are nicely outfitted and located right off the Viktualienmarkt. While the hotel caters mainly to longer-term business guests, they happily welcome short-term visitors. Prices vary with demand (and according to how far in advance you book)—if you can nab a double room for less than €180, it's a good deal; less than €160 is a great one (Sb-€95-160, Db-€115-190 though official rates much higher, breakfast-€14, air-con, Wi-Fi, parking-€16/day, Utzschneiderstrasse 3, tel. 089/885-6560, www.deraghotels.de, fiori@derag.de).

$$$ Hotel am Markt, is a lesser value right next to the Viktualienmarkt. It has old-feeling hallways but 32 decent rooms, and is a better deal if you skip the expensive breakfast (Sb-€91, Db-€131-143, Tb-€173-185, prices depend on room size, €12/person less without breakfast, Wi-Fi, Heiliggeiststrasse 6, tel. 089/225-014, www.hotel-am-markt.eu, service@hotel-am-markt.eu).

$$ At Hotel am Viktualienmarkt, everything about this 26-room hotel is small but well-designed, including the elevator and three good-value, tiny single rooms. It's on a small side street a couple of blocks from the Viktualienmarkt. Coming from the train station, you can take tram #16 to Reichenbachplatz nearly to the door (tiny Sb-€59, larger Sb-€89, Db-€129, Tb-€169, Qb-€179, Quint/b-€199; guest computer, Wi-Fi, Utzschneiderstrasse 14, tel. 089/231-1090, www.hotel-am-viktualienmarkt.de, reservierung@hotel-am-viktualienmarkt.de)

$$ Pension Lindner is clean and quiet, with nine pleasant pastel-bouquet rooms off a bare stairway. Frau Sinzinger offers a warm welcome and good buffet breakfasts, but rarely has room for last-minute bookings (S-€45, D-€75, Db-€100, T-€105, Tb-€130, €5 discount on doubles and triples if you pay cash, tiny elevator, Wi-Fi, Dultstrasse 1, tel. 089/263-413, www.pension-lindner. com, info@pension-lindner.com, Marion Sinzinger).

$$ Pension am Jakobsplatz, downstairs from Pension Lindner, has four basic but pleasant rooms. Two have fully private facilities, and the other two have a sink and shower but share a toilet. Showers here are in-room (Ss-€70-80, Sb-€80-90, Ds-€80-90, Db-€90-100, guest computer, Wi-Fi, Dultstrasse 1, tel. 089/2323-1556, mobile 0173-973-4598, www.pension-jakobsplatz.de, info@pension-jakobsplatz.de, Christoph Zenker and son Marco).

$$ Motel One Sendlinger Tor, across from the Sendlinger Tor tram and U-Bahn stop, is a huge 241-room, busy, inexpensive chain hotel with rushed-but-pleasant staff in a fine location. The stylish, modern rooms are fairly tight and lack some basic amenities (phones, minibars), but otherwise are a good value—and tend to sell out a few weeks in advance. Streetside rooms on upper floors have great views—I'd request one of these. When booking on their website, make sure to choose the Sendlinger Tor location—they have six other hotels in Munich (Sb-€87, Db-€119, breakfast-€7.50, air-con, Wi-Fi, guest iPad at front desk, parking-€15/day in hotel garage or €6/day in nearby public garage, Herzog-Wilhelm-Strasse 28, tel. 089/5177-7250, www.motel-one.com, muenchen-sendlingertor@motel-one.com).

AWAY FROM THE CENTER

$ The Tent—a venerable Munich institution officially known as the International Youth Camp Kapuzinerhölzl—offers 400 spots in three huge circus tents near Nymphenburg Palace. It never fills up, though you are encouraged to reserve online. Choose a mattress on a wooden floor (€7.50) or a bunk bed (€10.50), or pitch your own tent (€5.50/tent plus €5.50/person). Blankets, hot showers,

lockers (bring or buy a lock), a kitchen, and Wi-Fi are all included; breakfast is a few euros extra. It can be a fun but noisy experience—kind of a cross between a slumber party and Woodstock. It feels quite wholesome, but I wouldn't bring kids—it's really for young adults. There's a cool table-tennis-and-Frisbee atmosphere throughout the day, nightly campfires, and no curfew, though silence is requested after 1:00 (open early June-early Oct only, prices a little higher during Oktoberfest, cash only, pay guest computer, self-service laundry, bikes-€9/day, catch tram #17 from train station for 18 minutes to Botanischer Garten, direction: Amalien-burgstrasse, then go right down Franz-Schrank-Strasse—it's be-hind the trees at the end of the street, tel. 089/141-4300, www.the-tent.com, cu@the-tent.com).

MORE HOTELS IN MUNICH

If my listings above are full, here are some others to consider.

Within walking distance of the Viktualienmarkt, consider artsy **$$$ Hotel Olympic,** with 37 fresh, relaxing rooms (Db-€160-210, Hans-Sachs-Strasse 4, tel. 089/231-890, www.hotel-olympic.de, info@hotel-olympic.de); classy yet homey **$$$ Hotel Admiral** (Db-€139-349, Kohlstrasse 9, tel. 089/216-350, www.hotel-admiral.de); and **$$ Hotel Isartor,** with 68 comfortable but plain rooms (Db-€119-249, Baaderstrasse 2-4, tel. 089/216-3340, www.hotel-isartor.de).

Near Sendlinger Tor, alpine-bright and sunny **$$ Hotel Mueller**, offers 44 cozy rooms (Db-€109-369, Fliegenstrasse 4, tel. 89-232-3860, www.hotel-mueller-muenchen.de), while **$$ Carat Hotel** is a glossy slumber-mill popular with groups. Its street-side rooms have rare air-conditioning and its 48 apartments have kitchenettes (Db-€89-399, Lindwurmstrasse 13, tel. 089/230-380, www.carat-hotel-muenchen.de).

An easy tram or U-Bahn ride from Marienplatz, **$$$ Hotel Europa Muenchen** has four-star American-style comfort and amenities in an impersonal, blocky structure (Db-€132-156, Dachauerstrasse 115, U-1 to Stiglmaierplatz or U-2 to Theresien-strasse, tel. 089/542-420, www.hotel-europa.de).

Eating in Munich

Munich's cuisine is traditionally seasoned with beer. In beer halls, beer gardens, or at the Viktualienmarkt, try the most typical meal in town: *Weisswurst* (white-colored veal sausage—peel off the skin be-fore eating, often available only until noon) with *süsser Senf* (sweet mus-tard), a salty *Brezel* (pretzel), and *Weissbier* ("white" wheat beer). An-other traditional favorite is *Obatzda* (a.k.a. *Obatzter*), a mix of soft chees-es, butter, paprika, and often garlic or

onions that's spread on bread. *Brotzeit*, literally "bread time," gets you a wooden platter of cold cuts, cheese, and pickles and is a good option for a light dinner.

I'm here for the beer-hall and beer-garden fun (my first several listings). But when the *Wurst und Kraut* get to be too much for you,

Munich has plenty of good alternatives; I've listed my favorites later in this section.

Bavarian restaurants are smoke-free. The only ashtrays you'll see throughout Bavaria are outside.

BEER HALLS, BEER GARDENS, AND BAVARIAN FOOD

Nothing beats the Hofbräuhaus (the only place in town where you'll find oompah music) for those in search of the boisterous, clichéd image of the beer hall. Locals prefer the innumerable beer gardens. On a warm day, when you're looking for the authentic outdoor beer-garden experience, your best options are the Augustiner (near the train station), the small beer garden at the Viktualienmarkt (near Marienplatz), or the sea of tables in the English Garden.

Near Marienplatz

The **Hofbräuhaus** (HOAF-broy-howz) is the world's most famous beer hall. While it's grotesquely touristy and filled with sloppy backpackers and tour groups, it's still a lot of fun—a Munich must. Even if you don't eat here, check it out to see 200 Japanese people drinking beer in a German beer hall...across from a Hard Rock Café. Germans go for the entertainment—to sing "Country Roads," see how Texas girls party, and watch tourists try to chug beer.

You can drop by anytime for a large or light meal (my favorite: €8 for *Vier Stück gebratene Schweinswürstl auf Sauerkraut*—four small pork sausages with sauerkraut), or for just a drink. Even though the visitors outnumber the locals, the food here is good. Choose from four zones: the rowdy main hall on the ground floor, a quieter courtyard under the stars, a dainty restaurant with mellow music (zither, oboe, harp) on first floor up, or the giant festival hall (sometimes reserved for events) under a big barrel vault on the top floor. The festival hall has a free folk show every evening from 18:30 to 22:30.

Except for Weissbier, they only sell beer by the *Mass* (one-liter mug, €8)—and they claim to sell 10,000 of these liters every day. The Hofbräuhaus offers regular live oompah music. This music-every-night atmosphere is irresistible, and the fat, shiny-leather bands get even church mice to stand up and conduct three-quarter time with breadsticks (daily 9:00-23:30, music during lunch and dinner only—daily 12:00-16:00 and 18:00-23:30, 5-minute walk from Marienplatz at Platzl 9, tel. 089/2901-3610, www.hofbraeuhaus. de). For more on this Munich institution, see page 52.

Wirtshaus Ayingers, just across the street from the Hofbräuhaus, is good for those who've seen the Hofbräuhaus but would

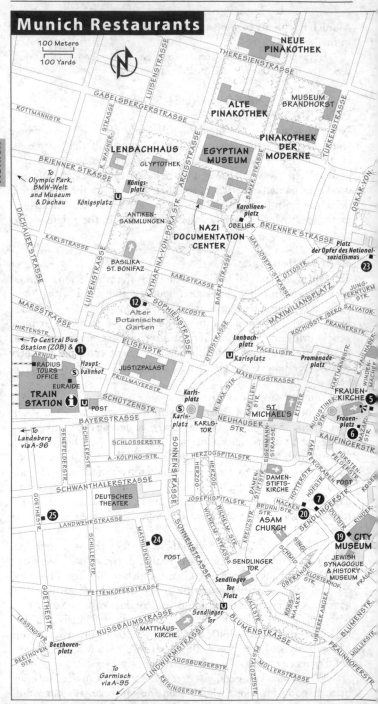

Munich Restaurants

100 Meters
100 Yards

MUNICH

MUNICH

1 Hofbräuhaus Beer Hall
2 Wirtshaus Ayingers
3 Haxnbauer
4 Jodlerwirt Pub
5 Andechser am Dom
6 Nürnberger Bratwurst Glöckl am Dom
7 Altes Hackerhaus
8 Ratskeller & Kantine im Rathaus
9 Der Pschorr Beer Hall
10 Spatenhaus Beer Hall
11 To Augustiner Beer Garden
12 Park Café
13 To Chinese Tower Beer Garden & Seehaus
14 Glockenspiel Café & Hugendubel Bookstore Café
15 Der Kleine Chinese
16 Blatt Salate
17 Viktualienmarkt & Die Münchner Suppenküche
18 Restaurant Opatija
19 Stadt Café
20 Prinz Myshkin Veggie Rest.
21 Schrannenhalle
22 Café Tambosi
23 Café Luitpold
24 La Vecchia Masseria
25 Altin Dilim
26 Dallmayr Deli
27 Heilig-Geist-Stüberl

rather eat somewhere less chaotic. It serves quality Bavarian food—especially the schnitzels—and beer from Aying, a village south of Munich. There's lively outside seating on the cobbles facing the touristic chaos or a simple woody interior (€14-18 main courses, daily 11:00-23:30, Platzl 1a, tel. 089/2370-3666, www.ayingers. de).

Haxnbauer is a stark, old, and elegant place filled with locals here for one thing: the best pork knuckle in town. You'll pay a little extra, but it's clearly the place for what looks like pork knee (half *Schweinshaxe*-€18, daily 11:00-23:00, two blocks from Hofbräuhaus at Sparkassenstrasse 6, tel. 089/216-6540).

Jodlerwirt ("Yodeling Innkeeper") is a tiny, cramped, and smart-alecky pub. The food is great, and the ambience is as Bavarian as you'll find. Avoid the basic ground-floor bar and climb the stairs into the action. Even if it's just you and the accordionist, it's fun. Good food and lots of belly laughs...completely incomprehensible to the average tourist (€8-17 main courses, Tue-Sat 19:00-late, food until 23:00, closed Mon except Oktoberfest and Dec, closed Sun except Oktoberfest, accordion act Tue-Sat 20:00-2:00 in the morning, between Hofbräuhaus and Marienplatz at Altenhofstrasse 4, tel. 089/221-249, www.jodlerwirt-muenchen.net).

Andechser am Dom, at the rear of the twin-domed Frauenkirche on a breezy square, is a trendy place serving Andechs beer and great food to appreciative regulars. Münchners favor the dark beer (ask for *dunkles*), but I love the light *(helles)*. The €13.50 *Gourmetteller* is a great sampler of their specialties, and the *Rostbratwurst* with kraut (€7.50) gives you the virtual *Nürnberger* bratwurst experience with the better Andechs beer (€8-20 main courses, daily 10:00-24:00, Weinstrasse 7a, reserve during peak times, tel. 089/2429-2920, www.andechser-am-dom.de).

Nürnberger Bratwurst Glöckl am Dom, around the corner from Andechser am Dom, is popular with tourists and offers a more traditional, fiercely Bavarian evening. Dine outside under the trees or in the dark, medieval, cozy interior. Enjoy the tasty little *Nürnberger* sausages with kraut (€8-20 main courses, daily 10:00-24:00, Frauenplatz 9, tel. 089/291-9450, www.bratwurst-gloeckl. de).

Altes Hackerhaus is popular with locals for its traditional *Bayerisch* (Bavarian) fare served with a slightly fancier feel in one of the oldest buildings in town. It offers a small courtyard and a fun forest of characteristic nooks festooned with old-time paintings, ads, and posters. This place is much-appreciated for its Hacker-Pschorr beer (€7-10 wurst dishes, €9-25 main courses, daily 10:00-24:00, Sendlinger Strasse 14, tel. 089/260-5026, www.hackerhaus. de).

Munich's **Ratskeller** fills the City Hall's vast cellar, and also has some tables in the courtyard (offering a 360-degree view of the architecture with the sky overhead). Traditionally, city halls had a fine restaurant in their cellar—a *Rathauskeller*. While touristy, locals still dine here to sit in elegant nooks and enjoy the timeless traditional atmosphere (€14-24 main courses, €13.50 3-course lunches with water, daily 10:00-24:00, Marienplatz 8, tel. 089/219-9890, www.ratskeller.com).

Der Pschorr, an upscale beer hall occupying a former slaughterhouse, has a terrace overlooking the Viktualienmarkt and serves a special premium version of what many consider Munich's finest beer. With organic "slow food" and chilled glasses, this place mixes modern concepts—no candles, industrial-strength conviviality—with traditional, quality, classic dishes. They tap classic wooden kegs every few minutes with gusto. The sound of the hammer lets patrons know they're getting it good and fresh (€15-25 main courses, €10 lunch specials, daily 10:00-24:00, food served at least until 22:00, Viktualienmarkt 15, at end of Schrannenhalle, tel. 089/442-383-940, www.der-pschorr.de).

The small **beer garden** at the center of the Viktualienmarkt taps you into about the best budget eating in town; it's just steps from Marienplatz (Mon-Sat until late, closed Sun, see page 40). There's table service wherever you see a tablecloth; to picnic, choose a table without one—but you must buy a drink from the counter. Countless stalls surround the beer garden and sell wurst, sandwiches, produce, and so on. This B.Y.O.F. tradition recalls a time when monastery beer gardens served beer but not food. This is a good spot to grab a typical Munich *Weisswurst*—and some beer.

Spatenhaus is the opera-goers' beer hall, serving more elegant food in a woodsy, traditional setting since 1896—maybe it's not even right to call it a "beer hall." You can also eat outside, on the square facing the opera and palace. It's pricey, but you won't find better-quality Bavarian cuisine. The upstairs restaurant serves a more international cuisine and is dressier—reservations are advised (€15-30 main courses, daily 9:30-24:00, on Max-Joseph-Platz opposite opera, Residenzstrasse 12, tel. 089/290-7050, www.spatenhaus.de).

Near the Train Station

Augustiner Beer Garden is a sprawling haven for local beer lovers on a balmy evening. A true under-the-leaves beer garden packed with Münchners, this is a delight. In fact, most Münchners consider Augustiner the

MUNICH

MUNICH

Munich's Beer Scene

In Munich's beer halls *(Brauhäuser)* and beer gardens *(Biergartens)*, meals are inexpensive, white radishes are salted and cut in delicate spirals, and surly beer maids pull mustard packets from their cleavage. Unlike with wine, spending more money on beer doesn't get you a better drink. Beer is truly a people's drink, and you'll get the very best here in Munich. The big question among connoisseurs (local and foreign) is, "Which brew today?"

Beer gardens go back to the days when monks brewed their beer and were allowed to sell it directly to the thirsty public. They stored their beer in cellars under courtyards kept cool by the shade of bushy chestnut trees. Eventually, tables were set up, and these convivial eateries evolved. The tradition (complete with chestnut trees) survives, and any real beer garden will keep a few tables (those without tablecloths) available for customers who buy only beer and bring their own food.

Huge liter beers (called *ein Mass* in German, or "ein pitcher" in English) cost about €8. (Men's rooms come with vomitoriums.) If you order a half-liter *(eine Halbe)*, the barmaid is likely to say, "Why don't you go home and come back when you are thirsty?" You can order your beer *helles* (light in color but not "lite" in calories), *dunkles* (dark), or ask for a *Weiss* or *Weizen* ("white" or wheat-based beer—cloudy and sweet) or a *Radler* (half lemon soda, half beer).

Most beer gardens have a deposit *(Pfand)* system for their big glass steins: You pay €1 extra, and when you're finished, you can take the mug and your deposit token *(Pfandmarke)* to the return man *(Pfandrückgabe)* for your refund, or leave it on the table and lose your money. If you buy a bottled beer, pour it into the glass before you check out; otherwise you'll pay two deposits

best beer garden in town—which may be why there are 5,000 seats. There's no music, it's away from the tourist hordes, and it serves up great beer, good traditional food, huge portions, reasonable prices, and perfect conviviality. The outdoor self-service ambience is best, making this place ideal on a nice summer evening (figure €15 for a main course and a drink). Parents with kids can sit at tables adjoining a sizable playground. There's also indoor and outdoor seating at a more expensive restaurant with table service (€12-19 main courses) by the entrance (daily 11:00-24:00, self-service outdoors

(one for the glass, the other for the bottle).

Many beer halls have a cafeteria system. The food is usually *selbstdienst* (self-service)—a sign may say *Bitte bedienen Sie sich selbst* (please serve yourself). If two prices are listed, *Schank* is for self-service, while *Bedienung* is for table service. If you have trouble finding cutlery, ask around for *Besteck*. In addition to the predictable *Wurst* (see page 931) and *Brotzeit* (salads and spreads—see page 933), look for these heavy specialties:

Fleischpfanzerl (a.k.a. **Fleischklösse** or **Frikadellen**): meatballs

Grosse Brez'n: gigantic pretzel

Hendl (or **Brathähnchen**): roasted chicken

Radi: radish that's thinly spiral-cut and salted

Schweinrollbraten: pork belly

Schweinshax'n (or just **Hax'n**): pork knuckle

Spareribs: spareribs

Steckerlfisch: a whole fish (usually mackerel) herbed and grilled on a stick

At a large *Biergarten*, assemble your dream feast by visiting various counters, marked by type of food (*Bier* or *Bierschänke* for beer, *Bratwürste* for sausages, *Brotzeiten* for lighter fare served cold, and so on). After the meal, reclaim your deposit and bus your dirty dishes (*Geschirr*)—look for *Geschirrrückgabe* or *Geschirrabgabe* signs.

Eating outside is made more pleasant by the *Föhn* (warm winds that come over the Alps from Italy), which gives this part of Germany 30 more days of sunshine than the North—and sometimes even an Italian ambience. (Many natives attribute the city's huge increase in outdoor dining to global warming.)

Beer halls take care of their regular customers. You'll notice many tables marked *Stammtisch* (reserved for regulars and small groups, such as the "Happy Saturday Club"). These have a long tradition of being launch pads for grassroots action. In the days before radio and television, aspiring leaders used beer halls to connect with the public. Hitler hosted numerous political rallies in beer halls, and the Hofbräuhaus was the first place he talked to a big crowd.

MUNICH

until 23:00, table service indoors until 22:00, Arnulfstrasse 52, 3 looooong blocks from station going away from the center—or take tram #16/#17 one stop to Hopfenstrasse, taxis always waiting at the gate, tel. 089/594-393, www.augustinerkeller.de).

Park Café, though in a park, is much more than a café. The indoor section is big and bold, with a clean yet rustic ambience, DJs or live music in the late evening, few tourists, and quality food (€9-20 main courses). When it's hot, everyone decamps to the beer garden out back in the Alter Botanischer Garden, where you can order off the menu or from the self-service counters. Don't forget to reclaim the deposit for your plate and mug when you leave (daily 11:00-24:00, beer garden opens at 11:30, a short walk north of the train station at Sophienstrasse 7, tel. 089/5161-7980, www.parkcafe089.de).

In the English Garden

For outdoor ambience and a cheap meal, spend an evening at the English Garden's **Chinese Tower Beer Garden** *(Chinesischer Turm Biergarten)*. You're welcome to B.Y.O. food and grab a table, or buy from the picnic stall *(Brotzeit)* right there. Don't bother to phone ahead—they have 6,000 seats. This is a fine opportunity to try a *Steckerlfisch*, sold at a separate kiosk (daily, long hours in good weather, usually live music, tel. 089/383-8730, www.chinaturm.de; take tram #18 from main train station or Sendlinger Tor to Tivolistrasse, or U-3 or U-6 to Giselastrasse and then bus #54 or #154 two stops).

Deeper into the English Garden, **Seehaus** is a 10-minute walk past the Chinese Tower. It's famous among Münchners for its idyllic lakeside setting and excellent Mediterranean and traditional cooking. It's dressy and a bit snobbish, and understandably filled with locals who fit the same description. Choose from classy indoor or lakeside seating (€17-27 main courses, daily 10:00-24:00; take U-3 or U-6 to Münchner Freiheit and walk 10 minutes, or get off at Dietlindenstrasse and then take bus #144 one stop to Osterwaldstrasse; Kleinhesselohe 3, tel. 089/381-6130).

Seehaus Beer Garden, adjacent to the fancy Seehaus restaurant, offers the same waterfront atmosphere in a less expensive, more casual setting. There's all the normal wurst, kraut, pretzels, and fine beer at typical prices (daily, long hours from 11:00 when the weather's fine).

NON-BEER HALL RESTAURANTS

Man does not live by beer alone. Well, maybe some do. But for the rest of us, I recommend the following alternatives to the beer-and-wurst circuit.

On and near Marienplatz

Kantine im Rathaus is your solid, fast, economical, and no-nonsense standby in the center. (It's actually the cafeteria for City Hall workers—they get a discount off the listed prices.) The entrance is just behind the New Town Hall tower—go through the arch under the tower into the courtyard and look for the sign on the right. There's seating in the courtyard or inside (€5-13 main courses, Mon-Fri 11:00-18:30, Sat 12:00-16:00, closed Sun, closes at 17:00 on weekdays Jan-April).

Glockenspiel Café is good for a coffee or a meal with a bird's-eye view down on the Marienplatz action—I'd come for the view more than the food (€12-24 main courses). Locals like the open terrace without a view, but regardless of the weather, I grab a seat overlooking Marienplatz (Mon-Sat 9:00-24:00, Sun 9:00-19:00, ride elevator from Rosenstrasse entrance, opposite glockenspiel at Marienplatz 28, tel. 089/264-256).

The **Hugendubel bookstore** has a Starbucks-style café on the top floor. It's quicker and less crowded than the Glockenspiel Café, and comes with the same great view (self-serve, take the glass elevator, Mon-Sat 9:30-20:00, closed Sun, tel. 089/2601-1987).

Der Kleine Chinese, two blocks downhill from Marienplatz, is popular, with inexpensive Asian standards (€5-7 main courses, order at counter and they'll bring it to your table, daily 11:00-22:00, Im Tal 28, tel. 089/2916-3536).

Blatt Salate is a self-serve salad bar on a side street between the Frauenkirche and the New Town Hall; it's a great little hideaway for a healthy quick lunch. You'll spend €12-14 for a yummy salad with fresh bread and a drink (vegetarian and meat salads and soups, Mon-Sat 11:00-19:00, closed Sun, Schäfflerstrasse 7, tel. 089/2102-0281).

Around the Viktualienmarkt

Restaurant Opatija, in the Viktualienmarktpassage a few steps from Marienplatz, is modern and efficient, bringing the Adriatic to Munich with a big, eclectic Italian and Balkan menu, plus traditional German favorites. Choose between the comfortable indoor section and the outdoor seating in a quiet, narrow courtyard. Prices are low, it's family-friendly, and they do takeout (good €7-8 pizzas, €7 pastas, €10-12 salad plates, €8-13 main courses, daily 11:30-22:30, kitchen closes at 21:30, enter the passage at Viktualienmarkt 6 or Rindermarkt 2, tel. 089/2323-1995).

Die Münchner Suppenküche ("Munich Soup Kitchen"), a self-service soup joint at the Viktualienmarkt, is fine for a small, cozy sit-down lunch at picnic tables under a closed-in awning. The chalkboard lists six soups of the day (€4-6 soup meals, Mon-Sat 9:00-18:00, closed Sun, near corner of Reichenbachstrasse and Frauenstrasse, tel. 089/260-9599).

Stadt Café is a lively café serving healthy fare, with great daily specials (€7-10), an inventive menu of Italian, German, and vegetarian dishes, salads, and a big selection of cakes by the slice. This informal, no-frills restaurant draws newspaper-readers, stroller moms, and tourists, too. Dine in the quiet cobbled courtyard, inside, or outside facing the new synagogue (blackboard has today's specials, daily 10:00-24:00, in same building as Munich City Museum, St.-Jakobs-Platz 1, tel. 089/266-949).

Prinz Myshkin Vegetarian Restaurant is an upscale vegetarian eatery in the old center. The menu is totally meatless and dictated by the season. You'll find a clever, appetizing selection of €14-20 main courses. The decor is modern, the arched ceilings are cool, and the outside seating is on a quiet street. Don't miss the enticing appetizer selection on display as you enter (they do a fine €14 mixed-appetizer plate). They also have vegetarian sushi, pastas, Indian dishes, and their own baker, so they're proud of their sweets (€7.50 weekday lunch specials, daily 11:30-23:00, Hackenstrasse 2, tel. 089/265-596).

Eateries on Sebastiansplatz: Looking for a no-schnitzel-or-dumplings alternative? Sebastiansplatz is a long, pedestrianized square between the Viktualienmarkt and the synagogue, lined with bistros handy for a healthy and quick lunch. Options range from French to Italian to Asian to salads. All serve €10 main courses on the busy cobbled square or inside—just survey the scene and choose. The **Schrannenhalle,** the former grain exchange overlooking the square, is also busy with creative, modern eateries and gourmet delis (Mon-Sat 10:00-20:00, closed Sun).

Near Odeonsplatz

Two venerable cafés near Odeonsplatz keep traditions alive.

Café Tambosi has an Italian-influenced menu, Viennese elegance inside, and a relaxing garden setting out back (daily 8:00-24:00, €9-20 main courses, Odeonsplatz 18, tel. 089/298-322).

Café Luitpold is where Munich's high society comes to sip its coffee and nibble on exquisite cakes. The café is proudly home to the original *Luitpoldtorte* (sponge cake with layers of marzipan and buttercream, covered in dark chocolate, €3.40 per slice). They say it's Munich's answer to Vienna's Sacher-Torte—though I prefer their strawberry-cream cake (Mon 8:00-19:00, Tue-Sat 8:00-23:00, Sun 9:00-19:00, Brienner Strasse 11, tel. 089/242-8750).

Near the Train Station

La Vecchia Masseria, between Sendlinger Tor and the train station hotels, serves Italian food inside amid a cozy Tuscan farmhouse decor, or outside in a beautiful flowery courtyard. Try the €25 *menu* (€6-8 pizza or pasta, €14-16 main courses, daily 11:30-23:30, reservations smart, Mathildenstrasse 3, tel. 089/550-9090).

Altin Dilim, a cafeteria-style Turkish restaurant, is a standout among the many hole-in-the-wall Middle Eastern places in the ethnic area just near the station (sporting a uniquely decorated hole in its own wall, no less). It feels like a trip to Istanbul—complete with a large, attractively displayed selection, ample seating, and a handy pictorial menu that helps you order. Pay at the counter (€4 *Döner Kebab*, €8-13 main courses, Mon-Sat 7:00-24:00, Sun 10:00-24:00, Goethestrasse 17, tel. 089/9734-0869).

PICNICS

For a truly elegant picnic (costing as much as a restaurant meal), **Dallmayr's** is the place to shop. The crown in their emblem reflects that no less than the royal family assembled its picnics at this historic and expensive delicatessen. Pretend you're a Bavarian aristocrat—King Ludwig himself, even—and put together a royal spread to munch in the nearby Hofgarten. Or visit the classy but pricey cafés that serve light meals on the ground floor and first floor (Mon-Sat 9:30-19:00, closed Sun, behind New Town Hall, Dienerstrasse 13-15, tel. 089/213-5110). For more information, see page 51.

A Budget Picnic: To save money, browse at Dallmayr's but buy at a **supermarket.** The ones that hide in the basements of department stores are on the upscale side: the **Kaufhof** stores at Marienplatz and Karlsplatz (Mon-Sat 9:30-20:00, closed Sun), or the even more upmarket **Karstadt** across from the train station (same hours). Cheaper options include the **REWE** in the basement at Fünf Höfe (Mon-Sat 7:00-20:00, closed Sun, entrance is in Viscardihof) or the **Lidl** at Schwantaler Strasse 31, near the train-station hotels (Mon-Sat 8:00-20:00, closed Sun).

Munich Connections

Munich is a super transportation hub (one reason it was the target of so many WWII bombs), with easy train and bus connections to most Bavarian destinations, as well as international trains.

BY TRAIN

For quick help at the main train station, stop by the service counter in front of track 18. For better English and more patience, drop by the EurAide desk at counter #1 in the *Reisezentrum* (see page 20). Train info: tel. 0180-599-6633, www.bahn.com.

From Munich to: Füssen (hourly, 2 hours, most with easy transfer in Kaufbeuren; for a Neuschwanstein Castle day trip, leave as early as possible), **Reutte,** Austria (every hour, 2.5-3.5 hours, change in **Füssen**), **Oberammergau** (nearly hourly, 2 hours, change in Murnau), **Salzburg,** Austria (2/hour, 1.5-2 hours), **Berchtesgaden** (at least hourly, 2.5-3 hours, change in Freilassing or Salzburg), **Nürnberg** (2-3/hour, 1-1.5 hours), **Cologne** (2/hour, 4.5 hours, some with 1 change), **Würzburg** (1-2/hour, 2 hours),

Rothenburg (hourly, 2.5-4 hours, 2-3 changes), **Frankfurt** (hourly, 3.5 hours), **Frankfurt Airport** (1-2/hour, 3.5 hours), **Leipzig** (8/day direct, 5.5 hours; more with change in Nürnberg or Naumburg, 5.5 hours), **Erfurt** (about 2/hour, 4.5-5 hours, change in Fulda), **Dresden** (every 2 hours, 6 hours, change in Leipzig or Nürnberg), **Hamburg** (hourly, 6-6.5 hours), **Berlin** (1-2/hour, 6-7 hours, some direct, otherwise change in Göttingen), **Vienna** (direct trains every 2 hours, 4 hours), **Venice** (every 2 hours, 7-7.5 hours, change in Verona, 1 direct night train, 9 hours), **Paris** (1/day direct, 6 hours, 6/day with transfer, 6-8.5 hours), **Prague** (2/day direct, 6 hours; better by bus—see below; no night trains), **Zürich** (3/day direct, 4.5 hours). Trains run nightly to Berlin, Vienna, Venice, Milan, Florence, Rome, Paris, Amsterdam, and Budapest (at least 6 hours to each city). To use a rail pass for any train to Italy, your pass must include all countries on the train route (i.e., Austria or Switzerland), or you'll have to buy the segment that's not included; Euro-City trains to Italy via Innsbruck also require passholders to make a reservation (not indicated in online schedules, and not required if you're buying a point-to-point ticket instead of using a pass).

BY BUS

For information on Munich's Central Bus Station (ZOB), see page 21. The Lufthansa airport bus (described later) leaves from the north side of the train station (exit by track 26). The Deutsche Bahn buses to **Prague** (only €4 with rail pass, 4/day, 5 hours) leave from Munich's Central Bus Station (ZOB).

Romantic Road Bus: The **Romantic Road bus** (mid-April-late Oct only) connects Munich's Central Bus Station to Füssen, Dinkelsbühl, Rothenburg, Würzburg, Frankfurt, and other destinations en route. This slower but more scenic alternative to the train allows a glimpse of towns such as Augsburg, Nördlingen, and Dinkelsbühl (no advance reservations needed, northbound bus departs Munich at 10:30, arrives Rothenburg at 15:45; southbound bus departs Munich at 17:55, arrives Füssen at 20:20). For more information on the bus, run by Deutsche Touring, see page 380.

BY PLANE

Munich's airport (code: MUC) is an easy 40-minute ride on the S-1 or S-8 **subway,** each of which runs every 20 minutes (starting at 4:00 in the morning and continuing until almost 2:00 in the morning) between the airport and Marienplatz and the train station. While you can buy a single ticket for €10.40, the €11.70 Munich *Gesamtnetz* day pass (a.k.a. the "Airport-City-Day-Ticket"), which covers public transportation all day, is worth getting if you'll be making just one more public transport journey that same day. (To buy it at a ticket machine, first press "MVV Münchner Verkehrs-

und Tarifverbund," which displays the array of ticket options. No need to validate the pass.) Groups of two or more should buy the €21.30 Munich *Gesamtnetz* partner day pass, which gives up to five adults the run of the system for the day (for more info on Munich transit passes, see page 23). The trip is also free with a validated and dated rail pass. The S-8 is a bit quicker and easier, as the S-1 line has two branches and some trains split—if on the S-1 to the airport, be certain your train is going to the *Flughafen*.

Another alternative is the **Lufthansa airport bus**, which links the airport with the main train station (€10.50, €17 round-trip, 3/ hour, 45 minutes, buses depart train station 5:15-19:55, buy tickets on bus; from inside the station, exit near track 26 and look for yellow *Airport Bus* signs; www.airportbus-muenchen.de). If you're traveling alone, going round-trip, and not using other public transport the same day, the bus saves a few euros. Avoid taking a taxi from the airport, as it's a long, expensive drive; it's better to take public transport and then switch to a taxi if needed. Airport info: tel. 089/97500, www.munich-airport.de.

BAVARIA AND TIROL

Germany: Füssen • King's Castles • Wieskirche •
Oberammergau • Linderhof Castle • Ettal Monastery •
Zugspitze • Reutte, Austria

In this picturesque corner of the Alps (2.5 hours west of Innsbruck), you'll find a timeless land of fairy-tale castles, painted buildings shared by cows and farmers, and locals who still dress in dirndls and lederhosen and yodel when they're happy.

This area straddles the border between Bavaria (part of Germany) and Tirol (part of Austria). On the German side, you can tour "Mad" King Ludwig II's ornate Neuschwanstein Castle, Europe's most spectacular. Stop by the Wieskirche, an ornately decorated Baroque church that puts the faithful in a heavenly mood, and browse through Oberammergau, Germany's woodcarving capital and home of the famous Passion Play (next performed in 2020). Yet another impressive castle (Linderhof), another fancy church (Ettal), and a sky-high viewpoint (the Zugspitze) round out southern Bavaria's top attractions. Then, just over the border in Austria, you can explore the ruined Ehrenberg Castle and scream down a mountain

on an oversized skateboard at one of the area's many luge runs. In this chapter, I'll first cover the German side (with the most sights), then the Austrian side (around Reutte in Tirol).

CHOOSING A HOME BASE

My hotel recommendations in this chapter cluster in three areas: Füssen and Oberammergau (in Germany), and Reutte (in Austria). When selecting a home base, here are a few factors to consider:

Füssen offers the easiest access to the region's biggest attraction, the "King's Castles" (Neuschwanstein and Hohenschwangau), and is the handiest base for train travelers. The town itself is a mix of real-world and cutesy-cobbled, and has some of the glitziest hotels in the area (as well as more affordable options).

Oberammergau is the best-known, most touristy, and cutest town of the bunch. World-famous for its once-per-decade Passion Play, it's much sleepier the other nine years. It's a long bus ride or a 45-minute drive from Oberammergau to the King's Castles. But three lesser, yet still worthwhile sights are close by: Ettal Monastery, Linderhof Castle, and the German lift to the Zugspitze.

Reutte is the least appealing town, and is less practical for train travelers, but the villages around it are home to some of the coziest, most pleasant rural accommodations in the region—making it a particularly good option for drivers. Reutte butts up against the ruined Ehrenberg Castle, and the King's Castles, Linderhof, and the Austrian approach to the Zugspitze are all within a 30-minute drive.

For specifics on public-transit logistics from each town, see "By Public Transportation," later.

PLANNING YOUR TIME AND GETTING AROUND BAVARIA

While Germans and Austrians vacation here for a week or two at a time, the typical speedy American traveler will find two days' worth of sightseeing. With a car and more time, you could enjoy three or four days, but the basic visit ranges anywhere from a long day trip from Munich to a three-night, two-day stay. If the weather's good and you're not going to Switzerland, be sure to ride a lift to an alpine peak.

By Car

This region is best by car, and all the sights are within an easy 60-mile loop from Füssen or Reutte. Even if you're doing the rest of your trip by train, consider renting a car for your time here (for local rental offices, see page 133).

Here's a good plan for a one-day circular drive from **Reutte** (from **Füssen,** you can start about 30 minutes later):

7:00	Breakfast
7:30	Depart hotel
8:00	Arrive at Neuschwanstein to pick up tickets for the two castles (Neuschwanstein and Hohenschwangau)

9:00	Tour Hohenschwangau
11:00	Tour Neuschwanstein
13:00	Drive to Oberammergau (with a 15-minute stop at the Wieskirche), and spend an hour there browsing the carving shops and grabbing a quick lunch
15:00	Drive to Ettal Monastery for a half-hour stop, then on to Linderhof Castle
16:00	Tour Linderhof
18:00	Drive along scenic Plansee Lake back to your hotel
19:00	Back at hotel
20:00	Dinner

Off-season (Oct-March), start your day an hour later, since Neuschwanstein and Hohenschwangau tours don't depart until 10:00; and skip Linderhof, which closes at 16:00.

The next morning, you could stroll through Reutte, hike to the Ehrenberg ruins, and ride a mountain luge on your way to Munich, Innsbruck, Switzerland, Venice, or wherever.

If you're based in **Oberammergau** instead, get an early start and hit Neuschwanstein and Hohenschwangau first. If the weather's good, hike to the top of Ehrenberg Castle (in Reutte). Drive along the Plansee and tour Linderhof and Ettal Monastery on your way back home.

By Public Transportation

Where you stay determines which sights you can see most easily. Train travelers use **Füssen** as a base, and bus or bike the three miles to the King's Castles and the Tegelberg luge or gondola. Staying in **Oberammergau** gives you easy access to Linderhof and Ettal Monastery, and you can day-trip to the top of the Zugspitze via Garmisch. **Reutte** is the least convenient base if you're carless, but travelers staying there can easily bike or hike to the Ehrenberg ruins, and can reach Neuschwanstein by bus (via Füssen), bike (1.5 hours), or taxi; if you stay at the recommended Gutshof zum Schluxen hotel (between Reutte and Füssen, in Pinswang, Austria) it's a 1- to 1.5-hour hike through the woods to Neuschwanstein.

Visiting sights farther from your home base is not impossible by local bus, but requires planning. The Deutsche Bahn (German Railway) journey planner at www.bahn.com does a great job of finding bus connections that work, on both sides of the border. (Schedules for each route are available at www.rvo-bus.de, but only in German.) Those staying in **Füssen** can day-trip by bus to Reutte and the Ehrenberg ruins, to the Wieskirche, or, with some effort, to Oberammergau. From **Oberammergau**, you can reach Neuschwanstein and Füssen by bus if you plan ahead. From **Reutte**, you can take the train to Ehrwald to reach the Zugspitze from the Austrian side, but side-trips to Oberammergau and Lin-

Füssen & Reutte Area

To Munich via Buchloe

Romantic Road to Landsberg & Rothenburg

ECHELSBACHER BRIDGE (GORGE)

Steingaden

To Kempten

A-7

WIES-KIRCHE

17

23

Ammer

Saulgrub

GERMANY

Forggen-see

Füssen
See detail map

Unterammergau

STECKENBERG

Oberammergau

See King's Castles Area map

Schwangau

LINDERHOF

Kofel

To Munich

Tegelberg

Ettal

NEUSCHWANSTEIN

Pinswang

TREETOP WALKWAY & LECH FALLS

HOHEN-SCHWANGAU

HAHNEN-KAMMBAHN

Reutte

Garmisch-Partenkirchen

187

To Mittenwald & Innsbruck

198

EHRENBERG RUINS

See Reutte map

Plansee

Eibsee

Lech River

179

Bichlbach

Lermoos

Ehrwald

Zugspitze 9718'

Stanzach

Namlos

Blindsee

Biberwier

NARROW ROAD

Fernpass

Fallerschein

REST STOP

Luge

AUSTRIA

Nassereith

Telfs

179

5 Kilometers

5 Miles

A-12

Stams

To Zürich

To Innsbruck

derhof are impractical. More transport details are provided later, under each individual destination.

Hitchhiking, though always risky, is a slow-but-doable way to connect the public-transportation gaps. For example, even reluctant hitchhikers can catch a ride from Linderhof back to Oberammergau, as virtually everyone leaving there is a tourist like you and heading that way.

Staying overnight in this region is magical, but travelers in a hurry can make it a day trip from **Munich.** If you can postpone leaving Munich until after 9:00 on weekday mornings, the **Bayern-Ticket** is a great deal for getting to Füssen or Oberammergau: It covers buses and slower regional trains throughout Bavaria for up to five people at a very low price (€23/day for the first person plus €4 for each additional person, for more information, see page 101 in the Munich chapter). If you're interested only in Ludwig's castles, consider an all-day organized bus tour of the Bavarian biggies as a side-trip from Munich (see page 33 in the Munich chapter).

Bavarian Craftsmanship

The scenes you'll see painted on the sides of houses in Bavaria are called *Lüftlmalerei*. The term came from the name of the house ("Zum Lüftl") owned by a man from Oberammergau who pioneered the practice in the 18th century. As the paintings became popular during the Counter-Reformation Baroque age, themes tended to involve Christian symbols, saints, and stories (such as scenes from the life of Jesus), to reinforce the Catholic Church's authority in the region. Some scenes also depicted an important historical event that took place in that house or town.

Especially in the northern part of this region (for example, in Rothenburg), you'll see *Fachwerkhäuser*—half-timbered houses. A timber frame outlines the wall, which was traditionally filled in with a mixture of wicker and clay. These are most often found inside fortified cities that were once strong and semi-independent (such as Rothenberg, Nürnberg, and Dinkelsbühl). Farther south, you'll see sturdy, white-walled masonry houses with woodwork on the upper stories and an overhanging roof. Many Bavarian homes and hotels have elaborate wooden paneling and furniture, often beautifully carved or made from special sweet-smelling wood.

By Bike

This is great biking country. Many hotels loan bikes to guests, and shops in Reutte and at the Füssen train station rent bikes for €10-15 per day. The ride from Reutte to Neuschwanstein and the Tegelberg luge (1.5 hours) is a natural.

HELPFUL HINTS

Sightseeing Pass: The Bavarian Palace Department offers a **14-day ticket** (called *Mehrtagesticket*) that covers admission to Neuschwanstein (but not Hohenschwangau) and Linderhof; the Residenz, Nymphenburg Palace, and Amalienburg Palace in Munich; the Imperial Palace in Nürnberg; the Residenz and Marienberg Fortress in Würzburg; and many other castles and palaces not mentioned in this book. The one-person pass costs €24, and the family/partner version (up to two adults plus children) costs €40. If you are planning to visit at least three of these sights within a two-week period, the pass will likely pay for itself. (For longer stays, there's also an annual pass available—€45/single, €65/family.) The pass is sold at all covered castles and online. For more information, see www.schloesser.bayern.de. Don't confuse this with the pointless combination ticket for Ludwig II's castles, which costs the same (€24) but only covers three castles—Neuschwanstein, Linderhof, and Herrencheimsee (farther east and not covered in this book).

Local Guest Tax: Hotels and B&Bs in the region are required to collect a local tax (called a *Kurtax*) of about €2 per person per night. This is usually included in the rates I've listed, but may be listed separately on your bill. Usually, this tax funds a card that provides discounts on attractions and free public transportation; details are in each city's "Tourist Information" sections.

Visiting Churches: At any type of church, if you'd like to attend a service, look for the *Gottesdienst* schedule. In every small German town in the very Catholic south, when you pass the big town church, look for a sign that says *Heilige Messe*. This is the schedule for holy Mass, usually on Saturday *(Sa.)* or Sunday *(So.)*.

Füssen, Germany

Dramatically situated under a renovated castle on the lively Lech River, Füssen (FEW-sehn) has been a strategic stop since ancient

times. Its main street was once part of the Via Claudia Augusta, which crossed the Alps in Roman times. Going north, early travelers could follow the Lech River downstream to the Danube, and then cross over to the Main and Rhine valleys—a route now known to modern travelers as the "Romantic Road." Today, while Füssen is overrun by tourists in the summer, few venture to the back streets...which is where you'll find the real charm. Apart from my self-guided walk and the Füssen Heritage Museum, there's little to do here—but it's a fine base for visiting the King's Castles and the other surrounding attractions.

Orientation to Füssen

Füssen's roughly circular old town huddles around its castle and monastery, along the Lech River. The train station, TI, and many shops are at the north end of town, and my recommended hotels and eateries are within easy walking distance. Roads spin off in all directions (to the lake, to Neuschwanstein, to Austria). Halfway between Füssen and the German border (as you drive, or a woodsy walk from town) is the **Lechfall,** a thunderous waterfall (with a handy WC).

TOURIST INFORMATION

The TI is in the center of town (July-mid-Sept Mon-Fri 9:00-18:00, Sat 10:00-14:00, Sun 10:00-12:00; mid-Sept-June Mon-Fri 9:00-17:00, Sat 10:00-14:00, closed Sun; one Internet terminal, free with Füssen Card—described next, 3 blocks down Bahnhofstrasse from station at Kaiser-Maximilian-Platz 1, tel. 08362/93850, www.fuessen.de). If necessary, the TI can help you find a room. After hours, the little self-service info pavilion near the front of the TI features an automated room-finding service with a phone to call hotels.

Be sure to ask your hotel for a **Füssen Card,** an electronic pass that your hotel tax entitles you to. The card gives you free use of public transit in the immediate region (including the bus to Neuschwanstein), as well as discounts at major attractions: €1 each on Neuschwanstein, Hohenschwangau, the Museum of the Bavarian Kings, and the Forggensee boat trip, and €2 on the Füssen Heritage Museum (plus discounts on the Tegelberg gondola, the Royal Crystal Baths, and the Hahnenkammbahn cable car near Reutte). Some accommodations won't tell you about the card unless you request it. You may be asked for a €3-5 deposit; be sure to return the card before you leave town. After the hotel activates the card, it can take an hour or two before it actually works at sights and on buses.

ARRIVAL IN FÜSSEN

By Train: From the unstaffed train station (lockers available, €2-3), continue two blocks in the same direction as the tracks to reach the center of town and the TI. Buses to Neuschwanstein, Reutte, and elsewhere leave from a parking lot next to the station. Plans are afoot to tear down and replace the old station building, so specifics may change.

By Car: Füssen is known for its traffic jams, and you can't drive into the old town. The most convenient lots (follow signs) are the underground P-5 (across street from old town entrance, €7/day) and the aboveground P-3 (off Kemptener Strasse, €9/day).

HELPFUL HINTS

Internet Access: ICS Internet Café has four computers, a printer...and a betting salon in back (€2.50/hour, daily 9:00-24:00, Luitpoldstrasse 8, tel. 08362/883-7073). The **city library** (Stadtbibliothek), inside the monastery complex that houses the Füssen Heritage Museum, has computers and Wi-Fi but limited hours (€1/30 minutes, free with Füssen Card; Tue-

Wed 13:00-17:00, Thu 13:00-19:00, Fri 10:00-17:00, closed Mon, Lechhalde 3, tel. 08362/903-144).

Bike Rental: Fahrrad-Station, sitting right where the train tracks end, outfits sightseers with good bikes and tips on two-wheeled fun in the area (prices per 24 hours: €10-city bike, €15-sport bike, €20-electric bike; March-Oct Mon-Fri 9:00-12:00 & 14:00-18:00, Sat 9:00-13:00, Sun 10:00-12:00, closed Nov-Feb, tel. 08362/505-9155, mobile 0176-2205-3080, www.ski-sport-luggi.de). For a strenuous but enjoyable 20-mile loop trip, see page 156.

Car Rental: Two rental agencies are about an €8 taxi ride from the center: **Schlichtling** (Mon-Fri 8:00-18:00, Sat 9:00-12:00, closed Sun, Hiebeler Strasse 49, tel. 08362/922-122, www.schlichtling.de) and **Auto Osterried/Europcar** (daily 8:00-19:00, past waterfall on road to Austria, Tiroler Strasse 65, tel. 08362/6381).

Local Guide: Silvia Beyer speaks English, knows the region very well, and can even drive you to sights that are hard to reach by train (€30/hour, mobile 0160-9011-3431, silliby@web.de).

Füssen Walk

For most, Füssen is just a home base for visiting Ludwig's famous castles. But the town has a rich history and hides some evocative corners, as you'll see when you follow this self-guided orientation walk. This 45-minute stroll is designed to get you out of the cutesy old cobbled core where most tourists spend their time. Throughout the town, "City Tour" information plaques explain points of interest in English (in more detail than I've provided).

• *Begin at the square in front of the TI, three blocks from the train station.*

ⓐ Kaiser-Maximilian-Platz

The entertaining "Seven Stones" fountain on this square, by sculptor Christian Tobin, was built in 1995 to celebrate Füssen's 700th birthday. The stones symbolize community, groups of people gathering, conviviality...each is different, with "heads" nodding and talking. It's granite on granite. The moving heads are not connected, and nod only with waterpower. While frozen in winter, it's a popular and splashy play zone for kids on hot summer days.

• *Walk half a block down the busy street (to the left, with the TI at your back). You'll soon see...*

❶ Hotel Hirsch and Medieval Towers

Recent renovations have restored some of the original Art Nouveau flavor to Hotel Hirsch, which opened in 1904.
In those days, aristocratic tourists came here to appreciate the castles and natural wonders of the Alps. Across the busy street stands one of two surviving towers from Füssen's medieval town wall (c. 1515), and next to it is a passageway into the old town.

• *Walk 50 yards farther down the busy street to another tower. Just before it, you'll see an information plaque and an archway where a small street called Klosterstrasse emerges through a surviving piece of the old town wall. Step through the smaller pedestrian archway, walk along Klosterstrasse for a few yards, and turn left through the gate into the...*

❷ Historic Cemetery of St. Sebastian (Alter Friedhof)

This peaceful oasis of Füssen history, established in the 16th century, fills a corner between the town wall and the Franciscan monastery. It's technically full, and only members of great and venerable Füssen families (who already own plots here) can join those who are buried (free, daily April-Sept 7:30-19:00, Oct-March 8:00-17:00).

Immediately inside the gate and on the right is the tomb of Domenico Quaglio, who painted the Romantic scenes decorating the walls of Hohenschwangau Castle in 1835. Across the cemetery, on the old city wall (beyond the church), is the World War I memorial, listing all the names of men from this small town killed in that devastating conflict (along with each one's rank and place of death). A bit to the right, also along the old wall, is a statue of the hand of God holding a fetus—a place to remember babies who died before being born. And in the corner, farther to the right, is a gated area with the simple wooden crosses of Franciscans who lived just over the wall in the monastery. Strolling the rest of the grounds, note the fine tomb art from many ages collected here, and the loving care this community gives its cemetery.

• *Exit on the far side, just past the dead Franciscans, and continue toward the big church.*

❸ Town View from Franciscan Monastery (Franziskaner-kloster)

From the Franciscan Monastery (which still has big responsibili-

BAVARIA & TIROL

ties, but only a handful of monks in residence), there's a fine view over the medieval town with an alpine backdrop. The Church of St. Magnus and the High Castle (the former summer residence of the Bishops of Augsburg) break the horizon. The tall, skinny smokestack (c. 1886) and workers' housing on the left are reminders that when Ludwig built Neuschwanstein, the textile industry (linen and flax) was very big here. Walk all the way to the far end of the monastery chapel and peek around the corner, where you'll see a gate that proclaims the *Ende der romantischen Strasse* (end of the Romantic Road).

• *Now go down the stairway and turn left, through the medieval "Bleachers' Gate" (marked 5½) to the...*

ⓔ Lech Riverbank

This low end of town, the flood zone, was the home of those whose work depended on the river—bleachers, rafters, and fishermen. In its heyday, the Lech River was an expressway to Augsburg (about 70 miles to the north). Around the year 1500, the rafters established the first professional guild in Füssen. Cargo from Italy passed here en route to big German cities farther north. Rafters would assemble rafts and pile them high with goods—or with people needing a lift. If the water was high, they could float all the way to Augsburg in as little as one day. There they'd disassemble their raft and sell off the lumber along with the goods they'd carried, then make their way home to raft again. Today you'll see no modern-day rafters here, as there's a hydroelectric plant just downstream.

• *Walk upstream a bit, appreciating the river's milky color, and head inland (turn right) immediately after crossing under the bridge.*

ⓕ Church of the Holy Spirit, Bread Market, and Lute-Makers

Climbing uphill, you pass the colorful Church of the Holy Spirit (Heilig-Geist-Spitalkirche) on the right. As this was the church of the rafters, their patron, St. Christopher (with the Baby Jesus on his shoulder), is prominent on the facade. Today it's the church of Füssen's old folks' home (it's adjacent—notice the easy-access skyway).

Farther up the hill on the right (almost opposite an archway into a big courtyard) is Bread Market Square (Brotmarkt), with a fountain honoring a famous 16th-century lute-making family, the Tieffenbruckers. In its day, Füssen (surrounded by forests) was a huge center of violin- and lute-making, with about 200 workshops. Today only three survive.

BAVARIA & TIROL

SELF-GUIDED WALK

- **A** Kaiser-Maximilian-Platz
- **B** Medieval Towers (2)
- **C** Historic Cemetery of St. Sebastian
- **D** Town View
- **E** Lech Riverbank
- **F** Church of the Holy Spirit, Bread Market & Lute-Makers
- **G** Benedictine Monastery
- **H** Füssen Heritage Museum
- **I** St. Magnus Basilica
- **J** High Castle

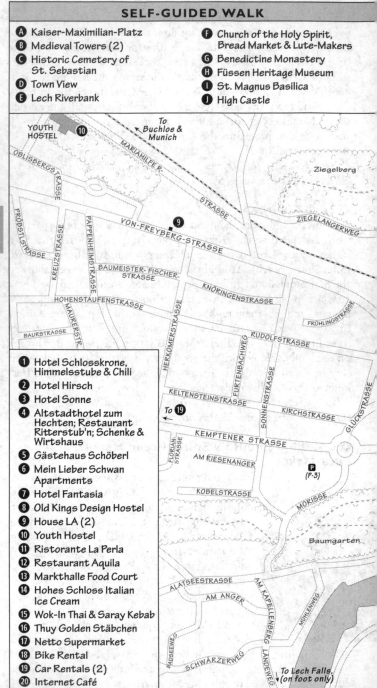

- **1** Hotel Schlosskrone, Himmelsstube & Chili
- **2** Hotel Hirsch
- **3** Hotel Sonne
- **4** Altstadthotel zum Hechten; Restaurant Ritterstub'n; Schenke & Wirtshaus
- **5** Gästehaus Schöberl
- **6** Mein Lieber Schwan Apartments
- **7** Hotel Fantasia
- **8** Old Kings Design Hostel
- **9** House LA (2)
- **10** Youth Hostel
- **11** Ristorante La Perla
- **12** Restaurant Aquila
- **13** Markthalle Food Court
- **14** Hohes Schloss Italian Ice Cream
- **15** Wok-In Thai & Saray Kebab
- **16** Thuy Golden Stäbchen
- **17** Netto Supermarket
- **18** Bike Rental
- **19** Car Rentals (2)
- **20** Internet Café

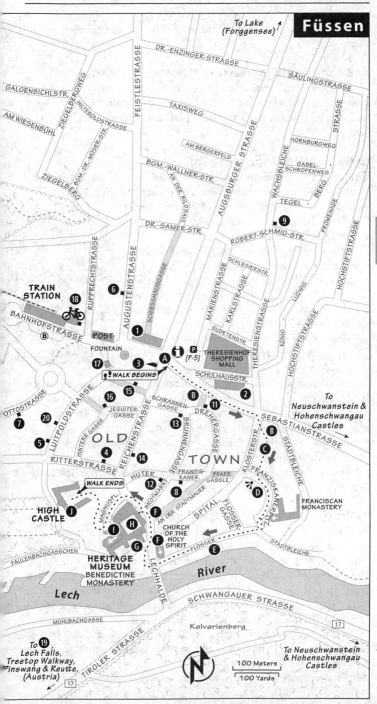

Füssen

To Lake
(Forggensee)

BAVARIA & TIROL

DR.-ENZINGER-STRASSE

SÄULINGSTRASSE

FEISTLESTRASSE

GALGENBICHLSTR.

TAXISWEG

AM WIESENBÜHL

ZIEGELBERGWEG

HILTEBOLDSTRASSE

BGM.-DR.-MOSER-STR.

AM BERGERFELD

HORNBURGWEG

GABEL-
SCHROFENWEG

ZIEGELBERG

BGM.-WALLNER-STR.

AN DER BILDSÄULE

AUGSBURGER STRASSE

WACHSBLEICHE

TEGEL · BERG

DR.-SAMER-STR.

ROBERT-SCHMID-STR.

❾

RUPPRECHTSTRASSE

SCHIESSHAUSGASSE

AUGUSTENSTRASSE

MARIENSTRASSE

SCHLESIERSTR.

KARLSTRASSE

THERESIENSTRASSE

HOCHSTIFTSTRASSE

LUDWIG · STRASSE

KÖNIG

PROMENADE

**TRAIN
STATION** ⓲

🚲

Ⓑ BAHNHOFSTRASSE

POST

FOUNTAIN

❻

❶

SUDETENSTR.

ⓐ ℹ️ P (P-5)

**THERESIENHOF
SHOPPING
MALL**

⓱ ❸

WALK BEGINS

SCHULHAUSSTR.

❷

To Neuschwanstein &
Hohenschwangau
Castles

OTTOSTRASSE

❼

⓴

❺

LUITPOLDSTRASSE

HINTERE GASSE

JESUITER-
GASSE

⓰ ⓯

REICHENSTRASSE

SCHRANNEN-
GASSE

Ⓑ

❶❶

DREHERGASSE

SEBASTIANSTRASSE

Ⓑ

OLD

❹

BRUNNENGASSE

⓭

❹ KLOSTERSTR.

Ⓒ

STADTBLEICHE

RITTERSTRASSE

TOWN

⓮

FRANZIS-
KANER.

PFARR-
GÄSSLE

FRANZISKANERPLATZ

Ⓓ

**FRANCISCAN
MONASTERY**

WALK ENDS

HUTER

⓬

BROTMARKT

❽

AN DER STADTMAUER

SPITAL

FLOSSER-
GÄSSELE

**HIGH
CASTLE** Ⓙ

MAGNUSPL.

Ⓘ Ⓗ

Ⓕ

Ⓖ Ⓕ

**CHURCH
OF THE
HOLY SPIRIT**

FLOSSER.

STADTBLEICHE

Ⓔ

FAULENBACHGASSCHEN

**HERITAGE
MUSEUM
BENEDICTINE
MONASTERY**

LECHHALDE

River

Lech

SCHWANGAUER STRASSE

MÜHLBACHGASSE

Kalvarienberg

17

To ⓳
Lech Falls,
Treetop Walkway,
inswang & Reutte,
(Austria)

17

TIROLER STRASSE

Ⓝ

100 Meters

100 Yards

To Neuschwanstein
& Hohenschwangau
Castles

• *Backtrack and go through the archway into the courtyard of the former...*

⑥ Benedictine Monastery (Kloster St. Mang)

From 1717 until secularization in 1802, the monastery was the power center of town. Today the courtyard is popular for concerts, and the building houses the City Hall and Füssen Heritage Museum.

⑦ Füssen Heritage Museum

This is Füssen's one must-see sight (€6, €7 combo-ticket includes painting gallery and castle tower; April-Oct Tue-Sun 11:00-17:00, closed Mon; shorter hours and closed Mon-Thu Nov-March; tel. 08362/903-146, www. museum.fuessen.de).

Pick up the loaner English translations and follow the one-way route. In the St. Anna Chapel, you'll see the famous *Dance of Death.* This was painted shortly after a plague devastated the community in 1590. It shows 20 social classes, each dancing with the Grim Reaper—starting with the pope and the emperor. The words above say, essentially, "You can say yes or you can say no, but you must ultimately dance with death." Leaving the chapel, you walk over the metal lid of the crypt. Upstairs, exhibits illustrate the rafting trade, and violin- and lute-making (with a complete workshop). The museum also includes an exquisite *Kaisersaal* (main festival hall), an old library, an exhibition on textile production, and a King Ludwig-style "castle dream room."

• *Leaving the courtyard, hook left around the old monastery and go up-hill. The square tower marks...*

⑧ St. Magnus Basilica (Basilika St. Mang)

St. Mang (or Magnus) is Füssen's favorite saint. In the eighth century, he worked miracles all over the area with his holy rod. For centuries, pilgrims came from far and wide to enjoy art depicting the great works of St. Magnus. Above the altar dangles a glass cross containing his relics (including that holy stick). Just inside the door is a chapel remembering a much more modern saint—Franz Seelos (1819-1867), the local boy who went to America (Pittsburgh and New Orleans) and lived such a righteous life that in 2000 he was beatified by Pope John Paul II. If you're in need of a miracle, fill out a request card next to the candles.

• *From the church, a lane leads high above, into the courtyard of the...*

❶ High Castle (Hohes Schloss)

This castle, long the summer residence of the Bishop of Augsburg, houses a painting gallery (the upper floor is labeled in English) and

a tower with a view over the town and lake (included in the €7 Füssen Heritage Museum combo-ticket, otherwise €6, same hours as museum). Its courtyard is interesting for the striking perspective tricks painted onto its flat walls.

From below the castle, the city's main drag (once the Roman Via Claudia, and now Reichenstrasse) leads from a grand statue of St. Magnus past lots of shops, cafés, and strolling people to Kaiser-Maximilian-Platz and the TI... where you began.

BAVARIA & TIROL

Sleeping in Füssen

Convenient Füssen is just three miles from Ludwig's castles and offers a cobbled, riverside retreat. All recommended accommodations are within a few handy blocks of the train station and the town center. Parking is easy, and some hotels also have their own lot or garage. Prices listed are for one-night stays in high season (mid-June-Sept). Most hotels give about 5-10 percent off for two-night stays—always request this discount—and prices drop by 10-20 percent off-season. Competition is fierce, so shop around. Be sure to ask your hotelier for a Füssen Card (see page 132).

BIG, FANCY HOTELS IN THE CENTER OF TOWN

$$$ Hotel Schlosskrone, with 64 rooms and all the amenities, is just a block from the station. It also runs two restaurants and a fine pastry shop—you'll notice at breakfast (Sb-€111, standard Db-€153, bigger Db-€173, Db with balcony-€179, Tb-€192, Qb-€208, various pricey suites also available, air-con in a few expensive rooms only, elevator, Wi-Fi, free sauna and fitness center, parking-€10/day, Prinzregentenplatz 2-4, tel. 08362/930-180, www.schlosskrone.de, rezeption@schlosskrone.de, Norbert Schöll and family).

$$$ Hotel Hirsch is a romantic, well-maintained, family-run, 53-room, old-style hotel that takes pride in tradition. Their standard rooms are fine, and their rooms with historical and landscape themes are a fun splurge (typical rates: Sb-€122, standard Db-€139-154, theme Db-€174-184, book direct on their website for best prices, family rooms, elevator, Wi-Fi, free parking, Kai-

Sleep Code

Abbreviations   (€1 = about $1.40)
S = Single, **D** = Double/Twin, **T** = Triple, **Q** = Quad, **b** = bathroom, **s** = shower only.
Price Rankings
   $$$ Higher Priced—Most rooms €130 or more.
    $$ Moderately Priced—Most rooms between €70-130.
     $ Lower Priced—Most rooms €70 or less.
Unless otherwise noted, credit cards are accepted, English is spoken, Wi-Fi is generally free, and breakfast is included. The prices listed here include local tax. Prices change; verify current rates online or by email. For the best prices, always book directly with the hotel.

ser-Maximilian-Platz 7, tel. 08362/93980, www.hotelfuessen.de, info@hotelhirsch.de).

$$$ Hotel Sonne, in the heart of town, has a modern lobby and takes pride in decorating (some would say overdecorating) its 50 stylish rooms (Sb-€109, Db-€135, fancier Db-€145-195, Tb-€149, bigger Tb-€199, Qb-€219, 5 percent discount if you book on their website, elevator, guest computer, Wi-Fi; free laundry machine, €3 if you need soap; free sauna and fitness center, parking-€6-8/day, kitty-corner from TI at Prinzregentenplatz 1, on GPS you may need to enter Reichenstrasse 37, tel. 08362/9080, www.hotel-sonne.de, info@hotel-sonne.de).

SMALLER, MID-PRICED HOTELS AND PENSIONS

$$ Altstadthotel zum Hechten offers 34 modern and nicely renovated rooms in a friendly, traditional building right under Füssen Castle in the old-town pedestrian zone. It's a good value, with lots of extras (laundry-€10-20/load, travel resource/game room with maps and books, borrowable hiking gear, fun miniature bowling alley in basement, recommended restaurant), a family-run feel, and borderline-kitschy decor (Sb-€74, Db-€108, bigger Db-€125, Tb-€148, Qb-€178, often less if you stay 3 nights, ask when you reserve for 5 percent off these prices with this book, also mention if you're very tall as most beds can be short, non-smoking, lots of stairs, guest computer, Wi-Fi, parking-€4/day on-site—or free a 5-minute walk away, in the heart of the old town at Ritterstrasse 6, tel. 08362/91600, www.hotel-hechten.com, info@hotel-hechten.com, Pfeiffer and Tramp families).

$$ Gästehaus Schöberl, run by the head cook at Altstadthotel zum Hechten, rents six attentively furnished, modern rooms a five-minute walk from the train station. One room is in the owners' house, and the rest are in the building next door (Sb-€55, Db-€80,

Tb-€105, two-room Qb-€140, cash only, Wi-Fi, free parking, Luitpoldstrasse 14-16, tel. 08362/922-411, www.schoeberl-fuessen. de, info@schoeberl-fuessen.de, Pia and Georg Schöberl).

$$ Mein Lieber Schwan, a block from the train station, is a former private house with four superbly outfitted apartments, each with a double bed, sofa bed, kitchen, and antique furnishings. The catch is the three-night minimum stay in high season (Sb-€77-88, Db-€89-100, Tb-€107-116, Qb-€124-133, price depends on apartment size, cash or PayPal only, no breakfast, Wi-Fi, free parking, laundry facilities, garden, from station turn left at traffic circle to Augustenstrasse 3, tel. 08362/509-980, www.meinlieberschwan. de, fewo@meinlieberschwan.de, Herr Bletschacher). Herr Bletschacher also has two slightly larger, more expensive apartments at Klosterstrasse 10, near the cemetery.

$$ Hotel Fantasia, recently converted from a home for nuns, has 16 rooms a short walk through the park from the train station (Sb-€69-89, Db-€99-129, Tb-€120-150, Qb-€160-170, Quint/b-€180-190, price depends on room size, 5 percent discount if you book on their website, Wi-Fi, parking-€5/day, Ottostrasse 1, tel. 08362/9080, www.hotel-fantasia.de, info@hotel-fantasia.de).

BUDGET BEDS

$ Old Kings Design Hostel shoehorns two eight-person dorms and three doubles into an old townhouse buried deep in the pedestrian zone. While the quarters are tight (all the rooms share two bathrooms), the Old World location, creative decor, and reasonable prices are enticing (dorm bed-€24, D-€57-60, breakfast-€5, Wi-Fi, kitchen, laundry-€4/load, reception open daily 7:30-12:00 & 16:00-21:00, Franziskanergasse 2, tel. 08362/883-7385, www. oldkingshostel.com, info@oldkingshostel.com).

$ House LA, run by energetic mason Lahdo Algül and hardworking Agata, has two branches. The backpacker house has 11 basic, clean, mostly four-bed dorm rooms at rock-bottom prices about a 10-minute walk from the station (dorm bed-€18, D-€46, breakfast-€3, pay guest computer, Wi-Fi, free parking, Wachsbleiche 2). A second building has five family apartments with kitchen and bath, each sleeping four to six people (apartment-€60-90, depends on number of people and season—mention Rick Steves for best price, breakfast-€3, Wi-Fi, free parking, 6-minute walk back along tracks from station to von Freybergstrasse 26; contact info for both: tel. 08362/607-366, mobile 0170-624-8610, www.housela. de, info@housela.de). Both branches rent bikes (€8/day) and have laundry facilities (€7/load).

$ Füssen Youth Hostel, with 138 beds in 32 institutional rooms, occupies a pleasant modern building in a grassy setting an easy walk from the center. There are ping-pong tables and a basketball net out front, but few other extras (bed in 2- to 6-bed dorm rooms-€23, bunk-bed Db-€51, €3 more for nonmembers, €2 extra for one-night stays, €4 extra for those over age 26, includes breakfast and sheets, laundry-€5/load, dinner-€5.50, lockers, Wi-Fi, free parking, office open daily 8:00-12:00 & 17:00-22:00, from station backtrack 10 minutes along tracks, Mariahilfer Strasse 5, tel. 08362/7754, www.fuessen.jugendherberge.de, fuessen@jugendherberge.de).

Eating in Füssen

Restaurant Ritterstub'n offers delicious, reasonably priced German grub, fish, salads, veggie plates, gluten-free options, and a fun kids' menu. They have three eating zones: modern decor in front, traditional Bavarian in back, and a courtyard. Demure Gabi serves while her husband cooks standard Bavarian fare (€8-16 main courses, smaller portions available for less, €6.50 lunch specials, €19 three-course fixed-price dinners, Tue-Sun 11:30-14:30 & 17:30-23:00, closed Mon, Ritterstrasse 4, tel. 08362/7759, www.restaurant-ritterstuben.de).

Schenke & Wirtshaus (inside the recommended Altstadthotel zum Hechten) dishes up hearty, traditional Bavarian dishes in a cozy setting. They specialize in pike *(Hecht)* pulled from the Lech River, served with a tasty fresh-herb sauce (€8-16 main courses, salad bar, daily 11:00-22:00, Ritterstrasse 6, tel. 0836/91600, www.hotel-hechten.com).

Ristorante La Perla is an Italian restaurant with fair prices, along a passageway through Füssen's town wall. Sit either in the classic interior, at streetside tables on a quiet Old Town lane, or in a back courtyard (€8-11 pizzas and pastas, €12-22 meat and fish dishes, daily 11:00-22:00, in winter closed 14:30-17:30 and all day Mon, Drehergasse 44, tel. 08362/7155).

The **Himmelsstube** is the restaurant inside Hotel Schlosskrone, right on Füssen's main traffic circle. It offers a €10 weekday lunch buffet and live Bavarian zither music most Fridays and Saturdays during dinner (€10-20 main courses). Choose between a traditional dining room and a pastel winter garden (both feel quite formal). If your hotel doesn't offer breakfast, consider their €13.50 breakfast or huge €17 Sunday brunch buffet (open Mon-Sat 7:30-10:30 & 11:30-14:30 & 18:00-22:00, Sun 7:30-13:00 & 18:00-22:00, Prinzregentenplatz 2-4, tel. 08362/930-180, www.schlosskrone.de). The hotel's second restaurant, **Chili,** serves Mediterranean dishes.

Restaurant Aquila serves modern German and Italian-influenced dishes in a simple indoor setting and at outdoor tables on the delightful little Brotmarkt square (€10-18 main courses, serious €10-11 salads, Wed-Mon 11:30-21:30, closed Tue, Brot-markt 9, tel. 08362/6253, www.aquila-fuessen.de).

Food Court: The fun **Markthalle** offers a wide selection of rea-sonably priced, wurst-free food. Located in an old warehouse from 1483, it's now home to a fishmonger, deli counters, a fruit stand, a bakery, and a wine bar. Buy your food from one of the vendors, park yourself at any one of the tables, then look up and admire the Renaissance ceiling (Mon-Fri 8:00-20:00, Sat 8:00-15:00, closed Sun, corner of Schrannengasse and Brunnengasse).

Brewpub near the Castles: If you have a car, consider heading to **Schloss Brauhaus,** in the village of Schwangau (described on page 158).

Gelato: **Hohes Schloss Italian Ice Cream** is a good *gelateria* on the main drag with a huge menu of elaborate sundaes and an inviting people-watching perch (Reichenstrasse 14).

Cheap Eats: **Wok-In,** in the Luitpold-Passage at Reichen-strasse 33, has little atmosphere but serves good Thai food to eat in or take out (Mon-Sat 11:00-22:00, Sun 12:00-21:00, tel. 08362/924-905). At the outer end of the passage, **Saray Kebab** is the town's favorite Middle Eastern takeaway joint (Luitpoldstrasse 1). The Vietnamese **Thuy Golden Stäbchen,** on a deserted back street, has low prices and outdoor tables with a castle view (Hin-teregasse 29).

Picnic Supplies: Bakeries and butcher shops *(Metzger)* abound and frequently have ready-made sandwiches. For groceries, try the discount **Netto** supermarket, underground at Prinzregentenplatz, the roundabout on your way into town from the train station, or the mid-range **REWE** in the Theresienhof shopping complex be-hind Hotel Hirsch (both supermarkets open Mon-Sat 7:00-20:00, closed Sun).

Füssen Connections

Bus schedules from Füssen can be very confusing. The website www.bahn.com is good for figuring out your options for a particu-lar day and route.

From Füssen to: Neuschwanstein (bus #73 or #78, departs from train station, most continue to Tegelberg lift station after cas-tles, 1/hour, 10 minutes, €2.10 one-way, buses #9606 and #9651 also make the trip; taxis cost €10 one-way); **Wieskirche** (bus #73, #9606, or #9651; 4-6 buses/day, 45-60 minutes); **Oberammergau** (bus #9606, 4-5/day, 1.5 hours, bus sometimes starts as #73 and changes number to #9606 en route—confirm with driver that bus is bound for Oberammergau); **Reutte** (bus #74 in Germany, chang-es number to #4258 in Austria, Mon-Fri 6/day, Sat-Sun 4/day, last bus 19:00, 30-50 minutes, €4.30 one-way); **Zugspitze** (possible as day trip via bus #74 to Reutte, then train to Ehrwald or Garmisch-Partenkirchen, allow up to 3.5 hours total to reach the top); **Munich** (hourly, 2 hours, some change in Buchloe); **Innsbruck** (fastest via bus #4258/#74 to Reutte, then train from Reutte to Innsbruck via Garmisch, 3/day, 4 hours; otherwise via Munich); **Salzburg** (roughly hourly, 4 hours on fast trains, 5 hours on slow trains eligible for Bayern-Ticket, change in Munich and sometimes in Buchloe); **Rothenburg ob der Tauber** (hourly, 5-6 hours, look for connections with only 3 changes—often in Augsburg, Treuchtlingen, and Steinach); **Frankfurt** (hourly, 5-6 hours, 1-2 changes). Train info: tel. 0180-599-6633, www.bahn.com.

Romantic Road Buses: The northbound Romantic Road bus departs Füssen at 8:00; the southbound bus arrives in Füssen at 20:20 (daily, mid-April-late Oct only, bus stop is at train station, www.romanticroadcoach.de). A rail pass gets you a 20 percent discount on the Romantic Road bus (without using up a day of a flexipass). The northbound bus arrives in Munich at 10:30 and in Rothenburg at 15:45. The bus is much slower than the train, especially to Rothenburg; the only reason to take the bus is that it gives you the briefest glimpse of the Wieskirche and other sights along the way, and requires no changes. Note that the northbound bus stops at the **Wieskirche** for 20 minutes, while the southbound bus stops there for 15 minutes—but after the church has closed. For more details on the bus, see page 380 in the Rothenburg and the Romantic Road chapter.

The Best of Bavaria

Within a short drive of Füssen and Reutte, you'll find some of the most enjoyable—and most tourist-filled—sights in Germany. The otherworldly "King's Castles" of Neuschwanstein and Hohenschwangau capture romantics' imaginations, the ornately decorated Wieskirche puts the faithful in a heavenly mood, and the little town of Oberammergau overwhelms visitors with cuteness. Yet another impressive castle (Linderhof), another fancy church (Ettal), and a sky-high viewpoint (the Zugspitze) round out southern Bavaria's top attractions.

The King's Castles: Neuschwanstein and Hohenschwangau

The most popular tourist destinations in southern Bavaria are the two "King's Castles" (Königsschlösser) near Füssen. The older Hohenschwangau, King Ludwig's boyhood home, is less famous but more historic. The more dramatic Neuschwanstein, which inspired Walt Disney, is the one everyone visits. I'd recommend visiting both and hiking above Neuschwanstein to Mary's Bridge. If you enjoy romantic hikes, also plan to walk down through the gorge below. Reservations are a magic wand that smooths out your visit. With fairy-tale turrets in a fairy-tale alpine setting built by a fairy-tale king, these castles are understandably a huge hit.

GETTING THERE

If arriving by **car,** note that road signs in the region refer to the sight as *Königsschlösser,* not Neuschwanstein. There's plenty of parking (all lots–€5). The first lots require more walking. The most convenient lot, by the lake (#4, *Parkplatz am Alpsee*), is up the small road past the souvenir shops and ticket center.

From **Füssen,** those without cars can catch **bus** #73 or #78 (hourly, generally departs Füssen's train station at :05 past the hour, €2.10 each way, 10 minutes, extra buses often run when crowded; a few departures of #9606 and #9651 also make this trip). A Bayern-Ticket (see page 101) or the local guest card available from your hotel (see page 288) lets you ride for free. You can also take a **taxi** (€10 one-way), ride a rental **bike** (two level miles), or—if you're in a pinch—**walk** (less than an hour). The bus drops you at the tourist office; it's a one-minute walk from there to the ticket office. When returning, note that buses #73 and #78 pointing left (with your back to the TI) are headed to Füssen, while the same numbers pointing right are going elsewhere.

From **Reutte,** take bus #4258 (number changes to #74 in Germany, fewer buses on Sat and Sun—only 4/day) to the Füssen train station, then hop on bus #73 or #78 to the castles. Overnight guests with an Aktiv-Card (described on page 177) can book a taxi to the castles (runs daily 9:00-18:00, ask your hotelier or Reutte TI).

Orientation to the King's Castles

Cost: Neuschwanstein and Hohenschwangau cost €12 apiece. A "Königsticket" combo-ticket for both castles costs €23, and a "Schwanenticket," which also covers the Museum of the

Bavarian Kings—described on page 153—costs €29.50. Children under age 18 (accompanied by an adult) are admitted free.

Hours: The ticket center, located at street level between the two castles, is open daily April-Sept 8:00-17:30, Oct-March 9:00-15:30. The first castle tour of the day departs an hour after the ticket office opens and the last normally departs 30 minutes after it closes: April-Sept at 9:00 and 18:00, Oct-March at 10:00 and 16:00.

Getting Tickets for the Castles: Every tour bus in Bavaria converges on Neuschwanstein, and tourists flush in each morning from Munich. A handy reservation system sorts out the chaos for smart travelers. (One out of every three castle tickets is reserved. Look left. Look right. If you want to be smarter than these two people, prebook.) Tickets, whether reserved in advance or bought on the spot, come with admission times. If you miss your appointed tour time, you can't get in. To tour both castles, you must do Hohenschwangau first (logical, since this gives a better introduction to King Ludwig's short life). You'll get two tour times: Hohenschwangau and then, two hours later, Neuschwanstein.

Arrival: Make the **ticket center** your first stop. If you have a reservation, stand in the short line for picking up tickets. If you don't have a reservation...welcome to the very long line. Arrive by 8:00 in summer, and you'll likely be touring at 9:00. During August, the busiest month, tickets for English tours can run out by around noon. Because day-trippers from Munich tend to take the morning train—with a bus connection arriving at the castles by about 11:15—if you need to buy a ticket on the spot, you'd be wise to try to make it here by 11:00 to beat this crowd.

Reservations: It's smart to reserve in peak season (June-Oct—especially in July-Aug, when slots can book up several days in advance). Reservations cost €1.80 per person per castle, and must be made no later than 17:00 on the previous day. It works best to book online (www.ticket-center-hohenschwangau. de); you can also reserve by phone (tel. 08362/930-830) or email (info@ticket-center-hohenschwangau.de). A few hotels can book these tickets for you with enough notice (ask). You must pick up reserved tickets an hour before the appointed entry time, as it takes a while to walk up to the castles. (It doesn't usually take an hour, though—so this might be a good time to pull out a sandwich or a snack.) Show up late and they may have given your slot to someone else (but then they'll likely help you make another reservation). If you know a couple of hours in advance that you're running late and can call the office, they'll likely rebook you at no charge.

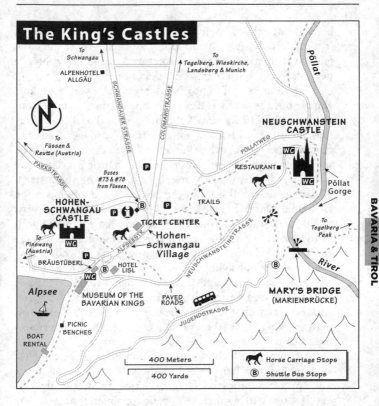

The King's Castles

Note that if you are staying in Reutte and depending on buses for transportation, you'll need to make your reservation for midday (noon or later) to give yourself ample time to arrive at Neuschwanstein.

Tips for Day-Tripping from Munich: Rather than buy point-to-point train tickets, it's a no-brainer to buy the Bayern-Ticket (described on page 101); not only is it cheaper, but it also covers the bus between Füssen and the castles (the only catch is that on weekdays, the pass isn't valid before 9:00). If coming by train, make a castle tour reservation and take a train leaving at least four hours before your reserved castle entry. (The train to Füssen takes over two hours, getting from Füssen to the castle ticket office by bus takes another half-hour, and you must be there an hour before your tour.) Trains from Munich leave hourly at :53 past the hour. So, if you take the 9:53 train, you can make a 14:00 castle tour. If you reserve a castle tour for 11:00, you'll need to pack breakfast and take the 6:53 train (confirm train times in advance).

Getting Up to the Castles: From the ticket booth, Hohenschwangau is an easy 10-minute climb (just zigzag up to the big yellow castle, following the signs), while Neuschwanstein is a moderately steep 30-minute hike in the other direction (also well-signed—the most direct and least steep approach begins across the street from the ticket center).

To minimize hiking to Neuschwanstein, you can take a **shuttle bus** (generally leaves every few minutes from in front of Hotel Lisl, just above ticket office and to the left, but occasionally full or on break) or a horse-drawn carriage (in front of Hotel Müller, just above ticket office and to the right), but neither gets you to the castle doorstep. The shuttle bus drops you off near Mary's Bridge (Marienbrücke), leaving you a steep, 10-minute downhill walk to the castle—so be sure to see the view from Mary's Bridge *before* hiking down (€1.80 one-way, €2.60 round-trip not worth it since you have to hike uphill to the bus stop for your return trip). **Horse-drawn carriages** (€6 up, €3 down) are slower than walking and stop below Neuschwanstein, leaving you a five-minute uphill hike. Here's the most economical and least strenuous plan: Ride the bus to Mary's Bridge for the view, hike down to Neuschwanstein, and then catch the horse carriage from the castle back down to the parking lot (total round-trip cost: €4.80). Carriages also run to Hohenschwangau (€4.50 up, €2 down).

Warning: Both the shuttle bus and the carriage can have long lines at peak times—especially if it's raining. You might wait up to 45 minutes for the bus, making it slower than walking. If you're cutting it close to your appointed time, you may need to hoof it.

Entry Procedure: For each castle, tourists jumble at the entry, waiting for their ticket number to light up on the board. When it does, power through the mob (most waiting there are holding higher numbers) and go to the turnstile. Warning: You must use your ticket while your number is still on the board. If you space out while waiting for a polite welcome, you'll miss your entry window and never get in.

Services: A TI (run by helpful Thomas), bus stop, ATM, WC (€0.50), lockers (€1), coin-op Internet terminal, and telephones cluster around the main intersection a couple hundred yards before you get to the ticket office (TI open daily April-Sept 10:00-17:30, Oct-March 10:00-16:00, tel. 08362/819-765, www.schwangau.de). While bathrooms inside the castles themselves are free, you'll pay €0.30-0.50 to use the WCs elsewhere.

Best Views: In the morning, the light comes in just above the mountains—making your initial view of Neuschwanstein hazy and disappointing (though views from the ticket center up to Hohenschwangau are nice). Later in the day, the sun

> # "Mad" King Ludwig (1845-1886)
>
> A tragic figure, Ludwig II (a.k.a. "Mad" King Ludwig) ruled Bavaria for 22 years until his death in 1886 at the age of 40. Bavaria was weak. Politically, Ludwig's reality was to "rule" either as a pawn of Prussia or a pawn of Austria. Rather than deal with politics in Bavaria's capital, Munich, Ludwig frittered away most of his time at his family's hunting palace, Hohenschwangau. He spent much of his adult life constructing his fanciful Neuschwanstein Castle—like a kid builds a tree house—on a neighboring hill upon the scant ruins of a medieval castle. Here and in his other projects (such as Linderhof Castle and the never-built Falkenstein Castle), even as he strove to evoke medieval grandeur, he embraced the state-of-the-art technology of the Industrial Age in which he lived. Neuschwanstein had electricity, running water, and a telephone (but no Wi-Fi).
>
> Ludwig was a true romantic living in a Romantic age. His best friends were artists, poets, and composers such as Richard Wagner. His palaces are wallpapered with misty medieval themes—especially those from Wagnerian operas.
>
> Although Ludwig spent 17 years building Neuschwanstein, he lived in it only 172 days. Soon after he moved in (and before his vision for the castle was completed), Ludwig was declared mentally unfit to rule Bavaria and taken away. Two days after this eviction, Ludwig was found dead in a lake. To this day, people debate whether the king was murdered or committed suicide.

BAVARIA & TIROL

drops down into the pasture, lighting up Neuschwanstein magnificently. Regardless of time of day, the best accessible Neuschwanstein view is from Mary's Bridge (or, for the bold, from the little bluff just above it)—an easy 10-minute hike from the castle. (Many of the postcards and posters you'll see are photographed from high in the hills, best left to avid hikers.)

Eating: Bring a packed lunch. The park by the Alpsee (the nearby lake) is ideal for a picnic, although you're not allowed to sit on the grass—only on the benches (you could also eat out on the lake in one of the old-fashioned rowboats, rented by the hour in summer). The restaurants in the "village" at the foot of Europe's Disney castle are mediocre and overpriced, feeding off the endless droves of hungry, shop-happy tourists. There are no grocery shops near the castles, but you can buy sandwiches and hot dogs across from the TI, and at the *Imbiss* (take-out window) next to Hotel Alpenstuben (between the TI and ticket center). For a sit-down meal, the yellow **Bräustüberl cafeteria** serves the cheapest grub, but isn't likely to be a highlight of your visit (€6-7 gut-bomb grill meals, often with live folk music, daily 11:00-17:00, close to end of road and lake). Up near Neuschwanstein itself (near the horse carriage drop-off) is another cluster of overpriced eateries.

After Your Castle Visit: If you follow my advice, you could be done with your castle tours in the early afternoon. With a car, you could try to squeeze in a nearby sight (such as Linderhof Castle, Ehrenberg Castle ruins, or Wieskirche). If you'd rather stick closer to this area, here are some ideas: The hike from Neuschwanstein up to **Mary's Bridge** is easy and rewarding; the hike back down to the valley through the **Pollät Gorge** is also highly recommended. With a **bike**, you could pedal through the mostly flat countryside that spreads out in front of Neuschwanstein (perhaps partway around Forggensee). And nearby—an easy drive or bus ride away—the Tegelberg area has both a high-mountain **cable car** and a fun **luge** ride. All of these options are described later in this chapter. Yet another option is to walk all the way around **Alpsee,** the lake below Hohenschwangau (about 1.5 hours, some steps).

Sights at the King's Castles

The two castles complement each other perfectly. But if you have to choose one, Neuschwanstein's wow factor—inside and out—is undeniable.

▲▲▲HOHENSCHWANGAU CASTLE

Standing quietly below Neuschwanstein, the big, yellow Hohenschwangau Castle was Ludwig's boyhood home. Originally built in the 12th century, it was ruined by Napoleon. Ludwig's father, King Maximilian II, rebuilt it in 1830. Hohenschwangau (hoh-en-SHVAHN-gow, loosely translated as "High Swanland") was used by the royal family as a summer hunting lodge until 1912. The Wittelsbach family (which ruled Bavaria for nearly seven centuries) still owns the place (and lived in the annex—today's shop—until the 1970s).

The interior decor (mostly Neo-Gothic, like the castle itself) is harmonious, cohesive, and original—all done in 1835, with paintings inspired by Romantic themes. As you tour the castle, imagine how the paintings must have inspired young Ludwig. For 17 years, he lived here at his dad's place and followed the construction of his dream castle across the way—you'll see the telescope still set up and directed at Neuschwanstein.

The excellent 30-minute tours give a better glimpse of Ludwig's life than the more-visited and famous Neuschwanstein Castle tour. Tours here are smaller (35 people rather than 60) and more relaxed. You'll explore rooms on two floors—the queen's rooms, and then, upstairs, the king's. (Conveniently, their bedrooms were connected by a secret passage.) You'll see photos and busts of Ludwig and his little brother, Otto; some Turkish-style flourishes (to please the king, who had been impressed after a visit to the Orient); more than 25 different depictions of swans (honoring the Knights of Schwangau, whose legacy the Wittelsbachs inherited); over-the-top gifts the Wittelsbachs received from their adoring subjects; and paintings of VIGs (very important Germans, including Martin Luther—who may or may not have visited here—and an infant Charlemagne).

One of the most impressive rooms is the Banquet Hall (also known as the Hall of Heroes); one vivid wall mural depicts a savage, yet bloodless, fifth-century barbarian battle. Just as the castle itself had running water and electricity despite its historic appearance, its Romantic decor presents a sanitized version of the medieval past, glossing over inconvenient details. You'll also see Ludwig's bedroom, which he inherited from his father. He kept most of the decor (including the nude nymphs frolicking over his bed), but painted the ceiling black and installed transparent stars that could be lit from the floor above to create the illusion of a night sky.

▲▲▲NEUSCHWANSTEIN CASTLE

Imagine "Mad" King Ludwig as a boy, climbing the hills above his dad's castle, Hohenschwangau, dreaming up the ultimate fairy-

tale castle. Inheriting the throne at the young age of 18, he had the power to make his dream concrete and stucco. Neuschwanstein (noy-SHVAHN-shtine, roughly "New Swanstone") was designed first by a theater-set designer...then by an architect. While it was built upon the ruins of an old castle and looks medieval, Neuschwanstein is modern iron-and-brick construction with a sandstone veneer—only about as old as the Eiffel Tower. It feels like something you'd see at a home show for 19th-century royalty. Built from 1869 to 1886, it's the epitome of the Romanticism popular in 19th-century Europe. Construction stopped with Ludwig's death (only a third of the interior was finished), and within six weeks, tourists were paying to go through it.

BAVARIA & TIROL

During World War II, the castle took on a sinister role. The Nazis used Neuschwanstein as one of their primary secret store-houses for stolen art. After the war, Allied authorities spent a year sorting through and redistributing the art, which filled 49 rail cars from this one location alone. It was the only time the unfinished rooms were put to use.

Today, guides herd groups of 60 through the castle, giving an interesting—if rushed—30-minute tour. (While you're waiting for your tour time to pop up on the board, climb the stairs up to the upper courtyard to see more of the exterior, which isn't covered on your tour.) Once inside, you'll go up and down more than 300 steps, visiting 15 lavish rooms with their original furnishings and fanciful wall paintings—mostly based on Wagnerian opera themes.

Ludwig's extravagant throne room, modeled in a Neo-Byzantine style to emphasize his royal status, celebrates six valiant Christian kings (whose mantle Ludwig clearly believed he had donned) under a huge gilded-bronze chandelier. The exquisite two-million-stone mosaic floor is a visual encyclopedia of animals and plant life. The most memorable stop may be the king's gilded-lily bedroom, with his elaborately carved canopy bed (with a forest of Gothic church spires on top), washstand (filled with water piped in from the Alps), and personal chapel. After passing through Ludwig's living room (decorated with more than 150 swans) and a faux grotto, you'll climb to the fourth floor for the grand finale: the Singers' Hall, an ornately decorated space filled with murals depicting the story of Parzival, the legendary medieval figure with whom Ludwig identified.

After the tour, before you descend to the king's kitchen, see the 13-minute video (runs continuously, English subtitles). This uses historical drawings and modern digital modeling to tell the story of how the castle was built, and illustrates all of the unfinished parts of Ludwig's vision (more prickly towers, a central chapel, a fancy view terrace, an ornate bathhouse, and more). Finally you'll see a digital model of Falkenstein—a whimsical, over-the-top, never-built castle that makes Neuschwanstein look stubby. Falkenstein occupied Ludwig's fantasies the year he died.

After the kitchen (state of the art for this high-tech king in its day), you'll see a room lined with fascinating drawings (described in English) of the castle plans, as well as a large castle model.

NEAR THE CASTLES

These activities are right around the castles—an easy way to round out your day if you have extra time.

▲▲Mary's Bridge (Marienbrücke)

Before or after the Neuschwanstein tour, climb up to Mary's Bridge to marvel at Ludwig's castle, just as Ludwig did. Jockey with a

United Nations of tourists for the best angle. This bridge was quite an engineering accomplishment 100 years ago. (Access to the bridge is closed in bad winter weather, but many travelers walk around the barriers to get there—at their own risk, of course.)

For an even more glorious castle view, the frisky can hike even higher: After crossing the bridge, you'll see very rough, steep, unofficial trails crisscrossing the hillside on your left. If you're willing to ignore the *Lebensgefahr* (danger of death) signs, you can scamper up to the bluff just over the bridge.

The trail connecting Neuschwanstein to Mary's Bridge is also scenic, with views back on Neuschwanstein's facade in one direction, and classic views of Hohenschwangau—perched on its little hill between lakes, with cut-glass peaks on the horizon—in the other.

▲Pöllat Gorge (Pöllatschlucht)

The river gorge that slices into the rock just behind Neuschwanstein's lofty perch is a more interesting and scenic—and less crowded—alternative to shuffling back down the main road. While it takes an extra 15 minutes or so, it's well worth it. You'll find the trailhead just above the Neuschwanstein exit, on the path toward Mary's Bridge (look for *Pöllatschlucht* signs; gorge trail closed in winter).

You'll begin by walking down a steep, well-maintained set of concrete stairs, with Germany's finest castle looming through the trees. Then you'll pop out along the river, passing a little beach (with neatly stacked stones) offering a view up at the grand waterfall that gushes beneath Mary's Bridge. From here, follow the river as it goes over several smaller waterfalls—and stroll for a while along steel walkways and railings that help make this slippery area safer. After passing an old wooden channel used to harness the power of all that water, you'll hit level ground; turn left and walk through a pleasantly untouristy residential settlement back toward the TI.

Museum of the Bavarian Kings (Museum der Bayerischen Könige)

About a five-minute walk from the castles' ticket center, in a former grand hotel on the shore of the Alpsee, this modern, well-presented exhibit documents the history of the Wittelsbachs, Bavaria's former royal family. On display are plenty of family portraits and busts, as

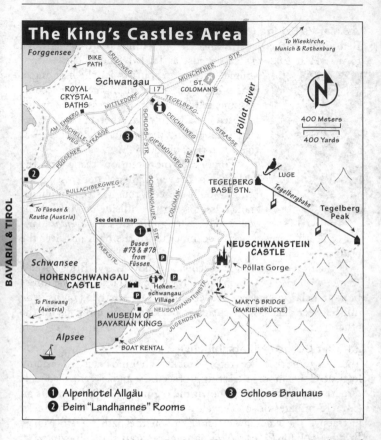

The King's Castles Area

To Wieskirche, Munich & Rothenburg

Forggensee

BIKE PATH

ROYAL CRYSTAL BATHS

Schwangau [17]

ST. COLOMAN'S

Pöllat River

N

400 Meters
400 Yards

LUGE

TEGELBERG BASE STN.

Tegelbergbahn

Tegelberg Peak

BULLACHBERGWEG

To Füssen & Reutte (Austria)

See detail map

Buses #73 & #78 from Füssen

NEUSCHWANSTEIN CASTLE

Pöllat Gorge

Schwansee

HOHENSCHWANGAU CASTLE

Hohenschwangau Village

MARY'S BRIDGE (MARIENBRÜCKE)

To Pinswang (Austria)

MUSEUM OF BAVARIAN KINGS

Alpsee

BOAT RENTAL

❶ Alpenhotel Allgäu
❷ Beim "Landhannes" Rooms
❸ Schloss Brauhaus

BAVARIA & TIROL

well as treasures including Ludwig II's outlandish royal robe and elaborately decorated fairy-tale sword, and the impressive dining set given as a golden-anniversary present to his cousin Ludwig III and his wife, the last reigning Wittelsbachs. After losing the throne, the family spoke out against the Nazis, and some were sent to concentration camps as a result. A free, dry audioguide lends some context to the family's history, in more detail than most casual visitors want. The museum is worth the price only if you're captivated by this clan and have some time to kill. (But trying to squeeze it between your two castle visits is rushing it—especially if you like to linger.)

Cost and Hours: €9.50; combo-ticket with Hohenschwangau-€20.50, with Neuschwanstein-€20, with both castles-€29.50; daily April-Sept 9:00-19:00, Oct-March 10:00-18:00; no reservations required, includes audioguide, mandatory lockers with refundable €1 deposit, Alpseestrasse 27, tel. 08362/926-4640, www.museumderbayerischenkoenige.de.

NEAR FÜSSEN AND THE CASTLES

Here are a few attractions that lie within a few miles of Füssen or Neuschwanstein. All can be reached by car, bike, or bus.

▲Tegelberg Gondola (Tegelbergbahn)

Just north of Neuschwanstein is a fun play zone around the mighty Tegelberg Gondola, a scenic ride to the mountain's 5,500-foot

summit. At the top on a clear day, you get great views of the Alps and Bavaria and the vicarious thrill of watching hang gliders and para-gliders leap into airborne ecstasy. Weather permitting, scores of adventurous Germans line up and leap from the launch ramp at the top of the lift. With someone leaving every two or three minutes, it's great for spectators. Thrill seekers with exceptional social skills may talk themselves into a tandem ride with a paraglider. From the top of Tegelberg, it's a steep and demanding 2.5-hour hike down to Ludwig's castle. (Avoid the treacherous trail directly below the gondola.) Around the gondola's valley station, you'll find a playground, a cheery eatery, the stubby remains of an ancient Roman villa, and a summer luge ride (described next).

Cost and Hours: €19 round-trip, €12.20 one-way; first ascent daily at 9:00; last descent April-Oct at 17:00, mid-Dec-March at 16:00, closed Nov-mid-Dec; 4/hour, 5-minute ride to the top, in bad weather call first to confirm, tel. 08362/98360, www.tegelbergbahn.de.

Getting There: From the castles, most #73 and #78 buses from Füssen continue to the Tegelbergbahn valley station (5-minute ride). It's a 30-minute walk or 10-minute bike ride from the castles.

▲Tegelberg Luge

Next to the gondola's valley station is a summer luge course *(Sommerrodelbahn)*. A summer luge is like a bobsled on wheels (for more details, see "Luge Lesson" on page 187). This course's stainless-steel track is heated, so it's often dry and open even when drizzly weather shuts down the concrete luges. A funky cable system pulls riders (in their sleds) to the top without a ski lift. It's not as long, fast, or scenic as Austria's Biberwier luge (described on page 188), but it's handy, harder to get hurt on, and half the price.

Cost and Hours: €3.50/ride, shareable 6-ride card-€15; hours vary but typically April-June Mon-Fri 13:00-17:00, Sat-Sun 10:00-17:00; July-Sept daily 10:00-18:00; may open for season earlier in spring or stay open later in fall if weather is good; in bad weather call first to confirm, waits can be long in good weather, no children under age 3, ages 3-8 may ride with an adult, tel. 08362/98360, www.tegelbergbahn.de.

▲Royal Crystal Baths (Königliche Kristall-Therme)

This pool/sauna complex just outside Füssen is the perfect way to relax on a rainy day, or to cool off on a hot one. The main part of the complex (downstairs), called the *Therme*, contains two heated indoor pools and a café; outside you'll find a shallow kiddie pool, a lap pool, a heated *Kristallbad* with massage jets and a whirlpool, and a salty mineral bath. The extensive saunas upstairs are well worth the few extra euros, as long as you're OK with nudity. (Swimsuits are required in the downstairs pools, but *verboten* in the upstairs saunas.) You'll see pool and sauna rules in German all over, but don't worry—just follow the locals' lead.

To enter the baths, first choose the length of your visit and your focus (big outdoor pool only, all ground-floor pools but not the saunas, or the whole enchilada—a flier explains all the prices in English). You'll get a wristband and a credit-card-sized ticket with a bar code. Insert that ticket into the entry gate, and keep it—you'll need it to get out. Enter through the yellow changing stalls—where you'll change into your bathing suit—then choose a storage locker (€1 coin deposit). When it's time to leave, reinsert your ticket in the gate—if you've gone over the time limit, feed extra euros into the machine.

Cost and Hours: Baths only-€11/2 hours, €17/4 hours, €21/all day; saunas-about €5-6 extra, towel rental-€3, bathrobe rental-€5, bathing suits sold but not rented; daily 9:00-22:00, Fri-Sat until 23:00; nude swimming everywhere Tue and Fri after 19:00; from Füssen, drive, bike, or walk across the river, turn left toward Schwangau, and then, about a mile later, turn left at signs for *Kristall-Therme*, Am Ehberg 16; tel. 08362/819-630, www.kristalltherme-schwangau.de.

Bike or Boat Around the Forggensee

On a beautiful day, nothing beats a **bike ride** around the bright-turquoise Forggensee, a nearby lake. This 20-mile ride is exclusively on bike paths (give it a half-day; it's tight to squeeze it into the afternoon after a morning of castle visits, but possible with an early start). Locals swear that going clockwise is less work, but either way has a couple of strenuous uphill parts. Still, the amazing views of the surrounding Alps will distract you from your churning legs—so this is still a great way to spend the afternoon. Rent a bike, pack a picnic lunch, and figure about a three-hour round-trip. From Füssen, follow *Festspielhaus* signs; once you reach the theater, follow *Forggensee Rundweg* signs.

You can also take a **boat ride** on the Forggensee, leaving either from the Füssen "harbor" *(Bootshafen)* or the theater *(Festspielhaus)*, a 20- to 30-minute walk north of town (€8/50-minute cruise, 6/day; €11/2-hour cruise, 3/day; runs daily June-mid-Oct, no boats off-season, tel. 08362/921-363, www.stadt-fuessen.de—click on "*Forggensee-Schiffahrt*"). Unless it's very crowded in the summer, you can bring your bike onto the boat and get off across the lake—shortening the total loop.

Treetop Walkway (Baumkronenweg Ziegelwies)

This elevated wooden "treetop path" lets you stroll for a third of a mile, high in the trees on a graceful yet sturdy suspension-bridge-like structure 60 feet in the air. The walkway crosses the Austria-Germany border and offers views of the surrounding mountains and the "wild" alpine Lech River, which can be a smooth glacier-blue mirror one day and a muddy torrent the next. Located east of Füssen, just past Lech Falls on the road to Reutte, the walkway can be accessed at either end. The Austrian end (closer to Reutte) has a large parking lot, a tiny ticket booth, and no WC. At the German end (closer to Füssen), parking is scarce and you enter/exit the walkway via a small museum about local flora and fauna. Stairs (kids can take the slide) lead down to a riverside trail that loops about a mile through a kid-friendly park, with a log raft to cross a little creek, a wonky little bridge, and a sandy stream great for wading. Those with more energy to burn can try the slightly longer mountain loop, accessed by a tunnel under the road.

Cost and Hours: €4, free for kids under age 16, daily May-Oct 10:00-17:00, closed Nov-April and in bad weather, last entry at 16:30, Tiroler Strasse 10, tel. 08362/938-7550, www.baumkronenweg.eu.

Sleeping near the King's Castles

These two places are in Schwangau, very near the castles. Though best for drivers, both are a quick taxi ride from the Füssen train station and also close to bus stops. In return for paying the Schwangau hotel tax, you get a card with the same benefits as the Füssen Card (see page 132).

$$ Alpenhotel Allgäu is a small, family-run hotel with 18 rooms in a bucolic setting. It's a 15-minute walk from the castle ticket office, not far beyond the humongous parking lot (small Sb without balcony-€54, Sb-€60, perfectly fine older Db-€89, newer

Db-€97, Tb-€141, book directly with hotel and ask about discount with cash and this book, all but one room have porches or balconies—some with castle views, family rooms, Wi-Fi, elevator, free parking, just before tennis courts at Schwangauer Strasse 37 in the town of Schwangau—don't let your GPS take you to Schwangauer Strasse 37 in Füssen, tel. 08362/81152, www.alpenhotel-allgaeu. de, info@alpenhotel-allgaeu.de, Frau Reiss).

$ **Beim "Landhannes,"** a 200-year-old working dairy farm run by Conny Schön, is a great value for drivers. They rent three creaky but sunny rooms, and keep flowers on the balconies, big bells and antlers in the halls, and cows in the yard (Sb-€35, Db-€70, €5 less per person for 3 or more nights, also rents apartments with kitchen with a 5-night minimum, cash only, Wi-Fi, free parking, nearby bike rental, poorly signed in the village of Horn on the Füssen side of Schwangau, look for the farm down a tiny lane through the grass 100 yards in front of Hotel Kleiner König, Am Lechrain 22, tel. 08362/8349, www.landhannes.de, info@landhannes.de).

Eating near the King's Castles

For pointers on quick, functional eateries in the immediate castle area, see "Orientation to the King's Castles," earlier.

If you have a car and want to eat at a good-value, non-touristy place without going into Füssen, consider **Schloss Brauhaus,** a sprawling microbrewery restaurant in the village of Schwangau, about 1.5 miles from the castles. They brew five types of beer (dark, light, wheat, and two seasonal brews) and serve classic German fare (€11-19 hearty meals). Choose between the woody-industrial interior—with big copper vats and a miniature bowling alley—or the outdoor *Biergarten*, with distant views of Neuschwanstein (food served Mon-Thu 14:00-21:00, Fri-Sun 11:00-21:00; beer served until 23:00; Gipsmühlweg 5 in Schwangau—watch for signs on the main street, Füssener Strasse, coming in from Füssen; tel. 08362/926-4680, www.schlossbrauhaus.de).

Wieskirche

Germany's greatest Rococo-style church, this "Church in the Meadow"—worth ▲▲—looks as brilliant now as the day it floated down from heaven. Overripe with decoration but bright and bursting with beauty, this church is a divine

droplet, a curly curlicue, the final flowering of the Baroque movement.

ORIENTATION

Cost and Hours: Donation requested, daily April-Oct 8:00-20:00, Nov-March 8:00-18:00. The interior is closed to sightseers for about an hour during services: Sun at 8:30 and 11:00; Tue, Wed, and Sat at 10:00; and Fri at 19:00 (17:00 in winter). Tel. 08862/932-930, www.wieskirche.de.

Getting There: By car, the Wieskirche is a 30-minute drive north of Neuschwanstein or Füssen. Head north, turn right at Steingaden, and follow the brown signs (parking-€2/2 hours minimum). With careful attention to schedules, you can day-trip here from Füssen by bus (4-6/day, 45-60 minutes), but it's a long round-trip for a church that most see in 10-15 minutes.

Trinket shops and snack stands (one sells freshly made doughnuts—look for *Wieskücherl* sign) clog the parking area in front of the church; take a commune-with-nature-and-smell-the-farm detour back through the meadow to the parking lot.

The Romantic Road bus tour stops here for 20 minutes on the northbound route to Frankfurt. Southbound buses stop here for 15 minutes, but it's after the church has closed for the day.

VISITING THE CHURCH

This pilgrimage church is built around the much-venerated statue of a scourged (or whipped) Christ, which supposedly wept in 1738. The carving—too graphic to be accepted by that generation's Church—was the focus of worship in a peasant's barn. Miraculously, it shed tears—empathizing with all those who suffer. Pilgrims came from all around. A tiny and humble chapel was built to house the statue in 1739. (You can see it where the lane to the church leaves the parking lot.) Bigger and bigger crowds came. Two of Bavaria's top Rococo architects, the Zimmermann brothers (Johann Baptist and Dominikus), were commissioned to build the Wieskirche that stands here today.

Follow the theological sweep from the altar to the ceiling: Jesus whipped, chained, and then killed (notice the pelican above the altar—recalling a pre-Christian story of a bird that opened its breast to feed its young with its own blood); the painting of Baby Jesus posed as if on the cross; the golden sacrificial lamb; and finally, high on the ceiling, the resurrected Christ before the Last Judgment. This is the most positive depiction of the Last Judgment around. Jesus, rather than sitting on the throne to judge, rides high on a rainbow—a symbol of forgiveness—giving any sinner the feeling that there is still time to repent, with plenty of mercy on hand. In the back, above the pipe organ, notice the closed door to paradise, and at the opposite end (above the main altar), the empty throne—waiting for Judgment Day.

Above the doors flanking the altar are murky glass cases with 18th-century handkerchiefs. People wept, came here, were healed, and no longer needed their hankies. Walk through either of these doors and up an aisle flanking the high altar to see votives—requests and thanks to God (for happy, healthy babies, and so on). Notice how the kneelers are positioned so that worshippers can meditate on scenes of biblical miracles painted high on the ceiling and visible through the ornate tunnel frames. A priest here once told me that faith, architecture, light, and music all combine to create the harmony of the Wieskirche.

Two paintings flank the door at the rear of the church. The one on the right shows the ceremonial parade in 1749 when the white-clad monks of Steingaden carried the carved statue of Christ from the tiny church to its new big one. The second painting (on the left), from 1757, is a votive from one of the Zimmermann brothers, the artists and architects who built this church. He is giving thanks for the successful construction of the new church.

If you can't visit the Wieskirche, visit one of the other churches that came out of the same heavenly spray can: Oberammergau's church, Munich's Asamkirche, Würzburg's Hofkirche Chapel (at the Residenz), the splendid Ettal Monastery (free and near Oberammergau), and, on a lesser scale, Füssen's basilica.

Driving from Wieskirche to Oberammergau: If doing this drive, you'll cross the **Echelsbacher Bridge,** which arches 230 feet over the Pöllat Gorge. Thoughtful drivers let their passengers walk across to enjoy the views, then meet them at the other side. Any kayakers? Notice the painting of the traditional village woodcarver (who used to walk from town to town with his art on his back) on the first big house on the Oberammergau side. It holds the Almdorf Ammertal shop, with a huge selection of overpriced carvings and commission-hungry tour guides.

Oberammergau

The Shirley Temple of Bavarian villages, and exploited to the hilt by the tourist trade, Oberammergau wears too much makeup. During its famous Passion Play (every 10 years, next in 2020), the crush is unbearable—and the prices at the hotels and restaurants can be as well. The village has about 1,200 beds for the 5,000 playgoers coming daily. But the rest of the time, Oberammergau—while hardly "undiscovered"—is a pleasant, and at times even sleepy, Bavarian village.

If you're passing through, Oberammergau is a ▲ sight—worth a wander among the half-timbered *Lüftlmalerei* houses frescoed

with biblical scenes and famous fairy-tale characters. It's also a relatively convenient home base for visiting Linderhof Castle, Ettal Monastery, and the Zugspitze (via Garmisch). A smaller (and less conveniently located) alternative to Füssen and Reutte, it's worth considering for drivers who want to linger in the area. A day trip to Neuschwanstein from Oberammergau is manageable if you have a car, but train travelers do better to stay in Füssen.

BAVARIA & TIROL

GETTING THERE

Trains run from Munich to Oberammergau (nearly hourly, 1.75 hours, change in Murnau). From Füssen, you can take the **bus** (#9606, 4-5/day, 1.5 hours). **Drivers** can get here from Reutte in less than 30 minutes via the pretty Plansee Lake, or from Munich in about an hour.

Orientation to Oberammergau

This village of about 5,000 feels even smaller, thanks to its remote location. The downtown core, huddled around the onion-domed church, is compact and invites strolling; all of my recommended sights, hotels, and restaurants are within about a 10-minute walk of each other. While the town's name sounds like a mouthful, it's based on the name of the local river (the Ammer) and means, roughly, "Upper Ammerland."

Tourist Information: The helpful, well-organized TI provides a wide range of glossy brochures, including maps and English information on area hikes (mid-July-mid-Sept Mon-Fri 9:00-18:00, Sat-Sun 9:00-13:00; mid-Sept-mid-July same hours but closed Sun; Nov-Dec also closed Sat; Eugen-Papst-Strasse 9A, tel. 08822/922-740, www.ammergauer-alpen.de).

Internet Access: Hotel Alte Post, right in the heart of town, offers access to the public. Pay at the hotel reception, then either use Wi-Fi or the terminals in the little room at the right end of the building (€3/hour, €5/day, daily 7:00-21:00, Dorfstrasse 19, tel. 08822/9100).

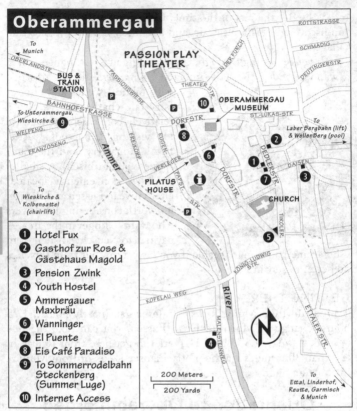

Oberammergau

To Munich
OBERLANDSTR.
BUS & TRAIN STATION
BAHNHOFSTRASSE
To Untermmergau, Wieskirche & ⑨
WELFENG.
FRANZOSENG.
Ammer
To Wieskirche & Kolbensattel (chairlift)
PASSIONSWIESE
PASSION PLAY THEATER
THEATER STR.
DORFSTR.
FREIKORF.
VERLEGER.
PAPST.
EUGEN
⑧
⑩
OBERAMMERGAU MUSEUM
ST.-LUKAS-STR.
To Laber Bergbahn (lift) & Wellenberg (pool)
②
①
DEDLER STR.
DAISEN.
③
⑦
⑥
DORFSTR.
ℹ
PILATUS HOUSE
STR.
CHURCH
TIROLER.
⑤
KÖNIG-LUDWIG STR.
River
KOFELAU WEG
MALENSTEINWEG
④
N
EITALER STR.
ROTTSTRASSE
SCHMADIG.
DEUTINGERSTR.
IN DER FUEH.
To Ettal, Linderhof, Reutte, Garmisch & Munich

200 Meters
200 Yards

① Hotel Fux
② Gasthof zur Rose & Gästehaus Magold
③ Pension Zwink
④ Youth Hostel
⑤ Ammergauer Maxbräu
⑥ Wanninger
⑦ El Puente
⑧ Eis Café Paradiso
⑨ To Sommerrodelbahn Steckenberg (Summer Luge)
⑩ Internet Access

ARRIVAL IN OBERAMMERGAU

The town's **train** station is a short walk from the center: Turn left, cross the bridge, and you're already downtown.

If you're **driving**, you'll find that there are two exits from the main road into Oberammergau—at the north and south ends. Either way, make your way to the free lot between the TI and the river. While there's ample street parking in town, most is time-limited and/or requires payment—be sure to read signs carefully. Hotels and sights are well-signed in the town.

Sights in Oberammergau

▲Local Arts and Crafts

The town's best sight is its woodcarving shops *(Holzschnitzerei)*. Browse through these small art galleries filled with very expensive whittled works. The beautifully frescoed **Pilatus House** at Ludwig-Thoma-Strasse 10 has an open workshop where you can watch woodcarvers and painters at work on summer afternoons (free; late

Woodcarving in Oberammergau

The Ammergau region is relatively poor, with no appreciable industry and no agriculture, save for some dairy farming. What they *do* have is wood. Carving religious and secular themes became a lucrative way for the locals to make some money, especially when confined to the house during the long, cold winter. And with a major pilgrimage site—Ettal Monastery—just down the road, there was a built-in consumer base eager to buy hand-carved crucifixes and other souvenirs. Carvers from Oberammergau peddled their wares across Europe, carrying them on their backs (on distinctive wooden backpack-racks called *Kraxe*) as far away as Rome.

Today, the Oberammergau Carving School (founded in 1887) is a famous institution that takes only 20 students per year out of 450 applicants. Their graduates do important restoration work throughout Europe. For example, much of the work on Dresden's Frauenkirche (see page 686) was done by these artists.

BAVARIA & TIROL

May-mid-Oct Tue-Sat 13:00-18:00, closed Sun-Mon; open weekends in Dec, closed rest of year, tel. 08822/949-511). Upstairs in the Pilatus House is a small exhibit of "reverse glass" paintings *(verre églomisé)* that's worth a quick glance.

▲Oberammergau Museum

This museum showcases local woodcarving, with good English explanations. The ground floor has a small exhibit of nativity scenes (*Krippe*—mostly made of wood, but some of paper or wax). In the back, find the small theater, where you can watch an interesting film in English about the 2010 Passion Play. Upstairs is a much more extensive collection of the wood carvings that helped put Oberammergau on the map, including a room of old woodcarving tools, plus a small exhibit on Roman archaeological finds in the region. Your ticket also lets you into the lobby of the Passion Play Theater, described next.

Cost and Hours: €6, includes museum and theater lobby; Easter-Oct and Dec-mid-Jan Tue-Sun 10:00-17:00; closed Mon, Nov, and mid-Jan-Easter; Dorfstrasse 8, tel. 08822/94136, www. oberammergaumuseum.de.

Passion Play Theater (Festspielhaus)

Back in 1633, in the midst of the bloody Thirty Years' War and with horrifying plagues devastating entire cities, the people of Oberammergau promised God that if they were spared from extinction, they'd "perform a play depicting the suffering, death, and resurrection of our Lord Jesus Christ" every decade thereafter. The town survived, and, heading into its 41st decade, the people of Oberammergau are still making good on the deal. For 100 days every 10 years (most recently in 2010), about half of the town's population (a cast of 2,000) are involved in the production of this extravagant five-hour Passion Play—telling the story of Jesus' entry into Jerusalem, the Crucifixion, and the Resurrection.

Until the next show in 2020, you'll have to settle for reading the book, seeing Nicodemus tool around town in his VW, or taking a quick look at the theater, a block from the center of town.

Visiting the Theater: With a ticket for the Oberammergau Museum (described earlier), you can enter the theater lobby, where there's a modest exhibit on the history of the performances. A long wall of photographs of past performers shows the many generations of Oberammergauers who have participated in this tradition. Climb the stairs and peek into the theater itself, which has an unusual indoor/outdoor design and a real-life alpine backdrop.

To learn more, you can take a 45-minute guided tour of the theater, organized by the museum (€6, or €8 if you also want to visit the museum; tours run Easter-Oct only, Tue-Sun at 11:00 in English, at 10:00 and 14:00 in German; tel. 08822/94136, www.oberammergaumuseum.de).

Oberammergau Church

The town church is typically Bavarian Baroque, but a poor cousin of the one at Wies. Being in a woodcarving center, it's only logical that all the statues are made of wood, and then stuccoed and gilded to look like marble or gold. Saints Peter and Paul flank the altar, where the central painting can be raised to reveal a small stage decorated to celebrate special times during the church calendar. In the central dome, a touching painting shows Peter and Paul bidding each other farewell (with the city of Rome as a backdrop) on the day of their execution—the same day, in the year A.D. 67. On the left, Peter is crucified upside-down. On the right, Paul is beheaded with a sword (open daily 8:00-19:30; a fine little €3 booklet explains it all).

Wander through the lovingly maintained **graveyard**, noticing the wide variety in headstones. A towering stone WWI memorial at the gate has an imposing look and sternly worded celebrations of the "heroes" of that war. But around the other side, below it on the outer fence, find the newer glass panel that modifies the sentiment:

"We honor and remember the victims of the violence that our land gave the world."

NEAR OBERAMMERGAU

These attractions are a long walk from town, but easy to reach by car or bike.

Mountain Lifts

Oberammergau has two mountain lifts of its own. At the east end of town is the **Laber Bergbahn**, a gondola that lifts you up to fine views over the town (www.laber-bergbahn.de). Across town to the west is the **Kolbensattel** chairlift—popular for skiers in winter and hikers in summer (www.kolbensattel.de). From the top, you can hike along the ridge to a series of mountain huts: In about 1.5 hours, you'll reach Pürschling; two hours later is Brunnenkopf (from which you could hike down to Linderhof Castle). Get tips and maps from the TI before doing any of these hikes. Also at Kolbensattel is the 1.5-mile-long Alpine Coaster—similar to a luge, but fixed to a track.

WellenBerg Swimming Pool

Near the Laber Bergbahn lift and a 25-minute walk from town is this sprawling complex of indoor and outdoor pools and saunas.

Cost and Hours: €7/3 hours, €12/day, €4 extra for sauna, daily 10:00-21:00, Himmelreich 52, tel. 08822/92360, www.wellenberg-oberammergau.de.

Sommerrodelbahn Steckenberg

The next town over, Unterammergau, hosts a stainless-steel summer luge track that's faster than the Tegelberg luge, but not nearly as wicked as the one in Biberwier. This one has double seats (allowing a parent to accompany kids) and two sticks—one for each hand; be careful of your elbows. Unlike other luges, children under age three are allowed, and you only pay one fare when a parent and child ride together.

Cost and Hours: €3/ride, €12/6 rides; daily May-early Oct 10:00-17:00, Sat-Sun until 18:00, closed off-season and when wet; Liftweg 1 in Unterammergau, clearly marked and easy 2.5-mile bike ride to Unterammergau along Bahnhofstrasse/Rottenbucherstrasse, take the first left when entering Unterammergau, tel. 08822/4027, www.steckenberg.de.

SPEEDWAY PUBLIC LIBRARY
SPEEDWAY, INDIANA

Sleeping in Oberammergau

Accommodations in Oberammergau tend to be affordable (compared to Füssen or Reutte) and friendly. All offer free parking. Prices listed are for summer (generally May-Oct) and include the €1.80 local tax.

$$ Hotel Fux—quiet, romantic, and well-run—rents eight large rooms decorated in the Bavarian *Landhaus* style (Sb-€67, Db-€93, extra bed-€22, guest computer and Wi-Fi, Mannagasse 2a, tel. 08822/93093, www.hotel-in-oberammergau.de, info@firmafux.de). They also have six apartments for stays of at least 3-4 days.

$$ Gasthof zur Rose is a big, central, classic, family-run place with 19 mostly small but comfortable rooms, with tiny bathrooms. At the reception desk, look at the several decades-worth of photos showing the family performing in the Passion Play (Sb-€62, Db-€84, Tb-€96, Qb-€108, guest computer and Wi-Fi, Dedlerstrasse 9, tel. 08822/4706, www.rose-oberammergau.de, info@rose-oberammergau.de, Frank family).

$$ Pension Zwink offers 10 small, quiet, woody rooms in a residential-feeling neighborhood just across the street from the town center (Sb-€40, Db-€70, Wi-Fi, Daisenbergerstrasse 10, tel. 08822/923-753, www.pension-oberammergau.de, info@pension-oberammergau.de).

$ Gästehaus Magold, homey and family-friendly, has three bright and spacious rooms—twice as nice as the cheap hotel rooms in town, and for much less money (Db-€60, cash only, non-smoking, cable Internet, also has two family apartments—minimum stay in summer, immediately behind Gasthof zur Rose at Kleppergasse 1, tel. 08822/4340, www.gaestehaus-magold.de, info@gaestehaus-magold.de, Christine).

$ Oberammergau Youth Hostel, on the river, was recently remodeled and is just a short walk from the center (€23/bed, includes breakfast and sheets, €3 extra for nonmembers, €2 extra for one-night stays, €4 extra for those over age 26, reception open 8:00-10:00 & 17:00-19:00, closed mid-Nov-Dec, Malensteinweg 10, tel. 08822/4114, www.oberammergau.jugendherberge.de, oberammergau@jugendherberge.de).

Eating in Oberammergau

Ammergauer Maxbräu, in the Hotel Maximilian on the edge of downtown, serves high-quality, thoughtfully presented Bavarian fare with a modern, international twist. The rustic-yet-mod interior—with big copper vats where they brew their own beer—is cozy on rainy day. And in nice weather, locals fill the beer garden out front (€10-19 main courses, daily 11:00-22:00, right behind the church, Ettaler Strasse 5, tel. 08822/948-740, www.maximilian-oberammergau.de).

Gasthof zur Rose, a couple of blocks off the main drag, serves reasonably priced Bavarian food in its dining room and at a few outdoor tables (€10-15 main courses, Tue-Sun 12:00-14:00 & 17:00-21:00, closed Mon, Dedlerstrasse 9, tel. 08822/4706, www.rose-oberammergau.de).

Wanninger is a café by day (coffee, cakes, €7-9 budget weekday lunches, €9-10 main courses) and a steakhouse by night (€18-26 steaks, €13-18 main courses; food served daily 12:00-22:00, Dorfstrasse 22, tel. 08822/836).

El Puente may vex Mexican food purists, but it's the most hopping place in town, with €7.50 cocktails attracting young locals and tourists alike. Come not for the burritos and enchiladas, but for the bustling energy (€11-15 burgers and Mexican standards, €20-24 steaks, Mon-Sat 18:00-23:30, closed Sun, Daisenbergerstrasse 3, tel. 08822/945-777, www.elpuente-oberammergau.de).

Dessert: **Eis Café Paradiso** serves up good Italian-style gelato along the main street; in nice weather, Germans sunbathe with their big sundaes on the generous patio out front (daily until 22:00 in summer, Dorfstrasse 4, tel. 08822/6279).

Oberammergau Connections

From Oberammergau to: Linderhof Castle (bus #9622, 8/day Mon-Fri, 5/day Sat-Sun, 30 minutes; many of these also stop at **Ettal Monastery**), **Hohenschwangau** (for Neuschwanstein) and **Füssen** (bus #9606, 3-4/day, 1.5 hours, some transfer or change number to #73 at Echelsbacher Brücke), **Garmisch** (bus #9606, nearly hourly, better frequency in morning, 40 minutes; also possible—but much longer—by train with a transfer in Murnau, 1.5 hours; from Garmisch, you can ascend the **Zugspitze**), **Munich** (nearly hourly trains, 2 hours, change in Murnau). Train info: tel. 0180-599-6633, www.bahn.com.

Linderhof Castle

This homiest of "Mad" King Ludwig's castles is a small, comfortably exquisite mini-Versailles—good enough for a minor god, and worth ▲▲. Set in the woods 15 minutes from Oberammergau and surrounded by fountains and sculpted, Italian-style gardens, it's the only palace I've toured that actually had me feeling envious.

ORIENTATION

Cost: €8.50, €5 for grotto only.

Hours: Daily April-mid-Oct 9:00-18:00, mid-Oct-March 10:00-16:00 (grotto closed mid-Oct-March); last tour 30 minutes before closing, tel. 08822/92030, www.linderhof.de.

Crowd-Beating Tips: July and August crowds can mean an hour's wait between when you buy your ticket and when you start your tour. It's most crowded in the late morning. During this period, you're wise to arrive after 15:00. Any other time of year, you should get your palace tour time shortly after you arrive. If you do wind up with time to kill, consider it a blessing—the gardens are fun to explore, and some of the smaller buildings can be seen quickly while you're waiting for your appointment. While it's possible to reserve ahead by fax or email for 10 percent extra (see the website for details), it's generally not necessary.

Getting There: Without a car, getting to (and back from) Linderhof is a royal headache, unless you're staying in Oberammergau. Buses from Oberammergau take 30 minutes (#9622, 8/day Mon-Fri, 5/day Sat-Sun). If you're driving, park near the ticket office (€2.50). Driving from Reutte, take the scenic Plansee route.

Sightseeing Tips and Procedure: The complex sits isolated in natural splendor. Plan for lots of walking and a two-hour stop to fully enjoy this royal park. Bring raingear in iffy weather. Your ticket comes with an entry time to tour the palace, which is a 10-minute walk from the ticket office. At the palace entrance, wait in line at the turnstile listed on your ticket (A through D) to take the required 30-minute English tour. Afterwards, explore the rest of the park; be sure not to miss the grotto (10-minute uphill hike from palace, brief but interesting free tour in English, no appointments—the board out front lists the time of the next tour). Then see the other royal buildings dotting the king's playground if you like. You can eat lunch at a café across from the ticket office.

VISITING THE CASTLE

The main attraction here is the **palace** itself. While Neuschwanstein is Neo-Gothic—romanticizing the medieval glory days of Bavaria—Linderhof is Baroque and Rococo, the frilly, overly ornamented styles more associated with Louis XIV, the "Sun King" of France. And, while Neuschwanstein is full of swans, here you'll see fleur-de-lis (the symbol of French royalty) and multiple portraits of Louis XIV, Louis XV, Madame Pompadour, and other pre-Revolutionary French elites. Though they lived a century apart, Ludwig and Louis were spiritual contemporaries: Both clung to the notion of absolute monarchy, despite the realities of the changing world around them. Capping the palace roofline is one of Ludwig's favorite symbols: Atlas, with the weight of the world literally on his shoulders. Oh, those poor, overburdened, misunderstood absolute monarchs!

Ludwig was king for 22 of his 40 years. He lived much of his last eight years here—the only one of his castles that was finished in his lifetime. Frustrated by the limits of being a "constitutional monarch," he retreated to Linderhof, inhabiting a private fantasy world where extravagant castles glorified his otherwise weakened kingship. You'll notice that the castle is small—designed for a single occupant. Ludwig, who never married or had children, lived here as a royal hermit.

The castle tour includes 10 rooms on the upper floor. (The downstairs, where the servants lived and worked, now houses the gift shop.) You'll see room after room exquisitely carved with Rococo curlicues, wrapped in gold leaf. Up above, the ceiling paintings have 3-D legs sticking out of the frame. Clearly inspired by Versailles, Linderhof even has its own (much smaller) hall of mirrors—decorated with over a hundred Nymphenburg porcelain vases and a priceless ivory chandelier. The bedroom features an oversized crystal chandelier, delicate Meissen porcelain flowers framing the mirrors, and a literally king-size bed—a two-story canopy affair draped in blue velvet. Perhaps the most poignant sight, a sad commentary on Ludwig's tragically solitary lifestyle, is his dinner table—preset with dishes and food—which could rise from the kitchen below into his dining room so he could eat alone. (Examine the incredibly delicate flowers in the Meissen porcelain centerpiece.)

The palace is flanked on both sides with grand, terraced **fountains** (peopled by gleaming golden gods) that erupt at the top and bottom of each hour. If you're waiting for your palace tour to begin, hike up to the top of either of these terraces for a fine photo-op. (The green gazebo, on the hillside between the grotto and the palace, provides Linderhof's best view.)

The other must-see sight at Linderhof is Ludwig's **grotto.** Exiting the gift shop behind the palace, turn right, then cut left through the garden to climb up the hill. You'll wait out front for the next tour (the time is posted on the board), then head inside. Inspired by Wagner's *Tannhäuser* opera, this artificial cave (300 feet long and 70 feet tall) is actually a performance space. Its rocky walls are made of cement poured over an iron frame. (While Ludwig exalted the distant past, he took full advantage of then-cutting-edge technology to bring his fantasies to life.) The grotto provided a private theater for the reclusive king to enjoy his beloved Wagnerian operas—he was usually the sole member of the audience. The grotto features a waterfall, fake stalactites, and a swan boat floating on an artificial lake (which could be heated for swimming). Brick ovens hidden in the walls could be used to heat the huge space. The first electricity in Bavaria was generated here, to change the colors of the stage lights and to power Ludwig's fountain and wave machine.

Other Sights at Linderhof: Several other smaller buildings are scattered around the grounds; look for posted maps and directional signs to track them down. Most interesting are the **Moroccan House** and **Moorish Kiosk.** With over-the-top decor seemingly designed by a sultan's decorator on acid, these allowed Ludwig to "travel" to exotic lands without leaving the comfort of Bavaria. (The Moorish Kiosk is more interesting; look for its gilded dome in the woods beyond the grotto.) At the far edge of the property is **Hunding's Hut,** inspired by Wagner's *The Valkyrie*—a rustic-cottage stage-set with a giant fake "tree" growing inside of it. And closer to the entrance—along the path between the ticket booth and the palace—is the **King's Cottage,** used for special exhibitions (often with an extra charge).

Ettal Monastery

In 1328, the Holy Roman Emperor was returning from Rome with what was considered a miraculous statue of Mary and Jesus. He was

in political and financial trouble, so to please God, he founded a monastery with this statue as its centerpiece. The monastery, located here because it was suitably off the beaten path, became important as a place of pilgrimage and today, Ettal is on one of the most-traveled tourist routes in Bavaria. Stopping here (free

and easy for drivers) offers a convenient peek at a splendid Baroque church. Restaurants across the road serve lunch. A visit is worth ▲.

ORIENTATION

Cost and Hours: The church is free and open daily 8:00-19:45 in summer, until 18:00 off-season, tel. 08822/740, www.kloster-ettal.de. It's best not to visit during Mass (usually Sun at 9:30 and 11:00). If you're moved to make a donation, you can use the self-serve credit-card machine (to the right as you enter)... or drop a coin in one of the old-fashioned collection boxes.

Getting There: Ettal Monastery dominates the village of Ettal—

20 + C + M + B + 14

All over Germany (and much of Catholic Europe), you'll likely see written on doorways a mysterious message: "20 + C + M + B + 14." This is marked in chalk on  Epiphany (Jan 6), the Christian holiday celebrating the arrival of the Magi to adore the newborn Baby Jesus. In addition to being the initials of the three wise men (Caspar, Melchior, and Balthazar), the letters also stand for the Latin phrase *Christus mansionem benedicat*— "May Christ bless the house." The little crosses separating the letters remind all who enter that the house has been blessed in this year (20+14). Epiphany is a bigger deal in Catholic Europe than in the US. The holiday includes gift-giving, feasting, and caroling door to door—often collecting for a charity organization. Those who donate get their doors chalked up in thanks, and these marks are left on the door through the year.

you can't miss it. Ettal is a few minutes' **drive** (or a delightful **bike** ride) from Oberammergau. Just park (€1/4 hours in larger lots; free in small, crowded lot near the *Klosterladen*, alongside the building) and wander in. Some Oberammergau-to-Linderhof **buses** stop here (see "Oberammergau Connections," earlier).

VISITING THE MONASTERY

As you enter the more than 1,000-square-foot **courtyard,** imagine the 14th-century Benedictine abbey, an independent religious community. It produced everything it needed right here. In the late Middle Ages, abbeys like this had jurisdiction over the legal system, administration, and taxation of their district. Since then, the monastery has had its ups and downs.

Secularized during the French Revolution and Napoleonic age, the Benedictines' property was confiscated by the state and sold. Religious life returned a century later. Today the abbey survives, with 50 or 60 monks. It remains a self-contained community, with living quarters for the monks, workshops, and guests' quarters. Along with their religious responsibilities, the brothers make their famous liqueur, brew beer, run a hotel, and educate 380 students in their private high school. The monks' wares are for sale at two shops (look for the *Klosterladen* by the courtyard or the *Kloster-Markt* across the street).

After entering the outer door, notice the **tympanum** over the inner door dating from 1350. It shows the founding couple, Emperor Louis the Bavarian and his wife Margaret, directing our attention to the crucified Lord and inviting us to enter the church contemplatively.

Stepping inside, the light draws our eyes to the **dome** (it's a double-shell design, 230 feet high) rather than to the high altar. Illusions—with the dome opening right to the sky—merge heaven and earth. The dome fresco shows hundreds of Benedictines worshipping the Holy Trinity...the glory of the Benedictine Order. This is classic "south-German Baroque."

Statues of the **saints** on the altars are either engaged in a holy conversation with each other or singing the praises of God. Broken shell-style patterns seem to create constant movement, with cherubs adding to the energy. Side altars and confessionals seem to grow out of the architectural structure; its decorations and furnishings become part of an organic whole. Imagine how 18th-century farmers and woodcutters, who never traveled, would step in here on Sunday and be inspired to praise their God.

The origin of the monastery is shown over the **choir arch:** An angel wearing the robe of a Benedictine monk presents the emperor with a marble Madonna and commissions him to found this monastery. (In reality, the statue was made in Pisa, circa 1300, and given to the emperor in Italy.)

Dwarfed by all the magnificence and framed by a monumental tabernacle is that tiny, most precious statue of the abbey—the miraculous **statue of Mary and the Baby Jesus.**

Nearby: The fragrant **demonstration dairy** *(Schaukäserei)* about a five-minute walk behind the monastery is worth a quick look. The farmhouse displays all the steps in the production line, starting with the cows themselves (next to the house), to the factory staff hard at work, and through to the end products, which you can sample in the shop (try the beer cheese). Better yet, enjoy a snack on the deck while listening to the sweet music/incessant clanging of cowbells (free; daily 10:00-17:00—but to see the most cheesemaking action, come in the morning, ideally between 10:00-11:00; Mandlweg 1, tel. 08822/923-926, www.schaukaeserei-ettal.de). To walk there from the monastery's exit, take a left and go through the passageway; take another left when you get to the road, then yet another left at the first street (you'll see it up the road, directly behind the abbey).

Zugspitze

The tallest point in Germany, worth ▲▲ in clear weather, is also a border crossing. Lifts from both Austria and Germany meet at the 9,700-foot summit of the Zugspitze (TSOOG-shpit-seh). You can straddle the border between two great nations

while enjoying an incredible view. Restaurants, shops, and telescopes await you at the summit.

SUMMITING THE ZUGSPITZE

German Approach: There are several ways to ascend from this side, but they all cost the same (€51 round-trip, €42 in winter, tel. 08821/7970, www.zugspitze.de).

If relying on **public transit,** you'll first head to Garmisch (for details on getting there from Füssen, see page 143; from Oberammergau, see page 167). From there, you'll ride a train to Eibsee (30 minutes, hourly departures daily 8:15-14:15), at which point you can choose: Walk across the parking lot and zip up to the top in a cable car (10 minutes, daily 8:00-16:15, departs at least every 30 minutes; in busy times departs every 10 minutes, but since each car fits only 35—which the electronic board suspensefully counts down as each passenger goes through the turnstile—you may have to wait to board), or transfer to a cogwheel train (45 minutes to the top, departs about hourly—coordinated with Garmisch train; once up top, you'll transfer from the train to a short cable car for the quick, 3-minute ascent to the summit).

Drivers can go straight to Eibsee (about 10 minutes beyond Garmisch—head through town following signs for *Fernpass/Reutte*, and watch for the Zugspitze turnoff on the left); once there, you have the same cable car vs. cog railway choice. (Even though they're not taking the train from Garmisch, drivers pay the same—€50 round-trip, plus another €3 for parking.)

You can choose how you want to go up and down at the spur of the moment: both ways by cable car, both by cog train, or mix and match. Although the train ride takes longer, many travelers enjoy the more involved cog-railway experience—at least one way. The disadvantage of the train is that more than half of the trip is through dark tunnels deep in the mountains; aside from a few fleeting glimpses of the Eibsee sparkling below, it's not very scenic.

Arriving at the top, you'll want to head up to the third floor (elevators recommended, given the high altitude)—follow signs for *Gipfel* (summit).

To get back down to Eibsee, the last cable car departs the summit at 16:45, and the last cogwheel train at 16:30. On busy days, you may have to reserve a return time once you reach the top—if it's crowded, look for signs and prebook your return to avoid getting stuck up top longer than you want. In general, allow plenty of time for afternoon descents: If bad weather hits in the late afternoon, cable cars can be delayed at the summit, causing tourists to miss their train connection from Eibsee back to Garmisch.

Hikers can enjoy the easy six-mile walk around the lovely Eibsee Lake (start 5 minutes downhill from cable-car station).

Austrian Approach: The Tiroler Zugspitzbahn ascent is less crowded and cheaper than the Bavarian one. Departing from above the village of Ehrwald (a 30-minute train trip from Reutte, train runs every 2 hours), the lift zips you to the top in 10 minutes (€39 round-trip, departures in each direction at :00, :20, and :40 past the hour, daily 8:40-16:40 except closed mid-April-late May and most of Nov, last ascent at 16:00, drivers follow signs for *Tiroler Zugspitzbahn*, free parking, Austrian  tel. 05673/2309, www.zugspitze.at). While those without a car will find the German ascent from Garmisch easier, the Austrian ascent is also doable: Either hop the bus from the Ehrwald train station to the Austrian lift (departures nearly hourly), or pay €8 for the five-minute taxi ride from Ehrwald train station.

◑ SELF-GUIDED TOUR

Whether you've ascended from the Austrian or German side, you're high enough now to enjoy a little tour of the summit. The two terraces—Bavarian and Tirolean—are connected by a narrow walkway, which was the border station before Germany and Austria opened their borders. The Austrian (Tirolean) side was higher until the Germans blew its top off in World War II to make a flak tower, so let's start there.

Tirolean Terrace: Before you stretches the Zugspitzplatt glacier. Each summer, a 65,000-square-foot reflector is spread over the ice to try to slow the shrinking. Since metal ski-lift towers collect heat, they, too, are wrapped to try to save the glacier. Many ski lifts fan out here, as if reaching for a ridge that defines the border between Germany and Austria. The circular metal building is the top of the cog-railway line that the Germans cut through the mountains in 1931. Just above that, find a small square building—the *Hochzeitskapelle* (wedding chapel) consecrated in 1981 by Cardinal Joseph Ratzinger (now the recently retired Pope Benedict XVI).

Both Germany and Austria use this rocky pinnacle for communication purposes. The square box on the Tirolean Terrace provides the Innsbruck airport with air-traffic control, and a tower nearby is for the German *Katastrophenfunk* (civil defense network).

This highest point in Germany (there are many higher points in Austria) was first climbed in 1820. The Austrians built a cable car that nearly reached the summit in 1926. (You can see it just over the ridge on the Austrian side—look for the ghostly, abandoned concrete station.) In 1964, the final leg, a new lift, was built connecting that 1926 station to the actual summit, where you stand now. Before then, people needed to hike the last 650 feet to the top. Today's lift dates from 1980, but was renovated after a 2003 fire. The Austrian station, which is much nicer than the German station, has a fine little museum—free with Austrian ticket, €2.50 if you came up from Germany—that shows three interesting videos (6-minute 3-D mountain show, 30-minute making-of-the-lift documentary, and 45-minute look at the nature, sport, and culture of the region).

Looking up the valley from the Tirolean Terrace, you can see the towns of Ehrwald and Lermoos in the distance, and the valley that leads to Reutte. Looking farther clockwise, you'll see Eibsee Lake below. Hell's Valley, stretching to the right of Eibsee, seems to merit its name.

Bavarian Terrace: The narrow passage connecting the two terraces used to be a big deal—you'd show your passport here at the little blue house and shift from Austrian shillings to German marks. Notice the regional pride here: no German or Austrian national banners, but regional ones instead—*Freistaat Bayern* (Bavaria) and *Land Tirol*.

The German side features a golden cross marking the summit...the highest point in Germany. A priest and his friends hauled it up in 1851. The historic original was shot up by American soldiers using it for target practice in the late 1940s, so what you see today is a modern replacement. In the summer, it's easy to "summit" the Zugspitze, as there are steps and handholds all the way to the top. Or you can just stay behind and feed the birds. The yellow-beaked ravens get chummy with those who share a little pretzel or bread. Below the terrace, notice the restaurant that claims—irrefutably—to be the "highest Biergarten in Deustchland."

The oldest building up here is the rustic tin-and-wood weather tower near the border crossing, erected in 1900 by the *Deutscher Wetterdienst* (German weather service). The first mountaineers' hut, built in 1897, didn't last. The existing one—entwined with mighty cables that cinch it down—dates from 1914. In 1985, observers clocked 200-mph winds up here—those cables were necessary. Step inside the restaurant to enjoy museum-like photos and paintings on the wall (including a look at the team who hiked up with the golden cross in 1851).

Near the waiting area for the cable cars and cogwheel train is a little museum (in German only) that's worth a look if you have some time to kill before heading back down. If you're going down on the German side, remember you must choose between the cable car (look for the *Eibsee* signs) or cog railway (look for *Talfahrt/Descent*, with a picture of a train; you'll board a smaller cable car for the quick trip to the train station).

Reutte, Austria

Reutte (ROY-teh, with a rolled *r*), a relaxed Austrian town of 6,000, is a 20-minute drive across the border from Füssen. While overlooked by the international tourist crowd, it's popular with Germans and Austrians for its climate. Doctors recommend its "grade 1" air.

Although its setting—surrounded by alpine peaks—is striking, the town itself is pretty unexceptional. But that's the point. I enjoy Reutte for the opportunity it offers to simply be in a real community. As an example of how the town is committed to its character, real estate can be sold only to those using it as a primary residence. (Many formerly vibrant alpine towns made a pile of money but lost their sense of community by becoming resorts. They allowed  wealthy foreigners—who just drop in for a week or two a year—to buy up all the land, and are now shuttered up and dead most of the time.)

Reutte has one claim to fame among Americans: As Nazi Germany was falling in 1945, Hitler's top rocket scientist, Werner von Braun, joined the Americans (rather than the Russians) in Reutte. You could say that the American space program began here.

Reutte isn't featured in any other American guidebook. The town center can be congested and confusing, and its charms are subtle. It was never rich or important. Its castle is ruined, its buildings have painted-on "carvings," its churches are full, its men yodel for each other on birthdays, and its energy is spent soaking its

Austrian and German guests in *Gemütlichkeit*. Most guests stay for a week, so the town's attractions are more time-consuming than thrilling.

Some travelers tell me this town is over-Reutte-d. Füssen's tidy pedestrian core and glitzy hotels make it an easier home base. But in my view, Reutte's two big trump cards are its fine countryside accommodations (the farther from the town center, the more rustic, authentic, and relaxing) and its proximity to one of my favorite ruined castles, Ehrenberg. Since you need a car to take best advantage of these pluses (as well as to reach the King's Castles quickly), Reutte is a good place for drivers to spend the night.

Orientation to Reutte

Reutte feels spread out, because it's really a web of several villages that fill a basin hemmed in by mountains and cut through by the Lech River. Drivers find its tangle of crisscrossing roads bewildering at first; know where you're going and follow signs (to your point of interest, hotel, or neighboring village) to stay on track.

Reutte proper, near the train station, has a one-street downtown where you'll find the TI, museum, and a couple of hotels and eateries. The area's real charm lies in the abutting hamlets, and that's where my favorite hotels and restaurants are located: **Breitenwang**, flowing directly from Reutte to the east, marked by its pointy steeple; **Ehenbichl**, a farming village cuddled up against the mountains to the south; **Höfen**, squeezed between an airstrip and a cable-car station, just across the river from Ehenbichl; and remote **Pinswang**, stranded in a forgotten valley halfway to Germany, just over the mountain from Neuschwanstein. Watching over it all to the south are the **Ehrenberg Castle** ruins—viewable from just about everywhere and evocatively floodlit at night—two miles out of town on the main Innsbruck road.

TOURIST INFORMATION

Reutte's TI is a block in front of the train station (Mon-Fri 8:00-12:00 & 14:00-17:00, no midday break July-Aug, Sat 8:30-12:00, closed Sun, Untermarkt 34, tel. 05672/62336, www.reutte.com). Go over your sightseeing plans, ask about a folk evening, and pick up city and biking/hiking maps, bus schedules, the *Sommerprogramm* events schedule (in German only), and a free town info booklet (with a good self-guided walk).

Guests staying in the Reutte area (and, therefore, paying the local hotel tax) are entitled to an **Aktiv-Card**—be sure to ask your hotel for one. The TI has a brochure explaining all of the perks of this card, including free travel on local buses (including the Reutte-Füssen route—but not Füssen-Neuschwanstein), low-cost taxi service to the castles (daily 9:00-18:00—ask your hotelier for details), and free admission to some otherwise very pricey attractions, including the recommended museum below Ehrenberg Castle, the Hahnenkammbahn mountain lift (summer only), and the Alpentherme bath complex (2 hours free each day). Also included are various guided hikes in the surrounding mountains (get schedule from TI), and discounts on mountain-bike tours, rafting trips, and paragliding.

ARRIVAL IN REUTTE

By Car: From the expressway, always take the south *(Süd)* exit into town (even if you pass the *Nord* exit first). For parking in town, blue lines denote pay-and-display spots (if you're staying more than 30 minutes, pay at the meter, then put the receipt in your windshield). There are a few spaces just outside the TI that are free for up to 30 minutes—handy for stopping by with a few questions en route to your out-of-town hotel. For longer stays, there's a free lot (P-1) just past the train station on Muhlerstrasse (about a 10-minute walk from the town center and TI).

While Austria requires a **toll sticker** *(Vignette)* for driving on its expressways (€8.50/10 days, buy at the border, gas stations, car-rental agencies, or *Tabak* shops), those just dipping into Tirol from Bavaria don't need one—even on the expressway-like bypass around Reutte.

By Train or Bus: From Reutte's tidy little train and bus station (no baggage storage, usually unstaffed), exit straight ahead and walk three minutes straight up Bahnhofstrasse. After the park on your left, you'll see the TI; my recommended town-center hotels are down the street just beyond the TI and its parking lot.

HELPFUL HINTS

Welcome to Austria: Remember, Reutte is in a different country. While Austrians use the same euro currency the Germans do, postage stamps and phone cards only work in the country where you buy them. If you have a German SIM card in your mobile phone, you're roaming (and paying higher rates) in Reutte.

To telephone from Germany to Austria, dial 00-43 and then the number listed in this section (omitting the initial zero). To call from Austria to Germany, dial 00-49 and then the number (again, omitting the initial zero).

Laundry: There isn't an actual launderette in town, but the recommended Hotel Maximilian lets non-guests use its laundry service (wash, dry, and fold-€16/load; hotel guests pay €12).

Bike Rental: Try **Intersport** (€15/day, Mon-Fri 9:00-18:00, Sat

9:00-17:00, closed Sun, Lindenstrasse 25, tel. 05672/62352), or check at the recommended Hotel Maximilian.

"Nightlife": Reutte is pretty quiet. For any action at all, there's a strip of bars, dance clubs, and Italian restaurants on Lindenstrasse.

Sights in and near Reutte

▲▲EHRENBERG CASTLE ENSEMBLE (FESTUNGSENSEMBLE EHRENBERG)

If Neuschwanstein was the medieval castle dream, Ehrenberg is the medieval castle reality. Once the largest fortification in Tirol,

its brooding ruins lie about two miles outside Reutte. What's here is actually an "ensemble" of four castles, built to defend against the Bavarians and to bottle up the strategic Via Claudia trade route, which cut through the Alps as it connected Italy and Germany. Half-forgotten and overgrown only a decade ago, they've been transformed into a fine attraction with hiking paths, a museum, guesthouse, and—soon—the longest pedestrian suspension bridge in the world. The European Union helps fund the project because it promotes the heritage of a multinational region—Tirol—rather than a country.

In Roman times, the Via Claudia—the road below Ehrenberg—was the main route between northern Italy (Verona) and southern Germany (Augsburg), and was broad enough for wheeled traffic. Historians estimate that in medieval times, about 10,000 tons of precious salt passed through this valley each year, so it's no wonder the locals built this complex of fortresses and castles to control traffic and levy tolls on all who passed.

The complex has four parts: the old toll buildings on the valley floor, where you park (the Klause); the oldest castle, on the hilltop directly above (Ehrenberg); a mightier castle on a slightly higher peak of the same hill (Schlosskopf); and a smaller fortification across the valley (Fort Claudia). All four were once a single complex connected by walls. Signs posted throughout the site help visitors find their way and explain some background on the region's history, geology, flora, and fauna, and colorful, fun boards relate local folktales.

Cost and Hours: The castle ruins themselves are free and always open, but the museum and suspension bridge charge admission (for details, see individual listings).

Getting There: The castles are on the road to Lermoos and

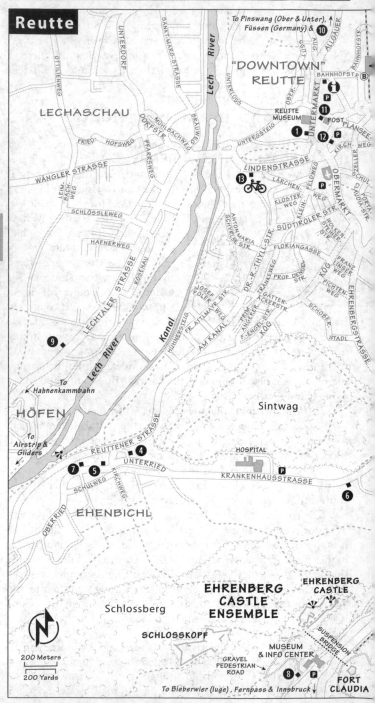

Reutte

To Pinswang (Ober & Unter),
Füssen (Germany) &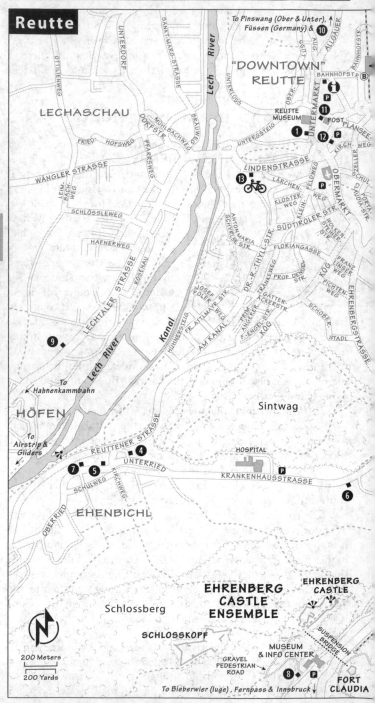

"DOWNTOWN" REUTTE

LECHASCHAU

REUTTE MUSEUM

POST

LINDENSTRASSE

HÖFEN

To Hahnenkammbahn

To Airstrip & Gliders

EHENBICHL

Sintwag

HOSPITAL

KRANKENHAUSSTRASSE

Schlossberg

EHRENBERG CASTLE ENSEMBLE

EHRENBERG CASTLE

SCHLOSSKOPF

MUSEUM & INFO CENTER

GRAVEL PEDESTRIAN ROAD

SUSPENSION BRIDGE

FORT CLAUDIA

To Bieberwier (luge), Fernpass & Innsbruck

200 Meters
200 Yards

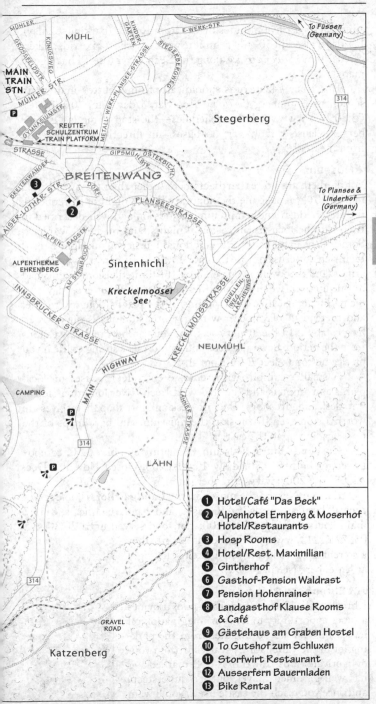

1. Hotel/Café "Das Beck"
2. Alpenhotel Ernberg & Moserhof Hotel/Restaurants
3. Hosp Rooms
4. Hotel/Rest. Maximilian
5. Gintherhof
6. Gasthof-Pension Waldrast
7. Pension Hohenrainer
8. Landgasthof Klause Rooms & Café
9. Gästehaus am Graben Hostel
10. To Gutshof zum Schluxen
11. Storfwirt Restaurant
12. Ausserfern Bauernladen
13. Bike Rental

Innsbruck, just five minutes by car from Reutte (parking-€2/day). It's also a pleasant 30- to 45-minute walk or a short bike ride; bikers can use the *Radwanderweg* along the Lech River (the TI has a good map).

Local bus #4250 runs sporadically from Reutte's main train station to Ehrenberg (5-7/day Mon-Sat, 1/day Sun, 10 minutes, €2.80; see www.vvt.at for schedules—the stop name is "Ehrenberger Klause"). However, no buses run directly *back* to Reutte from the castle.

▲Museum

While there are no real artifacts here (other than the sword used in A.D. 2014 to make me the honorary First Knight of Ehrenberg), the clever, kid-friendly museum is hands-on and well-described in English. The focus is on castles, knights, and medieval warcraft. Some of the exhibits trace the fictional journey of a knight named Heinrich to Jerusalem in the late 1300s. You can try on a set of armor (and then weigh yourself), see the limited vision knights had to put up with when wearing helmets, learn about everyday medieval life, empathize with victims of the plague, join a Crusade, and pretend to play soccer with gigantic stone balls once tossed by a catapult. In the armory section, you can heft replica weapons from the period. Several videos and soundtracks spring to life if you press a button (select *E* for English).

A smaller exhibit (with separate entry fee) focuses on local plants and animals and the still-wild Lech River (on other side of info desk and gift shop). The info desk and gift shop themselves are worth a stop even if you skip the museum, and have maps of the trails leading up to the castles.

Cost and Hours: Museum-€8, nature exhibit-€5.50, combo-ticket for both-€10.80, daily 10:00-17:00, closed Nov-mid-Dec, tel. 05672/62007, www.ehrenberg.at.

Eating: Next to the museum, the **Landgasthof Klause** serves typical Tirolean meals (€7-10 pastas and vegetarian meals, €11-17 main courses, daily 8:00-23:00, hot food served until 20:30, tel. 05672/62213, www.gasthof-klause.com). They also rent a few rooms if you'd like to stay right at Ehrenberg (see page 191).

▲▲Ehrenberg Ruins

Ehrenberg, a 13th-century rock pile, provides a super opportunity to let your imagination off its leash. Hike up 30 minutes from the parking lot in the valley for a great view from your own private ruins. The trail is well-marked and has well-groomed gravel, but it's quite steep, and once you reach the castle itself, you'll want good shoes to scramble over the uneven stairs. The castle is always open.

➋ **Self-Guided Tour:** From the parking lot, follow yellow signs up into the woods, tracking *Ruine Ehrenberg* or *Bergruine Ehrenberg*. At the top of the first switchback, notice the option to turn left and hike 45 minutes up to Schlosskopf, the higher castle (described next; this is an easier ascent than the very steep route you can take from closer to Ehrenberg). But we'll head right and continue up the path through the lower entrance bastion of Ehrenberg.

Emerging from the woods, you'll pop out at a saddle between two steep hills. As you face Reutte, the hill on the left is Schlosskopf (notice the steeper ascent here to reach the top), and to the right is Ehrenberg. Ehrenberg is the older of the two, built around 1290. Thirteenth-century castles were designed to stand boastfully tall. Later, with the advent of gunpowder, castles dug in. (Notice the 18th-century ramparts around the castle.)

Now continue twisting up the path to Ehrenberg Castle. As you approach its outer gate, look for the small **door** to the left. It's the night entrance (tight and awkward, and therefore safer against a surprise attack). But we'll head through the **main gate**—actually, two of them. Castles were designed with layered defenses—outer bastion down below, outer gate here, inner gate deeper within— which allowed step-by-step retreat, giving defenders time to regroup and fight back against invading forces.

After you pass through the outer gate, but before climbing to the top of the castle, follow the path around to the right to a big, grassy courtyard with commanding views and a fat, restored **turret**. This stored gunpowder and held a big cannon that enjoyed a clear view of the valley below. In medieval times, all the trees approaching the castle were cleared to keep an unobstructed view.

Look out over the valley. The pointy spire marks the village of **Breitenwang,** which was the site of a Roman camp in A.D. 46. In 1489, after a bridge was built across the Lech River at Reutte (marked by the onion-domed church), Reutte was made a market town and eclipsed Breitenwang in importance. Any gliders circling? They launch from just over the river in Höfen.

For centuries, this castle was the seat of government—ruling an area called the "judgment of Ehrenberg" (roughly the same as today's "district of Reutte"). When the emperor came by, he stayed here. In 1604, the ruler moved downtown into more comfortable quarters, and the castle was no longer a palace.

Now climb to the top of Ehrenberg Castle. Take the high ground. There was no water supply here—just kegs of wine, beer, and a cistern to collect rain. Up at the top, appreciate how strategic this lofty position is—with commanding views over Reutte and its broad valley, as well as the narrow side-valley where the highway to the south runs. But also notice that you're sandwiched between two higher hilltops: Schlosskopf in one direction and Falkenberg (across the narrow valley) in the other. In the days before gunpowder, those higher positions offered no real threat. But in the age of cannonballs, Ehrenberg was suddenly very vulnerable...and very obsolete.

Still, Ehrenberg repelled 16,000 Swedish soldiers in the defense of Catholicism in 1632. But once the Schlosskopf was fortified a few decades later, Ehrenberg's days were numbered, and its end was not glorious. In the 1780s, a local businessman bought the castle in order to sell off its parts. Later, in the late 19th century, when vagabonds moved in, the roof was removed to make squatting miserable. With the roof gone, deterioration quickened, leaving only this evocative shell and a whiff of history.

Scramble around the ruined walls a bit—nocking imaginary arrows—and head back down through the main gate, returning to the valley the way you came. If you have more energy and castle curiosity, you could try conquering the next castle over: Schlosskopf.

▲Schlosskopf

When Bavarian troops captured Ehrenberg in 1703, the Tiroleans climbed up to the bluff above it to rain cannonballs down on their former fortress. In 1740, a mighty new castle—designed to defend against modern artillery—was built on this sky-high strategic location: Schlosskopf ("Castle Head"). But it too fell into ruin, and by the end of the 20th century, the castle was completely overgrown with trees—you literally couldn't see it from Reutte. But today the trees have been shaved away, and the castle has been excavated. In 2008, the Castle Ensemble project, led by local architect Armin Walch, opened the site with English descriptions and view platforms. One spot gives spectacular views of the strategic valley. The other looks down on the older Ehrenberg Castle ruins, illustrating the strategic problems presented with the advent of cannon.

Getting There: There are two routes to Schlosskopf, both steep and time-consuming. The steeper of the two (about 30 minutes straight up) starts at the little saddle of land between the two castles (described earlier). The second, which curls around the back of the hill, is less steep but takes longer (45-60 minutes); this one begins from partway down the gravel switchbacks between Ehrenberg and the valley floor—just watch for *Schlosskopf* signs.

Suspension Bridge

At more than 1,200 feet, this suspended pedestrian bridge is set to be the longest of its type in the world (and should be completed by the time you visit). Plans call for it to hang more than 300 feet above the valley floor, connecting Ehrenberg with the previously difficult-to-reach Fort Claudia across the valley.

Cost and Hours: Likely €8, daily 8:00-22:00, tel. 05672/62007, www.highline179.com.

IN THE TOWN
Reutte Museum (Museum Grünes Haus)

Reutte's cute city museum offers a quick look at the local folk culture and the story of the castles. There are exhibits on Ehrenberg and the Via Claudia, local painters, and more—ask to borrow the English translations.

Cost and Hours: €3; May-Oct Tue-Sat 13:00-17:00, closed Sun-Mon; shorter hours and closed Sun-Tue off-season; closes Easter-end of April and Nov-early Dec; in the bright-green building at Untermarkt 25, around corner from Hotel Goldener Hirsch, tel. 05672/72304, www.museum-reutte.at.

▲▲Tirolean Folk Evening

Ask the TI or your hotel if there's a Tirolean folk evening scheduled. During the summer (July-Aug), nearby towns (such as Höfen on Tue) occasionally put on an evening of yodeling, slap dancing, and Tirolean frolic. These are generally free and worth the short drive. Off-season, you'll have to do your own yodeling. There are also weekly folk concerts featuring the local choir or brass band in Reutte's Zeiller Platz, as well as various groups in the surrounding communities (free, July-Aug only, ask at TI). For listings of these and other local events, pick up a copy of the German-only *Sommerprogramm* schedule at the TI.

Alpentherme Ehrenberg

This new, extensive swimming pool and sauna complex, a 15-minute walk from downtown Reutte, is a tempting retreat. The Badewelt section features two indoor pools and a big outdoor saltwater pool, as well as two waterslides. The all-nude Saunaparadies section (no kids under age 16) consists of three indoor saunas, three freestanding outdoor saunas, and a big outdoor swimming pool. They'll issue you a wristband that lets you access your locker and buy snacks on credit without needing a key or money. Those staying in the Reutte area can access the pools for two hours free with an Aktiv-Card (see "Tourist Information," earlier); it's a nice way to relax after hiking around castles all day.

Cost and Hours: Pools only-€9.50/2 hours, €11.50/4 hours, €13.50/day; sauna and pools-€19.50/3 hours, €25.50/day; towel rental-€3, robe rental-€5, swimsuits sold but not rented; daily 10:00-21:00, sauna until 22:00, closes for one week every May; Thermenstrasse 10, tel. 05672/72222, www.alpentherme-ehrenberg.at.

ACROSS THE RIVER, IN HÖFEN

Just over the Lech River are two very different ways to reach high-altitude views. To get here from Reutte, head up Lindenstrasse (where the cobbled Obermarkt ends), cross the bridge, and turn left down Lechtaler Strasse; as you enter the village of Höfen, you'll see the cable car to your right and the airstrip to your left.

▲Scenic Flights

For a major thrill on a sunny day, drop by the tiny airport in Höfen, where small single-prop planes and gliders take passengers on scenic flights. Although I've listed contact information below, your best bet is to show up at the airstrip on a good-weather afternoon and ask around. Prop planes can buzz the Zugspitze and Ludwig's castles and give you a bird's-eye peek at Reutte's Ehrenberg ruins (tel. 05672/632-0729 or mobile 0664-221-2233, www.flugsportverein-reutte.at). Or, to try something more angelic, how about gliding *(segelfliegen)?* For a modest price, you and a pilot get 30 minutes in a two-seat glider. Just watching the towrope launch the graceful glider like a giant slow-motion rubber-band gun is exhilarating (mobile 0676-945-1288, www.segelflugverein-ausserfern.at, Adrian Eberhardt).

Getting There: The prop planes and gliders are based out of two different restaurants that face the airstrip. From the main road, watch for the big building marked *Flugplatz* down below. The contact for the prop-plane pilots is the Fliegerklause café (closed Mon); for the gliders, head 100 yards farther down the road to the Thermic Ranch.

Hahnenkammbahn

This mountain lift swoops you in small, enclosed cars high above the tree line to an attractive restaurant and starting point for several hikes. In the alpine flower park, special paths lead you past countless varieties of local flora. Unique to this lift is a barefoot hiking trail *(Barfusswanderweg),* designed to be walked without shoes—no joke.

Cost and Hours: €12 one-way, €17.50 round-trip, runs June-Sept daily 9:00-16:30, also in good weather late May and Oct-early Nov, flowers best in late July, base station across the river in Höfen, tel. 05672/62420, www.reuttener-seilbahnen.at.

NEAR REUTTE
Sights Along the Lech River

The Lech River begins high in the Alps and meanders 75 miles (including right past Reutte) on its way to the Lechfall, where it becomes navigable, near Füssen. This stretch of the Lech River Valley (Lechtal) has been developed as a popular hiking trail, called the **Lechweg,** divided into 15 stages *(Strecken)*; part of the area has also

Luge Lesson

Taking a wild ride on a summer luge (pronounced "loozh") is a quintessential alpine experience. In German, it's called a *Sommerrodelbahn* ("summer toboggan run"). To try one of Europe's great accessible thrills (€3-8), take the lift up to the top of a mountain, grab a wheeled sled-like go-cart, and scream back down the mountainside on a banked course. Then take the lift back up and start all over again.

Luge courses are highly weather-dependent, and can close at the slightest hint of rain. If the weather's questionable, call ahead to confirm that your preferred luge is open. Stainless-steel courses are more likely than concrete ones to stay open in drizzly weather.

Operating the sled is simple: Push the stick forward to go faster, pull back to apply brakes. Even a novice can go very, very fast. Most are cautious on their first run, speed demons on their second...and bruised and bloody on their third. A woman once showed me her travel journal illustrated with her husband's dried five-inch-long luge scab. He had disobeyed the only essential rule of luging: Keep both hands on your stick. To avoid a bumper-to-bumper traffic jam, let the person in front of you get as far ahead as possible before you start. You'll emerge from the course with a windblown hairdo and a smile-creased face.

Key Luge Terms

Lenkstange	lever
drücken / schneller fahren	push / go faster
ziehen / bremsen	pull / brake
Schürfwunde	scrape
Schorf	scab

been designated as a nature park. A variety of glossy brochures—mostly in German and available at local TIs and hotels—explain the importance of the Lech to local culture and outline some enticing hikes.

Within the pristine Tiroler Lech Nature Park, a little outside Reutte, is an impressive wooden **lookout tower** from which you can observe the vibrant bird life in the wetlands along the Lech River (110 different species of birds nest here). Look for *Vogelerlebnispfad* signs as you're driving through the village of Pflach (on the road between Reutte and Füssen; www.naturpark-tiroler-lech.at).

BAVARIA & TIROL

▲▲Biberwier Luge Course

Near Lermoos, on the road between Reutte and Innsbruck, you'll find the Biberwier *Sommerrodelbahn*. At 4,250 feet, it's the longest summer luge in Tirol. The only drawbacks are its brief season, short hours, and a proclivity for shutting down sporadically—even at the slightest bit of rain. If you don't have a car, this is not worth the trouble; consider the luge near Neuschwanstein instead (see "Tegelberg Luge" on page 155). The ugly cube-shaped building marring the countryside near the luge course is a hotel for outdoor adventure enthusiasts. You can ride your mountain bike right into your room, or skip the elevator by using its indoor climbing wall.

Cost and Hours: €7.70/ride, cheaper with multi-ride tickets; daily early May-early Oct 9:00-16:30, closed off-season; tel. 05673/2323, www.bergbahnen-langes.at.

Getting There: It's 20 minutes from Reutte on the main road toward Innsbruck; Biberwier is the first exit after a long tunnel.

▲Fallerschein

Easy for drivers and a special treat for those who may have been Kit Carson in a previous life, this extremely remote log-cabin village, south of Reutte, is a 4,000-foot-high flower-speckled world of serene slopes and cowbells. Thunderstorms roll down the valley like it's God's bowling alley, but the pint-size church on the high ground, blissfully simple in a land of Baroque, seems to promise that this huddle of houses will survive, and the river and breeze will just keep flowing. The couples sitting on benches are mostly Austrian vacationers who've rented cabins here. Some of them, appreciating the remoteness of Fallerschein, are having affairs.

Getting There: From Reutte, it's a 45-minute drive. Take road 198 to Stanzach (passing Weisenbach am Loch, then Forchach), then turn left toward Namlos. Follow the L-21 Berwang road for about five miles to a parking lot. From there, it's a two-mile walk down a drivable but technically closed one-lane road. Those driving in do so at their own risk.

Sleeping in Fallerschein: **$ Michl's Fallerscheiner Stube** is a family-friendly mountain-hut restaurant with a low-ceilinged attic space that has basic beds for up to 17 sleepy hikers. The accommodations aren't fancy, but if you're looking for remote, this is it (dorm bed-€20, cheaper without breakfast, dinner-€11, sheets-€4, open May-Oct only, wildlife viewing deck, mobile 0676-727-9681, www.alpe-fallerschein.com, michaelknitel@alpe-fallerschein.com, Knitel family).

Sleeping in and near Reutte

While it's not impossible by public transport, staying here makes most sense for those with a car. Reutte is popular with Austrians and Germans, who visit year after year for one- or two-week vacations. Prices stay fairly even throughout the year and include a guest tax of €2 per person per day. Remember to ask for the Aktiv-Card, which is covered by your guest tax and includes lots of freebies (for details, see page 177). All of my recommendations have free parking and a great breakfast.

Most of my listings are in the "villages" around Reutte (such as Breitenwang, Ehenbichl, and Höfen), which basically feel like the suburbs. For locations, see the Reutte map. For even more options, check www.reutte.com (or ask the Reutte TI) for their list of private homes that rent out rooms. These average about €30 per person per night in a room with breakfast and facilities down the hall.

Remember, to call Reutte from Germany, dial 00-43 and then the number (minus the initial zero).

IN CENTRAL REUTTE

$$ Hotel "Das Beck" offers 17 clean, sunny rooms (many with balconies) filling a modern building in the heart of town close to the train station. This is the most practical option for those coming by train or bus. It's a great value, and guests are personally taken care of by Hans, Inge, Tamara, and Birgit. Their small café offers tasty snacks and specializes in Austrian and Mediterranean wines. Expect good conversation, overseen by Hans (Sb-€48-55, Db-€72-78, Tb-€96-99, price depends on room size—more for a balcony; family suites: Db-€90, Tb-€108, Qb-€125; these prices with this book in 2015 if you book direct, non-smoking, guest computer and Wi-Fi, Untermarkt 11, tel. 05672/62522, www.hotel-das-beck.at, info@hotel-das-beck.at).

IN BREITENWANG

Now basically a part of Reutte, the older and quieter village of Breitenwang has good *Zimmer* and a fine bakery. It's a 20-minute walk from the Reutte train station: From the post office, follow Planseestrasse past the onion-dome church to the pointy straight-dome church near the two hotels. The Hosps—as well as some other families renting private rooms—are along Kaiser-Lothar-Strasse, the first right past this church. Reutte's Alpentherme indoor pool complex, free for two hours a day with your Aktiv-Card, is just around the block.

If staying in Breitenwang and traveling by train, take advantage of the tiny Reutte-Schulzentrum Station, just a five-minute walk from these listings. All trains on the Garmisch-Reutte line stop here, but only on demand—which means you have to let the conductor know in advance where you want to get off. To board at Reutte-Schulzentrum, stand on the platform and flag the train down; you'll be able to buy a ticket from the conductor with no penalty.

$$ Alpenhotel Ernberg's 26 fresh wood-paneled rooms (most with terraces) are run with great care by friendly Hermann, who combines Old World elegance with modern touches. Nestle in for some serious coziness among the carved-wood eating nooks, tiled stoves, and family-friendly backyard (Sb-€55-65, Db-€90-100, price depends on demand, less for 2 nights, Wi-Fi, popular restaurant, Planseestrasse 50, tel. 05672/71912, www.ernberg.at, info@ernberg.at).

$$ Moserhof Hotel has 40 new-feeling rooms plus an elegant dining room (Sb-€61, Db-€100, larger Db-€110, these special rates promised in 2015 if you ask for the Rick Steves discount when you reserve and pay cash, extra bed-€35, most rooms have balconies, elevator, Wi-Fi, restaurant, sauna and whirlpool, Planseestrasse 44, tel. 05672/62020, www.hotel-moserhof.at, info@hotel-moserhof.at, Hosp family).

$ Walter and Emilie Hosp rent three simple rooms sharing one bathroom in a comfortable, quiet, and modern house two blocks from the Breitenwang church steeple. You'll feel like you're staying at Grandma's (S-€30, D-€60, less if you stay 2 nights, cash only, Kaiser-Lothar-Strasse 29, tel. 05672/65377).

IN EHENBICHL, NEAR THE EHRENBERG RUINS

These listings are a bit farther from central Reutte, a couple of miles upriver in the village of Ehenbichl. From central Reutte, go south on Obermarkt and turn right on Kög, which becomes Reuttener Strasse, following signs to *Ehenbichl*. These places are inconvenient by public transit (you'll need to brave infrequent local buses; see www.vvt.at for schedules). For taxi service, ask your hotelier for details.

$$ Hotel Maximilian offers 30 rooms at a great value. It includes table tennis, play areas for children (indoors and out), a pool table, and the friendly service of Gabi, Monika, and the rest of the Koch family. They host many special events, and their hotel has extras such as a sauna and a piano (Sb-€60, Db-€85-99 depending on demand—weekends usually more expensive, reserve directly with hotel by email and mention this book for best prices, family deals, elevator, guest computer, free Wi-Fi in common areas, pay Wi-Fi in rooms, laundry service-€12/load—non-guests pay €16, good restaurant open evenings only, Reuttener Strasse 1 in Ehenbichl—don't let your GPS take you to Reuttener Strasse in Pflach, tel. 05672/62585, www.maxihotel.com, info@hotelmaximilian.at).

They rent cars to guests only (€0.72/km, automatic transmission, book in advance) and bikes to anyone (€5/half-day, €10/day; or, for non-guests, €6/half-day, €12/day).

$$ Gintherhof is a working dairy farm that provides its guests with fresh milk, butter, and bacon. Kind, hardworking Annelies Paulweber offers a warm welcome, geranium-covered balconies, six cozy and well-appointed rooms with carved-wood ceilings, and a Madonna in every corner (Db-€77, Db suite-€81, €5/person less for 3 nights, cash only, family rooms, Wi-Fi, Unterried 7, just up the road behind Hotel Maximilian, tel. 05672/67697, www.gintherhof.com, info@gintherhof.com).

$$ Gasthof-Pension Waldrast, separating a forest and a meadow, is run by the farming Huter family and their dog, Picasso. The place feels hauntingly quiet and has no restaurant, but it's inexpensive and offers 10 pleasant, spacious rooms with generous sitting areas, castle-view balconies, and well-preserved furniture from the 1960s and '70s. They've restored a nearly 500-year-old mill on their property and happily show it to interested guests. This is my only listing within easy walking distance of the Ehrenberg Castle ruins (Sb-€45, Db-€77, Tb-€96, Qb-€115, 5 percent off second night or longer with this book if you reserve directly with hotel, cash only, non-smoking, Wi-Fi, Krankenhausstrasse 16, tel. 05672/62443, www.waldrasttirol.com, info@waldrasttirol.com, Gerd).

$$ Pension Hohenrainer, a quiet, no-frills place, has 12 rooms past their prime, with some castle-view balconies (Sb-€38-40, Db-€76-80, €5/person less for 3 nights, cash only, family rooms, guest computer, Wi-Fi, reception in Gasthof Schlosswirt across the street and through the field, follow signs up the road behind Hotel Maximilian into village of Ehenbichl, Unterried 3, tel. 05672/62544 or 05672/63262, mobile 0676-799-6902, www.hohenrainer.at, hohenrainer@aon.at).

AT THE EHRENBERG RUINS

$$ Landgasthof Klause café, just below the Ehrenberg ruins and next to the castle museum, rents 14 non-smoking, sleek, and modern rooms with balconies, as well as six apartments. You'll need a car to get anywhere besides Ehrenberg (Sb-€47, Db-€86, Tb-€111, ask for Rick Steves discount when you book, Wi-Fi, tel. 05672/62213, www.gasthof-klause.com, gasthof-klause@gmx.at).

ACROSS THE RIVER, IN HÖFEN

$$ Gästehaus am Graben, with 13 rooms, is a good value less than two miles from Reutte, with fine castle views and family rooms sleeping four to six (Db-€60-80, Qb-€120-140, price depends on room size and amenities, less if you stay 3 nights, non-smoking, Wi-Fi, closed April and Nov-mid-Dec; from downtown Reutte, cross bridge and follow main road left along river, or take bus #4268 to the Graben stop; Graben 1, tel. 05672/626-440, www.hoefen.at, info@hoefen.at, Reyman family).

IN PINSWANG

The village of Pinswang is closer to Füssen (and Ludwig's castles), but still in Austria. While this hotel works best for drivers, about half of the departures of yellow post bus #4258/#74, which runs between the Reutte and Füssen train stations, stop here (3-4/day, get off at Pinswang Gemeindeamt stop, verify details with hotel or at www.postbus.at, or use www.bahn.com and plug in "Pinswang Gemeindeamt" to find a workable train-bus connection).

$$ Gutshof zum Schluxen gets the "Remote Old Hotel in an Idyllic Setting" award. This family-friendly farm, with 34 rooms, offers rustic elegance. Its picturesque meadow setting will turn you into a dandelion-picker, and its proximity to Neuschwanstein will turn you into a hiker—the castle is just an hour's walk away. The hotel has new owners, and prices and services may change (Sb-€56, Db-€106, extra bed-€32, bike rental, restaurant, bar, between Reutte and Füssen in village of Pinswang, tel. 05677/89030, www. schluxen.at, info@schluxen.at).

To reach Neuschwanstein from this hotel by foot or bike, follow the dirt road up the hill behind the hotel. When the road forks at the top of the hill, go right (downhill), cross the Austria-Germany border (marked by a sign and deserted hut), and follow the narrow paved path to the castles. It's a 1- to 1.5-hour hike or a great circular bike trip (allow 30 minutes; cyclists can return to Schluxen from the castles on a different 30-minute bike route via Füssen).

Eating in Reutte

The nicer restaurants in Reutte are all in hotels. **Alpenhotel Ernberg,** the **Moserhof Hotel,** and **Hotel Maximilian** (evenings only) all have fine restaurants. On weekdays, Alpenhotel Ernberg serves good three-course business lunches for €11.

Storfwirt is a great place for a quick and cheap weekday lunch. This rustic cafeteria in downtown Reutte serves some 300 happy eaters every day. There's a salad bar, €6 pastas, and daily soup-and-main-course specials for €7-8 (always something for vegetarians, Mon-Fri 9:00-14:00, closed Sat-Sun). Their adjacent **deli** is a great place to shop for a Tirolean picnic; choose from the local meats, cheeses, and prepared salads in the glass case, pick up a schnitzel with potato salad (€4-6), or ask them to make you a sandwich to order. You can take your food away or eat at informal tables (deli open Mon-Fri 7:00-18:00, Sat 7:30-12:00, closed Sun;

Schrettergasse 15 but facing Tauschergasse—roughly next door to the big Müller pharmacy and post office, tel. 05672/62640, www. storfwirt.at, helpful manager Rainer).

Picnic Supplies: Along Mühlerstrasse near the intersection with Untermarkt, is the **Ausserfern Bauernladen** (farmer's shop), which sells only locally produced products. You can buy picnic fixings here (cheeses, spreads, and *Heuwürstchen* or *Cabanossi* sausages are good), or ask them to make you a rustic sandwich to eat at one of the tables (Wed-Fri 9:00-18:00, Sat 9:00-12:00, closed Sun-Tue, Obermarkt 3, mobile 0676-575-4588).

Billa supermarket also has everything you'll need for a picnic (across from TI, Mon-Fri 7:15-19:30, Sat 7:15-18:00, closed Sun).

Reutte Connections

From Reutte by Train to: Ehrwald (at base of Zugspitze lift, every 2 hours, 30 minutes), **Garmisch** (same train, every 2 hours, 1 hour), **Innsbruck** (every 2 hours, 2.5 hours, change in Garmisch), **Munich** (every 2 hours, 2.5 hours, change in Garmisch), **Salzburg** (every 2 hours, 5 hours, change in Garmisch and Munich). Austrian train info: tel. 051-717 (to get an operator, dial 2, then 2), www. oebb.at; German train info: tel. 0180-599-6633, www.bahn.com.

By Bus to: Füssen (#4258—but known as #74 in Germany, Mon-Fri 6/day, Sat-Sun 4/day, last bus at 17:30, 30-50 minutes, €4.30 one-way, buses depart from train station, pay driver).

Taxi service is available to hotel guests with an Acktiv-Card (described on page 177; ask your hotelier for further details).

ROUTE TIPS FOR DRIVERS

From downtown Reutte, *Fernpass* signs lead you out to the main Innsbruck road, which is also the best way to reach the Ehrenberg ruins. To reach the Ehrenberg Castle ruins, the Biberwier luge, the Zugspitze (either the Austrian ascent at Ehrwald or the German ascent at Garmisch), or Innsbruck, turn right for the on-ramp (marked Fernpass and Innsbruck) to highway 179. But if you're headed for Germany via the scenic Plansee Lake, Linderhof Castle, Ettal Monastery, or Oberammergau, continue straight (bypassing the highway on-ramp).

SALZBURG AND BERCHTESGADEN

Salzburg, just over the Austrian border, makes a fun day trip from Munich (1.5 hours by direct train). Thanks to its charmingly preserved Old Town, splendid gardens, Baroque churches, and one of Europe's largest intact medieval fortresses, Salzburg feels made for tourism. As a musical mecca, the city puts on a huge annual festival, as well as constant concerts. Salzburgers are forever smiling to the tunes of Mozart and *The Sound of Music*. It's a city with class. Vagabonds visiting here wish they had nicer clothes.

In the mountains just outside Salzburg is Berchtesgaden, a German alpine town that was once a favorite of Adolf Hitler's, but thrills a better class of nature lover today.

PLANNING YOUR TIME

While Salzburg's museums are, frankly, mediocre, the town itself is a Baroque showpiece of cobbled streets and elegant buildings— simply a touristy stroller's delight. Even if your time is short, consider allowing half a day for the *Sound of Music* tour. The *S.O.M.* bus tour kills a nest of sightseeing birds with one ticket (city overview, *S.O.M.* sights, and a fine drive by the lakes).

You'd probably enjoy at least two nights in Salzburg—nights are important for swilling beer in atmospheric local gardens and attending concerts in Baroque halls and chapels. Seriously consider one of Salzburg's many evening musical events (a few are free, some are as low as €22, and most average €40).

To get away from it all, bike down the river or hike across the Mönchsberg cliffs that rise directly from the middle of town. Or consider swinging by Berchtesgaden, just 15 miles away, in Germany. A direct bus gets you there from Salzburg in 45 minutes.

Salzburg, Austria

Even without Mozart and the von Trapps, Salzburg is steeped in history. In about A.D. 700, Bavaria gave Salzburg to Bishop Rupert

in return for his promise to Christianize the area. Salzburg remained an independent city (belonging to no state) until Napoleon came by in the early 1800s. Thanks in part to its formidable fortress, Salzburg managed to avoid the ravages of war for 1,200 years...until World War II. Allied bombing destroyed many buildings (especially around the train station), but the historic Old Town survived.

Today, eight million tourists crawl Salzburg's cobbles each year. That's a lot of Mozart balls—and all that popularity has led to a glut of businesses hoping to catch the tourist dollar. Still, Salzburg is both a must and a joy.

Orientation to Salzburg

Salzburg, a city of 150,000 (Austria's fourth-largest), is divided into old and new. The Old Town (Altstadt), between the Salzach River and Salzburg's mini-mountain (Mönchsberg), holds nearly all the charm and most of the tourists. The New Town (Neustadt), across the river, has the train station, a few sights and museums, and some good accommodations.

Welcome to Austria: Austria uses the same euro currency as Germany, but postage stamps and phone cards only work in the country where you buy them.

To **telephone** from Germany to Austria, dial 00-43 and then the number listed in this section (omitting the initial zero). To call from Austria to Germany, dial 00-49 and then the number (again, omitting the initial zero).

Austria requires a **toll sticker** *(Vignette)* for driving on its expressways (€8.50/10 days, buy at the border, gas stations, car-rental agencies, or *Tabak* shops). To avoid the A-1 toll road between the German border and Salzburg, you can exit the A-8 autobahn at Bad Reichenall while you're still in Germany, take B-20, and then B-21, which becomes B-1 as it crosses the border (this adds about 10 minutes to the drive). You'll be fine without a toll sticker on a drive to Hallstatt, provided you stick to the most direct route (B-158 via St. Gilgen), which doesn't use the autobahn.

TOURIST INFORMATION

Salzburg has three helpful TIs (main tel. 0662/889-870, www.
salzburg.info): at the **train station** (daily 9:00-18:00, May-

Sept until 19:00; tel.
0662/8898-7340); on **Mozartplatz** in the old center
(daily 9:00-18:00, July-
Aug until 19:00, closed
Sun Sept-March; tel.
0662/8898-7330); and at
the **Alpensiedlung parkand-ride** (May-Sept Thu-
Sat 10:00-16:30, generally closed Sun-Wed, closed Oct-April; tel.
0662/8898-7360).

At any TI, you can pick up a free city-center map (the €0.70
map has a broader coverage and more information on sights, and
is particularly worthwhile if biking out of town), the free bus map
(*Liniennetz;* shows bus stop names not on the city map), the Salzburg Card brochure (listing sights with current hours and prices),
and a bimonthly events guide. The TIs also book rooms (€2.20 fee
and 10 percent deposit). Inside the Mozartplatz TI is the privately
run Salzburg Ticket Service counter, where you can book concert
tickets (see "Music in Salzburg," page 241).

Salzburg Card: The TIs sell the Salzburg Card, which covers all your public transportation (including the Mönchsberg elevator and funicular to the fortress) and admission to all the city
sights (including Hellbrunn Palace and a river cruise). The card is
pricey, but if you'd like to pop into all the sights, it can save money
and enhance your experience (€26/24 hours, €35/48 hours, €41/72
hours, www.salzburg.info). To analyze your potential savings, here
are the major sights and what you'd pay without the card: Hohensalzburg Fortress and funicular-€11.30; Mozart's Birthplace and
Residence-€17; Hellbrunn Palace-€10.50; Salzburg Panorama
1829-€3; DomQuartier Museums-€12; Salzach River cruise-€15;
24-hour transit pass-€3.40. Busy sightseers can save plenty. Get
this card, feel the financial pain once, and the city will be all yours.

ARRIVAL IN SALZBURG

By Train: The Salzburg station, gleaming white after a multi-year
renovation, has all the services you need: train information, tourist
information, luggage lockers (€2-4.50) and a WC (€0.50, both by
platform 5), and a handy Spar supermarket (Mon-Sat 6:00-23:00,
Sun 8:00-23:00). Ticket counters for both the Austrian and German railways are off the main hall (Mon-Sat 5:30-21:15, Sun 6:30-
21:15). If you're looking for the TI, follow the green-and-white
information signs (the blue-and-white ones lead to a railway "Info-

Point"). A transit info desk, down the escalator from the TI or bus platforms, has information on local buses (Mon-Fri 6:00-18:45, Sat 7:30-14:45, closed Sun). Next to the train station is Forum 1, a sizable shopping mall.

Getting downtown from the station is a snap. Simply step outside, find **bus platform C** (labeled *Zentrum-Altstadt*), buy a ticket from the machine, and hop on the next bus. Buses #1, #3, #5, #6, and #25 all do the same route into the city center before diverging. For most sights and Old Town hotels, get off just after the bridge, at the fifth stop (either Rathaus or Hanuschplatz, depending on the bus). For my recommended New Town hotels, get off at Makartplatz (the fourth stop), just before the bridge.

Taxis don't make much sense to get from the train station into town, as they're expensive for short rides (€2.50 drop charge, about €8 for most rides in town).

To **walk** downtown (15 minutes), turn left as you leave the station, and walk straight down Rainerstrasse, which leads under the tracks past Mirabellplatz, turning into Dreifaltigkeitsgasse. From here, you can turn left onto Linzer Gasse for many of my recommended hotels, or cross the river to the Old Town. For a slightly longer but more dramatic approach, leave the station the same way but follow the tracks to the river, turn left, and walk the riverside path toward the fortress.

By Car: Mozart never drove in Salzburg's Old Town, and neither should you. The best place to park is the **park-and-ride** lot at the Alpensiedlung bus stop, near the Salzburg Süd autobahn exit. Coming on A-8 from Munich, cross the border into Austria. Take A-10 toward Hallein, and then take the next exit (Salzburg Süd) in the direction of Anif, and look for *P+R* signs. You'll pass Hellbrunn Castle (and the zoo) before arriving at the park-and-ride (€5/24 hours). From the parking lot, catch bus #3 or #8 into town. The TI, in a small building next to the lot, sells bus tickets for less than bus drivers (24-hour transit pass-€3.40 at TI, €5.50 from driver). Alternatively, groups of 2-5 people can buy a combo-ticket from the parking lot attendant, which includes the 24-hour parking fee and a 24-hour transit pass for the whole group (€14, €12 from July-Aug, group must stay together).

If you don't believe in park-and-rides, head to the easiest, cheapest, most central parking lot—the 1,500-car Altstadtgarage, in the tunnel under the Mönchsberg (€18/day, note your slot number and which of the twin lots you're in, tel. 0662/809-900).

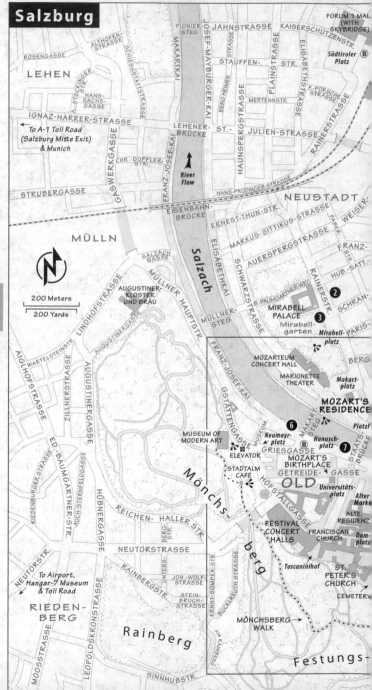

Salzburg

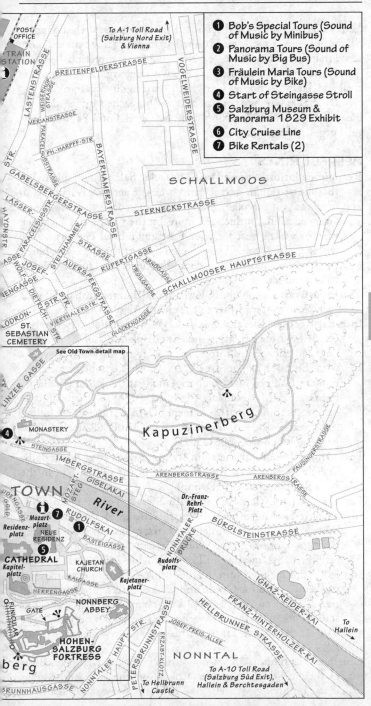

1. Bob's Special Tours (Sound of Music by Minibus)
2. Panorama Tours (Sound of Music by Big Bus)
3. Fräulein Maria Tours (Sound of Music by Bike)
4. Start of Steingasse Stroll
5. Salzburg Museum & Panorama 1829 Exhibit
6. City Cruise Line
7. Bike Rentals (2)

POST OFFICE
TRAIN STATION

To A-1 Toll Road (Salzburg Nord Exit) & Vienna

LASTENSTRASSE
BREITENFELDERSTRASSE
WEISERHOF STRASSE
MERIANSTRASSE
PARACELSUSSTRASSE
PH.-HARPFF-STR.
VOGELWEIDERSTRASSE
BAYERHAMERSTRASSE
GABELSBERGERSTRASSE
STR.
LASSER
HAYDNSTR
GASSE
WOLF-DIETRICH-STR.
JOSEF-MENGASSE
PARACELSUSSTR.
STELZHAMER-STRASSE
AUERSPERGSTRASSE
RUPERTGASSE
ARNOGASSE
YRGLGASSE
VIERTHALERSTR.
LODRON-GASSE
ST. SEBASTIAN CEMETERY
GLÖCKENGASSE

SCHALLMOOS
STERNECKSTRASSE
SCHALLMOOSER HAUPTSTRASSE

See Old Town detail map

LINZER GASSE
MONASTERY
STEINGASSE
IMBERGSTRASSE
MOZART STEG
GISELAKAI
TOWN
River
UDENGASSE
GOLD-
Mozart-platz
RUDOLFSKAI
Residenz-platz
NEUE RESIDENZ
BASTEIGASSE
CATHEDRAL
Kapitel-platz
KAJETAN CHURCH
KAIGASSE
Kajetaner-platz
HERRENGASSE
FUNICULAR
GATE
NONNBERG ABBEY
HOHEN-SALZBURG FORTRESS
berg
BRUNNHAUSGASSE
NONNTALER HAUPT-STR.
PETERSBRUNNSTRASSE
ERZABT-KLOTZ STR.
JOSEF-PREIS-ALLEE

Kapuzinerberg

ARENBERGSTRASSE
ARENBERGSTRASSE
FAUZINGERSTRASSE

Dr.-Franz-Rehrl-Platz
BÜRGLSTEINSTRASSE
NONNTALER BRÜCKE
Rudolfs-platz
IGNAZ-REIDER-KAI
FRANZ-HINTERHOLZER-KAI
HELLBRUNNER STRASSE
NONNTAL
To A-10 Toll Road (Salzburg Süd Exit), Hallein & Berchtesgaden

To Hellbrunn Castle

To Hallein

Your hotel may provide discounted parking passes. If staying in Salzburg's New Town, the Mirabell-Congress garage makes more sense than the Altstadtgarage (see page 244 for directions).

For more info on parking, see www.salzburg.info (under "Arrival and Traffic," choose "Car," then "Parking in Salzburg.")

By Plane: Salzburg's airport is easily reached by regular city buses #2, #10, and #27 (airport code: SZG, tel. 0662/85800, www.salzburg-airport.com).

HELPFUL HINTS

Recommendations Skewed by Kickbacks: Salzburg is addicted to the tourist dollar, and it can never get enough. Virtually all hotels are on the take when it comes to concert and tour recommendations, influenced more by their potential kickback than by what's best for you. Take any tour or concert advice with a grain of salt. If you book a concert through your hotel, you'll probably lose the discount I've negotiated for my readers who go direct.

Music Festival: The Salzburg Festival (Salzburger Festspiele) runs each year from mid-July to the end of August (see page 243).

Internet Access: The city has **free Wi-Fi** hotspots at Mirabell Gardens, Mozartplatz, and Kapitelplatz (choose *Salzburg surft* and click *Agree*, info at www.salzburg-surft.at). Travelers with this book can get free Wi-Fi or use a computer for a few minutes (long enough to check email) at the Panorama Tours terminal on Mirabellplatz (daily 8:00-18:00). If you need to print something, the **Ibis Internet Café** is at the train station, right next to the entrance (daily 8:00-22:00, €3/hour, €0.20/page, mobile 0676-8686-2502).

Post Office: The one at the train station is open long hours daily. There's another branch in the heart of the Old Town, in the New Residenz (closed Sat-Sun).

Laundry: A handy **launderette** with a few self-serve machines is at Paris-Lodron-Strasse 16, at the corner of Wolf-Dietrich-Strasse, near my recommended Linzer Gasse hotels—or take bus #2, #4, or #21 to the Wolf-Dietrich-Strasse stop (€10 self-service, €15 same-day full-service, Mon-Fri 7:30-18:00, Sat 8:00-12:00, closed Sun, tel. 0662/876-381). On evenings and weekends, head for **Green and Clean**, three stops beyond the train station on the #1 or #2 bus; board from platform D at station, get off at the Gaswerkgasse stop (about €9/load, daily 6:00-22:00, Ignaz-Harrer-Strasse 32, www.greenandclean.at).

Cinema: Das Kino is an art-house movie theater that plays films in their original language (a block off the river and Linzer Gasse on Steingasse, tel. 0662/873-100, www.daskino.at).

Smoking Policies: Unlike Germany, which can implement sweeping reforms overnight, conservative Austria has been slow to embrace the smoke-free movement. By law, big restaurants must offer smoke-free zones (and smoking zones, if they choose). Smaller places choose to be either smoking or non-smoking, indicated by red or green stickers on the door.

Market Days: Popular farmer's markets pop up at Universitätsplatz in the Old Town on Saturdays and around the Andräkirche in the New Town on Thursdays. On summer weekends, a string of craft booths with fun goodies for sale stretches along the river.

Morning Joggers: Salzburg is a great place for jogging. Within minutes you can be huffing and puffing "The hills are alive..." in green meadows outside of town. The obvious best bets in town are through the Mirabell Gardens along its riverbank pedestrian lanes.

Updates to This Book: For updates to this book, check www.ricksteves.com/update.

GETTING AROUND SALZBURG

By Bus: Most visitors take at least a couple of rides on Salzburg's extensive bus system. Everything in this book is within the *Kernzone* (core zone). At *Tabak/Trafik* shops and scarce ticket machines, you can buy €1.70 single-ride tickets or a €3.40 day pass *(24-Stunden-Karte)* good for 24 hours (€2.50 and €5.50 from the driver, respectively). If you'll be in Salzburg for at least five days, the €14.60 *Wochenkarte* makes sense (valid 7 calendar days, starting with the day you validate it). Remember to validate your ticket after purchase (insert it in the machines on board).

Get oriented using the free bus map *(Liniennetz)*, available at the TI. Many lines converge at Hanuschplatz, on the Old Town side of the river, in front of the recommended Fisch Krieg Restaurant. To get from the Old Town to the train station, catch bus #1 from the inland side of Hanuschplatz. From the other side of the river, find the Makartplatz/Theatergasse stop and catch bus #1, #3, #5, or #6. Busy stops like Hanuschplatz and Mirabellplatz have several bus shelters; look for your bus number to double-check where exactly you should stand.

For more information, visit www.svv-info.at, call 0662/632-900 (open 24 hours), or visit the office downstairs from bus platform C in front of the train station (Mon-Fri 6:00-18:45, Sat 7:30-14:45, closed Sun).

By Bike: Salzburg is great fun for cyclists. The following two bike-rental shops offer 20 percent off to anyone with this book—ask for it: **Top Bike** rents bikes on the river next to the Staatsbrücke (€6/2 hours, €10/4 hours, €15/24 hours, usually daily April-June and Sept-Oct 10:00-17:00, July-Aug 9:00-19:00, closed Nov-March, easy 24/7 return, show this book for 20 percent discount off these prices and free helmet, mobile 0676-476-7259, www.topbike.at, Sabine). **A'Velo Radladen** rents bikes in the Old Town, just outside the TI on Mozartplatz (€4.50/1 hour, €10/4 hours, €16/24 hours, more for electric or mountain bikes; daily 9:00-18:00, until 19:00 July-Aug, but hours unreliable, shorter hours off-season and in bad weather; passport number for security deposit, mobile 0676-435-5950, www.a-velo.at). Some of my recommended hotels and pensions also rent or loan bikes to guests.

By Funicular and Elevator: The Old Town is connected to the top of the Mönchsberg mountain (and great views) via funicular and elevator. The **funicular** *(Festungsbahn)* whisks you up into the imposing Hohensalzburg Fortress (included in castle admission, goes every few minutes—for details, see page 225). The **elevator** (Mönchsberg Aufzug) on the west side of the Old Town lifts you to the recommended Stadtalm Café, the Museum of Modern Art and its chic café, wooded paths, and more great views (€2.10 one-way, €3.40 round-trip, normally Mon 8:00-19:00, Tue-Sun 8:00-23:00).

By Buggy: The horse buggies *(Fiaker)* that congregate at Residenzplatz charge €40 for a 25-minute trot around the Old Town (www.fiaker-salzburg.at).

Tours in Salzburg

Walking Tours

Any day of the week, you can take a one-hour guided walk of the Old Town without a reservation—just show up at the TI on Mozartplatz and pay the guide. The tours are informative. While generally in English only, on slow days you may be listening to everything in both German and English (€9, daily at 12:15, Mon-Sat also at 14:00, tel. 0662/8898-7330). To save money, you can easily do it on your own using this chapter's self-guided walk (or download a free Rick Steves **audio tour** of my walk to your mobile device—see page 12).

Local Guides

Salzburg is home to over a hundred licensed guides. I have worked with three who are well worth recommending: **Christiana Schnee-weiss** ("Snow White") has been instrumental in both my guide-book research and my TV production in Salzburg, and has her own minibus for private tours outside of town (on foot: €135/2 hours, €165/3 hours; with minibus: €240/4 hours, €350-450/day, up to 6 people; mobile 0664-340-1757, other options explained at www.kultur-tourismus.com, info@kultur-tourismus.com). Two other excellent guides, both a joy to learn from, are **Sabine Rath** (€155/2 hours, €205/4 hours, €310/8 hours, mobile 0664-201-6492, www.tourguide-salzburg.com, info@tourguide-salzburg.com, ask about her creepy witch tours and her Empress Sisi tours) and **Anna Stellnberger** (€150/2 hours, €190/4 hours, €280/8 hours, mobile 0664-787-5177, anna.stellnberger@aon.at). Salzburg has many other good guides (for a list, see www.salzburgguides.at).

Boat Tours

City Cruise Line (a.k.a. Stadt Schiff-Fahrt) runs a basic 40-minute round-trip river cruise with recorded commentary (€15, 9/day July-Aug, 7/day May-June, fewer Sept-Oct and March-April, no boats Nov-Feb). For a longer cruise, ride to Hellbrunn (€18, daily April-Oct at 14:00) and return by bus. Boats leave from the Old Town side of the river just downstream of the Makartsteg bridge (tel. 0662/825-858, www.salzburghighlights.at). While views can be cramped, passengers are treated to a fun finale just before docking, when the captain twirls a fun "waltz."

▲▲The Sound of Music Tours

Salzburg is the joyful setting of *The Sound of Music*. The Broadway musical and 1965 movie tell the story of a stern captain who hires a governess for his unruly children and ends up marrying her. Though the movie took plenty of Hollywood liberties (see "*The Sound of Music* Debunked"), it's based on the actual von Trapp family from Austria. They really did come from Salzburg. Maria really was a governess who became the captain's wife. They did sing in the Festival Hall, they did escape from the Nazis, and they ended up after the war in Vermont, where Maria passed away in 1987.

Salzburg today has a number of *Sound of Music* sights—mostly locations where the movie was shot, but also some actual places associated with the von Trapps. Some of the main ones are:

- The Mirabell Gardens, with its arbor and Pegasus statue, where the kids sing "Do-Re-Mi."
- Festival Hall, where the real-life von Trapps performed, and where (in the movie) they sing "Edelweiss."
- St. Peter's Cemetery, the inspiration for the scene where the family hides from Nazi guards (it was actually filmed on a Hollywood set).
- Nonnberg Abbey, where the nuns sing "How Do You Solve a Problem like Maria?"
- Leopoldskron Palace, which serves as the von Trapps' idyllic lakeside home in the movie (though it wasn't their actual home).
- Hellbrunn Palace gardens, where the famous gazebo in "I am Sixteen" has found a home.

There are many more sights—the horse pond, the wedding

The Sound of Music Debunked

Rather than visit the real-life sights from the life of Maria von Trapp and family, most tourists want to see the places where Hollywood chose to film this fanciful story. Local guides are happy not to burst any *S.O.M.* pilgrim's bubble, but keep these points in mind:

- "Edelweiss" is not a cherished Austrian folk tune or national anthem. Like all the "Austrian" music in *The S.O.M.*, it was composed for Broadway by Rodgers and Hammerstein. It was the last composition that the famed team wrote together, as Hammerstein died in 1960—nine months after the musical opened.
- *The S.O.M.* implies that Maria was devoutly religious throughout her life, but Maria's foster parents raised her as a socialist and atheist. Maria discovered her religious calling while studying to be a teacher. After completing school, she joined the convent not as a nun, but as a novitiate (that is, she hadn't taken her vows yet).
- Maria's position was not as governess to all the children, as portrayed in the musical, but specifically as governess and teacher for the Captain's second-oldest daughter, also called Maria, who was bedridden with rheumatic fever.
- The Captain didn't run a tight domestic ship. In fact, his seven children were as unruly as most. But he did use a whistle to call them—each kid was trained to respond to a certain pitch.
- Though the von Trapp family did have seven children, the show changed all their names and even their genders. As an adult, Rupert, the eldest child, responded to the often-asked question, "Which one are you?" with a simple, "I'm Liesl!" Maria and the Captain later had three more children together.
- The family didn't escape by hiking to Switzerland (which is a five-hour drive away). Rather, they pretended to go on one of their frequent mountain hikes. With only the possessions in their backpacks, they "hiked" all the way to the train

church, the fountain in Residenzplatz. Since they're scattered throughout greater Salzburg, taking a tour is the best way to see them efficiently.

I took a *S.O.M.* tour skeptically (as part of my research)—and had a great time. The bus tour version includes a quick but good general city tour, hits the *S.O.M.* spots, and—something that's worthwhile even for non-*S.O.M.* fans—shows you a lovely stretch of the Salzkammergut Lake District. Warning: Many think rolling through the Austrian countryside with 30 Americans singing "Doe, a deer..." is pretty schmaltzy. Local Austrians don't understand all the commotion. (Many have never heard of the movie.) For more on *S.O.M.*, see the sidebar.

station (it was at the edge of their estate) and took a train to Italy. The movie scene showing them climbing into Switzerland was actually filmed near Berchtesgaden, Germany... home to Hitler's Eagle's Nest, and certainly not a smart place to flee to.

- The actual von Trapp family house exists...but it's not the one in the film. The mansion in the movie is actually two different buildings—one used for the front, the other for the back. The interiors were all filmed on Hollywood sets.
- For the film, Boris Levin designed a reproduction of the Nonnberg Abbey courtyard so faithful to the original (down to its cobblestones and stained-glass windows) that many still believe the cloister scenes were really shot at the abbey. And no matter what you hear in Salzburg, the graveyard scene (in which the von Trapps hide from the Nazis) was also filmed on the Fox lot.
- In 1956, a German film producer offered Maria $10,000 for the rights to her book. She asked for royalties, too, and a share of the profits. The agent claimed that German law forbids film companies from paying royalties to foreigners (Maria had by then become a US citizen). She agreed to the contract and unknowingly signed away all film rights to her story. Only a few weeks later, he offered to pay immediately if she would accept $9,000 in cash. Because it was more money than the family had seen in all of their years of singing, she accepted the deal. Later, she discovered the agent had swindled them—no such law existed.

Rodgers, Hammerstein, and other producers gave the von Trapps a percentage of the royalties, even though they weren't required to—but it was a fraction of what they otherwise would have earned. But Maria wasn't bitter. She said, "The great good the film and the play are doing to individual lives is far beyond money."

Two companies do *S.O.M.* tours by bus (Bob's and Panorama), while a third company does a bike version. It's best to reserve ahead. Note: Your hotel will be eager to call to reserve for you—to get their commission—but you won't get the discount I've negotiated.

Minibus Option: Most of **Bob's Special Tours** use an eight-seat minibus (and occasionally a 20-seat bus) and therefore have good access to Old Town sights, promote a more casual feel, and spend less time waiting to load and unload. Online bookings close three days prior to the tour date—after that, email, call, or stop by the office to reserve (€48 for adults—€42 with this book if you pay cash and book direct, €42 for kids aged 7-15 and students with ID, €36 for kids 6 and under—includes required car seat but must reserve in advance; daily at 9:00 and 14:00 year-round, tours leave from Bob's office along the river just east of Mozartplatz at Rudolfskai 38, tel. 0662/849-511, mobile 0664-541-7492, office@bobstours. com, www.bobstours.com). Nearly all of Bob's tours stop for a fun luge ride in Fuschl am See when the weather is dry (mountain bobsled-€4.50 extra, generally April-Oct, confirm beforehand).

For a private minibus tour consider **Christina Schneeweiss,** who does an *S.O.M.* tour with more history and fewer jokes (€240, up to 6 people, see "Local Guides," earlier).

Big-Bus Option: Panorama Tours depart from their smart kiosk at Mirabellplatz daily at 9:15 and 14:00 year-round (€40, €5 discount for *S.O.M.* tours with this book if you pay in cash and don't need hotel pickup, book by calling 0662/874-029 or 0662/883-2110, discount not valid for online reservations, www. panoramatours.com). Many travelers appreciate their more businesslike feel, roomier buses, and higher vantage point.

Bike Tours by "Fräulein Maria": For some exercise with your *S.O.M.* tour, you can meet your guide (likely a man) at the Mirabell Gardens (at Mirabellplatz 4, 50 yards to the left of palace entry). The main attractions that you'll pass during the eight-mile pedal include the Mirabell Gardens, the horse pond, St. Peter's Cemetery, Nonnberg Abbey, Leopoldskron Palace, and, of course, the gazebo. The tour is very family-friendly, and you'll get lots of stops for goofy photo ops (€26 includes bike, €18 for kids ages 13-18, €12 for kids under age 13, €2 discount for adults and kids with this book, daily May-Sept at 9:30, June-Aug also at 16:30, allow 3.5 hours, reservations required for afternoon tours and recommended for morning tours, mobile 0650-342-6297, www.mariasbicycletours.com). For €8 extra (€20 per family), you're welcome to keep the bike all day.

BEYOND SALZBURG

Both Bob's and Panorama Tours also offer an extensive array of other day trips from Salzburg (e.g., Berchtesgaden/Eagle's Nest, salt mines, Hallstatt, and Salzkammergut lakes and mountains). One efficient tour worth considering is Bob's full-day *Sound of Music/Hallstatt Tour,* which first covers everything in the standard four-hour *S.O.M.* tour, then continues for a four-hour look at the scenic, lake-speckled Salzkammergut, with free time to explore charming Hallstatt (€96, €12 discount if you show this book, pay cash, and book direct; doesn't include entrance fees to optional Hallstatt sights such as salt mine; departs daily at 9:00; Rudolfskai

38, tel. 0662/849-511, mobile 0664-541-7492, office@bobstours. com, www.bobstours.com).

Salzburg Old Town Walk

I've linked the best sights in the Old Town into this handy self-guided orientation walk (rated ▲▲▲). You can download a free Rick Steves **audio tour** of this walk; see page 12.

• *Begin at the Mozartsteg, the pedestrian bridge over the Salzach River.*

❶ Mozartsteg

Get your bearings: The river flows west to east. On the north bank is the New Town. The south side is the Old Town, dominated by a castle on a hill.

Take in the charming, well-preserved, historic core of Salzburg's Old Town. The skyline bristles with Baroque steeples and green, copper domes. Salzburg has 38 Catholic churches, plus two Protestant churches and a synagogue. The biggest green dome is the cathedral, which we'll visit shortly. Overlooking it all is the castle called the Hohensalzburg Fortress. Far to the right of the fortress, find the Museum of Modern Art—it looks like a mini-castle, but that's actually a water reservoir alongside the modern building.

The milky-green Salzach River thunders under your feet. It's called "salt river" not because it's salty, but because of the precious cargo it once carried. The salt mines of Hallein are just nine miles upstream. For 2,000 years, barges carried the precious salt from here to the wider world—to the Danube, the Black Sea, and on to the Mediterranean. As barges passed through here, they had to pay a toll on their salt. The city was born from the trading of salt (*salz*) defended by a castle (*burg*)—"Salz-burg."

• *Now let's plunge into Salzburg's Old Town. From the bridge, walk one block toward the hill-capping castle into the Old Town. Pass the traffic barriers (that keep this quiet town free of too much traffic) and turn right into a big square—Mozartplatz.*

❷ Mozartplatz

All the tourists around you probably wouldn't be here if not for the man honored by this statue—Wolfgang Amadeus Mozart. The great composer spent most of his first 25 years (1756-1781) in Salzburg. He was born just a few blocks from here. He and his father both served Salzburg's rulers before Wolfgang went on to seek his fortune in Vienna. The statue (considered a poor

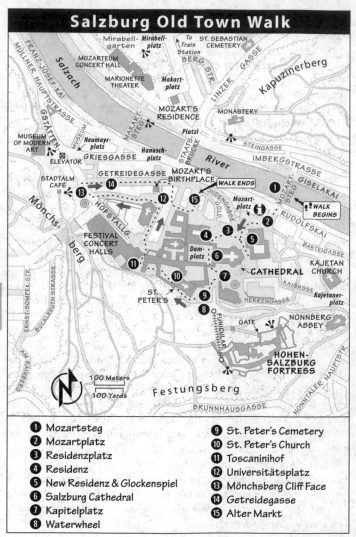

Salzburg Old Town Walk

1. Mozartsteg
2. Mozartplatz
3. Residenzplatz
4. Residenz
5. New Residenz & Glockenspiel
6. Salzburg Cathedral
7. Kapitelplatz
8. Waterwheel
9. St. Peter's Cemetery
10. St. Peter's Church
11. Toscaninihof
12. Universitätsplatz
13. Mönchsberg Cliff Face
14. Getreidegasse
15. Alter Markt

likeness) was erected in 1842, just after the 50th anniversary of Mozart's death. The music festival of that year planted the seed for what would become the now world-renowned Salzburg Festival.

Mozart stands atop the spot where the first Salzburgers settled. Two thousand years ago, the Romans had a salt-trading town here called Juvavum. In the year 800, Salzburg—by then Christian and home to an important abbey—joined Charlemagne's Holy Roman Empire as an independent city. The Church of St. Michael (whose tower overlooks the square) dates from that time. It's Salzburg's oldest, if not biggest, church.

You may see lots of conservative Muslim families vacationing here. While there are plenty of Muslims in Austria, many of the conservatively dressed women you'll see here are from the United Arab Emirates. Lots of wealthy families from the Middle East come here in the summer to escape the heat back home, to enjoy a break from their very controlled societies, or for medical treatment. Nearby Munich is a popular destination for hospital visits, and the entire family usually joins in for sightseeing and shopping.

• *Before moving on, note the TI (which also sells concert tickets). Also, looking back past Mozart's statue, you may catch a glimpse of a TV tower. This stands atop the 4,220-foot-high Gaisberg hill. The summit is a favorite destination for local nature lovers and strong bikers. Now walk toward the cathedral and into the big square with the huge fountain.*

❸ Residenzplatz

As Salzburg's governing center, this square has long been ringed with important buildings. The cathedral borders the south side. The Residenz—the former palace of Salzburg's rulers—is to the right (as you face the cathedral). To the left is the New Residenz, with its bell tower.

In the 1600s, this square got a makeover in the then-fashionable Italian Baroque style. The rebuilding started under energetic Prince-Archbishop Wolf Dietrich, who ruled from 1587 to 1612. Dietrich had been raised in Rome. He counted the Medicis as his cousins, and had grandiose Italian ambitions for Salzburg. Fortunately for him, the cathedral conveniently burned down in 1598. Dietrich set about rebuilding it as part of his grand vision to make Salzburg the "Rome of the North."

The fountain is as Italian as can be, an over-the-top version of Bernini's famous Triton Fountain in Rome. It shows Triton on top blowing his conch-shell horn. The water cascades down the basins and sprays playfully in the wind.

Notice that Salzburg's buildings are made from three distinctly different types of stone. Most common is the chunky grey conglomerate (like the cathedral's side walls) quarried from the nearby cliffs. There's also white marble (like the cathedral's towers and windows) and red marble (best seen in monuments inside buildings), both from the Alps near Berchtesgaden.

• *Turn your attention to...*

❹ The Residenz

This was the palace of Salzburg's powerful ruler, the prince-archbishop—that is, a ruler with both the political powers of a prince

Salzburg at a Glance

▲▲▲**Salzburg Old Town Walk** Old Town's best sights in handy orientation walk. **Hours:** Always open. See page 207.

▲▲**Salzburg Cathedral** Glorious, harmonious Baroque main church of Salzburg. **Hours:** May-Sept Mon-Sat 9:00-19:00, Sun 13:00-19:00; March-April, Oct, and Dec closes at 18:00; Jan-Feb and Nov closes at 17:00. See page 212.

▲▲**Getreidegasse** Picturesque old shopping lane with characteristic wrought-iron signs. **Hours:** Always open. See page 219.

▲▲**Hohensalzburg Fortress** Imposing castle capping the mountain overlooking town, with tourable grounds, several mini-museums, commanding views, and good evening concerts. **Hours:** Fortress museums open daily May-Sept 9:00-19:00, Oct-April 9:30-17:00. Concerts nearly nightly. See page 225.

▲▲**Salzburg Museum** Best place to learn more about the city's history. **Hours:** Tue-Sun 9:00-17:00, closed Mon. See page 221.

▲▲*The Sound of Music* **Tour** Cheesy but fun tour through the S.O.M. sights of Salzburg and the surrounding Salzkammergut Lake District, by minibus, big bus, or bike. **Hours:** Various options daily at 9:00, 9:15, 9:30, 14:00, and 16:30. See page 203.

▲▲**Mozart's Birthplace** House where Mozart was born in 1756, featuring his instruments and other exhibits. **Hours:** Daily 9:00-17:30, July-Aug until 20:00. See page 223.

▲▲**Hellbrunn Palace** Lavish palace on the outskirts of town featuring gardens with trick fountains. **Hours:** Daily May-Sept 9:00-17:30, July-Aug until 21:00, April and Oct 9:00-16:30, closed Nov-March. See page 237.

▲**DomQuartier Museums** Prince-Archbishop Wolf Dietrich's palace, a cathedral viewpoint, and adjoining buildings covering

and the religious authority of an archbishop. The ornate Baroque entrance attests to the connections these rulers had with Rome. You can step inside the Residenz courtyard to get a glimpse of the impressive digs.

To see the Residenz interior you must buy a DomQuartier ticket (see page 220). This admits you to the fancy chandeliered state rooms and an impressive collection of paintings.

Notice that the Residenz has a white-stone structure (called the Cathedral Terrace) connecting it with the cathedral. This sky-

religious art and Salzburg history. **Hours:** Tue-Sun 10:00-17:00, closed Mon except in July-Aug. See page 220.

▲**Salzburg Panorama 1829** A vivid peek at the city in 1829. **Hours:** Daily 9:00-17:00. See page 222.

▲**Mozart's Residence** Restored house where the composer lived. **Hours:** Daily 9:00-17:30, July-Aug until 20:00. See page 234.

▲**Mönchsberg Walk** "The hills are alive" stroll you can enjoy right in downtown Salzburg. **Hours:** Doable anytime during daylight hours. See page 231.

▲**Mirabell Gardens and Palace** Beautiful palace complex with fine views, Salzburg's best concert venue, and *Sound of Music* memories. **Hours:** Gardens—always open; concerts—free in the park May-Aug Sun at 10:30, in the palace nearly nightly. See page 233.

▲**Steingasse** Historic cobbled lane with trendy pubs—a tranquil, tourist-free section of old Salzburg. **Hours:** Always open. See page 235.

▲**St. Sebastian Cemetery** Baroque cemetery with graves of Mozart's wife and father, and other Salzburg VIPs. **Hours:** Daily April-Oct 9:00-18:00, Nov-March 9:00-16:00. See page 236.

St. Peter's Cemetery Atmospheric old cemetery with mini-gardens overlooked by cliff face with monks' caves. **Hours:** Cemetery—daily June-Aug 6:30-21:30, April-May 6:30-20:00, Sept 6:30-19:00, Oct-March 6:30-18:00. See page 216.

St. Peter's Church Romanesque church with Rococo decor. **Hours:** Daily April-Oct 8:00-21:00, Nov-March 8:00-19:00. See page 216.

way gave the prince-archbishops an easy commute to church and a chance to worship while avoiding the public.

• *At the opposite end of Residenzplatz from the Residenz is the...*

❺ New (Neue) Residenz

In the days of the prince-archbishops, this building hosted parties in its lavish rooms. These days, the New Residenz houses two important sights: the Salzburg Museum and the Salzburg Panorama

1829 (see page 222). It's also home to the Heimatwerk, a fine shop showing off local handicrafts like dirndls and locally made jelly.

The New Residenz bell tower has a famous glockenspiel. This 17th-century carillon has 35 bells (cast in Antwerp) and chimes

daily at 7:00, 11:00, and 18:00. It also plays little tunes appropriate to the season. The mechanism is a big barrel with adjustable tabs that turns like a giant music box, pulling the right bells in the right rhythm. (Twice-weekly tours let you get up close to watch the glockenspiel action: €3, April-Oct Thu at 17:30 and Fri at 10:30, no tours Nov-March, meet at Salzburg Panorama 1829, no reservations needed—just show up).

Notice the tower's ornamental top: an upside-down heart in flames surrounds the solar system, representing how God loves all of creation.

Residenzplatz sets the tone for the whole town. From here, a series of interconnecting squares—like you'll see nowhere else—make a grand procession through the Old Town. Everywhere you go, you'll see similar Italian architecture. As you walk from square to square, notice how easily you slip from noisy and commercial to peaceful and reflective.

• *Exit the square by walking under the prince-archbishop's skyway. You'll step into the Cathedral Square or Domplatz. A good place to view the cathedral facade is from the far end of the square.*

❻ Salzburg Cathedral (Salzburger Dom)

Salzburg's cathedral (rated ▲▲) was one of the first Italian Baroque buildings north of the Alps. The dome stands 230 feet high. Two domed towers flank the entrance. Between them is a false-front roofline. The windows are flanked with classical half-columns and topped with heavy pediments. The facade is ringed with a Baroque balustrade, decorated with garlands and masks, and studded with statues. The whole look reminded visitors that Salzburg was the "Rome of the North."

The church, rebuilt under Wolf Dietrich, was consecrated in 1628. Experts differ on what motivated the builders. As it dates from the years of Catholic-Protestant warfare, it may have been meant to emphasize Salzburg's commitment to the Roman Catholic cause. Or it may have represented a peaceful alternative to the religious strife. Regardless, Salzburg's archbishop was the top papal official north of the Alps, and the city was the pope's northern outpost. With its rich salt production, Salzburg had enough money to stay out of the conflict and earn the nickname "The Fortified Island of Peace."

The cathedral was the center of power for the prince-archbishop in his religious role, and the cathedral square is surrounded by government buildings for his role as secular prince. (You visit some of these rooms as part of the DomQuartier Museums tour; see page 220.)

In the square, the **statue of Mary** (1771) is looking away from the church, welcoming visitors. Photo tip: Try looking at the statue while standing in the rear of the square, immediately under the middle arch. From the right perspective, you'll see that she's positioned to be crowned Queen of Heaven by the two angels on the church facade.

As you approach the church, pause at the iron entrance doors. The dates on the doors are milestones in the church's history. In the year 774, the first church was consecrated by St. Virgil (see his statue), an Irish monk who became Salzburg's bishop. In 1598, the original church burned. It was replaced in 1628 by the one you see today. The year 1959 marks a modern milestone: The cathedral had been severely damaged by a WWII bomb that blew through the dome. In 1959, the renovation was complete.

• *Go inside. Take some time to let your eyes adjust.*

The Cathedral Interior

The interior is clean and white, without excess decoration. Because it was built in just 14 years (from 1614 to 1628), the church boasts harmonious architecture. And it's big—330 feet long, 230 feet tall—built with sturdy pillars and broad arches. When Pope John Paul II visited in 1998, some 5,000 people packed the place.

Cost and Hours: Free, but donation prominently requested; May-Sept Mon-Sat 9:00-19:00, Sun 13:00-19:00; March-April, Oct, and Dec until 18:00; Jan-Feb and Nov until 17:00; www. salzburger-dom.at.

Visiting the Cathedral: At the back pew, black-and-white photos show the bomb damage of October 16, 1944, which left a gaping hole where the dome once was. In the first chapel on the left is a dark bronze baptismal font. It dates from 1320—a rare survivor from the medieval cathedral. In 1756, little Wolfgang Amadeus Mozart was baptized here. For the next 25 years, this would be his home church. Amadeus, by the way, means "beloved by God."

As you make your way slowly up the nave, notice how you're drawn toward the light. Imagine being part of a sacred procession, passing from the relatively dim entrance to the bright altar with its painting of Christ's resurrection, bathed in light from the dome overhead. The church never had stained glass, just clear windows to let light power the message.

Under the soaring dome, look up and admire the exceptional stucco work, by an artist from Milan. It's molded into elaborate garlands, angels, and picture frames, some of it brightly painted. You're surrounded by the tombs (and portraits) of 10 archbishops.

You're also surrounded by four organs. (Actually, five. Don't forget the biggest organ, over the entrance.) Mozart served as organist here for two years, and he composed several Masses still played today. Salzburg's prince-archbishops were great patrons of music, with a personal orchestra that played religious music in the cathedral and dinner music in the Residenz. The tradition of music continues today. Sunday Mass here can be a musical spectacle—all five organs playing, balconies filled with singers and musicians, creating glorious surround-sound. Think of the altar in Baroque terms, as the center of a stage, with sunrays serving as spotlights in this dramatic and sacred theater.

• *You can visit the underwhelming crypt (downstairs from the left transept, free) with more tombs and a prayer chapel. As you leave the cathedral, check out the concert and Mass schedules posted near the entrance.*

To learn more about the church, you can visit the **Cathedral Museum** *as part of the DomQuartier Museums tour (see page 220). In summer, the* **Cathedral Excavations Museum** *(Domgrabungsmuseum, outside the church on Residenzplatz and down the stairs) shows off the church's medieval foundations and a few Roman mosaics—worthwhile only for Roman-iacs (€2.50, July-Aug daily 10:00-17:00, closed Sept-June, www.salzburgmuseum.at).*

Exiting the cathedral, turn left, heading in the direction of the distant fortress on the hill. You'll soon reach a spacious square with a golden orb.

❼ Kapitelplatz

The playful modern sculpture in the square shows a man atop a golden orb. Every year, a foundation commissions a different artist to create a new work of public art somewhere in the city; this one's from 2007. Kapitelplatz is a pleasant square—notice the giant chessboard that often draws a crowd.

Follow the orb-man's gaze up the hill to

Hohensalzburg Fortress. (I think he's trying to decide whether to shell out €11 for the funicular or save a few euros by hiking up.) Construction of the fortress began in 1077. Over the centuries, the small castle grew into a mighty, whitewashed fortress—so impressive that no army even tried attacking for over 800 years. These days, you can tour the castle grounds, visit some interior rooms and museums, and enjoy incredible views (see page 225). You can hike up (Festungsgasse leads up from Kapitelplatz) or, for €3 more, take the funicular. The funicular's rails actually date from as far back as the 1500s, when animals pulled cargo up to the fortress. Today's electric-powered funicular is from 1910.

Now walk across the square to the pond surrounded by a balustrade and adorned with a Trevi-fountain-like statue of Neptune. It looks fancy, but the pond was built as a horse bath, the 18th-century equivalent of a car wash. Notice the gold lettering above Neptune. It reads, "Leopold the Prince Built Me." But the artist added a clever twist. The inscription uses the letters "LLDVI," and so on. Those are also Roman numerals—add 'em up: L is 50, D is 500, and so on. It all adds up to 1732—the year the pond was built.

• *With your back to the cathedral, leave the square, exiting through the right corner. You'll pass by a sign on a building that reads* zum Peterskeller—*to St. Peter's Cemetery. But first, you reach a waterwheel.*

❽ Waterwheel

The waterwheel—overlooked by a statue of St. Peter—is part of a clever canal system that brings water to Salzburg from the foothills of the Alps, 10 miles away. The canal was built in the 13th century and is still used today. When the stream reached Salzburg, it was divided into five smaller canals for the citizens' use. The rushing water was harnessed to waterwheels which powered factories. There were more than 100 watermill-powered firms as late as the 19th century. The water also was used to fight fires, and every Thursday morning they flushed the streets. Hygienic Salzburg never suffered from a plague...it's probably the only major town in Austria with no plague monument. For more on the canal system, you might want to visit the nearby Alm River Canal exhibit (which you enter after exiting the funicular on the way down, see page 227).

This particular waterwheel (actually, it's a modern replacement) once ground grain into flour to make bread for the monks of St. Peter's Abbey. Nowadays, you can pop into the adjacent bakery—fragrant and traditional—and buy a fresh-baked roll for about a euro (Mon-Tue 8:00-17:30, Thu-Fri 7:00-17:30, Sat 7:00-13:00, closed Wed and Sun).

• *You've entered the borders of the former St. Peter's Abbey, a monastic complex of churches, courtyards, businesses (like the bakery), and a cemetery. Find the* Katakomben *sign and step through the wrought-iron gates into...*

❾ St. Peter's Cemetery

This collection of lovingly tended graves abuts the sheer rock face of the Mönchsberg (free, silence requested; open daily June-Aug 6:30-21:30, April-May 6:30-20:00, Sept 6:30-19:00, Oct-March 6:30-18:00; www.stift-stpeter.at). Walk in about 30 yards to the middle of the cemetery. You're surrounded by three churches, each founded in the early Middle Ages atop a pagan Celtic holy site. The biggest church, St. Peter's, sticks its big Romanesque apse into the cemetery

The graves surrounding you are tended by descendants of the deceased. In Austria (and many other European countries), gravesites are rented, not owned. Rent bills are sent out every 10 years. If no one cares enough to make the payment, your tombstone is removed.

The cemetery plays a role in *The Sound of Music*. The Captain and his large family were well-known in Salzburg for their musical talents. But when Nazi Germany annexed Austria in 1938, the von Trapps decided to flee so that the father would not be pressed into service again. In the movie, they hid here as they made their daring escape. The scene was actually filmed on a Hollywood set, inspired by St. Peter's Cemetery.

Look up the cliff, which has a few buildings attached—called (not quite accurately) "catacombs." Legendary medieval hermit monks are said to have lived in the hillside here. For a small fee, you can enter the *Katakomben* and climb lots of steps to see a few old caves, a chapel, and some fine city views (entrance at the base of the cliff, under the arcade; €2, visit takes 10 minutes; daily 10:00-12:00 & 13:00-18:00, Oct-April until 17:00).

Explore the arcade at the base of the cliff with its various burial chapels. Alcove #XXI has the tomb of the cathedral architect—forever facing his creation. #LIV (which is also the catacombs entry) has two interesting tombs marked by plaques on the floor. "Marianne" is Mozart's sister, nicknamed Nannerl. As children, Mozart and his sister performed together on grand tours of Europe's palaces. Michael Haydn was the brother of Joseph Haydn. He succeeded Mozart as church cathedral organist.

• *Exit the cemetery at the opposite end. Just outside, you enter a large courtyard anchored by...*

❿ St. Peter's Church (Stiftskirche St. Peter)

You're standing at the birthplace of Christianity in Salzburg. St. Peter's Abbey—the monastery that surrounds this courtyard—was founded in 696, barely two centuries after the fall of Rome.

The recommended Stiftskeller St. Peter restaurant in the courtyard (known these days for its Mozart Dinner Concert) brags that Charlemagne ate here in the year 803, making it (perhaps) the oldest restaurant in Europe. St. Peter's Church dates from 1147.

Cost and Hours: Free, daily April-Oct 8:00-21:00, Nov-March 8:00-19:00, www.stift-stpeter.at.

Visiting the Church: Enter the church, pausing in the atrium to admire the Romanesque tympanum (from 1250) over the inner doorway. Jesus sits on a rainbow, flanked by Peter and Paul. Beneath them is a stylized Tree of Life, and overhead, a Latin inscription reading, "I am the door to life, and only through me can you find eternal life."

Enter the nave. The once purely Romanesque interior (you may find a few surviving bits of faded 13th-century frescoes) now lies hidden under a sugary Rococo finish. It's Salzburg's only Rococo interior—all whitewashed, with highlights of pastel green, gold, and red. If it feels Bavarian, it's because it was done by Bavarian artists. The ceiling paintings feature St. Peter receiving the keys from Christ (center painting), walking on water, and joining the angels in heaven.

The monastery was founded by St. Rupert (c. 650-718). Find his statue at the main altar—he's the second gold statue from the left. Rupert arrived as a Christian missionary in what was then a largely pagan land. He preached the gospel, reopened the Roman salt mines, and established the city. It was he who named it "Salzburg."

Rupert's tomb is midway up the right aisle. It's adorned with a painting of him praying for his city. Beneath him is a depiction of Salzburg circa 1750 (when this was painted): one bridge, salt ships sailing the river, and angels hoisting barrels of salt to heaven.

• *Exit the courtyard at the opposite side from where you entered. The passageway takes you past dorms still used for student monks. At the T-intersection (where you bump into the Franziskanerkirche), turn left. Pass beneath the archway painted with a modern Lamentation scene (1926). You'll enter a square (Max-Reinhardt-Platz). Pause to admire the line of impressive Salzburg Festival concert halls ahead of you. Then turn left, through an arch, into a small square called...*

⓫ Toscaninihof

In this small courtyard, you get a peek at the back end of the large Festival Hall complex. The Festival Hall, built in 1925, has three theaters and seats 5,000 people. It's very busy during the Salzburg Music Festival each summer. As the festival was started in the 1920s (an austere time after World War I), Salzburg couldn't afford a new concert hall, so they remodeled what were once the prince-archbishop's stables and riding school.

The tunnel you see (behind the *Felsenkeller* sign) leads to the actual concert hall. It's generally closed, but occasionally, you can look through nearby doorways and see carpenters building stage sets for an upcoming show.

The von Trapp family performed in the Festival Hall. In the movie, this courtyard is where Captain von Trapp nervously waited before walking onstage to sing "Edelweiss." Then the family slipped away to begin their escape from the Nazis.

The Toscaninihof also has the entrance to the city's huge, 1,500-space, inside-the-mountain parking lot. The stone stairway in the courtyard leads a few flights up to a panoramic view. Continuing up farther you reach the recommended Stadtalm Café.

• *Return to Max-Reinhardt-Platz. Continue straight, heading downhill, along the right side of the big church. As you stroll, you'll pass by popular sausage stands, offering the best of the wurst. You'll pass by a public toilet, and enter Universitätsplatz.*

⑫ Universitätsplatz

This square hosts Salzburg's liveliest open-air produce market. It generally runs mornings, Monday through Saturday. It's at its best early Saturday mornings, when the farmers are in town. The fancy yellow facade overlooking the square marks the back end of Mozart's Birthplace, which we'll see shortly.

Find the fountain—it's about 30 yards along. As with public marketplaces elsewhere, it's for washing fruit and vegetables. This fountain—though modern in design—is still part of a medieval-era water system. The water plummets down a hole and on to the river. The sundial over the water hole shows both the time (easy to decipher) and the date (less obvious).

• *Continue toward the end of the square. Along the way, you'll pass several nicely arcaded medieval passageways (on the right), which lead to Salzburg's old main street, Getreidegasse. (Try weaving back and forth through some.)*

⑬ Mönchsberg Cliff Face

Rising 200 feet above you is the Mönchsberg, Salzburg's mountain. Today you see the remains of an aborted attempt in the 1600s to cut through the Mönchsberg. It proved too big a job, and when new tunneling technology arrived, the project was abandoned. The stones cut did serve as a quarry for the city's 17th-century growth spurt—the bulk of the cathedral, for example, is built of this economical and local conglomerate stone.

Early one morning in 1669, a huge landslide killed more than 200 townspeople who lived close to where the elevator is now (to the right). Since then the cliffs have been carefully checked each

spring and fall. Even today, you might see crews on the cliff, moni-
toring its stability.

At the base of the cliff are giant horse troughs, for the prince-
archbishops' former stables. Paintings show the various breeds and
temperaments of horses in the stable. Like Vienna, Salzburg had a
passion for the equestrian arts.

• *From here, turn right. You'll pass by the elevator up the Mönchsberg
(see page 231). Turn right again, entering a long pedestrian street.*

⓮ Getreidegasse

Old Salzburg's colorful main drag, Getreidegasse (rated ▲▲) has
been a center of trade since Roman times. Check out all the old
wrought-iron signs that advertise what's sold inside. This was the
Salzburg of prosperous medieval burghers, or businessmen. These
days it bustles with the tourist trade. The buildings date mainly
from the 15th century. They're tall and narrow, because this neighborhood was prime real estate, and there was nowhere to build but
up. Space was always tight, as the town was squeezed between
the river and the mountain, and lots of land was set aside for the
church. The architecture still looks much as it did in Mozart's
day—though many of the buildings themselves are now inhabited
by chain outlets.

Enjoy the traditional signs, and try to guess what they sold.
There are signs advertising spirits, a book maker, and a horn in-

dicating a place for the postal coach. A
brewery has a star for the name of the beer,
"Sternbrau." There's a window maker, a
key maker, a pastry shop, a tailor, a pretzel
maker, a pharmacy, a hat maker, and...ye
olde hamburger shoppe, McDonald's.

On the right at #39, **Sporer** serves up
homemade spirits (about €2/shot, Mon-
Fri 9:30-19:00, Sat 8:30-17:00, closed
Sun). This has been a family-run show for
a century—fun-loving, proud, and English-speaking. *Nuss* is nut,
Marille is apricot (typical of Austria), the *Kletzen* cocktail is like
a super-thick Baileys with pear, and *Edle Brande* are the stronger
schnapps. The many homemade firewaters are in jugs at the end of
the bar.

After noticing the building's old doorbells—one per floor—
continue down Getreidegasse. At #40, **Eisgrotte** serves good ice
cream (€1/scoop). Across from Eisgrotte, a tunnel leads to the recommended **Balkan Grill** (signed as *Bosna Grill*), the local choice
for the very best wurst in town. At #28 (a blacksmith shop since the
1400s), Herr Wieber, the ironworker and locksmith, welcomes the

curious. Farther along, you'll pass McDonald's (required to keep its arches Baroque and low-key).

At Getreidegasse #9, the knot of excited tourists marks the home of Salzburg's most famous resident. Mozart was born here in 1756. It was here that he composed most of his boy-genius works. Inside you see paintings of his family, letters, personal items (a lock of his hair, a clavichord he may have played), all trying to bring life to the Mozart story (see the description on page 223).

• *At Getreidegasse #3, turn right, into the passageway. You'll walk under a whale bone (likely symbolizing the wares of an exotic import shop) and reach the venerable Schatz Konditorei (worth a stop for coffee and pastry). At Schatz, turn left through the passage. When you reach Sigmund-Haffner-Gasse, glance to the left (for a nice view of the city hall tower), then turn right. Walk along Sigmund-Haffner-Gasse and take your first left, to reach a square called...*

⓯ Alter Markt

This is Salzburg's old marketplace. Here you'll find a sausage stand, the venerable and recommended Café Tomaselli, and a fun candy shop at #7. Next door is the beautifully old-fashioned Alte F. E. Hofapotheke pharmacy—duck in discreetly to peek at the Baroque shelves and containers (be polite, the people in line are here for medicine; no photography).

• *Our walk is over. If you're up for more sightseeing, most everything's a short walk from here. You can head up to the Hohensalzburg Fortress. Or visit sights across the river in the New Town—there's a pedestrian bridge nearby.*

Sights in Salzburg

IN THE OLD TOWN
▲DomQuartier Museums

The DomQuartier ticket admits you to a circular, indoor route through the Residenz (the ornate former palace), the cathedral (which you view from the organ loft), and a couple of adjoining buildings. These sights—largely (but not entirely) focused on religious art and the history of Salzburg's prince-archbishops—were felt to be too minor to stand on their own, but worthwhile when knitted into one whole. The tour includes a good audioguide. On the map, you can see how the interconnected museums ring the Domplatz.

Cost and Hours: €12, Tue-Sun 10:00-17:00, closed Mon except in July-Aug, last tickets sold at 16:00, includes audioguide, Residenzplatz 1, tel. 0662/8042-2109, www.domquartier.at.

Visiting the DomQuartier Museums: If you enter at the

Residenz (you can also enter at the cathedral), signs will guide you along the following circuit:

Once Salzburg's center of power, the **Residenz State Rooms** were the home of the prince-archbishop. Walking through these 15 chandeliered, stuccoed, and frescoed "stately rooms" *(Prunkräume),* you'll see elements of Renaissance, Baroque, and Classicist styles—200 years of let-them-eat-cake splendor.

The painting collection in the **Residenz Gallery**—not surprisingly in this bastion of Catholicism—is strongest in Baroque paintings. Rubens' *Allegory on Charles V* shows the pope's great champion with a sword in one hand and a scepter in the other. Rembrandt's teeny-tiny *Old Woman Praying* glows, despite her wrinkled face and broken teeth (the model was probably his mother). Other highlights include Federico Barocci's intense *Self-Portrait,* Bernardo Strozzi's *Sleeping Child,* and Boucher's rosy-cheeked *Dreaming Shepherdess.* Austria is represented by F. G. Waldmüller's cheery, sun-drenched *Children at the Window* and (Salzburg's own) Hans Makart's honest portrait of his first wife, *Amalie.*

In good weather, you can cross over to the cathedral the same way the prince-archbishops did—walking across their marble skyway (the **Cathedral Terrace**), high above the unwashed masses. (If it's raining, you'll be sent one floor down to the indoor walkway.)

Though you don't actually tour the **Cathedral** interior, you do glance down on the nave from high above. On this level you can visit two small museums: the Nordoratorium, with modern religious art, and the **Cathedral Museum,** with rich religious objects from the cathedral's long history.

The next section, **St. Peter's Abbey Museum,** introduces you to work and life at the abbey (which claims to be the oldest monastery north of the Alps), and displays curiosities from its collections.

Your final stop is a peek inside the **Franciscan Church** (Franziskanerkirche), a Gothic oddity in Baroque Salzburg. Admire the tall (conglomerate-stone) columns supporting an elaborate fan-vaulted ceiling. The altar area is surrounded by exuberantly decorated chapels. Find the unicorn.

▲▲Salzburg Museum

This is your best look at Salzburg's history. As the building was once the prince-archbishop's New Residence, many exhibits are in the lavish rooms where Salzburg's rulers entertained.

Cost and Hours: €7, €8.50 combo-ticket with Salzburg Panorama 1829; open Tue-Sun 9:00-17:00, closed Mon; includes so-so audioguide, tel. 0662/620-8080, www.salzburgmuseum.at.

Visiting the Museum: The centerpiece of the museum is the permanent exhibit called **The Salzburg Myth,** on the second floor. You'll learn how the town's physical beauty—nestled among the

Alps, near a river—attracted 19th-century Romantics who made it one of Europe's first tourist destinations, an "Alpine Arcadia." When the music festival began in the 1920s, Salzburg's status grew still more, drawing high-class visitors from across the globe.

After that prelude, the exhibit focuses on the glory days of the prince-archbishops (1500-1800), with displays housed in the impressive ceremonial rooms. Portraits of the prince-archbishops (in Room 2.07) show them to be cultured men, with sensitive eyes, soft hands, and carrying books. But they were also powerful secular rulers of an independent state that extended far beyond today's Salzburg (see the map in Room 2.08).

The heart of the exhibit is Room 2.11—a big, colorful hall where the Salzburg Diet (the legislature) met. The elaborate painted ceiling depicts heroic Romans who sacrificed for their country. Spend some time here with the grab-bag of interesting displays, including old guns, rock crystals, and medallions. A portrait shows the prince-archbishop who sums up Salzburg's golden age—Wolf Dietrich von Raitenau (1559-1617). Here he is at age 28, having just assumed power. Educated, well-traveled, a military strategist, and fluent in several languages, Wolf Dietrich epitomized the kind of Renaissance Man who could lead both church and state. He largely created the city we see today—the rebuilt cathedral, Residenz, Residenzplatz, and Mirabell Palace—done in the Italian Baroque style. Nearby exhibits flesh out Wolf Dietrich the man (his shoes and gloves) and the city he created with Italian architect Vincenzo Scamozzi. That city inspired visits and depictions by countless artists, who helped to create what the museum calls the "Salzburg Myth."

The first floor and the *Kunsthalle* in the basement house temporary exhibits.

▲Salzburg Panorama 1829

Also in the New Residence, the Salzburg Panorama 1829 displays a wrap-around painting of the city, giving a 360-degree look at Salzburg in the year 1829. From the Salzburg Museum entryway, find the underground "Panorama Passage" that leads to this unique exhibit. The passage itself is lined with archaeological finds (Roman and early medieval), helping set the stage for the Salzburg you're about to see.

In the early 19th century, before the advent of photography, 360-degree "panorama" paintings of great cities or events were popular. These creations were even taken on extended road trips. When this one was created, the 1815 Treaty of Vienna had just divied up post-Napoleonic Europe, and Salzburg had become part of the Habsburg realm. This photo-realistic painting served as a town portrait done at the emperor's request. The circular view, painted

Mozart's Salzburg

Salzburg was Mozart's home for the first 25 years of his brief, 35-year life. He was born on Getreidegasse and baptized in the cathedral. He played his first big concert, at age six, at the Residenz. He was the organist for the Cathedral, conducted the prince-archbishop's orchestra, and dined at (what's now called) Café Tomaselli. It was from Salzburg that he gained Europe-wide fame, touring the continent with his talented performing family. At age 17, Mozart and his family moved into lavish digs at (today's) Mozart's Residence.

As his fame and ambitions grew, Mozart eventually left Salzburg to pursue his dreams in Vienna. His departure from Salzburg's royal court in 1781 is the stuff of legend. Mozart, full of himself, announced that he was quitting. The prince-archbishop essentially said, "You can't quit; you're fired!" and as Mozart walked out, he was literally kicked in the ass.

by Johann Michael Sattler, shows the city as seen from the top of its castle. When complete, it spent 10 years touring the great cities of Europe, showing off Salzburg's breathtaking setting.

Today, the exquisitely restored painting, hung in a circular room, offers a fascinating look at the city as it was in 1829. The river was slower and had beaches. The Old Town looks essentially as it does today. Your ticket also lets you see the temporary exhibitions in the room that surrounds the Panorama.

Cost and Hours: €3, €8.50 combo-ticket with Salzburg Museum, open daily 9:00-17:00, Residenzplatz 9, tel. 0662/620-808-730, www.salzburgmuseum.at.

▲▲Mozart's Birthplace (Geburtshaus)

In 1747, Leopold Mozart—a musician in the prince-archbishop's band—moved into this small rental unit with his new bride. Soon they had a baby girl (Nannerl) and, in 1756, a little boy was born—Wolfgang Amadeus Mozart. It was here that Mozart learned to play piano and violin and composed his first boy-genius works. Even after the family gained fame, touring Europe's palaces and becoming the toast of Salzburg, they continued living in this rather cramped apartment.

Today this is the most popular Mozart sight in town—for fans, it's almost a pilgrimage. Shuffling through with the crowds, you'll peruse three floors of rooms with exhibits displaying paintings, letters, personal items, and lots of facsimiles, all attempting to bring life to the Mozart story. There's no audioguide, but everything's described in English.

Both Mozart sights in Salzburg—the Birthplace and the Residence—are equally good. If I had to choose, I'd go with the Birthplace as the best overall introduction (though it's more crowded), and consider the Residence extra credit. If you're truly interested in Mozart and his times, take advantage of the combi-ticket and see both. If Mozart isn't important to you, skip both museums and concentrate on the city's other sights and glorious natural surroundings.

Cost and Hours: €10, €17 combo-ticket with Mozart's Residence in New Town—see page 234, daily 9:00-17:30, July-Aug until 20:00, Getreidegasse 9, tel. 0662/844-313, www.mozarteum. at. Avoid the shoulder-to-shoulder crowds by visiting right when it opens or late in the day.

Visiting Mozart's Birthplace: You'll begin on the top floor in the actual apartment—five small rooms, including the bedroom where Mozart was born. The rooms are bare of any furnishings. Instead, you see portraits of the famous family and some memorabilia: Mozart's small-size childhood violin, some (possible) locks of his hair, buttons from his jacket, and a letter to his wife, whom he calls his "little rascal, pussy-pussy."

After leaving the actual apartments, you'll enter the museum portion. First up is an exhibition on Mozart's life after he left Salzburg and moved to Vienna: He jams with Haydn and wows the Viennese with electrifying concerts and new compositions (see a "square piano" which may have been his). Despite his fame, Mozart fell on hard times and died young and poor. But, as the museum shows, his legacy lived on. Computer terminals let you hear his music while following along on his handwritten scores.

Downstairs, the focus is on the operas he wrote (*Don Giovanni, The Magic Flute, The Marriage of Figaro*), with stage sets and video clips. The finale is an old clavichord on which Mozart supposedly composed his final work—the *Requiem,* which was played for his own funeral. (A predecessor of the more complicated piano, the clavichord's keys hit the strings with a simple teeter-totter motion that allows you to play very softly—ideal for composers living in tight apartment quarters.)

The lower-floor exhibit takes you on the road with the child prodigy, and gives a slice-of-life portrait of Salzburg during Mozart's time, including a bourgeois living room furnished much as the Mozart family's would have been.

ATOP THE CLIFFS ABOVE THE OLD TOWN

Atop the Mönchsberg—the mini-mountain that rises behind the Old Town—is a tangle of paved walking paths with great views, a hostel with a pleasant café/restaurant, a modern art museum, a neighborhood of very fancy homes, and one major sight (the Hohensalzburg Fortress, perched on the Festungsberg, the Mönchsberg's southern arm). You can walk up from several points in town, including Festungsgasse (near the cathedral), Toscaninihof, and the recommended Augustiner Bräustübl beer garden. At the west end of the Old Town, the Mönchsberg elevator whisks you up to the top for a couple euros. The funicular directly up to the fortress is expensive, and worthwhile only if you plan to visit the fortress, which is included in the funicular ticket.

▲▲Hohensalzburg Fortress (Festung)

Construction of Hohensalzburg Fortress was begun by Archbishop Gebhard of Salzburg as a show of the Catholic Church's power (see

sidebar). Built on a rock (called Festungsberg) 400 feet above the Salzach River, this fortress was never really used. That was the idea. It was a good investment—so foreboding, nobody attacked the town for over 800 years. The city was never taken by force, but when Napoleon stopped by, Salzburg wisely surrendered. After a stint as a military barracks, the fortress was opened to the public in the 1860s by Habsburg Emperor Franz Josef. Today, it remains one of Europe's mightiest castles, dominating Salzburg's skyline and offering incredible views, cafés, and a handful of mediocre museums. It's a pleasant place to grab an ice-cream cone and wander the whitewashed maze of buildings while soaking up some medieval ambience.

Cost: Your cost to enter the fortress depends on whether you get there on foot (the walk is easier than it looks), or, for €3 more, by funicular. Either way, your ticket includes all of the interior sights at the fortress: the Regency Rooms with audioguide (Tour A), the Fortress and Rainer Regiments museums (Tour B), the Marionette Exhibit, and a few minor sights.

On Foot: It's a steep but quick walk from Kapitelplatz (next to the cathedral), up Festungsgasse. (Alternatively, you can go up the Mönchsberg at the other end of the Old Town, then take the "Mönchsberg Walk," described on page 231, to the fortress; this is a much longer walk, but the Mönchsberg elevator takes care of some of the altitude gain.)

Arriving on foot, you'll pay €8 to enter (at the fortress gate), which includes all of the fortress sights plus the funicular ride

Battlefield Salzburg:
Popes vs. Emperors

Salzburg is so architecturally impressive today to a great degree because of the Roman Catholic Church. This town was on the frontline of a centuries-long power struggle between Church and emperor. The town's mighty Hohensalzburg Fortress—a symbol of the Church's determination to assert its power here—was built around 1100, just as the conflict was heating up.

The medieval church-state argument, called the "Lay Investiture Controversy," was a classic tug-of-war between a series of popes and Holy Roman Emperors. The prize: the right to appoint (or "invest") church officials in the Holy Roman Emperor's domain. (Although called "Holy," the empire was headed not by priests, but by secular—or "lay"—rulers.)

The Church impinged on the power of secular leaders in several ways: Their subjects' generous tithes went to Rome, leaving less for the emperor to tax. In many areas, the Church was the biggest landowner (people willed their land to the Church in return for prayers for their salvation). And the pope's appointees weren't subject to secular local laws. Holy Roman Emperors were plenty powerful, but not as powerful as the Church.

In 1075, Emperor Henry IV bucked the system, appointing his own set of church officials and boldly renouncing Gregory VII as pope. In retaliation, Gregory excommunicated both Henry and the bishops he'd appointed. One of Henry's chief detractors was Salzburg's pope-appointed archbishop, Gebhard, who started construction of Hohensalzburg Fortress in a face-off with the defiant emperor.

The German nobility seized on the conflict as an opportunity to rebel, seizing royal property and threatening to elect a new emperor. To placate the nobles, Henry sought to regain the Church's favor. In January of 1077, Henry traveled south to Italy—supposedly crossing the Alps barefoot and in a monk's hair-shirt—to Canossa, where the pope was holed up. The emperor knelt in the snow outside the castle gate for three days, begging the pope's forgiveness. (To this day, the phrase "go to Canossa" is used to refer to any act of humility.)

But the German princes continued their revolt, electing their own king (Henry's brother-in-law, Rudolf of Rheinfelden). Henry's reconciliation with the Church was brief: In short order he named an antipope (Clement III), killed Rudolf in battle, and invaded Rome. Archbishop Gebhard was forced out of Salzburg and spent a decade in exile, raising forces against Henry in an attempt to reclaim the Salzburg archdiocese.

The back-and-forth continued until 1122, when a power-sharing accord was finally reached between Henry's son, Emperor Henry V, and Pope Calistus II.

down—whether you want it or not. Within one hour of the muse-ums' closing time, the entry price is reduced to €4. After the mu-seums close, you can't enter on foot, but you can exit (the door will lock behind you) and walk down.

Via Funicular: Most visitors opt for the one-minute trip on the funicular *(Festungsbahn).* It starts from Festungsgasse (just off Kapitelplatz, by the cathedral) and comes up inside the fortress complex. The round-trip funicular ticket, which includes all the fortress sights, is €11.30 (family ticket-€26.20). If you board the funicular going up within one hour of the museums' closing time (i.e., May-Sept after 18:00 or Oct-April after 16:00), you pay only €8, or €6.50 if you don't want to take the funicular down; this is a good deal if you only want a glimpse of the museums. After the museums have closed, the funicular continues to run until about 21:30 or 22:00 (later if there's a concert) and costs €4 round-trip, or €2.50 one-way.

Hours: The museums in the fortress are open daily year-round (May-Sept 9:00-19:00, Oct-April 9:30-17:00). The grounds of the fortress stay open and the funicular continues to run even after the museums close, especially when there's a concert (300 nights a year).

Avoiding Crowds: You can avoid waits for the funicular as-cent with the Salzburg Card (which lets you skip to the head of the line) or by walking up. In summer, there are often long waits to get into Tour A (only 60 people are admitted at a time). To avoid crowds in general, visit early in the morning or late in the day.

Information: Tel. 0662/8424-3011, www.salzburg-burgen.at.

Concerts: The fortress serves as a venue for evening concerts (the Festungskonzerte), which are held in the old banquet rooms on the upper floor of the palace museum. A concert is a good way to see the fortress without noisy crowds. To visit the fortress in the evening for a concert, you'll need to take the funicular (see funicu-lar info above). For concert details, see page 241.

Café: The cafés to either side of the upper funicular station are a great place to nibble on apple strudel while taking in the jaw-dropping view.

☉ Self-Guided Tour:
The fortress is an eight-acre complex of some 50 buildings, with multiple courtyards and multiple rings of protective walls. Your ticket admits you to all of the interior exhibits.

• *At the top of the funicular, turn right, and bask in the **view** to the south (away from town) toward the Alps. Continue up through the for-*

Hohensalzburg Fortress

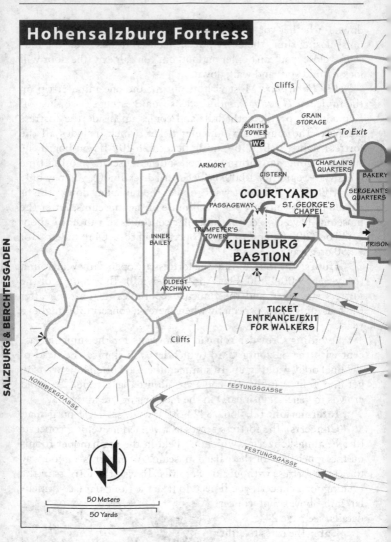

tress gates—two defensive rings for double protection. Emerging into the light, go left (uphill) to find the entrance to....

Tour A—The Regency Rooms: Here you see a few (mostly bare) rooms, following an audioguide included with your ticket. The Stable Rooms highlight various prince-archbishops and models showing the fortress' growth, starting in 1077. The last model (1810) shows it at its peak. The fortress was never overthrown, but it did make a negotiated surrender with Napoleon, and never saw action again. Your tour includes a room dedicated to the art of "enhanced interrogation" (to use American military jargon)—filled with tools of that gruesome trade.

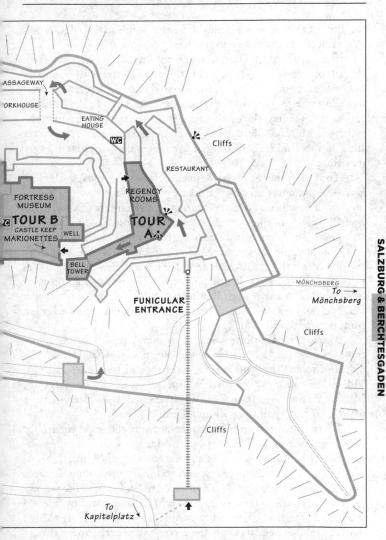

One of the most esteemed prisoners held here was Prince-Archbishop Wolf Dietrich, who lost favor with the pope, was captured by a Bavarian duke, and spent his last seven years in Hohensalzburg. It's a complicated story—basically, the pope counted on Salzburg to hold the line against the Protestants for several generations following the Reformation. Wolf Dietrich was a good Catholic, as were most Salzburgers. But the town's important businessmen and the region's salt miners were Protestant, and for Salzburg's financial good, Wolf Dietrich dealt with them in a tolerant and pragmatic way. Eventually the pope—who allowed zero tolerance for Protestants in those heady Counter-Reformation days—had Wolf Dietrich locked up and replaced.

The highlight of Tour A is the commanding city view from the top of a tower. To the north is the city. To the south are Salzburg's suburbs in a flat valley, from which rises the majestic 6,000-foot Untersberg massif of the Berchtesgaden Alps. To the east, you can look down into the castle complex to see the palace where the prince-archbishops lived. As you exit, pause at the "Salzburger Bull," a mechanical barrel organ used to wake the citizens every morning.

Tour B—The Fortress Museum (Festungsmuseum): This extensive museum covers the history of the fortress (including models of how it was constructed), everyday objects (dishes, beds, ovens), weapons (pikes, swords, pistols, cannons), old musical instruments, and more torture devices (including a chastity belt).

On the top floor are three pretty ceremonial rooms, including the one where the evening concerts are held. (Check out the colorfully painted tile stove in the far room.) The rest of the top floor is given over to the Rainer Regiments Museum, dedicated to the Salzburg soldiers who fought mountain-to-mountain on the Italian front during World War I.

Marionette Exhibit: Marionette shows are a Salzburg tradition (think of the "Lonely Goatherd" scene in *The Sound of Music*). Two fun rooms show off various puppets and scenery backdrops. Videos show glimpses of the Marionette Theater performances of Mozart classics (see page 243). Give the hands-on marionette a whirl, and find Wolf Dietrich in a Box.

Fortress Courtyard: The courtyard was the main square for the medieval fortress's 1,000-some residents, who could be self-sufficient when necessary. The square was ringed by the shops of craftsmen, blacksmiths, bakers, and so on. The well dipped into a rain-fed cistern. The church is dedicated to St. George, the protector of horses (logical for an army church) and decorated by fine red marble reliefs (1512). Behind the church is the top of the old lift (still in use) that helped supply the fortress. Under the archway next to it are the steps that lead back into the city, or to the paths across the Mönchsberg.

• *Just downhill from the chapel, find an opening in the wall that leads to a balcony with a view of Salzburg—the Kuenburg Bastion.*

Kuenburg Bastion: Survey Salzburg from here and think about fortifying an important city by using nature. The fortress sits atop a ridgeline with sheer cliffs on three sides, giving it a huge defensive advantage. Meanwhile, the town of Salzburg sits between the natural defenses of the Salzach River and the ridge. (The ridgeline consists of the Mönchsberg, the cliffs to the left, and Festungsberg, the little mountain you're on.) The fortress itself has three concentric rings of defense: the original keep in the center (where Tour B is located), the vast whitewashed walls (near you), and still more beefed-up fortifications (on the hillside below you, added against an expected Ottoman invasion). With all these defenses, the city only required a few more touches: the New Town across the river needed a bit of a wall arcing from the river to its hill. Back then, only one bridge crossed the Salzach into town, and it had a fortified gate. Cradled amid the security of its defenses—both natural and man-made—independent Salzburg thrived for nearly a thousand years.

• Our tour is over. To **walk**—either down to Salzburg or across the Mönchsberg (see "Mönchsberg Walk," next)—you'll want to take the exit at the east end of the complex. Get out your fortress-issued map and locate the route that leads to that exit.

To reach the **funicular**, just backtrack. If you take the funicular down, don't miss (at the bottom of the lift) the...

Alm River Canal Exhibit: At the base of the funicular, below the fortress, is this fine little exhibit on how the river was broken into five smaller streams—powering the city until steam took up the energy-supply baton. Pretend it's the year 1200 and follow (by video) the flow of the water from the river through the canals, into the mills, and as it's finally dumped into the Salzach River. (The exhibit technically requires a funicular ticket—but you can see it unofficially by slipping through the exit at the back of the amber shop, next door to the funicular terminal.)

Mönchsberg Sights
▲Mönchsberg Walk

The paved, wooded walking path along the narrow ridgeline between the Mönchsberg elevator and the fortress is less than a mile long and makes for a great 30-minute hike. There's some up and down, but the total elevation gain is about equal going in either direction.

The mountain is small, and frequent signposts direct you between all the key points, so it's hard to get lost. (Festung Hohensalzburg and Museum der Moderne Salzburg refer to the fortress and elevator ends of the mountain, respectively. The spots where you can go down the stairs into town are signed Altstadt.) The views of Salzburg are the main draw, but there's also a modern art museum, mansions to ogle, and a couple of places to eat or enjoy a scenic drink. Along the way, you'll see stunning views of Salzburg, rustic homes, a few unique little castle-like homes, occasional modern art sculptures in yards, a snack shack, the sheer cliff face with its layers of sediment, parts of the medieval wall, and information plaques on Salzburg's first settlers and on quarrying the cliffs.

You can do this walk in either direction. If you're planning to visit the fortress, do the walk first and the fortress last, saving €3 by skipping the funicular up: Take the Mönchsberg elevator, walk across to the fortress, pay the €8 entry price at the fortress gate, see the fortress, then take the funicular down—included in your fortress ticket.

The Mönchsberg **elevator** *(Aufzug)* starts from Gstättengasse/Griesgasse on the west side of the Old Town (€2.10 one-way, €3.40 round-trip, normally Mon 8:00-19:00, Tue-Sun 8:00-23:00).

You can also **climb** up and down under your own power; this saves a few more euros (no matter which direction you go). Paths or stairs lead up from the Augustiner beer hall (see page 258), Toscaninihof (near the Salzburg Festival concert halls), and Festungsgasse (at the base of the fortress).

Cafés: The elevator deposits you right at Mönchsberg 32, a sleek modern café/bar/restaurant adjacent to the modern art museum and a fine place for a drink or splurge meal (see page 256 for details). From there, it's a five-minute walk to the rustic, recommended Stadtalm Café, with wooden picnic tables and a one-with-nature allure. Next to the Stadtalm is a surviving section of Salzburg's medieval wall with an info plaque showing how the wall once looked.

Museum of Modern Art on Mönchsberg

The modern-art museum—a stark concrete-and-glass exhibition space—features temporary exhibits. It's located right at the top of the Mönchsberg elevator. Next to the museum is the "Sky Space," a cylindrical stone tower intended to let you contemplate the sky.

Cost and Hours: €8, Tue-Sun 10:00-18:00, Wed until 20:00, closed Mon.

IN THE NEW TOWN, NORTH OF THE RIVER

The following sights are across the river from the Old Town. I've connected them with walking instructions.

• *Begin at the Makartsteg pedestrian bridge, where you can survey the...*

Salzach River

Salzburg's river is called "salt river" not because it's salty, but because of the precious cargo it once carried—the salt mines of Hallein are just nine miles upstream. Salt could be transported from here all the way to the Danube, and on to the Mediterranean via the Black Sea. The riverbanks and roads were built when the river was regulated in the 1850s. Before that, the Salzach was much wider and slower moving. Houses opposite the Old Town fronted the river with docks and "garages" for boats. The grand buildings just past the bridge (with their elegant promenades and cafés) were built on reclaimed land in the late 19th century.

Scan the cityscape. Notice all the churches. Salzburg, nicknamed the "Rome of the North," has 38 Catholic churches (plus two Protestant churches and a synagogue). Find the five streams gushing into the river. These date from the 13th century, when the river was split into five canals running through the town to power its mills. The Stein Hotel (upstream, just left of next bridge) has a popular roof-terrace café (see page 236). Downstream, notice the Museum of Modern Art atop the Mönchsberg, with a view restaurant and a faux castle (actually a water reservoir). The Romanesque bell tower with the green copper dome in the distance is the Augustine church, site of the best beer hall in town (the Augustiner Bräustübl).

• *Cross the bridge, pass the recommended Café Bazar (a fine place for a drink), walk two blocks inland, and take a left past the heroic statues into...*

▲Mirabell Gardens and Palace (Schloss)

These bubbly gardens, laid out in 1730 for the prince-archbishop, have been open to the public since 1850 (thanks to Emperor Franz

Josef, who was rattled by the popular revolutions of 1848). The gardens are free and open until dusk. The palace is open only as a concert venue (explained later). The statues and the arbor (far left) were featured in *The Sound of Music*.

Walk through the gardens to the palace and find the statue of the horse (on the river side of the palace). Look back, enjoy the garden/cathedral/castle view, and imagine how the prince-archbishop must have reveled in a vista that reminded him of all his secular and religious power.

The rearing **Pegasus statue** (rare and very well-balanced) is the site of a famous *Sound of Music* scene where the kids all danced before lining up on the stairs with Maria (30 yards farther along). The steps lead to a small mound in the park (made of rubble from a former theater).

Nearest the horse, stairs lead between two lions to a pair of tough dwarves (early volleyball players with spiked mittens) welcoming you to Salzburg's **Dwarf Park.** Cross the elevated walk (noticing the city's fortified walls) to meet statues of a dozen dwarves who served the prince-archbishop—modeled after real people with real fashions in about 1600. This was Mannerist art, from the hyper-realistic age that followed the Renaissance.

There's plenty of **music** here, both in the park and in the palace. A brass band plays free park concerts (May-Aug Sun at 10:30). To properly enjoy the lavish Mirabell Palace—once the prince-archbishop's summer palace and now the seat of the mayor—get a ticket to a Schlosskonzerte (my favorite venue for a classical concert—see page 242).

• *Now go a long block southeast to Makartplatz, where, opposite the big and bright Hotel Bristol, you'll find...*

▲Mozart's Residence (Wohnhaus)

In the fall of 1773, when Wolfgang was 17—and his family was flush with money from years of touring—the Mozarts moved here from their cramped apartment on Getreidegasse. The exhibits are aimed a bit more toward the Mozart connoisseur than those at Mozart's Birthplace, but the place comes with a good introductory video, is less crowded, and includes an informative audioguide. The building itself, bombed in World War II, is a reconstruction.

Cost and Hours: €10, €17 combo-ticket with Mozart's Birthplace in Old Town—see page 223, daily 9:00-17:30, July-Aug until 20:00, allow an hour for visit, Makartplatz 8, tel. 0662/8742-2740, www.mozarteum.at. Behind the ticket desk is the free Mozart Sound and Film Collection, an archive of historic concerts on video (Mon-Tue and Fri 9:00-13:00, Wed-Thu 13:00-17:00, closed Sat-Sun).

Visiting Mozart's Residence: The exhibit—seven rooms on one floor—starts in the main hall, which was used by the Mozarts

to entertain Salzburg's high society. Here, you can see the museum's prize possession—Mozart's very own piano, as well as his violin. The family portrait on the wall (from around 1780) shows Mozart with his sister Nannerl at the piano, their father on violin, and their mother—who'd died two years earlier in Paris. A display of air guns and targets shows Mozart's fascination with a popular game of the time that they played in the garden. (Known crudely as licking an "arse," it speaks of Wolfgang's disdain for the rigors of high society.) Before moving on, consider spending time with the good introductory video in this room.

Room 2 trumpets the successes the Mozart family enjoyed while living here: portraits of Salzburg bigwigs they hung out with, letters from Mozart bragging about his musical successes, and the publication of Leopold's treatise on playing violin.

Room 3 is dedicated to father Leopold—*Kapellmeister* of the prince—a member of the archbishop's orchestra, musician, and composer in his own right. Was Leopold a loving nurturer of young Wolfgang or an exploiting Svengali?

Room 4 stars "Nannerl" (Maria Anna), Mozart's sister, who was five years older. Though both were child prodigies, playing four-hand show-pieces for Europe's crowned heads, Nannerl went on to lead a stable life as a wife and mother.

Room 5 boasts "Mozart's first printed work"—a sonata for clavichord and violin he wrote when he was eight. Room 6 shows many portraits of Mozart, some authentic, some not, but all a testament to his long legacy. By the time Mozart was 25, he'd grown tired of his father, this house, and Salzburg, and he went on to Vienna—to more triumphs, but ultimately, a sad end.

• *From here, you can walk a few blocks back to the main bridge (Staatsbrücke), where you'll find the Platzl, a square once used as a hay market. Pause to enjoy the kid-pleasing little fountain. Look down handsome Linzer Gasse (once the road to Linz and Vienna), with its attractive small shops. Near the fountain (with your back to the river), Steingasse leads darkly to the right.*

▲Steingasse Stroll

Heading up dim, narrow Steingasse, you get a rare glimpse of medieval Salzburg. It's not the church's Salzburg of grand squares and Baroque facades, but the people's Salzburg, of cramped quarters and humble cobbled lanes. Inviting cocktail bars along here come alive at night (see "Steingasse Pub Crawl" on page 259).

Stop at #9 and look across the river into the Old Town; the city's original bridge once connected Salzburg's two halves right here. According to the plaque (of questionable veracity) at #9, this is where Joseph Mohr, who wrote the words to "Silent Night," was born—poor and illegitimate—in 1792. There is no doubt, however, that the popular Christmas carol was composed and first sung in the village of Oberndorf, just outside of Salzburg, in 1818. Stairs lead from near here up to a 17th-century Capuchin monastery.

On the next corner, the wall is gouged out. This scar was left even after the building was restored, to serve as a reminder of the American GI who tried to get a tank down this road during a visit to the town brothel—two blocks farther up Steingasse. Within steps of here is the art cinema (showing movies in their original language) and four recommended bars (described on page 259).

At #19, find the carvings on the old door. Some say these are notices from beggars to the begging community (more numerous after post-Reformation religious wars, which forced many people out of their homes and towns)—a kind of "hobo code" indicating whether the residents would give or not. Trace the wires of the old-fashioned doorbells to the highest floors.

Farther on, you step through the old fortified gate (at #20) and find a commanding Salzburg view across the river. Notice the red dome marking the oldest nunnery in the German-speaking world (established in 712) under the fortress and to the left. The real Maria, who inspired *The Sound of Music*, taught in this nunnery's school. In 1927, she and Captain von Trapp were married in the church you see here (not the church filmed in the movie). He was 47. She was 22. Hmmmm.

From here look back, above the arch you just passed through, and up at part of the town's medieval fortification. The coat of arms on the arch is of the prince-archbishop who paid Bavaria a huge ransom to stay out of the Thirty Years' War (smart move). He then built this fortification (in 1634) in anticipation of rampaging armies from both sides.

Today, this street is for making love, not war. The Maison de Plaisir (a few doors down, at #24) has for centuries been a Salzburg brothel. But the climax of this walk is more touristic.

• *For a grand view, head back to the Platzl and the bridge, enter the Stein Hotel (left corner, overlooking the river), and ride the elevator to...*

Stein Terrasse

This café offers one of the best views in town. Hidden from the tourist crush, it's a trendy, professional, local scene. You can discreetly peek at the view, enjoy a drink or light meal, or come back later to gaze into the eyes of your travel partner as you sip a nightcap (small snacks, indoor/outdoor seating, daily 7:00-24:00).

• *Back at the Platzl and the bridge, you can head straight up Linzer Gasse (away from the river) into a neighborhood packed with recommended accommodations, as well as our final New Town sight, the...*

▲St. Sebastian Cemetery

Wander through this quiet oasis. Mozart is buried in Vienna, his mom's in Paris, and his sister is in Salzburg's Old Town (St. Peter's)—but Wolfgang's wife Constanze ("Constantia") and his father Leopold are buried here (from the black iron gate entrance on Linzer Gasse, walk 19 paces and look left). When Prince-Archbishop Wolf Dietrich had the cemetery moved from around the cathedral and put here, across the river, people didn't like it. To help popularize it, he had his own mausoleum built as its centerpiece. Continue straight past the Mozart tomb to this circular building (English description at door). In the corner to the left of the entrance is the tomb of the Renaissance scientist and physician Paracelsus, best known for developing laudanum as a painkiller.

Cost and Hours: Free, daily April-Oct 9:00-18:00, Nov-March 9:00-16:00, entry at Linzer Gasse 43 in summer; in winter go around the corner to the right, through the arch at #37, and around the building to the doorway under the blue seal.

NEAR SALZBURG
▲▲Hellbrunn Palace and Gardens

In about 1610, Prince-Archbishop Sittikus decided he needed a lavish palace with a vast and ornate garden purely for pleasure

(I imagine after meditating on stewardship and Christ-like values). He built this summer palace and hunting lodge, and just loved inviting his VIP guests from throughout Europe to have some fun with his trick fountains. Today, Hellbrunn is a popular sight for its formal garden (one of the oldest in Europe, with a gazebo made famous by *The Sound of Music*), amazing fountains, palace exhibits, and the excuse it offers to simply get out of the city.

Cost and Hours: €10.50 ticket includes fountain tour and palace audioguide, daily May-Sept 9:00-17:30, July-Aug until 21:00—but tours from 18:00 on don't include the castle (which closes in the evening), April and Oct 9:00-16:30, these are last tour times, closed Nov-March, tel. 0662/820-3720, www.hellbrunn.at.

Getting There: Hellbrunn is nearly four miles south of Salzburg.

By Bus: Take bus #25 from the train station or the Rathaus stop by the Staatsbrücke bridge (2-3/hour, 20 minutes). Get off at the Schloss Hellbrunn stop.

By Bike: In good weather, the trip out to Hellbrunn makes for a pleasant 30-minute bike excursion (see "Riverside or Meadow Bike Ride," later, and ask for a map when you rent your bike).

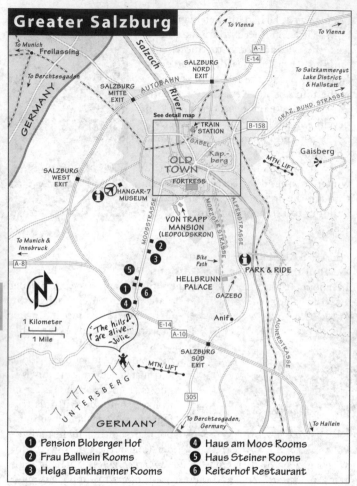

Greater Salzburg

1 Pension Bloberger Hof
2 Frau Ballwein Rooms
3 Helga Bankhammer Rooms
4 Haus am Moos Rooms
5 Haus Steiner Rooms
6 Reiterhof Restaurant

SALZBURG & BERCHTESGADEN

Visiting the Palace: Upon arrival, buy your **fountain tour** ticket and get a tour time (generally on the half-hour). The 40-minute English/German tours take you laughing and scrambling through a series of amazing 17th-century garden settings with lots of splashy fun and a guide who seems almost sadistic in the joy he has in soaking his group. (Hint: When you see a wet place, cover your camera.) If there's a wait until your tour, you can see the palace first.

With the help of the included audioguide, wander through the modest **palace** exhibit to the sounds of shrieking fountain-taunted tourists below. The palace was built in a style inspired by the Venetian architect Palladio, who was particularly popular around 1600, and it quickly became a cultural destination. This was the era when the aristocratic ritual was to go hunting in the morning (hence the wildlife-themed decor) and enjoy an opera in the evening. The first opera north of the Alps, imported from Italy, was performed here. The decor is Mannerist (between Renaissance and Baroque), with faux antiquities and lots of surprising moments—intentional irregularities were in vogue after the strict logic, balance, and Greek-inspired symmetry of the Renaissance. (For example, the main hall is not in the palace's center, but at the far end.) The palace exhibit also explains the impressive 17th-century hydraulic engineering that let gravity power the intricate fountains.

After the fountain tour you're also free to wander the delightful **garden**. Pop out to see the **gazebo** made famous by the "Sixteen Going On Seventeen" song from *The Sound of Music* (relocated here in the 1990s; look for *Sound-of-Music Pavilion* signs).

▲▲Riverside or Meadow Bike Ride

The Salzach River has smooth, flat, and scenic bike lanes along each side (thanks to medieval tow paths—cargo boats would float downstream and be dragged back up by horses). On a sunny day, I can think of no more shout-worthy escape from the city.

Perhaps the most pristine, meadow-filled farm-country route is the nearly four-mile path along Hellbrunner Allee; it's an easy ride with a worthy destination (Hellbrunn Palace, listed above): From the middle of town, head along the river on Rudolfskai, with the river on your left and the fortress on your right. After passing the last bridge at the edge of the Old Town (Nonntaler Brücke), cut inland along Petersbrunnstrasse, until you reach the university and Akademiestrasse. Beyond it find the start of Freisaalweg, which becomes the delightful Hellbrunner Allee bike path...which leads directly to the palace (paralleling Morzgerstrasse; see map on page 238). For a nine-mile ride, continue on to Hallein (where you can tour a salt mine—see next listing; if heading to Hallein directly from Salzburg, head out from the north bank of the river, i.e. the New Town side, which is more scenic).

Even a quickie ride across town is a great Salzburg experience. In the evening, the riverbanks are a world of floodlit spires. For bike rental information, see "Getting Around Salzburg—By Bike," earlier.

▲Hallein Salt Mine (Salzbergwerke)

You'll be pitched plenty of different salt-mine excursions from Salzburg, all of which cost substantial time and money. One's plenty. This salt-mine tour (in Bad Dürrnberg, just above the town of Hallein, 9 miles from Salzburg) is a good choice. Wearing white overalls and sliding down the sleek wooden chutes, you'll cross underground from Austria into Germany while learning about the old-time salt-mining process. The tour entails lots of time on your feet as you walk from cavern to cavern, learning the history of the mine by watching a series of video skits with an actor channeling Prince-Archbishop Wolf Dietrich. The visit also includes a "Celtic Village" open-air museum.

Cost and Hours: €19, €17 if purchased online, allow 2.5 hours for the visit, daily April-Oct 9:00-17:00, Nov-Dec and Feb-March 10:00-15:00—these are last tour times, closed Jan, English-speaking guides—but let your linguistic needs be known loud and clear, tel. 06132/200-8511, www.salzwelten.at.

Getting There: The convenient *Salz Erlebnis* ticket from Salzburg's train station covers your transport and admission in one money-saving round-trip ticket (€29, buy ticket at train station, no discount with rail pass; covers train to Hallein, then 11-minute ride on bus #41 to salt mines in Bad Dürrnberg, runs hourly, check schedules when buying tickets).

Hangar-7

This purpose-built hangar at the Salzburg airport (on the other side of the runways from the terminal) houses the car-and-aircraft collection of Dietrich Mateschitz, the flamboyant founder of the Red Bull energy-drink empire. Under the hangar's modern steel-and-glass dome are 20 or so glittering planes and racecars, plus three pretentious eateries, all designed to brandish the Red Bull "culture." To learn about the machines, you can borrow an iPod Touch with English information, or get information on the iPads posted by each exhibit.

Mateschitz (now in his 70s) remains Salzburg's big personality: He has a mysterious mansion at the edge of town, sponsors the local "Red Bull" soccer and hockey teams, owns several chic Salzburg eateries and cocktail bars, and employs 6,000 mostly good-looking people. He seems much like the energy drink that made him rich and powerful—a high-energy, anything's-possible cultural Terminator.

Cost and Hours: Free, daily 9:00-22:00, bus #10 from Hanuschplatz to the Pressezentrum/Kuglhof stop—don't get off at the airport terminal, Wilhelm-Spazier-Strasse 7a, tel. 0662/2197, www.hangar-7.com.

Eating: Two floors up, the Mayday Bar has light meals and an unusual, experimental menu (€10-15 dishes). On the first floor, you'll probably want to skip the Ikarus Restaurant—all it offers is a €160 fixed-price meal. On the ground floor, the Carpe Diem bar serves drinks (it's an outpost of the larger Carpe Diem bar in the Old Town, also owned by Mateschitz.)

Hallstatt and Berchtesgaden

Rustic Hallstatt, crammed like a swallow's nest into the narrow shore between a lake and a steep mountainside, is a 2.5-hour bus or train ride from Salzburg. It's my favorite town in the scenic Salz-kammergut Lake District and worth ▲▲. Berchtesgaden (covered in the next chapter) is equally scenic, and home to Hitler's Eagle's Nest and other interesting sights. Both of these towns make for busy but worthwhile side-trips from Salzburg, and both are easy enough to do on your own. But if you're on a tight schedule, taking a bus tour can be a good use of your time and money (for details, see page 206).

Music in Salzburg

Music lovers come to Salzburg in late July and August for the Sal-zburg Festival, but there are also smaller, less expensive festivals at other times of year. The regular programs at the city's theaters and concert halls are often accessible to visitors. And all year long, you can enjoy pleasant, if touristy concerts held in historic venues around town—or a musical Mass on Sunday morning. To help case out your options, pick up the events calendar brochure at the TI (free, bimonthly) or check www.salzburg.info (under "Art & Cul-ture," click on "Music"). I've never planned in advance, and I've enjoyed great concerts with every visit.

NIGHTLY MUSICAL EVENTS

The following concerts are mostly geared to tourists and can have a crank-'em-out feel, but still provide good value, especially outside festival times.

Concerts at Hohensalzburg Fortress (Festungskonzerte)

Nearly nightly concerts—Mozart's greatest hits for beginners—are held in the "prince's chamber" of the fortress atop the hill, featur-ing small chamber groups (€32-40 plus €4 for the funicular, open seating after the first six more expensive rows; at 19:30, 20:00, or 20:30; doors open 30 minutes early, reserve at tel. 0662/825-858 or via www.salzburghighlights.at, pick up tickets at the door). The medieval-feeling chamber has windows overlooking the city, and the concert gives you a chance to enjoy the grand city view and a stroll through the castle courtyard. For €52, you can combine the concert with a four-course dinner (starts 2 hours before concert). Purists may object to hearing Baroque music in an incongruously Gothic setting.

Concerts at the Mirabell Palace (Schlosskonzerte)

The nearly nightly chamber music concerts at the Mirabell Palace are performed in a lavish Baroque setting. They come with more sophisticated programs and better musicians than the fortress concerts...and Baroque music flying around a Baroque hall is a happy bird in the right cage (open seating after the first five pricier rows, €31-37, usually at 20:00—but check flier for times, doors open one hour ahead, tel. 0662/848-586, www.salzburger-schlosskonzerte.at).

Mozart Dinner Concert

For those who'd like some classical music but would rather not sit through a concert, the elegant Stiftskeller St. Peter restaurant (see page 253) offers a traditional candlelit meal with Mozart's greatest hits performed by a string quartet and singers in historic costumes gavotting among the tables. In this elegant Baroque setting, tourists clap between movements and get three courses of food (from Mozart-era recipes) mixed with three 20-minute courses of crowd-pleasing music—structured much as such evenings were in Baroque-era times (€56, €9 discount for Mozart lovers who reserve direct by phone or email and mention this book, music starts nightly May-Sept at 20:00, Oct-April at 19:00, arrive 30 minutes before that, dress is "smart casual," to reserve email office@skg.co.at or call 0662/828-695, www.mozart-dinner-concert-salzburg.com).

WEEKLY MUSICAL EVENTS

Friday and Saturday: Mozart Piano Sonatas

These short (45-minute) and fairly inexpensive concerts in St. Peter's Abbey are ideal for families (€22, €11 for kids, €55 for a family of four, almost every Fri and Sat at 19:00 year-round, in the abbey's Romanesque Hall—a.k.a. Romanischer Saal, enter from inner courtyard 20 yards left of St. Peter's Church, mobile 0664-423-5645, www.agenturorpheus.at, then click on "Konzerte" and "Salzburg—Mozart Klaviersonaten").

Sunday Morning: Free Brass Band Concerts

Traditional brass bands play in the Mirabell Gardens (May-Aug Sun at 10:30).

Sunday Morning: Music at Mass

Each Sunday morning, three great churches offer a Mass, generally with glorious music. The **Salzburg Cathedral** is likely your best bet for fine music to worship by. The 10:00 service generally features a Mass written by a well-known composer performed by choir, organist, or other musicians. The worship service is often followed at 11:30 by a free organ concert (music program at www.kirchen.net/dommusik). Nearby (just outside Domplatz, with the pointy green spire), the **Franciscan Church** is the locals' choice and is enthusiastic about its musical Masses (at 9:00, www.franziskanerkirche-salzburg.at—click on "Programm"). **St. Peter's Church** sometimes has music (at 10:15, www.stift-stpeter.at—click on "Kirchenmusik," then "Jahresprogramm").

MARIONETTE THEATER

Salzburg's much-loved marionette theater offers operas with spellbinding marionettes and recorded music. A troupe of 10 puppeteers—actors themselves—brings to life the artfully created puppets at the end of their five-foot strings. The 180 performances a year alternate between *The Sound of Music* and various German-language operas (with handy superscripts in English). While the 300-plus-seat venue is forgettable, the art of the marionettes enchants adults and children alike. For a sneak preview, check out the videos playing at the marionette exhibit at Hohensalzburg Fortress—and on their website.

Cost and Hours: €20-35, kids-€15, May-Sept nearly nightly at 19:30 plus matinees on some days, also a few shows in Dec, no shows Oct-Nov or Jan-April, near Mozart's Residence at Schwarzstrasse 24, tel. 0662/872-406, www.marionetten.at.

SALZBURG FESTIVAL (SALZBURGER FESTSPIELE)

Each summer, from mid-July to the end of August, Salzburg hosts its famous Salzburg Festival, founded in 1920 to employ Vienna's musicians in the summer. This fun and festive time is crowded—a total of 200,000 tickets are sold to festival events annually—but there are usually plenty of beds (except for a few August weekends). Events take place primarily in three big halls: the Opera and Orchestra venues in the Festival House, and the Landestheater, where German-language plays are performed. Tickets for the big festival events are generally expensive (€50-600) and sell out well in advance (bookable from January). But many "go to the Salzburg Festival" by seeing smaller, non-festival events that go on during the festival weeks. For these unofficial events, same-day tickets are normally available—ask at the TI for details. For specifics on this year's festival schedule and tickets, visit www.salzburgfestival.at.

Music lovers in town during the festival who don't have tickets (or money) can still enjoy **Festival Nights,** a free series of videos of previous festival performances, projected on a big screen on Kapitelplatz (behind the cathedral). It's a fun scene, with plenty of folding chairs and a food circus of temporary eateries. For info and schedules, go to www.salzburg.info and search for "Festival Nights."

OTHER ANNUAL FESTIVALS

The Salzburg Festival stages a week of concerts over the **Whitsunday** holiday weekend in early June (a school holiday in Austria and Bavaria). Offerings and prices are similar to those in July-August.

Mozart Week (Mozartwoche) is a high-quality, more affordable option held each year in late January. Run by the Mozarteum Foundation, it features up to three daily performances of works by both the great composer and his contemporaries (www.mozarteum.at; click on "Mozart Week" for details).

Sleeping in Salzburg

I've listed the rates you'll typically find in May, June, the first half of July, September, and October. Rates rise significantly (20-30 percent) during the music festival (mid-July-Aug), during Advent (the four weeks leading up to Christmas, when street markets are at full blast), and around Easter. Rates are lower in the off-season. Many places charge 10 percent extra for a one-night stay. Remember, to call Salzburg from Germany, dial 00-43 and then the number (minus the initial zero).

IN THE NEW TOWN, NORTH OF THE RIVER

These listings cluster around Linzer Gasse, a lively pedestrian shopping street that's a 15-minute walk or quick bus ride from the train station (for directions, see "Arrival in Salzburg," earlier) and a 10-minute walk to the Old Town. If you're coming from the Old Town, simply cross the main bridge (Staatsbrücke). Linzer Gasse is straight ahead. If driving, exit the highway at Salzburg-Nord, follow Vogelweiderstrasse straight to its end, and turn right. Parking is easy at the nearby Mirabell-Congress garage (€15/day, your hotel may be able to get you a €1-2 discount, Mirabellplatz).

$$$ Altstadthotel Wolf-Dietrich, around the corner from Linzer Gasse on pedestrians-only Wolf-Dietrich-Strasse, has 40 well-located, tastefully plush rooms (half of them overlook St. Sebastian Cemetery; a third are in an annex across the street). Prices include a huge breakfast spread and an afternoon *Kaffee-und-Kuchen* snack (roughly Sb-€90, Db-€150, Tb-€175, rates vary with demand, family deals, readers of this book who reserve direct get a 10 percent discount on prevailing price—insist on this discount deducted from whatever price is offered that day; non-smoking, elevator, guest computer and Wi-Fi, annex rooms have air-con, pool with loaner swimsuits, sauna, free DVD library, Wolf-Dietrich-Strasse 7, tel. 0662/871-275, www.salzburg-hotel.at, office@salzburg-hotel.at).

$$ Hotel Trumer Stube, well-located three blocks from the river just off Linzer Gasse, has 20 small, attractive rooms (Sb-

Sleep Code

Abbreviations   **(€1 = about $1.40, country code: 43)**
S = Single, **D** = Double/Twin, **T** = Triple, **Q** = Quad, **b** = bathroom, **s** = shower only
Price Rankings
 $$$ **Higher Priced**—Most rooms €125 or more.
  $$ **Moderately Priced**—Most rooms between €75-125.
   $ **Lower Priced**—Most rooms €75 or less.
Unless otherwise noted, credit cards are accepted, breakfast is included, Wi-Fi is generally free, and English is spoken. Salzburg levies a hotel tax of €1 per person, per night, which is generally not included in the rates I've quoted. Prices can change without notice; verify current rates online or by email. For the best prices, always book directly with the hotel.

€72.50, Db-€120, Tb-€151, Qb-€177; email and ask for the best Rick Steves cash-only rate, €7.50/person less if you skip breakfast; non-smoking, elevator, Wi-Fi, look for the flower boxes at Bergstrasse 6, tel. 0662/874-776, www.trumer-stube.at, info@trumer-stube.at, Vivienne).

$$ Hotel Krone 1512, about five blocks from the river, offers 23 decent, simply furnished rooms in a building that dates to medieval times. Back-facing rooms are quieter than the streetside ones. Cheapskates can save by requesting the near-windowless "student" double. Stay awhile in their pleasant cliffside garden (Sb-€79, Db-€108-122, Tb-€152, Qb-€198, €14/person less if you skip breakfast—bakeries and cafés nearby, family deals, guests with this book who reserve direct get about 8 percent off—plus another 4 percent if you pay with cash, elevator, guest computer and Wi-Fi, Linzer Gasse 48, tel. 0662/872-300, www.krone1512.at, hotel@krone1512.at, run by Ukrainian-Austrian-Canadian Niko).

$$ Gästehaus im Priesterseminar Salzburg occupies two floors of a dormitory for theological students that have been turned into a superbly located hotel. The 47 high-ceilinged rooms ring the stately Baroque courtyard of a grand building. Each room has a Bible and a cross (and no TV), but guests are not required to be in a contemplative frame of mind (Sb-€60, Db-€106-120 depending on size, Db suite-€138, one-night stay-€4/person extra, 3-night minimum in July-Aug, elevator; guest computer, cable Internet, and Wi-Fi—must borrow router and leave deposit; kitchen, laundry facilities; reception closes Mon-Sat at 18:00, Sun at 15:00—arrange ahead if arriving later; Dreifaltigkeitsgasse 14, tel. 0662/8774-9510, www.gaestehaus-priesterseminar-salzburg.at, gaestehaus@priesterseminar.kirchen.net).

$$ Hotel Schwarzes Rössl is a university dorm that becomes a student-run hotel each July, August, and September. The location couldn't be handier. It looks like a normal hotel from the outside, and its 56 rooms, while a bit spartan, are as comfortable as a hotel on the inside (S-€60, Sb-€70, D-€88, Db-€106, Tb-€135, ask for Rick Steves discount, good breakfast, guest computer, Wi-Fi in common areas, no rooms rented Oct-June, just off Linzer Gasse at Priesterhausgasse 6, tel. 0662/874-426, www.academiahotels.at, schwarzes.roessl@academiahotels.at).

$$ Institute St. Sebastian is in a somewhat sterile but very clean historic building next to St. Sebastian Cemetery. From October through June, the institute houses female students from various Salzburg colleges and also rents 40 beds for travelers (men and women). From July through September, the students are gone, and they rent all 118 beds (including 20 twin rooms) to travelers. The building has spacious public areas, a roof garden, a piano that guests are welcome to play, and some of the best rooms and dorm beds in town for the money. The immaculate doubles come with modern baths and head-to-toe twin beds (S-€48, Sb-€53, D-€68, Db-€85, Tb-€105, Qb-€118, one-night stay-€3/person extra, elevator, non-smoking, Wi-Fi, self-service laundry-€4/load; reception closes at 21:00 or in the afternoon off-season; Linzer Gasse 41, enter through arch at #37, tel. 0662/871-386, www.st-sebastian-salzburg.at, office@st-sebastian-salzburg.at). Students like the €24 bunks in 4- to 10-bed dorms (free lockers). You'll find self-service kitchens on each floor (fridge space is free; request a key). If you need parking, request it when you book.

On Rupertgasse

These two similar hotels are about five blocks farther from the river on Rupertgasse—a breeze for drivers but with more street noise than the places on Linzer Gasse. They're both modern and well-run, with free on-site parking, making them good values if you don't mind being a 15-20-minute walk or quick bus ride from the Old Town. From the station, take bus #2 to the Vogelweiderstrasse stop; from Hanuschplatz, take #4 to Grillparzerstrasse.

$$ Bergland Hotel is charming and classy, with 18 comfortable neo-rustic rooms. It's a modern building, spacious and solid (Sb-€65, Db-€95-105 depending on size, big Db suites-€130, non-smoking, elevator, pay guest computer, Wi-Fi, Rupertgasse 15, tel. 0662/872-318, www.berglandhotel.at, office@berglandhotel.at, Kuhn family).

$$ Hotel Jedermann, a few doors down, is simpler and larger. It's tastefully done and comfortable, with an artsy painted-concrete ambience, a backyard garden, and 30 rooms (Sb-€75, Db-€95, Tb-€120, Qb-€160, non-smoking, elevator, pay guest computer, cable Internet and Wi-Fi, Rupertgasse 25, tel. 0662/873-2410, www.

hotel-jedermann.com, office@hotel-jedermann.com, Herr und Frau Gmachl).

Near the Train Station

$$ Motel One Salzburg-Mirabell, part of a German chain, is an inexpensive hotel right along the river. Its 119 cookie-cutter rooms are small, with spongy carpets, but the staff is helpful and the lounge is inviting. It's six blocks (or a two-stop bus ride) from the train station, and a 15-minute riverside walk or short bus ride from the Old Town (Sb-€78, Db-€101, €7.50/person less if you skip breakfast, elevator, Wi-Fi, guest iPad at front desk, parking-€12/day, Elisabethkai 58, bus #1 or #2 from platform D at station to St.-Julien-Strasse—use underpass to cross road safely, tel. 0662/885-200, www.motel-one.com, salzburg-mirabell@motel-one.com).

IN THE OLD TOWN

These two hotels are nicely located near Mozartplatz. While this area is car-restricted, your hotel can give you a code that lets you drive in to unload, pick up a map and parking instructions, and head for the €18-per-day garage in the mountain (punch the code into the gate near Mozartplatz). You can't actually drive into the narrow Goldgasse, but you can park to unload at the end of the street.

$$$ Hotel am Dom, on the narrow Goldgasse pedestrian street, offers 15 chic, upscale rooms, some with their original wood-beam ceilings. Manager Josef promises his best rates to readers of this book who reserve direct and pay cash (Sb-€110-130, standard Db-€130-180, "superior" Db-€150-200, rates vary with demand, air-con, non-smoking, elevator; guest computer, cable Internet, and Wi-Fi; Goldgasse 17, tel. 0662/842-765, www.hotelamdom.at, office@hotelamdom.at).

$$$ Hotel Weisse Taube has 30 comfortable rooms in a quiet dark-wood 14th-century building, well-located about a block off Mozartplatz (typically Sb-€99, Db with shower-€129-139, bigger Db with bath-€159, extra bed-€30-35, 10 percent discount with this book if you reserve directly with hotel and pay cash, elevator, Wi-Fi, tel. 0662/842-404, Kaigasse 9, www.weissetaube.at, hotel@weissetaube.at).

HOSTELS

The Institute St. Sebastian, listed earlier, also has cheap dorm beds.

$ International Youth Hotel, a.k.a. the "Yo-Ho," is the most lively, handy, and American of Salzburg's hostels. This backpacker haven is a youthful and easygoing place that speaks English first; has cheap meals, 186 beds, lockers, tour discounts, and no curfew; plays *The Sound of Music* free daily at 19:00; runs a lively bar; and

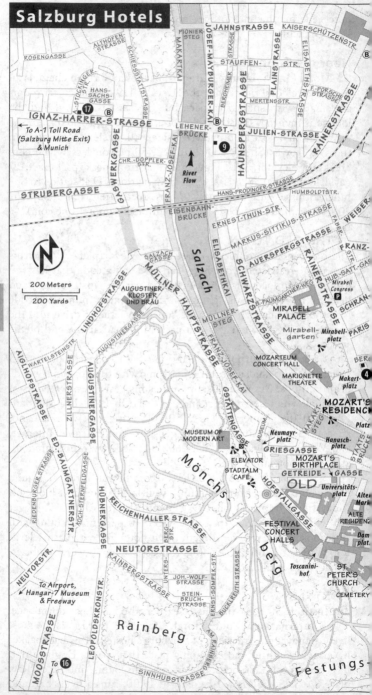

Salzburg Hotels

SALZBURG & BERCHTESGADEN

To A-1 Toll Road
(Salzburg Mitte Exit)
& Munich

To Airport,
Hangar-7 Museum
& Freeway

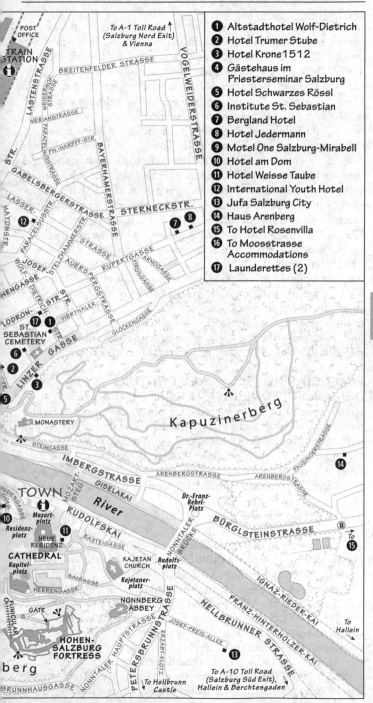

1. Altstadthotel Wolf-Dietrich
2. Hotel Trumer Stube
3. Hotel Krone 1512
4. Gästehaus im Priesterseminar Salzburg
5. Hotel Schwarzes Rössl
6. Institute St. Sebastian
7. Bergland Hotel
8. Hotel Jedermann
9. Motel One Salzburg-Mirabell
10. Hotel am Dom
11. Hotel Weisse Taube
12. International Youth Hotel
13. Jufa Salzburg City
14. Haus Arenberg
15. To Hotel Rosenvilla
16. To Moosstrasse Accommodations
17. Launderettes (2)

SALZBURG & BERCHTESGADEN

welcomes anyone of any age. The noisy atmosphere and lack of a curfew can make it hard to sleep (€18-21/person in 4- to 8-bed dorms, €21-22 in dorms with bathrooms, S-€40, D-€65, Ds-€75, T-€72, Q-€88, Qs-€93, includes sheets, breakfast-€3.50, pay guest computer, Wi-Fi, laundry-€4/load, 6 blocks from station toward Linzer Gasse and 6 blocks from river at Paracelsusstrasse 9, tel. 0662/879-649, www.yoho.at, office@yoho.at).

$ **Jufa Salzburg City,** quietly set amidst modern university buildings a short walk from the Old Town, is an upscale, privately run, 132-room "hostel" that actually has mostly double and quad rooms with very spartan furnishings. It has pleasant public spaces and offers lots of extras—including Ping-Pong, foosball, and a cafeteria with inexpensive meals—but the hotel-style rooms cost as much as those at better-located lodgings (bed in 8-person dorm-€22, Db-€110, Qb-€172, higher prices during festival, includes sheets, guest computer, Wi-Fi in common areas only, *The Sound of Music* plays daily at 20:00, laundry-€5/load, limited parking-€5/day, just around the east side of the castle hill at Josef-Preis-Allee 18; from train station, take bus #5 or #25 to the Justizgebäude stop, then continue one block past the bushy wall, cross Petersbrunnstrasse, find shady Josef-Preis-Allee, and walk a few minutes to the end—the hostel is the big orange/green building on the right; tel. 05/708-3613, www.jufa.eu/en, salzburg@jufa.eu).

FOUR-STAR HOTELS IN RESIDENTIAL NEIGHBORHOODS AWAY FROM THE CENTER

If you want to pay a little extra for plush furnishings, spacious public spaces, generous balconies, gardens, and free parking—and don't mind a longish walk or bus ride to the Old Town—consider the following places. These two modern hotels are set near each other in a residential area. While not ideal for train travelers, drivers in need of no-stress comfort for a home base should consider these (see map on page 248).

$$$ **Haus Arenberg** rents 16 big, breezy rooms—most with generous balconies—in a modern, ranch-style mansion with a quiet garden. Though in one of Salzburg's toniest neighborhoods, with Porsches lining the narrow hillside lanes, it's relaxed and unpretentious. Figure a 15-minute downhill walk to the center of town (along atmospheric Steingasse) and 20 minutes back up, or take bus #6, #7, or #10 to the Volksgarten stop and hike five minutes uphill (Sb-€85, Db-€135, Tb-€159, Qb-€165, no elevator, Wi-Fi, library, electric bikes-€12/day, Blumensteinstrasse 8, tel. 0662/640-097, www.arenberg-salzburg.at, info@arenberg-salzburg.at, Leobacher family). If driving here, get detailed directions.

$$$ **Hotel Rosenvilla,** farther out than Haus Arenberg, offers 15 bright, attentively furnished rooms surrounded by a leafy

garden, around the corner from a stop for the bus into town (Sb-€79, Db-€135, bigger Db-€145, Db suite-€168, no elevator, Wi-Fi, electric bikes-€12/day, Höfelgasse 4, tel. 0662/621-765, www.rosenvilla. com, hotel@rosenvilla.com, take bus #7 from Hanuschplatz to the Finanzamt stop, Stefanie).

PENSIONS ON MOOSSTRASSE

These are generally roomy and comfortable, and come with a good breakfast, free parking, farm-fresh scents, and mountains in the distance. They offer much more for your money than lodgings in town. Each is mere steps from a bus stop and the 15-minute ride from town is easy: with a €3.40 24-hour transit pass *(24-Stunden-Karte)* and frequent service, it shouldn't keep you away (see map on page 238). I've listed prices for two nights or more—if staying only one night, expect a small surcharge.

Moosstrasse runs southwest from the Old Town (behind the Mönchsberg). It was laid out a century ago through reclaimed marshland and lined with farm lots on each side. Some farm families continue to work the land, while others concentrate on offering rooms.

Handy bus #21 connects Moosstrasse to the center frequently (Mon-Fri 4/hour until 19:00, Sat 4/hour until 17:00, evenings and Sun 2/hour, last bus leaves downtown around 23:00). To get to these pensions from the train station, take any bus heading toward the center to Makartplatz, where you'll change to #21. If you're coming from the Old Town, catch bus #21 from Hanuschplatz, just downstream of the Staatsbrücke bridge, by the Fisch Krieg Restaurant. Buy your ticket from the streetside machine and punch it when you board the bus. The stop you get off at for each place is included in the listings below. Follow along with the stops on the map in the bus and press the button as soon as you hear yours announced—the bus only stops when requested.

If you're driving from the center, go through the tunnel, continue straight on Neutorstrasse, and take the fourth left onto Moosstrasse. Drivers exit the autobahn at *Süd* and then head in the direction of *Grodig*.

Reiterhof, at Moosstrasse 151 by the Hammerauer Strasse bus stop, is a popular, reasonably priced restaurant near these listings.

$$ Pension Bloberger Hof, while more a hotel than a pension, is comfortable and friendly, with a peaceful, rural location and 20 farmer-plush, good-value rooms. Inge and her daughter Sylvia offer a 10 percent discount to those who have this book, reserve direct, and pay cash (Sb-€70-80, Db-€85, big new Db with bal-

SALZBURG & BERCHTESGADEN

cony-€110, Db suite-€140, extra bed-€20, 10 percent extra for one-night stays, dinner for guests available Mon-Sat 18:00-21:00, no dinner on Sun, family apartment with kitchen, non-smoking, guest computer and Wi-Fi, free loaner bikes, free station pickup if staying 3 nights, Hammerauer Strasse 4, bus stop: Hammerauer Strasse, tel. 0662/830-227, www.blobergerhof.at, office@blobergerhof.at).

$ Frau Ballwein offers eleven cozy, charming, and fresh rooms in a delightful, family-friendly farmhouse. Some rooms have balconies with an intoxicating view (Sb-€47, Db-€63, Tb-€85, Qb-€95, 2-bedroom apartment for up to 5 people-€115, no surcharge for one-night stays, cash only, farm-fresh breakfasts amid her hanging teapot collection, non-smoking, Wi-Fi, 2 free loaner bikes, Moosstrasse 69a, bus stop: Gsengerweg, tel. 0662/824-029, www.haus-ballwein.at, haus.ballwein@gmx.net).

$ Helga Bankhammer rents four inexpensive, nondescript rooms in a farmhouse, with a real dairy farm out back (D-€52, Db-€54, no surcharge for one-night stays, family deals, non-smoking, Wi-Fi, laundry-about €7/load, Moosstrasse 77, bus stop: Marienbad, tel. 0662/830-067, www.privatzimmer.at/helga.bankhammer, bankhammer@aon.at).

$ Haus am Moos has nine nicely furnished rooms in a relaxed country atmosphere, with a garden, swimming pool, breakfast buffet with mountain views, and a tiny private chapel (Sb-€32, Db-€60, extra bed-€15, family rooms, no surcharge for one-night stays, non-smoking, guest computer and Wi-Fi, Moosstrasse 186a, bus stop: Lehrbauhof, tel. 0662/824-921, www.ammoos.at, ammoos186a@yahoo.de, Strasser family).

$ Haus Steiner's six rooms are straightforward and quiet, with older modern furnishings; there's a minimum two-night stay (Sb-€36, Db-€60, Tb-€90, non-smoking, guest computer and Wi-Fi, Moosstrasse 156c, bus stop: Hammerauer Strasse, tel. 0662/830-031, www.haussteiner.com, info@haussteiner.com, Rosemarie Steiner).

Eating in Salzburg

IN THE OLD TOWN

Gasthaus zum Wilden Mann is *the* place if the weather's bad and you're in the mood for a hearty, cheap meal at a shared table in one well-antlered (and non-smoking) room. Notice the century-old flood photos on the wall. For a quick lunch, get the *Bauernschmaus,* a mountain of dumplings, kraut, and peasant's meats (€13). While they have a few outdoor tables, the atmosphere is all indoors, and the menu is more geared to cold weather. Owner Robert—who runs the restaurant with Schwarzenegger-like energy—enjoys fostering a convivial ambience and encouraging strangers to share tables. I simply love this place (€10-14 main courses, specials posted on the wall, kitchen open Mon-Sat 11:00-21:00, closed Sun, 2 minutes from Mozart's Birthplace, enter from Getreidegasse 22 or Griesgasse 17, tel. 0662/841-787, www.wildermann.co.at).

St. Paul's Stub'n Beer Garden is tucked secretly away under the fortress with a decidedly untouristy atmosphere. The food is better than at beer halls, and a young, bohemian-chic clientele fills its two troll-like rooms and its idyllic tree-shaded garden. *Kasnock'n* is a tasty dish of *Spätzle* with cheese served in an iron pan. It includes a side salad for €9 (€10 with ham)—it's enough for two. Reservations are smart (€9-17 main courses, Mon-Sat 17:00-22:00, open later for drinks only, closed Sun, Herrengasse 16, tel. 0662/843-220, paulstubm.blogspot.com, Bernard).

Zirkelwirt serves reasonably priced Austrian standards (schnitzel, goulash, *Spätzle* with kraut) and big €8-9 salads in an updated *Gasthaus* dining room and exotic plant-screened terrace. Just a block off Mozartplatz, it's a world away from the tourism of Old Town (€9-13 main courses, daily 11:00-24:00, Pfeifergasse 14, tel. 0662/842-796, www.zumzirkelwirt.at).

Saran Essbar, in the middle of Old Town, is the product of hardworking Mr. Saran (from the Punjab), who cooks and serves with his heart. This delightful little eatery casts a rich orange glow under medieval vaults. Its fun menu is small (Mr. Saran is committed to both freshness and value), mixing Austrian (great schnitzel and strudel) and South Asian cuisine (€12-17 main courses, vegetarian options, cash only, no reservations, daily 11:00-15:00 & 17:00-22:00, longer hours during festival, a block off Mozartplatz at Judengasse 10, tel. 0662/846-628, www.saranessbar.at).

Café Tomaselli (with its Kiosk annex and terrace seating across the way) has long been Salzburg's top place to see and be seen. While pricey, it is good for lingering and people-watching. Tomaselli serves light meals and lots of drinks, keeps long hours daily, and has fine seating on the square, a view terrace upstairs, and indoor tables. Despite its fancy inlaid wood paneling, 19th-century portraits, and chandeliers, it's surprisingly low-key (€4-8 light meals, daily 7:00-20:00, until 22:00 during festival, Alter Markt 9, tel. 0662/844-488, www.tomaselli.at).

Vietnam Pho 18, fragrant with fresh cilantro, is where the Nguyen family dishes up Vietnamese noodle soups and other Asian standards in a six-table restaurant a long block from the cathedral (€7-9 main courses, eat in or take out, Sat-Thu 11:30-15:00 & 17:00-20:00, Fri 11:30-15:00, Kapitelgasse 11, mobile 0660-257-5588).

Stiftskeller St. Peter has been in business for more than 1,000 years—it was mentioned in the biography of Charlemagne. These

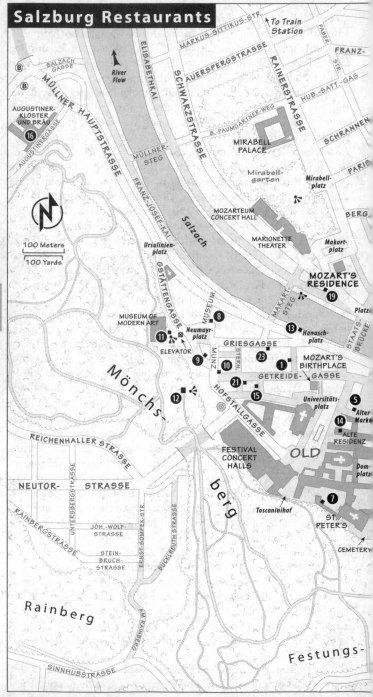

Salzburg Restaurants

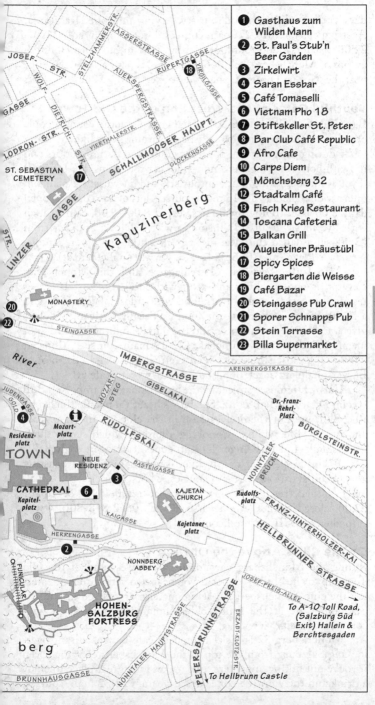

1. Gasthaus zum Wilden Mann
2. St. Paul's Stub'n Beer Garden
3. Zirkelwirt
4. Saran Essbar
5. Café Tomaselli
6. Vietnam Pho 18
7. Stiftskeller St. Peter
8. Bar Club Café Republic
9. Afro Cafe
10. Carpe Diem
11. Mönchsberg 32
12. Stadtalm Café
13. Fisch Krieg Restaurant
14. Toscana Cafeteria
15. Balkan Grill
16. Augustiner Bräustübl
17. Spicy Spices
18. Biergarten die Weisse
19. Café Bazar
20. Steingasse Pub Crawl
21. Sporer Schnapps Pub
22. Stein Terrasse
23. Billa Supermarket

SALZBURG & BERCHTESGADEN

days it's classy and high-end touristy, serving uninspired traditional Austrian cuisine (€18-27 main courses, kitchen open daily 11:30-22:00 or later, indoor/outdoor seating, next to St. Peter's Church at foot of Mönchsberg, tel. 0662/841-268, www.haslauer.at). They host the Mozart Dinner Concert described on page 242.

Youthful Cafés at the West End of the Old Town

Bar Club Café Republic, a hip hangout for local young people opposite the base of the Mönchsberg elevator, feels like a theater lobby during intermission. It serves good food both outdoors and in (with both smoking- and non-smoking rooms inside). It's ideal if you want something mod, untouristy, and un-wursty (Asian and international menu, €10-16 main courses, lots of hard drinks, open daily 8:00-late, trendy breakfasts served 8:00-18:00, Sun brunch with live music 10:00-13:00, music with a DJ Fri and Sat from 23:00, salsa dance club Tue night from 21:00—no cover, Anton-Neumayr-Platz 2, tel. 0662/841-613, www.republic-cafe.at).

Afro Cafe, between Getreidegasse and the Mönchsberg elevator, is non-smoking and a hit with local students. It serves tea, coffee, cocktails, and tasty food with a dose of '70s funk and a healthy sense of humor. The food isn't really African, but does give a nod to the continent, as do the murals and the leopard-spot menus (€8.20 weekday lunches, €12-19 main courses, Mon-Sat 9:00-24:00, closed Sun, between Getreidegasse and cliff face at Bürgerspitalplatz 5, tel. 0662/844-888, www.afrocafe.at).

Carpe Diem is a project by the local Donald Trump, Red Bull tycoon Dietrich Mateschitz. Salzburg's beautiful people, fueled by Red Bull, present themselves here in the chic ground-floor café and trendy "lifestyle bar" (smoking allowed), which serves quality cocktails and fine finger food in cones (café open daily 8:30-24:00). Upstairs is an expensive, non-smoking restaurant boasting a Michelin star (€26-37 main courses, €4.50 cover charge, €19.50 lunch special, restaurant open Mon-Sat 12:00-14:00 & 18:30-22:00, closed Sun; Getreidegasse 50, tel. 0662/848-800, www. carpediemfinestfingerfood.com).

On the Cliffs Above the Old Town

Riding the Mönchsberg elevator from the west end of the Old Town up to the clifftop deposits you near two very different eateries: the chic Mönchsberg 32 at the modern art museum, and the Stadtalm Café at the funky old mountaineers' hut—each with commanding city views.

Mönchsberg 32 is a sleek, modern café/bar/restaurant overlooking Salzburg from the top of the Mönchsberg elevator. Even if you're not hiking anywhere, this makes for a great place to enjoy a drink and the view (€5 coffee or ice cream, €22-32 main courses,

€3 cover charge, €14 lunch special, Tue-Sun 9:00-24:00, closed Mon except during festival, popular breakfasts served until 16:00, buy a one-way elevator ticket—they give customers a free pass to descend, tel. 0662/841-000. www.m32.at).

Stadtalm Café sits high above the Old Town on the edge of the cliff, with cheap prices, good traditional food, and great views. Nearby are the remnants of the old city wall. If hiking across the Mönchsberg, make this a stop (€10-12 main dishes, €9-10 salads, cliff-side garden seating or cozy-mountain-hut indoor seating—one indoor view table is booked for a decade of New Year's celebrations, daily May-Sept 10:00-22:00, Oct-April 10:00-18:00, hours are weather-dependent, 5 minutes from top of Mönchsberg elevator, also reachable by stairs from Toscaninihof, Mönchsberg 19C, tel. 0662/841-729, www.stadtalm.at, Peter).

Eating Cheaply in the Old Town

Fisch Krieg Restaurant, on the river where the fishermen used to sell their catch, is a great value. They serve fast, fresh, and inexpensive fish in a casual dining room—where trees grow through the ceiling—as well as great riverside seating (€2.50-€3 fishwiches to go, €8-9 self-serve main courses, salad bar, Mon-Fri 8:30-18:30, Sat 8:30-13:00, closed Sun, Hanuschplatz 4, tel. 0662/843-732, www.fisch-krieg.at).

Toscana Cafeteria Mensa is the university lunch canteen, very basic but fast and cheap—with drab indoor seating and a great courtyard for good weather. Choose between two daily soup- and main-course specials, each around €5-6 and one always meatless; there's free tap water (Mon-Thu 8:30-17:00, Fri 8:30-15:00, hot meals served 11:30-13:30 only, closed Sat-Sun, closed early Aug-mid-Sept, behind the Old Residenz, in the courtyard opposite Sigmund-Haffner-Gasse 16, tel. 0662/8044-6909).

Sausage stands *(Würstelstände)* serve the town's favorite "fast food." The best stands (like those on Universitätsplatz) use the same boiling water all day, which gives the weenies more flavor. For a list of helpful terms, see page 931. The 60-year-old **Balkan Grill,** run by chatty Frau Ebner, is a Salzburg institution, selling just one type of spicy sausage—*Bosna*—with your choice of toppings (€3.40; survey the five options—described in English—and choose a number; take-out only, steady and sturdy local crowd, Mon-Sat 11:00-19:00, Sun 15:00-19:00, hours vary with demand, Jan-Feb closed Sun, hiding down the tunnel at Getreidegasse 33 across from Eisgrotte).

Picnics: Picnickers will appreciate the well-stocked **Billa super-**

market at Griesgasse 19a, next to the Hanuschplatz bus stop (Mon-Fri 7:40-20:00, Sat 7:40-18:00, Sun 11:00-15:00). The smaller **Spar supermarket** in the train station is open long hours (Mon-Sat 6:00-23:00, Sun 8:00-23:00). The bustling morning **produce market** (Mon-Sat, closed Sun) on Universitätsplatz, behind Mozart's Birthplace, is fun, but expensive.

AWAY FROM THE CENTER

Augustiner Bräustübl, a huge 1,000-seat beer garden within a monk-run brewery in the Kloster Mülln, is rustic and raw. On busy

nights, it's like a Munich beer hall with no music but the volume turned up. When it's cool outside, enjoy a historic indoor setting in any of several beer-sloshed and smoke-stained halls (one of which is still for smokers). On balmy evenings, it's like a Renoir painting—but with beer breath and cigarette smoke—outdoors under chestnut trees. Local students mix with tourists eating hearty slabs of grilled meat with their fingers or cold meals from the self-serve picnic counter, while children frolic on the playground kegs. For your beer: Pick up a half-liter or full-liter mug, pay the lady (*schank* means self-serve price, *bedienung* is the price with waiter service), wash your mug, give Mr. Keg your receipt and empty mug, and you will be made happy. Waiters only bring beer; they don't bring food—instead, go up the stairs, survey the hallway of deli counters, grab a tray, and assemble your own meal (or, as long as you buy a drink, you can bring in a picnic—many do). Classic pretzels from the bakery and spiraled, salty radishes make great beer even better. Locals agree that the hot food here is not as good as the beer. Stick with the freshly cooked meat dishes: I made the mistake of choosing schnitzel, which was reheated in the microwave. For dessert—after a visit to the strudel kiosk—enjoy the incomparable floodlit view of old Salzburg from the nearby Müllnersteg pedestrian bridge and a riverside stroll home (daily 15:00-23:00, Augustinergasse 4, tel. 0662/431-246, www.augustinerbier.at).

Getting There: It's about a 15-minute walk along the river (with the river on your right) from the Old Town side of the Staatsbrücke bridge. After passing the Müllnersteg pedestrian bridge, just after Café am Kai, follow the stairs up to a busy street, and cross it. From here, either continue up more stairs into the trees and around the small church (for a scenic approach to the monastery), or stick to the sidewalk as it curves around to Augustinergasse.

Either way, your goal is the huge yellow building. Don't be fooled by second-rate gardens serving the same beer nearby. You can also take a bus from Hanuschplatz (#7, #8, #21, #24, #27, or #28) two stops to the Landeskrankenhaus stop, right in front of the beer garden.

NORTH OF THE RIVER, NEAR LINZER GASSE HOTELS

Spicy Spices is a trippy vegetarian-Indian restaurant where Suresh Syal (a.k.a. "Mr. Spicy") serves tasty curry and rice, samosas, organic salads, vegan soups, and fresh juices. It's a *namaste* kind of place, where everything's proudly organic (€7.50 specials served all day, €9 with soup or salad, €0.50 extra for takeout—refunded if you return the container, Mon-Fri 10:30-21:30, Sat-Sun 12:00-21:30, Wolf-Dietrich-Strasse 1, tel. 0662/870-712).

Biergarten die Weisse, close to the hotels on Rupertgasse and away from the tourists, is a longtime hit with the natives. If a beer hall can be happening, this one—modern yet with antlers—is it. Their famously good beer is made right there; favorites include their fizzy wheat beer (Die Weisse Original) and their seasonal beers (ask what's on offer). Enjoy the beer with their good, cheap traditional food in the great garden seating, or in the wide variety of indoor rooms—sports bar, young and noisy, or older and more elegant (€10-14 main courses, Mon-Sat 10:00-24:00, closed Sun, Rupertgasse 10, bus #2 to Bayerhamerstrasse or #4 to Grillparzer-strasse, tel. 0662/872-246, www.dieweisse.at).

Café Bazar, overlooking the river between the Mirabell Gardens and the Staatsbrücke bridge, is as close as you'll get to a Vienna coffee house in Salzburg. Their outdoor terrace is a venerable spot for a classy drink with an Old-Town-and-castle view (reasonable prices, light meals, Mon-Sat 7:30-23:00, Sun 9:00-18:00, Oct-May closes Mon-Sat at 19:30, Schwarzstrasse 3, tel. 0662/874-278).

Steingasse Pub Crawl

For a fun post-concert activity, drop in on a couple of atmospheric bars along medieval Steingasse (described on page 235). This is a local and hip scene—yet is accessible to older tourists: dark bars filled with well-dressed Salzburgers lazily smoking cigarettes and talking philosophy to laid-back tunes (no hip-hop). These four places are all within about 100 yards of each other. Start at the Linzer Gasse end of Steingasse. As they are quite different, survey all before choosing your spot (all open until the wee hours). Most don't serve food, but **Reyna,** a convenient four-table pizzeria and Döner Kebab shop at #3, stays open late.

Pepe Cocktail Bar, with Mexican decor and Latin music,

serves cocktails and nachos (Wed-Sun 19:00-until late, closed Mon-Tue, live DJs on Sat, Steingasse 3, tel. 0662/873-662, www. pepe-cocktailbar.at).

Saiten Sprung wins the "Best Atmosphere" award. The door is kept closed to keep out the crude and rowdy. Just ring the bell and enter its hellish interior—lots of stone and red decor, with mountains of melted wax beneath age-old candlesticks and an ambience of classic '70s and '80s music. Stelios, who speaks English with Greek charm, serves cocktails and fine wine, though no food (Mon-Sat 21:00-until late, closed Sun except in Dec, Steingasse 11, tel. 0662/881-377).

Fridrich, two doors down, is an intimate little place under an 11th-century vault, with lots of mirrors and a silver ceiling fan. Bernd Fridrich is famous for his martinis and passionate about Austrian wines, and has a tattered collection of vinyl that seems hell-bent on keeping the 1970s alive. Their Yolanda cocktail (grapefruit and vodka) is a favorite. He and his partner Ferdinand serve little dishes designed to complement the focus on socializing and drinking, though their €13 "little of everything dish" can be a meal for two (€6-13 appetizers, Thu-Tue from 18:00, closed Wed except during festival, Steingasse 15, tel. 0662/876-218, www. gastlokal-fridrich.at).

Selim's Bar, with cozy seating both inside and out, has a cool, conversation-friendly atmosphere with mellow music. A few years back, Tom Cruise and Cameron Diaz filmed a movie scene here. Gentlemanly Selim, who came here long ago from Algeria, also works as a dance instructor (no food, Mon-Sat 18:00-late, also open Sun in July-Aug and Dec, across street from cinema at Steingasse 10, mobile 0664-433-8447).

Salzburg Connections

BY TRAIN

By train, Salzburg is the first stop over the German-Austrian border. This means that if Salzburg is your only stop in Austria, and you're using a rail pass that covers Germany (including the Bayern-Ticket) but not Austria, you don't have to pay extra or add Austria to your pass to get here. Deutsche Bahn (German Railway) ticket machines at the Salzburg train station make it easy to buy tickets to German destinations.

From Salzburg by Train to: Berchtesgaden (roughly hourly, 1.5 hours, change in Freilassing, faster and prettier by bus—see "Getting There" in the Berchtesgaden section), **Füssen** (roughly hourly, 4 hours on fast trains, 5 hours on slow trains eligible for Bayern-Ticket, change in Munich and sometimes in Buchloe), **Reutte** (roughly hourly, 5 hours, change in Augsburg and Kempten, or in Munich and Garmisch), **Nürnberg** (hourly with change in Munich, 3 hours), **Hallstatt** (every 30-90 minutes, 50 minutes to Attnang-Puchheim, short wait, then 1.5 hours to Hallstatt; also works well by bus—see below), **Innsbruck** (hourly, 2 hours), **Vienna** (3/hour, 2.5-3 hours), **Melk** (almost hourly, 2.5 hours, transfer in Amstetten), **Munich** (2/hour, 1.5 hours on fast trains, 2 hours on slower trains eligible for Bayern-Ticket), **Frankfurt** (4/day direct, 6 hours), **Ljubljana** (3/day, 4.5 hours, some with change in Villach), **Prague** (4/day, 6.5 hours with change in Linz or 7.5 hours with change in Landshut), **Venice** (5/day, 6-8 hours, change in Innsbruck or Villach, short night train option). German train info: tel. 0180-599-6633, from Austria call 00-49-180-599-6633, www.bahn.com. Austrian train info: tel. 051-717 (to get an operator, dial 2, then 2), from Germany call 00-43-51-717, www.oebb.at.

BY BUS

To reach **Berchtesgaden,** bus #840 is easier than the train (about hourly Mon-Fri, 6-8/day Sat-Sun, 45 minutes, buses leave from platform G across street from Salzburg train station and also stop in Mirabellplatz and near Mozartplatz).

The bus trip to **Hallstatt** via Bad Ischl is cheaper, more scenic (with views of the Wolfgangsee), and only slightly slower than the train via Attnang-Puchheim—but the bus trip isn't covered by rail passes (bus #150 to Bad Ischl—Mon-Fri nearly hourly, Sat-Sun every 1-2 hours, 1.5 hours, leaves from platform F outside Salzburg train station, also stops at Mirabellplatz and Hofwirt, tel. 0810-222-333, www.postbus.at; at Bad Ischl station, change to the train—20-minute ride to Hallstatt, then ride the boat across the lake—or continue by bus to the Lahn section of Hallstatt with a change in Gosaumühle).

ROUTE TIPS FOR DRIVERS

From Salzburg to Innsbruck: To leave town driving west, go through the Mönchsberg tunnel and follow blue *A-1* signs for Munich. It's 1.5 hours from Salzburg to Innsbruck.

From Salzburg to Hallstatt: To avoid tolls, stick to the most direct route (B-158 via St. Gilgen). If you're in a hurry, get on the Munich-Vienna autobahn (follow blue A-1 signs, toll sticker required), head for Vienna, exit at Thalgau (#274), and follow signs to Hof, Fuschl, and St. Gilgen. The Salzburg-Hallstatt road passes two luge rides, St. Gilgen (pleasant but touristy), and Bad Ischl (the center of the Salzkammergut, with a spa, the emperor's villa if you need a Habsburg history fix, and a good TI, tel. 06132/277-570).

Berchtesgaden

This alpine ski region, just across the border from Salzburg in a finger of German territory that pokes south into Austria, is famous for its fjord-like lake and its moun-taintop Nazi retreat. Long before its association with Hitler, Berchtes-gaden (BERKH-tehs-gah-dehn) was one of the classic Romantic corners of Germany. In fact, Hitler's propa-gandists capitalized on the Führer's love of this region to establish the notion that the native Austrian was truly German at heart. Today visitors

cruise up the romantic Königssee to get in touch with the soul of Bavarian Romanticism; ride a bus up to Hitler's mountain retreat (5,500 feet); see the remains of the Nazis' elaborate last-ditch bunkers; ride an old miners' train into the mountain to learn all about salt mining; and hike along a secluded gorge to a high waterfall.

Remote little Berchtesgaden (pop. 7,500) can be inundated with Germans during peak season, when you may find yourself in a traffic jam of tourists desperately trying to turn their money into fun.

GETTING THERE

Berchtesgaden is only 15 miles from Salzburg. The quickest way there **from Salzburg** is by bus #840 from the Salzburg train sta-tion (runs about hourly Mon-Fri, 6-8/day Sat-Sun, usually at :15 past the hour, 45 minutes, buy tickets from driver, €9.80 *Tageskarte* day pass covers your round trip plus most local buses in Berchtes-gaden—except bus #849 up to the Eagle's Nest, last bus back leaves Berchtesgaden at 18:15; check schedules at www.svv-info.at—click "Timetables," then under "Find a timetable" select "Timetable book page," then enter "840"). On my last visit, bus #840 left from platform G across the street from the Salzburg train station (along-side the building with the H&M and Müller shops; as you exit the station's front door, go right). You can also catch bus #840 from the middle of Salzburg—after leaving the station, it stops a few minutes later on Mirabellplatz, and then in Salzburg's Old Town (on Rudolfskai, near Mozartplatz).

Coming **from Munich**, it's simplest to reach Berchtesgaden by train (almost hourly, 2.5-3 hours, change in Freilassing or Salz-burg). You can also get to Berchtesgaden from Salzburg by train via Freilassing, but it takes twice as long as the bus and isn't as scenic. The train is an option, though, if you need to get between Salzburg and Berchtesgaden in the evening or early morning, when no buses run.

PLANNING YOUR TIME

The Nazi and Hitler-related sites outside Berchtesgaden are the town's main draw and need a half-day to see. David and Christine Harper's tour of the sites is a good value and worth planning around (afternoons only, see "Tours in Berchtesgaden").

To do the Nazi sites on your own by bus, try this plan (confirm times in advance): 9:15—depart Salzburg on bus #840; 10:00—arrive Berchtesgaden station, look at murals in main hall; 10:15—bus #838 departs for Obersalzberg Documentation Center, arrives 10:27, visit bunkers and museum; 11:50—ride bus #849 from Documentation Center up to Eagle's Nest, look around and eat lunch; 13:30—take bus #849 down from Eagle's Nest; 14:14—ride bus #838 from Documentation Center to Berchtesgaden station. You could return to Salzburg on the 15:15 bus, or stay in Berchtesgaden to visit other attractions. On weekdays, consider an earlier start, leaving Salzburg on the 8:15 bus.

If you have time for more than the Nazi sites, Berchtesgaden also has tourable salt mines (similar to the ones at Hallein—see page 239) and a romantic, pristine lake called Königssee (extremely popular with less-adventurous Germans). Visiting either can take up to a half-day. While combining either of these with the Nazi sites is easy for drivers, it's challenging for those coming by public transport. Bus travelers wanting to fill up the rest of the day might be happier spending an hour walking through Berchtesgaden's Old Town, or going for a short hike in the Almbach Gorge (described later).

If you're visiting Berchtesgaden on your way between Salzburg and points in Germany, you can leave luggage in lockers at the Berchtesgaden train station during your visit.

Orientation to Berchtesgaden

Berchtesgaden's train station is worth a stop for its luggage lockers (along the train platform), WC (free, also near platform), and history (specifically, its vintage 1937 Nazi architecture and the murals in the main hall). The oversized station was built to accommodate (and intimidate) the hordes of Hitler fans who flocked here in

hopes of seeing the Führer. The building next to the station, just beyond the round tower, was Hitler's own V.I.P. reception area.

Berchtesgaden's central bus terminal (ZOB) is just in front of the train station. There are bakeries and a few forgettable restaurants nearby (consider bringing a picnic). The old center of Berchtesgaden, bypassed by most tourists, is up the hill behind the station (use the bridge over the tracks).

TOURIST INFORMATION

The TI is on the other side of the roundabout from the train station, in the yellow building with green shutters (mid-June-Sept Mon-Fri 8:30-18:00, Sat 9:00-17:00, Sun 9:00-15:00; Oct-mid-June Mon-Fri 8:30-17:00, Sat 9:00-12:00, closed Sun; German tel. 08652/9670, from Austria call 00-49-8652-9670, www.berchtesgadener-land.info). Pick up a local map, and consider the 30-page local-bus schedule (*Fahrplan*, €0.30) if you'll be hopping more than one bus.

GETTING AROUND BERCHTESGADEN

None of the sights I list are within easy walking distance from the station, but they're all connected by convenient local buses, which use the station as a hub (all these buses—except the special bus #849 between the Obersalzberg Documentation Center and the Eagle's Nest chalet—are free with the *Tageskarte* day pass from Salzburg; timetables at www.rvo-bus.de, or call 08652/94480). You'll want to note departure times and frequencies while still at the station, or pick up a schedule at the TI.

From the train station, buses #840 (the same line as the bus from Salzburg) and #837 go to the salt mines (a 20-minute walk otherwise). Bus #840 also goes to the Almbach Gorge. Bus #838 goes to the Obersalzberg Documentation Center, and bus #841 goes to the Königssee.

Tours in Berchtesgaden

Eagle's Nest Historical Tours

For 20 years, David and Christine Harper—who rightly consider this visit more an educational opportunity than simple sightseeing—have organized thoughtful tours of the Hitler-related sites near Berchtesgaden. Their bus tours, usually led by native English speakers, depart from the TI opposite the Berchtesgaden train station. Tours start by driving through the remains of the Nazis' Obersalzberg complex, then visit the bunkers underneath the Documentation Center, and end with a guided visit to the Eagle's Nest (€53/person, €1 discount with this book, English only, daily at 13:15 mid-May-late Oct, 4 hours, 30 people maximum, reserva-

Berchtesgaden and Nearby

To Vienna

To Vienna

AUTOBAHN A-1

Freilassing

To Munich

TRAIN STATION

A-1

158

2 Kilometers

2 Miles

A-8

Salzburg

To Salzkammergut & Hallstatt

20

HELLBRUNN CASTLE

AUSTRIA

A-10

Untersberg

SALZBURG SÜD EXIT

Bad Reichenhall

21

305

Bus #840 Between Salzburg & Berchtesgaden

Hallein

GERMANY

Dürrnberg

ALMBACH GORGE

SALT MINE

20

Oberau

305

Bus #840 / 837 to Salt Mines

SALT MINES

Unterau

Ober-salzberg

Berchtesgaden

Bus #838

NAZI DOCUMENTATION CENTER

Bus #841

Kehlstein

A-10

Königssee

Shuttle Bus #849 Only

HITLER'S EAGLE'S NEST

Watzmann

Königssee

To Villach (Austria), Italy & Slovenia

St. Bartholomä

SALZBURG & BERCHTESGADEN

tions strongly recommended, private tours available, German tel. 08652/64971, from Austria call 00-49-8652-64971, www.eagles-nest-tours.com). While the price is €53, your actual cost for the guiding is only about €26, as the tour takes care of your transport and admissions, not to mention relieving you of having to figure out the local buses up to Obersalzberg. Coming from Salzburg, you can take the 10:15 or 11:15 bus to Berchtesgaden, eat a picnic lunch, take the tour, then return on the 18:15 bus from Berchtesgaden, which gets you back to Salzburg 45 minutes later. If you're visiting near the beginning or end of the season, be aware that tours will be canceled if it's snowing at the Eagle's Nest (as that makes the twisty, precipitous mountain road too dangerous to drive). David and Christine also arrange off-season tours, though the Eagle's Nest isn't open for visitors in winter (€120/up to 4 people; see website for details).

If you'd like to use the morning (before the tour) to sightsee in and around Berchtesgaden, here are two good plans. One is to leave Salzburg on the 8:15 bus (Mon-Fri only), arrive at the salt mines as they open at 9:00 (when there's no line), see the mines, then take the bus or walk (either along the river or through the old town) up to the TI, where the Harpers' tour begins. The other is to leave Salzburg on the 8:15 or 9:15 bus, get off at the Kugelmühle stop to hike the Almbachklamm, then continue on a later bus, arriving in Berchtesgaden at 12:00 or 13:00. Bringing a picnic isn't essential, but it beats a rushed restaurant lunch.

Bus Tours from Salzburg

While Salzburg-based tour companies (including Bob's Special Tours, www.bobstours.com, and Panorama tours, www.panoramatours.com) offer half- and full-day tours to Berchtesgaden, I don't recommend them except as a last resort. They take you to (but not into) the sights described here—meaning that you pay the tour price of €48-96 for the same transport that you can buy yourself for €9.50. Even on the full-day tours, you cannot see both the Eagle's Nest and the Obersalzberg Documentation Center—you have to choose between them. Take David and Christine Harper's tour instead, or visit the Documentation Center and Eagle's Nest on your own by bus, using the plan suggested earlier (under "Planning Your Time").

Sights near Berchtesgaden

▲▲▲NAZI SITES

Early in his career as a wannabe tyrant, Adolf Hitler had a radical friend who liked to vacation in Berchtesgaden, and through him Hitler came to know and love this dramatic corner of Bavaria. Berchtesgaden's part-Bavarian, part-Austrian character held a special appeal to the Austrian-German Hitler. In the 1920s, just out of prison, he checked into an alpine hotel in Obersalzberg, three miles uphill from Berchtesgaden, to finish work on his memoir and Nazi primer, *Mein Kampf*. Be-

cause it was here that he claimed to be inspired and laid out his vision, some call Obersalzberg the "cradle of the Third Reich."

In the 1930s, after becoming the German Chancellor, Hitler chose Obersalzberg to build his mountain retreat, a supersized alpine farmhouse called the Berghof. His handlers crafted Hitler's image here—surrounded by nature, gently receiving alpine flowers from adoring little children, lounging around with farmers in lederhosen...no modern arms industry, no big-time industrialists, no ugly extermination camps. In reality, Obersalzberg was home to much more than Hitler's alpine chalet. It was a huge compound of 80 buildings—fenced off from the public after 1936—where the major decisions leading up to World War II were hatched. Hitler himself spent about a third of his time at the Berghof, hosted world leaders in the compound, and later had it prepared for his last stand.

Some mistakenly call the entire area "Hitler's Eagle's Nest." But that name actually belongs only to the Kehlsteinhaus, a small mountaintop chalet on a 6,000-foot peak that juts up two miles south of Obersalzberg. (A visiting diplomat humorously dubbed it the "Eagle's Nest," and the name stuck.) In 1939, it was given to the Führer for his 50th birthday. While a fortune was spent building this perch and the road up to it, Hitler, who was afraid of heights, visited only 14 times. Hitler's mistress, Eva Braun, though, liked to hike up to the Eagle's Nest to sunbathe.

In April of 1945, Britain's Royal Air Force bombed the Obersalzberg compound nearly flat, but missed the difficult-to-target Eagle's Nest entirely. Almost all of what survived the bombing at Obersalzberg was blown up in 1952 by the Allies—who wanted to leave nothing as a magnet for future neo-Nazi pilgrims—before they turned the site over to the German government. The most extensive surviving remains are of the Nazis' bunker system, intended to serve as a last resort for the regime as the Allies closed in. In the 1990s, a museum, the Obersalzberg Documentation Center, was built on top of one of the bunkers. The museum and bunker, plus the never-destroyed Eagle's Nest, are the two Nazi sites worth seeing near Berchtesgaden.

Obersalzberg Documentation Center and Bunker

To reach the most interesting part of this site, walk through the museum and down the stairs into the vast and complex bunker system. Construction began in 1943, after the Battle of Stalingrad ended the Nazi aura of invincibility. This is a professionally engineered underground town, which held meeting rooms, offices, archives for the government, and lavish living quarters for Hitler—all connected by four miles of tunnels cut  through solid rock by slave labor. You can't visit all of it, and what you can see was stripped and looted bare after the war. But enough is left that you can wander among the concrete and marvel at megalomania gone mad.

The museum above, which has almost no actual artifacts, is designed primarily for German students and others who want to learn and understand their still-recent history. There's little English, but you can rent the €2 English audioguide.

Cost and Hours: €3 covers both museum and bunker; April-Oct daily 9:00-17:00; Nov-March Tue-Sun 10:00-15:00, closed Mon; last entry one hour before closing, allow 1.5 hours for visit, German tel. 08652/947-960, from Austria tel. 00-49-8652-947-960, www.obersalzberg.de.

Getting There: Hop on bus #838 from Berchtesgaden's train station (daily, roughly hourly, 12 minutes, 5-minute walk from Obersalzberg stop).

Eagle's Nest (Kehlsteinhaus)

Today, the chalet that Hitler ignored is basically a three-room, reasonably priced restaurant with a scenic terrace, 100 yards below the summit of a mountain. You could say it's like any alpine hiking hut, just more massively built. On a nice day, the views are magnificent. If it's fogged in (which it often is), most people won't find it worth coming up here (except on David and Christine Harper's tours—described earlier—which can make the building come to life even without a view). Bring a jacket, and prepare for crowds in summer (less crowded if you go early or late in the day).

From the upper bus stop, a finely crafted tunnel (which will have you humming the *Get Smart* TV theme song) leads to the original polished-brass elevator, which takes you the last 400 feet up to the Eagle's Nest. Wander into the fancy back dining room (the best-preserved from Hitler's time), where you can see the once-sleek marble fireplace chipped up by souvenir-seeking troops in 1945.

Cost and Hours: Free, generally open mid-May-late Oct, snowfall sometimes forces a later opening or earlier closing.

Getting There: The only way to reach the Eagle's Nest—even if you have your own car—is by specially equipped bus #849, which leaves from the Documentation Center and climbs steeply up the one-way, private road—Germany's highest (every 25 minutes, 15 minutes, €16.10 round-trip, *Tageskarte* day passes not valid, buy ticket from windows, last bus up 16:00, last bus down 16:25, free parking at Documentation Center).

OTHER SIGHTS NEAR BERCHTESGADEN
▲Salt Mines (Salzbergwerk Berchtesgaden)

At the Berchtesgaden salt mines, you put on traditional miners' outfits, get on funny little trains, and zip deep into the mountain. For two hours (which includes time to get into and back out of your miner's gear), you'll cruise subterranean lakes; slide speedily down two long, slick, wooden banisters; and learn how they mined salt so long ago. Call ahead for crowd-avoidance advice; when the weather gets bad, this place is mobbed with a two-hour wait for the next open tour. Tours are in German, but English-speakers get audioguides.

Cost and Hours: €16, daily May-Oct 9:00-17:00, Nov-April 11:00-15:00—these are last-entry times, German tel. 08652/600-20, from Austria dial 00-49-8652-600-20, www.salzzeitreise.de.

Getting There: The mines are a 20-minute walk or quick bus ride (#837 or #840) from the Berchtesgaden station; ask the driver to let you off at the Salzbergwerk stop. (Since buses coming from Salzburg pass here on the way into Berchtesgaden, you can also simply hop off at the mines before getting into town, instead of backtracking from the station.) If you have extra time, you can take a longer, more interesting 35-minute walk from the station to the mines through Berchtesgaden's Old Town.

▲Königssee

Three miles south of Berchtesgaden, the idyllic Königssee stretches like a fjord through pristine mountain scenery to the dramatically situated Church of St. Bartholomä and beyond. To get to the lake from Berchtesgaden, hop on bus #841 (about hourly from train station to boat dock, 10 minutes), or take the scenically woodsy, reasonably flat 1.25-hour walk (well-signed). Drivers pay €4 to park.

Most visitors simply glide scenically for 35 minutes on the silent, electronically propelled **boat** to the church, enjoy that peaceful setting, then glide back. Boats, going at a sedate Bavarian speed and filled with Germans chuckling at the captain's commentary, leave with demand—generally 2-4 per hour (late April-mid-Oct, no boats off-season, €14 round-trip, German tel. 08652/96360, from Austria dial 00-49-8652-96360, www.seenschifffahrt.de). At a rock cliff midway

SALZBURG & BERCHTESGADEN

through the journey, your captain stops, and the first mate pulls out a trumpet to demonstrate the fine echo.

The remote, red-onion-domed **Church of St. Bartholomä** (once home of a monastery, then a hunting lodge of the Bavarian royal family) is surrounded by a fine beer garden, rustic fishermen's pub, and inviting lakeside trails. The family next to St. Bartholomä's lives in the middle of this national park and has a license to fish—so very fresh trout is the lunchtime favorite.

While the Königssee is lovely once you're on the water, all the preliminaries are a bit tedious. The bus from Berchtesgaden

drops you next to a complex with WCs, ATMs, and a TI; across the parking lot rise the golden arches of McDonald's. From there, a brick path leads five minutes downhill to the lakeshore through a thicket of souvenir stores selling marmot-fat ointment, quartz chunks, carved birdhouses, and "super-pretzels." At the ticket windows, you'll get a set departure time (expect a wait, as boats fill up). Rowboat rental is also an option (€7-10/hour), but the church is too far up the lake to reach easily by muscle power alone.

Almbach Gorge (Almbachklamm)

This short, popular hike is a good option for nature-lovers who come to see Berchtesgaden's Nazi sites, then want to fill up the rest of the day hiking along a stream-filled gorge with a minimum of fuss and crowds. Though not a world-class attraction (and not for children, due to drop-offs), it can easily make for an enjoyable two or three hours. Most visitors do it as roughly a four-mile roundtrip, though you can go farther if you wish.

Leave bus #840 at the Kugelmühle stop (12 minutes towards Salzburg from Berchtesgaden) and check the next bus times—two hours between buses is enough for a quick visit, three hours for a leisurely one. Walk five minutes along Kugelmühlweg (following the *Almbachklamm* signs) to the trailhead. First you'll see the **Gasthaus zur Kugelmühle,** which serves reasonably priced meals (daily 11:30-19:30, tel. 08650/461, from Austria dial 00-49-8650-461, www.gasthaus-kugelmuehle.de). In front of the restaurant is an old wooden apparatus for shaping marble blocks into round toy spheres (hence the name—*Kugel* means ball, *Mühle* means mill). Just beyond is a gate where you pay €3 to enter the gorge; pick up a map and get hiking advice here (daily May-Oct 9:00-18:00; gorge closed in winter).

A rushing stream cascades through the gorge, which the trail crosses and recrosses on numbered steel bridges. The trail is well-maintained and exciting, and accessible to anyone who is reasonably fit, sure-footed, and wearing sturdy shoes. However, it's not safe or appropriate for young children because the path has some steep, unguarded drop-offs that could land kids into the cold water. Expect some narrow and slippery parts, and take advantage of the hand rails and steel cables strung along some portions for support. You can just walk up as far as you have time for, but the high Sulzer waterfall by bridge #19 is a traditional turn-around point. The walk there and back can be done in two hours at a good clip, but allowing three hours makes for a more pleasant visit.

BADEN-BADEN AND THE BLACK FOREST

Baden-Baden • Freiburg • Staufen • Best of the Black Forest

Combine Edenism and hedonism as you explore this most romantic of German regions and dip into its mineral spas. The Black Forest ("Schwarzwald" in German) is a range of hills stretching along the French border 100 miles from Switzerland north to Karlsruhe (the highest peak is the 4,900-foot Feldberg). Because this region's thick forests allowed little light in, people called it "black."

Until the last century, the Schwarzwald was cut off from the German mainstream. The poor farmland drove medieval locals to become foresters, glassblowers, and clockmakers. Today, the Black Forest offers clean air, cuckoo clocks, cheery villages, and countless hiking possibilities. This is where Germans come to recuperate from their hectic workaday lives, as well as from medical ailments—often compliments of Germany's generous public health system. Key words you'll see everywhere are *Bad* (or *Baden*), meaning "bath"; and *Kur*, loosely, "cure." Either term is synonymous with "spa" and directs you to a place to relax, soak, and recover. The region is also known for its favorite dessert, *Schwarzwälder Kirschtorte*—Black Forest cake, a mouthwatering concoction with alternating layers of schnapps-soaked chocolate cake, cherries, and whipped cream.

Germans use the term Schwarzwald to refer to the entire southwestern corner of Germany rather than just its forested parts. The region's two major (and very different) towns are Baden-Baden in the north and Freiburg in the south. Neither feels particularly woodsy—instead, their proximity to France lends both cities a sunny elegance. Baden-Baden is Germany's grandest 19th-century spa resort. Stroll through its elegant streets and casino. Soak in its

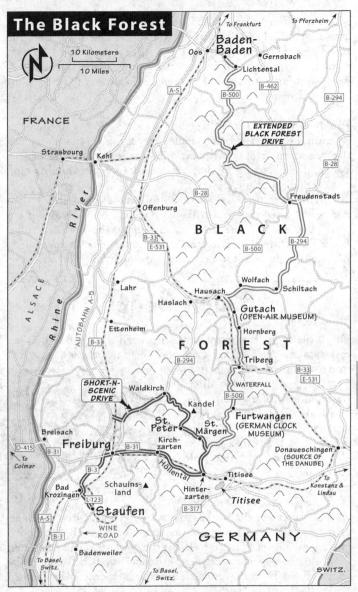

The Black Forest

10 Kilometers
10 Miles

To Frankfurt
To Pforzheim

Baden-Baden

Oos
Gernsbach
Lichtental

A-5
B-500
B-462
B-294

FRANCE

EXTENDED BLACK FOREST DRIVE

Strasbourg
Kehl

B-28

B-28

Offenburg
Freudenstadt

B L A C K

B-33
E-531
B-500
B-294

Lahr
Wolfach
Schiltach

Hausach

Haslach
Gutach
(OPEN-AIR MUSEUM)

Ettenheim
Hornberg

F O R E S T

B-294

Triberg

B-33
E-531

SHORT-N-SCENIC DRIVE
Waldkirch
WATERFALL
B-500

Kandel
Furtwangen
(GERMAN CLOCK MUSEUM)

Breisach
St. Peter
St. Märgen

B-31
Kirch-zarten

Freiburg

Donaueschingen
(SOURCE OF THE DANUBE)

D-415
B-31

B-3
Höllental
Titisee
To Konstanz & Lindau

To Colmar

Bad Krozingen
Schauins-land
Hinter-zarten
Titisee

L-123
A-5
Staufen
B-317

B-3
WINE ROAD
G E R M A N Y

Badenweiler

To Basel, Switz.
To Basel, Switz.
SWITZ.

RHINE River
ALSACE
AUTOBAHN A-5

famous baths. Freiburg is the Black Forest's de facto capital and main university town. For a small-town experience, hang your hat in cozy Staufen.

Back up in the hills, a pair of worthwhile museums show off two different sides of the local culture—the Vogtsbauernhof Black Forest Open-Air Museum near Gutach, and the German Clock

Museum in Furtwangen. You'll also find plenty of opportunity for lazy drives and hikes. The area's two biggest tourist traps are the tiny Titisee (a lake not quite as big as its parking lot) and Triberg, a small town filled with cuckoo-clock shops and a sprinkling of worthwhile attractions. Skip these places in favor of the attractions listed in this chapter.

PLANNING YOUR TIME

By **train,** Freiburg and Baden-Baden are easy, as is a short foray into the forest from either town. Save a day and two nights for Baden-Baden. Tour Freiburg by day, but consider sleeping in charming and overlooked Staufen.

With more time and a **car,** do the whole cuckoo thing: two nights and a relaxing day in Baden-Baden, a busy day doing the small-town forest medley south (with stops at the Vogtsbauernhof Black Forest Open-Air Museum and Furtwangen's German Clock Museum), a quick visit to Freiburg, and a night in Staufen.

Baden-Baden

Of all the high-class resort towns I've seen, Baden-Baden is the easiest to enjoy in jeans with a picnic. The town makes a great first stop in Germany (1.5 hours from Frankfurt's airport, a few direct trains, most with transfer).

Baden-Baden was the playground of Europe's high-rolling elite around 150 years ago. Royalty and aristocracy came from all corners of the continent to take the *Kur*—a soak in the (supposedly) curative mineral waters—and enjoy the world's top casino. Wrought-iron balconies on handsome 19th-century apartment buildings give Baden-Baden an elegant, almost Parisian feel. The town acquired its hyphenated double name—short for "Baden in Baden" (that is, Baden in the state of Baden)—in 1931, to distinguish it from other places named Baden (German for "baths").

The town remains popular today. How popular? Hoteliers in typical convention towns expect that 85 percent of their guests will need single rooms and 15 percent will need doubles. As spouses insist on coming to conventions held in Baden-Baden, hoteliers here flip-flop those figures, anticipating that 85 percent of the demand will be for doubles.

Along with conventioneers, this lush resort town attracts a middle-class crowd of tourists in search of a slower pulse, and Germans enjoying the fruits of their generous health-care system.

Orientation to Baden-Baden

Baden-Baden, with 55,000 residents, is made for strolling with a poodle. Except for the train station and a few accommodations, everything that matters is clustered within a 10-minute walk between the baths and the casino.

Although you'll barely notice if you just stick around the center, Baden-Baden is actually a long, skinny town, strung over several miles along the narrow valley of the Oosbach River (conveniently accessed by bus #201—see "Getting Around Baden-Baden," later). The train station is at the lower (northern) end of the valley, in a suburb called Baden-Oos, three miles from downtown; the Lichtentaler Abbey marks the upper end of the valley. The casino and town center are about halfway between, at the point where a small side valley joins the Oosbach valley. The church, castle, baths, and oldest sections of town are a few blocks uphill on the north slope of this side valley.

TOURIST INFORMATION

Baden-Baden's understaffed main TI is in the ornate Trinkhalle building. The TI has enough recommended walks and special events to keep the most energetic vacationer happy. Pick up the free monthly events program, *Baden-Baden Aktuell* (German only), which includes a good, fine-print, fold-out map. Hikers like the TI's *Panoramaweg* map (€1.50, German only). If you're headed into the countryside with a car, consider two other sources: the accessible cartoon-style €1 *Outline Map*, which helps you get your bearings for the region; and the €6 Black Forest guidebook. Mon-Sat 10:00-17:00, Sun 14:00-17:00, WC-€0.50, tel. 07221/275-200, www.baden-baden.de.

The main TI shares space with a genteel-feeling café and an agency that sells tickets to performances in town (theater, opera, orchestra, and musicals; Tue-Sat 10:00-18:00, Sun 14:00-17:00, closed Mon, tel. 07221/932-700, www.tickets-baden-baden.de, ticketservice@baden-baden.de).

Another TI is at the B-500 autobahn exit (Mon-Sat 9:00-18:00, Sun 9:00-13:00, Schwarzwaldstrasse 52).

ARRIVAL IN BADEN-BADEN

By Train: The train station has lockers (at platform 1, €2-4) and a handy *Reisezentrum* that sells tickets (long hours daily). To get downtown, walk out of the train station and catch bus #201 (€2.30

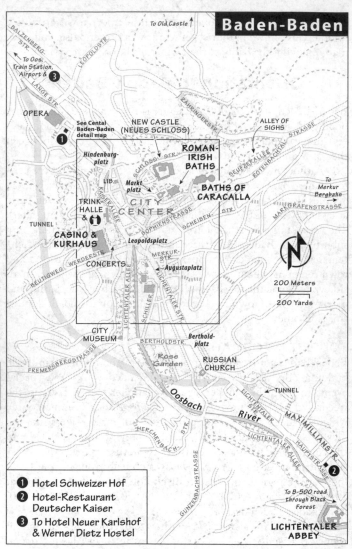

Baden-Baden

1 Hotel Schweizer Hof
2 Hotel-Restaurant Deutscher Kaiser
3 To Hotel Neuer Karlshof & Werner Dietz Hostel

BADEN-BADEN & THE BLACK FOREST

single ticket; see "Getting Around Baden-Baden," later). If you're staying in the town center, get off in about 15 minutes at Leopoldsplatz. Allow about €16 for a taxi from the train station to the center.

By Car: Because most traffic goes underneath Baden-Baden (through long underground tunnels), finding your way to your hotel can be counterintuitive. Most hotels I recommend are in the town center; to reach them, first follow the blue *Therme* signs to the baths neighborhood, then look for green signs directing you to each individual hotel. Ask your hotelier for parking tips (you'll likely wind up at one of the big garages in the town center). For outlying accommodations, I've listed specific driving directions (see each listing under "Sleeping in Baden-Baden," later).

By Plane: Baden-Baden's airport is served by Ryanair from London, Air Berlin from Berlin, and a few smaller airlines (www. badenairpark.de). To get downtown by bus, catch bus #205 to the train station (ask driver at airport for three-zone ticket—€3.30— to cover entire trip; hourly Mon-Fri, less frequent on weekends, 45 minutes), then transfer to bus #201 to get downtown (every 10 minutes, 15-minute trip).

HELPFUL HINTS

Shopping: The big **Wagener Galerie** shopping mall at Lange Strasse 44 has just about everything, including a modern supermarket on the top floor (Mon-Sat 9:00-19:00, closed Sun) and a post office on the ground floor (Mon-Fri 9:00-19:00, Sat 9:00-14:00, closed Sun).

Horse Races: Book well in advance if you'll be visiting Baden-Baden during its three annual horse races (usually in May, Aug, and Oct; races are held in nearby town of Iffezheim, check dates at www.baden-racing.com).

Baden-Baden in Bloom: Gardening events throughout the year draw people to the town, particularly in June when the roses are in full bloom. Ask the TI for more information.

Internet Access: The **Internetcafe and Callshop,** just north of the shopping mall, is your best bet for Internet (€2/hour, Mon-Sat 10:00-20:00, closed Sun, Lange Strasse 54, tel. 07221/398-400).

Laundry: **Klara Ross Wäscherei** is a dry-cleaning shop in the town center that also does laundry (full service, same-day or next morning turnaround). Friendly Klara speaks Russian, but no English (€12/load; Mon-Tue and Thu-Fri 8:00-12:00 & 14:00-18:00, Wed and Sat 8:00-12:00, closed Sun; Eichstrasse 14, take bus #201 to Augustaplatz stop, tel. 07221/22676).

Bike Rental: You can rent bikes a few bus stops away from the town center (€12-25/day, must show ID and leave cash deposit, call ahead to reserve, daily 8:30-21:00, delivery-€10; Eisenbahnstrasse 1a, tel. 0172/721-4280, www.rent-a-sportsman. de). Take bus #201 (or walk 15 minutes) toward the train station, get off at Verfassungsplatz, and cross the busy street; the rental office is behind the Olive restaurant. Active Klaus also offers lessons in the sport of Nordic walking.

Train Info: The **Derpart** travel agency, between Leopoldsplatz and the casino, posts a train schedule outside. They charge a €5 fee to sell you a ticket—which is pricey, but saves you a trip to the station (Mon-Fri 9:00-18:00, Sat 10:00-14:00, closed Sun, Sophienstrasse 1B, tel. 07221/21050).

GETTING AROUND BADEN-BADEN

Within town, only one bus really matters: **Bus #201** runs straight through Baden-Baden, connecting the train station in Oos, the town center (Leopoldsplatz is the most central stop), and the Lichtentaler Abbey at the southeast end of town (every 10 minutes until 20:00, then about every 20 minutes until around midnight; buy tickets from driver or try the German-only machines at some stops, €2.30/person single ticket, Citysolo day pass for 1 adult-€6, and Cityplus day pass for up to 5 adults-€9.50, bus info at www.kvv. de). Tickets are sold without a date-stamp and must be validated in the machine on board. Single tickets are valid for 90 minutes in one direction; day passes expire at 3:00 in the morning. With bus #201, you don't need to mess with downtown parking.

Bus #208, though infrequent, can serve as a fun sightseeing bus. Hop on at Leopoldsplatz, and you'll take a big scenic drive (actually a kind of figure-eight with three loops) through Baden-Baden, returning to the center 55 minutes later (leaves Leopoldsplatz 5 times a day Mon-Fri; twice on Sat; no buses run Sun). **Buses #204** and **#205** end at the recommended Merkur funicular (about twice hourly). Bus #205 also runs from the train station to the airport (hourly Mon-Fri, less often Sat-Sun, 45 minutes).

Baden-Baden Walk

This self-guided walk starts at the casino, loops through the Old Town to both of the famous baths, and ends back at the river, where you can stroll up to the abbey. In other words, it covers everything.
• *Start on the steps of the...*

Casino

The impressive building called the Kurhaus is wrapped around a grand casino. Built in the 1850s in wannabe-French style, it was declared "the most beautiful casino" by Marlene Dietrich. You can tour it in the morning, and gamble away the afternoon and evening.

To get a visual overview of the town from the casino, stand on the steps between the second and third big white columns from the entrance, and survey the surroundings from left to right: Find the ruined castle near the top of the hill, then the rock-climbing cliffs, the new castle (top of town) next to the salmon-colored spire of the Catholic church (the famous baths are just behind that), the Merkur peak (marked by a TV tower, 2,000 feet above sea level, easy to reach by bus and funicular), and the bandstand in the Kurhaus garden. The Baden-Baden orchestra plays here most Sundays from March through October, but not in August (free, usually at 16:00).

• *Now walk about 100 yards to your left, to the...*

Trinkhalle

Beyond the colonnade is the old Trinkhalle—a long entrance hall decorated with nymphs and romantic legends (explained in the book *Trinkhalle Baden-Baden: Its Tales and Legends,* sold inside for €10). It's now home to the main TI, a recommended café, and a ticket agency. Wander around its fancy portico, studying the romantic paintings that spa-

goers a century ago could easily relate to. For a sample of the warm spring water, go inside and look for the tap by the TI desk (cups available in café for €0.20).

• *From the Trinkhalle, walk down the steps, tip your hat to Kaiser Wilhelm (no moustache jokes now), and cross the river. Walk one block inland, then go left on the pedestrian Lange Strasse. A block past the* "Bad" Hotel zum Hirsch *sign, take a hard right, and climb up Hirschstrasse until you hit a big church.*

Catholic Church and Marktplatz

Baden-Baden's Catholic church looks over the marketplace that has marked the center of town since Roman times. You're stand-

ing upon the "emperor's spa." Though it's not open to the public, every year city workers don oxygen masks and descend, through the square metal hatch in the cobbles, to clean its sumptuous marble.

Enter the church (the door on the left side is usually open). Because it sits atop the spa, the church is muggy and warm all year. There are no heaters inside; the floor stones are designed to transmit the natural spa heat in the winter. Notice a musty smell? The air in the nave is at a steady 85 percent humidity level. That means the wooden pews have to be replaced every 50 years, and all the art consists of copies (originals are stored safely in the regional museum).

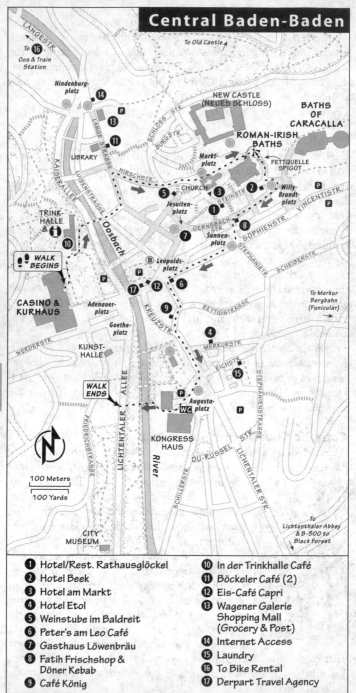

Central Baden-Baden

To Old Castle

To **16** Oos & Train Station

LANGESTR.

Hindenburg-platz

14

NEW CASTLE (NEUES SCHLOSS)

BATHS OF CARACALLA

13

SCHLOSS STR.

BURGSTR.

ROMAN-IRISH BATHS

11

LANGE STRASSE

LIBRARY

HIRSCHSTR.

Marktplatz

FETTQUELLE SPIGOT

KAISERALLEE

LUISENSTRASSE

5

CHURCH

3

STEINSTR.

2

Willy-Brandt-platz

Jesuiten-platz

1

Oosbach

7

GERNSBACH STR.

8

SONNEN-platz

SOPHIENSTR.

VINCENTISTR.

TRINK-HALLE & **i**

10

STEPHANIEStr.

SCHEIBENSTR.

WALK BEGINS

B Leopolds-platz

6

CASINO & KURHAUS

Adenauer-platz

17 **12**

KREUZSTR.

9

RETTIGSTRASSE

To Merkur Bergbahn (Funicular)

Goethe-platz

WERDERSTR.

4

MERKURSTR.

KUNST-HALLE

EICHSTR.

15

WALK ENDS

LICHTENTALER ALLEE

Augusta-WC platz

STEPHANIENSTRASSE

FRIEDRICHSTRASSE

KONGRESS HAUS

River

SCHILLERSTR.

DU-RUSSEL STR.

LICHTENTALER STR.

N

100 Meters

100 Yards

CITY MUSEUM

To Lichtenthaler Abbey & B-500 to Black Forest

1 Hotel/Rest. Rathausglöckel	**10** In der Trinkhalle Café
2 Hotel Beek	**11** Böckeler Café (2)
3 Hotel am Markt	**12** Eis-Café Capri
4 Hotel Etol	**13** Wagener Galerie Shopping Mall (Grocery & Post)
5 Weinstube im Baldreit	**14** Internet Access
6 Peter's am Leo Café	**15** Laundry
7 Gasthaus Löwenbräu	**16** To Bike Rental
8 Fatih Frischshop & Döner Kebab	**17** Derpart Travel Agency
9 Café König	

Back outside, you can see the edge of the "new castle" towering above the square. It's owned by a Kuwaiti woman who hopes to open a fabulous five-star hotel in 2017 at a cost of €500 million (if she can clear the hurdles that come with renovating a historic building).

• *Now we'll explore the area around Baden-Baden's namesake and claim to fame...*

The Baths Area

Walk to the back of the church, under a modern art installation holding jugs three stories high (reminders of the Roman spa that once stood here), and down the cobbled lane behind the Roman-Irish Bath complex. Because the soil is spa-warmed, the vegetation is lush—Mediterranean pines and orange trees. At the end (top of stairs), enjoy the **viewpoint;** Baden-Baden's high-rent district—nicknamed "Paradise"—climbs the hills opposite.

Take the steps down to the water spigot that taps the underground spring called the **Fettquelle** ("rich water source"). It's 105 degrees—very hot—as hot as a spa open to the public can legally be. Bring a cup if you want a taste. Until recently, this was a practical source of hot water for Baden-Baden residents. Older locals remember being sent here to fetch hot water for their father's shave.

Find the handless **statue** on the lawn 50 yards farther. She's got her rear to the modern fun baths (Baths of Caracalla) and is eyeing the luxurious old-school Roman-Irish Bath (both described later).

• *Return halfway to the Fettquelle spigot and take the stairs down into the parking level (signposted* Römische Badruinen*) to the small...*

Ancient Spa Museum

This spa, now in ruins, was built for Roman soldiers to use. It's just one room—most of which you can see through the big windows—and worth the admission only if you want to use the included audioguide to learn the story of the ancient spa, including how it was engineered. As it was only for soldiers, this spa is just a simple terra-cotta structure with hollow walls and elevated floors to let the heat circulate.

Cost and Hours: €2.50, mid-March-mid-Nov daily 11:00-12:00 & 15:00-16:00, closed mid-Nov-mid-March, Römerplatz 1, www.badruinen.de.

• *Leaving the museum, jog left, then right, and head down...*

Gernsbacher Strasse

Walking down Gernsbacher Strasse, consider the 2,000-year heritage of guests who have been housed, fed, and watered here at the spa. Fyodor Dostoyevsky, Mark Twain, Johannes Brahms, and Russian princes all called this neighborhood home in its 19th-century heyday. Germany's oldest tennis and golf clubs were created here (for the English community) in the 19th century.

The late 20th-century German health-care system was very, very good for Baden-Baden—the government provided lavishly for spa treatment for its tired citizens. Times have changed, and now doctors must make the case to insurance companies that their patients are more than tired...they must actually be sick to have their visit subsidized. And the insurance company then dictates where they'll go. The government will still pay for up to three weeks of recreation at a spa like this, but patients must go to the spa that is recommended and sleep in its clinic. If they want to sleep in a hotel, the jig is up—and they lose their government funding.

• *After two blocks, you hit Sonnenplatz. Jog left, and at the corner, continue right down Sophienstrasse, where a signpost directs you toward* Lichtentaler Allee.

Sophienstrasse

This street enjoys the reliable shade of a long row of tall chestnut trees. In the 1870s, when it was lined exclusively by hotels, this was the town's aristocratic promenade. Back then there were 15,000 bedrooms for rent in Baden-Baden (triple what the city has today).

• *Sophienstrasse leads into...*

Leopoldsplatz

Until 1985, this square was a main traffic hub, with 30,000 cars muscling through it each day. Now a 1.5-mile-long tunnel takes the east-west traffic under the city, and the peace and quiet you'd expect in a spa town has returned. Actually, Baden-Baden had to get rid of the noise and pollution caused by the traffic in order to maintain its top rating as a spa resort—lose that, and Baden-Baden would lose half its business. The main city bus stop is just off the square, on Luisenstrasse.

• *From Leopoldsplatz, head left on Lichtentaler Strasse. You'll pass the venerable and recommended Café König (on right), jewelry stores, and plenty of high-end shops. Head for the big fountain in the distance, which marks Augustaplatz (public WC nearby). At the fountain, go right, through the park, and over the petite bridge, where you'll come to a sweet riverside path called Lichtentaler Allee (described under "Sights in Baden-Baden," next). From here the casino is to your right. A stroll to the left—down Lichtentaler Allee—takes you to the rose garden, City Museum (an elegant old mansion with a humble but well-displayed col-*

lection of artifacts and etchings showing the history of the spa town), and out to Lichtentaler Abbey. You choose which way to go. My walk is done.

Sights in Baden-Baden

THE BATHS

Baden-Baden's top sights—two much-loved but very different baths—stand side by side in a park at the top of the Old Town. The Roman-Irish Bath is traditional, stately, indoors, contemplative, and extremely relaxing...just you, the past, and your body. The perky, fun, and modern Baths of Caracalla are less expensive, both indoor and outdoor, and more social. Caracalla is better in the sunshine; the Roman-Irish is fine anytime. Some hotels sell discounted tickets (10-15 percent off) to one or both of the baths—ask at your hotel.

At either bath, you'll get an electronic wristband, which you'll need when you're ready to leave. If you overstay your allotted time, you pay extra. You can relax while your valuables are stowed in very secure lockers. The baths share a huge underground Bäder-Garage, which has a reduced price for the first two hours (then €1/hour) if you validate your parking ticket before leaving either bath (garage entrance on Rotenbachtalstrasse).

Most years, one bath (but never both) closes for two weeks of maintenance in June or July; this is announced prominently at www.carasana.de.

▲▲▲Roman-Irish Bath (Friedrichsbad)

The highlight of most visits to Baden-Baden is a sober 17-step ritual called the Roman-Irish Bath. This bathhouse pampered the rich

and famous in its elegant surroundings when it opened in 1877. Today, this steamy world of marble, brass columns, tropical tiles, herons, lily pads, and graceful nudity welcomes gawky tourists as well as locals.

Cost and Hours: €25/3 hours, €12 more gets you a soap-and-brush massage and another half-hour, another €12 for final crème massage; daily 9:00-22:00; last entry 3 hours before closing if you're getting a massage, 2 hours before otherwise, check website for other massage options, consider booking in advance; kids under 14 not allowed, Römerplatz 1, tel. 07221/275-920, www.friedrichsbad.eu. It's possible to speed through the bath in less than an hour, but you'll probably want to slow down and enjoy the experience.

Dress Code: Everyone in these baths is always nude. On

Mondays, Thursdays, and Saturdays, men and women use separate and nearly identical facilities—but the sexes can mingle briefly in the pool under the grand dome in the center of the complex (yes, everyone's nude there, too). Shy bathers should avoid Tuesdays, Wednesdays, Fridays, Sundays, and holidays, when all of the rooms are mixed—including the steam and massage rooms. If you're concerned, you needn't be; there's no ogling going on. It's a very classy and respectful ritual, and a shame to miss just because you're intimidated by nudity.

Procedure: Read this carefully before stepping out naked: In your changing cabin, load all your possessions onto the fancy hanger. Then hang it in the locker across the way, and close the locker by pressing on the button with your wristband. As you enter (in the "body crème" room), check your weight on the digital scale. Do this again as you leave to see how much you sweated off—you'll lose about a kilo...all in sweat. The complex routine is written (in English) on the walls with recommended times—simply follow the room numbers from 1 to 17. Instructions are repeated everywhere. For the first couple of stops only, you will use plastic slippers (marked with European sizes, see page 979 for conversions) and a towel (given to you by the attendant for the hot-room lounges) for hygienic reasons and because the slats are too hot to sit on without the towel.

Start by taking a shower. Grab a towel and put on plastic slippers before hitting the warm-air bath for 15 minutes and the hot-air bath for 5 minutes. Shower again. If you paid extra, take the rough and slippery soap-brush massage—which may finish off with a good Teutonic spank. Play Gumby in the shower; lounge under sunbeams in one of several thermal steam baths; and glide like a swan under a divine dome in the mixed-gender royal pool. Don't skip the invigorating cold plunge. Dry in more warmed towels and lie on a bed for 30 minutes, thinking prenatal thoughts, in the mellow, yellow silent room. At the end, there's a reading room with refreshing drinks, chaise lounges, and plenty of magazines. You don't appreciate how clean you are after this experience until you put your dirty socks back on. Ewwww (bring a clean pair).

All you need is money. You'll get an electronic wristband, locker, and towel; hair dryers are available, and clocks are prominently displayed throughout. If you wear glasses, consider leaving them in your locker (it's more relaxing without them). Otherwise, you'll find trays throughout for you to park your specs.

Afterward, before going downstairs, sip just a little of the terrible but "magic" hot water *(Thermalwasser)* from the elegant fountain, and stroll down the broad royal stairway, feeling, as they say, five years younger—or, at least, 2.2 pounds (a kilo) lighter.

▲▲Baths of Caracalla (Caracalla Therme)

For a more modern experience, spend a few hours at the Baths of Caracalla, a huge palace of water, steam, and relaxed people.

More like a mini-water park, and with more bathers clothed more of the time, this is a fun and accessible experience, and is recommended for those who'd prefer less nudity.

Cost and Hours: €15/2 hours, €18/3 hours, €21/4 hours, €130.50 for 10 2-hour entries for multiple visits or to split among your group, discounts with hotel guest card *(Kurkarte)*; massages—€30/25 minutes, €58/50 minutes, must also pay for admission, check website for other massage options, consider booking in advance; daily 8:00-22:00, last entry at 20:00, no kids under age 7, kids aged 7-14 must be with parents (it's not really a splashing and sliding kind of pool). Tel. 07221/275-940, www.caracalla.de.

Procedure: At this bath, you need to bring a towel (or rent one for €6 plus a €10 deposit) and a swimsuit (shorts are OK for men, no swimsuit rental available but you can buy one in the shop).

Find a locker, change clothes, strap the band around your wrist, and go play. Your wristband gets you into another poolside locker if you want to lock up your glasses. If you buy something to drink, you'll pay on exit (it's recorded on your wristband). Bring your towel to the pool (there are plenty of places to stow it). The baths are an indoor/outdoor wonderland of steamy pools, waterfalls, neck showers, Jacuzzis, hot springs, cold pools, lounge chairs, saunas, a wellness lounge/massage area, a cafeteria, and a bar. After taking a few laps around the fake river, you can join some kinky Germans for water spankings (you may have to wait a few minutes to grab a vacant waterfall). Then join the gang in the central cauldron. The steamy "inhalation" room seems like purgatory's waiting room, with a misty minimum of visibility, filled with strange, silently aging bodies.

Nudity is limited to one zone upstairs. The grand spiral staircase leads to a naked world of saunas, tanning lights, cold plunges, and sunbathing outside on lounge chairs. At the top of the stairs everyone stows their suit in a cubbyhole and wanders around with their towel (some are modest and wrapped; others just run around buck naked). There are three eucalyptus-scented saunas of varying temperatures (80, 90, and 95 degrees) and two saunas in outdoor log cabins (with mesmerizing robotic steam-makers). Follow the instructions on the wall. Towels are required, not for modesty but to separate your body from the wood benches. The highlight is the arctic bucket in the shower room. Pull the chain. Only rarely will you feel so good. And you can do it over and over.

MORE SIGHTS IN BADEN-BADEN
▲▲Casino and Kurhaus

Baden-Baden's grand casino occupies a classy building called the Kurhaus. Built in the 1850s, it was inspired by the Palace of Versailles and is filled with rooms honoring French royalty who never actually set foot in the place. But many other French people did. Gambling was illegal in 19th-century France... just over the border. The casino is licensed on the condition that it pay 80 percent of its earnings to the state. The amount of revenue it generates to help the state fund social services is a  secret, but insiders estimate that it's more than $18 million a year. The staff of 180 is paid by tips from happy gamblers.

You can visit the casino on a guided tour in the mornings, when it's closed to gamblers, but it is most interesting to see in action, after 14:00. You can gamble if you want, but a third of the visitors come only to people-watch under the chandeliers. The scene is more subdued than at an American casino; anyone showing emotion is more likely a tourist than a serious gambler. Lean against a gilded statue and listen to the graceful reshuffling of personal fortunes. Do some imaginary gambling or buy a few chips at the window near the entrance (an ATM is downstairs).

Cost and Hours: €5 entry, €2 minimum bet, €14,000 maximum bet; open daily 14:00-2:00 in the morning, Fri-Sat until 3:00 in the morning, livelier after dinner and liveliest after 22:00; no athletic shoes, coat and collared shirt required for men and ties are encouraged—tie and coat can be rented for €11 with €11 deposit, collared shirt can be purchased for €18, nice jeans OK; passport required—driver's license isn't enough, under 21 not admitted, no photos, pick up game rules as you enter, tel. 07221/30240, www. casino-baden-baden.de.

Lower rollers and budget travelers can try their luck downstairs at the casino's slot machines, called *Automatenspiel* (€1 entry or included in €5 casino admission, opens at 12:00—otherwise same hours and age restrictions, passport required, no dress code).

Tours: The casino gives 30-minute German tours every morning (€7, €1 discount with hotel guest card—*Kurkarte*; departures every half-hour 9:30-11:30, no 9:30 tour Nov-March; some guides may add short English summaries if asked, tel. 07221/30240).

Even peasants wearing T-shirts, shorts, and sandals, with their cameras and kids in tow, are welcome on tours.

▲▲Strolling Lichtentaler Allee

Imagine yourself in top hat and tails as you promenade down the famous Lichtentaler Allee, a pleasant, picnic-perfect 1.5-mile-long lane. You'll stroll through a park along the babbling brick-lined Oosbach River, past old mansions and under hardy oaks and exotic trees (street-lit all night). By the elitist tennis courts, make sure to cross the footbridge into the free Art Nouveau rose garden (Gönneranlage, 400 labeled kinds of roses bloom May-Oct—best in early summer, great tables and benches). If you wish, continue all the way to the historic Lichtentaler Abbey, a Cistercian convent founded in 1245. Either walk round-trip, or take city bus #201 one-way (runs along the main street, parallel to the promenade, on the other side of the river). Many bridges cross the river, making it easy to shortcut to bus #201 anytime. Biking is another option (see "Helpful Hints" earlier), but you'll have to stay on the road in the bike lane, since the footpath is only for pedestrians.

Russian Baden-Baden

The town's Russian link dates back to 1793, when the future Czar Alexander I took Louise, Princess of Baden, as his wife. Later, many Russians, including Dostoyevsky and Tolstoy, flocked here after gambling was banned in their motherland. Some lost their fortunes, borrowed a pistol, and did themselves in on the "Alley of Sighs" (Seufzerallee, near the Caracalla baths).

The **Russian Orthodox church** is just south of the town center—step in (€1 donation requested, daily April-Oct 10:00-18:00, Nov-March 10:00-17:00, services Sat evening and Sun morning, Lichtentaler Strasse 76, near rose garden across river from Lichtentaler Allee, or take bus #201 to Bertholdplatz stop).

While the church dates from about 1900 and was quiet for generations, a current boom in the Russian population here makes it livelier than ever. Even the Soviet period did little to dim the allure of this spa town in the Russian imagination. In the 1990s, Russians of German ethnic origin were allowed to emigrate to Germany, and many decided to settle in Baden-Baden. More recently, ultra-wealthy Russians seeking safe property investments have poured their rubles into Baden-Baden: Many of the town's top hotels are now Russian-owned, and direct flights from Moscow land at Baden-Baden's airport. While more Americans visit Baden-Baden each year, Russian tourists stay longer and account for more overnights. You'll see Russian on multilingual signs around town.

▲Funicular to the Summit of Merkur

This delightful trip to a hilltop overlooking Baden-Baden is easy, quick, and a good reason to explore beyond the main drag. Catch bus #204 or #205 from the city center (departing 2/hour from Leopoldsplatz) and ride 11 minutes through the ritzy "Paradise" neighborhood to the end of the line at the base of the Merkur Bergbahn. Take the funicular to the 2,000-foot summit.

At the top, you can enjoy a meal or drink (restaurant open until 18:00 or later), and, if the weather's good (with winds from the south or west), you can watch the paragliders leap into ecstasy. Take the funicular back down, or risk getting lost and take the lane back to the base of the funicular (2.5 miles, signposted *Merkurbahn Talstation*). From the bottom of the funicular, buses depart back to Baden-Baden twice hourly.

Cost and Hours: €2 each way, departs frequently, daily 10:00-22:00, ticket office closes at 18:00, tickets also available at machines at both departure points, restaurant tel. 07221/31640.

Mini-Black Forest Walks

Baden-Baden is at the northern end of the Black Forest. If you're not going south, but want a taste of Germany's favorite woods, consider one of several hikes from town. The TI has details and can suggest routes. If you're serious about hiking, invest in the TI's good (but German-only) €1.50 *Panoramaweg* map, which outlines a 30-mile trail leading all the way around Baden-Baden's perimeter and the nearby Geroldsau valley (it's easy to do just part of the trail, since you're never far from the town center or a bus stop).

Sleeping in Baden-Baden

While Baden-Baden has some grand hotels, my recommended places are mostly small (20-30 rooms), family-run, and more budget-friendly (though all accommodations are pricey in this posh town). Hotel am Markt is a particularly great value and worth reserving in advance. Note that most hotels here don't have 24-hour reception desks; most close for the night at 21:00 or earlier, though they can wait up for you if they know you're arriving later. It's wise to call ahead with your specific arrival details if you'll be coming after 17:00.

While weekends and summer are generally more expensive, demand—and prices—change from day to day based on conventions, theater performances, and other events.

All hotels and pensions are required to extract an additional €3.50 per person, per night "spa tax," so don't get upset when this is added to the bill. This comes with a "guest card" *(Kurkarte)*, offering small discounts on tourist admissions around town (including

Sleep Code

Abbreviations   **(€1 = about $1.40, country code: 49)**
S = Single, **D** = Double/Twin, **T** = Triple, **Q** = Quad, **b** = bathroom, **s** = shower only.
Price Rankings
 $$$ **Higher Priced**—Most rooms €100 or more.
   $$ **Moderately Priced**—Most rooms between €80-100.
     $ **Lower Priced**—Most rooms €80 or less.
Unless otherwise noted, credit cards are accepted, English is spoken, breakfast is included, and Wi-Fi is generally free. Prices change; verify current rates online or by email. For the best prices, always book directly with the hotel.

the casino and the Caracalla Spa). If you're coming into town by car or foot, look for the helpful green signs that direct you to each hotel by name.

IN THE CENTER, NEAR THE BATHS

These well-located options stick you right in the heart of Baden-Baden, in a pleasant, stepped pedestrian zone a short saunter from the baths.

$$$ Hotel Rathausglöckel is a 16th-century guesthouse that has undergone a tasteful 21st-century renovation. Oliver (a German-American) and his Ukrainian wife Zoia have turned this classic little place into one of the town's most inviting hotels. Steep stairs lead to 15 antique-furnished rooms (plus a few grand suites) and an inviting rooftop deck (Sb-€85-90, Db-€124-139, junior suite-€147-150, multi-room suite-€160-200, higher prices are for weekends and events, 10 percent discount for Rick Steves readers if you book directly with the hotel, guest computer, Wi-Fi, church bells every 15 minutes 6:15-22:00, parking-€10/day, Steinstrasse 7-9, tel. 07221/90610, www.rathausgloeckel.de, info@rathausgloeckel.de).

$$$ Hotel Beek rents 15 comfortable but worn rooms from a pastry shop/café on the ground floor. It's well situated, facing the baths on a little square in a pedestrian zone. The reception (on street bordering right side of café) closes at 18:00, so be sure to call ahead if you'll be arriving later (Sb-€85, Db-€135, balcony-€7 extra, Db suite-€165, elevator, Wi-Fi, parking-€15/day, on Römerplatz at Gernsbacher Strasse 44, tel. 07221/36760, www.hotel-beek.de, info@hotelbeek.de).

$$ Hotel am Markt is Baden-Baden's best little hotel. Family-run, with 23 rooms, it offers all the modern comforts a commoner could want in a peaceful, central, nearly traffic-free location, two cobbled blocks from the baths. For romantics, the church

bells blast charmingly through each room every quarter-hour from 6:15 until 22:00; for others, they are a nuisance. Otherwise, quiet rules. The ambience makes it a joy to have breakfast or just kill time on the small terrace (S-€36, Sb-€52, Db-€92, Tb-€125, extra bed-€20, elevator, guest computer, Wi-Fi; first-come, first-served parking-€5/day; Marktplatz 18, tel. 07221/27040, www.hotel-am-markt-baden.de, info@hotel-am-markt-baden.de, run for three generations by sisters Frau Jung, Frau Bogner-Schindler, and Frau Baum).

IN THE MODERN TOWN

$$$ Hotel Etol is in the quiet courtyard of a renovated industrial complex, which celebrates its history as a tile and bathtub factory from around the year 1900. You'll climb the stairs to reach most of the 18 rooms, but natural light, tasteful design, friendly staff, and a central location make this a winning choice (Sb-€78-85, Db-€105-130, family rooms, extra bed-€30, book directly and mention Rick Steves for a discount off these prices—except during events, Wi-Fi, parking-€5/day, Merkurstrasse 7, 2-minute walk from Augustaplatz stop of bus #201, tel. 07221/973-470, www.hotel-etol.de, info@hotel-etol.de).

$$$ Hotel Schweizer Hof's 39 rooms mix classic style and modern comfort. It's about a five-minute walk north of the pedestrian district, on a little square next to the opera house (Sb-€72-87, Db-€102-125, suite-€125-155, higher prices are during opera events, elevator, guest computer, Wi-Fi, parking-€10/day, Lange Strasse 71-73—for location see map on page 276, bus #201 stop: Alter Bahnhof/Festspielhaus—then walk 50 yards past the opera house, drivers follow *Festspielhaus/Casino* signs, tel. 07221/30460, www.schweizerhof.de, mail@schweizerhof.de).

OUTSIDE THE CENTER

The following listings are a few stops from the center on bus #201 (for locations, see the map on page 276).

$ Hotel-Restaurant Deutscher Kaiser, a good choice for those looking to spend less, is a traditional guesthouse with 14 spacious and surprisingly modern rooms, run by no-nonsense Frau Peter. Herr Peter cooks fine local-style dinners for hotel guests (Wed-Sun 18:00-20:00, closed Mon-Tue). It's just before the Eckerlestrasse bus stop (bus #201, 6/hour, 10 minutes from center, 20 minutes from train station) or a 25-minute stroll from the city center down polite Lichtentaler Allee—cross the river at the green *Restaurant Deutscher Kaiser* sign, then turn right (S-€35, Sb-€47-51, D-€46-49, Db-€65-84, family rooms, check website for discounts, guest computer, Wi-Fi, free and easy public parking nearby, Hauptstrasse 35, tel. 07221/72152, www.hoteldk.de, info@

hoteldk.de). Drivers: From the autobahn, skip the town center by following *Congress* signs into Michaelstunnel. Take the tunnel's first exit, then another right at the end of the exit (direction: Lichtental). Outside, the hotel is about a half-mile down on the left. From the Black Forest, follow *Zentrum* signs. Just 50 yards after the Aral gas station, turn left down the small road to Hauptstrasse.

$ Hotel Neuer Karlshof is in the Baden-Baden train station building, up a flight of stairs from the Coffee Fellows café (where you'll check in). Four of the eight new and attractive rooms are trackside and have some train noise—despite multipaned windows—light sleepers beware. If you can get a room on the quiet side, it's a great deal for a short stay (Sb-€65, Db-€85, Db suite-€119, extra bed-€25, Wi-Fi, free parking, Ooser Bahnhofstrasse 4, tel. 07221/971-5697, www.hotel-neuer-karlshof.de, info@hotel-neuer-karlshof.de).

$ Werner Dietz Hostel, between the station and the center, is big, modern, and has the cheapest beds in town (€22.70/bed in 4- to 6-bed dorm, €3.50 less for second and subsequent nights, €4.50 more if you're over 26, nonmembers pay €3.50 extra, single- or double-room surcharge-€11, includes sheets and breakfast, 23:30 curfew, pay guest computer, outdoor swimming pool next door, Hardbergstrasse 34, tel. 07221/52223, www.jugendherberge-baden-baden.de, info@jugendherberge-baden-baden.de). To reach the hostel from the train station or downtown, take bus #201 to Grosse Dollenstrasse (also announced as *Jugendherberge*); it's a steep, well-marked 10-minute climb from there. Drivers should call the hostel for careful directions.

Eating in Baden-Baden

DINING WITH ELEGANCE AND ATMOSPHERE

Weinstube im Baldreit, with both a cozy cellar and a leafy back courtyard, is ideal on a hot evening. Dining here, I feel like a pampered salamander in a Monet terrarium. While her French husband Philippe cooks wonderful regional dishes, Nicole is happy to translate the daily specials chalked in German on the board. The priority here is near-gourmet food at great prices. Reservations are smart (€8-23 main courses, Tue-Sat 17:00-22:00, closed Sun-Mon; from Lange Strasse 10, walk up the higgledy-piggledy street called Küferstrasse, follow *Weinstube* signs, and enter at the top of the lane where the green ivy abounds, Küferstrasse 3, tel. 07221/23136).

Hotel Rathausglöckel's homey, air-conditioned restaurant features traditional cuisine and seasonal specialties in a dining room with understated Old World elegance. Reservations are smart, especially for the limited outdoor seating upstairs, but flexible Michele will work with you (€10-20 main courses, Mon-Tue and Thu-Sat 18:00-23:00, Sun 12:00-15:00 & 18:00-23:00, closed Wed, Steinstrasse 7-9, tel. 07221/90610).

QUICK AND SIMPLE MEALS NEAR LEOPOLDSPLATZ

Peter's am Leo Café is a fun self-service café offering big breakfasts, sandwiches, salads, pastries, and a few outdoor tables with views over Baden-Baden's central square. This is where commoners pile their plates high (€5-8 lunch specials, Mon-Sat 6:30-19:00, Sun 8:00-19:00, on Leopoldsplatz at Sophienstrasse 10, tel. 07221/392-817).

On Jesuitenplatz: This thriving people zone, between Leopoldsplatz and the baths (at the bottom of Gernsbacher Strasse), has several options. The square is dominated by **Gasthaus Löwenbräu,** a sloppy, rude Bavarian-style *Biergarten* slinging good beer and basic schnitzel fare under a vine-covered trellis (€8-11 snacks and wurst plates, €13-28 main courses, daily 10:00-24:00). Across the street, several decent restaurants offer curbside tables—great for people-watching. One block up Gernsbacher Strasse from here (at Sonnenplatz 1), the Fatih Frischshop and *Döner Kebab* stand serve up deli items and takeaway food—perfect for a picnic (Mon-Sat 7:00-19:00 or later, closed Sun).

PRIME PEOPLE-WATCHING CAFÉS

Baden-Baden's many cafés are variations on a genteel theme. They serve chocolates, coffee, cakes (including the famous *Schwarzwälder Kirschtorte*—Black Forest cake), and light meals. Figure around €5-6 to savor a slice of cake and cup of coffee, or €5-8 for light food (such as sandwiches and salads). Most cafés are closed for dinner. While you have no shortage of options in this town, I like these four.

Café König is *the* place to bring your poodle and spend too much for an elegant cup of coffee and a slice of Black Forest cake (€3.70, €2.90 to go). Look for the sign with the squiggly script and the pink-and-gray awning (daily 8:30-18:30, counter opens Mon-Sat at 9:30 and Sun at 10:30, fine shady patio, between Leopoldsplatz and Augustaplatz at Lichtentaler Strasse 12, tel. 07221/23573).

In der Trinkhalle, a café that shares the handsome Trinkhalle building with the TI, has comfy leather sofas, international newspapers and magazines, and a casino-view terrace (Sun-Thu 10:00-18:00, Fri-Sat 10:00-24:00, Kaiserallee 3, tel. 07221/302-905).

Böckeler Café, a good but less fancy option, has an extensive dessert counter (Black Forest cake-€3.55, €2.95 to go), an ice-cream sundae menu, light meals, a modern interior, and outdoor tables along a lively pedestrian street (Mon-Fri 8:30-18:30, Sat 8:30-18:00, Sun 9:30-18:00, Lange Strasse 40-42, tel. 07221/949-594).

Eis-Café Capri is popular with locals and tourists alike. It has plenty of outdoor seating and is a perfect spot for a cup of coffee or a decadent ice-cream dessert (daily 8:00-20:00, later in summer, Sophienstrasse 1B, tel. 07221/23751).

Baden-Baden Connections

From Baden-Baden by Train to: Freiburg (direct fast trains every 1-2 hours, 45 minutes; cheaper regional trains take 1.5 hours with change in Offenburg), **Triberg** (hourly, 1.5 hours), **Munich** (hourly, 4 hours, change in Mannheim or Karlsruhe), **Frankfurt** (hourly, 1.5-2 hours, direct or with a change in Karlsruhe), **Frankfurt Airport** (roughly hourly, 1.5 hours, mostly with a change in Mannheim or Karlsruhe), **Bacharach** (hourly, 3 hours, 1-3 changes), **Strasbourg,** France (every 1-2 hours, usually 1.5 hours with a change in Appenweier), **Bern** or **Zürich,** Switzerland (every 1-2 hours, 3 hours, change in Basel). Train info: Tel. 0180-599-6633, www.bahn.com.

Freiburg

Freiburg (FRY-boorg) is the capital of the Schwarzwald. This "sunniest town in Germany," with 30,000 students, lacks must-see attractions but offers the pleasures of a university town: small shops, cozy cafés, fine food, and fewer tourists than Baden-Baden. Exuding an "I could live here" appeal, Freiburg is surrounded by lush forests and filled with creative and environmentally aware people. Bikers and hikers seem to outnumber cars, the town center is laced with cute miniature canals, and silent, efficient trams run everywhere. The city merits a visit, if only to appreciate its thriving center and very human scale. Freiburg's striking red-sandstone cathedral is worth a peek, and its own little mountain offers sunset views over the rooftops.

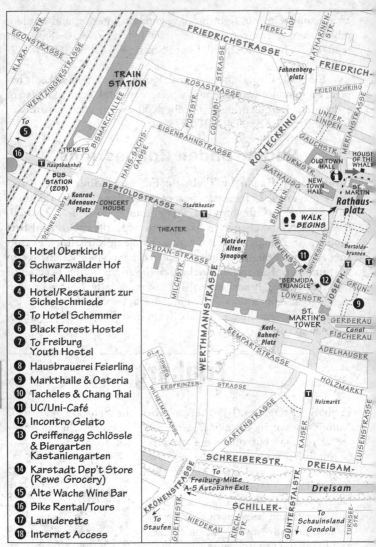

1. Hotel Oberkirch
2. Schwarzwälder Hof
3. Hotel Alleehaus
4. Hotel/Restaurant zur Sichelschmiede
5. To Hotel Schemmer
6. Black Forest Hostel
7. To Freiburg Youth Hostel
8. Hausbrauerei Feierling
9. Markthalle & Osteria
10. Tacheles & Chang Thai
11. UC/Uni-Café
12. Incontro Gelato
13. Greiffenegg Schlössle & Biergarten Kastaniengarten
14. Karstadt Dep't Store (Rewe Grocery)
15. Alte Wache Wine Bar
16. Bike Rental/Tours
17. Launderette
18. Internet Access

BADEN-BADEN & THE BLACK FOREST

Orientation to Freiburg

With about 230,000 people, Freiburg is a happening midsize city. Most points of interest to visitors are concentrated in the compact Old Town (Altstadt), bounded to the west by the train station and to the east by Freiburg's mountain, Schlossberg, and circled by a ring road. You can walk from one end of this zone to the other in about 20 minutes. The town's centerpiece, always in view, is the spiny spire of its cathedral.

TOURIST INFORMATION

Freiburg's helpful TI, on Rathausplatz, has free city maps (and sells better maps for €1), various city and regional guidebooks, and lots of information on the Black Forest region (June-Sept Mon-Fri 8:00-20:00, Sat 9:30-17:00, Sun 10:30-15:30; Oct-May Mon-Fri 8:00-18:00, Sat 9:30-14:30, Sun 10:00-12:00; room-booking service for region-€3 plus deposit; tel. 0761/388-1880, www.freiburg.de).

The TI runs weekly **walking tours** in English (€9, Sat at 11:30,

1.5 hours) and rents an entertaining, two-hour **audioguide** that covers the top sights (€9/2.5 hours, €11/4 hours, €13/overnight, €5/ extra headset).

ARRIVAL IN FREIBURG

The bustling train station has lockers (near track 1, €3-5), a WC (downstairs, €1), and a useful *Reisezentrum* that dispenses rail info and sells tickets (long hours daily). The bus station is next door (under the bridge; follow signs for "ZOB"—the German initials for central bus station).

To get to the city center, you can take a taxi (€9), tram, or walk. To access **trams** from the train platform, take the escalators up to the tram stop on the bridge above the tracks. Cross to the other side and take tram #1, #3, or #5 to get downtown. Get off at the second stop, Bertoldsbrunnen.

To reach the city center by **foot** (about 15 minutes), walk straight through the train station, cross the busy street (watch out for bikes), and continue ahead up the tree-lined boulevard called Eisenbahnstrasse (passing the post office). Within three blocks, you'll cross the ring road, then continue straight (on the pedestrian-only Rathausgasse) to Rathausplatz. This is where you'll find the TI (in the bright-red building), and where my self-guided walk begins. Most of my recommended accommodations are within a 10-minute walk of here.

HELPFUL HINTS

Laundry: An outdated self-service launderette, **Miele**, is at Adelhauser Strasse 24 (€4.50/load, Mon-Fri 8:00-20:00, Sat 7:00-17:00, closed Sun, in passageway behind hair salon at corner with Marienstrasse, tel. 0761/35656).

Internet Access: The **Internetcafe and Callshop,** near the end of Kaiser-Joseph-Strasse, is your best bet for getting online (€1.90/hour, Mon-Sat 9:00-22:00, Sun 11:00-21:00, Friedrichring 15, tel. 0761/704-9830).

Supermarket: Pick up picnic supplies at **REWE** (Mon-Sat 9:30-20:00, closed Sun, in basement of Karstadt department store on Kaiser-Joseph-Strasse, near the cathedral).

Bike Rental/Tours: Radstation Freiburg am Hauptbahnhof, across the tracks from the train station, rents bikes and has free route maps (€8/4 hours, €15/24 hours, subsequent days-€8, show ID and leave €50 cash deposit per bike, daily May-Sept 9:30-19:00, Oct-April 9:30-18:00, or by appointment; 2-hour tours €150/4 people, includes bike rental; from station, cross tram bridge over train tracks to round building on left and go downstairs, look for *Fahrradverleih* signs; Wentzingerstrasse 15, tel. 0761/202-3426, www.freiburg-aktiv.de).

Local Guides: Iris Bürklin leads good tours around Freiburg (€99/2 hours, mobile 0162-595-6876, www.iris-freiburg.de, contact@iris-freiburg.de). **Black Forest Tours,** run by Simone Brixel, offers walking, hiking, and mountain bike tours of Freiburg and the Black Forest (€120/1.5 hours, tel. 0761/5147-0551, www.the-black-forest.com, simone@the-black-forest.com).

GETTING AROUND FREIBURG AND SURROUNDINGS

The city center (which includes most of my recommended hotels) is completely walkable. Trams are also useful to reach outlying sights, such as the Schauinsland lift (€2.20/ride, €5.50/24-hour pass, €10.50/24-hour pass for 2-5 people, buy tickets from machine at train station or inside cars, and have some change handy). For local transport info in English, see www.vag-freiburg.de.

To visit **Staufen, St. Peter,** or **St. Märgen** by regional train and bus, you'll need a two-zone ticket (€3.80 each way) or a 24-hour regional pass (€11 for 1 adult, €21 for 2-5 adults, available from ticket machines). If you're staying in one of those towns, your hotel tax includes a KONUS card, giving you free access to all public transit in the region (see page 317); unfortunately, this does not apply if you're sleeping in Freiburg.

Freiburg Walk

This self-guided orientation walk, starting at Rathausplatz (and the TI), leads you through the top sights in the old center of Freiburg in about an hour.
• *Begin on the square in front of the Town Hall buildings.*

Rathausplatz

The relaxing square with the fountain used to be an enclosed courtyard—the cloister of the neighboring Franciscan Church of St.

Martin. Today it's fronted by twin city administration buildings: the bright-red Old Town Hall (on the right, with the TI inside) and the white-and-pink New Town Hall (on the left).

Embedded in the cobbles in front of both of the Town Hall buildings are mosaic coats of arms representing each of Freiburg's **sister cities.** Many of them—including Padua (Italy),

Madison (Wisconsin), and Isfahan (Iran) are university towns, like Freiburg. The town has been a university center since the mid-15th century, and the prestigious university is still the town's biggest employer.

• *Curl around the far side of St. Martin's Church and head up Franziskanerstrasse. As you walk, you'll notice the first of many small canals lining the street.*

Bächle

BADEN-BADEN & THE BLACK FOREST

These tiny streams, running down nearly every street in the pedestrianized core since the 13th century, are Freiburg's trademark. Originally they were designed to keep fires from spreading (in case of fire, the canals could be quickly dammed to flood the street). It worked— Freiburg had no major fires after it introduced its *Bächle*. The canals also provided a constantly replenishing source of water for people and cattle. These days, the canals are just fun:  A sunny day turns any kid-at-heart into a puddle-jumper. Toddlers like to dangle their feet in the water to cool off when it's hot. Freiburg still employs two *Bächleputzer* to scrub the canals clean each day with steel brooms. Local lore says that if you fall into a *Bächle*, you are destined to marry a Freiburger.

At the end of the church, look at the facade of the red building on the left, the **House of the Whale,** featuring the first of many whimsical little statues that decorate Freiburg. Look closely at the right-hand gargoyle on the facade. The veiny growth hanging from her neck is a goiter (a result of iodine deficiency). These were so common in the Middle Ages that the local folk costume includes a tightly fitting band around the neck to disguise a goiter.

• *Continue ahead one block, until you reach the wide cross-street called...*

Kaiser-Joseph-Strasse

Since the Middle Ages, this has been the center of commerce in Freiburg, and is now lined with its biggest department stores and malls.

Look before crossing the street: Virtually silent trams glide along here constantly. With some 220 miles of tram and bus lines,

Freiburg is very proud of its reputation as a "green" city. Only 40 percent of trips taken in Freiburg are by car, and the percentage of locals who own bikes rivals that of pedal-happy Amsterdam. The city is home to a large solar-panel factory, and it started the annual Intersolar trade fair (which has since outgrown the town and moved to Munich, Mumbai, Shanghai, and California).

Looking down the street to the right, you can see one of the two surviving towers of Freiburg's former town wall, **St. Martin's Tower** (or as some call it, McDonald's Tower—thanks to the not-subtle-enough golden arches that try to fit into its facade). If you were to head in that direction, then cut up the street to the right just before you reached the tower, you'd wind up in the colorful student quarter called the "Bermuda Triangle" that visitors of any age enjoy exploring (described later, under "Eating in Freiburg"). The tower is dedicated to the beloved saint who famously offered half of his cape to a beggar; he's celebrated with children's parades all over Germany every November 11. The top of the tower once held the town prison; so those who went to jail were euphemistically said to have "put on St. Martin's cape."

· *Jog a half-block to the right and continue straight to the...*

Münsterplatz and Market

This main square of Freiburg hosts a bustling outdoor produce and crafts market six mornings a week (Mon-Fri 7:30-13:00, Sat 7:30-14:00, biggest on Wed and Sat, no market on Sun). On the north side of the cathedral (to the left), vendors sell local produce; in front of the cathedral's door, flowers and herbs; and to the south (right), imported produce. Around the left side, you'll also find stands selling Freiburg's distinctive type of bratwurst—long, red, and skinny, called a *lange Rote*. If you order one, they'll ask you *Mit oder ohne?*—"with or without" onions.

The market goes way back. On the giant pillar to the left of the cathedral's main door, look for the **engravings** with different years (e.g., ADMCCLXX—that's A.D. 1270) next to oval and circular shapes. These were the officially decreed sizes for a loaf of bread; customers could bring their purchases here to be sure they weren't being cheated. Notice that the size of the loaf shrunk between 1270 and 1317. The price stayed the same, but the bread got smaller...medieval inflation.

In the alcove in front of the cathedral entrance are more official measures. For example, to the left, you'll see the standard measures for a basket (the circle plus the line), an "elbow" (the line), and a barrel (the square with a diagonal line). On the right are even more measures, dictating home-construction supplies (the proper size of bricks, roof tiles, floor tiles, and beams). Nearby, the inscription boasts that since the 16th century, Freiburg has enjoyed the right to hold a large-scale market twice a year (a rare privilege in the Holy Roman Empire).

• *Now's a good time to visit the* **cathedral** *(for details, see my self-guided cathedral tour on page 302). When you're done, exit the cathedral out the side door (around the right side of the building) to continue this walk.*

Münsterplatz, Side View

For many visitors, the most memorable part of the cathedral is its many **gargoyles.** Find the "mooning" gargoyle (facing the entrance, walk around the right side and look at the second butt-ress)...and wait for rain.

Do an about-face and salute the Habsburgs, who are represented by the statues and the coat of arms on the **Historical Merchant House** (Historisches

Kaufhaus, from 1532). This was the trading and customs center in the 16th century, and briefly housed the state parliament after the war. You'll notice lots of red buildings in town. During the Middle Ages around here, a red paint job on a building indicated it was a place where you'd be required to pay a tax or fee.

To the left as you face the Merchant House, you'll see the gray building that houses the **City History Museum** (with a pair of interesting models in the cellar—see page 305), then the yellow building marked *Alte Wache.* A former police station, this was recently turned into a wine bar and is a fine place to sample local wines, either indoors or out on the square (€2-6 glasses, Mon-Fri 10:00-19:00, Sat 10:00-18:00, until 22:00 in good weather, closed Sun, Münsterplatz 38, tel. 0761/202-870). Most of the wine made here uses grape varieties that originated in Burgundy. This corner of Germany enjoys some of the country's balmiest weather, thanks to the so-called "Burgundy Gate"—a gap between the Vosges and Jura mountains, which channels in warm Mediterranean air from the south of France. Winds coming through the "gate" also carry with them Burgundian sediments, enriching the German soil.

• *Go up the narrow lane (called Buttergasse) to the left of the Merchant House. Then turn left and head up...*

Schusterstrasse

This pleasant street is typical of old Freiburg, lined with a *Bächle,* with historic labels on many of the houses and mosaic seals (made of Rhine River stones) in front of most doors. For example, the building at #35 (on the left) is labeled *Haus zur kleinen Meise* (House of the Little Titmouse), with a knife mosaic out front. While the house labels date from the Middle Ages, the mosaics are typically more modern, paid for by today's merchants to match the purpose of the building. This one is a knife shop. The mosaics are portable, so if the vendor moves shop, he can just lift his up and take it with him.

• *Cross Herrenstrasse and continue up the narrow lane called Münzgasse. Turn right along...*

Konviktstrasse

Named not for a convict but for a convent, this is another typical Freiburg street. Chain stores and chain restaurants are forbidden along this storybook lane, and in the springtime it is draped with fragrant purple wisteria. Walk slowly to take it all in, or consider stopping in a nearby café.

• *Konviktstrasse brings you to a major street right in front of the...*

Swabian Gate (Schwabentor)

This second of Freiburg's surviving gates is named for the Swabians, the historical rivals of the Freiburgers (the gate leads to where you'd head to meet them). Just below the big painting, at the apex of the arch, look for the little figure pulling a thorn out of his foot. This is the last thing Freiburgers would see before leaving town, to remind them to stay on the right path and avoid the "thorns" of sinful living.

• *Freiburg's little mountain, Schlossberg, is nearby. It's best at sunset, but if you want to head up now, simply climb the stairs at the Schwabentor, use the pedestrian over-pass to cross the busy road, and take the free elevator on up (see page 305).*

Or, for some back-street experiences, stick with me for a few more minutes. Cross the busy Oberlinden, passing the Schwabentor, and then make a hard right onto the downhill road, toward the little river.

Riverside Freiburg

This is the main branch of the much bigger river that splits into all those little canals at the top of town. Walking down this incline, you can see how the street level of town was actually raised to create a steeper incline to power the canals. While this was once the smelly tanners' and millers' quarter, now it's a delightfully low-key neighborhood. Follow the pleasant river for a while, and soon you'll reach two recommended eateries: Across the canal (on the left) is the picturesque Sichelschmiede; a few more steps up on the left is the modern-inside, rollicking-outside Hausbrauerei Feierling microbrewery, with an inviting beer garden across the street (on the right). If you keep on past these two, you'll end up at the broad square called Augustinerplatz, with the entrance (uphill and to the right) to the **Augustiner Museum.** Continuing along the little street called Grünwälderstrasse (directly across from the Augustiner Museum entrance) brings you to even more eateries, including the wonderful Markthalle food circus on the left (all described later, under "Eating in Freiburg").

• *Our Freiburg walk is finished. Now go splash in those canals.*

Sights in Freiburg

▲▲Cathedral (Münster)

The lacy spire rocketing up from Freiburg's skyline marks its impressive main church. While Germany has bigger and better cathedrals, Freiburg's has some interesting details that make it worth a visit.

Cost and Hours: Cathedral interior—free, usually Mon-Fri 10:00-12:00 & 12:30-17:00, Sat 10:00-11:30 & 12:30-17:00, Sun 13:00-17:00. Tower—€2, Mon-Sat 10:00-16:45, Sun 13:00-16:00, enter from outside church on right and pay at top. Choir—free, open shorter hours and Sat-Sun only in winter; free organ concerts every Sat April-Dec at 11:30.

● Self-Guided Tour: Begin out front. The exterior **scaffolding** is a semipermanent feature of the church. The cathedral's distinctive pink color comes from a soft local sandstone that's easy to work, but also extremely fragile. Decorations need to be replaced every 30 to 60 years. Keeping the church from falling apart is a never-ending task—elderly locals who've lived here their entire lives report having never seen the church without at least some scaffolding.

The frilly **tower** *(Münsterturm)* is as tall as the church is long (127 yards)...but not worth the 329-step ascent. Up in the tower are 16 different bells, each one with a different name and purpose. Traditionally, Catholics could not eat meat on Fridays, so instead they'd eat *Spätzle* (German egg noodles)—giving the oldest bell, rung just before lunchtime on Fridays, its nickname, the "*Spätzle* Bell." Other bells include one that tolls each night at 20:00 (originally to remind townspeople that the city gates were closing), and a "Tax Bell" that rings twice weekly in November and December, when taxes traditionally came due.

Before heading inside, spend a few minutes looking around the ornately decorated **entryway** (outside the door itself, but inside the gated area). The 418 colorfully painted statues (recently restored and now protected with netting from destructive pigeons) ooze with medieval church symbolism. Each has an identifying symbol. As you look back out to the square, the first figure on the left is St. Catherine, holding a wheel. The breaking wheel (also called the "Catherine Wheel") was a torture device used during the Middle Ages; a victim's limbs were stretched along a cart wheel and crushed.

Two particularly memorable characters have become mascots of Freiburg. First is the so-called **"praying devil."** In the tympanum (over the door), look for Jesus on the cross. Just below him and a bit to the right is a pot-bellied devil, greedily rubbing his hands together as he watches the Archangel Michael weigh the goodness of a person's soul (while two other devils try to fix the results). Then, along the left wall, notice the strange little character under the third statue from the right—playing his nose like a trumpet.

Now go **inside.** Go right and look along the back wall, where you'll find a photo of Freiburg after it was devastated by WWII bombs. The city made it through most of the war virtually unscathed—until November 27, 1944, when, in a space of just 20 minutes, about 80 percent of Freiburg's buildings were destroyed by an Allied bombing run. Miraculously, the cathedral was one of the few structures that survived. Some credit divine intervention, while others claim the bombers intentionally avoided it; either way, the steeple's latticework top and underground lead anchors probably saved it, since shockwaves from explosions all around it would have leveled a solid, less-supported tower.

The **stained-glass windows** are originals, from the 13th and 14th centuries, which were hidden away and protected during World War II. Each one is marked with the seal of a local merchant who sponsored it (go on a scavenger hunt to find the pretzel, from the baker; the barrel, from the cooper; the scissors, from the tailor; and the hammer, tongs, and snake—representing fire—from the blacksmith).

Now stroll down the **nave** toward the altar. After its thriving market and Black Forest silver mine made Freiburg rich, this cathedral was built on the site of an earlier church. Begun in about 1200, most of the structure was finished relatively quickly (it has the only Gothic steeple in Germany that was actually completed during Gothic times, in 1330), but it still demonstrates various styles. The earliest part of the church, at the **transept,** is Romanesque (notice the rounded tops to the windows); but as Gothic engineering swept neighboring France, Freiburg's cathedral builders began to incorporate that style (see the telltale pointed arches elsewhere in the church).

Many churches from this era have 12 **pillars** lining the nave, each one with the statue of an apostle. But after the primary construction on this cathedral was finished, a large choir was added beyond the altar, so two more pillars were built—bringing the total to 14. The new pillars were granted to Paul and Jesus himself. Look at the statues on the two pillars flanking the altar: On the right is Jesus, and on the left is Thomas—pointing two fingers because of his insistence on touching Jesus before he'd believe in the Resurrection. Thomas' privileged position in this church is based on the philosophy that non-believers should be closest to Christ.

You can take a quick spin around the **choir** (if it's open) to see some ornately decorated chapels, the crypt, and a closer look at the painting over the altar (enter to the right of the altar). When you're finished, head outside using the side door (right transept), and you'll be back out on Münsterplatz. The tower entrance is nearby.

Augustiner Museum

Freiburg's top museum displays local fine art and medieval artifacts around the reconstructed shell of an Augustinian church. The highlights are close-up looks at some of the cathedral's original 13th-century medieval statuary (first floor) and 16th-19th-century stained glass (second floor). The top floor shows off regional 19th-century paintings and a unique eye-level view of some gargoyles; a second wing is scheduled to open in a few years. The interactive media stations (choose "English") provide excellent information.

Cost and Hours: €6, ticket serves as day pass to all city museums, Tue-Sun 10:00-17:00, closed Mon, audioguide-€2, entrance on Augustinerplatz, tel. 0761/201-2531, www.freiburg.de/museen.

Eating: The museum café (open same hours) sells coffee, cakes, light lunches, and beer and wine around a lovely courtyard.

Nearby: The area around Augustinerplatz is the heart of the **Gerberau district,** popular with locals. It's quieter and filled with little galleries and restaurants that are less expensive than on Münsterplatz (several are recommended later, under "Eating in Freiburg").

City History Museum

Telling the story of Freiburg, this museum is worthwhile if only to see the two town models in the cellar. One shows medieval Freiburg circa 1590, with the city wall and all five city gates intact. Notice the little wall around the cathedral (today's Münsterplatz). This was the town cemetery, and the little house huddled next to the grand church was the *Beinhaus* (charnel house, where exhumed remains were stored). The other model, from the early 1700s, shows how the French King Louis XIV turned the city into a gigantic fortress—one of Europe's largest at the time (see next listing). Upstairs you'll find a beautiful ceiling—with Baroque babies swinging from the rafters—and other exhibits and artifacts documenting town history.

Cost and Hours: €3, covered by €6 city museum day pass, Tue-Sun 10:00-17:00, closed Mon, Münsterplatz 30, tel. 0761/201-2515.

Schlossberg (Castle Hill)

Schlossberg towers over the east end of Freiburg's Old Town. A monstrous 18th-century fort once stood here on "Castle Hill," built by the French to control the citizens of Freiburg during a period of French occupation. The giant fortress garrisoned as many as 150,000 soldiers at once. (The debate about where the border between France and Germany should be was only put to

rest after World War II.) The French destroyed the fortress when they retreated, leaving behind virtually no traces of the fort, except for a few stony walls. Today Schlossberg is Freiburg's playground, popular for its views over the city. A modern lookout tower (100 feet high) stands where the French Fort d'Aigle (eagle tower) once stood.

To get to the top of Schlossberg, you can either hike or (easier) take a free elevator up. From the Schwabentor, the half-timbered tower at the east end of the Old Town, look for the pedestrian walkway over the busy ring road. Once across, if you want to walk, bear left and hike up the steep switchbacks for 10 minutes. Or, to take the elevator *(Aufzug)*, continue straight through the cave-like tunnel to access it. At the top of the elevator and trail, you'll come to the pricey Greiffenegg Schlössle restaurant, and (in good weather) an affordable beer garden just above; both have knockout views, especially at sunset (and are described later, under "Eating in Freiburg").

For even better views, keep hiking to higher and higher perches. About a seven-minute hike above the restaurant is a broad, flat plateau with benches overlooking the town's rooftops. From there, you can hike about five more minutes up to a stubby stone bastion; or, for the highest vantage point, trek about 20 minutes up to the modern lookout tower. You can loop up to the tower and back on different paths. For the most straightforward approach to the tower, begin at the plateau with your back to the benches, walk the level path to the left, then veer right uphill at the big metal cross (look for the silver signs—these can be easy to miss—with a picture of the tower).

Schauinsland

Freiburg's own mountain, little more than an oversized hill, is nine miles southeast of the center. The viewpoint at its 4,000-foot summit, which won't wow anyone from Colorado, offers the handiest panorama view of the Schwarzwald for those without wheels. The gondola system that takes you up—one of Germany's oldest—was designed for Freiburgers relying on public transportation. At the top, you'll find a view restaurant, pleasant circular walks, and the Schniederlihof, a 1592 farmhouse museum. A tower on a nearby peak offers an even more commanding Black Forest view.

Cost and Hours: €12 round-trip for gondola, €25.50 family ticket includes 2 adults and up to 4 kids, daily July-Sept 9:00-18:00, Oct-June 9:00-17:00; catch tram #2—direction: Günterstal—from town center until the final stop, then take bus #21 to the Talstation stop; city center to gondola takes 25 minutes, gondola ride lasts 20 minutes; tel. 0761/451-1777, www.schauinslandbahn.de.

Hikes

If you want to hike, consider the St. Peter-St. Märgen trail described on page 320, which is cheaper and quicker to reach from Freiburg than the Schauinsland.

Sleeping in Freiburg

Though I prefer nights in sleepy Staufen (where you'll get better value for your money—see page 317), Freiburg is livelier and easier for non-drivers. If you have a car, hotels can usually get €10/day deals in city parking garages (normally €23/day). All my listings are in or near Freiburg's Old Town. In this university town, the busiest months with the highest rates are May, June, September, and October. Most hotels don't have 24-hour reception desks. If you think you'll be arriving after 20:00, call ahead and make arrangements.

$$$ Hotel Oberkirch is pricey but ideally situated. Nine of its 26 rooms sit right on the main square (facing the cathedral and above a restaurant); the rest are in a nearby building on Schusterstrasse, a pleasant pedestrian street. Each of the Old World rooms is different; some are a bit dated, but all are clean and comfortable (Schusterstrasse rooms: Sb-€99-129, Db-€149-169; main-square rooms: Sb-€121-149, Db-€165-199; up to €20 extra during busy times, family rooms, elevator, Wi-Fi, laundry service, Schusterstrasse 11, main-square rooms at Münsterplatz 22, tel. 0761/202-6868, www.hotel-oberkirch.de, info@hotel-oberkirch.de).

$$$ Schwarzwälder Hof, just a block behind the cathedral, has 40 surprisingly modern rooms over a reasonably priced restaurant. Guests get a free regional transport card *(Regiokarte),* valid as far as St. Peter and Staufen—a deal worth about €11/person per day (Sb-€68-85, Db-€99-125, Tb-€125-150, prices depend on room size and amenities; elevator, guest computer, Wi-Fi, Herrenstrasse 43, from station take tram #1 in direction: Littenweiler three stops to Oberlinden, tel. 0761/3803-0, www.shof.de, info@shof.de, Engler family).

$$$ Hotel Alleehaus has 19 comfy, creaky-floored rooms at the south edge of the Old Town. While close to the action, it's on a quiet, leafy street in a big, old house—think Art Nouveau with a hint of ramshackle. It feels like home and is warmly run by Bernd and his team (S-€48, Sb-€70-80, twin Db-€105, larger Db-€115, Tb-€145, Qb-€165, Wi-Fi, Marienstrasse 7, tel. 0761/387-600, www.hotel-alleehaus.de, wohlfuehlen@hotel-alleehaus.de). From the station, walk 20 minutes or take tram #3 (direction: Vauban) or #5 (direction: Rieselfeld) three stops to Holzmarkt; then walk along Holzmarkt, which becomes Wallstrasse, and turn right on Marienstrasse.

$$ Hotel zur Sichelschmiede rents six small rooms with attractive, traditional decor above a recommended restaurant in the cutest part of town, overlooking a canal (Sb-€69, Db-€89, Wi-Fi, Insel 1, tel. 0761/35037, www.sichelschmiede.de, info@sichelschmiede.de, Gerdi Stark and family).

$ **Hotel Schemmer,** though literally on the wrong side of the tracks, is close to public transport and a workable option if you're on a tight budget. It has 16 basic rooms on five floors (no elevator). Rooms with a private bath, which face the back, are quieter than shared-bath rooms, which front a busy street (S-€45, Sb-€55, D-€58, Db-€71, Tb-€99, Qb-€120, Wi-Fi, Eschholzstrasse 63; take tram #1, #3, or #5 one stop to Eschholzstrasse; on foot, follow the tracks 10 minutes from the station, turn left on Eschholzstrasse, and walk a block; tel. 0761/207-490, www.hotel-schemmer.de, kontakt@hotel-schemmer.de).

HOSTELS

$ **Black Forest Hostel** has 105 of the cheapest beds in Freiburg. Run by friendly Tania and Cori, with a young, bohemian attitude, it's bare-bones simple (€17-20/bed in 10- to 21-bed rooms, €21-27/bed in 3- to 8-bed rooms, S-€35, D-€58, sheets-€4, sleeping bags OK, cash only, no curfew, lockers, guest computer for a fee, self-service kitchen, laundry-€5, free parking nearby, Kartäuser Strasse 33—look for anchor sign and go down driveway; 20-minute walk from station or take tram #1—direction: Littenweiler—to Oberlinden stop, then walk 5 more minutes; tel. 0761/881-7870, www.blackforest-hostel.de, backpacker@blackforest-hostel.de). If full, they might direct you to the much larger, more distant $ **Freiburg Youth Hostel** at Kartäuser Strasse 151 (tel. 0761/67656, www.jugendherberge-freiburg.de, info@jugendherberge-freiburg.de).

Eating in Freiburg

Many of Freiburg's best eateries are conveniently concentrated within a block or two of the square called Augustinerplatz. Browse your options here and choose your favorite. Or consider a picnic at the Schlossberg viewpoint (buy supplies at the REWE supermarket—see page 296).

IN THE GERBERAU DISTRICT

These two places are just downhill from Augustinerplatz, along the town creek.

Hausbrauerei Feierling is a rollicking microbrewery that also serves good meals. On warm summer evenings, their *Biergarten* across the street offers cool, leafy shade and a bustling atmosphere. If you're dining inside, try the cozy upstairs seating, looking down over the big copper vats and order the local brew—*Inselhopf* (€6-13 main courses and wurst plates, daily 11:00–24:00, indoor section closed in afternoons when weather is hot, Gerberau 46, tel. 0761/243-480).

Sichelschmiede is a good option rain or shine. Its timbered alcoves and cluttered interior give it a cozy living-room feel, and its creekside seating can't be beat. Come here for easygoing seasonal regional cuisine, good value, and a family-friendly ambience (€8–20 main courses, daily 12:00–22:00, Insel 1, tel. 0761/35037; also rents rooms—see "Sleeping in Freiburg"). Don't confuse it with the neighboring, lesser-value restaurant that shares the outdoor terrace.

ALONG GRÜNWÄLDERSTRASSE

This street, connecting Augustinerplatz to the shopping and university zone, is lined with tempting choices.

Markthalle is a wonderful food court where you can peruse cuisines from around the world—German, French, Swiss, Italian, Indian, Brazilian, Chinese, Arabic, and more (most meals around €5-10, eat at stand-up tables or find scarce stools, Mon-Thu 11:00–20:00, Fri-Sat 11:00–24:00, closed Sun, live music or DJ on weekends after 20:00—no cover, Grünwälderstrasse 4). At the front of the complex is a restaurant called **Osteria,** offering a seasonal menu of mostly German food in a charming atmosphere (€7-18 lunches, €10-25 main courses, Tue-Sat 9:00–22:00, closed Sun-Mon, Grünwälderstrasse 2, tel. 0761/32054).

Tacheles appeals to student-size appetites (big) and budgets (small). Who knew that schnitzel could be prepared in 300 different ways? Here at the self-proclaimed "*Schnitzel Paradies,*" they serve up big schnitzels (€1.20 extra for *Pute*—turkey—instead of the usual pork), a salad, and your choice of a side dish (french fries, *Spätzle,* and so on) for a mere €7.50 before 18:00 on weekdays (€8.50 evenings and weekends). Non-schnitzel specials, including vegetarian options, run €7 to €9. The pub downstairs, a favorite hangout, can be crowded and smoky; instead, opt for the quiet courtyard seating upstairs (daily 11:30–23:00 or later, Grünwälderstrasse 17, tel. 0761/319-6669). There's a disco in the cellar on Friday and Saturday nights between 23:00 and 5:00 in the morning (with DJ, free entry).

Chang Thai, two doors down from Tacheles, is where students satisfy their Asian-food cravings (€5-9 weekday lunches, €6-10 main courses, Mon-Sat 12:00–23:00, Sun 13:00–22:30, Grünwälderstrasse 21, tel. 0761/137-9684).

IN THE "BERMUDA TRIANGLE" NEIGHBORHOOD

Night owls flock around St. Martin's Tower (Martinstor), in the area affectionately called Freiburg's "Bermuda Triangle." Take the street to your right just before going through the gate, and get sucked in. Look at the Burger King ahead of you; mischievous

Puck does a little dance and plays the pan pipes. He's a fitting mascot for a district known for its fun, colorful bars.

At **UC/Uni-Café,** join the cerebral grad-student crowd for cheap breakfast options (all day while they last), crêpes, salads, and light meals. Enjoy the spacious outdoor seating, or pop inside and order the cocktail of the week (€6-9 salads, €5-6 sandwiches, €5 *Flammkuchen*—German-style pizza, daily 8:00-23:00, Niemensstrasse 7, at Universitätsstrasse, tel. 0761/383-355).

Gelato: Drop by **Incontro,** where you'll be greeted with a robust *"Buona sera!"* before choosing your favorite flavor (€1/scoop, free Wi-Fi, daily 10:00-23:00, Niemensstrasse 3).

ON FREIBURG'S SCHLOSSBERG

For directions on getting to these scenic eateries, see page 305.

Greiffenegg Schlössle offers dynamite rooftop views over Freiburg, but the meals are expensive, and worth it only if you

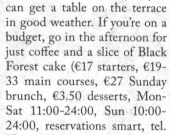

can get a table on the terrace in good weather. If you're on a budget, go in the afternoon for just coffee and a slice of Black Forest cake (€17 starters, €19-33 main courses, €27 Sunday brunch, €3.50 desserts, Mon-Sat 11:00-24:00, Sun 10:00-24:00, reservations smart, tel. 0761/32728, www.greiffenegg.de). The self-service open-air **Biergarten Kastaniengarten,** just above the restaurant, is a nice casual option (€6-9 main courses, open April-Oct in good weather, same hours). If the weather is iffy, before ascending look for the *Biergarten geöffnet* ("beer garden open") sign near the base of the elevator.

Freiburg Connections

The full name of the town—and the station—is Freiburg im Breisgau, often abbreviated as "Freiburg (Brsg)" on schedules.

By Train to: Staufen (at least hourly until about 24:00, 30 minutes, most require transfer at Bad Krozingen), **Baden-Baden** (direct fast trains every 1-2 hours, 45 minutes; cheaper regional trains take 1.5 hours with change in Offenburg), **Munich** (hourly, 4.5 hours, most with 1 change), **Basel,** Switzerland (about 3/hour, 40 minutes; 1 hour on cheaper regional train), **Bern,** Switzerland (about 2/hour, 2 hours, some transfer in Basel), **Frankfurt** (hourly, 1.5-2 hours, most direct), **Frankfurt Airport** (hourly, 2 hours, most with 1 change). Train info: Tel. 0180-599-6633, www.bahn.com.

Staufen

Hemmed in by vineyards and watched
over by the ruins of a protective castle,
Staufen (SHTOW-fehn, rhymes with
"now then") is small and off the beaten
path—except on weekends, when it's a
popular destination for Germans, who
fill hotels and parking spots. Staufen's
quiet pedestrian zone of colorful old
buildings is bounded by a happy creek
that actually babbles. The hotels in
Staufen make a peaceful and delightful home base for your exploration of

Freiburg and the southern trunk of the Black Forest. You can also
make Staufen a half-day outing from Freiburg.

Orientation to Staufen

Staufen (pop. 7,500) is simple to master. The main square is an
easy 10-minute walk from the train station, and everything I list is
along the way (or just off it). Though Staufen feels small, its high
school, courthouse, and shopping district serve all the villages in
the Münstertal valley. Staufen hosts a modest annual music festival, the Staufener Musikwoche, around the beginning of August;
check TI website for information.

TOURIST INFORMATION
Staufen's helpful TI, on the main square in the Rathaus, has Internet access for €4 per hour (April-Oct Mon-Fri 9:00-12:30 &
14:00-17:30, Sat 10:00-12:00, closed Sun; Nov-March Mon-Fri
9:00-12:00 plus Mon, Wed, and Fri 14:00-17:00, closed Sat-Sun;
tel. 07633/80536, www.muenstertal-staufen.de). In summer, they
offer weekly **walking tours** (€5, April-Oct Wed at 16:30).

Local Guide: Marianne Pfadt, a German who speaks English with a charming Scottish brogue, enjoys taking visitors on a
casual but insightful tour around the back streets of her hometown
(€50/1.5-hour walk, tel. 07633/982-529, siegfried.pfadt@t-online.
de).

ARRIVAL IN STAUFEN
The **train station** is often unstaffed and has no lockers. To get to
town, exit the station with your back to the pond and angle right
up Bahnhofstrasse. Turn right onto Hauptstrasse, which leads
through the town center to the Rathaus and TI.

If you're arriving by **car**, be sure you're going to Staufen im Breisgau, and follow signs for *Stadtmitte* to find the town center. If your hotel is in the pedestrian zone, it's OK to drive there to park. If you're day-tripping, you'll find a handy parking lot right at the entrance to the center (and at the start of my self-guided walk).

Staufen Walk

Few small German towns are as enjoyable to explore as Staufen. It's tourist-friendly without being a tourist trap—a real town with real shops and residents, but still accessible to visitors. This self-guided walk will help you get your bearings. It begins at the start of the cobbled pedestrian zone, near the parking lot; if you're coming from the train station, this is the first part of the old center you'll reach.

• *Begin at the Wine Cooperative building, near the big tree, fountain, and giant wine press.*

Wine Co-op Square

As you can see from the vineyards blanketing its little castle hill, this is a wine-growing region. Wine production (along with taxes levied on silver, which was mined deeper in the Black Forest) once brought Staufen wealth...and it still helps out. People "taking the cure" at the rehab centers in nearby Bad Krozingen come to this square to take a break from their treatment and sip local wines. The building labeled *Winzergenossenschaft* is Staufen's **bottling cooperative,** where several local vintners produce and sell their wines. They offer free tastes and sell affordable bottles (most bottles €5-10, Mon-Fri 9:00-18:00, Sat 9:00-14:00, Sun 10:00-15:00 except closed Sun Jan-Feb, Auf dem Rempart 2, tel. 07633/5510, www.wg-staufen.de). Or, if you'd just like a glass of wine in the summer, you can sit out front at the little **wine garden** (€2-3/glass, Mon-Fri 14:00-22:00, Sat-Sun 11:00-22:00). The Gutedel grape, also known as Chasselas, is common in this area.

At the benches between the fountain and the gigantic wine press, look for the photo of a red-sandstone courthouse that once stood here. That building, like much of Staufen, was devastated by an Allied bombing late in World War II (February 8, 1945)—you'll see other photos of the damage scattered around town.

• *Now walk up Staufen's main street called...*

Hauptstrasse

Like its big sister Freiburg, Staufen has little canals called *Bächle* running along its main street (originally made for fire protection and now enjoyed for their own sake). The charm of this colorful drag is governed by strict building codes: Only certain colors can be used, and the shutters are uniform. But locals grumble that sometimes the rules go too far. Notice the rain gutters that empty out onto the cobbles. These used to run underground, but were brought aboveground to be more authentically medieval—and now the streets turn into an ice rink in cold weather.

But the careful restrictions aren't just for the tourists. You'll notice that most of the shops even along this main street aren't trinket boutiques, but real services. Staufen's downtown is thriving, and you'll see bakers, butchers, pharmacies (such as the old-time *Apotheke* on the right, at #52), and other everyday shops. In fact, some Freiburgers like to come to Staufen on Saturday mornings, to shop where the stores are smaller and the owner-clerks are friendlier.

Just before you reach the main square, on the left (at #47), look for the red **Gasthaus zum Löwen.** In the early 16th century, a popular and successful doctor/scientist/fortune-teller/alchemist named Johann Georg Faust was brought to Staufen to produce gold for the town. He lived and worked in this very house, experimenting with chemical processes until an accidental explosion killed him around the year 1540. This being the Middle Ages, the townspeople assumed that the devil must have had a hand in his death, and legends began to swirl. Over time, these stories grabbed the attention of various writers, including Goethe (sometimes regarded as the "German Shakespeare"). In Goethe's seminal work *Faust,* the title character sells his soul to a demon named Mephistopheles in exchange for unlimited earthly powers. You might see a costumed Mephistopheles leading tours (in German only) through the streets of Staufen. The building is now run as a guesthouse, and believe it or not, you can sleep in Faust's very room—it's a double with a private bath (€108; tel. 07633/908-9390, www.fauststube-im-loewen. de).

Across the street, at #56 (marked *Stubenhaus Stadtmuseum*), you can duck into one of Staufen's oldest **courtyards.** Go down the half-timbered passage (and past the cheesy Restaurant Käsestube) to get inside. Historically, the building overlooking this courtyard was used by the local guilds to host special events...and it can still be rented out today. The courtyard itself is filled with occasional concerts (usually advertised by posters nearby).

• *Continue out to Staufen's main square.*

BADEN-BADEN & THE BLACK FOREST

Marktplatz (Market Square)

Looking around the square, notice the accidentally clever design: Four streets converge, but are offset, so as you approach you see not other streets—but buildings. This makes the square feel especially cozy.

The soldier atop the **fountain** holds the shield of Staufen, with its symbol: three golden goblets on a red field. The medieval word *Stuff* meant "goblet"; Staufen was named for its castle hill, which resembles an upside-down goblet.

Dominating the square is the **Town Hall** *(Rathaus).* The left part (Gothic) is older than the right part (Renaissance), but the whole thing was restored in 2007. The coats of arms represent the various powers that have controlled Staufen over the centuries. The golden seashell at the top of the right peak indicates that this was a stop along the Camino de Santiago, the medieval pilgrimage route that leads all the way to the northwest corner of Spain. Inside the Town Hall are the TI and a very humble town **museum** (Stadtmuseum, upstairs, a few town artifacts, German only, free, open Mon 8:00-12:00 & 14:00-18:00, Tue-Fri 8:00-12:00, Sun 14:00-17:00, closed Sat).

The Town Hall restoration left the building looking beautiful...but is also threatening to destroy Staufen. Notice the troubling **cracks** running along the building

facade adjoining the Town Hall (you'll see similar cracks all over town). The restoration included the installation of a heat pump—an environmentally friendly solution intended to set a good example for townsfolk. Engineers drilled deep into the ground behind the Town Hall, built heat exchangers, and for a few weeks everything worked perfectly. But then cracks began to appear. Apparently, the drilling punctured a layer of anhydrite, a mineral that soaks up groundwater and turns into a bigger-moleculed mineral called gypsum—and the ground beneath Staufen is rising at rates of up to a centimeter each month. While experts scramble to stop it (if they can), more and more precious old buildings show still-growing cracks—250 homes in all have been damaged so far. The costs are huge, and it's not clear who will pay them.

• *Before moving on, put your back to the Town Hall and look out toward the busy street in the distance. The yellow building on the right with the big* CAFE *sign is the recommended Café Decker, the best place in town for cakes and chocolates. Five minutes' walk beyond that is Staufen's fascinating little cemetery (explained later).*

But first, if you'd like to see a side of Staufen most tourists miss, walk through...

Staufen's Back Streets *(Hinterstädtle)*

Leave Marktplatz on the little lane (called Freihofgasse) between the Kornhaus and the Volksbank. Stick with this lane as it curls around to the left (passing a butcher shop on the right) and goes through a residential neighborhood. Then continue moseying straight along Spitalstrasse, the oldest quarter of town. Until a few decades ago, this was a poor neighborhood; wealthier folk (including well-heeled retirees) lived in villas on the hillside above. But in the 1980s, gentrification began to turn many of the once-humble cottages in this area into fancy town houses. Today it's a hodgepodge of spiffed-up yuppie homes and ramshackle older ones. As you stroll, you'll enjoy the constant sound of running water from little fountains (most marked *Kein Trinkwasser*—"not drinking water"). After passing a few art galleries, look for the former town wall (on the right). Where the street does a little jog and hits a bigger road, the big building on the left (marked *Renoviert A.D. 1978* on the upper window, and *Re: 1830* above the door) was a hospice *(Spital)*, which wealthy townspeople financed to house people who were ill and too poor to care for themselves.

Turn left and head for the church. This area has some fun boutique shops: Around the right side of the church is a local **coffee roaster** (Coffee & More Kaffeerösterei, buy a bag of coffee to go or sip a cup here on the square, Mon-Fri 9:30-18:00, Sat 9:30-14:00, Sun 12:00-17:30, St. Johannesgasse 14, tel. 07633/981-824), and around the left side is a **chocolatier** (Chocolaterie Axel Sixt, €5.50/100 grams—mix and match, Mon-Tue and Thu-Fri 9:00-12:30 & 15:00-18:00, Wed 9:00-12:30, Sat 9:00-13:00, closed Sun, Kirchstrasse 11, tel. 07633/801-255). Choose your poison. The church itself is big and empty-feeling.

You could follow the paved street right back to Marktplatz. Or, to savor residential Staufen, face the church, look left, and notice the big doorway at #9, marked *Jägergasse*. Go into the passage and continue through local neighborhoods. Watch kids having fun at the playground or peek over fences into somebody's garden patch. You can turn left at Meiergasse, or keep going straight as the path narrows—both options lead you right back to the cobbled pedestrian zone...you've come full-circle.

• *If you still have time and energy, consider poking around Staufen's evocative cemetery, just across the river, or hiking up to its hilltop castle (both described next).*

To reach the cemetery, leave Market Square toward Café Decker, Staufen's largest chocolate shop. Cross the big bridge next to the shop, turn right, and walk a short distance between the river and the busy road. When you reach the small footbridge on your right, turn left, cross the busy road, and walk down Wettelbrunner Strasse. A few steps down the street on the left, a small onion-domed chapel marks Staufen's cemetery.

Sights in Staufen

Cemetery (Friedhof)

Staufen has one of the more atmospheric and unexpectedly pleasant little cemeteries I've seen. It's a good place for a contempla-

tive walk, and to ponder German burial customs. Ornate headstones stand in a garden of trees and plants, giving it a comforting feel. As in much of Europe, plots in the cemetery are not purchased, only leased. When your lease is up, someone else moves in. Notice that some headstones have several added-on plaques identifying the remains of many generations of tenants. You may see people here lovingly tending to the graves, tidying the ivy and planting flowers: Tenants' survivors are responsible for maintenance. Some graves have huge trees growing right up out of them, like towering headstones reminding visitors that mortality is nothing new.

Nearby: On your way back to Market Square, you'll see Staufen's **pottery museum,** in the building labeled Keramik-Museum (€2.50, Wed-Sat 14:00-17:00, Sun 11:00-13:00 & 14:00-17:00, closed Mon-Tue and Dec-Jan, Wettelbrunner Strasse 3, tel. 07633/6721, www.landesmuseum.de).

For another detour, go down the street on the right side of the Hotel Kreuz-Post, where you'll find the Schladerer **liquor distillery** and its outlet shop—look for the *Verkauf* sign (Mon-Fri 9:30-12:30 & 14:00-18:00, Sat 9:30-13:00, closed Sun, tours every Wed at 14:00, book in advance at TI, tel. 07633/8320, www.schladerer.de).

Castle

Staufen's own little vineyard-covered mountain is topped by the remains of a castle (once the residence of the Lords of Staufen) that was destroyed by Swedish troops in 1632. The most direct route to visit these ruins is to charge right on up, but you can also take one of the less-steep roundabout trails.

Sleeping in Staufen

Unless otherwise noted, your hotel will add a local tax of €1.50 per person per night to the rates below. In Staufen—as in other small Black Forest towns—this comes with a big return for those relying on public transportation: the KONUS card *(KONUS Gästekarte)*, which covers all transit for the entire Black Forest region (south to Switzerland, west to France, and north to Baden-Baden). This includes unlimited use of all buses, regional trains, and local transit (such as buses or trams in Freiburg or Baden-Baden), but doesn't cover express ICE or IC trains. (Unfortunately, hotel guests in Freiburg or Baden-Baden don't get the KONUS card.) For more details, see www.blackforest-tourism.com/info/KONUS.

All of the following listings have free parking.

$$$ Hotel-Gasthof Kreuz-Post, in the pedestrian zone directly ahead of the Town Hall (on the left), is the town splurge. It rents 12 colorful, tidy rooms over a well-regarded but pricey restaurant (Sb-€90-105, Db-€110-145, price depends on room size, some rooms have elevator access, Wi-Fi, Hauptstrasse 65, tel. 07633/95320, www.kreuz-post-staufen.de, info@kreuz-post-staufen.de).

$$ Gasthaus Krone, the town's top value, sits in the middle of Staufen's main pedestrian drag like it owns it. Charming, friendly, and with nine comfortable rooms, it's a winner. Try here first (Sb-€70, Db-€95, Tb-€125, some rooms with balconies, Wi-Fi, Hauptstrasse 30, tel. 07633/5840, www.die-krone-staufen.de, info@die-krone.de, Lahn family—father Kurt reminds me of Dan Rather).

$$ Zum Hirschen, also family-run and with a storybook location on the main pedestrian street, has 15 rooms, a roof deck, and a traditional restaurant on the ground floor (Sb-€68, Db-€89-118, Tb-€118-128, some rooms with balconies, elevator, Wi-Fi, Hauptstrasse 19, tel. 07633/5297, www.hirschen-staufen.de, hotel@hirschen-staufen.de, Dieter and Isabelle). Their top floor is a two-bedroom suite with room for up to six people (€168 for 4 people).

$ Gästehaus Kaltenbach is a great deal in a rural-feeling location. It's a 10-minute, moderately uphill walk from the station or town center; they'll pick you up if you arrive by train with luggage. English teacher Gabriele Kaltenbach and her policeman-turned-farmer husband Günter rent six rooms in a huge farmhouse with horses out back. They have maps of local hiking trails (Sb-€34, Db-€68, cheaper with 3-night stay, guest computer, Wi-Fi, laundry facilities, yard with swing set; Bötzenstrasse 37, tel. 07633/95310, www.gaestehaus-kaltenbach.de, info@gaestehaus-kaltenbach.de). From the station, walk toward town and after a block look for the Bacchus statue at the corner of Bahnhofstrasse and Hauptstrasse. Head up Sixtgasse behind the statue, with the vineyards on your left, continue straight through the barrier along Im Rondell, then turn left at the T-intersection onto Bötzenstrasse.

Eating in Staufen

Many of the hotels listed earlier also have their own good restaurants. For fine dining, head for **Gasthaus Krone,** which proudly uses regional products (€19-30 main courses, €30-45 three-course fixed-price menu, 11:30-14:00 & 18:00-22:30 except closed Fri lunch and all day Sat, Hauptstrasse 30, tel. 07633/5840). For a mid-range option, try **Gasthaus zum Löwen** (tables right on the main square next to Town Hall, or eat in the comfy interior, €9-13 lunch specials, €15-27 main courses, fixed-price meals from €35-39, daily 10:00-22:00, Rathausgasse 8, tel. 07633/908-9390). Across the square, the informal **Kornhaus** is a less-expensive, family-friendly option (€9-15 main courses, seasonal menu, daily 11:00-23:00, Hauptstrasse 57, tel. 07633/5401).

Dessert: Every sweet-tooth in Staufen adores **Café Decker** for its 50 types of chocolates (€6.30/100 grams) and long display case showing off a wide array of cakes (around €3/slice to go, or €4 to eat there). The dining room is genteel, but don't miss the inviting rooftop terrace, with views over Staufen's babbling brook (also €5-10 full breakfasts and €8-11 light lunch specials including dessert, Mon-Sat 6:30-18:00, Sun 13:30-18:00, Hauptstrasse 70, tel. 07633/5316).

Staufen Connections

Getting to Staufen can be tricky. It's on a tiny branch line (called the Münstertalbahn) that connects to the main line at Bad Krozingen. After about 24:00 trains stop serving Staufen. Keep in mind that the Staufen train station is rarely staffed. Plan ahead by checking schedules online (www.vag-freiburg.de or www.bahn.com), asking at the Freiburg train station (pick up a printed schedule), or checking at the Staufen TI.

From Staufen by Train to: Freiburg (at least hourly until about 24:00, 30 minutes, a few direct, most require transfer in Bad

Krozingen; covered by a single €3.80 two-zone local transport ticket, available from ticket machines, covered by KONUS Card).

Best of the Black Forest

Baden-Baden, Freiburg, and Staufen are appealing towns and fine places to stay overnight. But to let the Black Forest live up to its

name, spend a few daytime hours delving into the countryside in this land of cuckoo clocks and healthy hikes. Using public transport, you can day-trip from Freiburg to the small towns of St. Märgen and St. Peter, and enjoy the two-hour hike between them. Drivers can choose between a short excursion out and back from Freiburg or, with a day to connect Baden-Baden and Freiburg, a longer drive that takes in some fun museums and activities. Everything that can be done from Freiburg can also be done from Staufen (just add another 30 minutes or so each way). Fair warning: The Black Forest is what I'd call "gently scenic." Do it before you delve into the bigger, better Alps in Switzerland or Bavaria; otherwise, you might be underwhelmed.

Black Forest Loop by Public Transportation

FREIBURG-ST. MÄRGEN-ST. PETER DAY TRIP

This pleasant train-and-bus excursion focuses on a pair of charming upland towns nestled in the idyllic Black Forest landscape: St. Märgen and St. Peter. You can connect the two towns by bus, or hike the five miles between St. Märgen and St. Peter in about two hours without stops; the walk requires no more than average fitness and offers lots of picnic benches. The trail runs partly (but not entirely) through woods, so you may want to bring along a hat, water, and sunscreen. Both towns have restaurants, and each has modest sights worth about a half-hour of your time.

PLANNING YOUR TIME

Here's a relaxed plan: 9:40—Train leaves Freiburg; 10:30—Arrive St. Märgen, see museum if open; 11:30—Start hike to St. Peter, with leisurely picnic lunch along the way; 14:00—Arrive St. Peter, take a quick look at the abbey church; 15:00—Bus leaves for the

45-minute ride back to Freiburg. On weekends, leave Freiburg at 9:10.

Before you start, buy two €3.80 two-zone local transport tickets or a 24-hour regional pass (€11 for 1 adult, €21 for 2-5 adults, available from ticket machines). These cover your transport from Freiburg to St. Märgen, and from St. Peter back to Freiburg. Though not absolutely necessary, it's not a bad idea to pick up the *Hochtouren/St. Märgen* 1:25,000 hiking map, which shows the route in detail; buy it from bookstores in Freiburg or at the St. Märgen TI.

❍SELF-GUIDED TOUR

From Freiburg to St. Märgen: Take the train from Freiburg to Kirchzarten (13 minutes). At Kirchzarten, change to bus #7216, which winds 25 minutes up to St. Peter and then another 10 minutes to St. Märgen. This connection works hourly on weekdays and once every two hours on weekends; confirm times in advance at www.bahn.com or at the Freiburg train station. In St. Märgen, the bus drops you in the village center, near the Rathaus, abbey, supermarket, and bakery—a last chance to picnic-shop (shops closed Sat afternoon and all day Sun).

St. Märgen: St. Märgen (pop. 1,900) is a pleasant, sleepy town dominated by its Augustinian abbey (nice, but less impressive than the abbey in St. Peter). The St. Märgen **TI** is in the back of the *Rathaus* (open Mon-Fri 8:00-12:00, closed Sat-Sun; tel. 07652/1206-8390; www.hochschwarzwald.de).

The only real sightseeing in town is the **Kloster Museum St. Märgen,** attached to (and named for) the Augustinian cloister. This small but delightful collection is worth a peek, but it can be toured only with a guide. While there's not a word of English, the highlights include Black Forest clocks (from ancient clocks using stones as counterweights, to more familiar cuckoo clocks, all displayed chronologically) and the *Reise ins Uhrenland* exhibit, which describes how Black Forest clock vendors spread far and wide around the world to sell these affordable timepieces. You'll see Black Forest clocks decorated for customers in many different countries. If you're not going to Furtwangen's German Clock Museum, this is a decent substitute. Rounding out the collection are landscape paintings, local history exhibits, and ecclesiastical art, including folk pieces and paintings on glass (€4 for German tour at 10:15 and 11:45 on Sun year-round plus Wed-Thu in May-Oct; €5 for English tour, six-person minimum, arrange in advance; Rathausplatz 1, tel. 07652/1206-8390, www.kloster-museum.de).

Hiking from St. Märgen to St. Peter: From the St. Märgen bus stop, follow the signposts marked *St. Peter (Höhenweg)*. The first 40 minutes of the walk go gently uphill, with an elevation gain of about 500 feet. Walk through the village, and by Hotel Hirsch, make a left turn up a small paved road. (When the trail branches left and changes to dirt, you can detour right 100 yards to the Rankmühle, a picturesque old house.) Eventually you'll reach a small chapel, the Kapfenkapelle.

The trail is level for the next half hour, with views down into the valley. At a clearing in the woods, you'll find another chapel, the Vogesenkapelle. This chapel was built in 1938 by a local man who had fought during World War I in France's Vosges mountains (*Vogesen* in German, just across the Rhine valley from the Schwarzwald). On a clear winter evening at sunset in the Vosges, the man was able to see all the way to the Black Forest—and could even make out his own farm. He vowed then to build a chapel near his home if the Black Forest was spared the horrors of the war.

From the Vogesenkapelle, the path leads down about 45 minutes through farms and residential neighborhoods on the outskirts of St. Peter, and deposits you just below the abbey at the main St. Peter bus stop. Explore the town (described next), or hop on bus #7216 back to Kirchzarten (1-2/hour) where you can catch a train to Freiburg.

Although you can also do this hike in reverse—from St. Peter to St. Märgen—it's more strenuous (as St. Märgen is 500 feet higher than St. Peter) and a little harder to follow.

St. Peter: St. Peter (pop. 2,500) is one of those healthy, go-take-a-walk-in-the-clean-air places that doctors actually prescribe for people from all over Germany. The well-organized little **TI**, under the archway across from the Benedictine Abbey, can give you details on the region or recommend a countryside walk (TI open Mon-Fri 9:00-12:00 & 15:00-17:00, closed Sat-Sun except July-Aug open Sat 10:00-12:00, Klosterhof 11, tel. 07652/1206-8371).

To find a public WC and reasonably priced eating options, go through the archway to the square.

The town of St. Peter is dominated by its giant, namesake **Benedictine abbey**—red sandstone outside, with an interior dripping with white Rococo curlicues. Duck into the church, finished in 1727, for a glimpse at a classic Rococo interior. While it's not the finest in Germany—you'll see bigger and better in Bavaria—it's the best in the Black Forest. The most interesting feature, the attached library, can be entered only with a German-language tour (church—free, daily 8:00-19:00; library tour—€6; runs Tue at 11:00, Thu at 14:30, Sun at 11:30; enter at Geistliches Zentrum next door to church, tel. 07660/91010).

Returning to Freiburg: Just below St. Peter's abbey is the town's main bus stop, called Zähringer Eck, where you can catch bus #7216 back to Kirchzarten (1-2/hour); from there, catch the train to Freiburg.

SLEEPING IN ST. MÄRGEN AND ST. PETER

Accommodations in both towns come with the same KONUS card public-transit deal as Staufen (see page 317)—you could easily stay up here and day-trip down into the valley.

In St. Märgen: **$ Gasthaus Pension Rössle** is centrally located with 19 rooms (Sb-€37, Db-€70, less for 3 nights or more, cash only, Wagensteigstrasse 7, tel. 07669/213, www.roessle-st-maergen.de, roessle-st-maergen@t-online.de).

In St. Peter: **$ Gasthof Hirschen** is a traditional, old 18-room guesthouse conveniently situated on the main square (Sb-€39-44, Db-€66-85, Tb-€87-110, Qb-€120-136, pay Wi-Fi, Bertholdsplatz 1, tel. 07660/941-380, www.gasthof-hirschen.de, info@gasthof-hirschen.de). **$ Pension Kandelblick,** your budget option, has five basic rooms a 10-minute walk from the abbey and main square (D/Ds-€50-60, cash only, Seelgutweg 5, a block off the main drag at the St. Märgen end of town, tel. 07660/1259, haus-kandelblick@web.de).

Short-and-Scenic Black Forest Drive

FREIBURG-ST. MÄRGEN-ST. PETER LOOP DRIVE

This pleasant loop takes you through the most representative chunk of the area, including the towns of St. Märgen and St. Peter. This basically passes through much the same scenery as the day trip described above, but by car.

⊙SELF-GUIDED TOUR

Leave Freiburg on Schwarzwaldstrasse (signs to *Donaueschingen*), which becomes scenic road B-31 up the dark Höllental ("Hell's Valley"). Here the cliffs on either side begin to close in. Just before you enter the narrowest part of the canyon, you'll pass an area known as Himmelreich ("heaven"). This valley was made to order for bandits—those surviving the Höllental felt like they'd reached heaven when they reached this point.

As you enter the narrowest part of the valley, watch for the *Hirschensprung* sign, then look up to the top of the cliff on the right to see a bronze statue of a deer *(Hirsch)* preparing to leap *(sprung)* over the chasm to escape a hunter, a feat memorialized in a local legend.

After the moody, narrow stretch of the valley, you'll hit a straightaway, and then the road begins a series of switchbacks up and out of the canyon. En route, you're sure to see signs to over-rated, overcrowded Titisee. This famous lake, with a giggle-inducing name, is improbably popular among Germans. One glance and you'll be wondering why they even bothered to develop this dull spot into a tourist attraction—and yet it's a huge hit. Don't let morbid curiosity take you to Titisee...or you'll squander valuable Black Forest time. (After all, you can't spell "tourist trap" without "T. T.")

Instead, at Hinterzarten (just before Titisee), turn onto B-500 toward Furtwangen and St. Märgen. Soon you'll come to a fork in the road, where you can choose between heading straight to Furt-wangen (and its German Clock Museum—a detour from this route but worth a visit if you have a car and plenty of time, described on page 328); or turning off for St. Märgen, then St. Peter (both described earlier).

At St. Märgen, visit the museum in the Augustinian cloister—if it's open—and in St. Peter, check out the Rococo church in the former Benedictine abbey. If you have at least three hours, you could park in St. Märgen, do the walk from St. Märgen to St. Peter, and then take the bus back from St. Peter to St. Märgen.

After passing through St. Peter, stick with the main B-31 road (toward Kirchzarten) to head back down to Freiburg. Or, for a longer drive, continue up about 15 minutes from St. Peter through idyllic Black Forest scenery to the pass over Mount Kandel (head for Glottertal; just outside St. Peter, turn right at Elmehof to follow brown signs to *Kandel*). At the summit is the Berghotel Kandel, with parking and fine views on either side of the ridge. For even better views, take a short hike to the 4,000-foot peak (Kandelgip-fel), where on a nice day, you can watch paragliders psych themselves up and take off.

On the other side of the pass, the road winds steeply down through a dense forest to Waldkirch, where a fast road takes you down to the Freiburg Nord autobahn entrance. From here you can return to Freiburg, or drive on to Baden-Baden.

Extended Black Forest Drive

BETWEEN BADEN-BADEN AND FREIBURG

For a more thorough (and more interesting) look at the Black Forest, try this drive. Some of these sights are reasonably accessible by public transportation, as noted, but can't be done as efficiently as by car. The two major museums of this area—both worth visiting—focus on different characteristics of the Black Forest: farming (the

Vogtsbauernhof Black Forest Open-Air Museum) and clockmaking (Furtwangen's German Clock Museum).

GETTING AROUND

Here are the directions for taking in all of the attractions listed here, whether you're heading from Baden-Baden to Freiburg, or vice versa.

By Car from Baden-Baden to Freiburg: Head south from Baden-Baden on B-500, a.k.a. the Schwarzwald-Hochstrasse, which takes you along a ridge through 30 miles of pine forests (and becomes B-28—take it east, signs to Freudenstadt). Eventually you'll reach Freudenstadt, the workaday capital of the northern Black Forest. Wind your way through the sprawl of Freudenstadt, and hop on B-294 southbound toward Triberg. Just after Wolfach and before Hausach, turn south onto B-33/E-531 to Gutach, where you'll visit the Vogtsbauernhof Black Forest Open-Air Museum. Next, continue south on B-33/E-531, turning off to visit Triberg. Leaving Triberg, head south on B-500 to Furtwangen and its impressive German Clock Museum. From Furtwangen, continue south on B-500. From this road, you have two options for joining up with different scenic areas (both described earlier, under "Short and Scenic Black Forest Drive"): Turn off for St. Märgen, then St. Peter. From here, you could take the slower and higher-altitude route to Freiburg via Mount Kandel and Waldkirch. For a more direct, but still scenic approach, continue a bit farther south on B-500 to Hinterzarten, where you can turn right onto B-31 and follow the claustrophobic Höllental ("Hell's Valley"). Either option brings you to Freiburg's backyard.

By Car from Freiburg to Baden-Baden: Begin by following the "Short-and-Scenic Black Forest Drive," described earlier, but continue north on B-500 to Furtwangen for a visit to its German Clock Museum, then Triberg. From Triberg, head north on B-33/E-531 (toward Hausach) to the open-air museum in Gutach, then continue north and pick up B-294 to Freudenstadt, and on to the Schwarzwald-Hochstrasse (B-28, then B-500), which dumps you right on Baden-Baden's back porch.

SIGHTS BETWEEN BADEN-BADEN AND FREIBURG
▲Vogtsbauernhof Black Forest Open-Air Museum

This museum, the Schwarzwälder Freilichtmuseum Vogtsbauernhof, offers the best look at this region's traditional folk architecture. Built around one grand old farmhouse, the museum is a collection of several old farm buildings, some of which house exhibits on the local dress and lifestyles. While English information is sparse, the place gives you a good sense of traditional rural life in the Black Forest.

Cost and Hours: €8; April-Oct daily 9:00-18:00, until 19:00 in Aug, last entry one hour before closing, closed Nov-March; audioguide-€3 (available in English), guidebook-€8; just outside the town of Gutach, tel. 07831/93560, www.vogtsbauernhof. de.

Getting There: Drivers will find it just south of the town of Hausach (not to be confused with nearby Haslach) on B-33/E-531; while technically in Gutach, the museum is actually in the countryside. Parking costs €4 (first 45 minutes free), or just €1.50 if you're visiting the museum (if so, take your parking ticket to the museum entrance rather than paying at the machine, and get it validated when you buy your museum ticket).

Without a car, take the **train** to Hausach (reached via a branch line from Offenburg, on the main Baden-Baden-to-Freiburg line). From the Hausach station, take bus #7150 to the museum (5 minutes) or walk 35 minutes; the whole trip takes 1.5-2 hours from Freiburg or 1-1.5 hours from Baden-Baden.

Demonstrations and Tours: In July and August, you might see costumed docents posted at certain parts of the museum. At other times, it can be pretty sleepy, but occasional live presentations give it some zip; look for a schedule of today's demonstrations on the chalkboard at the entry hall, or ask when you buy your ticket. English tours are available, but you need to reserve two to three weeks in advance.

Visiting the Museum: From the parking lot, it's a five-minute walk past eateries (described later) and under the railroad tracks to reach the ticket windows and main building. Pick up the map of the complex when you buy your ticket. The various buildings are identified out front (find English on the spinning language board), but the explanations inside are in German only. The following light commentary will bring some meaning to your visit.

The museum is named for its biggest building, the *Vogtsbauernhof,* or "farmhouse of the district governor"—the first, and only original, building on the premises, around which the rest of the complex grew. (As with all open-air folk museums, the other structures were moved here from around the region and then reconstructed.) Built in 1612 and occupied until 1965, this giant farmhouse has distinctive Black Forest features that you'll also see (on a smaller scale) in the surrounding buildings. The characteristic "semi-hipped" roof is wider than the frame of the house, which creates ample dry storage space under the eaves all around the perimeter of the building. In case of a storm, the farmer and livestock could rush in quickly for shelter.

The house is built into the side of a hill, allowing easy ramp access to any of its levels—including the vast "attic." From here, hay would be unloaded into the middle level, and then could easily be dropped down as needed to where the livestock lived below.

People and animals lived under one roof. Explore the people's quarters. In that age of poor nutrition, people didn't grow as tall—you'll see short beds and short doorways made for short people. The kitchen occupied the center of the building, where its stove radiated heat to the surrounding living areas. Notice the lack of a chimney, and the blackened walls in the kitchen—the stove was open to the roof to allow smoke to flow through the house, dry out the air (which was otherwise made uncomfortably humid by the animals), and sift out through the thatch. The two-story kitchen allowed farmers to smoke meat above while they cooked meals below. The soot also helped to coat and preserve the wood frame. Windows were a sure sign of wealth and status—the bigger the windows, the more prosperous the family.

Surrounding the main *Vogtsbauernhof* building are several smaller ones to explore. The **farm mill** is popular during its live grain-grinding demonstrations, when water power sets the giant gears in motion (daily at 11:15, 12:15, and 14:15, in German only). The **day laborer's cottage** once housed a family with 14 kids; two brothers lived here right up until 1993. Even though it has electricity, it's undeniably simple. The **bakery and distillery** has a communal oven where families from the community baked their bread all at once—an efficient use of limited resources. The "knock-and-drop" **saw mill,** which runs only sporadically (on special request for groups), systematically—little by little—saws planks of wood from huge trunks.

Eating: The shops and restaurants scattered between the parking lot and museum entrance are awfully touristy, but are a fair source for local specialties. Skip the indoor restaurants and instead try your *Frikadelle* (a spiced pork-and-beef patty) or *Schupfnudeln* (potato-based noodles, fried up with sauerkraut) at the outdoor stands. Don't be shy to try a little of everything; the friendly ladies ladling the portions will fill up your plate with whatever you point to and charge about €7. Be sure to indulge in a creamy slice of *Schwarzwälder Kirschtorte* (€3). Closer to the museum, in the main building, is the pricey but convenient Hofengel ("House Angel") restaurant (€5-10 salads, €7-10 light dishes, €12-15 main courses).

Triberg

Deep in the Black Forest, Triberg is a midsize town that exploits its cuckoo-clock heritage to the hilt. Despite the kitsch, it's a pleasant place to stretch your legs under giant cuckoo-clock facades. Triberg's two main attractions—the Black Forest Museum and Triberg Waterfall—are near each other, with convenient eateries clustering around the lowest reaches of the waterfall. Touristy as Triberg is, it offers an easy way for travelers without cars to enjoy the Black Forest. The **TI** is located in the Black Forest Museum (Mon-Fri 9:00-17:00, also open Sat-Sun 11:00-17:00 summer only, tel. 07722/866-490, www.triberg.de).

Getting to Triberg: Drivers on B-500 will go right through the center of town. By **train,** it's a scenic trip from **Freiburg** (hourly, 1.5-2 hours, change in Offenburg) or **Baden-Baden** (hourly, 1.5 hours).

▲Black Forest Museum (Schwarzwaldmuseum)

Don't confuse this museum with the nearby Vogtsbauernhof Black

Forest Open-Air Museum. Triberg's Black Forest Museum gives a fine look at the local culture. It's well-explained; as you explore its three floors, you'll find insightful exhibits on various aspects of Black Forest cultural heritage, with a special emphasis on engineering (clock-making, railways, locally built SABA radios) and crafts (wood-carving, glassmaking).

The main hall contains dozens of dolls wearing traditional dress from the region, including the distinctive maidens' hats, piled with gigantic cranberries (married women's hats have black puffballs). Player pianos, barrel organs, orchestrions ("orchestras-in-a-box"), and other music-making machines—which were built here alongside cuckoo clocks—were extremely popular in the days before radio or record players, when it was the only cheap way to listen to music. Rounding out the museum are exhibits on farming (a replica of a farmer's traditional quarters), mineral mining, winter sports, and creepy masks used to celebrate Germanic Mardi Gras, called Fasnacht.

Cost and Hours: €5, pick up the free one-page English "Short Tour" at the entrance, a few additional posted explanations in English, April-Sept daily 10:00-18:00; Oct-March Tue-Sun 10:00-17:00, closed Mon; Wallfahrtstrasse 4, tel. 07722/4434, www.schwarzwaldmuseum.de.

Triberg Waterfall (Triberger Wasserfall)

Triberg's other claim to fame is Germany's highest waterfall, where the Gutach River tumbles 500 feet in several bounces. Although it seems odd to pay to see a waterfall, this one really is impressive—

especially if you have time to walk through its steep, misty gorge. Three entrances lead to the waterfall, at different altitudes (scattered along the twisty main road toward Furtwangen). While the lowest entrance—"Haupteingang," in the town center, across from the Black Forest Museum—is most convenient, drivers might want to stop by the middle entrance ("Scheffelplatz," a 5-minute downhill walk to the middle of the falls). If you're traveling in a group, it's handy to drop the gang off at Scheffelplatz to hike down, while the driver loops down into town to meet them at the lower entrance. If you don't want to pay, you can get a partial glimpse of the falls through the trees near the lower entrance.

Cost and Hours: €4, less in winter, daily May-Sept 9:00-19:00, Oct-April 10:00-18:00, free entry at other times.

▲▲Furtwangen's German Clock Museum (Deutsches Uhrenmuseum)

The unremarkable town of Furtwangen hosts the most interesting museum in the Black Forest: the excellent German Clock Museum. More than a chorus of cuckoo clocks, this museum is practically evangelical in tracing the development of clocks from the Dark Ages to the Space Age. Because it's modern and well-presented in English, this exhibit makes the history of timekeeping more fascinating than it has any right to be.

Cost and Hours: €5, €10 family ticket, daily April-Oct 9:00-18:00, Nov-March 10:00-17:00, Robert-Gerwig-Platz 1, tel. 07723/920-2800, www.deutsches-uhrenmuseum.de.

Getting There: It's hiding out in the town center of Furtwangen; as you approach the town, closely track the low-profile signs to *Deutsches Uhrenmuseum* or simply *Uhrenmuseum*. It's related—and attached—to the local technical university.

Tours: Tours run daily at 11:00 and cost €2 (German only, but call ahead to see if an English tour is possible). In the afternoon, if it's quiet, someone might be able to demonstrate one or two of the interactive pieces for you.

Visiting the Museum: As you enter, borrow the thorough English translations of the descriptions, then match them to the pictures on the posted information to find the right text. Appropriately enough, the collection is displayed chronologically, starting on the first floor (upstairs), then working its way down through the split-level building—follow the *Rundgang* (tour) signs.

Floor 1: Starting with Stonehenge (which is thought to be a celestial calendar) and early sundials, the exhibit takes in the full breadth of timepiece history. In the display case of celestial clocks, find the highly detailed **astronomical-geographical clock** from 1787, which used just 24 gears to tell not only the time, but also the position of the stars in the night sky, which saint's day it was, and the phase of the moon.

Black Forest clockmakers achieved a breakthrough when they simplified the timekeeping mechanism so that it could be built almost entirely of wood, allowing the clocks to be sold at a much lower price (leading to a worldwide boom in clock sales). In this collection, you can watch **Black Forest clocks** evolve from rough-hewn wood to delicately painted white lacquer faces. You'll see that locals also figured out how to make musical clocks with wooden flutes and bellows—much more affordable than bells or other metal instruments.

The vast collection of **cuckoo clocks** (*Kuckucksuhren* in German) explains the evolution of the Black Forest's most iconic product. The cuckoo clock as we know it was created for a contest in 1850 by Friedrich Eisenlohr, a railway architect who modeled his *Bahnhäusleuhr* clock after a railroad house. While the clocks strike us as quaint and kitschy now, consider how Eisenlohr's idea of shaping a clock like a little house revolutionized the cuckoo-clock-making industry. Cuckoo clocks became very popular—especially among tourists during the late 19th-century heyday of the romantic Grand Tour era—and were eventually copied by clockmakers in Switzerland. (If you even hint that cuckoo clocks are Swiss, proud Black Forest natives will quickly set you straight.)

On the way downstairs, ogle the gigantic **"Astronomical World Clock"** by August Noll. In addition to the giant clock dial,

notice the smaller dials to show different time zones—a new concept in the slow-travel era when this was created. The clock has many details to examine—and even more if its mechanical gears are whirring. If a tour is going on, you might get to see this giant clock in action, with Jesus blessing the 12 apostles as they shuffle past. (If it's not too busy, you can try asking the front desk to turn it on for you.) Next, head downstairs to...

Floor -1: Now in the 20th century, the exhibit shows off pocket watches with precious details (including, at #19, a French watch with decimalized time—one branch of the metric system that never took off). Wristwatches became popular first among women, who didn't have pockets, but were later adopted by men in World

The Black Forest Clockmaker Diaspora

Black Forest clockmakers specialized in affordable, everyday timepieces. Because they could be produced and sold cheaply, Black Forest clocks became popular around the world. Between 1800 and 1850 alone, 15 million Black Forest clocks were sold worldwide. This demand—combined with a need for steady employment among a growing population—persuaded many Black Forest natives to leave home and sell clocks in foreign lands.

From the 1770s through the early 1900s, roving Black Forest clockmakers (called *Uhrenhändler*) traveled far. They'd load their wares onto a wood-frame rucksack and cry, *Ins Uhrenland!*— "To clock country!"...that is, wherever people were buying clocks. Once they found a good market abroad, they'd settle in, set up shop, and create a lucrative little business. Many clockmakers were away from home for months, or even years—and quite a few married into their adopted local communities. (Emigrants from this part of Germany likely started out as clock-sellers.)

Most of these *Uhrenhändler* sold simple "shield clocks" (*Schilduhr*), with a simple face that hid the mechanical workings. The face of the clock could be painted to match the local tastes of the buyer, whether in England, France, Italy, Spain, Russia, Turkey, China, Australia...or the US. But no matter how far from home the clockmakers wandered, and no matter how different the clocks looked, they were still Black Forest at heart.

War I for easy access while using a rifle. The exhibit on Black Forest clockmaking in the 20th century demonstrates that, even as technology advanced, local clockmakers specialized in straightforward, affordable, everyday timepieces. Quartz technology allowed for far greater accuracy at a much lower price, which made clocks cheap and effectively crippled the industry. Furtwangen no longer makes clocks today, but it's still a respected industrial town.

Ponder this: If Germany is known for its engineering prowess, you can thank clocks. As technology evolved, technical know-how came to be applied to more and more complicated machines. And so, in a way, precision BMWs are the direct descendant of the rough wooden cuckoo clocks that have been made in the Black Forest for centuries.

Floor -2: The bottom level brings the story up to the modern day, from punch-clocks to atomic clocks that strive for ever more precise timekeeping. One fascinating exhibit explains how faster and faster transportation in the late 19th century brought about the need for standardized time across locales. In the past, each town used its own, local solar time. As the railroad advanced, this made a wreck of train schedules and connections (since different towns and countries were a few minutes off from each other). The innovation of the telegraph sealed it: The world's clocks needed to be in sync. Only in the 1870s did scientists begin to pursue standardization, leading in 1884 to the creation of the prime meridian (to use as a starting point for calculating world time zones). Germany didn't adopt a standardized time zone until 1893.

The grand finale is an upbeat combo of mechanical musical instruments, from player pianos to giant wind-up carnival organs. Notice it's in a soundproof room; to hear some of the thunderous music, you can ask at the desk for someone to turn one on for you. Hearing the amazing variety of sounds, it's fun to imagine how the simple "cuck-oo" of a clock with a little wooden bird evolved into a self-playing musical band in a box.

ROTHENBURG AND THE ROMANTIC ROAD

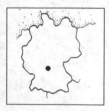

The Romantic Road takes you through Bavaria's medieval heartland, a route strewn with picturesque villages, farmhouses, onion-domed churches, Baroque palaces, and walled cities. The route, which runs from Würzburg to Füssen, is the most scenic way to connect Frankfurt with Munich. No trains run along the full length of the Romantic Road, but Rothenburg (ROH-tehn-burg), the most interesting town along the route, is easy to reach by rail. Drivers can either zero in on Rothenburg or take some extra time to meander from town to town en route. For nondrivers, a tour bus travels the Romantic Road once daily in each direction.

Countless travelers have searched for the elusive "untouristy Rothenburg." There are many contenders (such as Michelstadt, Miltenberg, Bamberg, Bad Windsheim, and Dinkelsbühl), but none holds a candle to the king of medieval German cuteness. Even with crowds, overpriced souvenirs, Japanese-speaking night watchmen, and, yes, even *Schneeballen*, Rothenburg is best. Save time and mileage and be satisfied with the winner.

Rothenburg ob der Tauber

In the Middle Ages, when Berlin and Munich were just wide spots on the road, Rothenburg ob der Tauber was a "free imperial city" beholden only to the Holy Roman Emperor. During Rothenburg's heyday, from 1150 to 1400, it was a strategic stop on the trade routes between northern and southern Europe. Because of its privileged position, along with the abundant resources of its surrounding countryside (textile-producing sheep and fertile farmlands), Rothenburg thrived. With a whopping population of 6,000, it was one of Germany's largest towns. But as with many of Europe's best time-warp towns, Rothenburg's fortunes tumbled. With no money to fix up its antiquated, severely leaning buildings, the town was left to languish in this state. Today, it's the country's best-preserved medieval walled town, enjoying tremendous tourist popularity without losing its charm.

Rothenburg's great trade these days is tourism: Two-thirds of the 2,000 people who live within its walls are employed to serve you. While roughly 2 million people visit each year, most come only on day trips. Rothenburg is yours after dark, when the groups vacate and the town's floodlit cobbles wring some romance out of any travel partner.

Too often, Rothenburg brings out the shopper in visitors before they've had a chance to see the historic town. True, this is a fine place to do your German shopping. But appreciate Rothenburg's great history and sights, too.

Germany has several towns named Rothenburg, so make sure you're going to **Rothenburg ob der Tauber** (not "ob der" any other river); people really do sometimes drive or ride the train to nondescript Rothenburgs by accident.

PLANNING YOUR TIME

Rothenburg in one day is easy. If time is short, you can make just a two- to three-hour midday stop in Rothenburg, but the town is really

ally best appreciated after the day-trippers have gone home. Ideally, spend at least one night in Rothenburg (hotels are cheap and good).

With two nights and a full day, you'll be able to see more than the essentials and actually relax a little. I'd spend your day this way: Start with my self-guided town walk, including a visit to St. Jakob's Church (for the carved altarpiece) and the Imperial City Museum (historic artifacts). Spend the afternoon visiting the Medieval Crime and Punishment

Museum and taking my Schmiedgasse-Spitalgasse shopping stroll, followed by a walk on the wall (from Spitaltor to Klingentor). Cap your day with the entertaining Night Watchman's Tour (at 20:00). Locals love *"Die Blaue Stunde"* (the blue hour)—the time just before dark when city lamps and the sky hold hands. Be sure to be out enjoying the magic of the city at this time.

For nature lovers, there are plenty of relaxing walks and bike rides in the forested environs around the town.

Rothenburg is very busy through the summer and in the Christmas Market month of December. Spring and fall are a joy, but it's pretty bleak in November and from January through March—when most locals are hibernating or on vacation. Legally, shops are only allowed to remain open 40 Sundays a year; this means that many close on Sundays during the slow off-season months.

Orientation to Rothenburg

To orient yourself in Rothenburg, think of the town map as a human head. Its nose—the castle garden—sticks out to the left, and the skinny lower part forms a neck, with the youth hostel and a recommended hotel being the Adam's apple. The town is a delight on foot. No sights or hotels are more than a 15-minute walk from the train station or each other.

Most of the buildings you'll see were in place by 1400. The city was born around its long-gone fort or castle—built in 1142, destroyed in 1356—which was located where the castle garden is now. You can see the shadow of the first town wall, which defines the oldest part of Rothenburg, in its contemporary street plan. Two gates from this wall still survive: the Markus Tower and the White Tower. The richest and biggest houses were in this central part. The commoners built higgledy-piggledy (read: picturesque) houses farther from the center, but still inside the present walls.

Although Rothenburg is technically in Bavaria, the region around the town is called by its medieval name, Franken (Franconia).

TOURIST INFORMATION

The TI is on Market Square (May-Oct and Dec Mon-Fri 9:00-18:00, Sat-Sun 10:00-17:00; off-season Mon-Fri 9:00-17:00, Sat 10:00-13:00, closed Sun; Marktplatz 2, tel. 09861/404-800, www.tourismus.rothenburg.de, run by Jörg Christöphler). If there's a

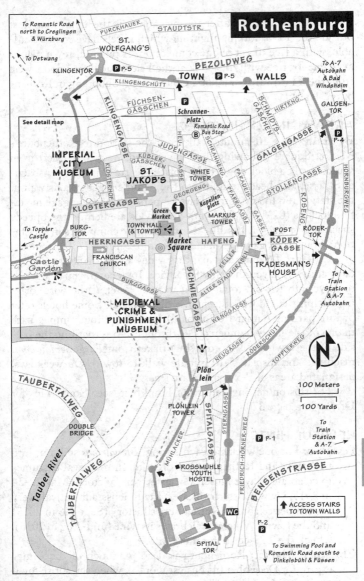

long line, just raid the rack where they keep all the free pamphlets. The free city map comes with a walking guide to the town. The yearly *Events 2015* booklet covers the basics in English. Also look for current concert listing posters here (and at your hotel), and in 2015, an English-language booklet to accompany your walk around the town wall. The TI has one free public computer with Internet access (15-minute maximum).

Visitors who arrive after closing can check the handy map (just outside the TI's door) highlighting which hotels have rooms available, with a free direct phone connection. A pictorial town map is available for free with this book at the Friese shop, two doors west from the TI (toward St. Jakob's Church; see "Shopping in Rothenburg," later).

ARRIVAL IN ROTHENBURG

By Train: It's a 10-minute walk from the station to Rothenburg's Market Square (following the brown *Altstadt* signs, exit left from station, walk a block down Bahnhofstrasse, turn right on Ansbacher Strasse, and head straight into the Middle Ages). Taxis wait at the station (€6 to any hotel). Day-trippers can leave luggage in station lockers (€2-3, on platform). Free WCs are behind the Speedy snack bar on track 1. If killing time, there are computers in the station's Spielothek gaming room (daily 8:00-24:00, €1/30 minutes).

By Car: Driving and parking rules in Rothenburg change constantly—ask your hotelier for advice. In general, you're allowed to drive into the old town to get to your hotel. Otherwise, driving within the old walled center is discouraged. Some hotels offer private parking (either free or paid). To keep things simple, park in one of the lots—numbered P-1 through P-5—that line the outside of the town walls (€5/day, buy ticket from *Parkscheinautomat* machines and display, 5-10 minute walk to town). On weekdays, designated areas of P-5 and P-4 are free.

For tips on getting here from Frankfurt, see "Route Tips for Drivers" on page 370.

HELPFUL HINTS

Festivals: For one weekend each spring, *Biergartens* spill out into the street and Rothenburgers dress up in medieval costumes to celebrate Mayor Nusch's Meistertrunk victory (May 22-24 in 2015, www.meistertrunk.de). The Reichsstadt festival every September celebrates Rothenburg's history (Sept 4-6 in 2015) and the town's Winefest celebrates its wine (mid-Aug in 2015). Check the TI website for more info.

Christmas Market: Rothenburg is dead for much of the winter except for December (its busiest month), when the entire town cranks up the medieval cuteness with concerts and costumes, shops with schnapps, stalls filling squares, hot spiced wine, giddy nutcrackers, and mobs of ear-muffed Germans. Christmas markets are big all over Germany, and Rothenburg's is considered one of the best. The market takes place each year during Advent. Try to avoid Saturdays and Sundays, when big-city day-trippers really clog the grog.

Internet Access: All recommended hotels have Wi-Fi. The **TI** has one free terminal for brief use. At the station, Spielothek am Bahnhof has several terminals.

Mailing Your Goodies Home: You can get handy yellow €2.50 boxes at the old town **post office** (Mon-Tue and Thu-Fri 9:00-13:00 & 14:00-17:30, Wed 9:00-13:00, Sat 9:00-12:00, closed Sun, inside photo shop at Rödergasse 11). The main post office is in the shopping center across from the train station.

Laundry: A handy launderette, **Waschsalon Then,** is near the station (€5.50/load, includes soap, English instructions, Mon-Fri 8:00-18:00, closed Sat-Sun, off Ansbacher Strasse at Johannitergasse 9, tel. 09861/2775).

Bike Rental: Consider renting a bike to enjoy the nearby countryside; you can follow the route described on page 357. Two shops, both outside the old town (and both open Mon-Fri 9:00-18:00, Sat 9:00-13:00, closed Sun) rent bikes: **Rad & Tat** is a bit cheaper and closer (€10/6 hours, €14/24 hours; electric bike-€26/day; Bensenstrasse 17, tel. 09861/87984, www.mietraeder.de); leave the old town toward the train station, but take a right on Erlbacher Strasse, cross the tracks, and look across the street from the Lidl supermarket. **Fahrradhaus Krauss** is farther out (€12/day; electric bike-€25/day, must reserve ahead; no helmets, Ansbacher Strasse 85, tel. 09861/3495, www.fahrradhaus-krauss.de); to reach it from the old town, head toward the train station, then continue along Ansbacher Strasse.

Taxi: For a taxi, call 09861/2000 or 09861/7227.

Haircuts: At **Salon Wack** (pronounced "vahk," not "whack"), Horst and his team speak English and welcome both men and women (wash and cut: €21 for men, €32-39 for women; Tue-Fri 8:00-12:00 & 13:30-18:00, Sat 8:30-14:00, closed Sun-Mon, off Wenggasse at Goldene Ringgasse 8, tel. 09861/7834).

Swimming: Rothenburg has a fine swimming complex, with a heated outdoor pool *(Freibad)* from mid-May to mid-September, and an indoor pool and sauna the rest of the year. It's about a 15-minute walk south of Spitaltor along the main road toward Dinkelsbühl (adults-€3.50, kids-€2; outdoor pool daily 9:00-20:00; indoor pool Mon-Thu 9:00-21:00, Fri-Sun 9:00-18:00; Nördlinger Strasse 20, tel. 09861/4565).

Tours in Rothenburg

▲▲Night Watchman's Tour

This tour is flat-out the most entertaining hour of medieval wonder anywhere in Germany. The Night Watchman (a.k.a. Hans-Georg Baumgartner) jokes like a medieval Jerry Seinfeld as he lights his lamp and takes tourists on his rounds, telling slice-of-gritty-life tales of medieval Rothenburg (€7, teens-€4, free for kids 12 and under, mid-March-Dec nightly at 20:00, in English, meet at Market Square, www.nightwatchman.de). This is the best evening activity in town.

▲Old Town Historic Walk

The TI offers 1.5-hour guided walking tours in English (€7, Easter-Oct and Dec daily at 14:00, no English tours off-season, departs from Market Square). Just show up and pay the guide directly—there's always room. Take this tour for the serious side of Rothenburg's history, and to make sense of the town's architecture; you won't get as much of that on the fun—and completely different—Night Watchman's Tour. It would be a shame not to take advantage of this informative tour just because you took the other.

Local Guides

A local historian can really bring the ramparts alive. Prices are standardized (€68/1.5 hours, €86/2 hours). Reserve a guide by emailing the TI (info@rothenburg.de; more info at www.tourismus.rothenburg.de—look under "Tourism Service," then "Guided Tours"). I've had good experiences with **Martin Kamphans,** who also works as a potter (tel. 09861/7941, www.stadtfuehrungen-rothenburg.de, post@stadtfuehrungen-rothenburg.de) and **Daniel Weber** (www.toot-tours.com, d.weber@reiseleitung-rothenburg.de).

Town Wall Walk

It's free to walk along Rothenburg's town wall, and 20 info plaques provide good English descriptions. An English booklet with the same info should be available at the TI in 2015. For details see "Walk the Wall" on page 354.

Rothenburg Walks

My self-guided circular "Rothenburg Town Walk" weaves the town's top sights together, takes about an hour without stops, and starts and ends on Market Square. (Note that this is roughly the same route followed by city guides on their daily Old Town Historic Walk, described earlier.) It flows right into my "Schmeidgasse-Spitalgasse Shopping Stroll," which traces a straight shot from Market Square to Spitaltor, passing traditional shops and eateries on the way.

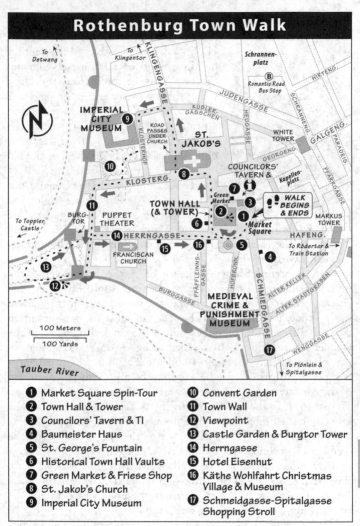

Rothenburg Town Walk

1. Market Square Spin-Tour
2. Town Hall & Tower
3. Councilors' Tavern & TI
4. Baumeister Haus
5. St. George's Fountain
6. Historical Town Hall Vaults
7. Green Market & Friese Shop
8. St. Jakob's Church
9. Imperial City Museum
10. Convent Garden
11. Town Wall
12. Viewpoint
13. Castle Garden & Burgtor Tower
14. Herrngasse
15. Hotel Eisenhut
16. Käthe Wohlfahrt Christmas Village & Museum
17. Schmeidgasse-Spitalgasse Shopping Stroll

ROTHENBURG TOWN WALK

This walk links Market Square to St. Jakob's Church, the Imperial City Museum, the castle garden, and Herrngasse Street.

• *Start the walk on Market Square.*

Market Square Spin-Tour

Stand at the bottom of Market Square (10 feet below the wooden post on the corner—watch for occasional cars) and spin 360 degrees clockwise, starting with the Town Hall tower. Now do it again, this time more slowly, following these notes:

Town Hall and Tower: Rothenburg's tallest spire is the Town Hall tower (Rathausturm). At 200 feet, it stands atop the old Town

Hall, a white, Gothic, 13th-century building. Notice the tourists enjoying the best view in town from the black top of the tower (see listing on page 352 for details on climbing the tower). After a fire in 1501 burned down part of the original building, a new Town Hall was built alongside what survived of the old one (fronting the square). This half of the rebuilt complex is in the Renaissance style from 1570. The double eagles you see decorating many buildings here are a repeated reminder that this was a "free imperial city" belonging directly to the (Habsburg) Holy Roman Emperor, a designation that came with benefits.

Meistertrunk Show: At the top of Market Square stands the proud Councilors' Tavern (clock tower from 1466). In its day, the city council—the rich guys who ran the town government—drank here. Today, it's the TI and the focus of most tourists' attention when the little doors on either side of the clock flip open and the wooden figures (from 1910) do their thing. Be on Market Square at the top of any hour (between 10:00 and 22:00) for the ritual gathering of the tourists to see the less-than-breathtaking re-enactment of the Meistertrunk ("Master Draught") story:

In 1631, in the middle of the Thirty Years' War, the Catholic army took the Protestant town and was about to do its rape, pillage, and plunder thing. As was the etiquette, the mayor had to give the conquering general a welcoming drink. The general enjoyed a huge tankard of local wine. Feeling really good, he told the mayor, "Hey, if you can drink this entire three-liter tankard of wine in one gulp, I'll spare your town." The mayor amazed everyone by drinking the entire thing, and Rothenburg was saved.

While this is a nice story, it was dreamed up in the late 1800s for a theatrical play designed (effectively) to promote a romantic image of the town. In actuality, if Rothenburg was spared, it happened because it bribed its way out of a jam. It was occupied and ransacked several times in the Thirty Years' War, and it never recovered—which is why it's such a well-preserved time capsule today.

For the best show, don't watch the clock; watch the open-mouthed tourists gasp as the old windows flip open. At the late shows, the square flickers with camera flashes.

Bottom of Market Square: This was the most-prestigious address in town, so it's ringed by big homes with big carriage gates.

One of the finest is just downhill from the bottom end of the square—the **Baumeister Haus,** featuring a famous Renaissance facade with statues of the seven virtues and the seven vices. The statues are copies; the originals are in the Imperial City Museum (described later on this walk).

Keep circling to the big 17th-century **St. George's fountain.** It had long metal gutters that could slide to route the water into the villagers' buckets. Rothenburg had an ingenious water system. Built on a rock, the town had one real source above the town, which was plumbed to serve a series of fountains; water flowed from high to low through Rothenburg. Its many fountains had practical functions beyond providing drinking water (some were stocked with fish on market days and during times of siege). Water was used for fighting fires, and because of its plentiful water supply—and its policy of requiring relatively wide lanes as fire breaks—the town never burned entirely, as so many neighboring villages did.

Two fine half-timbered buildings behind the fountain show the old-time lofts with warehouse doors and pulleys on top for hoisting. All over town, lofts were filled with grain. A year's supply was required by the city so they could survive any siege. The building behind the fountain is an art gallery showing off work by members of the local artists' association (free, Tue-Sun 14:00-18:00, closed Mon). To the right is Marien Apotheke, an old-time pharmacy mixing old and new in typical Rothenburg style.

The broad street running under the Town Hall tower is **Herrngasse.** The town originated with its castle (built in 1142 but now long gone; only the castle garden remains). Herrngasse connected the castle to Market Square. The last leg of this circular walking tour will take you from the castle garden up Herrngasse and back here.

For now, walk a few steps down Herrngasse and stop by the arch under the Town Hall tower (between the new and old town halls). On the wall to the left of the gate are the town's measuring rods—a reminder that medieval Germany was made of 300 independent little countries, many with their own weights and measures. Merchants and shoppers knew that these were the local standards: the rod (4.3 yards), the *Schuh* ("shoe," roughly a foot), and the *Ell* (from elbow to fingertip—four inches longer than mine...try it). Notice the protruding cornerstone. These are all over town—originally to protect buildings from reckless horse carts. In German if you're going recklessly fast they say, "You're scratching the cornerstone."

• *Careen around that stone and under the arch to find the...*

▲Historical Town Hall Vaults (Historiengewölbe)

This eclectic and grade-schoolish little museum gives a waxy but interesting look at Rothenburg during the Catholics-vs.-Protestants Thirty Years' War. With helpful English descriptions, it offers a look at "the fateful year 1631," a replica of the mythical Meistertrunk tankard, an alchemist's workshop, and a dungeon complete with three dank cells and some torture lore.

Cost and Hours: €2.50, daily May-Oct 9:30-17:30, shorter hours April and Nov-Dec, closed Jan-March, tel. 09861/86751.

• *Leaving the museum, turn left (past a much-sketched-and-photographed venerable door) and find a posted copy of a centuries-old map showing the territory of Rothenburg.*

Map of Rothenburg City Territory

In 1537 Rothenburg actually ruled a little country—one of about 300 petty dukedoms like this that made up what is today's Germany. The territory spanned a 12-by-12-mile area (about 400 square kilometers), encompassing 180 villages—a good example of the fragmentation of feudal Germany. While not to scale (Rothenburg is actually less than a mile wide), the map is fun to study. In the 1380s, Mayor Toppler purchased much of this territory. In 1562 the city sold off some of its land to neighboring dukes, which gave it the money for all the fine Renaissance buildings that embellish the town to this day.

• *Continue through the courtyard and into a square called...*

Green Market (Grüner Markt) to St. Jakob's Church

Once a produce market, this parking lot fills with Christmas stands during December. Notice the clay-tile roofs. These "beaver tail" tiles became standard after thatched roofs were outlawed to prevent fires. Today, all of the town's roofs are made of these. The little fences protect people from snow falling off the roof. The free public WC is on your left and the recommended Friese gift shop is on your right. Continue straight ahead to St. Jakob's Church.

▲▲St. Jakob's Church (St. Jakobskirche)

Rothenburg's main church is home to Tilman Riemenschneider's breathtaking, wood-carved *Altar of the Holy Blood*.

Cost and Hours: €2, daily April-Oct 9:00-17:15, Dec 10:00-16:45, Nov and Christmas-March 10:00-12:00 & 14:00-16:00, on Sun wait to enter until services end at 10:45, free helpful English info sheet, concerts and tour schedule posted on the door; guided tours in English for no extra charge on Sat at 15:30 April-Oct. The worthwhile audioguide (€2, 45 minutes) lets you tailor your education, offering a dual commentary—historical and theological—for a handful of important stops in the church.

Visiting the Church: Start by viewing the exterior of the church. Next, enter the church, where you'll see the main nave first, then climb above the pipe organ (in the back) to finish with the famous carved altar.

Exterior: Outside the church, under the little roof at the base of the tower, you'll see 14th-century statues (mostly original) showing Jesus praying at Gethsemane, a common feature of Gothic churches. The sculptor is anonymous—in the Gothic age (pre-Albrecht Dürer), artists were just nameless craftspeople working only for the glory of God. Five yards to the left (on the wall), notice the nub of a sandstone statue—a rare original, looking pretty bad after 500 years of weather and, more recently, pollution. Most original statues are now in the city museum. The better-preserved statues you see on the church are copies.

Before entering, notice how the church was extended to the west and actually built over the street. The newer chapel was built to accommodate pilgrims and to contain the sumptuous Riemenschneider carved altarpiece.

If it's your wedding day, take the first entrance—marked by a very fertile Eve and, around the corner, Adam showing off an impressive six-pack. Otherwise, head toward the church's second (downhill) door. Before going inside, notice the modern statue at the base of the stairs. This is **St. James** (a.k.a., Sankt Jakob in German, Santiago in Spanish, and Saint-Jacques in French). You can tell this important saint by his big, floppy hat, his walking stick, the gourd on his hip (used by pilgrims to carry water), and—most importantly—the scallop shell in his hand. St. James' remains are entombed in the grand cathedral of Santiago de Compostela, in the northwestern corner of Spain. The medieval pilgrimage route called the Camino de Santiago (recently back in vogue) passed through here on its way to that distant corner of Europe. Pilgrims would wear the scallop shell as a symbol of their destination (where that type of marine life was abundant). To this day, the word for "scallop" in many languages carries the name of this saint: *Jakobsmuschel* in German, *coquille Saint-Jacques* in French, and so on.

Inside the Church: Built in the 14th century, this church has been Lutheran since 1544. The interior was "purified" by Romantics in the 19th century—cleaned of everything Baroque or not original and refitted in the Neo-Gothic style. (For example, the baptismal font—in the middle of the choir, and the pulpit above the second pew *look* Gothic, but are actually Neo-Gothic.) The stained-glass windows behind the altar, which are most colorful in the morning light, are originals from the 1330s. Admiring this church, consider what it says about the priorities of a town of just a few thousand people, who decided to use their collective wealth to build such a place. The size of a church is a good indication of the town's wealth back then. Medallions and portraits of Rothenburg's leading families and church leaders line the walls above the choir in the front of the church.

The **main altar**, from 1466, is by Friedrich Herlin. Below Christ are statues of six saints—including St. James (a.k.a. Jakob), with the telltale shell on his floppy hat. Study the painted panels—ever see Peter with spectacles (below the carved saints)? Go around the back of the altarpiece and look at the doors. In the upper left, you'll see a painting of Rothenburg's Market Square in the 15th century, looking much like it does today, with the exception of the full-Gothic Town Hall (as it was before the big fire of 1501). Notice Christ's face on the veil of Veronica (center of back side, bottom edge). It follows you as you walk from side to side—this must have given the faithful the religious heebie-jeebies four centuries ago.

The **Tabernacle of the Holy Eucharist** (left of the main altar) is a century older. It stored the wine and bread used for Holy Communion. Before the Reformation this was a Roman Catholic church, which meant that the bread and wine were considered to be the actual body and blood of Jesus (and therefore needed a worthy repository). Notice the unusual Trinity: The Father and Son are bridged by a dove, which represents the Holy Spirit. Stepping back, you can see that Jesus is standing on a skull—clearly "overcoming death."

Now, as pilgrims did centuries ago, climb the stairs at the back of the church that lead up behind the pipe

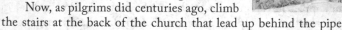

organ to a loft-like chapel. Here you'll find the artistic highlight of Rothenburg and perhaps the most wonderful wood carving in all of Germany: the glorious 500-year-old, 35-foot-high *Altar of the Holy Blood*. Tilman Riemenschneider, the Michelangelo of German woodcarvers, carved this from 1499 to 1504 (at the same time Michelangelo was working on his own masterpieces). The altarpiece was designed to hold a rock-crystal capsule—set in the cross you see high above—that contains a precious scrap of tablecloth stained in the shape of a cross by a drop of communion wine.

The altar is a realistic commotion, showing that Riemenschneider—a High Gothic artist—was ahead of his time. Below, in the scene of the Last Supper, Jesus gives Judas a piece of bread, marking him as the traitor, while John lays his head on Christ's lap. Judas, with his big bag of cash, could be removed from the scene (illustrated by photos on the wall nearby), as was the tradition for the four days leading up to Easter.

Everything is portrayed exactly as described in the Bible. In the relief panel on the left, Jesus enters the walled city of Jerusalem. Notice the exacting attention to detail—down to the nails on the horseshoe. In the relief panel on the right, Jesus prays in the Garden of Gethsemane.

Before continuing on, take a moment to simply linger over the lovingly executed details: the curly locks of the apostles' hair and beards, and the folds of their garments; the delicate vines intertwining above their heads; Jesus' expression, at once tender and accusing.

• *Leave the church. Walk around the corner to the right and under the chapel (built over the road). Go two blocks down Klingengasse and stop at the corner of the street called Klosterhof. Looking farther ahead of you down Klingengasse, you see the...*

Klingentor

This cliff tower was Rothenburg's water reservoir. From 1595 until 1910, a 900-liter (240-gallon) copper tank high in the tower pro-

vided clean spring water—pumped up by river power—to the privileged. To the right of the Klingentor is a good stretch of wall rampart to walk. To the left, the wall is low and simple, lacking a rampart because it guards only a cliff.

Now find the shell decorating a building on the street corner next to you. Remember, that's the symbol of St. James, indicating that this building is associated with the church.

• *Turn left down Klosterhof, passing the shell and, on your right, the colorful, recommended Altfränkische Weinstube am Klosterhof pub, to reach the...*

▲▲Imperial City Museum (Reichsstadt-Museum)

You'll get a vivid and artifact-filled sweep through Rothenburg's history at this excellent museum, housed in a former Dominican convent. Cloistered nuns used the lazy Susan embedded in the wall (to the right of the museum door) to give food to the poor without being seen.

Cost and Hours: €5, daily April-Oct 9:30-17:30, Nov-March 13:00-16:00, pick up English info sheet at entrance, additional English descriptions posted, Klosterhof 5, tel. 09861/939-043, www.reichsstadtmuseum.rothenburg.de.

Visiting the Museum: As you follow the *Rundgang/Tour* signs to the left, watch for the following highlights:

Immediately inside the entry, a glass case shows off the 1616

Prince Elector's tankard (which inspired the famous legend of the Meistertrunk, created in 1881 to drive tourism) and a set of golden Rothenburg coins. Down the hall, find a modern city model and trace the city's growth, its walls expanding like rings on a big tree. Around the corner (before going upstairs), you'll see medieval and Renaissance sculptures, including original sandstone statues from St. Jakob's Church and original statues of the seven vices and seven virtues that decorated the Baumeister Haus. Upstairs in the nuns' dormitory are ornate locks, tools for various professions, and a valuable collection of armor and weapons. You'll then see old furniture and the Baroque statues that decorated the organ loft in St. Jakob's Church from 1669 until the 19th century, when they were cleared out to achieve "Gothic purity."

The Gemäldegalerie (painting gallery) is lined with Romantic paintings of Rothenburg, which served as the first tourist promotion, and give visitors today a chance to envision the city as it appeared in centuries past.

Back downstairs, circle around the cloister to see an exhibit of Jewish culture in Rothenburg through the ages *(Judaika);* a 14th-century convent kitchen *(Klosterküche)* with a working model of the lazy Susan (give it a swing) and a massive chimney (step inside and look up); and the grand finale (in the *Konventsaal*), the *Rothenburger Passion.* This 12-panel series of paintings, showing scenes leading up to Christ's Crucifixion, dates from 1492.

• *Leaving the museum, go around to the right and into the Convent Garden (when locked at night, continue straight to the T-intersection and turn right).*

Convent Garden

This spot is a peaceful place to work on your tan...or mix a poisoned potion. Monks and nuns—who were responsible for concocting herbal cures in the olden days, finding disinfectants, and coming up with ways to disguise the taste of rotten food—often tended herb gardens. Smell (but don't pick) the *Pfefferminze* (peppermint), *Heidewacholder* (juniper/gin), *Rosmarin* (rosemary), *Lavandel* (lavender), and the tallest plant, Hopfen (hops...monks were the great medieval brewers). Don't smell the plants that are poisonous (potency indicated by the number of crosses, like stars indicating spiciness on a restaurant menu). Appreciate the setting, taking in the fine architecture and expansive garden—all within the city walls, where land was at such a premium. It's a reminder of the power of the pre-Reformation Church.

Cost and Hours: Free, daily April-Oct 8:00-19:30, closed Nov-March.

• *Exit opposite from where you entered, angling left through the nuns' garden, eventually leaving via an arch along the far wall. Turn right and go downhill to the...*

Town Wall

This part of the wall takes advantage of the natural fortification provided by the cliff (view through bars, look to far right), and is therefore much shorter than the ramparts.

• *Angle left along the wall. Cross the big street (Herrngasse, with the Burgtor tower on your right—which we'll enter from outside momentarily) and continue downhill on Burggasse a block until you hit the town wall. Turn right, go through a small tower gate, and park yourself at the town's finest viewpoint.*

Castle Garden Viewpoint

From here enjoy a fine view of fortified Rothenburg. You're looking at the Spitaltor end of town (with the finest gate and the former hospital). After this tour, consider the TI's guided stroll that leads from Market Square down to this end of town, where you get on the wall and walk the ramparts 180 degrees to the Klingentor (which we saw in the distance just after St. Jakob's Church earlier on this tour). The droopy-eyed building at the far end of town (today's youth hostel) was the horse mill—which provided grinding power when the water mill in the valley below was not working (due to drought or siege). Stretching below you is the fine park-like land around the Tauber River, nicknamed the "Tauber Riviera."

• *Now explore deeper into the park.*

Castle Garden (Burggarten) and the Burgtor Tower

The garden before you was once a fortress (destroyed in the 14th century). Today, it's a picnic-friendly park. The chapel (50 yards straight into the park, on the left) is the only bit of the original castle to survive. In front of that building is a memorial to local Jews killed in a 1298 slaughter. A few steps beyond that is a grapevine trellis that provides a fine picnic spot. If you walk all the way out to the garden's far end, you'll find a great viewpoint (well past the tourists, and considered the best place to kiss by romantic local teenagers).

• *When you're ready to leave, circle around to the fortified gate behind you to exit.*

Leaving the park, approach the ornate fortified tower, the Burgtor. Look around (WC to the left—circa 1975) and imagine being locked out in the year 1400. This tower was accessed by a wooden drawbridge (see the chain slits above). Above the inner gate, notice the openings in the "pitch nose" mask—designed to allow defenders to pour boiling Nutella on attackers. High above is the town coat of arms: a red *(roten)* castle *(Burg)*.

Go through the gate and study the big wooden door with the tiny "eye of the needle" door cut into it. If trying to get into town after curfew, you could bribe the guard to let you through this door (which was small enough to keep out any fully armed attackers). Note also the square-shaped hole and imagine the massive timber that once barricaded the gate.

• *Now, climb up the big street, Herrngasse, as you return to your staring point.*

Herrngasse

Many towns have a Herrngasse, where the richest patricians and merchants (the *Herren*) lived. Predictably, it's your best chance to see the town's finest old mansions. Strolling back to Market Square, you'll pass on the right—the Franciscan church (from 1285, oldest in town). Up a few doors, across the street, the mint-green house at #18 is the biggest patrician house on this main drag. The front door was big enough to allow a carriage to drive through it; a human-sized door cut into it was used by those on foot. The family, which has lived here for three centuries, disconnected the four old-time doorbells. The gift shop (at #11 on right) offers a chance to poke into one of these big landowners' homes and appreciate their structure: living quarters in front above carriage-size doors, courtyard out back functioning as a garage, stables, warehouse, servants' quarters, and a private well.

Farther up, on the right, is Hotel Eisenhut, Rothenburg's fanciest hotel and worth a peek inside. Finally, passing the Käthe Wohlfahrt Christmas shop (described under "Shopping in Rothenburg") you'll be back where you started—and the end of this tour—Market Square.

• *This square is also the starting point for my "Schmeidgasse-Spitalgasse Shopping Stroll," described next. This stroll ends at the tower called Spitaltor, a good access point for a walk on the town walls.*

▲▲SCHMEIDGASSE-SPITALGASSE SHOPPING STROLL

After doing the basic town walk and visiting the town's three essential interior sights (Imperial City Museum, Medieval Crime and Punishment Museum, and St. Jakob's Church), your next priority might be Rothenburg's shops and its town wall. I'd propose this fun walk, which goes from Market Square in a straight line south (past the best selection of characteristic family-run shops) to the city's most impressive fortification (Spitaltor).

Standing on Market Square, with your back to the TI, you'll see a street sloping downward towards the south end of town. That's where you're headed. This street changes names as you walk, from **Obere Schmeidgasse** (upper blacksmith street) to **Spitalgasse** (hospital street), and runs directly to the **Spitaltor** tower and gate. From Spitaltor you can access the town wall and walk the ramparts 180 degrees around the city to Klingentor.

Here's a brief run-down on some of the places I found interesting along this walk, with the street number and "left" or "right" to indicate the side of the street. As you stroll down this delightful lane, feel welcome to pop in and explore any shop along this cultural and historical scavenger hunt.

Market Square to Burgasse

The fine Renaissance **Baumeister** (master builder) **Haus** at #3 (left) is where the man who designed and built the city hall lived. As it's a Renaissance building, its facade celebrates a secular (rather than religious) morality with statues representing the seven virtues and the seven vices. Which ones do you recognize?

At #5 (left) **Hotel Golden Greifen** was once the home of the illustrious Mayor Toppler (who died here in 1408). By the looks of its door (right of the main entrance), the mayor must have had an impressive wine cellar. Note the fine hanging sign (much nicer than "hanging out your shingle") of a gilded griffin. Business signs in a mostly illiterate medieval world needed to be easy for all to read. The entire street is ornamented with fun signs such as this. Nearby, a pretzel marks the bakery, and the crossed swords advertise the weapon maker.

Shops on both sides of the street at #7 display examples of **Schneeballen** gone wild. These "snowballs," once a humble way to bake extra flour into a simple treat, are now iced and dolled up a million ways—none of which would be recognizable to the kids who originally enjoyed them. Long ago locals used a fork to pierce the middle, but today's tourists eat them like an apple. Watch them crumble.

Waffenkammer, at #9 (left) is "the weapons chamber," where Johannes Wittmann is working hard to make a wonderland in which young-at-heart tourists can shop for (and try out) various medieval weapons, armor, and medieval clothing. Fun photo ops abound, especially downstairs—where you can try on a set of chain mail and pose with a knight in shining armor on horseback.

At #18 (right), **Metzgerei Trumpp**, a top-end butcher, is a carnivores' heaven. Check out the endless wurst offerings in the window. Locals who love bacon opt for fat slices of pork with crackling skins.

Burgasse to Plönlein

The next corner, **Burggasse**, with an old fountain, St. John's Church, and the Medieval Crime and Punishment Museum (just down the lane to the right), marks the site of Rothenburg's first town wall. Below the church (on the right) is a cute little doggie park complete with a doggie WC.

The **Jutta Korn** shop, on the right at #4, showcases the work of a local artisan who designs her own jewelry. At #6 (right) **Lichthäuser** sells "lighthouses" made in town, many modeled after local buildings. The **Kleiderey**, an offbeat clothing store at #7 (left), is run by Tina, the Night Watchman's wife. The clothing is inspired by their southeast Asian travels.

At #13 (left), look opposite to find a narrow lane **(Ander Eich)** which leads to a little viewpoint in the town wall. Overlooking the "Tauber Riviera," it's a popular romantic perch in the evening.

The **Sumiko Ishii** souvenir shop, on the left at #15, is a reminder that the big future in tourism is visitors from Asia, and German shops are catering to that crowd.

Continuing along, at #17 (left), the **Lebe Gesund Vegetarian** shop is all about healthy living. This charming little place (run by tasty sample-dealing Universalist Christians who like to think of Jesus as a vegan) seems designed to offer forgiveness to those who loved the butchers' shop but are ready to repent.

On the right at #18, the **Da Vinci Lounge** café is decorated as if out of *A Clockwork Orange*. Its modern interior is a stark contrast to this medieval city.

The **Käthe Wohlfahrt** shop at #19 (left) is just another of the six or eight around town, all selling German clichés with gusto. Also on the left, at #21, the **An Ra** Shop is where Annett Rafoth designs and sells her flowery cloths. You can pop in to see the actual work in the back. (There's more of An Ra across the street at #26.)

At **Kunsthandlung Leyrer** (on the left, at #23), Peter Leyrer would love to show you his etchings. He is one of the last artisans using Albrecht Dürer's copper-plate technique to print his art. After he retires (in 2017), his 3,500 copper plates from all over Germany will go to a museum. Peter and his wife print the black-and-white etchings and then apply watercolor.

At this point, stop and take a moment to notice the "vernacular architecture" (developed to meet local needs), with the cute gables and higgledy-piggledy rooflines, tiny doors closing narrow slits between homes, and the fountain that's hooked into pipes plumbed in the 1590s. In the Medieval Ages, nothing was standard. Everything was built to order.

At #29 (left), **Glocke Weinladen am Plönlein** is an inviting shop of wine glasses and related accessories. The **Gasthof Glocke,** next door, with its wine-barrel-sized cellar door just waiting for some action, is a respected restaurant and home to the town's last vintner—a wonderful place to try local wines, as they serve a flight of five tiny glasses (several different flights: half-dry, dry, red, and sweet dessert wines) for those ready to appreciate this production.

Plönlein to Spitalhof

The next corner, on the right, is dubbed **Plönlein** and is famously picturesque. Plönlein is named for the carpenters' plumb-line— a string that dangles exactly straight down when anchored by a plumb (a lead weight; the Latin word for lead is *plumbum*). The line helps carpenters build things straight, but of course, here, nothing is made "to plumb." If this scene brings you back to your childhood, that's because Rothenburg was the inspiration for the village in the 1940 Disney animated film, *Pinocchio*.

Walk a few more yards and look far up the lane **(Neugasse)** to the left. You'll see some cute pastel buildings with uniform windows and rooflines—clues that the buildings were rebuilt after WWII bombings hit that part of town. Straight ahead, the **Siebers Tower** (named for the sifting that was once done in this quarter), marks the next layer of expansion to the town wall.

Also on the left, notice the corner where the old wall was knocked down and the extension built to the south. Continue through the tower. The former tannery is now a pub featuring **Landwehr Brau,** the local brew.

At #16 (right), the **Antique Shop,** which smells like an antique shop should, is fun to browse through. Keep your eyes peeled for a 500-year-old pamphlet printed by Martin Luther that promoted the reforming of the Church.

Farther down, on the left at #25, **Hotel-Cafe Gerberhaus** is a fine stop for a coffee and cake, with a delicate dining room and a peaceful courtyard hiding out back under the town wall.

Spitalhof and Spitaltor

From here, the town runs out of energy and the remaining stretch is a bit glum. This is **Spitalhof**—the former Hospital Quarter— with some nice architecture and the town's retirement home. Stick with me and continue a few short blocks down the main drag to **Spitaltor,** the tower marking the end of town (and a good place to begin a ramparts ramble, if you're up for it).

In any walled city, the gate—made of wood—was the weak point. A bastion is an architectural shield, built beyond the wall proper to protect its wooden doors from cannon fire. Spitaltor is a double bastion, built around 1600 with the advent of stronger artillery. Walk through the gate (taking note of the stairs to the right—that's where you could begin your wall walk). Notice how the entry is curved: Any cannon that got past the first door and tried to blow the second door down would be vulnerable to cannon fire from the ramparts and arrows from the slits above.

Outside the fortified gate is the ditch or dry moat (water and alligators were mostly added by Hollywood) that kept artillery at a distance. Standing outside the wall, ponder this sight as if approaching the city 400 years ago. The wealth of a city was shown by its walls and towers. (Stone was costly—in fact, the German saying for "filthy rich" is "stone rich".)

Circle around to the right. Look up at the formidable tower. The guardhouse atop it, one of several in the wall, was manned 24/7. Above the entry gate, notice the emblem: Angels bless the double eagle of the Holy Roman Emperor, which blesses the town (symbolized by the two red towers).

Cross the wooden bridge ahead and take a right. Past the first arch, you can access the cannon gallery upstairs in the double bastion—with stone ramps rather than stairs so that horse-drawn caissons bearing ammunition could make deliveries easily (free, always open, worth exploring but very dark). To the right of the second arch are the stairs that lead to the ramparts (from where you can start your ramparts walk around the east side of town—for more details, see "Walk the Wall" on page 354). Or you can hike back up the street you just walked down to return to the town center.

Sights in Rothenburg

ON AND NEAR MARKET SQUARE
▲Town Hall Tower

From Market Square you can see tourists on the crow's nest capping the Town Hall's tower. For a commanding view from the town's tallest perch, climb the steps of the tower. It's a rigorous but interesting 214-step climb that gets narrow and steep near the top—watch your head.

Cost and Hours: €2, pay at the top, daily in season 9:00-12:30 & 13:00-17:00, enter from the grand steps overlooking Market Square.

▲▲Medieval Crime and Punishment Museum (Mittelalterliches Kriminalmuseum)

Specializing in everything connected to medieval criminal justice, this exhibit (well-described in English) is a cut above all of the tacky and popular torture museums around Europe. In addition to

ogling spiked chairs, thumb-
screws, and shame masks,
you'll actually learn about medieval police and criminal law.
The museum is more eclectic
than its name, and includes
exhibits on general history, su-
perstition, biblical art, and so
on.

Cost and Hours: €5, daily
April 11:00-17:00, May-Oct 10:00-18:00, Nov and Jan-Feb 14:00-
16:00, Dec and March 13:00-16:00, last entry 45 minutes before
closing, fun cards and posters, Burggasse 3-5, tel. 09861/5359,
www.kriminalmuseum.rothenburg.de.

Visiting the Museum: It's a one-way route. Just follow the
yellow arrows and you'll see it all. From the entrance, head downstairs to the **cellar** to begin your education. Torture was common
in the Middle Ages—not to punish, but to get a confession (medieval "justice" required a confession). Just the sight of the tools
for enhanced interrogation was often enough to make an innocent
man confess. You'll see the rack, "stretching ladder," thumb screws,
spiked leg screws, and other items that would make Dick Cheney
proud. Medieval torturers also employed a waterboarding-like
technique—but here, the special ingredient was holy water.

Upstairs, on the **first and second floors,** the walls are lined
with various legal documents of the age, while the dusty glass cases
show off law-enforcement tools—many of them quite creative.
Shame was a big tool back then; wrongdoers would be creatively
shamed before their neighbors. The town could publically humili-
ate those who ran afoul of the law by tying them to a pillory in the
main square and covering their faces in an iron mask of shame. The
mask's fanciful decorations indicated the crime: Chicken feathers
meant promiscuity, horns indicated that a man's wife slept around
(i.e., cuckold), and a snout suggested that the person had acted pig-
gishly. A gossip might wear a mask with giant ears (heard everything), eyeglasses (saw everything), and a giant, wagging tongue
(couldn't keep her mouth shut). For more serious offenses, criminals were branded—so that even if they left town, they'd take that
shame with them for the rest of their lives. When all else failed,
those in charge could always turn to the executioner's sword.

To safely capture potential witches, lawmen used a device resembling a metal collar—with spikes pointing in—that was easy to
get into, but nearly impossible to get out of. A neck violin—like a
portable version of a stock—kept the accused under control. (The
double neck violin could be used to lock together a quarrelsome
couple to force them to work things out.) The chastity belts were

used to ensure a wife's loyalty (giving her traveling husband peace of mind) and/or to protect women from attack at a time when rape was far more commonplace.

The exit routes you through a courtyard garden to a last building with temporary exhibits (included in your admission and often interesting) and a café. (If you must buy a *Schneeball*, do it here—where they are small, inexpensive, and fairly edible—and help support the museum.)

▲German Christmas Museum (Deutsches Weihnachtsmuseum)

This excellent museum, upstairs in the giant Käthe Wohlfahrt Christmas Village shop, tells the history of Christmas decorations. There's a unique and thoughtfully described collection of tree stands, mini-trees sent in boxes to WWI soldiers at the front, early Advent calendars, old-time Christmas cards, Christmas pyramids, and a look at the evolution of Father Christmas as well as tree decorations through the ages—including the Nazi era and when you were a kid. The museum is not just a ploy to get shoppers to spend more money, but a serious collection managed by professional curator Felicitas Höptner.

Cost and Hours: €4 but you can visit the museum at the €2.50 student rate with this book in 2015—if you promise to learn something, April-Dec daily 10:00-18:00, Jan-March Sat-Sun 10:00-18:00 and irregularly on weekdays, last entry at 17:00, Herrngasse 1, tel. 09861/409-365, www.christmasmuseum.com.

▲Tradesman's House (Alt-Rothenburger Handwerkerhaus)

If all of the higgledy-piggledy buildings make you curious about how people lived way back when, stop into this restored 700-year-old home to see the everyday life of a Rothenburger in the town's heyday. You'll crouch under low ceilings as you explore a house that doesn't have a single right angle—kitchen (with soot-blackened ceilings); tight, shared bedrooms; and attic workshop. Ponder the rugged reality of medieval *Bürger* life. While the house itself is fascinating, information (in any language) is scarce; pick up the free, paltry English handout, or shell out €0.50 for a better one.

Cost and Hours: €3, Easter-Oct Mon-Fri 11:00-17:00, Sat-Sun 10:00-17:00, closed off-season, two blocks east of Market Square, near Markus Tower at Alter Stadtgraben 26, tel. 09861/2098.

ALONG THE WALL
▲▲Walk the Wall

Just longer than a mile and a half around, providing great views and a good orientation, this walk can be done by those under six

feet tall in less than an hour. The hike requires no special sense of balance. Most of the walk is covered and is a great option in the rain. Photographers will stay very busy, especially before breakfast or at sunset, when the lighting is best and the crowds are gone.

While the wall circles the city, the best fortifications are in Spitaltor (south end; described at the end of my "Schmeidgasse-Spitalgasse Shopping Stroll," earlier). The most-easily-hiked elevated and covered ramparts are essentially the eastern half (from Spitaltor at the south end of town to Klingentor in the north). The western side of the city is also a delight to walk—with great views outward, but you'll be at street level for most of the way. You can enter or exit the ramparts at nearly every tower.

The names you see along the way belong to people who donated money to rebuild the wall after World War II, and those who've more recently donated €1,000 per meter for the maintenance of Rothenburg's heritage.

Information: The TI has installed a helpful series of English-language plaques at about 20 stops along the route. They plan to have a companion English booklet available at the TI in 2015—ask. The booklet will give more meaning to your ramparts ramble, and you won't have to search out the info plaques (which are at ground level).

When to Go: While enjoyable, the wall-top walkway can get crowded midday. For a less congested alternative, see the next listing.

▲The Allergic-to-Tourists Wall and Moat Walk

For a quiet and scenic break from the tourist crowds and a chance to appreciate the marvelous fortifications of Rothenburg, consider this hike: From the Castle Garden, go right and walk outside the wall to the Klingentor. At the Klingentor, climb up to the ramparts and walk on the wall past the Galgentor to the Rödertor. Then descend, leave the old town, and hike through the park (once the moat) down to Spitaltor. Explore the fortifications here before hiking a block up Spitalgasse, turning left to pass the youth hostel, popping back outside the wall, and heading along the upper scenic reaches of the river valley and above the vineyards back to the Castle Garden. Note that on the west (cliff-top) side of town, some of the outside-the-walls sections are steeper and harder to hike than the wall-top walkway.

St. Wolfgang's Church

This fortified Gothic church (which feels like a pale imitation of St. Jakob's) is built into the medieval wall at the Klingentor. While it sounds intriguing—and looks striking from the outside—its dungeon-like passages and shepherd's-dance exhibit are pretty lame.

Cost and Hours: €2, April-Oct Wed-Mon 10:00-13:00 & 14:30-17:00, closed Tue, closed off-season.

NEAR ROTHENBURG

▲A Walk in the Countryside

This pleasant stroll—easy and downhill at the start, with an uphill return at the end—takes you through the tranquil countryside below Rothenburg, including stops at a characteristic little "castle," a *Biergarten,* and a historic church.

From the *Burggarten* (castle garden), head into the Tauber Valley. As you come through the Burgtor into the castle garden, veer left to find the path that leads out of the garden; after leaving the wall, at the first big fork, turn right and head down and around the garden, keeping the castle and town on your right. The trail becomes quite steep, taking you down to the wooden covered bridge on the valley floor. Across the bridge, the road goes left to Toppler Castle and right (downstream, with a pleasant parallel footpath) to Detwang.

Toppler Castle (Topplerschlösschen) is cute, skinny, sky-blue, and 600 years old. It was the castle/summer home of the medi-

eval Mayor Toppler. The tower's top looks like a house—a sort of tree fort for grownups. It's in a farmer's garden, and it's open whenever he's around and willing to let you in (€1.50, normally Fri-Sun 13:00-16:00, closed Mon-Thu and Nov, one mile from town center at Taubertalweg 100, tel. 09861/7358). People say the mayor had this valley-floor escape built to get people to relax about leaving the fortified town...or to hide a mistress. After leaving the castle, you can continue straight along the same road to reach the big bridge in the valley just below town; from here, various roads and paths lead steeply back up into town.

Or, to extend your stroll, walk back to the small footbridge and follow the river downstream (passing the recommended Unter den Linden beer garden) to the peaceful village of **Detwang.** One of the oldest villages in Franconia (one of Germany's medieval dukedoms), Detwang dates from 968. Like Rothenburg, it has a Riemenschneider altarpiece in its **Church of Sts. Peter and Paul.**

Founded more than a millennium ago, this church has a dimly lit Romanesque interior with some Gothic frills. Riemenschneider's *Altar of the Holy Cross* depicts the moment when Christ, upon the cross, takes his last breath. While the central figures carry the same level of detail and emotion as any of Riemenschneider's work, the side panels (praying in Gethsemane on the left, the Resurrection on the right) exhibit a bit less mastery than the altarpiece in St. Jakob's. Originally carved for a church in Rothenburg, the altar was later trimmed to fit this smaller space. Notice the soldier on the right looking at an angle into thin air. Before being scooted in, his gaze fell on the dying Christ. Angels and other figures were cut out entirely (€1.50, daily 8:30-12:00 & 13:30-17:00, shorter hours and closed Mon off-season).

From Detwang, you can hike steeply back up into Rothenburg (arriving at the northern edge of town), or backtrack to the wooden footbridge—or all the way to Toppler Castle—and head up from there.

Franconian Bike Ride

To get a fun, breezy look at the countryside around Rothenburg, rent a bike (see "Helpful Hints" on page 336). For a pleasant half-day pedal, escape the old town through the Rödertor, bike along Topplerweg to Spitaltor, and follow the curvy road down into the river valley. Turn right at the yellow *Leutzenbronn* sign to cross the double-arcaded bridge. From here a peaceful road follows the river downstream to **Detwang,** passing the cute Toppler Castle (described earlier). From Detwang, follow the main road to the old mill, and turn left to follow the *Liebliches Taubertal* bike path signs as far up the Tauber River (direction: Bettwar) as you like. After 2.5 miles, you'll arrive in the sleepy farming town of **Bettwar,** where you can claim a spot among the chickens and the apple trees for a picnic or have a drink at one of the two restaurants in town.

Franconian Open-Air Museum (Fränkisches Freilandmuseum)

A 20-minute drive from Rothenburg—in the undiscovered "Rothenburgy" town of Bad Windsheim—is an open-air folk museum that, compared with others in Europe, is a bit humble. But it tries very hard and gives you the best look around at traditional rural Franconia.

Cost and Hours: €6, daily March-Oct 9:00-18:00, Nov-mid-Dec 10:00-16:00, closed mid-Dec-March, check website for schedule, last entry one hour before closing, tel. 09841/66800, www.freilandmuseum.de.

Shopping in Rothenburg

Be warned...Rothenburg is one of Germany's best shopping towns. Do it here and be done with it. Lovely prints, carvings, wine glasses, Christmas-tree ornaments, and beer steins are popular. Rödergasse is the old town's everyday shopping street. There's also a modern shopping center across the street from the train station.

For an appealing string of family-run shops, follow my "Schmeidgasse-Spitalgasse Shopping Stroll" (described earlier, under "Rothenburg Walks"). Below are two shops not on that walk:

Käthe Wohlfahrt Christmas Headquarters

Rothenburg is the headquarters of the **Käthe Wohlfahrt** Christmas trinkets empire, which is spreading across the half-timbered reaches of Europe. Rothenburg has six or eight Wohlfahrts. Tourists flock to the two biggest, just below Market Square (Herrngasse 1 and 2). Start with the **Christmas Village** (Weihnachtsdorf) at Herrngasse 1. This Christmas wonderland is filled with enough twinkling lights (196,000—mostly LEDs) to require a special electrical hookup. You're greeted by instant Christmas mood music (best appreciated on a hot day in July) and tourists hungrily filling little woven shopping baskets with goodies to hang on their trees (items handmade in Germany are the most expensive). Let the spinning flocked tree whisk you in, and pause at the wall of Steiff stuffed animals, jerking uncontrollably and mesmerizing little kids. Then head downstairs to find the vast and sprawling "made in Germany" section, surrounding a slowly spinning 15-foot tree decorated with a thousand glass balls. The fascinating **Christmas Museum** upstairs is described earlier, under "Sights in Rothenburg." The smaller shop (across the street at Herrngasse 2) specializes in finely crafted wooden ornaments. Käthe opened her first storefront here in Rothenburg in 1977. The company is now run by her son Harald Wohlfahrt, who lives in town (all stores open Mon-Sat 9:00-18:00, May-Dec also most Sun 10:00-17:00).

Friese Shop

Cuckoo with friendliness, trinkets, and souvenirs, the Friese shop has been open for more than 50 years—and they've been welcoming my readers for more than 30 of those years (20 steps off Market Square, west of TI, on corner across from free public WC). They give shoppers with this book tremendous service: a 10 percent discount and a free pictorial map (normally €1.50). Anneliese Friese, who runs the place with her son Bernie and granddaughter Dolores (a.k.a. "Mousy"), charges only her cost for shipping and lets tired travelers leave their bags in her back room for free (Mon-Sat 9:00-18:00, Sun 10:00-18:00, Grüner Markt 8, tel. 09861/7166).

Sleep Code

Abbreviations   (€1 = about $1.40, country code: 49)
S = Single, **D** = Double/Twin, **T** = Triple, **Q** = Quad, **b** = bath-
room, **s** = shower only.
Price Rankings
  $$$ **Higher Priced**—Most rooms €85 or more.
   $$ **Moderately Priced**—Most rooms between €60-85.
    $ **Lower Priced**—Most rooms €60 or less.
Unless otherwise noted, credit cards are accepted, English
is spoken, breakfast is included, and Wi-Fi is generally free.
Prices can change; verify current rates online or by email. For
the best prices, always book directly with the hotel.

Sleeping in Rothenburg

Rothenburg is crowded with visitors, but most are day-trippers.
Except for the rare Saturday night and during festivals (see page
336), finding a room is easy throughout the year. Competition
keeps quality high. If you want to splurge, you'll snare the best
value by paying extra for the biggest and best rooms at the hotels I
recommend. In the off-season (Nov and Jan-March), hoteliers may
be willing to discount.

Train travelers save steps by staying in the area toward the
Rödertor (east end of town). Hotels and guesthouses will sometimes pick up tired heavy-packers at the station. If you're driving,
call ahead to get directions and parking tips. Save some energy to
climb the stairs: No hotels listed here have elevators.

Keep your key when out late. As Rothenburg's hotels are small
and mostly family-run, they often lock up early (at about 22:00)
and take one day a week off, when you'll need to let yourself in.

IN THE OLD TOWN

$$$ Hotel Herrnschlösschen prides itself on being the small-
est (8 rooms) and most exclusive hotel in Rothenburg. If you're
looking for a splurge, this is your best bet. This 1,000-year-old
building has a beautiful Baroque garden and every amenity you'd
ever want (including a sauna), but you'll pay for them (deluxe Db-
€210, junior suite-€265, senior suite-€325, see website for sea-
sonal discounts, Wi-Fi, Herrngasse 20, tel. 09861/873890, www.
herrnschloesschen.de, info@herrnschloesschen.de).

$$$ Hotel Kloster-Stüble, deep in the old town near the cas-
tle garden, is one of my classiest listings. Rudolf does the cooking,
while Erika—his energetic first mate—welcomes guests. Twenty-
one rooms fill two medieval buildings, connected by a modern

atrium. The hotel is just off Herrngasse on a tiny side street (Sb-€58-78, traditional Db-€88-108, bigger and more modern Db-€134-144, Tb-€108-146, see website for suites and family rooms, kids 5 and under free, guest computer, Wi-Fi in most rooms, Heringsbronnengasse 5, tel. 09861/938-890, www.klosterstueble.de, hotel@klosterstueble.de).

$$$ Hotel Spitzweg is a rustic-yet-elegant 1536 mansion (never bombed or burned) with 10 big rooms, new bathrooms, open beams, and endearing hand-painted antique furniture. It's run by gentle Herr Hocher, whom I suspect is the former Wizard of Oz—now retired and in a very good mood (Sb-€65-70, Db-€90-100, Tb-€115, Qb apartment-€160, non-smoking, inviting old-fashioned breakfast room, free parking, Wi-Fi at son-in-law's nearby hotel, Paradeisgasse 2, tel. 09861/94290, www.hotel-spitzweg.de, info@hotel-spitzweg.de).

$$$ Gasthof Goldener Greifen, once Mayor Toppler's home, is a big, traditional, 600-year-old place with 14 spacious rooms and all the comforts. It's run by a helpful family staff and creaks with rustic splendor (Sb-€48, small Db-€65, big Db-€85-98, Tb-€105-139, Qb-€125-158, price depends on size, 10 percent less for 3-night stays, non-smoking, Wi-Fi, full-service laundry-€8, free loaner bikes for guests, free and easy parking, half a block downhill from Market Square at Obere Schmiedgasse 5, tel. 09861/2281, www.gasthof-greifen-rothenburg.de, info@gasthof-greifen-rothenburg.de, Brigitte, daughter Ursula, and Klingler family). The family also runs a good restaurant, serving meals in the back garden or dining room.

$$$ Hotel Gerberhaus mixes modern comforts into 20 bright and airy rooms that still maintain a sense of half-timbered elegance. Enjoy the pleasant garden in back (Sb-€65-85, Db-€79-130, Tb-€139-150, Qb-€145-185, Quint/b-€195-205, prices depend on room size; apartment-€130/2 people, €195/4 people; 10 percent off the second and subsequent nights and a *Schneeball* if you book direct and pay cash, non-smoking, 4 rooms have canopied 4-poster *Himmel* beds, guest computer, Wi-Fi, laundry-€7, close to P-1 parking lot, Spitalgasse 25, tel. 09861/94900, www.gerberhaus.rothenburg.de, gerberhaus@t-online.de, Inge).

$$ Hotel Altfränkische Weinstube am Klosterhof is *the* place for well-heeled bohemians. Mario, Hanne, and their lovely daughter Viktoria rent seven cozy rooms above their dark and evocative pub in a 600-year-old building. It's an upscale *Lord of the Rings* atmosphere, with modern plumbing, open-beam ceilings, and some canopied four-poster beds (Sb-€75, Db-€69, bigger Db-€82, Db suite-€108, Tb-€108, Wi-Fi, off Klingengasse at Klosterhof 7, tel. 09861/6404, www.altfraenkische.de, altfraenkische-weinstube@web.de). Their pub is a candlelit classic—and a favorite with lo-

Rothenburg Hotels

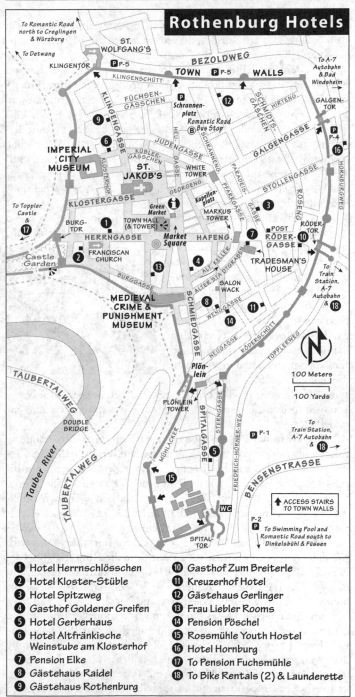

To Romantic Road north to Creglingen & Würzburg

To Detwang

ST. WOLFGANG'S

KLINGENTOR

P-5

BEZOLDWEG

TOWN

P-5

WALLS

To A-7 Autobahn & Bad Windsheim

KLINGENSCHÜTT

FÜCHSEN-GÄSSCHEN

Schrannen-platz

Romantic Road Bus Stop

GALGEN-TOR

KLINGENGASSE

JUDENGASSE

SCHMIDT'S-GÄSSCHEN

HIRTENG.

GALGENGASSE

P-4

IMPERIAL CITY MUSEUM

KLOSTERHOF

KÜBLER-GÄSSCHEN

ST. JAKOB'S

HEUGASSE

WHITE TOWER

SCHRANNENG.

PARADIES-GASSE

STOLLENGASSE

HORNBURGWEG

To Toppler Castle &

KLOSTERGASSE

Georgeng.

Green Market

Kapellen-platz

MARKUS TOWER

PFARRG.

ROSENG.

To A-7 Autobahn &

BURG-TOR

HERRNGASSE

TOWN HALL (& TOWER)

Market Square

HAFENG.

ALT KELLER

POST

RÖDER-GASSE

RÖDER-TOR

Castle Garden

FRANCISCAN CHURCH

BURGGASSE

ALTER STADTGRABEN

TRADESMAN'S HOUSE

To Train Station, A-7 Autobahn &

MEDIEVAL CRIME & PUNISHMENT MUSEUM

SCHMIEDGASSE

SALON WACK

WENGGASSE

NEUGASSE

RÖDERSCHÜTT

TOPPLERWEG

100 Meters

100 Yards

TAUBERTALWEG

Plönlein

PLÖNLEIN TOWER

MÜHLACKER

SPITALGASSE

STERNGASSE

FRIEDRICH-HÖRNER-WEG

To Train Station, A-7 Autobahn &

P-1

DOUBLE BRIDGE

Tauber River

TAUBERTALWEG

WC

BENSENSTRASSE

ACCESS STAIRS TO TOWN WALLS

P-2

SPITAL-TOR

To Swimming Pool and Romantic Road south to Dinkelsbühl & Füssen

ROTHENBURG & THE ROMANTIC ROAD

1 Hotel Herrnschlösschen
2 Hotel Kloster-Stüble
3 Hotel Spitzweg
4 Gasthof Goldener Greifen
5 Hotel Gerberhaus
6 Hotel Altfränkische Weinstube am Klosterhof
7 Pension Elke
8 Gästehaus Raidel
9 Gästehaus Rothenburg

10 Gasthof Zum Breiterle
11 Kreuzerhof Hotel
12 Gästehaus Gerlinger
13 Frau Liebler Rooms
14 Pension Pöschel
15 Rossmühle Youth Hostel
16 Hotel Hornburg
17 To Pension Fuchsmühle
18 To Bike Rentals (2) & Launderette

cals, serving hot food to Hobbits (see listing later, under "Eating in Rothenburg"). It also hosts the Wednesday evening English Conversation Club (see "Meet the Locals" on page 369).

$$ Pension Elke, run by spry Erich Endress and his son Klaus, rents 12 comfy rooms above the family grocery store. Guests who jog are welcome to join Klaus on his half-hour run around the city every evening at 19:30 (S-€35, Sb-€45, D-€45-55, Db-€65-67, price depends on room size, extra bed-€18, 10 percent discount with this book through 2015 if you stay at least 2 nights, cash only, guest computer, Wi-Fi; reception in grocery store until 19:00, otherwise go around back and ring bell at top of stairs; near Markus Tower at Rödergasse 6, tel. 09861/2331, www.pension-elke-rothenburg.de, info@pension-elke-rothenburg.de).

$$ Gästehaus Raidel rents eight rooms in a 500-year-old house filled with beds and furniture all handmade by friendly, soft-spoken Norry Raidel himself. The ramshackle ambience makes me want to sing the *Addams Family* theme song—but the place has a rare, time-passed family charm. Norry, who plays in a Dixieland band, has invented a fascinating hybrid saxophone/trombone called the Norryphone...and loves to jam (Sb-€45, Db-€69, Tb-€90, Qb

suite-€120, cash only, Wi-Fi, Wenggasse 3, tel. 09861/3115, Norry asks you to use the reservations form at www.romanticroad.com/raidel).

$$ Gästehaus Rothenburg has seven tastefully modern, fresh, and comfortable rooms and a peaceful terrace behind St. Jakob's Church. It's run by friendly Gunnar, who likes to join his guests for a drink on the terrace to improve his English (Sb-€52-59, Db-€69-75, Tb-€88-95, family suite, extra bed-€25, non-smoking, Wi-Fi, Klingengasse 21, tel. 09861/92380, www.gaestehaus-rothenburg.de, info@gaestehaus-rothenburg.de).

$$ Gasthof Zum Breiterle offers 20 comfortable rooms with wooden accents above their restaurant near the Rödertor (Sb-€55, Db-€75-85, Tb-€95, apartment-€140, reception in restaurant, pay Wi-Fi, free parking, Rödergasse 30, tel. 09861/6730, www.breiterle.de/, info@breiterle.de, Mike and Nicole).

$$ Kreuzerhof Hotel offers nine fine rooms surrounding a courtyard on a quiet side street near the Rödertor (Sb-€48, Db-€75, large Db-€92, Tb-€95, Qb-€124, 6-bed room-€159, family deals, non-smoking, guest computer, Wi-Fi, laundry-€6, parking in courtyard-€3/day, Millergasse 2-6, tel. 09861/3424, www.kreuzerhof.eu, info@kreuzerhof.eu, Heike and Walter Maltz).

$$ Gästehaus Gerlinger, a fine value, has five comfortable rooms in a pretty 16th-century house with a small terrace for guests (Sb-€49, Db-€62, Tb-€78, cash only, non-smoking, Wi-Fi, easy parking, Schlegeleinsweth 10, tel. 09861/87979, mobile 0171-690-0752, www.pension-gerlinger.de, info@pension-gerlinger.de, Hermann).

$ Frau Liebler rents two large, modern, ground-floor rooms with kitchenettes. They're great for those looking for real privacy close to the action. On the top floor is an attractive two-bedroom apartment (Db-€48, apartment-€60, extra bed-€12, 10 percent discount for 2 or more nights with this book in 2015, breakfast-€6, cash only, non-smoking, Wi-Fi, laundry-€5, behind Christmas shop at Pfäffleinsgässchen 10, tel. 09861/709-215, www. gaestehaus-liebler.de). Frau Liebler also has three more apartments a couple blocks away.

$ Pension Pöschel is simple, with six plain rooms in a concrete but pleasant building and an inviting garden out back. Only one room has a private shower and toilet (S-€30, D-€50, Db-€55, T-€65, Tb-€70, small kids free, cash only, non-smoking, Wi-Fi, Wenggasse 22, tel. 09861/3430, mobile 0170-700-7041, www. pensionpoeschel.de, pension.poeschel@t-online.de, Bettina).

$ Rossmühle Youth Hostel rents 186 beds in two buildings. While it mostly has four- to six-bed dorms, this institutional yet charming hostel also has 15 doubles. Reception is in the droopy-eyed building—formerly a horse-powered mill, it was used when the old town was under siege and the river-powered mill was inaccessible (dorm bed-€25, bunk-bed Db-€58, guests over 26 pay €4 extra unless traveling with a family, nonmembers pay €4 extra, includes breakfast and sheets, all-you-can-eat dinner-€7, Wi-Fi, self-serve laundry including soap-€5, close to P-1 parking lot, entrance on Rossmühlgasse, tel. 09861/94160, www.rothenburg. jugendherberge.de, rothenburg@jugendherberge.de).

OUTSIDE THE WALL

$$$ Hotel Hornburg, a grand 1903 mansion, is close to the train station, a two-minute walk outside the wall. With groomed grounds, gracious and colorful sitting areas, and 10 spacious, tastefully decorated rooms, it's a good value (Sb-€69-90, Db-€78-115, Tb-€110-135, price depends on size of room, non-smoking, family-friendly, dogs welcome—ask for pet-free room if you're allergic, guest computer, Wi-Fi; Hornburgweg 28, at intersection with Mannstrasse—across from parking lot P-4; tel. 09861/8480, www. hotel-hornburg.de, info@hotel-hornburg.de, Gabriele and Martin).

$$ Pension Fuchsmühle is a guesthouse in a renovated old mill on the river below the castle end of Rothenburg, across from the Toppler Castle. It feels rural, but is a pleasant (though steep)

15-minute hike to Market Square, and a €10 taxi ride from the train station. Alex and Heidi Molitor, a young couple with kids, offer eight bright, modern light-wood rooms. The building's electric power comes from the millwheel by the entrance, with excess sold to the municipal grid (Sb-€43, Db-€65, Tb-€83, Qb-€112, 3-room suite-€145/5 people or €165/6 people, less if you stay more than one night, healthy farm-fresh breakfast-€7.50, Wi-Fi, free parking, laundry-€12, flashlights provided for your walk back after dark, Taubertalweg 101, tel. 09861/92633, www.fuchsmuehle.de, info@fuchsmuehle.de).

Eating in Rothenburg

Many restaurants take a midafternoon break, and stop serving lunch at 14:00 and dinner as early as 20:00. My recommendations are all within a five-minute walk of Market Square. While all survive on tourism, many still feel like local hangouts. Your choices are typical German or ethnic. You'll see regional Franconian *(frankisch)* specialties advertised, such as the German ravioli called *Maultaschen* and Franconian bratwurst (similar to other brats, but a bit more coarsely ground, with less fat, and liberally seasoned with marjoram).

TRADITIONAL GERMAN RESTAURANTS
Reichsküchenmeister is a forgettable big-hotel restaurant, but on a balmy evening, its pleasant tree-shaded terrace overlooking St. Jakob's Church and reliably good dishes are hard to beat (€13-23 main courses, €7-10 *Flammkuchen*—German-style pizza, steaks, vegetarian options, daily 11:00-23:00, Kirchplatz 8, tel. 09861/9700).

Hotel Restaurant Kloster-Stüble, on a small street off Herrngasse near the castle garden, is a classy place for delicious and beautifully presented traditional cuisine, including homemade *Maultaschen*. Chef Rudy cooks while head waitress Erika makes sure communication goes smoothly. Choose from their shaded terrace, sleek- and-stony modern dining room, or woody traditional dining room (€10-16 main courses, Thu-Mon 11:00-14:00 & 18:00-21:00, closed Tue-Wed, Heringsbronnengasse 5, tel. 09861/938-890).

Gasthof Goldener Greifen, in a historic building with a peaceful garden out back, is just off the main square. The Klingler family serves quality Franconian food at a good price...and with a smile. The wood is ancient and polished from generations of happy use, and the ambience is practical rather than posh (€8-17 main courses, €12-15 three-course daily specials, affordable kids' meals,

Mon-Sat 11:30-21:00, Obere Schmiedgasse 5, tel. 09861/2281, Ursula).

Altfränkische Weinstube am Klosterhof seems designed for gnomes to celebrate their anniversaries. At this very dark pub, classically candlelit in a 600-year-old building, Mario whips up gourmet pub grub (€7-15 main courses, hot food served Wed-Mon 18:00-22:30, closed Tue, off Klingengasse at Klosterhof 7, tel. 09861/6404). If you'd like dinner company, drop by on Wednesday evening, when the English Conversation Club has a big table reserved from 18:00 on (see "Meet the Locals," page 369). You'll eat well and with new friends—both travelers and locals.

Zum Pulverer ("The Powderer") is a very traditional *Weinstube* (wine bar) just inside the Burgtor gate that serves a menu of affordable and well-executed regional fare, some with modern flourishes. The interior is a cozy wood-hewn place that oozes history, with chairs carved in the shape of past senators of Rothenburg (€6-14 dishes, Wed-Mon 17:00-22:00, closed Tue, Herrengasse 31, tel. 09861/3293).

Alter Keller is a modest, tourist friendly restaurant with an extremely characteristic interior and outdoor tables on a peaceful square just a couple blocks off Market Square. The menu has German classics at reasonable prices—*Spätzle*, schnitzel, trout, and roasts—as well as steak (€8-14 main dishes, steaks higher-priced but reasonable, Wed-Sun 11:00-22:00, closed Mon-Tue, Alter Keller 8, tel. 09861/2268).

A NON-FRANCONIAN SPLURGE

Hotel Restaurant Herrnschlösschen is the local favorite for gourmet presentation and a departure from Franconian fare. They offer a small menu of international and seasonal dishes with a theme. There's always a serious vegetarian option and a €50 fixed-price meal with matching wine. It's perhaps the most elegant dining in town, whether in the classy dining hall or in the shaded Baroque garden out back. Reservations are a must (€20-28 main dishes, Herrngasse 20, tel. 09861/873-890, Ulrika).

BREAKS FROM PORK AND POTATOES

Pizzeria Roma is the locals' favorite for €6-8 pizza and pastas, with good Italian wine. The Magrini family moved here from Tuscany in 1970 (many Italians immigrated to Germany in those years), and they've been cooking pasta for Rothenburg ever since (Thu-Tue 11:30-24:00, closed Wed and mid-Aug-mid-Sept, Galgengasse 19, tel. 09861/4540, Ricardo).

Bosporus Café, just off Market Square, serves cheap and tasty Turkish food to eat in or take away. Their *Döner Kebabs* must be the

ROTHENBURG & THE ROMANTIC ROAD

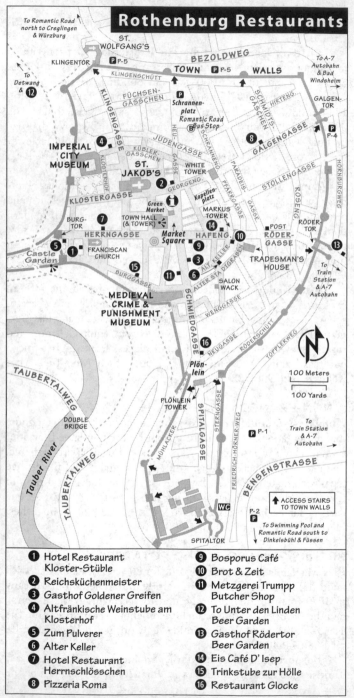

Rothenburg Restaurants

1. Hotel Restaurant Kloster-Stüble
2. Reichsküchenmeister
3. Gasthof Goldener Greifen
4. Altfränkische Weinstube am Klosterhof
5. Zum Pulverer
6. Alter Keller
7. Hotel Restaurant Herrnschlösschen
8. Pizzeria Roma
9. Bosporus Café
10. Brot & Zeit
11. Metzgerei Trumpp Butcher Shop
12. To Unter den Linden Beer Garden
13. Gasthof Rödertor Beer Garden
14. Eis Café D' Isep
15. Trinkstube zur Hölle
16. Restaurant Glocke

best €3.50 hot meal in Rothenburg (daily 9:00-21:00, until 19:00 Oct-March, Hafengasse 2, Oktay).

SANDWICHES AND SNACKS

Brot & Zeit (a pun on *Brotzeit,* "bread time," the German term for snacking), conveniently located a block off Market Square, is like a German bakery dressed up as a Starbucks. In a bright, modern atmosphere just inside the super-picturesque Markus Tower, they sell take-away coffee, sandwiches, and a few hot dishes, making it a good one-stop shop for grabbing a meal to go or to eat inside at its few small tables (€5 hot meals, cheaper sandwiches, Mon-Sat 6:00-18:30, Sun 7:30-18:00, Hafengasse 24, tel. 09861/936-8701).

Bakery and Butcher Sandwiches: While any bakery in town can sell you a sandwich for a couple of euros, I like to pop into **Metzgerei Trumpp**, a high-quality butcher shop serving up cheap and tasty sausages on a bun with kraut to go (Mon-Sat 8:00-18:00, closed Sun, a block off Market Square at Schmiedgasse 18).

Grocery Stores: A small grocery store is in the center of town at Rödergasse 6 (Mon-Fri 7:30-19:00, Sat 7:30-18:00, May-Dec also Sun 10:00-18:00, closed Sun Jan-April). Larger supermarkets are outside the wall: Exit the town through the Rödertor, turn left through the cobbled gate, and cross the parking lot to reach the Edeka supermarket (Mon-Fri 8:00-20:00, Sat 8:00-18:00, closed Sun); or head to the even bigger Kaufland across from the train station (Mon-Sat 7:00-20:00, closed Sun).

BEER GARDENS *(BIERGARTENS)*

Rothenburg's *Biergarten*s can be great fun, but they're open only when the weather is balmy.

Unter den Linden, a family-friendly (with sandbox and swing), slightly bohemian *Biergarten* in the valley along the river, is worth the 20-minute hike on a pleasant evening (daily 10:00-22:00 in season with decent weather, sometimes later, self-service food and good beer, €13 breakfast buffet Sundays until noon, call first to confirm it's open, Kurze Steige 7, tel. 09861/5909). As it's in the valley on the river, it's cooler than Rothenburg; bring a sweater. Take a right outside the Burgtor, then a left on the footpath toward Detwang; it's at the bottom of the hill on the left.

Gasthof Rödertor, just outside the wall through the Rödertor, runs a backyard *Biergarten* that's popular with locals. It's great for a rowdy crowd looking for pizza, classic beer garden fare, and good beer. Their passion is potatoes—the menu is dedicated to spud cuisine. Try a plate of *Schupfnudeln*—potato noodles with sauerkraut and bacon (May-Sept daily 17:30-23:00 in good weather, table service only—no ordering at counter, Ansbacher Strasse 7, look for wooden gate, tel. 09861/2022). If the *Biergarten* is closed, their indoor restaurant, with a more extensive menu, is a good value (€8-13 main courses, Tue-Sun 11:30-14:00 & 17:30-21:30, closed Mon).

DESSERT

Eis Café D'Isep, with a pleasant "Venetian minimalist" interior, has been making gelato in Rothenburg since 1960, using family recipes that span four generations. They proudly serve up cakes, drinks, fresh-fruit ice cream, and fancy sundaes. Their sidewalk tables are great for lazy people-watching (daily 9:30-22:30, closed early Oct-mid-Feb, one block off Market Square at Hafengasse 17, run by Paolo and Paola D'Isep and son Enrico).

Pastries: Rothenburg's *Bäckereien* (bakeries) offer succulent pastries, pies, and cakes...but skip the bad-tasting *Rothenburger Schneeballen.* Unworthy of the heavy promotion they receive, *Schneeballen* are bland pie crusts crumpled into a ball and dusted with powdered sugar or frosted with sticky-sweet glop. There's little reason to waste your appetite on a *Schneeball* when you can enjoy a curvy *Mandelhörnchen* (almond crescent cookie), a triangular *Nussecke* ("nut corner"), a round

Florentiner cookie, a couple of fresh *Krapfen* (like jelly doughnuts), or even just a soft, warm German pretzel.

WINE-DRINKING IN THE OLD CENTER

Trinkstube zur Hölle ("Hell") is dark and foreboding, offering a thick wine-drinking atmosphere, pub food, and a few main courses (€12-20). It's small and can get painfully touristy in summer (Mon-Sat 17:00-24:00, food until 21:30, closed Sun, a block past Medieval Crime and Punishment Museum on Burggasse, look for the devil hanging out front, tel. 09861/4229).

Altfränkische Weinstube am Klosterhof (listed earlier, under "Traditional German Restaurants") is the liveliest place, and a clear favorite with locals for an atmospheric drink or late meal. When every other place is asleep, you're likely to find good food, drink, and energy here.

Restaurant Glocke, a *Weinstube* (wine bar) with a full menu, is run by Rothenburg's oldest and only surviving winemakers, the Thürauf family. The very extensive wine list is in German only because the friendly staff wants to explain your options in person. Their special €5 wine flight lets you sample five Franconian wines

(€8-18 main courses, Mon-Sat 11:00-23:00, closed Sun, Plönlein 1, tel. 09861/958-990).

MEET THE LOCALS WEDNESDAY NIGHTS

For a rare chance to mix it up with locals who aren't selling anything, bring your favorite slang and tongue twisters to the **English**

Conversation Club at Mario's Altfränkische Weinstube am Klosterhof (Wed 18:00-24:00, restaurant listed earlier). This group of intrepid linguists has met more than 1,000 times. Hermann the German and his sidekick Wolfgang are regulars. Consider arriving early for dinner, or after 21:00, when the beer starts to sink in, the crowd grows, and everyone seems to speak that second language a bit more easily.

Rothenburg Connections

BY TRAIN

If you take the train to or from Rothenburg, you'll transfer at Steinach. A tiny branch train line shuttles back and forth hourly between Steinach and Rothenburg (14 minutes, generally departs Steinach at :35 and Rothenburg at :06). Train connections in Steinach are usually quick and efficient (trains to and from Rothenburg generally use track 5; use the conveyor belts to haul your bags smartly up and down the stairs).

If you plan to arrive in Rothenburg in the evening, note that the last train from Steinach to Rothenburg departs at about 22:30. All is not lost if you arrive in Steinach after the last train—there's a subsidized taxi service to Rothenburg (cheaper for the government than running an almost-empty train). To use this handy service, called AST *(Anrufsammeltaxi)*, make an appointment with a participating taxi service (call 09861/2000 or 09861/7227) at least an hour in advance (2 hours ahead is better), and they'll drive you from Steinach to Rothenburg for the train fare (€4/person) rather than the regular €25 taxi fare.

The Rothenburg station has a touch-screen terminal for fare and schedule information and ticket sales. If you need extra help, visit the combined ticket office/travel agency in the station building (€1-4 surcharge for most tickets, €0.50 charge for questions without ticket purchase, Mon-Fri 9:00-18:00, Sat 9:00-13:00, closed Sun, tel. 09861/7711). The station at Steinach is entirely unstaffed, but also has touch-screen ticket machines. As a last resort, call for train info at tel. 0180-599-6633, or visit www.bahn.com.

From **Rothenburg (via Steinach) by Train to: Würzburg** (hourly, 70 minutes), **Nürnberg** (hourly, 1.5 hours, change in Ansbach), **Munich** (hourly, 2.5-4 hours, 2-3 changes), **Füssen** (hourly, 5 hours, often with changes in Treuchtlingen and Augsburg), **Frankfurt** (hourly, 2.5-3 hours, change in Würzburg), **Frankfurt Airport** (hourly, 3-3.5 hours, change in Würzburg), **Berlin** (hourly, 5-6 hours, 3 changes). Remember, all destinations require a change in Steinach.

BY BUS

The **Romantic Road bus** stops in Rothenburg once a day (mid-April-late Oct) on its way from Frankfurt to Munich and Füssen (and vice versa). The bus stop is at Schrannenplatz, a short walk north of Market Square. See the schedule and tour description at the end of this chapter.

ROUTE TIPS FOR DRIVERS

The three-hour autobahn drive from **Frankfurt Airport** (and other points north) to Rothenburg is something even a jet-lagged zombie can handle. It's a 75-mile straight shot to Würzburg on the A-3 autobahn; just follow the blue autobahn signs toward *Würzburg*. Then turn south on A-7 and take the *Rothenburg o.d.T.* exit (#108). For a back-roads alternative, see "The Romantic Road" section, next.

The Romantic Road

The countryside between Frankfurt and Munich is Germany's medieval heartland. Walls and towers ring half-timbered towns, and flowers spill over the window-sills of well-kept houses. Glockenspiels dance from town halls by day, while night watchmen still call the hours after dark. Many travelers bypass these small towns by fast train or autobahn. But consider an extra day or two to take in the slow pace of small-town German life. With a car, you can wander through quaint hills and rolling villages, and stop wherever the cows look friendly or a town fountain beckons.

In the 1950s, towns in this region joined together to work out a scenic driving route for visitors that they called the Romantic Road (*Romantische Strasse*, www.romanticroad.de). Because local

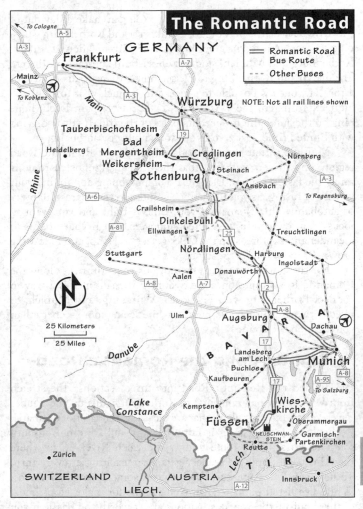

The Romantic Road

To Cologne
A-3
A-5
GERMANY
Frankfurt
A-7
Mainz
To Koblenz
A-3
Main
Würzburg

Romantic Road
Bus Route
Other Buses

NOTE: Not all rail lines shown

Tauberbischofsheim
Bad
Heidelberg
Mergentheim
Creglingen
Weikersheim
Rothenburg
Steinach
Nürnberg
Ansbach
A-3
To Regensburg
Rhine
A-6
Crailsheim
Treuchtlingen
A-81
Dinkelsbühl
Ellwangen
25
Stuttgart
Nördlingen
Harburg
Ingolstadt
Aalen
Donauwörth
A-8
A-7
2
25 Kilometers
A-8
25 Miles
Ulm
Augsburg
Dachau
B A V A R I A
17
Danube
Landsberg
am Lech
Munich
Lake
Buchloe
A-95
A-8
Constance
Kaufbeuren
17
To Salzburg
Kempten
Wies-
kirche
Füssen
Oberammergau
NEUSCHWAN-
Garmisch-
STEIN
Partenkirchen
Reutte
Zürich
T I R O L
SWITZERLAND
AUSTRIA
Innsbruck
LIECH.
A-12

train service was poor, they also organized a bus along the route for tourists, from Würzburg in the north to Füssen in the south.

The Romantic Road is the oldest and most famous of Germany's two dozen signposted scenic routes. Others celebrate toys, porcelain, architecture (Swabian Baroque or brick Gothic), clocks, and baths—and there are even two separate *Spargelstrassen* (asparagus roads). The "Castle Road" that runs between Rothenburg and Mannheim sounds intriguing, but it's nowhere near as interesting.

Now that the A-7 autobahn parallels the old two-lane route, the Romantic Road itself has become less important, but its destinations are still worthwhile. For drivers, the Romantic Road is basically a set of scenic stepping stones to Rothenburg, which is the most exciting town along the way. You can make a day out of the drive between Würzburg (or Frankfurt) and Rothenburg, stopping in the small towns along the Tauber River Valley. If linking Rothenburg and Munich, stop in Dinkelsbühl and/or Nördlingen. The drive from Rothenburg to Füssen on two-lane roads makes for a full day, but it's possible to squeeze in a quick visit to Dinkelsbühl, Nördlingen, the Wieskirche, or Landsberg am Lech, hopping on the autobahn to speed up parts of the trip. If you're driving with limited time, just zero in on Rothenburg by autobahn.

Multiple, often parallel roads crisscross the Romantic Road region, and drivers will find that the official, signposted route is rarely the fastest option. Using GPS or a mapping app to find your way is confusing, as you'll usually be routed to the nearest highway or autobahn. This is smart if your time is tight and you want to focus on a few carefully selected stopovers. But if your goal is to meander and explore, skip the GPS, get a good map, and follow the brown *Romantische Strasse* signs.

For those without a car, the tour bus that still runs along the Romantic Road route once a day during the summer is a way to connect Rothenburg with Frankfurt, Würzburg, and Munich, or to go between Munich and Füssen, while seeing more scenery than you'd get on the train.

Sights Along the Romantic Road

I've divided the Romantic Road into three sections. The stretch from Würzburg (or Frankfurt) to Rothenburg runs up the Tauber River Valley, offering views that are pleasant, though not dramatic. Rothenburg to Augsburg is fairly flat and dull. From Augsburg south to Füssen, the route follows the Lech River up to where the Alps begin, and the scenery gets more exciting at every turn. To help you find your way, I've included some driving directions. While I've listed public-transit connections for major stops, most of these out-of-the-way destinations aren't worth the hassle if you lack a car. The Romantic Road bus is an option, but can be disappointing (see end of chapter).

FROM WÜRZBURG (OR FRANKFURT) TO ROTHENBURG

To take this scenic back-road approach from Frankfurt, take A-3, then turn south on A-81, get off at the Tauberbischofsheim exit, and follow signs for *Bad Mergentheim*. Or stay on A-3 to the Heidingsfeld-Würzburg exit and follow *Stuttgart/Ulm/Road 19* signs south to Bad Mergentheim. From Würzburg, follow *Ulm/Road 19* signs to Bad Mergentheim.

Bad Mergentheim

This town, one of the less "romantic" stops along this route, holds a unique footnote in Germanic history: In 1525, the Teutonic Knights (called the *Deutschorden*, or "German Order") lost their lands in East Prussia (today's Poland) and the Baltic states. The order's leadership retreated to their

castle at Bad Mergentheim, which became their headquarters for the next three centuries. Today the building houses the **German Order Museum**—practically a pilgrimage for German historians, but underwhelming for casual visitors, who will find it dry and with limited English (www.deutschordensmuseum.de).

Leaving Bad Mergentheim, continue east. Turn into Weikersheim off the main road, following *Stadtmitte* and *Schloss* signs, then bear right to park in the large free lot. From there it's a couple of minutes' walk to the town square.

▲Weikersheim

This picturesquely set town, nestled between hills, has a charming little main square offering easy access to a fine park and an impressive palace.

Weikersheim's **palace** (Schloss Weikersheim), across a moat-turned-park from the main square, was built in the late 16th cen-

tury as the Renaissance country estate of a local count. With its bucolic location and glowing sandstone texture, it gives off an almost British, *Downton Abbey*-esque vibe. The palace **interior** boasts an unusual triangular floor plan but is only viewable by guided tour; unfortunately, tours are only offered in German, though you may be able to borrow an English handout (€6.50, includes garden, hourly tours, daily April-Oct 9:00-18:00, Nov-March 10:00-12:00 & 13:00-17:00, tel. 07934/992-950, www.schloss-weikersheim.de).

I'd skip the tour and instead focus on exploring the fine Baroque **gardens** (€3.50 ticket includes admission to gardens and a few paltry museum exhibits, same hours as palace—see above, borrow free English audioguide, €5 deposit required). From the ticket office, cut through the courtyard and pop out at the finely manicured gardens, originally laid out in the early 18th century and populated by an army of whimsical stony statues (most of them mythological figures). Along the balustrade separating the palace from the gardens are the most-photographed statues, the so-called "Dwarves' Gallery." At the far end of the complex is an *orangerie*, offering fine views back over the gardens to the palace.

The **rose garden**, to the right as you face the palace, is free (but likely not at its best, as it's been recovering from an infestation). A gate off the rose garden leads to a spooky "alchemy garden" with plants used by medieval witches.

If you have time after your garden visit, the pleasant **town square** and cobbled old town are worth exploring. The Gänsturm ("Goose Tower"), which used to be the city gate, now houses a small town history museum (free, April-Oct open only on Sun 13:30-17:00, otherwise call to arrange, Hauptstrasse 42, tel. 07934/1209, www.weikersheim.de). The **city park** (*Stadtpark*, enter off town square) is a fine and free picnic spot, and from it you can peer over the hedge into the palace gardens.

Creglingen

While Creglingen itself isn't worth much fuss (TI tel. 07933/631, www.creglingen.de), two quick and rewarding sights sit across the road from each other a mile south of town.

The peaceful 14th-century **Herrgottskirche Church**, worth ▲, is graced with Tilman Riemenschneider's greatest carved altarpiece, completed sometime between 1505 and 1510. The church was built on the site where a local farmer found a seemingly miraculous communion host in a field. Centuries later, Riemenschneider graced the space with an impressive altar nearly 30 feet high—tall enough that its tip pokes up between the rafters. While Riemenschneider's altars in Rothenburg and Detwang (see pages 342 and 356) are focused on Jesus, the star here is Mary, captured in the moment she ascends to heaven. Angels—with their angular wings jutting out in all directions—whisk Mary off into the sky as the 12 apostles watch in wonder. Just above Mary, appreciate the remarkably intricate tangle of vines. Higher up is the heavenly coronation of Mary, who is surrounded by God and Jesus (distinguished by the bushiness of their beards) and the Holy Spirit. The side panels show important scenes from Mary's life: on the left, the Visitation of St. Anne and Annunciation, and on the right, Jesus' birth and presentation in the temple. The church's other, colorful (non-Riemenschneider) altars are also worth a peek, as is the huge mural (on the right wall

of the apse) of St. Christopher—patron saint of travelers—carrying Jesus on his back (€2; April-Oct daily 9:15-18:00; Nov-Dec and Feb-March Tue-Sun 13:00-16:00, closed Mon; closed Jan; tel. 07933/338, www.herrgottskirche.de).

The **Fingerhut Museum**, showing off thimbles (literally, "finger hats"), is far more interesting than it sounds. You'll step from case to case to squint at the collection, which numbers about 4,000 (but still fits in a single room) and comes from all over the world; some pieces are centuries old. There are only a few English descriptions, but they're not really necessary anyway. Owner Thorvald Greif got a head start from his father, who owned a thimble factory (€2, April-Oct Tue-Sun 10:00-12:30 & 14:00-17:00, Nov-Dec and March Tue-Sun 13:00-16:00, closed Mon year-round and Jan-Feb, tel. 07933/370, www.fingerhutmuseum.de).

FROM ROTHENBURG TO AUGSBURG

Dinkelsbühl and Nördlingen (via B-25) are the main attractions between Rothenburg and Augsburg. From Donauwörth, taking the B-2 highway (which parallels the Romantic Road here) can speed up your trip.

▲Dinkelsbühl

Rothenburg's little sister is cute enough to merit a short stop. A moat, towers, gates, and a beautifully preserved medieval wall all

surround this town. Dinkelsbühl is pretty, and a bit less touristy than Rothenburg, but also less exciting. There's not much to say about the place, but it's a delight to simply stroll for an hour or two.

Park at one of the free lots outside the town walls, which are well-signed from the main road (you can park inside the walls, but there's a one-hour limit—not quite enough for a satisfying visit).

To orient yourself, head for the tower of **St. Georg's Cathedral,** at the center of town. This 15th-century church has fine carved altarpieces and a surprisingly light, airy interior. On good-weather summer weekends, you can climb to the top of the tower (€1.50, Fri-Sun 14:00-17:00, enter from outside).

Back outside the church, follow the signs around the corner (first into Ledermarkt, then Altrathausplatz) to the **TI,** which offers a free "Tour of the Town" brochure with a map and short walking tour; they can also help find rooms (May-Oct Mon-Fri 9:00-18:00, Sat-Sun 10:00-17:00; Nov-April daily 10:00-17:00; tel. 09851/902-470, www.dinkelsbuehl.de). In the TI, take a minute to watch the TV monitor showing the stork nest on top of the old Town Hall (also visible at www.storch24.de).

The TI doubles as the ticket office for the fine **City History Museum** (Haus der Geschichte) in the same building (€4, thorough English audioguide, same hours as TI, kids' play area). This shiny, up-to-date museum fills three floors with an exhibit that delves deeply into local history—perhaps too deeply for a casual visitor (though historians will be in heaven). Learn about Dinkelsbühl's location along important north-south travel routes in early times, its role in the Thirty Years' War, and how the tug-of-war between Catholics and Protestants ended in a power-sharing agreement and the loss of the town's medieval prosperity. Rounding out the museum are exhibits on local painters and printers, and temporary exhibits. The self-service movie theater shows short film clips about Dinkelsbühl (in English, plus old silent clips). On the top floor is the large, recently restored town model (Stadtschaue) with only the walls and a few key buildings set up on a medieval street plan.

Entertainment in Dinkelsbühl: You can accompany Dinkelsbühl's **Night Watchman** on his one-hour rounds at 21:00 (in German only, free, May-Oct daily, Nov-April Sat only, meet at St. Georg's Cathedral, not as fun as Night Watchman Tour in Rothenburg). The Kinderzeche **children's festival** turns Dinkelsbühl wonderfully on end for over a week in mid-July, celebrating the success of the local children who pleaded with the Swedish army during the Thirty Years' War, convincing them to spare the town (www.kinderzeche.de).

Sleeping in Dinkelsbühl: Dinkelsbühl has a good selection of hotels, many of them lining the main drag in front of the church. But prices are high—you'll find more choices and lower prices in either Rothenburg or Nördlingen. **$$$ Hezelhof Hotel** is a splurge with 53 sleek, modern rooms in an old shell (Sb-€99-119, Db-€128-168, price varies with room category, elevator, Wi-Fi, pay parking, Segringer Strasse 7, tel. 09851/555-420, www.hezelhof.com, info@hezelhof.com). **$$$ Weisses Ross** ("White Horse") is the traditional choice, with 12 rooms (old bones, but decently maintained). It's attached to a historic restaurant that faces a sleepy square a couple of blocks off the main drag (Sb-€62, Db-€88-98, family room with 4 beds-€110-150, Wi-Fi, free parking, Steingasse 12/17, tel. 09851/579-890, www.hotel-weisses-ross.de, Hotel-Weisses-Ross@t-online.de).

Dinkelsbühl's unique **$ youth hostel,** which fills a picturesque medieval granary, is closed for renovation through summer of 2016 (Koppengasse 10—just steps from the Schweinemarkt, where Romantic Road buses stop once a day in each direction; tel. 09851/9509, www.dinkelsbuehl.jugendherberge.de).

Dinkelsbühl Connections: No trains run to Dinkelsbühl, so you'll have to switch to a bus to get there (in Crailsheim, Ellwangen, or Nördlingen) or take the once-a-day Romantic Road bus.

▲Nördlingen

Though less cute than Dinkelsbühl, Nördlingen is a real workaday town that also has one of the best city walls in Germany, not

to mention a surprising geological history. For centuries, Nördlingen's residents puzzled over the local terrain, a flattish plain called the Ries, which rises to a low circular ridge that surrounds the town in the distance. In the 1960s, geologists figured out that Nördlingen lies in the middle of an impact crater blasted out 15 million years ago by a meteor, which hit earth with the force of 250,000 Hiroshima bombs.

Weekday (all day) and Saturday morning parking at the entrances to the old town (and inside) is limited to 1.5 hours, which isn't really enough time to see the town. Unless visiting on Saturday afternoon or Sunday, drivers should use the big, free lots at the Delninger Tor and the Baldinger Tor or the free parking garage at the Berger Tor.

After parking, head through one of the gates in the wall and into the center of town by zeroing in on the tower of **St. Georg's Church** (yes, the same saint as in Dinkelsbühl). The inside is stripped-down austere—a far cry from the frilly Wieskirche two hours to the south. It's clear that Nördlingen and Wies straddle the Protestant-Catholic boundary.

Climb Nördlingen's **church tower** (which locals call "the Daniel") for sweeping views over the almost perfectly circular Old Town. The rickety 350-step climb up the tower (€3, daily 10:00-18:00, Oct-April until 16:00, enter from outside the church—next to church entrance) rewards you with the very best view of the city walls and crater. You'll twist up a tight stone staircase, then tackle several flights of wooden ones—passing a giant wheel once used to winch materials up into the tower. Higher up is a modern winch used today. From the top, take a slow 360-degree spin; it's easy to visualize how the trees on the horizon sit upon the rim of the meteorite crater.

The small square next to the church's main entrance is called Marktplatz, and just behind the step-gabled Rathaus (Town Hall) is the **TI,** which gives out free town maps with a basic town walking tour brochure (Easter-Oct Mon-Thu 9:30-18:00, Fri 9:30-16:30, Sat 10:00-14:00, closed Sun except July-Aug Sun 10:00-

Maypoles

Along the Romantic Road and throughout Bavaria, you'll see colorfully ornamented maypoles *(Maibaum)* decorating town squares. Many are painted in Bavaria's colors, white and blue. The decorations that line each side of the pole symbolize the craftspeople and businesses of that community (similar to the Chamber of Commerce billboards that greet visitors to small American towns today). Originally these allowed passing traders to quickly determine whether their services were needed in that town. The decorations are festively replaced each May Day (May 1). Traditionally, rival communities try to steal each other's maypole. Locals guard their new pole night and day as May Day approaches. Stolen poles are ransomed only with lots of beer for the clever thieves.

14:00, shorter hours and closed Sat-Sun Nov-Easter, Marktplatz 2, tel. 09081/84116, www.noerdlingen.de).

Now walk out the bottom of Marktplatz and down Baldinger Strasse (past the Rathaus). At the traffic light, turn right and then left, past the skippable Stadtmuseum (town history, obscure local artists, and very little English), to the **Ries Crater Museum** (Rieskrater-Museum). Ask them to play the two 10-minute English films, which explain meteors and the formation of the solar system. The exhibits are well-presented, but only described in German. For English information, you must shell out €3.30 to borrow a dry and detailed English guidebook, or pay €1 for basic photocopied explanations. Unfortunately, the language barrier makes this sight less rewarding than it could be (€4, May-Oct Tue-Sun 10:00-16:30, Nov-April Tue-Sun 10:00-12:00 & 13:30-16:30, closed Mon year-round, Eugene-Shoemaker-Platz 1, tel. 09081/84710, www.noerdlingen.de).

If you can spare the time, walk all the way around on the top of the **town wall**, which is even better preserved than Rothenburg's or Dinkelsbühl's. Circle back to Baldinger Strasse and continue to the Baldinger Tor (tower). This is one of five towers where you can climb the stairs to the walkway along the wall. From here, stroll atop the wall back to the lot where your car is parked (or, for a longer walk, first detour to the City Wall Museum—described next). The city started building the wall in 1327 and financed it with a tax on wine and beer; it's more than a mile and a half long, has 16 towers and five gates, and offers great views of backyards and garden furniture.

For those with extra time, a **City Wall Museum** (Stadtmauermuseum) is in the Löpsinger Tor. You can climb 108 steps to the tower's top level, pausing at each level to peruse endearing exhibits about the wall and town history (€2, April-Oct Tue-Sun 10:00-16:30, closed Mon and Nov-March). If you have the time or energy for only one climb, the view from the church tower is far better—and far higher.

Sleeping in Nördlingen: Several small hotels surrounding St. Georg's Church vie for your business with mediocre but reasonably priced rooms. Of these, try **$$ Hotel Altreuter,** over an inviting bakery/café (Sb-€38-54, Db-€56-68, prices depend on room size, non-smoking, lots of stairs, Marktplatz 11, tel. 09081/4319, www.hotel-altreuter.de, mail@hotel-altreuter.de).

Nördlingen Connections: Nördlingen is reachable by train (change in Donauwörth).

Harburg

You can't miss this town, thanks to the impressively intact, 900-year-old castle that looms high on a bluff over the river. Unusually well-preserved from the Middle Ages (not a Romantic Age rebuild), it's still owned by the noble Wallerstein family. Locals enjoy repeating the story of how, years ago, Michael Jackson tried to buy this place—which he termed "the castle of my dreams."

Augsburg

Founded more than 2,000 years ago by Emperor Augustus, Augsburg enjoyed its heyday in the 15th and 16th centuries. Today, it's Bavaria's third-largest city (population 278,000). It lacks must-see sights, but the old town is pleasant, especially the small streets below the main square, where streams diverted from the River Lech run alongside pedestrians (www.augsburg.de).

FROM AUGSBURG TO FÜSSEN

From Augsburg, you can either continue south to Füssen on two-lane B-17, or you can hop on A-8, which brings you quickly into Munich (in about an hour).

Landsberg am Lech

Like many towns in this area, Landsberg (on the River Lech) has its roots in the salt trade. Every four years, the town returns to its medieval roots and hosts the Ruethenfest. The town was shaped by the architect Dominikus Zimmerman (of Wieskirche fame). Adolf Hitler wrote *Mein Kampf* while serving his prison sentence here after the Beer Hall Putsch of 1923 (when Hitler and his followers unsuccessfully attempted to take over the government of Bavaria).

About 30 miles south of Landsberg, the nondescript village of **Rottenbuch**, near the Wieskirche, has an impressive church in a lovely setting.

▲▲Wieskirche

This is Germany's most glorious Baroque-Rococo church, beautifully restored and set in a sweet meadow. Romantic Road buses (described next) stop here for about 20 minutes—but the church is open only during the northbound Füssen-to-Frankfurt run. Southbound buses stop here for an exterior-only photo op (see the full Wieskirche description on page 158 of the Bavaria and Tirol chapter, which also covers Füssen).

The Romantic Road Bus

From mid-April to late October, the Deutsche Touring company runs daily tour buses that roughly follow the Romantic Road. One bus per day goes from Frankfurt to Munich to Füssen, and another goes from Füssen to Munich to Frankfurt. While this bus tour was once a traveler's dream, it has become less special in recent years—with higher prices, just one daily departure (compared to hourly train connections on these same routes), slow travel times, and fewer (and shorter) sightseeing stops than before. Even so, the bus is still worthwhile if you have no car but want to catch a fleeting glimpse of the towns along the Romantic Road, or if you're planning an overnight stay in a town that's poorly served by train (such as Dinkelsbühl). The bus also offers the convenience of a direct connection between towns where you'd have to transfer if traveling by train, such as between Rothenburg and the cities of Munich and Frankfurt.

The Frankfurt-Rothenburg leg passes through the small towns in the Tauber River Valley (Bad Mergentheim, Weikersheim, and Creglingen), but only stops to pick up and drop off passengers. The Rothenburg-Munich leg includes a 45-minute stop in Dinkelsbühl and 30 minutes in Augsburg—just enough for a glimpse of each. Between Füssen and Munich, the bus stops at the Wieskirche for 20 minutes—on the northbound bus, that's just enough time to peek into the church (the southbound bus stops after the church is closed). Be warned that in case of delays, these stops can be shortened.

Frankfurt to Rothenburg costs €45, Rothenburg to Munich is €38, and Munich to Füssen is €27 (each about the same as the train). The entire ride (Frankfurt to Füssen) costs €108. Pay by cash on the bus. Students and seniors—without a rail pass—get a 10

Romantic Road Bus Schedule

The Romantic Road bus runs daily from mid-April to late October. Every day, one bus goes north to south (Frankfurt to Munich to Füssen), and another follows the reverse route south to north (Füssen to Munich to Frankfurt). You can begin or end your journey at any of these stops. The following times include only the main stops, based on the 2014 schedule. In Munich, the bus stops at the central bus station (ZOB), not the train station. The bus also stops in other towns, including Bad Mergentheim, Weikersheim, Creglingen, Nördlingen, Harburg, Augsburg, the Wieskirche, and Hohenschwangau. Check the full schedule at www.romanticroadcoach.de for any changes.

North to South

Depart Frankfurt	8:00
Arrive Würzburg	9:40
Depart Würzburg	9:55
Arrive Rothenburg	11:55
Depart Rothenburg	12:50
Arrive Dinkelsbühl	13:40
Depart Dinkelsbühl	14:25
Arrive Munich	17:55
Depart Munich	17:55
Arrive Wieskirche	19:25
Depart Wieskirche	19:40
Arrive Füssen	20:20

South to North

Depart Füssen	8:00
Arrive Wieskirche	8:35
Depart Wieskirche	8:55
Arrive Munich	10:30
Depart Munich	10:30
Arrive Dinkelsbühl	14:15
Depart Dinkelsbühl	15:00
Arrive Rothenburg	15:45
Depart Rothenburg	16:35
Arrive Würzburg	18:05
Depart Würzburg	18:20
Arrive Frankfurt	20:00

percent discount. You can get a 20 percent discount on your bus ticket if you have a German rail pass, Global Pass, or Select Pass (if Germany is one of your selected countries). You don't have to activate the use of a travel day of a flexipass to get this discount; if bus drivers say it takes a travel day, set them straight.

Bus reservations are almost never necessary. But they are free and easy, and, technically, without one you can lose your seat to someone who has one (reserve online at www.romanticroadcoach. de; info tel. 09851/555-3800). The main ticket office is in Frankfurt (see page 435); there's also a ticket office at the ZOB in Munich.

Bus stops are not well-signed, but their location in each town is listed on the bus brochure and website. Look for a small *Touring* or *Romantische Strasse* sign.

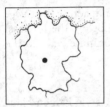

WÜRZBURG

A historic mid-sized city, Würzburg (VEWRTS-boorg) is worth a stop to see its impressive prince-bishop's Residenz and the palace's sculpted gardens. Surrounded by vineyards and filled with atmospheric *Weinstuben* (wine bars), this tourist-friendly town is easy to navigate by foot or streetcar. Today, 25,000 of its 130,000 residents are students—making the town feel young and very alive. It's also popular both with bike tourists (who enjoy the four-day pedal between Bamberg and here) and with river cruises.

While the town isn't all that charming (thanks to its unmistakable post-WWII-rebuild vibe), Würzburg's palace is one of Germany's most enjoyable to tour, and its rebuilt old center is quiet and welcoming. While you're here, be sure to stroll the city's atmospheric bridge. Lined with stone statues, surrounded by vineyard-laced hills, and with a stout fortress looming overhead, it feels like a low-rent version of Prague's famous Charles Bridge.

PLANNING YOUR TIME

Würzburg has a few hours' worth of sightseeing. Begin at the Residenz (prince-bishop's palace), then take my self-guided walk through town to the Old Main Bridge. With more time, cross the bridge and hike up to the hilltop Marienberg Fortress.

Orientation to Würzburg

Würzburg's old town core huddles along the bank of the Main (pronounced "mine") River. The tourists' Würzburg is bookended by the opulent Residenz (at the east end of downtown) and the

---

Würzburg's Beginnings

The city was born centuries before Christ at an easy-to-ford part of the Main River under an easy-to-defend hill. A Celtic fort stood where the fortress stands today. Later, three Irish missionary monks came here to Christianize the local barbarians. In A.D. 686, they were beheaded, and their relics put Würzburg on the pilgrimage map. About 500 years later, when the town was the seat of a bishop, Holy Roman Emperor Frederick Barbarossa came here to get the bishop's OK to divorce his wife. The bishop said, "No problem," and the emperor thanked him by giving him secular rule of the entire region of Franconia. From then on, the bishop was also a prince, and the prince-bishop of Würzburg answered only to the Holy Roman Emperor.

---

hill-capping Marienberg Fortress (at the west end, across the river). You can walk from the Residenz to the river (below the fortress) in about 15 minutes; the train station is a 15-minute walk to the north.

TOURIST INFORMATION

Würzburg's helpful TI is in the yellow Rococo-style Falken Haus on Market Square (May-Oct Mon-Fri 10:00-18:00, Sat-Sun 10:00-14:00; April and Nov-Dec same hours but closed Sun; Jan-March Mon-Fri 10:00-16:00, Sat 10:00-14:00, closed Sun; Market Square, tel. 0931/372-398, www.wuerzburg.de). The TI gives out a free city map, books rooms for free, and has plenty of tips about biking along the Main River. If you're continuing on the Romantic Road (see previous chapter), the TI has information on routes and accommodations along the *Romantische Strasse*, including a very helpful route plan in English.

Sightseeing Passes: Ambitious sightseers might benefit from the **Würzburg Welcome Card,** which offers minimal discounts on a few sights and restaurants—but you'll have to visit at least four sights to make it pay off (€3, valid for 7 days, available at TI). Würzburg's Residenz and Marienberg Fortress are covered by Bavaria's 14-day *Mehrtagesticket* (sold at all participating sights; details on page 130).

ARRIVAL IN WÜRZBURG

By Train: Würzburg's train station is user-friendly and filled with services, including lockers (€3-5) and a handy *Reisezentrum* that sells tickets (long hours daily). Walk out of the train station to the small square in front. An information board with a **city map** provides a quick orientation (on small building to the right). Farther right are **WCs** (€1), the **post office,** and the **Romantic Road bus stop** (look for *Touring* sign and schedule—usually platform 13).

To reach your hotel or the Residenz, you can either walk or take a tram (a tram is valuable if you're hauling luggage from the station, but otherwise the city is very walkable).

From the tram cul-de-sac in front of the station, **tram** #1, #2, #3, or #5 will take you one stop to the Juliuspromenade stop, near most recommended hotels. Trams #1, #3, and #5 continue into town: The next stop (Dom) is close to Market Square, the TI, and the recommended Hotel Zum Winzermännle. After that is the Rathaus stop, near the river and the recommended Hotel Alter Kranen. By **foot,** cross over the busy Röntgenring and head up the shop-lined Kaiserstrasse. To reach the Residenz, it's simplest to walk (15 minutes), but you can get part of the way by taking tram #1, #3, or #5 to the Dom stop.

By Car: Drivers entering Würzburg can keep it simple by following signs to the *Residenz* and parking in the vast cobbled square that faces the palace.

HELPFUL HINTS

Festivals: Würzburg—always clever when it comes to trade—tightly schedules its three annual festivals in summer: Mozart (late May-June, with concerts in the Residenz, www.mozartfest-wuerzburg.de), wine (late May-early June, www.weindorf-wuerzburg.de), and the Kiliani Volksfest (first three weeks in July, www.wuerzburg.de/kiliani).

Internet Access: Log Inn Internet Café is near Market Square, down the street behind the Marienkapelle (€3/hour, Mon-Sat 9:00-23:00, Sun 12:00-20:00, Häfnergasse 5). Free Wi-Fi is available in the **library** courtyard that shares space with the TI. Computers are upstairs (€2.40/hour, same hours as TI).

Supermarket: Kupsch, at Domstrasse 10, is just a few doors from City Hall (Mon-Sat 7:00-20:00, closed Sun). Another branch is on Kaiserstrasse, near the train station and recommended hotels.

Bike Rental: Ludwig Körner rents bikes right in the old town, a five-minute walk north of Market Square (€12/24 hours, €9/additional day, Mon-Fri 9:00-18:00, Sat 9:00-14:00, closed Sun, Bronnbachergasse 3, tel. 0931/52340).

Taxi: For a taxi, call 0931/19410.

Launderette: A **Waschhaus** with English instructions is right at the Wörthstrasse stop for the #2 and #4 trams, five stops from Juliuspromenade in the direction of Zellerau (Mon-Sat 7:00-

WÜRZBURG

1. Hotel Würzburger Hof
2. Hotel Barbarossa
3. Hotel Zum Winzermännle
4. City Hotel Schönleber
5. Hotel Dortmunder Hof
6. Hotel Alter Kranen
7. Sankt Josef Hotel
8. Babelfish Hostel
9. Youth Hostel
10. Bürgerspital Weinstuben, Weinhaus & Hockerle
11. Wirtshaus Lämmle
12. Backöfele
13. Weinstube Maulaffenbäck
14. Pasta e Olio
15. Dean & David on Marktplatz
16. Sternbäck
17. Alte Mainmühle
18. Alter Kranen Brauerei-Gasthof & Biergarten
19. Fischbar zum Krebs
20. Stehcafe
21. Bratwurststand am Markt
22. Café Michel
23. Goldene Gans Biergarten
24. Internet Café
25. Grocery
26. Bike Rental
27. Launderette

22:00, Sun 9:00-18:00, Frankfurter Strasse 13a, tel. 0931/416-773).

Tourist Train: While most everything in the city is easily walkable, the tourist train is worth considering for a quick 40-minute loop through town with English headphone commentary (€8, buy tickets on board, leaves at the top of each hour in front of the Residenz, May-Oct 10:00-16:00, June-Sept until 17:00,

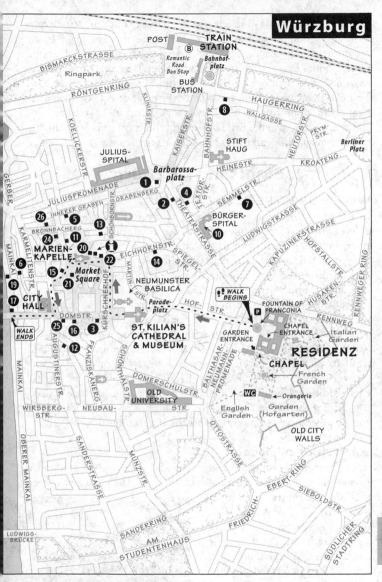

fewer departures and sometimes weekends only off-season,
www.city-tour.info).

GETTING AROUND WÜRZBURG

You can easily walk to everything but the hilltop Marienberg Fortress (doable, but a steep hike). For public transit, the same tickets work on all city bus and tram lines (including the bus up to the fortress). Your options include a short-trip ticket (*Kurzstrecke Eins +4*-€1.25, good for up to four stops; this is all you need to get to my recommended hotels), a single ticket (*Einzelfahrschein*-€2.45, good for 1.5 hours in one direction with transfers), or a day pass (*Tages-karte Solo*-€4.75 for one person, also valid Sun if purchased on Sat). You can buy tickets from the bus driver or at streetside machines near tram stops (marked *Fahrausweise*). Most tickets come pre-stamped; if not, use the little box inside the tram or bus to validate it. For transit info, call 0931/362-320 or visit www.vvm-info.de.

Sights in Würzburg

WÜRZBURG'S RESIDENZ

In the early 18th century, Würzburg's powerful prince-bishop decided to move from his hilltop residence at Marienberg, across the river, into new digs down in the city. His opulent, custom-built, 360-room palace and its associated sights—the chapel (Hofkirche) and garden—are the main attractions of today's Würzburg. The Residenz is impressive, yet quickly taken in; it's less overwhelming to visit than many other European royal palaces.

Getting There: Don't confuse the Residenz (a 15-minute walk southeast of the train station) with Marienberg Fortress (on the hilltop across the river). The Residenz is the far more important sight to visit. Easy parking is available in front of the Residenz (open 24/7, get ticket as you enter, €1.50/hour for first 2 hours, €1/each additional hour, pay at machine marked *Kasse* before leaving). Enter the palace through the main door at the middle of the sprawling complex (directly behind the big fountain).

▲▲Residenz Palace

This Franconian Versailles features grand rooms, 3-D art, and a massive fresco by Giovanni Battista Tiepolo. The palace has three sections: the central main rooms (open to all), the North Wing (open to all), and the South Wing (with the dazzling Mirror Cabinet, viewable only with a tour). I've described all three sections of the palace on my self-guided tour, below.

Cost and Hours: €7.50, includes guided tour, daily April-Oct 9:00-18:00, Nov-March 10:00-16:30, last entry 30 minutes before closing, no photos, tel. 0931/355-170 or 0931/355-1712, www.residenz-wuerzburg.de.

Sightseeing Strategies and Tours: A guided tour is included with your ticket and covers the main rooms (vestibule, Tiepolo fresco, White Hall, Imperial Hall), along with the otherwise inaccessible South Wing (tours last 45-60 minutes; English tours daily at 11:00 and 15:00, April-Oct also at 16:30; never full, just show up and wait in the vestibule; more tours in German: 2-3/hour). The English tour, while good, isn't worth planning your day around. To see everything worthwhile in the Residenz, follow my self-guided tour (or consider the €5 English guidebook), and then jump onto any German tour heading into the South Wing from the Imperial Hall. You can do the history rooms behind the gift shop on your own.

Services: You'll find free WCs on the right as you exit the ticket office.

⊘ Self-Guided Tour

The following self-guided tour gives you the basics to appreciate the palace, whether visiting it on your own or with a tour.

• *Begin at the entrance.*

Vestibule

This indoor area functioned as a grand circular driveway, exclusively for special occasions—just right for six-horse carriages to drop off their guests at the base of the stairs. This area is relatively dark and serves as a good springboard for the dazzling palace that awaits.

Garden Hall

Before climbing the formal staircase, pop into the adjacent Garden Hall, where the garden and the palace meet. The ceiling was painted by Johann Zick in 1750. Notice how he portrays his subjects without Greek-style idealism; they're shown realistically and in high contrast—quite edgy for the time.

• *Return to the vestibule, dress up in your imagination...and ascend the stairs.*

Grand Staircase

The elegant stairway comes with low steps, enabling high-class ladies to glide up gracefully, heads tilted back to enjoy Europe's largest and grandest fresco opening up above them. Hold your lady's hand high and get into the ascending rhythm. Enjoy the climb.

• *As you reach the top of the stairs, look up at the...*

Tiepolo Fresco

In 1752, the Venetian master Giovanni Battista Tiepolo was instructed to make a grand fresco illustrating the greatness of Europe, Würzburg, and the prince-bishop. And he did—completing the world's largest fresco (more than 7,000 square feet) in only 13 months. (The prince-bishop was in a rush to finish furnishing his new home in time for a visit from Habsburg Empress Maria Theresa.) Tiepolo was a master of three-dimensional illusion—and here, he employs one of his favorite tricks, with actual 3-D feet and other features breaking the frame of his faux 3-D frescoes.

The ceiling celebrates the esteemed prince-bishop, who smirks in the medallion with a red, ermine-trimmed cape. This guy had a healthy ego. The ceiling features Apollo (in the sunburst) and a host of Greek gods, all paying homage to the P-B. Ringing the room are the four continents, each symbolized by a woman on an animal and pointing to the prince-bishop. Walk the perimeter of the room to study and enjoy the symbolism of each continent one by one:

America—desperately uncivilized—sits naked with feathers in her hair on an alligator among severed heads. (Notice the cannibal BBQ going on just to the right. Eeew.) She's being served hot chocolate, a favorite import and nearly a drug for Europeans back then. The black cloud hovering ominously above her head symbolizes (with great subtlety) how unenlightened Europeans of the time considered this savage continent to be.

Africa sits on a camel in a land of trade (notice the blue vase, the ivory tusk, and the kneeling servant with wafting frankincense) and fantasy animals (based on secondhand reports, and therefore inaccurate—the ostrich has human-like legs). Father Nile, with his blue cloak, represents the river by pouring water from a jug.

Asia rides her elephant (with the backward ear) in the birthplace of Christianity (notice the crosses on the hill) and the alphabet (carved into the block beneath the obelisk).

Europe, who rides a bull, is shown as the center of high culture. And here, Lady Culture points her brush not at Rome, but at Würzburg. A few portraits are hiding out in this area. The big dog is sniffing the purple-clad architect of the Residenz building. And Tiepolo includes a self-portrait as well: Find the burgundy-clad fellow in the corner just to the left, between the heads of the two white statues.

The White Hall

This hall—with four big paintings portraying various prince-bishops—is actually gray (to provide better contrast) and was kept plain to punctuate the colorful rooms on either side. Also completed at a breakneck pace to meet the Maria Theresa deadline, it's a Rococo-stucco fantasy. (The word "Rococo" comes from the Portuguese word for the frilly rocaille shell.) The stucco decorations (particularly in the corners) have an armor-and-weapons theme, as this marked the entrance to the prince-bishop's private apartments—which had to be carefully guarded. Even the cloth-like yellow decorations above those weapons, draped high in the corners, are made of painted stucco. As you observe the stucco, dripping with symbolism that celebrates the prince-bishop, notice how the Rococo style is free from the strict symmetry of the Baroque. Also notice the stove, which heated the room. There's one in each room, all stoked from service hallways behind. The four gold cupids symbolize the seasons.

• *Straight ahead is the palace gift shop, which leads to a few other interesting rooms. Instead, from the White Hall, continue to your left, following signs for* Rundgang/Circuit.

The Imperial Hall

Enjoy the artistic ensemble of this fine room in its entirety and feel its liveliness. This glorious hall—which was smartly restored—is the ultimate example of Baroque: harmony, symmetry, illusion, and the bizarre; lots of light and mirrors facing windows; and all with a foundation of absolutism (a divine monarch, inspired by Louis XIV). Take a moment to marvel at all the 3-D tricks in the ceiling. Here's another trick: As you enter the room, look left and check out the dog in the fresco (at the top of the pillar). When you get to the window, have another look...notice that he has gotten older and fatter while you were crossing the hall.

The room features three scenes: On the ceiling, find Father Main (the local river—I call him "Dirty Old Man River") amusing himself with a nymph, whose blue shroud breaks the frame as it flows and flutters down the wall (subtly shifting from 3-D illusion to three actual dimensions). The two walls tell more history. On one (to the right as you enter), the bishop presides over the marriage (in 1156, but with more modern dress) of a happy Barbarossa (whose bride was actually 12 years old, unlike the woman in the painting, who looks considerably older; for more on Barbarossa, see the "Würzburg's Beginnings" sidebar, earlier). The bishop's power is demonstrated through his oversized fingers (giving the benediction) and through the details of his miter (tall hat), which—unlike his face—is not shown in profile, to allow you to see his coat of arms. Opposite that (left wall as you enter) is the pay-off: Barbarossa, now the Holy Roman Emperor, gives the bishop Franconia and the secular title of prince. Notice the bishop touching Barbarossa's scepter with two fingers, performing an oath of fealty. From this point onward, the prince-bishop rules. Also in the Imperial Hall, the balcony offers a great vantage point for surveying the Italian section of the garden.

The North Wing (Northern Imperial Apartments)

This wing is a string of lavish rooms—evolving from fancy Baroque to fancier Rococo—used for the prince-bishop's VIP guests. It's a straight shot, with short English descriptions in each room, to the **Green Lacquered Room** in the far corner. This room is named for its silver-leaf walls, painted green. The Escher-esque inlaid floor was painstakingly restored after WWII bombings. Have fun multiplying in the mirrors before leaving.

Keep going through a few more small rooms, which serve as a gallery for paintings, and then step out into the **hallway**. In this area, look for the little four-foot-tall doors that were used by tiny servants who kept the stoves burning, unseen from inside the walls. Also in the hallway are photos of the building's destruction in the 1945 firebombing of Würzburg, and its subsequent restoration. While about three-quarters of the Residenz was destroyed during World War II, the most precious parts—the first rooms on this tour, including the Tiepolo frescoes—were unscathed, partly because these important halls were located in a stout stone structure rather than a more fragile wooden one. A temporary roof saved the palace from total ruin, but it was not until the late 1970s that it was returned to more or less its original condition.

The South Wing (by Tour Only)

From the Imperial Hall, you'll need to join a passing tour to visit the South Wing (included with admission; tours in German go more frequently; this part of the guided tour takes about 15 minutes). Here's what you'll see:

The South Wing is dark and woody and feels more masculine than the North Wing. In this wing's string of rooms, you'll first come to the waiting room (antechamber), the audience chamber/throne room (with circa-1700 Belgian tapestries showing scenes from the life of Alexander the Great), and the Venetian Room (which was a bedroom; note the three tapestries, made around 1740 in Würzburg). The rooms become progressively more ornate until you reach the South Wing's climax: the Mirror Cabinet.

The 18th-century **Mirror Cabinet** was where the prince-bishop showed off his amazing wealth. It features six lavish pounds of gold leaf, lots of Asian influence, an allegory of one of the four continents in each corner, and painted figures on the reverse side of glass. Because it couldn't be removed, it was destroyed by WWII bombing raids in 1945. The doors in this room are original, but everything else was restored in the 1980s based on photos taken by the Nazis, who knew that regardless of how the war turned out, Germany would be rebuilding.

The **Art Gallery** room is next, with portraits of different prince-bishops who ruled until the early 1800s, when Napoleon said, "Enough of this nonsense" and secularized politics in places like Franconia.

You can leave the escorted tour at this point and explore the **history exhibit**, including Napoleonic-age furniture and a barbaric carousel where children competed to lop off papier-mâché heads and noses—illustrating child-oriented violent games long before videogames were known (all described in English). This route eventually leads to the **gift shop**.

• *Finish your tour of the Residenz at the Court Chapel (described next). To get there, head back down the stairs to the vestibule and go outside. Turn left, and walk about 20 steps to the southern wing of the big complex. An arch leads left into a courtyard, from which a humble door leads into the magnificent chapel. Follow signs to* Court Chapel/Hofkirche.

▲▲Court Chapel (Hofkirche)

This sumptuous chapel was for the exclusive use of the prince-bishop (private altar upstairs with direct entrance to his residence) and his

court (ground floor). The decor and design are textbook Baroque. Architect Johann Balthasar Neumann was stuck with the existing walls. His challenge was to bring in light and create symmetry—essential to any Baroque work. He did it with mirrors and hidden windows. All the gold is real—if paper-thin—gold leaf. The columns are "manufactured marble," which isn't marble at all but marbled plaster. This method was popular because it was uniform, and the color could be controlled. Pigment was mixed into plaster, which was then rolled onto the stone or timber core of the column. This half-inch veneer was then polished. You can tell if a "marble" column is real or fake by resting your hand on it. If it warms up, it's not marble.

The faded painting in the dome high above the altar shows three guys in gold robes losing their heads (for more on these martyred Irish monks, see the "Würzburg's Beginnings" sidebar). The two side paintings are by the great fresco artist Tiepolo. Since the fresco plaster wouldn't dry in the winter, Tiepolo spent his downtime painting with oil.

Cost and Hours: Free, same hours as Residenz.

Residenz Garden

One of Germany's finest Baroque gardens is a delightful park cradling the palace. It has three sections: English, Austrian, and Italian. The Austrian section, just inside the gate, features statues of Greek gods (with lots of kidnapping action); carefully trimmed, remarkably conical, 18th-century yew trees; and an orangery (at the far back). The English section (to the right) is like a rough park. The Italian section, directly behind the palace around to the left, is grand—à la Versailles—but uses terraces to create the illusion of spaciousness (since it was originally hemmed in by the town wall).

Behind the Austrian section's orangery is the replanted palace kitchen garden.

Cost and Hours: Free, open daily until dusk—20:00 at the latest, enter through gate at right of Residenz building. WCs are to the right as you come in the main entrance, next to the orangery.

Würzburg Walk

This one-hour self-guided walk gets you from the Residenz, which you may want to tour first, to the Old Main Bridge (Alte Mainbrücke) via the key old-town sights. (If you're not touring the Residenz before taking this walk, you can start at St. Kilian's Cathedral.)

• *Begin at the fountain in front of the Residenz palace.*

Fountain of Franconia

In 1814, the prince-bishop got the boot, and the region of Franconia was secularized and given to the Bavarian Wittelsbach dynasty. Technically, Franconia is a part of Bavaria, but calling a Franconian a Bavarian is like calling a Scot an Englishman. This statue—a gift from the townspeople to their then-new royal family—turns its back to the palace and faces the town. It celebrates the artistic and intellectual genius of Franconia with statues of three great hometown boys (a medieval bard, the woodcarver Tilman Riemenschneider, and the Renaissance painter Matthias Grünewald).

• *If Franconia hopped down and ran 300 yards ahead down Hofstrasse, she'd hit the twin-spired cathedral. Meet her there. As you walk, think about how the city was essentially destroyed in 1945 and later rebuilt. At the cathedral, circle around the right, and enter the church through its side door (before the underground passage and across from the modern cathedral museum).*

St. Kilian's Cathedral (Dom)

This building's core is Romanesque (1040-1188), with Gothic spires and Baroque additions to the transepts. It was built as a Catholic church and stayed that way after the Reformation.

Cost and Hours: Free, daily 8:00-19:00, tel. 0931/3866-2870, www.dom-wuerzburg.de.

Visiting the Church: The cathedral was destroyed in World War II and rebuilt in the 1960s with a passion for mixing historic and modern styles. Before 1945, the entire church was

slathered in Baroque stucco decor, as the apse is today. The nave has a cohesive design, progressing from the menorah (representing the Old Testament) in the back, past tombstones of centuries of prince-bishops and a crucified Jesus (above the high altar), to the apse, where a resurrected Christ, riding a golden disc, welcomes you into a hopeful future. The skulls of Würzburg's three favorite saints—those Irish monks martyred in the seventh century—lie in a box within the altar (see "Würzburg's Beginnings" sidebar, earlier).

Halfway along the nave (on the left side, as you face the altar) is a fine memorial to the 15th-century Prince-Bishop Rudolf von

Scherenberg, whose name means "scissors man" (see his coat of arms). Scherenberg ruled until he was 94 years old. Carved by Tilman Riemenschneider, this tombstone is an example of late-Gothic realism. Back then, it was outrageous to portray an old bishop as...an old bishop (looking at the tombstone, you can tell he needs dentures). The next prince-bishop, whose tomb is to the right of Scherenberg's, saw how realistic his predecessor's was, and insisted on having an idealized portrait (also by Riemenschneider) done to his satisfaction before he died. (He's looking implausibly dashing.)

• *Leave the church the way you entered—behind Mr. Scissors, through the low-key side door, and up four steps. Outside, look up at the three martyrs (before they were beheaded), high on the building opposite. Walk a few steps downhill (to the left) and notice, embedded in the cathedral wall, the tomb of the great local artist Riemenschneider, placed here after the church's cemetery was moved. If you're interested in a fresh take on religious art, go into the modern Cathedral Museum across the way. Otherwise, skip ahead and continue downhill through the tunnel on your way to the basilica.*

Cathedral Museum (Museum am Dom)

This museum features a refreshing, poignant juxtaposition of old and new religious art, managing to be provocative in a constructive way. It pairs 11th- to 18th-century works with modern interpretations, sprinkles it all with a Christian theme, and wraps it in a shiny modern building. With an emphasis on more cutting-edge contemporary works, it does an impressive job of respecting "religious art" for both its artistic and spiritual sides.

Cost and Hours: €3.50, €4.50 combo-ticket includes Cathedral Treasury, April-Oct Tue-Sun 10:00-18:00, Nov-March Tue-Sun 10:00-17:00, closed Mon, tel. 0931/3866-5600, www. museum-am-dom.de.

• *Upon leaving the museum, hook right through a tunnel, which emerges on a delightful urban scene. Straight ahead, Domstrasse leads down to the spire of the City Hall and the Old Main Bridge (where this walk will end). But we're looping right. Go a block up Kurschner Hof, where a staircase leads into the...*

Neumünster Basilica

Like the cathedral, this church has a Romanesque body with a Baroque face. Climb the stairs to take a look inside, appreciating the church's rounded Romanesque nave decorated (like the outside) with bubbly Baroque stucco.

Return to Kurschner Hof and continue up the street, noticing the vineyards in the distance. Appreciate this quiet pedestrian zone. Locals wouldn't have it any other way—electric trolleys, bikes, and pedestrians in a vital and thriving commercial zone.

• *Enter the square on the left with the lacy, two-tone church.*

Upper Market Square

Imagine this square during the wine fest in June—with 75 vintners showing off their best wines—or during the Christmas market, when the square is full of quaint stalls selling holiday goodies. The fancy yellow-and-white, Rococo-designed Falken Haus (House of the Falcon) dates from 1751, when the landlady gave a wandering band of stucco artists a chance to show their stuff (inside are the TI and library).

• *Head farther downhill, passing the church on your right, into the main Market Square. Find the obelisk.*

Market Square (Marktplatz)

Würzburg's Marktplatz is a great scene. The obelisk, built in 1805, has a relief showing romantic maidens selling fruits, a hare, and other items. To this day, the square is host to a bustling produce and flower market (May-Oct Tue-Wed and Fri-Sat 8:00-16:00). Facing the church, find the modern statue nicknamed "Market Barbara" *(Markt Barbel)*, which recalls a traditional merchant woman. From there, stretching toward the church, a line often leads to the recommended **Bratwurststand am Markt**, where sausage sandwiches are made and sold to an eager local crowd. (Watch the wiener-folding action through the side window.) Beyond that, nestled under the church, is the recommended **Stehcafe**, a venerable choice for a quick coffee and cake while people-watching.

Marienkapelle

The two-tone late-Gothic church was the merchants' answer to the prince-bishop's cathedral. Since Rome didn't bankroll the place, it's ringed with "swallow shops" (like swallows' nests cuddled up against a house)—enabling the church to run little businesses. The sandstone statues (in the small alcoves partway up the columns; they're replicas of Riemenschneider originals) depict the 12 apostles and Jesus. The famous Adam and Eve statues (flanking the side entrance to the church) show off Riemenschneider's mastery of the human body. Continue around the church to the west portal, where the carved Last Judgment (above the main doors) shows kings, ladies, and bishops—some going to heaven, others making up the chain gang bound for hell, via the monster's mouth. (This was commissioned by those feisty town merchants tired of snooty bluebloods.) Continue around to the next entry (which faces a *Biergarten* under chestnut trees) to see the Annunciation, with a cute angel Gabriel telling Mary (who is a virgin, symbolized by the lilies) the good news. Notice how God whispers through a speaking tube as Baby Jesus slips down and into her ear.

• *Go back around to the market (Adam-and-Eve side) and leave—passing the obelisk—in the direction of the yellow building. Follow Schustergasse, a pedestrian lane lined with shops that leads back to Domstrasse (with tram tracks). The cathedral is on your left, while the City Hall and Old Main Bridge are to the right. Head right to the City Hall's tower.*

City Hall (Rathaus)

Würzburg's City Hall is relatively humble because of the power of the prince-bishop. As you face the building, go around the left side to find the *Gedenkraum 16 März 1945* (free, always open). This commemorates the 20-minute Allied bombing raid on March 16, 1945, and the resulting firestorm that destroyed (and demoralized) Würzburg six weeks before the end of World War II. The damage was almost as bad as in Dresden: Nearly every downtown building was reduced to a shell, with roofs, floors, and windows gone. Most residents survived in bomb shelters, but 5,000 died—largely women and children. Check out the sobering model of the devastated town, and read the interesting panels about the rise of Nazism and the brutality of war and the hope brought by a spirit of reconciliation.

• *As you leave City Hall, notice the horizontal lines cut into the archway on your right. These mark the floodwaters (Hochstand des Maines) of the years 1342, 1682, and 1784. Now, find the bridge.*

Old Main Bridge (Alte Mainbrücke)

This isn't the town's "main" (as in primary) bridge; rather, it spans the Main (pronounced "mine") River, which flows through Frankfurt and into the Rhine.

The bridge, from 1133, is the second-oldest in Germany. The 12 statues lining the bridge are Würzburg saints and prince-bishops. Walk to the St. Kilian statue (with the golden sword)—one of the three monks who are shown being beheaded in the Residenz Palace's chapel. Squint up at Kilian, still with his head on, pointing to God.

Beyond Kilian you may see river cruise ships moored by the next bridge. The rising popularity of river cruising (from Amsterdam to Budapest) is bringing lots of crowds and business to towns like Würzburg.

High above the city, capping the hill beyond the bridge, is the Marienberg Fortress (described at the end of this walk). And downstream are three stacks marking a power plant. Between here and there find the old crane, built in 1770 to further the city's desirability as a river trading port. Along the embankment near the crane are a recommended beer garden (named for the crane) and a fish-and-chips boat—and lots of people picnicking (see "Eating in Würzburg," later).

The hillside (beyond the crane) is blanketed with grapevines destined to become the fine Stein Franconian wine. Goethe, the great German author often compared to Shakespeare, ordered 900 liters of this vintage annually. A friend once asked Goethe what he thought were the three most important things in life. He said, "Wine, women, and song." The friend then asked, "If you had to give one up, which would it be?" Without hesitating, Goethe answered "Song." Then, when asked what he would choose if he had to give up a second item, Goethe paused and said, "It depends on the vintage."

• *Your walking tour is over. From here, consider having lunch at the recommended Alte Mainmühle restaurant, with a terrace overlooking the bridge (at the near end). On warm summer evenings, the restaurant sets up a little wine stand at the start of the bridge—worth returning to at sunset to buy a glass of wine to sip while you do laps around the bridge. Or you can continue on to the fortress on the hill above you.*

Marienberg Fortress (Festung Marienberg)

This 13th-century fortified retreat was the original residence of Würzburg's prince-bishops (before the opulent Residenz across the river was built). After being stormed by the Swedish army during the 17th-century Thirty Years' War, the fortress was expanded in Baroque style.

Cost and Hours: Grounds—free; Prince's Garden—free, mid-April-Oct daily 9:00-17:30, closed off-season; Prince's Building Museum—€4.50, €6 combo-ticket includes Mainfränkisches Museum, mid-March-Oct Tue-Sun 10:00-17:00, closed Mon and off-season, tel. 0931/355-170, www.schloesser.

bayern.de; Mainfränkisches Museum—€4, €6 combo-ticket includes Prince's Building Museum, April-Oct Tue-Sun 10:00-17:00, Nov-March Tue-Sun 10:00-16:00, closed Mon year-round, tel. 0931/205-940, www.mainfraenkisches-museum.de.

Tours and Information: A 45-minute English-language tour brings the fortress to life from mid-March to October (€3.50, Sat-Sun at 15:00, no tours off-season, buy tickets at museum shop in the inner courtyard). The €2.90 *Marienberg Castle* booklet, available throughout the fortress, is well-written and has basic information on both museums.

Getting There: To walk there, cross the Old Main Bridge and follow small *Festung Marienberg* signs to the right uphill for a heart-thumping 20 minutes. Or, take bus #9 (direction: Festung) to the last stop (Schönborntor) and walk through the tunnel to enter the fortress (runs daily 10:00-18:00 every 45 minutes, times listed at stops, departs from Residenzplatz and Juliuspromenade). Consider taking the bus up and walking down (follow *Fussweg zur Altstadt* signs). Taxis wait near the Old Main Bridge for anyone feeling lazy (€10).

Visiting the Fortress: The **fortress grounds** provide fine city views and a good place for a picnic. You can wander freely through the fortress courtyards and peek into the bottom of the original keep (tower stronghold at the center of the complex) and the round church, where carved relief monuments to former bishops decorate the stone floor. For the best views of the town, go through the archway off the inner courtyard (next to church entrance) into the **Prince's Garden**—look for the *Fürstengarten* sign.

The fortress houses two museums: The **Mainfränkisches Museum,** which highlights the work of Tilman Riemenschneider, Germany's top woodcarver and onetime mayor of Würzburg, is in the red-and-white building at the back of the fortress, near the bus stop. Riemenschneider fans will also find his work throughout Würzburg's many churches (I've described two pieces in the cathedral on page 394). A visitor's guide (in English) directs the way, but it provides little real information.

The **Prince's Building Museum** (Fürstenbaumuseum) is in the inner courtyard. The first floor shows off relics of the prince-bishops (some signs in English), and the second floor focuses on the history of Würzburg (German only). You'll wander through big, mostly empty rooms with a few sparse exhibits and grand Würzburg views through hazy windows.

Sleep Code

Abbreviations   (€1 = about $1.40, country code: 49)
S = Single, **D** = Double/Twin, **T** = Triple, **Q** = Quad, **b** = bath-
room, **s** = shower only.
Price Rankings
 $$$ **Higher Priced**—Most rooms €120 or more.
   $$ **Moderately Priced**—Most rooms between €80-120.
    $ **Lower Priced**—Most rooms less than €80.
Unless otherwise noted, credit cards are accepted, English
is spoken, breakfast is included, and Wi-Fi is generally free.
Prices change; verify current rates online or by email. For the
best prices, always book directly with the hotel.

Sleeping in Würzburg

Würzburg's hotels and hostels are a stress-free option for a first
or last night when flying into or out of Frankfurt. Trains run at
least hourly between Würzburg and Frankfurt's airport; the journey takes 1.5 hours. Hotels will generally discount the prices listed
during slow months—November to April, and sometimes in August as well.

As Würzburg is a convention town, it has ample chain hotels that can be a great value in slow times—consider doing a Web
search for the dates you're in town. My listings are smaller places
with more personality and charm, and rates that are less likely to
fluctuate. In these hotels, quieter rooms are in back, front rooms
have street noise, and all rooms are entertained by church bells.

Most of these listings are less than a 10-minute walk from the
train station and perfectly situated for sightseeing. To reach nearly
all of them, head up Kaiserstrasse from the station to Barbarossaplatz (with the circular awning) or take the tram to the Juliuspromenade stop (one stop after the station). Hotel Zum Winzermännle
and Alter Kranen are closer to the river; consider riding a tram to
the Dom or the Rathaus stops, respectively. If you're driving, you'll
likely have to park in a garage near your hotel (about €8/day) as
street parking is scarce.

$$$ Hotel Würzburger Hof has an elegant lobby and 34
large, Baroque, borderline froufrou rooms right at the Julius-
promenade tram stop. They have two types of rooms: smaller
but perfectly fine "comfort" rooms and larger "superior" rooms—
I've noted the price for each (Sb-€99/€120, Db-€149/€199, Tb-
€219/€249, elevator, guest computer, Wi-Fi, good windows that
dampen street noise, Barbarossaplatz 2, tel. 0931/53814, www.
hotel-wuerzburgerhof.de, info@hotel-wuerzburgerhof.de).

$$ Hotel Barbarossa, tucked away on top of a tall medical-office building above the busy Barbarossaplatz intersection, has a more modern, youthful sensibility than the others listed here and is a good value. Its 17 rooms combine sleek minimalism and a respect for traditional design (Sb-€68-78, Db-€88-98, rooftop terrace, elevator, Wi-Fi, Theaterstrasse 2, fourth floor, tel. 0931/3291-9091, www.hotelbarbarossa-wuerzburg.de, info@ hotelbarbarossa-wuerzburg.de, run by hardworking Christine).

$$ Hotel Zum Winzermännle has 28 bright rooms along a busy pedestrian street in the city center, but its double-paned windows keep things quiet. The atmosphere is simple but tastefully done, in a hotel the Fick family has run for three generations (Sb-€69, Db-€89-99, Tb-€120-140, elevator, Wi-Fi, reception up one floor from street, Domstrasse 32, tel. 0931/54156, www. winzermaennle.de, info@winzermaennle.de, friendly Alexandra and her parents).

$$ City Hotel Schönleber has 33 simple, up-to-date rooms fronting a busy street (S-€45, Sb-€75, D-€70, small twin Db-€79, Db-€89-105 depending on size, Tb-€138, ask for a 10 percent discount when you book directly with the hotel, elevator, guest computer, Wi-Fi, parking in nearby garage-€8/day, from Barbarossaplatz angle left down Theaterstrasse to #5, tel. 0931/304-8900, www. cityhotel-schoenleber.de, reservierung@cityhotel-schoenleber.de, Ulrich Kölbel).

$$ Hotel Dortmunder Hof has 13 simple, bright, slightly musty rooms on a quiet back street. Mellow jazz tunes sometimes play in the cozy restaurant and wine bar, where you'll check in and enjoy a warm welcome (Sb-€48-59, Db-€80-89, Tb-€115-125, family deals, discount if you stay more than one night, wonderful breakfast, elevator, Wi-Fi in common areas and lower-floor rooms, reception in wine bar to right of entrance; from train station, turn right onto Juliuspromenade, then jog left a block onto Innerer Graben, Innerer Graben 22, tel. 0931/56163, www.dortmunder-hof. de, info@dortmunder-hof.de, Hennig-Rink family).

$$ Hotel Alter Kranen has 16 standard rooms with a tidy, business-class vibe right along the river (but only three rooms have views—try requesting one when you reserve). This hotel is farther from the train station than the others listed here, but a bit handier to the Market Square/Old Main Bridge action (Sb-€69, Db-€99, extra bed-€35, cheaper if you stay more than one night, air-con in top-floor rooms only, elevator, Wi-Fi, Kärrnergasse 11, tel. 0931/35180, www.hotel-alter-kranen.de, mail@hotel-alter-kranen.de).

$$ Sankt Josef Hotel, a lesser value, has 33 dated but comfortable rooms. It's located on a street with a pleasant neighborhood feel (Sb-€55-60, Db-€90-100, no elevator, Wi-Fi, reserve ahead for parking-€8/day, reception up one floor from street, from Barbarossaplatz follow Theaterstrasse and take your first left onto Semmelstrasse, Semmelstrasse 28-30, tel. 0931/308-680, www. hotel-st-josef.de, hotel.st.josef@t-online.de, Casagrande family).

Hostels: **$ Babelfish Hostel,** across the street from the station, welcomes travelers of all ages to its 18 rooms. This laid-back place is clean, modern, and feels safe (dorm beds-€17-23 in 4- to 10-bed rooms, Sb-€45, Db-€62—some with kitchenettes, includes sheets, breakfast-€5, guest computer, Wi-Fi, laundry-€5/load, free lockers, kitchen, roof deck, wheelchair-accessible, reception on second floor, Haugering 2, tel. 0931/304-0430, www.babelfish-hostel.de, info@babelfish-hostel.de).

$ Würzburg's official **youth hostel** *(Jugendherberge),* across the river in a former prison, has 238 beds (€26/bed in 4- to 8-bed rooms, a few S-€29, Sb-€32, D-€28/person, Db-€29/person, includes sheets and breakfast, towel rental-€1.50, one-night stays-€2 extra, non-members-€3.50 extra, over 26 years old-€4 extra, slightly cheaper Nov-March, family rooms, Wi-Fi in lobby, no curfew—but get night code; 20-minute walk from station: cross Old Main Bridge and turn left on Saalgasse to Fred-Joseph-Platz 2; or take tram #3 or #5 to Löwenbrücke stop, then follow *Jugendherberge* signs; tel. 0931/42590, www.wuerzburg.jugendherberge.de, wuerzburg@jugendherberge.de).

Eating in Würzburg

IN THE CENTER
Bürgerspital

In medieval times, rich Würzburgers founded charitable foundations to support the city's elderly and poor. They began making and selling wine to fund their charity work, and this tradition continues today. Still occupying grand Baroque complexes, the foundations have restaurants, wine shops, and extensive wine cellars. These are not basic soup kitchens, but well-respected, quite elegant eateries that also happen to support a good cause. The oldest and best-known of these foundations is the Bürgerspital, which now cares for about a hundred local seniors. It's a large complex (on the corner of Theaterstrasse and Semmelstrasse) that provides three options:

Weinstuben Bürgerspital is a candlelit but informal restaurant that serves beautifully presented Franconian specialties. Depending on the weather, you'll dine outside in a fine old courtyard or indoors in traditional or modern rooms (€10-18 main courses, daily 11:00-24:00, enter at Theaterstrasse 19, tel. 0931/352-880).

Weinhaus Bürgerspital, an unintimidating wine shop/tasting room on a busy corner, serves up wine (flights available) and small dishes (€8-13) in a contemporary setting. The staff is happy to educate you on the basics of Franconian wine (Mon 9:00-18:00, Tue-Sun 9:00-24:00, Theaterstrasse 19, tel. 0931/350-3403).

Hockerle, a funky little pub tucked away next door, is my favorite of the three. This unique place, stuck in a time warp, serves wine on tap to locals and outgoing tourists who bring in their own food. The regulars start drinking early (no food, wines listed on blackboard, Mon-Fri 9:00-18:00, Sat 9:00-15:00, closed Sun).

Other Eateries

Wirtshaus Lämmle is just right for a wine garden serving traditional Franconian dishes under chestnut trees with a view of the back side of the Marienkapelle (€9-12 main courses, salads, vegetarian options, Mon-Sat 10:00-24:00, Sun 11:00-16:00, Marienplatz 5, tel. 0931/54748).

Backöfele is a fun hole-in-the-wall (literally, though it's quite big once you enter). Named "The Oven" for its entryway, this place is a hit with Germans, offering a rustic menu full of traditional meat and fish dishes. You can sit inside or in the delightful, glassed-in, cobbled courtyard (€8-20 main courses, daily 12:00-23:00, reservations smart; a couple of blocks beyond City Hall, Ursulinergasse 2; tel. 0931/59059).

Weinstube Maulaffenbäck, hidden in an alley near Market Square with a few outdoor tables, is a characteristic place for cheap Franconian meals and good wine. If you order wine, you're welcome to bring your own food—they'll provide the plate and fork. This is an old tradition unique to Würzburg. If you choose to follow this custom, consider stopping at the butcher shop next door (owned by the same family, open until 18:00) to pick up great cold cuts before finding a table (€4-10 main courses, Mon-Sat 10:00-22:00, closed Sun, Maulhardgasse 9, tel. 0931/52351).

Pasta e Olio, a couple of blocks east of Market Square, is a fun and popular stand-up pasta lunch counter. Because Signora Aucone makes pasta fresh daily, the menu is limited, but usually includes a pasta dish, lasagna, a vegetarian option, and mixed antipasti. Place your order cafeteria style, then eat standing at one of the tables (€4-5 plates, Mon-Fri 11:00-17:00, Sat 11:00-16:00, closed Sun, no WC, Eichhornstrasse 6, tel. 0931/16699). Lots of other cheap, fast, stand-up lunch places—serving various cuisines—are nearby, between here and the Market Square.

Dean & David on Marktplatz is a favorite for a fast, inexpensive, and healthy meal with views of the market action. They have a pleasant modern interior and tables on the square (€6-8 plates, super-fresh salads, veggie dishes, curries, soups, wok plates, sandwiches, smoothies, daily 10:00-21:00, look for modern building kitty-corner from church, Marktplatz 4, tel. 0931/4522-8303).

Sternbäck is an inviting *kneipe* (pub) with rickety tables spilling onto a busy square. This is where locals from all walks of life gather for a drink and cheap eats. The hip, friendly staff can recommend something that will satisfy you (€5-10 plates, Franconian classics, curries, salads, daily 9:00-22:00, breakfast served until 13:00, Sternplatz 4, tel. 0931/54056).

ON THE RIVERFRONT

Alte Mainmühle, on the bridge in a converted mill, is a great place to end your walking tour or enjoy a sunset. On a warm day, nothing beats a cold beer on their deck, which overlooks the river and the fortress—choose from their sunny top-floor terrace or the shade below. (They also run a wine stand on the Old Main Bridge on summer evenings.) If dining inside, I'd sit upstairs rather than in the lower level. They have fresh fish specials and traditional fare with a Franconian twist. Their homemade sourdough bread *(Natursauerteigbrot)* is a delicious nod to their milling history (€7-9 wurst plates, €8-22 main courses, daily 11:00-22:00, Mainkai 1, tel. 0931/16777).

Alter Kranen Brauerei-Gasthof is a youthful eatery with a big beerhall interior and outdoor tables around the old crane overlooking the river (€9-16 traditional plates, try the local brew—Würzburger Hofbräu, table service only, daily 11:00-24:00, a couple of blocks down from the Old Main Bridge at Kranenkai 1, tel. 0931/9913-1545). They kick off evenings with a popular happy hour (cheap beer and cocktails from 17:00-19:00). Their cheaper *Biergarten* cafeteria is next door (and listed next).

Biergarten Alter Kranen is the Alter Kranen Brauerei-Gasthof's adjacent and cheaper beer garden, with a cafeteria serving rustic dishes like currywurst and bratwurst with fries. Tables fill a park-like area on a rampart overlooking the river (€5 main dishes, daily 12:00-23:00, may close in bad weather).

Fischbar zum Krebs, a fun-loving little fish-and-chips boat, is permanently tied up just below the Old Main Bridge. With a commotion of funky tables and plastic chairs, and lots of riverside park benches nearby, it caters to a youthful crowd and is the cheapest meal on the water. They serve local fish—trout, pike-perch, and carp—with English-style malt vinegar and sea salt. Place your order at the counter onboard. You'll have to fetch your own beer, and if ordering beer or wine you have to stay on the boat (€3-6, daily 15:00-22:00, May-Oct only).

Riverfront Picnic: A park-like stretch of riverbank from the Old Main Bridge to the crane is made-to-order for picnicking. There are plenty of benches and a long, inviting concrete embankment to spread out your meal. It comes with beer-drinking students, the down-and-out collecting their bottles, and great views of the river, bridge, and castle.

PLACES FOR A MEMORABLE SNACK OR DRINK

Stehcafe is a fixture, anchored like a Hansel-and-Gretel barnacle to the foot of the church on Market Square. Locals enjoy coffee, cakes, and great people-watching from its humble stand-up tables (daily 6:30-18:00, Marktgasse 3).

Through the day a crowd lines up at **Bratwurststand am Markt,** a nondescript stand on Market Square where you can get a yummy yet simple €2 sausage sandwich with or without mustard (*"mit"* or *"ohne"*—your choice). The line may be long but it moves quickly (Mon-Sat 9:30-6:00, closed Sun, near the obelisk, look for the yellow-and-white awning near the covered walkway).

Café Michel, right on Upper Market Square and next to the TI, is a family-oriented bakery and teahouse with quiet indoor seating and tables on the square. They offer soups, sandwiches, and an impressive selection of cakes and strudels (daily 8:00-18:00, Marktplatz 11).

Goldene Gans Biergarten is a sloppy riverside beer garden on the west side of the river, with wooden benches, shaded views of the Old Main Bridge, bad food, and good beer (€5-10 main courses, daily 11:00-23:00—weather permitting, closed off-season; to the left about a block after you cross the Old Main Bridge).

Würzburg Connections

From Würzburg by Train to: Rothenburg (hourly, 70 minutes, transfer in Steinach; 45 minutes to Steinach, then 15 minutes to Rothenburg; tiny Steinach-Rothenburg train leaves usually from track 5 shortly after the Würzburg train arrives), **Frankfurt Airport** (1-2/hour, 1.5 hours), **Frankfurt** (1-2/hour, 70 minutes, or 2 hours on cheaper RE trains), **Nürnberg** (2-3/hour, 1-1.5 hours), **Munich** (1-2/hour, 2 hours), **Cologne** (hourly, 2.5 hours, some with change in Frankfurt), **Leipzig** (hourly, 3.5-4 hours, transfer in Fulda or Bamberg), **Berlin** (hourly, 4 hours, change in Göttingen or Fulda). Train info: Tel. 0180-599-6633, www.bahn.com.

WÜRZBURG

SPEEDWAY PUBLIC LIBRARY
SPEEDWAY, INDIANA

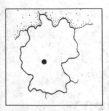

FRANKFURT

Frankfurt, while low on Old World charm, offers a good look at today's no-nonsense, modern Germany. There's so much more to this country than castles and old cobbled squares. Ever since the early Middle Ages, when—as the city's name hints—this was a good place to ford the river, people have gathered here to trade. Frankfurt is a pragmatic city, and its decisions are famously based on what's good for business. Destroyed in World War II? Make that an opportunity to rebuild for trade better than ever. And that's what they did.

With trade came people from around the world. Cosmopolitan Frankfurt—nicknamed "Bankfurt"—is a business hub of the united Europe and home to the European Central Bank. Especially in the area around the train station, you'll notice the fascinating multiethnic flavor of the city. A quarter of its 700,000 residents carry foreign passports. Though it's often avoided by tourists who consider it just a sterile business and transportation hub, Frankfurt's modern energy, fueled in part by the entrepreneurial spirit of its immigrant communities, makes it a unique and entertaining city well worth a look.

PLANNING YOUR TIME

You might fly into or out of Frankfurt am Main, or at least pass through, as this glossy city links the best wine-and-castles stretch of the Rhine to the north with the fairy-tale Romantic Road to the south. Even two or three hours in Frankfurt leaves you with some powerful impressions: The city's main sights can be enjoyed in a half-day by using its train station (a 12-minute ride from the airport) as a springboard. At a minimum, head up to the top of the

Main Tower for commanding city views and wander through the pedestrian zone to the Old Town area (Römerberg). My self-guided walk provides a framework for your explorations. With more time or an overnight, Frankfurt has plenty of museums and other attractions to choose from.

Orientation to Frankfurt

Frankfurt, with its forest of skyscrapers perched on the banks of the Main (pronounced "mine") River, has been dubbed Germany's

"Mainhattan." The city is Germany's trade and banking capital, leading the country in high-rises (mostly bank headquarters)...and yet, a third of Frankfurt is green space.

The convention center *(Messe)* and the red light district are near the train station. Just to the east is the skyscraper banking district and the shopping and pedestrian area around the distinctive Hauptwache building. Beyond that is what remains of Frankfurt's Old Town, around Römerberg, the city's central market square. A short walk across the river takes you to a different part of town: Frankfurt's top museums line the south bank of the Main, and nearby is Sachsenhausen, a residential neighborhood and schmaltzy restaurant zone.

TOURIST INFORMATION

Frankfurt has several TIs. The handiest is inside the **train station**'s main entrance (Mon-Fri 8:00-21:00, Sat-Sun 9:00-18:00, tel. 069/212-38800, www.frankfurt-tourismus.de). Another TI is on **Römerberg square** (Mon-Fri 9:30-17:30, Sat-Sun 9:30-16:00); there's also one at the **airport.** At any TI, buy the city/subway map (the basic €0.50 version is fine). The train station and Römerberg TIs rent iPods loaded with a multimedia city tour (€7.50/4 hours, €10/day; you can download it to your own mobile device from iTunes for €4.50). The TI also offers city bus tours and weekend walking tours (see "Tours in Frankfurt," later).

Discount Deals: Two discount passes compete for your attention, both sold at local TIs. The **Museum Ticket** gets you free entry into 34 museums (€18, valid 2 days). The **Frankfurt Card** gives you a transit pass (including connections to and from the airport), 50 percent off all major museums, and 20 percent off the city bus tour, which virtually pays for the pass (1 person: €9.90/1 day, €14.50/2 days; 2-5 people: €20/1 day, €29.50/2 days). These are both potentially good deals and worth considering if you'll be taking public transportation and visiting several sights.

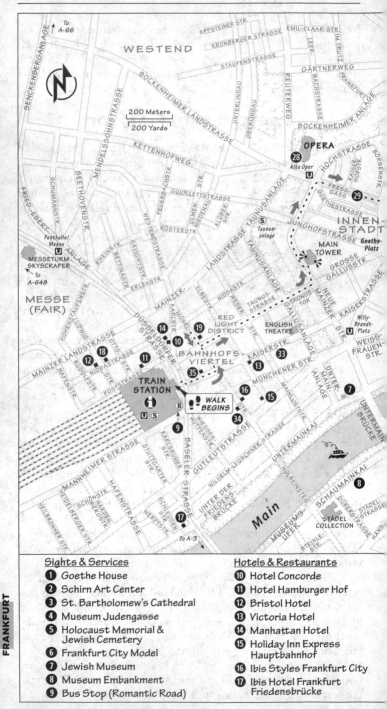

Sights & Services

1 Goethe House
2 Schirn Art Center
3 St. Bartholomew's Cathedral
4 Museum Judengasse
5 Holocaust Memorial & Jewish Cemetery
6 Frankfurt City Model
7 Jewish Museum
8 Museum Embankment
9 Bus Stop (Romantic Road)

Hotels & Restaurants

10 Hotel Concorde
11 Hotel Hamburger Hof
12 Bristol Hotel
13 Victoria Hotel
14 Manhattan Hotel
15 Holiday Inn Express Hauptbahnhof
16 Ibis Styles Frankfurt City
17 Ibis Hotel Frankfurt Friedensbrücke

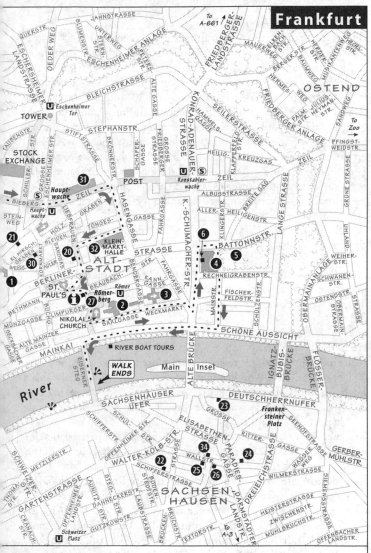

Frankfurt

18 Hotel Topas

19 Five Elements Hostel

20 Hotel Neue Kräme

21 Hotel Zentrum

22 Maingau Hotel

23 Haus der Jugend Hostel

24 Dauth-Schneider Restaurant

25 Atschel Restaurant

26 Fichtekränzi Restaurant

27 Römerberg Eateries

28 Restaurant Opera

29 Fressgass' ("Feeding St.") & Das Wirtshaus Rest.

30 Leib & Seele Restaurant

31 Galeria Kaufhof's Leonhard's Cafeteria

32 Kleinmarkthalle Eateries

33 Kaiserstrasse Eateries

34 Launderettes (2)

35 Internet Access

ARRIVAL IN FRANKFURT

By Train: Frankfurt's main train station (Hauptbahnhof) bustles with travelers. The TI is in the main hall just inside the front door, the least expensive lockers are along track 24 (€3.50-5), and the post office is across from track 24 (closed Sun). Pay WCs and showers are down the stairway by tracks 9 and 10. Inquire about train tickets in the *Reisezentrum,* off the main hall (long hours daily).

Getting out of the station can be a bit tricky. Use the underground passageway *(Bahnhofspassage)* and follow the signs, or better yet, exit straight out the main door or the side doors near tracks 1 and 24 to reach a crosswalk. The station is a five-minute walk from the convention center *(Messe),* a three-minute subway ride or 20-minute walk from Römerberg, and a 12-minute shuttle train ride from the airport.

By Plane: See "Frankfurt Connections," at the end of this chapter.

By Car: Follow signs for *Frankfurt,* then *Messe,* and finally *Hauptbahnhof* (train station). The Hauptbahnhof garage (€29/day) is under the station, near most recommended hotels. For information on parking elsewhere in Frankfurt, visit www.parkhausfrankfurt.de.

HELPFUL HINTS

Museum Hours: Most museums are closed Monday. Many stay open until 20:00 on Wednesday.

Festivals and Events: Frankfurt keeps a busy and fun-loving calendar of events. When you're there, be sure to check out what's happening.

Internet Access: The **Internet & Call Shop** is your best bet for online access near the train station (€2/hour, daily 8:00-23:00, Kaiserstrasse 70).

Laundry: Miele Wash World is near the station and looks a bit worn (Mon-Sat 6:00-23:00, closed Sun, Moselstrasse 17, by the corner of Münchener Strasse, signs in English). In Sachsenhausen, by the recommended Fichtekränzi restaurant, is an **SB-Waschsalon** (Mon-Sat 6:00-23:00, closed Sun, Wallstrasse 8, instructions in German only).

Supermarket: The small but well-stocked **REWE** supermarket is near the station, across the street from the recommended Hotel Concorde (Mon-Sat 7:00-22:00, closed Sun, Karlstrasse 4, use Kaiserstrasse exit from underground passageway). A larger branch is in the basement of the MyZeil shopping center near the Hauptwache, in the center of town (Mon-Sat 7:00-24:00, closed Sun). On Sundays (when many stores are closed), you'll find a pharmacy and a grocery store in the underground section of the station (open until 20:00).

Theater: **English Theatre Frankfurt** is the most active English-language theater on the Continent, hosting companies from the UK and the US. The quality is good and the delightful theater is small, so it books up well in advance (Gallusanlage 7, tel. 06924/231-620, www.english-theatre.de).

Helpful Website: For those interested in an insider's take on Frankfurt, read tour guide Jodean Ator's blog (www.frankfurtonfoot.com).

GETTING AROUND FRANKFURT

By Public Transportation: Frankfurt's subway (U-Bahn) and suburban train (S-Bahn) network is easy to use, but trams are more convenient and give you a better look at the city. For all forms of public transit, buy your tickets *(Fahrkarten)* from an RMV machine. Tickets are issued with a validating stamp already on them, and are valid only immediately after they're bought. Choose the option to type in your destination, choose your ticket type, and then pay (carry cash, some machines won't accept US credit cards). If you don't see your destination listed, type "Frankfurt" first, along with the name of your stop. Choose *Einzelfahrt* for a regular single ticket (€2.60), *Kurzstrecke* for a short ride (€1.60—valid destinations listed on machines), *Tageskarte Frankfurt* for an all-day pass (€6.60 without the airport, €8.50 with), or *Gruppentageskarte* for an all-day group ticket (up to 5 adults, €9.90 without the airport, €15 with). If you'll be going to or from the airport, note that the one-day Frankfurt Card (described earlier, under "Tourist Information") costs only €1.40 more than the all-day transit pass and also includes sightseeing discounts. An individual one-way ticket to the airport costs €4.35 (no group rate for airport-only trips). For more information in English, see www.rmv.de.

By Taxi: A taxi stand is just outside the main entrance of the train station to your left. A typical ride, such as to Römerberg square, should cost you €7 (up to €10 in slow traffic).

Tours in Frankfurt

Hop-On, Hop-Off Bus Tours

Double-decker hop-on, hop-off buses give you an orientation to Frankfurt, pausing at 16 stops in a one-hour loop. Buy tickets at the TI or on the bus (€19/one-day pass, discount if bought online, departures daily 10:00-17:00, every 30 minutes from near St. Paul's Church, www.citysightseeing-frankfurt.com). The same ticket also covers a bus tour called the Skyline Tour (focuses on city architecture, 2-4/day) and CitySightseeing's walking tour (1/day). Tickets purchased after 15:00 are valid for the following day as well.

River Boat Tours

These tours are relaxing but pretty boring (with no medieval castles in sight). You can go an hour in either direction or take a grand two-hour ride (departures from near the Eiserner Steg bridge). You'll see the impressive skyline, but a river ride in the Romantic Rhine gorge is far more interesting.

Walking Tours

Frankfurt on Foot's three-hour walks, led by longtime Frankfurt residents (and Ohio natives) Jodean Ator and her husband David, hit the major sights and make Frankfurt's history meaningful (€12, €1 discount with this book, basic walk leaves daily at 10:30 from Römer/Paulskirche tram stop—just show up, private walking tours possible, mobile 01520-846-4200, www.frankfurtonfoot.com, info@frankfurtonfoot.com). Their flexible **"Frankfurt Layover Tour"** is ideal for those with long layovers at the Frankfurt Airport and includes pickup and drop-off at the airport. Check out their website, which is packed with sightseeing suggestions, historical info, and Jodean's insightful blog.

The **TI** offers daily walking tours of the historic center at 14:30 (€14) and two-hour themed walks on weekends (topics vary from history and architecture to banking and apple wine; check ahead on www.frankfurt-tourismus.de; also €14, April-Oct Sat-Sun at 10:30, Nov Sun only at 10:30, no tours Dec-March). You get a 20 percent discount on both walks with the Frankfurt Card. Tours depart from the Römerberg TI, and the guides speak both English and German during the walks. Reserve ahead by phone or email (info@infofrankfurt.de).

Local Guide

Elisabeth Lücke is a brilliant guide who loves her city and shares it very well (€65/hour, cash only, reserve in advance, tel. 06196/45787, mobile 0173-913-3157, www.elisabeth-luecke.de, elisabeth.luecke@t-online.de). She enjoys tailoring tours (for example, to the IG Farben building, a.k.a. the "Pentagon of Europe") for military personnel once based around here.

Frankfurt Walk

This self-guided sightseeing walk, worth ▲▲, shows you both the new Frankfurt and the old. Starting at the train station, it takes you past junkies and brothels, up the Main Tower, through the modern shopping and eating districts, and into the lively square at the center of the Old Town (where you could continue on to the Holocaust Memorial), before finishing on a bridge overlooking the city and its river.

Train Station

Frankfurt has Germany's busiest train station: 350,000 travelers make their way to 24 platforms to catch 1,800 trains every day.

Hop a train and you can be in either Paris or Berlin in four hours. While it was big news when it opened in the 1890s, it's a dead-end terminus station, which, with today's high-speed trains, makes it outdated. Complaining that it takes an extra 20 minutes to stop here, railway officials threatened to have the speedy ICE trains bypass Frankfurt altogether unless it dug a tunnel to allow for a faster pass-through stop. But this proved too expensive, and—while some trains stop only at the pass-through airport station—most fast trains begrudgingly serve downtown Frankfurt.

Leaving through the station's front door, walk directly away from the station to the traffic island facing the pedestrian Kaiserstrasse, and turn to look back at the building's Neo-Renaissance facade—a style popular with Industrial Revolution-era architects. This classic late 19th-century glass-and-iron construction survived World War II. High above, a statue of Apollo carries the world—but only with some heavy-duty help: Green copper figures representing steam power and electricity pitch in. The 1890s were a confident age, when people believed that technology would solve the world's problems.

• With your back to the station, look down...

Kaiserstrasse

This grand 19th-century boulevard features appropriately elegant facades that were designed to dress up the approach to what was a

fine new station. Towering above and beyond the 100-year-old buildings are the skyscrapers of Frankfurt's banking district. Until a few years ago, the street was rife with local riff-raff. But city officials have directed that crowd a couple of blocks to the left, and Kaiserstrasse is fast becoming a people-friendly eating zone.

Warning: This walk now goes into a neighborhood of hard-drug users and prostitutes. If you use common sense, it's not dangerous, but it can be unnerving, and is creepy at any time of day. If you'd rather go directly to the Main Tower, walk straight down

Kaiserstrasse four blocks to the park and skip ahead to "Frankfurt's Banking District" on page 415.

• *Walk down Kaiserstrasse, one block away from the station. If you're game, jog left on Moselstrasse and walk a block to the corner of Taunusstrasse. This is where the city contains and controls its sex-and-drug scene. To the right, Taunusstrasse is lined half with brothels and half with bank towers. And across Taunusstrasse and farther down Moselstrasse is a heroin-maintenance clinic, known here as a "drug-consumption room."*

▲Junkies

A half-block down Moselstrasse, on the left, you'll probably see a gang congregating at Café Fix (#47, daily 11:00-23:00, no photos). This is one of several **"junkie cafés"** in Frankfurt.

In the 1980s Frankfurt was plagued by one of the largest open drug markets in Europe. Its parks (and police) were overwhelmed with needle addicts. Then Frankfurt decided to get creative, take the crime out of the equation, and go for a pragmatic harm-reduction approach.

In 1992, Frankfurt began offering "pump rooms" to its hard-drug users. The idea: provide a safe haven for addicts (mostly heroin, but also crack and methadone) to hygienically maintain their habit. Heroin addicts still buy their stuff on the street, but inject it here with clean needles, with medical help standing by, and a place to stay if needed. It's strictly not for first-time users and no dealing or sharing of drugs is allowed. These centers provide a safe and caring place for addicts to go to maintain their habit and get counseling and medical help. These days, overdose deaths are down 75 percent in general, and there's never been a death in a drug-consumption room. Locals consider the program a success and are accustomed to wasted people congregating in neighborhoods like this one. While unsightly, the compassionate harm reduction approach that much of Europe uses to deal with this problem saves lives. Meanwhile, the US continues to suffer about double the heroin-related deaths per capita as Europe.

• *Now for the sex. Take a right on Taunusstrasse and walk to Elbestrasse.*

▲▲ Brothels

From Taunusstrasse, look or turn left down Elbestrasse, where you'll find a row of high-rise brothels, or **"eros towers."** With all the businessmen coming into town, Frankfurt found there was no effective way to outlaw prostitution. So the city (like any German city over a certain population threshold) decided to corral prostitution in what it calls a "tolerance area."

About 20 five-story brothels fill original, late-19th-century apartment flats within a block of this spot. Perfectly legal since 2002, prostitution is big business here. The women, who are mostly from Eastern Europe, Latin America, and Thailand (only about 2 percent are from Germany), essentially run their own little businesses. They charge around €20 for services and rent their rooms for about €130 a day. It's said that they cover their rent by the end of the businessmen's lunch break (look at the bank towers nearby). German sex workers get health care just like any other workers and pay taxes (on €14 billion of declared income each year).

Crazy Sexy, at Elbestrasse 51, is the biggest of these brothels, with 180 rooms. The first three floors are for women. The fourth floor is for transvestites. (I was told, "A sex change is expensive, and many of these 'she-males' or 'lady boys' are making money to pay for their operation.")

Climbing through a few of these towers may be one of the more memorable experiences of your European trip. But while hiking through the towers feels safe, the aggressive women at the neighboring strip shows can be unsettling.

Ever since the Middle Ages, Frankfurt's thriving prostitution industry has gone hand-in-hand with its trade fairs. Today, prostitution thrives with the *Messe* (convention center). Both hotels and prostitutes double their prices during big trade fairs. Prostitutes note that business varies with the theme of the trade show—the auto show is boom time and the butchers' convention is famously hungry, but Frankfurt's massive book fair is a bust.

To the right of Taunusstrasse, at Elbestrasse 31, is a strip joint called **Pik-Dame.** Old-timers are nostalgic about this lone remnant from "the good old days" just after World War II, when 30,000 US soldiers stationed in Frankfurt provided a stimulus for this neighborhood's economy. Later, the troops left and the Russian mob moved in, replacing any old-time gentility with a criminal and thuggish edge. (Note that there's another drug-consumption center across the street from Pik-Dame.)

• *Enough sex and drugs. Continue down Taunusstrasse out of the red light district and into the banking district. Look up and see why this city (on the Main River) is nicknamed "Mainhattan." Cross the street to the park and go to the statue of the poet Schiller (a Romantic poet and friend of Goethe), on your left.*

▲Frankfurt's Banking District

This park is part of a circular greenbelt that circles the old center and marks the site of Frankfurt's medieval moat and fortifications. These walls (along with many castles on the Rhine) were destroyed by the French in 1806. Napoleon was on his way to Russia, and, since he had the upper hand, he figured it was wise to preemptively destroy any German fortifications that might haunt him if the Germans turned against France in the future.

The park is the center of Frankfurt's banking district. The post-WWII Marshall Plan was administered from here—requiring fancy money-handling. And the mighty deutsche mark was born in a 1930s-era building facing this square (in the low Art Deco building on the left of the square as you entered, behind the greenery from where you now stand). After World War II, Germany's economy was in chaos. In 1948, the US gave it a complete currency transfer—like a blood transfusion—literally printing up the new deutsche marks and shipping them across the Atlantic to inject them from here directly into the German economy. As if catching water from a fountain, banks naturally grew up around this square.

But Frankfurt was "Bankfurt" long before World War II. This was the Rothschilds' hometown. Born in Frankfurt's Jewish ghetto in 1744, Mayer Rothschild went from being a pauper to the richest banker in the world in one lifetime. His five sons set up businesses in Rome, London, Paris, and Vienna, and in two generations the Rothschild banking dynasty was established. (Their former palace now houses Frankfurt's Jewish Museum, described on page 424.) Today, locals call Frankfurt's legion of bankers "penguins," as they all dress the same. Tour guides here talk of banks as part of the cultural soil (the way French Riviera guides talk of the big yachts).

Beyond the statue of Schiller stand the twin towers of the Deutsche Bank (not to be confused with the DB—Deutsche Bahn—tower to your left). This country's #1 bank, its assets are greater than the annual budget of the German government. If money makes the world go round, the decisions that spin Germany are made in Frankfurt. But, with the recent economic crisis, a third of these skyscraper offices are empty.

Make a 360-degree spin and survey all the bank towers. Notice the striking architecture. By law, no German worker can be kept out of natural light for more than four hours, so work environments are filled with windows. And, as you can see, Germans like their skyscrapers with windows that open.

• *Find the skyscraper with the red-and-white candy cane on top. That's your destination—the Main Tower. To reach it, continue straight along Taunustor a block, then turn left on Neue Mainzer Strasse and look for the tower symbol on the doors on the right.*

▲▲Main Tower

Finished in 2000, this tower houses the Helaba Bank and offers the best (and only public) viewpoint from the top of a Frankfurt skyscraper. A 55-second, ear-popping elevator ride to the 54th floor (watch the meter on the wall as you ascend) and then 50 stairs take you to the rooftop, 650 feet above the city.

Cost and Hours: €6.50; April-Sept Sun-Thu 10:00-21:00, Fri-Sat 10:00-23:00; Oct-March Sun-Thu 10:00-19:00, Fri-Sat 10:00-21:00; enter at Neue Mainzer Strasse 52, between Taunustor and Junghofstrasse, tel. 069/3650-4740, www.maintower.de.

⊙ **Self-Guided Spin-Tour:** Here, from Frankfurt's ultimate viewpoint, survey the city by circling clockwise, starting with the biggest skyscraper (with the yellow emblem).

Designed by Norman Foster (of Berlin Reichstag and London City Hall fame), the **Commerzbank building** was finished in 1997. It's 985 feet high, with nine winter gardens spiraling up its core and windows that open. It's considered the first ecological skyscraper...radically "green" in its day. Just to the left is Römerberg—the Old Town center (the half-timbered houses huddled around the red-and-white church with a green spire; we'll visit there soon).

The **Museum Embankment** (see page 425) lines Schaumainkai on the far side of the Main River, just beyond the new Taunus Tower.

The Rhine-Main **airport,** off in the distance (like a city in the forest), is the largest employment complex in Germany, with 70,000 workers. Frankfurt's massive train station dominates the foreground. From the station, the grand Kaiserstrasse cuts through the city to Römerberg.

The **Frankfurt fair** *(Messe),* marked by the brown skyscraper with the pointy top, is a huge convention center—the size of 40 soccer fields. It sprawls behind the skyscraper that looks like a classical column sporting a visor-like capital. (The protruding lip of the capital is heated so that icicles don't form, break off, and impale people on the street below.) Frankfurt's fair originated in 1240, when the emperor promised all participating merchants safe passage. The glassy black twin towers of the Deutsche Bank in the foreground (nicknamed "Debit and Credit") are typical of mid-1980s mirrored architecture.

The **West End,** with vast green spaces and the telecommunications tower, is Frankfurt's priciest residential quarter. The city's most enjoyable zone cuts from the West End to the right. Stretching from the classic-looking Opera House below are broad and people-filled boulevards made to order for eating and shopping. Find the "Beach Club" filling the rooftop of a parking garage with white tents, two pools, and colorful lounge chairs. This is a popular family zone by day and a chic club after dark.

From here, you can see how the city walls, demolished in 1806, left a string of green zones arcing out from the river. This defined the city limits in the 19th century.

Take a moment from this vantage point to trace the rest of this walk: from the Opera House, along the tree-lined eating and shopping boulevards to St. Paul's Church and Römerberg. After side-tripping from Römerberg out to the cathedral, we'll finish on Eiserner Steg, the iron pedestrian bridge over the Main River.

Now look east, farther out along the river to the glistening twin towers (standing all alone). At 600 feet tall, these are the striking new headquarters of the **European Central Bank.**

As you leave the Main Tower, step into the **Helaba Bank** lobby (next door over from base of elevator). A black-and-white mosaic filling the wall shows cultural superstars of 20th-century Frankfurt, from composer Paul Hindemith to industrialist and humanitarian Oskar Schindler to Anne Frank (see the key on the post nearby for a who's who).

• *Leave the Main Tower and continue walking along Neue Mainzer Strasse (crossing Junghofstrasse) for a couple of blocks, to where you see a large square open to your left. Across the square is the Opera House.*

Frankfurt's Good-Living People Zone

Opera House (Alte Oper): Finished in 1880, Frankfurt's opera house celebrated German high culture and the newly created nation. Mozart and Goethe flank the entrance, reminders that this is a house of both music and theater. On a hot day, people of all ages cool their heels in the refreshing fountain in the plaza out front. The original opera house was gutted in World War II. Over the objections of a mayor nicknamed "Dynamite Rudi," the city rebuilt it in the original style, and it opened in 1981. Underneath is a U-Bahn station (Alte Oper).

• *Facing the Opera, turn right down Frankfurt's famous...*

Fressgass': The official names for this pedestrian street are Grosse Bockenheimer Strasse and Kalbächer Gasse...but every-

one in Frankfurt calls it the Fressgass', roughly "Feeding Street." Herds of bank employees come here on their lunch breaks to fill their bellies before returning for another few hours of cud-chewing at their computers. It's packed gable-to-gable with eateries and shoulder-to-shoulder with workers wolfing €3 sandwiches, plates of Asian food, and more. It also offers great people-watching. Join in if you're hungry—or wait for more eating options in a couple of blocks.

• *Fressgass' leads to a square called Rathenauplatz, but it's known as Goethe Platz for its central statue. Cross the square and continue straight—the pedestrian street is now called Biebergasse—another block to the...*

Hauptwache: The small, red-and-white building—which has given its name to the square (and the subway station below it)—was built in 1730 to house the Frankfurt city militia. Now it's a café. The square, entirely closed to traffic, is one of the city's hubs.

• *To the right, at the south side of the square, is the Protestant Kath-arinenkirche, which was destroyed in the bombing raids of March 1944 and rebuilt after the war. Straight ahead of you is a boulevard called the...*

Zeil: This tree-lined pedestrian drag is Frankfurt's main shopping street. Crowds swirl through the Galeria Kaufhof department store, the Zeil Galerie, and the MyZeil shopping center (the one with the glassy hole in its wall) along the left side of the street. MyZeil has a huge glass atrium shaped like two massive funnels—and can be a mesmerizing sight on a rainy day. A really long escalator (behind the much shorter twin set by the door) leads straight to the top-floor food court (with good, free WC).

Lunch and Views from Department Store Rooftops: The Galeria Kaufhof has a recommended rooftop cafeteria, Leonhard's (good for lunch or just the views). If you do go up, walk to Zeil Galerie from Leonhard's for an even higher (free) view observatory. There are supermarkets in the basements of both the Zeil Galerie and the MyZeil shopping center; the REWE supermarket in the MyZeil is cheaper and open longer hours (Mon-Sat 8:00-24:00, closed Sun) and has a bakery with seating.

• *Continue down Zeil a block to the fountain at the next intersection. Turn right on Hasengasse. In the distance is the lacy red-brick spire of the cathedral. Halfway there, after about two blocks, find the low-key green entrance to Kleinmarkthalle on the right. Enter the market (public WC downstairs at entry).*

Kleinmarkthalle: This delightful, old-school market was saved from developers by a local outcry, and to this day it's a neighborhood favorite. Explore and sample your way through the ground floor. It's an adventure in fine eating (with a line of simple eateries upstairs, too) and a delight for photographers. The far wall is filled with a fun piece of art offering a bird's-eye view of Frankfurt over a charming montage of the many ways locals love their hometown.

• *Exit the Kleinmarkthalle opposite where you entered. Angle right, and climb six steps into a square (Leibfrauenberg) with a red-brick fountain and the 14th-century Church of Our Lady (rebuilt after World War II). On the far side is Lebkuchen-Schmidt, a fun shop selling traditional gin-*

gerbread, a local favorite. Turn left and head downhill on Neue Kräme, then cross Berliner Strasse to Paulsplatz.

▲St. Paul's Church (Paulskirche)

To your right, the former church dominating the square is known as the "cradle of German democracy." It was here, during the polit-

ical upheaval of 1848, that the first freely elected National Assembly met and the first German Constitution was drafted, paving the way for a united Germany in 1871. Following its destruction by Allied bombs in 1944, the church became the first historic building in the city to be rebuilt. This was a symbolic statement from the German people that they wanted to be free (as they had demonstrated here in 1848), democratic...and no longer fascist. Around the outside of the building, you'll see reliefs honoring

people who contributed to the German nation, including Theodor Heuss, the first president, and John F. Kennedy, who spoke here on June 25, 1963.

Step inside. Displays described in English tell the story of 1848. Check out the circular mural, from the 1980s. Called *The March of Members of Parliament,* it was controversial when unveiled. Commissioned to honor the political heroes of 1848, the portraits are cartoonish figures, with faces hinting of contemporary politicians. Political leaders seem to sneer at the working class, and two naked men who look like they're having sex represent the forces of democracy and monarchy fighting within Germany. Upstairs is a 900-seat assembly hall with no decor except the flags of the 16 states of the Federal Republic of Germany.

Cost and Hours: Free, daily 10:00-17:00.

• *Walk across the square. If you need a break, a variety of eateries offer inviting seating that's perfect for some fun people-watching. Then, cross the next street and tram tracks and you'll enter what's left of Frankfurt's Old Town.*

▲Römerberg

Frankfurt's market square was the birthplace of the city. This is the site of the first trade fairs (12th century), bank (1405), and stock exchange (1585). Now, crowds of tourists convene here. Römerberg's central statue is the goddess of justice without her customary blindfold. She oversees the town hall, which itself oversees trade. The Town Hall *(Römer)* houses the *Kaisersaal,* or Imperial Hall, where Holy Roman Emperors celebrated their coronations.

Today, the *Römer* houses the city council and mayor's office. Marriages must be performed in a civil ceremony here to be legal, so you'll see lots of brides and grooms celebrating outside the City Hall. The cute row of half-timbered homes (rebuilt in 1983) opposite the *Römer* is typical of Frankfurt's quaint old center before the square was completely destroyed in World War II. The Gothic red-and-white Old Nikolai Church (Alte Nikolaikirche, with fine stained glass from the 1920s by a local artist) dates from the 13th century and was restored after the war. Hosting everything from Christmas markets to violent demonstrations, this square is the beating heart of Frankfurt.

In the center of the square, the metal plaque that looks like a large manhole cover reminds us that a Nazi book-burning took place in the square on May 10, 1933. Around the edge of the plaque is a quote from the German poet Heinrich Heine, who presciently pointed out that it's a short step from burning books to burning people.

• *Facing the Town Hall, the river and the bridge where this walk ends are just two blocks to the left. But first, we'll take a short detour. Circle around the Old Nikolai Church to Saalgasse.*

Saalgasse

Literally "Hall Street," Saal- gasse is lined by postmodern buildings echoing the higgle- dy-piggledy houses that stood here until World War II. In the 1990s, famous architects from around the world were each given a ruined house of the same width and told to design a

new structure to reflect the one that stood there before the war. As you continue down the street, guess which one is an upside-down half-timbered house with the stars down below. (Hint: Animals are on the "ground floor.")

When you see the big, red St. Bartholomew's Cathedral (de- scribed next), turn left.

St. Bartholomew's Cathedral (Kaiserdom)

This Catholic church—still bright and airy like the original—is

FRANKFURT

made of modern concrete with paint to imitate mortar and medieval bricks. Holy Roman Emperors were elected here starting in 1152 and crowned here between 1562 and 1792. The cathedral was gutted by fire in 1867 and had to be rebuilt. It was seriously damaged in World War II, but repaired and reopened in 1953. Though the cathedral is free, you must pay to access two sights within the church: a museum (not particularly interesting) and a 328-step tower climb with city views at the top.

Enter on the side opposite the river. Frescoes from the 15th century survive (flanking the high altar and ringing the choir). They show 27 scenes from the life of St. Bartholomew. The Electors Chapel (to the right of the altar, with fine modern glass) is where the electors convened to choose the Holy Roman Emperor in the Middle Ages. Everything of value that could be moved was taken out of the church before the WWII bombs came. The delightful sandstone Chapel of Sleeping Mary (to the left of the high altar), carved and painted in the 15th century, was too big to move—so it was fortified with sandbags. The altarpiece and stained glass next to it survived the bombing. As you wander, appreciate the colorful and extravagant tombstones embedded in the walls when the church's cemetery was emptied.

Cost and Hours: Cathedral—free, Sat-Thu 9:00-20:00, Fri 13:00-20:00; museum—€3, Tue-Fri 10:00-17:00, Sat-Sun 11:00-17:00, closed Mon, enter from church vestibule, www. dommuseum-frankfurt.de; tower—€3, daily 9:00-18:00, tel. 069/7808-9255, www.domturm-frankfurt.de.

• *From here, you can continue on a couple of blocks to visit the Holocaust Memorial and/or the Frankfurt City Model (both free and described later, under "Sights in Frankfurt"). Or, to complete this walk, head down to the river, turn right, and go along the pleasant riverfront park to the next bridge. Walk to its center.*

Eiserner Steg Bridge

This iron bridge, the city's second oldest, dates to 1869. (The oldest is just upstream: the Alte Brucke, site of the first "Frank ford"—a fifth-century crossing.) From the middle of the bridge, survey the skyline and enjoy the lively scene along the riverbanks of Frankfurt.

• *For a quick ride back to your starting point, return to Römerberg and take the U-Bahn or tram #11 or #12 to the Hauptbahnhof.*

Sights in Frankfurt

NEAR RÖMERBERG

▲Goethe House (Goethehaus)

Johann Wolfgang von Goethe (1749-1832), a scientist, minister, poet, lawyer, politician, and playwright, was a towering figure in the early Romantic Age. His birthplace, now a fine museum, is a five-minute walk northwest of Römerberg. It's furnished as it was in the mid-18th century, when the boy destined to become the "German Shakespeare" grew up here.

Borrow a laminated card at the bottom of the stairs for a refreshingly brief commentary on each of the 16 rooms. Since nothing's roped off and there are no posted signs, it's easy to picture real people living here. Goethe's father dedicated his life and wealth to cultural pursuits, and his mother told young Johann Wolfgang fairy tales every night, stopping just before the ending so that the boy could exercise his own creativity. Goethe's family gave him all the money he needed to travel and learn. His collection of 2,000 books was sold off in 1795. In recent decades, more than half of these have been located and repurchased by the museum (you'll see them in the library). This building honors the man who inspired the Goethe-Institut, which is dedicated to keeping the German language strong.

Cost and Hours: €7, Mon-Sat 10:00-18:00, Sun 10:00-17:30, €3 high-tech but easy-to-use and informative audioguide, €1.50 English booklet has same info as free laminated cards—worthwhile only as a souvenir; 15-minute walk from Hauptbahnhof up Kaiserstrasse, turn right on Am Salzhaus to Grosser Hirschgraben 23; tel. 069/138-800, www.goethehaus-frankfurt.de.

Schirn Art Center (Schirn Kunsthalle)

Opened in 1986, this facility has quickly become one of Europe's most respected homes of modern and contemporary art. Rotating exhibits pay homage to everything and everyone from Kandinsky and Kahlo to contemporary artists, movements, and topics.

Cost and Hours: €7-10 depending on exhibits, Tue and Fri-Sun 10:00-19:00, Wed-Thu 10:00-22:00, closed Mon, Römerberg, tel. 069/299-8820, www.schirn.de.

IN THE FORMER JEWISH GHETTO

During the early Middle Ages, the most important Jewish communities north of the Alps were along the Rhine, in towns like Cologne, Speyer, Worms, and Frankfurt. Even after the center of Jewish life moved east to Poland and Lithuania, Frankfurt had a large and prominent Jewish community, including the Rothschilds (the famous banking family).

You can get a feel for Frankfurt's Jewish history with a visit to the Holocaust Memorial at the old Jewish cemetery, down Battonnstrasse from the Museum Judengasse (museum closed in 2015). Both are a short walk (or one tram stop) east of Römerberg and St. Bartholomew's Cathedral.

For more detail on the city's Jewish community, visit the Jewish Museum (described later), located near the river.

▲Holocaust Memorial, Jewish Cemetery, and Museum Judengasse

This memorial to Frankfurt's Jewish community—devastated by the Holocaust—marks the site of the old Jewish ghetto and where

the city's main Börneplatz Synagogue once stood. Commemorating 12,000 murdered Jews, it's a powerful and evocative collection of images.

Around the old Jewish cemetery is the Wall of Names, with a tiny tombstone for each Frankfurt Jew deported and murdered by the Nazis (with destination and date of death if known). Pebbles atop each tomb represent Jewish prayers. The memorial gives each victim the dignity of a tombstone and of being named, while a databank inside the adjacent Museum Judengasse keeps their memory alive with a record of everything known about each person (museum closed in 2015).

By peeking through the locked black-metal gate into the cemetery, you can see a few tombstones that survived the Nazi rampage. In the tree-filled square is a stone tower, built with foundation stones from homes excavated from the Jewish ghetto. The gravel is designed to evoke train tracks and the deportation of so many people to concentration camps.

The paved section marks the footprint of the Börneplatz Synagogue, destroyed on November 9, 1938—a night traditionally known as Kristallnacht. (Because people's lives were also destroyed on that night along with lots of windows and glass, the preferred name is "Pogrom Night.") A plaque on the wall opposite recalls this terrible event. In the wake of World War II, American troops made Frankfurters memorialize each synagogue they destroyed with a plaque like this.

▲Frankfurt City Model (in the City Planning Office)

This model, though unrelated to the Jewish story, is next to the Holocaust Memorial in the same building as the (closed) Museum Judengasse. Step past the receptionist and into the atrium to see a current model of Frankfurt and its skyscrapers (marked

Planungsdezernat). The city's planning department fills its atrium with an ever-evolving model of Frankfurt's inner city (a 30-by-20-foot layout on a 1:500 scale of the city). Since 1960 this model has helped planners track and envision the development of the city and its many massive building projects—even seeing where shadows of new buildings will fall. Red buildings are those under construction.

Cost and Hours: Free, Mon-Fri 8:30-18:00, closed Sat-Sun, Kurt-Schumacherstrasse 10.

NEAR THE RIVER, ON THE NORTH BANK
Jewish Museum (Jüdisches Museum)

This museum is housed in the former Rothschild family palace, along the river between Römerberg and the train station. Exhibits on the middle floor trace in detail Jewish life in Frankfurt from the early Middle Ages to World War II, with special emphasis on Jews' 19th-century struggle for equal rights as citizens of Frankfurt. The top floor focuses on Jewish life and customs.

Cost and Hours: €7, Tue-Sun 10:00-17:00, Wed until 20:00, closed Mon; Untermainkai 14/15, tel. 069/2123-5000, www.juedischesmuseum.de.

Riverside Promenade

Just across the road from the Jewish Museum is a lovely riverside promenade—a perfect place to rest your feet and watch people and planes go by.

ACROSS THE RIVER, ON THE SOUTH BANK
Schaumainkai and Frankfurt's Museum Embankment (Museumsufer)

The Schaumainkai riverside promenade (across the river from Römerberg over the Eiserner Steg pedestrian bridge, and then to the right) is great for an evening stroll or people-watching on any sunny day. Keep your eyes peeled for nude sunbathers. Every other Saturday, the museum strip street is closed off for a sprawling flea market.

Nine museums in striking buildings line the Main River along Schaumainkai. In the 1980s, Frankfurt decided that it wanted to buck its "Bankfurt" and "Krankfurt" (*krank* means "sick") image. It went on a culture kick and devoted 11 percent of the city budget to the arts and culture. The result: Frankfurt has become a city of art. These nine museums (covering topics such as architecture, film, world cultures, and great European masters—the Städel Collection) and a dozen others are all well-described in the TI's *Museum-sufer* brochure.

Cost and Hours: All museums here are covered by the two-day €18 Museum Ticket sold at TIs and participating museums—see page 407; most museums open Tue-Sun 10:00-17:00, Wed until 20:00, closed Mon; www.kultur-frankfurt.de.

Sleeping in Frankfurt

Planning to sleep in Frankfurt is a gamble, since the city's numerous trade fairs *(Messe)* send hotel prices skyrocketing—a €70 double can suddenly shoot up to €300. Visit www.messefrankfurt.com (and select "The Company," then "Our Publications," then "Calendar of Trade Fairs") for an exact schedule. During these trade fairs, skip Frankfurt altogether and stay in Würzburg, Bacharach, or St. Goar.

When trade fairs aren't in town, room prices in most Frankfurt hotels fluctuate €10-50 with the day of the week. If you'll be staying overnight in Frankfurt during a non-convention summer weekend, you can land a great place relatively cheaply. Frankfurt hotels are business-oriented, so many are empty and desperate for guests from Friday night to Monday morning. The lower prices listed here are for weekends, and the higher prices for weekdays. Although the ranges listed here are typical, varying demand may skew them higher or lower.

Keep overnights in Frankfurt to a minimum: Pleasant Rhine and Romantic Road towns are just a quick drive or train ride away, offering a mom-and-pop welcome that you won't find here in the big city.

NEAR THE TRAIN STATION

The following places are within a few blocks of the train station and its fast and handy train to the airport (to sleep even closer to the airport, see "Sleeping at or near Frankfurt Airport," page 436). The Hamburger Hof, Bristol, and Topas hotels are on the north (and most sedate) side of the station. The Manhattan and Concorde hotels are along the busy streets just to the northeast of the station. The Victoria, Holiday Inn Express, Ibis Styles, and Five Elements hostel are in the multiethnic neighborhood east of the station. The Ibis Hotel Frankfurt is south of the station, close to the Main River and within walking distance of the Museum Embankment (Museumsufer). For locations, see the map on page 409.

All these listings are well-run and feel safe and respectable. I like staying in this colorful and convenient neighborhood (which gets more gentrified every year). But the red light district is close

---

Sleep Code

Abbreviations   (€1 = about $1.40, country code: 49)
S = Single, **D** = Double/Twin, **T** = Triple, **Q** = Quad, **b** = bathroom, **s** = shower only.

Price Rankings

  $$$ **Higher Priced**—Most rooms €110 or more.
  $$ **Moderately Priced**—Most rooms between €75-110.
  $ **Lower Priced**—Most rooms €75 or less.

Unless otherwise noted, credit cards are accepted, English is spoken, breakfast is included, and Wi-Fi is generally free. Prices change; verify current rates online or by email. For the best prices, always book directly with the hotel.

---

by, with gritty clubs and hard-drug users. Don't wander into seedy-feeling streets, and use care and common sense after dark.

$$$ Hotel Concorde, across the street from the station and then a few doors down Karlstrasse in a restored 1890s building, offers 45 air-conditioned rooms and four-star comfort and professionalism, all at a reasonable price (Sb-€55-120, Db-€80-140, optional €12/person breakfast—free when you book directly with the hotel, air-con, elevator, Wi-Fi, Karlstrasse 9, tel. 069/242-4220, www.hotelconcorde.de, info@hotelconcorde.de, Marc is manager). Exit the station by track 24, cross the street and head right, walking past the Manhattan Hotel (listed later) and around the corner to the Concorde. The REWE supermarket is across the street.

$$$ Hotel Hamburger Hof, right next to the train station but in a quiet and safe-feeling location, has a classy, shiny lobby and 62 modern rooms. The side facing the station is cheerfully sunny, while rooms on the other side are quieter (Sb-€65-110, Db-€95-130, Tb-€115-150, air-con, elevator, guest computer, Wi-Fi, Poststrasse 10-12, tel. 069/2713-9690, www.hamburgerhof.com, info@hamburgerhof.com). Exit the station by track 24, cross the street, turn left, and walk to the end of the block.

$$$ Bristol Hotel is a swanky 145-room place that serves up style and flair, from its nod to Pacific Rim architecture to its teak-furnished breakfast room and relaxing patio café. It's just two blocks from the station and enjoys quiet and respectable surroundings (Sb-€60-95, larger Sb-€75-110, Db-€95-130, larger Db-€105-140, elevator, huge breakfast buffet, guest computer, Wi-Fi, Ludwigstrasse 15, tel. 069/242-390, www.bristol-hotel.de, info@bristol-hotel.de). Exit the station by track 24, cross the street, turn left, then right on Ottostrasse, then left on Niddastrasse to Ludwigstrasse.

$$$ Victoria Hotel, two blocks from the station along the grand Kaiserstrasse, has 73 smartly redone rooms (with lots of pillows) and feels a world apart from the red light district a block away (Sb-€65-99, Db-€90-130, Db suite-€130-170, air-con, elevator, guest computer, Wi-Fi, Kaiserstrasse 59, entrance on Elbestrasse, tel. 069/273-060, www.victoriahotel.de, victoria-hotel@t-online. de). From the station, go down the escalators to the underground passageway below the station and follow the *Kaiserstrasse* signs.

$$ Manhattan Hotel, with 55 rooms, is a few doors from the station on a busy street. Friendly manager Robert tries to greet all of his guests personally (Sb-€85-149, Db-€99-179, mention this book when booking directly with the hotel to get a 10 percent discount during non-convention times in 2015, one child under 12 free, elevator, guest computer, Wi-Fi, Düsseldorfer Strasse 10, tel. 069/269-5970, www.manhattan-hotel.com, info@manhattan-hotel.com). Exit the station by track 24, cross the street, and go right until you see the hotel; to cross Düsseldorfer Strasse safely, walk up to the tram stop.

$$ Holiday Inn Express Hauptbahnhof has 116 fresh, new, inexpensive rooms two blocks from the station, in a quiet location just off Münchener Strasse in the Turkish district (Sb/Db-€69-99, air-con, elevator, Wi-Fi, Elbestrasse 7, tel. 069/8700-3883, www. fmhos.com, frankfurt@fmhos.com). From the front of the station, use the crosswalk by the tram stop and follow the tracks down Münchener Strasse two blocks to Elbestrasse and turn right.

$$ Ibis Styles Frankfurt City is a small step up from the Ibis Hotel (mentioned next) and is centrally located just a few blocks from the station. Its 96 funky, colorful rooms help you forget that this is a popular chain hotel (Sb-€75-80, Db-€85-95, Tb-€105-115, air-con, elevator, guest computer, Wi-Fi; Moselstrasse 12, tel. 069/6925-6110, www.ibisstyles.com, H7561@accor.com). From the front of the station, use the crosswalk by the tram stop and follow the tracks down Münchener Strasse one block to Moselstrasse and turn right.

$$ Ibis Hotel Frankfurt Friedensbrücke is a good value, with 233 rooms on a quiet riverside street away from the station (Sb/Db-€59-90, Tb-€124, breakfast-€10/person, elevator, guest computer, Wi-Fi, parking-€10/day, Speicherstrasse 4, tel. 069/273-030, www.ibishotel.com, h1445@accor.com). Exit the station by track 1 and follow busy Baseler Strasse three blocks, then turn right before the river; it's across the street from the green office tower and park.

$ Hotel Topas, a respectable budget choice with 31 rooms, is a block north of the train station. Ask for a back-facing room, as they're quieter and cooler in summer (Sb-€49-59, Db-€59-75, elevator, Wi-Fi, Niddastrasse 88, tel. 069/2380-5820, www. hoteltopas.de, hoteltopas@t-online.de). From the station, follow the same directions as for the Bristol Hotel (listed earlier), two doors away.

Hostel: **$ Five Elements** has 160 beds a block from the train station. It's clean and modern and feels very safe. But because it's smack in the middle of the red light district, families might feel more comfortable elsewhere. Here, too, prices skyrocket during conventions (€20-30/bed in 4-, 6-, and 8-bed dorms, check website for single and double room rates, always saves rooms for last-minute vagabonds who book 1-3 days in advance—€19/person; prices include breakfast, sheets and lockers; elevator, kitchen, guest computer, Wi-Fi, laundry-€4.50/load, Moselstrasse 40, tel. 069/2400-5885, www.5elementshostel.de, welcome@5elementshostel.de). From the station, exit the underground passage onto Taunusstrasse and go one block to the corner of Moselstrasse; the hostel is across the intersection to your left.

ELSEWHERE IN FRANKFURT

If you're in Frankfurt for one night, stay near the station—but if you're in town for a few days and want to feel like you belong, choose one of the following listings. Hotel Neue Kräme and Hotel Zentrum are near Römerberg, and the Maingau Hotel and the hostel are in the Sachsenhausen district (see "Eating in Frankfurt," later). For locations, see the map on page 409.

$$ Hotel Neue Kräme is a quiet little 21-room oasis tucked away above the center of Frankfurt's downtown action, just steps from Römerberg. Friendly David welcomes guests in this bright and cheerful blue-and-white place (Sb-€69-75, Db-€79-95, 5-person apartment with kitchen across street-€105-120, mention this book when booking directly to get these prices, elevator, Wi-Fi, Neue Kräme 23—look for blue-and-white hotel sign out front, tel. 069/284-046, www.hotel-neuekraeme.de, info@hotel-neuekraeme.de).

$$ Hotel Zentrum, hidden on the upper floors of a downtown building, has 30 good rooms in a great location near the Hauptwache (Sb-€75-85, Db-€85-105, Tb-€115-135, Qb-€155-180, mention this book when booking directly to get these prices, elevator, guest computer, Wi-Fi, Rossmarkt 7, tel. 069/5050-0190, www.hotel-zentrum.de, info@hotel-zentrum.de).

$$ Maingau Hotel, located across the river in the Sachsenhausen district, is on a quiet residential street facing a neighborhood park. The 79 rooms are simple and bright. If you're looking for a little tranquility in an authentic residential setting, stay here (Sb-€68-78, Db-€88-98, nicer Db-€98-108, elevator, expensive Wi-Fi, parking-€16/day, restaurant next door serves fancy dinners and €27-40 fixed-price meals, limited selection in hotel lobby bistro, Schifferstrasse 38-40, tel. 069/609-140, www.maingau.de, info@maingau.de). From the station, take tram #16 to the Lokalbahnhof/Textorstrasse stop; the hotel is three blocks away.

Hostel: The **$ Haus der Jugend**, with 434 beds, is right along the river and is the only place I list where prices don't go up during conferences (€19-27/bed in 3-, 4-, 8-, and 10-bed dorms; Sb-€38-42, Db-€64-74, nonmembers-€3.50/day extra, guests older than 26 pay extra, prices include sheets and breakfast; elevator, guest computer, pay Wi-Fi, lunch or dinner-€6, laundry-€2/load, 2:00 curfew, Deutschherrnufer 12, tel. 069/610-0150, www.jugendherberge-frankfurt.de, info@hellofrankfurt.de). From the station, exit through the front door, turn right to the bus platforms, and take bus #46 (3/hour, direction: Mühlberg) to the Frankensteiner Platz stop, which is one door from the hostel.

Eating in Frankfurt

Instead of beer-garden ambience, Frankfurt entices visitors and locals to its Sachsenhausen district, across the river, where you'll find lots of characteristic apple-wine pubs (and plenty of other options). This cobbled and cozy neighborhood is the city's traditional eating-and-drinking zone—a great place to spend a warm summer evening.

Apfelwein, drunk around here since Charlemagne's time 1,200 years ago, became more popular in the 16th century, when local grapes were diseased. It enjoyed another boost two centuries later, when a climate change made grape-growing harder. Apple wine is about the strength of beer (5.5 percent alcohol), but like wine, it can be served spiced and warm in winter. This hard cider can be an acquired taste—good luck enjoying it. You'll see locals, who've spent a lifetime learning to like it, grasping their apple wine in *geripptes*—characteristic hatched glasses (which go back to its early days, when this tax-free drink was slurped by greasy-fingered sausage munchers on the streets).

Sachsenhausen is also a good place to sample local cuisine. The culinary pride of Frankfurt is *Grüne Sosse,* a green sauce made of sour cream blended with seven herbs (parsley, chives, watercress, sorrel, borage, chervil, and burnet); it's frequently served with beef, schnitzel, or halved hard-boiled eggs. Another widely available local specialty (for the adventurous) is *Handkäse mit Musik* ("hand cheese with music"—the "music" comes tomorrow), an aged, cylindrical ricotta-like cheese served with onions and vinegar. You can also satisfy your craving for *Leiterchen* here ("mini-ladders," or spare ribs—surprisingly meaty and salty).

APPLE-WINE PUBS IN SACHSENHAUSEN

The three apple-wine pubs I've listed below all have indoor and outdoor seating in a woodsy, rustic setting. Not just for tourists, these characteristic places are truly popular with Frankfurters, too. To reach them, take bus #46 from the train station (direction: Mühlberg) to Frankensteiner Platz. Or to walk from downtown, cross the river on the pedestrian-only Eiserner Steg or the Alte Brücke. For locations, see the map on page 409.

Dauth-Schneider has lots of tables outside on the shady, tree-covered square, a large indoor section, and a big and accessible menu. It's my first choice for eating outside on a balmy evening (€8-16 main courses, daily 12:00-24:00, Neuer Wall 5-7, tel. 069/613-533). Families appreciate the big city playground across the square from the outdoor tables.

Atschel, across the street and a few doors down, is my Sachsenhausen choice for eating inside. They serve "Frankfurter Schnitzel" with green sauce and other local standards in a handsome dining room and cozy back garden (€8-14 main courses, daily 12:00-24:00, Wallstrasse 7, tel. 069/619-201).

Fichtekränzi, opposite Atschel, is open evenings only. It offers the typical specialties and some lighter fare, both in its cozy, bench-filled beer hall and outside under the trees. The atmosphere is relaxed—expect to share a table and make some new friends (€9-15 main courses, cash only, daily from 17:00, Wallstrasse 5, tel. 069/612-778).

Pub Crawl: Irish pubs and salsa bars clutter the pedestrian zone around Grosse Rittergasse and Frankensteiner Strasse; if you're looking for a place to do a pub crawl, this is it.

DINING DOWNTOWN
On or near Römerberg

Römerberg, Frankfurt's charming, traffic-free, and historic market square, is the focal point of any visit. As you can imagine, it's lined with the typical array of touristy and over-priced restaurants. Still, if you'd like to eat here (especially nice if eating outside), your best bets are listed below.

Weinstube im Römer, in the bottom of the Town Hall, is a classic old place serving good schnitzel and the local Frankfurt white wine, a Riesling, still produced in vineyards owned by the city (€10-12 plates, Tue-Sun 16:00-23:00, closed Mon, Römerberg 19, tel. 069/291-331).

Alte Limpurg, a very simple and basic option with the cheapest menu on the square, is easy to spot: Look for the big sausages displayed out front. Choose from the comfy pub inside or order from the sausage window and enjoy sitting on the square (daily 9:00-24:00, Römerberg 17, tel. 069/287-393).

Cafebar im Kunstverein, while a few steps off the square and without the memorable views, is a fine value and serves more locals than tourists in a kind of retro elegance under medieval vaults (€8-13 plates, homemade cakes, daily 11:00-19:00, adjacent modern art gallery at Markt 44, tel. 069/8477-0863).

In the Old Center near the Hauptwache

Restaurant Opera is a great place for a dressy splurge, with white tablecloths and formal service both inside, under gilded arches and circa-1900 décor, or out on a terrace over the opera's grand entry (€20-30 plates, €15-20 salads, daily 11:00-15:00 & 18:00-23:00, Opernplatz 1, tel. 069/134-0215).

Das Wirtshaus is the traditional favorite on the Fressgass' restaurant row, with classic German dishes and local beers on tap. Sit in its characteristic interior or outside to enjoy the pedestrian action (€10-15 plates, daily/seasonal menus, daily 10:00-23:00, Grosse Bockenheimer Strasse 29, tel. 069/284-399).

Leib & Seele is a modern place a block toward the river from the Hauptwache. Its name means "body and soul," and this local favorite serves lots of hearty and creative salads, serious vegetarian plates, and traditional dishes in a woody, modern pub interior with fine outside tables (€6 lunch specials, €10-12 dinners, daily 10:00-24:00, Kornmarkt 11, tel. 069/281-529).

Galeria Kaufhof's Leonhard's Cafeteria is a huge, sleek, modern cafeteria serving good buffet-style food (at restaurant prices), and has nice city views from its top-floor perch. It's super-efficient, with lots of healthy options, air conditioning, and sofas on the rooftop terrace for those just having a drink (€4-7 salads, €7-8 pizza and pastas, Mon-Sat 9:30-21:00, closed Sun).

Kleinmarkthalle (described on my self-guided walk, earlier) is one of the most charming and inviting indoor market halls you'll find anywhere in Germany, and a great place for a simple lunch. Strolling its ground floor, you can graze through a world of amazing free samples (call that the first course). Once you've made your selection (fish, Italian, oyster bar), find a place to sit down at the far end opposite the entrance or go upstairs (Mon-Fri 8:00-18:00, Sat 8:00-16:00, closed Sun). If you want to picnic, consider the adjacent square, Liebfrauenberg, near the fountain.

Kleinmarkthalle Markt-Stubb (lunch only) is the only real restaurant in the market hall. It's upstairs at the east end and is a hit with local seniors for its traditional home cooking (€10 meals, fresh-from-market ingredients, Mon-Sat 9:00-16:00, closed Sun).

Kleinmarkthalle Weinterrasse is a lively wine garden upstairs at the market hall, serving every wine but apple to locals. It stays open for two hours after the market is closed (Mon-Fri 10:00-20:00, Sat 10:00-18:00, closed Sun).

NEAR THE TRAIN STATION, ON AND NEAR KAISERSTRASSE

A grand boulevard connecting the train station with the old center, Kaiserstrasse is a venerable street of once-dazzling buildings (circa 1880) that's been cleaned up recently (the sex and drugs have been corralled a block or two to the north). It's emerging as a fun eating-and-drinking zone—especially if you need a break from traditional German fare. The parallel Münchener Strasse is less upscale and comes with a cheaper and less-trendy selection of ethnic eateries (such as the Turkish place described below). And the train station itself is a veritable mall of shops and restaurants with long hours. If eating on Kaiserstrasse, I'd recommend strolling the entire Linden tree-lined, four-block stretch (from the station to Gallusanlage) to enjoy the scene and survey your options (as things are steadily evolving upward in quality). Here are a few places to consider (starting nearest the station).

Der Fette Bulle Hamburger Restaurant (the "Fat Bull") is a trendy burger place with a modern and fun interior and good seating on the street. If you're in the mood for a fancy burger, this is the place (€10-12 meals, cheaper lunch specials, dinner salads, daily 11:00-23:00, tel. 069/9075-7004). Across the street (at #64) is **Kaiserpassage,** a fun mini-souk busy with Asian and Arabic eateries.

Merkez Kebab Haus, a block to the right down Elbestrasse, is the best place for Turkish food. With a wood-fired grill, it's a cut above the usual *Döner Kebab* shop, with an inviting ambience and good service, but at a great price (*Döner Kebabs* cost only €4.50; €9-15 main dishes, salads, and desserts—most on view at the counter; wonderful *sütlac*—rice pudding, daily 8:00-24:00, Münchener Strasse 33, tel. 069/233-995).

Urban Kitchen (at #53) is a chic and modern place serving creative global food from a fun and healthy menu to a cool crowd (€10-12 plates, €7 lunch specials, daily 11:00-23:00, tel. 069/2710-7999).

BonaMente Steakhaus (at #51) is the local choice for red meat, with a sleek and modern steakhouse ambience inside and good on-the-street tables. The portions are big, and so is the selection (€13-32 plates, daily 11:30-24:00, Kaiserstrasse 51, tel. 069/2562-7566).

L'Emir, hidden inside a cheap hotel on the corner of Weserstrasse (at #17), is a good Lebanese place. Choose from their endless appetizer options or try their popular lamb dishes (€7-18 plates, daily 12:00-24:00, tel. 069/2400-8686).

Bagel Brothers (at #49) can make a bagel sandwich any way you like it for cheap (€3-4, Mon-Fri 7:30-14:00, Sat-Sun 9:00-18:00).

The **Indigo Restaurant** is a block down Weserstrasse to the north. It is a bit closer to the red light district, but their Indian food is rumored to be some of the best in town. This is a good place for takeout (€8-11 main courses, daily 12:00-14:00 & 17:30-22:30, Taunusstrasse 17, tel. 069/2648-8878). Back on the main drag, **Maharaja** (at #41) is another good Indian option.

Thai Snack (at #38) is good for those who want quick and in-expensive meals. Dine inside the small, modern interior or eat your food streetside (daily 11:30-22:00, tel. 069/2695-7957).

Dean & David (at #33) is a favorite for a fast, inexpensive, and healthy meal with views of the skyscrapers of "Bankfurt." It has a pleasant modern interior and wonderful streetside tables (€6-8 plates, super-fresh salads, veggie dishes, curries, soups, wok plates, sandwiches, smoothies, daily 10:00-21:00, tel. 069/800-88363).

Frankfurt Connections

BY TRAIN

German Destinations: Rothenburg (hourly, 2.5-3 hours, changes in Würzburg and Steinach; the tiny Steinach-Rothenburg train often leaves from track 5, shortly after the Würzburg train arrives), **Würzburg** (1-2/hour, 70 minutes, or 2 hours on cheaper RE trains), **Nürnberg** (1-2/hour, 2 hours), **Munich** (hourly, 3.5 hours), **Baden-Baden** (hourly, 1.5-2 hours, direct or transfer in Karlsruhe), **Bacharach** (hourly, 1.5-2 hours, change in Mainz or Bingen), **Freiburg** (hourly, 1.5-2 hours), **Cochem** (1-2/hour, 2.5 hours, change in Koblenz), **Cologne** (direct ICE trains hourly, 1-1.5 hours; cheaper, less frequent IC trains take 2.5 hours and show you more of the Rhine), **Leipzig** (every 2 hours direct on ICE, 3.5 hours; a few additional on IC, 4 hours), **Berlin** (hourly, 4 hours), **Hamburg** (hourly, 4 hours). Train info: Tel. 0180-599-6633, www.bahn.com.

International Destinations: Amsterdam (3/day direct, 4 hours; more with changes, 5.5-7 hours), **Bern** (hourly, 4 hours, some with change in Basel), **Zürich** (hourly, 4 hours, most change in Basel), **Brussels** (at least hourly, 3-5 hours, most change in Cologne), **Copenhagen** (10/day, 9 hours, change in Hamburg), **Paris** (every 1-2 hours, 4-6 hours, most with 1 change), **Vienna** (6/day direct, 7 hours), **Prague** (6/day, 6 hours, change to bus in Nürnberg).

BY ROMANTIC ROAD BUS

The bus departs promptly at 8:00 (mid-April-late Oct) from the Deutsche Touring bus stop by the front corner of the Frankfurt train station. Exit the station through the main entrance and turn right; look for the platform (usually 7-9) with signs saying *Touring* and *Romantische Strasse*. You can either pay cash when you board, or buy your ticket at the Deutsche Touring office, which is across the street from the south (track 1) side of the station (Mon-Fri 7:30-19:30, Sat-Sun 7:30-13:00 or longer; Mannheimer Strasse 15, tel. 069/4609-2780, www.romanticroadcoach.de). It's free to book a seat in advance on their website, but it's not necessary. Frankfurt to Rothenburg costs €45, to Munich is €82, and all the way to Füssen is €108 (20 percent discount with rail pass). For more information, see page 380.

BY PLANE
Frankfurt Airport

Frankfurt's airport *(Flughafen),* just a few stops by S-Bahn from the city center, has its own long-distance train station, which makes it a snap to connect from a flight here to other German cities. For flight information in English, visit www.frankfurt-airport.com, call 01805-372-4636, or contact your airline (airport code: FRA).

There are two separate terminals (know your terminal—check your ticket or the airport website). **Terminal 1,** a multi-level maze of check-in counters and shops, is linked to the train station. **Terminal 2** is small and quiet, with few services. A Skytrain connects the two terminals in less than five minutes. Pick up the free brochure *Your Airport Guide* for a map and detailed information (available at the airport and at most Frankfurt hotels).

The airport has three **baggage-storage** desks (*Gepäckausbewahrung,* €7/day per bag; the branch in Terminal 1B, level 1 is open 24 hours, others daily 6:00-22:00). There is a **post office** (in Terminal 1B, level 1, Mon-Fri 9:00-19:00, Sat-Sun 11:00-18:00), a **pharmacy** (in Terminal 1B, level 2, and also in Terminal 2, daily 7:00-21:00), a 24-hour **medical clinic** (on level 1 between terminals 1B and 1C), public **showers** (Terminal 1B, level 2, near the pharmacy, €6, shampoo and towel included, open 24 hours), and free **Wi-Fi.** A good-sized, fairly priced **supermarket** is handy for last-minute shopping for European treats (Terminal 1C, level 0, daily 6:00-22:00; tricky to find: Go down the escalators from the underpass on level 1 between terminals 1B and 1C, or up the escalators from train platforms 1-3). Take advantage of the **luggage carts,** ingeniously designed to ride on the airport's escalators (and even all the way up to, but not into, the Skytrain; €2 deposit is refunded when you return your cart). But heed the instructions on the carts and at the escalator entrances. There are **customs desks** in both terminals for VAT refunds (daily 7:00-21:00; after hours, ask the information desk to page a customs officer for you). There's even McBeer at three McDonald's; one allegedly is among Europe's largest. McWelcome to Germany.

Frankfurt Airport Train Station

The airport's train station has two parts, both reachable from Terminal 1. Regional S-Bahn trains to downtown Frankfurt and nearby towns and suburbs depart from platforms 1-3. Long-distance trains leave from the slightly more distant *Fernbahnhof*, platforms 4-7.

Getting Between the Airport and Downtown Frankfurt: The airport is a 12-minute train ride on the **S-Bahn** from Frankfurt's main train station, or Hauptbahnhof (4/hour, €4.35, ride included in €9.90 Frankfurt Card and €8.50 individual/€15 group version of all-day *Tageskarte Frankfurt* transit pass, but not in cheaper group version of *Tageskarte Frankfurt*). Figure about €25 for a **taxi** from the airport to any of my recommended hotels.

From Frankfurt Airport by Long-Distance Train: Train travelers can validate rail passes or buy tickets at the *Reisezentrum* on the level above the long-distance train platforms. Handy ticket machines are easy to use and allow you to print a schedule even if you aren't buying a ticket—great for those traveling with a rail pass. Destinations include **Rothenburg** (hourly, 3-3.5 hours, change in Würzburg and Steinach), **Würzburg** (1-2/hour, 1.5 hours), **Nürnberg** (1-2/hour, 2.5 hours), **Munich** (1-2/hour, 3.5 hours), **Baden-Baden** (roughly hourly, 1.5 hours, change in Karlsruhe and/or Mannheim), **Cologne** (1-2/hour, 1 hour; trains along Rhine go less often and take 2.5 hours), **Bacharach** (hourly, 1-1.5 hours, most change in Mainz, some depart from regional platforms), **Berlin** (1-2/hour, 4.5-5 hours, most with 1 change). There are also many **international connections** from here (such as Paris, London, Brussels, Amsterdam, Zürich, Bern, and Prague).

Sleeping at or near Frankfurt Airport

Because train connections to Frankfurt Airport are so good, if your flight doesn't leave too early, you can sleep in another city and still make it to the airport for your flight. If you wake up in Cologne, Baden-Baden, Würzburg, or Bacharach, you can still catch a late-morning or midday flight; you can often make it from Nürnberg, Rothenburg, Freiburg, the Mosel, and even Munich for an early-afternoon flight. But plan ahead and leave room for delays; don't take the last possible connection.

Because of these easy connections—and since downtown Frankfurt is just 12 minutes away by frequent train—it makes little sense for train travelers to sleep at the airport. Drivers who want to stay near the airport the night before returning a rental car can stay in Kelsterbach, just across the expressway from the airport, at the **$$ Ibis Frankfurt Airport Hotel** (Sb/Db without breakfast-€79-99, Langer Kornweg 9a-11, tel. 06107/9870, www. ibishotel.com). If you're desperate, the **$$$ Sheraton Frankfurt** is conveniently connected to Terminal 1 and has 1,008 international business-class rooms (Db-€179 and up, check website or the hotel desk in the airport for lower rates, tel. 069/69770, www.sheraton. com/frankfurt, salesfrankfurt@sheraton.com).

"Frankfurt" Hahn Airport

This smaller airport, misleadingly classified as a "Frankfurt" airport for marketing purposes, is a nearly two-hour drive away in the Mosel region. Regular buses connect Frankfurt Hahn Airport to Bullay (for trains to Cochem), Trier, Mainz, Cologne, and Frankfurt (more info at www.hahn-airport.de). Hahn Airport is popular with low-cost carriers (such as Ryanair). To avoid any confusion, double-check the three-letter airport code on your ticket (FRA for Frankfurt Airport, HHN for Frankfurt Hahn).

RHINE VALLEY

Best of the Rhine • Bacharach • Oberwesel • St. Goar • Koblenz

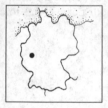

The Rhine Valley is storybook Germany, a fairy-tale world of legends and robber-baron castles. Cruise the most turret-studded stretch of the romantic Rhine as you listen for the song of the treacherous Loreley. For hands-on thrills, climb through the Rhineland's greatest castle, Rheinfels, above the town of St. Goar. Connoisseurs will also enjoy the fine interior of Marksburg Castle. Spend your nights in a castle-crowned village, either Bacharach or St. Goar.

PLANNING YOUR TIME

The Rhineland is magical, but doesn't take much time to see. Both Bacharach and St. Goar are an easy 1.5-hour train ride (€20) or a one-hour drive from Frankfurt Airport, and they make a good first or last stop for travelers flying in or out.

The blitziest tour of the area is an hour looking at the castles from your train window—use the narration in this chapter to give it meaning. The non-stop express runs every hour, connecting Koblenz and Mainz in 50 scenic minutes. (Super-express ICE trains between Cologne and Frankfurt bypass the Rhine entirely.) For a better look, cruise in, tour a castle or two, sleep in a medieval town, and take the train out.

Ideally, if you have two nights to spend here, sleep in Bacharach, cruise the best hour of the river (from Bacharach to St. Goar), and tour Rheinfels Castle. If rushed, focus on Rheinfels Castle and cruise less. With more time, add a visit to Koblenz or Oberwesel, or ride the riverside bike path. With another day, mosey through the neighboring Mosel Valley or day-trip to Cologne (both covered in different chapters).

There are countless castles in this region, so you'll need to be selective in your castle-going. Aside from Rheinfels Castle, my favorites are Burg Eltz (see page 501 in next chapter; well preserved with medieval interior, set evocatively in a romantic forest the next valley over), Marksburg Castle (page 451; rebuilt medieval interior, with commanding Rhine perch), and Rheinstein Castle (page 455; a 19th-century duke's hunting palace overlooking the Rhine). Of these, Marksburg is the easiest to reach by train.

If possible, visit the Rhine between April and October. The low season (winter and spring) is lower here than in some other parts of Germany. Many hotels and restaurants close from November to February or March. Only one riverboat runs, sights close or have short hours, and neither Bacharach nor St. Goar have much in the way of Christmas markets.

CHOOSING A HOME BASE

Bacharach and St. Goar, the best towns for an overnight stop, are 10 miles apart, connected by milk-run trains, riverboats, and a riverside bike path. Bacharach is a much more interesting town, but St. Goar has the famous castle. In general, the Rhine is an easy place for cheap sleeps. B&Bs and *Gasthäuser* with €25-30 beds abound (and normally discount their prices for longer stays). Rhine-area hostels offer €20 beds to travelers of any age. Each town's TI is eager to set you up, and finding a room should be easy any time of year (except for Sept-Oct winefest weekends). Note: Rhine Valley towns often have guesthouses and hotels with similar names—when reserving, double-check that you're contacting the one in your planned destination.

Best of the Rhine

Ever since Roman times, when this was the empire's northern boundary, the Rhine has been one of the world's busiest shipping rivers. You'll see a steady flow of barges with 1,000- to 2,000-ton loads. Tourist-packed buses, hot train tracks, and highways line both banks.

Many of the castles were "robber-baron" castles, put there by petty rulers (there were 300 independent little countries in medieval Germany, a region about the size of Montana) to levy tolls on passing river traffic. A robber baron would put his castle on, or even in, the river. Then, often with the help of chains and a tower on the opposite bank, he'd stop each ship and get his toll. There were 10 customs stops in the 60-mile stretch between Mainz and Koblenz alone (no wonder merchants were early proponents of the creation of larger nation-states).

Some castles were built to control and protect settlements, and others were the residences of kings. As times changed, so did the lifestyles of the rich and feudal. Many castles were abandoned for more comfortable mansions in the towns.

Most Rhine castles date from the 11th, 12th, and 13th centuries. When the pope successfully asserted his power over the German emperor in 1076, local princes ran wild over the rule of their emperor. The castles saw military action in the 1300s and 1400s, as emperors began reasserting their control over Germany's many silly kingdoms.

The castles were also involved in the Reformation wars, in which Europe's Catholic and Protestant dynasties fought it out using a fragmented Germany as their battleground. The Thirty Years' War (1618-1648) devastated Germany. The outcome: Each ruler got the freedom to decide if his people would be Catholic or Protestant, and one-third of Germans died. (Production of Gummi Bears ceased entirely.)

The French—who feared a strong Germany and felt the Rhine was the logical border between them and Germany— destroyed most of the castles as a preventive measure (Louis XIV in the 1680s, the Revolutionary army in the 1790s, and Napoleon in 1806). Many were rebuilt in the Neo-Gothic style in the Romantic Age—the late 1800s—and today are enjoyed as restaurants, hotels, hostels, and museums.

GETTING AROUND THE RHINE

The Rhine flows north from Switzerland to Holland, but the scenic stretch from Mainz to Koblenz hoards all the touristic charm. Studded with the crenellated cream of Germany's castles, it bustles with boats, trains, and highway traffic. Have fun exploring with a mix of big steamers, tiny ferries *(Fähre)*, trains, and bikes.

By Boat: While some travelers do the whole Mainz-Koblenz trip by boat (5.5 hours downstream, 8.5 hours up), I'd just focus on the most scenic hour—from St. Goar to Bacharach. Sit on the boat's top deck with your handy Rhine map-guide (or the kilometer-keyed tour in this chapter) and enjoy the parade of castles, towns, boats, and vineyards.

Two boat companies take travelers along this stretch of the Rhine. Boats run daily in both directions from early April through October, with only one boat running off-season.

Most travelers sail on the bigger, more expensive, and romantic **Köln-Düsseldorfer (K-D) Line** (recommended Bacharach-St. Goar trip: €12.60 one-way, €15.20 round-trip, bikes-€2.80/day, €2 extra if paying with credit card; discounts: up to 30 percent if over

Rhine Overview

Düsseldorf

Rhine

Cologne

UNROMANTIC RHINE

Bonn

•Aachen

Remagen

BELG.

Koblenz

BURG ELTZ

Cochem

St. Goar

Beilstein

Oberwesel

Bingen

Bacharach

BEST OF THE RHINE

See detail map

Frankfurt

Wies-baden

Main R.

Mainz

Frankfurt

Mosel R.

Neckar R.

LUX.

Lux. City

Trier

Hahn

Heidelberg

GERMANY

Berlin

GERMANY

N

50 Kilometers

50 Miles

FRANCE

60, 20 percent if you present a connecting train ticket, free with rail passes but starts the use of a day of a flexipass; tel. 06741/1634 in St. Goar, tel. 06743/1322 in Bacharach, www.k-d.com). You'll see K-D's abridged schedule in this chapter. Complete, up-to-date schedules are posted at any Rhineland station, hotel, TI, and www.k-d.com. (Confirm times at your hotel the night before.) Purchase tickets at the dock up to five minutes before departure. The boat is never full. Romantics will enjoy the old-time paddle-wheeler *Goethe*, which sails each direction once a day (noted on schedule, confirm time locally).

The smaller **Bingen-Rüdesheimer Line** is slightly cheaper than the K-D, doesn't offer any rail pass deals, and makes three trips in each direction daily from early April through October (Bacharach-St. Goar: €12 one-way, €14 round-trip, bikes-€2/day, buy tickets at ticket booth or on boat, ticket booth only open just before boat departs, 30 percent discount if over 60; departs Bacharach at 10:10, 12:00, and 15:00; departs St. Goar at 11:00, 14:10, and 16:10; tel. 06721/14140, www.bingen-ruedesheimer.de).

By Car: Drivers have these options: 1) skip the boat; 2) take a round-trip cruise from St. Goar or Bacharach; 3) draw pretzels and let the loser drive, prepare the picnic, and meet the boat; 4) rent a bike, bring it on the boat for €2.80, and bike back; or 5) take the boat one-way and return to your car by train. When exploring by car, don't hesitate to pop onto one of the many little ferries that shuttle across the bridgeless-around-here river.

By Ferry: As there are no bridges between Koblenz and Mainz, you'll see car-and-passenger ferries (usually family-run for generations) about every three miles. Bingen-Rüdesheim, Lorch-Niederheimbach, Engelsburg-Kaub, and St. Goar-St. Goarshausen are some of the most useful routes (times vary; St. Goar-St. Goarshausen ferry departs each side every 15-20 minutes, Mon-Sat 5:30-24:00, Sun 6:30-24:00; one-way fares: adult-€1.60, car and driver-€4, pay on the boat; www.faehre-loreley.de). For a fun little jaunt, take a quick round-trip with some time to explore the other side.

By Bike: You can bike on either side of the Rhine, but for a designated bike path, stay on the west side, where a 35-mile path runs between Koblenz and Bingen. The six-mile stretch between St. Goar and Bacharach is smooth and scenic, but mostly along the highway. The bit from Bacharach to Bingen hugs the riverside and is car-free. Either way, biking is a great way to explore the valley. Many hotels provide free or cheap bikes to guests; some also rent to the public (including Hotel Hillen in Bacharach and Hotel an der Fähre in St. Goar).

Consider biking one-way and taking the bike back on the riverboat, or designing a circular trip using the fun and frequent shuttle ferries. A good target might be Kaub (where a tiny boat shuttles sightseers to the better-from-a-distance castle on the island) or Rheinstein Castle.

By Train: Hourly milk-run trains hit every town along the Rhine (St. Goar-Bacharach in both directions about :20 after the hour, 10 minutes, €3.60; Bacharach-Mainz, 1 hour; Mainz-Koblenz, 1.5 hours). Express trains speed past the small towns, taking only 50 minutes non-stop between Mainz and Koblenz. Some train schedules list St. Goar but not Bacharach as a stop, but any schedule listing St. Goar also stops at Bacharach. Tiny stations are not staffed—buy tickets at machines. Though generally user-friendly, the ticket machines are not all created equal. Some claim to only take exact change; others may not accept US credit cards. When buying a ticket, be sure to select "English" and follow the instructions carefully. For example, the ticket machine may give you the choice of validating your ticket for that day or a day in the near future—but only for some destinations (when you're not given this option, your ticket will automatically be validated for the day of purchase).

The **Rheinland-Pfalz-Ticket** day pass covers travel on milk-run trains to anywhere in this chapter—plus the Mosel and Trier chapters (and also Remagen, but not Frankfurt, Cologne, or Bonn). It can save heaps of money, particularly on longer day trips or if there's more than one in your party (1 person-€23, up to 4 additional people-€4/each, buy from station ticket machines, good after 9:00 Mon-Fri and all day Sat-Sun, valid on trains labeled *RB, RE,* and *MRB*). For a day trip between Bacharach and Burg Eltz (normally €30 round-trip; Burg Eltz described in next chapter), even one person saves with a Rheinland-Pfalz-Ticket, and a group of five adults saves more than €100—look for travel partners at breakfast.

Rhine Blitz Tour by Train or Boat

One of Europe's great train thrills is zipping along the Rhine enjoying this self-guided blitz tour, worth ▲▲▲. Or, even better, do it relaxing on the deck of a Rhine steamer, surrounded by the wonders of this romantic and historic gorge. This quick and easy tour (you can cut in anywhere) skips most of the syrupy myths filling normal Rhine guides. You can follow along on a train, boat, bike, or car. By train or boat, sit on the left (river) side going south from Koblenz. While nearly all the castles listed are viewed from this side, train travelers need to clear a path to the right window for the times I yell, "Cross over!"

You'll notice large black-and-white kilometer markers along the riverbank. I erected these years ago to make this tour easier to follow. They tell the distance from the Rhine Falls, where the Rhine leaves Switzerland and becomes navigable. (Today, river-barge pilots also use these markers to navigate.) We're tackling just 36 miles (58 km) of the 820-mile-long (1,320-km) Rhine. Your Rhine Blitz Tour starts at Koblenz and heads upstream to Bingen. If you're going the other direction, it still works. Just hold the book upside-down.

You can download a free Rick Steves **audio tour** of this Rhine sightseeing jaunt—it works in either direction (see page 12).

Km 590—Koblenz: This Rhine blitz starts with Romantic Rhine thrills, at Koblenz. Koblenz isn't terribly attractive (it was hit hard in World War II), but its place at the historic Deutsches Eck ("German Corner")—the tip of land where the Mosel River joins the Rhine—gives it a certain patriotic charm. A cable car links the Deutsches Eck with the yellow Ehrenbreitstein Fortress across the river. (For more on Koblenz, see page 486.)

Km 586—Lahneck Castle (Burg Lahneck): Above the modern autobahn bridge over the Lahn River, this castle *(Burg)* was built in 1240 to defend local silver mines. The castle was ruined by

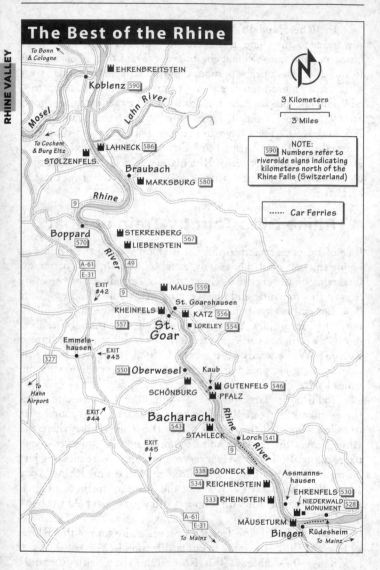

The Best of the Rhine

To Bonn & Cologne

EHRENBREITSTEIN

Koblenz 590

Lahn River

Mosel

To Cochem & Burg Eltz

LAHNECK 586
STOLZENFELS

Braubach

MARKSBURG 580

Rhine

9

Boppard 570

STERRENBERG
LIEBENSTEIN 567

A-61
E-31

49

9

EXIT #42

MAUS 559

St. Goarshausen

RHEINFELS
KATZ 556

St. Goar

LORELEY 554

557

Emmels-hausen

EXIT #43

327

550 Oberwesel

Kaub

To Hahn Airport

SCHÖNBURG

GUTENFELS 546
PFALZ

EXIT #44

Bacharach
543

STAHLECK

Lorch 541

9

EXIT #45

538 SOONECK
534 REICHENSTEIN

Assmanns-hausen

533 RHEINSTEIN

EHRENFELS 530
NIEDERWALD MONUMENT 528

A-61
E-31

MÄUSETURM

Bingen
Rüdesheim
To Mainz

To Mainz

NOTE:
590 Numbers refer to riverside signs indicating kilometers north of the Rhine Falls (Switzerland)

3 Kilometers
3 Miles

······ Car Ferries

the French in 1688 and rebuilt in the 1850s in Neo-Gothic style. Burg Lahneck faces another Romantic rebuild, the yellow Schloss Stolzenfels (out of view above the train, a 10-minute climb from tiny parking lot, closed Mon and Dec, www.schloss-stolzenfels. de). Note that a *Burg* is a defensive fortress, while a *Schloss* is mainly a showy palace.

Km 580—Marksburg Castle: This castle stands bold and white—restored to look like most Rhine castles once did, with their slate stonework covered with stucco to look as if made from

K-D Line Rhine Cruise Schedule

Boats run from early April through October (usually 5/day, but 3-4/day in early April and most of Oct). From November through March, one boat runs daily for groups, but individuals can tag along if they know you're coming—call the boat directly (tel. 0172/1360-335) or the main office in Cologne (tel. 0221/2088-318) to confirm. The times listed below are based on the 2014 schedule. Check www.k-d.com for the latest.

Koblenz	Boppard	St. Goar	Bacharach
—	9:00	10:20	11:30
*9:00	*11:00	*12:20	*13:30
—	13:00	14:20	15:30
—	14:00	15:20	16:30
14:00	16:00	17:20	18:30
13:10	11:50	10:55	10:15
—	12:50	11:55	11:15
—	13:50	12:55	12:15
18:10	16:50	15:55	15:15
*20:10	*18:50	*17:55	*17:15

*These sailings are on the 1913 paddle-wheeler Goethe.

a richer stone. You'll spot Marksburg with the three modern chimneys behind it, just before the town of Spay. This is the best-looking of all the Rhine castles and the only surviving medieval castle on the Rhine. Because of its commanding position, it was never attacked in the Middle Ages (though it was captured by the US Army in March of 1945). It's now open as a museum with a medieval interior second only to the Mosel Valley's Burg Eltz. (A self-guided tour for Marksburg appears on page 451; Burg Eltz is covered in the next chapter.) The three modern smokestacks vent Europe's biggest car-battery recycling plant just up the valley.

If you haven't read the sidebar on river traffic (later in this chapter), now's a good time.

Km 570—Boppard: Once a Roman town, Boppard has some impressive remains of fourth-century walls. Look for the Roman towers and the substantial chunk of Roman wall near the train station, just above the main square. You'll notice that a church is a big part of each townscape. Many small towns have two towering churches. Four centuries ago, after enduring a horrific war, each prince or king decided which faith his subjects would follow (more often Protestant to the north and east, Catholic to the south and west). While church attendance in Germany is way down, the towns here, like Germany as a whole, are still divided between Catholic and Protestant.

If you visit Boppard, head to the fascinating Church of St. Severus below the main square. Find the carved Romanesque crazies at the doorway. Inside, to the right of the entrance, you'll see Christian symbols from Roman times. Also notice the painted arches and vaults (originally, most Romanesque churches were painted this way). Down by the river, look for the high-water *(Hochwasser)* marks on the arches from various flood years. (You'll find these flood marks throughout the Rhine and Mosel valleys.)

Km 567—Sterrenberg Castle and Liebenstein Castle: These are the "Hostile Brothers" castles across from Bad Salzig. Take the wall between the castles (actually designed to improve the defenses of both castles), add two greedy and jealous brothers and a fair maiden, and create your own legend. Burg Liebenstein is now a fun, friendly, and affordable family-run hotel (9 rooms, Db-€135-140, suite-€165, giant king-and-the-family room-€240, easy parking, tel. 06773/308 or 06773/251, www.castle-liebenstein.com, info@burg-liebenstein.de, Nickenig family).

Km 560: While you can see nothing from here, a 19th-century lead mine functioned on both sides of the river, with a shaft actually tunneling completely under the Rhine.

Km 559—Maus Castle (Burg Maus): The Maus (mouse) got its name because the next castle was owned by the Katzenelnbogen family. (*Katz* means "cat.") In the 1300s, it was considered a state-of-the-art fortification...until 1806, when Napoleon had it blown up with then-state-of-the-art explosives. It was rebuilt true to its original plans in about 1900. Today, the castle is open only for concerts and weddings, with occasional guided tours (20-minute walk up, tel. 06771/9100, www.burg-maus.de).

Km 557—St. Goar and Rheinfels Castle: Cross to the other side of the train. The pleasant town of St. Goar was named for a sixth-century hometown monk. It originated in Celtic times (i.e., really old) as a place where sailors would stop, catch their breath, send home a postcard, and give thanks after surviving the seductive and treacherous Loreley crossing. St. Goar is worth a stop to explore its mighty Rheinfels Castle. (For more on St. Goar, see page 475; for a self-guided castle tour, see page 478.)

Km 556—Katz Castle (Burg Katz): Burg Katz (Katzenelnbogen) faces St. Goar from across the river. Together, Burg Katz (built in 1371) and Rheinfels Castle had a clear view up and down the river, effectively controlling traffic (there was absolutely no duty-free shopping on the medieval Rhine). Katz got Napoleoned in 1806 and rebuilt in about 1900.

Today, the castle is shrouded by intrigue and controversy. In 1995, a wealthy and eccentric Japanese man bought it for about $4 million. His vision: to make the castle—so close to the Loreley that Japanese tourists are wild about—an exotic escape for his countrymen. But the town wouldn't allow his planned renovation of the historic (and therefore protected) building. Stymied, the frustrated investor abandoned his plans. Today, Burg Katz sits empty...the Japanese ghost castle.

Below the castle, notice the derelict grape terraces—worked since the eighth century, but abandoned in the last generation. The Rhine wine is particularly good because the local slate absorbs the heat of the sun and stays warm all night, resulting in sweeter grapes. Wine from the steep side of the Rhine gorge—where grapes are harder to grow and harvest—is tastier and more expensive.

About Km 555: A statue of the Loreley, the beautiful-but-deadly nymph (see next listing for legend), combs her hair at the end of a long spit—built to give barges protection from vicious ice floes that until recent years raged down the river in the winter. The actual Loreley, a cliff (marked by the flags), is just ahead.

Km 554—The Loreley: Steep a big slate rock in centuries of legend and it becomes a tourist attraction—the ultimate Rhinestone. The Loreley (flags on top, name painted near shoreline), rising 450 feet over the narrowest and deepest point of the Rhine, has long been important. It was a holy site in pre-Roman days. The fine echoes here—thought to be ghostly voices—fertilized legend-tellers' imaginations.

Because of the reefs just upstream (at km 552), many ships never made it to St. Goar. Sailors (after days on the river) blamed their misfortune on a *wunderbares Fräulein,* whose long, blond hair almost covered her body. Heinrich Heine's *Song of Loreley* (the CliffsNotes version is on local postcards) tells the story of a count sending his men to kill or capture this siren after she distracted his horny son, who forgot to watch where he was sailing and drowned. When the soldiers cornered the nymph in her cave, she called her father (Father Rhine) for help. Huge waves, the likes of which you'll never see today, rose from the river and carried Loreley to safety. And she has never been seen since.

But alas, when the moon shines brightly and the tour buses are parked, a soft, playful Rhine whine can still be heard from the Loreley. As you pass, listen carefully ("Sailors...sailors...over my bounding mane").

Km 552—The Seven Maidens: Killer reefs, marked by red-and-green buoys, are called the "Seven Maidens." OK, one more goofy legend: The prince of Schönburg Castle (*über* Oberwesel—

Rhine River Trade and Barge-Watching

The Rhine is great for barge-watching. There's a constant parade of action, and each boat is different. Since ancient times, this has been a highway for trade. Today, Europe's biggest port (Rotterdam) waits at the mouth of the river.

Barge workers are almost a subculture. Many own their own ships. The captain lives in the stern, with his family. The family car is often parked on the stern. Workers live in the bow.

In the Rhine town of Kaub, there was once a boarding school for the children of the Rhine merchant marines—but today it's closed, since most captains are Dutch, Belgian, or Swiss. The flag of the boat's home country flies in the stern (Dutch—horizontal red, white, and blue; Belgian—vertical black, yellow, and red; Swiss—white cross on a red field; German—horizontal black, red, and yellow; French—vertical red, white, and blue). Logically, imports go upstream (Japanese cars, coal, and oil) and exports go downstream (German cars, chemicals, and pharmaceuticals). A clever captain manages to ship goods in each direction. Recently, giant Dutch container ships (which transport five times the cargo) have been driving many of the traditional barges out of business, presenting the German economy with another challenge.

Going downstream, tugs can push a floating train of up to five barges at once, but upstream, as the slope gets steeper (and the stream gradient gets higher), they can push only one at a time. Before modern shipping, horses dragged boats upstream (the faint remains of towpaths survive at points along the river). From 1873 to 1900, workers laid a chain from Bonn to Bingen, and boats with cogwheels and steam engines hoisted themselves

described next) had seven spoiled daughters who always dumped men because of their shortcomings. Fed up, he invited seven of his knights to the castle and demanded that his daughters each choose one to marry. But they complained that each man had too big a nose, was too fat, too stupid, and so on. The rude and teasing girls escaped into a riverboat. Just downstream, God turned them into the seven rocks that form this reef. While this story probably isn't entirely true, there was a lesson in it for medieval children: Don't be hard-hearted.

Km 550—Oberwesel: Cross to the other side of the train. The town of Oberwesel, topped by the commanding Schönburg Castle (now a hotel), boasts some of the best medieval wall and tower remains on the Rhine. (For more on Oberwesel, see page 470).

Notice how many of the train tunnels along here have entrances designed like medieval turrets—they were actually built in the Romantic 19th century. OK, back to the riverside.

Km 546—Gutenfels Castle and Pfalz Castle, the Classic Rhine View: Burg Gutenfels (now a privately owned hotel) and

upstream. Today, 265 million tons travel each year along the 530 miles from Basel on the German-Swiss border to the Dutch city of Rotterdam on the Atlantic.

Riverside navigational aids are of vital interest to captains who don't wish to meet the Loreley (see page 447). Boats pass on

the right unless they clearly signal otherwise with a large blue sign. Since ships heading downstream can't stop or maneuver as freely, boats heading upstream are expected to do the tricky do-si-do work. Cameras monitor traffic all along and relay warnings of oncoming ships by posting large triangular signals before narrow and troublesome bends in the river. There may be two or three triangles per signpost, depending upon how many "sectors," or segments, of the river are covered. The lowest triangle indicates the nearest stretch of river. Each triangle tells whether there's a ship in that sector. When the bottom side of a triangle is lit, that sector is empty. When the left side is lit, an oncoming ship is in that sector.

The **Signal and River Pilots Museum** (Wahrschauer- und Lotsenmuseum), located at the signal triangles at the upstream edge of St. Goar, explains how barges are safer, cleaner, and more fuel-efficient than trains or trucks (free, May-Sept Wed and Sat 14:00-17:00, outdoor exhibits always open).

the shipshape Pfalz Castle (built in the river in the 1300s) worked very effectively to tax medieval river traffic. The town of Kaub grew rich as Pfalz raised its chains when boats came, and lowered them only when the merchants had paid their duty. Those who didn't pay spent time touring its prison, on a raft at the bottom of its well. In 1504, a pope called for the destruction of Pfalz, but the locals withstood a

six-week siege, and the castle still stands. Notice the overhanging outhouse (tiny white room between two wooden ones). Pfalz (also known as Pfalzgrafenstein) is tourable but bare and dull (€3 ferry from Kaub, €3 entry, April-Oct Tue-Sun 10:00-18:00, closed Mon; shorter hours in March; Nov and Jan-Feb Sat-Sun only;

closed Dec; last entry one hour before closing, mobile 0172-262-2800, www.burg-pfalzgrafenstein.de).

In Kaub, on the riverfront directly below the castles, a green statue (near the waving flags) honors the German general Gebhard von Blücher. He was Napoleon's nemesis. In 1813, as Napoleon fought his way back to Paris after his disastrous Russian campaign, he stopped at Mainz—hoping to fend off the Germans and Russians pursuing him by controlling that strategic bridge. Blücher tricked Napoleon. By building the first major pontoon bridge of its kind here at the Pfalz Castle, he crossed the Rhine and outflanked the French. Two years later, Blücher and Wellington teamed up to defeat Napoleon once and for all at Waterloo.

Immediately opposite Kaub (where the ferry lands, marked by blue roadside flags) is a gaping hole in the mountainside. This marks the last working slate mine on the Rhine.

Km 544—"The Raft Busters": Just before Bacharach, at the top of the island, buoys mark a gang of rocks notorious for busting up rafts. The Black Forest, upstream from here, was once poor, and wood was its best export. Black Foresters would ride log booms down the Rhine to the Ruhr (where their timber fortified coal-mine shafts) or to Holland (where logs were sold to shipbuilders). If they could navigate the sweeping bend just before Bacharach and then survive these "raft busters," they'd come home reckless and horny—the German folkloric equivalent of American cowboys after payday.

Km 543—Bacharach and Stahleck Castle (Burg Stahleck): Cross to the other side of the train. The town of Bacharach is a great stop (described on page 455). Some of the Rhine's best wine is from this town, whose name likely derives from "altar to Bacchus." Local vintners brag that the medieval Pope Pius II ordered Bacharach wine by the cartload. Perched above the town, the 13th-century Burg Stahleck is now a hostel. Return to the riverside.

Km 541—Lorch: This pathetic stub of a castle is barely visible from the road. Check out the hillside vineyards. These vineyards once blanketed four times as much land as they do today, but modern economics have driven most of them out of business. The vineyards that do survive require government subsidies. Notice the small car ferry, one of several along the bridgeless stretch between Mainz and Koblenz.

Km 538—Sooneck Castle: Cross back to the other side of the train. Built in the 11th century, this castle was twice destroyed by people sick and tired of robber barons.

Km 534—Reichenstein Castle and **Km 533—Rheinstein Castle:** Stay on the other side of the train to see two of the first castles to be rebuilt in the Romantic era. Both are privately owned, tourable, and connected by a pleasant trail. (See my listing for Rheinstein Castle on page 455.) Go back to the river side.

Km 530—Ehrenfels Castle: Opposite Bingerbrück and the Bingen station, you'll see the ghostly Ehrenfels Castle (clobbered by the Swedes in 1636 and by the French in 1689). Since it had no view of the river traffic to the north, the owner built the cute little *Mäuseturm* (mouse tower) on an island (the yellow tower you'll see near the train station today). Rebuilt in the 1800s in Neo-Gothic style, it's now used as a Rhine navigation signal station.

Km 528—Niederwald Monument: Across from the Bingen station on a hilltop is the 120-foot-high Niederwald monument, a memorial built with 32 tons of bronze in 1877 to commemorate "the re-establishment of the German Empire." A lift takes tourists to this statue from the famous and extremely touristy wine town of Rüdesheim.

From here, the Romantic Rhine becomes the industrial Rhine, and our tour is over.

Sights Along the Rhine

▲▲MARKSBURG CASTLE

Medieval invaders decided to give Marksburg a miss thanks to its formidable defenses. This best-preserved castle on the Rhine can be toured only with a guide on a 50-minute tour. In summer, tours in English normally run daily at 13:00 and 16:00. Otherwise, you can join a German tour (3/hour in summer, hourly in winter) that's almost as good—there are no explanations in English in the castle itself, but your ticket includes an English handout. It's an awesome castle, and between the handout and my self-guided tour, you'll  feel fully informed, so don't worry about being on time for the English tours.

Cost and Hours: €6, family card-€15, daily April-Oct 10:00-17:00, Nov-March 11:00-16:00, last tour departs one hour before closing, tel. 02627/206, www.marksburg.de.

Getting There: Marksburg caps a hill above the village of Braubach, on the east bank of the Rhine. By **train,** it's a 10-minute trip from Koblenz to Braubach (1-2/hour); from Bacharach or St. Goar, it takes 1-2 hours, depending on the length of the layover in Koblenz (€11.80 one-way). The train is quicker than the **boat** (downstream from Bacharach to Braubach-2 hours, upstream return-3.5 hours; €25.40 one-way, €32.60 round-trip). Consider taking the downstream boat to Braubach, and the train back. If traveling with luggage, store it in the convenient lockers in the underground passage at the Koblenz train station (Braubach has no enclosed station—just platforms—and no lockers).

Once you reach Braubach, **walk** into the old town (follow *Altstadt* signs—coming out of tunnel from train platforms, it's to your right); then follow the *Zur Burg* signs to the path up to the castle. Allow 20 to 30 minutes for the climb up. Scarce **taxis** charge at least €10 from the train platforms to the castle. A green **tourist train** circles up to the castle, but there's no fixed schedule, so don't count on it (Easter–mid-Oct Tue-Sun, no trains Mon or off-season, €3 one-way, €5 round-trip, leaves from Barbarastrasse, tel. 06773/587, www.ruckes-reisen.de). Even if you take the tourist train, you'll still have to climb the last five minutes up to the castle from its parking lot (cars-€2).

۞ Self-Guided Tour: The tour starts inside the castle's first gate.

Inside the First Gate: While the dramatic castles lining the Rhine are generally Romantic rebuilds, Marksburg is the real McCoy—nearly all original construction. It's littered with bits of its medieval past, like the big stone ball that was swung on a rope to be used as a battering ram. Ahead, notice how the inner gate—originally tall enough for knights on horseback to gallop through—was made smaller, and therefore safer from enemies on horseback. Climb the Knights' Stairway, carved out of slate, and pass under the murder hole—handy for pouring boiling pitch on invaders. (Germans still say someone with bad luck "has pitch on his head.")

Coats of Arms: Colorful coats of arms line the wall just inside the gate. These are from the noble families who have owned the castle since 1283. In that year, financial troubles drove the first family to sell to the powerful and wealthy Katzenelnbogen family (who made the castle into what you see today). When Napoleon took this region in 1803, an Austrian family who sided with the French got the keys. When Prussia took the region in 1866, control passed to a friend of the Prussians who had a passion for medieval things—typical of this Romantic period. Then it was sold to the German Castles Association in 1900. Its offices are in the main palace at the top of the stairs.

Romanesque Palace: White outlines mark where the larger original windows were located, before they were replaced by easier-to-defend smaller ones. On the far right, a bit of the original plaster survives. Slate, which is vulnerable to the elements, needs to be covered—in this case, by plaster. Because this is a protected historic building, restorers can use only the traditional plaster methods... but no one knows how to make plaster that works as well as the 800-year-old surviving bits.

Cannons: The oldest cannon here—from 1500—was back-loaded. This was advantageous because many cartridges could be pre-loaded. But since the seal was leaky, it wasn't very powerful. The bigger, more modern cannons—from 1640—were one piece and therefore airtight, but had to be front-loaded. They could easily hit targets across the river from here. Stone balls were rough, so they let the explosive force leak out. The best cannonballs were stones covered in smooth lead—airtight and therefore more powerful and more accurate.

Gothic Garden: Walking along an outer wall, you'll see 160 plants from the Middle Ages—used for cooking, medicine, and witchcraft. *Schierling* (hemlock, in the first corner) is the same poison that killed Socrates.

Inland Rampart: This most vulnerable part of the castle had a triangular construction to better deflect attacks. Notice the factory in the valley. In the 14th century, this was a lead, copper, and silver mine. Today's factory—Europe's largest car-battery recycling plant—uses the old mine shafts as vents (see the three modern smokestacks).

Wine Cellar: Since Roman times, wine has been the traditional Rhineland drink. Because castle water was impure, wine—less alcoholic than today's beer—was the way knights got their fluids. The pitchers on the wall were their daily allotment. The bellows were part of the barrel's filtering system. Stairs lead to the...

Gothic Hall: This hall is set up as a kitchen, with an oven designed to roast an ox whole. The arms holding the pots have notches to control the heat. To this day, when Germans want someone to hurry up, they say, "give it one tooth more." Medieval windows were made of thin sheets of translucent alabaster or animal skins. A nearby wall is peeled away to show the wattle-and-daub construction (sticks, straw, clay, mud, then plaster) of a castle's inner walls. The iron plate to the left of the next door enabled servants to stoke the heater without being seen by the noble family.

Bedroom: This was the only heated room in the castle. The canopy kept in heat and kept out critters. In medieval times, it was impolite for a lady to argue with her lord in public. She would wait for him in bed to give him what Germans still call "a curtain lecture." The deep window seat caught maximum light for needlework and reading. Women would sit here and chat (or "spin a yarn") while working the spinning wheel.

Hall of the Knights: This was the dining hall. The long table is an unattached plank. After each course, servants could replace it with another pre-set plank. Even today, when a meal is over and Germans are ready for the action to begin, they say, "Let's lift up the table." The action back then consisted of traveling minstrels who sang and told of news gleaned from their travels.

Rhein in Flammen

During the annual "Rhine in Flames" festival, spectacular displays of fireworks take place along the most scenic stretches of the Rhine, while beautifully illuminated ships ply the river, offering up-close views of the fireworks above. Held on five days between May and September, the festival rotates between several Rhine towns. Traditional wine festivals and other local celebrations are often timed to coincide with the Rhein in Flammen (in 2015: Bonn—May 2, Rüdesheim—July 4, Koblenz—Aug 8, Oberwesel—Sept 12, St. Goar—Sept 19; www.rhein-in-flammen.com).

Notice the outhouse—made of wood—hanging over thin air. When not in use, its door was locked from the outside (the castle side) to prevent any invaders from entering this weak point in the castle's defenses.

Chapel: This chapel is still painted in Gothic style with the castle's namesake, St. Mark, and his lion. Even the chapel was designed with defense in mind. The small doorway kept out heavily armed attackers. The staircase spirals clockwise, favoring the sword-wielding defender (assuming he was right-handed).

Linen Room: About the year 1800, the castle—with diminished military value—housed disabled soldiers. They'd earn a little extra money working raw flax into linen.

Two Thousand Years of Armor: Follow the evolution of armor since Celtic times. Because helmets covered the entire head, soldiers identified themselves as friendly by tipping their visor up with their right hand. This evolved into the military salute that is still used around the world today. Armor and the close-range weapons along the back were made obsolete by the invention of the rifle. Armor was replaced with breastplates—pointed (like the castle itself) to deflect enemy fire. This design was used as late as the start of World War I. A medieval lady's armor hangs over the door. While popular fiction has men locking up their women before heading off to battle, chastity belts were actually used by women as protection against rape when traveling.

The Keep: This served as an observation tower, a dungeon (with a 22-square-foot cell in the bottom), and a place of last refuge. When all was nearly lost, the defenders would bundle into the keep and burn the wooden bridge, hoping to outwait their enemies.

Horse Stable: The stable shows off bits of medieval crime and punishment. Cheaters were attached to stones or pillories. Shame masks punished gossipmongers. A mask with a heavy ball had its victim crawling around with his nose in the mud. The handcuffs with a neck hole were for the transport of prisoners. The pictures on the wall show various medieval capital punishments. Many times the accused was simply taken into a torture dungeon to see all these tools, and, guilty or not, confessions spilled out of him. On that cheery note, your tour is over.

▲▲RHEINSTEIN CASTLE (SCHLOSS BURG RHEINSTEIN)

This castle seems to rule its chunk of the Rhine from a commanding position. While its 13th-century exterior is medieval as can be, the interior is mostly a 19th-century duke's hunting palace. Visitors wander freely (with an English flier) among trophies, armor, and Romantic Age decor.

Cost and Hours: €5; mid-March-Oct daily 9:30-18:00; Nov-mid-March Sat-Sun only 10:00-17:00, last entry 30 minutes before closing, tel. 06721/6348, www.burg-rheinstein.de.

Getting There: This castle (at km 533 marker, 2 km upstream from Trechtingshausen on the main B-9 highway) is easy by **car** (small, free parking lot on B-9, steep 5-minute hike from there), or **bike** (35 minutes upstream from Bacharach, stick to the great riverside path, after km 534 marker look for small *Burg Rheinstein* sign and Rösler-Linie dock). It's less convenient by **boat** (no K-D stop nearby) or **train** (nearest stop in Trechtingshausen, a 30-minute walk away).

Bacharach

Once prosperous from the wine and wood trade, charming Bacharach (BAHKH-ah-rahkh, with a guttural *kh* sound) is now just a pleasant half-timbered village of 2,000 people working hard to keep its tourists happy. Businesses that have been "in the family" for eons are dealing with succession challenges, as the allure of big-city jobs and a more cosmopolitan life lure away the town's younger generation. But Bacharach retains its time-capsule quaintness.

Orientation to Bacharach

Bacharach cuddles, long and narrow, along the Rhine. The village is easily strollable—you can walk from one end of town to the other along its main drag, Oberstrasse, in about 10 minutes. Bacharach widens at its stream, where more houses trickle up its small valley (along Blücherstrasse) away from the Rhine. The hillsides above town are occupied by vineyards, scant remains of the former town walls, and a castle-turned-youth hostel.

TOURIST INFORMATION

The bright new TI, on the main street a block-and-a-half from the train station, will store bags for day-trippers (April-Oct Mon-Fri 9:00-17:00, Sat-Sun 10:00-15:00; Nov-March Mon-Fri 9:00-13:00, closed Sat-Sun; from train station, exit right and walk down main street with castle high on your left, TI will be on your right at Oberstrasse 10; tel. 06743/919-303, www.bacharach.de or www.rhein-nahe-touristik.de, Herr Kuhn and his team).

HELPFUL HINTS

Shopping: The **Jost** German gift store, across the main square from the church, carries most everything a souvenir-shopper could want—from beer steins to cuckoo clocks—and can ship purchases to the US (March-Oct Mon-Fri 9:00-18:00, Sat-Sun 10:00-18:00, shorter hours in winter, closed Jan-Feb; Blücherstrasse 4, tel. 06743/909-7214). They offer discounts to my readers (€10 minimum purchase): 10 percent with cash, 5 percent with credit card.

Internet Access: The **TI** has one computer (€0.50/15 minutes).

Post Office: It's inside a newsagents' shop, across from the church and Altes Haus, at Oberstrasse 56.

Picnics: You can pick up picnic supplies at **Nahkauf,** a basic grocery store (Mon-Fri 8:00-12:30 & 14:00-18:00, Sat 8:30-12:30, closed Sun, Koblenzer Strasse 2). For a gourmet picnic, call the recommended **Rhein Hotel** to reserve a "picnic bag" complete with wine, cheese, small dishes, and a hiking map (€12/person, arrange a day in advance, tel. 06743/1243).

Bike Rental: While many hotels loan bikes to guests, the only real bike-rental business in the town center is run by Erich at **Hotel Hillen** (€12/day, €10/half-day, daily 9:00-19:00, Langstrasse 18, tel. 06743/1287).

Parking: It's simple to park along the highway next to the train tracks or, better, in the big lot by the boat dock (€4 from 9:00 to 18:00, pay with coins at *Parkscheinautomat* and put ticket on dashboard, free overnight).

Local Guides: Get acquainted with Bacharach by taking a walking tour. These guides enjoy sharing their town with visitors: **Thomas Gundlach** is a charming local who's licensed as a guide and happily gives 1.5-hour town walks to individuals or small groups for €25. He can also drive up to three people around the region in his car (€70/6 hours, €120/long day, mobile 0179-353-6004, thomas_gundlach@gmx.de). Also good is **Birgit Wessels** (€45/1.5-hour walk, tel. 06743/937-514, wessels.birgit@t-online.de). The **TI** books 1.5-hour tours in English (€70/group). Or take my self-guided town walk or walk the walls—both are described next.

Bacharach Town Walk

• *Start this self-guided walk at the Köln-Düsseldorfer ferry dock (next to a fine picnic park).*

Riverfront: View the town from the parking lot—a modern landfill. The Rhine used to lap against Bacharach's town wall, just over the present-day highway. Every few years the river floods, covering the highway with several feet of water. Flat land like this is rare in the Rhine Valley, where towns are often shaped like the letter "T," stretching thin along the riverfront and up a crease in the hills beyond.

Reefs farther upstream forced boats to unload upriver and reload here. Consequently, in the Middle Ages, Bacharach was the biggest wine-trading town on the Rhine. A riverfront crane hoisted huge kegs of prestigious "Bacharach" wine (which, in practice, was from anywhere in the region). The tour buses next to the dock and the flags of the biggest spenders along the highway remind you that today's economy is founded on tourism.

Look above town. The **castle** on the hill is now a youth hostel. Two of the town's original 16 towers are visible from here (up to five if you look really hard). The bluff on the right, with the yellow flag, is the **Heinrich Heine Viewpoint** (the end-point of a popular hike). Old-timers remember when, rather than the flag marking the town as a World Heritage site, a swastika sculpture 30 feet wide and tall stood there. Realizing that it could be an enticing target for Allied planes in the last months of the war, locals tore it down even before Hitler fell.

Nearby, a stele in the park describes the Bingen to Koblenz stretch of the Rhine gorge.

• *Before entering the town, walk upstream through the...*

Riverside Park: New elements of the park are designed to bring people to the riverside and combat flooding. The park was originally laid out in 1910 in the English style: Notice how the trees were planted to frame fine town views, highlighting the most picturesque bits of architecture. The dark, sad-looking monument—its

1. Rhein Hotel & Stüber Rest.
2. Hotel zur Post
3. Hotel/Rest. Kranenturm
4. Pension im Malerwinkel
5. Pension Binz
6. Hotel Hillen & Bike Rental
7. Pension Lettie
8. To Pension Winzerhaus
9. Irmgard Orth B&B
10. Jugendherberge Stahleck Hostel
11. Altes Haus Restaurant
12. Gasthaus Jägerstube
13. Posthof Bacharach Restaurant
14. Kleines Bräuhaus Rheinterrasse
15. Bacharacher Pizza & Kebap Haus
16. Eis Café Italia
17. Restaurant Zeus
18. Bastian's Weingut zum Grüner Baum
19. Weingut Karl Heidrich
20. Grocery

"eternal" flame long snuffed out—is a **war memorial.** The German psyche is permanently scarred by war memories. Today, many Germans would rather avoid monuments like this, which revisit the dark periods before Germany became a nation of pacifists. Take a close look at the monument. Each panel honors sons of Bacharach who died for the Kaiser: in 1864 against Denmark, in 1866 against Austria, in 1870 against France, in 1914 during World War I. The military Maltese cross—flanked by classic German helmets—has a W at its center, for Kaiser Wilhelm. Review the family names here: You may later recognize them on today's restaurants and hotels.

• *Look (but don't go) upstream from here to see the...*

Trailer Park and Campground: In Germany, trailer vacationers and campers are two distinct subcultures. Folks who travel in motorhomes, like many retirees in the US, are a nomadic bunch, cruising around the countryside and paying a few euros a night

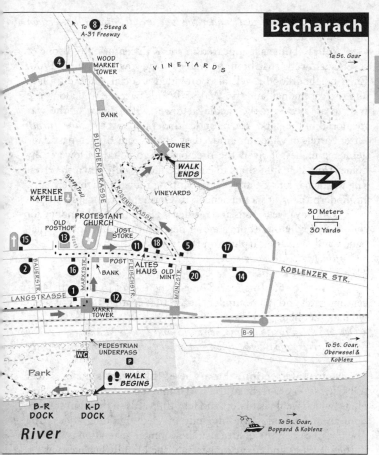

Bacharach

To **8**, Steeg & A-31 Freeway

WOOD MARKET TOWER

4

To St. Goar →

VINEYARDS

BANK

BLÜCHERSTRASSE

TOWER

WALK ENDS

Steg Trail

WERNER KAPELLE

ROSENSTRASSE

VINEYARDS

OLD POSTHOF

PROTESTANT CHURCH

13

JOST STORE

15

11 **18** **5**

17

2

16

POST

BANK

ALTES HAUS

OLD MINT

20

14

KOBLENZER STR.

BAUERSTR.

MARKTSTR.

FLEISCHSTR.

MÜNZSTR.

LANGSTRASSE

1

12

MARKT TOWER

30 Meters

30 Yards

PEDESTRIAN UNDERPASS

WC

P

B-9

To St. Goar, Oberwesel & Koblenz →

Park

WALK BEGINS

B-R DOCK

K-D DOCK

To St. Goar, Boppard & Koblenz →

River

to park. Campers, on the other hand, tend to set up camp in one place—complete with comfortable lounge chairs and TVs—and stay put for weeks, even months. They often come back to the same spot year after year, treating it like their own private estate. These camping devotees have made a science out of relaxing. Tourists are welcome to pop in for a drink or meal at the campground café (see "Activities in Bacharach," later).

• *Continue to where the park meets the playground, and then cross the highway to the fortified riverside wall of the Catholic church, decorated with...*

High-Water Marks: These recall various floods. Before the 1910 reclamation project, the river extended out to here, and boats would use the rings in this wall to tie up.

• *From the church, go under the 1858 train tracks and hook right past the yellow floodwater yardstick and up the stairs onto the town wall. Atop the wall, turn left and walk under the long arcade. After 30 meters, on your left, notice a...*

Well: Rebuilt as it appeared in the 17th century, this is one of seven such wells that brought water to the townsfolk until 1900. Each neighborhood's well also provided a social gathering place and the communal laundry. Walk 50 yards past the well along the wall to an alcove in the medieval tower with a view of the war memorial in the park. You're under the crane tower *(Kranenturm)*. After barrels of wine were moved overland from Bingen past dangerous stretches of river, the precious cargo could be lowered by cranes from here into ships to continue more safely down the river. The Rhine has long been a major shipping route through Germany. In modern times, it's a bottleneck in Germany's train system. The train company gives hotels and residents along the tracks money for soundproof windows (hotels along here routinely have quadruple-pane windows...and earplugs on the nightstand).

• *Continue walking along the town wall. Pass the recommended Rhein Hotel just before the...*

Markt Tower: This marks one of the town's 15 original 14th-century gates and is a reminder that in that century there was a big wine market here.

• *Descend the stairs, pass another well, and follow Marktstrasse away from the river toward the town center, the two-tone church, and the town's...*

Main Intersection: From here, Bacharach's main street (Oberstrasse) goes right to the half-timbered red-and-white Altes Haus (which we'll visit later) and left 400 yards to the train station. Spin around to enjoy the higgledy-piggledy building styles. The town has a case of the doldrums: The younger generation is moving to the big cities and many long-established family businesses have no one to take over for their aging owners. Bacharach's only pub recently closed. In the winter the town is particularly dead.

• *To the left (south) of the church, a golden horn hangs over the old...*

Posthof: Throughout Europe, the postal horn is the symbol of the postal service. In olden days, when the postman blew this, traffic stopped and the mail sped through. This post station dates from 1724, when stagecoaches ran from Cologne to Frankfurt and would change horses here, Pony Express-style. As you enter, notice the cornerstones at the Posthof entrance, protecting the venerable building from reckless carriage wheels. Inside the old oak doors (on the left) is the actual door to the post office that served Bacharach for 200 years. Find the mark on the wall labeled *Rheinhöhe 3/1-4/2 1850*. This recalls an historic flood caused by an ice jam at the Loreley just downstream. Notice also the fascist eagle (from 1936; a swastika once filled its center).

Step into the courtyard—once a carriage house and inn that

accommodated Bacharach's first VIP visitors, and now home to the recommended Posthof Bacharach restaurant, with a fine view of the church and a ruined chapel above.

Two hundred years ago, Bacharach's main drag was the only road along the Rhine. Napoleon widened it to fit his cannon wagons. The steps alongside the church lead to the castle.

• *Return to the church, passing the recommended Italian ice-cream café (**Eis Café Italia**), where friendly Mimo serves his special invention: Riesling wine-flavored gelato.*

Protestant Church: Inside the church (daily May-Sept 10:00-18:00, April and Oct 10:00-17:00, closed Nov-March, English info on table near door), you'll find Grotesque capitals, brightly painted in medieval style, and a mix of round Romanesque and pointed Gothic arches. The church was fancier before the Reformation wars, when it (and the region) was Catholic. Bacharach lies on the religious border of Germany and, like the country as a whole, is split between Catholics and Protestants. To the left of the altar, some medieval (pre-Reformation) frescoes survive where an older Romanesque arch was cut by a pointed Gothic one.

If you're considering bombing the town, take note: A blue-and-white plaque just outside the church's door warns that, according to the Hague Convention, this historic building shouldn't be targeted in times of war.

• *Continue down Oberstrasse to the...*

Altes Haus: Dating from 1368, this is the oldest house in town. Notice the 14th-century building style—the first floor is made of stone, while upper floors are half-timbered (in the ornate style common in the Rhine Valley). Some of its windows still look medieval, with small, flattened circles as panes (small because that's all that the glass-blowing technology of the time would allow), pieced together with molten lead (like medieval stained glass in churches). Frau Weber welcomes visitors to enjoy the fascinating ground floor of the recommended Altes Haus restaurant, with its evocative old photos and etchings (consider eating here later).

• *Keep going down Oberstrasse to the...*

Old Mint (Münze): The old mint is marked by a crude coin in its sign. As a practicality, any great trading town needed coinage, and since 1356, Bacharach minted theirs here. Across from the mint, the recommended **Bastian** family's wine garden is a lively place after dark. Above you in the vineyards stands a lonely white-and-red tower—your final destination.

• *At the next street, look right and see the mint tower, painted in the medieval style, and then turn left. Wander 30 yards up Rosenstrasse to the **well**. Notice the sundial and the wall painting of 1632 Bacharach with its walls intact. Study the fine slate roof over the well: The town's* *roof tiles were quarried and split right here in the Rhineland. Now climb the tiny-stepped lane behind the well up into the vineyard and to the...*

Tall Tower: The slate steps lead to a small path through the vineyard that deposits you at a viewpoint atop the stubby remains of the medieval wall and a tower. The town's towers jutted out from the wall and had only three sides, with the "open" side facing the town. Towers were covered with stucco to make them look more impressive, as if they were made of a finer white stone. If this tower's open, hike up to climb the stairs for the best view. (The top floor has been closed to give nesting falcons some privacy.)

Romantic Rhine View: A grand medieval town spreads before you. For 300 years (1300-1600), Bacharach was big (population 4,000), rich, and politically powerful.

From this perch, you can see the chapel ruins and six surviving **city towers.** Visually trace the wall to the castle. The castle was actually the capital of Germany for a couple of years in the 1200s. When Holy Roman Emperor Frederick Barbarossa went away to fight the Crusades, he left his brother (who lived here) in charge of his vast realm. Bacharach was home to one of seven electors who voted for the Holy Roman Emperor in 1275. To protect their own power, these prince elec-

tors did their best to choose the weakest guy on the ballot. The elector from Bacharach helped select a two-bit prince named Rudolf von Habsburg (from a no-name castle in Switzerland). However, the underestimated Rudolf brutally silenced the robber barons along the Rhine and established the mightiest dynasty in European history. His family line, the Habsburgs, ruled much of Central and Eastern Europe from Vienna until 1918.

Plagues, fires, and the Thirty Years' War (1618-1648) finally did in Bacharach. The town has slumbered for several centuries. Today, the castle houses commoners—40,000 overnights annually by youth hostelers.

In the mid-19th century, painters such as J. M. W. Turner and writers such as Victor Hugo were charmed by the Rhineland's romantic mix of past glory, present poverty, and rich legend. They put this part of the Rhine on the old Grand Tour map as the "Romantic Rhine." Victor Hugo pondered the ruined 15th-century chapel that you see under the castle. In his 1842 travel book, *Excursions Along the Banks of the Rhine,* he wrote, "No doors, no roof or windows, a magnificent skeleton puts its silhouette against the sky. Above it, the ivy-covered castle ruins provide a fitting crown. This is Bacharach, land of fairy tales, covered with legends and sagas."

If you're enjoying the Romantic Rhine, thank Victor Hugo and company.

• *Our walk is done. To get back into town, just retrace your steps. Or, to extend this walk, take the level path away from the river that leads along the once-mighty wall up the valley to the next tower, the...*

Wood Market Tower: Timber was gathered here in Bacharach and lashed together into vast log booms known as "Holland rafts" (as big as a soccer field) that were floated downstream. Two weeks later the lumber would reach Amsterdam, where it was in high demand as foundation posts for buildings and for the great Dutch shipbuilders. Notice the four stones above the arch—these guided the gate as it was hoisted up and down.

• *From here, cross the street and go downhill into the parking lot. Pass the recommended Pension im Malerwinkel on your right, being careful not to damage the old arch with your head. Follow the creek past a delightful little series of half-timbered homes and cheery gardens known as "Painters' Corner"* (Malerwinkel). *Resist looking into some pervert's peep show (on the right) and continue downhill back to the village center.*

Activities in Bacharach

Walk Along the Old Town Walls

A well-maintained and clearly marked walking path follows the remains of Bacharach's old town walls and makes for a good hour's workout. The TI has maps that show the entire route. The path starts near the train station, then climbs up to the youth hostel, descends into the side valley, and then continues up the other side to the tower in the vineyards before returning to town. To start the walk at the train station, find the house at Oberstrasse 2 and climb up the stairway to its left. Then follow the *Stadtmauer-Rundweg* signs. Good bilingual signposts tell the history of each of the towers along the wall—some are intact, one is a private residence, and others are now only stubs.

Camping Sonnenstrand

This campground, a 10-minute walk upstream from Bacharach, has a sandy beach with water as still as a lake, and welcomes non-campers who want to poke around (especially if you buy a drink at their café). It's a chance to see Euro-style camping, which comes with a sense of community. Campers are mostly Dutch, Belgian, and German, with lots of kids (and a playground). The terrace café overlooking the campsites and the river is the social center and works well for a drink or meal (inside or outside with river view, daily 13:00-21:00, €5-10 salads and main dishes, tel. 6743/1752, www.camping-rhein.de).

Sleeping in Bacharach

None of the hotels listed here have elevators. The only listings with parking are Pension im Malerwinkel, Pension Winzerhaus, and the youth hostel. For the others, you can drive in to unload your bags and then park in the public lot (see "Helpful Hints," earlier). If you'll arrive after 20:00, let your hotel know in advance (many hotels with restaurants stay open late, but none have 24-hour reception desks).

$$$ Rhein Hotel, overlooking the river with 14 spacious and comfortable rooms, is classy, well-run, and decorated with modern flair. Since it's right on the train tracks, its river- and train-side rooms come with quadruple-paned windows and air-conditioning. This place has been in the Stüber family for six generations (Sb-€55, Db-€96, Tb-€125, Qb-€145, these prices good with this book in 2015 when you book directly with the hotel, cheaper for longer stays and off-season, special packages available including big three-course dinner for stays longer than one night, inquire about "picnic bags" upon check-in, non-smoking, free loaner bikes, Wi-Fi, directly inland from the K-D boat dock at Langstrasse 50, tel. 06743/1243, www.rhein-hotel-bacharach.de, info@rhein-hotel-bacharach.de). Their recommended Stüber Restaurant is considered the best in town.

$$ Hotel zur Post, refreshingly clean and quiet, is conveniently located right in the town center with no train noise. Its 12 rooms are a good value. Run by friendly and efficient Ute, the hotel offers more solid comfort than old-fashioned character, though the lovely wood-paneled breakfast room has a rustic feel (Sb-€40-45, Db-€70-75, Qb-€110, Wi-Fi, Oberstrasse 38, tel. 06743/1277, www.hotel-zur-post-bacharach.de, h.zurpost@t-online.de).

$$ Hotel Kranenturm, offering castle ambience without the climb, combines hotel comfort with delightful *Privatzimmer* funkiness right downtown. Run by hardworking Kurt Engel and his intense but friendly wife, Fatima, this 16-room hotel is part of the medieval town wall. The rooms in its former *Kranenturm* (crane tower) have the best views. While just 15 feet from the train tracks, a combination of medieval sturdiness, triple-paned windows, and included earplugs makes the riverside rooms sleepable (Sb-€40-46, small Db-€59-65, regular Db-€64-70, Db in huge tower rooms with castle and river views-€73-82, Tb-€85-95, Qb great for families with small kids-€100-115, lower prices are for 3-night stay, cash preferred, €2

Sleep Code

Abbreviations   (€1 = about $1.40, country code: 49)

S = Single, **D** = Double/Twin, **T** = Triple, **Q** = Quad, **b** = bathroom, **s** = shower only.

Price Rankings

$$$ **Higher Priced**—Most rooms €90 or more.

$$ **Moderately Priced**—Most rooms between €60-90.

$ **Lower Priced**—Most rooms €60 or less.

Staff at all hotels speak at least some English. Unless otherwise noted, breakfast is included, credit cards are accepted, and Wi-Fi is generally free. Prices change; verify current rates online or by email. For the best prices, always book directly with the hotel.

---

extra with credit card, Rhine views come with train noise, back rooms are quiet, non-smoking, showers can be temperamental, good breakfast, guest computer, Wi-Fi in common areas, closed in winter, Langstrasse 30, tel. 06743/1308, www.kranenturm.com, hotel-kranenturm@t-online.de). Kurt, a good cook, serves €10-19 main courses in their recommended restaurant.

$$ Pension im Malerwinkel sits like a grand gingerbread house that straddles the town wall in a quiet little neighborhood so charming it's called "Paint-  ers' Corner" *(Malerwinkel)*. The Vollmer family's 20-room place is super-quiet and comes with a picturesque garden on a brook, views of the vineyards, and easy parking—all just a few minutes from the town center (Sb-€43; Db-€68 for one-night stay, €63/night for 2 nights, €60/ night for 3 nights or more; family rooms, cash only, no train noise, non-smoking, Wi-Fi, bike rental-€6/day, parking; from Oberstrasse, turn left at the church, walkers can follow the path to the left just before the town gate but drivers must pass through the gate to find the hotel parking lot, Blücherstrasse 41-45; tel. 06743/1239, www.im-malerwinkel.de, pension@im-malerwinkel.de, Armin and Daniela).

$$ Pension Lettie, run by effervescent and eager-to-please Lettie, rents four bright rooms. Lettie speaks English (she worked for the US Army before they withdrew) and does laundry for €14/ load (Sb-€40, Db-€60, Tb-€90, Qb-€95, Quint/b-€107, these prices with this book in 2015 when you reserve directly with the hotel, discounts for stays of 2 nights or more, 10 percent extra if paying with credit card, non-smoking, small in-room refrigerator, buffet breakfast with waffles and bacon, no train noise, Wi-Fi, Kranenstrasse 6, tel. 06743/947-5656, pension.lettie@t-online.de).

$$ Pension Binz offers four worn, bare-bones rooms in a good location with no train noise (Sb-€40, Db-€65, Tb-€83, no Internet access, Koblenzer Strasse 1, tel. 06743/1604, mailto:pension.binz@freenet.de, Carla speaks a little English). Their large apartment requires a minimum three-night stay (sleeps 4, €65/night).

$ Hotel Hillen, a block south of Hotel Kranenturm, has less charm and similar train noise (with the same ultra-thick windows). It offers five spacious rooms and good hospitality from friendly owners Iris and Erich (Sb-€40, D-€45, Ds-€50, Db-€55, Tb-€70, Qb-€85, these prices when you reserve directly with this book in 2015, 10 percent discount for stays of 2 nights or longer, cash only, family rooms, closed mid-Nov-Easter, Langstrasse 18, tel. 06743/1287, hotel-hillen@web.de). They also rent bikes (see page 442).

$ Pension Winzerhaus, a 10-room place run by friendly Sybille and Stefan, is just outside the town walls, directly under the vineyards. The rooms are simple, clean, and modern, and parking is a breeze (Sb-€35, Db-€55, Tb-€75, Qb-€96, 10 percent off in 2015 when you book direct and show this book at check-in, cash only, non-smoking, free Wi-Fi, free loaner bikes for guests, parking, will pick up at train station but then you won't get the room discount, Blücherstrasse 60, tel. 06743/1294, www.pension-winzerhaus.de, winzerhaus@gmx.de).

$ Irmgard Orth B&B rents three bright rooms, two of which share a bathroom on the hall. Charming Irmgard speaks almost no English, but is exuberantly cheery and serves homemade honey with breakfast (S-€22-25, D-€38, Db-€38-40, higher price is for one-night stay, cash only, non-smoking, no Internet access, Spurgasse 2, tel. 06743/1553, speak slowly).

$ Jugendherberge Stahleck hostel is a 12th-century castle on the hilltop—350 steps above Bacharach—with a royal Rhine view. Open to travelers of any age, this is a gem with 168 beds and a private modern shower and WC in most rooms. The hostel offers hearty €8.50 all-you-can-eat buffet dinners (18:00-19:30 nightly), and in summer, its pub serves cheap local wine and snacks all day until late. If you're arriving at the train station with luggage, it's a €10 taxi ride to the hostel—call 06743/1653 (€21.50 dorm beds with breakfast and sheets, non-members-€3.50 extra, generally 6-10 beds per room, couples can share one of five €54 Db,

pay guest computer and Wi-Fi, laundry-€6; reception open 7:30-20:00, call if arriving later and check in at bar until 21:30; curfew at 22:00, tel. 06743/1266, www.diejugendherbergen.de, bacharach@diejugendherbergen.de, Michael and Andrea). If driving, don't go in the driveway; park on the street and walk 200 yards.

Eating in Bacharach

RESTAURANTS

Bacharach has no shortage of reasonably priced, atmospheric restaurants offering fine indoor and outdoor dining. Two of my recommended hotels—Rhein and Kranenturm—have particularly good restaurants.

The Rhein Hotel's **Stüber Restaurant** is Bacharach's best top-end choice. Chef Andreas Stüber, his family's sixth-generation chef, creates regional plates prepared with a slow-food ethic. The menu changes with the season and is served at river- and track-side seating or indoors with a spacious wood-and-white-tablecloth elegance. Consider the €11 William Turner pâté starter plate, named after the British painter who liked Bacharach (€18 main courses, €33 fixed-price meals, always good vegetarian and vegan options, daily 17:00-21:15 plus Sat-Sun 11:30-14:15, closed mid-Dec-Feb, call to reserve on weekends or for an outdoor table when balmy, family-friendly with a play area, facing the K-D boat dock below town center, Langstrasse 50, tel. 06743/1243). Their Posten Riesling is well worth the splurge and pairs well with both the food and the atmosphere.

Hotel Kranenturm is another good value, with hearty dinners. Kurt cooks and Fatima serves. Kurt prides himself on his trout, lamb, and *Sauerbraten* (marinated beef with potato dumplings and red cabbage), good main-course salads, and seasonal white-asparagus dishes. If you're a trainspotter, sit on their informal trackside terrace and trade travel stories with new friends over dinner, letting screaming trains punctuate your conversation. If you prefer charming old German decor, sit inside their pleasant dining room (€10-19 main courses, Tue-Sun 17:00-21:00, closed Mon and in winter).

Altes Haus, the oldest building in town (see page 461), serves classic German dishes within Bacharach's most romantic atmosphere. Find the cozy little dining room with photos of the opera singer who sang about Bacharach, adding to its fame (€10-20 main courses, Thu-Tue 12:00-15:00 & 18:00-21:30, longer hours on weekends, closed Wed and Dec-Easter, dead center by the Protestant church, tel. 06743/1209).

CASUAL OPTIONS

Gasthaus Jägerstube is every local's non-touristy, good-value hangout. It's a no-frills place with no outdoor seating, run by a former East German family determined to keep Bacharach's working class well-fed and watered. Next to the WC is a rare "party cash box." Regulars drop money into their personal slot throughout the year, Frau Tischmeier banks it, and by year's end...there's plenty in the little savings account for a community party (€9-18 main courses, March-Nov Wed-Mon 11:00-21:30, Dec-Feb Wed-Mon 15:00-23:00, closed Tue year-round, Marktstrasse 3, tel. 06743/1492, Tischmeier family).

The **Posthof Bacharach** restaurant and café in the Posthof courtyard has nice outdoor seating and a medieval feel, with a view of the ruined chapel above (€10-12 main courses, daily Easter-Oct 12:00-21:00, closed Nov-Easter, Oberstrasse 45-49, tel. 06743/947-1830).

Kleines Brauhaus Rheinterrasse is a funky microbrewery serving meals, fresh-baked bread, and homemade beer under a 1958 circus carousel that overlooks the town and river. Annette serves while Armin brews and the kids run free in this family-friendly place (Tue-Sun 12:00-22:00, closed Mon, at the downstream end of town, Koblenzer Strasse 14, tel. 06743/919-179). The little flea market in the old trailer nearby seems to fit right in.

Bacharacher Pizza and Kebap Haus, on the main drag in the town center, is the town favorite for €4 *Döner Kebabs*, cheap pizzas, and salads. Imam charges the same to eat in or take out (daily 10:00-23:00, Oberstrasse 43, tel. 06743/3127).

Camping Sonnenstrand, a 10-minute walk from town, has a café with great river views inside and out (see listing on page 463).

Gelato: **Eis Café Italia,** on the main street, is run by friendly Mimo Calabrese, who brought gelato to town in 1976. He's known for his refreshing, not-too-sweet Riesling-flavored gelato. Eat in or take it on your evening stroll (no tastes offered, homemade, Waldmeister flavor is made with forest herbs—top secret, April-mid-Oct daily 10:00-22:00, closed mid-Oct-March, Oberstrasse 48).

BACHARACH AFTER DARK

Bacharach goes to bed early, so if you're looking for a little after-dinner action, your options are limited. But a handful of local bars/restaurants and two wine places (listed in "Wine-Tasting" below) are welcoming and can be fun in the late hours.

Gasthaus Jägerstube (described earlier) is a good pick for those who want to mix with a small local crowd. **Restaurant Zeus** is new in town, but its long hours and nice outdoor seating add a spark to the city center after dark (daily 11:00-24:00, Koblenzer Strasse 11, tel. 06743/909-7171). For something a bit off the beaten path try **Jugendherberge Stahleck**—Bacharach's youth hostel—where the pub serves munchies and cheap wine with priceless views until late in summer (listed earlier, under "Sleeping in Bacharach").

WINE-TASTING

Bacharach is proud of its wine. Two places in town—Bastian's rowdy and rustic Grüner Baum, and the more sophisticated Weingut Karl Heidrich—offer visitors an inexpensive tasting memory. Each creates carousels of local wines that small groups of travelers (who don't mind sharing a glass) can sample and compare. Both places offer light plates of food if you'd like a rustic meal.

At **Bastian's Weingut zum Grüner Baum,** groups of 2-6 people pay €22.50 for a wine carousel of 15 glasses—14 different white wines and one lonely red—and a basket of bread. Your mission: Team up with others who have this book to rendezvous here after dinner. Spin the Lazy Susan, share a common cup, and discuss the taste. The Bastian family insists: "After each wine, you must talk to each other" (daily 12:00-22:00, closed in winter, just past Altes Haus, tel. 06743/1208). To make a meal of a carousel, consider the €10 *Käseteller* (seven different cheeses—including *Spundekäse,* the local soft cheese—with bread and butter). Along with their characteristic interior, they have two nice terraces (front for shade, back for sun).

Weingut Karl Heidrich is a fun family-run wine shop and *Stube* in the town center (at Oberstrasse 16), where Markus and daughter Magdalena proudly share their family's centuries-old wine tradition, explaining its fine points to travelers. They offer a variety of carousels with six wines, English descriptions, and bread (€12)—ideal for the more sophisticated wine-taster—plus light meals and a €10 meat-and-cheese plate (Thu-Tue 11:00-22:00, closed Wed and Nov-mid-April, will ship to the US, tel. 06743/93060).

Bacharach Connections

TRAIN CONNECTIONS FROM THE RHINE

Milk-run trains stop at Rhine towns each hour starting as early as 6:00, connecting at Mainz and Koblenz to trains farther afield. Trains between St. Goar and Bacharach depart at about :20 after the hour in each direction (€3.60, buy tickets from the machine in the unstaffed stations, carry cash since some machines won't accept US credit cards).

The durations listed below are calculated from Bacharach; for St. Goar, the difference is only 10 minutes. From Bacharach (or St. Goar), to go anywhere distant, you'll need to change trains in Koblenz for points north, or in Mainz for points south. Milk-run connections to these towns depart hourly, at about :20 past the hour for northbound trains, and at about :30 past the hour for southbound trains. Train info: Tel. 0180-599-6633, www.bahn.com.

From Bacharach by Train to: St. Goar (hourly, 10 minutes), **Moselkern** near Burg Eltz (hourly, 2 hours, change in Koblenz), **Cochem** (hourly, 1.5 hours, change in Koblenz), **Trier** (hourly, 2.5 hours, change in Koblenz), **Cologne** (hourly, 2 hours with change in Koblenz, 2.5 hours direct), **Frankfurt Airport** (hourly, 1-1.5 hours, change in Mainz or Bingen), **Frankfurt** (hourly, 1.5-2 hours, change in Mainz or Bingen), **Rothenburg ob der Tauber** (every 2 hours, 4.5 hours, 3-4 changes), **Munich** (hourly, 5 hours, 2 changes), **Berlin** (hourly, 6.5-7.5 hours, 1-3 changes), **Amsterdam** (hourly, 5-7 hours, change in Cologne, sometimes 1-2 more changes).

ROUTE TIPS FOR DRIVERS

This area is a logical first (or last) stop in Germany. If you're using Frankfurt Airport, here are some tips.

Frankfurt Airport to the Rhine: Driving from Frankfurt to the Rhine or Mosel takes about an hour (follow blue autobahn signs from airport—major cities are signposted).

The Rhine to Frankfurt: From St. Goar or Bacharach, follow the river to Bingen, then autobahn signs to *Mainz,* then *Frankfurt.* From there, head for the airport *(Flughafen)* or downtown (signs to *Messe,* then *Hauptbahnhof,* to find the parking under Frankfurt's main train station—see "Arrival in Frankfurt—By Car" on page 410).

Oberwesel

Oberwesel (**oh**-behr-vay-zehl), with more commerce than St. Goar and Bacharach combined, is just four miles from Bacharach. Oberwesel was a Celtic town in 400 B.C., then a Roman military station. It's worth a quick visit, with a charming main square, a fun-to-walk medieval wall, and the best collection of historic Rhine artifacts I've found within the Rhine Valley. From the river, you'll notice its ship's masts rising from terra firma—a memorial to the generations of riverboat captains and sailors for whom this town is famous. Like most towns on the Rhine, Oberwesel is capped by a castle (Schönburg, now a restaurant, hotel, and youth hostel with a small museum). The other town landmark is its 130-foot-tall crenellated Ochsenturm, standing high and solitary overlooking the river.

Oberwesel is an easy stop by boat, train, bike, or car from

Bacharach. There's free parking by the river (as is often the case in small towns, you must display a cardboard clock—see page 968).

Exploring Oberwesel is a breeze when you follow my self-guided walk, below. Start out by picking up a map from the **TI** on the main square (closed Sun, 10-minute walk from the train station at Rathausstrasse 3—from the station turn right and follow Liebfrauenstrasse to Marktplatz, tel. 06744/710-624, www.oberwesel. de). Maps are also available at the Kulturhaus and Stadtmuseum Oberwesel, and posted around town—just snap a photo of one to use as a guide.

Oberwesel Walk

I've laced together Oberwesel's sights with this self-guided walk. Allow at least an hour without stops. Here's an overview: Starting at the Marktplatz, you'll visit the museum and hike the lower wall to the Ochsenturm (Oxen Tower) at the far end of town, then climb to the top of the town and walk the upper wall, passing through the Stadtmauergarten and Klostergarten (former monastery) before returning to the Marktplatz, where you can get a bite to eat at one of several cafés.

• *Begin at the Marktplatz in front of the TI.*

Marktplatz: For centuries this has been Oberwesel's social and commercial center. That tradition continues today in the Marktplatz's tourist-friendly cafés and wine bars. If you're here in the summer, you can't miss the oversized wine glass declaring that Oberwesel is a winegrower's town. Around harvest time, the city hosts a huge wine festival and elects a "Wine Witch." Why? It's pure marketing. After World War II, the Rhine's wine producers were desperate to sell their wine, so they hosted big parties and elected a representative. All of the other towns picked wine queens, but Oberwesel went with a witch instead.

• *Continue along the main drag, passing several cafés, until you see the entrance (marked* Eingang*) for the museum on the left.*

Kulturhaus and Stadtmuseum Oberwesel: This is the region's best museum on local history and traditions, with lots of artifacts and interesting exhibits. The ground floor retraces the history of Oberwesel, from the Romans to the 19th-century Romantics. Upstairs you'll learn how salmon were once fished here, and timber traders lashed together huge rafts of wood and floated them to the Netherlands to sell. You'll see dramatic photos of the river when it was jammed with ice, and review wine witches from the past few decades (€3, April-Oct Tue-Fri 10:00-17:00, Sat-Sun 14:00-17:00; Nov-March Tue-Fri 10:00-14:00; closed Mon, borrow the English descriptions, Rathausstrasse 23, tel. 06744/7147-26, www. kulturhaus-oberwesel.de).

• *Return to the Marktplatz, turn toward the river and walk to the...*

Town Wall: The walls in front of you are some of the best-preserved walls in the Middle Rhine Valley, thanks to the work of a group of local citizen volunteers.

• *Climb to the top of the wall, and start walking downstream (left), toward the leaning tower.*

Hospital Tower (Hospitalgassenturm) and Vineyards: This tower was initially constructed to rest on the wall. But it was too heavy. In an attempt to "fix it," they straightened out the top.

Notice the vineyards along the banks of the Rhine. They've been part of the landscape here for centuries. Recently, many vintners have been letting the vineyards go untended, as they are just too expensive to keep up. The hope is that a young generation will bring new energy to the Rhinelands vineyards. But the future of these fabled vineyards remains uncertain.

• *Continue walking until you come to the...*

Hospital Chapel (Werner-Kapelle): This chapel was built into the wall in the 13th century and remains part of the hospital district to this day. The sick lay in bed here with their eyes on the cross, confident that a better life awaited them in heaven. Today this chapel serves the adjacent, more modern hospital (free, daily 9:00-17:00).

• *Continue walking along the wall to reach the next tower. Climb up if you'd like.*

Steingassenturm: This tower is named for the first paved road in town, just ahead. Inside the tower, notice the little holes about six feet up. This is where they placed the scaffolding during construction. If you climb to the top, consider how many Romantic painters and poets in centuries past enjoyed this same view.

As Victor Hugo wrote, "This is the warlike Oberwesel whose old walls are riddled with the havoc of shot and shells. Upon them you easily recognize the trace of the huge cannon balls of the bishops of Treves, the Biscayans of Louis XIV, and the revolutionary grape shot of France. At the present day Oberwesel resembles an old veteran soldier turned winemaker, and what excellent wine he produces."

• *Carry on toward the two towers in the distance. Just before the break in the wall, stop to take in the view.*

View of the Katzenturm (Cat Tower) and Ochsenturm (Oxen Tower): These were among the 16 towers that once protected Oberwesel. The farthest tower, Ochsenturm, was built in the 14th century as a lookout and signal tower, but its eight-sided design and crenellated top were also a status symbol for the archbishop, declaring his power to all who passed here along the Rhine. The tower still impresses passersby today.

Take a moment here, with all the ships and trains going by,

to think about transportation on the Rhine across the centuries. The Rhine has been a major transportation route since Roman times, when the river marked the northern end of the empire. The Rhineland's many castles and fortifications, like the one above Oberwesel, testify to its strategic importance in the Middle Ages. The stretch from Koblenz to Bingen was home to no fewer than 16 greedy dukes and lords—robber barons running two-bit dukedoms, living in hilltop castles and collecting tolls from merchant vessels passing by in the river below.

Between you and the river are: a bike lane (once a towpath for mighty horses pulling boats upstream), a train line (one of the first

in Germany), and the modern road (built in the 1950s). Until modern times there was just one small road through Oberwesel—the one you walked along to get to the center of town.

Have you heard the trains passing by? Increasing rail traffic has made nearly constant train noise quite an issue for Rhinelanders. It's estimated that, on average, a train barrels down each side of the Rhine every three minutes. That's 500 trains a day. Landowners complain that it's nearly impossible to sell a piece of property along this stretch due to the train noise.

• *A set of stairs will take you down to street level. Notice the white church on the hilltop to your left—that's where you're headed, if you'd like to continue this walk with a visit to the upper town walls. To get there, walk straight ahead along Niederbachstrasse. Go under the arch and make an immediate left to walk through the Kölnischer Torturm (Cologne Gate Tower). Follow Kölnische Turmgasse two blocks to find a staircase to your right, leading up to the church. Ascend the stairs and stop at the top to enjoy the view.*

St. Martin's Church: Built in the 14th century, this is one of two major churches in town and is known to townspeople as the "white church." Although it looks like sandstone, it's actually made of more readily available slate. Notice the picturesque little church-caretaker's house to the left, then ascend the small set of stairs to the church.

• *Walk around the left side of the church and peek inside. Then continue through the cemetery and around the back to the gardens overlooking the Rhine.*

Gardens: The church garden to the right, with the green cross, was planted in the 17th century. The garden to the left is much more modern; step into it to enjoy this secret oasis. Before leaving the garden, turn around and notice the tower attached to the back of the church. Set on a hilltop, the tower was part of the town's defensive wall—built long before the church. Later, when it came time to build a church, the townsfolk incorporated the tower into the new structure.

• *Now exit the gardens and angle right. Walk up the stairs, through the gate, cross the street, and merge onto the dirt path bordering the outside of the upper town wall. Follow the wall to the first of two towers.*

Michelfeldturm I and II: This stretch is the oldest part of the town wall. Of the 23 original towers, 16 remain today. If you're looking for a summer home along the Rhine, here's a real-estate tip. The city leases these towers for €1 for 100 years. The hitch? You have to agree to restore them. Notice the house set atop the first tower.

• *Continue walking until you come to the next tower.*

Kuhhirtenturm (Cowherder's Tower): This is now a private home with a fanciful drawbridge. If the bridge is down you'll know they're home. According to local folklore, a teenage son of the tower's owners once had a rowdy graduate party here. With all of the noise, neighbors complained. But when the police came, they just hoisted up the drawbridge and partied on.

• *Enjoy the views along this last stretch of the wall. To the left you'll see the Rauthaus (Town Hall), with the clock on top. That's where this walk ends. Pass the Pulverturm (Powder Tower) and start downhill, stopping just beyond the miniature house.*

View of the Castle (Schönburg): You can't help but take in the castle view from here. There's been a castle in Oberwesel since the 10th century. Destroyed by the French in 1689, it stood in ruins for 200 years before being rebuilt. Today it houses a hotel/restaurant, youth hostel, and small museum. While there's not much to see at the castle itself, the hike to reach it (along the Elfenley trail) is scenic.

• *Turning away from the castle, continue downhill and take the first set of stairs to your left, bordering a vineyard. At the bottom of the stairs follow the path past the beautiful backyard gardens. Continue down another small set of stairs, passing a well on your left, and then immediately ascend another set of stairs (along Rasselberg). When you reach the ivy-lined wall, enter the gardens to your left.*

Stadtmauergarten (Town Wall Gardens): These beautiful gardens were made possible by a wealthy local who left town to pursue his fortune but never forgot where he came from. Upon his retirement, he returned to Oberwesel to establish a private foundation and spent his last years back in his old childhood home...our next stop.

• *Exit the gardens, turn left, and walk downhill. At the dead-end, turn right and walk until you see the cross (on the left) at the next intersection. Take a left and walk to the entrance of the monastery.*

Klostergarten (Monastery Garden): For 600 years Franciscan monks lived, worked, and prayed here. During Napoleon's reign this monastery was vacated and later fell victim to fire. The poor took refuge in what was left and built their homes inside the former cloister, sacristy, and other remnants. At its peak, after World War II, about 70 people were living here. Only a dozen remain today in this very unique (and cramped) living space.

• *Feel free to enter and explore a bit, but be respectful and remember that this is a private residence. When you reach the information board (in English) beside the church entrance, you know you're done. Retrace your steps back to the entrance and walk downhill until you reach the Marktplatz.*

St. Goar

St. Goar (sahnkt gwahr) is a classic Rhine tourist town. Its hulk of a castle overlooks a half-timbered shopping street and leafy riverside park, busy with sightseeing ships and contented strollers. Rheinfels Castle, once the mighti-est on the Rhine, is the single best Rhineland ruin to explore. While the town of St. Goar itself is less interest-ing than Bacharach, be sure to explore beyond the shops: Thoughtful little placards scattered around town explain factoids (in English)  about each street, lane, and square. St. Goar also makes a good base for hiking or biking the region. A tiny car ferry will shuttle you back and forth across the busy Rhine from here. (If you run out of things to see, a great pastime in St. Goar is simply chatting with friendly Heike at the K-D boat kiosk.) For train connections, see "Bacharach Connections," earlier.

Orientation to St. Goar

St. Goar is dominated by its mighty castle, Rheinfels. The village—basically a wide spot in the road at the foot of Rheinfels' hill—isn't much more than a few hotels and restaurants. From the riverboat docks, the main drag—a dull pedestrian mall without history—cuts through town before ending at the road up to the castle.

TOURIST INFORMATION

The helpful St. Goar TI, which books rooms and stores bags for free, is on the pedestrian street, three blocks from the K-D boat dock and train station (May-Sept Mon-Fri 9:00-18:00, Sat 10:00-13:00, closed Sun; April and Oct Mon-Fri 9:00-12:30 & 13:30-17:00, closed Sat-Sun; Nov-March Mon-Thu 9:00-12:30 & 13:30-17:00, Fri 9:00-14:00, closed Sat-Sun; from train station, go downhill around church and turn left, Heerstrasse 86, tel. 06741/383, www.st-goar.de).

HELPFUL HINTS

Picnics: St. Goar's waterfront park has benches perfect for a picnic. You can buy picnic fixings on the pedestrian street at the tiny **St. Goarer Stadtladen** grocery store (Tue-Fri 8:00-18:00, Sat 8:00-13:00, closed Sun-Mon, Heerstrasse 106) or at the recommended **Café St. Goar**.

Shopping: The Montag family runs two shops (one specializes in steins and the other in cuckoo clocks), both at the base of the castle hill road. The stein shop under Hotel Montag has Rhine guides and fine steins. The other shop boasts "the largest free-hanging cuckoo clock in the world" (both open daily 8:30-18:00, shorter hours Nov-April). Montag's shops offer 10 percent off any of their souvenirs (including Hummels; €10 minimum purchase) for travelers who show this book prior to checkout. They'll ship your souvenirs home—or give you a VAT form to claim your tax refund at the airport if you're carrying your items with you. A couple of other souvenir shops are across from the K-D boat dock.

Internet Access: The **TI** is your best bet (€0.50/10 minutes).

Bike Rental: Hotel an der Fähre rents bikes for a fair price, but you need to call head to reserve (€10/day, Heerstrasse 47, tel. 06741/980-577).

Parking: A free lot is at the downstream end of town, by the harbor. For on-street parking by the K-D boat dock and recommended hotels, use coins to get a ticket from the machine *(Parkschein-automat)* and put it on the dashboard (€4/day, Mon-Sat 10:00-18:00, Sun 12:00-18:00, coins only, free overnight). Make sure you press the button for a day ticket.

RHINE VALLEY

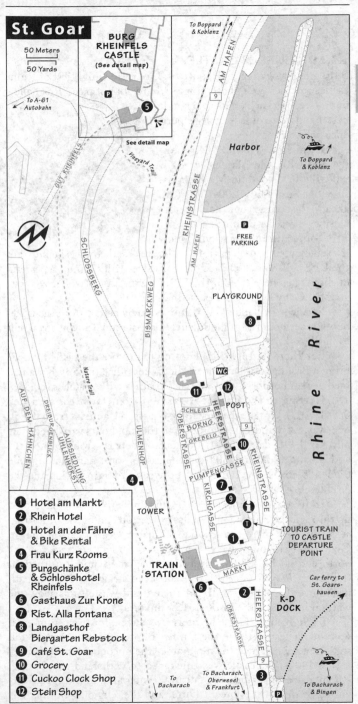

St. Goar

50 Meters
50 Yards

To A-61
Autobahn

BURG RHEINFELS CASTLE
(See detail map)

See detail map

Vineyard Trail

To Boppard
& Koblenz

AM HAFEN

Harbor

To Boppard
& Koblenz

FREE PARKING

Rhine River

PLAYGROUND

WC

POST

SCHLEIER

BORNG

GREBELG

PUMPENGASSE

KIRCHGASSE

HEERSTRASSE

OBERSTRASSE

RHEINSTRASSE

AM HAFEN

SCHLOSSBERG

BISMARCKWEG

GUT RHEINFELS

AUF DEM HÄHNCHEN

DREIBURGENBLICK

AUSSIEDLUNG UHLENHORST

Nature Trail

ULMENHOF

TOWER

TRAIN STATION

MARKT

TOURIST TRAIN TO CASTLE DEPARTURE POINT

K-D DOCK

Car ferry to St. Goarshausen

To Bacharach

To Bacharach, Oberwesel & Frankfurt

To Bacharach & Bingen

❶ Hotel am Markt
❷ Rhein Hotel
❸ Hotel an der Fähre & Bike Rental
❹ Frau Kurz Rooms
❺ Burgschänke & Schlosshotel Rheinfels
❻ Gasthaus Zur Krone
❼ Rist. Alla Fontana
❽ Landgasthof Biergarten Rebstock
❾ Café St. Goar
❿ Grocery
⓫ Cuckoo Clock Shop
⓬ Stein Shop

Sights in St. Goar

▲▲▲RHEINFELS CASTLE

Sitting like a dead pit bull above St. Goar, this mightiest of Rhine castles rumbles with ghosts from its hard-fought past. This hollow but interesting shell offers your single best hands-on ruined-castle experience on the river.

Cost and Hours: €4, family card-€10, mid-March-Oct daily 9:00-18:00, Nov-mid-March possibly Sat-Sun only 11:00-17:00 (call ahead), last entry one hour before closing—weather permitting.

Tours and Information: Follow my self-guided tour on page 480. The free castle map is helpful, but the €2 English booklet is of no real value. If it's damp, be careful of slippery stones. Tel. 06741/7753, in winter 06741/383, www.st-goar.de. Gaby Loch is the castle manager.

Services: A handy WC is immediately across from the ticket booth (check out the guillotine urinals—stand back when you pull to flush).

Let There Be Light: If planning to explore the castle tunnels, bring a flashlight or buy one at the ticket office (€3.50). For a real medieval atmosphere, they also sell candles with matches (€0.50).

Getting to the Castle: A **taxi** up from town costs €5 (tel. 06741/7011). Or take the kitschy "tschu-tschu" **tourist train** (€2.50 one-way, €4 round-trip, 8 minutes to the top, hours vary but generally April-Oct daily 9:30-17:00, usually departs from town at :15 and :45 and at :00 and :30 from the castle, some narration, mobile 0171-445-1525). The train waits between the train station and the K-D dock.

To **hike** up to the castle, you can simply follow the main road up through the railroad underpass at the top end of the pedestrian street. But it's more fun to take the nature trail: Start at the St. Goar train station. Take the underpass under the tracks at the north end of the station, climb the steep stairs uphill, turn right (following *Burg Rheinfels* signs), and keep straight along the path just above the old city wall. Small red-and-white signs show the way, taking you to the castle in 15 minutes.

Background: Burg Rheinfels *was* huge—for five centuries, it was the biggest castle on the Rhine. Built in 1245 to guard a toll station, it soon earned the nickname "the unconquerable fortress." In the 1400s, the castle was thickened to withstand cannon fire. Rheinfels became a thriving cultural center and, in the 1520s, was visited by the artist Albrecht Dürer and the religious reformer Ul-

St. Goar's Rheinfels Castle

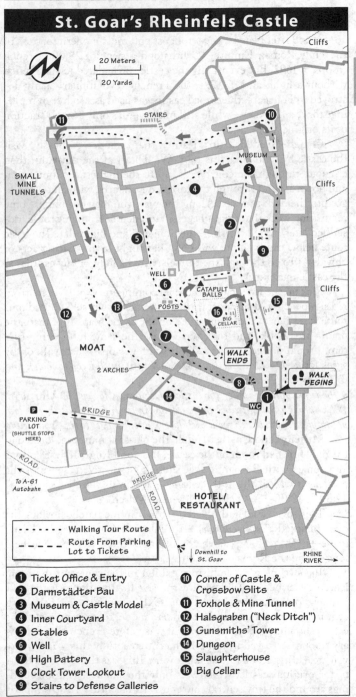

Cliffs

20 Meters
20 Yards

STAIRS

SMALL
MINE
TUNNELS

MUSEUM

Cliffs

Cliffs

WELL

CATAPULT
BALLS

POSTS

BIG
CELLAR

MOAT

WALK
ENDS

WALK
BEGINS

2 ARCHES

WC

BRIDGE

PARKING
LOT
(SHUTTLE STOPS
HERE)

ROAD

To A-61
Autobahn

BRIDGE

ROAD

HOTEL/
RESTAURANT

Downhill to
St. Goar

RHINE
RIVER

- - - - - Walking Tour Route

———— Route From Parking
Lot to Tickets

1. Ticket Office & Entry
2. Darmstädter Bau
3. Museum & Castle Model
4. Inner Courtyard
5. Stables
6. Well
7. High Battery
8. Clock Tower Lookout
9. Stairs to Defense Galleries

10. Corner of Castle &
Crossbow Slits
11. Foxhole & Mine Tunnel
12. Halsgraben ("Neck Ditch")
13. Gunsmiths' Tower
14. Dungeon
15. Slaughterhouse
16. Big Cellar

rich Zwingli. It saw lots of action in the Thirty Years' War (1618-1648), and later became the strongest and most modern fortress in the Holy Roman Empire. It withstood a siege of 28,000 French troops in 1692. But eventually the castle surrendered to the French without a fight, and in 1797, the French Revolutionary army destroyed it. For years, the ruined castle was used as a source of building stone, and today—while still mighty—it's only a small fraction of its original size.

⊘ Self-Guided Tour: Rather than wander aimlessly, visit the castle by following this tour. We'll start at the museum, then circulate through the courtyards, up to the highest lookout point, and down around through the fortified ramparts, with an option to go into the dark tunnels. Along the way, you may encounter some renovation work that might necessitate a detour from our route (described later). We'll finish in the dungeon and big cellar. The basic route below can be done without a flashlight or any daring acts of chivalry. (To go through the tunnels, bring a light or buy candles at the castle museum.)

Pick up the free map and use its commentary to navigate from red signpost to red signpost through the castle. My self-guided tour route is similar to the one marked on the castle map. That map, the one in this book, and this tour all use the same numbering system. (You'll notice that I've skipped a few stops—just walk on by signs for ❷ *Darmstädter Bau,* ❺ *Stables,* ⓫ *Fuchsloch (foxhole),* and ⓭ *Gunsmiths' Tower.*)

• *The ticket office is under the castle's clock tower, labeled* ❶ Uhrturm. *Walk through the entranceway and continue straight, passing several points of interest (which we'll visit later), until you get to the* ❸ *museum.*

Museum and Castle Model: The pleasant museum, located in the only finished room of the castle, has good English descriptions and comes with Romantic Age etchings that give a sense of the place as it was in the 19th century (daily mid-March-Oct 10:00-12:30 & 13:00-17:30; closed Nov-mid-March).

The seven-foot-tall carved stone immediately inside the door (marked *Flammensäule*)—a tombstone from a nearby Celtic grave—is from 400 years before Christ. There were people here long before the Romans...and this castle.

The sweeping castle history exhibit in the center of the room is well-described in English. The massive fortification was the only Rhineland castle to withstand Louis XIV's assault during the 17th century. At the far end of the room is a model reconstruction of the castle, showing how much bigger it was before French Revolutionary troops destroyed it in the 18th century. Study this. Find where you are. (Hint: Look for the tall tower.) This was the living quarters of the original castle, which was only the smallest ring of buildings around the tiny central courtyard (13th century). The ramparts were added in the 14th century. By 1650, the fortress was largely complete. Since its destruction by the French in the late 18th century, it's had no military value. While no WWII bombs were wasted on this ruin, it served St. Goar as a stone quarry for generations. The basement of the museum shows the castle pharmacy and an exhibit of Rhine-region odds and ends, including tools, an 1830 loom, and photos of icebreaking on the Rhine. While once routine, icebreaking hasn't been necessary here since 1963.

• *Exit the museum and walk 30 yards directly out, slightly uphill into the castle courtyard, where you'll see a sign for the inner courtyard (*❹ Innenhof*).*

Medieval Castle Courtyard: Five hundred years ago, the entire castle encircled this courtyard. The place was self-sufficient

and ready for a siege, with a bakery, pharmacy, herb garden, brewery, well (top of yard), and livestock. During peacetime, 300-600 people lived here; during a siege, there would be as many as 4,000. The walls were plastered and painted white. Bits of the original 13th-century plaster survive.

• *Continue through the courtyard under the* Erste Schildmauer *(first shield wall) sign, turn left, and walk straight to the two old wooden upright posts. Find the pyramid of stone catapult balls on your left.*

Castle Garden: Catapult balls like these were too expensive not to recycle—they'd be retrieved after any battle. Across from the balls is a well (❻ *Brunnen*)—essential for any castle during the age of sieges. Look in. Thirsty? The old posts are for the ceremonial baptizing of new members of the local trading league. While this guild goes back centuries, it's now a social club that fills this court with a huge wine party every year on the third weekend of September.

• *Climb uphill to the castle's highest point by walking along the cobbled path (look for the* To the Tower *sign) up past the high battery (*❼ Hohe Batterie*) to the castle's best viewpoint—up where the German flag waves (signed* ❽ Uhrturm*).*

Highest Castle Tower Lookout: Enjoy a great view of the river, the castle, and the forest. Remember, the fortress once covered five times the land it does today. Notice how the other castles (across the river) don't poke above the top of the Rhine canyon. That would make them easy for invading armies to see.

From this perch, survey the Rhine Valley, cut out of slate over millions of years by the river. The slate absorbs the heat of the sun, making the grapes grown here well-suited for wine. Today the slate is mined to provide roofing. Imagine St. Goar himself settling here 1,500 years ago, establishing a place where sailors—thankful to have survived the treacherous Loreley—would stop and pray. Imagine the frozen river of years past, when the ice would break up and boats would huddle in manmade harbors like the one below for protection. Consider the history of trade on this busy river—from the days when castles levied tolls on ships, to the days when boats would be hauled upstream with the help of riverside towpaths, to the 21st century when 300 ships a day move their cargo past St. Goar. And imagine this castle before the French destroyed it... when it was the mightiest structure on the river, filled with people and inspiring awe among all who passed.

• *Return to the catapult balls, walk downhill and through the tunnel, and veer left through the arch marked* ❾ zu den Wehrgängen (*"to the Defense Galleries"*). *Pause here, just before the stairs, to look up and see the original 13th-century core of the castle. Now go down two flights of stairs. Turn left and step into the dark, covered passageway. From here, we'll begin a rectangular walk taking us completely around (counterclockwise) the perimeter of the castle.*

Covered Defense Galleries with "Minutemen" Holes: Soldiers—the castle's "minutemen"—had a short commute: defensive positions on the outside, home in the holes below on the left. Even though these living quarters were padded with straw, life was unpleasant.

• *Continue straight through the dark gallery, up the stairs, and to the corner of the castle, where you'll see a red signpost with the number* ❿. *Stand with your back to the corner of the wall.*

Corner of Castle: Gape up. That's the original castle tower. A three-story, half-timbered building originally rose beyond the tower's stone fortification. The two stone tongues near the top just around the corner (to the right) supported the toilet. (Insert your own joke here.) Turn around and face the wall. The three crossbow slits were once steeper. The bigger hole on the riverside was for hot pitch.

• *Continue out along the back side of the castle. At the corner, turn left.*

Thoop...You're Dead: Look ahead at the smartly placed crossbow slit. While you're lying there, notice the stonework. The little round holes were for the scaffolds they used as they built up, which indicate that this stonework is original. Notice also the fine stonework on the chutes. More boiling pitch...now you're toast, too.

• *Pick yourself up and keep going along the castle perimeter. Pass under the first of three arches and pause at the gray railing to enjoy the view. Look up the valley and uphill where the sprawling fort stretched (as far as the tiny farm on the ridge, a half-mile away). Below, just outside the wall, is land where invaders would gather. The mine tunnels are under there, waiting to blow up any attackers.*

Now continue under two more arches, jog left, go down five steps and into an open field, and walk toward the wooden bridge. The "old" wooden bridge is actually modern.

Dark Tunnel Detour: For a short detour through a castle tunnel—possible only if you have a light—turn your back to the main castle (with the modern bridge to your left) and face the stone dry-moat labeled ❶❷ *Halsgraben "Neck Ditch."* (You'll exit in a few minutes at the high railing above the red #12 sign.) Go 20 yards down the path to the right, and enter the tunnel at the bottom of the wall, following the red *Grosser Minengang* sign. At the end of the short, big tunnel, take two steps up and walk eight level steps, turn left, and follow the long uphill ramp (this is where it's pitch-black, and adults will need to watch their heads). At the end, a spiral staircase takes you up to the high-railing opening you saw earlier, and then back to the courtyard.

• *When ready to leave this courtyard, angle left (under the zum Verliess/ Dungeon sign, before the bridge) through two arches and through the rough entry to the* ❶❹ *Verliess (dungeon) on the left.*

Dungeon: This is one of six dungeons. You just walked through an entrance prisoners only dreamed of 400 years ago. They came and went through the little square hole in the ceiling. The holes in the walls supported timbers that thoughtfully gave as many as 15 residents something to sit on to keep them out of the filthy slop that gathered on the floor. Twice a day, they were given bread and water. Some prisoners actually survived longer than two years in here. While the town could torture and execute, the castle had permission only to imprison criminals in these dungeons. Consider this: According to town records, the two men who spent the most time down here—2.5 years each—died within three weeks of regaining their freedom. Perhaps after a diet of bread and water, feasting on meat and wine was simply too much.

• *Continue through the next arch, under the white arrow, then turn left and walk 30 yards to the* ❶❺ *Schlachthaus.*

Slaughterhouse: Any proper castle was prepared to survive a six-month siege. With 4,000 people, that's a lot of provisions. The cattle that lived within the walls were slaughtered in this room. The castle's mortar was congealed here (by packing all the organic waste from the kitchen into kegs and sealing it). Notice the drainage gutters. "Running water" came through from drains built into the walls (to keep the mortar dry and therefore strong...and less smelly).

• *Back outside, climb the modern stairs to the left (look for the zum Ausgang sign). A skinny, dark passage leads you into the...*

Big Cellar: This ❶❻ *Grosser Keller* was a big pantry. When the castle was smaller, this was the original moat—you can see the rough lower parts of the wall. The original floor was 13 feet deeper. The drawbridge rested upon the stone nubs on the left. When the castle expanded, the moat became this cellar. Halfway up the walls on the entrance side of the room, square holes mark spots where timbers made a storage loft, perhaps filled with grain. In the back, an arch leads to the wine cellar (sometimes blocked off) where finer wine was kept. Part of a soldier's pay was wine...table wine. This wine was kept in a single 180,000-liter stone barrel (that's 47,550 gallons), which generally lasted about 18 months.

The count owned the surrounding farmland. Farmers got to keep 20 percent of their production. Later, in more liberal feudal times, the nobility let them keep 40 percent. Today, the German government leaves the workers with 60 percent...and provides a few more services.

• *You're free. Climb out, turn right, and leave. I don't know what the women get, but the men's room at the exit comes with rather unnerving guillotine urinals. For coffee on a terrace with a great view, visit Schlosshotel Rheinfels, opposite the entrance.*

Sleeping in St. Goar

For parking advice, see "Helpful Hints," earlier.

$$ Hotel am Markt, run by Herr and Frau Marx and their friendly staff, is a good deal with all the modern comforts. It features 17 rustic rooms in the main building (think antlers with a pastel flair), plus 10 classier rooms right next door, and a good restaurant. It's a decent value and a stone's throw from the boat dock and train station (Sb-€50, standard Db-€65, bigger river view Db-€80, closed Nov-Feb, guest computer, Wi-Fi, parking-€5/day, Markt 1, tel. 06741/1689, www.hotelammarkt1.de, hotel.am.markt@t-online.de).

$$ Rhein Hotel, two doors down from Hotel am Markt and run with enthusiasm by young and energetic Gil Velich, has 10 quality rooms in a spacious building (Sb-€50-55, quiet viewless Db-€65-70, river-view balcony Db-€85-90, larger view/balcony Db-€95-100, Qb-€120-140—great for families, extra bed-€20, higher prices are for Fri-Sat nights, non-smoking, Wi-Fi, laundry-€15/load, closed mid-Nov-Feb, Heerstrasse 71, tel. 06741/981-240, www.rheinhotel-st-goar.de, info@rheinhotel-st-goar.de).

$ Hotel an der Fähre is a simple place (with a slight aroma of cigarette smoke in the lobby) on the busy road at the end of town, immediately across from the ferry dock. It rents 12 cheap but decent rooms (S-€35, Sb-€45, D-€45, Db-€55-€60, extra bed-€15, cash only, street noise but double-glazed windows, Wi-Fi, closed Nov-Feb, Heerstrasse 47, tel. 06741/980-577, www.hotel-stgoar.de, hotel_anderfaehre@web.de, Max & Alessia). They also offer rental bikes (see "Helpful Hints," earlier).

$ Frau Kurz has been housing my readers since 1988. With

the help of her daughter, Jeanette, she offers St. Goar's best B&B, renting three delightful rooms (sharing 2.5 bathrooms) with bathrobes, a breakfast terrace with castle views, a garden, and homemade marmalade (S-€30, D-€56, 2-night minimum, D-€52 with stay of 4 nights or more, cash only, non-smoking, free and easy parking, no Internet access, ask about apartment with kitchen if staying at least 5 days, Ulmenhof 11, tel. 06741/459, www.gaestehaus-kurz.de, fewokurz@kabelmail.de). It's a steep five-minute hike from the train station: Exit left from the station, take an immediate left under the tracks, and go part-way up the zigzag stairs, turning right through an archway onto Ulmenhof; #11 is just past the tower.

Eating in St. Goar

Hotel am Markt serves tasty traditional meals with plenty of game and fish (specialties include marinated roast beef and homemade cheesecake) at fair prices with good atmosphere and service. Choose cozy indoor seating, or dine outside with a river and castle view (€9-15 main courses, March-Oct daily 8:00-21:00, closed Nov-Feb, Markt 1, tel. 06741/1689).

Burgschänke is easy to miss on the ground floor of Schlosshotel Rheinfels (the hotel across from the castle ticket office—enter through the souvenir shop). It offers the only reasonably priced lunches up at Rheinfels Castle, is family-friendly, and has a Rhine view from its fabulous outdoor terrace (€7-9 pastas and *Flammkuchen*, €15-18 regional dishes, daily 11:00-17:30 plus Tue-Sat 18:30-22:00, tel. 06741/802-806).

The **Schlosshotel Rheinfels** dining room is your Rhine splurge, with an incredible indoor view terrace in an elegant, dressy setting. Call to reserve or arrive early if you're coming for breakfast or want a window table (€16 buffet breakfast, €19-28 main courses, €29-45 multi-course fixed-price meals, daily 7:00-11:00, 12:00-14:00 & 18:30-21:00, tel. 06741/8020).

Gasthaus Zur Krone is the local choice for traditional German food in a restaurant off the main drag. There's no river view, but it's cozy and offers some outdoor seating (€7-14 main courses, Thu-Tue 11:00-14:30 & 18:00-21:00, closed Wed, next to the train station and church at Oberstrasse 38, tel. 06741/1515).

Ristorante Alla Fontana, tucked away on a back lane and busy with locals, serves the best Italian food in town at great prices in a lovely dining room or on a leafy patio (€5-9 pizza and pasta, Tue 17:30-22:00, Wed-Sun 11:30-14:00 & 17:30-22:00, closed Mon, reservations smart, Pumpengasse 5, 06741/96117).

Landgasthof Biergarten Rebstock is hidden on the far end of town on the banks of the Rhine. They serve schnitzel (€7-12) and plenty of beer and wine. A nice playground nearby keeps the kids busy (April-Oct long hours daily—weather permitting, Am Hafen 1, tel. 06741/980-0337).

Café St. Goar is the perfect spot for a quick lunch or the German tradition of coffee and *kuchen*. They sell open-face sandwiches (€3-5), strudel (€2), tiny cookies (€2/bag), and a variety of cakes to satisfy any appetite. Grab something for a picnic or enjoy the seating on the pedestrian-only street out front (Mon-Sat 6:00-20:00, Sun 12:00-20:00, Heerstrasse 95, tel. 06741/1635).

Koblenz

The main town on this stretch of the Romantic Rhine is Koblenz—situated where the Mosel River flows into the Rhine. The word "Koblenz" comes from the Roman word for confluence—a reminder that 2,000 years ago, this was the northern border of the Roman Empire. The city has long been a strategic base. A transportation hub with a key bridge and a mighty fortress, it was heavily bombed in World War II. The city feels rebuilt today and has little of the charm that most are looking for when they visit the Rhineland. All I would do here is check out the modern center (Zentralplatz, with its Forum Confluentes and Rhineland museum), trek out to the Deutsches Eck ("German Corner") for a little Deutschland patriotism, ride the cable car over the Rhine (from the Deutsches Eck to the castle), and tour the Ehrenbreitstein Fortress, if only for the views.

Arrival in Koblenz: Drivers should go directly to the Deutsches Eck and park. If arriving by **train,** walk (or catch bus #1) from the station through the town center to the Deutsches Eck, with a stop at Zentralplatz on the way. KD Rhine sightseeing **boats** stop right at the Deutsches Eck (3-4/day, 3.25 hours upstream to St. Goar, 2.25 hours downstream from St. Goar, www.k-d.com).

Tourist Information: The TI is located within the Forum Confluentes cultural center on Zentralplatz (daily 10:00-18:00, tel. 0261/19433, www.koblenz-touristik.de).

Sights in Koblenz

Zentralplatz and Forum Confluentes

The city's once bombed-out center now sparkles with sleek modern architecture. On the main square, **Zentralplatz,** you'll find the striking new **Forum Confluentes.** This bright, modern cultural center houses the TI, an art museum, and the Mittelrhein Museum, with a fun look at Romantic-era portrayals of Rhine towns and exhibits on the Rhineland culture (museum-€6, Tue-Sun 10:00-18:00, closed Mon, Zentralplatz 1, tel. 0261/129-2520, www.mittelrhein-museum.de). It's a short walk from here to the Deutsches Eck.

Deutsches Eck

The actual tip of land where the two rivers meet is the legendary "Deutsches Eck"—the "German Corner." For many Germans,

this spot stirs their nationalistic spirit. While *"Deutschland über alles"* ("Germany above all"—a line from the German national anthem) is often associated with Hitler and German expansionism in the 20th century, the phrase actually refers to the fragmentation of German-speaking states before unity in 1871. The *Song of Germany* celebrated the notion of the little German states uniting in one German nation.

When Germany finally was united, it was the Johnny-come-lately of European superpowers and scrambled to establish its legitimacy. The allure of this strategic spot made it a natural staging ground for their purpose. Notice how the flags of the many German states all converge on the flag of a united Germany at the tip of the peninsula. While, historically, there was a lack of clarity about the French/German border (and under Napoleon, it was actually right here), today the "German Corner" is seen not as a border but as the heart of a great nation. Beyond the flag-lined plaza is a reconstructed memorial to Kaiser Wilhelm. Germans come here to feel good about their country while enjoying the organ-grinders and buskers playing accordions in this park-like atmosphere.

Seilbahn Cable Car

Koblenz's cable car runs above the Rhine River, stretching a half-mile from the Deutsches Eck to the Ehrenbreitstein Fortress high above. As you glide over the river you'll get fine views of the point where the Rhine and the Mosel rivers converge. This is the only convenient way to get from the city to the fortress.

Cost and Hours: €6 one-way, €9 round-trip, €11.80 round-trip combo-ticket with fortress entry; mid-April-Oct daily 10:00-18:30 plus June-Sept Fri-Sun until 22:00; Nov-mid-April daily 10:00-17:00; tel. 0261/2016-5850, www.seilbahn-koblenz.de.

Ehrenbreitstein Fortress

While a castle has stood on this strategic point much longer, what you see today is not your classic Rhine castle standing tall, but a squat and sprawling, bombshell-hardened 19th-century fortress. The exhibit is gangly and poorly signposted, with little English describing a vast space that is, by nature, not very inviting. As you enter you'll get a map with 20 points of (little) interest. But the views are grand and it's a chance to roam free in a castle.

Cost and Hours: €6, €11.80 combo-ticket with round-trip cable-car ride, daily mid-April-Oct 10:00-18:00, off-season until 17:00, tel. 0261/6675-4000.

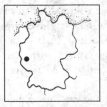

MOSEL VALLEY

Cochem • Burg Eltz • Beilstein

The misty Mosel is what some visitors hope the Rhine will be—peaceful, sleepy, romantic villages slipped between impossibly steep vineyards and the river; fine wine; a sprinkling of castles (Burg Eltz is tops); and lots of friendly small pensions. Boat, train, and car traffic here is a trickle compared to the roaring Rhine. While the swan-speckled Mosel (MOH-zehl in German; Moselle/moh-ZEHL in French) moseys 300 miles from France's Vosges mountain range to Koblenz (where it dumps into the Rhine), the most scenic piece of the valley lies between the towns of Bernkastel-Kues and Cochem. I'd savor only this section. Cochem and Trier (see next chapter) are easy day trips from each other (45-60 minutes by train, 55 miles by car). Cochem is the handiest home base, unless you have a car and want the peace of Beilstein.

GETTING AROUND THE MOSEL VALLEY

By Train and Bus: Fast trains zip you between Koblenz, Cochem, Bullay, and Trier in a snap. Other destinations require changing to a slow train or bus. Beilstein is a 20-minute ride on bus #716 from Cochem (May-Oct almost hourly Mon-Fri, 5-7/day on weekends, less frequent Nov-March; last bus departs between 21:00-22:00 except Sun 18:00-19:00, €3.65). Burg Eltz is a scenic 1.5-hour hike or €28 taxi ride from the tiny Moselkern train station (or about a €55 taxi ride from Cochem). For bus times, pick up printed schedules at train stations and TIs, or check the regional transit website (www.vrminfo.de) or Germany's train timetable (www.bahn.com).

By Boat: Thanks to its many locks, Mosel cruises feel more like canal-boat rides than the cruises on the mighty Rhine. The Kolb Line has the most frequent departures, and cruises the most scenic stretch of the Mosel (tel. 02673/1515, www.moselfahrplan.de). A simple and fun outing is the one-hour cruise between **Cochem** and **Beilstein,** passing through the Fankel lock (4-5/day in each direction May-Oct, weekends only in April, no boats off-season, first departure from Cochem at about 10:30, last departure from Beilstein at about 17:30, €12 one-way, €16 round-trip). Another option is the boat in the other direction (downstream) from **Cochem** to **Karden** (3/day, runs mid-July-Aug daily; May-mid-July and Sept-

Oct Wed and Sat-Sun only; no boats off-season; 35 minutes, €10 one-way, €13 round-trip). From Karden, you can get to Burg Eltz via a long hike (2 hours, steep in places), train-and-hike combination, weekend bus (May-Oct only, 4/day, www.burg-eltz.de), or taxi ride—though it's generally easier to reach Burg Eltz from the Moselkern train station. Kolb also runs one-hour **sightseeing cruises** and two-hour **dancing cruises** from Cochem (€10 sightseeing cruises 5/day Easter-Oct; €17 dancing cruises with live music daily at 20:15 mid-July-Aug; Tue and Sat only May-mid-July; Tue, Thu, and Sat Sept-Oct).

The K-D (Köln-Düsseldorfer) line sails the lower Mosel, between **Cochem** and **Koblenz**—but only Friday to Sunday, and only once a day in each direction (€31 one-way, June-Sept only, none off-season, Koblenz to Cochem 9:45-15:00, Cochem to Koblenz 15:40-20:00; free with a German rail pass but begins the use of a flexipass day, possible discounts with Eurail pass—ask; tel. in Cochem 02671/980-023, www.k-d.com).

Each year in May or June, the Mosel locks close for 10 days of maintenance, and none of the boats listed here run.

By Car: Two-lane roads run along both riverbanks. While these riverside roads are a delight, the river valley is very windy. Shortcuts overland can "cut the corners" and save you serious time—especially between Burg Eltz and Beilstein (see page 507) and if you're driving between the Mosel and the Rhine (note the Brodenbach-Boppard shortcut). Both Koblenz and Trier have car-rental agencies. A mile-long, 500-foot-high, €270 million expressway bridge (called Hochmoselbrücke) is being built near the town of Ürzig, just southwest/upstream of Cochem and Beilstein.

By Bike: Biking along the Mosel is the rage among Dutch and German tourists. You can rent bikes in most Mosel towns (I've listed options in both Cochem and Beilstein). A fine bike path follows the river from Koblenz to Zell (with some bits sharing the road with cars). Allow one hour between Cochem and Beilstein. Many pedal one-way, then relax on a return cruise or train ride.

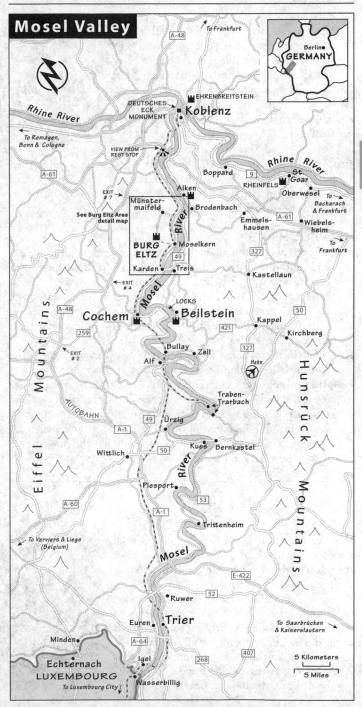

Mosel Valley

MOSEL VALLEY

To Frankfurt

A-48

Berlin
GERMANY

Rhine River

To Remagen,
Bonn & Cologne

DEUTSCHES
ECK
MONUMENT

EHRENBREITSTEIN

Koblenz

VIEW FROM
REST STOP

A-61

Rhine River

Boppard

9

St. Goar

RHEINFELS

Oberwesel

To
Bacharach
& Frankfurt

Wiebels-
heim

EXIT
7

Alken

Münster-
maifeld

Brodenbach

Emmels-
hausen

A-61

See Burg Eltz Area
detail map

BURG
ELTZ

Moselkern

Karden

49

Treis

Kastellaun

To
Frankfurt

327

Mosel River

EXIT
4

Cochem

A-48

259

EXIT
2

LOCKS

Beilstein

421

Kappel

50

Kirchberg

327

Hahn

Eiffel Mountains

Hunsrück Mountains

AUTOBAHN

Bullay

Alf

Zell

Traben-
Trarbach

49

A-1

Ürzig

50

Kues

Bernkastel

Wittlich

Piesport

River

53

A-1

Trittenheim

To Verviers & Liege
(Belgium)

Mosel

E-422

Ruwer

52

Trier

Euren

To Saarbrücken
& Kaiserslautern

Minden

A-64

Igel

268

407

Echternach

LUXEMBOURG

Wasserbillig

To Luxembourg City

5 Kilometers

5 Miles

MOSEL VALLEY

By Ferry: About a dozen small car-and-passenger ferries *(Fähre)* cross the Mosel between Koblenz and Trier.

By Plane: The confusingly named Frankfurt Hahn Airport, a popular hub for low-fare airlines such as Ryanair, is actually located near the Mosel (airport code: HHN, www.hahn-airport. de). You can ride bus #750 from the airport to Bullay (about €7.90, runs every 2 hours, 50 minutes; then 10-minute train ride from Bullay to Cochem). Groups of five or more need to book ahead for this bus (tel. 01805-066-735, www. airportshuttle-mosel.de/AirportHahn/).

HELPFUL HINTS

Wine Festivals: Throughout the Mosel region on summer weekends and during the fall harvest, wine festivals with oompah bands, dancing, and colorful costumes are powered by good food and wine. You'll find a wine festival in some nearby village any weekend, June through September. The tourist season lasts from April through October. Things close down tight through the winter.

Carry Cash: Be prepared to pay cash for nearly everything in the Mosel Valley, including food, hotels, and transportation.

Helpful Guidebook: Look for the booklet *The Castles of the Moselle* (€3.10, at local TIs), with information on castles from Koblenz to Trier (including Burg Eltz, Cochem, and Metternich in Beilstein). The booklet not only has historical and structural information, but also some drawings of what the now-ruined castles once looked like.

Cochem

With a majestic castle and picturesque medieval streets, Cochem (KOHKH-ehm) is the hub of the middle Mosel. With 5,000 inhabitants, it's a larger, more bustling town than Beilstein, Bacharach, or St. Goar. Duck into a damp wine cellar to sample the local white wine (*Weinprobe* means "wine-tasting"). Stroll pleasant paths along the idyllic riverbank, play life-size chess, or just grab a bench and watch Germany at play. River-cruise passengers clog the old town during the day, but evenings are peaceful.

Orientation to Cochem

Long and skinny Cochem stretches along both banks of the Mosel. The main part of town, on the west bank, sits below vineyards and the town's showpiece castle. From the river, the town bunny-hops up various small valleys.

TOURIST INFORMATION

The information-packed TI is by the bridge at the main bus stop. Most of the pamphlets (free map with town walk, town history flier) are kept behind the desk—ask. The TI also has information on special events, wine-tastings held by local vintners, public transportation to Burg Eltz, and area hikes. You can also pick up the informative, six-foot-long, €3.50 *Mosellauf* poster/brochure here (mid-July-Oct Mon-Sat 9:00-17:00, Sun 10:00-15:00; May-mid-July Mon-Fri 9:00-17:00, Sat 9:00-15:00, closed Sun; Nov-April Mon-Fri 9:00-13:00 & 14:00-17:00, closed Sat-Sun; Endertplatz 1, tel. 02671/60040, www.ferienland-cochem.de). Their thorough 24-hour room listings in the display cases on the wall outside come with a free phone connection.

ARRIVAL IN COCHEM

By Train: Cochem's train station is often unstaffed and has no lockers, but you can leave your bags at the Gleis 9 café off the station hall (€2/bag, Mon-Fri 8:30-19:30, Sat-Sun 10:00-19:30). Make a hard right out of the station and walk about 10 minutes along cobbled Ravenéstrasse to the TI and bus station (both on your left, before the bridge). To get to the main square (Markt) and colorful medieval town center, continue under the bridge (€0.50 WC), then angle right and follow Bernstrasse.

By Car: Drivers can park in a lot behind the train station (€4/day, reach it by circling around on Ravenéstrasse and Pinnerstrasse). There's also a multistory garage just up Endertstrasse from the bridge (€8/day).

HELPFUL HINTS

Festival: Cochem's biggest wine festival is held the last weekend in August. High season for wine aficionados lasts from August through October.

Internet Access: The very pleasant **Espresso I-O** café has free Wi-Fi (Mon-Fri 7:00-18:00—opens later during school holidays, Sat-Sun 11:00-18:00, between TI and train station at Ravenéstrasse 18-20).

Bike Rental: Consider taking a bike on the boat or train, and pedaling back. **Radverleih Schaltwerk,** between the station and TI, offers helmets with rentals (€9/day, €10/day for mountain bikes, €24/day for electric bikes; Mon-Fri 9:00-12:00 & 14:00-18:00, Sat 9:00-12:30, Sun 10:00-12:30—except closed Sun Nov-March; drop-off possible until 18:00, Ravenéstrasse 18-20, tel. 02671/603-500). The ticket office at the **K-D boat dock** also rents bikes (€9/day, €18/day for electric bikes; daily May-Sept 9:30-18:00, tel. 02671/980-023).

Sights in Cochem

Cochem Castle (Reichsburg Cochem)

This pretty, pointy castle on a hill above town is the work of overly imaginative 19th-century restorers. Like many castles along the

Rhine and Mosel, Cochem's was blown up by French troops in 1689. For almost two hundred years it stood in ruins—much like Beilstein's—until it caught the attention of Louis Ravené, a rich Berliner who'd made a fortune in the steel industry. He bought the castle dirt-cheap in 1868 and spared no expense in turning it into a luxurious private residence furnished with tasteful antiques. Today, the castle can only be visited on a 40-minute tour (these run frequently throughout the day and are in German only, but guides pass out a helpful English info sheet that makes the visit worthwhile). You'll see seven beautiful rooms, complete with antlers on the wall and hidden doors leading to secret passages. The other 43 rooms are empty, as Ravené's descendants took most of their stuff in 1942 when they were forced to sell the castle to the Nazi government (which then used it as a training center for lawyers). The castle is now owned by the town of Cochem.

Cost and Hours: €5, daily mid-March-mid-Nov, first tour at 9:00, last tour at 17:00, mid-Nov-mid-March tours run irregularly—see schedule on website, tel. 02671/255, www.reichsburg-cochem.de.

Falcon Show: Below the entrance, the resident falconer frequently shows off his flock—check the notice at the gate to see if the birds are in fine feather (€4, 40-minute show, Tue-Sun at 11:00, 13:00, 14:30, and 16:00, no shows Mon, look for *Falknerei* sign, mobile 0160-9912-7380, www.falknerei-reichsburg-cochem.de).

Eating: Restaurant Burgschänke serves lunch and offers scenic views of the Mosel Valley (€5-€10 meals, mid-March-Oct daily 10:00-18:00, closed Nov-mid-March, tel. 02671/255).

MOSEL VALLEY

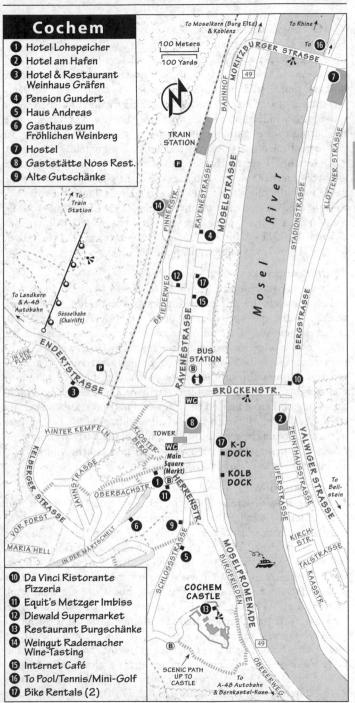

Cochem

1 Hotel Lohspeicher
2 Hotel am Hafen
3 Hotel & Restaurant Weinhaus Gräfen
4 Pension Gundert
5 Haus Andreas
6 Gasthaus zum Fröhlichen Weinberg
7 Hostel
8 Gaststätte Noss Rest.
9 Alte Gutschänke

10 Da Vinci Ristorante Pizzeria
11 Equit's Metzger Imbiss
12 Diewald Supermarket
13 Restaurant Burgschänke
14 Weingut Rademacher Wine-Tasting
15 Internet Café
16 To Pool/Tennis/Mini-Golf
17 Bike Rentals (2)

100 Meters
100 Yards

To Moselkern (Burg Eltz) & Koblenz
To Rhine
To 16

TRAIN STATION

To Train Station

To Landkern & A-48 Autobahn

Sesselbahn (Chairlift)

IN DER PLAIN

ENDERTSTRASSE

HINTER KEMPELN

KELBERGER STRASSE

JAHNSTRASSE

VOR FORST

MARIA HELL

IN DER MÄRTSCHELT

KLOSTERBERG

OBERBACHSTR.

HERRENSTR.

SCHLOSSSTRASSE

MORITZBURGER STRASSE

BAHNHOF

MOSELSTRASSE

RAVENESTRASSE

PINNERSTR.

BRIEDERWEG

MOSELSTRASSE

Mosel River

STADIONSTRASSE

KLOTTENER STRASSE

BERGSTRASSE

VALWIGER STRASSE

ZEHNTHAUSSTRASSE

UFERSTRASSE

KIRCHSTR.

TALSTRASSE

KAASSTR.

To Beilstein

BUS STATION

BRÜCKENSTR.

WC

TOWER

WC

Main Square (Markt)

K-D DOCK

KOLB DOCK

MOSELPROMENADE

BURGFRIEDEN

COCHEM CASTLE

SCENIC PATH UP TO CASTLE

To A-48 Autobahn & Bernkastel-Kues

OBERERWEG

Getting There on Foot: *Zur Burg* signs point the way up. From the old town's main square (Markt), with your back to the tower, the quickest way is to walk a block straight ahead on Herrenstrasse and then turn right up Schlossstrasse (10- to 15-minute huff and puff). A 25-minute scenic route is to continue along Herrenstrasse, which changes its name to Burgfrieden and then turns into a path winding up to the castle from behind. Even if you ride the bus up to the castle (explained next), this trail is the prettiest way to get back down (look for the *Zur Mosel* sign below the castle).

Getting There by Bus: If you've already *probed* a little *Wein* and would rather ride up, consider the shuttle bus that runs to the castle from the bus station (next to the TI)—though you still have to walk the last five minutes uphill (bus #781, €2.50 one-way, €4 round-trip, 1-3/hour, May-Oct only, first bus up at 10:10, last bus down at 18:00, look for *Reichsburg Shuttle-Bus* sign at bus station, tel. 02671/7647, www.reichsburg-cochem.de).

Chairlift and Hikes

For great views, ride the *Sesselbahn* (chairlift), which ascends the hill on the opposite side of town from the castle (€4.30 one-way, €6.30 round-trip, April-Oct 10:00-18:00, July-Aug until 19:00, closed off-season, tel. 02671/989-065, www.cochemer-sesselbahn. de). There's a pricey restaurant at the top, along with a short, rocky path that leads to the Pinnerkreuz overlook. Instead of riding to the top, you can scramble up the narrow path under the lift for 20 minutes of heart-pounding, aerobic excitement. Or take the trail up to the same point from behind the train station (find trailhead behind station parking lot). For the best of all worlds, ride the lift up, take in the view from the restaurant, then follow the path to the station *(Bahnhof)*, then down through the forest and then the vineyards to a wine-tasting at Weingut Rademacher.

Wine-Tasting

At **Weingut Rademacher,** near the train station, you can taste four local wines for €2.90. There's no charge for tasting if you buy at least three bottles (usually open May-Sept Mon-Tue and Thu-Sat 10:00-19:30, closed Wed and Sun, different hours during festivals, call ahead to confirm, open by arrangement Oct-April, Pinnerstrasse 10, tel. 02671/4164, www.weingut-rademacher.de). Other wine cellars in town also offer tastings. For a unique treat, look for the Roter-Weinbergs-Pfirsich Likör—a local cordial made from the small, tart "red peaches" that are unique to the Mosel Valley.

If you have a car, consider going upriver to the town of **Zell,** famous for its Schwarze Katze ("Black Cat") wine. English-speaking Peter Weis runs **F. J. Weis** winery and gives a clever, entertaining tour of his 40,000-bottle-per-year wine cellar. The tour includes a wine-tasting and usually runs daily at 17:00, but it's important to call ahead to reserve a spot (€18, open April–mid-Nov daily 10:30–18:00, closed mid-Nov–March except with advance notice, tel. 06542/41398, mobile 0172-780-7153, www.weingut-fjweis. de, f.j.weis@t-online.de). You will find his *Weinkeller* south of the town of Zell. It's 200 yards past the bridge toward Bernkastel, riverside at Notenau 30. Peter also rents two luxurious apartments with kitchen facilities (Db–€71, less for 3 or more nights, extra person–€12, breakfast–€7.50).

Swimming, Tennis, and Golf

Cochem's Moselbad and Freizeit Zentrum offers an array of family-friendly activities: an indoor wave pool, an outdoor pool, a sauna, tennis courts, and mini-golf. The downside: It's 30 minutes on foot from the center of town.

Cost and Hours: Indoor pool–€8/3 hours, Mon 13:00–22:00, Tue-Fri 9:00–22:00, Sat-Sun 10:00–19:00; other activities have different hours and prices; 10 minutes beyond youth hostel at Moritz-burger Strasse 1, tel. 02671/97990, www.moselbad.de.

Cruise

The Kolb Line offers one-hour sightseeing cruises and schmaltzy two-hour "Tanz Party" dancing cruises with live music (see "Getting Around the Mosel Valley—By Boat," page 489).

Sightseeing Train

A little green-and-yellow tourist train leaves from under the bridge at the TI and does a 25-minute sightseeing loop through town. Since the commentary is only in German (ask for English flier), and Cochem is such a pedestrian-friendly town anyway, this is worth it only if you're bored and lazy.

Cost and Hours: €5.50, includes a glass of wine, 1-2/hour, April-Oct daily 10:00–17:00, Nov-March weekends only.

Sleeping in Cochem

Cochem is a good base for train travelers. Most listings are within a 10- to 15-minute walk or a €6 taxi ride. August is very tight on rooms, with various festivals and generally inflated prices. Cochem has no launderette.

$$$ Hotel Lohspeicher, an upscale-rustic hotel just off the main square on a street with tiny steps, is for those willing to pay a bit extra for quality lodgings in the thick of things. Its nine high-ceilinged rooms have modern comforts, and the owner is a gourmet chef (Sb–€70, Db–€90-125, prices depend on room size, includes big breakfast in a fine stone-and-timber room, elevator, Wi-Fi, fancy restaurant—closed Feb-mid-March, parking–€9/

MOSEL VALLEY

Sleep Code

Abbreviations   (€1 = about $1.40, country code: 49)
S = Single, **D** = Double/Twin, **T** = Triple, **Q** = Quad, **b** = bathroom, **s** = shower only.
Price Rankings
 $$$ **Higher Priced**—Most rooms €80 or more.
  $$ **Moderately Priced**—Most rooms between €50-80.
   $ **Lower Priced**—Most rooms €50 or less.
Unless otherwise noted, credit cards are accepted, English is spoken, breakfast is included, and Wi-Fi is generally free. Prices change; verify current rates online or by email. For the best prices, always book directly with the hotel.

day, Obergasse 1, tel. 02671/3976, www.lohspeicher.de, service@lohspeicher.de, Ingo).

$$$ Hotel am Hafen, across the bridge from the TI, offers a mellow atmosphere with views over the river to Cochem. Some of the 20 rooms have balconies (Sb-€70-85, Db-€85, slightly nicer Db-€108, deluxe Db-€120, €10 less Nov-June or for 2 nights, guest computer, Wi-Fi, free parking, closed Dec-Jan, Uferstrasse 3, tel. 02671/97720, www.hotel-am-hafen.de, hotel-am-hafen.cochem@t-online.de).

$$ Hotel & Restaurant Weinhaus Gräfen, run by the friendly and helpful Vatlav family, has a mix of 12 comfortable rooms (some very small but others quite large), a nicely decorated terrace, and a recommended restaurant downstairs (Sb-€40, Db-€76, Tb-€90, elevator, Wi-Fi, discounted parking at nearby public garage-€14 for up to 4 days; near chair lift at Endertstrasse 27, tel. 02671/4453, www.weinhaus-graefen.de, info@weinhaus-graefen.de).

$$ Pension Gundert's 12 rooms fill a handsome 1904 row house two convenient blocks from the station, along the street leading into town. Guests enjoy a pleasant roof terrace overlooking the river. The Gundert family and the pension manager are very helpful, and work hard to provide an enjoyable stay (Sb-€36-45, Db-€59-78, breakfast buffet, family deals, Wi-Fi, free parking, local wines/beers and non-alcoholic drinks available in kitchen on roof terrace, Ravenéstrasse 34, tel. 02671/910-224, www.pension-gundert.de, info@pension-gundert.de).

$ Haus Andreas has 10 clean rooms at fair prices in the old town (Sb-€30, Db-€50-70, Tb-€75, lower prices are for at least 3 nights, cash only, pay Wi-Fi, parking-€2/day, Schlossstrasse 9, reception is often across the street in shop at #16, tel. 02671/1370 or 02671/5155, www.hausandreas.de, info@hausandreas.de, kind Frau Pellny speaks a little English). From the main square, take

Herrenstrasse (go straight if coming from the station); after a block, angle right up the steep hill on Schlossstrasse.

$ Gasthaus zum Fröhlichen Weinberg, also in the old town, is a relaxed jumble of nine clean, inexpensive rooms, some with low ceilings and tiny bathrooms and most with sunny balconies, topped by a fun roof garden with a view over town. It's run by a mother-and-daughter team (Sb-€25, Db-€55-60, ask about family rooms, lower prices for longer stays, cash only, lots of stairs, Wi-Fi, parking-€3.50/day, Schlaufstrasse 11, tel. 02671/4193, www.zum-froehlichen-weinberg.de, info@zum-froehlichen-weinberg.de). From the main square, go up Oberbachstrasse (in the far-right corner if coming from the station) and then left up tiny Schlaufstrasse.

Hostel: Cochem's **$ hostel** is a huge, family-friendly complex just across the river from the train station, with 148 beds, picnic tables, grill pit, playground, game room, bar, restaurant, and a sundeck over the Mosel (dorm bed in 4- to 6-bed rooms-€22.50, Db-€56, includes sheets and breakfast, box lunches-€4.90/person, pay guest computer and Wi-Fi, fills up—reserve in advance, Klottener Strasse 9, tel. 02671/8633, www.diejugendherbergen.de/cochem, cochem@diejugendherbergen.de). From the train station, walk straight down to the river, turn left, and use the stairway to cross the modern bridge to the hostel.

Eating in Cochem

In addition to the following listings, both the castle and the chairlift have cafés serving lunch (see "Sights in Cochem," earlier), the Hotel Lohspeicher has a very fancy, very expensive gourmet restaurant (see "Sleeping in Cochem," earlier), and there are plentiful pizza, Turkish, and Asian options in the old town.

Gaststätte Noss is one of several restaurants along the riverside promenade. It's open later than most and supplies meat from its own butcher shop—a plus in Germany. Don't confuse it with the hotel of the same name (€10-20 main courses, cheaper daily specials; March-Nov Fri-Wed 10:00-21:30, also open Thu Aug-Sept only; Dec-Jan Fri-Wed 10:00-15:00 & 17:30-21:30, closed Thu and Feb; Moselpromenade 4, tel. 02671/7067).

Alte Gutschänke, better known as "Arthur's place," is where locals go for a glass of wine in a cozy cellar. Seating is at long, wooden, get-to-know-your-neighbor tables (extensive wine list and very basic pub food, Easter-Oct Tue-Fri from 18:00, Sat-Sun from 14:00, closed Mon and in winter, just uphill from the old town's Markt square at Schlossstrasse 6, tel. 02671/8950).

Hotel & Restaurant Weinhaus Gräfen is where you can meet the locals while enjoying freshly prepared traditional food (€8-€18 main courses, €14 daily fixed-price meals, daily 10:00-22:00 except closed last 2 weeks of Nov and Feb, below recommended hotel at Endertstrasse 27, tel. 02671/4453).

Da Vinci Ristorante Pizzeria serves good, reasonably priced Italian fare at its hard-to-miss location just across the bridge from the TI. Grab a seat on the covered terrace for city, river, and castle views while rubbing elbows with locals and fellow travelers (€6-10 pizzas, €7-20 main courses, Tue-Sun 12:00-14:00 & 17:30-22:00, closed Mon except mid-July-Aug, cash only, Bergstrasse 1, tel. 02671/916-195).

Equit's Metzger Imbiss is a great and inexpensive alternative for lunch or an early dinner. Local butcher Thomas Equit offers tasty sausages, schnitzel, and other regional dishes—as well as burgers—for a reasonable price. The interior is modern, clean, and very inviting. In summer, the big front windows are opened up, and you'll feel like you're sitting right on the main square (€4-8 main courses, daily 10:00-20:00, cash only, Markt 10, tel. 02671/910-710).

Picnics: The **Diewald supermarket** stocks everything you need for a fabulous picnic (Mon-Fri 7:30-20:00, Sat 8:00-18:00, closed Sun). Located between the train station and TI, it's just off Ravenéstrasse, up a little side street at #33, behind a clothing store.

Cochem Connections

From Cochem by Train to: Moselkern (for hike to Burg Eltz; hourly, 16 minutes), **Trier** (2/hour, 45-60 minutes), **Frankfurt Airport** (hourly, 2-2.5 hours, change in Koblenz and sometimes Mainz), **Cologne** (1-2/hour, 2-2.5 hours, most change in Koblenz), **Bacharach** (hourly, 2 hours, change in Koblenz), **Rothenburg** (every 1-2 hours, 5-7 hours, 3-4 changes), **Berlin** (roughly hourly, 7-8 hours, 1-3 changes), **Paris** (best routings roughly every 2 hours, 4-5 hours, transfer in Saarbrücken or in Trier and Luxembourg).

Train info: Tel. 0180-599-6633, www.bahn.com. Bus info: Tel. 02671/8976, www.vrminfo.de.

Burg Eltz

My favorite castle in all of Europe—worth ▲▲▲—lurks in a mysterious forest. It's been left intact for 700 years and is decorated and furnished throughout much as it was 500 years ago. Thanks to smart diplomacy, clever marriages, and lots of luck, Burg Eltz (pronounced "boorg elts") was never destroyed (it survived one five-year siege). It's been in the Eltz family for 850 years. The scenic 1.5-hour walk up the Elz Valley to the castle makes a great half-day outing if you're staying anywhere along the Mosel—and a worthwhile day trip if you're staying on the Rhine. For details on the various ways to reach the castle, see "Getting to Burg Eltz" on page 503.

MOSEL VALLEY

ORIENTATION

Cost and Hours: €9 castle entry (includes guided tour and treasury), April-Oct daily from 9:30, last tour departs at 17:30, closed Nov-March. Pick up the free English descriptions at entry. Tel. 02672/950-500, www.burg-eltz.de, burg@eltz.org.

Tours: The only way to see the castle is with a 45-minute tour (included in entry price). Guides speak English and thoughtfully collect English speakers into their own tours—well worth waiting for (usually a 30-minute wait at most; visit treasury in the meantime).

Bring Cash: The castle (including the parking lot and café) doesn't accept credit cards—only cash. There's no ATM, so make sure you bring enough. (There's only one exception: If you spend at least €50 at the ticket desk—which is hard for most visitors to do—they accept Visa and MasterCard.)

VISITING THE CASTLE

Elz is the name of a stream that runs past the castle through a deep valley before emptying into the Mosel. The first record of a *Burg* (castle) on the Elz is from 1157. By about 1490, the castle looked like it does today, with the homes of three big landlord families gathered around a tiny courtyard within one formidable fortification. Today, the excellent 45-minute tour winds you through two of those homes, while the third is still the residence of the castellan (the man who maintains the castle). This is where members of the Eltz family stay when they're not at one of their other feudal

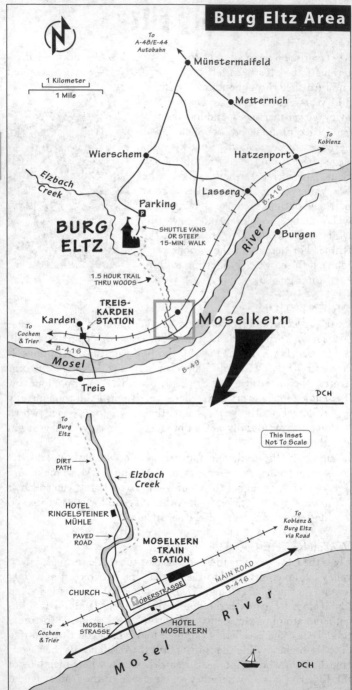

Burg Eltz Area

MOSEL VALLEY

N

1 Kilometer
1 Mile

To A-48/E-44
Autobahn

Münstermaifeld

Metternich

To Koblenz

Wierschem

Hatzenport

Lasserg

B-416

Elzbach
Creek

Parking
P

BURG
ELTZ

SHUTTLE VANS
OR STEEP
15-MIN. WALK

Burgen

River

1.5 HOUR TRAIL
THRU WOODS

TREIS-
KARDEN
STATION

Moselkern

Karden

To Cochem
& Trier

B-416

Mosel

B-49

Treis

DCH

To
Burg
Eltz

This Inset
Not To Scale

DIRT
PATH

Elzbach
Creek

HOTEL
RINGELSTEINER
MÜHLE

To
Koblenz &
Burg Eltz
via Road

PAVED
ROAD

MOSELKERN
TRAIN
STATION

MAIN ROAD

B-416

CHURCH

OBERSTRASSE

River

To
Cochem
& Trier

MOSEL-
STRASSE

HOTEL
MOSELKERN

Mosel River

DCH

holdings. The elderly countess of Eltz—whose family goes back 33 generations here (you'll see a photo of her family)—enjoys flowers. Each week for 40 years, she's had grand arrangements adorn the public castle rooms.

It was a comfortable castle for its day: 80 rooms made cozy by 40 fireplaces and wall-hanging tapestries. Many of its 20 toilets were automatically flushed by a rain drain. The delightful **chapel** is on a lower floor. Even though "no one should live above God," this chapel's placement was acceptable because it filled a bay window, which flooded the delicate Gothic space with light. The three families met—working out common problems as if sharing a condo complex—in the large "conference room." A carved jester and a rose look down on the big table, reminding those who gathered that they were free to discuss anything ("fool's freedom"—jesters could say anything to the king), but nothing discussed could leave the room (the "rose of silence"). In the **bedroom,** have fun with the suggestive decor: the jousting relief carved into the canopy, and the fertile and phallic figures hiding in the lusty green wall paintings.

Near the exit, the **treasury** fills the four higgledy-piggledy floors of a cellar with the precious, eccentric, and historic mementos of this family that once helped elect the Holy Roman Emperor and, later, owned a sizable chunk of Croatia (Habsburg favors). The silver and gold work—some of Germany's best—is worth a close look with the help of an English flier.

Eating at Burg Eltz: The **castle café** serves lunch, with soups and bratwurst-and-fries cuisine for €4-7 (April-Oct daily 9:30-17:30, cash only).

Sleeping near Burg Eltz: Although I prefer the bustle of Cochem or the charm of Beilstein, staying in tiny, sleepy Moselkern is a workable option. You can start off to Burg Eltz right after breakfast to beat the heat on a warm day. **$$ Hotel Moselkern**, set alongside the river a five-minute walk from the train station, has 25 comfortable rooms in a solid, 1970s-era building. All of the

rooms have balconies, most of them overlooking the river (Sb-€38-43, Db-€76-86, higher prices are for July-Sept, elevator, Wi-Fi, restaurant with outdoor seating, free parking, bowling alley in basement, tel. 02672/1303, www.hotel-moselkern.de, hotelmoselkern@t-online.de, Rother family).

GETTING TO BURG ELTZ

The castle is a pleasant 1.5-hour **walk** from the nearest train station, in the little village of Moselkern—the walk is not only easy, it's the most fun and scenic way to visit the castle.

Alternatively, if the weather is bad, or you prefer not to walk, you can take a **taxi** (or, on summer weekends only, the **bus**) to the castle from the village of Karden (see "By Bus from the Treis-Karden Station," later).

Cars (and taxis) park in a lot near, but not quite at, Burg Eltz. From the lot, hike 15 minutes downhill to the castle or wait (10 minutes at most) for the red castle shuttle bus (€2 each way).

Each of your options is explained below.

Hiking from Moselkern

The hike between the Moselkern train station and Burg Eltz runs through a magical pine forest, where sparrows carry crossbows, and maidens, disguised as falling leaves, whisper "watch out." You can do the hike in 70 minutes at a steady clip, but allow an extra 20 minutes or so to enjoy the scenery. The trail is mostly gentle, except for a few uneven parts that are slippery when wet and the steep flight of stairs leading up to the castle at the end. But the overall rise from the river to the castle is less than 400 feet.

Getting to Moselkern: To start the hike, take the slow milk-run train (hourly) to Moselkern from Cochem (16 minutes, €4.65). If you're returning to Cochem, buy a €9.30 round-trip ticket; groups of at least three can get an €18.90 *Minigruppenkarte* (covers round-trips for up to 5 people, not valid before 9:00 on weekdays). You can also reach Moselkern from towns on the Rhine (including Cologne and Bacharach) with a change at Koblenz.

Storing Luggage: The Moselkern train station is unstaffed and has no lockers, phones, or taxis. If you need to store luggage, you can leave it at Hotel Moselkern, on the river a five-minute walk from the station (see "Sleeping near Burg Eltz," earlier); call the hotel in advance to make sure someone will be there when you arrive (tel. 02672/1303). While there's no charge for storage, consider thanking them by eating at their reasonably priced restaurant (food served Mon-Fri 17:00-22:00, Sat-Sun 11:00-22:00) or buying a drink at the hotel bar.

The Hike: The path up to the castle begins at the other end of Moselkern village from the station. Turn right from the station along Oberstrasse, cross the intersection with Weinbergsstrasse, and continue straight along narrow Oberstrasse. In about five minutes, you'll pass the village church. Keep going straight a few houses past the church; then, as the street ends, turn right through the underpass. On your left is the Elzbach stream that you'll follow all the way up to the castle. Follow the road straight along the stream through a mostly residential neighborhood. Just before the road crosses the stream on a stone bridge, take either the footpath (stay right) or the bridge—they join up again later.

After about a 30-minute walk from the train station, the road ends at the parking lot of the Hotel Ringelsteiner Mühle. Stay to the right of the hotel and continue upstream along the easy-to-follow trail, which starts out paved but soon changes to dirt—from here, it's another 45 minutes through the forest to the castle.

Hiking from Karden (with Optional Boat Trip)

If you don't mind a longer hike, consider a boat ride to the village of Karden, then walk to Burg Eltz from there. (Karden is also on the train line between Cochem and Moselkern.) This two-hour hike is steep in places, and harder to follow and less shady than the hike from Moselkern.

Getting to Karden: Kolb Line riverboat cruises run between Cochem and Karden three times a day in midsummer and less frequently in spring and fall (described on page 489). Make sure to get off the boat in Karden (not in Treis, across the river). If you come by train, get off at the Treis-Karden stop, which is in Karden but serves both villages.

Storing Luggage: If you need to store luggage before the hike, the elegant Schloss-Hotel Petry, across from the Treis-Karden station, is happy to guard your bags if you eat at their restaurant (€10-22 main courses, lunch daily 11:30-14:00, St. Castorstrasse 80, tel. 02672/9340, www.schloss-hotel-petry.de).

The Hike: The path from Karden to Burg Eltz starts at the far end of Karden village, beyond the white-towered St. Castor's church (follow *Burg Eltz* signs). Get a trail map (available locally), and be prepared for full sun when the hike travels through open fields.

Shortcuts: To ride the boat but avoid the lengthy hike to Burg Eltz, you can either hop the hourly train from Treis-Karden to Moselkern and take the shorter 1.5-hour hike from there (described earlier); take the bus from the Treis-Karden station straight up to Burg Eltz on weekends (May-Oct only, described next); or take a taxi from Karden to the castle (see later).

By Bus from the Treis-Karden Station

From May through October on Saturdays and Sundays only, bus #330 runs to Burg Eltz from the Treis-Karden railway station (4/day, 35 minutes; leaves Treis-Karden station at 8:59, 10:59, 14:59, and 16:59; returns from Burg Eltz at 10:15, 12:15, 16:15, and 18:15; confirm times at Cochem TI, with bus operator at tel. 02671/8976, or at www.vrminfo.de).

MOSEL VALLEY

By Taxi

You can taxi to the castle from **Cochem** (30 minutes, about €55 one-way for up to 4 people, Cochem taxi tel. 02671/8080), **Moselkern** (€28 one-way, taxi tel. 02672/1407), or **Karden** (€30 one-way, taxi tel. 02672/1407). Remember: Even with a taxi, you'll still have a 15-minute walk from the parking lot to the castle. If you're planning to taxi from Moselkern, call ahead and ask the taxi to meet your train at Moselkern station. Consider taxiing up to Burg Eltz and then enjoying the hike downhill back to the train station in Moselkern.

By Car

Be Careful: Signs direct drivers to two different "Burg Eltz" parking lots—some deceptively take drivers far from the castle, while others get you right there. From Koblenz, leave the river at Hatzenport, following the white *Burg Eltz* signs through the towns of Münstermaifeld and Wierschem. From Cochem, follow the *Münstermaifeld* signs from Moselkern. The castle parking lot (€2/day, daily 9:00-18:30) is just over a mile past Wierschem. (Note that the *Eltz* signs at Moselkern lead to Hotel Ringelsteiner Mühle and the trailhead for the hike to the castle—see next. To drive directly to the castle, ignore the *Eltz* signs until you reach Münstermaifeld.)

Drive/Hike Combo: If you're traveling by car but would enjoy walking part of the path from Moselkern up to the castle, drive to Moselkern, follow the *Burg Eltz* signs up the Elz Valley, park at the Hotel Ringelsteiner Mühle (€3, buy ticket from machine), and hike about 45 minutes up the trail to the castle (full hike described earlier).

Shortcut to Beilstein: If driving from Burg Eltz to Beilstein, you'll save 30 minutes with this shortcut: Cross the river at Treis-Karden, go through town, and bear right at the swimming pool (direction: Bruttig-Fankel). This overland route deposits you in Bruttig, a scenic three-mile riverside drive from Beilstein.

Beilstein

Just upstream from Cochem is the quaintest of all Mosel towns. Cozy Beilstein (BILE-shtine) is Cinderella-land—touristy but tranquil, except for its territorial swans. Beilstein has zero food shops, zero ATMs (make sure to bring cash), one bus stop, one mailbox, and 180 residents who run

about 30 guesthouses and eateries. It's nicknamed the "Sleeping Beauty of the Mosel" because until about 1900, it was inaccessible except by boat. Beilstein has no TI, but there is an information board by the bus stop, and cafés and guesthouses can give you town info.

PLANNING YOUR TIME

Car travelers use Beilstein as a base, day-tripping from here to Cochem, Trier, Burg Eltz, and the Rhine. Overnighting in Beilstein without a car is doable, as long as you check the bus schedule in advance and plan carefully. If you're staying in Cochem and using public transportation, you can day-trip to Beilstein: Take the bus to Beilstein, follow my self-guided walk up to the castle, have lunch, and then return by boat. While the town is peaceful and a delight in the evening, midday crowds in peak season can trample all its charm and turn it into a human traffic jam. But in the winter (mid-Nov until Easter), Beilstein is dead as a doornail.

GETTING TO BEILSTEIN

Beilstein has no train station, but it's easy to reach from Cochem—either on **bus #716** (May-Oct almost hourly Mon-Fri, 5-7/day on weekends, less frequent Nov-March; last bus departs between 21:00-22:00 except Sun 18:00-19:00, €3.65, www.vrminfo.de), by **taxi** (about €20), or by one-hour **river cruise** (4-5/day in each direction May-Oct, weekends only in April, no boats off-season, first departure from Cochem at about 10:30, last departure from Beilstein at about 17:30, €12 one-way, €16 round-trip). If **driving,** there's a free lot along the river just upstream from town, under the castle hill. The parking spaces closer-in cost €1/hour during the day (4-hour maximum, use coins to buy ticket from *Parkscheinautomat* machine by town info board).

Two helpful tips: When looking up schedules on www.bahn.com (the Deutsche Bahn website), Beilstein's bus stop appears as "Moselstrasse (Beilstein)." On weekends when bus #716 runs infrequently and the Ellenz Fähre ferry is running (see next page for cost and hours), you can reach Beilstein from Cochem via bus #711 along the other side of the river. (This alternative is slightly more expensive, and the ferry's irregular hours and early closing time complicate it, so I prefer taking the direct #716 bus.) If you go this way, take bus #711 to the Ellenz Fähre stop, then ride the ferry across the river to Beilstein.

Beilstein Walk

Explore the narrow lanes, ancient wine cellar, resident swans, and ruined castle by following this short self-guided walk.

• *Stand along the riverfront, by the town info board.*

Beilstein's Riverfront

In 1963, the big road and the Mosel locks were built, making the river peaceful today. Before then, access to Beilstein was limited to a tiny one-way lane and the small ferry. Originally, the ferry was motorless and the cables that tether it allowed the craft to cross the river powered only by the current and an angled rudder. Since the river was tamed by locks, the current is so weak that the ferry needs its motor. Today, the funky little **Ellenz Fähre** ferry shuttles people (€1.50), bikes, and cars constantly (Easter-Oct daily 10:00-12:00 & 13:00-18:00, no ferries off-season, wave to summon ferry if captain has paused on opposite bank).

The campground across the river is typical of German campgrounds—nearly all of its residents set up their trailers and tents at Easter and use them as summer homes until October, when the regular floods chase them away for the winter. If you stood where you are now through the winter, you'd have cold water up to your crotch five times.

Look inland. The town was given market rights in 1310 and was essentially an independent city-state for centuries (back when there

were 300 such petty kingdoms and dukedoms in what we now call "Germany"). The Earl of Beilstein ruled from his castle above town. He built the Altes Zollhaus in 1634 to levy tolls from river traffic. Today, the castle is a ruin, the last monk at the once-mighty monastery (see the big church high on the left) retired in 2009, and the town's economy is based only on wine and tourists.

Beilstein is so well-preserved because it was essentially inaccessible by road until about 1900. And its tranquility is a result of Germany's WWI loss, which cost the country the regions of Alsace and Lorraine (now part of France, these provinces have flip-flopped between the two nations since the Thirty Years' War). Before World War I, the Koblenz-Trier train line—which connects Lorraine to Germany—was the busiest in the country, tunneling through the grape-laden hill across the river in what was the longest train tunnel in Germany. The construction of a supplemental line designed to follow the riverbank (like the lines that crank up the volume on the Rhine) was stopped in 1914. After Alsace and Lorraine went to France in 1918, the new line no longer made any sense, and the plans were scuttled.

• Follow the main "street" up into town. You'll notice blue plaques on the left marking the high-water (Hochwasser) points of historic floods. At the first corner, after the Wirtshaus Alte Stadtmauer, go left and find house #13 in the corner.

Former Synagogue

In the 1300s, several Jewish families were invited to Beilstein after being persecuted and expelled from towns on the Rhine. By 1840,

a quarter of the town's 300 inhabitants were Jewish. The synagogue (which dates from 1310) and the adjacent rabbi's home were at #13. The medallion above the door shows the Star of David embedded in the double-headed eagle of the Holy Roman Emperor, indicating that the Jews would be protected by the emperor. This was perhaps of some comfort, but not reliable. Of the town's many Jews, most moved away (to larger German towns or abroad) in the 1800s and early 1900s. Others assimilated, marrying Gentiles and raising their children as Christians (among these was the Lipmann family, whose descendants run the riverfront hotels). By 1933, only one Jewish family was left in Beilstein to deal with the Nazis. There are no practicing Jews in town today. The cemetery above the castle is another interesting Jewish sight (see "Beilstein's Castle," later).

• Continue right (uphill) from the synagogue, and then with the church high above, go right again. You'll reach a long flight of stairs (marked Klostertreppe) that leads to the monastery. Look up (it's not worth actually going up the stairs).

Although the last Carmelite monk retired several years ago, Rome maintains a handsome but oversized-for-this-little-town **Catholic church** that runs a restaurant with a great view. It's a screwy situation that seems to make locals uncomfortable when you ask them about it.

• Continue back to the main street, called...

Bachstrasse ("Creek Street")

The town's main drag runs straight inland through Beilstein, passing through the tunnel you see to the left. It covers up the brook that once flowed through town and used to provide a handy 24/7 disposal service. Today, Bachstrasse is lined with wine cellars. The only way for a small local vintner to make any decent money these days is to sell his wine directly to customers in inviting little places like these.

• Cross Bachstrasse and walk a few steps ahead to the...

Market Square (Marktplatz)

For centuries, neighboring farmers sold their goods on Marktplatz. The *Zehnthaus* (tithe house) was the village IRS, where locals would pay one-tenth *(Zehnte)* of their produce to their landlord (either the Church or the earl). Pop into the **Zehnthauskeller.** Stuffed with peasants' offerings 400 years ago, it's now packed with vaulted medieval ambience. It's fun at night for candlelit wine-tasting, soup and cold cuts, and schmaltzy music (often live Fri and Sat). The adjacent **Bürgerhaus** (above the fountain) had nothing to do with medieval fast food. First the village church, then the residence of the *Bürger* (like a mayor), and later the communal oven and the village grade school, today it's where locals hold a big party or wedding (upstairs) and a venue for local craftspeople to show their goodies (below). **Haus Lipmann** (on the riverside, now a recommended hotel and restaurant) dates from 1727. It was built by the earl's family as a residence after the French destroyed his castle. Haus Lipmann's main dining hall was once the knights' hall.

• *Leave the square going uphill and follow the main street through the tunnel and up to the top end of town. Then bear right up the stairs (follow signs for* Burgruine Metternich) *to...*

Beilstein's Castle

Beilstein once rivaled Cochem as the most powerful town on this part of the Mosel. Like so much around here, it was destroyed by

the French in 1689. Its castle (officially named Burg Metternich) is a sorry ruin today, but those who make the steep 10-minute climb are rewarded with a postcard Mosel view and a chance to hike even higher to the top of its lone surviving tower (€2.50, Easter-Oct daily 9:00-18:00, closed Nov-Easter, last entry 30 minutes before closing, view café/restaurant, tel. 02673/93639, www.burgmetternich. de).

For more exercise and an even better **viewpoint,** exit through the turnstile at the rear of the castle. Take the uphill (left-hand) road, and after 100 yards, fork right. Here you'll find the ultimate "castle/river bend/carpets of vineyards" photo op. The derelict roadside vineyard is a sign of recent times—the younger generation is

abandoning the family plots, opting out of all that hard winemaking work.

From this viewpoint, continue another 100 yards farther up the road to the small but evocative **Jewish cemetery** (*Jüdische Friedhof*).

To reach the viewpoint and the cemetery without going through the castle, continue up the road past the castle entrance, then follow the signs for *Jüdische Friedhof.*

• From here, you can return to the castle gate, ring the bell (Klingel), *and show your ticket to get back in and retrace your steps; or continue on the road, which curves and leads downhill (a gravel path at the next bend on the left leads back into town).*

MOSEL VALLEY

Activities in Beilstein

Biking and Boating

Boats come and go all day for extremely relaxing river trips (for details, see page 489). While scenic, these rides can take longer than you'd like because of the locks. I prefer a riverside bike ride (perhaps combined with a boat trip). Biking is very popular along the Mosel, and roads are accompanied by smooth and perfectly flat bike lanes. The lanes are separate from the car traffic, letting you really relax as you pedal through gorgeous riverside scenery. To rent a quality bike in Beilstein, visit **Herr Nahlen** (€8/day, April-Oct daily 9:00-12:00, return bikes between 16:00 and 19:00, no rentals Nov-March, reservations smart for groups, Bachstrasse 47, tel. 02673/1840, www.fahrradverleih-in-beilstein.de).

Five-Hour Trip to Zell and Back: You could rent a bike in Beilstein, catch the 9:20 boat to Zell (2.5-hour ride), enjoy that pretty town, and cycle 15 miles back to Beilstein along the sleepy and windy riverside bike path.

Hour-and-a-Half Loop: For a shorter bike trip, ride the little ferry across the river from Beilstein, explore the campground, continue left past Poltersdorf, cycle under vineyards to Senhals, cross the bridge to Senheim, and return to Beilstein on the other side of the river. At the edge of Mesenich, leave the road and take the peaceful bike lane along the river, explore another campground, and head for Beilstein, with its castle in the distance encouraging you home.

Sleeping in Beilstein

Beilstein's hotels shut down from at least December through mid-March. All of the listings here are just steps from the bus stop and boat dock, except for Hotel Lipmann am Klosterberg. Only Hotel Gute Quelle accepts credit cards.

$$$ Hotel Haus Lipmann is your chance to live in a medieval mansion with hot showers and TVs. A prizewinner for atmosphere, it's been in the Lipmann family since 1795. The creaky wooden staircase and the elegant dining hall, with long wooden tables surrounded by antlers, chandeliers, and feudal weapons, will get you in the mood for your castle sightseeing, but the riverside terrace may mace your momentum. There are six guest rooms in the main building and six larger rooms in an equally old building next door. The entire family—Marion (née Lipmann) and her husband Jonas Thölén, their hardworking son David, and his wife Anja—hustle for their guests (Db-€100-130, usually €20 higher Fri-Sat, higher prices are for Mosel views, discount for 2 or more nights, extra bed-€30, family deals, cash only, €19 half-board—sensible here, closed Nov-Easter, guest computer, Wi-Fi, Marktplatz 3, tel. 02673/1573, www.hotel-haus-lipmann.com, hotel.haus.lipmann@t-online.de).

$$$ Hotel Lipmann Am Klosterberg, run by Marion's brother Joachim and his wife Marlene, is a big, modern place with 16 comfortable rooms at the extremely quiet top of town (Sb-€55-75, Db-€85-110, closed mid-Nov-Easter, elevator, Wi-Fi, easy free parking, Auf dem Teich 8, up the main street 200 yards inland, tel. 02673/1850, www.hotel-lipmann.de, lipmann@t-online.de).

$$$ Hotel Lipmann Altes Zollhaus, run by Joachim Lipmann's daughter Julia, packs all the comforts into eight tight, bright riverfront rooms (Sb-€50, Db-€85, Wi-Fi, free parking at Hotel Lipmann Am Klosterberg, also has a restaurant—see "Eating in Beilstein," later).

$$ The welcoming **Gasthaus Winzerschenke an der Klostertreppe** is a great value, with five rooms right at the bottom of the stairs to the cloister (Db-€65, bigger Db-€75, cash only, discount for 4-night stays, closed Nov-Easter, Wi-Fi, go up main street and take second left onto Fürst-Metternich-Strasse, reception in restaurant, tel. 02673/1354, www.winzerschenke-beilstein.de, winzerschenke-beilstein@t-online.de, young and eager Stefanie and Christian Sausen).

$$ Hotel Gute Quelle offers half-timbers, a good restaurant, and 13 inviting rooms up a narrow stairway, plus seven more in an annex across the street (Sb-€42, Db-€68-84, less if staying 4 nights, credit cards accepted, closed Dec-mid-March, Wi-Fi, Marktplatz 34, tel. 02673/1437, www.hotel-gute-quelle.de, info@hotel-gute-quelle.de, helpful Susan speaks Irish). The hotel also has five bigger, very quiet, family-sized rooms in an adjacent building (Tb/Qb €110-120).

Eating in Beilstein

You'll have no problem in Beilstein finding a characteristic dining room or a relaxing riverview terrace.

Restaurant Haus Lipmann serves good, fresh food with daily specials on a glorious, leafy riverside terrace. For a wonderful trip memory, enjoy a slow meal here while watching the lazy riverside action and the changing light on the distant vineyards (€8-22 main courses, Easter-Oct daily 10:00-22:00, last meal order at 20:00, closed Nov-Easter).

The restaurant at **Hotel Lipmann Altes Zollhaus** serves specialties cooked on a lava-stone grill (€8-27 main courses, Thu-Tue 10:00-22:00, closed Wed). The adjoining **Alte Stadtmauer** restaurant is run by Joachim Lipmann's daughter Kristina (€8-27 main courses, Wed-Mon 10:00-22:00, closed Tue and mid-Nov-Easter).

The **Zehnthauskeller** on the Marktplatz is *the* place for wine-tasting, a light meal, and lively *Schlager* music (kitschy German folk-pop). Hang with old locals on holiday, sitting under a dark medieval vault or out in the Marktplatz (soup, *Flammkuchen*— German version of white pizza, €9-11 cold plates, Easter-Oct Tue-Sun 11:00-23:00, closed Mon and Nov-Easter, run by Joachim Lipmann's daughter Sabine).

The recommended **Hotel Gute Quelle** runs a popular restaurant with classic, well-presented German dishes (€11-17 main courses, €9 daily specials, daily 11:00-21:00, closed Dec-mid-March, Marktplatz 34).

TRIER

Germany's oldest city lies at the head of the scenic Mosel Valley, near the border with Luxembourg. An ancient Roman capital, Trier brags that it was inhabited by Celts for 1,300 years before Rome even existed. Today, Trier (TREE-air) is thriving and feels very young. A short stop here offers you a look at Germany's oldest Christian church, one of its most enjoyable market squares, and its best Roman ruins.

Founded by Augustus in 16 B.C., Trier was a Roman town called Augusta Treverorum for 400 years. When Emperor Diocletian (who ruled A.D. 285-305) divided his overextended Roman Empire into four sectors, he made Trier the capital of the west: roughly modern-day Germany, France, Spain, and England. For most of the fourth century, this city of 80,000—with a four-mile wall, four great gates, and 47 round towers—was a favored residence of Roman emperors. Emperor Constantine lived here, spending lavishly on urban projects. As a military town in a god-forsaken corner of the empire, Trier received lots of perks from Rome to make it livable for those assigned here. But when the last emperor checked out in A.D. 395, the money pretty much dried up, and that was the end of Trier's ancient glory days. In the late 400s, when Rome fell to the barbarians, so did Trier.

Roman Trier was much bigger than medieval Trier. The pedestrian center of town—containing nearly all of your sightseeing and browsing—is defined by the medieval wall (which encloses only half the area the Roman wall did). Trier's Roman sights include the huge city gate (Porta Nigra), basilica, baths, and amphitheater.

Trier's main draw is the chance to experience Germany's Roman and early Christian history. If you're more interested in wine-tasting and scenery, stay elsewhere on the Mosel River (see previous chapter).

Orientation to Trier

The mid-size city of Trier, with about 100,000 people, has a broad, rectangular footprint hemmed in by the Mosel River and gentle hills. Many visitors never even see the river, and stick to the city's central core: From the landmark Porta Nigra, the main drag (Simeonstrasse) runs south to the Market Square (Hauptmarkt) and beyond. Most sights—including the cathedral and its museum, the Basilica/Imperial Throne Room, and the Archaeological Museum—are within a five-minute walk of this artery. The train station is about a 10-minute walk east of the Porta Nigra.

TRIER

TOURIST INFORMATION

Trier's cramped and busy TI is just through the Porta Nigra. The TI sells an easily readable map for €1.50, but cheapskates can squint at the free and sufficient small-print map. The TI also sells a useful little guide to the city called *Trier: History and Monuments* (€4). Also consider the booklet *Walking Tours Through Trier* (€3), which has little information on sights but a great map and suggested walking routes (Roman, medieval, Jewish, rainy day). The TI also offers tours (see "Tours in Trier," later) and has a free room-booking service (May-Oct Mon-Sat 9:00-18:00, Sun 10:00-17:00; Nov-Dec and March-April Mon-Sat 9:00-18:00, Sun 10:00-15:00; Jan-Feb Mon-Sat 10:00-17:00, Sun 10:00-13:00; tel. 0651/978-080, www.trier-info.de).

Discount Deals: The **Antique Card** can save you a few euros. The €9 version covers the Archaeological Museum (otherwise €6) and any two of Trier's four Roman sights (Porta Nigra, Imperial Baths, Viehmarkt Baths, and amphitheater—otherwise €3 each). The €14 version covers the museum and all four Roman sights (available at TI and participating sights). The **Trier Card** allows free use of city buses and 25 percent discounts on city walks, bus tours, and museums, but offers only a 10 percent discount on the Roman sights. It's not worth it if you're staying in the center of this small, walkable town (€9.90, €21.90 family card, valid 3 days, sold at TI).

ARRIVAL IN TRIER

By Train: The *Reisezentrum* at the train station can answer your train-schedule questions and book tickets (long hours daily). The

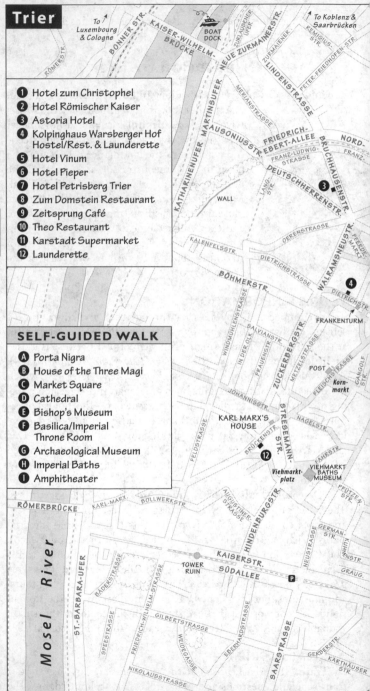

Trier

1. Hotel zum Christophel
2. Hotel Römischer Kaiser
3. Astoria Hotel
4. Kolpinghaus Warsberger Hof Hostel/Rest. & Launderette
5. Hotel Vinum
6. Hotel Pieper
7. Hotel Petrisberg Trier
8. Zum Domstein Restaurant
9. Zeitsprung Café
10. Theo Restaurant
11. Karstadt Supermarket
12. Launderette

TRIER

SELF-GUIDED WALK

A. Porta Nigra
B. House of the Three Magi
C. Market Square
D. Cathedral
E. Bishop's Museum
F. Basilica/Imperial Throne Room
G. Archaeological Museum
H. Imperial Baths
I. Amphitheater

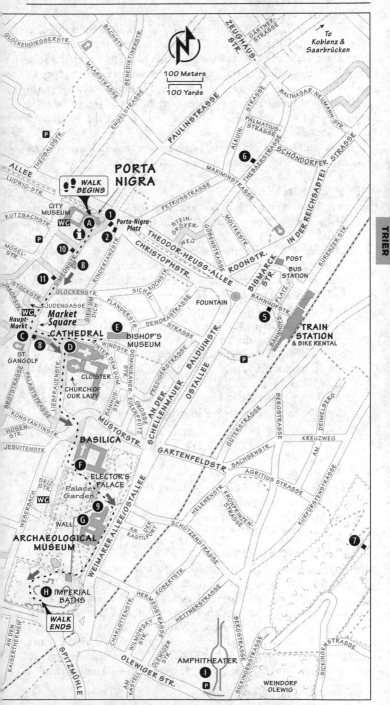

station also has lockers (€2.50-3.50), a WC (€0.50, coins only), and bike rental (see "Helpful Hints," later). To reach the town center from the train station, walk 10 boring minutes and four blocks up Theodor-Heuss-Allee to the big black Roman gate (Porta Nigra), and turn left under the gate to find the TI. From here, the main pedestrian mall (Simeonstrasse) leads right to the sights: Market Square and the cathedral (a 5-minute walk), and the basilica (5 more minutes).

By Car: Drivers get off at Trier Verteilerkreis and follow signs to *Zentrum*. Parking is near the gate and TI.

HELPFUL HINTS

Internet Access: Free Wi-Fi is available at the **Coffee Fellows** café on the ground floor of the House of the Three Magi (see page 520).

Laundry: A well-maintained self-service **launderette** is just beyond Karl Marx's House (€8.50/load, daily 8:00-22:00, last load at 20:30, instructions in English, Brückenstrasse 19). **Kolpinghaus Warsberger Hof** (see "Sleeping in Trier," later) has laundry facilities for non-guests (€4/load, daily 9:00-18:00, Dietrichstrasse 42).

Bike Rental: A local citizens' group called **Bürgerservice** rents bikes for reasonable daily rates. Find them at the train station, just off track 11 (€12/up to 24 hours, spiffy 27-gear bikes-€14, show ID and leave €30 as deposit; mid-April-Sept daily 9:00-18:00; Oct-mid-April Mon-Fri 10:00-18:00, Sat 10:00-14:00, closed Sun; tel. 0651/148-856, www.bues-trier.de).

Tours in Trier

Walking Tours

The TI offers a €6, 75-minute walking tour in English daily at 13:00 (April-Oct, may also be offered Nov-March—ask) and can put you in touch with local guides who do private tours (€90/2 hours, tel. 0651/978-0821).

Hop-On, Hop-Off Bus Tour

The hop-on, hop-off CitySightseeing bus leaves Porta Nigra every 30 minutes. The route has seven stops—including the amphitheater, Basilica/Imperial Throne Room, and Karl Marx's House—and takes you as far as Petrisberg, a recreational area with great views over the city and the Mosel Valley. Tickets are valid for 24 hours; buy them onboard, at any stop, or at the TI at Porta Nigra (€12, April-Oct daily 2/hour 10:00-17:00, recorded commentary in 8 languages, tel. 00352/3565-75888, www.city-sightseeing.com).

Tourist Train

If you're tired and want a city overview, consider riding the hokey little red-and-yellow tourist train, the Römer-Express, for its 35-minute loop of Trier's major old-town sights (€9, April-Oct daily 2/hour 10:00-18:00; March and Nov-Dec Mon-Fri hourly 10:00-17:00, Sat-Sun 2/hour 10:00-17:00; Jan-Feb Sat-Sun hourly 10:00-17:00—weather permitting; recorded narration in English, departs from TI, buy tickets from driver or at TI, tel. 0651/9935-9525, www.roemer-express.de).

Sights in Trier

I've laced together the historic city's top sights on this fascinating walk, offering a taste of Trier old, new, and in-between.

• Start at the...

TRIER

▲Porta Nigra

Roman Trier was built as a capital. Its architecture mirrored the grandeur of the empire. Of the four-mile town wall's four huge gates, only this northern gate survives. This is the most impressive Roman fortification in Germany, and it was built without mortar—only iron pegs hold the sandstone blocks together. While the other three gates were destroyed by medieval metal and stone scavengers, this  "black gate" (originally lighter sandstone, but darkened by time) survived because it became a church. St. Simeon—a pious Greek recluse—lived inside the gate for seven years. After his death in 1035, the St. Simeon monastery was established, and the Roman gate was made into a two-story church—lay church on the bottom, monastery church on top. The 12th-century Romanesque apse— the round part at the east end—survives. You can climb around inside the gate, but there's little to see other than a fine town view. You can enter through the adjacent City Museum (described below). As you go in, look for pictures of how the gate looked during various eras, including its church phase.

Cost and Hours: €3, €7.20 for both Porta Nigra and City Museum, daily April-Sept 9:00-18:00, March and Oct 9:00-17:00, Nov-Feb 9:00-16:00, last entry 30 minutes before closing, www.trier-info.de.

Nearby: The remaining arcaded courtyard and buildings of the monastery of St. Simeon, next to the Porta Nigra, are now home to the TI and a **City Museum** (Stadtmuseum Simeonstift). The museum's mildly interesting collection seems to be largely made up of anything old that turned up in townspeople's basements. The third level, however, holds a fascinating model—painstakingly constructed over 19 years—of Trier as it looked in 1800. Families will appreciate the entertaining audioguide designed especially for children—there's one for adults, too (€5.50, includes audioguide, €7.20 combo-ticket with Porta Nigra, Tue-Sun 10:00-17:00, closed Mon, tel. 0651/718-1459, www.museum-trier.de).

The busy road beyond the Porta Nigra follows what was a dry moat outside the Roman wall. In the 19th century, Trier's wealthy built their mansions along this belle époque promenade. Today, it's a people's park lined with fine old buildings, interrupted by newer construction where WWII bombs hit.

• *Trier's main pedestrian drag, which leads from the gate into the town center, is named for St. Simeon. As you walk to Market Square, you'll follow the main north-south axis of the grid-planned Roman town. The small pink house (on the left, at #8, next to pharmacy) was where Karl Marx lived from age one until he left for college at age 17—nearly his entire childhood. (Marx enthusiasts can visit a museum in the house where he was born, described on page 529.) Farther down Simeonstrasse, on your left at #19, is the...*

House of the Three Magi (Dreikönigenhaus)

Now home to a coffee shop and café, this colorful Venetian-style building was constructed in the 13th century as a keep. Before the age of safe banking, rich men hoarded their gold and silver inside their homes...and everyone knew it. Understandably paranoid, they needed fortified houses like this one. Look for the floating door a story above the present-day entrance. A wooden staircase to this door—once the only way in or out—could be pulled up when necessary.

• *Continue down the pedestrian street. As you walk, ignore street-level storefronts—instead, look up to appreciate the variety and richness of the town's architecture. Eventually you'll reach the...*

▲▲Market Square (Hauptmarkt)

Trier's Hauptmarkt is a people-filled swirl of fruit stands, flowers, painted facades, and fountains (plus stairs down to a handy public WC). This is one of Germany's most in-love-with-life market squares.

For an orientation to the sights, go to the square's centerpiece, a market cross, and stand on the side of the cross closest to the big gray-stone **cathedral** a block away. This cathedral (described later in more detail) was the seat of the archbishop. In medieval times, the cathedral was its own walled city, and the archbishop of Trier was one of the seven German electors who chose the Holy Roman Emperor. This gave the archbishop tremendous political, as well as spiritual, power.

The pink-and-white building (now an H&M clothing store) on the corner of the lane leading to the cathedral was a **palace** for the archbishop. Notice the seal above the door: a crown flanked by a crosier (representing the bishop's ecclesiastical power) and a sword (demonstrating his political might). This did not sit well with the townspeople of Trier. The square you're standing in was the symbolic battlefield of a centuries-long conflict between Trier's citizens and its archbishop.

The stone market **cross** (a replica of the A.D. 958 original, now in the City Museum) was the archbishop's way of bragging about the trading rights granted to him by King Otto the Great. This was a slap in the face to Trier's townspeople. They'd wanted Trier to be designated a "free imperial city," with full trading rights and beholden only to the Holy Roman Emperor, not a local prince or archbishop.

Look across the square. Facing the cathedral is the 15th-century **Town Hall** (Steipe). The people of Trier wanted a town hall, but the archbishop wouldn't allow it—so they built this "assembly hall" instead, with a knight on each second-story corner. The knight on the left, facing Market Square, has his mask up, watching over his people. The other knight, facing the cathedral and the archbishop, has his mask down and his hand on his sword, ready for battle.

Just below the knights are four brightly painted 16th-century statues of Christian figures nestled between the arches (right to left): St. Paul, with his sword, was patron saint of Trier's university in the 15th century. St. Peter, with his bushy beard and key, is the patron saint of Trier. St. Helena, Emperor Constantine's mom and a devout Christian, lived in Trier and brought many super relics here from the Holy Land, giving the town lasting importance. And St. James, with his staff and scallop shell, is the patron saint of pilgrims—a reminder that Trier was the staging point for northern European pilgrims heading south on the spiritual trek to Santiago de Compostela (in northwest Spain).

Elsewhere on the square are more indications of tension between the archbishop and the townsfolk. Look to the left, at the tall white steeple with yellow trim. This is the Gothic tower of the **Church of St. Gangolf,** the medieval townspeople's church and fire-watchman's post. (From medieval times until the present day, a bell has rung nightly at 22:00, reminding drunks to go home. When the automatic bell-ringer broke a few years back, concerned locals flooded the mayor with calls.) In 1507, Trier's mayor built this new Gothic tower to make the people's church higher than the cathedral. A Bible verse in Latin adorns the top in gold letters: "Stay awake and pray." In retaliation, the archbishop raised one tower of his cathedral (all he could afford). He topped it with a threatening message of his own, continuing the Town Hall's verse: "For you never know the hour when the Lord will come."

Look farther to the left, to the Renaissance **St. Peter's Fountain** (1595). This fountain symbolizes thoughtful city government, with allegorical statues of justice (sword and scale), fortitude (broken column), temperance (wine and water), and prudence (a snake and, formerly, a mirror—but since the mirror was stolen long ago, she's now empty-handed). The ladies represent idealized cardinal virtues—but notice the rude monkeys hiding on the column behind them, showing the naughty way things are really done. The recommended **Zum Domstein** restaurant is next to the fountain.

The rest of the square is a textbook of architectural styles. Look for the Art Deco hotel that now houses a McDonald's (forced to keep its presence low-key). The half-timbered houses at the north end of the square (toward the Porta Nigra) mark Trier's 14th-century Jewish ghetto. Judengasse ("Jews' Alley") led under these facades into a gated ghetto where 60 families earned enough from moneylending to buy protection from the archbishop. But the protection only went so far—in 1418 Trier's Jews were expelled. (They tried to collect interest owed them by the prince, but rather than pay up, he sent them packing.) The buildings lining Judengasse today, while quaint, date only from the 18th century.

• *When you're finished on the square, head down Sternstrasse to the...*

▲▲Cathedral (Dom)

This is the oldest Christian church in Germany. After Emperor Constantine legalized Christianity in the Roman Empire in A.D. 312, his mother, Helena (now a saint), allowed part of her palace in Trier to be used as the first church on this spot. In A.D. 326, to celebrate the 20th anniversary of his reign, Constantine began the construction of two great churches: St. Peter's in Rome and this huge cathedral in Trier—also called St. Peter's.

Cost and Hours: Cathedral—free, daily April-Oct 6:30-18:00, Nov-March 6:30-17:30. Treasury—€1.50, April-Oct and Dec Mon-Sat 10:00-17:00, Sun 12:30-17:00; Nov and March Mon 13:30-16:00, Tue-Sat 11:00-16:00, Sun 12:30-16:00, same hours Jan-Feb except closed Mon.

Information: The Dom Information Office (on the square facing the church) runs a gift shop, has a handy WC (€0.50), and provides services for Santiago de Compostela-bound pilgrims (Easter-Oct and Dec Mon-Sat 9:30-17:30, Sun 12:00-17:30; Nov and Jan-Easter Mon-Wed 10:00-17:30, Thu-Fri 9:30-17:30, Sat 10:00-15:00, closed Sun; tel. 0651/979-0790, www.trierer-dom. de).

➋ **Self-Guided Tour:** Begin your visit in the cathedral's large front **courtyard.** As you face the cathedral, look in the corner behind you and to your left (near the pink palace); you'll see a large patch of light-colored bricks in an L shape in the ground. The original Roman cathedral was more than four times its present size; these light-colored bricks mark one corner of this massive "double cathedral." (The opposite corner was at the back of the smaller Church of Our Lady, waaay across the courtyard.) The plaque by the corner shows the floor plan of the original Roman cathedral (from A.D. 380).

The cathedral's mighty **facade** is 12th-century Romanesque. To the right is the more delicate 13th-century Gothic facade of the Church of Our Lady, which we'll visit later.

As you walk toward the cathedral entrance, you'll pass an evocative bit of Roman scrap stone (just outside the door on the left). This was part of a 60-ton ancient granite column quarried near Frankfurt—one of four columns used in the fourth-century Roman church.

Enter the cathedral (€0.50 English info brochure in racks on right). The many **altars** lining the nave are dedicated not to saints, but to bishops. These ornate funeral altars were a fashionable way for the powerful archbishop-electors to memorialize themselves. Even the elaborate black-and-white altar at the back of the church (above where you entered) is not a religious shrine, but a memorial for a single rich archbishop. (His black 1354 tomb dominates the center of that chapel.)

The "pilgrim's walk" (the stairway to the right of the altar) leads to the chapel at the far east end of the church that holds the cathedral's most important relic: the supposed **Holy Robe of Christ,** thought to have been found by St. Helena on a pilgrimage to Jerusalem (rarely on view, but you can see its reliquary; look for photos of the robe itself as you approach, after the first flight of stairs).

Midway along the "pilgrim's walk," you'll find the entrance to the **treasury** *(Schatzkammer)*, displaying huge bishops' rings, medieval Bibles, St. Andrew's sandal (in a box topped with a golden foot), and a holy nail supposedly from the Crucifixion. At the base of the steps below the treasury, pause and look back up at the statues of St. Helena and Emperor Constantine.

Down the stairs, the door on your immediate left marked *Kreuzgang* leads to the peaceful 12th-century Domkreuzgang **cloister** between the Dom and the Church of Our Lady.

When you're ready to leave the cathedral, head back toward the main door, where you'll see two controversially modern (1972) paintings at the back of the church, representing the Alpha (Paradise/Creation, to the left) and the Omega (the Last Judgment, to the right). The archbishop pushed this artwork through, arguing that a living church needs contemporary art, and overriding objections from the congregation's conservative old guard.

Once outside the cathedral, go left to find the entrance to the adjoining **Church of Our Lady** (Liebfrauenkirche), which dates from 1235 and claims to be the oldest Gothic church in Germany. This church was built when Gothic was in vogue, so French architects were brought in—and paid with money borrowed from the bishop of Cologne when funds ran dry. Pop in to see the recently renovated interior, filled with colorful, modern stained glass.

Exit the Church of our Lady and go right, passing the cathedral entrance, and then turn down the first street on your right (Windstrasse). As you walk with the cathedral on your right, you'll be able to see the different **eras of its construction.** The big red cube that makes up the back half of the present-day cathedral is all that remains of the enormous, original fourth-century Roman construction (at one time twice as tall as what you see here). Arched bricks in the facade show the original position of Roman windows and doors. Around this Roman nucleus, chunks were grafted on over a millennium and a half of architectural styles: the front half of the cathedral facing the big courtyard, added in the 11th century; the choir on the back, from the 12th century; and the transept and round Baroque shrine on the far back, from the 18th century.

If you look at the original Roman construction squarely, you'll see that it's not perfectly vertical. Locks were built along the Mosel River in the 1960s, depleting groundwater—which was the only thing preserving the church's original wooden foundation. When dry, the foundation disintegrated, and the walls began to settle. Architects competed to find a way to prevent the cathedral from collapsing. The winning solution: a huge steel bracket above the main nave, holding the walls up with cables.

• *Just past the cathedral on Windstrasse (to the left) is the...*

▲Bishop's Museum (Museum am Dom)

This museum focuses on the history of the cathedral. Its highlight is the pieced-together remains of exquisite ceiling frescoes from St. Helena's palace. The vivid reds, greens, and blues of the restored works depict frolicking cupids, bejeweled women, and a philosopher clutching his scroll. The 15 panels are displayed in such a way that you feel mysteriously transported back to when they were made, in A.D. 320. The frescoes were discovered in 50,000 pieces while cleaning up from WWII bombs. Incredibly, with the help of computers (and using patterns from the wattle-and-daub work on the back sides of the pieces), the jigsaw puzzle was put back together. There are no English descriptions, but you can—and should—borrow the book in English that explains the frescoes and their restoration (also on sale for €3.60). Elsewhere in this small, modern museum, you'll see an interesting model of the original Roman church, stone capitals, gold chalices, vestments, and icons.

Cost and Hours: €3.50, Tue-Sat 9:00-17:00, Sun 13:00-17:00, Bischof-Stein-Platz 1, tel. 0651/710-5255, www.bistum-trier.de/museum.

• *Return to the front of the cathedral and head two blocks south (passing the Church of Our Lady, under an arch capped by a Crucifixion scene—indicating that you're leaving the archbishop's walled ecclesiastical city). Bear left on An der Meerkatz, to the 200-foot-by-100-foot...*

▲▲Basilica/Imperial Throne Room (Konstantin Basilica)

This building is the largest intact Roman structure outside Rome. It's best known as a basilica, but it actually started out as a throne room. The last emperor moved out in A.D. 395, and petty kings set up camp in the building throughout the Middle Ages. By the 12th century, the archbishops had taken it over, using the nave as a courtyard and converting the apse into a five-story palace. The building became a Lutheran church in 1856, and it remains the leading Protestant church in Trier. It was badly damaged by WWII bombs (as illustrated by photographs at the cashier's desk), and later restored.

Cost and Hours: Free, €2.50 *Basilica of Trier* English booklet brings the near-empty shell to life; April-Oct daily 10:00-18:00; Nov-Dec Tue-Sat 10:00-12:00 & 14:00-16:00, Sun 12:00-13:00, closed Mon; shorter hours Jan-March; tel. 0651/42570, www.konstantin-basilika.de.

Visiting the Basilica: Standing inside the vast structure, you see the genius of Roman engineering. Notice the 65-foot-wide round arch over the apse. The small rectangular holes between the windows were chimneys, which vented the hot air that circulated below the floor, heating the place. It's a huge expanse to span without columns. Each of the squares in the ceiling above you measures 10 feet by 10 feet—as big as your hotel room. While today's roof cheats, using concrete girders, the Roman original was all wood, relying on triangular trusses above the flat ceiling. Today's windows match the Roman originals—small frosted panes held in place by a wooden frame. The place is enormous. (A little model in the back near the entry shows the Porta Nigra fitting comfortably inside this building.)

Picture this throne room in ancient times, decorated with golden mosaics, rich marble, colorful stucco, and busts of Constantine and his family filling the seven niches. The emperor sat in majesty under a canopy on his altar-like throne. The windows in the apse around him were smaller than the ones along the side walls, making his throne seem even bigger.

Posters along the far wall (with English text) give a full rundown on the building's history, including artist reconstructions that help you envision how the basilica was used through the ages.

Nearby: A pink Rococo wing, the Elector's Palace, was added to the basilica in the 18th century to house the archbishop-elector; today, it houses local government offices (closed to the public).

• *The Rococo wing faces a fragrant, picnic-riffic garden. Beyond the garden are three more sights: the Archaeological Museum (with a handy café for lunch—see "Eating in Trier," later), the remains of a Roman bath, and a 16,000-seat Roman amphitheater. Cut across the garden toward Weimarer Allee (the main street in the distance) and veer right, passing through the medieval city wall to the entrance of the...*

▲▲Archaeological Museum (Rheinisches Landesmuseum)

This is clearly Trier's top museum, with arguably the best collection of Roman art in Germany. The museum tells the town's story from prehistoric times to today. The best pieces are all from the Roman period, including funeral art, mosaics, coins, and a fine model of Roman Trier.

Cost and Hours: €6, Tue-Sun 10:00-17:00, last entry at 16:30, closed Mon, tel. 0651/97740, www.landesmuseum-trier.de. Get a map as you enter, and pick up the free English audioguide in the museum shop. Brief English overviews are posted in each room.

⊙ Self-Guided Tour: *Rundgang* signs guide you through the museum's 19 exhibition rooms in a logical order. I'll focus just on the museum's most important collections.

Start by walking down the round staircase and out to the gaudy copy of a **Roman funerary monument** in the courtyard. (The original still stands in a nearby Mosel River Valley village.) You'll see more funerary monuments like this in a minute. For pagan Roman big shots, the closest thing to eternal life was to be remembered after they died. Consequently, those who could afford it erected big memorials to their own lives and accomplishments along the road leading into Trier. When Roman Trier went Christian in A.D. 320, these pagan ideals were no longer respected. The memorials were scavenged for their stones, which were then used as a foundation for a nearby fortress and forgotten. In 1890, a resident of the modern village sitting on the ruins of that Roman fortress dug up one of these stones, the museum paid a handsome price for it, and everyone in the village went wild digging up old Roman stones to cash in.

From here, go down to basement level and through three rooms of displays on prehistoric Trier, then back up and through two rooms on the Romanization of the area's Celtic population. In Room 6, a big room at the back of the courtyard, find the rich collection of **funerary art;** originally these were all painted like the courtyard replica. Browse around, finding glimpses of everyday Roman life: the tax collector at work, the boys with their Latin teacher, a woman visiting a beauty salon, and a ship laden with barrels of Mosel wine. Behind the wine ship, a wall painting shows how the mausoleum-lined road into Roman Trier might have looked. Archaeologists have learned a lot about life in this corner of the Roman Empire by studying these artifacts.

The **Roman mosaics** in Room 8 (just beyond the wine ship) are another highlight. On one wall is a mosaic of four horses surrounding the superstar charioteer Polydus, discovered intact at the Imperial Baths. Mosaic floors were the *Sports Illustrated* covers of the Roman world.

Room 11 displays a **map** showing Trier's position in the Roman Empire. You can see how Gaul (roughly modern France) was divided into three parts, with Trier in the northern ("Belgian") section. Roads led from Trier south toward Rome via modern-day Lyon and Marseille.

Upstairs, in Room 12, don't miss the huge **model** of Roman Trier—a thriving city of 80,000. Notice the grid street plan, and pick out the sights you're visiting today: Porta Nigra, the cathedral, basilica, baths, and amphitheater.

Back down a flight, in the small, darkened Room 13, is an exhibit of **coins** through the centuries of Roman rule. In 1993, some Trier construction workers dug up a bag holding 2,600 golden Roman coins; the coins are in the central display case. Experts used the emperor's face on each coin to date the finds. Look closely and you can follow the steady progression of emperors and their coins from Nero (A.D. 54) to Septimius Severus (A.D. 211). It's impressive that over 150 years of coinage were in circulation when this bag was lost.

Finally, Rooms 15-16 show how medieval Trier was built on the ruins of the Roman town. A model lets you see how the Porta Nigra looked as a church.

• *Exit the Archaeological Museum, walk right (paralleling the main Weimarer Allee through the trees), then follow the* Tourist Route *signs through the archway in the wall to the modern, red-brick entry arcade of the...*

Imperial Baths (Kaiserthermen)

Built by Constantine, these were destined to be the biggest of Trier's three Roman baths and the most intricate baths of the Roman world. Trier's cold northern climate, the size of the complex, and the enormity of Constantine's ego meant that these Imperial Baths required a two-story subterranean complex of pipes, furnaces, and slave galleys to keep the water at a perfect 47 degrees Celsius (120 degrees Fahrenheit). But the grandiose vision was never finished. When  Constantine left Trier in A.D. 316, the huge and already costly project was scuttled. Later the site was used as a military barracks. The giant courtyard—originally for exercising and lounging—became a parade ground for the Praetorian Guard.

Stepping into the unfinished building section, you can imagine the intended pools (cold, tepid, and hot) and the heated floor. Thirty years of construction left nearly a mile of underground tunnels and foundation work, which are fun to explore. Imagine the engineering, slave labor, and wood that would have been necessary to make all this work, if it had ever been completed. A literal river of water was planned to flow into the baths via an aqueduct. And the surrounding land would ultimately have been deforested as it supplied enough wood to keep the ovens going to heat the water.

Cost and Hours: €3, daily April-Sept 9:00-18:00, March and Oct 9:00-17:00, Nov-Feb 9:00-16:00, last entry 30 minutes before closing, good €2.50 English booklet, tel. 0651/436-2550, www.trier-info.de.

• *To finish your tour of Trier's Roman sights, hike from the baths about 10 minutes farther to the amphitheater. If you're beat, you can skip it (just look at amphitheater photos in shop postcard racks), head back to Market Square, and enjoy the town.*

To reach the amphitheater, backtrack through the arch in the wall, follow the signs through the pedestrian underpass, then follow Hermesstrasse as it curves up the hill, and then turn left on Olewigerstrasse.

Amphitheater

Roman Trier's amphitheater, built around A.D. 200, seated at least 16,000. The city was largely inhabited by Celts who learned Latin and wanted to adopt the Roman lifestyle. And any self-respecting Roman town needed an amphitheater. While Trier's amphitheater had some gore, the scene here wasn't mainly Roman degenerates egging on gladiators—it was more often used for less-bloody spectacles, assemblies, and religious festivals.

You'll enter where grand processions did. Pick up the free map when you buy your ticket. To tour the site, go left up the stairs to a handy illustrated diagram of ancient Trier that helps put the amphitheater into context with the city. After enjoying this high vantage point, continue along the left side of the amphitheater for a few yards, then turn left on the downhill path. Enter the amphitheater through one of its grand entries (called *vomitoria*, these were named for the way crowds could spew out quickly after events). Then descend a staircase in the center of the amphitheater into the cellar, where gear for the spectacles was kept (it's below the water table, so it's always wet). After Rome fell, the amphitheater was used as a refuge from barbarian attacks, a quarry, and a vineyard.

Cost and Hours: €3, daily April-Sept 9:00-18:00, March and Oct 9:00-17:00, Nov-Feb 9:00-16:00, last entry 30 minutes before closing, tel. 0651/73010, www.trier-info.de. It's OK to picnic discreetly in the amphitheater grounds (free WC inside entrance).

MORE SIGHTS IN TRIER
Karl Marx's House

Communists can lick their wounds at Karl Marx's birthplace, a 1727 house with two floors of exhibits in German. While the influential economist/philosopher is a fascinating and important figure, this place has almost no historic artifacts. Visiting this "museum" is like reading a book in a foreign language, while standing up. The included English audioguide gives more meaning to the displays, but even that is pretty tedious. When Marx was one year old, his lawyer father purchased the house at Simeonstrasse 8 and moved the family there.

Cost and Hours: €4, includes audioguide and free brochure; April-Oct daily 10:00-18:00; Nov-March Tue-Sun 11:00-17:00, Mon 14:00-17:00; from Market Square follow signs for 10 minutes to Brückenstrasse 10, tel. 0651/970-680, www.fes.de/Karl-Marx-Haus.

Viehmarkt Baths Museum

A beautiful modern glass building covers the ruins of a Roman bath, mixed with stone monastery foundations and medieval waste-wells. It's certainly historic, but almost meaningless unless you have a good guide and a freakish interest in Roman stones. You can see nearly everything without paying just by looking in from the entry and through the many windows. The best thing about going here is walking down Fahrstrasse to the museum—a block away, you'll pass a cool fountain showing Trier craftsmen at work.

Cost and Hours: €3, Tue-Sun 9:00-17:00, closed Mon, last entry at 16:30, Viehmarktplatz, tel. 0651/994-1057, www.trier-info.de.

Sleeping in Trier

I've listed prices for high season, which often includes times when there's a festival in town. Rates generally drop from November through February or March.

NEAR THE PORTA NIGRA

$$$ Hotel zum Christophel offers top comfort in 11 mostly large and classy rooms next to the Porta Nigra, with a kind owner. It's an easy roll from the train station with your luggage (Sb-€75, Db-€95-115, Tb-€115; price varies with room size, season, and day of week; family deals, elevator, Wi-Fi, parking-€6/day, Am Porta-Nigra-Platz 1, tel. 0651/979-4200, www.zumchristophel.de, info@zumchristophel.de).

$$$ Hotel Römischer Kaiser, next door, is also nice, but a lesser value—charging more for a polished lobby and 43 comparable rooms (Sb-€79-86, Db-€111-116, Tb-€146-156; price varies with season—most expensive in May, Sept-Oct, and during festivals; family rooms, elevator, Wi-Fi, free parking, Am Porta-Nigra-Platz 6, tel. 0651/977-0100, www.friedrich-hotels.de, rezeption@friedrich-hotels.de).

$$ Astoria Hotel, three blocks beyond the Porta Nigra when coming from the train station, is a 15-room family-run place in a quiet area just beyond the tourist crowds. Rooms are colorfully decorated, and a rose-filled terrace beckons outside the light and cheery breakfast room (Sb-€58-62, Db-€79-88, lower prices are for weekdays, cheaper Nov-March, no elevator, Wi-Fi, parking-€5.70/day, Bruchhausenstrasse 4, tel. 0651/978-350, www.astoria-hotel.de, info@astoria-hotel.de, American-born Paula and her husband Sudhir like to offer guests a choice of welcome drinks).

Sleep Code

Abbreviations **(€1 = about $1.40, country code: 49)**
S = Single, **D** = Double/Twin, **T** = Triple, **Q** = Quad, **b** = bathroom, **s** = shower only.
Price Rankings
 $$$ **Higher Priced**—Most rooms €90 or more.
  $$ **Moderately Priced**—Most rooms between €55-90.
   $ **Lower Priced**—Most rooms €55 or less.
Unless otherwise noted, credit cards are accepted, English is spoken, breakfast is included, and Wi-Fi is generally free. Prices change; verify current rates online or by email. For the best prices, always book directly with the hotel.

TRIER

NEAR MARKET SQUARE

$ Kolpinghaus Warsberger Hof, run by a Catholic foundation, is a clean, simple hostel and budget hotel two blocks from Market Square, with 168 beds and an inexpensive restaurant. This is your best value for cheap sleeps in town (€23/bed in 4- to 6-bed dorms, includes sheets, S-€34-38, D-€60-68, showers down the hall, no elevator, Wi-Fi in reception area, public laundry-€4/load, limited courtyard parking-€7/day—reserve ahead, Dietrichstrasse 42, tel. 0651/975-250, www.kolpinghaus-warsberger-hof.de, info@kolpinghaus-warsberger-hof.de).

NEAR THE TRAIN STATION

$$$ Hotel Vinum, with 31 rooms directly across from the train station, is owned and run by the Lutheran Church and has a wine theme (all guests get a free bottle). It's conveniently located if you're not bothered by the square's train-station ambience (Sb-€56, Db-€87-107, price depends on room size, elevator, Wi-Fi, parking-€7.50/day, Bahnhofsplatz 7, tel. 0651/994-740, www.hotelvinum.de, info@hotelvinum.de).

$$$ Hotel Pieper, a good value, is run by the friendly Becker family. They rent 20 comfortable rooms furnished with dark wood. Some rooms have air-conditioning (Sb-€60, Db-€95, Tb-€120, buffet breakfast, no elevator, Wi-Fi, free parking; 8-minute walk from station, 2 blocks off main drag at Thebäerstrasse 39; tel. 0651/23008, www.hotel-pieper.com, info@hotel-pieper-trier.de). From the station, follow Theodor-Heuss-Allee (toward Porta Nigra) to the second big intersection, angle right onto Göbenstrasse, and continue as the road curves and becomes Thebäerstrasse.

OUTSIDE THE CENTER

$$$ Hotel Petrisberg Trier, up a steep road behind the amphitheater, is top-quality, reasonably priced, and ideal if you have a car. It's on a hillside overlooking the city, exuding old-school elegance without being stuffy. The Pantenburg family takes great care to spoil all their guests: Helpful Helmut runs the place, brother Wolfgang whips up tasty egg breakfasts, and his niece Christina—the 1999 Trier Wine Queen—sometimes works reception. A pleasant footpath brings you downhill to the cathedral in 20 minutes (35 rooms, Sb-€70-75, Db-€100-105, higher prices are for weekends, extra bed-€40, elevator, Wi-Fi, free parking, taxi from train station-€8, Sickingenstrasse 11-13, tel. 0651/4640, www.hotel-petrisberg.de, info@hotel-petrisberg.de).

Eating in Trier

Zum Domstein, right on Market Square, serves standard German fare at decent prices and also has a special, pricier menu of dishes based on ancient Roman recipes. The Roman menu was inspired during renovations, when the owner discovered a Roman column in her cellar. (In Trier, you can't put a rec room in your basement without tripping over Roman ruins.) The finished cellar dining room incorporates the column, plus a mini-museum of Roman crockery (€12-20 main courses, €10-12 lunch specials, €17-31 Roman dishes usually served in cellar 18:00-21:00, open daily 8:30-24:00, last orders at 21:30, Am Hauptmarkt 5, tel. 0651/74490).

Zeitsprung Café, at the rear of the Archaeological Museum building, has good-value lunches and salads in a pretty setting overlooking the Elector's Palace and fountain (€8-10 main courses and daily specials; May-Sept daily 9:00-19:00; Oct-April Tue-Sun 9:00-18:00, closed Mon; closed first 2 weeks of Jan, outdoor seating available, Weimarer Allee 1, tel. 0651/994-5820).

At **Theo,** right at Porta Nigra, locals and tourists enjoy reasonably priced regional dishes and daily specials. The outdoor patio, with a huge sunshade sail, has a pleasant view overlooking the square (€8-15 main courses, daily 11:30-22:00, Simeonstrasse 59, tel. 0651/44888).

The recommended **Kolpinghaus Warsberger Hof hostel** runs an inexpensive eatery with a pub in the big yellow pastel building a few doors down Dietrichstrasse from Market Square (€10-120 main courses, fixed-price lunch deals Mon-Fri, open daily for lunch 11:30-14:00, dinner Wed-Sat only 18:00-22:00, nice enclosed terrace, kid-friendly).

Picnics: One of several supermarkets in the center is in the basement of the **Karstadt** department store on Simeonstrasse (Mon-Sat 9:30-20:00, closed Sun).

Trier Connections

From Trier by Train to: Cochem (2/hour, 45-60 minutes), **Cologne** (at least hourly, 2.5-3 hours, some change in Koblenz), **St. Goar/Bacharach** (hourly, 2.5 hours, change in Koblenz), **Frankfurt Airport** (hourly, 3 hours, change in Koblenz and sometimes Mainz), **Paris** (roughly hourly, 3-3.5 hours, best with change in Saarbrücken or Luxembourg). Train info: Tel. 0180-599-6633, www.bahn.com.

TRIER

COLOGNE AND THE UNROMANTIC RHINE

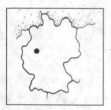

Romance isn't everything. Cologne (Köln—pronounced "kurln"—in German) is an urban Jacuzzi that keeps the Rhine churning. It's home to Germany's greatest Gothic cathedral, one of the country's best collections of Roman artifacts, a world-class art museum, and a healthy dose of German urban playfulness.

Peaceful Bonn, which offers good people-watching and fun pedestrian streets, used to be the capital of West Germany. The small town of Remagen had a bridge that helped defeat Hitler in World War II, and unassuming Aachen, near the Belgian border, was once the capital of Europe.

Cologne

Germany's fourth-largest city, Cologne has a compact, lively center. The Rhine was the northern boundary of the Roman Empire, and, 1,700 years ago, Constantine—the first Christian emperor—made what was then called "Colonia" the seat of a bishopric. (Five hundred years later, under Charlemagne, Cologne became the seat of an archbishopric.)

With 40,000 people within its walls, Cologne was the largest German city and an important cultural and religious center throughout the Middle Ages. Today, the city is most famous for its toilet water: Eau de Cologne was first made here by an Italian chemist in 1709.

During World War II, bombs destroyed 95 percent of Cologne—driving its population from 800,000 down to an estimated 30,000 at its lowest ebb. But with the end of the war, the city immediately began putting itself back together (the population rebounded to about 400,000 by Christmas of 1945). Today, it's a bustling commercial and cultural center that still respects its rich past.

PLANNING YOUR TIME

Cologne makes an ideal on-the-way stop; it's a major rail junction, and its top sights are clustered near the train station. With a couple of hours, you can toss your bag in a locker, take my self-guided town walk, zip through the cathedral, and make it back to the station for your train. If you're planning that short of a stop, make sure you'll be here when the whole church is open (in between its services—times are listed on page 542). More time (or an overnight) allows you to delve into a few of the city's fine museums and take in an old-time beer pub.

Orientation to Cologne

Cologne's core was bombed out, then rebuilt in mostly modern style with a sprinkling of quaint. The city has two areas that matter to visitors: One is the section right around the train station and cathedral. Here you'll find most sights, all my recommended hotels, plus the TI and plenty of eateries and services. Hohe Strasse, Cologne's pedestrian shopping street, begins near the cathedral. The other area—called the "old town"—is between the river and the Alter Markt, a few blocks to the south. After the war, this section was chosen to be rebuilt in the old style, and today pubs and music clubs pack the restored buildings.

TOURIST INFORMATION

Cologne's energetic TI, opposite the cathedral entrance, has a basic €0.50 city map and can find you a room (Mon-Sat 9:00-20:00, Sun 10:00-17:00, Kardinal-Höffner-Platz 1, tel. 0221/2213-0400, www.koelntourismus.de).

ARRIVAL IN COLOGNE

Cologne couldn't be easier to visit—its three important sights cluster within two blocks of the TI and train station. This super pedestrian zone is a constant carnival of people.

By Train: Cologne's busy train station has everything you need: drugstore, bookstore, food court, juice bar, grocery store, pricey 24-hour "McClean" WC (€1) with showers (€7, €20 deposit), travel center (*Reisezentrum*, long hours daily), and high-tech lockers (€3/2 hours, €6/24 hours, accepts coins and €5 and €10 bills, put money in and wait 30 seconds for door to open, your luggage—up to four pieces—is transferred to storage via an underground conveyor belt and retrieved when you reinsert your ticket; next to *Reisezentrum*). Exiting the front of the station (the end near track 1), you'll find yourself smack-dab in the shadow of the cathedral. Up the steps and to the right is the cathedral's main entrance (TI across street).

By Car: Drivers should follow signs to *Zentrum*, then continue to the huge Parkhaus am Dom garage under the cathedral (€1.80/hour, €18/day). The lot outside the garage has a cheaper day rate (€3/hour, €12/day). There's also the Parkhaus am Heumarkt, centrally located at the south end of the old town area (€2.50/hour, €16/day).

By Boat: If you're arriving on a K-D Line boat, exit the boat to the right, then walk along the waterside park until just before the train bridge, when the cathedral comes into view on the left.

HELPFUL HINTS

Closed Day: Note that most museums are closed on Monday (though the cathedral remains open). The cathedral is off-limits to sightseers during services, which are more frequent on Sundays. For information on Cologne's museums, visit www.museenkoeln.de.

Sightseeing Discount Cards: Cologne has two different cards, only one of which is worth considering. The **MuseumCard** is valid for two consecutive days (or a Sunday and Tuesday, as museums close Monday). It covers all local public transportation on the first day and includes the Roman-Germanic Museum, Museum Ludwig, and Wallraf-Richartz Museum, plus several lesser museums (but not the cathedral sights). If you're visiting all three of these museums, this card will save you money (€18/person, €30 family pass includes 2 adults and 2 kids up to 18, available at participating museums, www.museenkoeln.de).

The **KölnCard**, offering small discounts on some museums, is a waste of money; though it covers the city's transit system, you can easily reach the top sights on foot (€9/1 person, €19/2-5 people, valid 24 hours, www.koelntourismus.de).

Festivals: Though **Carnival** is celebrated all over Germany, Cologne's celebration is famously exuberant. Join the locals as they dress up, feast, and exchange *Bützje*—innocent pursed-lip kisses. Festivities start on the Thursday before Ash Wednesday and culminate with a huge parade on the following Monday ("Rose Monday," or *Rosenmontag*, Feb 16 in 2015). The parade draws musicians from all over Germany, and families line the parade route to grab pieces of candy tossed off the floats (www.koelnerkarneval.de). Cologne's **Kölner Lichter** festival lights up the sky the second weekend in July with fireworks, music, and lots of boats on the river (July 11 in 2015, www.koelner-lichter.de). It's part of the Rhein in Flammen regional festival, which hosts five additional events in the Rhine Valley (see page 454).

Internet Access: A small call shop and Internet café is a block from the station at Marzellenstrasse 3-5 (€2.50/hour, also sells cheap phone cards, Mon-Sat 9:00-24:00, Sun 11:00-24:00 tel. 0221/1399-6200).

Bike Rental: Convenient bike rental is available at two branches of the friendly **Radstation.** One is tucked under the train-track arcade (Mon-Fri 5:30-22:30, Sat 6:30-20:00, Sun 8:00-20:00; from the station, exit out the back by track 11 to Breslauer Platz, turn right, cross street, and look toward the train tracks). The other is along the river a 10-minute walk from the station, on Markmannsgasse, 100 yards upstream from the K-D Line dock (daily April-Oct 10:00-18:00). Both locations have the same prices and contact info (€5/3 hours, €10/day; tel. 0221/139-7190, mobile 0171-629-8796, www.radstationkoeln.de). Consider biking the path along the Rhine River up past the convention center *(Messe)* to the Rheinpark for a picnic. Or try a guided bike tour (described under "Tours in Cologne," next).

Tours in Cologne

Bus Tours

The TI sells tickets and is the departure point for city bus tours offered by two competing companies (€13 for 1.5-hour round-trip tour; €15 for hop-on, hop-off tour; departures at least hourly in summer, most have recorded commentary in both German and English, but Kölner CityTour has live guides every 2 hours—see www.cityfahrten.de).

Bike Tours

Radstation (listed earlier, under "Bike Rental") offers German/English guided city tours by bike (€17.50, 3-3.5 hours, daily April-Oct at 13:30, includes bike rental, rain poncho provided just in case, about 10 people per guide, reservations smart, tel. 0221/139-7190, mobile 0171-629-8796, www.radstationkoeln.de).

Cologne Walk

Cologne lends itself to a fine orientation walk, worth ▲▲. The old town, towering cathedral, and most of the sights cluster near the train station. Starting at the train station, this self-guided walk takes less than an hour and provides a good introduction.

Bahnhofsvorplatz

Stepping out of the train station, you're confronted with a modern hodgepodge of post-WWII architecture and the towering icon of Cologne, its cathedral. The city feels rebuilt—because it was. The Allies bombed Cologne hard in retaliation for Germany's bombing of London. Your gaze is grabbed by the cathedral. While it was built according to the original 13th-century plans, and the left (east) part was completed in the 13th century, the right half wasn't built until after German unification, in the 1880s.

· *Climb the steps and circle right, to the people-filled square facing the cathedral.*

Cathedral Plaza (Roncalli Platz)

In centuries past, a clutter of half-timbered huts crowded around the cathedral. They were all cleared out in the late 1800s so the great building would have a suitable approach.

This has been a busy commercial zone since ancient times. The Roman arch was discovered nearby and set up here as a reminder of the town's Roman roots. This north gate of the Roman city, from A.D. 50, marks the start of Cologne's nearly 2,000-year-old main shopping street, Hohe Strasse.

Look for the life-size replica tip of a spire. The real thing is 515 feet above you. The cathedral facade, while finished in the 1880s, is exactly what was envisioned by the original church planners in 1280. (For more on the cathedral, see page 542.)

· *Continue around the right side of the church, passing modern buildings and public spaces. Step up to the window of the Roman-Germanic Museum to see a...*

Roman Mosaic

Through the Roman-Germanic Museum's generous window, you can get a free look at the museum's prize piece—a fine mosaic floor. Once the dining-room floor of a rich Roman merchant, this is actually in its original position (the museum was built around it). It shows scenes from the life of Dionysus...wine, women, and song, Roman-style. The mosaic is quite sexy, with several scenes show-

COLOGNE & THE UNROMANTIC RHINE

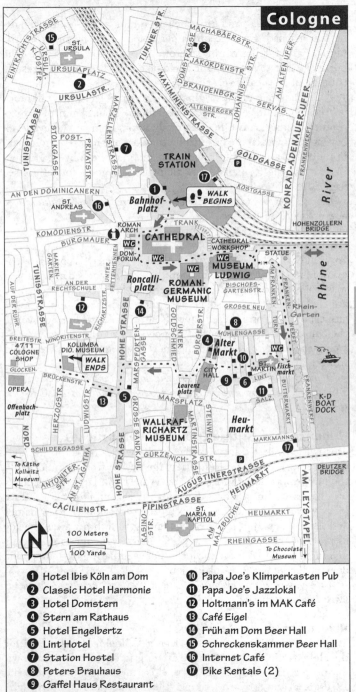

COLOGNE & THE UNROMANTIC RHINE

- ① Hotel Ibis Köln am Dom
- ② Classic Hotel Harmonie
- ③ Hotel Domstern
- ④ Stern am Rathaus
- ⑤ Hotel Engelbertz
- ⑥ Lint Hotel
- ⑦ Station Hostel
- ⑧ Peters Brauhaus
- ⑨ Gaffel Haus Restaurant
- ⑩ Papa Joe's Klimperkasten Pub
- ⑪ Papa Joe's Jazzlokal
- ⑫ Holtmann's im MAK Café
- ⑬ Café Eigel
- ⑭ Früh am Dom Beer Hall
- ⑮ Schreckenskammer Beer Hall
- ⑯ Internet Café
- ⑰ Bike Rentals (2)

ing a satyr seducing and ultimately disrobing a half-goddess, half-human maenad. First he offers her grapes, then he turns on the music. After further wining and dining—all with an agenda—the horny satyr finally scores. The cupid on a lion's back symbolizes the triumph of physical love.

The mosaic is at the original Roman street level. The tall monument above and left of the mosaic is the mausoleum of a first-century Roman army officer. Directly across from you (at eye level, beyond the mosaic) are beautifully carved stone reliefs—an indication of what a fine city Roman Cologne must have been. If you'd like to visit the Roman-Germanic Museum's good collection, see page 548.

• *Walk 20 steps beyond the mosaic farther along the cathedral and look down to see the...*

Cathedral Workshop

Any church of this size is a work in progress. There is constant renovation, repair, and care. Sandstone blocks are stacked and waiting to be shaped and plugged in wherever needed. The buttresses above are the church's showiest, because they face the bishop's palace, city center, and original entrance (south transept). For 500 years, the church was left unfinished, simply capped off midway. You're facing the functional part of the church, where services were held from the 1300s until the late 1800s.

• *From the cathedral, walk past the Museum Ludwig (described on page 549, and with a convenient WC in the lobby) and continue left onto the...*

Hohenzollern Bridge (Hohenzollernbrücke)

This is the busiest railway bridge in the world (30 trains an hour all day long). A classic Industrial Age design from around 1900, the bridge was destroyed in World War II and later rebuilt in its original style. These days, the bridge is a landmark for its "love locks"—couples come here, mark a little padlock with their names and the date, chain it to the bridge railing, and throw away the key as proof of their everlasting love. Citing safety concerns, officials had threatened to remove the locks, but eventually gave in to public demands to let the love-tokens stay.

• *Walk back in the direction of Museum Ludwig, then head down the stairs toward the river.*

Riverfront

The statue (to your left) honors Kaiser Wilhelm II, who paid for the Hohenzollernbrücke (named after his family). Stairs lead down to a people-friendly riverside park. This is urban planning from the 1970s: Real and forward-looking. The riverside, once a noisy highway, is now a peaceful park. All that traffic still courses through the city, but flows unnoticed below you in a tunnel. A bike-and-pedestrian path follows the riverside in each direction, and families let their children frolic in the fountain.

Turn right, walking away from the bridge, and walk for a few blocks along the Frankenwerft, Cologne's riverside restaurant district, until you are even with the tower of the Romanesque church. (Cologne's famous chocolate museum, described on page 549, is a five-minute walk farther downstream.)

Notice a strip of sockets for a metal flood wall (on the inland side of the grassy stretch; an eight-foot-high structure can be erected here when needed). Locals see a definite change in climate here: They say that "floods of the century" now happen every decade, thunderstorms are 10 times more prevalent, and for the first time, this part of Europe has witnessed small tornadoes.

• *At the foot of the church is the Fischmarkt, a tiny square.*

Fischmarkt and "Old Town"

Right below Great St. Martin Church, this little square—once the fish market—faces the river. It's ringed by medieval-looking build-

ings from the 1930s. In the early 20th century, Cologne's entire old town was a scruffy, half-timbered, prostitute-ridden slum. To the disgusted Nazis, prostitutes were human dirt. Their vision for old towns all over Germany: Clear out the clutter, boot the riffraff, and rebuild in the clean, tidy, stone-and-stucco style you see here. After World War II, Cologne decided to rebuild in a faux-medieval style to approximate what had once been. This square and the streets around the church are from that period.

• *Walk inland, circling around the right (downstream) side of the church. From the church's front door, a passageway leads away from the river directly to Alter Markt (Old Market Square).*

Alter Markt and City Hall

The ornate City Hall tower symbolized civic spirit standing strong against the power of the bishops in the 15th century. Circle around the tower to see the City Hall's fine Renaissance porch—the only historic facade left standing after the 1945 bombings. Its carvings stress civic independence. The busts of emperors bring to mind Cologne's strong Roman past; the lions symbolize the evil aspect of church authority. Above the door, the mayor kills the lion (thus establishing independence from church government for his city). This scene is flanked by Biblical parallels: the angel saving Daniel from the lions (on right), and Samson fighting lions (on left). Beware of flying rice—the City Hall is often busy with civil wedding parties (Mon-Sat).

• *From the City Hall, pass through Laurenzplatz and walk two blocks farther away from the river to Hohe Strasse.*

Shopping, Church Art, and Eau de Cologne

Jog left onto the town's busy pedestrian shopping street. **Hohe Strasse** thrived during the Middle Ages, when Cologne was a major player in the heavyweight Hanseatic League of northern European merchant towns. The street was rebuilt after its complete destruction in World War II and was the first pedestrian shopping mall in Germany. Today it's a rather soulless string of chain stores—most interesting for its seas of shoppers (the big Media-Markt electronics store, Germany's version of Best Buy, is ahead on the left).

Now take your first right on Brückenstrasse to the modern white building, set atop the ruins of a bombed-out Gothic church. This is the **Kolumba Diocesan Museum** (described on page 548). Inside, from the corner, you can grab a free peek at what was the church interior.

Across busy Tunisstrasse stands Cologne's circa-1960s **Opera House** (a big deal in Germany when built—it's now being remodeled). And across the street from that, on the right, is a historic building at **Glockengasse 4.** When Cologne's houses were renumbered in a single series during the Napoleonic era in 1796, this building was given the number 4711—which the perfume-making firm based here later adopted as its trademark. A shop on the ground floor has Cologne water running in a fountain by the door—sample this year's new fragrances for free at the counter. Just up the stairs is a small, free exhibit (Mon-Fri 9:30-18:30, Sat 9:30-18:00, closed Sun, tel. 0221/2709-9910, www.glockengasse.de).

Sights in Cologne

▲▲▲COLOGNE CATHEDRAL (DOM)

The Gothic Dom—Germany's most exciting church—looms immediately up from the train station in one of Germany's starkest juxtapositions of the modern and the medieval. The church is so big and so important that it has its own information office, the Domforum, in a separate building across the street (described on page 548, under "More Cathedral Sights").

Cost and Hours: Free, open daily May-Oct 6:00-21:00, Nov-April 6:00-19:30—but

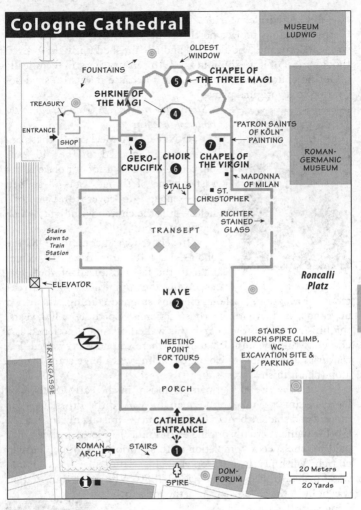

Cologne Cathedral

MUSEUM LUDWIG

OLDEST WINDOW

FOUNTAINS

CHAPEL OF THE THREE MAGI

❺

SHRINE OF THE MAGI

TREASURY

❹

ENTRANCE

SHOP

"PATRON SAINTS OF KÖLN" PAINTING

❸

GERO-CRUCIFIX

CHOIR

❻

CHAPEL OF THE VIRGIN

❼

ROMAN-GERMANIC MUSEUM

STALLS

MADONNA OF MILAN

ST. CHRISTOPHER

Stairs down to Train Station

RICHTER STAINED GLASS

TRANSEPT

ELEVATOR

Roncalli Platz

NAVE

❷

STAIRS TO CHURCH SPIRE CLIMB, WC, EXCAVATION SITE & PARKING

MEETING POINT FOR TOURS

PORCH

TRANKGASSE

CATHEDRAL ENTRANCE

❶

ROMAN ARCH

STAIRS

SPIRE

DOM-FORUM

20 Meters

20 Yards

tourist visits are not permitted during services (generally Mon-Sat at 6:30, 7:15, 8:00, 9:00, 12:00, and 18:30; Sun at 7:00, 8:00, 9:00, 10:00, 12:00, 17:00, and 19:00; confirm times at Domforum office or www.koelner-dom.de).

Tours: The one-hour English-only tours are reliably excellent (€8, Mon-Sat at 10:30 and 14:30, Sun at 14:30, meet inside front door of Dom, tel. 0221/9258-4730). Your tour ticket also gives you free entry to the 20-minute English video in the Domforum directly following the tour.

❍ **Self-Guided Tour:** If you don't take the guided tour, follow this seven-stop walk (note that stops 3-7 are closed off during confession Sat 14:00-18:00, and any time services are under way).

❶ Cathedral Exterior: The cathedral—the most ambitious Gothic building project north of France in the 13th century—was stalled in the Middle Ages and not finished until 1880. Even though most of it was built in the 19th century, it's still technically a Gothic church (not "Neo-Gothic") because it was finished according to its original plans.

• *Step inside the church. Grab a pew in the center of the nave.*

❷ Nave: If you feel small, that's because you're supposed to. The 140-foot-tall ceiling reminds us of our place in the vast scheme of things. Lots of stained glass—enough to cover three football fields—fills the church with light, which represents God.

The church was begun in 1248. The choir—the lofty area from the center altar to the far end ahead of you—was inaugurated in 1322. Later, during the tumultuous wars of religious reformation, Catholic pilgrims stopped coming. This dried up funds, and eventually construction stopped. For 300 years, the finished end of the church was walled off and functioned as a church, while the unfinished nave (where you now sit) waited. For centuries, the symbol of Cologne's skyline was a huge crane that sat atop the unfinished west spire.

With the rise of German patriotism in the early 1800s, Cologne became a symbol of German unity. And the Prussians—the movers and shakers behind German unity—mistakenly considered Gothic (which actually originated in France) a German style. They paid for the speedy completion of this gloriously Gothic German church. With nearly 700 workers going at full speed, the church was finished in just 38 years (1842-1880). The great train station was built in the shadow of the cathedral's towering spire.

The glass windows at the east end of the church (in the chapels and high above) are medieval. The glass surrounding you in the nave is not as old, but it's precious nevertheless. The glass on the left is early Renaissance. Notice the many coats of arms, which depict the lineage of the donors. One of these windows would have cost as much as two large townhouses. The glass on the right—a gift from Ludwig I, grandfather of the "Mad" King Ludwig who built the fairy-tale castles—is 19th-century Bavarian. Compare both the colors and the

realism of the faces between the windows to see how techniques advanced and tastes changed over the centuries.

While 95 percent of Cologne was destroyed by WWII bombs, the cathedral held up fairly well. (It was hit by 15 bombs, but the skeletal Gothic structure flexed, and it remained standing.) In anticipation of the bombing, the glass and art treasures were taken to shelters and saved.

The "swallow's nest" organ above you was installed to celebrate the cathedral's 750th birthday in 1998. Attaching it to the wall would have compromised the cathedral's architectural integrity, so the organ is actually suspended from precarious-looking steel wires.

The guys in the red robes are cathedral cops, called *Schweizer* (after the Swiss guard at the Vatican); if a service is getting ready to start, they hustle tourists out (but you can stay for the service if you like).

• *Leave the nave by stepping through the gate on the left, into the oldest part of the church. As you enter, look down.*

This 19th-century mosaic shows a saint holding the Carolingian Cathedral, which stood on this spot for several centuries before this one was built.

❸ **Gero-Crucifix:** Ahead of you on the left, the Chapel of the Cross features the oldest surviving monumental crucifix from north of the Alps. Carved in the 970s with a sensitivity that was 300 years ahead of its time, it shows Jesus not suffering and not triumphant—but with eyes closed...dead. He paid the price for our sins. It's quite a twofer: great art and powerful theology in one. The cathedral  has three big pilgrim stops: this crucifix, the Shrine of the Magi, and the *Madonna of Milan.*

• *Continue to the front end of the church, stopping to look at the big golden reliquary in the glass case behind the high altar.*

❹ **Shrine of the Magi:** Relics were a big deal in the Middle Ages. Cologne's acquisition of the bones of the Three Kings in the 12th century put it on the pilgrimage map and brought in enough money to justify the construction of this magnificent place. By some stretch of medieval Christian logic, these relics also justified the secular power of the German king. This reliquary, made in about 1200 of gilded silver, jewels, and enamel, is the biggest and most splendid I've seen. On the long sides, Old Testament prophets line the bottom, and 12 New Testament apostles—with a wingless angel in the center—line the top. The front looks like three stacked coffins, showing scenes of Christ's flagellation, Crucifixion, and Resurrection.

Inside sit the bones of the Magi...three skulls with golden crowns. So what's the big deal about these three kings (of Christmas-carol fame)? They were the first to recognize Jesus as the Savior and the first to come as pilgrims to worship him—inspiring medieval pilgrims and countless pilgrims since. For a thousand years, a theme of this cathedral has been that life is a pilgrimage...a search for God.

• *Opposite the shrine, at the far-east end of the church, is the...*

❺ Chapel of the Three Magi: The center chapel, at the church's far end, is the oldest. It also features the church's oldest window (center, from 1265). The design is typical: a strip of Old Testament scenes on the left with a parallel strip of New Testament scenes on the right that matches theologically and visually (such as, on bottom panels: to the left, the birth of Eve; to the right, the birth of Mary with her mother Anne on the bed).

Later glass windows (which you saw lining the nave) were made from panes of clear glass that were painted and glazed. This medieval window, however, is actually colored glass, which is assembled like a mosaic. It was very expensive. The size was limited to what pilgrim donations could support. Notice the plain, budget design higher up.

• *Peek into the center zone between the high altar and the carved wooden central stalls. (You can't usually get inside, unless you take the tour.)*

❻ Choir: The choir is surrounded by 13th- and 14th-century art with carved oak stalls, frescoed walls, statues painted as they would have been, and original stained glass high above. Study the fanciful oak carvings. The woman cutting the man's hair is a Samson-and-Delilah warning to the sexist men of the early Church.

• *The nearby chapel holds one of the most precious paintings of the important Gothic School of Cologne.*

❼ Chapel of the Virgin: *The Patron Saints of Cologne* was painted around 1440, probably by Stefan Lochner. Notice the photographic realism and believable depth. There are literally dozens of identifiable herbs in the grassy foreground. During the 19th century, the city fought to move the painting to a museum. The Church went to court to keep it. The judge ruled that it could stay in the cathedral—as long as a Mass was said before it every day. For more than a hundred years, that happened at 18:30. Now, 21st-century comfort has trumped 19th-century law: In winter, services take place in the warmer Sacrament Chapel instead. (If you like this painting, you'll enjoy the many other fine works from the School of Cologne at the Wallraf-Richartz Museum—see page 549.)

Overlooking the same chapel (between the windows), the delicate *Madonna of Milan* sculpture (1290), associated with miracles, was a focus of pilgrims for centuries. Its colors, scepter, and crown were likely added during a restoration in 1900. The reclining medieval knight in the cage at the back of the chapel (just before the gate) is a wealthy but childless patron who donated his entire county to the cathedral.

As you head for the exit, look into the transept on your left. The stained-glass windows above you are a random and abstract pattern of 80 colors, "sampled" from the church's more-historic windows. The local artist Gerhard Richter designed these windows to create a "harmony of colors" in 2007.

Before leaving, look above the tomb with the cage and find the statue of St. Christopher (with Jesus on his shoulder and the pilgrim's staff). He's facing the original south transept entry to the church. Since 1470, pilgrims and travelers have looked up at him and taken solace in the hope that their patron saint is looking out for them.

• *Go in peace.*

More Cathedral Sights
Church Spire Climb (Dom-Turm)

An exterior entry (to the right of the church as you face the west facade) takes you into a modern excavation site, where you can see an arch and the foundations from the cathedral's predecessor (free), and pay to climb the cathedral's dizzying south tower. For a workout of 509 steps, you can enjoy a fine city view. From the *Glockenstube* (only 400 steps up), you can see the Dom's nine huge bells, including *Dicke Peter* (24-ton Fat Peter), claimed to be the largest free-swinging church bell in the world.

Cost and Hours: €3, €6 combo-ticket also includes treasury, daily May-Sept 9:00-18:00, March-April and Oct until 17:00, Nov-Feb until 16:00.

Treasury

The treasury sits outside the cathedral's left transept (when you exit through the front door, turn right and continue right around the building to the gold pillar marked *Schatzkammer*). The six dim, hushed rooms are housed in the cathedral's 13th-century stone cellar vaults. Spotlights shine on black cases filled with gilded chalices and crosses, medieval reliquaries (bits of chain, bone, cross, and cloth in gold-crusted glass capsules), and plenty of fancy bishop garb: intricately embroidered miters and vestments, rings with fat gemstones, and six-foot gold crosiers. Displays come with brief English descriptions, but the little €4.50 *Cologne Cathedral* book sold inside the adjacent cathedral shop *(Domladen)* provides extra information.

Cost and Hours: €5, €6 combo-ticket also includes spire climb, daily 10:00-18:00, last entry 30 minutes before closing, tel. 0221/1794-0530.

Domforum

This helpful visitors center, across from the entrance of the cathedral, is a good place to support the Vatican Bank (notice the Pax Bank ATM just outside the entrance), or just to take a break from the crowds outside. The staff offers plenty of cathedral information, and the welcoming lounge has €1-2.50 coffee and juice. The English "multi-vision" video about the church starts slow but gets a little better (runs Mon-Sat at 11:30 and 15:30, Sun at 15:30 only, 20 minutes, €2 or included with church tour).

Cost and Hours: Free, Mon-Fri 9:30-18:00, Sat 9:30-17:00, Sun 13:00-17:00, may close for special events, clean WC downstairs—€0.50, tel. 0221/9258-4720, www.domforum.de.

Kolumba Diocesan Museum

This museum contains some of the cathedral's finest art. A stop on my self-guided walk, it's on Kolumbastrasse, which runs between Minoritenstrasse and Brückenstrasse a few blocks southwest of the cathedral. Built around the Madonna in the Ruins church, the museum is conceived as a place of reflection. There are no tours or information or noise. It's just you and the art in a modern building built upon the rubble of war. The daring modernist rebuild is a statement: We lost the war. Just accept it.

Cost and Hours: €5, Wed-Mon 12:00-17:00, closed Tue, tel. 0221/933-1930, www.kolumba.de.

NEAR THE CATHEDRAL

▲▲Roman-Germanic Museum (Römisch-Germanisches Museum)

One of Germany's top Roman museums offers minimal English information among its elegant and fascinating display of Roman artifacts: glassware, jewelry, and mosaics. All these pieces are evidence of Cologne's status as an important site of civilization long before the cathedral was ever imagined. The permanent collection is downstairs and upstairs; temporary exhibits are on the ground floor. Upstairs, you'll see an original, reassembled arched gate to the Roman city with the Roman initials for the town, CCAA, still legible, and incredible glassware that Roman Cologne was famous for producing. The museum's main attraction, described near the start of my self-guided walk, is the in-situ Roman-mosaic floor—which you can see from the street for free through the large window.

Cost and Hours: €9, includes special exhibits, Tue-Sun 10:00-17:00, closed Mon, Roncalliplatz 4, tel. 0221/2212-4590, www.museenkoeln.de/rgm.

▲▲Museum Ludwig

Next door and more enjoyable, this museum—in a slick and modern building—offers a stimulating trip through the art of the last century, including American Pop and post-WWII art. The ground floor shows special exhibits. Upstairs (on the right) is the Haubrich collection. Josef Haubrich managed to keep his impressive collection of German Expressionist art out of Nazi hands (they considered it "decadent art") and eventually gave it to the city. The collection includes works by the great German Expressionists Max Beckmann, Otto Dix, and Ernst Ludwig Kirchner. Their paintings capture the loss of idealism and innocence following World War I and helped take art into the no-holds-barred modern world. The first floor also has a fine Picasso collection. The top floor is mostly contemporary and abstract paintings.

Cost and Hours: €11, Tue-Sun 10:00-18:00, closed Mon, audioguide-€3, free WC in entry hall, exhibits are fairly well-described in English, pricey cafeteria, Heinrich-Böll-Platz, tel. 0221/2212-6165, www.museum-ludwig.de.

FARTHER FROM THE CATHEDRAL

These museums are several blocks south of the cathedral.

▲▲Wallraf-Richartz Museum

Housed in a cinderblock of a building near the City Hall, this minimalist museum features a world-class collection of old masters, from medieval to northern Baroque and Impressionist. You'll see the best collection anywhere of Gothic School of Cologne paintings (1300-1550), offering an intimate peek into those times. Also included are German, Dutch, Flemish, and French works by masters such as Albrecht Dürer, Peter Paul Rubens, Rembrandt, Frans Hals, Jan Steen, Vincent van Gogh, Pierre-Auguste Renoir, Claude Monet, Edvard Munch, and Paul Cézanne.

Cost and Hours: €8-13, price varies depending on special exhibits, Tue-Sun 10:00-18:00, Thu until 21:00, closed Mon, on Obenmarspforten, tel. 0221/2212-1119, www.wallraf.museum.

▲Imhoff Chocolate Museum (Schokoladenmuseum)

Chocoholics love this place, cleverly billed as the "MMMuseum." Three levels of displays—well-described in English—follow the cocoa bean from its origin to the finished product. Local historians,

noting the "dumbing-down" of this generation of tourists, complain that this museum gets more visitors than all of Cologne's other museums combined. You'll see displays on the history, culture, and business of chocolate from the Aztecs onward, step into a hot and muggy greenhouse to watch the beans grow, and follow sweet little treats as they trundle down the conveyor belt in the functioning chocolate factory, the museum's highlight. The top-floor exhibit on chocolate advertising is fun. Some find that the museum takes chocolate too seriously, and wish the free samples weren't so meager—you'll have to do your indulging in the fragrant, choc-full gift shop.

Cost and Hours: €8.50, Tue-Fri 10:00-18:00, Sat-Sun 11:00-19:00, closed Mon except in Dec, last entry one hour before closing, Am Schokoladenmuseum 1a, tel. 0221/931-8880, www.schokoladenmuseum.de. The museum is a pleasant 10-minute walk south on the riverfront, between the Deutzer and Severins bridges.

Käthe Kollwitz Museum

This contains the largest collection of the artist's powerful Expressionist art, welling from her experiences living in Berlin during the tumultuous first half of the 20th century.

Cost and Hours: €4, Tue-Fri 10:00-18:00, Sat-Sun 11:00-18:00, closed Mon, Neumarkt 18-24, tel. 0221/227-2899, www.kollwitz.de.

Getting There: From Hohe Strasse, walk west on Schildergasse for about 10 minutes to Neumarkt; go past the Neumarkt Gallerie shopping center to Neumarkt Passage, enter Neumarkt Passage, and walk to the glass-domed center courtyard, where you'll take the glass elevator to the fifth floor.

Sleeping in Cologne

Cologne is *the* convention town in Germany. Consequently, hotels are either jam-packed, with their rooms going for €180-200, or empty and hungry for guests. Unless otherwise noted, prices listed are the non-convention weekday rates. Prices are soft, so ask the hotel for its best offer. During conventions, rates double or even triple. Outside of convention times, the TI can always get you a discounted room in a business-class hotel (free by phone or Internet, walk-ins pay a €3 booking fee).

Sleep Code

Abbreviations   (€1 = about $1.40, country code: 49)
S = Single, **D** = Double/Twin, **T** = Triple, **Q** = Quad, **b** = bathroom, **s** = shower only.

Price Rankings

  $$$ **Higher Priced**—Most rooms €110 or more.

    $$ **Moderately Priced**—Most rooms between €85-110.

     $ **Lower Priced**—Most rooms €85 or less.

Unless otherwise noted, credit cards are accepted, English is spoken, breakfast is included, and Wi-Fi is generally free. Prices change; verify current rates online or by email. For the best prices, always book directly with the hotel.

An updated list of convention dates is posted at www.koelnmesse.de (choose English, then click on "Trade fairs and events," then "Trade fairs in Cologne"). Unlisted smaller conventions can also lead to small price increases, and big conventions in nearby Düsseldorf can also fill rooms and raise rates in Cologne.

All the options listed here are an easy roll from the train station with your luggage.

IN FRONT OF THE STATION

$$$ Hotel Ibis Köln am Dom, a 71-room chain hotel, offers predictability and tidiness, and you can't beat the location—inside the station building—though it lacks personality (Sb-€89-120, Db-€104-190; €12/person less if you skip breakfast; air-con, elevator, guest computer, Wi-Fi, Bahnhofsvorplatz, entry across from station's *Reisezentrum*, tel. 0221/912-8580, www.ibishotel.com, h0739@accor.com).

$$ Classic Hotel Harmonie's 72 business-class rooms include some very small, nicely priced singles as well as luxurious "superior" rooms, which have hardwoods and swanky bathrooms with heated floors. It's plenty pricey during conventions, but becomes affordable on weekends and is a downright steal when business is slow (Sb-€60-90, Db-€80-110, price depends on room category, more expensive rooms have air-con, elevator, Wi-Fi, limited parking-€18/day, Ursulaplatz 13-19, tel. 0221/16570, www.classic-hotel-harmonie.de, info@classic-hotel-harmonie.de). It's a five-minute walk northwest of the station: Exit by track 1 and walk straight to the roundabout, then go right on Marzellenstrasse and bear left on Ursulaplatz, toward the church.

BEHIND THE STATION

$$ Hotel Domstern is a 16-room boutique hotel with fresh, pleasant rooms above a colorful lobby, located in a fine townhouse just steps from the station (Sb-€72-79, Db-€105, extra bed-€20, elevator, Wi-Fi, parking-€10/day; from the train station, take the Breslauer Platz exit by track 11 and walk two blocks up Domstrasse to #26; tel. 0221/168-0080, www.hotel-domstern.de, info@hotel-domstern.de).

IN THE TOWN CENTER

$$$ Stern am Rathaus has eight new rooms on three floors, over a small, modern restaurant in a quiet location just around the corner from Alter Markt and the City Hall (Sb-€89, Db-€115, Qb suite-€135, extra bed-€25, air-con, no elevator, Wi-Fi, cable Internet in rooms, parking-€12/day; Bürgerstrasse 6, tel. 0221/2225-1750, www.stern-am-rathaus.com, info@stern-am-rathaus.com).

$$ Hotel Engelbertz is a fine, family-run, 40-room enterprise. It's an eight-minute walk from the station and cathedral at the end of the pedestrian mall (non-convention-time specials in 2015 for readers with this book who reserve directly with the hotel: last-minute Sb-€59 and Db-€85 if you reserve on same day or day before, Sb-€68 and Db-€95 with advance reservation; regular rate Sb-€65-79 and Db-€89-114, convention rates up to Db-€220, elevator, pay Wi-Fi, public parking-€14-18/day; just off Hohe Strasse at Obenmarspforten 1-3, coming from station turn left at Hohe Strasse 96; tel. 0221/925-4860, www.hotel-engelbertz.de, info@hotel-engelbertz.de).

$$ Lint Hotel, a small place with 18 modern rooms and hardwood floors, is comfortably located in a little alley between Fischmarkt and Alter Markt. It's expensive during conventions and in high season, but offers affordable deals at other times (Sb-€59-79, Db-€79-99, €10 breakfast with homemade Bircher Muesli, no elevator, Wi-Fi, parking-€16/day, Lintgasse 7, tel. 0221/920-550, www.lint-hotel.de, contact@lint-hotel.de).

BUDGET ROOMS

$ Station Hostel, with 200 beds, is a five-minute walk from the train station and full of young travelers (dorm bed-€17-24, S-€32, Sb-€39, twin-bed D-€48, Db-€55, Tb-€75, prices go up during conventions and summer weekends but usually no more than €6/person, includes sheets, towel-€1, key deposit-€1, breakfast-€3-4, kitchen, elevator, no curfew, guest computer, Wi-Fi, laundry-€4/load, tel. 0221/912-5301; exit station on cathedral side, walk straight 1 block, turn right on Marzellenstrasse to #44-56; www.hostel-cologne.de, station@hostel-cologne.de).

Eating in Cologne

The city's distinct type of beer, called *Kölsch,* is pale, hoppy, and fermented in a way more typical of wheat-based beers than of pilsner, lending it a slight sweetness. Beer-hall menus tend to be similar, with the real defining feature being which brand of beer they serve (usually Gaffel, Päffgen, Peters, or Früh). Beers come in delicate glasses (by Bavarian standards) and are shuttled around in small wreath-like trays *(Bierkränze).* Cologne's waiters, called *Köbes,* have a reputation for grumpiness, and some beer halls have a sloppy, sticky-tabled feeling, but others have helpful and attentive service and attractive interiors. This is the place to satisfy your cravings for blood sausage *(Blutwurst)* and kidneys *(Nierchen)*...or, for something a little more mainstream, look for the tasty *Rheinischer Sauerbraten* with *Klössen* (dumplings) and applesauce. Pub after pub advertises yard-high beer glasses and yard-long bratwurst.

NEAR ALTER MARKT

The area around Alter Markt, a square a few blocks from the cathedral, is home to dozens of beer halls, most with both outdoor and indoor seating. Wander from Alter Markt through Heumarkt (an adjacent square) and down Salzgasse to Frankenwerft (along the river) to catch the flavor. The following places are open daily from about 11:00 to 24:00.

Peters Brauhaus, at the top of Alter Markt, is a reliable eating choice with an unusually nice interior and outdoor seating across the street (€11-19 main courses, kids' menu, Mühlengasse 1, tel. 0221/257-3950).

In **Gaffel Haus,** at the bottom of the square, look for the wall filled with coats of arms of Cologne's old guilds *(Gaffeln)*—see how many crafts you can guess by their pictures (€10-20 main courses, near Lintgasse at Alter Markt 20-22, tel. 0221/257-7692).

If you're more interested in music and beer than in food, check out **Papa Joe's Klimperkasten,** a dark pub packed with memorabilia and live jazz daily (€5-13 pub meals, Gaffel on tap, live piano jazz Sept-May Sun-Thu from 20:00, Alter Markt 50-52, tel. 0221/258-2132). A couple of minutes' walk away is its rowdier sibling, **Papa Joe's Jazzlokal** (live bands Mon-Sat from 20:30, Sun from 19:30—but closed Sun June-Aug, Buttermarkt 37, tel. 0221/257-7931, www.papajoes.de for jazz schedule—American jazz and Dixieland have a big following in Germany). The pubs on the Frankenwerft, along the river across from the K-D boat dock, tend to be a bit more expensive.

NEAR THE TRAIN STATION AND CATHEDRAL

Holtmann's im MAK, a museum café with sophisticated locals enjoying light fare, is a good option for a non-*Brauhaus* lunch. If you eat here on a Sunday morning, be sure to sit outside and enjoy a free organ concert al fresco—the courtyard abuts a church (€9-11 main courses, Tue-Sun 11:00-17:00, closed Mon, on other side of Hohe Strasse from the cathedral in Museum of Applied Arts—Museum für Angewandte Kunst—at An der Rechtschule 1, inside front door and down the stairs, no museum ticket needed, tel. 0221/2779-8860).

Café Eigel, just off Hohe Strasse near the recommended Hotel Engelbertz, is a good option for *Kaffee und Kuchen* (afternoon cake and coffee) or for a light lunch (including salads and omelets). It's been in the same location for 50 years, but has been remodeled in a fresh, sleek, modern style. Enjoy delicious pastries in the airy atrium, and be sure to pick up some homemade chocolates (€8-10 main courses, €3-4 slices of cake, Mon-Fri 9:00-19:00, Sat 9:00-18:00, Sun 14:00-18:00, Brückenstrasse 1-3, tel. 0221/257-5858).

Früh am Dom, close to the cathedral, is the closest beer hall to the station, offering three floors of touristy, traditional German drinking and dining options. Head to the back wall to check out a painting of what the city looked like in 1534 (€10-23 main courses, daily 8:00-24:00, Am Hof 12-14, tel. 0221/261-3211).

Schreckenskammer is a down-home joint and might be the least touristy beer hall in central Cologne. It's located just behind the St. Ursula church, near the recommended Harmonie hotel and the Station Hostel. The sand on the floor, swept out and replaced each morning, buffs the hardwood and also keeps it clean. The *kammer* is small and cozy, so be prepared to share a table and make new friends over a *Kölsch* or two. Most meals (choose from the *Tageskarte,* or daily specials) start with a complimentary cup of *Brühe* (broth). Don't mistake this as an act of hospitality—it only serves to make you thirstier. This eatery is really popular, so arrive early or make a reservation (€9-19 main courses, Tue-Sat 11:00-13:45 & 16:30-22:30, closed Sun-Mon, Ursulagartenstrasse 11-15, tel. 0221/132-581).

Cologne Connections

From Cologne by Train to: Bonn (5/hour, 20-30 minutes), **Remagen** (2-3/hour, 30-50 minutes), **Aachen** (2-3/hour, 50-60 minutes), **Frankfurt** (direct ICE trains almost hourly, most leave from Cologne's Köln-Messe-Deutz station—a 2-minute trip across river by S-Bahn, 1-1.5 hours; slower, cheaper, less frequent IC trains along Rhine are better for enjoying scenery, 2.5 hours), **Frankfurt Airport** (1-2/hour, 1 hour; trains along Rhine go less often and take 2.5 hours), **Bacharach/St. Goar** (hourly; 2 hours with change in Koblenz, 2.5 hours direct), **Cochem** (1-2/hour, 2-2.5 hours; most change in Koblenz), **Trier** (at least hourly, 2.5-3 hours, some change in Koblenz), **Würzburg** (at least hourly, 2.5 hours, some with change in Frankfurt), **Hamburg** (hourly, 4 hours), **Munich** (2/hour, 4.5 hours, some with 1 change), **Berlin** (hourly, 4.5 hours), **Paris** (5/day direct, 3.5 hours, Thalys train—requires seat reservation), **Amsterdam** (7/day direct, 3 hours). Train info: Tel. 0180-599-6633, www.bahn.com.

The Unromantic Rhine

HIGHLIGHTS
▲Bonn

Bonn was chosen for its sleepy, cultured, and peaceful nature as a good place to plant West Germany's first post-Hitler government. Since the two Germanys became one again in 1989, Berlin has taken back its position as capital.

Today, Bonn is sleek, modern, and, by big-city standards, remarkably pleasant and easygoing. The pedestrian-only old town stretching out from the station will make you wonder why the US can't trade in its malls for real, people-friendly cities. The market square and Münsterplatz—filled with

The Unromantic Rhine

Düsseldorf•
Rhine
Cologne•
Brühl•
•**Aachen**
•**Bonn**
Bad Godesberg
Remagen•
River
Koblenz•
Mosel

30 Kilometers
30 Miles

BEST OF RHINE

street musicians—are a joy. People-watching doesn't get much better, though the actual sights are disappointing.

The **TI** is a five-minute walk from the station (Mon-Fri 10:00-18:00, Sat 10:00-16:00, Sun 10:00-14:00, go straight on Windeckstrasse, next to Karstadt department store, tel. 0228/775-000, www.bonn.de).

If you're a classical-music fan, you can stop by **Beethoven's Birthplace,** with its sparse exhibits (free tours Mon, Thu, and Sat at 14:30, family-only tours on Sun and first Sat of month; entry-€6, includes tour; April-Oct daily 10:00-18:00, shorter hours Nov-

March, last entry 25 minutes before closing; free English brochure, Bonngasse 18-26, tel. 0228/981-7525, www.beethoven-haus-bonn. de).

▲Remagen

Midway between Koblenz and Cologne are the scant remains of the Bridge at Remagen, of WWII (and movie) fame. But the memorial and the bridge stubs are enough to stir the emotions of Americans who remember when, in 1945, it was the only bridge still standing on the Rhine, allowing the Allies to pour across the river and race toward Berlin. The bridge was built during World War I to help supply the German forces on the Western Front. (Ironically, one war later, General Eisenhower said the bridge was worth its weight in gold for its service *against* Germany.) An American unit captured the bridge on March 7, 1945, just after two failed attempts to demolish it (Hitler executed four generals for this failure). Ten days after US forces arrived, the bridge did collapse, killing 28 American soldiers. Today you can pay your respects here and visit the **Peace Museum,** which tells the bridge's fascinating story in English (€3.50, daily 10:00-17:00, May-Oct until 18:00, closed mid-Nov-early March; it's on the Rhine's west bank, south side of Remagen town, follow *Brücke von Remagen* signs; tel. 02642/42893, www.bruecke-remagen.de). Remagen **TI:** Tel. 02642/905-9924.

▲Aachen (Charlemagne's Capital)

This city was the capital of Europe in A.D. 800, when Charles the Great (Charlemagne) called it Aix-la-Chapelle. The remains of his rule include an impressive Byzantine- and Ravenna-inspired church, with his sarcophagus and throne. Enjoy the town's charming historic pedestrian center and festive Christmas market. See the headliner newspaper museum and great fountains, including a clever arrange-'em-yourself version.

LOWLIGHTS
Heidelberg

This famous old university town attracts hordes of Americans. Any surviving charm is stained almost beyond recognition by commercialism. It doesn't make it into Germany's top three weeks.

Mainz, Wiesbaden, and Rüdesheim

These towns are all too big or too famous. They're not worth your time. Mainz's Gutenberg Museum is also a disappointment.

NÜRNBERG

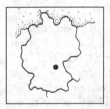

Nürnberg ("Nuremberg" in English), Bavaria's second city, is known for its glorious medieval architecture, important Germanic history museum, haunting Nazi past, famous Christmas market (Germany's biggest), and little bratwurst (Germany's tiniest and perhaps most beloved). Nürnberg (NEWRN-behrg) was one of Europe's leading cities in about 1500, and its large Imperial Castle marked it as a stronghold of the Holy Roman Empire.

Today, though Nürnberg has a half-million residents, the charming Old Town—with its red-sandstone Gothic buildings—makes visitors feel like they are in a far smaller city. Thanks to an enlightened city-planning vision that rebuilt in a modern yet people-friendly style after the war, and policies that ensured that lots of residents chose to live in the center, Nürnberg's downtown is lively and inviting day and night.

PLANNING YOUR TIME

Nürnberg is an easy add-on to any itinerary that includes Munich, Würzburg, or Rothenburg (each about an hour away by frequent trains), and a handy stop on the way to Frankfurt, Berlin, or Dresden. Keep in mind that nearly all museums (except those relating to World War II) are closed on Monday.

For the sightseer, Nürnberg is a city of the First Reich (Holy Roman Empire sights in the Old Town) and the Third Reich (Nazi-period sights that lie outside the town center).

If you're staying just one night (or day-tripping from elsewhere), follow my self-guided walk from the train station through the Old Town up to the castle, then visit the Nazi sites. If you have two days (most worthwhile if you have a serious interest in German history, especially the Nazi years), spend one day at the Nazi Documentation Center (and the nearby Rally Grounds) and the other in the Old Town, with time for its outstanding history museum (the Germanic National Museum).

Orientation to Nürnberg

Nürnberg's Old Town is surrounded by a three-mile-long wall and moat, and, beyond that, a ring road. At the southeast corner of the ring is the train station; across the street, just inside the ring, is the medieval Frauentor gate. Sights cluster along Königstrasse downhill from the Frauentor to the small Pegnitz River, then back uphill through the main market square (Hauptmarkt) to the Imperial Castle (Kaiserburg). The former Nazi Rally Grounds are southeast of the center (easily accessible by tram or bus).

TOURIST INFORMATION

Nürnberg's handy and helpful TI is across the ring road from the station, in the modern building just opposite the Frauentor (Mon-Sat 9:00-19:00, Sun 10:00-16:00, Königstrasse 93, tel. 0911/233-6132, www.tourismus.nuernberg.de). Pick up the free *See and Enjoy* city-guide booklet (with updated sights hours and prices) and get information about bus and walking tours. The TI also books rooms (no fee) and sells transit passes and the Nürnberg Card (see below). The TI has a small branch office at #18 on the Hauptmarkt (Mon-Sat 9:00-18:00, also open Sun May-Oct and during the Christmas market 10:00-16:00).

Discount Day Pass: When you buy a ticket at any of Nürnberg's city-run museums—including the Nazi Documentation Center, Nürnberg Trials Courtroom, Albrecht Dürer House, Toy Museum, and the City Museum—you can pay an additional €2.50 for a day pass that lets you visit all the others free of charge on the same day (www.museen.nuernberg.de).

Nürnberg Card: If you're staying at least two days, this card is a good value and gets you into a much wider range of sights (€25/2 days, €5 for kids ages 6-11, sold at TI and most hotels, covers all local public transit and admission to all city-run museums, the Germanic National Museum, Imperial Castle, German Railway Museum, and more—plus small discounts on bus and walking tours).

ARRIVAL IN NÜRNBERG

By Train: Nürnberg's stately old Hauptbahnhof—with a shiny new interior—is conveniently located just outside the old city walls and ring road. The busy station has WCs, lockers, ATMs, and lots of

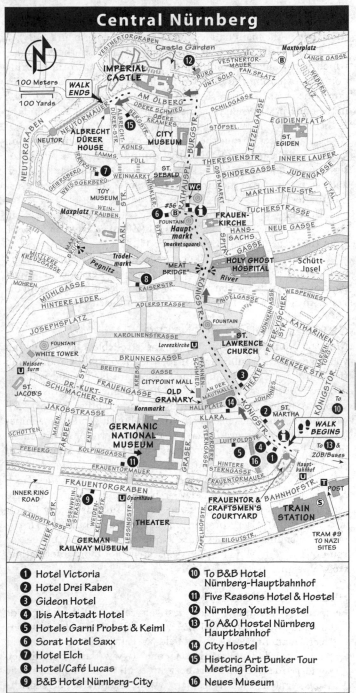

Central Nürnberg

① Hotel Victoria
② Hotel Drei Raben
③ Gideon Hotel
④ Ibis Altstadt Hotel
⑤ Hotels Garni Probst & Keiml
⑥ Sorat Hotel Saxx
⑦ Hotel Elch
⑧ Hotel/Café Lucas
⑨ B&B Hotel Nürnberg-City
⑩ To B&B Hotel Nürnberg-Hauptbahnhof
⑪ Five Reasons Hotel & Hostel
⑫ Nürnberg Youth Hostel
⑬ To A&O Hostel Nürnberg Hauptbahnhof
⑭ City Hostel
⑮ Historic Art Bunker Tour Meeting Point
⑯ Neues Museum

NÜRNBERG

shops. You can get train information and buy tickets at the *Rei-sezentrum* in the main hall (center of building, long hours daily).

To reach the **Frauentor** (the medieval city's southern gate)—which is near most recommended hotels and is also the starting point for exploring the Old Town—follow signs for *Ausgang/City* down the escalator, then signs to *Königstor/Frauentor* and *Altstadt* in the underpass. When you emerge, the TI is on your right and the Frauentor tower is on your left.

To go directly from the station to the **Nazi Documentation Center** and the **former Nazi Rally Grounds**, follow the pink *Tram* signs in the underpass to the stop in front of the Postbank Center, and catch tram #9 in the direction of Doku-Zentrum (leaves every 10 minutes).

By Long-Distance Bus: The city's long-distance buses all congregate at the central bus terminal (ZOB), a five-minute walk from the Frauentor at Bahnhofstrasse 11.

By Car: A handful of public garages are located within the city walls (most around €15/day and well-signed); cheaper on-street parking is available if you're willing to look for it in the neighborhoods that lie a 5- to 10-minute walk from the city walls.

GETTING AROUND NÜRNBERG

Most of Nürnberg's sights are in the strollable Old Town, but you'll need to use public transit for the Nazi Rally Grounds and the Nürnberg Trials Courtroom, which are far beyond walking distance. Nürnberg has the typical German lineup of trams, buses, U-Bahns (subways), and S-Bahns (faster suburban trains). All work on the same tickets, which you can buy at vending machines (marked *VAG Fahrausweise*) on the tram platform or before entering the U- or S-Bahns, or on board (buses only). A **single ticket** *(Einzelfahrkarte)* costs €2.50 (good for 90 minutes of travel in one direction, including transfers). A **day ticket** is €5.30 (*TagesTicket Solo*, good for one calendar day or both Sat and Sun; the €9.10 *TagesTicket Plus* covers 2 adults and up to 4 children; day tickets also sold at TI). Everything in this chapter is within zone *(Preisstufe)* 2. Vending machines time-stamp single and day tickets, so you don't need to validate them separately. For more information, see www.vgn.de.

HELPFUL HINTS

Festivals: Two summer music festivals cater to different crowds in late July: **Klassik Open Air** is a series of free classical concerts and fireworks show held at Luitpoldhain park, near the Nazi Documentation Center (www.klassikopenair.de), and **Bardentreffen Nürnberg** hosts all kinds of world-music acts right in the city center (www.bardentreffen.de/english-infos). Two **city fairs** happen every spring and fall, also at Luitpoldhain park, with rides, traditional costumes, and the works (www.volksfest-nuernberg.de). The annual **Christmas market** *(Christkindlesmarkt),* with more than two million visitors annually, engulfs the Hauptmarkt (starts the Fri before the first Sun in Advent—November 27 in 2015, www. christkindlesmarkt.de).

Internet Access: Telepoint, in the passage underneath the train station, is wholesome, with no gaming (€1.50/hour, Mon-Sat 8:30-23:00, Sun 9:30-23:00, tel. 0160/753-0240).

Laundry: A **Schnell & Sauber** coin launderette with instructions in English is at Allersberger Strasse 89 (daily 6:00-22:00, until 23:00 in summer, near Schweiggerstrasse stop for tram #9, two stops from train station in same direction as Nazi Documentation Center; from tram stop, head 200 yards away from downtown along Allersberger Strasse to see launderette on left).

Tours in Nürnberg

Walking Tours

English-language tours of Nürnberg's Old Town leave daily at 13:00 in peak season from the branch TI at Hauptmarkt 18 (mid-April-early Jan, €10, kids under 14 free, 2.5 hours, no reservation needed, buy ticket from TI or guide, www.nuernberg-tours.de).

Historic Art Bunker Tours

This intriguing tour takes you deep into the sandstone cellars under Castle Hill to learn how the city protected most of its art treasures (plus some plundered from elsewhere in Europe) from WWII's most devastating bomb attacks (see page 572). The bunkers themselves are largely empty now, except for the photos posted at each stop of the tour. You'll get some background on the pieces kept here, and hear a lot about the air raids themselves and the citywide rebuilding process that followed. While most live guides give the tour only in German, the good included audioguide is in English (€5, daily at 14:30, Sat also at 17:30, 1.25 hours, buy tickets and meet at the Brauereiladen brewery shop—under the *Nürnberger Altstadthof* sign—at Bergstrasse 19, tel. 0911/227-066, www. felsengaenge-nuernberg.de).

Bus Tours

These tours, which include some walking, leave daily at 10:00 (May-Oct and Dec) from the Old Granary (Mauthalle) at Hallplatz, two blocks up from the Frauentor TI (€17, buy ticket on bus or at TI, 2.5 hours, in German and English, tel. 0911/202-290, www.neukam.de).

NÜRNBERG

Tourist Train

A goofy little tourist train makes the rounds in the Old Town (€7, 40 minutes, live narration in German only, written information in English, schedule posted at fountain, leaves Hauptmarkt April-Oct about hourly 10:30-16:00, March and Nov weekends only, no trips Dec-Feb, www.nuernberg-tourist.de).

Private Guides

For a good and charming local guide, call **Doris Ritter** (€135/3 hours, tel. 0911/518-1719, mobile 0176-2421-5863, ritter.doris@t-online.de). The **Geschichte für Alle** ("History for All") association can set you up with good private guides who are enthusiastic about the town's history (office open Mon-Thu 9:00-12:30 & 14:00-17:00, Fri 9:00-14:00, closed Sat-Sun; tel. 0911/307-360, www.geschichte-fuer-alle.de, info@geschichte-fuer-alle.de). Guides can also be booked through the TI (tel. 0911/233-6123, fuehrung@ctz-nuernberg.de).

Nürnberg Old Town Walk

Many of Nürnberg's top sights are conveniently clustered along a straight-line thoroughfare connecting the train station (Hauptbahnhof) with the main market square (Hauptmarkt) and the Imperial Castle (Kaiserburg). For a good orientation, take the following self-guided stroll, worth ▲▲. Plan on an hour, not including stops.

• *Begin at the Frauentor (where you emerge from the Hauptbahnhof underpass). Review the lay of the land on the 10-foot-tall city map posted in front of the tunnel (find the four towers). This walk will take you from the red dot at the bottom to the* Burg *(castle) at the top.*

Frauentor

This tower guards one of the four medieval entrances to Nürnberg's Old Town. Of the three miles of wall that once surrounded the city, 90 percent survives. The sandstone was quarried locally, and you can still see the little dimples made by the construction tongs as they hoisted the stones into place. Many Central European cities (such as Vienna) tore down their walls to make way for expansion in the 1800s, and Nürnberg nearly did the same. Now the city is glad it didn't: It's better for tourism.

• *Between the walls just next to the gate, you'll see the entrance to the...*

Craftsmen's Courtyard (Handwerkerhof)

This hokey collection of half-timbered houses was built in 1971 to celebrate craftsmanship and to honor the 500th birthday of Nürnberg's favorite son, Albrecht Dürer. Nürnberg didn't have abundant

natural resources or a navigable waterway, so its citizens made their living through trade and crafts (such as making scientific instruments, weapons, and armor). Dürer, arguably Germany's best painter, was considered the ultimate craftsman.

While a bit kitschy, this courtyard—originally a holding zone for carriages waiting to enter the "free imperial city"—is good for picking up a medieval vibe as you enter the Old Town. It's packed with replicas of medieval shops, where artisans actually make—and, of course, sell—leather, pottery, and brass goods. In the Middle Ages, this area between the walls was not a medieval mall but a *Passkontrolle*—a customs and security checkpoint zone where all visitors had to register before they could enter the town.

At the back of the courtyard, step through the old gate and out onto a bridge over what was the moat. The bridge marks one of four entries into the medieval town. Admire the double eagle over the entry—a reminder to all who approached that this was a free city under the direct control of the Habsburgs, who were the Holy Roman Emperors. Look over at the mighty round Frauentor tower. It was originally square, but was made round after the development of better cannons (so balls would glance off rather than hit it head-on). Imagine cannons lined up under the eaves of the tower, set to defend the city. When local kids look at the mighty train station (across the street), they remember that the first train in Germany choo-chooed from Nürnberg in 1835.

• *When you're finished poking around the courtyard, head into town (with the train station at your back) on...*

Königstrasse

Though it had always been one of the four primary entrances to Nürnberg, this street became the city's main drag only after the train station was built in the early 20th century. It's lined with key sights, several recommended hotels and restaurants, and some wonderful Gothic and Neo-Gothic architecture.

Nürnberg hit its peak in the 14th century. In 1356 Emperor Charles IV issued a decree from Nürnberg called the Golden Bull, which regularized many aspects of imperial government. From then on, throughout the Middle Ages, German emperors were elected in Frankfurt, crowned in Aachen, and were supposed to hold their first Imperial Diet (a gathering of German nobles and VIPs) right here in Nürnberg, though not all bothered to follow through on such democratic and inclusive notions.

Nürnberg's low point came during World War II. By the end

of the war, 90 percent of the Old Town was destroyed. Damaged buildings were repaired in the original Gothic style. But some structures were beyond repair. Instead of replicating these exactly as they had been, or replacing them with modern-style buildings, postwar Nürnberg architects compromised. Look 50 yards down the street to #71. This is a good example of the city's "traditional modern" ethic of rebuilding in a modern style while preserving the medieval city's footprint and using traditional building materials (such as native sandstone). The blemishes on the older sandstone buildings all around are patched bullet scars from 1945.

Ahead, on the left, is the small **Clara Church** (Klarakirche). Step inside—first into a candlelit spiritual decompression chamber, and then into the modern and peaceful nave. The rear door leads to the old cloister area—a tranquil oasis and another good example of how the city retooled with respect to history as it rebuilt. In the Middle Ages, Nürnberg had nine monasteries like this one. When the Reformation hit, Nürnberg turned Lutheran, and most of its monasteries were converted into practical municipal buildings such as hospitals and homes for the poor. As the monasteries fell, so did Nürnberg's importance: The city was now Lutheran, but the emperors were still Catholic. They moved the increasingly frequent Imperial Diet meetings—once Nürnberg's claim to fame—to more Catholic-friendly Regensburg. (Today, this church is an "ecumenical free church"—meaning it's neither Lutheran nor Catholic and welcomes worshippers of all stripes.)

Across the way, above the recommended Istanbul Restaurant, look for Mary on the second-story corner. Statues like this grace houses all over Nürnberg.

• *Continue down Königstrasse to Hallplatz, where the pedestrian stretch begins, and stop at the metal arch on the left. This is the...*

Monument to German WWII Refugees

This minimalist metal doorway remembers the German refugees of World War II and the hospitality of the Bavarians who took them in. Walk through the doorway and find a metal plaque in the pavement 30 steps beyond. It lists regions to the east once populated by Germans. In the years after the war, nearly a third of Bavaria's population was made up of German citizens who had fled west—or who'd been expelled from lands lost in the east. As a new generation of Germans comes into its own, memorials like this reflect a delicate challenge: to remember those who suffered in the war without forgetting that Germany was the aggressor.

• *If you want to visit the excellent Germanic National Museum (described on page 574) now, detour left at Hallplatz and walk 200 yards. Otherwise, continue down the main drag and check out the...*

Old Granary (Mauthalle)

Medieval Nürnberg had 11 of these huge granaries to ensure that residents would have enough food in case of famine or siege. The grain was stored up above in the attic (behind all those little dormer windows, which provided ventilation). Today, the cellar is home to a lively beer hall, Barfüsser. There are better places to eat in town, but pop in for a look or a drink.

Continue down pedestrian-only Königstrasse. Check out the Brezen Kolb stand (in the tiny red box), which sells pretzels local-style: as sandwiches with butter and cold cuts—never with mustard.

Look ahead beyond the big church to notice another fine example of "traditional modern" architecture, and feel the energy of this healthy urban center. This drag used to have more cars and trams than any other street in town. But when the U-Bahn came in the 1970s, this part of the street became traffic-free.

• *After another two blocks, you'll see...*

▲▲St. Lawrence Church (Lorenzkirche)

This once-Catholic, now-Protestant church is a massive house of worship. It was never a cathedral because Nürnberg never had a bishop (a fact locals were very proud of—a bishop would have threatened their prized independence). The name Königstrasse ("King's Street")—where you've been walking—is a misnomer. When royals processed into town, they actually preferred to come through the west gate, so they could approach its magnificent facade head-on.

Cost and Hours: €1 donation requested, Mon-Sat 9:00-17:00, Sun 12:00-16:00, www.lorenzkirche.de.

➲ **Self-Guided Tour:** Stand in front of St. Lawrence's west portal, its **main door.** Flip around and imagine the Holy Roman Emperor parading—right past Starbucks—toward this magnificent Oz-like church.

Study the 260-foot-tall **facade** (completed c. 1360). Adam and Eve flank the doors (looking for a sweater). In the first row above the left door, are two scenes: an intimate take on Jesus' birth on top, and the visit from the Magi on the bottom (with the Star of Bethlehem shining from above). Over the right door are the slaughter of the innocents (with a baby skewered by a Roman sword—classic medieval subtlety), and below that the presentation of Jesus in the temple and the flight to Egypt. Above those scenes is the Passion story (from left to right: trial, scourging, carrying the cross, Crucifixion, deposition, entombment, Resurrection, and, above that row, people rising from their graves). In the next row up, the saved (Peter—with his huge key—and company) stand on the left, while the sorry chain gang of the damned (including some kings and bishops) is shuttled off literally into the jaws of hell on the right. Above it all stands the triumphant resurrected Christ, with the sun and moon at his feet, flanked by angels tooting horns to announce Judgment Day.

• Step inside (enter around right side).

The **interior** wasn't completely furnished until more than a century after the church was built—just in time for the Reformation (so the Catholic decor adorned a now-Lutheran church). Most of the decorations inside were donated by wealthy Nürnbergers trying to cut down on their time in purgatory. Through the centuries, this art survived three separate threats: the iconoclasm of the Reformation, the whitewashing of the Baroque age, and the bombing of World War II. While Nürnberg was the first "free imperial city" to break with the Catholic Church and become Lutheran, locals didn't go wild (like Swiss Protestants did) in tearing down the rich, Mary-oriented decor of their fine churches. Luther (who, despite some flaws, was still very cool for his time) told the iconoclasts, "Tear the idols out of your heart, and you'll understand that these statues are only pieces of wood."

Suspended over the altar, the sculptural *Annunciation* is by a Nürnberg citizen and one of Central Europe's best woodcarvers, Veit Stoss. Carved in 1517, it shows the angel Gabriel telling Mary that she'll be giving birth to the Messiah. Startled, she drops her prayer book. This is quite Catholic (notice the rosary frame with beads, and a circle of roses—one for each Hail Mary, and with a medallion depicting the "Joys of Mary"). The dove sits on Mary's head, and God the Father—looking as powerful as a Holy Roman Emperor—looks down. The figures are carved from the wood of linden trees. The piece survived the Reformation covered in a sack, revealed only on special occasions. Around back, enjoy more details—Mary's cascading hair, and the sun and the moon. Nearby, the altar painting at the very front of the church (behind the altar) shows the city of Nürnberg in 1483 (before the city's square towers were made round).

To the left of the altar, the frilly **tabernacle** tower is the "house of sacraments" that stored the consecrated Communion wafer. After the Mass, leftovers needed a worthy—even heavenly—home, and this was it. The cupboard behind the gold grate was the ap-

propriate receptacle for what Catholics considered literally "the body of Christ." The theme of the carving is the Passion. The scenes ascend in chronological order: Last Supper, Judas' kiss, arrest, Crucifixion, and so on. Everything is carved of stone except for the risen Christ (way up high). He was living, and so was this—it's made of wood.

The man holding the tabernacle on his shoulders is the artist who created it, Adam Kraft (with his curly black beard, chisel in hand). In the Middle Ages, artists were faceless artisans, no more important than a blacksmith or a stonemason. But in the 1490s, when this was made, the Renaissance was in the air, and artists like Kraft began putting themselves into their works. Kraft's contemporary, the painter Albrecht Dürer, actually signed his works—an incredible act in Germany at that time (for more on Dürer, see page 573). In anticipation of the Allied bombs of World War II, this precious work was encased in protective concrete, except for the top 22 feet—which was the only part destroyed when the church was hit.

Adam Kraft is looking up at a **plaque** honoring American philanthropist brothers Samuel and Rush Kress, who donated nearly a million Deutschmarks in 1950 to help rebuild the church. The plaque is in English, but it's hard to read, as it's written in an old-style black-letter font. Though the church was devastated by WWII bombs, everything movable had been hidden away in bunkers right here in Nürnberg (which we'll pass later), including the stained glass you see today.

• *Wander slowly to the rear of the church.*

As you walk, notice the many **side chapels,** each a private chapel for a leading Nürnberg family. Also note the dozen or so wooden boxes with finely carved symbols representing various trades and craft guilds. After Mass, these were manned by a leading master of that trade who shamed parishioners into donating to needy widows and others in his organization. In a society without welfare, this was a way to cope. At the rear of the church, old **photos** show WWII destruction and reconstruction scenes.

• *Head back outside.*

Near St. Lawrence Church: Tower House and Fountain

As you exit the church, look for the castle-like building on the corner across from the church facade. This is the only remaining **tower house** in Nürnberg. When it was built, in 1200, there was no city wall, and locals had to defend their own homes. It's basically a one-family castle. The ornate church-like structure protruding halfway up the wall is a reminder that while rich families could afford their own chapel, not even the very wealthy could live above God. Their personal chapels had to be "outside" the house. The house also sports a sundial. While it only bothers to show daylight hours, it still works (as long as you adjust for the fact that they didn't have daylight saving time back then).

• *Walk downhill, toward the river.*

American moralists might shield their eyes from the kinky 16th-century **Fountain of the Seven Virtues** (Tugendbrunnen). Otherwise, play a game: Circle the sprightly fountain and try to identify the classic virtues by the symbolism: justice (on top), faith, love, hope (anchor), courage (lion), moderation, patience. Are any birds sipping? Notice that there's no religious symbolism here, as this fountain was made during the Renaissance, when artists celebrated secular values.

• *Continue down the street toward the river. Caution: On your left, you'll pass **Kaiserstrasse**—the most expensive shopping street in town (with a little shop filled with insanely expensive Steiff teddy bears). When you get to the bridge, look to the right to see the...*

Holy Ghost Hospital (Heilig-Geist-Spital)

This river-spanning hospital was donated to Nürnberg in the 14th century by the city's richest resident, eager to do his part to help the poor—and hopefully skip purgatory altogether. (A modern statue of this donor hangs out on the second-story corner of the Spital Apotheke, the first building after the bridge.) He funded this very scenic hospital to care for ill, disabled, and elderly Nürnbergers. The wing over the river dates from the 16th century. The dove beneath the middle window under the turret represents the Holy Ghost, the hospital's namesake.

Cross to the other side of the bridge, and look at the next bridge over (the Fleischbrücke—**"Meat Bridge"**). This is the narrowest point of the river. When it was built in 1596, this was considered the most high-tech bridge in Central Europe, an engineering feat inspired by Venice's single-span Rialto Bridge. Flooding along the river was a big concern until a fix was constructed after World War II.

Note that there are a few handy lunch spots in the arcade between the two bridges (see "Eating in Nürnberg," later). The arrival of a big Starbucks, just beyond the Meat Bridge, is credited with cleaning up what had been a dodgy part of the riverbank. (In this land of cake-and-coffee, the Dunkin' Donuts and Starbucks chains—wildly popular among younger Germans—are shaking up tradition.)

Continue across the bridge and study the monument depicting characters from a 15th-century satire called *The Ship of Fools (Das Narrenschiff)*. It's adapted to follies that plague modern society: violence, technology, and apathy. Hey, how about the quiet, people-friendly ambience created by making this big city traffic-free in the center? Do a slow 360-degree spin and imagine this back home.

• *Now enter the...*

▲▲Hauptmarkt (Main Market Square)

When Nürnberg began booming in the 13th century, it consisted of two distinct walled towns separated by the river. As the towns

grew, they merged and the middle wall came down. This square, built by Holy Roman Emperor Charles IV, became the center of the newly united city. Though Charles is more often associated with Prague (he's the namesake for the Charles Bridge and Charles University), he also loved Nürnberg—and visited 60 times during his reign.

The **Frauenkirche** church on the square is located on the site of a former synagogue (inside, there's a Star of David on the floor). When Nürnberg's towns were separate, Jewish residents were required to live in this swampy area close to the river and outside the walls. When the towns merged and the land occupied by the Jewish quarter became valuable, Charles IV allowed his subjects to force out the Jews. Six hundred were killed in the process—a somber reminder that anti-Semitism predated the Nazis. Charles IV, the most powerful man in Europe in his time, oversees the square

from a perch high on the church facade. He's waiting for noon, when the electors dance around him.

Year-round, the Hauptmarkt is lively with fruit, flower, and souvenir stands. For a few weeks before Christmas, it hosts Germany's largest **Christmas market**.

Walk across the square to the pointy gold **Beautiful Fountain** (Schöner Brunnen). Medieval tanneries, slaughterhouses, and the hospital you just saw dumped their by-products into the river. So this fountain brought clean drinking water into the square. Of course, it's packed with allegorical meaning. Step up to the iron railing. The outermost figures ringing the bottom represent the earthly arts (such as philosophy, music, and astronomy). On the pillars sitting behind each of these characters are the four church fathers and the four evangelists, showing that religion is higher than the arts. On the column itself, the lowest figures are the seven electors of the Holy Roman Emperor and nine heroes: three Christian (including King Arthur and Charlemagne); three Jewish (such as King David); and three heathen (such as Julius Caesar). At the very top are eight prophets, hovering above—but granting legitimacy to—worldly power. On the side of the fountain facing the McDonald's, you'll probably see tourists fussing over a gold ring. If you believe in such silly tour-guide tales, spinning this ring three times brings good luck...OK, go ahead and spin it.

Sausage connoisseurs will want to take a short side-trip from here: Head a block down Tuchgasse (directly opposite the church) to find the **Schwarz Bakery** at #2, a paradise for lovers of sausage and dark bread (i.e., Nürnbergers). Step in and inhale. This old-school place, still family-run, selects the best wursts and breads from producers in the surrounding countryside, and brings the bounty into the city. They can make the German sandwich of your dreams. When Franconians travel, what they miss most is their homeland's dark bread and variety of high-quality sausages.

• *Return to the fountain on the Hauptmarkt. (Note that bus #36, which goes directly to the Nazi Documentation Center, departs from a stop just around the corner.) Now climb uphill, heading for the Imperial Castle. After a block, you'll pass **Bratwursthäusle** (on the left), a popular sausage restaurant (see "Eating in Nürnberg," later). For another local taste treat—my favorite in town—step inside, pay €2.50 at the half-door, take your receipt to the beechwood grill, and trade it for three sausages in a bun.*

*Hiking farther uphill, you'll pass **St. Sebald** (Sebaldkirche), Nürnberg's second great Gothic church. About 100 yards farther up the hill, on the left, you'll see the...*

City Museum (Stadtmuseum Fembohaus)

This fine museum, packed with historic artifacts, fills a former merchant's house dating from the late Renaissance. If you decide to visit, be sure to pick up the included headphones as you enter to enjoy the enlightening videos. A 50-minute slideshow gives a fun and thoughtful overview of the city, its history, and its great sights (ground-floor theater, on the hour). On the first floor up, the photographs of pre- and postwar Nürnberg and short WWII film clips are interesting. The museum also has several town models on display, including a huge one on the top floor.

Cost and Hours: €5, Tue-Fri 10:00-17:00, Sat-Sun 10:00-18:00, closed Mon, Burgstrasse 15, tel. 0911/231-2595, www.museen.nuernberg.de.

• *Now hike the rest of the way up to the Imperial Castle. The cobbled path forks at the castle's base. The right fork leads to the castle garden and youth hostel. The left fork leads to the castle courtyard (see big, round tower high above). For now, take the left fork and visit the...*

▲Imperial Castle (Kaiserburg)

In the Middle Ages, Holy Roman Emperors stayed here when they were in town, and the imperial regalia, including the imperial cross, imperial sword, and crown, were stored here from 1424 until 1796. While this huge complex has 45 buildings, only a few are open to the public. The part on the right, which housed the stables and stockpiles of grain, is now a youth hostel.

Cost and Hours: €5.50 for castle only, €3.50 for Deep Well and Sinwell Tower, €7 combo-ticket; covered by Nürnberg Card; €2 audioguide has more background than you likely want—most displays have sufficient English explanations, tickets sold in office at top end of courtyard; daily April-Sept 9:00-18:00, Oct-March 10:00-16:00; tel. 0911/244-6590, www.kaiserburg-nuernberg.de.

Visiting the Castle: Your visit is a no-way-to-get-lost, one-way route—just follow the *Rundgang* signs.

The **Lower Hall** is empty of furniture because, in the 12th century, the imperial court was mobile. Royal roadies would arrive and set things up before the emperor got there. The **Romanesque church** has a triple-decker design: lower nobility on the lower floor, upper nobility above that, and the emperor worshipping from the topmost balcony.

The **Upper Hall** is most interesting, with a thorough explanation and artifacts that show what the heck the Holy Roman Empire actually was. Then comes a series of creaky-floored **former living quarters,** with painted ceilings (many dismantled and stored in bunkers during the war—they're that precious), and a copy of the imperial crown (the original is in Vienna). The final exhibit is on **old weapons.**

After leaving the main exhibit area you can visit a few more parts of the castle; the most interesting are the castle well and gardens (separate or combo-ticket required for Deep Well and Sinwell Tower; see earlier).

The **Deep Well** is indeed deep—165 feet. Visits are simple, fun, and possible only accompanied by a guide (10-minute tours leave on the hour and half-hour). You'll see water poured way, waaay down—into an incredible hole dug in the 14th century. Then the guide lowers a small candle until it almost disappears into the water table. A climb up the **Sinwell Tower** offers only a higher city view and lots of exercise.

When you're finished, walk out around the round tower to enjoy a commanding **city view** from the rampart just behind it. Then curve downhill and through a gate onto the back side of the castle, where you'll find the fine **garden** *(Burggarten)*. Wrapped around the back of the castle, it offers great views of the town's 16th-century fortifications and former moat. From here, simply walk counterclockwise through the park-like ramparts (completely circling the castle).

• *When you reach an arch on the left, exit the gardens. On the right and directly below you, about a block away, is a lively cobbled square called...*

Tiergärtnertorplatz

Near the top of the square, inspect the giant rabbit. While it looks like roadkill with mice gnawing at it, it's actually a modern interpretation of *The Hare,* one of the best-known paintings by medieval Nürnberg artist Albrecht Dürer. (The original painting is in Vienna.)

• *About 20 yards beyond the well on the square, at Obere Schmiedgasse 52, is the...*

▲▲Historic Art Bunker

Behind these doors, a series of cellars are buried deep inside the rock of Castle Hill. This is where precious artworks were carefully safeguarded from the WWII air raids that devastated the city. Unfortunately, the only way to visit the bunker is with a once-daily tour (see "Tours in Nürnberg," earlier).

Nürnberg was bombed relatively late in the war, which allowed its citizens time (and experience gained from already-bombed cities to the north) to prepare for the aerial attack they knew would be coming. While many other cities sent their most important works away from the urban centers (obvious targets), Nürnberg was able to safely shelter everything right here. The art wasn't just stashed in the bunker, but carefully battened up inside wooden crates and padded with sandbags, safeguarded in a climate-controlled environment behind layer upon layer of thick fireproof doors.

Rich in art, Nürnberg had long been known as the "treasure chest of the German Empire." The pieces stored here included regalia of the Holy Roman Empire and the city's own treasures, evacuated from nearby buildings (such as the tabernacle in St. Lawrence Church, as well as all of that church's stained glass). Other pieces had been plundered by the Nazis from conquered lands, such as the Veit Stoss Altar from Kraków, Poland (later recovered by the "Monuments Men," as described in Robert Edsel's 2009 book and the 2014 movie based on it).

• *Turning back to the rabbit statue on the square, notice that it faces a half-timbered building (at the square's bottom). That's the...*

▲Albrecht Dürer House (Albrecht-Dürer-Haus)

Nürnberg's most famous resident lived in this house for the last 20 years of his life. Albrecht Dürer (1471-1528), a contemporary of Michelangelo, studied in Venice and brought the Renaissance to stodgy medieval Germany. He did things that were unthinkable to other northern European artists of his time—such as signing his works, and painting things like rabbits simply for study (not on commission).

Nothing in the museum is original (all the paintings are replicas—the only Dürer originals in Nürnberg are in the Germanic National Museum, described next). But the museum does a fine job of capturing the way Dürer actually lived, and it includes a replica of the workshop, with a working printing press, where he painted and printed his woodcuts. Another room is a gallery with copies of Dürer's most famous paintings and woodcuts.

Cost and Hours: €5, covered by discount day pass, includes Agnes (Mrs. Dürer)-led audioguide, Mon-Wed and Fri 10:00-17:00, Thu 10:00-20:00, Sat-Sun 10:00-18:00, closed Mon Oct-June, Albrecht-Dürer-Strasse 39, tel. 0911/231-2568, www.museums.nuremberg.de.

• *You've walked from the southern gate of Nürnberg to the northern gate, and your tour is over. If heading from here to the Nazi sites, catch bus #36 (from its stop around the corner from the fountain on the Hauptmarkt) or hop into a taxi.*

Or, for more sightseeing on your way back to the Frauentor, four more museums are listed in the next section.

More Sights in Nürnberg

IN AND NEAR THE OLD TOWN
▲▲▲Germanic National Museum (Germanisches Nationalmuseum)

This sprawling, sweeping museum is dedicated to the cultural history of the German-speaking world. It's gorgeously presented,

nicely lit, and well-described by its audioguide. For German history buffs, this museum alone makes a visit to Nürnberg worthwhile. It occupies an interconnected maze of buildings, old and new, in the southern part of the Old Town, near the station and recommended hotels. Approaching the museum along Kartäusergasse, you'll walk along the "Way of Human Rights." Designed by an Israeli artist, its pillars trumpet each of the provisions of the United Nations' Universal Declaration of Human Rights.

Cost and Hours: €8, free Wed after 18:00, worthwhile audioguide-€2; open Tue-Sun 10:00-18:00, Wed until 21:00, closed Mon; two blocks west of Königstrasse at Kartäusergasse 1, enter on far side of building, tel. 0911/13310, www.gnm.de.

Eating: The cafeteria, while pricey, is top quality, with elegant and artfully presented dishes.

Visiting the Museum: Before leaving the ticket desk, pick up the English floor plan/brochure, and use it to pick out a few things you're particularly interested in.

The **entry hall** is dominated by a wall displaying street signs from East Germany—complete with a little politically motivated spray paint—dating from the time when the Soviets had renamed the main drag in many towns *Strasse der Befreiung* ("Street of the Liberation" from the Nazis and capitalism).

The museum's star attraction is its **German art collection** (in the Renaissance/Baroque exhibit just upstairs from the entrance hall). It includes works by Dürer (the only originals in town), Cranach, and Tilman Riemenschneider.

Other "must-sees" include the oldest surviving globe in the world, crafted by Nürnberg's own Martin Behaim (since it dates from 1492, the Americas are conspicuously missing), and the delicate wooden *Nürnberg Madonna* (1515). This intimate, anonymous carving of the favorite hometown girl was the symbol of the city during the 19th-century Romantic Age. For those interested in the Reformation, there's a wonderful Martin Luther section.

Of Nürnberg's 200 churches, only one escaped the WWII bombs. The historic core of the museum building, an old monastery, is filled with original, surviving **statues** from the city's bombed-out churches and fountains.

The rest of this huge museum covers a vast spectrum of German culture, from fine arts to prehistory to science to musical instruments, plus regular temporary exhibits.

▲German Railway Museum (DB Museum)

Germany's first railway was built in Nürnberg in 1835, and the Deutsche Bahn (German Railway) runs a huge museum just outside the Old Town telling the story of German trains from 1835 to 1989. The "Serving Dictatorship" exhibit explains the role of the train system during the Nazi regime. A big, hands-on kids' section is full of games and model railroads, while the petting zoo of real engines and carriages appeals to all ages.

Cost and Hours: €5, €4 with valid train or city transit ticket, free with valid rail pass; Tue-Fri 9:00-17:00, Sat-Sun 10:00-18:00, closed Mon; Lessingstrasse 6—from Germanic National Museum take the footbridge over the old moat, cross the ring road, and walk a block down Lessingstrasse; tel. 0180-444-2233, www. dbmuseum.de. Pick up the free English booklet as you enter, and consider getting the English audioguide (€1).

Neues Museum

Nürnberg's "new museum" of contemporary art fills a striking modern building right by the town wall (near the train station), with two quiet, bright, and air-conditioned floors of wacky, stimulating, abstract installations and artwork.

Cost and Hours: €4, €1 on Sun; open Tue-Sun 10:00-18:00, Thu until 20:00, closed Mon; behind recommended Hotel Victoria on Klarissenplatz, tel. 0911/240-2069, www.nmn.de.

Toy Museum (Spielzeugmuseum)

This museum's chronological/thematic display makes for a breezy history lesson, starting from the wooden toys on the ground floor that exemplify German woodworking traditions, culminating with the corporate-branded toys three floors up (the entire top floor is a play zone). For many, the highlight is the miniature replica of the Omaha train station (third floor up).

Cost and Hours: €5 or covered by discount day pass, children €0.50, Tue-Fri 10:00-17:00, Sat-Sun 10:00-18:00, closed Mon, no photos, Karlstrasse 13-15, near Albrecht Dürer House, tel. 0911/231-3164, www.museen.nuernberg.de. Get an English audioguide (€1), or consider the good little €1.50 booklet.

NAZI SITES

Though the city tries to present itself as the "City of Human Rights," its reputation as Hitler's favorite place for a really big party is hard to shake. To understand Nürnberg's place in the Nazi era, visit Hitler's vast Nazi Party Rally Grounds (Reichsparteitagsgelände) and the excellent museum—the Nazi Documentation Center—set amid the mute remains of the Third Reich.

The courtroom where the Nürnberg Trials were held is across town from the Documentation Center and Rally Grounds, and has much less to offer visitors.

Planning Your Time: With half a day, spend two hours in the museum, peek into the courtyard of the Congress Hall, and walk to Zeppelin Field and back. History buffs can easily spend an entire day here. The map in this book is enough to guide you around the site, but you can buy a more detailed map and guide from the museum counter for €3. Also consider the small English-language book (€7). For lunch there's a disappointing café in the museum and the excellent Guttmann's beer garden at the lake (midway between the museum and the Zeppelin Field).

If you opt to also visit the courtroom and its exhibit, allow two hours for your visit, including travel time from the train station.

Getting to the Nazi Documentation Center and Rally Grounds: The sprawling complex is wrapped around a pond called Dutzendteich, southeast of the Old Town. Take tram #9, which leaves from the front of the Postbank Center at the train station (Hauptbahnhof) every 10 minutes (direction: Doku-Zentrum, 10-minute trip). From the Hauptmarkt (around the corner from the fountain, on Waaggasse) or Rathaus (City Hall), you can also hop on bus #36, which ends at the Doku-Zentrum stop. Both options go about every 10 minutes and cost the same (€2.50 one-way; it's better to purchase the €5.30 day ticket). Stepping off either the tram or bus, you'll see the Documentation Center.

▲▲▲Nazi Documentation Center (Dokumentationszentrum)

Visitors to Europe's Nazi and Holocaust sites inevitably ask the same question: How could this happen? This superb museum does its best to provide an answer. It meticulously traces the evolution of the National Socialist (Nazi) movement, focusing on how it both energized and terrified the German people (the exhibit's title is "Fascination and Terror"). Special attention is paid to Nürnberg's role in the Nazi movement, including the construction and use of the Rally

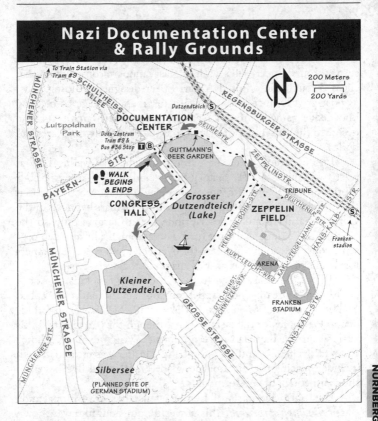

Nazi Documentation Center & Rally Grounds

Grounds, where Hitler's largest demonstrations took place. This is not a WWII or Holocaust museum; those events are almost an afterthought. Instead, the center frankly analyzes the Nazi phenomenon, to understand how it happened—and to prevent it from happening again.

Cost and Hours: €5 or covered by discount day pass, includes essential audioguide, Mon-Fri 9:00-18:00, Sat-Sun 10:00-18:00, last entry at 17:00, Bayernstrasse 110, tel. 0911/231-7538, www.museen.nuernberg.de.

Visiting the Documentation Center: The museum is housed in one small wing of Hitler's cavernous, unfinished Congress Hall—the largest surviving example of Nazi architecture. The building was planned to host the mammoth annual Nazi Party gatherings. Today, it has been symbolically cut

NÜRNBERG

open by its modern entryway—exposing the guts and brains of the Nazi movement.

The museum's purpose-built structure is sometimes called "a spear through Speer"—it's a jolt of glassy modern construction that slices through the original Albert Speer-designed building. (Just as post-WWII doctors didn't want to take advantage of medical knowledge gained through Nazi torture, modern architects who designed the museum didn't want to utilize anything the Nazis had built.)

Inside the museum, the exhibit is a one-way walk; allow at least two hours. WWII history buffs should allow an extra hour for the various 10-minute videos that play continuously throughout the exhibit, offering excellent insights into the mass hypnosis of the German nation. Exhibit descriptions are in German only, so the English audioguide is a must (turns on automatically at video presentations; dial room numbers for overviews and specific numbers for details of displays—if rushed, listen to the overviews only).

The introductory video has you following two kids on skateboards on a dreamy now-and-then tour of the entire complex. You'll see copies of *Mein Kampf* (the sale of which has been forbidden in Germany for the last 70 years, though the ban may end this year, when the Bavarian government's copyright expires). Photos show Hitler-mania and how the cult of Hitler was created, which included placing the dictator alongside Goethe and Beethoven in the pantheon of great Germans.

You'll also see parts of Leni Riefenstahl's 1934 propaganda classic *Triumph of the Will*. This powerful four-hour film was shown in all German schools and theaters, bringing a visual celebration of the power of the Nazi state to every person in Germany.

At the end, you'll sit in a small theater to watch footage of the Nürnberg Trials. The last stop (before the long ramp back to the start) is a catwalk giving you a look into the core of the unfinished Congress Hall (an artist's sketch of the hall filled with 50,000 cheering Nazis is on a nearby wall; for more on the Congress Hall, see the listing, later).

In addition to housing a museum, the Documentation Center has an important function in a society determined to learn from the horrible deeds of its dark past. For example, students at police and military academies are required to attend special programs taught in classrooms right on this site.

▲Rally Grounds (Reichsparteitagsgelände)

The Rally Grounds occupy four square miles behind the museum. Albert Speer, Hitler's favorite architect, designed this immense complex of buildings for the Nazi rallies. Not many of Hitler's ambitious plans were completed, but you can visit the courtyard of the Congress Hall, Zeppelin Field (where Hitler addressed his followers), and a few other remains. The easiest way to see them is to follow the circular route around the lake that's shown in the map on page 577 and on the museum's free bilingual area plan *(Geländeplan)*. The numbers on the plan correspond to the information pillars that you'll find on-site (this information also available at www.kubiss.de).

Figure an hour round-trip from the Documentation Center for the full circuit. If you have less time, just look into the courtyard of the Congress Hall from the perch at the end of your museum visit and then walk the short way around the lake directly to the Zeppelin Field and back. If you're really short on time, skip this walk, as you'll get the best sense of the Rally Grounds and how they were used simply from the videos and exhibits inside the Documentation Center.

I've listed the main sites here in the order you reach them while circling the lake.

Congress Hall (Kongresshalle)

This huge building—big enough for an audience of 50,000—was originally intended to be topped with a roof and skylight. The Nazi Documentation Center occupies part of the hall. To see the vast, Colosseum-like courtyard, turn right as you leave the Documentation Center, and walk along the side of the  building. Dip through the archway into the courtyard to appreciate its dimensions. Notice the stacked stones still awaiting further construction, untouched since the 1930s. Part of the hall is now used by the Nürnberg symphony orchestra.

• *Turn around and return to the main path. When you get to the end, turn right again and continue walking with the Congress Hall on your right. Continue past the end of the building, and then turn left (under the* Kommen Sie gut nach Hause *sign) onto the...*

Great Road (Grosse Strasse)

At 200 feet wide, the Great Road was big enough to be used as a runway by the Allies after the war. Now it's a parking lot for trucks serving the nearby conference center. The road points toward Nürnberg's Imperial Castle—Hitler's symbolic connection to the Holy Roman Empire (the First Reich). The lights you see in the distance hover above the Franken Stadium (a 1928 soccer field before Hitler used it for Nazi rallies and, most recently, a host venue of the 2006 World Cup).

Ahead and to the right was to be the site of the **German Sta-**

Nazis in Nürnberg

It's no coincidence that Nürnberg appealed to Hitler. For one thing, it was convenient: Nürnberg is centrally located in Germany, making it a handy meeting point for Nazi supporters. Hitler also had a friend here, Julius Streicher (a.k.a. the "Franconian Führer"), who fanned the flames of Nazism and anti-Semitism through his inflammatory newspaper *Der Stürmer* (*The Storm Trooper*).

But of far greater importance was the fact that Nürnberg was steeped in German history. Long before the rise of Nazism, the city—one-time home of Albrecht Dürer and the Holy Roman Emperor, and packed with buildings in the quintessential German Gothic style—was nicknamed the "most German of German cities." As one of the most important cities of medieval Europe, Nürnberg appealed to Hitler as a way to legitimize his Third Reich by invoking Germany's glorious past. Hitler loved the idea of staging his rallies within sight of the Imperial Castle, a symbol of the "First Reich" (the Holy Roman Empire).

When Hitler took power in 1933, he made Nürnberg the site of his *Reichsparteitage*—**Nazi Party Rallies.** Increasingly elaborate celebrations of Nazi culture, ideology, and power took place here annually for the next six years. The chilling images from Leni Riefenstahl's documentary *Triumph of the Will* were filmed at the 1934 rallies and then shown in every theater and schoolroom in the country. At the 1935 rallies, the Nazis devised the first laws—which came to be known as the **Nürnberg Laws**—that legally defined Jews as second-class citizens.

Hitler and his favorite architect, Albert Speer, designed staggeringly massive buildings (such as a stadium seating 400,000 spectators) to host the proceedings. Only a few of the plans were completed before World War II broke out in 1939, forcing the construction budget to be reassigned to the war effort. Today, it's possible to walk around the still-unfinished remains of Hitler's megalomaniacal super-structures. The Rally Grounds were the ultimate example of Hitler's preferred architecture style: stark, huge, and Neoclassical. (Historians are ambivalent about using the term "Nazi architecture," as so much of it was stolen from other styles and then simply enlarged. For example, Hitler was enamored by the Roman Colosseum. Inspired by that, he had his Congress Hall built double the scale.)

As the war drew to a close, the world puzzled over what to do with the Nazi officers who had overseen some of the most gruesome atrocities in the history of humankind. It was finally decided that they should be tried as war criminals by an international tribunal (spearheaded by the United States and based on the Anglo-American code of law). These trials took place right here, in the **Nürnberg Trials Courtroom.** The Nürnberg Trials—the first-ever international war-crimes tribunal—brought about a new concept of international law, which continues today in The Hague, Netherlands.

dium (Deutsches Stadion)—the biggest in the world (with 400,000 seats). They got as far as digging a foundation before funding was redirected to the war effort. Today, the site is a park surrounding the big lake, Silbersee—which filled the hole for the never-built stadium's foundation.

• *From here, you can detour across the road to an information sign about the stadium. Otherwise, follow the Dutzendteich lakeshore to the left for about 15 minutes until you hit a parking lot. To your right is the huge...*

Zeppelin Field (Zeppelinwiese)

This was the site of the Nazis' biggest rallies, including those (in)famously filmed by Leni Riefenstahl. You can climb up on the grandstand and stand on the platform in front of the Zeppelin Tribune, where Hitler stood to survey the masses (up to 150,000 people at a time). The Tribune is based on the design of the ancient Greek Pergamon Altar (now in Berlin's Pergamon Museum); it was originally topped by a towering swastika,

which was blown up by the Allies at the end of the war. Warning: Clowning around on the speaking platform with any Nazi gestures is illegal and taken seriously by the police.

• *From Zeppelin Field, continue the rest of the way around the lake, past Guttmann's beer garden (a good lunch option), and back to the Documentation Center (and the bus and tram stop).*

Nürnberg Trials Courtroom and Museum (Memorium Nürnberger Prozesse)

Across town from the Documentation Center and Rally Grounds is the courtroom where the Nürnberg Trials were held.

In 1945, in Room 600 of Nürnberg's Palace of Justice, 21 Nazi war criminals stood trial before an international tribunal of judges appointed by the four victorious countries. It was during these trials that the world learned of the full scale of the Holocaust, and heard first-hand accounts from victims and perpetrators alike. The trials were also legally novel, setting a precedent for international law that has since been followed in a number of post-atrocity tribunals (think South Africa, Rwanda, Bosnia). Legally speaking, before the Nürnberg Trials, there was no such thing as a "crime against humanity."

After a year of trials and deliberations, 12 Nazis were sentenced to death by hanging, 3 were acquitted, and the rest were sent to prison. One of the death sentences was for Hitler's right-hand man, Hermann Göring. He asked to be shot by firing squad—a proper military execution—but his request was denied. Instead, two hours before his scheduled hanging, Göring committed suicide with poison he had smuggled into his cell, infuriating many who thought that this death was too easy for him.

Cost and Hours: €5 or covered by discount day pass, includes audioguide; Wed-Mon 10:00-18:00, closed Tue, last entry at 17:00; tel. 0911/3217-9372, www.memorium-nuremberg.de.

Getting There: The building is a five-stop subway ride from the Hauptbahnhof: Take the U-1 subway line (direction Fürth Hardhöhe) to Bärenschanze, exit the station following signs for *Sielstrasse*, and continue 200 yards along the main street (Fürther Strasse) to the huge court building, turning right at the corner with the tall signs showing the four national flags. It's at Bärenschanzstrasse 72.

Visiting the Courtroom and Museum: There are two parts to the experience here: the courtroom (upstairs from the entrance)

and the museum (farther up on the top floor). You can usually enter the courtroom itself, but as it's still in occasional use, you could find it closed, especially if you come on a weekday. You're pretty much assured of getting to see the courtroom on a Saturday or Sunday. If it's important to you, call the museum (no more than a week in advance) to ask about the court schedule.

Unfortunately, the museum displays are almost all in German, and there's little here in the way of artifacts. The included audioguide gives exact translations of all the printed information, but it's outrageously long-winded.

Sleeping in Nürnberg

Prices spike during major conventions in the spring and fall, and in December—when the Christmas market brings visitors from around the world. Nürnberg gets a lot of business travelers, so some hotels drop their rates on weekends. July and August are generally low season and come with the lowest prices.

Budget travelers beyond traditional backpacker-age should consider private rooms offered by the Five Reasons and A&O hostels, where travelers of any age will feel comfortable. For hotel locations, please see the map on page 559.

Sleep Code

Abbreviations   **(€1 = about $1.40, country code: 49)**
S = Single, **D** = Double/Twin, **T** = Triple, **Q** = Quad, **b** = bathroom, **s** = shower only.
Price Rankings
  $$$ Higher Priced—Most rooms €100 or more.
   $$ Moderately Priced—Most rooms between €70-100.
    $ Lower Priced—Most rooms €70 or less.
Unless otherwise noted, credit cards are accepted, English is spoken, Wi-Fi is generally free, and breakfast is included. Prices change; verify current rates online or by email. For the best prices, always book directly with the hotel.

NEAR THE FRAUENTOR, ON KÖNIGSTRASSE

These hotels clustered along Königstrasse, just inside the Frauentor and the city walls, are convenient to both the train station and city sightseeing. From the station, you can roll your luggage here in five minutes without a single stair.

$$$ Hotel Victoria offers friendly staff and 62 fresh, new-feeling rooms behind its historic 1896 facade just inside the Frauentor. The standard rooms are a better value than the slightly bigger business rooms (standard rooms: Sb-€80-100, Db-€100-120; business rooms-€10 extra, air-con-€30 extra, best to book on website, discounts on slow weekends, fabulous breakfast, elevator, Wi-Fi, parking garage-€12/day, Königstrasse 80, tel. 0911/24050, www. hotelvictoria.de, book@hotelvictoria.de).

$$$ Hotel Drei Raben is an artsy and fun splurge, with a super-stylish lobby, 22 comfortable rooms, a huge breakfast buffet (eggs or cappuccino by request), and lots of elegant and whimsical touches. In this "theme hotel" you might get the Dürer room, the soccer room, the toys room, or even the graffiti room (Sb/Db-€120 or €150 depending on size; spacious suites with freestanding bathtubs: Db-€225; nearby apartment also available, air-con, elevator, guest computer, Wi-Fi, valet parking-€15/day, Königstrasse 63, tel. 0911/274-380, www.hoteldreiraben.de, info@hoteldreiraben. de).

$$$ Gideon Hotel, overlooking the main pedestrian drag, has less personality than the Drei Raben, but plenty of style. Its 27 rooms, many quite spacious, are decked out in a chic black, white, and red decor, and can often be had at a good value. In nice weather, breakfast is served on the lovely rooftop terrace (official rates-€280, Db-€315—but you'll likely pay closer to Sb-€90, Db-€100; air-con, elevator, Wi-Fi, parking-€16/day at Parkhaus Katharinenhof, Königstrasse 45 but enter around the corner on Theatergasse, tel. 0911/660-0970, www.gideonhotels.de, info@gideonhotels.de).

$$ Ibis Altstadt Hotel, sandwiched between a bunch of fast-food joints, offers 61 good-value cookie-cutter rooms in a convenient location (normal rates: Sb-€65-90, Db-€75-100, depending on demand; extra bed-€25-30; €10/person less if you skip breakfast, family deals, air-con, elevator, guest computer, Wi-Fi, parking-€14/day, Königstrasse 74, tel. 0911/232-000, www.ibishotel.com, h1069@accor.com).

NEAR THE FRAUENTOR, ON LUITPOLDSTRASSE

These two affordable, family-run hotels are next door to each other, around the corner from the ones just described, set amidst a harmless sprinkling of casinos, strip clubs, and sex shops. Either hotel will do just fine if you're watching your budget. To avoid street noise, ask for a room on the back side (especially for Friday or Saturday night). The Keiml has nicer rooms, but the Probst has an elevator.

$$ Hotel Garni Probst has been run for nearly 70 years by the hardworking Probst family. They rent 45 decent if dated rooms on floors 2-4 of an older apartment building (Ss-€40-45, Sb-€50-56, Db-€70-75, Tb-€87-93, lower prices generally for summer and on weekends, elevator to third floor, pay Wi-Fi, Luitpoldstrasse 9, tel. 0911/203-433, www.hotel-garni-probst.de, info@hotel-garni-probst.de).

$ Hotel Keiml is run by gracious Frau Keiml, who has been welcoming guests here since 1975. She rents 22 bright and homey rooms up two long flights of stairs (no elevator) in another former apartment building (Sb-€45, Db-€65-70, street-side Tb-€85, these prices with this book and cash in 2015, Wi-Fi, Luitpoldstrasse 7, tel. 0911/226-240, www.hotel-keiml.de, info@hotel-keiml.de).

CLOSER TO THE CASTLE

These accommodations are closer to the castle at the far side of the Old Town. Getting here is an €8 taxi ride or a long hike from the station. You can get partway by taking the U-Bahn (line #1) to Lorenzkirche and exiting toward Kaiserstrasse.

$$ Sorat Hotel Saxx, from its sleek lobby up to its 103 rooms, is professionally run. Most rooms aren't terribly big, but they're stylish, fresh, often well-priced, and in the middle of town, right on the Hauptmarkt (prices vary with demand but usually Sb-€69-79, Db-€88-98, breakfast-€9.50, family rooms, pricier "business suites" are bigger and face the square, elevator, Wi-Fi, parking-€15/day, at Hauptmarkt 17 but enter at Waaggasse 7, tel. 0911/242-700, www.sorat-hotels.com, saxx-nuernberg@sorat-hotels.com).

$$ Hotel Elch, the oldest hotel in town (with 500-year-old exposed beams adding to its classic elk-friendly woodiness), is buried deep in the Old Town near the castle. It rents 12 charming and well-equipped rooms (Sb-€60-74, Db-€79-95, rates depend on demand, extra bed-€26, new business-class rooms next door are more expensive, Wi-Fi, parking-€12/day, near St. Sebald Church at Irrerstrasse 9, tel. 0911/249-2980, www.hotel-elch.com, info@hotel-elch.com).

$$ Hotel Lucas occupies three floors above a busy, similarly named café a short walk from the Hauptmarkt (market square). The 11 rooms and seven river-view apartments next door are modern and cheerful, making this a great home base if you don't mind that there's no elevator (Sb-€60-75, Db-€85-100, extra person-€25, lower prices are for Fri-Sun; Wi-Fi, Kaiserstrasse 22, tel. 0911/227-845, www.hotel-lucas.de, info@hotel-lucas.de). Coming from the train station with luggage, I'd hop on the U-1 subway line for one stop to Lorenzkirche. Exit following the *Kaiserstrasse* signs to emerge a couple of doors from the hotel.

JUST BEYOND THE CITY WALLS

$ B&B Hotel Nürnberg-City isn't a B&B by any stretch, but its 135 pleasant rooms are a solid value. Though it feels a tad more institutional than most hotels, its accommodations are a few steps above most hostels' private rooms (Sb-€54, Db-€60, family rooms, breakfast-€7.50, air-con, elevator, wheelchair-accessible rooms, pay guest computer, Wi-Fi, limited parking-€5/day, right across from city walls at Frauentorgraben 37, from station take U-2 one stop to Opernhaus, tel. 0911/378-510, www.hotelbb.de, nuernberg-city@hotelbb.com). They have a second location (B&B Hotel Nürnberg-Hbf) with the same room rates, about 500 yards from the station at Marienstrasse 10 (tel. 0911/367-760, nuernberg-hbf@hotelbb.com).

HOSTELS

$ Five Reasons Hotel & Hostel is the best kind of budget accommodation: clean, bright, centrally located, and run with care. None of the 15 rooms here have their own bath, but the shared bathrooms are some of the swankiest hostel bathrooms I've seen (dorm bed-€18-26, D-€54, breakfast-€3-6, elevator, Wi-Fi, limited free parking, facing the town walls around the corner from the Germanic History Museum at Frauentormauer 42, tel. 0911/9928-6625, www.five-reasons.de, booking@five-reasons.de).

$ Nürnberg Youth Hostel, with 355 beds, is romantically situated at the top of the Old Town inside the castle complex (at the far right as you face it). It's scenic but expensive for a hostel, and can be crowded with groups of school-age kids in the summer. All rooms have their own bath. For the best views, request

NÜRNBERG

the eighth- or ninth-floor tower rooms (bed in sex-segregated 4- to 6-bed dorm-€34; Db-€89, Qb-€124, nonmembers pay €3.50 more, €4 extra if over 26, includes breakfast and sheets, lunch or dinner-€7, Wi-Fi, Burg 2, tel. 0911/230-9360, www.nuernberg. jugendherberge.de, nuernberg@jugendherberge.de). To reach the hostel from the train station, take the U-3 subway three stops to Maxfeld, then walk (level, 10 minutes) or take the #46 bus two stops back to Maxtor.

$ A&O Hostel Nürnberg Hauptbahnhof, just outside the medieval city center on busy Bahnhofstrasse, has 116 rooms and boasts a rooftop bar. Vast and institutional, it caters to a wide range of travelers, from backpackers to families. To avoid street noise, ask for a room facing the courtyard (bed in 4- or 6-bunk dorm-€11-22, Sb/Db-€43-55, breakfast-€7, sheets-€3, towel-€1, private rooms include sheets and towels, €3 extra to pay with a credit card, fans but no air-con, pay guest computer, Wi-Fi, bar and lounge in lobby, parking-€12.50/day in garage or €7.50 in lot, Bahnhofstrasse 13-15, tel. 0911/309-168-4400, www.aohostels.com, booking@ aohostels.com).

$ City Hostel is a last-ditch backpacker option, though its location is unbeatable. Offering only the most basic necessities, it's a lesser value compared to the other hostel options listed here—except during festivals and conventions, since its prices stay the same year-round (bed in 3- to 9-bunk dorm-€17-23 depending on size of room, Db-€50, breakfast-€4, includes sheets, pay guest computer, pay Wi-Fi, Klaragasse 12, tel. 0911/8019-2146, www.city-hostel-nuernberg.de, info@city-hostel-nuernberg.de).

Eating in Nürnberg

SOUTH OF THE RIVER, NEAR THE STATION

Königstrasse, the main pedestrian boulevard leading from the train station into the old center, is lined with enticing places to eat. All along this street you'll find department stores, many with efficient cafeterias, popular restaurant chains, and memorable one-offs. The following places are my favorites on or just off Königstrasse, working from the station to the center.

Hans im Glück Burgergrill and Bar is a trendy hangout packed with mostly young locals enjoying a wide selection of burgers with "real bread," good fries, and aromatic pots of rosemary at each table. There's fun, high-energy seating inside or out (€7-8 burgers, €8-9 salads, daily 12:00-24:00, near station next to recommended Hotel Victoria at Königstrasse 74, tel. 0911/9928-3661).

Istanbul Restaurant is a local favorite for Turkish food and fresh *ayran* (yogurt drinks), with friendly service and great outdoor seating for people-watching (€3.50 *döner kebabs*, €9-13 Turkish-

Central Nürnberg Restaurants

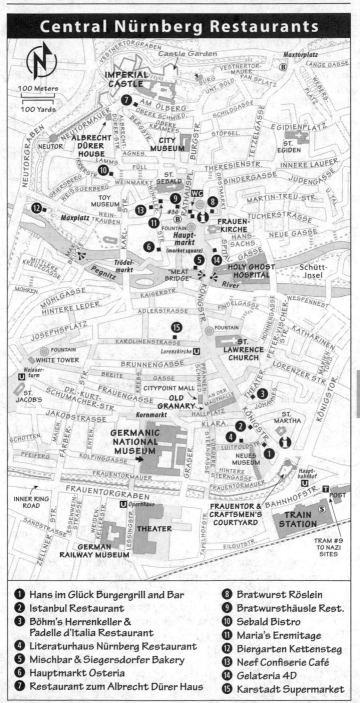

1. Hans im Glück Burgergrill and Bar
2. Istanbul Restaurant
3. Böhm's Herrenkeller & Padelle d'Italia Restaurant
4. Literaturhaus Nürnberg Restaurant
5. Mischbar & Siegersdorfer Bakery
6. Hauptmarkt Osteria
7. Restaurant zum Albrecht Dürer Haus
8. Bratwurst Röslein
9. Bratwursthäusle Rest.
10. Sebald Bistro
11. Maria's Eremitage
12. Biergarten Kettensteg
13. Neef Confiserie Café
14. Gelateria 4D
15. Karstadt Supermarket

style grill plates, daily 8:00-24:00, air-con on upper floor, König-strasse 60, tel. 0911/2124-8330).

Böhm's Herrenkeller is cozy, with a hunting-room ambience. It's proudly traditional but not kitschy, serving classic Franconi-an standards at good prices. Try the €13 Schäufele (oven-roasted pork shoulder with dumplings and salad) or the fixed-price menus, which are a fine value (€7-18 main courses, €10 three-course week-day lunch specials, €25 three-course meals, Mon-Sat 11:30-15:00 & 17:30-24:00, closed Sun, a block off Königstrasse across from the Old Granary at Theatergasse 9, tel. 0911/224-465).

Padelle d'Italia is a cut above your average pizza-and-pas-ta joint, serving good classic Italian dishes, with splittable large portions and daily seasonal specials. Reserve ahead for dinner (€7-10 pizzas, €10 pastas, €15-20 *secondi*, Mon-Sat 11:30-14:00 & 17:30-23:00 except open all day Fri-Sat, closed Sun, next to Böhm's Herrenkeller at Theatergasse 17, tel. 0911/274-2130, www.padelleditalia.de).

Literaturhaus Nürnberg is a Parisian-style café run by the local book club and popular for readings. It serves theme breakfasts (daily until 15:00) and creative international dishes for €9-14. Lo-cals like to order several varied plates, tapas-style, or just enjoy its bookish café ambience for drinks and desserts (daily 9:00-22:00, 2 blocks from Frauentor just off Königstrasse at Luitpoldstrasse 6, tel. 0911/234-2658).

Quick Lunches between Museum Bridge and Meat Bridge: This covered arcade has several little modern, healthy places in a row next to a Starbucks, with good seating inside or overlooking the river. My favorites are **Mischbar,** where "everything's mixed" (€7 salads, curries, soups, smoothies, fresh-squeezed juices), and the **Siegersdorfer** bakery, serving traditional rye breads and toppings (their *Aufstriche* samplers give you 3 or 5 toppings and a selection of dark breads).

Hauptmarkt Osteria is a basic pizza place with splittable €9 pizzas (plenty for two), pastas, and a nice garden out back (daily 11:00-24:00, a block off the Hauptmarkt at Winklerstrasse 3, tel. 0911/224-655).

Picnicking in the Center: There's a Frida supermarket in the basement of the CityPoint mall, behind the Mauthalle and near recommended hotels (Mon-Sat 9:30-20:00, closed Sun) and a more upscale supermarket in the subbasement of the Karstadt de-partment store at the Lorenzkirche U-Bahn entrance (enter store at Karolinenstrasse 6 and take the escalators down two flights, Mon-Sat 9:30-20:00, closed Sun).

The Nürnberger Bratwurst

Nürnberg is famous for its pinkie-sized bratwurst (called, like a city resident, a "Nürnberger"). Local butchers churn out 1.3 billion of the little buggers every year. Nürnbergers—the people—insist that size doesn't matter; they maintain that *in der Kürze liegt die Würze* ("in the shortness lies the tastiness"). All over town, signs read *3 im Weckle* (or *im Weggle*), meaning "three Nürnberger bratwurst in a blankie" (a good snack for about €2.50). Restaurant menus often offer them in 6-, 8-, or 10-weenie servings accompanied by *Beilagen* (side dishes, generally potato salad and/or kraut). Six Nürnberger with sauerkraut and bread will run you about €7. Old-timers go for mustard, while children like ketchup.

NORTH OF THE RIVER, NEAR THE CASTLE

At **Restaurant zum Albrecht Dürer Haus,** you can dine with a view of half-timbered buildings and town-wall towers at a reasonable price. The dark-wood interior has three floors, and there are also outside tables. The menu is updated Franconian—traditional dishes such as *Schäufele* (shoulder), but creatively tweaked (€7-13 main courses, Tue-Sun 11:00-23:00, closed Mon, Obere Schmiedgasse 58, tel. 0911/2114-4940).

Bratwurst Röslein is a huge, no-nonsense, traditional beer hall with top-quality classics pouring out of a big open kitchen. It's a fixture on the sausage scene, where you can top off your meal with a fried apple dessert (€7.20 for six sausages and kraut, daily 11:00-23:00, a block above the Hauptmarkt at Rathausplatz 6, tel. 0911/214-860).

Bratwursthäusle is a high-energy, woody place with a leafy terrace (and enjoyable people-watching). Its cozy interior—small, crowded, and touristy—feels like a big farmhouse with tables gathered around an open grill. The menu is very limited, with little more than bratwurst, sides (pretzels, tasty potato salad, kraut), and some nasty pickled animal parts. You come here for the best bratwurst in town—all made in-house by the *Häusle's* own butcher, cooked on a beechwood grill, and dished up with efficient service (Mon-Sat 10:00-21:30, closed Sun, midway between Hauptmarkt and the castle on the main drag, Rathausplatz 1, tel. 0911/227-695). For a bratwurst sandwich to go, head inside, pay €2.50 at the half-door on your right, take your receipt to the grill...and in seconds, you'll be on your way with Nürnberg's "Little Mac" (three *Nürnberger* in a fresh roll).

Sebald Bistro is ideal for an elegant meal without sausage or dumplings. They serve excellent modern German dishes in a classy setting, with nice tables outside under the trees (€9 lunch specials,

€15-20 main dishes, daily specials, Mon-Sat 11:00-24:00, Sun 12:00-23:00, a block west of St. Sebald Church at Weinmarkt 14, tel. 0911/381-303).

Maria's Eremitage, primarily a wine shop, serves just one special plate a day—available from noon until it's sold out—at small stand-up tables just inside the door from a leafy mini-plaza that's shared by the flower shop run by the owner's husband (€6 plates and fine wine by the glass, closed Tue and Sun, just under St. Sebald Church at Winklerstrasse 24, mobile 0160-591-9139).

Biergarten Kettensteg is a sloppy place with good drinks and simple traditional plates set like a riverside oasis under trees (basic €7-10 plates, daily 11:00-23:00, mobile 01512-589-3484, Biergar and just inside the town wall at the Kettensteg bridge, Maxplatz 35). While here, notice the mix of medieval fortification, Industrial Age brickwork, and an early iron bridge. This was the industrialized, downstream end of town where you'd find watermills, stinky industries like tanners, and the graphite industry. (In Germany, Nürnberg is famous for its pencils.)

Sweets: **Neef Confiserie Café** is every Nürnberger's go-to spot for an afternoon coffee-and-cake break. You can even get a marzipan version of the town's famous three-sausages-in-a-bun (Mon-Fri 8:30-18:00, Sat 8:30-17:00, closed Sun, Winklerstrasse 29, tel. 0911/225-0179).

Of the many *Eiscafés* in town, **Gelateria 4D** is the most likely to have locals lined up at the counter for a scoop—and it's worth the wait (just off Hauptmarkt on the corner of Königstrasse and Spitalgasse, long hours daily).

Nürnberg Connections

From Nürnberg by Train to: Rothenburg (hourly, 1.5 hours, change in Ansbach and Steinach), **Würzburg** (2-3/hour, 1-1.5 hours), **Munich** (2-3/hour, 1-1.5 hours), **Frankfurt** (1-2/hour, 2 hours), **Frankfurt Airport** (1-2/hour, 2.5 hours), **Dresden** (hourly, 4.5-5 hours, may change in Leipzig or Hof), **Leipzig** (every 2 hours direct, 3.5 hours; more with transfer in Naumburg), **Berlin** (hourly, 4.5 hours), **Salzburg** (hourly with change in Munich, 3 hours), **Prague** (4 slow trains/day, 5 hours; better to take express bus, nearly hourly, 4 hours, covered by rail passes, leaves from front door of train station). Train info: Tel. 0180-599-6633, www.bahn.com.

LUTHERLAND

Erfurt • Wartburg Castle • Wittenberg

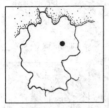

Martin Luther—pious monk, fiery orator, and religious whistle-blower—came from a humble, pastoral corner of Germany's heartland. In the charming university town of Erfurt, Luther was a student before casting his former life aside to become a monk. At Wartburg Castle, he hid out to translate the New Testament. And he eventually made his home in Wittenberg, where he worked as a university professor, nailed his 95 theses to the church door, and enjoyed married life with Katharina von Bora.

Located in the present-day states of Saxony and Thuringia, this chapter's three destinations—Erfurt, Wartburg Castle, and Wittenberg—form the cradle of the Protestant Reformation. Luther's groundbreaking work here set into motion a chain of events that would split Western Christian faith, plunge Europe into a century of warfare, cause empires to rise and fall, and inspire new schools of art and thought.

OK, I'll admit it—I'm a Lutheran. So I have a special reason for enjoying this area. But anyone with an appreciation for history will likely be interested as well. Erfurt is pleasant for a stroll, and Wartburg is a fine castle, even apart from their Luther connections. And Wittenberg's excellent Luther sights can make even an atheist appreciate the dramatic impact this dreamer had on European history—and the enduring example he set for those who dare to speak truth to power.

If you're connecting the Luther towns, you'll almost certainly pass through the city of Leipzig, which also has a few Luther ties and is worth a visit in its own right (see next chapter).

Throughout the region that I call "Lutherland," keep an eye out for the Luther rose, a symbol of the great Reformer: a black

cross in a red heart (symbolizing the Crucifixion) inside a white rose (the peace and joy of faith), all within a golden ring that symbolizes the infinite nature of heaven.

PLANNING YOUR TIME

Lutherland is easy to visit on the way between the Frankfurt/Würzburg area to the west and the Berlin/Dresden area to the east. Luther pilgrims may want several days to linger at the historic sights. But if you're short on time and have a limited appetite for Luther lore, here's a concise two-day plan for splicing this area into your itinerary:

Day 1: Ride the train to Eisenach, throw your bag in a locker, and visit Wartburg Castle. In the evening, continue by train 30 minutes to Erfurt, where you'll enjoy a charming evening and sleep.

Day 2: Spend the morning sightseeing in Erfurt; at midday, head to Wittenberg, see the sights there, and then take an evening train to Berlin. (If you'd also like to visit Leipzig, do it today and stay the night, then see Wittenberg on the morning of Day 3 en route to Berlin.)

Background on Martin Luther

A basic understanding of Martin Luther's life and times is essential to fully appreciate this region. The following overview explains the most important events that shaped the man known as The Great Reformer.

Luther lived a turbulent life. In early adulthood, the newly ordained Catholic priest suffered a crisis of faith, before finally emerging as "born again." In 1517, he openly protested against Church corruption and was later excommunicated. Defying both the pope and the emperor, he lived on the run as an outlaw, watching as his ideas sparked peasant riots. He still found time to translate the New Testament from Greek to modern German, write hymns such as "A Mighty Fortress is Our God," and spar with fellow Reformers.

Early Life (Erfurt)

Luther was born on November 10, 1483, in Eisleben, south of Berlin. His dad owned a copper smelter, affording Luther a middle-class upbringing—a rarity in the medieval hierarchy of nobles, clergy, and peasants.

Luther enrolled at the University of Erfurt in 1501. There he earned a liberal-arts degree, entered law school, and earned himself two nicknames—"the philosopher" for his wide-ranging mind, and "the king of hops" for his lifelong love affair with beer. In 1505, he received his master's degree, graduating second in his class.

Then came July 2, 1505. While riding through the countryside, Luther was caught up in an intense thunderstorm, and a bolt of lightning knocked him to the ground. Luther cried out, "St. Anne, save me, and I will become a monk!" Surviving the storm, Luther was determined to make good on his promise. He returned to Erfurt, sold his possessions, and told his friends, "After this day, you will see me no more." The next morning, he knocked on the door of Erfurt's Augustinian Monastery and dedicated his life to Christ.

But Luther soon realized that pious

monastic life did not suit his inquisitive nature. He returned to academia, was ordained a priest in 1507 in Erfurt's cathedral, and by 1508 was teaching theology part-time at the university in nearby Wittenberg.

In 1509, Luther set out to travel to Rome on foot, a pilgrimage that would change him forever. Upon arriving in the Eternal City, he was dismayed to find rich, corrupt priests and bishops selling "indulgences," which supposedly guaranteed entry to heaven to those able to pay the price. This was the Rome of Pope Julius II, who was in the midst of an expensive, over-the-top remodel of Vatican City—and the lucrative sale of indulgences helped refill the papal treasury. At the time of Luther's visit, Michelangelo was lying aloft on his back in the Sistine Chapel, executing detailed frescoes on the ceiling, while Raphael was slathering nearby hallways with his own Renaissance masterpieces.

This traffic in indulgences and luxury clashed violently with Luther's deeply held belief that people's faith, not their pocketbook, would determine the final destination of their souls. Indulgences were an insult to his worldview—and, to Luther, a betrayal of the Christian faith.

Professor and Preacher (Wittenberg)

After returning to Germany in 1512, Luther received his doctorate and got a job teaching theology at the university in Wittenberg—the progressive city that would be his home for the rest of his life. The prince elector of Saxony, Frederick the Wise, had decided to make this backwater town his royal seat, so he set about building a castle, grand church, and university, and invited the region's best and brightest to populate his dynamic new burg. Here, Luther mingled with other great thinkers (including fellow professor Philipp Melanchthon) and artists (most notably Lucas Cranach the Elder).

During these early years in Wittenberg, Luther lived in a monastery and spent hours alone in his room. Consumed with the notion that he was a sinner, he devoured the Bible, looking for an answer and finding it in Paul's letter to the Romans. Luther concluded that God makes sinners righteous through their faith in Jesus Christ, not by earning it through good deeds. As this concept of grace took hold, Luther said, "I felt myself to have been born again."

Energized, he began a series of Bible lectures at Wittenberg's twin-towered Town Church of St. Mary. The pews were packed as Luther quoted passages directly from the Bible. Speaker and audience alike began to see discrepancies between what the Bible said and what the Church was doing. Coincidentally, a friar happened to arrive in Wittenberg around this time, selling letters of

Catholic and Protestant Differences

The differences between Protestant and Catholic doctrines have split Christians for centuries, ever since the Luther-sparked "protest" against Catholic corruption and rigidity. Both faiths see Jesus Christ as the central figure in bringing salvation, but they take different approaches.

Protestants emphasize the direct relationship between the individual and God, established through Bible study and personal prayer. With this one-on-one connection at the core of their worship, church rituals and doctrines aren't all that essential, and Protestant clergy (who can marry) are lay people or pastors hired to facilitate worship.

To Catholics, church rituals and an ordained clergy are key conduits for creating and maintaining an individual's connection to God. Catholics receive forgiveness for their sins through the act of Confession, which must be conducted with a priest. Unlike Protestants, they venerate saints and the Virgin Mary, and consider official pronouncements by the pope to be the word of God. Catholic priests must be celibate, and the Church recognizes organizations of monks and nuns.

indulgence that promised "forgiveness for all thy sins, transgressions, and excesses, howsoever enormous they may be"...a bargain at twice the price.

Outraged at the idea that God's grace could be bought, Luther thought the subject should be debated openly. On October 31, 1517, he nailed his now-famous 95 "theses" (topics for discussion) to the door of Wittenberg's Castle Church. The theses questioned indulgences and other Church practices and beliefs. Thesis #82 boldly asked: "If the pope redeems a number of souls for the sake of miserable money with which to buy a church, why doesn't he empty Purgatory for the sake of holy love?" With the newfangled printing presses belonging to Lucas Cranach, Luther's propositions were turned into pamphlets that became the talk of Germany. In much the same way that computers contributed to the fall of the USSR and social media made the Arab Spring possible, a revolutionary new technology—printing—empowered Reformation-age Christians who wanted to break from Rome.

Excommunication (Wartburg Castle)

Luther didn't set out to start a new church; he wanted to reform the existing one. He preached throughout the region, spreading his provocative ideas and publicly debating his positions in such venues as Leipzig's town hall. In 1520, a furious Pope Leo X sent the rebellious monk a papal bull threatening excommunication. Luther burned the edict on the spot, and soon after, Leo X formally excommunicated him.

Luther was branded a heretic and ordered to Rome to face charges, but he refused to go. Finally, the most powerful man in Europe, Emperor Charles V, stepped in to arbitrate, calling an Imperial Diet (congress) at Worms in 1521. Luther made a triumphal entry into Worms, greeted by cheering crowds. The Diet convened, and Luther took his place in the center of the large hall, standing next to a stack of his writings. Inquisitors grilled him while the ultra-conservative Charles looked on. Luther refused to disavow his beliefs.

The infuriated emperor declared Luther an outlaw, banned his writings, and put a price on his head. But after leaving Worms,

Luther disappeared. Rumor was that Luther had been kidnapped, but in fact he'd escaped (with the help of Frederick the Wise) to Wartburg Castle. There Luther spent 10 months disguised as the bearded "Junker Jörg" (Squire George), fighting depression and translating the Bible's New Testament from the original Greek into German. This "September Testament" (the German precursor to the King James Version) was revolutionary, bringing the Bible to the masses and shaping the modern German language.

Meanwhile, Luther's ideas caught on back home in Wittenberg, where his followers had continued to pursue reform. By the time Luther returned to the city in 1522, popular uprisings led by more radically minded proto-Protestants were undermining law and order.

Later Life (Wittenberg)

In 1525, Luther's friend and follower Thomas Müntzer used Luther's writings to justify an uprising known as the Peasant Revolt. Poor farmers attacked their feudal masters with hoes and pitchforks, fighting for more food, political say-so, and respect. Some 5,000 peasants died, and Müntzer was executed. Luther decried the violence, preaching that Church corruption did not justify outright societal rebellion.

In 1525, the 41-year-old ex-priest married a 26-year-old ex-nun, Katharina von Bora, "to please my father and annoy the pope." (Their

wedding set the precedent of allowing Protestant clergy to marry.) They moved into the former Wittenberg monastery where Luther had once lived (today's Luther House), where they let out rooms to students. Luther turned his checkbook over to "my lord Katie," who ran the family farm, raised their 6 children and 11 adopted orphans, and hosted Luther's circle of friends at loud, chatty dinner parties.

Luther traveled, spreading the Protestant message. In 1529, at Marburg Castle (just north of Frankfurt), he attended a summit of leading Protestants to try and forge an alliance against Catholicism. They agreed on everything except a single theological point: whether Christ was present in the wine and bread of Communion in a physical sense (according to Luther) or symbolic sense (per the Swiss Reformer Ulrich Zwingli). The disagreement doomed the Protestant movement to splinter into dozens of sects.

In 1534, Luther finished translating the entire Bible. Lucas Cranach illustrated it with woodcuts and published it on his printing presses. Luther also wrote a German Mass, catechisms, and several hymns, including the still-beloved "A Mighty Fortress is Our God."

In his fifties, Luther's health declined and he grew bitter, a fact made clear in such writings as "Against the Papacy at Rome Founded by the Devil" and "Of the Jews and Their Lies." A general tone of anti-Semitism pollutes his later work. Tragically, these words were later invoked to justify anti-Semitic speech and actions during the early days of Nazism.

Martin Luther died on February 18, 1546, and was buried in Wittenberg. Pilgrims still bring flowers. To read more about Luther's lasting legacy, see the sidebar on page 636. To watch a 30-minute documentary on Luther and the Reformation—shot on location at the big Luther sights in Germany (which I hosted and helped produce for the Lutheran Church)—go to www.elca.org, select "Video," then "Opening the Door to Luther."

LUTHERLAND

Erfurt

A half-timbered, many-steepled medieval townscape with a shallow river gurgling through its middle, Erfurt (AIR-foort) is an inviting destination. The capital of the Thuringia region, this is where Martin Luther spent his early years. While its Luther sights aren't as exciting as those at Wartburg Castle or Wittenberg, the town itself more than makes up for it. You can see the monastery where Luther became a monk and the cathedral where he became a priest, stroll across an atmospheric medieval bridge lined with characteristic shops, ogle an unearthed treasure-trove in one of Europe's oldest surviving synagogues, hike up to the citadel for views over town, or just bask in Erfurt's quaintness.

Sitting on an important medieval trade route, Erfurt boomed in the Middle Ages thanks largely to its production of woad, a plant-based blue dye. In the 16th century, trade with India flooded the market with less expensive dyes made from true indigo, and Erfurt's fortunes tumbled, leaving it a well-preserved backwater for centuries. It enjoyed another boom after the creation of a united Germany in 1871. Unlike the nearby cities of Berlin, Dresden, and Leipzig, Erfurt emerged from World War II relatively unscathed. This imbues Erfurt with a delightful time-capsule quality—rare for an eastern German city of its size.

These days, Erfurt is very popular among German tourists and Martin Luther pilgrims, but largely undiscovered by American visitors (meaning English information can be hard to come by). Erfurt provides a handy launch pad for visiting Wartburg Castle, where Luther hid out while translating the New Testament (in Eisenach, 30-45 minutes west by train).

PLANNING YOUR TIME

Erfurt deserves a day's visit, and possibly an overnight. You can get the gist of the town in a few hours: Take my self-guided walking tour, then drop into your choice of other sights—the twin churches are enjoyable, the citadel offers great views over town, Luther fans appreciate the Augustinian Monastery, and the truly old Old Synagogue interests historians.

Orientation to Erfurt

Although it has about 200,000 people, Erfurt feels smaller—particularly its downtown core, where you'll spend most of your time. Erfurt's Old Town, huddled picturesquely at a bend in the Gera River, is loosely bound by a ring road. The train station sits just beyond the southeastern edge of the ring, and the cathedral and citadel perch at the western edge. The Old Town core is about a short walk (or speedy tram ride) from the train station; once there, virtually all points of interest are within a 10-minute walk of each other.

TOURIST INFORMATION

Erfurt's TI is right in the town center, between the Merchants' Bridge and Town Hall. It has piles of brochures and Erfurt souvenirs for sale. The basic €0.10 map is good enough for a short visit. They also sell a self-guided tour booklet and rent an audioguide—see "Helpful Hints," later—(Mon-Sat 10:00-18:00, Sun 10:00-16:00, closes earlier Sat-Sun off-season; Benediktplatz 1, tel. 0361/66400, www.erfurt-tourismus.de). The TI's website helps put visitors in touch with residents renting private rooms.

ARRIVAL IN ERFURT

The Erfurt Hauptbahnhof **(main train station)** has a few shops and eateries, and luggage lockers (below track 2). There's no city TI at the station, but a regional (Thuringia) TI is directly across the square from the main door.

From the station, you can walk into the heart of town in about 10-15 minutes (a few minutes farther to Domplatz or the Augustinian Monastery), or you can hop a tram part of the way.

To **walk,** exit through the main door and bear left until you reach Bahnhofstrasse, with the tram tracks. Turn right and head five short blocks until you pop out at the shopping square called Anger (marked by a glassy modern building). This is the starting point for my self-guided walk; most of the hotels I list are within a 10-minute walk of Anger.

Or, to take a **tram,** exit out the side of the station, toward *Ausgang Bahnhofstrasse*; you'll run right into the tram stops. You can take trams #3, #4, or #6 to Anger, then to Domplatz; tram #1 goes first to Anger, then continues to the Augustinerkloster (Augustinian Monastery and recommended hotels). Tram #5 also goes to Augustinerkloster.

GETTING AROUND ERFURT

For most visitors, the only reason to use Erfurt's trams is to haul luggage to or from the station (particularly to lodgings near the Augustinian Monastery) or to reach the Egapark gardens. One ride costs €1.90; a day pass is €4.90. There are coin-op ticket machines (instructions in English) both at the stops and on the trams.

HELPFUL HINTS

Tours: You'll see tour groups all over town, but there are no regularly scheduled English tours; instead, follow my self-guided walk, buy the TI's self-guided tour booklet (€2.50), or rent the audioguide (€7.50/4 hours). **Petra Bischoff** is a good local guide for Erfurt and the region (€90/2 hours, mobile 0172-354-7021, bischoff-kultur@web.de, www.bischoff-kultur.de).

Musical Events: Erfurt has a long tradition of classical music—

LUTHERLAND

especially pipe organ music. There are evening organ concerts at the Preachers' Church (€5, May-Sept Wed at 20:00), plus open-air opera performances on the steps of the cathedral in the summer, a summer organ festival, and a Bach festival each spring. Visit the TI or its website for a listing of musical events.

Erfurt Walk

The best "sight" in Erfurt is the town itself, with its charming, half-timbered core. This self-guided walk (which takes about an hour, not including sightseeing breaks) begins at the main shopping zone and ends at the big square with the cathedral (Domplatz); along the way, it passes nearly every sightseeing option in town.

• Begin in the main shopping square, called Anger. To get here from the train station, follow my walking directions (earlier), or ride any tram one stop to the Anger stop.

Anger: The word *Anger* means "commons," evoking the grazing land that once sprawled just outside the city walls. Dur-

ing Erfurt's medieval heyday, this space was used as a marketplace. Much later, after Germany's unification in 1871, the new wealth that flowed into town was poured into construction around this square. Study the fine late-19th-century and early-20th-century facades. More recently, many of these buildings have been turned into shopping spaces.

In the middle of the square, notice the statues of the Maus and the Elefant—two beloved characters from Germany's public-television children's channel, **KiKA** (short for "Kinder Kanal"), which is based in Erfurt. When German families come here, their kids can't wait to pose with figures like these—you'll see them scattered around town.

The palatial yellow building, across the tram tracks from the glassy, modern building, hosts the **Anger Museum** (described later, under "Sights in Erfurt"). No, this doesn't highlight the ill temper of Germanic people. This building was restored to showcase the city's marginally interesting collections of paintings, applied arts, and medieval artifacts.

LUTHERLAND

• *Turn your back to the glassy shopping mall, turn left, and walk along the tram tracks with the red-and-white-striped post office on your left side. You'll reach a church with a statue in front, depicting...*

Martin Luther: Luther came to Erfurt in 1501 to enroll at the university. After graduating, the smart young student pursued

a doctorate at the prestigious law faculty, but after a close call with a lightning storm, Luther had a change of heart and became a monk at Erfurt's Augustinian Monastery for several years. This walk passes a few blocks from the monastery. The church in front of you is where Johann Sebastian Bach's parents were married in 1668.

• *To the right of the statue, notice the...*

Rostbratwurst **Stand:** Locals are extremely proud of what they stress is *"originale" Thüringer* bratwurst—a long, skinny, relatively low-fat pork sausage amply seasoned with pepper, marjoram, and other spices. When you buy one, grab a roll and hold it open, and they'll insert the wurst straight from the grill. While there's ketchup standing by, purists put only the locally made Born brand mustard *(Senf)* on their weenie.

• *As you munch, go around the left side of the church, then turn left up Meienbergstrasse, and walk for a couple of blocks—passing a row of Döner Kebab joints—to...*

Wenigemarkt: This "Little Market Square" is one of Erfurt's most charming, encircled with al fresco cafés and watched over by the fortified tower of the Methodist church of St. Aegidius (which you can climb for a town view).

• *Head toward that church tower, and go through the large gateway in the green building just to its right. Jog left with the cobbled lane, and you'll pop out at...*

The "Er-Ford": Notice the ramp that goes right down into the Gera River, out the other side, then

continues through the far branch of the river. Like any German town with "-furt" in its name, Erfurt is named for a shallow point where ancient travelers could ford a river. (The "Er" part comes from an old German word for "dirty"—the water was muddied when people would cross.) In centuries past,

LUTHERLAND

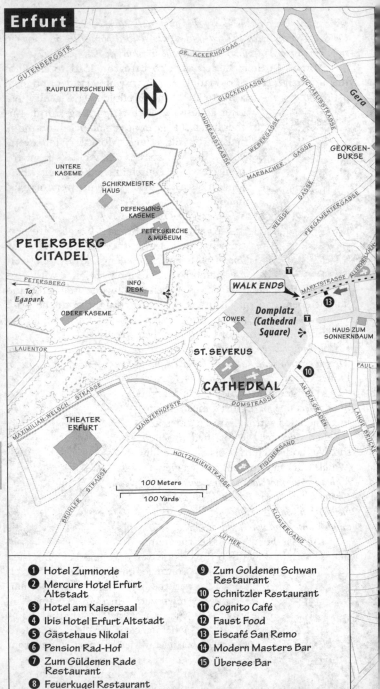

Erfurt

LUTHERLAND

1. Hotel Zumnorde
2. Mercure Hotel Erfurt Altstadt
3. Hotel am Kaisersaal
4. Ibis Hotel Erfurt Altstadt
5. Gästehaus Nikolai
6. Pension Rad-Hof
7. Zum Güldenen Rade Restaurant
8. Feuerkugel Restaurant
9. Zum Goldenen Schwan Restaurant
10. Schnitzler Restaurant
11. Cognito Café
12. Faust Food
13. Eiscafé San Remo
14. Modern Masters Bar
15. Übersee Bar

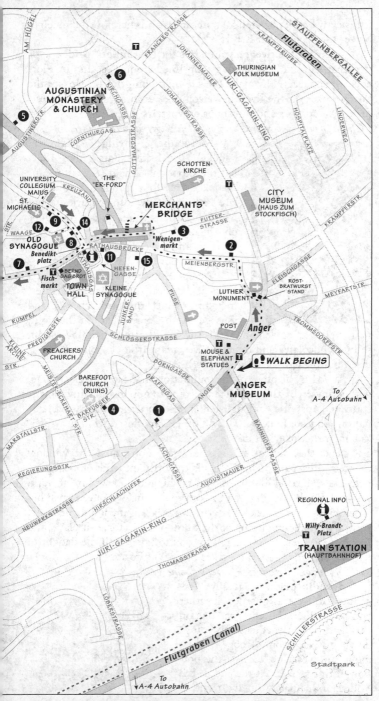

STAUFFENBERGALLEE

Flutgraben

KRÄMPFERUFER

FRANCKESTRASSE

AM HÜGEL

THURINGIAN
FOLK MUSEUM

JOHANNESMAUER

JURI-GAGARIN-RING

HOSPITALPLATZ

LINDERWEG

6

KIRCHGASSE

**AUGUSTINIAN
MONASTERY
& CHURCH**

JOHANNESSTRASSE

5

AUGUSTINERSTR.

CORNTHURGAS

GOTTHARDSTRASSE

SCHOTTEN-
KIRCHE

T

CITY
MUSEUM
(HAUS ZUM
STOCKFISCH)

KRÄMPFERSTR.

UNIVERSITY
COLLEGIUM
MAIUS

KREUZGA.

THE
"ER-FORD"

**MERCHANTS'
BRIDGE**

FUTTER-
STRASSE

ST.
MICHAELIS

STR.

12   **9**   **14**

WAAGE.

**OLD
SYNAGOGUE**

Benedikt-
platz

8

3 Wenigen-
markt

2

RATHAUSBRÜCKE

ELFISCHGASSE

MEYFARTSTR.

ROST-
BRATWURST
STAND

7

11

15

MEIENBERGSTR.

BERND
DAS BROT

HEFEN-
GASSE

T

Fisch-
markt

TOWN
HALL

KLEINE
SYNAGOGUE

PILSE

LUTHER
MONUMENT

JUNKER-
SAND

TROMMSDORFFSTR.

RUMPEL

PREDIGERSTR.

SCHLÖSSERSTRASSE

POST

Anger

KLEINE
ARCHE

PREACHERS'
CHURCH

BORNGASSE

T

MOUSE &
ELEPHANT
STATUES

T

WALK BEGINS

STR.

BARFOOT
CHURCH
(RUINS)

GRAFENGAS.

ANGER

**ANGER
MUSEUM**

To
A-4 Autobahn

MEISTERECKEHART STR.

BARFÜSSER
STR.

4

1

MARSTALLSTR.

LACHSGASSE

REGIERUNGSSTR.

HIRSCHLACHUFER

AUGUSTMAUER

BAHNHOFSTRASSE

REGIONAL INFO

NEUWERKSTRASSE

JURI-GAGARIN-RING

Willy-Brandt-
Platz

T

TRAIN STATION
(HAUPTBAHNHOF)

THOMASSTRASSE

LÖBERSTRASSE

SCHILLERSTRASSE

Flutgraben (Canal)

Stadtpark

To
A-4 Autobahn

LUTHERLAND

this sleepy brook powered 50 water mills and therefore did much to power the economy of Erfurt.

Spanning the river on your left is the **Merchants' Bridge.** Notice that—unlike the famous shop-lined Ponte Vecchio in Florence—people actually make their homes along this bridge (see the flower boxes on the lived-in balconies). As in ages past, the residents live upstairs and run shops downstairs.

• *Climb the narrow staircase on your left to get onto the bridge.*

Merchants' Bridge (Krämerbrücke): The bridge dates from 1325, but the shops that line it (*Krämer* means "shopkeeper") first sprouted around the late 15th and early 16th centuries, about Martin Luther's time. Today, the shops on the bridge are quaint, albeit a bit touristy, and a pleasure to browse. Window-shop your way across the bridge.

Across from the steps, at #19, is a shop dealing in Thuringian specialties, including wine, mustard, cheese, and sausage. Across from that (on the right, marked by the golden helmet) is the **Goldhelm Schokolade shop,** selling chocolates and delicious ice cream (the chocolate flavor is tasty, but the caramel is *wunderbar*).

At #31 is the office of the foundation that cares for the bridge, with a tiny, free exhibit. You're welcome to pop in and climb downstairs and upstairs. An English flier describes their work (small donation requested, daily 10:00-18:00 except closed Mon in winter, kraemerbruecke.erfurt.de).

Near the end, at #2 on the right, don't miss the window marked **Theatrum Mundi.** This is the brilliant work of local puppetmaker Martin Gobsch—go in, say hi, and observe him at work. It's well worth popping in a €1 coin to see the evil queen open her green eyes and pull back her arm to reveal an intricately detailed, fully articulated rendering of the Snow White story—it plays for a few minutes, just long enough for you to take in all the delightful details. Happily, the prince takes Snow White away.

• *At the end of Merchants' Bridge, you emerge at...*

Benediktplatz: Originally Merchants' Bridge was guarded at either end by fortified churches; the one on this end—St. Benedict's—was torn down by Napoleonic troops, but its name survives. The TI is at the bottom of this square. At the end of the bridge, immediately on the right, is

Backstube, a bakery proudly selling handmade breads in the traditional style (with a tasty selection of still-warm rolls and drinks).

• *Let's take a detour up...*

Michaelisstrasse: Historically the core of the university district, today this drag hosts some of the town's most popular restaurants and bars. After a block, go down the first lane on the left, then look left to find the entrance to the **Old Synagogue**—one of Europe's earliest surviving synagogues, displaying a rediscovered treasure in its cellar (see "Sights in Erfurt," later).

Back on Michaelisstrasse, at Zum Güldenen Krönbacken (#10), go through the fine arch. Walk 20 paces to a planter filled with leafy **woad plants.** Growing to four feet, and with yellow flowers, woad (*Waid* in German) was converted into a highly valuable, brilliant blue dye, which buoyed Erfurt's economy in the Middle Ages. This courtyard is one place where the woad was processed and warehoused. After being mashed up, the plant was fermented with urine for two months. (How they worked out this procedure, I don't care to know.) The mixture was dried, then ground into a fine powder that was literally worth its weight in gold. Leading woad merchants were local tycoons.

Continuing up Michaelisstrasse, you'll come to an intersection shared by a church and an old pink building—both related to the

University of Erfurt. Founded in 1379, the university was the third in present-day Germany and counts Martin Luther and Johannes Gutenberg as alums. The pink building, called the Collegium Maius, was the town's first university building (though it's mostly a reconstruction—the original was one of Erfurt's few WWII casualties in the last months of the war). Medieval students had a rough life: They got up at 4:00 in the morning to attend Mass, ate just two meals a day (breakfast at 10:00 and dinner at 16:00), and bathed once a month. On the upside, students were rationed one liter of beer per meal (it was purer than the water). Notice the modern stained-glass windows above the door depicting the four traditional areas of study: theology (cross and fish), law (weights), medicine (snake on staff), and philosophy (eye).

• *Head back to Benediktplatz and the TI, and turn right (in the direction you were originally going) toward...*

Fischmarkt: On the left just before you reach the square, in front of the Town Hall, look for another KiKA character—a morose, SpongeBob-looking slice of bread named **Bernd das Brot.** In what surely ranks among the most dramatic art heists in European history, this statue was stolen in 2009 by squatters protesting an eviction notice. They even put a tongue-in-cheek ransom video on YouTube. Several days later, Bernd was discovered by kids in an abandoned building, and returned to his rightful home.

Just past Bernd, enter the **square** itself, dominated by the Town Hall building. The statue in the center of the square holds a flag and shield, both with the city symbol—a wheel in a shield. Erfurt, which was never a free city, spent much of its history as part of the Archbishop of Mainz's holdings, so this wheel is based on that city's symbol.

The stately **Town Hall,** built in 1880 in the Neo-Gothic style, welcomes visitors (free and open daily, WC inside). In the lobby, the fine staircase ahead of you leads up two stories to the festival hall. Along the stairs and in the hall are melodramatic 19th-century Romantic paintings of Wagnerian opera themes and city history (all thoughtfully described in English).

Back out on the square, survey the building **facades** and enjoy the variety of architectural styles taking you from the 13th to 20th century. Notice in particular two fine Renaissance facades owned by wealthy woad merchants hell-bent on showing off their wealth: Zum Breiten Herd (1584, celebrates the five senses: to look, listen, smell, taste, and touch, from left to right); and the Red Oxen (#7, from 1562, with a round arch and "gossip stones" where women would sit flanking the doorway and gossip while keeping an eye on the city).

Finally, notice the modern addition to the Town Hall, built around 1930 in the bold and early-modern Bauhaus style. The German Bauhaus movement marked the beginning of functionalism—the "form follows function" aesthetic that became the norm for our age. The statues here, which also date from the 1930s, show bad human characteristics (greed, narcissism, laziness, stupidity, and so on). The Nazi-era relief celebrates solid, traditional family roles.
• *Stand with the Town Hall at your back. Now follow the tram lines ahead and to your right up...*

Marktstrasse: At the tall white steeple (after passing Werner's Head Shop on your left—pop in if you need a gift for your mother), look left down the street to see **Haus zum Sonneborn** (a yellow house with brown timbers and trim). At this popular venue for weddings, notice the intertwined golden rings on the grate over the window to the right of

the door, and to the left, the cage (whose symbolism is obvious). Lovers are trying to start a new custom by locking padlocks inscribed with their initials on this cage.

• *A block farther down Marktstrasse, on the left, is the recommended* **Eiscafé San Remo,** *with Italian-style gelato. Soon after, you'll reach...*

Domplatz (Cathedral Square): This vast square, often full of market stalls, is dominated by twin churches: the **cathedral** (on the left) and **St. Severus** (right).

While Erfurt's history is tied to religion, the atheistic East German government successfully smothered the faith: These days, just 7 percent of Erfurters profess to be Catholic, 14 percent are Protestant, and the rest are unchurched. On the hill to the right, you can see the base of **Petersberg Citadel,** a gigantic fortress that's free to explore and offers sweeping views over Erfurt. (The churches and citadel are described later, under "Sights in Erfurt.")

The street leading away from Domplatz to the right, **Andreasstrasse,** was called "the longest street in Erfurt" during communist times. The bright red-brick building behind the wall was a prison run by the Stasi, East Germany's secret police, reserved for those who were caught trying to escape to the West. Why was it the longest street? "It takes five minutes to go in, and five years to get out."

• *Our tour is finished. Visit the churches and citadel, then enjoy exploring the town. Or, if you're ready to head back to the train station, you can ride tram #3, #4, or #6 three stops to the Hauptbahnhof.*

Sights in Erfurt

MARTIN LUTHER SIGHTS
▲Augustinian Monastery and Church
(Augustinerkloster und Augustinerkirche)

On July 17, 1505, a young student knocked on the door of this monastery and declared that he wished to become a monk. Martin Luther lived here for several years—even after becoming a priest and a part-time professor—until he settled in Wittenberg in 1512. Inside the still-active complex, you can see the church, a small museum of Luther artifacts, and the cell where Monk Martin lived.

Visiting the church is easy, and while the museum and cell are more accustomed to German-speaking groups, they do try to accommodate English speakers (sometimes with an escort). As the exhibits are explained in English, visiting on your own works fine.

Cost and Hours: Church—free, daily 9:00-18:00, Augustinerstrasse 10, tel. 0361/576-600, www.augustinerkloster.de.

Tours: €7.50, one-hour guided tours in German depart roughly at the top of each hour (Mon-Sat 10:00-16:00, Sun at 11:00). Tours include the church, peaceful cloister, exhibition, and Luther's cell.

Visiting the Monastery: The Augustinians were a "begging order" and life here was just the basics: "ora et labora" (pray and work). That's why this monastery, while important, had no great spire and just a humble cloister. Entering through the door, you emerge into a tranquil, park-like **courtyard.** On the right, the modern building (housing offices and a conference center) marks the site of an earlier library, where 267 people suffocated while hiding in the cellar to escape WWII bombs. The new building is connected by an elevated walkway to the main part of the complex, with two major sights: the church and the Martin Luther museum and cell.

The **church,** dating from the late 13th century, is where Martin Luther worshipped as a monk. The stained-glass windows (c. 1330) include (in the lower left corner) a motif of lions (symbolizing Jesus) flanking a rose (Mary). This window, which monks used as a focal point for meditation, must have made a deep impression on Luther: He later adopted a similar rose icon for his personal coat of arms. In front of the main altar, the tomb of Johannes Zacharias, a prominent priest, was a place where monks (including Luther) would meditate overnight—lying on their backs, with their arms outstretched. The deeply introspective Luther struggled with all this piety, and eventually he returned to academic life.

Oddly enough, it was Zacharias who had the Czech reformer Jan Hus burned in 1415 for his proto-Reformation ideas. Just before his execution, Hus had defiantly cried, "You can burn me—I'm just a little goose—but in one century a white swan will come and defeat your thinking." A century later, Luther, meditating on that tomb, kindled the ideas of the Reformation. As a priest, Luther performed the Mass here and would sit on the bench under the arch on the right.

Today, this monastery and church form a center of ecumenism, and it was in that spirit that Pope Benedict XVI came here in 2011.

To see the **museum and cell,** you can either join a German-language tour, or ask to visit on your own. You'll find exhibits about the history of the Bible and a working model of a 15th-century printing press. It was the combination of humanism, Gutenberg, and

Luther that resulted in affordable Bibles in the vernacular rather than Latin. Another room dedicated to Martin Luther contains a few original artifacts, as well as replicas of his straw bed, gown, book, lute, and so on. The room is lined with small cells where monks would meditate. (The monks all slept together on the main floor.) The lattice windows allowed others to look in on the monks to be sure they were behaving appropriately. The cell at the far corner (called the Lutherzelle) was Martin Luther's. Inside the cell is a writing table, similar to the one Luther used for carrying out the monastic task of copying Bibles.

The **cloister** is simple, in keeping with Augustinian values. In the adjoining chapter hall, monks would convene for meetings and to confess before each other.

Georgenburse

A couple of blocks away, just across the stream, is the dorm where Luther lived as a student. The renovated building is basically one big room with information about university life and the U. of E.'s most famous alum, Luther.

Cost and Hours: €3.50; Mon, Wed, and Fri 9:00-14:00; Tue and Thu 13:00-17:00; closed Sat-Sun; Augustinerstrasse 27, tel. 0361/576-600, www.augustinerkloster.de.

▲Preachers' Church (Predigerkirche)

This church, founded by the Catholic Dominicans in the 14th century, whose mission was teaching and preaching, is now Erfurt's main Protestant church. Its architecture is stunning (it has undergone multiple rebuildings). Colorful keystones honor guilds that paid to build the original church in Gothic times (find symbols for the baker, hatter, goldsmiths, and *schneider*—that's a tailor...indicated by scissors). You'll see a rare surviving wall, which separated people from the clergy before the Reformation. The finely carved choir stalls date from 1320. And the windows behind the altar are an abstract kaleidoscope of colors—pieced together from the original medieval glass windows shattered in World War II. The church also has a glorious circa-1650 Baroque pipe organ that you can hear in action (see "Music in Erfurt," later).

Cost and Hours: Free, April-Oct Tue-Sat 11:00-16:00, Sun 12:00-16:00, closed Mon and Nov-March, Predigerstrasse 4.

OTHER SIGHTS IN THE TOWN CENTER

▲Old Synagogue (Alte Synagogue)

One of the oldest surviving synagogues in Europe, the original identity of this building was forgotten for several centuries before being rediscovered in the 1980s. Today it has been restored to highlight its medieval heyday, while preserving its other layers of history. The exhibit inside explains the history of the building, examines the relationship between Jews and Christians in medieval Erfurt, and shows off a cache of coins and jewelry that was discovered nearby.

Cost and Hours: €8, includes audioguide, Tue-Sun 10:00-18:00, closed Mon, last entry at 17:30, mandatory bag check, no photos, Waagegasse 8, tel. 0361/655-1520, www.juedisches-leben.erfurt.de.

Background: With sections dating back to around 1100, this building was the religious center of Erfurt's bustling medieval Jewish community. Erfurt's Jews mixed freely with their Christian neighbors. In fact, the synagogue's location was one of the most desirable in town, situated near the main trading routes.

All of that changed during the Black Death pandemic of 1348-1349, which killed a third of Europe's population. In the hysteria that ensued, Jewish communities, including Erfurt's, were accused of spreading the disease and faced appalling persecution. Hundreds of Erfurt Jews died and the rest were expelled in a single horrible day of violence.

The Jews returned to Erfurt in the 1350s, but from that point on they were relegated to a ghetto. By about 1450 the Jews had again moved out of Erfurt. The abandoned synagogue building was taken over by the town and sold. Over the next several centuries, it was used first as a warehouse, then (in the late 19th century) as a restaurant, bowling alley, and dance hall. Finally, in the 1980s, historians realized that it had once been a synagogue, and it was restored.

Visiting the Synagogue: On the **ground floor**, models illustrate how the original synagogue building grew over time. The rail high on the wall once held lamps. The octagon in the center of the room marks the location of the bema, a raised platform for reading the Torah. A projection on the wall shows the niche where the Torah was kept.

Now go **upstairs.** Nothing here is original—it looks more like the colorfully decorated dance hall that was here from 1876 through the 1930s. The balcony ringing the room was the so-called "dragon's watch," where mothers could keep an eye on their daughters dancing with would-be suitors. Imagine young Nazis waltzing here, oblivious to the fact that they were partying in a former synagogue. Among the replicas of parchment scrolls and important books is a copy of the biggest handwritten Hebrew Bible in the world (notice that the illustrations are made up of tiny Hebrew characters). The originals are in a Berlin museum.

Finally, head into the **cellar.** In 1998, a remarkable collection

LUTHERLAND

of gold, silver, and jewels—some 60 pounds—was discovered in the cellar of a nearby building. Called the "Erfurt Treasure," this almost certainly belonged to a wealthy local Jew who was killed in the 1349 pogrom. Display cases show off brooches, tableware, and golden decorations for a belt and other garments. The wheel-shaped necklace was used for perfume. (They've reformulated this original medieval perfume—you can ask to sniff it at the ticket desk upstairs.) The museum's prize piece is a finely detailed golden wedding ring from the early 14th century. Around the ring's central pillar is the hard-to-see inscription *mazel tov,* indicating that this belonged to a Jewish woman. Squint to see the clasped hand that allows the ring to be adjusted. Nearby are mannequins dressed as a Jewish bride and groom from that period—wearing rich materials and draped in gold. The stacks of coins come from all over Europe, especially from France. The 50-pound bag with chunks of silver is marked with the seal of an Erfurt goldsmith.

Anger Museum

This modern, well-presented museum, almost completely lacking in English information, displays paintings, applied arts, and arti-

facts from the Middle Ages. The ground-floor medieval collection includes wood-carved statues, altarpieces, and a huge collection of shields. The Heckelarium is a small room slathered with frescoes by painter Erich Heckel (1883-1970). Part of the early-1900s art movement called Die Brücke, Heckel strove to create a bridge between two emotional, artistic styles: dramatic Romanticism and edgy Expressionism. The first floor features the good applied arts collection (Kunsthandwerke, featuring historical room interiors with period furnishings, a treasury of precious items, and a collection of glass and porcelain) and a painting gallery (mostly Romantic canvases by largely unknown artists). Temporary exhibits fill the top floor.

Cost and Hours: €6, Tue-Sun 10:00-18:00, closed Mon, Anger 18, tel. 0361/655-1651, www.angermuseum.de.

DOMPLATZ AND NEARBY

Erfurt's grandest square is watched over by three giant structures: a pair of churches on the small hill called Domberg (the cathedral on the left, St. Severus on the right) and the Petersberg Citadel.

Climb up the 70 steps to enter the two churches, whose entrances face each other. Both churches are Catholic and Gothic,

LUTHERLAND

dating from the 14th century and later expanded after a fire in the 15th century.

▲▲Cathedral (Dom)

The seat of a bishopric founded in the eighth century by St. Boniface, Erfurt's cathedral is the church where Martin Luther was ordained a priest. It sticks out from the hill on a massive substructure to level out the foundation. Inside you'll find a gorgeously carved choir and a few interesting pieces of ecclesiastical art.

Cost and Hours: Free, May-Oct Mon-Sat 9:30-18:00, Sun 13:00-18:00; Nov-April until 17:00, tel. 0361/646-1265, www.dom-erfurt.de.

Visiting the Cathedral: Upon entering, turn left to reach the **choir,** with its intricately carved oak seats. Designs on the benches,

built about 50 years after the Black Death, demonstrate that anti-Semitic feelings were still running high. To the left near the entrance to the choir (about waist-high), find the carving depicting a duel between two knights—one on a horse, the other on a swine. The *Schweinereiter* (swine knight) caricature, wearing a Jewish helmet, was intended to both insult Jews (particularly because the Jewish faith considers pigs unclean) and to emphasize the triumph of Christianity over Judaism. Opposite, on the right, are a series of intimate and playful carved scenes from the world of winemaking. Look up to take in the stained-glass windows (c. 1370-1410), depicting Old and New Testament stories, and missionaries in the region of Thuringia.

Directly across from the main entrance, find the remarkably old (c. 1160) bronze candelabra shaped like a man holding up a pair of candles, fighting off evil with light. Nearby, the light hanging from the ceiling was stolen from the Jewish synagogue during the 1349 pogrom. Behind the candelabra in a simple niche is another exquisite example of 12th-century art—Mary and Jesus on the throne of wisdom.

Filling the wall to the right, a giant **fresco**

shows St. Christopher using Erfurt's namesake ford to walk Christ to safety (notice this cathedral's steeples over his shoulder). Pictorial depictions such as this helped make the saints' stories real to medieval congregations.

Below St. Christopher is a **tomb** relief panel showing the Duke of Gleichen flanked by two women. This gravestone gave rise to a popular (but almost certainly fabricated) local tale: Supposedly "the only man allowed to have two wives," this influential knight went to the Holy Land to fight in the Crusades, was captured and enslaved, and was forced to toil in the garden of the sultan. He married the sultan's daughter in exchange for her help in escaping, then brought her back with him to Erfurt...where he introduced her to his first wife. (Awwk-waaard.) The new bride was accepted by the first one, the knight received special dispensation

from the pope to be a bigamist, and the valley where the three of them lived in wedded bliss is still called Freudenthal ("Happy Valley").

Church of St. Severus (Severikirche)

This early Gothic "hall church" has five parallel naves (notice the two narrow ones flanking the main nave) and no perpendicular

transept. To the left of the fine Baroque organ is a 14th-century sarcophagus containing the remains of the church's namesake. (Some of the relics of St. Severus, bishop of Ravenna, were brought to Erfurt in the ninth century.) On the sides of the tomb, see the scenes of Severus' life (a poor craftsman being designated as the chosen one by a white dove over his head—representing the Holy Spirit—and then being "crowned" the bishop of Ravenna) and the Three Magi bringing gifts to the Baby Jesus.

Cost and Hours: Free, same hours as cathedral.

▲Petersberg Citadel (Zitadelle Petersberg)

This sprawling fortress complex, occupying the hill just above Domplatz, is an enjoyable place to go for a stroll and enjoy views over the rooftops of Erfurt. Built from the 17th to the 19th century, this is one of the best-preserved citadels of its kind in Europe.

While the grounds are extensive, you can have a satisfying quick visit: Walk up the ramp from Domplatz, pausing at the gatehouse to visit the Military History Museum (a couple of rooms with mannequin soldiers and other displays, well-explained in English). As you continue up into the main courtyard of the castle complex, the glassy building on your right is a visitors center with a helpful info desk,  a view café, and panoramic terrace offering sweeping views over Domplatz and the rest of Erfurt. The visitors center hands out a helpful, free map and mini-guide of the entire complex. Across the field from the center is a large church building with an exhibit of interesting "concrete art" (modern art with 3-D optical illusions). You can visit the underground tunnels only on a guided German tour (ask at info desk).

Cost and Hours: Free; grounds—always open; info desk and Military History Museum—daily April-Oct 11:00-18:30, Nov-March 11:00-16:00; church/art exhibit—Wed-Sun 10:00-18:00, closed Mon-Tue; tel. 0361/601-5384.

ON OR NEAR THE RING ROAD
Thuringian Folk Museum
(Museum für Thüringer Volkskunde)

This former hospital contains artifacts and old photos illustrating everyday folk life in the region of Thuringia. You'll climb up rickety stairs to see representations of various walks of life, including church, school, bars, farming, shops, kitchen, and home life. The top floor features clothing and dress-up dolls from the 19th through the early 20th century. While charming, the museum has not a word of English.

Cost and Hours: €6, Tue-Sun 10:00-18:00, closed Mon, Juri-Gagarin-Ring 140A, tel. 0361/655-5607, www.volkskundemuseum-erfurt.de.

City Museum (Stadtmuseum)

Filling the historic Haus zum Stockfisch town house, this old-fashioned collection shows off items relating to the history of Erfurt, and recently added a permanent exhibit on Martin Luther. You'll also see a model of the town, dusty cases of artifacts, military uniforms, collections of guns and typewriters (both manufactured in Erfurt), and a film about the growth of Erfurt over time. Look for the wall of street signs from Erfurt's time as part of the former German Democratic Republic (communist East Germany). Under the communists, Erfurt's main drags were renamed Karl-Marx-Allee, Waffenbrüderschaft ("Brothers in Arms"—i.e., the Warsaw Pact), Völkerfreundschaft ("Peoples' Friendship"—a favorite buzzword of Stalin's), and October 7 Street (celebrating the date, in 1949, when the republic was officially formed). In a display case, you can compare banknotes from West Germany and East Germany.

Cost and Hours: €6, Tue-Sun 10:00-18:00, closed Mon, Johannesstrasse 169, tel. 0361/655-5651, www.stadtmuseum-erfurt. de.

ON THE OUTSKIRTS OF TOWN
Egapark

When the flowers are blooming (April through October), garden lovers travel from all over Germany to this sprawling green space at the western edge of town. You can stroll through various gardens (perennials, roses, dahlias, irises, sculptures, Japanese rock and water), visit the houses (for butterflies, tropical plants, and more), climb the observation tower, and tour the museum.

Cost and Hours: €8, €2 after 17:30, €3 Nov-Feb, more during special events; daily March-Oct 9:00-18:00—until 18:30 May-mid-Sept, Nov-Feb 10:00-16:00; Gothaer Strasse 38, ride tram #2 from the train station, tel. 0361/564-3737, www.egapark-erfurt.de.

Sleeping in Erfurt

Like many other former East-German cities, Erfurt is short on characteristic little family-run inns. Except for the fun, informal Rad-Hof, the accommodations here are sterile business-class hotels offering predictable comfort in the Old Town core. The Rad-Hof and Gästehaus Nikolai are far enough from the station that you might want to bring your luggage there by tram (three stops on the #1 or #5 to Augustinerkloster). Erfurt hoteliers enjoy grumbling about a hefty 5 percent "cultural tax" that is levied on all overnights in town; this tax is not included in the rates listed below.

$$$ Hotel Zumnorde, buried deep in the Anger shopping district, has 54 spacious, somewhat overpriced rooms (Sb-€95-130, Db-€115-180; rate depends on demand and room size; air-con in some rooms, elevator, Wi-Fi, parking-€11/day, Anger 50-51 but enter on the side street at Weitergasse 26, tel. 0361/56800, www. hotel-zumnorde.de, info@hotel-zumnorde.de).

$$$ Mercure Hotel Erfurt Altstadt, part of the Europe-wide business-class chain, has 141 rooms on a nondescript street between the Anger shopping district and the main sightseeing zone (Sb-€70-140, Db-€70-148, breakfast-€17, elevator, guest computer, Wi-Fi, parking-€12/day, Meienbergstrasse 26-27, tel. 0361/59490, www.mercure.com, h5375@accor.com).

$$ Hotel am Kaisersaal offers 36 business-class rooms in an inviting location, just a few steps off the charming Wenigermarkt

Sleep Code

Abbreviations   (€1 = about $1.40, country code: 49)
S = Single, **D** = Double/Twin, **T** = Triple, **Q** = Quad, **b** = bathroom, **s** = shower only

Price Rankings

$$$ Higher Priced—Most rooms €110 or more.

  $$ Moderately Priced—Most rooms between €70-110.

    $ Lower Priced—Most rooms €70 or less.

Unless otherwise noted, credit cards are accepted, English is spoken, and Wi-Fi is generally free. Prices can change without notice; verify current rates online or by email. For the best prices, always book directly with the hotel.

restaurant square (Sb-€89, Db-€104, Tb-€119, rates can flex with demand, includes small breakfast, bigger breakfast-€10, elevator, Wi-Fi, parking-€9/day, Futterstrasse 8, tel. 0361/658560, www.hotel-am-kaisersaal.de, info@hotel-am-kaisersaal.de).

$$ Ibis Hotel Erfurt Altstadt offers 105 centrally located rooms with cookie-cutter comfort. Considering the dearth of characteristic hotels in town, if you're going to sleep in an Ibis, it might as well be here (Sb-€69, Db-€79, often €6 more on weekends, see online deals, extra bed-€15, breakfast-€10, air-con, elevator, guest computer, free Wi-Fi in lobby, pay Wi-Fi in rooms, garage parking-€8/day, Barfüsserstrasse 9, tel. 0361/66410, www.ibishotel.com, h1648@accor.com).

$$ Gästehaus Nikolai, run by the Augustinian Monastery, is along the river, just up the street from the monastery. Its 17 old-fashioned rooms have TVs and phones (Sb-€65, Db-€92, Qb-€133, extra bed-€24, limited free parking, Augustinerstrasse 30, tel. 0361/598-170, www.gaestehaus-nikolai.de, gaestehaus-nikolai@augustinerkloster.de).

$ Pension Rad-Hof is a wonderful oasis run with justifiable pride by bike aficionados Sigrid and Dieter. Located next to the Augustinian Monastery, this characteristic B&B has six homey rooms (all decorated with musical instruments) on two floors around a chirpy garden courtyard. While the lodgings aren't fancy, this place has more character than the rest of Erfurt's hotels combined (Sb-€30-50, Db-€60, Tb-€80, Qb with double bed and two bunks-€100, €3/person more for one-night stays, cash only, guest computer, Wi-Fi, bike rental-€6/day, Kirchgasse 1B, tel. 0361/602-7761, www.rad-hof.de, erfurt@rad-hof.de).

Eating in Erfurt

A Thuringian staple is the distinctive potato dumpling called a *Kloss* (plural: *Klösse*). About the size of a tennis ball, these are soft and light, though generally drenched in gravy, and served with meat dishes and sometimes in soups. Many Erfurt menus include an array of dumpling dishes. Thuringians are also proud of their own special type of peppery sausage.

Most of Erfurt's restaurants are quite plain-Jane—don't expect culinary variety here. Since little distinguishes one place from the next, the stakes are low—just look for an ambience that appeals.

Zum Güldenen Rade ("At the Golden Wheel") has Erfurt's most appealing beer garden out back—under trees and surrounded by half-timbers (with both table service and self-service sections). There's also indoor seating. Understandably touristy, it offers classic German and Thuringian cuisine (including a few vegetarian *Klösse* options; €12-15 main courses, €2-3 self-service bratwurst, daily 11:00-24:00, Marktstrasse 50, tel. 0361/561-3506).

Feuerkugel serves up good, traditional Thuringian cooking, supposedly from "Oma Käthe" (Granny Katie). Its cozy, warm, woody interior is particularly inviting (€9-12 main courses, including €10 *Klösse* dishes, daily 11:00-24:00, Michaelisstrasse 3-4, tel. 0361/789-1256).

Zum Goldenen Schwan ("At the Golden Swan") is a brewpub with several rooms, both new and old. Sit inside, near the big copper brewing vats, or head outside to the beer garden (€8-16 wurst plates and main courses, daily 11:00-24:00, Jan-March from 17:00 Mon-Fri, Michaelisstrasse 9, tel. 0361/262-3742).

Schnitzler, true to its name, serves schnitzel. When I asked how many different versions of schnitzel were on the menu, they shrugged and said, "Enough." I lost count at around 30. It's right on Domplatz, with a nondescript interior and outdoor tables looking toward the cathedral and St. Severus (€9-12 schnitzel dishes—huge and splittable, also other options, daily 11:00-23:00, Domplatz 32, tel. 0361/644-7557).

Cognito offers a fresh, healthy, self-service alternative right next to the Merchants' Bridge. This student-vibe place dishes up €5-10 soups, curries, and salads, as well as coffee drinks. You can get it to go, or enjoy the comfortable, hip lounge interior on two floors (Mon-Sat 8:00-22:00, Sun 9:00-21:00, Hefengasse 1, tel. 0361/660-4666).

Fast Food: To grab a *Thüringer* bratwurst in a hurry, stop by **Faust Food,** which grills up sausages and other quick meaty options at low prices (€3 or less). Get yours to go, or grab a table inside or out. A hit with students, it's on a forgotten lane in the middle of town—so near all the tourists, yet so far away (Tue-Sat 11:00-23:00, Sun 11:00-19:00, closed Mon, Waagegasse 1, tel. 0361/786-9969).

Ice Cream: **Eiscafé San Remo,** on Marktstrasse just a block off Domplatz, has a loyal following for its Italian-style gelato (daily until 21:30, Marktstrasse 21, tel. 0361/643-0449).

Late-Night Drinks: **Modern Masters** is the favorite in this student town for cocktails after dark in a sophisticated yet uns-nooty atmosphere (no food—only drinks, Tue-Sat from 18:00, closed Sun-Mon, right at the start of Michaelisstrasse at #48). Its historic interior is cool and inviting, and its outdoor tables are great for people-watching.

Übersee (literally "Over the Water") is a livelier restaurant and bar with tables on a terrace over the river, just upstream from the Merchants' Bridge. It has an eclectic international menu and tables that sprawl through two adjacent buildings—one new, one old—and out onto the best riverfront terraces in town (€8-9 salads, €8-13 main courses, Mon-Sat 9:00-24:00, Sun 10:30-24:00, Kürschner-gasse 8).

Erfurt Connections

From Erfurt by Train to: Eisenach and **Wartburg Castle** (2/ hour, 30 minutes on IC or ICE train, 45 minutes on regional train), **Leipzig** (hourly, 1.5-2 hours), **Wittenberg** (every 2 hours, 2 hours, most transfer in Naumburg; also possible in 2.5 hours with ad-ditional changes), **Dresden** (nearly hourly direct, 2.5 hours; more possible with change in Leipzig, 3 hours), **Berlin** (hourly, 2.5-3 hours, transfer in Leipzig or Naumburg/Saale), **Frankfurt** (hourly, 2.5 hours), **Würzburg** (every 2 hours direct, 2-2.5 hours; more with transfer in Fulda), **Nürnberg** (at least hourly, 3-3.5 hours, most transfer in Fulda, a few in Lichtenfels or Würzburg), **Munich** (about 2/hour, 4.5-5 hours, transfer in Würzburg or Fulda). Train info: Tel. 0180-599-6633, www.bahn.de.

Wartburg Castle

Just west of Erfurt is another important Martin Luther sight: Wartburg Castle (VART-boorg), perched over the town of Eisen- ach (EYE-zehn-nahkh).

When Luther spoke out against Church corruption, he made enemies of the pope and emperor, and put his life in jeopardy. Luther fled to this eas- ily defended castle, and—hidden away in a small room—he diligently translated the New Testament from original Greek sources. Although Luther's translation was not the first version of the Bible printed in German, it was so widely circulated that it helped shape the development of standard written Ger- man—making Wartburg, in a sense, the birthplace of the modern German language.

The town of **Eisenach,** squatting in the valley below Wart- burg, is worth a quick visit for those with extra time. The TI is on the main square, called the Markt (Mon-Fri 10:00- 18:00, Sat-Sun 10:00-17:00, Markt 24, tel. 03691/79230, www.eisenach.info). A build- ing where Martin Luther lived for three years while attend- ing high school here has been turned into a museum (Luther- haus), as has the house once

thought to be the birthplace of Johann Sebastian Bach (Bachhaus).

LUTHERLAND

PLANNING YOUR TIME

Wartburg Castle works well either as a side-trip from Erfurt or on the way between Erfurt and points west (such as Frankfurt or Würzburg). You can try to time your visit around the castle's hour- long, once-daily English tour (at 13:30, April-Oct only). But the tour isn't essential unless you're here to see the castle's few fine late- 19th-century rooms. Otherwise, you can see the castle courtyard and museum, including the room where Luther worked, at any time during open hours.

GETTING THERE

First head for the town of Eisenach, which is 30-45 minutes west of Erfurt on the main train line. (The Eisenach train station has lockers in the main hall.) From the station, you can take the bus, catch a taxi, or hike up to Wartburg.

Bus #10 (€1.50) runs from the parking lot across the street from the station up to Wartburg at the top of each hour (Easter-Oct only, daily 9:00-17:00, 20-minute trip).

A taxi costs about €10. Either way, you'll still have a steep 10-minute climb from the parking lot or bus stop up the stairs to Wartburg itself.

If you walk all the way from the train station to Wartburg, allow at least 45 minutes and expect an elevation gain of about 650 feet. Exiting the station, turn right and walk about 10 minutes into the Eisenach town center; then hike up into the hills (following signs for *Wartburg*; get more detailed directions at TI).

Drivers can park in the lot by the castle bus stop (€5).

Returning to Eisenach: Bus #10 departs Wartburg at :25 past each hour for the train station (Easter-Oct 9:25-17:25). Walking downhill to Eisenach is quick (20-25 minutes) and pleasant if you have strong knees. The broad dirt path starts at the bend in the road below the castle bus stop and takes you through the woods back into town: Follow signs for *Markt* to reach the main square, then wind your way through town to the station.

ORIENTATION

Cost and Hours: Castle courtyard—free, open daily April-Oct 8:30-20:00, Nov-March 9:00-17:00; museum—€5, same hours as courtyard, last entry April-Oct at 17:30, Nov-March at 16:00; tel. 03691/2500, www.wartburg.de.

Tours: €9 (€5 extra to take photos), includes museum entry. A one-hour English tour departs daily at 13:30. Tours in German run every 10-20 minutes (April-Oct 8:30-17:00, Nov-March 9:00-15:30). The castle offers a tiny-print, somewhat-hard-to-follow English handout to English-speaking visitors on a German tour.

Eating: The café in the castle courtyard serves *Flammkuchen* (German flatbread) and cakes. Halfway up the stairs from the parking lot, the self-serve Wartburg-Terrasse has €5-10 dumpling-based dishes (closed Nov-March). The wurst stands by the parking lot and bus stop close around 18:00.

OVERVIEW

Dramatically capping a forested ridgeline high above Eisenach, Wartburg Castle is famous among Luther lovers as a place that gave shelter and solace to an on-the-skids (and recently excommunicated) young scholar who was determined to translate the New Testament into his own living language. Pilgrims come here to see the room where Martin Luther carried out that important work.

But Luther aside, Wartburg is a fine fortress in its own right, with a few opulent rooms that were lavishly redecorated during a surge of German pride in the late 1880s (viewable on guided tour only). In the castle courtyard, you can climb the tower *(Südturm)* for €0.50 by inserting coins into the turnstile.

BACKGROUND

Wartburg has an impressive history. In 1130, the castle became the seat of Thuringia's landgraves (counts who ruled the region on behalf of the Holy Roman Empire). Most of the castle's days were peaceful (read: dull), but it was an important center of power—and notable as the site of a contest of minstrels in 1207, a story later famously dramatized by Richard Wagner in his opera *Tannhäuser*.

Around this same time, Wartburg became the home of St. Elisabeth (1207-1231). Elisabeth, a daughter of the Hungarian king, was sent to Wartburg for a po-

litically expedient marriage at the age of 14. The match turned out to be a happy one, and the couple had three children, but her husband died while returning from a crusade, leaving Elisabeth a widow at the age of 20. According to an often-told legend, the pious, kindly Elisabeth was known to sneak scraps of food out of the house to give to poor people on the street. One evening, her cruel confessor saw her leaving the house and stopped her. Seeing her full apron (which was loaded with bread for the poor), he demanded to know what she was carrying. "Roses," she replied. "Show me," he growled. Elisabeth opened her apron, the bread was gone, and rose petals miraculously cascaded out onto the floor. Elisabeth died only four years after her husband, but in her short life, she founded hospitals and did other charitable work, and she remains a popular symbol of charity not only in Germany, but also in her native Hungary.

In May of 1521, Luther came to the castle, disguised as a bearded man named Junker Jörg (Squire George). He spent the next year secretly translating the New Testament from Greek into German. His short visit helped put Wartburg on the map.

In October of 1817, shortly after German-speaking armies helped defeat Napoleon, recently formed fraternal organizations from around the region came together at this castle to celebrate German unity. It was one of the first occasions when German speakers began to band together and forge a common pride. In fact, the flag of one of those fraternities (from Jena) was later adopted as the flag of a united Germany, which still flies all over the country.

VISITING THE CASTLE

In the **museum,** placards tell a bit of the story of the castle, paintings show how it looked before reconstruction, and artifacts recall the life of St. Elisabeth. You get the chance to peek into one small "royal bedroom" that shows the sumptuous 19th-century restoration work, and there's also a collection of historical cutlery. One room displays a few paintings of Luther and his family (mostly mass-produced

ones from Lucas Cranach's workshop). Find the images of Luther's parents—note the family resemblance. Compare the portraits of Luther at various stages in his life—in the garb of an Augustinian monk, wearing the cap of a distinguished professor, in the bearded disguise of Junker Jörg—as well as the portraits of some of his notable contemporaries.

After the museum exhibit comes the highlight for Luther pilgrims: Walk along the gallery with low timber arches to find the

humble **Luther Room** (Lutherstube). This was the site of one of the greatest intellectual revolutions in human history: For 10 months, Luther hunkered down at a desk here and used original Greek sources to translate the New Testament into everyday German. For centuries Christian worship had been passed through the obscure Latin-speaking filter of the Roman Catholic Church. Luther's translation—even though it wasn't the first in German—was the version that gave Germans, even peasants, direct access to the Word of God. Luther's work also helped to codify the evolving German language—setting the foundation for the tongue still being spoken by the people around you. The furnishings you see aren't original and were placed in the room long after Luther's time.

The guided **tour** visits about 10 rooms in the part of the castle

LUTHERLAND

that was restored in the 19th century, and ends in the museum. Highlights include Elisabeth's Bower (with spectacular glittering Neo-Byzantine mosaics from the early 1900s); the Elisabeth Gallery (decorated with beautiful frescoes about the life of St. Elisabeth); the Hall of Minstrels (with walls decorated with the text of a poem about Wartburg's famous contest of minstrels—this room was the setting for part of Wagner's *Tannhäuser*); and the vast Banquet Hall (decorated in an exuberant Historicist style rivaling the creations of "Mad" King Ludwig, who had a replica of this room created at his Neuschwanstein Castle).

Eisenach Connections

From Eisenach by Train to: Erfurt (2/hour, 30 minutes on IC or ICE train, 45 minutes on regional train), **Leipzig** (hourly, 2-2.5 hours), **Wittenberg** (every 2 hours, 2.5 hours, most transfer in Naumburg; also possible in 3 hours with additional changes), **Frankfurt** (hourly, 2 hours), **Würzburg** (hourly, 2 hours, transfer in Fulda). Train info: Tel. 0180-599-6633, www.bahn.de.

Wittenberg

You need only look at its official name—Lutherstadt Wittenberg—to know this small city's claim to fame. The adopted hometown of Martin Luther, and the birthplace of his Protestant Reformation, little Wittenberg has a gigantic history that belies its straightforward townscape. With a pair of historic churches—St. Mary's, where Luther preached, and the Church of All Saints (Castle Church), where he famously hammered his 95 theses to the door—and an excellent museum about Luther's life (Luther House), this town can be a worthwhile stop even to those unfamiliar with The Great Reformer. The notable painter Lucas Cranach the Elder, a contemporary and friend of Luther who also lived and worked in Wittenberg, left behind a slew of fine paintings and woodcuts, and you can see where he lived as well.

Centuries of Germans have celebrated Wittenberg for its ties to Luther. In 1983, which marked Martin Luther's 500th birthday, Wittenberg was part of communist East Germany, whose atheistic regime was tear-

LUTHERLAND

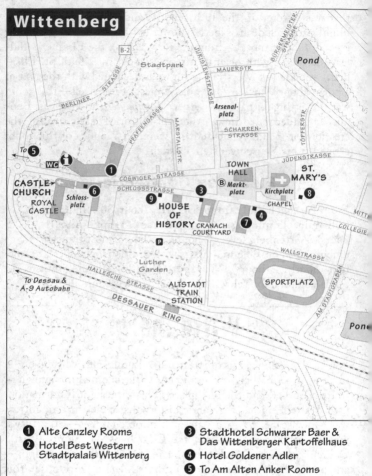

Wittenberg

1 Alte Canzley Rooms
2 Hotel Best Western Stadtpalais Wittenberg
3 Stadthotel Schwarzer Baer & Das Wittenberger Kartoffelhaus
4 Hotel Goldener Adler
5 To Am Alten Anker Rooms

LUTHERLAND

ing down proud old churches elsewhere. But ignoring the Luther anniversary would have made the East German government, already unpopular, seem too woefully out of touch. (The government also sensed an opportunity to attract Luther tourists flush with much-needed hard Western currency.) So the communists swallowed hard and rehabilitated the memory of Luther, tidying up the sights devoted to him.

This may be why Wittenberg emerged from communism in better shape than most East German towns. And, thanks partly to the steady stream of Luther pilgrims, the town has since been spruced up even more. Wittenberg is already gearing up for the banner year of 2017—the 500th anniversary of Martin Luther's

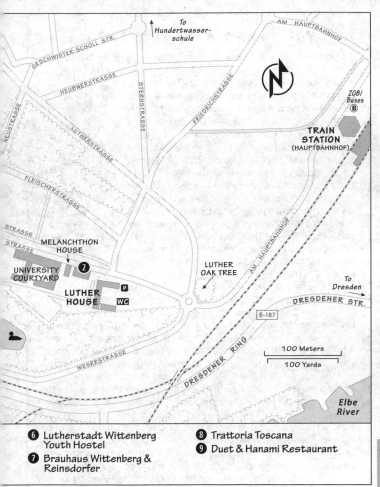

6 Lutherstadt Wittenberg Youth Hostel

7 Brauhaus Wittenberg & Reinsdorfer

8 Trattoria Toscana

9 Duet & Hanami Restaurant

95 theses. Local authorities have secured EU funds to support the festivities, so you may find a lot of construction in your way.

You'll see Luther pilgrims as you walk through town. Wittenberg is also a stop for riverboat cruise groups heading from Hamburg to Dresden and Prague. But Wittenberg is not very touristy. Its pedestrianized main street feels quiet—sometimes almost deserted. Though pleasant and nicely manicured, the town offers little to do beyond appreciating its Protestant history.

PLANNING YOUR TIME

Wittenberg's sights are easy to see quickly—you can have a satisfying visit in just four or five hours. The town is a stop on the main high-speed train line from Berlin to Leipzig and beyond, and this

Wittenberg in the Early 1500s

As you explore Wittenberg, mentally time-travel to the days of Luther—the first few decades of the 16th century. The Renaissance was percolating to the south, in Italy (where Michelangelo and Raphael were hard at work redecorating the Vatican), and a spirit of new ideas was also beginning to take hold in Germany. The influential prince elector Frederick III "the Wise" (1463-1525), who had inherited half of Saxony from his father, chose sleepy Wittenberg as his royal seat. He built a stout castle here in 1492 (not open to visitors, but viewable from the park just beyond the town gate), and began remaking this humble fishing village into a proper Renaissance town. (That explains Wittenberg's relatively intuitive grid of streets, compared with the twisty medieval muddle of many other German towns.) Frederick the Wise hired Lucas Cranach the Elder to be his official court painter. Cranach—along with his wife, Barbara, and son Lucas Cranach the Younger—lived in a gigantic mansion on Market Square (today a museum; his statue—pictured above—is in the courtyard). Frederick also founded a university here (in 1502) and stocked it with some of the brightest minds of his time, including the promising young theologian Martin Luther and the brilliant classical-languages specialist Philipp Melanchthon. Cranach, Luther, Melanchthon, and others were good friends who regularly socialized and swapped ideas.

Although he remained a devout Catholic until the end of his life, Frederick the Wise supported Luther and the Reformers in their darkest hour, likely saving them from obscurity or worse. Wittenberg would not be famous if not for Luther—but, most likely, if not for Frederick the Wise, Luther would not be famous, either.

makes it an ideal day-trip from Berlin (45 minutes by speedy ICE; 1.5 hours on cheaper trains) or Leipzig (30 minutes by ICE, 1 hour on cheaper trains). It also works as an on-the-way destination (store bags in a locker at the station).

Orientation to Wittenberg

Literally "White Hill," Wittenberg (Germans say VIT-tehn-behrk, pop. 49,000) sits atop a gentle rise above the Elbe River. The tourists' Wittenberg is essentially a one-street town: Its main drag runs about three-quarters of a mile from the Luther House (where the street is called Collegienstrasse) to the Castle Church (where it's called Schlossstrasse). The rest of the Old Town consists only of a few side streets. The modern part of town sprawls mostly to the north and east. (Don't confuse Wittenberg with Wittenberge, a town north of Berlin.)

TOURIST INFORMATION

Wittenberg's TI is at the far end of town from the train station, across the street from Castle Church (April-Oct Mon-Fri 9:00-18:00, Sat-Sun 10:00-16:00; Nov-March daily 10:00-16:00 except closed Sat-Sun Jan-March; tel. 0800-202-0114 or 03491/498-610, www.lutherstadt-wittenberg.de). You can watch a 25-minute, English-language film about Martin Luther (free, runs anytime on request), or rent a town audioguide (€6/day, 2 hours of commentary). There's a pay WC next door.

ARRIVAL IN WITTENBERG

Wittenberg's **main train station** (listed on schedules as Lutherstadt Wittenberg) is a dull 10-minute walk from the Luther Museum and a 25-minute walk from the TI and Castle Church. (The smaller Lutherstadt Wittenberg Altstadt station, while closer to the Old Town, only serves trains on a small branch line.)

The main station building sits oddly in the middle of the tracks. Inside is a *Reisezentrum;* outside, along track 4, are a few lockers. Beside the tracks, in an open area under a white, tent-like structure, is the bus station (ZOB), taxi stand, and more services, including a public transit info office that gives out free town maps (Mon-Fri 8:00-18:00, Sat 8:00-12:00, closed Sun).

Bus #300 runs from the station to Marktplatz in the center of the Old Town—stops are not announced, so ask the driver to alert you when you reach the Markt (€1.35, day pass-€2.65, buy tickets from driver; about 2/hour, leaves from platform C, direction: Apollendorf, www.vetter-bus.de). From Marktplatz, it's a five-minute walk to the TI.

A **taxi** from the station to the TI costs about €6 (if no taxis are waiting, call 03491/666-666). To **walk,** head left from the station, walk beneath the overpass, and look for signs directing you to the city center. Drivers will find plenty of free on-street **parking** just outside the mostly pedestrianized town center.

HELPFUL HINTS

Festivals: Various festivals dot Wittenberg's calendar, including a three-day celebration of the wedding of Luther and Katharina (second weekend in June), a pottery and craft market (last weekend in Sept), and special events for **Reformation Day** (Oct 31, when Luther nailed his 95 theses to the church door).

In 2015, the town marks its **"Cranach Year,"** primarily by exhibiting various Cranach paintings on loan from museums throughout Europe.

Tours: Most walking-tour options (you'll likely see costumed Martin Luthers and Katharina von Boras leading groups through town) are in German only. For an English tour, hire your own local guide—gracious **Katja Köhler** does a great job telling Wittenberg's story (€80/2-hour tour, €130/4-hour tour, mobile 0177-688-8218, katjakoehler@gmx.net).

English Worship Services: Local Lutherans offer English-language services in historic Wittenberg churches during the summer (May-Oct Wed-Fri at 16:30 in small Corpus Christi chapel next to Town Church of St. Mary, Sat at 17:00 in either Castle Church or Town Church of St. Mary, confirm times at www.wittenbergenglishministry.com).

Classical Concerts: It seems like there's always a concert on in one of the town's churches. If you're spending the night, check at the TI to find out when and where you can enjoy some classical music. As the 2017 festivities approach, Wittenberg will become enlivened, with more musical performances and special events.

Sights in Wittenberg

MARTIN LUTHER SIGHTS

I've organized these sights roughly in order from the TI end of town (with the Castle Church) to the Luther House end of town. If you're walking from the train station, you'll come across these sights in reverse order.

▲▲Castle Church (Schlosskirche)

This Church of All Saints was the site of one of the most important moments in European history: Martin Luther nailing his 95 the-

ses to the church door. That door—and most of the church as it existed in Luther's time—are long gone (destroyed in 1760, during the Seven Years' War). But in the late 19th century, as Germany was uniting as a nation for the first time, the church and the door were rebuilt in the Romantic style as a temple to Luther and his fellow Reformers.

As part of the town's huge sprucing up for the 500th anniversary of the nailing of the theses, the church and its tower are being renovated—which means the interior is closed until early 2017.

▲Market Square (Marktplatz)

This wide square is much the same today as it was in Luther's time. An all-purpose space back then, it was used for everything

from tournaments to executions. The square is dominated by the Renaissance-style **Town Hall** (Rathaus). Notice the seven small doors at the right side of the building, which led to a shopping gallery back when the building's cellar hosted a little marketplace (today the Town Hall houses a 20th-century Christian art collection). In one corner of the square you'll find a metal model of Wittenberg's Old Town. In the middle of the square are 19th-century **statues** of Martin Luther (pictured here) and Philipp Melanchthon (pictured on next page).

The main street through town is lined by delightful gurgling **canals,** as in a few other German cities, like Freiburg and Augsburg. When Luther first moved to Wittenberg, he was disgusted by these, which carried drinking water (on the way into town) and smelly sewage (on the way out). Years later, they were covered over by the modern street. But recently they were opened up to the air to evoke the ambience of Luther's time.

Opposite the Town Hall, find three brass plaques *(Stolpersteine)* in the sidewalk outside the houses at #3 and #2; they mark the former homes of Wittenbergers murdered in the Nazi years (there are more than a dozen similar plaques in Wittenberg; for more on the *Stolpersteine,* see page 795).

Cranach Courtyard (Cranachhof)

Find the big beige Renaissance building at Schlossstrasse 1, in one corner of the square, with a pharmacy (the Lucas-Cranach-

Apotheke) on the ground floor. This building, circling a surprisingly large courtyard, was the residence of the artist Lucas Cranach the Elder. Enter the courtyard to see a statue of Cranach sketching at the far end (see the photo on page 626).

As the official court painter for Frederick the Wise, Cranach was one of the most esteemed men in town, but he was also an entrepreneur who dabbled in endeavors like printing and running a pharmacy. Cranach and Luther were fast friends. The artist was

Philipp Melanchthon (1497-1560)

While everyone who comes to Wittenberg has heard of Martin Luther, many are surprised to find another important figure celebrated here with almost equal reverence: Philipp Melanchthon. The Garfunkel to Luther's Simon, Melanchthon was a brainy university professor who also played a critical role in the Protestant Reformation. Born Philipp Schwartzerdt in southern Germany, he later changed his name to its Greek translation, Melanchthon ("black soil"). Although he was short, young, sickly, and notoriously unattractive, Melanchthon impressed everybody in Wittenberg with his keen intellect. In fact, when Melanchthon became disillusioned with Wittenberg and threatened to move away, Frederick the Wise persuaded him to stay by arranging a marriage for him (to the mayor's daughter, no less). While Luther was no intellectual slouch, Melanchthon was even more brilliant—he taught several topics (specializing in ancient languages, pedagogy, and theology) and encouraged women to pursue university study. Particularly gifted with languages, he provided Luther with invaluable assistance when translating the Bible into German from the original Greek texts.

the only painter who had permission to do portraits of Luther and his family (Cranach and his school produced and reproduced some 2,000 Luther portraits), and he was one of the first printers of Luther's writings. Cranach's house is also where Luther's future bride, Katharina von Bora, lived when she first came to Wittenberg.

For decades, this space sat in ruins (see the pre-1989 photo in the entry arch.) But it's been converted into a kind of cultural center, hosting artists' studios, a small bar, a gift shop, comfortable hotel rooms, and—at the far end of the courtyard—an old-fashioned print shop. Operated by a quirky printer who speaks some English and enjoys explaining the importance of Luther's statement, "This is a German nation—the people speak German," the shop uses traditional methods to create postcards and replicas of works by Luther and Cranach (closed Sun).

▲▲Town Church of St. Mary (Stadtkirche St. Marien)

Peeking up over a row of buildings at the end of Market Square, this is the oldest building in town and the most historic place to be surrounded by Luther lore. For most of his life, this was Luther's home church—where he was married, where his children were

baptized, and where he preached over 2,000 times. Inside this church, what many consider to be the first-ever Protestant service took place, on Christmas Day in 1521 (although Martin Luther wasn't in attendance—he was hiding out at Wartburg Castle). The readings were in German (not Latin), communion was taken by everyone (not just priests), and hymns were sung by the congregation—actually quite radical at the time. It's also home to several engaging pieces of early Protestant artwork by Lucas Cranach and his son. The church is being restored, but should reopen by the time of your visit.

Cost and Hours: Free; Easter-Oct Mon-Sat 10:00-18:00, Sun 11:30-18:00; Nov-Easter Mon-Sat 10:00-16:00, Sun 11:30-16:00; www.stadtkirchengemeinde-wittenberg.de.

➔ Self-Guided Tour: From the **outside,** notice that the tops of the twin towers don't quite match the rest of the building. Formerly pointy Gothic steeples, these were knocked down to fortify the towers with cannons during a 1546 battle. They were later rebuilt in the round Renaissance style you see today.

• *Step inside.*

The focal point of the church is the colorful, engaging, almost

whimsical **altar painting** by Lucas Cranach the Elder, the Younger, and their school (completed in 1547, the year after Luther died). The gang's all here: All the big-name early Protestants and their buddies have showed up to re-enact classic ecclesiastical scenes. In the spirit of the Reformation, these aren't saints or royals—they're just people.

The bottom panel shows Martin Luther preaching from a pulpit as he points to the congregation—evocative of his mission to make worship more engaging for the people. The fluttering loincloth of Jesus helps to convey the message from preacher to parishioner. But notice that, true to life, some of those people aren't paying attention—they're chatting and looking around. The woman watching Luther most intently is his wife, Katharina.

The panel on the left shows Philipp Melanchthon (who was not a priest) baptizing a baby. The early Reformers believed that lay people—not exclusively priests—could perform baptisms. In the foreground, the extravagantly dressed woman with her back to us is Cranach's wife, Barbara. Supposedly, she grew frustrated that her husband was always painting Luther, Katharina, and others, but never her. "Fine," he said. "I'll include you in the altarpiece."

On the right panel, Johannes Bugenhagen (among Reformers, he ranks third after Luther and Melanchthon) is hearing confession from two very different people. Over the head of the obviously distraught and repentant man on the left, Bugenhagen holds the key of heaven—the sinner has done right by confessing and will reap eternal rewards. The man on the right, however, is trying to buy his way into heaven—but his hands are tied and the key of heaven is behind him, indicating he can't purchase paradise.

The central panel features the Last Supper, with the Reformers standing in for the apostles. Notice the round table—in Protestantism, all are equal. People from all walks of life are actively engaging each other. It's easy to pick out Judas in the foreground, who wears yellow (as evildoers often do in Cranach paintings). On the opposite side of the table, Martin Luther (clad in black, wearing the bearded disguise of Junker Jörg) is being handed a chalice by Lucas Cranach the Younger. In contrast to Catholic worship at the time, Protestant services invited everybody to participate in communion.

• *Now circle around behind the altar.*

Look at the lower panel, which looks like it's been defaced by some no-good teenagers. It was...centuries ago. Around Luther's time, students of theology came here at the end of their studies and scratched their names or initials into the painting: on the left, in the river of knowledge, if they'd done well—or on the right, in hell, if they'd flunked. Looking carefully among the damned (higher up, on a skull), you can find the name "Johannes Luther"—Martin's son. (Thankfully, he had more success after he switched to law.)

• *Return to the front of the altar.*

The **baptismal font** is where Luther's own children were baptized. Notice the tube extending from the basin directly down toward the ground. This allowed water, after having washed away sin, to be drained directly into what was a sandy floor, so it could be transmitted, unimpeded, to hell. Around the lower legs of the font, notice the many evil demons attempting to reach the baby being baptized up top—but their progress is blocked by the righteous saints.

• *Head to the back-right corner (behind and to the right of the main altar).*

Find the smaller painting, *The Vineyard of the Lord*, by Lucas Cranach the Younger. This work's political motives are obvious: On the right, the Reformers tend to the garden of the Lord (that's Martin Luther raking and Philipp Melanchthon pulling water from the

well—just as the Reformers went back to the original source to translate their Bible). On the left, the pope and his cronies (in their excessively opulent robes) trash all their hard work. Subtle. In the lower-left corner, everyone lines up to receive their reward from Jesus. The pope (wearing yellow, again symbolizing evil) has already received his, but keeps his hand outstretched, expecting more than his share. In the lower right, the Reformers (in their simple black robes) pray reverently.

Directly to the left of the altar is a modern sign marking the former location of the **pulpit** from which Martin Luther preached for many years (the original pulpit is now in the Luther House).

• *Leave the church, noticing the organ over the main door.*

Luther's greatest musical hit, "A Mighty Fortress is Our God," was first sung here. The grand **organ** dates from the communist period (1983), and booms out short and free organ concerts (May-Oct Fri at 18:00).

• *Back outside the church, head left (counter-clockwise) around the church.*

At the back corner of the church, look up at the bottom of the roofline to find the relief of a pig, called the **Judensau** ("Jewish sow"). This bit of medieval anti-Semitic propaganda was designed

to intimidate Wittenberg's Jews, who lived in the area just behind the church. Look carefully at the pig—which is considered unclean in the Jewish faith: Jewish children are suckling from it, and a rabbi seems to be peering inquisitively into its rear end. When restoring the church, church authorities asked the Jewish community in Berlin what they should do with this painful remnant of a less-enlightened time. Rather than cover it, they suggested leaving it here as a part of the town's heritage, and adding a modern monument: Look for the plaque in the cobbles directly below the pig, where four paving stones look as if they're being pried apart by something bubbling up from beneath. The message: You can't hide uncomfortable facts; they will find a way to see the light of day. The adjacent cedar tree was donated by students in Tel Aviv.

Behind you, go through the gap between the buildings near the pig to see one of Wittenberg's 16th-century **fountains.** Part of Frederick the Wise's improvements, this network of fountains (with wooden pipes) still works—but nobody knows quite how.

LUTHERLAND

▲▲Luther House (Lutherhaus)

The town's premier sight—and a must-see even for non-Lutherans—Luther's former home has been converted into an excellent museum displaying original paintings, manuscripts, and other Luther-era items—including the pulpit from which Luther preached, famous portraits of Luther and the other Reformers by Lucas Cranach, and Luther's original New Testament and Bible translations into High German. Everything is fully described in English, and touch-screen stations let the interested dig deeper.

Cost and Hours: €6, €8 combo-ticket with Melanchthon House; April-Oct daily 9:00-18:00; Nov-March Tue-Sun 10:00-17:00, closed Mon; Collegienstrasse 54, tel. 03491/420-3118, www.martinluther.de.

❂ Self-Guided Tour: From the street, step through the passage (at #59) into the inner courtyard to see the giant, turreted building. Not really a "house," this was originally a monastery. Luther lived here first as a monk and again later, after he had married Katharina von Bora (the building was a wedding gift from John the Steadfast, the prince elector who took Luther under his wing). Katharina rented out rooms to students, and kept the family fed and watered by cultivating a garden, brewing beer, and even breeding cattle. In the middle of the courtyard is a **statue of Katharina**. Erected on her 500th birthday in 1999, the sculpture symbolizes her leaving her former life at a nunnery and beginning a new one with Martin Luther.

Head inside through the gateway on your right. From the ticket desk, go straight into the first room to see a simplified model of Wittenberg during Luther's time; paintings by Lucas Cranach (including a portrait of Frederick the Wise, the prince elector who supported Luther); and a woodcut print of a knights' tournament at Market Square.

The next room juxtaposes several **historic items**. Flanking the door are an indulgence chest (actually filled with 21st-century coins) and an original letter of indulgence *(Ablassurkunde)*, from 1492. Those who bought indulgences would supposedly be rescued from their sins...while generating substantial income for the Catholic Church. And that "sin tax" was applied directly to an ambitious building project at the Vatican: On the right, see the engraving of St. Peter's Basilica, with its spectacular dome still under construc-

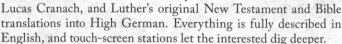

tion. Archbishop Albrecht of Mainz (Luther's direct superior) and Pope Leo X (both pictured at right), stunningly influential and wealthy, were part of a finely tuned business of salvation sales.

In contrast to the opulence of the Vatican, see Martin Luther's original linden-wood **pulpit** from the Town Church of St. Mary. Notice how relatively humble it is—imagine him climbing up to the top and bringing the Reformation message to a packed church. Nearby is the first printed version of Luther's troublemaking 95 theses (printed in Basel, Switzerland, in 1517; his friend Cranach printed a later version).

Continue into the **refectory,** where students would sit around a long table to dine. At the far end of this great hall is Cranach's wonderful painting *The Ten Commandments* (1516). This was originally designed for the Town Hall so that anybody could see it;

and today, as then, it's handy for a review of Sunday school lessons. See if you can identify each of the 10 commandments being broken (and followed)—and note that the same nobleman (in yellow and black) is responsible for half the sins. In each panel, an eerie-eyed demon prods the sinners.

On the **first floor** up are original printings of four major Luther works, what may be his robe, and a rare painting of a relatively young Martin Luther by Cranach (1520). Find the Cranach-printed 1522 first edition of Luther's German translation of the New Testament, illustrated with Cranach woodcuts. See the "community chest," the first systematized charity for poor people—Protestants began steering donations to the needy rather than into Church coffers. (Compare this to the Church's indulgence chest we saw earlier.) Other items illuminate the revolutionary changes brought about by Luther—such as the German hymn books (from the 1520s) and the shared chalice. (Before Luther's time, both singing and communion were practiced exclusively by priests.)

Pass through a lecture hall dominated by a fancy gilded lectern into the actual private **residence** of the Luther family (which still smells like the 16th century). Look for his-and-hers Cranach paintings of Martin and Katharina, three years after their wedding. Imagine the lifestyle of these newlyweds—he a former monk and

Luther's Legacy

It'd be difficult to overstate the impact Luther and the Protestant Reformation he led had on European history.

Even during Luther's lifetime, the Reformation raged across northern Europe. In Holland, Protestant extremists marched into Catholic churches, lopped off the heads of holy statues, stripped gold-leaf angels from the walls, and shattered stained-glass windows in a fit of anti-Catholic iconoclasm. Switzerland—with its deep roots in democracy and self-rule—was a haven for free thinkers, led by Ulrich Zwingli (1484-1531) and the exiled Frenchman John Calvin (1509-1564), who established a theocratic government and inspired French followers called Huguenots. When England's charismatic King Henry VIII (r. 1509-1547) was excommunicated for divorcing Catherine of Aragon so he could marry Anne Boleyn, Henry "divorced" England from the Catholic Church, established the Church of England (or "Anglican Church") and "dissolved" (destroyed) England's many countryside abbeys.

The Vatican responded to these Protestant revolutions with the Counter-Reformation, which was an attempt to put the universal Catholic Church back together using a carrot-and-stick approach. On the one hand, the Church worked diligently to eliminate corruption from within, reach out to alienated members, do missionary work, and inspire the faithful with exalted Church art. This "Counter-Reformation" art, Baroque and bubbly, gave

priest, she a former nun. While the idealistic Luther took little or no payment for preaching and writing, and depended on the charity of wealthy local supporters, Katharina was a businesswoman who balanced the books and kept this huge household going. Look for the lockbox they used to protect their valuables. Katharina kept the key so Luther wouldn't give everything they owned to the poor.

The centerpiece is the **"Lutherstube"**—the room with benches, a stove, and the table where Luther engaged in spirited conversations with his colleagues. Notice the names scratched into the ceiling, left behind by visiting VIPs (on the door, protected by glass, is the John Hancock of Russian Czar Peter the Great). Luther's adjoining study contains a collection of his beer mugs (Luther loved his suds).

In the final room, see Luther's translation of the complete Bible from 1534, printed and illustrated by Cranach with 266 woodcuts, and a tiny hymnal from 1533. Luther, who believed that

worshippers a glimpse of the heaven that awaited those who remained faithful. On the other hand, when need be, the Church resorted to propaganda, intimidation, and outright force—as doled out by the dreaded Inquisition.

The Reformation spawned a century of Catholics-versus-Protestants wars, with each side convinced that God favored them. The Treaty of Augsburg (1555), which allowed each German prince to choose the religion of his territory, brought a lull in the fighting, but it didn't last long. The Thirty Years' War (1618-1648) pitted mercenary soldiers from just about every European country against each other.

When these wars finally ended, Western civilization realized what it should have known from the start: Catholics and Protestants would have to live together. The Peace of Westphalia (1648) decreed that the leader of each country would decide the religion of his nation. Ultimately this divided Europe in half: the generally Protestant north (Scandinavia, the Low Countries, northern Germany, and England), and the predominantly Catholic south (Spain, Portugal, Italy, and southern Germany).

It's clear that Luther's legacy lives on. If you are a Lutheran, Presbyterian, Methodist, Baptist, Episcopalian—or any one of a number of other Protestant faiths—you're the spiritual descendant of this German monk.

music should be an important part of worship, composed hymns that are still sung today.

The **top floor** features a small treasury and an intriguing exhibit of images showing how Luther has been represented in the centuries after his death. At the very end, check out the 1982 East German print showing Luther conversing at a table with Che Guevara and other revolutionaries. The East German government decided that it was OK to tell Luther's story—as long as it was linked to the ideals of socialist revolution.

The **cellar** (reached through the museum's backyard) contains an exhibit about the everyday running of the Luther household.

Luther Sights near Luther House

Several other Reformation sights cluster along Collegienstrasse, at the Luther House end of town:

Leaving the Luther House, turn right down Collegienstrasse with your back toward the town center (toward the ring road). At the big roundabout (see map), at the edge of the park on the left, is the famous **"Luther Oak" tree** marking the spot where Luther burned the papal bull that threatened him with excommunication.

About a block toward Market Square from the Luther House are two other buildings of interest to Lutherans. At #60 (with the

LUTHERLAND

rounded gables) is the **Melanchthon House** (Melanchthonhaus)—given to Philipp Melanchthon to persuade him to stay in Wittenberg when he threatened to move elsewhere, and now a museum about his life. Nothing survives from Melanchthon's household, but the museum tries hard to bring him to life, and everything is described in English (€4, €8 combo-ticket with Luther House; April-Oct daily 10:00-18:00; Nov-March Tue-Sun 10:00-17:00, closed Mon; tel. 03491/420-3110).

At #62a, duck through the doorway into the **university courtyard.** These are some of the original buildings where Luther, Melanchthon, and their colleagues worked. Wall plaques ringing the courtyard celebrate famous professors and alums.

Luther Garden

This orchard of ecumenism, a short walk just south of the market square, is a leafy statement that Christian communities—Protestant, Catholic, and Orthodox—can cooperate. Hundreds of trees from as many Christian communities from all over the world have been planted, and each has a sister tree planted in its community of origin.

OTHER WITTENBERG SIGHTS
▲▲House of History (Haus der Geschichte)

Those intrigued by the communist chapter of Wittenberg's history will enjoy this museum's three floors of everyday items from East German times (1949-1989). The *Wende* (German reunification) in 1989 erased an entire culture, and in the space of a few years East German toys, food brands, cars, schoolbooks, and much more were replaced by Western ones—awakening nostalgia even in those who otherwise welcomed the end of communism. Over  the past two decades, a dedicated staff has collected thousands of items that memorialize the world of their youth. The museum also includes a few rooms showing furnishings and fashions from the 1920s and 1930s, and an exhibit (German only) on the life of Russian troops posted to East Germany.

Cost and Hours: €6, audioguide-€2, photo permission-€2, daily 10:00-18:00, Schlossstrasse 6, tel. 03491/409-004, www.pflug-ev.de.

Hundertwasserschule

This formerly drab communist-era public school, on the northeast outskirts of town, was redecorated in 1993 with wildly colorful and imaginative flair by Austrian architect Friedensreich Hundertwasser. Most intriguing to architecture buffs, it's a long 25- to 30-minute walk from the city center (interior closed to the public but exterior viewable anytime, officially called "Luther-Melanchthon-Gymnasium," Schillerstrasse 22a, www.hundertwasserschule.de).

Cruises and Biking the Elbe River Valley

While you can pay to take a brief cruise on the Elbe River, there's not much to see other than a panoramic view of town (for details, ask at the TI). The Elbe Valley also attracts many bicycle tourists, following the bike path called the Elberadweg (for more on this cycling route, see www.elberadweg.de).

Sleeping in Wittenberg

Wittenberg has a wide range of charming hotels at fine prices. My listings (except Am Alten Anker) are right in the heart of the Old Town. Air-conditioning and elevators are rare. The prices listed here are for high season (April-Oct). The Schwarzer Baer and Goldener Adler are particularly good values.

$$$ Alte Canzley, right next to the TI and across from the Castle Church, has eight enormous, well-equipped if somewhat dated rooms above a restaurant in a historic building from 1391. The three straightforward double rooms are more affordable (Sb-€75-99, Db-€89-119), while the five apartments have kitchens (Sb-€109-129, Db-€119-145; price depends on size, extra bed-€35, cheaper Nov-March, air-con, elevator, cable Internet in rooms, Wi-Fi in common areas and some rooms, free parking, sauna-€10, Schlossplatz 3-5, tel. 03491/429-110, www.alte-canzley.com, info@alte-canzley.de).

$$$ Hotel Best Western Stadtpalais Wittenberg is a professional-feeling place with 78 business-class rooms offering bland, predictable comfort right on the main drag, near the Luther House (Sb-€79-102, Db-€100-125, rate depends on demand, some rooms have air-con, Wi-Fi, parking-€6.50/day, Collegienstrasse 56-57, tel. 03491/4250, www.stadtpalais.bestwestern.de, info@stadtpalais.bestwestern.de).

$$ Stadthotel Schwarzer Baer ("Black Bear") has 32 modern, comfortable rooms—all differently and stylishly decorated—in a period building with hardwood floors right off Market Square (Sb-€65, Db-€85, elevator, Wi-Fi, free parking, Schlossstrasse 2, tel. 03491/420-4344, www.stadthotel-wittenberg.de, info@stadthotel-wittenberg.de).

$$ Hotel Goldener Adler rents 17 straightforward rooms over a restaurant and antique shop fronting Market Square. The rooms, along a long back corridor, are in a modern addition to the older main part of the building (Sb-€46-52, small twin Db-€60, bigger Db-€70, Db with tub-€75, extra bed-€15, cash only, closed Nov-March, lots of stairs with no elevator, Wi-Fi in common areas—reaches some rooms, free parking, Markt 7, tel. 03491/404-137, www.goldeneradler-wittenberg.de, hotel@goldeneradler-wittenberg.de).

$ Am Alten Anker, above a restaurant in a drab area at the far end of town (about a 15-minute walk beyond the TI, or a 30-minute walk or quick taxi ride from the train station), has 21 basic but comfortable rooms at a reasonable price (Sb-€38, Db-€60, €5 less per person if you skip breakfast, Wi-Fi, Dessauer Strasse 286, tel. 03491/768-760, www.amaltenanker.de, info@amaltenanker.de).

$ Lutherstadt Wittenberg Youth Hostel, an official HI hostel, has 152 beds in 3- to 6-bed dorms, each with its own bath. This modern hostel is perfectly located, filling a sleek building by the Castle Church (€21/bunk, Sb-€31, Db-€49, nonmembers-€3.10 more, over age 26-€3 more, includes breakfast, elevator, pay Wi-Fi, self-serve laundry-€5, doors close at 22:00, lunch or dinner-€5, tucked behind Castle Church at Schlossstrasse 14-15, tel. 03491/505-205, www.jugendherberge-wittenberg.de, wittenberg@jugendherberge.de).

Eating in Wittenberg

You'll find a fun variety of good, affordable restaurants within a couple of blocks of Market Square. The last three are ideal for lunch.

Brauhaus Wittenberg is the beer lovers' choice. From Market Square, you'll enter a classic old courtyard with a fun-loving beer garden; at the end, go inside to find comfortable seating on two levels, surrounding big copper vats where they brew their own "Wittenberger Original" pilsner. The menu includes big portions of tasty German standards (€7-16 meals, most dishes €10-12, daily 11:00-22:30, Markt 6, tel. 03491/433-130).

Das Wittenberger Kartoffelhaus serves up hearty, heavy skillets piled high with potatoes, potatoes, potatoes, prepared in fun and creative ways. The interior is cozy and brimming with kitschy decor, and the outdoor seating is on the relaxing pedestrian drag, just off Market Square (€4-9 baked potatoes, €11-15 main courses, Schlossstrasse 2, daily 11:00-24:00, tel. 03491/411-200).

Trattoria Toscana is a popular choice for Italian meals. Tucked in a "Little Italy" corner of town behind the Town Church of St. Mary, it has a fancy interior, romantic piazza seating, a fun

Italian staff, and down-to-earth prices (€6-8 pizzas and pastas, €8-18 main courses, kid-friendly, daily 11:00-24:00, Mittelstrasse 1, tel. 03491/433-188).

Duet is a great choice for a fast, central, light meal indoors or out. At lunchtime, they dish up five or six soups with bread; at least two are vegetarian. Choose one (€3-5/bowl), or ask English-speaking Jeannette for the unadvertised €6 three-bowl sampler. In the evening they switch to raclette (€9-16)—a fun Swiss dish of melted cheese and potatoes (order and pay at counter in back, Mon 11:00-15:00, Tue-Sat 11:00-15:00 & 18:00-22:00, closed Sun, Schlossstrasse 9, tel. 03491/695-095).

Hanami, next door to Duet, specializes in Vietnamese cooking. Like many Asian restaurants in eastern Germany, the Vietnam connection dates back to the communist days (€5-7 main courses and Vietnamese soups, usually daily 11:00-22:00 in summer but shorter hours when it's slow, Schlossstrasse 8, tel. 03491/459-7068).

Reinsdorfer is good for a quick lunch on the go—there's a bakery on one side of the shop (€1.50-2 sandwiches made to order) and a butcher's counter on the other (€2-3 grilled sausages and prepared side dishes sold from the counter's back end, take out or eat at simple tables, Mon-Fri 8:00-18:00, Sat 8:00-12:00, closed Sun, Markt 6).

Wittenberg Connections

From Wittenberg by Train to: Berlin (hourly on ICE, 45 minutes; also every 2 hours on slower regional train, 1.5 hours), **Leipzig** (6/day on ICE, 30-40 minutes; also hourly on regional trains, 1 hour, some with transfer in Bitterfeld), **Erfurt** (every 2 hours, 2 hours, most transfer in Naumburg; also possible in 2.5 hours with additional changes), **Eisenach** and Wartburg Castle (every 2 hours, 2.5 hours, most transfer in Naumburg; also possible in 3 hours with additional changes), **Dresden** (1-2/hour, 2-3.5 hours, transfer in Leipzig and sometimes also Bitterfeld), **Frankfurt** (every 2 hours, 4 hours, transfer in Naumburg), **Hamburg** (nearly hourly direct on ICE, 2.5-3 hours; also possible about hourly with transfer in Berlin, 2.5-3.5 hours), **Nürnberg** (every 2 hours direct on ICE, 4.5 hours). Train info: Tel. 0180-599-6633, www.bahn.de.

LUTHERLAND

LEIPZIG

Music, education, and business are Leipzig's claims to fame. Johann Sebastian Bach spent his adult years at the St. Thomas Church here, and today the city is home to the Gewandhaus Orchestra and a famous boys' choir. Luminaries such as Goethe gave the city's university (established in the 1400s) a reputation as one of Germany's best. Before World War II, Leipzig was known for its textile, piano making, and printing industries.

Although the city is one of the most architecturally drab destinations in this book and attracts more business travelers than tourists, there's plenty to do in Leipzig (LYPE-tsikh). It's one of the best places to learn about the communist era in East Germany (known as "DDR"): the excellent Stasi Museum documents the atrocities of the DDR's secret police, and the exhibits at the Contemporary History Forum contrast life in the East and West. Music lovers make a pilgrimage to Bach's tomb at the St. Thomas Church and the excellent Bach Museum across the street. Art lovers enjoy exploring the Museum of Fine Arts, beer lovers make it a point to taste the Bayerischer Bahnhof's unique Gose brew, history buffs trek to the Napoleonic battle site and monument at the edge of town, and those turned on by hipster hangouts flock to the Karli district just south of downtown.

PLANNING YOUR TIME

Conveniently located between east (Berlin, Dresden) and west (Frankfurt, Nürnberg), Leipzig easily fills a day or more. But even a visit of just a few hours can be satisfying. If your train comes through Leipzig, throw your bag in a locker at the station and enjoy a short tour. With limited time, focus on the city center—the best options are the Bach sights (St. Thomas Church and Bach Museum) and the Cold War sights (Augustusplatz, Stasi Museum, Contemporary History Forum, St. Nicholas Church). With more time, visit the City History Museum or the worthwhile outlying sights: the lively Karli restaurant and nightlife zone and the Monument to the Battle of the Nations.

Orientation to Leipzig

The city's most important sights lie within or very near the ring road—called simply the Ring—which follows what once was the city wall. You can walk across this compact downtown core (called Mitte—the "Middle") in about 15 minutes. At the center is Market Square (Markt); at the east end is the communist-style Augustusplatz, with the main university buildings and venues for the opera and orchestra. The gigantic main train station (Hauptbahnhof) rises at the northeastern edge of the Ring.

The central core has little cobbled charm—it's mostly shopping malls and massive old buildings. For more local color, head to the "Karli," a stretch of Karl-Liebknecht-Strasse that's a 20-minute walk or 5-minute tram ride due south from downtown. Several other worthwhile attractions are a tram ride from downtown: the Monument to the Battle of the Nations, the Bayerischer Bahnhof brewpub, and the Spinnerei artists' complex.

TOURIST INFORMATION

Leipzig's TI, next to the Museum of Fine Arts, hands out several good, free brochures and a free map; sells books and souvenirs; books rooms; and provides information about local tours (Mon-Fri 9:30-18:00, Sat 9:30-16:00, Sun 9:30-15:00; closed Sat-Sun Nov-Feb; Katharinenstrasse 8, tel. 0341/710-4260, www.leipzig.travel).

The skippable **Leipzig Card** covers local transit, entrance fees into a few sights (including the City History Museum), and yields minor discounts at most others (€10/1 day, €20/3 days, buy at TI or some transit offices).

Tours: The TI offers a **guided tour** of the city that combines an hour of walking and a 1.5-hour bus ride. While it's generally in German, they'll add English on request (€15, March-Dec daily at 13:30, departs from TI, smart to reserve ahead on weekends).

Engaging **Gisa Schönfeld** is a good local guide (€80/2 hours, mobile 0176-210-67204, gisa.schoenfeld@gmail.com). Guides can also be booked through the TI's Leipzig Erleben service (tel. 0341/710-4280, www.leipzig-erleben.com).

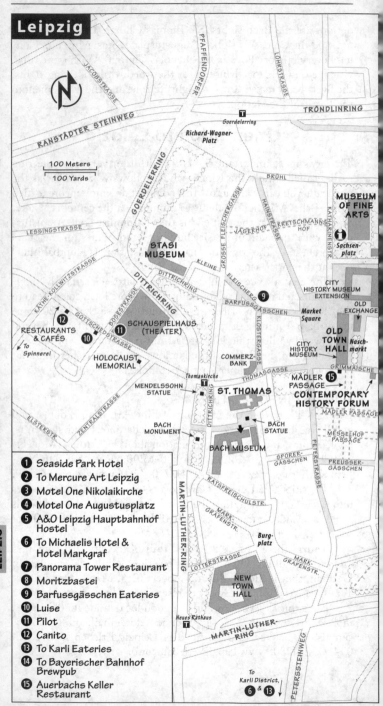

Leipzig

100 Meters
100 Yards

1. Seaside Park Hotel
2. To Mercure Art Leipzig
3. Motel One Nikolaikirche
4. Motel One Augustusplatz
5. A&O Leipzig Hauptbahnhof Hostel
6. To Michaelis Hotel & Hotel Markgraf
7. Panorama Tower Restaurant
8. Moritzbastei
9. Barfussgässchen Eateries
10. Luise
11. Pilot
12. Canito
13. To Karli Eateries
14. To Bayerischer Bahnhof Brewpub
15. Auerbachs Keller Restaurant

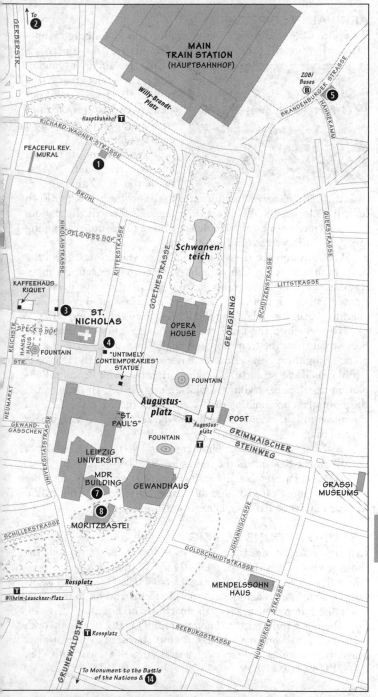

GERBERSTR.

To ❷

MAIN
TRAIN STATION
(HAUPTBAHNHOF)

Willy-Brandt-
Platz

ZOB/
Buses
Ⓑ

BRANDENBURGER STRASSE

HAHNEKAMM

❺

Hauptbahnhof Ⓣ

RICHARD-WAGNER-STRASSE

PEACEFUL REV.
MURAL

❶

BRÜHL

NIKOLAISTRASSE

OELSNERS HOF

RITTERSTRASSE

GOETHESTRASSE

Schwanen-
teich

QUERSTRASSE

SCHÜTZENSTRASSE

LITTSTRASSE

KAFFEEHAUS
RIQUET

❸

ST.
NICHOLAS

OPERA
HOUSE

GEORGIRING

REICHSSTR.

SPECK'S HOF

HANSA
HAUS

FOUNTAIN

❹

"UNTIMELY
CONTEMPORARIES"
STATUE

FOUNTAIN

NEUMARKT

GEWAND-
GÄSSCHEN

UNIVERSITÄTSSTRASSE

"ST.
PAUL'S"

Augustus-
platz

FOUNTAIN

Ⓣ

Ⓣ Augustus-
platz

POST

Ⓣ

GRIMMAISCHER
STEINWEG

LEIPZIG
UNIVERSITY

MDR
BUILDING
❼

FOUNTAIN

GEWANDHAUS

JOHANNISGASSE

GRASSI
MUSEUMS

❽

MORITZBASTEI

SCHILLERSTRASSE

GOLDSCHMIDTSTRASSE

Ⓣ

Rossplatz

Ⓣ
Wilhelm-Leuschner-Platz

MENDELSSOHN
HAUS

NÜRNBURGER STRASSE

GRUNEWALDSTR.

Ⓣ Rossplatz

SEEBURGSTRASSE

To Monument to the Battle
of the Nations & ⓮

LEIPZIG

ARRIVAL IN LEIPZIG

By Train: One of Europe's biggest train stations, **Leipzig Hauptbahnhof** is breathtaking, even a bit intimidating. As you arrive,

count the six giant arches along the concourse at the end of the tracks. Under your feet are two stories of shops with hundreds of stores open until 22:00.

Two cavernous, mirror-image arrival halls (Westhalle and Osthalle) are linked by the *Reisezentrum* (ticket office) and Burger King. Both halls have lockers; a WC is opposite track 22. To exit the station, take any elevator or escalator down one floor, to the upper shopping level, and follow signs for *Tram* or *City*.

Out through the front door you'll find waiting taxis and the busy, multilane Ring. Cross the busy street to the Hauptbahnhof tram stop. From here, **trams** fan out across the city (generally, trams head north from the first set of platforms, and south—including to Augustusplatz and the Karli—from the second set).

To **walk** into the town center (about 15 minutes), cross the busy street (past the tram stop and public-transit kiosk), and keep going straight on Nikolaistrasse. After one block, turn right onto Brühl (you'll see a colorful mural honoring the 1989 Peaceful Revolution up ahead). Walking a block along Brühl, you can't miss the giant glass box holding the Museum of Fine Arts; the TI is on the museum's far side, and the main Market Square is two blocks beyond that.

By Bus: Long-distance buses come and go from the bus depot (ZOB) on the east side of the train station.

By Car: Parking is fairly easy in Leipzig, which has a number of garages (most €10/day) and affordable on-street parking (€1.50 for first hour then €1/hour, cheaper outside Ring).

GETTING AROUND LEIPZIG

Leipzig's tram system is easy to use and essential for all but the shortest visit. Each ride costs €2.40 (or €1.60 for a *Kurzstrecke*—"short stretch"—of four stops or less). A day ticket costs €6. Tickets are available from machines at tram platforms and on most trams. You must stamp your ticket in the machines on board.

The main train station (Hauptbahnhof) is the tram network's main hub. A secondary hub is one stop south, at Augustusplatz (most trams connect these two central stops). Transit info: Tel. 0341/19449, www.lvb.de.

HELPFUL HINTS

Events: Market Square hosts a lively **farmers market** each Tuesday and Friday. The city is celebrating its 1,000th birthday in 2015—expect plenty of civic-oriented concerts and festivals (check the TI's site—www.leipzig.travel).

Laundry: Tipptopp Schnellreinigung is a coin launderette in the Karli district (daily 8:00-21:00, no English but staff can assist Mon-Fri 8:00-18:00, Karl-Liebknecht-Strasse 76, by the Karl-Liebknecht-/Karl-Eisner-Strasse stop for trams #10 and #11, tel. 0341/252-2794).

Sights in Leipzig

I've grouped sights into four categories: typical downtown sights (including the Museum of Fine Arts), Cold War sights, Bach-related sights, and sights outside the Ring.

WITHIN THE TOWN CENTER

These sights are all in the heart of town (Mitte), within the Ring.

▲▲Old Town Hall (Altes Rathaus) and City History Museum (Stadtgeschichtliches Museum)

The Renaissance-style Old Town Hall, overlooking the bustling Market Square, houses the good City History Museum upstairs. The audioguide is necessary for non-German speakers to fully appreciate the lower level of the museum.

Cost and Hours: €6, audioguide-€1, Tue-Sun 10:00-18:00, closed Mon, Markt 1, tel. 0341/965-1320, www.stadtgeschichtliches-museum-leipzig.de.

Visiting the Museum: You'll enter through a grand hall, lined with ornate benches and giant portraits of judges who presided here. The extremely detailed town model shows Leipzig in 1823. Smaller exhibit rooms branching off from the central hall cover the city's history chronologically from prehistoric times through the Middle Ages.

Start to the left of the entry, where you'll find good sections on the Reformation (with portraits of reformers by Cranach, and the wedding ring Martin Luther gave his wife) and the early trade fairs that enriched the city. At the opposite end of this floor is an exhibit on Bach, with the best portrait of the composer in existence.

The exhibit upstairs, which takes you into the Industrial Age and up to the present, is more engaging. Don't miss the film clip that lets you take a vicarious tram ride through 1930s Leipzig. You can also climb into the attic to see loud, grainy film clips showing the December 1943 bombing of the city, which destroyed this very attic (the lower floors survived).

Nearby: Behind the Town Hall is the ornately decorated Baroque **Old Exchange (Alte Börse)** building, now used as a meeting hall. The statues in the top corners symbolize important facets of Leipzig life: on the left, Apollo, representing art; and on the right, Mercury, for trade and commerce. The statue standing in front depicts Goethe, who studied law here (1765-1768) before dropping out to become a writer. It worked out well for him. Goethe set a scene from *Faust* in a restaurant in the nearby Mädler Passage (at the far end of the long square from the Alte Börse, and explained next).

▲▲Galleries and Passages

Leipzig once had the higgledy-piggledy cobbles-and-red-rooftops charm of many other German cities. But in the late 19th century, prosperous city leaders decided to modern-ize—tearing down the quaint medieval town-scape and replacing it with bulky buildings. After some WWII bomb damage and decades of communist neglect, the city center was a wasteland, but in just a generation, Leipzigers have dramatically remade their city. One fea-ture they preserved—and expanded—was the tradition of shopping galleries that burrow through the middle of many buildings. As you wander the city center, don't miss door-ways that lead into these areas (usually lined with shops); some are nondescript, but many  are more beautiful than what's on the outside. The TI has a free brochure to help you locate these galleries. Two particularly worth seeking out are Speck's Hof/Hansa Haus (enter across the street from St. Nicholas Church or from near the Old Exchange behind the Old Town Hall) and Mädler Passage (enter roughly across the street from the Old Town Hall).

Just inside **Mädler Passage,** at the end nearest the Old Town Hall, statues in front of the famous and touristy Auerbachs Keller restaurant enact a scene from *Faust* that Goethe set here: The bril-liant thinker Faust (wearing a scholar's gown and floppy hat) has made a deal with Mephistopheles (gesturing skyward) to experi-ence as much as possible of the world—but if anything so impresses Faust that he refuses to move on, the devil gets his soul. Mephistopheles brings Faust to Auerbachs Keller to show him the simple pleasures of revelry with friends ("Before all else, I bring thee hither/Where boon companions meet together,/To let thee see how smooth life runs away./Here, for the folk, each day's a holiday"). Across the passage are drunken students who have been bewitched by Mephistopheles.

Inside the **Hansa Haus** passage is a cool "sound fountain"—a bronze bowl of water with brass handles, which, if rubbed just right with dampened hands, produce a loud ringing that reverberates as the water bubbles—give it a shot. Below, a sunken "art clock" sundial shows the time with a green laser. The inscription around the basin has a line from a beloved children's book: "Just as you have eyes to see light with, and ears to hear to sounds with, so you have a heart to appreciate time."

Cafés

Leipzig has some classic cafés with old-timey interiors that are worth a peek. Consider dropping by **Kaffeehaus Riquet** (decorated with elephants, daily 9:00-20:00, Schuhmachergässchen 1) and **arko** (a chain now occupying the elegant former home of Kaffee Richter, Petersstrasse 43).

Museum of Fine Arts (Museum der Bildenden Künste)

Located in a fancy glass house in the center of town, this museum displays Leipzig's eclectic collection of fine arts. Instead of being organized chronologically, items are displayed thematically—juxtaposed by some clever curator to create a "dialogue" between otherwise unrelated works. While this treatment thrills a certain breed of museumgoer, it's sometimes alienating to lowbrows (like me). Worse, there's very little English (aside from a thick catalog), so the audioguide is essential.

Cost and Hours: €5, special exhibits extra—usually €8, €11 combo-ticket covers everything, audioguide-€2, Tue and Thu-Sun 10:00-18:00, Wed 12:00-20:00, closed Mon, a short block north of Market Square at Katharinenstrasse 10, tel. 0341/216-990, www. mdbk.de.

Visiting the Museum: Within the vast, glassy building, the basement features temporary exhibits; the first floor displays excellent works by local sculptor Max Klinger, as well as other 20th-century and Leipzig art; the second floor has mostly Dutch and Flemish works from the 15th to 18th centuries; and the third floor shows predominantly Romanticism, 19th-century works, and contemporary pieces.

The museum's highlight is Leipzig artist **Max Klinger's** (1857-1920) sculpture of Beethoven (1902, restored 2004). The marble and bronze piece—depicting the great composer pensively hunched over on a throne, nude, legs crossed, with Prometheus'

Leipzig History

Although it's the biggest city in Saxony, Leipzig has long been overshadowed by its glamour-girl sister, Dresden. While Dresden was the prettified capital of the rulers of Saxony, Leipzig was its down-and-dirty economic engine.

Leipzig first boomed in the 15th century. Its trade fairs attracted medieval vendors and businesspeople from throughout the region, and rich deposits of silver in the nearby Erzgebirge hills boosted the mining industry. While Dresden's glories were funded by princes who collected, then squandered, their subjects' wealth, Leipzig was imbued with a strong civic sensibility—its citizens took pride in voluntarily funding musicians and artists. Among the beneficiaries was an organist, choirmaster, and composer named Johann Sebastian Bach, who went largely unappreciated in his lifetime but whose works were later rediscovered and popularized by another Leipzig composer, Felix Mendelssohn.

Leipzig's university attracted great minds. Martin Luther came here to work with local printers and publishers to distribute his writings and to debate one of the Catholic Church's chief theologians (an event called the Leipzig Disputation) in what is today's New Town Hall. And Goethe, the "German Shakespeare"—who studied law at Leipzig U. before following his muse into literature—set a famous scene from his verse drama *Faust* at a cellar restaurant here. Current German Chancellor Angela Merkel is an alumna.

Leipzig's cityscape is a victim of its own success. In the late 19th century, the city boomed once again when it innovated the idea of a "sample fair." Instead of toting along their full inventory, vendors brought samples of their wares, allowing them to take orders and sell in much larger volumes. Never architecturally oriented, the newly flush people of Leipzig tore down most of their characteristic medieval Old Town. The city center—defined by a busy ring road that marks the former course of the city wall—features large, hulking buildings that are visually dull but shot

eagle in clouds at his feet—took Klinger some 15 years to complete. Installed as the centerpiece of a 1902 Vienna Secession exhibit devoted to Beethoven, the sculpture was surrounded by Gustav Klimt's famous *Beethoven Frieze* (still displayed in Vienna). On the same floor, look for Expressionist works by another Leipzig artist, Max Beckmann, including *Portrait of a Carpet Dealer* (1946). The rest of the collection features minor works by major artists (such as Frans Hals' *The Mulatto* and Rembrandt's *Head of an Old Man*) and some genuinely interesting pieces from lesser-known artists. For example, Paul de la Roche's evocative *Napoleon at Fontainebleau* shows the pudgy, diminutive Frenchman dejected after learning that he's lost Paris.

through with fun-to-explore passages.

After World War II, Leipzig became the second city, after East Berlin, of communist East Germany (DDR). The infamous Berlin Wall was built under DDR premier Walter Ulbricht, a Leipzig native. But the city's size and historical importance didn't protect it from communist neglect. Damaged by WWII bombs, postwar Leipzig fell into abhorrent disrepair. Making matters worse, an open-pit coal mine at the edge of town and belching Trabant cars covered everything in soot. People who lived here in the 1980s say they never wore white clothes outside, because they'd turn gray in minutes.

The people of Leipzig were also at the forefront of the so-called "Peaceful Revolution" that toppled the communist regime. The famous scenes of Berliners joyfully partying atop the Wall were made possible by protests that first began in Leipzig in 1982 and eventually came to a head in the series of civil-disobedience actions that caught the regime completely off-guard in 1989. Expecting an armed insurrection, DDR leaders were so flummoxed by the peaceful tone of the protests that they simply allowed them to continue. A month later, the Wall was history. (For more, see the sidebar on page 655.)

As Germany moved toward reunification, DDR television broadcast a provocative documentary asking: Can ragtag Leipzig be salvaged? (Their conclusion: No.) But salvaged it was—and then some. Pictures from just 20 years ago show a different city. The area within the ring road has been rejuvenated with shiny new shopping malls and university buildings. In other zones—such as the colorful stretch south of downtown called the Karli—trendy young entrepreneurs have turned decrepit buildings into a world of funky, engaging bars and restaurants. Leipzig may lack half-timbered and lederhosen charm, but its welcome urban contrast and fascinating history earn it a place on many itineraries.

▲Augustusplatz

This somewhat severe square is home to Leipzig's university and its two most respected musical institutions. Renamed Karl-Marx-Platz during the DDR period, the square became a showcase for the communist aesthetic. In September of 1989, protesters against the communist regime gathered here—and were dispersed by the police. Today it's a busy people zone and a hub for trams around the city.

◒ Self-Guided Spin Tour: Begin between the fountain with the obelisk and the tram stops, and face the tallest skyscraper.

This skyscraper, the **MDR building** (named after the radio and TV station that's based here), was erected in the 1970s as part

of the university. You can ride to the 29th floor and pay €3 to go out on the rooftop terrace for the best view in town (Mon-Sat 9:00-24:00, Sun until 23:00, tel. 0341/710-0590, www.panorama-leipzig.de). Enjoy a similar view from the Panorama Tower restaurant on the same floor (affordable €9 three-course lunch served Mon-Fri 11:00-14:30). Hiding behind this building (not quite visible from here) is the **Moritzbastei.** This bastion is all that survives from Leipzig's former city wall, which was torn down in the early 19th century to build the ring road. Today it hosts a happening student pub.

Stretching to the right is a complex of glassy buildings housing **Leipzig University**—the second oldest in present-day Germany. The pointed facade marks the new **University Church of St. Paul's**—replacing the 13-century church dynamited by the communists in 1968. The new church pays homage to the site's former purpose but will be used for secular assemblies as well as religious services.

At either end of this square, two of Leipzig's main cultural institutions are housed in communist-era buildings. At the south end (to the left) is the **Gewand-haus,** home to the city's world-renowned orchestra. (If you step into the lobby, you'll see models of the three different buildings that have housed the orchestra, including the original location in the clothmakers' guild hall—which is what *Gewandhaus*

means.) At the north (right) end is the **Opera House.**

Facing the Opera House, the tall building on the left with the two bell-ringers is Leipzig's earliest "skyscraper." To the right, down the street in the far distance (red building with tiny black spire), you can see the Grassi Museum complex (see page 661).

If you're intrigued by quirky public art, head a few steps up the pedestrianized shopping street, Grimmaische Strasse (to the left as you face the Opera House), and find the sculpture *Untimely Contemporaries* (a pun that works better in German), with insulting, exaggerated caricatures of hypocritical DDR figures. For example, the teacher (on the right) clutches a mallet used to pound communist ideology into her students; the fourth guy over, with the too-big laurel wreath covering his eyes, is detonating St. Paul's Church.

COLD WAR SIGHTS

These attractions are scattered around the city center, but are all within about a 10-minute walk of each other.

▲St. Nicholas Church (Nikolaikirche)

Leipzig's oldest church (1165) played a pivotal role in recent German history. In the 1980s, prayer meetings held here every Monday gradually became a forum for those deeply dissatisfied with the

communist status quo. As anti-communist sentiment grew, the church became a major staging ground for the Peaceful Revolution that would ultimately topple the regime. During these protests, people would bravely go inside the church to meet—not knowing what would happen to them when they came back out.

The church sits in what was once a market square—appropriate, since its namesake, St. Nicholas, is the patron saint of traders. The unusual but dull interior belies the church's importance in recent history. In the 1780s, the church was redecorated in a very clean, bright Neoclassical style, with a pastel pink-and-green color scheme and fluted columns that sprout green fronds at the top. Above the door is the largest organ in Saxony, which booms out concerts each Saturday at 17:00 (€2).

Outside and behind the church, find the single column with green leaves at the top. This column, echoing the decoration inside the church, is dedicated to the people of Leipzig and memorializes the anti-communist protests that began here.

Cost and Hours: Free, daily 10:00-18:00 (closes during Sunday services), Nikolaikirchhof 3, tel. 0341/124-5380, www.nikolaikirche-leipzig.de.

▲Contemporary History Forum (Zeitgeschichtliches Forum)

Funded by the German government, this center examines life in a divided Germany (1945-1990), focusing mainly on the East but dipping into the West to provide contrast. The statue out front represents Germany's two 20th-century dictatorships: the flat-palmed *Sieg Heil!* Nazi salute and the proletariat's raised communist fist.

The poor fellow has his head scrunched down, hoping to somehow get through it all.

Cost and Hours: Free, Tue-Fri 9:00-18:00, Sat-Sun 10:00-18:00, closed Mon, Grimmaische Strasse 6, tel. 0341/22200, www.hdg.de/leipzig.

Visiting the Museum: The exhibit is modern and well-presented, although there's little in English (translations sometimes available at the gift-shop counter where you enter—ask).

Ride the elevator (with patriotic DDR songs and voice clips piped in) up to the second floor, where the circular permanent ex-

hibit spins off from a central timeline. Displays include actual photographs, propaganda posters, a mock-up of a DDR-era apartment, film footage of DDR authorities destroying churches and Soviet tanks putting down a 1953 protest at Berlin's Brandenburg Gate, a van used by the secret police to transport prisoners, an original "You are leaving the American sector" sign from an East/West border crossing, a simple airplane used to escape to the West, heads from several Stalin statues, protest signs from the fall of 1989, and the long table where the East German politburo met to hash out their plans for the country.

While the permanent exhibit is all on the second floor, temporary exhibits, which can give a stimulating peek at contemporary German life, fill the third floor.

▲▲Stasi Museum in the "Runde Ecke"

In the notorious so-called "Round Corner" building, the communist secret police (Stasi) detained and interrogated those suspected of being traitors to the state. That same building—once the Stasi headquarters—now houses a humble but worthwhile exhibit about the Stasi's activities. A citizens' committee created the museum in 1990—just months after their protests helped spark the fall of the Wall—as a temporary exhibit to document Stasi atrocities, with the goal of preventing such things from happening again. More than two decades later, the museum and its committee are still going strong. The museum is not fancy—basically one long hallway and a few rooms, with dusty

LEIPZIG

The Peaceful Revolution

While the fall of the Berlin Wall got all the press, the end of communism in East Germany arguably began seven years earlier and a hundred miles to the south, in Leipzig.

In 1982, parishioners at Leipzig's St. Nicholas Church began gathering on Monday evenings to pray for peace and a better world. This continued until 1989, when a series of events sparked citizens to action. That spring, the Tiananmen Square protests in China inspired East Germans who felt similarly oppressed. And that summer, Hungary opened its border to the West, offering an enticing glimmer of hope to East Germans.

By September of 1989, the St. Nicholas prayer meetings started taking on an increasingly political bent, and more people joined, regardless of religious belief. DDR government officials watched with concern; after the October 2 gathering, they warned that deadly force would be authorized to put down any uprisings.

On October 7, Mikhail Gorbachev came to Berlin to celebrate the 40th anniversary of the founding of the DDR. He made a cryptic remark implying that the people of Eastern Europe had a right to bring about change. A huge demonstration ensued in Leipzig on October 9. An estimated 100,000 protesters carried banners bellowing *Wir sind das Volk!* (We are the people!). The Stasi (secret police) embedded undercover agents in the crowds to stoke the protesters to violence—but it didn't work. One official said, "We were ready for anything... except candles and prayer." With no excuse for clamping down on the demonstration, DDR officials for the first time allowed a major protest to continue—a turning point in the struggle to topple the Berlin Wall.

On October 16, an estimated 320,000 people participated in demonstrations. Two days later, DDR premier Erich Honecker and several other top officials resigned. The government was in disarray, and within two and a half weeks, people were dancing on top of the Berlin Wall.

While cameras were rolling in Berlin, the heroics in Leipzig were hardly documented. But today Leipzig remains fiercely proud of the crucial role it played in ousting the communists through nonviolent means. Around town, look for "89" plaques that explain sites relating to the Peaceful Revolution.

hand-lettered exhibits—but fascinating to those interested in this dark chapter of German history. And it's chilling to see all this while walking through the actual perpetrators' offices.

Cost and Hours: Free, €4 for the excellent and essential audioguide, daily 10:00-18:00, Dittrichring 24, tel. 0341/961-2443, www.runde-ecke-leipzig.de.

Background: Initially formed as a means of investigating and prosecuting Nazi crimes, the DDR government's Ministerium für Staatssicherheit ("Ministry for State Security")—nicknamed the "Stasi" for short—quickly became a means of suppressing dissent as civil liberties dwindled in communist Germany. Modeled after the Soviet Union's secret police, the Stasi actively recruited informants from every walk of life, often intimidating them into cooperating by threatening their employment, their children's education, or worse. The Stasi eventually gathered an army of some 600,000 "unofficial employees" *(inoffizielle Mitarbeiter)*, nearly 200,000 of whom were still active when communism fell in 1989. These "employees" were coerced into reporting on the activities of their coworkers, friends, neighbors, and even their own immediate family members. Preoccupied with keeping track of "nonconformist" behavior, the Stasi collected whatever bits of evidence they could about suspects—including saliva, handwriting, odors, and voice recordings—and wound up with vast amounts of files. In late 1989, Stasi officials attempted to destroy their files—but not before government officials decreed that their documentation be preserved as evidence of their crimes. These days, German citizens can come here to read the files that were once kept on them. (Locals now struggle with the agonizing decision: Request a full view of their record—and likely find out that friends and loved ones had been reporting on them—or never know the truth.) For a film that brilliantly captures the paranoid Stasi culture, see the 2006 Oscar winner *The Lives of Others*.

Visiting the Museum: As the museum exhibits are entirely in German, rent the audioguide before you start: Go partway down the hall and ask in the office on your left. Then return to the entrance to view the permanent exhibit.

The exhibit's title, "Power and Banality," invokes scholar Hannah Arendt's notion of the "banality of evil"—the idea that if horrific acts are systematized and repeated, they become routine and therefore more acceptable to the perpetrator. The first section of the exhibit documents the pivotal protest of October 9, 1989 (see sidebar on page 655), with shields and batons, and photos of the candles that stymied riot police who were expecting Molotov cocktails. It's an important reminder that the West can't take sole credit for the freedoms won that year—Leipzigers rightly take pride in what they helped accomplish as ordinary citizens, often at great risk to themselves. And it's hard to believe how recently this all happened—even for the Leipzigers who gathered again last fall to mark the 25th anniversary of their triumph.

Inside, **surveillance cameras** mounted overhead and a wall of monitors suggest just how closely the secret police observed the East German people. In the hallway, look for the copy of a 14-year-old student's essay questioning aspects of communist life, and its extensively documented consequences (audioguide #15). It's chilling to see how this free-thinking assignment was on track to bar this schoolboy from university and ruin his life; fortunately, he wrote it in 1989, just before the Wall fell.

The **former offices** contain several items and tools used by the Stasi, such as a camera that could easily be concealed in a briefcase, microphones that could be hidden just about anywhere, disguises

(including a fake beer belly with a hidden camera), and forged documents. One display case holds several jars with pale yellow cloths impregnated with "odor samples." Stasi agents would sit suspects on cloths to interrogate them, then save the sweat-drenched swatch for trained dogs to identify the scent. (For example, the dog would sniff an anti-DDR propaganda leaflet, then smell several odor samples and bark at the one that matched.) The police also used under-car mirrors to check for potential escapees at border crossings. The **replica prison cell**, with original fixtures, illustrates what life was like in a detention center. All mail and packages coming into the country were searched for contraband—inspectors would steam them open, read them, then reseal them. Stasi mail inspectors stole millions in West German marks (sent to East German relatives) and confiscated piles of cassette tapes containing Western pop music—which officials then reused to record interrogation sessions.

Snooping on citizens was a huge industry. Eventually the Stasi outgrew this building. As you exit the museum, walk to the right to see the Stasi headquarters expansion—a dreadfully ugly, typically DDR, gray and brown prefabricated annex.

LEIPZIG

BACH SIGHTS

These sights cluster along the west side of the Ring.

▲St. Thomas Church (Thomaskirche)

At this historic church, Martin Luther introduced Leipzig to Protestantism, and Johann Sebastian Bach con-
ducted the boys' choir. The most famous boys'
choir in Germany—the Thomanerchor—still
performs here.

Cost and Hours: Free, daily 9:00-18:00,
from 9:30 in winter, Thomaskirchhof 18, tel.
0341/222-240, www.thomaskirche.org.

Concerts: The St. Thomas boys' choir
performs Fridays at 18:00 and Saturdays at
15:00, unless they are traveling (€2).

Visiting the Church: Before entering the
church, look (just outside the church door)
for the **statue of Bach** standing in front of his
favorite instrument, a pipe organ. Bach was
the leader of the boys' choir here from 1723 until 1750. While

here, Bach was remarkably prolific
—for a time, he even composed a new
cantata every week. Examine the details
of his portrait: He's holding a rolled-up
sheet of music, which he used as a baton.
Notice the button open on his vest—he
could stick the "baton" into his shirt,
if necessary, to free up his hands. His
jacket pocket is turned out—Bach was
famously always scrounging for more
money to feed his huge family and the
boys in the choir. His dedication to the
arts led him to advocate tirelessly for the
funding of local musicians.

Inside, the clean, white, stripped-down Neo-Gothic interior
evokes the Protestant aesthetic of uncluttering the congregation's
communion with God. On Pentecost in 1539, Martin Luther came
here to perform Leipzig's first Protestant service. Look up at the
19th-century **stained-glass window** on the wall above the door
through which you entered. In the panel to the left, Martin Luther
is flanked by his supporter prince elector Frederick the Wise (on
the left) and fellow reformer Philipp Melanchthon (on the right).

The **main altar** actually comes from a different historic church,
St. Paul's on Augustusplatz, which was demolished by the communist regime in 1968 to make way for the expansion of university
buildings (for the rebuilt version of that church, see page 651).

LEIPZIG

In front of the altar is the **tomb of Bach**—or is it? Largely unappreciated in his own time and forgotten shortly after his death, Bach was buried in a humble graveyard. But after he was rediscovered in the 19th century, aficionados tracked down what they thought were his remains. Three cadavers that could have been Bach were compared to portraits of the composer to determine which one was most likely to be the real Bach.

Facing the altar, look up and to the left (opposite the pulpit) to see the new **organ,** built in 2000 but designed to sound like a much older, Bach-era organ.

Sights Near the Church

On the Ring side of the church (to the right as you leave, around the corner, and across the street), look for the **statue of Felix Men-**

delssohn (1809-1847). Mendelssohn came to Leipzig at age 26 to conduct the Gewandhaus Orchestra, which he led to great success, putting Leipzig on the world musical map. Mendelssohn is remembered today primarily as a composer, but perhaps his greatest contribution was to popularize the works of Bach, which had become unfashionable after his death. If not for Mendelssohn, the name "Bach" would probably mean nothing to you today. Because he was Jewish, Mendelssohn's statue was torn down and used for scrap metal by the Nazis; this copy was re-erected here in 2008.

The busy ring road just beyond the Mendelssohn statue was the fortified city wall that once marked the end of town. When the wall was torn down in the 19th century, the west portal of St. Thomas Church suddenly stood in full view of the townsfolk, who were inspired to add the fancy Neo-Gothic facade you see today.

Turn around and go a bit farther along the park (with the Ring on your right) to find another, much older **monument to Bach.** Mendelssohn was so dedicated to honoring the genius of the Baroque composer that he personally funded the construction of this monument. In the reliefs around the pillar, see Bach depicted as an organist, a good Christian, and a teacher (of the boys' choir).

Across the Ring from here, and a block up Gottschedstrasse (which is also lined with some great restaurants—see "Eating in Leipzig," later), you'll find a **Holocaust memorial,** with 140 chairs

Johann Sebastian Bach (1685-1750)

Johann Sebastian Bach was a man of many musical trades—composer, musical director, organist, organ builder, and violinist. Born in 1685, he lived immersed in music from the very beginning. His father was the director of the town musicians (because the family was so musically talented, people from Erfurt—where Bach senior was from—used the word *Bache* to describe any musician). After his parents' early deaths, Bach lived with his older brother, Johann Christoph, who helped him develop his musical skill.

In 1723, Bach was selected as the cantor of St. Thomas Church in Leipzig. He spent the last 27 years of his life in the city, working as the director of music for the city's four main churches and directing the St. Thomas boys' choir, the Thomanerchor. Responsible for providing Sunday music at the churches, in just five years Bach composed some 150 cantatas, two great Passions, and numerous other sacred pieces for his choir to perform.

In addition to shepherding the 50 boys in the choir, Bach, who married twice, had a number of his own children—seven with his first wife and another thirteen with the second. Of the twenty children, only nine survived into adulthood. And of those, six had musical careers of their own.

on the site of the city's former main synagogue. The empty seats encourage people to "stand up" for what's right.

▲▲Bach Museum

Across the little square from St. Thomas is this small but very well-presented museum about Leipzig's favorite composer. Its good interactive exhibits, all described in English, are mostly displayed in 12 rooms on one manageable floor. With the help of the excellent, included audioguide, this museum is an absolute delight for music lovers.

At the entry is a replica of a famous portrait-bust of the great composer. Inside and up the stairs, the family tree makes it clear that he came from a very musical family. In the listening studio, touch the organ pipes to hear music, or settle in at a station to listen on headsets to one of Bach's many compositions. You'll see the actual organ console where Bach played his favorite instrument, an iron chest that came from his household, and original manuscripts. The orchestra exhibit explains Baroque music by letting you press buttons to isolate the different instruments. The Leipzig room

While living in Leipzig, Bach began directing a group of university-student musicians who were more interested in convivial entertainment than somber church music. Their crowd-pleasing performances of his secular compositions drew attention to the composer's work, elevating his status in Leipzig.

Later in life, Bach became more withdrawn and reflective, composing complex, abstract Baroque pieces. He enjoyed entertaining guests with private concerts in his personal music room. But his eyesight began failing near the end of his life, and he died in 1750 after suffering a stroke. He was buried in an unmarked grave and soon forgotten.

In 1829, the musician and composer Felix Mendelssohn received from his grandmother a copy of Bach's manuscript for *St. Matthew Passion*. When Mendelssohn conducted and performed Bach's profoundly expressive music in Berlin, it was an instant hit. Mendelssohn's concert sparked a newfound appreciation for Bach's music that began in Germany, took over Europe, and soon spread around the world.

In the mid-1800s, several Bach fans and Leipzig scholars succeeded in rediscovering what they thought to be Bach's remains and moved them to Leipzig's Johanneskirche. After that church was destroyed by WWII bombs, the composer's remains were laid to rest, for a third time, at St. Thomas Church—where appreciative pilgrims and Bach admirers still bring flowers to honor the man whom *The New York Times* named "the most influential composer of all time."

shows sites in town associated with the composer—including a model of the residence (in the boarding school for his 50 choirboys) where he lived with his huge family. Film clips show the many cinematic depictions of Bach.

Cost and Hours: €8, includes audioguide, Tue-Sun 10:00-18:00, closed Mon, Thomaskirchhof 15-16, tel. 0341/913-7207, www.bach-leipzig.de.

OUTSIDE THE RING
▲Grassi Museums (Museen im Grassi)

This trio of museums, one tram stop from Augustusplatz, beautifully presents three different subjects: applied arts, anthropology, and musical instruments. For Germans, this complex would rank ▲▲▲ and could easily fill the better part of a day—but since there's

LEIPZIG

virtually nothing here unique to Leipzig, foreigners may find it less interesting than other options in town.

The **Museum of Applied Arts** (Museum für Angewandte Kunst) features decorative items from both European and Asian cultures. The excellent **Museum of Anthropology** (Völkerkunde-museum) displays an impressive range of artifacts gathered from around the world, arranged by geographical region. And the **Museum of Musical Instruments** (Museum für Musikinstrumente) boasts a fine collection. As the exhibits are almost entirely in German, invest in the excellent English audioguide that covers all three museums.

Cost and Hours: Applied Arts-€5, Anthropology-€8, Musical Instruments-€6, combo-ticket for everything-€15, Tue-Sun 10:00-18:00, audioguide-€1, closed Mon; take tram #4, #7, #12, or #15 from the station or Augustusplatz to Johannisplatz 5-11; tel. 0341/222-9100, www.grassimuseum.de.

▲▲The Karli

Just south of the Ring, Karl-Liebknecht-Strasse—"Karli" for short— hosts a funky zone of boutiques, cafés, restaurants, and nightclubs (a.k.a. the Südmeile—"South Mile").

Renamed "Adolf-Hitler-Strasse" during the Führer's reign, today's Karli would make Hitler spin in his grave. Parts of the street feel like a squatter's haven, filled with run-down buildings housing lots of fun eateries and nonconformist hangout spots, all slathered with artistic graffiti. But you'll also see many fine period buildings, and some of yesterday's hippies are now environmentally aware parents biking down the sidewalk with their children.

After the generally stern architecture of downtown Leipzig, a stroll here is good for the soul and flat-out fun. You can walk here from downtown (across the Ring, south of the New Town Hall), but it doesn't get interesting until the Hohe Strasse tram stop. The core of the zone is the four-block stretch between the Südplatz and Karl-Liebknecht-/Kurt-Eisner-Strasse stops. For more details, see the description under "Eating in Leipzig," later.

Getting There: Ride tram #10 or #11 about 5 minutes south from downtown (to the Hohe Strasse, Südplatz, or Karl-Liebknecht-/Kurt-Eisner-Strasse stops).

▲Monument of the Battle of the Nations (Völkerschlachtdenkmal)

This gigantic, heavy-handed monument—Europe's biggest—commemorates a pivotal battle in 1813 that involved forces from all over Europe. While it's on the

outskirts of town and a bit anticlimactic (it looks like a giant pedestal missing a statue on top), the monument is worth an ogle for its sheer size and chillingly patriotic design, especially if you're a history buff.

The year 2013 marked the 200th anniversary of the battle and the 100th anniversary of the monument. Today, nicknamed "Volki" by Leipzig's youth, it's most appreciated as a venue for concerts and outdoor events.

Cost and Hours: €6 ticket covers both monument and museum, daily April-Oct 10:00-18:00, Nov-March 10:00-16:00, audioguide-€1, Strasse des 18 Oktober 100, tel. 0341/241-6870, www.voelkerschlachtdenkmal.eu.

Getting There: Ride tram #15 from the Hauptbahnhof or Augustusplatz (direction: Meusdorf) to the Völkerschlachtdenkmal stop, which is right next to the big park surrounding the monument. "You can't miss it" is an understatement.

Background: In October 1813, the Battle of the Nations (*Völkerschlacht*, also called the Battle of Leipzig) pitted Napoleon's army against a united force of Prussian, Austrian, Russian, and Swedish fighters. With more than a half-million men involved and casualties approaching 100,000, it was the largest battle in European history until World War I. The Battle of the Nations marked the turning point in the fight against Napoleon, who was routed and forced to retreat to France. It was the ultimate victory of predominantly German forces against French invaders.

A century later—during a surge of nationalism following the unification of the modern nation of Germany—Leipzig city leaders built this 300-foot-tall memorial on the site of the bloodiest warfare. Looming over a huge reflecting pool, the concrete monument has a granite facade and is decorated inside and out with gigantic, heroic (almost mythical) statues of faceless soldiers and other archetypes celebrating German might. Not surprisingly, it later became a favorite backdrop for Hitler's speeches. The Soviet puppet government of East Germany wasn't thrilled with its German nationalistic overtones, but decided to let it stand as a monument to German-Russian cooperation.

Visiting the Monument: A visit here has several parts: viewing the massive monument (ideally from the far end of the reflect-

LEIPZIG

ing pool); entering the atmospheric crypt; riding the elevator up to the viewing platform; and visiting the Forum 1813 museum.

On the **exterior,** the Archangel Michael straddles the main door with the same tiresome message that accompanies most military monuments: "God with us." Circling the rounded top of the monument, a dozen stoic 40-foot-tall soldiers lean menacingly on their swords—which they will use, if necessary, to protect their nation.

Buy your ticket at the building to the left, and then head through the main door and ride the elevator up to floor 3 and the **crypt.** The atmospheric atrium is ringed by 16 soldiers with their heads respectfully bowed to honor the sacrifice of those lost in battle. Above them, four gigantic 30-foot-tall statues represent the virtues of the German people during wartime: bravery (flexing muscles), faith (an idealistic child),  power (a mother nursing two young children—more fodder for the battlefield), and sacrifice (holding out a piece of fruit). Rocketing up 225 feet from the crypt is a dome decorated with hundreds of life-sized cavalry triumphantly returning from battle. From the crypt or atrium, continue up the elevator to the **viewing balcony** for a commanding open-air view. From there you can climb more steps to summit the monument and stand on the tip-top **platform,** enjoying more sweeping (if distant) views over Leipzig.

Back on the ground, the Forum 1813 **museum,** in the smaller building to the right of the monument, narrates the story of the battle with paintings, models, uniforms, weapons, lots of artifacts from 1813, and a large diorama (all in German, but explained by the English audioguide).

Spinnerei

Formerly Europe's largest cotton mill—in the 19th century, it was a self-contained community of both factories and homes—this industrial complex has been converted into a sprawling artistic venue with some 10 galleries and dozens of artists' studios. Many showcase the "New Leipzig" art movement (contemporary eastern German art from after reunification). Gallery-hoppers, or anyone interested in the gentrification of old industrial wastelands, may find this place (with the slogan "from cotton to culture") worth a visit.

Cost and Hours: Most galleries are free to enter, but hours are variable—most are open Mon-Fri from 11:00, 12:00 or 13:00 until 17:00 or 18:00, Sat until 16:00, most closed Sun-Mon and some also on Tue, check schedules at www.spinnerei.de.

LEIPZIG

Getting There: It's about three miles southwest of the town center. Ride tram #8 or #15 from the Hauptbahnhof to the Lindenau Bushof stop. Exit the tram, turn left, walk to the corner, and turn right on Saalfelder Strasse. After crossing the bridge, turn right onto Spinnereistrasse.

Nightlife in Leipzig

Music lovers can look into performances at the **Opera House** or **Gewandhaus,** home of the city's orchestra (both on Augustusplatz). Nearby, the **Moritzbastei** is a popular-with-students place for cultural events (described later, under "Eating in Leipzig"; check events schedule at www.moritzbastei.de).

Leipzig's most happening nightlife zone is the **Karli,** loaded with cutting-edge restaurants, cafés, bars, and nightspots (see "Eating in Leipzig," later). A well-established venue here is **die naTo,** a cultural center presenting theater, film, and music as well as a bar with drinks and food (events nightly from 18:30, Karl-Liebknecht-Strasse 48, tel. 0341/391-5539, www.nato-leipzig.de).

Sleeping in Leipzig

Thanks to the one-two punch of being both a convention town and a post-communist one, Leipzig is short on the characteristic, family-run little pensions I favor in other parts of Germany. With one exception, I've listed functional, business-oriented hotels—anonymous and low on character, but offering predictable comfort. Rates are typically higher on weeknights than weekends, and soft both in midsummer (July-Aug) and winter (Nov-March). Prices skyrocket during conventions and fairs—concentrated during the months of April-June and Sept-Oct (for a schedule, see www.leipziger-messe.com).

WITHIN OR NEAR THE RING

$$ Seaside Park Hotel has an anonymous, business-class vibe but an extremely convenient location (albeit nowhere near any seashore), just across the busy Ring from the train station and an easy walk to anywhere in the town center. With 288 rooms and a lot of marble, mirrors, and brass in the lobby, it feels elegant for the price. But many rooms come with a catch: open-plan bathrooms, with the shower or tub visible from the whole room, won't work for those who want to wash in private (Sb-€100-110, Db-€110-120, rates vary with demand, breakfast-€16, air-con, elevator, free guest computer, expensive Wi-Fi, parking-€12.50/day, restaurant, Richard-Wagner-Strasse 7, tel. 0341/98520, www.parkhotelleipzig.de, info@parkhotelleipzig.de).

Sleep Code

Abbreviations   **(€1 = about $1.40, country code: 49)**
S = Single, **D** = Double/Twin, **T** = Triple, **Q** = Quad, **b** = bathroom, **s** = shower only.
Price Rankings
   $$$ Higher Priced—Most rooms €120 or more.
    $$ Moderately Priced—Most rooms between €80-120.
     $ Lower Priced—Most rooms €80 or less.
Unless otherwise noted, credit cards are accepted, English is spoken, and Wi-Fi is generally free. Prices can change without notice; verify the hotel's current rates online or by email. For the best prices, always book directly with the hotel.

$$ Mercure Art Leipzig, part of a stylish European chain, has 72 comfortable, minimalist rooms, decorated with bright paintings by a local artist. It's in a dull urban neighborhood one tram stop (or a 10-minute walk) north of the train station, but the prices are reasonable for what you get (Sb-€75, Db-€85; bigger "art loft" Sb-€95, Db-€105; breakfast-€14.50, air-con, elevator, Wi-Fi, parking-€12.50/day; from station ride tram #10, #11, or #16 one stop north to Wilhelm-Liebknecht-Platz, hotel is across street, on other side of triangular park; Eutritzscher Strasse 15, tel. 0341/303-840, www.mercure.de, h8847@accor.com).

$ Motel One Nikolaikirche, part of a German chain, is the best deal in town for well-located comfort. The most central hotel in Leipzig (facing St. Nicholas Church), its 194 rooms are cookie-cutter predictable, have spongy carpets, and lack some basic amenities (phones, minibars)—but that's what keeps the prices low. Still, the rooms are surprisingly stylish, and the staff is professional (Sb-€69, Db-€79, €20-50 more during fairs, breakfast-€7.50; no Tb rooms, but a child up to age 12 can sleep on a couch bed for free; iPad at reception for guest use, Wi-Fi, walkable from train station at Nikolaistrasse 23, tel. 0341/337-4370, www.motel-one.com, leipzig-nikolaikirche@motel-one.com). A second Motel One, located just off Augustusplatz, offers the same style and prices and also has family rooms (Ritterstrasse 4, tel. 0341/252-7980, www.motel-one.com, leipzig-augustusplatz@motel-one.com).

$ A&O Leipzig Hauptbahnhof Hostel fills the former post office with 163 rooms, ranging from dorms to private rooms. Vast and institutional, it caters to a wide range of travelers, from backpackers to families. Ask for a room away from the street (dorm bunk-€10-26, Sb-€39-55, Db-€40-70, ask about family specials, breakfast-€7, sheets-€3, towel-€1, private rooms include sheets and towels, credit-card surcharge-€3, pay guest computer, free Wi-Fi in common areas, pay Wi-Fi in rooms, elevator, bar and lounge in lobby, Brandenburger Strasse 2, tel. 0341/2507-94900, www.aohostels.com, booking@aohostels.com). From the train station, take the Wintergartenstrasse exit (by track 23); you'll see the hostel to the left, across the street from the bus parking lot.

IN THE KARLI DISTRICT

This area, along Karl-Liebknecht-Strasse, has Leipzig's best bar and nightclub scene, and some of its most appealing restaurants. Staying here puts you close enough to the sightseeing while helping you escape the relatively characterless downtown for a funkier, more colorful people zone. These listings are just off the main drag, so night noise is minimal, though you may hear rowdy people and rumbling trams in the distance—ask for a quieter back room. To get here from the train station (or Augustusplatz), ride south on tram #10 (direction: Lössnig) or #11 (direction: Markkleeberg-Ost).

$$$ Michaelis Hotel is a class act, with 65 rooms, sophisticated decor, good service, and rooms that are a particularly good value in July and August (Mon-Fri: Sb-€99, Db-€129; Sat-Sun: Sb-€89, Db-€119; even cheaper July-Aug and Jan-Feb: Sb-€79, Db-€99; extra bed-€30, breakfast included, guest computer, cable Internet in rooms, Wi-Fi in lobby, parking-€6/day, tram stop: Hohe Strasse—then walk 100 yards ahead and it's on the left, Paul-Gruner-Strasse 44, tel. 0341/26780, www.michaelis-leipzig.de, info@michaelis-leipzig.de).

$$ Hotel Markgraf is simple but professionally run, offering 57 straightforward rooms with sterile comfort at fair rates just a half block from the Südplatz tram stop—close but not *too* close to the Karli action (Sb-€59-104, Db-€69-114, rates depend on demand, extra bed-€18, breakfast-€13, Wi-Fi, elevator, sauna, parking-€10/day, tram stop: Südplatz, Körnerstrasse 36, tel. 0341/303-030, www.markgraf-leipzig.de, hotel@markgraf-leipzig.de).

Eating in Leipzig

NEAR AUGUSTUSPLATZ AND THE UNIVERSITY

Getting "High" for Lunch: The towering MDR skyscraper (described on page 651), just off Augustusplatz, is capped with the elegant **Panorama Tower restaurant,** serving modern, international cuisine in a classy setting with a dramatic view. While dinner can be pricey, they serve a very affordable lunch (three courses for €9, available Mon-Fri 11:00-14:30; take elevator to 29th floor, tel. 0341/710-0590, www.panorama-leipzig.de).

Student Grub: Behind the skyscraper, **Moritzbastei** is a maze of vaulted cellars that were once part of the city fortifications. After

LEIPZIG

World War II, these passages were covered with dirt until a group of students—including, reportedly, Angela Merkel—organized to excavate them. Today the complex is filled mostly with students enjoying its indoor and outdoor seating, bars, basic €3-5 bar food, sandwiches, weekday lunch specials, and live entertainment (Mon-Fri 10:00-24:00, Sat 12:00-24:00, Sun 9:00-24:00, often closed Sun mornings in summer, Universitätsstrasse 9, tel. 0341/702-590).

DOWNTOWN "RESTAURANT ROWS"

Two downtown streets to either side of the busy Dittrichring are lined with restaurants that cater to the lunch-break crowd and are also open for dinner. **Barfussgässchen** ("Barefoot Lane"), just inside the Ring, is closer to Market Square and has a higher concentration of bars and eateries. But unless you're exhausted and ready to sit down at the first place you see, I'd recommend walking another five minutes across the Ring and checking out **Gottschedstrasse,** which has somewhat better variety and value. Choose the cuisine and ambience you like best: Thai, tapas, Italian, Vietnamese, trendy lounge, and so on. Just about the only thing you won't find is a German beer hall.

Gottschedstrasse

Luise is a big, lively, red-and-yellow bar with happening outdoor seating (€7-11 main courses, daily 9:00-24:00, breakfast served until 15:00, at Gottschedstrasse and Bosestrasse at Bosestrasse 4, tel. 0341/961-1488).

   Pilot, attached to the Central Theater, is hip yet accessible, with eclectic German and international food in a relaxed setting with mismatched used furniture (€7-9 salads, €8-13 main courses, daily 9:00-24:00, at Gottschedstrasse and Bosestrasse at Bosestrasse 1, tel. 0341/126-8117).

   Canito is a classy wine bar serving light antipasti meals, with live piano music, a wall of wines, and a Mediterranean deli case in back (€8-15 dishes, Tue-Wed 10:00-19:00, Thu-Sat 10:00-23:00, closed Sun-Mon, Gottschedstrasse 13, tel. 0341/993-8011).

Barfussgässchen

If dining here, consider these tasty options: **Spizz** (a jazz bar with an easy menu serving popular pasta and offering lots of outside seating on the market square); **Coffe Baum** (which claims to be the oldest coffeehouse in Germany and is now a quality restaurant serving traditional Saxon and German food as well as lots of coffees and cakes); **Umaii Ramenbar** (big €6.50 Asian noodle soups at lunch); and the **100 Wasser Café Bar** (a mod pub offering breakfast until late, light meals, and drinks at Barfussgässchen 15).

IN THE KARLI

While it takes a bit more effort to reach this area, the payoff is substantial: a several-block stretch of artfully dilapidated, graffitoed buildings on Karl-Liebknecht-Strasse hosting eccentric and upscale boutiques, bars, restaurants, and venues for concerts and other artistic happenings. Leipzig's avant-garde epicenter is accessible to visitors of any age. You can walk here from downtown (across the Ring, south of the New Town Hall), but I'd hop on tram #10 (direction: Lössnig) or #11 (direction: Markkleeberg-Ost) at the train station or Augustusplatz, ride to the Karl-Liebknecht-/Kurt-Eisner-Strasse stop, and walk back until you find something you like.

Most eateries here are bars with decent food and indoor or outdoor seating. You'll have your choice of neighborhood hangouts: a classic smoky pub with a beer garden out back (**Volkshaus**, #30-32); a French brasserie (**Maître**, #62); an "Ostalgic" Czech beer hall (**Gaststätte Kollektiv**, #72); an edgy Russian-themed bar (**Café Puschkin**, #74); a Caribbean place (**La Cosita**, #89); a Spanish tapas bar (**Pata Negra**, #75); and so on (all open daily). There's even a stand-up hamburger joint with a nice selection of made-to-order burgers—and even sweet-potato fries—filling a circa-1900 public toilet kiosk (**Burgermeister der Grill**, #56, at Südplatz tram stop). In good weather, food trucks gather under the "Mrs. Hippie" gateway, marking a courtyard with boutiques and occasional events.

CHARACTERISTIC LEIPZIG BRAUHAUS

Bayerischer Bahnhof is the city's main draw for beer pilgrims eager to sample the local brew, Gose (GOH-zeh). Originating

in the town of Goslar, this extremely acidic-tasting light brew (to which coriander is added in the final stage) became a Leipzig favorite. But through the tumultuous 20th century, the recipe was all but lost, and Gose was forgotten. In the 1980s, a Berlin brewer dusted off the recipe and started making Gose once more. Its fizziness makes Gose especially refreshing on a hot day and also helps it mix well with various shots and flavors (you'll see a list on the menu; for example, the *Frauenfreundliche*—"women friendly"—has a shot of cherry syrup). Adding a shot isn't a bad idea, as first-timers sometimes find Gose sour and a bit salty.

True to its name, the restaurant is actually inside one wing of the old Bayerische Bahnhof ("Bavarian train station," where trains from Bavaria first reached all the way north to Saxony). Built in 1842, this station is in the midst of an extensive renovation to become part of the city's S-Bahn system, allowing it to retain its title as the "world's oldest functioning train station." Besides beer, the restaurant also has a full menu of tasty beer-hall dishes. Choose between several brewpub seating sections—some with a view of the giant copper vats—or the delightful beer garden (daily 11:00-24:00, Bayerischer Platz 1, ride tram #16 from Hauptbahnhof or Augustusplatz a few minutes to Bayerischer Platz and head for the forlorn-looking train station, tel. 0341/124-5760).

Leipzig Connections

Leipzig is a major rail hub for eastern Germany; if you're traveling between towns in the western part of the country (Frankfurt, Würzburg, Nürnberg) and towns in the east (Berlin, Dresden), you'll likely pass through here. If traveling to the Luther towns or Dresden, you can save some money (but not time) with the Sachsen-Ticket, which is valid on slower RE trains.

From Leipzig by Train to: Berlin (hourly direct, 1.5 hours), Dresden (1-2/hour direct, 1.5 hours), Erfurt (hourly direct, 1.5-2 hours), Eisenach and Wartburg Castle (hourly direct, 2-2.5 hours), Wittenberg (6/day on ICE, 30-40 minutes; also hourly on regional trains, 1 hour, some with transfer in Bitterfeld), Frankfurt (every 2 hours direct on ICE, 3.5 hours; a few additional on IC, 4 hours), Würzburg (about every 2 hours, 3.5-4 hours, transfer in Fulda or Bamberg), Hamburg (hourly, 3-3.5 hours, some direct, others transfer in Berlin), Nürnberg (every 2 hours direct, 3.5 hours, a few more with a transfer in Naumburg), Munich (8/day direct, 5.5 hours; more with change in Nürnberg or Naumburg, 5.5 hours), Prague (about every 1-2 hours, 3.5-5 hours, transfer in Dresden). Train info: Tel. 0180-599-6633, www.bahn.com.

DRESDEN

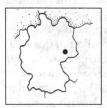

Dresden surprises visitors, with fanciful Baroque architecture in a delightful-to-stroll cityscape, a dynamic history that mingles tragedy with inspiration, and some of the best museum-going in Germany. Today's Dresden is a young and vibrant city, crawling with proud locals, cheery tourists, and happy-go-lucky students who have no memory of communism. This intriguing and fun city winds up on far fewer American itineraries than it deserves to. Don't make that mistake.

At the peak of its power in the 18th century, this capital of Saxony ruled most of present-day Poland and eastern Germany from the banks of the Elbe River. Dresden's answer to Louis XIV was Augustus the Strong. As both prince elector of Saxony and king of Poland, he imported artists from all over Europe, peppering his city with fine Baroque buildings and filling his treasury with lavish jewels and artwork. Dresden's grand architecture and dedication to the arts—along with the gently rolling hills surrounding the city—earned it the nickname "Florence on the Elbe."

Sadly, these days Dresden is better known outside Germany for its destruction in World War II. American and British bomber crews firebombed the city on the night of February 13, 1945. More than 25,000 people were killed—in just one night—and 75 percent of the historical center was destroyed. American Kurt Vonnegut, who was a POW in Dresden during the firebombing, later memorialized the event in his novel *Slaughterhouse-Five*.

As you walk through Dresden, you may see some circa-1946 photos on display. The city's heritage of destruction is hard to ignore. An inscription in the middle of Altmarkt square calling Dresden "a place of remembrance" asks passersby to recall that "thousands of victims' bodies were burnt here" in the February 1945 air raids and concludes: "Thus the horrors of war, unleashed by Germany upon the whole world, came back to be visited upon our city."

During the Cold War, Dresden was in what was facetiously called the "Valley of the Clueless"—the part of East Germany where you couldn't get Western television. Under the communists, Dresden patched up some of its damaged buildings, left many others in ruins, and replaced even more with modern, ugly sprawl.

After the Berlin Wall fell and Germany was reunited, new funding became available for Dresden. The city built apartment complexes and shopping centers, and rebuilt the Royal Palace and Frauenkirche. Bombed-out blocks and derelict parking lots became huge department stores with deep underground garages. Even though the city plan still feels bombed out—with big gaps, wide boulevards, and old streetscapes gone—the transformation has been astonishing, and all the most important historic buildings have been reconstructed.

The bombs missed most of the New Town, across the river. Much like the outer precincts of the former East Berlin, this well-worn area retains its prewar character and has emerged as the city's fun and lively people zone—especially the Outer New Town, north of Bautzner Strasse. Most tourists never cross the bridge away from the famous Old Town museums, but a visit to Dresden isn't complete without a wander through the New Town.

PLANNING YOUR TIME

Dresden, conveniently located about halfway between Prague and Berlin, is well worth even a quick stop. If you're short on time, Dresden's top sights can be seen in a midday break from your Berlin-Prague train ride (each less than 2.5 hours away). Catch the early train, throw your bag in a locker at the main train station, follow my self-guided walk, and visit some museums before taking an evening train out. If possible, reserve ahead to visit one of Dresden's top sights, the Historic Green Vault (for details, see page 693).

If you have more time, Dresden merits spending at least one night. The city is a handy home base for a quick bike ride to the "Blue Wonder" bridge, a paddleboat cruise along the Elbe, or getting back to nature in the Saxon Switzerland National Park.

Orientation to Dresden

With a half-million residents, Dresden is big. The Old Town (Altstadt) hugs a curve on the Elbe River, so most of its sights are within easy strolling distance along the south bank of the river. South of the Old Town (a 5-minute tram ride or 15-minute walk away) is the main train station (Hauptbahnhof). North of the Old Town, across the river, you'll find the more residential New Town (Neustadt). While the New Town boasts no great sights, it's lively, colorful, and fun to explore—especially after dark, when the funky, cutting-edge Outer New Town (Äussere Neustadt) sets the tempo for Dresden's nightlife scene.

TOURIST INFORMATION

Dresden has a good TI at Neumarkt 2 (Mon-Fri 10:00-19:00, Sat 10:00-18:00, Sun 10:00-15:00; enter under *Passage* sign across from door D of Frauenkirche, and go down escalators). A smaller, less useful TI kiosk is in the main train station (daily 8:00-20:00, under tracks 3-4). The TIs share a phone number and a website (tel. 0351/501-501, www.dresden.de/tourismus).

At either TI, ask for a map of the transit system, which includes an adequate street map. Both TIs sell a better €2.50 city map and offer a room-booking service (€3/person). They also book tickets to events. To find out about live entertainment and cultural events, skim the monthly *Theater Konzert Kunst* (free, in German only). Dresden's city website, www.dresden.de, has good information, including a free downloadable city guide and map.

Discount Deals: The two-day **Dresden Card** includes entry to the state-run Zwinger, Royal Palace, and Albertinum museums (but not the Historic Green Vault), use of the city's transit system, and small discounts for many other museums. Think of it as a combo-ticket for the three state-run museums, which pays for itself if you visit two of them and ride the trams a few times (€30, €55 family ticket covers 2 adults and up to 4 children). The one-day version (€10, €14 family) includes public transit, but offers only discounts at sights—not free admission. It can still pay off, especially for families. The **Dresden Regio-Card** also covers outlying areas for three or five days. Cards are sold at both TIs and state-run museums (www.dresden.de/dresdencard).

ARRIVAL IN DRESDEN

Dresden has two major train stations: Dresden Hauptbahnhof and Dresden-Neustadt. Most trains stop at both stations (coming from Berlin, first at Neustadt, then at Hauptbahnhof; from Prague, it's the other way around). If you're coming for the day and want the easiest access to sights, use the Hauptbahnhof. S-Bahn trains, as well as trams #3, #10, and #11, connect the two stations (see "Getting Around Dresden," later, for transit details).

By Train at the Hauptbahnhof: Dresden's main train station has a chic new roof designed by Norman Foster (of Berlin's Reichstag Dome fame). In the bright, white arrivals hall, you'll find a

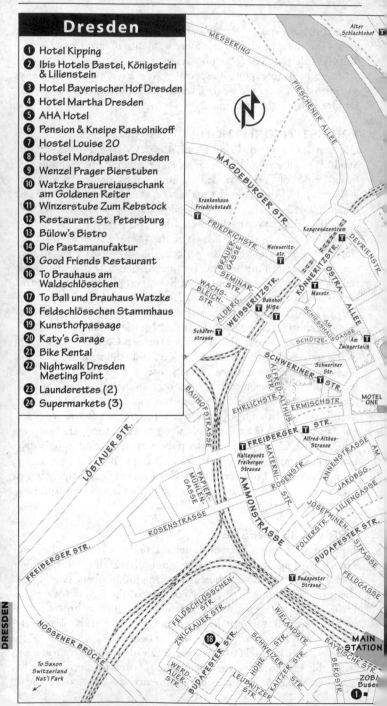

Dresden

1. Hotel Kipping
2. Ibis Hotels Bastei, Königstein & Lilienstein
3. Hotel Bayerischer Hof Dresden
4. Hotel Martha Dresden
5. AHA Hotel
6. Pension & Kneipe Raskolnikoff
7. Hostel Louise 20
8. Hostel Mondpalast Dresden
9. Wenzel Prager Bierstuben
10. Watzke Brauereiausschank am Goldenen Reiter
11. Winzerstube Zum Rebstock
12. Restaurant St. Petersburg
13. Bülow's Bistro
14. Die Pastamanufaktur
15. Good Friends Restaurant
16. To Brauhaus am Waldschlösschen
17. To Ball und Brauhaus Watzke
18. Feldschlösschen Stammhaus
19. Kunsthofpassage
20. Katy's Garage
21. Bike Rental
22. Nightwalk Dresden Meeting Point
23. Launderettes (2)
24. Supermarkets (3)

DRESDEN

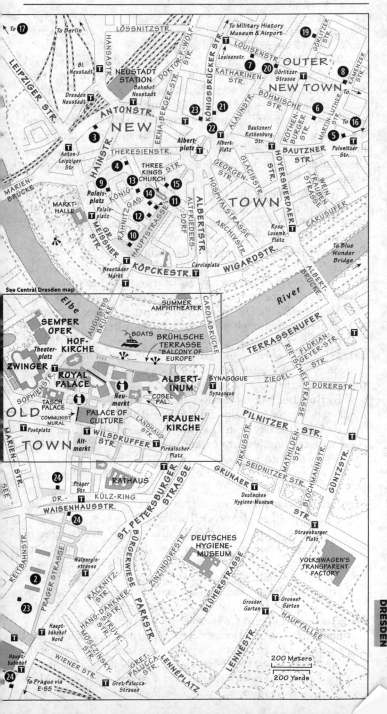

To 17
To Berlin
LÖSSNITZSTR.
To Military History Museum & Airport
19 GÖRLITZER STR.
HANSASTR.
DOKTOR-F.-WOLF-STR.
KÖNIGSBRÜCKER STR.
Louisenstr.
LOUISENSTR.
OUTER
7
KATHARINEN-STR.
20 Görlitzer Strasse
NEW TOWN
8
LEIPZIGER STR.
Bl. Neustadt
NEUSTADT STATION
Bahnhof Neustadt
ALAUNSTR.
BÖHMISCHE STR.
6
KAMENZER STR.
To 16
Dresden Neustadt
ANTONSTR.
23
21
ROTHEN-BURGER STR.
MARTIN-LUTHER-STR.
5
Pulsnitzer Str.
NEW
22
Bautzner/ Rothenburg. Str.
Anton-/ Leipziger Str.
3
HAINSTR.
THERESIENSTR.
Albert-platz
Albert-platz
HOVERSWERDAER STR.
BAUTZNER STR.
WEIN TRAUBEN STR.
4
THREE KINGS CHURCH
GEORGENSTR.
TOWN
CARUSUFER
MARIEN-BRÜCKE
9
PALAIS-platz
13
KÖNIG-STR.
14
15
ALTFRIEDERS-DORF
ALBERTSTR.
HOSPITALSTRASSE
ARCHIVSTR.
GLACISSTR.
Rosa-Luxemb.-Platz
To Blue Wonder Bridge
MARKT-HALLE
Palais-platz
RAHNITZ GAS.
11
12
HAUPTSTRASSE
10
Neustädter Markt
KÖPCKESTR.
Carolaplatz
WIGARDSTR.
ALBERT-BRÜCKE

GR. MEISSNER STR.

See Central Dresden map

Elbe
AUGUSTUS-BRÜCKE
SUMMER AMPHITHEATER
CAROLABRÜCKE
River
SEMPER OPER
HOF-KIRCHE
BOATS
BRÜHLSCHE TERRASSE "BALCONY OF EUROPE"
TERRASSENUFER
FLORIAN GEYER-STR.
RIESA-STR.
RIETSCHELSTRASSE
Theater-platz
ZWINGER
ROYAL PALACE
ALBERT-INUM
SYNAGOGUE
ZIEGEL-STR.
DÜRERSTR.
SOPHIENSTR.
Neu-markt
Synagogue
TASCH PALACE
COSEL PAL.
COMMUNIST MURAL
PALACE OF CULTURE
FRAUEN-KIRCHE
PILNITZER STR.
OLD
LANDHAUS-STR.
ZIRKUSSTR.
MATHILDEN-STR.
MARIEN STR.
Postplatz
WILSDRUFFER STR.
Altmarkt
Pirnaischer Platz
SEIDNITZER STR.
TOWN
BLOCHMANNSTR.
GÜNTZSTR.

24
RATHAUS
Prager Str.
ST. PETERSBURGER STRASSE
GRUNAER STR.
DR.-KÜLZ-RING
WAISENHAUSSTR.
Deutsches Hygiene-Museum
24
Strassburger Platz
MARIEN SEE STR.
REITBAHNSTR.
Walpurgis-strasse
BÜRGERWIESE PARKSTR.
ZINZENDORFSTR.
BLÜHERSTRASSE
DEUTSCHES HYGIENE-MUSEUM
VOLKSWAGEN'S TRANSPARENT FACTORY
PRAGER STRASSE
2
RACKNITZ-STR.
HANS-DANKNER-STR.
STRÜVE-STR.
Grosser Garten
Grosser Garten
23
Haupt-bähnhof Nord
MOSCZINSKY-STR.
HAUPTALLEE
WIENER STR.
GRET-PALUCCA-STR.
LENNÉPLATZ
LENNÉSTR.
Haupt-bahnhof
24
To Prague via E-55
GRET-Palucca-Strasse
200 Meters
200 Yards

DRESDEN

Reisezentrum (Mon-Fri 5:45-21:00, Sat-Sun 7:00-21:00). Under tracks 1 and 2 are pay WCs and lockers.

To reach the beginning of my self-guided walk quickly by **tram**, exit the station following the *Ausgang 1* signs, cross the tram tracks, and hop on tram #8 to Theaterplatz in the Old Town (five stops). If you'd rather **walk,** the 20-minute stroll to the Old Town gives you an insightful glimpse of the communist era as you head down Prager Strasse (described on page 702). From the station, exit toward *Ausgang 2/City/Prager Strasse,* and continue straight along Prager Strasse, then Seestrasse and Schlossstrasse until you emerge at the river.

To reach other points from the station by tram, note your line number and ask for help finding your platform. Lines #9 and #11 (linking to the New Town) depart from the Hauptbahnhof Nord tram stop: Exit the arrivals hall via *Ausgang 2*, then veer right under an archway through the long, glassy building.

By Train at Neustadt: The Neustadt train station serves the New Town north of the river and is near some recommended hotels. It has pay lockers and WCs, and a *Reisezentrum* (daily 7:00-20:00). To reach the Old Town from Neustadt Station, take tram #11 (direction: Zschertnitz) four stops to Postplatz.

By Plane: From Dresden's airport (airport code: DRS, tel. 351/881-3360, www.dresden-airport.de), S-Bahn line #2 runs frequently to both train stations for the price of a regular public-transport ticket.

By Bus: Long-distance buses arrive at, and leave from, a cluster of stops located just behind the Hauptbahnhof.

By Car: The city center has several well-marked parking garages with reasonable daytime rates (€6/day 8:00-20:00 on Mon-Sat, €3/day on Sun).

HELPFUL HINTS

Sightseeing Strategies: Note that many of Dresden's top museums are closed either Monday or Tuesday.

The Historic Green Vault admits a limited number of people every half-hour. If you haven't reserved ahead, try to line up early to buy a same-day ticket (ticket office opens at 10:00; for details, see page 693). Once you have your Historic Green Vault visit time, plan the rest of your day around it (it's conveniently located right in the center of the Old Town).

Entertainment, Organ Concerts, and Masses: The city has lots going on. Ask about events across the river at the big amphitheater (concerts, movies, sports broadcasts; almost nightly June-Aug). Both big churches—the Catholic Hofkirche and the Lutheran Frauenkirche—have a worship service or Mass with pipe organ music every evening (check schedule at TI and/or church); the Hofkirche also hosts free pipe-organ concerts (usually Wed and Sat evenings; check schedule at door).

Internet Access: Mondial in the Outer New Town has terminals (Mon-Fri 10:00-24:00, Sat-Sun 11:00-24:00, Louisenstrasse 42, at corner of Görlitzer Strasse).

Laundry: Coin-operated launderettes are common in Dresden. These both have English instructions: **Dani's Waschsalon** is roughly between the Hauptbahnhof train station and the Ibis hotels on Prager Strasse, on the ground floor of a very tall apartment building (Mon-Sat 6:00-23:00, closed Sun, Reitbahnstrasse 35, enter on northeast side of building, mobile 0179/363-5074). In the New Town, **Eco-Express SB-Waschsalon** is just off Albertplatz (Mon-Sat 6:00-23:00, last load at 22:15, closed Sun, Königsbrücker Strasse 2).

Bike Rental: Roll on Dresden rents bikes and will gladly deliver and pick up the bike at your hotel for a small fee (€8/day, Mon-Fri 10:00-13:00 & 16:00-19:00, Sat 10:00-13:00, Sun usually 10:00-12:00 in summer only, drop off until 20:30; in New Town, near Albertplatz tram stop at Königsbrücker Strasse 4a, mobile 0152-2267-3460, www.rollondresden.de, info@rollondresden.de). Reservations can be made by email.

Supermarkets: Flanking the Prager Strasse tram stop are big shopping centers with basement supermarkets. In the huge Altmarkt Galerie mall to the north is a discount Aldi (Mon-Sat 9:30-21:00, closed Sun) and a mid-priced REWE (Mon-Sat 9:00-21:00, closed Sun). The Karstadt department store to the south has a more upscale supermarket (Mon-Sat 9:30-20:00, closed Sun). Another REWE is immediately behind the Hauptbahnhof (Mon-Sat 7:00-22:00, closed Sun).

Festivals: In mid-June, the Outer New Town holds its **Stadtteilfest Bunte Republik Neustadt,** a huge three-day counter-cultural block party celebrating the neighborhood's tongue-in-cheek status as an independent republic. The last weekend of June sees the **Elbhangfest,** with parades, concerts, and dance performances (www.elbhangfest.de).

GETTING AROUND DRESDEN

As soon as you master the **trams,** you'll understand why so many Dresdeners never get around to learning how to drive. Trams are cheap, easy, and go every couple of minutes. Buy the day pass and commit to using trams for almost everything. Tram lines and numbers are clearly marked on city maps, and handy electronic boards at each stop say which trams are on the way and how many minutes until they arrive. Buy tickets from machines at platforms or on trams (€2.20 for a single *Einzelfahrkarte* ticket for rides up to 1 hour; €5 for a 4-pack of *Kurzstrecke* tickets for rides up to 4 stops in length; machines accept coins only). A day ticket *(Tageskarte)* is valid for one calendar day (€6, €8.50 family). Validate your ticket by date-stamping it in the little boxes on train platforms and on board buses and trams (for the day ticket, stamp it only the first time you ride). Free use of public transit is included with the Dresden Card (described earlier). For transit information, see www.vvo-online.de.

Taxis are reasonable, plentiful, and generally honest (roughly €6 per ride in town, tel. 0351/211-211). But once you commit yourself to the trams, you'll ignore the taxis for in-town rides.

Tours in Dresden

Walking Tours

Dresden Walks is a cooperative of local English-speaking guides who offer daily 1.5-hour walks of the Old Town. While generally covering the same ground as my self-guided walk (and no interiors), this tour is a fine way to get more in-depth background from a guide who can answer your questions. Tours go every day at 12:00; just show up and pay the guide (€12, meet at green sign on stairs at Schlossplatz—near the south end of Augustus Bridge, mobile 0163-716-9886, www.dresdenwalks.com).

Nightwalk Dresden, a late-night tour of the city's Outer New Town, is much more than a pub crawl; it's a journey through the unique culture of a virtually undiscovered part of the city—that just happens to include two or three stops for drinks along the way. This tour makes the prewar (and pre-reunification) Outer New Town come to life. You'll learn about the neighborhood's "street-art" scene and bohemian character (alive and well despite recent gentrification), get a sense of the wry humor that kept locals afloat through the gray communist times, and be pointed to fascinating urban details that you'd otherwise miss. Tours run in English and German simultaneously (€15, daily at 21:00—best to call ahead, 3 hours; starts in Neustadt on the north end of Albertplatz, by the artesian well—see website for map; mobile 0172/781-5007, www.nightwalk-dresden.de).

The **Kurt Vonnegut Tour** and the **Street Art Tour,** both run by Nightwalk Dresden, show you Dresden through the prism of *Slaughterhouse-Five* and the city's graffiti scene, respectively. Both tours meet near the equestrian statue in front of the Semperoper on Theaterplatz, but require advance booking through the contact info listed above for Nightwalk (Vonnegut: €12, Mon-Fri at 11:00 or 14:00, 2 hours; Street Art: €15, Tue-Sat at 14:00, 3 hours).

Hop-On, Hop-Off Bus Tours

Red-and-white double-decker buses (labeled *Stadtrundfahrt*) connect 22 of the city's main sights (including the Blue Wonder bridge and the Military Museum) in a 1.5-hour loop (€20, €2 more lets you ride for a second day; in summer 2-4/hour, first bus starts from Theaterplatz at 9:30, last bus finishes at 18:30; Nov-March 1-2/hour 10:00-16:30, tel. 0351/899-5650, www.stadtrundfahrt-dresden.de).

Local Guides

Liane Richter (€80/2-hour tour, lianerichter@gmx.net) and **Anke Winkler** (€90/2-hour tour, mobile 0151-1196-8770, info@dresden-citytour.de) are two good local guides who enjoy sharing the story of their hometown and region.

Old and New Dresden Walk

Dresden's major Old Town sights are conveniently clustered along a delightfully strollable promenade next to the Elbe River. From there, the city's oldest bridge leads into the energetic New Town. Lace these sights together by taking this self-guided walk, worth ▲▲▲. You'll get to know the four eras that have most shaped the city: Dresden's Golden Age in the mid-18th century under Augustus the Strong; the city's destruction by firebombs in World War II; the communist regime (1945-1989); and the current "reconstruction after reunification" era.

This walk takes about 90 minutes, not counting museum stops. It passes by three major sights (Zwinger, Royal Palace with Green Vault treasuries, and Frauenkirche), each of which is described later in the chapter. If you visit the sights, this walk will fill your day. Your stroll ends in the New Town, a great area for evening exploring or dining.

• *Begin at Theaterplatz (a convenient drop-off point for tram #8 from the Hauptbahnhof).*

❶ Theaterplatz

In the middle of the square, face the equestrian statue of King John, an intellectual mid-19th-century ruler who recognized and preserved Saxon culture—and paid for the opera house behind the statue. The Saxon State Opera House is nicknamed the **Semperoper** after its architect, Gottfried Semper (visits only with a tour, see page 701). Three opera houses have stood in this spot: The first was destroyed by a fire in 1869, the second by firebombs in 1945. The rebuilt Semperoper continues to be a world-class venue. Notice how the two greatest figures in German literary culture—Goethe and Schiller—flank the entry, welcoming all who enter to German high culture.

As you face the Opera House, the big building to your left is the vast Zwinger complex (your next stop). The smaller Neoclassi-cal building farther to your left is a former guardhouse called the Schinkelwache. If it looks out of place, that's because it was designed in a Prussian Classicist style by the architect Karl Fried-rich Schinkel, who was also responsible for some of Berlin's most impressive Neoclassical buildings. Today the Schinkel-wache functions as a popular café and the opera's box office.

Behind you, across the square from the Opera House, are the Hofkirche, with its distinctive green-copper, onion-domed steeple, and the sprawling Royal Palace (with shiny new clock; both worth visiting and described later).

All the buildings you see here—Dresden's Baroque trea-sures—are thorough reconstructions. The originals were destroyed in a single night by American and British bombs, with only walls and sometimes just foundations left standing. For decades, Dres-den has been rebuilding.

• *As you walk up the path between the Semperoper and the Zwinger, notice the small statue of composer Carl Maria von Weber to your left. Weber's* Der Freischütz *was the last opera performed in the building before its destruction in 1945—and the first opera performed when the building reopened in 1985.*

In the little corner by the recommended Alte Meister Café (see "Eat-ing in Dresden," later), go up the stairs and turn left up the path. This takes you to a balcony overlooking the Zwinger's grand courtyard. (But first, enjoy the adorable fountain on your left.) From the banister, look down on the Nymphs' Bath—which we'll visit momentarily. Then cross over to absorb the breathtaking view of the grand Zwinger courtyard. As you stand on the balcony, imagine yourself as one of Dresden's 18th-century burghers, watching one of Augustus' wild parties in the court-yard below.

Take the small stairs at the top of the Nymphs' Bath down to its pool.

The **Nymphs' Bath**, perhaps the city's favorite fountain, is where aristocrats relaxed in the 18th century among cascading wa-terfalls and an open-air grotto, ringed by sexy sandstone nymphs. It's textbook Baroque, with its pilasters evoking falling water and

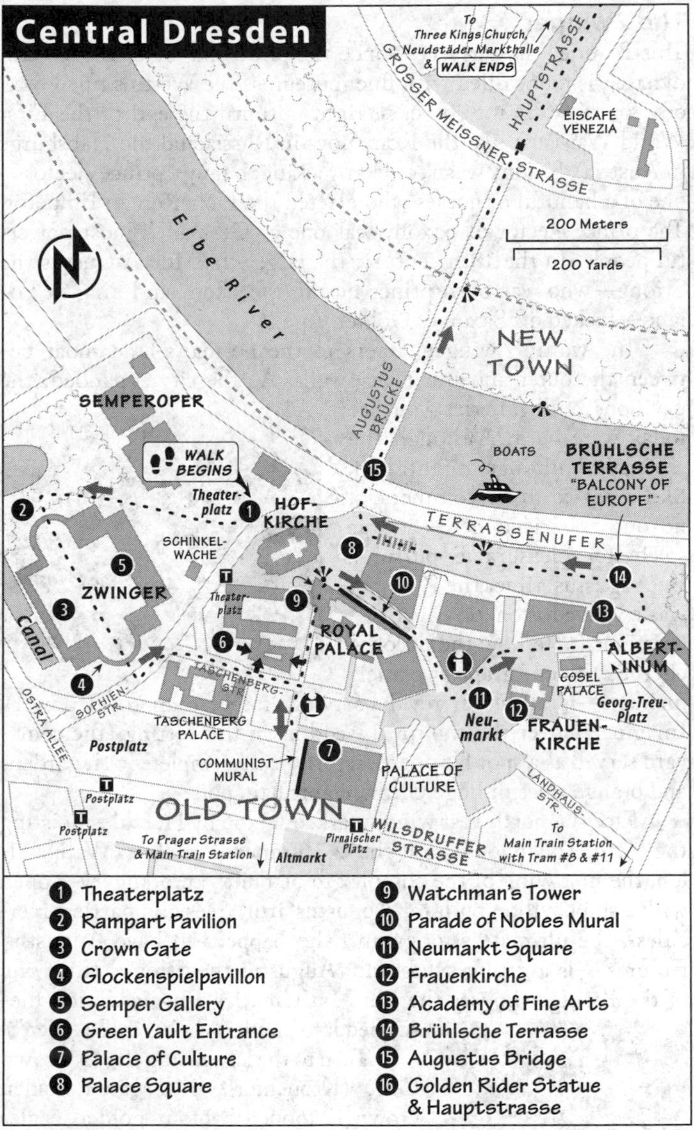
Central Dresden
To Three Kings Church, Neudstäder Markthalle & WALK ENDS
GROSSER MEISSNER STRASSE
HAUPTSTRASSE
EISCAFÉ VENEZIA
200 Meters
200 Yards
Elbe River
NEW TOWN
AUGUSTUS BRÜCKE
SEMPEROPER
WALK BEGINS
BOATS
BRÜHLSCHE TERRASSE "BALCONY OF EUROPE"
Theaterplatz
HOFKIRCHE
TERRASSENUFER
SCHINKELWACHE
ZWINGER
Canal
Theaterplatz
ROYAL PALACE
ALBERTINUM
COSEL PALACE
Georg-Treu-Platz
TASCHENBERG-STR.
SOPHIEN-STR.
OSTRA ALLEE
TASCHENBERG PALACE
Postplatz
Neumarkt
FRAUENKIRCHE
COMMUNIST MURAL
PALACE OF CULTURE
LANDHAUS-STR.
Postplatz
Postplatz
OLD TOWN
To Prager Strasse & Main Train Station
Altmarkt
Pirnaischer Platz
WILSDRUFFER STRASSE
To Main Train Station with Tram #8 & #11
1 Theaterplatz
2 Rampart Pavilion
3 Crown Gate
4 Glockenspielpavillon
5 Semper Gallery
6 Green Vault Entrance
7 Palace of Culture
8 Palace Square
9 Watchman's Tower
10 Parade of Nobles Mural
11 Neumarkt Square
12 Frauenkirche
13 Academy of Fine Arts
14 Brühlsche Terrasse
15 Augustus Bridge
16 Golden Rider Statue & Hauptstrasse

a wind machine conveniently blowing open the robes of eager-to-frolic maidens.

• *From the pool, cross through the glassy orangery and into the huge courtyard of the Zwinger complex. Stand in the middle to survey the four wings—marked by a clock, a crown, Hercules holding the earth high, and a grand and stern facade (through which you entered).*

DRESDEN

The Zwinger

This Baroque masterpiece—once the pride and joy of the Wettin dynasty, is today filled with fine museums. The Wettins ruled Saxony for more than 800 years, right up until the end of the First World War (just like the Romanovs in Russia and the Habsburgs in Austria). Saxony wasn't ruled by a king, but by a prince elector—one of a handful of nobles who elected the Holy Roman Emperor. The prince elector of Saxony was one of Germany's most powerful people. In the 18th century, the larger-than-life Augustus the Strong—who was both prince elector of Saxony and king of Poland—kicked off Saxony's Golden Age.

The word "Zwinger" refers to the no-man's-land moat between the outer and inner city walls. As the city expanded, the

pavilions and galleries you see today were built. Although the Zwinger buildings might look like a palace to us commoners, no one ever lived here—it was solely for pleasurable pursuits. By Augustus' time, the Zwinger was a venue for Saxon court celebrations (note how the decor—cherubs, wine grapes, comely maidens—is all about royal partying, rather than royal power). Imagine an over-the-top royal wedding in this setting. The courtyard served as a spot for open-air festivities, complete with gardens and orange trees in huge Chinese porcelain pots.

Face the northwest wing, marked up top by Hercules hoisting the earth. You're looking at the ❷ **Rampart Pavilion** (Wallpavillon, the first wing of the complex to be built), an orangery capped with a sun pavilion built for Augustus' fruit trees and parties. Hercules—the ultimate strongman (who happens to have Augustus' features)—is a fitting symbol for Augustus the Strong. This wing of the Zwinger houses the fun **Mathematics-Physics Salon** (described later, under "Sights in Dresden").

Turn to the left, facing the ❸ **Crown Gate** (Kronentor). The gate's golden crown is topped by four golden eagles supporting a smaller crown—symbolizing Polish royalty (since Augustus was also king of Poland).

Turn again to the left to see the ❹ **Glockenspielpavillon.** The glockenspiel near the top of the gate has 40 bells made of Meissen porcelain (bells chime every 15 minutes and play a sweet 3-minute melody at 10:15, 14:15, and 18:15). If you're here when they play, listen to the delightful chimes of the porcelain—far sweeter than a typical metal bell. This wing of the Zwinger also houses Augustus the Strong's **Porcelain Collection** (see "Sights in Dresden").

Turn once more to the left (with the Crown Gate behind you) to see the stern facade of the ❺ **Semper Gallery.** This Zwinger wing was added to the original courtyard 100 years later by Gottfried Semper (of Opera House fame). It houses Dresden's best painting collection, the **Old Masters Gallery** (see "Sights in Dresden").

Throughout the city, you'll see the local sandstone looking really sooty. It's not from pollution or firebombing (as many visitors presume), but natural oxidation that turns the stone black in about 50 years. Once restored, the statues are given a silicon treatment that lets the stone breathe but keeps it from going black.

You are surrounded by three of Dresden's top museums. Anticipating WWII bombs, Dresdeners preserved their town's art treasures by storing them in underground mines and cellars in the countryside. This saved these great works from Allied bombs...but not from the Russians. Nearly all of the city's artwork ended up in Moscow until after Stalin's death in 1953, when it was returned by the communist regime to win over their East German subjects. Today, Russians invade only as tourists (who generally steamroll in with Putin-esque smiles in aggressive tour groups of 50).

When you're finished with the museums, exit the Zwinger through the Glockenspielpavillon. Halfway through the corridor, look for the **timelines** telling the history of the Zwinger in German: to the right, its construction, and to the left, its destruction and reconstruction. Notice the Soviet spin: On February 13, 1945, gangs of Anglo-American bombers obliterated *(vernichteten)* the city. On May 8, 1945, the Soviet army liberated *(befreite)* Dresden from "fascist tyranny" *(faschistischen Tyrannei),* and from 1945 to 1964, the Zwinger was rebuilt with the "power of the workers and peasants" *(Arbeiter- und Bauern-Macht).*

• *As you exit the corridor, cross the street and the tram tracks and jog left, walking down the perpendicular street called Taschenberg, with the yellow Taschenberg Palace on your right (built for Augustus' mistress, it eventually housed the crown prince). Ruined until 1990, today it's a five-star hotel. The yellow-windowed sky bridge ahead connects the Taschenberg with the prince electors'* **Royal Palace.** *The gate on your left is one of several entrances to the* ❻ **Green Vault** *treasuries (described later, under "Sights in Dresden").*

Go under the sky bridge. Ahead of you and to the right, the blocky modern building is the...

DRESDEN

Augustus the Strong (1670-1733)

Friedrich Augustus I of the Wettin family exemplified royal excess, and made Dresden one of Europe's most important cities of culture. Legends paint Augustus as a macho, womanizing, powerful, ambitious, properly Baroque man—a real Saxon superstar. A hundred years after his death, historians dubbed Augustus "the Strong." Today, tour guides love to impart silly legends about Augustus, who supposedly fathered 365 children and could break a horseshoe in half with his bare hands.

As prince elector of Saxony, Augustus wheeled and dealed—and pragmatically converted from his Saxon Protestantism to a more Polish-friendly Catholicism—to become King Augustus II of Poland. (You'll notice the Protestant Frauenkirche is fancier than a typical Lutheran church, while the Catholic Hofkirche is a bit low-key, as Augustus was finessing it both ways to be acceptable to both realms.) Like most Wettins, Augustus the Strong was unlucky at war, but a clever diplomat and a lover of the arts.

The Polish people blame Augustus and his successors—who were far more concerned with wealth and opulence than with sensible governance—for Poland's precipitous decline after its own medieval Golden Age. According to Poles, the Saxon kings did nothing but "eat, drink, and loosen their belts" (it rhymes in Polish).

Whether you consider them the heroes of history, or the villains, Augustus and the rest of the Wettins—and the nobles who paid them taxes—are to thank for Dresden's rich architectural and artistic heritage.

❼ Palace of Culture (Kulturpalast)

Built by the communist government in 1969, today this hall is used for concerts. Notice the exterior mural depicting communist themes: workers, strong women, well-cared-for elders, teachers and students, and—of course—the red star and the seal of former East Germany. The bronze doors on the street side give a Marxist interpretation of the history of Dresden. Little of this propagandist art, which once inundated the lives of locals, survives in post-communist Germany (what does survive, like this, is protected). The palace is currently closed for restoration work.

• *Now turn left (with the Palace of Culture behind you). Walk along the palace wall (noticing the postwar construction on your right, a mix of new and old) toward the two small copper domes. After passing through a tunnel with (mostly Russian) musicians taking advantage of the fine acoustics, you emerge onto* ❽ **Palace Square**. *Ahead and to the left is the* **Katholiche Hofkirche** *(described later, under "Sights in Dresden") with another elevated passage, designed to allow royalty to go to church without the hassle of dealing with the public. Now turn around and face* *the gate you just came through. You're looking at the palace complex entry (with the ❾ **Watchman's Tower** above on the right—see listing, later). To the left, next to one of the palace's entrances, you'll see a long, yellow mural called the...*

❿ Parade of Nobles (Fürstenzug)

This mural is painted on 24,000 tiles of Meissen porcelain. Longer than a football field, it illustrates seven centuries of Saxon royalty.

It was built to commemorate Saxon history and heritage after Saxony became a part of Germany in 1871. The artist carefully studied armor and clothing through the ages, accurately tracing the evolution of weaponry and fashions for seven centuries. (This is great for couples—try this for a switch: As you stroll, men watch the fashions, women the weaponry.)

The very last figure (or the first one you see, coming from this direction) is the artist himself, Wilhelm Walther. In front of him are commoners (miners, farmers, carpenters, teachers, students, artists), and then the royals, with 35 names and dates marking more than 700 years of Wettin rule. Stop at 1694. That's August II (Augustus the Strong), the most important of the Saxon kings. His horse stomps on the rose (symbol of Martin Luther, the Protestant movement, and the Lutheran church today) to gain the Polish crown. The first Saxon royal is Konrad der Grosse ("the Great"). And waaay up at the very front of the parade, an announcer with a band and 12th-century cheerleaders excitedly herald the arrival of this wondrous procession. The porcelain tiles are originals (from 1907)—they survived the Dresden bombing. They were fired three times at 2,400 degrees Fahrenheit when created...and then fired again during the 1945 firestorm, at only 1,800 degrees.

• *When you're finished looking at the mural, dogleg right and walk into the big square, where a statue of Martin Luther stands tall.*

⓫ Neumarkt

This "New Market Square" was once a central square ringed by the homes of rich merchants. After many years of construction, it is once again alive with people and cafés. The statue of Martin Luther shows him holding not just any Bible, but the German version of the Word of God, which he personally translated so that regular people could wrestle with it directly (this is basically what the Protestant Reformation was all about). When translating, Luther used his native Saxon dialect of German, forming the basis for what's now considered "High German." So besides being the Great Reformer, Luther is considered the father of the modern German language. (For more on Luther—who came from this part of Germany and spent most of his life in nearby Erfurt and Wittenberg—see page 593.) Toppled in 1945, Luther has been cleaned up and is back on his feet again.

• *The big church looming over the square is the...*

⑫ Frauenkirche (Church of Our Lady)

This church is the symbol and soul of the city. When completed in 1743, this was Germany's tallest Protestant church (310 feet high).

Its unique central-stone-cupola design gave it the nickname "the stone bell." While it's a great church, this building garners the world's attention primarily because of its tragic history and phoenix-like resurrection: On the night of February 13, 1945, the firebombs came. When the smoke cleared the next morning, the Frauenkirche was smoldering but still standing. It burned for two days before finally collapsing. After the war, the Frauenkirche was left a pile of rubble and turned into a peace monument. Only after reunification was the decision made to rebuild it completely and painstakingly. It reopened to the public in 2005 (see listing later, under "Sights in Dresden").

A big hunk of the bombed **rubble** stands in the square (near door E, river side of church) as a memorial. Notice the small metal relief of the dome that shows where this piece came from.

• *From the chunk of church find the nearby dome nicknamed "the lemon juicer." This caps the exhibition hall of the* ⑬ *Academy of Fine Arts. Walk past that to the small, grassy Georg-Treu-Platz, which is surrounded by imposing architecture. The grand neo-Renaissance building ahead and to the right is the Albertinum. Long the home of the Saxon armory, it was rebuilt in the 1880s in Neo-Renaissance style. Today it's an art gallery with the city's best collection of 19th- and 20th-century art (described under "Sights in Dresden," later). Walk through the square and climb the ramparts, now a park.*

Find a bulge in the promenade 30 yards to the left. Belly up to that banister for an Elbe River view. Each summer, the city sets up a popular amphitheater on the bank directly across the Elbe (offering nearly nightly events—such as concerts and movies—from June through August). The Heute *("today") sign announces what's on tonight.*

⑭ Brühlsche Terrasse

This delightful promenade overlooking the river was once a defensive rampart—look along the side of the terrace facing the Elbe River to see openings for cannons. Later, it was given as a reward

to a Saxon minister named Brühl, who had distinguished himself as a tax collector, raising revenue for Frederick Augustus II's state treasury. In the early 1800s, it was turned into a public park, with a leafy canopy of linden trees, and was given the odd nickname "The Balcony of Europe."

• *For more river views, stroll the length of the promenade to the next grove of linden trees.*

Dresden claims to have the world's largest and oldest fleet of historic paddleboat steamers: nine riverboats from the 19th century. The hills in the distance (to the left) are home to vineyards, producing some of Germany's northernmost wine. Because only a small amount of land is suitable for grape growing, the area's respected, expensive wine (mostly white) is consumed almost entirely by locals.

• *Below you to the left is the...*

⑮ Augustus Bridge

This bridge (Augustusbrücke) has connected Dresden's old and new towns since 1319, when it was the first stone bridge over the

river. During massive floods in August of 2002, the water reached nearly to the top of the arches. The remaining black marks under the arches show the high-water mark.

At the far end of the Augustus Bridge, you can see the golden equestrian statue, a symbol of Dresden. It's Augustus the Strong, nicknamed the Golden Rider (Goldene Reiter). Beyond that is the spire of the Three Kings Church.

• *We're back near where we started out, which makes this a good stopping point if you want to end this walk here. But for a balanced Dresden visit, you need to cross the river. Don't worry about having to walk all the way back; this walk wraps up at a tram stop from where you can effortlessly whisk back to the Old Town or the main train station.*

To continue, walk across the bridge (on its right side), enjoying the Elbe scene. Before leaving the bridge, stop at the last pedestrian turnout.

Enjoy the **grand city view** from the bridge: the glass "lemon juicer" dome of the Academy of Fine Arts, capped by a trumpeting gold angel, and the other venerable facades, domes, and spires of regal Dresden. This is known as the "Canaletto view" for the Italian painter (Bernardo Bellotto, nephew of the Venetian master) who spent 12 years here immortalizing city vistas while on the Wettin payroll as a court painter; you'll see his canvases when you visit the Old Masters Gallery (described later). Note also the historic paddleboats and how the "Balcony of Europe" is actually a rampart. The broad riverbank, called the Elbe Meadow, provides flood protection.

Downstream (far right), the interesting mosque-shaped building in the distance, originally a tobacco factory designed to advertise Turkish cigarettes, is now an office building with restaurants.

• *At the end of the bridge, cross the street toward the stone building with five arched windows, then cross Grosse Meissner Strasse and head toward the golden statue.*

⓰ The Golden Rider and Hauptstrasse

Since its construction in 1736, the gleaming statue of Augustus the Strong—the Golden Rider—has faced east, toward Augustus' kingdom of Poland and trade routes to Warsaw and Kiev.

The broad, inviting, and tree-lined Hauptstrasse stretches from here into the New Town (Neustadt). On the left is Watzke, a popular (and recommended) peoples' brewery/restaurant. On the right is Eiscafé Venezia, an ice-cream parlor since 1979 and a reminder of the communist heritage here. A monument in the wall (just past the ice-cream palace) marks the 30th anniversary of the creation of the communist "German Democratic Republic" (or DDR) in 1949. With that important anniversary, in 1979, Hauptstrasse was opened as a showpiece of DDR urban design—a landscaped utopian workers' district with the best shops, affordable apartments, and delicious ice cream—everything a communist worker could aspire to.

Stroll down Hauptstrasse a few blocks (past two more recommended restaurants) until you reach the towering Three Kings Church (Dreikönigskirche) on the left. Immediately across Hauptstrasse from the church stands the Neustädter Markthalle. This neighborhood market hall, a 19th-century iron and steel structure, is busy with fun shops selling local handicrafts and hosting fun eateries (Mon-Sat 8:00-20:00, closed Sun).

While three-quarters of Dresden's Old Town was decimated by Allied firebombs, much of the New Town survived. Some of Dresden's 18th-century apartment buildings still stand, such as those facing the charming square that lies under the church's tower, a few steps down An der Dreikönigskirche from where you're standing (note that several recommended restaurants face this square—see "Eating in Dresden," later).

Hauptstrasse ends where this walk ends: at the grand Albertplatz (flanked by twin Art Nouveau fountains).

• *From here you can stop for a meal, or hop on a handy tram (for a quick return to the Frauenkirche or main train station, take tram #3 or #7; tram #8 goes to the Zwinger and Royal Palace before also heading to the station). Just beyond Albertplatz lies the Outer New Town, a bohemian district of swap shops, pubs, cafés, and galleries (described on page 707).*

Sights in Dresden

MUSEUMS IN THE OLD TOWN

Dresden's three most established museums are in the center of the Old Town: the Zwinger, the Royal Palace, and the Albertinum. Each has some sort of combo-ticket that covers its different collections. For each museum, tickets are valid all day, so you can come and go as you please. (Different ticketing conditions apply at the Historic Green Vault, however; see listing below.) The Dresden Card includes admission or discounts to all three museums, and use of public transport as well (see page 673).

The Zwinger Museums

Three museums are located off the Zwinger courtyard: the Old Masters Gallery (with the stern facade), Mathematics-Physics Salon (under Hercules holding the earth), and Porcelain Collection (under the clock). All exhibits are well-described in English, but their audioguides will enrich your visit much more.

Cost and Hours: €6 for each museum; €10 combo-ticket covers all three; museums share the same hours: Tue-Sun 10:00-18:00, closed Mon; tel. 0351/4914-2000, www.skd.museum. At each museum you'll need to show your ticket and check your bag; photographs are *verboten* anywhere inside.

▲▲Old Masters Gallery (Gemäldegalerie Alte Meister)

Dresden's best collection of paintings, housed in the Zwinger's Semper Gallery, features works by Raphael, Titian, Rembrandt, Rubens, Vermeer, and more. It feels particularly enjoyable for its "quality, not quantity" approach to showing off great art. Old-timers remember the Old Masters Gallery as the first big public building reopened after the war, in 1956. While the building is undergoing a years-long renovation project, the major works are always on display.

Visiting the Museum: As you enter, pick up a map from the ticket desk (in the basement) to help you navigate. I've listed some of the highlights of the collection here, but to give meaning and context to the paintings, use the excellent €3 audioguide (free headsets for easier listening by request).

Bernardo Bellotto's paintings of mid-18th-century Dresden offer a great study of the city, showing the Hofkirche (still under construction) and the newly completed Frauenkirche. It's fun to compare them with how the city looks today. Bellotto's uncle and teacher was Antonio Canal (a.k.a. Canaletto), famous for his paintings of Venice (a few of which are also on display).

Look for the work of another Venetian master, **Giorgione,** who died in 1510 while in the middle of painting his sumptuous *Sleeping Venus* (Titian stepped in to finish it). Giorgione's idealized Venus sleeps soundly, at peace with plush nature.

You'll know when you've entered the Baroque world of **Peter Paul Rubens**—everything is richly textured, vividly colored, and lushly emotional. Belgian Baroque works are also on display.

The mood shifts with the humbler, quieter art of the Dutch Masters, including **Rembrandt**. Included in the fine collection of his works is a jaunty self-portrait—with wife Saskia on his lap and a glass of ale held aloft. Another Northern master, **Vermeer,** is represented by his pristine and rare *Girl Reading a Letter at an Open Window*.

August the Strong and his son, August III, supported much of the purchasing of art for this collection. Their agents traveled across Europe to add to their holdings, but they also systematically included German works of the **late-Gothic** and **early-Renaissance** periods. You'll see exquisite canvases by Hans Holbein the Younger, Lucas Cranach, and minor works by Albrecht Dürer.

August charged his agents with finding him a good painting by the Renaissance genius **Raphael,** and they succeeded. The masterful *Sistine Madonna* features the Madonna and Child, two early Christian martyrs (Saints Sixtus and Barbara), and wispy angel faces in the clouds. Mary is in motion, offering the Savior to a needy world. Note Mary's pensive gaze—this Madonna was originally part of a larger altarpiece, and her eyes were once directed at a painting of the Crucifixion. These days, the gaze of most visitors is directed at the pair of whimsical angels in the foreground—which Raphael added after the painting was completed, just to fill the empty space. These lovable tykes—of T-shirt and poster fame—

are bored...just hanging out, oblivious to the exciting arrival of the Messiah just behind them. They connect the heavenly world of the painting with you and me.

Mathematics-Physics Salon
(Mathematisch-Physikalischer Salon)

This fun collection (at the end of the courtyard with the Hercules-topped pavilion; enter through left corner) features scientific gadgets from the 16th to 19th century, including measuring, timekeeping, and surveying instruments, as well as globes and telescopes—all displayed like dazzling works of art. Anyone with a modest scientific bent will find something of interest; be sure to pick up the included audioguide.

Visiting the Museum: As you enter, most of the exhibits are in long halls to the left and right. Near the far end of the right hall, look for the mechanical adding machine devised by French mathematician Blaise Pascal, which could do sums like a modern calculator. A clever touch-screen replica lets you try it out and shows how the machine "carried the tens." In the left hall, beware the mechanical bear who plays the drums—pretty exciting stuff in 1625 (a video shows the wind-up "action").

The back room *(Neuer Saal)* has a large collection of old globes. The upper floor, reached only by elevator, displays "Instruments of the Enlightenment": telescopes (the salon was originally part of the Saxon state observatory); an early 18th-century vacuum pump; and "burning mirrors" that were valued for their ability to focus the sun's rays and, like a magnifying glass, create high-temperature light beams for use in scientific experiments. (I imagine a few 18th-century bugs were burnt along the way.)

▲Porcelain Collection (Porzellansammlung)

Every self-respecting European king had a porcelain works, and the Wettins had the most famous one, at Meissen (a charming town 10 miles north of here on the Elbe River). They inspired other royal courts to get into the art form. They also collected porcelain from around the world—from France to Japan and China.

Augustus the Strong was obsessed with the stuff...he liked to say he had "porcelain sickness" (for more on his porcelain fixation, see "Saxony's White Gold" sidebar). Here you can enjoy some of his symptoms, under chandeliers in elegant galleries flooded with natural light from the huge windows over the Zwinger courtyard. Today it's the largest specialist ceramics collection in the world.

Visiting the Museum: The royal porcelain collection fills the end of the Zwinger marked by the clock tower. Before entering, look closely at the clock with 40 white porcelain bells. The two crossed swords in the center, Augustus' coat of arms, eventually became the famous trademark (one of the world's oldest) of the royal

Saxony's White Gold

In the early 18th century, porcelain was considered "white gold"—an incredibly valuable and difficult-to-produce material. Only the Chinese had perfected the secret of its manufacture—which they jealously guarded. To acquire his initial collection, Augustus the Strong famously traded 600 soldiers (and their horses) for 150 Chinese vases belonging to Friedrich Wilhelm I of Prussia. Hungry for more, Augustus commissioned an alchemist named Johann Friedrich Böttger to solve the mystery of making the finicky stuff. Böttger was reluctant—he'd already failed at creating actual gold—but Augustus persuaded him by locking him up until he complied. Eventually Böttger came up with a recipe for "true" porcelain, and the Saxon prince electors became pioneers in European porcelain production.

Meissen porcelain factory. The collection is in two wings (some to the left, but with the lion's share to the right). Upstairs, behind the clock, is a café with fine courtyard view tables.

Peruse the long halls of vases, the choice collection of Asian porcelain, and the outstanding collection of locally produced Meissen wares. A special attraction is the hall of white Meissen porcelain animals—peacocks, eagles, lions, monkeys, and lapdogs.

Royal Palace (Residenzschloss)

This palace, the residence of the Saxon prince electors and kings, was one of the finest Renaissance buildings in Germany before its

destruction in World War II. It's currently being rebuilt in a years-long project, with galleries opening to the public as they are completed. For now, the big draw here is the Saxon treasuries: the Historic Green Vault (Augustus' goodies displayed in reconstructed Baroque halls) and the New Green Vault (more royal treasures in contemporary display cases). Other attractions include the Royal Armory, displaying sumptuous armor for horse and rider; the Turkish Chamber, one of the oldest collections of Ottoman art outside Turkey;

and the Watchman's Tower, the reconstructed main tower of the palace complex.

Cost and Hours: €12 covers the palace complex, special exhibitions, and audioguide—but not the Historic Green Vault. The Historic Green Vault requires a separate, timed-entry ticket (€12 same-day, includes audioguide, €2 surcharge to book in advance—

see "Reservations," later). A €23 combo-ticket covers everything, including the Historic Green Vault. Hours for the entire complex: Wed-Mon 10:00-18:00, closed Tue.

Orientation: The palace complex has three entrances, each leading to a glass-domed inner courtyard, where you'll find the ticket windows and restrooms. Inside, the ground floor is home to the Baroque halls of the Historic Green Vault; the first floor up has the New Green Vault, and the top floor houses the Giant's Hall, with the bulk of the Royal Armory, and the Turkish Chamber.

Information: Tel. 0351/4914-2000, www.skd.museum.

▲▲▲Historic Green Vault (Historisches Grünes Gewölbe)

This famed, glittering Baroque treasury collection was begun by Augustus the Strong in the early 1700s. Over the years it evolved into the royal family's extravagant trove of ivory, silver, and gold knickknacks, displayed in rooms as opulent as the collection itself.

Reservations: To protect these priceless items, the number of visitors each day is carefully controlled. If you must get in at a certain time, or if you'll be here at a busy time (weekend, holiday, or any time in December), book your entry time well in advance. You'll be given a 15-minute entry window (strictly enforced; once inside, you can stay as long as you like). You can book online and print your own ticket (www.skd.museum), or reserve by email (besucherservice@skd.museum) and either pick up your ticket on site or receive it via email.

If you haven't booked ahead, your chances of getting a same-day slot are usually pretty good, especially if you show up in the morning (90 tickets are available every half-hour). The number of spots still available *(Karten)* and for what entry time *(Einlasszeit)* are indicated on screens over each ticket desk.

Visiting the Historic Green Vault: Your visit is designed to wow you in typically Baroque style—starting easy and crescendo-ing to a climax, taking a quick break, and finishing again with a second climax. Following the included audioguide, you'll spend about an hour progressing through nine rooms. The treasures are not behind glass. Inside, you feel it's an almost sacred space—no guiding, no photos, and people speaking in no more than whispers.

The **Amber Cabinet** serves as a reminder of just how many different things you can do with fossilized tree sap (in a surprising range of colors), and the **Ivory Room** does the same for elephant tusks, with some strikingly delicate hand-carved sculptures. The **White Silver Room,** painted its original vermillion color, holds a chalice carved from a rhino horn, and the **Silver-Gilt Room** displays tableware and gold-ruby glass.

The wide variety of items in the largest room—the aptly named **Hall of Precious Objects**—includes mother-of-pearl sculptures, ostrich-egg and snail-shell goblets, and a model of the Hill of Calvary atop a pile of pearls and polished seashells.

The oak cupboards that line the **Coats of Arms Room** are emblazoned with copper-and-gold heraldry boasting of the various territories in Augustus the Strong's domain.

The vault's highlight is the grandly decorated **Jewel Room**— essentially, Saxony's crown jewels. The incredible pieces in here are fine examples of the concept of *Gesamtkunstwerk*—an artwork whose perfection comes from the sum of its parts. The *Moor with Emerald Tier*—a "Moor" clad in jewels and gold (and a Native American headdress)—was designed to carry a chunk of rock embedded with large gems. Nearby, an ornately decorated obelisk trumpets the greatness of Augustus the Strong.

The exhibit concludes in the relatively subdued **Bronze Room,** with its eight-foot-tall equestrian statue of Augustus the Strong (designed to compete with similar depictions of his rival, the French Sun King Louis XIV), as well as a statue of Apollo surrounded by six women. The last room is filled with Renaissance bronze statues, including Giambologna's *Mercury*.

Your audioguide also describes treasures in the "pre-vault" (where you pick up and drop off the audioguide). Don't miss the photos of the vault before the war and the small room in the corner with Reformation treasures, including Martin Luther's signet ring.

▲▲New Green Vault (Neues Grünes Gewölbe)

This collection shows off more Saxon treasure, but in a modern setting. Pick up the essential and included audioguide before climbing the steps. The collection is arranged chronologically from the Renaissance to the 19th century in nine rooms with the same floor plan as the Historic Green Vault one floor below. The focus here isn't the rooms themselves, but the treasures in glass cases.

Visiting the New Green Vault: In the **Hall of Works of Art** (the first room you enter), a twisted **ivory column** from 1589 is actually a very elaborate clock (the golden Cupid on top points to the hour with a wand), and includes a music box featuring a dining scene carved inside an ivory sphere, ship-in-a-bottle-style.

In the **Micro-Cabinet,** a magnifying glass helps you marvel at an earring from 1589 featuring a cherry pit carved with 113 minute faces.

The precious centerpiece of the **Crystal Cabinet** is a serving bowl in the shape of a galley ship, with intricate scenes carved on the side—it's hard to imagine anyone filling it with gravy (and they probably never did; items like this were made just for showing off).

The **First Elector's Room** features Renaissance treasures, such as an ivory frigate with delicately carved, nearly transparent sails and golden rigging, all of it supported by a heroic Neptune, riding his sea horses.

The **Room of Royal Precious Objects** holds a collection of irregular pearls carved into amusing figures, such as a fat fiddler and an ice skater. The nobles of this era were fascinated with gems and precious stones, which they prized much more than the craftsmanship exhibited in the Renaissance items we saw earlier.

The **Dinglinger Hall** features the masterpieces of court jeweler, Johann Melchior Dinglinger. His golden coffee service is pure gold (circa 1700), iced with enamel to imitate porcelain and crusted with thousands of precious stones. At the other end of the room is his ornate, captivating ensemble from 1708 depicting the Grand Mogul Aurengzeb, who sits enthroned on his birthday awaiting his presents (including a white elephant). Like royal Legos, the 132 figurines and 32 gift items, all of pure gold glazed with enamel, are movable for the king's pleasure.

The **Traveling Treasures Room** contains the leather cases the king used to pack his favorite playthings to Poland, and in the **Neuber Room,** the Dresden Green diamond sparkles all on its own—one huge green stone decorated with more than 400 twinkling white diamonds.

▲▲ Royal Armory in the Giant's Hall (Rüstkammer im Riesensaal)

Dazzling, original, centuries-old armor fills one long room called the Giant's Hall. The biggest space in the palace, it was the scene of medieval war games. Today, its exhibits recall those breathtaking pageants of the 16th century with jousting models (something rich boys did when there was no war to fight). This is the largest collection of 16th-century Europe's leading armor designer, Anton Peffenhauser, and it's an unusual chance to see armor displayed in dynamic fighting stances (instead of stiffly standing). The parade armor of King Erick XIV of Sweden—slathered in Herculean symbolism from 1565—is considered the "Sistine Madonna" of the collection. Stand before it and imagine this coming at you. The black, no-nonsense, Darth Vader suits at the end of the hall were actually used in the Thirty Years' War (around 1620). Near the back of the room, check out the wee training suits of armor for little electoral princes.

▲Turkish Chamber (Türkisches Cammer)

From the 16th through 19th century, Western European elites were crazy about all things Turkish, and Augustus the Strong was no exception. Augustus collected Ottoman art with a passion, even dressing up as a sultan in his own court. This fascinating collection of Ottoman art started as war booty from the Habsburgs (given as thanks for Saxon support in holding off invasions), and then

DRESDEN

grew over several centuries through diplomatic gifts, trades, and shopping trips to Constantinople. A highlight is the 20-yard-long, three-poled ornamented silk tent from the 17th century—the most complete three-masted Ottoman tent on display in Europe. Don't miss the "Relief of Vienna 1683" painting, showing the epic battle when, for the first time, Ottoman forces were turned back—with the help of the Saxons—from Christian lands.

Watchman's Tower (Hausmannsturm)

This palace tower is completely rebuilt (and feels entirely modern). You can climb past an underwhelming coin collection, see the re-built medieval clock mechanism from behind, peruse an extensive series of dome-damage photos, and earn a good city view after a long climb. In bad weather, the view terrace is closed, and you'll peer through small windows—a big disappointment. If you've climbed the Frauenkirche dome (which affords the best view in town—for a fee), or are planning to, skip this.

▲▲Albertinum

This museum's excellent collections feature artwork from the Romantic period (late 18th and early 19th centuries) to the present.

The included audioguide does a beautiful job of explaining the artwork. The museum's ticket desk is in the building's old courtyard, which has been roofed over into a cavernous, minimalist, white atrium.

Cost and Hours: €10, Tue-Sun 10:00-18:00, closed Mon, entrances on the Brühlsche Terrasse and on Georg-Treu-Platz, tel. 0351/4914-2000, www.skd. museum.

Visiting the Museum: Most visitors come to see the New Masters Gallery on the museum's top floor. Moving down from there, contemporary and turn-of-the-20th-century art is on the first floor, and sculpture on the ground floor, opposite the ticket desk.

New Masters Gallery (Galerie Neue Meister): On the top floor, take a counterclockwise walk around this chronologically organized collection, showcasing mostly German (and some French) paintings from the Romantic era, 20th-century Modernism, and contemporary art.

In Caspar David Friedrich's 19th-century landscapes, notice that people are small and blend into the background, reminding us that German Romanticism is all about the exploration of man's place as a part of nature—not as its dominating force. Friedrich's Norwegian counterpart and friend, Johan Christian Dahl—who moved to Dresden later in life—captures his adopted hometown in his lovely *View of Dresden at Full Moon*, which seems not so different from today's reconstructed city. (The buildings across the river aren't on fire; the glow is from the hearths inside these rooms.)

Take a breather with Ludwig Richter's bucolic scenes of the Italian countryside, then move into the top-notch Modernist wing, with works by Paul Gauguin (Polynesian women), Vincent van Gogh *(Still Life with Quinces)*, Max Liebermann (insightful portraits), Oskar Kokoschka (vibrantly colored, almost garish portraits), Claude Monet, Edouard Manet, and more. Some of the lesser-known works are also worth a good look, such as Max Slevogt's evocative paintings of North Africa.

Give yourself a moment to really take in Otto Dix's haunting, frank images—particularly his stirring triptych *War*, rooted in his firsthand experience fighting in the trenches of France and Flanders during World War I. This vision, modeled after a medieval altarpiece, has a circular composition that's kept moving by the grotesque pointing skeleton. In this fetid wasteland, corpses are decomposing, and helmets and gas masks make even the intact bodies seem inhuman. Dix painted this in the 1930s, when Adolf Hitler was building a case for war (ostensibly to reclaim territory Germany lost after World War I). The Führer didn't care for Dix's pacifist message, dismissing the artist from his teaching job at Dresden's art academy and adding Dix's works to his collection of "degenerate art."

The collection wraps up with works by Paul Klee, Pablo Picasso, some harrowing Expressionistic works, and Gerhard Richter's recent acrylics under glass. New media (sound and video) are also represented.

Mosaiksaal, Klingersaal, and Contemporary Art: On the first floor up, the Mosaiksaal features sculpture from the Classicist era on up to Ernst Rietschel's mid-19th-century depictions of historically important Germans.

The Klingersaal shows slinky fin-de-siècle paintings and sculptures. Look for Gustav Klimt's atmospheric *Buchenwald*, a tranquil beech forest that shimmers with color, achieving startling depth. In Ferdinand Hodler's portrait of *Madame de R.*, the subject regards us with a steely gaze; Oskar Zwintscher's *Lady with Cigarette* is equally unfazed by our presence.

Running along the other side of this floor is a hall of contemporary, mostly 20th-century German art. Along the short sides of the building, connecting the Klingersaal and Mosaiksaal to the contemporary exhibits, are *Schaudepots*—viewable display storerooms jammed full of sculptures that didn't find a permanent home in the public exhibits. These give a glimpse into the vastness of the Albertinum's collection. (There are two more *Schaudepots* on the ground floor, one in the kids' activity room.)

Sculpture Collection (Skulpturensammlung): Gathered in one huge *Skulpturhalle* on the ground floor, this easy-on-the-eyes collection covers 5,000 years of Western sculpture, with a special focus on the last 200 years. There are several plaster casts by Auguste Rodin, including a *Thinker*. Look also for Edgar Degas' *Little Dancer Aged Fourteen* (one of 29 bronzes cast from the wax original). At the contemporary end of the spectrum is Tony Cragg's *Ever After* (2010), a 10-foot-tall wooden sculpture that appears to be melting; look closely to see profiles of human faces emerge on the left side.

CHURCHES IN THE OLD TOWN
▲▲Frauenkirche (Church of Our Lady)

When this landmark Lutheran church was first built in the 18th century, it was financed largely by local donations—Protestant

pride. Destroyed by Allied firebombing in World War II, it sat in ruins for decades. Rebuilding of the church finally began in 1992, following carefully considered guidelines: Stay true to the original design; use as much original material as possible; avoid using any concrete or rebar; maximize modern technology; and make it a lively venue for 21st-century-style worship. The remnants of the destroyed church were fitted together like a giant jigsaw puzzle, with about a third made of the darker original stones—all placed lovingly in their original spots. The reconstruction cost more than €100 million, 90 percent of which came from donors around the world.

Cost and Hours: Free but donation requested, 45-minute audioguide-€2.50 (available inside and to the left), Mon-Fri 10:00-12:00 & 13:00-18:00, open between services and concerts on Sat-Sun; worship services with organ music Mon-Fri at 12:00 and 18:00, check at church for Sat-Sun schedule, enter through door D, www.frauenkirche-dresden.de.

Climbing the Dome: Get a great view over the city by hiking to the top of the dome. After an elevator takes you half of the way, you still have a long ramp to climb (€8—consider it a donation to the church, March-Oct Mon-Sat 10:00-18:00, Sun 12:30-18:00; Nov-Feb until 16:00 daily, enter through door G, follow signs to *Kuppelaufstieg*).

Visiting the Church: The Frauenkirche is as worthwhile for its glorious **interior** as for its tragic, then uplifting, recent history. Stepping inside, you're struck by the shape—not so wide (150 feet) but very tall (inner dome 120 feet, under a 225-foot main dome). The color scheme is pastel, in an effort to underline the joy of faith and enhance the festive ambience of the services and ceremonies held here. The curves help create a feeling of community. The seven entrances are perfectly equal (as people are, in the eyes of God). When the congregation exits, the seven exits point to all quarters—a reminder to "go ye," the Great Commission to spread the Word everywhere. The glassed-in "box seats" are just that. Like the rich get their own sections in a stadium, generous patrons of the church got their own VIP worship areas.

The Baroque sandstone **altar** shows Jesus praying in the Gar-den of Gethsemane the night before his Crucifixion. Soldiers, led

by Judas, are on their way, but Christ is firmly in the pres-ence of God and his angels. Eighty percent of today's altar is from original materi-al—in the form of 2,000 in-dividual fragments that were salvaged and pieced back together by restorers. If this feels more ornate than your typical Lutheran church, it's because of the taste of the king—who had to be Catholic to rule Poland.

The **Cross of Nails** at the high altar is from Coventry, Eng-land—Dresden's sister city. Two fire-blackened nails found in the smoldering rubble of Coventry's bombed church are used as a symbol of peace and reconciliation. Coventry was bombed as

thoroughly as Dresden (so thoroughly, it gave the giddy Luftwaffe a new word for "bomb to smithereens"—to "coventrate"). From the de-stroyed town of Coventry was born the Com-munity of the Cross of Nails, a worldwide network promoting peace and reconciliation through international understanding.

Near the exit stands the church's **twisted old cross,** which fell 300 feet and burned in the rubble. Lost until restorers uncovered it from the pile of stones in 1993, it stands exactly on the place it was found, still relatively intact. A copy—a gift from the British people in 2000 on the 55th anniversary of the bombing—crowns the new church. It was crafted by an English coppersmith whose father had dropped bombs on the church on that fateful night. Visitors are invited to light a candle before this cross and enter a wish for peace in the guest book.

Before you leave the church, go downstairs to the **cellar,** which is a maze of rooms and exhibits. In a separate room (on the left as you climb into the crypt) is a modest exhibit about the history of the building. There is a modern-feeling, very stark chapel under vaulted ceilings in the center. A side room has old grave markers, from prewar times when the crypt was here. In each stairwell, plaques list the names of donors who helped resurrect this church from the rubble.

▲Katholiche Hofkirche (Catholic Church of the Royal Court)

Why does Dresden, a stronghold of local boy Martin Luther's Protestant Reformation, boast such a beautiful Catholic cathedral? When Augustus the Strong died, his son wanted to continue as king of Poland, like his father. The pope would allow it only if Augustus Junior built a Catholic church in Dresden. Now, thanks to Junior's historical kissing-up, the mere 5 percent of locals who are Catholic get to enjoy this fine church. The elevated passageway connecting the church with the palace allowed the royal family to avoid walking in the street with commoners.

Cost and Hours: Free, Mon-Tue 9:00-18:00, Wed-Thu 9:00-17:00, Fri 13:00-17:00, Sat 10:00-17:00, Sun 12:00-16:00, Mass daily at 18:00—check at church for complete schedule and for pipe organ concert times (usually Wed and Sat), enter through side door facing palace, tel. 0351/484-4712, www.kathedrale-dresden.de.

Visiting the Church: Inside the cathedral, on the right side of the main nave, is the fine Baroque **pulpit,** carved from linden wood and hidden in the countryside during World War II. The church was designed with a grand ambulatory that kept ritual Roman Catholic processions within the church, to avoid provoking the Lutheran populace.

The glorious 3,000-pipe **organ** filling the back of the nave is played for the public for free on Wednesdays and Saturdays at 11:30 (and occasionally at other times as well, posted at door).

The **Memorial Chapel** (on the left as you face the rear) is dedicated to those who died in the WWII firebombing and to all victims of violence. Its evocative, abstract *pietà* altarpiece was constructed in 1976 of white Meissen porcelain. Mary offers the faithful the crown of thorns made from Dresden's rubble, as if to remind us that Jesus—on her lap, head hanging lifeless on the left—died to save humankind. Jesus' open heart shows us his love, offers us atonement for our sins, and proves that reconciliation is more powerful than hatred. The altar (freestanding, in front) shows five flaming heads. It seems to symbolize how Dresdeners suffered...in the presence of their suffering savior. The dates on the high altar (30-1-33 and 13-2-45) mark the dark period between Hitler's rise to power and the night Dresden was destroyed.

The adjacent **Benno Chapel** recalls the only Saxon saint (see his 11th-century bishop's hat on the altar).

The room with the gift shop is the only part of church that still survives of the architect's original vision and the style of the day—helpful in imagining the intended, initial look of the entire place.

The basement houses the **royal crypt,** including the heart of the still-virile Augustus the Strong—which, according to legend, still beats when a pretty woman comes near (crypt open only during one 45-minute German tour of the church each day, usually Mon-Thu at 14:00 and Fri-Sun at 13:00, confirm times at 0351/484-4712).

MORE SIGHTS IN DRESDEN
Semperoper
This elegant opera house watches over Theaterplatz in the heart of town.

Tours: The opulent interior can only be visited with a tour.

German-language tours (with an English handout) go regularly throughout the day, with one English tour generally daily at 14:00 or 15:00, sometimes at 10:45. It's wise to reserve in advance by phone, email, or online (€10, €3 extra to take photos, 1 hour, tour schedule depends on rehearsal schedule, tel. 0351/320-7360, www.semperoper-erleben.de).

Performances: Tickets, which go on sale a year in advance, are hard to come by. You can book in advance online or by phone (tel. 0351/491-1705, www.semperoper.de). If you're here in winter, enjoy the opera's heating system, beloved by locals (before its rebuilding, the opera was warmed by filling it with hundreds of soldiers, who'd be sent out just before the audience was admitted).

Box Office: You can reserve space on a tour or buy performance tickets from a real person at the box office in the Schinkelwache, the small building across the square (Mon-Fri 10:00-18:00, Sat-Sun 10:00-13:00).

Prager Strasse

This street, connecting the Hauptbahnhof train station and the historic center, was in ruins until the 1960s, when communist

planners redeveloped it as a pedestrian mall. The design is typical of Soviet-bloc architecture—there are similar streets in Moscow—and it reflects communist ideals: buildings are big, blocky, and functional, without extraneous ornamentation. As you stroll down Prager Strasse, imagine these buildings without much color or advertising (which were unnecessary back in the no-choices days of communism). Today, the street is filled with corporate logos, shoppers with lots of choices, and a fun summertime food circus. The street has developed into exactly what the communists envisioned for it, but never quite achieved: a pedestrian-friendly shopping area, where people can stroll and relax, with residential space above. The huge department stores, like the vast Altmarkt-Galerie, charge the German norm, which means things are expensive here, as local workers still earn only about 80 percent of what Germans make farther to the west.

German Hygiene Museum (Deutsches Hygiene-Museum)

This family-oriented museum is devoted to the wonders of the human body (don't take the word "hygiene," its historical title, too

literally). Visitors with strong stomachs get a kick out of this highly interactive museum, but those easily grossed out should stay away—or at least plan meal times accordingly.

Cost and Hours: €7 includes audioguide, €11 family ticket, 16 and under free, Tue-Sun 10:00-18:00, closed Mon; Lingnerplatz 1, take tram #1, #2, #4, or #12 to the Deutsches Hygiene-Museum stop or tram #10 or #13 to Grosser Garten, then walk one long block; tel. 0351/484-6400, www.dhmd.de.

Visiting the Museum: The building, which is huge, was completed in 1930 in a severe functional style. (A few years later, it briefly became a center for Nazi eugenics and "racial studies.") The permanent exhibit on the upper floor is divided into six themed sections (Life and Death; Eating and Drinking; Sexuality; Memory, Thinking, and Learning; Movement; and Beauty, Skin, and Hair). A highlight is the "transparent woman" *(Gläserne Frau)*, a life-size plastic model with bones, veins, and interior organs visible. Check out the little wooden anatomical figures with removable parts (complete with strategically placed fig leaves), X-ray machines from the 1930s, and graphic wax models of venereal diseases. The museum offers some English explanations, but most exhibits speak (or shriek) for themselves.

Your ticket also gets you into Dresden's **children's museum,** in the basement, which stays with the general theme by focusing on the five senses.

Volkswagen's Transparent Factory (Gläserne Manufaktur)

You don't need to be automotively inclined to enjoy a pilgrimage to the recently built VW assembly plant on the southeastern edge of town. Two floors of this fas-
cinating, transparent building are open to visitors interested in the assembly of the high-end VW Phaeton sedan, one of the carmaker's *luxus-schlitten* (luxury sleds). If you buy a Phaeton here, you can set yourself on the platform (BYO folding chair) and follow it through

every moment of the 36-hour "birth" process.

Visitors have two options: Just gaze at the slowly moving assembly line from the building's atrium for free, or pay to take a 75-minute tour, which lets you see the process at close range. (Tours are limited to 15 participants and can fill up, so you're encouraged to call ahead and book a spot.) Informative touch-screen terminals in the atrium describe the plant's operations in English, and a mini-movie theater shows classic old VW commercials.

Cost and Hours: Atrium—free, Mon–Fri 8:30–19:00, Sat–Sun 9:00–18:00. Guided tour—€7; English tours generally Mon-Fri at 12:00, 15:00, and 17:00 except no 17:00 tour Jan-March, Sat at 12:00 and 15:00, Sun at 15:00; German tours at least hourly. Open hours and tour times can vary due to special events; check the website or call ahead to confirm. An expensive café is on site (tel. 0351/420-4411, www.glaesernemanufaktur.de).

Getting There: Take tram #1, #2, or #4 (from the Old Town) or tram #10 (from the Hauptbahnhof) to the Strassburger Platz stop. You'll see the plant on one corner of the intersection; enter off Lennestrasse.

▲New Town (Neustadt) and Outer New Town (Äussere Neustadt)

A big sign across the river from the old center declares, "Dresden continues here"—directed at tourists who visit the city without ever crossing the river into the New Town and Outer New Town. Don't be one of them: While there are no famous sights here, it's the only part of Dresden that looks as it did before World War II. Today, it's thriving with cafés, shops, clubs, and—most important—actual Dresdeners. On a warm summer evening, experiencing the vibe here is a must. A fine destination is the Kunsthofpassage, a lovely, fun, inviting series of courtyards with shops and eateries. For more on this neighborhood, see "Nightlife in Dresden," later.

Military History Museum (Militärhistorisches Museum der Bundeswehr)

This huge museum covers more than 800 years of German military history and focuses on the causes and consequences of war and violence. At over 180,000 square feet, it's the largest museum in Germany. The museum is housed in Dresden's Neoclassical former arsenal building, forcefully severed by a Daniel Libeskind-designed wedge of glass and steel (signaling the break from Germany's militaristic past and its hope for a transparent government and peaceful future).

Cost and Hours: €5, includes audioguide; Mon 10:00-21:00, Tue and Thu-Sun 10:00-18:00, closed Wed; onsite café; take tram #7 or #8 to Stauffenbergallee stop (beyond the New Town), then follow the diagonal, tree-lined path through the park to Olbrichtplatz 2; tel. 0351/823-2803, www.mhmbundeswehr.de.

Visiting the Museum: The museum is long on design, and uses creative arrangements and juxtapositions to get visitors thinking in unconventional and critical ways about war and the military. Rather than glorifying soldiers and their bravery, the museum dissects our ideas about war, asks where those ideas come from, encourages us to question them, and ultimately sends a pacifist message.

The exhibits, which are fully labeled in English, are too vast to see in a single visit. Start by taking the elevator to the fourth floor, which has a view of Dresden's Old Town and two visually arresting pieces designed to start you thinking about the subject of war. Next, head down to the third floor to consider the question of how people remember war—and whether they glorify the memory or push it into the background—in an exhibit organized like a set of library stacks.

The bulk of the museum's exhibits are on the lower three floors. Three comprehensive, chronological exhibits tell the story of German military activity from 1300 to 1914 (ground floor), from

1914 to 1945 (first floor up), and after 1945 (including the founding of the Bundeswehr, also on the first floor). Sprinkled among the ground, first, and second floors are thematic exhibits showing how topics such as toys, music, language, fashion, and animals intersect with the military world.

NEAR DRESDEN

Dresden is the starting point for two pleasant excursions—a peaceful half-day's walk or bike ride up the Elbe River, and a day of hiking in dramatic "Saxon Switzerland."

Along the Elbe River to the Blue Wonder Bridge

This quick excursion is a fine way to get out of the city—even if it only takes you as far as its suburbs. Your goal is the Blue Wonder bridge, which, though handsome and famous, is less a destination than a convenient place to stop, have something to eat or drink in the nearby beer garden, and head back the other way.

The **Blue Wonder** (a.k.a. Loschwitz Bridge) is a cantilever truss bridge that connects the Dresden suburbs of Loschwitz and Blasewitz. When the bridge was completed in 1893, these were among the most expensive pieces of real estate in Europe—note the ultra-posh villas near the bridge. The bridge is indeed a wonder

in that it survived World War II completely untouched, and it is, in fact, blue (well, more gray really). Its name is actually a pun on the German expression, "to witness a blue wonder" *(ein Blaues Wunder erleben)*—to experience a nasty surprise.

Underneath the bridge, a delightful beer garden awaits: **Schiller Garten,** a vast, 300-year-old complex of gastronomic delights and cold suds that pours an unfiltered *Zwickel* beer brewed specially for this garden by Feldschlösschen (Dresden's best brewery). The garden has a self-service buffet (in the building marked *Lichtspiel*) serving good grilled food, and also hosts a rudimentary playground and a digital departure board for the nearby Schillerplatz tram stop (€3-6 dishes and snacks, daily 11:00-24:00, weather dependent). If you're looking for something fancier, try the sit-down restaurant in the half-timbered house (€7-10 wurst plates, €10-18 main dishes, daily 11:00-24:00). Both the garden and restaurant have been supplied by their own butcher and pastry kitchen since 1764 (tel. 0351/811-990, www.schillergarten.de).

Getting to the Blue Wonder: If you have enough time and nice weather, you could slow down and do this outing on **foot** (about one hour each way) or by **bike** (about 30 minutes each way;

for bike rental, see "Helpful Hints," earlier). The 3.5-mile path gives you a great slice-of-life glimpse of Germans at play as you hug the riverbank—past several tempting beer gardens—all the way from central Dresden to the bridge. If the weather's warm, pack a swimsuit. The closer you get to the bridge the more opportunities you'll find for swimming and boating (several places rent kayaks, Jet Skis, and so on).

You can also make the trip by **boat**: The Saxon Steamboat Company (Sächsische Dampfschiffahrt) runs steam-powered paddle boats along the Elbe (about 6/day May-Oct, 3-4/day mid-April and Oct-Nov, no boats Nov-mid-April; from Dresden to Blasewitz: €7, 40 minutes, board at Brühlsche Terrasse; from Blasewitz to Dresden: €6, 30 minutes, board by Schiller Garten; round-trip-€11; check schedule in advance—low water levels on the Elbe can limit traffic, tel. 0351/866-090, www.saechsische-dampfschiffahrt.de).

Finally, **trams** #6 (from the New Town) and #4 (from the Old Town) take you to Schillerplatz, about 50 yards from the Blue Wonder, in about 30 minutes. The tram ride is interesting, as it travels a path through communist prefabricated housing and strip-mall urban sprawl before taking you through an enviable collection of villas and large 19th-century homes. On tram #6, keep your eyes peeled at the Trinitatis Platz stop for a beautiful bombed church, which sits amid a sea of dreary prefab architecture. You can take your bike on the tram for €3 (choose the *Fahrradtageskarte* button for your bike fare).

Saxon Switzerland National Park

Consider a break from big-city sightseeing to spend a half-day taking a *wunderbar* hike through this scenic national park.

Twenty miles southeast of Dresden (an easy 40-minute S-Bahn ride away), the Elbe River cuts a scenic swath through the beech forests and steep cliffs of Saxon Switzerland (Sächsische Schweiz) National Park. You'll share the trails with serious rock climbers and equally serious Saxon grandmothers. Allow five hours (including lunch) to enjoy this day trip.

Getting to the Park: Take S-Bahn line 1 from either the Hauptbahnhof or Neustadt station (direction: Bad Schandau) and get off at the Kurort Rathen stop (1-2/hour, 40 minutes; €5.90 each way, or buy regional day passes, also good for Dresden city transport: €13.50, €18.50/family, €27/group of up to 5 adults). Before leaving the platform at Kurort Rathen, note the return times (on the yellow poster). Then follow the road downhill five minutes through town to the dock, and take the two-minute ferry across the Elbe (€1.50 round-trip, pay on board, runs continuously). When the ferry docks on the far (north) side of the river, turn your back

DRESDEN

on the river and walk 100 yards through town, with the little creek on your right. Turn left after the **Sonniges Eck Restaurant** (tasty lunch option); as you round the corner be sure to look up at the restaurant's green wall for the black sign marking the high-water mark of the June 2013 flood...and another mark way above it marking the height of the 2002 flood. Then walk up the lane—the trail begins with stairs on your left just past Hotel Amselgrundschlösschen (follow *Bastei* signs).

Visiting the Park: A 30-minute walk uphill through the woods leads you to the **Bastei Bridge** and stunning views of gray sandstone sentries rising several hundred feet above forest ridges. Elbe Valley sandstone was used to build Dresden's finest buildings (including the Frauenkirche and Zwinger), as well as Berlin's

famous Brandenburg Gate. The multiple-arch bridge looks straight out of *The Wizard of Oz*—built in 1851 specifically for Romantic Age tourists, and scenic enough to be the subject of the first landscape photos ever taken in Germany. Take the time to explore the short 50-yard spur trails that reward you with classic views down on the Elbe 900 feet below. Watch the slow-motion paddleboat steamers leave V-shaped wakes as they chug upstream toward the Czech Republic, just around the next river bend. If you're not afraid of heights, explore the maze of catwalks through the scant remains of the **Felsenberg Neurathen,** a 13th-century Saxon fort perched precariously on the bald stony spires (€1.50, entrance 50 yards before Bastei Bridge).

Just a five-minute uphill hike beyond the bridge is the **Berg Hotel Panorama Bastei,** with a fine restaurant, a snack bar, and memorable views. The best photo op of the bridge itself is from the spur trail to the right just after you've crossed the bridge. Return to the Elbe ferry down the same trail.

Nightlife in Dresden

OUTER NEW TOWN (ÄUSSERE NEUSTADT)

To really connect with Dresden as it unfolds, you need to go to the Outer New Town. This area was built, with elegant facades, in the 19th century to accommodate workers of the Industrial Age. (That's when this neighborhood became hallowed ground, at least for some: The planet's first milk chocolate was made right here, in 1839.) Despite the devastation wreaked upon the area south of the river, this neighborhood wasn't bombed in World War II— but during communist times it became so dilapidated that officials made plans to just tear it all down. Today locals recall a time when no one ventured out on balconies fearing they'd fall off. A popular slogan for people disillusioned with the DDR was, "We create ruins without any weapons." After the end of the DDR in 1989, the area sprouted the first entrepreneurial cafés and bistros. Now it's a bohemian-chic mix of cheap apartments, galleries, cafés, bars, and swap shops. While gentrification is kicking in, it remains a popular neighborhood for young people and progressive families, reminiscent of Berlin's Prenzlauer Berg in its pre-yuppie days. This is a fun place to eat dinner, then join the action, which picks up after 22:00. Eateries range from the merely creative to the truly unconventional. The clientele is young, hip, pierced, and tattooed. You'll find mini-*Biergartens* (but not your grandfather's oompah bands) and see young adults hanging out on the curb, nursing beer bottles. The neighborhood feels more exuberant than rough.

One of the best ways to experience this scene, and to learn a bit more about the neighborhood's history at the same time, is to take the Nightwalk Dresden (listed under "Tours in Dresden," earlier).

If exploring on your own, rather than seek out particular places in this continuously evolving scene, I'd suggest just getting to the epicenter—at the corner of Görlitzer Strasse and Louisenstrasse—and wandering. From the Old Town, take tram #7 or #8 to Louisenstrasse, or tram #6 or #11 to Bautzner/Rothenburger Strasse. Night trams bring you back to the center even in the wee hours.

Here are a few places and bars worth checking out:

Kunsthofpassage is a series of fanciful, imaginatively decorated courtyards surrounded by boutiques, eateries, a craft-beer pub, and art galleries. On one wall the downspouts have been reworked into a fountain made of musical-instrument shapes. The opposite wall sports large metal shavings. This is a delightful fantasy world, tucked improbably between lively urban streets (just as interesting by day; enter at Görlitzer Strasse 21, 23, or 25, or at Alaunstrasse 70; www.kunsthof-dresden.de).

Katy's Garage really was once a garage ("Katy" wasn't a woman but a Land Rover), and is now a funky *Biergarten* on the corner of Alaunstrasse and Louisenstrasse (open long hours daily).

Kneipe Raskolnikoff, a Russian-flavored place with cosmonaut Yuri Gagarin on its chimney and a stand of bamboo in the back garden, gives off a Moscow-meets-Maui ambience. It's more a pub than a restaurant, with a small menu of Russian specialties and lots of drinks (€7-13 main courses, daily 10:00-24:00, a half-block off Lutherplatz at Böhmische Strasse 34, tel. 0351/804-5706).

Sleeping in Dresden

Hotels in Dresden tend to be large. Characteristic, family-run places are rare. (Many smaller buildings were destroyed during World War II, and communists didn't do "quaint" very well.) The rates listed are for peak season: For hotels, that's May, June, September, and October. Prices soften at midsummer and drop in winter. Peak season for hostels is July and August (especially weekends). Of the listings below, only Hotel Kipping, the Martha Dresden, and the Bayerischer Hof include breakfast in their prices.

IN OR NEAR THE OLD TOWN

$$$ Aparthotels an der Frauenkirche rents 100 units in five beautifully restored houses (many with views) in the heart of the Old Town. Designed for longer stays but also welcoming one- or two-nighters, these modern, comfortable apartments come with kitchens and lots of amenities. Two buildings ("Neumarkt" and "Altes Dresden") overlook the pleasant Neumarkt square in front of the Frauenkirche, another is on the touristy Münzgasse restaurant street, a fourth is on Schössergasse, and the fifth is a bit closer to the Hauptbahnhof on less-interesting Altmarkt square (rates for up to 2 people: studio-€95-155, 2-room apartment-€125-195, 3-room apartment-€135-180, extra person-€30, rates depend on unit size and amenities, cheaper for longer stays and off-season—roughly Nov and Jan-March, breakfast-€13 at nearby café, elevator in all buildings, Wi-Fi, parking at nearby garage-€15-20/day, Münzgasse building has smoking rooms—otherwise non-smoking, reception for Neumarkt and Altmarkt units is in gift shop at Neumarkt 7, reception for Münzgasse apartments is at Münzgasse 10, reception for Schössergasse at Schössergasse 16/Sporergasse 7, for locations see map on page 713, tel. 0351/438-1111, www.aparthotels-frauenkirche.de, info@aparthotels-frauenkirche.de, Drescher family).

$$ Hotel Kipping, with 20 quiet, tidy rooms 100 yards behind the Hauptbahnhof, is professionally run by the friendly and proper Kipping brothers (Rainer and Peter). The original building was one of very few in this area to survive the 1945 firebombing—in fact, people took shelter here during the attack (Sb-€65-105, Db-€80-120; suite: Sb-€85-125, Db-€100-140; includes breakfast, extra bed-€25; higher prices are for weekends, May-June, and Sept-Oct; elevator, Wi-Fi, free parking, air-con in most rooms; exit the station following signs for *Bayerische Strasse* near track 1, it's at Winckelmannstrasse 6, from here trams #3 and #8 whisk you to the Old Town; tel. 0351/478-500, www.hotel-kipping.de, reception@hotel-kipping.de). Their restaurant serves good dinners (closed Sun). For location, see the map on page 674.

DRESDEN

Sleep Code

Abbreviations   (€1 = about $1.40, country code: 49)
S = Single, **D** = Double/Twin, **T** = Triple, **Q** = Quad, **b** = bathroom, **s** = shower only.
Price Rankings
  $$$ Higher Priced—Most rooms €120 or more.
   $$ Moderately Priced—Most rooms between €80-120.
    $ Lower Priced—Most rooms €80 or less.
Unless otherwise noted, credit cards are accepted, English is spoken, breakfast is *not* included, and Wi-Fi is generally free. Prices change; verify current rates online or by email. For the best prices, always book directly with the hotel.

$$ Hotels Bastei, Königstein, and **Lilienstein** are cookie-cutter members of the Ibis chain, goose-stepping single-file up Prager Strasse (listed in order from the station to the center). Each place is practically identical, and all together they have 918 rooms. Nobody will pretend they have charm, but they're a decent value in a convenient location between the Hauptbahnhof and the Old Town (see map on page 674). They're historic, too—a chance to experience communist designers' revolutionary, if warped, vision of urban life (Sb-€59-99, Db-€69-109, extra bed-€25, kids 12 and under free, prices vary with demand—book online for best deal, breakfast-€10, elevator, guest computer, pay Wi-Fi, air-con, bikes-€10/day, public parking-€3.50-€6/day, reservations for all: Tel. 0351/4856-2000; individual receptions: Tel. 0351/4856-5445, tel. 0351/4856-6445, and tel. 0351/4856-7445, respectively; www.ibis-dresden.de, reservierung@ibis-dresden.de).

$$ Motel One Dresden am Zwinger looms over a corner of Postplatz, right in cherub-fountain-spitting distance of the Zwinger. Some of its 288 aqua-and-brown, posh-feeling but small rooms peek right into the palace's courtyard. The outdoor lounge soothes with mini-fountains, swing-chairs, and an inviting vibe that echoes the words across the hotel's roofline: "A life without joy is like a long trip without an inn" (Sb-€69, Db-€79, €20 more for bigger room, breakfast-€7.50, Wi-Fi, parking-€12/day; Postplatz 5—from left side of main station either hop tram #8 direction: Hellerau, tram #9 direction: Kaditz Riegelplatz, or tram #11 direction: Bühlau; see map on page 713, tel. 0351/438-380, www.motel-one.com, dresden-am-zwinger@motel-one.com).

$ Ibis Budget Dresden City, with 203 small, simple rooms, is conveniently situated right by the Postplatz tram stop, steps from the major sights. At these prices, it's a steal. The catch is that your shower and sink are in the room, with only the frosted glass of the shower stall screening you off. The toilet does have a separate enclosure (Sb-€39-49, Db-€49-69, prices vary with demand and how far in advance you book, breakfast-€7.50, air-con, Wi-Fi, parking-€9/day—but they can point you to cheaper parking nearby; Wilsdruffer Strasse 25—hop tram #8, #9, or #11 from main station—see tram details for Motel One, above; see map on page 713, tel. 0351/8339-3820, www.ibisbudget.com, h7514@accor.com).

IN THE NEW TOWN

The first two hotels are comfy splurges in the tidy residential neighborhood between the Neustadt train station and the Augustus Bridge. The third hotel, plus the two cheap and funky hostels, are buried in the happening Outer New Town zone (see "Nightlife in Dresden," earlier). For locations, see the map on page 674.

$$$ Hotel Bayerischer Hof Dresden, 100 yards toward the river from the Neustadt train station, offers 50 spacious rooms and elegant, inviting public spaces in a grand old building on a busy street. Be sure to ask for a room facing the quiet courtyard (Sb-€95, Db-€132, Db suite-€159, extra bed-€40, includes breakfast, non-smoking rooms, elevator, free guest computer, Wi-Fi, free parking, Antonstrasse 33-35, yellow building to the right and across from station, tel. 0351/829-370, www.bayerischer-hof-dresden.de, info@bayerischer-hof-dresden.de).

$$ Hotel Martha Dresden is a better value than the Bayerischer Hof, with 50 no-nonsense rooms in a quiet location a five-minute walk from Neustadt train station. The two old buildings that make up the hotel have been smartly renovated and connected in back with a glassed-in winter garden and a pleasant outdoor breakfast terrace. It's a 10-minute walk to the historical center (four Sb with private bath down hall-€55, Sb-€79-86, Db-€113, "superior" Db-€121, extra bed-€27, includes breakfast, elevator, free guest computer, Wi-Fi, parking-€5/day; leaving Neustadt Station, veer right and cross the street, walking past the tram stops and head down Hainstrasse, then take the first left on Theresienstrasse, then around the first corner to the first building on the right, Nieritzstrasse #11; tel. 0351/81760, www.hotel-martha-dresden.de, rezeption@hotel-martha-dresden.de).

$ AHA Hotel has an unassuming facade on a big, noisy street, but inside you'll find a homey and welcoming ambience. The 30 neat and spacious rooms all come with kitchenettes; most have balconies. It's a bit farther from the center, but its friendliness, coziness, and good value make it a winner, as long as you request the more expensive rooms on the quieter back side (Sb-€50-60, Db-€73-83, huge Db-€80-90, extra bed-€15-20, breakfast-€9, non-smoking rooms, elevator, free guest computer, Wi-Fi; Bautzner Strasse 53, 10 minutes by foot east of Albertplatz or take tram #11 from Hauptbahnhof Nord or Neustadt Station to Pulsnitzer Strasse stop; tel. 0351/800-850, www.ahahotel-dresden.de, kontakt@ ahahotel-dresden.de).

$ **Pension Raskolnikoff** is your chance to live in relative comfort amid the Neustadt alternative scene. Eight rooms—all different and creatively designed—are on the top floors and in the back building of this café and art-gallery complex on a quiet side street. Originally slated for demolition at the end of the DDR years, the building was taken over by an artists' cooperative, two of whose members are the current owners (Sb-€45, Db-€62, big Db-€72, extra bed-€17, lots of stairs, no breakfast but bakery around corner and good €9 breakfast served a few doors down at Lloyd's, free guest computer, Wi-Fi; Böhmische Strasse 34, take tram #11 from Hauptbahnhof Nord or Neustadt Station to Bautzner/Rothenburger Strasse, then walk one block up Rothenburger Strasse and turn right on Böhmische Strasse; tel. 0351/804-5706, www. raskolnikoff.de, pension@raskolnikoff.de).

HOSTELS

$ **Hostel Louise 20** rents 78 beds in the middle of the Outer New Town action. Though located in this wild-and-edgy nightlife district, it feels safe, solid, clean, and comfy. The bright, IKEA-furnished rooms, guest kitchen, cozy common room, and friendly staff make it a good place for cheap beds, even for those older than the backpacker crowd (S-€32-40, D-€42-48, small dorm-€17-18/bed, cheapest weekdays and winter outside December, sheets-€2.50, breakfast-€6, Wi-Fi in common areas, pay guest computer, launderette down street, in the courtyard at Louisenstrasse 20, tel. 0351/889-4894, www.louise20.de, info@louise20.de).

$ **Hostel Mondpalast Dresden** is young and laid-back, with 94 beds above a trendy bar in a historic building (it's the city's oldest hotel) the heart of the Outer New Town. Its super-groovy vibe is good for backpackers with little money and an appetite for late-night fun (dorm bed-€13-20, S-€34-39, Sb-€44, D-€44-48, Db-€52-56, higher prices are for Fri-Sat, sheets-€2, breakfast-€6.50, Wi-Fi, pay guest computer, lockers, kitchen, bike rental-€7/day, launderette across street, near Kamenzer Strasse at Louisenstrasse 77, take tram #11 from Hauptbahnhof or Neustadt Station to Pulsnitzer Strasse stop, tel. 0351/563-4050, www.mondpalast.de, info@mondpalast.de).

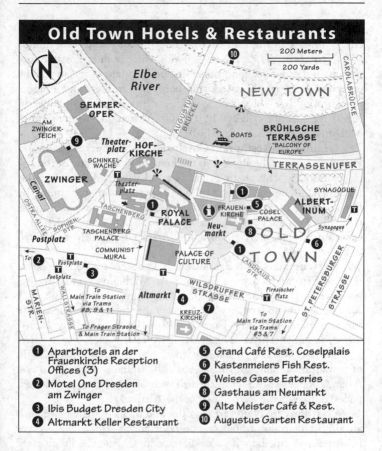

Old Town Hotels & Restaurants

200 Meters
200 Yards

1 Aparthotels an der Frauenkirche Reception Offices (3)
2 Motel One Dresden am Zwinger
3 Ibis Budget Dresden City
4 Altmarkt Keller Restaurant
5 Grand Café Rest. Coselpalais
6 Kastenmeiers Fish Rest.
7 Weisse Gasse Eateries
8 Gasthaus am Neumarkt
9 Alte Meister Café & Rest.
10 Augustus Garten Restaurant

Eating in Dresden

Nearly every Old Town restaurant seems bright, shiny, and modern. Old Town restaurants tend to be nice but touristy, and a bit expensive, with main courses ranging from €9 to €17. For cheaper prices and authentic local character, leave the famous center, cross the river, and wander through the New Town.

Many Dresden restaurants serve a soup called *Soljanka*, which is Russian in origin and usually includes finely chopped meat and pickled vegetables in a light tomato-based broth. A special local dessert sold all over town is *Dresdner Eierschecke,* an eggy cheesecake with vanilla pudding, raisins, and almond shavings.

IN THE OLD TOWN

Altmarkt Keller (a.k.a. Sächsisch-Böhmisches Bierhaus), a few blocks from the river on Altmarkt square, is a festive beer cellar that serves nicely presented Saxon and Bohemian food (from sepa-

DRESDEN

rate menus) and has good Czech beer on tap. The lively crowd, cheesy brass-band music (live Sat 19:00-22:00), and jolly murals add to the fun. While the on-square seating is fine, most choose the vast-but-stout air-conditioned cellar. The giant mural inside the entryway portrays the friendship between Dresden and Prague, proclaiming that "the sunshine of life is drinking and being merry" (€9-17 main courses, daily 11:00-24:00, Altmarkt 4, to the right of McDonald's, tel. 0351/481-8130).

Grand Café Restaurant Coselpalais, which serves Saxon and French cuisine in the shadow of the Frauenkirche, is one of the few places near the church that offers a good value. Indoors is a Baroque, chandeliered dining experience; outdoors there's unusually fine courtyard seating—great for an elegant meal or tea and pastries (€11-17 main courses, cheaper daily specials, huge selection of cakes on display, daily 10:00-24:00, An der Frauenkirche 12, tel. 0351/496-2444).

Kastenmeiers Fish Restaurant is a good bet if you're loaded, fond of fish, and want an elegant near-Michelin-star dining experience in the old town center. Under stony modern vaults, it's surrounded by modern artwork and very romantic (€50 four-course surprise menu, €20 first courses, €30 main dishes, daily 12:00-23:00, Tzschirnerplatz 3, tel. 0351/4848-4801).

Weisse Gasse's "restaurant row" offers a high-energy mix of restaurant chains and bars (Spanish, Italian, steak, Japanese, Asian, and ice cream) with seating inside and out along a cobbled, pedestrianized lane a block east of the Altmarkt.

Gasthaus am Neumarkt, a calm and inviting little place with an almost tearoom ambience one floor above street level, serves hearty Saxon cuisine with a passion for local wine (€6 lunch plate with coffee, regular dishes €10-15, always fish, meat, and vegetarian, Mon-Fri 11:00-15:00, nightly from 18:00, be sure to go upstairs, just off Neumarkt at An der Frauenkirche 13, enter on Salzgasse, tel. 0351/3236-7210).

Alte Meister Café and Restaurant, with delightful garden seating, is a handy bet between the Opera House and the Zwinger (daily 12:00-23:00, facing the Opera at Theaterplatz 1, tel. 0351/481-0426).

IN THE NEW TOWN

Venture to these eateries—across the Augustus Bridge from the Old Town—for lower prices and a more local scene. Also consider places in the Outer New Town (see under "Nightlife in Dresden").

Just Across Augustus Bridge

Augustus Garten is a lazy, crude-yet-inviting beer garden with super-cheap self-service food (pork knuckle, wurst, kraut, cheap beer, and lots of mustard). You'll eat among big bellies—and few tourists—with a good view back over the river to the Old Town, but only in good weather (€5-10 main courses, daily 11:00-24:00 if warm, otherwise closed, tel. 0351/404-5531). As you walk across the bridge from the Old Town, it's on your immediate right.

On Königstrasse

Wenzel Prager Bierstuben serves country Bohemian cuisine in a woodsy bar that spills out into an airy, glassed-in gallery—made doubly big by its vast mirror. Stepping inside, you'll be immediately won over by the interior. There's also peaceful streetside seating. The menu is fun and Bohemian, with three varieties of Czech Staropramen beer on tap (€10-11 main-dish-with-small-beer specials on Tue-Thu, €10-17 main courses, daily 11:00-22:00, Königstrasse 1, tel. 0351/804-2010).

On Hauptstrasse

Watzke Brauereiausschank am Goldenen Reiter, just over the Augustus Bridge and facing the Golden Rider statue, is run by a local brewery. A hit with Dresdeners (and a world away from the touristy kitsch of the Old Town), it serves beer-hall fare, including pork knuckle *(Haxe)*, lots of kraut, and its own unfiltered beer (nightly meal specials with beer-€11, daily 11:00-24:00, Hauptstrasse 1, tel. 0351/810-6820).

Winzerstube Zum Rebstock is a charming pub serving Saxon cuisine with seasonal specials in a small romantic interior or in a leafy and quiet "Baroque garden" courtyard (€10-14 main dishes, daily 12:00-22:00, Hauptstrasse 17, tel. 0351/563-3544).

Restaurant St. Petersburg is like a cross between a pub and a Russian salon, with heavy red-velvet furniture and mini-chandeliers under fluorescent lighting inside, and charming tables outside on what had been the showpiece East German boulevard. They serve classic Russian and Ukrainian dishes, such as *pelmeni*—filled dumplings (cheap lunch plates, €15 main dishes, daily 11:30-14:30 & 17:00-24:00, Hauptstrasse 11, tel. 0351/563-3233).

Under the Three Kings Church Steeple

At the top of Hauptstrasse, in an 18th-century zone that survived World War II intact, several good eateries cluster around the towering spire of the Three Kings Church (Dreikönigskirche).

Bülow's Bistro, in the fancy Hotel Bülow Palais, shares the same kitchen as the Michelin star-quality Caroussel Restaurant. It's just seven tables off the hotel lobby, yet offers elegantly presented international dishes and one of the nicest dining experiences in town—reservations are smart (€10 lunch plates, 3-course

DRESDEN

dinner-€35, first courses-€10, main dishes-€20, daily 11:00-23:00, Königstrasse 14, tel. 0351/800-3140).

Die Pastamanufaktur, a fun and romantic little place for pasta lovers, has a pleasantly simple interior and nice seating out back with its own little fountain (€5-9 dishes, daily 10:00-22:00, Karl-Liebknecht-Strasse 56, tel. 0351/323-7797).

Good Friends is a favorite for slightly upscale Thai and Vietnamese food (€8-13 main courses, €6 lunches on weekdays, daily 12:00-15:00 & 17:30-22:30, An der Dreikönigskirche 8, tel. 0351/646-5814).

Outer New Town
The trendy Outer New Town is thriving with creative and youthful places to eat and drink. While the scene is always changing, see "Nightlife in Dresden," earlier, for several suggestions.

BEER HALLS
All of Dresden's famous beer halls were destroyed in the war, and the communists refused to rebuild them. But after unification, ambitious Dresdeners began re-creating this tradition. Beer halls usually serve their own brew and meaty German cuisine. Germans love to eat and talk, so beer halls are great places to meet locals and get a taste of life beyond the tourist areas. All of these places are outside the city center but easily and quickly reached by public transportation.

Brauhaus am Waldschlösschen is fun and lively, with nightly music that really gets going after 21:00. It's worth the extra effort it takes to reach this place. The self-service beer garden on the terrace overlooks the Elbe River Valley, with Dresden's Old Town in the distance (half-chicken-€4, pork knuckle with kraut-€7.50, Mon-Thu €10-11 daily specials include a large beer). Indoors and under a shady awning, the restaurant serves traditional Saxon cuisine with some fine salads (€9-13 main courses, daily 11:00-24:00, Am Brauhaus 8b, tram #11 to Waldschlösschen—it's in a squarish building above the tram stop, tel. 0351/652-3900).

Ball und Brauhaus Watzke, the oldest of the beer halls, started life as a ballroom (it still holds public balls once a month). It sits pleasantly on the banks of the Elbe, with nice views of the Old Town. Watzke serves traditional beer-hall food in huge portions and features €11 main-course-with-beer specials on some weekdays (€8-13 main courses, daily 11:00-24:00, Kötzschenbroderstrasse 1, tram #4 or #9 to Altpieschen, tel. 0351/852-920).

Feldschlösschen Stammhaus was the original brewery and hops warehouse for Feldschlösschen beer, but the company moved to another part of Dresden in the 1970s. It's worth the trek from downtown—this is a cozy, energy-filled spot in a sea of East German prefab apartments. Traditional fare dominates the menu, but they sneak fresh vegetables into some dishes and serve homemade bread (€8-12 main courses, €8 lunch and dinner specials include a beer, daily 11:00-24:00, Budapester Strasse 32, bus #62—direction: Dölzschen—from Prager Strasse tram platforms to Agentur für Arbeit stop—yes, there is a beer hall next to the unemployment office, tel. 0351/471-8855).

Dresden Connections

From Dresden by Train to: Leipzig (1-2/hour direct, 1.5 hours), **Berlin** (every 2 hours, more with transfer in Leipzig, 2.5 hours), **Erfurt** (nearly hourly direct, 2.5 hours; more possible with change in Leipzig, 3 hours), **Wittenberg** (1-2/hour, 2-3.5 hours, transfer in Leipzig and sometimes also Bitterfeld), **Prague** (every 2 hours, 2.5 hours), **Hamburg** (4/day direct, 4.5 hours; otherwise about hourly with change in Leipzig or Berlin, 4-4.5 hours), **Frankfurt** (hourly, 5 hours), **Nürnberg** (hourly, 4.5-5 hours, may change in Leipzig or Hof), **Munich** (every 2 hours, 6 hours, transfer in Nürnberg), **Vienna** (2/day direct, 7 hours; plus 1 night train/day, 9 hours), **Budapest** (4/day, 9.5 hours; plus 1 night train, 11.5 hours). There are overnight trains from Dresden to Zürich, the Rhineland, and Munich. Train info: Tel. 0180-599-6633, www.bahn.com.

BERLIN

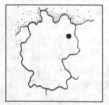

No tour of Germany is complete without a look at its historic and reunited capital. Over the last two decades, Berlin has been a construction zone. Standing on ripped-up tracks and under a canopy of cranes, visitors witnessed the rebirth of a great European capital. Although construction continues, today the once-divided city is thoroughly woven back together. Berlin has emerged as one of Europe's top destinations: captivating, lively, fun-loving, all-around enjoyable—and easy on the budget.

Of course, Berlin is still largely defined by its tumultuous 20th century. The city was Hitler's capital during World War II, and in the postwar years, it became the front line of a new global war—one between Soviet-style communism and American-style capitalism. The East-West division was set in stone in 1961, when the East German government boxed in West Berlin with the Berlin Wall. The Wall stood for 28 years. In 1990, less than a year after the Wall fell, the two Germanys—and the two Berlins—officially became one. When the dust settled, Berliners from both sides of the once-divided city faced the monumental challenge of reunification.

When the Wall came down, the East was a decrepit wasteland and the West was a paragon of commerce and materialism. Since then, city planners have seized on the city's reunification and the return of the national government to make Berlin a great capital once again. A quarter-century later, the roles are reversed: It's eastern Berlin where you feel the vibrant pulse of the city, while western Berlin seems like yesterday's news. Berliners joke that they don't need to travel anywhere because their city's always changing. Spin a postcard rack to see what's new. A 10-year-old guidebook on Berlin covers a different city.

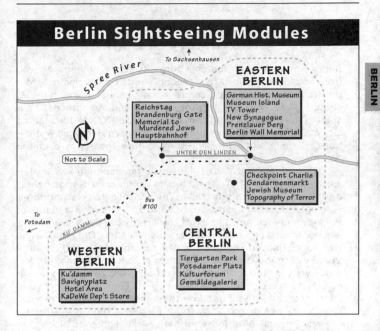

Berlin Sightseeing Modules

To Sachsenhausen

Spree River

EASTERN BERLIN

German Hist. Museum
Museum Island
TV Tower
New Synagogue
Prenzlauer Berg
Berlin Wall Memorial

Reichstag
Brandenburg Gate
Memorial to
 Murdered Jews
Hauptbahnhof

N

Not to Scale

UNTER DEN LINDEN

Checkpoint Charlie
Gendarmenmarkt
Jewish Museum
Topography of Terror

Bus
#100

To
Potsdam

KU'DAMM

CENTRAL BERLIN

Tiergarten Park
Potsdamer Platz
Kulturforum
Gemäldegalerie

WESTERN BERLIN

Ku'damm
Savignyplatz
Hotel Area
KaDeWe Dep't Store

But even as the city busily builds itself into the 21st century, Berlin has made a point of acknowledging and remembering its past. A series of thought-provoking memorials installed throughout the city center—such as the Memorial to the Murdered Jews of Europe—directly confront some of Germany's most difficult history of the last century. Lacing these sights into your Berlin sightseeing is a way to learn from those horrific times.

As you appreciate the thrill of walking over what was the Wall and through the well-patched Brandenburg Gate, it's clear that history is not contained in some book; it's an evolving story in which we play a part. In Berlin, the fine line between history and current events is excitingly blurry.

But even for non-historians, Berlin is a city of fine experiences. Explore the fun and funky neighborhoods emerging in the former East, packed with creative hipster eateries and boutiques trying to one-up each other. Go for a pedal or a cruise along the delightful Spree riverfront. In the city's world-class museums, walk through an enormous Babylonian gate amid rough-and-tumble ancient statuary, and peruse canvases by Dürer, Rembrandt, and Vermeer. Nurse a stein of brew in a rollicking beer hall, or dive into a cheap *Currywurst.*

On the outskirts of town, at Potsdam, glide like a swan through the opulent halls of an imperial palace or, at Oranienburg, ponder the darkest chapter of this nation's past at the Sachsen-

The History of Berlin

Berlin was a humble, marshy burg—its name perhaps derived from an old Slavic word for "swamp"—until prince electors from the Hohenzollern dynasty made it their capital in the mid-15th century. Gradually their territory spread and strengthened, becoming the powerful Kingdom of Prussia in 1701. As the leading city of Prussia, Berlin dominated the northern Germanic world—both militarily and culturally—long before there was a united "Germany."

The only Hohenzollern ruler worth remembering was Frederick the Great (1712-1786). The ultimate enlightened despot, he was both a ruthless military tactician (he consolidated his kingdom's holdings, successfully invading Silesia and biting off a chunk of Poland) and a cultured lover of the arts (he actively invited artists, architects, and other thinkers to his lands). "Old Fritz," as he was called, played the flute, spoke six languages, and counted Voltaire among his friends. Practical and cosmopolitan, Frederick cleverly invited to Prussia Protestants who were being persecuted elsewhere in Europe—including the French Huguenots and Dutch traders. Prussia became the beneficiary of these groups' substantial wealth and know-how. Frederick the Great left Berlin—and Prussia—a far more modern and enlightened place than he found it. Thanks largely to him, Prussia was well-positioned to become a magnet of sorts for the German unification movement in the 19th century.

When Germany first unified, in 1871, Berlin (as the main city of its most powerful constituent state, Prussia) was its natural capital. Even in the disarray of post-WWI Germany, Berlin thrived as an anything-goes, cabaret-crazy cultural capital of the Roaring '20s. During World War II, the city was Hitler's headquarters—and the place where the Führer drew his final breath. When the Soviet Army reached Berlin in 1945, the protracted fighting left the city

hausen Concentration Camp Memorial (both covered in the next chapter).

Berlin today is like the nuclear fuel rod of a great nation. It's vibrant with youth, energy, and an anything-goes-and-anything's-possible buzz (Munich feels spent in comparison). Berlin is both extremely popular and surprisingly affordable. As a booming tourist draw, Berlin now welcomes more visitors annually than Rome.

PLANNING YOUR TIME

On all but the shortest trips through Germany, I'd give Berlin three nights and at least two full days, and spend them this way:

Day 1: Begin your day getting oriented to this huge city. For a quick and relaxing once-over-lightly tour, jump on one of the many hop-on, hop-off buses that make two-hour narrated orienta-

in ruins.

After World War II, Berlin was divided by the victorious Allied powers. The American, British, and French sectors became West Berlin, and the Soviet sector, East Berlin. In 1948 and 1949, the Soviets tried to starve the 2.2 million residents of the Western half in an almost medieval-style siege, blockading all roads in and out. But they were foiled by the Berlin Airlift, with the Western Allies flying in supplies from Frankfurt 24 hours a day for 10 months.

Years later, with the overnight construction of the Berlin Wall in 1961, an Iron (or, at least, concrete) Curtain literally cut through the middle of the city, completely encircling West Berlin. For details, see "The Berlin Wall (and Its Fall)" on page 786.

While the wild night when the Wall came down (November 9, 1989) was inspiring, Berlin still faced a fitful transition to reunification. Two cities—and countries—became one at a staggering pace. Reunification had its downside, and the Wall survives in the minds of some people. Some "Ossies" (impolite slang for Easterners) miss their security. Some "Wessies" miss their easy ride (military deferrals, subsidized rent, and tax breaks for living in an isolated city surrounded by the communist world). For free spirits, walled-in West Berlin was a citadel of freedom within the East.

But in recent years, the old East-West division has faded more and more into the background. Ossi-Wessi conflicts no longer dominate the city's political discourse. The city government has been eager to charge forward, with little nostalgia for anything that was associated with the East. Big corporations and the national government have moved in, and the dreary swath of land that was the Wall and its notorious "death strip" has been transformed (as the cash-starved city has been selling off lots of land to anyone determined to develop it). Berlin is a whole new city—ready to welcome visitors.

tion loops through the city. Use the bus to get off and on at places of interest (such as Potsdamer Platz). Then walk from the Reichstag (reservations required), under the Brandenburg Gate, and down Unter den Linden following my "Best of Berlin" self-guided walk. Tour the German History Museum, and cap your sightseeing day by catching a one-hour boat tour (or pedaling a rented bike) along the park-like banks of the Spree River from Museum Island to the Chancellery.

Day 2: Spend your morning touring the great museums on Museum Island (note that the island's biggest draw, the Pergamon Museum, is partly closed, with the Pergamon Altar out of view until 2019). Dedicate your afternoon to sights of the Third Reich and Holocaust: After lunch, hike via Potsdamer Platz to the Topography of Terror exhibit and along the surviving Niederkirchnerstrasse stretch of the Wall to Checkpoint Charlie. You could also head up to the Berlin Wall Memorial for a more in-depth survey of that infamous barrier, or swing by the Jewish Museum. Finish your day in the lively East—ideally in the once glum, then edgy, now fun-loving and trendy Prenzlauer Berg district.

Berlin merits additional time if you have it. There's much more in the city (such as the wonderful Gemäldegalerie art museum). And nearby are some very worthwhile side-trips: the concentration camp memorial at Sachsenhausen, the palaces at Potsdam (both covered in the next chapter), and the historic town of Wittenberg (which is gearing up for the 500th birthday of the Reformation in 2017; see the Lutherland chapter).

Orientation to Berlin

Berlin is huge, with 3.4 million people. The city is spread out and its sights numerous, so you'll need to be well-organized to experience it all smartly. The tourist's Berlin can be broken into three main digestible chunks:

Eastern Berlin has the highest concentration of notable sights and colorful neighborhoods. Near the landmark Brandenburg Gate, you'll find the Reichstag building, Pariser Platz, and poignant memorials to the victims of Hitler (Jews, Roma and Sinti, and homosexuals). From the Brandenburg Gate, the famous Unter den Linden boulevard runs eastward through former East Berlin, passing the German History Museum (a history lover's favorite) and Museum Island (Pergamon Museum, Neues Museum, and Berlin Cathedral) on the way to Alexanderplatz (TV Tower). The intersection of Unter den Linden and Friedrichstrasse has reclaimed its place as the center of the city. South of Unter den Linden are the delightful Gendarmenmarkt square, most Nazi sites (including the Topography of Terror), some good Wall-related sights (Museum of the Wall at Checkpoint Charlie and East Side Gallery), the Jewish Museum, and the colorful Turkish neighborhood of Kreuzberg. North of Unter den Linden are these worth-a-wander neighborhoods: Oranienburger Strasse (Jewish Quarter and New Synagogue), Hackescher Markt, and Prenzlauer Berg (several recommended hotels and a very lively restaurant/nightlife zone). Just west of Prenzlauer Berg is the Berlin Wall Memorial (with an intact surviving section of the Wall). Eastern Berlin's pedestrian-friendly Spree riverbank is also worth a stroll (or a river cruise).

Central Berlin is dominated by the giant Tiergarten park. South of the park are Potsdamer Platz and the Kulturforum museum cluster, which includes the Gemäldegalerie, New National Gallery (closed until at least 2017), Musical Instruments Museum, and Philharmonic Concert Hall. To the north, the huge Hauptbahnhof (main train station) straddles the former Wall in what was central Berlin's no-man's-land.

Western Berlin centers on the Bahnhof Zoo (Zoo train station, often marked "Zoologischer Garten" on transit maps) and the grand Kurfürstendamm boulevard, nicknamed "Ku'damm" (transportation hub, tours, information, shopping, and recommended hotels). The East is all the rage. But the West, while staid in comparison, is bouncing back—with big-name stores and destination restaurants that keep the area buzzing. During the Cold War, this "Western Sector" was the hub for Western visitors. Capitalists visited the West, with a nervous side-trip beyond the Wall into the grim and foreboding East. (Cubans, Russians, Poles, and Angolans stayed behind the Wall and did their sightseeing in the East.)

TOURIST INFORMATION

With any luck, you won't have to use Berlin's TIs—they're for-profit agencies working for the city's big hotels, which colors the information they provide. TI branches, appropriately called "info-stores," are unlikely to have the information you need (tel. 030/250-025, www.visitberlin.de). You'll find them at the **Hauptbahnhof** train station (daily 8:00-22:00, by main entrance on Europaplatz), **Ku'damm** (Kurfürstendamm 22, in the glass-and-steel Neues Kranzler Eck building, Mon-Sat 9:30-20:00, closed Sun), and at the **Brandenburg Gate** (daily 9:30-19:00).

Skip the TI's €1 map, and instead browse the walking tour companies' brochures—many include nearly-as-good maps for free. Most hotels also provide free city maps. While the TI does sell the three-day Museum Pass Berlin (described next), it's also available at major museums. If you take a walking tour, your guide is likely a better source of nightlife or shopping tips than the TI.

Museum Passes: The three-day, €24 **Museum Pass Berlin** is a great value. It gets you into more than 50 museums, including the national museums and most of the recommended biggies (though not the German History Museum), on three consecutive days. Sights covered by the pass include the five Museum Island museums (Old National Gallery, Neues, Altes, Bode, and Pergamon), Gemäldegalerie, and the Jewish Museum Berlin, along with other more minor sights.

As you'll routinely spend €10-14 per admission, this pays for itself in a hurry. And you'll enjoy the ease of popping in and out of museums that you might not otherwise want to pay for. Buy it at the TI or any participating museum. The pass generally lets you skip the line and go directly into the museum. The €18 **Museum Island Pass** (Bereichskarte Museumsinsel; does not include special exhibits) covers all the venues on Museum Island (otherwise €10-14 each) and is a fine value—but for just €6 more, the three-day Mu-

seum Pass Berlin gives you triple the days and many more entries. TIs also sell the **WelcomeCard,** a transportation pass that includes discounts for the following recommended sights (and more): Berlin Cathedral, DDR Museum, German History Museum, Museum of the Wall at Checkpoint Charlie, Jewish Museum Berlin, and The Kennedys Museum (pass described later, under "Getting Around Berlin").

Local Publications: Various magazines can help make your time in Berlin more productive (available at the TI and/or many newsstands). *Berlin Programm* is a comprehensive German-language monthly, especially strong in high culture, that lists upcoming events and museum hours (€2.20, www.berlin-programm.de). *Exberliner Magazine,* an English monthly (published mostly by expat Brits who love to poke fun at expat Americans), is very helpful for curious travelers. With a youthful focus, it gives a fascinating insider's look at this fast-changing city (€3 but often given away at theaters or on the street, www.exberliner.com).

ARRIVAL IN BERLIN
By Train at Berlin Hauptbahnhof
Berlin's newest and grandest train station is Berlin Hauptbahnhof

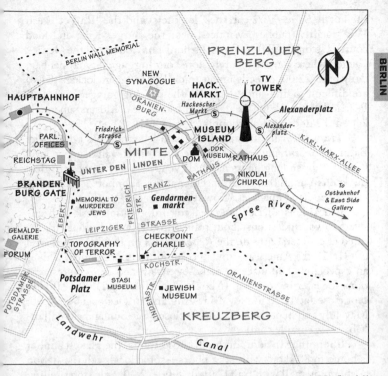

(main train station, a.k.a. "der Bahnhof", abbreviated Hbf). All long-distance trains arrive here, at Europe's biggest, mostly underground train station. This is a "transfer station"—unique for its major lines coming in at right angles—where the national train system meets the city's S-Bahn train system.

The gigantic station can be intimidating, but it's laid out logically on five floors (which, confusingly, can be marked in different ways). Escalators and elevators connect the **main floor** (*Erdgeschoss*, EG, a.k.a level 0); the two **lower levels** (*Untergeschoss*, UG1 and UG2, a.k.a. levels -1 and -2); and the two **upper levels** (*Obersgeschoss*, OG1 and OG2, a.k.a. levels +1 and +2). Tracks 1-8 are in the lowest underground level (UG2), while tracks 11-16 (along with the S-Bahn) are on the top floor (OG2). Shops and services are concentrated on the three middle levels (EG, OG1, and UG1). The south entrance (toward the Reichstag and downtown, with a taxi stand) is marked *Washingtonplatz*, while the north entrance is marked *Europaplatz*.

Services: On the main floor (EG), you'll find the **TI** (facing the north/*Europaplatz* entrance, look left) and the **"Rail & Fresh WC"** facility (public pay toilets, near the Burger King and food court). Up one level (OG1) is a 24-hour **pharmacy** and the Gepäck Center, where you can securely store your **luggage** (€5/day per bag, daily 6:00-22:00, directly under track 14). Luggage lockers (€4-6) are difficult to find since they're in the parking garage (levels P-1, P-2, and P-3; look for the garage entrance near Kaisers supermarket on the underground shopping level UG1).

Train Information and Tickets: The station has a Deutsche Bahn *Reisezentrum* information center on the first upper level (OG1/+1, open long hours daily). If you're staying in western Berlin, keep in mind that the info center at the Bahnhof Zoo station is just as good and much less crowded.

EurAide is an English-speaking information desk with answers to your questions about train travel around Europe. It's located at counter 12 inside the *Reisezentrum* on the first upper level (OG1/+1). It's American-run, so communication is simple. This is an especially good place to make fast-train and *couchette* reservations for later in your trip (March-Dec Mon-Fri 11:00-19:00 except closes at 18:30 in Nov, May-Aug and in Dec opens at 10:00, May-July and Sept open till 20:00, closed Sat-Sun and closed Jan-Feb; www.euraide.com).

Shopping: In addition to all those trains, the Hauptbahnhof is home to 80 shops with long hours—some locals call the station a "shopping mall with trains" (daily 8:00-22:00, only stores selling travel provisions are open Sun). The Kaisers supermarket (UG1, follow signs for tracks 1-2) is handy for assembling a picnic for your train ride.

Getting into Town: Taxis and buses wait outside the station, but the S-Bahn is probably the best means of connecting to your destination within Berlin. The crosstown express S-Bahn line connects the station with my recommended hotels in a few minutes. It's simple: All S-Bahn trains are on tracks 15 and 16 at the top of the station (level OG2/+2). All trains on track 15 go east, stopping at Friedrichstrasse, Hackescher Markt (with connections to Prenzlauer Berg), Alexanderplatz, and Ostbahnhof; trains on track 16 go west, toward Bahnhof Zoo and Savignyplatz. (Your train ticket or rail pass into the station covers your connecting S-Bahn ride into town; your outbound ticket includes the transfer via S-Bahn to the Hauptbahnhof.)

If you're sleeping at one of my recommended hotels in eastern Berlin's Prenzlauer Berg neighborhood, take any train on track 15 two stops to Hackescher Markt, exit to Spandauer Strasse, go left, and cross the tracks to the tram stop. Here you'll catch tram #M1 north (direction Schillerstrasse; see map on page 820).

To reach my recommended hotels in western Berlin, catch

any train on track 16 to Savignyplatz, and you're a five-minute walk from your hotel (see map on page 826). Savignyplatz is one stop after **Bahnhof Zoo** (rhymes with "toe"; a.k.a. Bahnhof Zoologischer Garten), the once-grand train hub now eclipsed by the Hauptbahnhof. Nowadays Bahnhof Zoo is useful mainly for its shops, uncrowded train-information desk, and BVG public-transit office (outside the entrance, amid the traffic); expect it to be a massive construction zone in 2015.

The Berlin Hauptbahnhof is not well-connected to the city's U-Bahn (subway) system—yet. The station's sole U-Bahn line—U55—goes only two stops, to the Brandenburger Tor station, and doesn't yet really connect to the rest of the system. It's part of a planned extension of the U5 line to Alexanderplatz that's far from completion. But for transit junkies, it is an interesting ride on Europe's shortest subway line.

By Plane

For information on reaching the city center from Berlin's airports, see "Berlin Connections" at the end of this chapter.

HELPFUL HINTS

Medical Help: "Call a doc" is a nonprofit referral service designed for tourists (tel. 01805-321-303, phone answered 24 hours a day, www.calladoc.com). Payment is arranged between you and the doctor, and is likely more affordable than similar care in the US. The US Embassy also has a list of local English-speaking doctors (tel. 030/83050, germany.usembassy.gov).

Museum Tips: Some major Berlin museums are closed on Monday—if you're in town on that day, review hours carefully before making plans. If you plan to see several museums, you'll save money with the Museum Pass Berlin, which covers nearly all the city sights for three days—including everything covered by the one-day Museum Island Pass (see "Tourist Information—Museum Passes," earlier).

Addresses: Many Berlin streets are numbered with odd and even numbers on the same side of the street, often with no connection to the other side (for example, Ku'damm #212 can be across the street from #14). To save steps, check the white street signs on curb corners; many list the street numbers covered on that side of the block.

Cold War Terminology: Cold War history is important here, so it's helpful to learn a few key terms. What Americans called "East Germany" was technically the German Democratic Republic—the Deutsche Demokratische Republik, or **DDR** (day-day-AIR). You'll still see those initials around what was once East Germany. The formal name for "West Germany" was the Federal Republic of Germany—the Bundesrepublik Deutschland (BRD)—and is the name now shared by all of reunited Germany.

Late-Hours Sightseeing: Berlin's museums typically close at 18:00, but many stay open later at least one day a week, allowing smart planners to stretch their sightseeing day. Four of the biggies are open late every day: the Reichstag (until midnight, last entry at 22:00), the Museum of the Wall at Checkpoint Charlie (until 22:00), the Topography of Terror (until 20:00), and the Jewish Museum Berlin (Tue-Sun until 20:00, 22:00 on Mon). All of the Museum Island museums are open until 20:00 on Thursdays.

Outdoor monuments such as the Berlin Wall Memorial and the Memorial to the Murdered Jews of Europe are accessible, safe, and pleasantly lit late into the night, though their visitor centers close earlier. Many of Berlin's art galleries are also open late, so consider the Mitte neighborhood or Fasanenstrasse for an evening gallery stroll.

Internet Access: You'll find Wi-Fi in most hotels and hostels, as well as at small Internet cafés all over the city. Bahnhof Zoo, Friedrichstrasse, and Hauptbahnhof train stations have coin-operated Internet terminals.

Bookstore: Berlin Story, a big, cluttered, fun bookshop (not to be confused with the Story of Berlin museum on Ku'damm), has a knowledgeable staff and the best selection anywhere in town of English-language books and helpful magazines on Berlin. They also stock an amusing mix of knickknacks and East Berlin nostalgia souvenirs (Mon-Sat 10:00-19:00, Sun 10:00-18:00, Unter den Linden 40, tel. 030/2045-3842, www.berlinstory.de).

Other Berlin Souvenirs: If you're taken with the city's unofficial mascot, the *Ampelmännchen* (traffic-light man), you'll find a world of souvenirs slathered with his iconic red and green image at **Ampelmann Shops** (various locations, including along Unter den Linden at #35, near Gendarmenmarkt at Markgrafenstrasse 37, near Museum Island inside the DomAquarée mall, in the Hackesche Höfe, and at Potsdamer Platz).

Laundry: Berlin has several self-service launderettes with long hours (wash and dry-€4-9/load). Near my recommended hotels in Prenzlauer Berg, try **Waschsalon 115** (daily 6:00-22:00, exact change required, free Wi-Fi, Torstrasse 115, around the corner from the recommended Circus hostel) or **Eco-Express Waschsalon** (daily 6:00-22:00, last load at 21:00, handy pizzeria next door, Danziger Strasse 7). The **Schnell & Sauber Waschcenter** chain has a location in Prenzlauer Berg (daily 6:00-23:00, exact change required, Oderberger Strasse 1).

Shell Games: Believe it or not, there are still enough idiots on the street to keep the con men with their shell games in business. Don't be foolish enough to engage with any gambling on the street.

Updates to This Book: For updates to this book, check www.ricksteves.com/update.

GETTING AROUND BERLIN

The city is vast. Berlin's sights spread far and wide. Right from the start, commit yourself to the city's fine public-transit system.

By Public Transit: Subway, Train, Tram, and Bus

Berlin's consolidated transit system uses the same ticket for its many modes of transportation: U-Bahn (*Untergrund-Bahn*, Berlin's subway), S-Bahn (*Stadtschnellbahn*, or "fast urban train," mostly aboveground and with fewer stops), *Strassenbahn* (trams), and buses. For all types of transit, there are three lettered zones (A, B, and C). Most of your sightseeing will be in zones A and B (the city proper)—but you'll need to buy a ticket that also covers zone C if you're going to Potsdam, Sachsenhausen, Schönefeld airport, or other outlying areas.

Ticket Options:

• The €2.60 **basic single** ticket *(Einzelfahrschein)* covers two hours of travel in one direction. It's easy to make this ticket stretch to cover several rides...as long as they're in the same direction.

• The €1.50 **short-ride** ticket *(Kurzstrecke Fahrschein)* covers a single ride of six bus stops or three subway stations (one transfer allowed). You can save a little bit on short-ride tickets by buying them in groups of four (€5.60).

• The €8.80 **four-trip** ticket *(4-Fahrten-Karte)* is the same as four basic single tickets at a small discount.

• The **day pass** *(Tageskarte)* is good until 3:00 the morning after you buy it (€6.70 for zones AB, €7.20 for zones ABC). For longer stays, consider a seven-day pass *(Sieben-Tage-Karte;* €28.80 for zones AB, €35.60 for zones ABC), or the WelcomeCard (described below), which is good for up to five days and also includes sightseeing discounts. The *Kleingruppenkarte* lets groups of up to five travel all day (€16.20 for zones AB, €16.70 for zones ABC).

• If you've already bought a ticket for zones A and B, and later decide that you also want to go to zone C (such as to Potsdam), you can buy an **"extension ticket"** *(Anschlussfahrschein)* for €1.60 per ride in that zone.

• If you plan to cover a lot of ground using public transportation during a two- or three-day visit, the **WelcomeCard** (available at TIs) is usually the best deal. For longer stays, there's even a five-day option. It covers all public transportation and gives you up to 50 percent discounts on lots of minor and a few major museums (including Checkpoint Charlie), sightseeing tours (including 25 percent off the recommended Original Berlin Walks), and music and theater events (www.visitberlin.de/welcomecard). If you plan to stay inside the city, the Berlin-only option makes more sense (covers transit zones AB, €19.50/48 hours, €26.70/72 hours). For trips beyond the city center, you might want to get the Berlin-with-Potsdam option (zones ABC, €21.50/48 hours, €28.70/72 hours). If you're a museum junkie, consider the **WelcomeCard+Museumsinsel** (€40.50/72 hours), which combines travel in zones A and B with unlimited access to the five museums on Museum Island. Families get an extra price break: The ABC version (€42.50/72 hours) is valid for one adult and up to three kids younger than 15.

Buying Tickets: You can buy U-Bahn/S-Bahn tickets from machines at stations. (They are also sold at BVG pavilions at train stations and the TI, from machines on board trams, and on buses from drivers, who'll give change.) *Erwachsener* means "adult"— anyone 14 or older. Don't be afraid of the automated machines: First select the type of ticket you want, then load the coins or paper bills. (Coins work better, so keep some handy.) As you board the bus or tram, or enter the subway system, punch your ticket in a clock machine to validate it (or risk a €60 fine; for an all-day or multiday pass, stamp it only the first time you ride). Be sure to travel with a valid ticket. Tickets are checked frequently, often by plainclothes inspectors. Within Berlin, Eurail passes are good only on S-Bahn connections from the train station when you arrive and to the station when you depart.

Transit Tips: The S-Bahn crosstown express is a river of public transit through the heart of the city, in which many lines converge on one basic highway. Get used to this, and you'll leap within a few minutes between key locations: Savignyplatz (hotels in western Berlin), Bahnhof Zoo (Ku'damm, bus #100), Hauptbahnhof (all major trains in and out of Berlin—unless construction has temporarily re-routed some), Friedrichstrasse (a short walk north of the heart of Unter den Linden; this station has the interesting Palace of Tears exhibit, described on page 799), Hackescher Markt (Museum Island, restaurants, nightlife, connection to Prenzlauer Berg hotels and eateries), and Alexanderplatz (eastern end of Unter den Linden).

Sections of the U-Bahn or S-Bahn sometimes close temporarily for repairs. In this situation, a bus route often replaces the train (*Ersatzverkehr,* or "replacement transportation"; *zwischen* means "between").

Berlin's public transit is operated by BVG (except the S-Bahn, run by Deutsche Bahn). Schedules, including bus timetables, are available on the helpful BVG website (www.bvg.de). Get and use the excellent *Discover Berlin by Train and Bus* map-guide published by BVG (at subway ticket windows).

By Taxi
Cabs are easy to flag down, and taxi stands are common. A typical ride within town costs €8-10, and a crosstown trip (for example, Bahnhof Zoo to Alexanderplatz) will run about €15. Tariff 1 is for a *Kurzstrecke* ticket (see below). All other rides are tariff 2 (€3.40 drop plus €1.80/kilometer for the first 7 kilometers, then €1.28/kilometer after that). If possible, use cash—paying with a credit card comes with a hefty surcharge (about €4, regardless of the fare).

Money-Saving Taxi Tip: For any ride of less than two kilometers (about a mile), you can save several euros if you take advantage of the **Kurzstrecke** (short-stretch) rate. To get this rate, it's important that you flag the cab down on the street—not at or even near a taxi stand. Also, you must ask for the *Kurzstrecke* rate as soon as you hop in: Confidently say *"Kurzstrecke, bitte"* (KOORTS-sh-treh-keh, BIT-teh), and your driver will grumble and flip the meter to a fixed €4 rate (for a ride that would otherwise cost €7).

By Bike
Flat Berlin is a very bike-friendly city, but be careful—Berlin's motorists don't brake for bicyclists (and bicyclists don't brake for pedestrians). Fortunately, some roads and sidewalks have special red-painted bike lanes. Don't ride on the regular sidewalk—it's *verboten* (though locals do it all the time). Better yet, to get out of the city on two wheels, rent a bike, take it on the subway (requires extra €1.70 ticket) to the pleasant Potsdam/Wannsee parkland area west of town, then ride through forests and along skinny lakes to the vast Grünewald park, then back into the city. (Back during the Cold War, Grünewald was the Wessies' playground, while Ossies communed with nature at the Müggelsee east of town.) Bike shops can suggest a specific route.

Fat Tire Bikes rents good bikes at two handy locations—East (at the base of the TV Tower near Alexanderplatz—facing the entrance to the tower, go around to the right) and West (at Bahnhof Zoo—leaving the station onto Hardenbergplatz, turn left and walk 100 yards along the side of the station to the big bike sign). Both locations have the same hours and rates (€7/4 hours, €12/day, cheaper rate for two or more days, trekking and e-bikes also available, free luggage storage, Alexanderplatz location also has Internet access, daily May-Sept 9:30-20:00, March-April and Oct-Nov 9:30-18:00, shorter hours or by appointment only Dec-Feb, leave ID, tel. 030/2404-7991, www.berlinbikerental.com).

In eastern Berlin, **Take a Bike**—near the Friedrichstrasse S-Bahn station—is owned by a lovely Dutch-German couple who know a lot about bikes and have a huge inventory. They can help you find the perfect fit (3-gear bikes: €8/4 hours, €12.50/day, €19/2 days, slightly cheaper for longer rentals, more for better bikes, helmets, daily 9:30-19:00, Neustädtische Kirchstrasse 8, tel. 030/2065-4730, www.takeabike.de). To find it, leave the S-Bahn station via the Friedrichstrasse exit, turn right, go through a triangle-shaped square, and hang a left on Neustädtische Kirchstrasse.

All around town, simple **Rent a Bike** stands are outside countless shops, restaurants, and hotels. Most charge €10 to €12 a day, and are super-convenient, given their ubiquitous availability—just keep in mind that bikes rented through these stands don't necessarily come with the reliable quality, advice, helmets, or maps that are commonly offered by full-service rental shops.

Tours in Berlin

BUS TOURS
▲▲▲Hop-on, Hop-off Buses

Several companies offer the same routine: a €15-17 circuit of the city with unlimited hop-on, hop-off privileges all day (about 15 stops at the city's major sights) on buses with cursory narration in English and German by a live, sometimes tired guide or a boring recorded commentary in whatever language you want to dial up. In season, each company has buses running at least four times per hour. They are cheap and great for photography—and Berlin really lends itself to this kind of bus-tour orientation. You can hop off at any major tourist spot (Potsdamer Platz, Museum Island, Brandenburg Gate, the Kaiser Wilhelm Memorial Church, and so on). Go with a live guide rather than the recorded spiel (so you get a few current asides). When choosing seats, check the sun/shade situation—some buses are entirely topless, and others are entirely covered. My favorites are topless with a shaded covered section in the back (April-Oct daily 10:00-18:00, last bus leaves all stops at around 16:00, 2-hour loop; for specifics, look for brochures in your hotel lobby or at the TI). Keep your ticket so you can hop off and on (with the same company) all day. In winter (Nov-March), most buses come only twice an hour, and the last departure is at around 15:00. Brochures explain extras offered by each company.

BEX Sightseeing Berlin

This company offers a long list of bus tours (including hop-on, hop-off) in and around Berlin; their 2.5-hour "City Circle Yellow" tour is a good introduction. You can hop on and off at any of 18 stops, or simply stay on for the full tour (€24, ticket good 2 days; 6/hour April-Oct daily 10:00-18:00, Fri-Sat until 19:00; Nov-March daily until 17:00; recorded English commentary provided over earphones, departs from Ku'damm 216, buy ticket on bus, tel. 030/880-4190, www.berlinerstadtrundfahrten.de).

City Bus #100

For do-it-yourselfers, Berlin's city bus #100 is a cheap, quick, workable alternative to the commercial hop-on, hop-off bus tours—and you can follow along with my self-guided bus tour on page 739.

▲▲▲WALKING TOURS

Berlin's fascinating and complex recent history can be challenging to appreciate on your own, making the city an ideal place to explore with a walking tour. Equal parts historian and entertainer, a good Berlin tour guide makes the city's dynamic story come to life.

But unlike many other European countries, Germany has no regulations controlling who can give city tours. This can make guide quality hit-or-miss, ranging from brilliant history buffs who've lived in Berlin for years while pursuing their PhDs, to new arrivals who memorize a script and start leading tours after being in town for just a couple of weeks. In general you have the best odds of landing a great guide by using one of the more established companies I recommend in this section.

Most outfits offer walks that are variations on the same themes: general **introductory** walk, **Third Reich** walk (Hitler and Nazi sites), and day trips to **Potsdam** and the **Sachsenhausen Concentration Camp Memorial**. Most tours cost about €12-15 and last about three to four hours (longer for the side-trips to Potsdam and Sachsenhausen—for details, see the next chapter); public-transit tickets and entrances to sights are extra. I've included some basic descriptions for each company, but for details—including prices and specific schedules—see the various websites or look for brochures in town (widely available at TIs, hotel reception desks, and many cafés and shops).

Brewer's Berlin Tours

Specializing in longer, more in-depth walks that touch on the entire span of Berlin's past, this company was started by the late, great Terry Brewer, who once worked for the British diplomatic service in East Berlin. Terry left the company to his guides, a group of historians who get very excited about Berlin. Their in-depth tours through the city are intimate, relaxed, and can flex with your in-

Berlin at a Glance

▲▲▲**German History Museum** The ultimate swing through Germany's tumultuous story. **Hours:** Daily 10:00-18:00. See page 774.

▲▲▲**Pergamon Museum** World-class museum of classical antiquities on Museum Island, partially closed through 2019 (including its famous Pergamon Altar). **Hours:** Daily 10:00-18:00, Thu until 20:00. See page 769.

▲▲▲**Reichstag** Germany's historic parliament building, topped with a striking modern dome you can climb (reservations required). **Hours:** Daily 8:00-24:00, last entry at 22:00. See page 741.

▲▲▲**Brandenburg Gate** One of Berlin's most famous landmarks, a massive columned gateway, at the former border of East and West. **Hours:** Always open. See page 746.

▲▲**Memorial to the Murdered Jews of Europe** Holocaust memorial with almost 3,000 symbolic pillars, plus an exhibition about Hitler's Jewish victims. **Hours:** Memorial always open; information center open Tue-Sun 10:00-20:00, Oct-March until 19:00, closed Mon. See page 749.

▲▲**Unter den Linden** Leafy boulevard through the heart of former East Berlin, lined with some of the city's top sights. **Hours:** Always open. See page 752.

▲▲**Neues Museum** Egyptian antiquities collection (on Museum Island) and proud home of the exquisite 3,000-year-old bust of Queen Nefertiti. **Hours:** Daily 10:00-18:00, Thu until 20:00. See page 770.

▲▲**Gendarmenmarkt** Inviting square bounded by twin churches (one with a fine German history exhibit), a chocolate shop, and a concert hall. **Hours:** Always open. See page 776.

▲▲**Topography of Terror** Chilling exhibit documenting the Nazi perpetrators, built on the site of the former Gestapo/SS headquarters. **Hours:** Daily 10:00-20:00. See page 779.

▲▲**Museum of the Wall at Checkpoint Charlie** Kitschy but moving museum with stories of brave Cold War escapes, near the former site of the famous East-West border checkpoint; the surrounding street scene is almost as interesting. **Hours:** Daily 9:00-22:00. See page 784.

▲▲**Jewish Museum Berlin** Engaging, accessible museum celebrating Jewish culture, in a highly conceptual building. **Hours:** Daily 10:00-20:00, Mon until 22:00. See page 785.

▲▲Gemäldegalerie Germany's top collection of 13th- through 18th-century European paintings, featuring Holbein, Dürer, Cranach, Van der Weyden, Rubens, Hals, Rembrandt, Vermeer, Velázquez, Raphael, and more. **Hours:** Tue-Fri 10:00-18:00, Thu until 20:00, Sat-Sun 11:00-18:00, closed Mon. See page 805.

▲▲Berlin Wall Memorial A "docu-center" with videos and displays, several outdoor exhibits, and lone surviving stretch of an intact Wall section. **Hours:** Visitor Center April-Oct Tue-Sun 9:30-19:00, Nov-March until 18:00, closed Mon; outdoor areas accessible 24 hours daily. See page 794.

▲▲Prenzlauer Berg Lively, colorful neighborhood with hip cafés, restaurants, boutiques, and street life. **Hours:** Always open. See page 798.

▲Old National Gallery German paintings, mostly from the Romantic Age. **Hours:** Tue-Sun 10:00-18:00, Thu until 20:00, closed Mon. See page 772.

▲DDR Museum Quirky collection of communist-era artifacts. **Hours:** Daily 10:00-20:00, Sat until 22:00. See page 776.

▲New Synagogue Largest prewar synagogue in Berlin, damaged in World War II, with a rebuilt facade and modest museum. **Hours:** March-Oct Sun-Mon 10:00-20:00, Tue-Thu 10:00-18:00, Fri 10:00-17:00—until 14:00 in March and Oct; Nov-Feb Sun-Thu 10:00-18:00, Fri 10:00-14:00; closed Sat year-round. See page 792.

▲Potsdamer Platz The "Times Square" of old Berlin, long a postwar wasteland, now rebuilt with huge glass skyscrapers, an underground train station, and—covered with a huge canopy—the Sony Center mall. **Hours:** Always open. See page 802.

▲Deutsche Kinemathek Film and TV Museum An entertaining look at German film and TV, from *Metropolis* to Dietrich to Nazi propaganda to the present day. **Hours:** Tue-Sun 10:00-18:00, Thu until 20:00, closed Mon. See page 803.

▲Kaiser Wilhelm Memorial Church Evocative destroyed church in heart of the former West Berlin, with modern annex. **Hours:** Church—daily 9:00-19:00; Memorial Hall in bombed tower—Mon-Fri 10:00-18:00, Sat 10:00-17:30, shorter hours Sun. See page 811.

▲Käthe Kollwitz Museum The black-and-white art of the Berlin artist who conveyed the suffering of her city's stormiest century. **Hours:** Daily 11:00-18:00. See page 812.

terests. Their Best of Berlin introductory tour, billed at six hours, can last for eight (daily at 10:30). They also do a shorter 3.5-hour tour (free, tip expected, daily at 13:00) and an all-day Potsdam tour (Wed and Sat, May-Oct). All tours depart from Bandy Brooks ice cream shop at the Friedrichstrasse S-Bahn station (tel. 030/2248-7435, mobile 0177-388-1537, www.brewersberlintours.com).

Insider Tour

This well-regarded company runs the full gamut of itineraries: introductory walk (daily), Third Reich, Cold War, Jewish Berlin, Sachsenhausen, and Potsdam, as well as pub crawls and a day trip to Dresden. Their tours have two meeting points (some tours convene at both, others at just one—check the schedule): in the West at the McDonald's across from Bahnhof Zoo, and in the East at AM to PM Bar at the Hackescher Markt S-Bahn station (tel. 030/692-3149, www.insidertour.com).

Original Berlin Walks

Their flagship introductory walk, Discover Berlin, offers a good overview in four hours (daily year-round, meet at 10:00 at Bahnhof Zoo, April-Oct also daily at 13:30). They offer a Third Reich walking tour (4/week in summer); tours to Potsdam and Sachsenhausen; and themed walks on Jewish Life in Berlin, Cold War Berlin, and Queer Berlin (each 1/week April-Oct only). Readers of this book get a €1 discount per tour in 2015. All tours meet at the taxi stand in front of the Bahnhof Zoo train station; the Discover Berlin, Jewish Life, and Sachsenhausen tours also have a second departure point opposite the Hackescher Markt S-Bahn station, outside the Weihenstephaner restaurant (tour info: tel. 030/301-9194, www.berlinwalks.de).

Berlin Underground Association
(Berliner Unterwelten Verein)

Much of Berlin's history lies beneath the surface, and this group has an exclusive agreement with the city to explore and research what is hidden underground. Their one-of-a-kind Dark Worlds tour of a WWII air-raid bunker features a chilling explanation of the air war over Berlin (Thu-Sun at 11:00 and Mon at 11:00 and 13:00). The From Flak Towers to Mountains of Debris tour enters the Humboldthain air defense tower (Thu, Sat, Mon, and Tue at 15:00). The Subways and Bunkers in the Cold War tour visits a completely stocked and fully functional nuclear emergency bunker in former West Berlin (Thu-Sun at 13:00). Additional tour times and days are added in summer; check the schedule online (tours generally cost €10-11 and last about 1.5 hours). Meet in the hall of the Gesundbrunnen U-Bahn/S-Bahn station—follow signs to the

Humboldthain/Brunnenstrasse exit, and walk up the stairs to their office (tel. 030/4991-0517, www.berliner-unterwelten.de).

BERLIN

Alternative Berlin Tours

Specializing in cutting-edge street culture and art, this company emphasizes the bohemian chic that flavors the city's ever-changing urban scene. Their basic three-hour tour (daily at 11:00, 13:00, and 15:00) is tip-based; other tours cost €12-20 (all tours meet at Starbucks on Alexanderplatz under the TV Tower, mobile 0162-819-8264, www.alternativeberlin.com).

"Free" Tours

You'll see companies advertising supposedly "free" introductory tours all over town. Designed for and popular with students (free is good), it's a business model that has spread across Europe: English-speaking students (often Aussies and Americans) deliver a memorized script before a huge crowd lured in by the promise of a free tour. What the customers don't know is that the guide must turn over about €3 per person to the company, so tour leaders expect to be "tipped in paper" (€5 minimum per person is encouraged). The "free" intro tour is then used to push other tours that do charge a fee. While the guides can be highly entertaining, the better ones typically move on to more serious tour companies before long. These tours are fine for poor students with little interest in real history. But as with many things, when it comes to walking tours, you get what you pay for.

The "free" tour companies also offer **pub crawls** that are wildly popular with visiting college students. For details, see page 818.

Local Guides

Berlin guides are generally independent contractors who work with the various tour companies (like those listed here). Many of them are Americans who came to town as students and history buffs, fell in love with the city, and now earn their living as guides. Some lead private tours on their own (generally charging around €50-60/hour or €200-300/day, confirm by email when booking). The following guides are all good: **Nick Jackson** (an archaeologist and historian who makes museums come to life, mobile 0171-537-8768, www.jacksonsberlintours.com, info@jacksonsberlintours.com, nick.jackson@berlin.de); **Lee Evans** (makes 20th-century Germany a thriller, mobile 0177-423-5307, lee.evans@berlin.de); and **Bernhard Schlegelmilch** (mobile 0176-6422-9119, www.steubentoursberlin.com, info@steubentoursberlin.com).

BIKE TOURS
Fat Tire Bike Tours
Choose among five different tours, which run (except where noted) from April through October (most €24, 4-6 hours, 6-10 miles): **City Tour** (March-Nov daily at 11:00, May-Sept also daily at 16:00, Dec-Feb Wed and Sat at 11:00), **Berlin Wall Tour** (Mon, Thu, Sat, and Sun at 10:30), **Third Reich Tour** (Wed, Fri, Sat, and Sun at 10:30), **"Raw" Tour** (countercultural, creative aspects of contemporary Berlin, Tue, Fri, and Sun at 10:30), and **Gardens and Palaces of Potsdam Tour** (€46, Wed, Sat, and Sun at 10:00; also on Fri June-Aug). For any tour, meet at the TV Tower at Alexanderplatz (reserve ahead except for City Tour, tel. 030/2404-7991, www.fattirebiketours.com).

BOAT TOURS
Spree River Cruises
Several boat companies offer one-hour, €13 trips up and down the river. A relaxing hour on one of these boats can be time and money well spent. You'll listen to excellent English audioguides, see lots of wonderful new government-commissioned architecture, and enjoy the lively park action fronting the river. Boats leave from various docks that cluster near the bridge at the Berlin Cathedral (just off Unter den Linden). I enjoyed  the Historical Sightseeing Cruise from **Stern und Kreisschiffahrt** (mid-March-Nov daily 10:00-19:00, leaves from Nikolaiviertel Dock—cross bridge from Berlin Cathedral toward Alexanderplatz and look right, tel. 030/536-3600, www.sternundkreis.de). Confirm that the boat you choose comes with English commentary.

TOUR PACKAGES FOR STUDENTS
Andy Steves (Rick's son) runs **WSA Europe**, offering three-day and longer guided and unguided packages—including accommodations, sightseeing, and unique local experiences—for budget travelers across 11 top European cities, including Berlin (from €99, see www.wsaeurope.com for details).

Bus #100 Tour

FROM BAHNHOF ZOO TO ALEXANDERPLATZ

While hop-on, hop-off bus tours are a great value, Berlin's city bus #100 laces together the major sights in a kind of poor man's self-guided bus tour. Bus #100 stops at Bahnhof Zoo, the Berlin Zoo, Victory Column, Reichstag, Unter den Linden, Brandenburg Gate, Pergamon Museum, and Alexanderplatz. An electronic board inside the bus displays the upcoming stop. As a basic, single bus ticket is good for up to two hours of travel in one direction and buses leave every few minutes, hopping on and off works great. The #100 route is smooth until the Reichstag, but from there, construction projects can cause random detours, making it frustrating to follow the last part of this route (which is better on foot anyway).

Starting in the West from Bahnhof Zoo, here's a quick review of what you'll see: Leaving the train station, you'll spot the bombed-out hulk of the **Kaiser Wilhelm Memorial Church,** with its jagged spire and postwar sister church. Then, on the left, the elephant gates mark the entrance to the venerable and much-loved **Berlin Zoo** and its aquarium. After a left turn, you cross the canal and pass Berlin's **embassy row.** The first interesting embassy is Mexico's, with columns that seem to move as you're driving by (how do they do that?). The big turquoise wall marks the communal home of all five Nordic embassies. This building is very "green," run entirely on solar power.

The bus then enters the 400-acre **Tiergarten** park, packed with cycling paths, joggers, and—on hot days—nude sunbathers. Straight ahead, the **Victory Column** (Siegessäule; with the gilded angel) towers above this vast city park that was once a royal hunting ground. A block beyond the Victory Column (on the left) is the 18th-century late-Rococo **Bellevue Palace.** Formerly the official residence of the Prussian (and later German) crown prince, and at one time a Nazi VIP guesthouse, it's now the residence of the federal president (whose power is mostly ceremonial—the chancellor wields the real clout). If the flag's out, he's in.

Driving along the Spree River (on the left), you'll see buildings of the **national government.** The huge brick "brown snake" complex (across the river) was built to house government workers—but it didn't sell, so now its apartments are available to anyone. A metal Henry Moore sculpture entitled *Butterfly* (a.k.a. "The Drinker's Liver") floats in front of the slope-roofed House of World Cultures (Berliners have nicknamed this building "the pregnant oyster" and "Jimmy Carter's smile"). The modern tower (next, on the left) is a carillon with 68 bells (from 1987). Through the trees on the left you'll see the **Chancellery**—Germany's "White House." The big open space is the **Platz der Republik,** where the Victory Column (which you passed earlier) stood until Hitler moved it. The Haupt-bahnhof (Berlin's vast main train station, marked by its tall tower with the *DB* sign) is across the field between the Chancellery and the **Reichstag** (Germany's parliament—the old building with the new dome, described on next page).

The next string of attractions are best seen on foot (see the "Best of Berlin Walk," next). But if you stay on the bus, you'll zip by them in this order:

Unter den Linden, the main east-west thoroughfare, stretches from the **Brandenburg Gate** (behind you) through Berlin's historic core (ahead) to the TV Tower in the distance (Alexanderplatz, where this bus finishes). You'll pass the **Russian Embassy** and the Aeroflot airline office (right). Crossing **Friedrichstrasse,** look right for a Fifth Avenue-style conga line of big, glitzy department stores. Later, on the left, are the **German History Museum, Museum Island**, and the **Berlin Cathedral;** across from these (on the right) is the construction site of the **Humboldt-Forum Berliner Schloss** (with the Humboldt-Box visitors center). Then you'll rumble to a final stop at what was the center of East Berlin in communist times: **Alexanderplatz.**

Best of Berlin Walk

This two-mile, self-guided walk starts in front of the Reichstag, takes you under the Brandenburg Gate and down Unter den Linden, and finishes up on Alexanderplatz, near the TV Tower. I describe minor sights along the way, and also point out major ones that you'll want to see later or by taking a break from the walk (find their details later in the chapter, under "Sights in Eastern Berlin"). If you have just one day in Berlin, or want a good orientation to the city, simply follow this walk (two hours at a brisk pace, not counting museum visits), and you'll have seen the core of Berlin and its most important sights. If you have more time and want to use this walk as a spine for your sightseeing, entering sights and museums as you go, consider doing Part 1 and Part 2 on different days. Part 1 goes from the Reichstag and takes you partway down Unter den Linden, with stops at the Brandenburg Gate, Memorial to the Murdered Jews of Europe, and Friedrichstrasse, the glitzy shopping street, along the way. Part 2 continues down Unter den Linden, from Bebelplatz to Alexanderplatz, and features Museum Island and the Spree River, the Berlin Cathedral, and the iconic TV Tower. This walk can also be downloaded as a free Rick Steves audio tour; see page 12.

PART 1: THE REICHSTAG TO UNTER DEN LINDEN

During the Cold War, the Reichstag stood just inside the West Berlin side of the Wall. And even though it's been 25 years since the Wall came down, you may still feel a slight tingle down your spine as you walk across the former death strip, through the once *verboten* Brandenburg Gate, and into the former communist east.

• *Start your walk directly in front of the Reichstag building (see map on page 742), at the big, grassy park called...*

Platz der Republik

Stand about 100 yards in front of the grand Reichstag building and spin left to survey the surroundings. At the **Reichstag U-Bahn stop** is a big federal building overlooking the Spree River. The huge **main train station** (Hauptbahnhof) is in the distance (see the tower marked *DB,* for Deutsche Bahn—the German rail company). Farther left is the mammoth white concrete-and-glass **Chancellery,** nicknamed the "washing machine" by Berliners for its hygienic, spin-cycle appearance. It's the office of Germany's most powerful person, the chancellor (currently Angela Merkel). To remind the chancellor whom he or she works for, Germany's Reichstag (housing the parliament) is about six feet taller than the Chancellery.

• *Dominating the Platz der Republik is a giant domed building, the...*

▲▲▲Reichstag

The parliament building—the heart of German democracy—has a short but complicated and emotional history. When it was inaugu-

rated in the 1890s, the last emperor, Kaiser Wilhelm II, disdainfully called it the "chatting home for monkeys" *(Reichsaffenhaus).* It was placed outside the city's old walls—far from the center of real power, the imperial palace. But it was from the Reichstag that the German Republic was proclaimed in 1918. Look above the door, surrounded by stone patches from WWII bomb damage, to see the motto and promise: *Dem Deutschen Volke* ("To the German People").

In 1933, this symbol of democracy nearly burned down. The Nazis—whose influence on the German political scene was on the rise—blamed a communist plot. A Dutch communist, Marinus van der Lubbe, was eventually convicted and guillotined for the crime. Others believed that Hitler himself planned the fire, using it as a handy excuse to frame the communists and grab power. Even though Van der Lubbe was posthumously pardoned by the Ger-

BERLIN

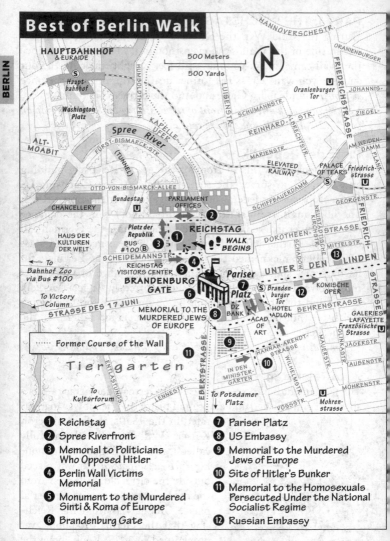

Best of Berlin Walk

500 Meters
500 Yards

1. Reichstag
2. Spree Riverfront
3. Memorial to Politicians Who Opposed Hitler
4. Berlin Wall Victims Memorial
5. Monument to the Murdered Sinti & Roma of Europe
6. Brandenburg Gate
7. Pariser Platz
8. US Embassy
9. Memorial to the Murdered Jews of Europe
10. Site of Hitler's Bunker
11. Memorial to the Homosexuals Persecuted Under the National Socialist Regime
12. Russian Embassy

man government in 2008, most modern historians concede that he most likely was guilty, and had acted alone—the timing was just incredibly fortuitous for the Nazis, who shrewdly used his deed to advance their cause.

The Reichstag was hardly used from 1933 to 1999. Despite the fact that the building had lost its symbolic value, Stalin ordered his troops to take the Reichstag from the Nazis no later than May 1, 1945 (the date of the workers' May Day parade in Moscow). More than 1,500 Nazi soldiers made their last stand here—extending

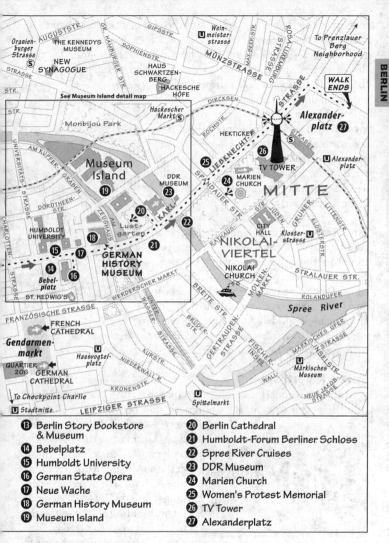

13 Berlin Story Bookstore & Museum
14 Bebelplatz
15 Humboldt University
16 German State Opera
17 Neue Wache
18 German History Museum
19 Museum Island

20 Berlin Cathedral
21 Humboldt-Forum Berliner Schloss
22 Spree River Cruises
23 DDR Museum
24 Marien Church
25 Women's Protest Memorial
26 TV Tower
27 Alexanderplatz

World War II by two days. On April 30, after fierce fighting on its rooftop, the Reichstag fell to the Red Army.

For the building's 101st birthday in 1995, the Bulgarian-American artist Christo wrapped it in silvery gold cloth. It was then wrapped again—in scaffolding—and rebuilt by British architect Lord Norman Foster into the new parliamentary home of the Bundestag (Germany's lower house, similar to the US House of Representatives). In 1999, the German parliament convened here for the first time in 66 years. To many Germans, the proud resurrection of the Reichstag symbolizes the end of a terrible chapter in their country's history.

The **glass cupola** rises 155 feet above the ground. Its two sloped ramps spiral 755 feet to the top for a grand view. Inside  the dome, a cone of 360 mirrors reflects natural light into the legislative chamber below. Lit from inside after dark, this gives Berlin a memorable nightlight. The environmentally friendly cone—with an opening at the top—also helps with air circulation, expelling stale air from the legislative chamber (no joke) and pulling in fresh, cool air.

Visitors with advance reservations can climb the spiral ramp up into that cupola. If you haven't booked a slot, you can cross the street to the white booth to check the screen showing available entry times for the next three days (for details on making reservations and visiting, including a self-guided dome tour, see page 763).

• *Facing the Reichstag, you can take a short side-trip to the river by circling around to the left of the building.*

Spree Riverfront

Admire the wonderful architecture incorporating the Spree River into the people's world. It's a poignant spot because this river was

once a symbol of division—the East German regime put nets underwater to stymie those desperate enough for freedom to swim to the West. When kings ruled Prussia, government buildings went right up to the water. But today, the city is incorporating the river thoughtfully into a people-friendly cityscape. From the Reichstag, a delightful riverside path leads around the curve, past "beach cafés," to the riverbank behind the Chancellery. For a slow, low-impact glide past this zone, consider a river cruise (see page 738; we'll pass the starting point—on Museum Island—later on this walk). The fine bridges symbolize the connection of East and West.

• *Back in front of the Reichstag, face the building and walk to the right. Near the road in front of the Reichstag, enmeshed in all the security apparatus and crowds, is a memorial of slate stones embedded in the ground.*

Memorial to Politicians Who Opposed Hitler

This row of slabs, which looks like a fancy slate bicycle rack, is a memorial to the 96 members of the Reichstag (the equivalent of our

members of Congress) who were persecuted and murdered because their politics didn't agree with Chancellor Hitler's. They were part of the Weimar Republic, the weak and ill-fated attempt at post-WWI democracy in Germany. These were the people who could have stopped Hitler...so they became his first victims. Each slate slab memorializes one man—his name, party (mostly KPD—Communists, and SPD—Social Democrats), and the date and location of his death—generally in concentration camps. (*KZ* stands for "concentration camp.") They are honored here, in front of the building in which they worked.

• *Walk along the side of the Reichstag, on busy Scheidemannstrasse, toward the rear of the building. At the intersection with Ebertstrasse, cross to the right (toward the park). Along a railing is a small memorial of white crosses. This is the...*

Berlin Wall Victims Memorial

This monument commemorates some of the East Berliners who died trying to cross the Wall. Many of them perished within

months of the Wall's construction on August 13, 1961. Most died trying to swim the river to freedom. The monument used to stand right on the Berlin Wall behind the Reichstag. Notice that the last person killed while trying to escape was 20-year-old Chris Guef-

froy, who died nine months before the Wall fell in 1989. (He was shot through the heart in no-man's land.) For more on the Wall, see "The Berlin Wall (and Its Fall)" sidebar on page 786.

• *Continue along Ebertstrasse (away from the Reichstag) for a few more steps and turn into the peaceful lane on the right (into Tiergarten park— more about it in a minute). Within a short distance, on your right, is the...*

Monument to the Murdered Sinti and Roma (Gypsies) of Europe

Unveiled in 2012, this memorial remembers the roughly 500,000 Sinti and Roma victims of the Holocaust. "Sinti" and "Roma" (the main tribes and politically correct terms for the group more commonly called "Gypsies") were as persecuted by the Nazis as were the Jews. And they lost the same percentage of their population to Hitler. The opaque glass wall, with a timeline in English and German, traces the Nazi abuse and atrocities.

Enter through the rusty steel portal. On the other side is a circular reflecting pool surrounded by stone slabs, some containing the names of the death camps where hundreds of thousands of Sinti and Roma perished. In the water along the rim of the pool is the heart-wrenching poem "Auschwitz," by composer and writer Santino Spinelli, an Italian Roma. Dissonant music evoking the tragedy of the Gypsy genocide adds to the atmosphere.

"Do you speak English?" beggar ladies—bussed in by traffickers from Romania—hit up visitors here at their own memorial. But it's a chance to appreciate, or at least ponder, the plight and struggles of a fragmented community with a nomadic heritage that refuses to conform to modern norms and has no organizational center or effective leadership.

• *Retrace your steps to Ebertstrasse and turn right, toward the busy intersection dominated by the imposing Brandenburg Gate. You're at one edge of...*

Tiergarten Park

Take this chance to get oriented. Facing the Brandenburg Gate is the park called Tiergarten (considered the "green lungs of Berlin"); its center is marked by the Victory Column (Siegessäule), which originally stood where you started this tour. Hitler had the column moved in the 1930s to its present position in the Tiergarten as the first step in creating the grandiose axis he envisioned for postwar Berlin. (For more on the Tiergarten and Victory Column, see page 800.)

Now face the Brandenburg Gate. It stands at one end of Unter den Linden, the Champs-Elysées of Berlin. In the distance, the red-and-white spire of the TV Tower marks the end of this walk (which, from here, is essentially a straight line with a few little detours).

• *As you cross the street toward the gate, notice the double row of cobblestones beneath your feet—it goes about 25 miles around the city, marking where the Wall used to stand. Then walk under the gate that, for a sad generation, was part of a wall that divided this city.*

▲▲▲Brandenburg Gate (Brandenburger Tor)

The historic Brandenburg Gate (1791) was the grandest—and is the last survivor—of 14 gates in Berlin's old city wall (this one led to the neighboring city of Brandenburg). The gate was the symbol of Prussian Berlin—and later the symbol of a divided Berlin.

The Brandenburg Gate, Arch of Peace

Two hundred years ago, the Brandenburg Gate was designed as an arch of peace, crowned by the Goddess of Peace and showing Mars sheathing his sword. The Nazis misused it as a gate of triumph and aggression. Today a Room of Silence, built into the gate, is dedicated to the peaceful message of the original Brandenburg Gate (daily 11:00-18:00, shorter hours in winter). As you consider the history of Berlin in this silent and empty room—which is carefully not dedicated to any particular religion—you may be inspired to read the prayer of the United Nations:

"Oh Lord, our planet Earth is only a small star in space. It is our duty to transform it into a planet whose creatures are no longer tormented by war, hunger, and fear, no longer senselessly divided by race, color, and ideology. Give us courage and strength to begin this task today so that our children and our children's children shall one day carry the name of man with pride."

It's crowned by a majestic four-horse chariot, with the Goddess of Peace at the reins. Napoleon took this statue to the Louvre in Paris in 1806. After the Prussians defeated Napoleon and got it back (1813), she was renamed the Goddess of Victory.

The gate sat unused, part of a sad circle dance called the Wall, for more than 25 years. Now postcards all over town show the

ecstatic day—November 9, 1989—when the world rejoiced at the sight of happy Berliners jamming the gate like flowers on a parade float. Pause a minute and think about struggles for freedom—past and present. (There's actually a special room built into the gate for this purpose—see the sidebar.) Around the gate, look at the information boards with pictures of how this area changed throughout the 20th century. There's a TI within the gate (S-Bahn: Brandenburger Tor).

The gate sits on a major boulevard running east to west through Berlin. The western segment, called Strasse des 17 Juni (named for a workers' uprising against the DDR government on June 17, 1953), stretches for four miles from the Brandenburg Gate and Victory Column to the Olympic Stadium. But we'll follow this city axis in the opposite direction, east, along Unter den Linden. The walk takes us into the core of old imperial Berlin and past the site where the palace of the Hohenzollern family, rulers of Prussia and then Germany, once stood. The palace is a phantom sight, long gone, but its occupants were responsible for just about all you'll see. Alexanderplatz, which marks the end of this walk, is near the base of the giant TV Tower hovering in the distance.

• *Pass all the way through the gate and stand in the middle of...*

▲Pariser Platz

"Parisian Square," so named after the Prussians defeated Napoleon in 1813, was once filled with important government buildings—all bombed to smithereens in World War II. For decades, it was an unrecognizable, deserted no-man's-land—cut off from both East and West by the Wall. But now it's rebuilt, and the banks, hotels, and embassies that were here before the bombing have reclaimed their original places—with a few additions, including a palace of coffee: Starbucks. The winners of World War II enjoy this prime real estate: The American, French, British, and Soviet (now Russian) embassies are all on or near this square.

As you face the gate, to your right is the French Embassy, and to your left is the **US Embassy.** This reopened in its historic pre-WWII location in 2008. (While Germany was divided, the embassy had been relocated to Bonn, with only a "mission" in West Berlin, as the US refused to officially recognize Berlin as the capital of East Germany.) The rebuilt building has been controversial: For safety's sake, Uncle Sam wanted more of a security zone around the building, but the Germans wanted to keep Pariser Platz a welcoming people zone. (Throughout the world, American embassies are the most fortified buildings in town.) The compromise: The extra security the US wanted is built into the structure. Easy-on-the-eyes barriers keep potential car bombs at a distance, and its front door is on the side farthest from the Brandenburg Gate.

Turn your back to the gate. On the right, jutting into the square, is the ritzy **Hotel Adlon**, long called home by visiting stars and VIPs. In its heyday, it hosted such notables as Charlie Chaplin, Albert Einstein, and Greta Garbo. It was the setting for Garbo's most famous line, "I vant to be alone," uttered in the film *Grand Hotel.* Damaged by the Russians just after World War II, the original hotel was closed with the construction of the nearby Wall in 1961 and later demolished. Today's grand Adlon was rebuilt in 1997. It was here that Michael Jackson shocked millions by dangling his baby, Blanket, over the railing (second balcony up).

• *Between the hotel and the US Embassy are two buildings worth a quick visit: the DZ Bank building (by Frank Gehry) and the glassy Academy of Arts. Enjoy the fun-loving scene on the square, and when you're ready to move on, work your way over to these two buildings; we'll enter both, then leave Pariser Platz through the Academy of Arts.*

DZ Bank Building: This building's architect, Frank Gehry, is famous for Bilbao's Guggenheim Museum, Prague's Dancing House, Seattle's Experience Music Project, Chicago's Millennium Park, and Los Angeles' Walt Disney Concert Hall. Gehry fans might be surprised at the bank building's low profile. Structures on Pariser Platz are designed so as not to draw attention away from the Brandenburg Gate. But to get your fix of wild and colorful Gehry, step into the lobby. Built in 2001 as an office complex and conference center, its undulating interior is like a big, slithery fish. Gehry explained, "The form of the fish is the best example of movement. I try to capture this movement in my buildings." For more of the architect's vision, read the nearby plaque.

• *Leaving the DZ Bank, turn right and head into the next building, the...*

Academy of Arts (Akademie der Künste): The glassy arcade is open daily (10:00-22:00, WC in basement, café serving light meals). Just past the café is the office where Albert Speer, Hitler's architect, planned the rebuilding of postwar Berlin into "Welthauptstadt Germania"—the grandiose "world capital" of Nazi Europe. Pass through the glass door to see Speer's favorite statue, *Prometheus Bound* (c. 1900). This is the kind of art that turned Hitler on: a strong, soldierly, vital man, enduring hardship for a greater cause. Anticipating the bombs, Speer had the statue bricked up in the basement here where it lay, undiscovered, until 1995.

This building provides a handy and interesting passage to the Holocaust memorial on the other side.

• *Exit the building out the back. Across the street, to the right, stretches the vast Holocaust memorial.*

▲▲Memorial to the Murdered Jews of Europe (Denkmal für die Ermordeten Juden Europas)

This Holocaust memorial, consisting of 2,711 gravestone-like pillars (called "stelae") and completed in 2005, was the first formal,

German government-sponsored Holocaust memorial. Using the word "murdered" in the title was intentional and a big deal. Germany, as a nation, was officially admitting to a crime. Jewish-American architect Peter Eisenman won the competition for the commission.

Cost and Hours: The memorial is free and always open. The information center is open Tue-Sun 10:00-20:00, Oct-March until 19:00, closed Mon year-round; last entry 45 minutes before closing, S-Bahn: Brandenburger Tor or Potsdamer Platz, tel. 030/2639-4336, www.stiftung-denkmal.de. The €4 audioguide augments the experience.

Visiting the Memorial: The pillars, made of hollow concrete, stand in a gently sunken area, which can be entered from any side. The number of pillars isn't symbolic of anything; it's simply how many fit on the provided land. The pillars are all about the same size, but of differing heights. The memorial's location—where the Wall once stood—is coincidental. Nazi propagandist Joseph Goebbels' bunker was discovered during the work and left buried under the northeast corner of the memorial.

Once you enter the memorial, notice that people seem to appear and disappear between the columns, and that no matter where you are, the exit always seems to be up. The memorial is thoughtfully lit at night and guarded.

The monument was criticized for focusing on just one of the groups targeted by the Nazis, but the German government has now erected memorials to other victims—such as the Roma/Sinti memorial we just visited, and a memorial to the regime's homosexual victims, also nearby (kitty-corner from where you entered the Jewish memorial and across Ebertstrasse, just inside the park). It's also been criticized because there's nothing intrinsically Jewish about it. Some were struck that there's no central gathering point or place for a ceremony. Like death, you enter it alone.

There is no one intended interpretation. Is it a symbolic cemetery, or an intentionally disorienting labyrinth? It's up to the visitor to derive the meaning, while pondering this horrible chapter in human history.

Memorial Information Center: The pondering takes place under the sky. For the learning, go under the field of concrete pillars to the state-of-the-art information center. Inside, a thought-provoking exhibit (well-explained in English) studies the Nazi system of extermination and humanizes the victims, while also providing space for silent reflection. In the Starting Hall, exhibits trace the historical context of the Nazi and WWII era,  while six portraits—representing the six million Jewish victims— look out on visitors. The Room of Dimensions has glowing boxes in the floor containing diaries, letters, and final farewells penned by Holocaust victims. The Room of Families presents case studies of 15 Jewish families from around Europe, to more fully convey the European Jewish experience. Remember: Behind these 15 stories are millions more tales of despair, tragedy, and survival. In the Room of Names, a continually running soundtrack lists the names

Imagining Hitler in the 21st Century

More than six decades after the end of World War II, the bunker where Hitler killed himself lies hidden underneath a Berlin parking lot. While the Churchill War Rooms are a major sight in London, no one wants to turn Hitler's final stronghold into a tourist attraction.

Germans tread lightly on their past. It took 65 years for the Germany History Museum to organize its first exhibit on the life of Hitler. Even then, the exhibit was careful not to give neo-Nazis any excuse to celebrate—even the size of the Hitler portraits was kept to a minimum.

The image of Hitler has been changing in Germany. No longer is he exclusively an evil mass murderer; sometimes he is portrayed as a nervous wreck, such as in the 2004 film *Downfall*, or as an object of derision. He's even a wax figure in the Berlin branch of Madame Tussauds.

But 21st-century Germans still treat the subject with extraordinary sensitivity. The Bavarian state won't allow any version of Hitler's political manifesto—*Mein Kampf*—to be published in German within Germany, even one annotated by historians (this may soon change, though, as the government's 70-year copyright expires at the end of 2015). Any visit to Hitler's mountain retreat in Berchtesgaden includes a stop at the Nazi Documentation Center, where visitors see Nazi artifacts carefully placed in their historical context.

Many visitors to Berlin are curious about Hitler sites, but few artifacts of that dark period survive. The German Resistance Memorial is worthwhile, but not really geared toward non-German visitors (see page 801). Hitler's bunker is completely erased from view, though the location is marked by a small information board. The best way to learn about Hitler sites is to take a Third Reich tour offered by one of the many local walking-tour companies (see "Tours in Berlin," page 732), or to visit the Topography of Terror, a fascinating exhibit located in a rebuilt hall on the same spot where the SS and Gestapo headquarters once stood (see page 778).

It's a balancing act, and Germans are still in the process of figuring out how to confront their regrettable past.

and brief biographical sketches of Holocaust victims; reading the names of all those murdered would take more than six and a half years. The Room of Sites documents some 220 different places of genocide. You'll also find exhibits about other Holocaust monuments and memorials, a searchable database of victims, and a video archive of interviews with survivors.

• *Wander through the gray pillars, but eventually emerge on the corner with the Information Center. Cross Hannah–Arendt–Strasse and go a half block farther. Walk alongside the rough parking lot (on the left side of street) to the info plaque over the...*

Site of Hitler's Bunker

You're standing atop the buried remains of the *Führerbunker*. In early 1945, as Allied armies advanced on Berlin and Nazi Germany lay in ruins, Hitler and his staff retreated to a bunker complex behind the former Reich Chancellery. He stayed there for two months. It was here, as the Soviet army tightened its noose on the capital, that Hitler and Eva Braun, his wife of less than 48 hours, committed suicide on April 30, 1945. A week later, the war in Europe was over. The info board presents a detailed cutaway illustration of the bunker complex plus a timeline tracing its history and ultimate fate (the roof was removed and the bunker filled with dirt, then covered over).

• *From here, you can visit the next memorial (which is important, but visually underwhelming and a bit of a detour), or you can continue the walk. To do either, first head back to Hannah-Arendt-Strasse. To rejoin the walk, turn right, go one block, then head up Wilhelmstrasse back to Unter den Linden. To see the memorial, go left one block at Hannah-Arendt-Strasse, cross the street, and head down a path into Tiergarten park. There, look for a large, dark gray concrete box...*

Memorial to the Homosexuals Persecuted Under the National Socialist Regime

At this stark memorial find the small window through which you can watch a black-and-white film loop of same-sex couples kissing. The message: Life and love are precious, regardless of who we are. The law against homosexuality in Germany had been on the books since 1850, and Hitler enforced it with brutality. Signage by the sidewalk explains the memorial in English and German.

• *Now return to Unter den Linden by backtracking a couple of blocks down Hannah-Arendt-Strasse, then turning left on Wilhelmstrasse. Because Wilhelmstrasse was a main street of the German government during WWII, it was obliterated by bombs, and all its buildings are new today. The pedestrianized part of the street is home to the British Embassy. The fun, purple color of its wall is the colors of the Union Jack mixed together.*

When you get back on Unter den Linden, stand in the median, in front of Hotel Adlon.

▲▲Unter den Linden

Unter den Linden is the heart of the former East Berlin. In the good old days, this was one of Europe's grand boulevards. In the 15th century, this carriageway led from the palace to the hunting grounds (today's big Tiergarten). In the 17th century, Hohen-

zollern princes and princesses moved in and built their palaces here so they could be near the Prussian king.

Named centuries ago for its thousands of linden trees, this was the most elegant street of Prussian Berlin before Hitler's time, and the main drag of East Berlin after his reign. Hitler replaced the venerable trees—many 250 years old—with Nazi flags. Popular discontent drove him to replant the trees.

Today, Unter den Linden is no longer a depressing Cold War cul-de-sac, and its pre-Hitler strolling café ambience has returned. It is divided, roughly at Friedrichstrasse, into a business section, which stretches toward the Brandenburg Gate, and a cultural section, which spreads out toward Alexanderplatz. Frederick the Great wanted to have culture, mainly the opera and the university, closer to his palace and to keep business (read: banks) farther away, near the city walls.

• *Begin walking toward the giant TV Tower. In front of Hotel Adlon is the Brandenburger Tor S-Bahn station. Cover a bit of Unter den Linden underground by climbing down its steps and walking along the platform.*

Ghost Subway Station: The Brandenburger Tor S-Bahn station is one of Berlin's former ghost subway stations. During the

Cold War, most underground train tunnels were simply blocked at the border. But a few Western lines looped through the East and then back into the West. To make a little hard Western cash, the Eastern government rented the use of these tracks to the West, but all but one of the stations in East Berlin were strictly off-limits. For 28 years, these stations were unused, as Western trains slowly passed through and passengers saw only eerie DDR (East German) guards and lots of cobwebs. Literally within days of the fall of the Wall, these stations were reopened, and today they are a time warp, looking much as they did when built in 1931, with dreary old green tiles and original signage on ticket kiosks.

• *Walk along the track (the walls are lined with historic photos of the Reichstag through the ages) and exit on the other side, to the right. You'll pop out at the Russian Embassy's front yard.*

Russian Embassy: This was the first big postwar building project in East Berlin. It's built in the powerful, simplified Neoclassical style that Stalin liked. While not as important now as it was a few years ago, it's as immense as ever. It flies the Russian white, blue, and red. Find the hammer-and-sickle motif decorating the window frames—a reminder of the days when Russia was the USSR.

• *At the next intersection (Glinkastrasse), cross to the other side of Unter den Linden. At #40 is the entertaining...*

Berlin Story Bookstore and Museum: Berlin Story is two shops side by side (on the left are Cold War souvenirs and the museum; on the right, the bookstore). The bookshop has just about the best range anywhere of English-language titles on Berlin (Mon-Sat 10:00-19:00, Sun 10:00-18:00). They have also created a beefy little museum covering the main points of modern Berlin history and a video about the Wall. It offers a vivid swing through the tumultuous story of this city (€5, or €4 with this book, includes good audioguide, daily 10:00-20:00, until 19:00 in Jan-Feb).

• *A few steps farther down is the...*

Intersection of Unter den Linden and Friedrichstrasse: This is perhaps the most central crossroads in Berlin. And for several years, it will be a mess as Berlin builds a new connection in its already extensive subway system. All over Berlin, you'll see big, colorful **water pipes** running aboveground. Wherever there are large construction projects, streets are laced with these drainage pipes. Berlin's high water table means that any new basement comes with lots of pumping out.

Looking at the jaunty DDR-style pedestrian lights at this intersection is a reminder that very little of the old East survives. Construction has been a theme since the Wall came down. The West lost no time in consuming the East; consequently, some have felt a wave of *Ost*-algia for the old days of East Berlin. At election time, a surprising number of formerly East Berlin voters still opt for the extreme left party, which has ties to the bygone Communist Party—although the East-West divide is no longer at the forefront of most voters' minds.

One symbol of that communist era has been given a reprieve: the DDR-style pedestrian lights you'll see along Unter den Linden (and throughout much of the former East Berlin). The perky red and green men—called *Ampelmännchen*—were recently threatened with replacement by far less jaunty Western-style signs. But, after a 10-year court battle, the wildly popular DDR signals were kept after all.

When the little green *Ampelmännchen* says you can go, cross the construction zone that has taken over this stretch of Unter den Linden, and note the Ampelmann souvenir store across the street.

• *Before continuing down Unter den Linden, look farther down...*

Friedrichstrasse: Before the war, this zone was the heart of Berlin. In the 1920s, Berlin was famous for its anything-goes love of life. This was the cabaret drag, a springboard to stardom for young and vampy entertainers like Marlene Dietrich. (Born in 1901, Dietrich starred in the first major German talkie—*The Blue Angel*—and then headed straight to Hollywood.) Over the last few years, this boulevard—lined with super-department stores (such as Galeries Lafayette) and big-time hotels (such as the Hilton and Regent)—is attempting to replace western Berlin's Ku'damm as the grand commerce-and-café boulevard of Berlin. More recently, western Berlin is retaliating with some new stores of its own. And so far, Friedrichstrasse gets little more than half the pedestrian traffic that Ku'damm gets in the West. Why? Locals complain that this area has no daily life—no supermarkets, not much ethnic street food, and so on.

Consider detouring to Galeries Lafayette, with its cool marble-and-glass, waste-of-space interior (Mon-Sat 10:00-20:00, closed Sun; check out the vertical garden on its front wall, belly up to its amazing ground-floor viewpoint, or have lunch in its recommended basement food court). The short walk there along Friedrichstrasse provides some of Berlin's most jarring old-versus-new architectural contrasts—be sure to look up as you stroll.

• *If you continued down Friedrichstrasse, you'd wind up at the sights listed under "South of Unter den Linden," on page 776—including Checkpoint Charlie (a 10-minute walk from here).*

We've reached the end of Part 1 of the Best of Berlin Walk. This is a good place to take a break, if you wish, and pick up Part 2 another time. But if you're up for ambling on, head down Unter den Linden a few more blocks, past the large equestrian statue of Frederick the Great, then turn right into Bebelplatz.

PART 2: BEBELPLATZ TO ALEXANDERPLATZ

• *Starting at Bebelplatz, head to the center of the square, and find the glass window in the pavement. We'll begin with some history and a spin tour.*

Bebelplatz

For centuries, up until the early 1700s, Prussia had been likened to a modern-day Sparta—it was all about its military. Voltaire famously said, "Whereas some states have an army, the Prussian army has a state." But Frederick the Great—who ruled from 1740 to 1786—established Prussia not just as a military power, but also as a cultural and intellectual heavyweight. This square was the center of the cultural capital that Frederick envisioned. His grand palace was just down the street (explained later).

Imagine that it's 1760. Pan around the square to see Frederick's contributions to Prussian culture. Everything is draped with Greek-inspired Prussian pomp.

Sure, Prussia was a modern-day Sparta. But Frederick also built an **"Athens on the Spree"**—an enlightened and cultured society.

To visually survey the square, start with the university across the street and spin counterclockwise:

Humboldt University, across Unter den Linden, is one of Europe's greatest. Marx and Lenin (not the brothers or the sisters) studied here, as did the Grimms (both brothers) and more than two dozen Nobel Prize winners. Einstein, who was Jewish, taught here until taking a spot at Princeton in 1932 (smart guy). Used-book merchants set up their tables in front of the university.

Turn 90 degrees to the left. The former **state library** (labeled *Juristische Fakultät*) is where Vladimir Lenin studied law during much of his exile from Russia. Bombed in WWII, the library was rebuilt by the East German government in the original style only because Lenin studied here. If you climb to the second floor of the library and go through the door opposite the stairs, you'll see a 1968 vintage stained-glass window depicting Lenin's life's work with almost biblical reverence. On the ground floor is Tim's Espressobar, a great little café with light food, student prices, and garden seating (€3 plates, Mon-Fri 8:00-20:00, Sat 9:00-17:00, closed Sun, handy WC).

Next to the library, the square is closed by one of Berlin's swankiest lodgings—**Hotel de Rome,** housed in a historic bank building with a spa and lap pool fitted into the former vault.

The round, Catholic **St. Hedwig's Church,** nicknamed the "upside-down teacup," is a statement of religious and cultural tolerance. The pragmatic Frederick the Great wanted to encourage the integration of Catholic Silesians after his empire annexed their region in 1742, and so the first Catholic church since the Reformation was built in Berlin. (St. Hedwig is the patron saint of Silesia, a region now shared by Germany, Poland, and the Czech Republic.) Like all Catholic churches in Berlin, St. Hedwig's is not on the street, but stuck in a kind of back lot—indicating inferiority to Protestant churches. You can step inside the church to see the cheesy DDR government renovation (generally daily until 17:00).

The **German State Opera** was bombed in 1941, rebuilt to bolster morale and to celebrate its centennial in 1943, and bombed again in 1945. It's currently undergoing an extensive renovation.

Now look down through the glass you're standing on: The room of empty bookshelves is a memorial repudiating the notorious Nazi **book burning.** It was on this square in 1933 that staff and students from the university threw 20,000 newly forbidden books (authored by Einstein, Hemmingway, Freud, and T. S. Eliot, among others) into a huge bonfire on the orders of the Nazi propaganda minister, Joseph Goebbels. In fact, Goebbels himself tossed books onto the fire, condemning writers to the flames. He declared, "The era of extreme Jewish intellectualism has come to an end, and the German revolution has again opened the way for the true essence of being German."

The Prussian heritage of Frederick the Great was one of culture and enlightenment. Hitler chose this square to thoroughly squash those ideals, dramatically signaling that the era of tolerance and openness was over. Hitler was establishing a new age of intolerance where German-ness was correct and diversity was evil.

A plaque nearby reminds us of the prophetic quote by the German poet Heinrich Heine. In 1820, he wrote, "Where they burn books, in the end they will also burn people." The Nazis despised Heine because he was a Jew who converted to Christianity. A century later, his books were among those that went up in flames on this spot.

This monument reminds us of that chilling event in 1933, while also inspiring vigilance against the anti-intellectual, scare-mongering forces of today that would burn the thoughts of people they fear to defend their culture from diversity.

• *Cross Unter den Linden to the university side. Just past the university is a Greek-temple-like building set in the small chestnut-tree-filled park. This is the...*

Neue Wache

This is the emperor's "New Guardhouse" (Neue Wache), from 1816. Converted by communist authorities in 1960 to a memorial to the

victims of fascism, the structure was transformed again, after the Wall fell, into a national memorial. Look inside, where a replica of the Käthe Kollwitz statue, *Mother with Her Dead Son,* is surrounded by thought-provoking silence. It marks the tombs of Germany's unknown soldier and an unknown concentration camp victim. The inscription in front reads, "To the victims of war and tyranny." Read the entire statement in English (on wall, left of entrance). The memorial, open to the sky, incorporates the elements—sunshine, rain, snow—falling on this modern-day *pietà*.

• *After the Neue Wache, the next building you'll see is Berlin's pink-yet-formidable Zeughaus (arsenal). Dating from 1695, it's considered the oldest building on the boulevard, and now houses the excellent **German History Museum**—well worth a visit, and described in detail on page 774.*

Continuing down Unter den Linden, you'll cross a bridge to reach...

Museum Island (Museumsinsel)

This island is filled with some of Berlin's most impressive museums (all part of the Staatliche Museen zu Berlin). The earliest building—the Altes Museum—went up in the 1820s, and the rest of the complex began taking shape in the 1840s under King Friedrich Wilhelm IV, who envisioned the island as an oasis of culture and learning. The island's imposing Neoclassical buildings host five grand museums: the **Pergamon Museum** (classical antiquities;  this is undergoing restoration—and is only partially open till at least 2019); the **Neues Museum** ("New Museum," famous for its Egyptian collection with the bust of Queen Nefertiti); the **Old National Gallery** (Alte Nationalgalerie, 19th-century art, mostly German Romantic and Realist paintings); the **Altes Museum** ("Old Museum," more antiquities); and the **Bode Museum** (European statuary and paintings through the ages, coins, and Byzantine art). The museums of Museum Island, worth the better part of a sightseeing day, are described in more detail on page 767.

• *For now, we'll continue on our walk. Before leaving Museum Island, check out a few of its other landmarks. First is the big, inviting park in the middle of the island, called the...*

Lustgarten

For 300 years, the island's big central square has flip-flopped between being a military parade ground and a people-friendly park, depending upon the political tenor of the time. During the revolutions of 1848, the Kaiser's troops dispersed a protesting crowd that had assembled here, sending demonstrators onto footpaths. Karl Marx later commented, "It is impossible to have a revolution in a country where people stay off the grass."

Hitler enjoyed giving speeches from the top of the museum steps overlooking this square. In fact, he had the square landscaped to fit his symmetrical tastes and propaganda needs.

In 1999, the Lustgarten was made into a park (read the history posted in the corner opposite the church). On a sunny day, it's packed with people relaxing and is one of Berlin's most enjoyable public spaces.

• *The huge church on Museum Island is the...*

Berlin Cathedral (Berliner Dom)

This century-old church's bombastic Wilhelmian architecture is a Protestant assertion of strength. It seems to proclaim, "A mighty fortress is our God." The years of Kaiser Wilhelm's rule, from 1888 to 1918, were a busy age of building. Germany had recently been united (1871), and the emperor wanted to give his capital stature and legitimacy. Wilhelm's buildings are over-the-top statements: Neoclassical, Neo-Baroque, and Neo-Renaissance, with stucco and gold-tiled mosaics. This cathedral, while Protestant, is as ornate as if it were Catholic. With the emperor's lead, this ornate style came into vogue, and anyone who wanted to be associated with the royal class built this way. (Aside from the cathedral, the other big examples of Wilhelmian architecture in Berlin are the Reichstag—which we saw earlier—and the Kaiser Wilhelm Memorial Church, described on page 811.) The church is most impressive from the outside, and there's no way to even peek inside without a pricey ticket.

Inside, the great reformers (Luther, Calvin, and company) stand around the brilliantly restored dome like stern saints guarding their theology. Frederick I (Frederick the Great's gramps) rests in an ornate tomb (right transept, near entrance to dome). The 270-step climb to the outdoor dome gallery is tough but offers pleasant, breezy views of the city at the finish line. The crypt downstairs is not worth a look.

Cost and Hours: €7 includes access to dome gallery, not covered by Museum Island ticket, Mon-Sat 9:00-20:00, Sun 12:00-20:00, until 19:00 Oct-March, closes early—around 17:30—on some days for concerts, interior closed but dome open during services, audioguide-€3, tel. 030/2026-9136, www.berliner-dom.de. The cathedral hosts many organ concerts (often on weekends, tickets always available at the door— prices range from free up to €50, but are often around €10).

• *Kitty-corner across Unter den Linden from the Berlin Cathedral is a huge construction site, known as the...*

Humboldt-Forum Berliner Schloss

For centuries, this was the site of the Baroque palace of the Hohenzollern dynasty of Brandenburg and Prussia. Much of that palace actually survived World War II but was replaced by the communists with a blocky, Soviet-style "Palace" of the Republic—East

Berlin's parliament building/entertainment complex and a showy symbol of the communist days. The landmark building fell into disrepair after reunification, and by 2009 had been dismantled.

After much debate about how to use this prime real estate, the German parliament decided to construct the Humboldt-Forum Berliner Schloss, a huge public venue filled with museums, shops, galleries, and concert halls behind a facade constructed in imitation of the original Hohenzollern palace. With a €1.2 billion price tag, many Berliners consider the reconstruction plan a complete waste of money. Funding disappointments are delaying the project and confusing the public. The latest news is that it should be finished by 2019.

In the meantime, the temporary **Humboldt-Box** has been set up. Until it gets in the way and has to be demolished, it will help the public follow the construction of the Humboldt-Forum.

• *Head to the bridge just beyond the Berlin Cathedral, with views of the riverbank. Consider...*

Strolling and Cruising the Spree River

With the reunification of Berlin, the Spree River has become people-friendly and welcoming. A park-like trail leads from the Berlin Cathedral to the Hauptbahnhof, with impromptu "beachside" beer gardens with imported sand, BBQs in pocket parks, and lots of locals walking their dogs, taking a lazy bike ride, or jogging.

You may notice "don't drop anchor" signs. There are still un-exploded WWII bombs around town, and many are in this river. Every month, several bombs are found at construction sites. Their triggers were set for the hard ground of Scottish testing grounds, and because Berlin sits upon soft soil (the name of the city likely comes from an old word for "swamp"), an estimated one of every ten bombs didn't explode.

The recommended **Spree River boat tours** depart from the riverbank near the bridge by the Berlin Cathedral. For details, see page 738.

• *Before crossing the bridge (and leaving Museum Island), look down the river in the distance. To the right, the pointy twin spires of the 13th-century Nikolai Church mark the center of medieval Berlin. This* **Niko-laiviertel** *(*Viertel *means "quarter") was restored by the DDR and became trendy in the last years of communism. To the left is the gilded* **New Synagogue** *dome, rebuilt after WWII bombing (described on page 792).*

Now look down along the riverbank (directly across from the backside of the Berlin Cathedral), for the...

▲DDR Museum

Exhibits in this interesting and entertaining museum give you a taste of everyday life in the former East Germany (DDR), with lots of hands-on exhibits and artifacts (for details, see page 776).

• *From the bridge, continue walking straight toward the TV Tower, down the big boulevard, which here changes its name to...*

Karl-Liebknecht-Strasse

The first big building on the left after the bridge is the **Radisson Blu Hotel** and shopping center, with a huge aquarium in the center. The elevator goes right through the middle of a deep-sea world. (You can see it from the unforgettable Radisson hotel lobby—tuck in your shirt and walk past the guards with the confidence of a guest who's sleeping there.) It's a huge glass cylinder rising high above the central bar (best seen from the left corner as you enter). Here in the center of the old communist capital, it seems that capitalism has settled in with a spirited vengeance.

In the park immediately across the street (a big jaywalk from the Radisson) are grandfatherly statues of **Marx** and **Engels** (nicknamed the "old pensioners"). Surrounding them are stainless-steel monoliths with evocative photos illustrating the struggles of the workers of the world.

Farther along, where Karl-Liebknecht-Strasse intersects with Spandauer Strasse, look right to see the red-brick **city hall**. It was built after the revolutions of 1848 and arguably the first democratic building in the city.

Continue toward **Marien Church** (from 1270), with its spire mirroring the TV Tower. Inside, an artist's rendering helps you follow the interesting but very faded old "Dance of Death" mural that wraps around the narthex inside the door.

• *Immediately across the street from the church, detour a half-block down little Rosenstrasse to find a beautiful memorial set in a park.*

Women's Protest Memorial: This is a reminder of a successful and courageous protest against Nazi policies. In 1943, when "privileged Jews" (men married to Gentile women) were arrested, their wives demonstrated en masse on this street, home to Berlin's oldest synagogue (now gone). They actually won the freedom of their men. Note the Berliner on the bench nearby. As most Berliners did, he looks the other way, even when these courageous women demonstrated that you could speak up and be heard under the Nazis.

• *Back on Karl-Liebknecht-Strasse, look up at the 1,200-foot-tall...*

TV Tower (Fernsehturm): Built (with Swedish know-how) in 1969 for the 20th anniversary of the communist government, the tower was meant to show the power of the atheistic state at a time when DDR leaders were having the crosses removed from church domes and spires. But when the sun hit the tower—the greatest spire in East Berlin—a huge cross was reflected on the mirrored ball. Cynics called it "God's Revenge." East Berliners dubbed the

tower the "Tele-Asparagus." They joked that if it fell over, they'd have an elevator to the West.

The tower has a fine view from halfway up, offering a handy city orientation and an interesting look at the flat, red-roofed sprawl of Berlin—including a peek inside the city's many courtyards, called *Höfe* (€13, daily March-Oct 9:00-24:00, Nov-Feb 10:00-24:00, www.tv-turm.de). The retro tower is quite trendy these days, so it can be crowded (your ticket comes with an assigned entry time). Consider a kitschy trip to the observation deck for the view and lunch in its revolving restaurant (mediocre food, €12 plates, horrible lounge music, reservations smart for dinner, tel. 030/242-3333, www.tv-turm.de).

• *Walk four more minutes down the boulevard past the TV Tower and toward the big railway overpass. Just before the bridge, on the left, is the half-price ticket booth called* **Hekticket**—*stop in to see what's on (for details, see page 816).*

Walk under the train bridge and continue for a long half-block (passing the Galeria Kaufhof mall). Turn right onto a broad pedestrian street, and go through the low tunnel into the big square where blue U-Bahn station signs mark...

Alexanderplatz

This square was the commercial pride and joy of East Berlin. The Kaufhof department store (now Galeria Kaufhof) was the ultimate shopping mecca for Easterners. It, along with the two big surviving 1920s "functionalist" buildings, defined the square. Alexanderplatz is still a landmark, with a major U-Bahn/S-Bahn station. The once-futuristic, now-retro "World Time Clock," installed in 1969, is a nostalgic favorite and remains a popular meeting point.

Stop in the square for a coffee and to people-watch. You may see the dueling human hot-dog stands. These hot-dog hawkers wear ingenious harnesses that let them cook and sell tasty, cheap German sausages on the fly. (Grillwalker is the original company; Grillrunner is the copycat.) While the square can get a little rough at night, it's generally a great scene.

• *Our orientation stroll is finished. From here, you can hike back a bit to catch the riverboat tour or visit Museum Island or the German History museums, take in the sights south of Unter den Linden, venture into the colorful Prenzlauer Berg neighborhood, or consider extending this foray into eastern Berlin by way of Karl-Marx-Allee. These options are covered in detail in the next section.*

Sights in Eastern Berlin

Many of Berlin's top sights and landmarks (including **Brandenburg Gate,** the **Memorial to the Murdered Jews of Europe, Pariser Platz, Unter den Linden,** and **Alexanderplatz**) are described in detail in the self-guided walk (see above). Additional sights mentioned in passing along that walk (including the **Reichstag, German History Museum, DDR Museum,** and the museums of **Museum Island**)—as well as other points of interest in the eastern part of Berlin—are detailed below.

▲▲▲REICHSTAG

Germany's historic parliament building—completed in 1894, burned in 1933, sad and lonely in a no-man's land throughout the Cold War, and finally rebuilt and topped with a glittering glass cupola in 1999—is a symbol of a proudly reunited nation. Its exterior and history are stirring (read the description on page 741 of my self-guided walk), and it's fascinating to climb up the twin ramps that spiral through its dome. Because of security concerns, getting in requires a reservation.

Cost and Hours: Free, but reservations required—see below, daily 8:00-24:00, last entry at 22:00, metal detectors, no big luggage allowed, Platz der Republik 1; S- or U-Bahn: Friedrichstrasse, Brandenburger Tor, or Bundestag; tel. 030/2273-2152, www.bundestag.de.

Reservations: To visit the dome, you'll need to **reserve online** (free); spots often book up several days in advance. Go to www.bundestag.de, click "English" and—from the "Visit the Bundestag" menu—select "Online registration." On this page, select "Visit to the dome" to choose your preferred date and time (you can request up to three different time slots). You'll be sent an email link to a website where you'll enter details for each person in your party. After completing this form, another email will confirm your request, and a final email will contain your reservation (with a letter you must print out and bring with you).

If you're in Berlin without a reservation, try dropping by the tiny visitors center on the Tiergarten side of Scheidemannstrasse, across from Platz der Republik. A screen in its window shows which hourly slots, over the next three days, still have tickets available (open daily April-Oct 8:00-20:00, Nov-March 8:00-18:00; go between 8:00-10:00 to avoid lines; you must book no less than

BERLIN

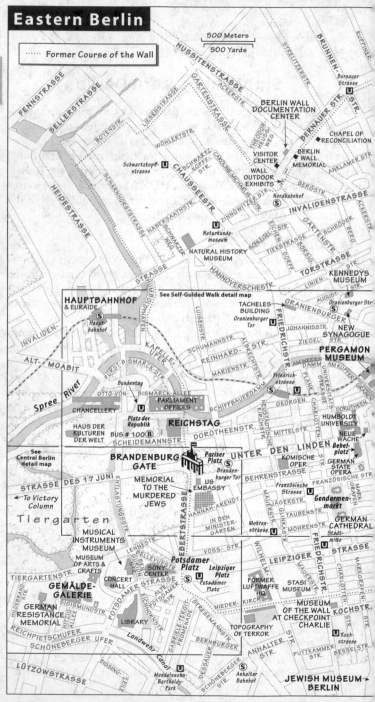

Eastern Berlin

····· Former Course of the Wall

500 Meters
500 Yards

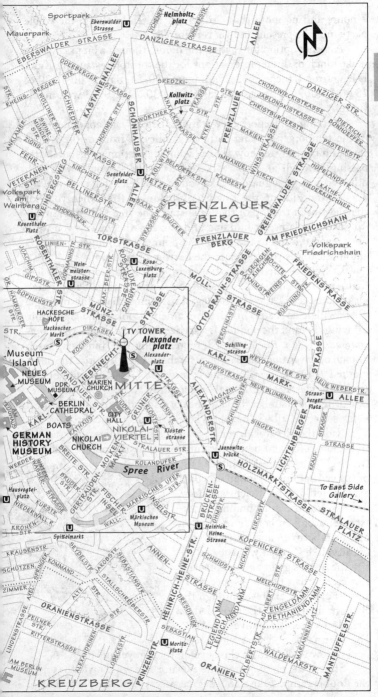

BERLIN

2 hours and no more than 2 days out; when booking, the whole party must be present and ID is required).

Another option for visiting the dome, though a bit pricey, is to make lunch or dinner reservations for the rooftop restaurant, Käfer Dachgarten (lunches €22-25, dinners €30-34, daily 9:00-16:30 & 18:30-24:00, last access at 22:00, call 030/2262-9933 well in advance).

Getting In: Report a few minutes before your appointed time to the temporary-looking entrance facility in front of the Reichstag, and be ready to show ID and your reservation print-out. After passing through an airport-like security check, you'll wait with other visitors for a guard to take you to the Reichstag entrance.

Tours: Pick up the English **"Outlooks" flier** when you exit the elevator at the top of the Reichstag. The free GPS-driven **audioguide** explains the building and narrates the view as you wind up the spiral ramp to the top of the dome; the commentary starts automatically as you step onto the bottom of the ramp.

◑ Self-Guided Tour: The open, airy lobby towers 100 feet high, with 65-foot-tall colors of the German flag. See-through glass doors show the **central legislative chamber.** The message: There will be no secrets in this government. Look inside. Spreading his wings behind the podium is a stylized German eagle, the *Bundestagsadler* (a.k.a. the "fat hen"), representing the Bundestag (each branch of government has its own symbolic eagle). Notice the doors marked *Ja* (Yes), *Nein* (No), and *Enthalten* (Abstain)...an homage to the Bundestag's traditional "sheep jump" way of counting votes by exiting the chamber through the corresponding door (for critical votes, however, all 631 members vote with electronic cards).

Ride the elevator to the base of the glass **dome.** Pick up the free audioguide and take some time to study the photos and read the circle of captions (around the base of the central funnel) for an excellent exhibit telling the Reichstag story. Then study the surrounding architecture: a broken collage of new on old, torn between antiquity and modernity, like Germany's history. Notice the dome's giant and unobtrusive sunscreen that moves as necessary with the sun. Peer down through the skylight to look over the shoulders of the elected representatives at work. For Germans, the best view from  here is down—keeping a close eye on their government.

Start at the ramp nearest the elevator and wind up to the top of the **double ramp.** Take a 360-degree survey of the city as you hike:

The big park is the **Tiergarten,** the "green lungs of Berlin." Beyond that is the **Teufelsberg** ("Devil's Hill"). Built of rubble from the destroyed city in the late 1940s, it was famous during the Cold War as a powerful ear of the West—notice the telecommunications tower on top. Knowing the bombed-out and bulldozed story of their city, locals say, "You have to be suspicious when you see the nice, green park."

Find the **Victory Column** (Siegessäule), glimmering in the middle of the park. Hitler moved it in the 1930s from in front of the Reichstag to its present position in the Tiergarten as part of his grandiose vision for postwar Berlin. Next, scenes of the new Berlin spiral into view—**Potsdamer Platz,** marked by the conical glass tower that houses Sony's European headquarters. Continue circling left, and find the green chariot atop the **Brandenburg Gate.** Just to its left is the curving fish-like roof of the **DK Bank** building, designed by the unconventional American architect Frank Gehry. The **Memorial to the Murdered Jews of Europe** stretches south of the Brandenburg Gate. Next, you'll see **former East Berlin** and the city's next huge construction zone, with a forest of 300-foot-tall skyscrapers in the works. Notice the **TV Tower,** the **Berlin Cathedral**'s massive dome, and the golden dome of the **New Synagogue.**

Follow the train tracks in the distance to the left toward Berlin's huge main train station, the **Hauptbahnhof.** Complete your spin-tour with the blocky, postmodern **Chancellery,** the federal government's headquarters. Continue spiraling up. You'll come across all the same sights again, twice, from a higher vantage point.

MUSEUM ISLAND (MUSEUMSINSEL)

Some of Berlin's top museums are concentrated on this aptly named, centrally located island, just up Unter den Linden from the

Brandenburg Gate. For more on the island itself, see page 758 in my self-guided walk; for specifics on each individual museum, read on.

A formidable renovation is under way on Museum Island. When complete (it's hoped in 2019), a new visitors center—the James-Simon-Galerie—will link the Pergamon Museum with the Altes Museum, the Pergamon will get a fourth wing, tunnels will lace the complex together, and this will become one of the grandest museum zones in Europe. In the meantime, pardon their dust.

Cost: The €18 Museum Island Pass combo-ticket—covering all five museums—is a far better value than buying individual entries, which range from €10 to €14. All five muse-

Museum Island

ums are also included in the city's €24 Museum Pass Berlin (both passes described on page 723). Special exhibits are extra.

Hours: The Pergamon and Neues museums are open daily 10:00-18:00, with later hours on Thursday (until 20:00); the Old National Gallery, Bode Museum, and Altes Museum are open the same hours, except closed Monday.

When to Go: Mornings are busiest, and you're likely to find long lines any time of day on Saturday or Sunday. The least-crowded time is Thursday evening, when the museums are open late. However, only the Pergamon Museum tends to have serious lines—for the other museums here, the timing of your visit isn't as critical.

Crowd-Beating Tips: Avoid the lines for the Pergamon Museum by purchasing a timed ticket online, or if you already have a Museum Pass Berlin or a Museum Island Pass (or plan to buy one), book a free timed-entry reservation (www.smb.museum). Both passes allow you to skip ticket-buying lines at the other museums on the island, but online booking is your only option for getting right to the head of the Pergamon's line.

Getting There: The nearest S-Bahn station is Hackescher

Markt, about a 10-minute walk away. From hotels in the Prenzlauer Berg, ride tram #M-1 to the end of line, and you're right at the Pergamon Museum.

Information: Tel. 030/266-424-242, www.smb.museum.

Eating Nearby: For lunch in the neighborhood, follow the elevated train tracks away from the Pergamon down Georgenstrasse (see recommendations on page 828), or cross the Friedrichsbrücke bridge and follow signs for five minutes to Hackescher Markt, with its multitude of eateries.

Just for Fun: Germany's formidable leader, Angela Merkel, could live in the expansive digs at the Chancellery. But her husband (who's a professor here) and she have long lived in an apartment overlooking Museum Island. You'll see a couple of policemen providing modest protection in front of her place on Am Kupfergraben, directly across the bridge from the Pergamon Museum.

▲▲▲Pergamon Museum (Pergamonmuseum)

The star attraction of this world-class museum, part of Berlin's Collection of Classical Antiquities (Antikensammlung), is the

fantastic and gigantic Pergamon Altar...which is off-limits to visitors until 2019, as the museum undergoes major renovation. But its Babylonian Ishtar Gate (slathered with glazed blue tiles from the sixth century B.C.) still makes it worth visiting, and its ancient Mesopotamian, Roman, and early Islamic treasures are also impressive. The north wing is already closed (its Greek and Roman sculptures, plus some vases and bronze figurines, can be seen at the Altes Museum; the north wing's Hellenistic architecture and artworks, however, won't be seen again until 2019).

Visting the Museum: Make ample use of the superb audioguide (included with admission—it will broaden your experience.

From the entry hall, head up the stairs and all the way back to 575 B.C., to the Fertile Crescent—Mesopotamia (today's Iraq). The Assyrian ruler Nebuchadnezzar II, who amassed a vast em-

pire and enormous wealth, wanted to build a suitably impressive processional entryway to his capital city, Babylon, to honor the goddess Ishtar. His creation, the blue **Ishtar Gate,** inspired awe and obedience in anyone who came to his city. This is a reconstruction, using

BERLIN

some original components. The gate itself is embellished with two animals: a bull and a mythical dragon-like combination of lion, cobra, eagle, and scorpion. The long hall leading to the main gate—designed for a huge processional of deities to celebrate the new year—is decorated with a chain of blue and yellow glazed tiles with 120 strolling lions (representing the goddess Ishtar). To get the big picture, find the model of the original site in the center of the hall.

Pass through the gate, and flash-forward 700 years to the ancient Roman city of Miletus. Dominating this room is the 95-foot-wide, 55-foot-high **Market Gate of Miletus,** destroyed by an earthquake centuries ago and now painstakingly reconstructed here in Berlin. The exquisite mosaic floor from a Roman villa in Miletus has two parts: In the square panel, the musician Orpheus strokes his lyre to charm the animals; in stark contrast, in the nearby rectangular mosaic (from an adjacent room), hunters pursue wild animals.

These main exhibits are surrounded by smaller galleries. Upstairs is the **Museum of Islamic Art.** It contains fine carpets, tile work, the Aleppo Room (with ornately painted wooden walls from an early 17th-century home in today's Syria; since it was commissioned by a Christian, it incorporates Arabic, Persian, and biblical themes), and the Mshatta Facade (walls and towers from one of the early eighth-century Umayyad "desert castles," from today's Jordan).

▲▲Neues (New) Museum

Oddly, Museum Island's so-called "new" museum features the oldest stuff around. There are three collections here: the Egyptian Collection (with the famous bust of Queen Nefertiti), the Museum of Prehistory and Early History, and some items from the Collection of Classical Antiquities (artifacts from ancient Troy—famously excavated by German adventurer Heinrich Schliemann—and Cyprus).

After being damaged in World War II and sitting in ruins for some 40 years, the Neues Museum has been gorgeously rebuilt. Everything is well-described by posted English information and the fine audioguide (included with admission), which celebrates new knowledge about ancient Egyptian civilization and offers fascinating insights into workaday Egyptian life as it describes the vivid papyrus collection, slice-of-life artifacts, and dreamy wax portraits decorating mummy cases (for more on the museum, see www. neues-museum.de).

Visiting the Museum: Pick up a floor plan showing the suggested route, then head up the central staircase.

The top draw here is the Egyptian art—clearly one of the world's best collections. But let's face it: The main reason to visit is to enjoy one of the great thrills in art appreciation—gazing into the still young and beautiful face of Queen Nefertiti. If you're in a pinch for time, make a beeline to her (floor 2, far corner of Egyptian Collection in Room 210).

To tour the whole collection, start at the top (floor 3), which is where you'll find the **prehistory section.** The entire floor is filled with Stone Age, Ice Age, and Bronze Age items. You'll see early human remains, tools, spearheads, and pottery.

The most interesting item on this floor (in corner Room 305) is the tall, conehead-like **Golden Hat,** made of paper-thin hammered gold leaf. Created by an early Celtic civilization in Central Europe, it's particularly exquisite for something so old (from the Bronze Age, around 1000 B.C.). The circles on the hat represent the sun, moon, and other celestial bodies—leading archaeologists to believe that this headwear could double as a calendar, showing how the sun and moon sync up every 19 years.

Down on floor 2, you'll find **early history** exhibits on migrations, barbarians, and ancient Rome (including larger-than-life statues of Helios and an unidentified goddess) as well as a fascinating look at the Dark Ages after the fall of Rome.

Still on floor 2, cross to the other side of the building for the **Egyptian** section. On the way, you'll pass through the impressive Papyrus Collection—a large room of seemingly empty glass cases. Press a button to watch a 3,000-year-old piece of primitive "paper" (made of aquatic reeds) imprinted with primitive text trundle out of its protective home.

Then, finally, in a room all her own, is the 3,000-year-old bust of **Queen Nefertiti** (the wife of King Akhenaton, c. 1340 B.C.)—the most famous piece of Egyptian art in Europe. (Note that she's

BERLIN

had it with the paparazzi—photos of her are strictly *verboten*.) Called "Berlin's most beautiful woman," Nefertiti has all the right beauty marks: long neck, symmetrical face, and the perfect amount of makeup. And yet, she's not completely idealized. Notice the fine wrinkles that show she's human (though these only enhance her beauty). Like a movie star discreetly sipping a glass of wine at a sidewalk café, Nefertiti seems somehow more dignified in person. The bust never left its studio, but served as a master model for all other portraits of the queen. (That's probably why the left eye was never inlaid.) Stare at her long enough, and you may get the sensation that she's winking at you. Hey, beautiful!

How the queen arrived in Germany is a tale out of *Indiana Jones*. The German archaeologist Ludwig Borchardt uncovered her in the Egyptian desert in 1912. The Egyptian Department of Antiquities had first pick of all the artifacts uncovered on their territory. After the first takings, they divided the rest 50/50 with the excavators. When Borchardt presented Nefertiti to the Egyptians, they passed her over, never bothering to examine her closely. Unsubstantiated rumors persist that Borchardt misled the Egyptians in order to keep the bust for himself—rumors that have prompted some Egyptians to call for the return of Nefertiti (just as the Greeks are lobbying the British to return the Parthenon frieze currently housed in the British Museum). Although this bust is not particularly representative of Egyptian art in general—and despite increasing claims that her long neck suggests she's a Neoclassical fake—Nefertiti has become a symbol of Egyptian art by popular acclaim.

The Egyptian Collection continues with other sculptures, including kneeling figures holding steles (inscribed stone tablets). You'll also see entire walls from tombs and (in the basement—floor 0) a sea of large sarcophagi.

▲Old National Gallery (Alte Nationalgalerie)

This gallery, behind the Neues Museum and Altes Museum, is designed to look like a Greek temple. Spanning three floors, it focuses on art (mostly paintings) from the 19th century: Romantic Ger-

man paintings (which I find most interesting) on the top floor, and French and German Impressionists and German Realists on the first and second floors. You likely won't recognize any specific paintings, but it's still an enjoyable stroll through German culture from the century in which that notion first came to mean something. The included audioguide explains the highlights.

Visiting the Museum: Start on the third floor, with Romantic canvases and art of the Goethe era (roughly 1770-1830), and work your way down. Use the audioguide to really delve into these romanticized, vivid looks at life in Germany in the 19th century and before. As you stroll through the Romantic paintings—the museum's strength—keep in mind that they were created about the time (mid-late 19th century) that Germans were first working toward a single, unified nation. By glorifying pristine German landscapes and a rugged, virtuous people, these painters evoked the region's high-water mark—the Middle Ages, when "Germany" was a patchwork of powerful and wealthy merchant city-states. Linger over dreamy townscapes with Gothic cathedrals and castles that celebrate medieval German might. Still lifes, genre paintings (e.g.,

of everyday scenes, often with subtle social commentary), and portraits ranging from idealized tow-headed children to influential German leaders (such as Otto von Bismarck, pictured) strum the heartstrings of anyone with Teutonic blood. The Düsseldorf School excelled at Romantic landscapes (such as Carl Friedrich Lessing's *Castle on a Rock*). Some of these canvases nearly resemble present-day fantasy paintings. Perhaps the best-known artist in the collection is Caspar David Friedrich, who specialized in dramatic scenes celebrating

grandeur and the solitary hero. His *The Monk by the Sea (Der Mönch am Meer)* shows a lone figure standing on a sand dune, pondering a vast, turbulent expanse of sea and sky.

On the second floor, you'll find one big room of minor works by bigger-name French artists, including Renoir, Cézanne, Manet, Monet, and Rodin. Another room is devoted to the Romantic Hans von Marées, the influential early Symbolist Arnold Böcklin, and other artists of the "German Roman" (Deutschrömer) movement—Germans who lived in, and were greatly influenced by, Rome. Artists of the Munich School are represented by naturalistic canvases of landscapes or slice-of-life scenes.

On the first floor, 19th-century Realism reigns. While the Realist Adolph Menzel made his name painting elegant royal gatherings and historical events, his *Iron Rolling Mill (Das Eisenwalzwerk)* captures the gritty side of his moment in history—the emergence of the Industrial Age—with a warts-and-all look at steelworkers toiling in a hellish factory. The first floor also hosts a sculpture collection, with works by great sculptors both foreign (the Italian Canova, the Dane Thorvaldsen) and German (Johann Gottfried Schadow's delightful *Die Prinzessinnen*, showing the dynamic duo of Prussian princesses, Louise and Frederike). Also on the first floor, near the sculptures, look for a low-key room left unrestored so visitors can recall the days when the DDR ran this museum.

Bode Museum

At the "prow" of Museum Island, the Bode Museum (designed to appear as if it's rising up from the river) is worth a brief stop. Just inside, a grand statue of Frederick William of Brandenburg on horseback, curly locks blowing in the wind, welcomes you into the lonely halls of the museum. This fine building contains a hodgepodge of collections: Byzantine art, historic coins, ecclesiastical art, sculptures, and medals commemorating the fall of the Berlin Wall and German reunification. For a free, quick look at its lavish interior, climb the grand staircase to the charming café on the first floor.

Altes (Old) Museum

Perhaps the least interesting of the five museums, this building features the rest of the Collection of Classical Antiquities—namely, Etruscan, Roman, and Greek art. It also contains Greek and Roman sculptures, vases, and some bronze figurines from the currently closed north wing of the Pergamon Museum.

NEAR MUSEUM ISLAND
▲▲▲German History Museum
(Deutsches Historisches Museum)

This fantastic museum is a two-part affair: the pink former Prussian arsenal building and the I. M. Pei-designed annex. The main building (fronting Unter den Linden) houses the permanent collection, offering the best look at German history under one roof, anywhere. The modern annex features good temporary exhibits surrounded by the work of a great contemporary architect. While this city has more than its share of hokey "museums" that slap together WWII and Cold War bric-a-brac, then charge too much for admission, this thoughtfully presented museum—with more than 8,000 artifacts telling not just the story of Berlin, but of all Germany—is clearly the top history museum in town.

Cost and Hours: €8, daily 10:00-18:00, Unter den Linden 2, tel. 030/2030-4751, www.dhm.de.

Audioguide: For the most informative visit, invest in the excellent €3 audioguide, with six hours of info to choose from.

Getting In: If the ticket-buying line is long at the main entrance, try circling around the back to the Pei annex (to reach it, head down the street to the left of the museum—called Hinter dem Giesshaus), where entry lines are usually shorter (but audioguides are available only at the main desk).

Visiting the Museum: The permanent collection packs two huge rectangular floors of the old arsenal building with historical objects, photographs, and models—all well-described in English and intermingled with multimedia stations to help put everything in context. From the lobby, head upstairs to the **first floor** and work your way chronologically down. This floor traces German history from 1 B.C. to 1918, with exhibits on early cultures, the Middle Ages, Reformation, Thirty Years' War, German Empire, and World War I. You'll see a Roman floor mosaic, lots of models of higgledy-piggledy medieval towns and castles, tapestries, suits of armor, busts of great Germans, a Turkish tent from the Ottoman siege of Vienna (1683), flags from German unification in 1871 (the first time "Germany" existed as a nation), exhibits on everyday life in the tenements of the Industrial Revolution, and much more.

History marches on through the 20th century on the **ground floor,** including the Weimar Republic, Nazism, World War II, Allied occupation, and a divided Germany. Propaganda posters trumpet Germany's would-be post-WWI savior, Adolf Hitler. Look for the model of the impossibly huge, 950-foot-high, 180,000-capacity

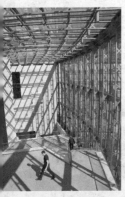

domed hall Hitler wanted to erect in the heart of Berlin, which he planned to re-envision as Welthauptstadt Germania, the "world capital" of his far-reaching Third Reich. Another model shows the sobering reality of Hitler's grandiosity: a crematorium at Auschwitz-Birkenau concentration camp in occupied Poland. The exhibit wraps up with chunks of the Berlin Wall, reunification, and a quick look at Germany today.

For architecture buffs, the big attraction is the **Pei annex** behind the history museum, which complements the museum with often-fascinating temporary exhibits. From the old building, cross through the courtyard (with the Pei glass canopy overhead) to reach the annex. A striking glassed-in spiral staircase unites four floors with surprising views and lots of light. It's here that you'll experience why Pei—famous for his glass pyramid at Paris' Louvre—is called the "perfector of classical modernism," "master of light," and a magician of uniting historical buildings with new ones.

▲DDR Museum

The exhibits here offer an interesting look at life in the former East Germany (DDR) without the negative spin most museums give. It's well-stocked with kitschy everyday items from the communist period, plus photos, video clips, and concise English explanations. The exhibits are interactive—you're encouraged to pick up and handle anything that isn't behind glass.

Cost and Hours: €7, daily 10:00-20:00, Sat until 22:00, just across the Spree from Museum Island at Karl-Liebknecht-Strasse 1, tel. 030/847-123-731, www.ddr-museum.de.

Visiting the Museum: You'll crawl through a Trabant car (designed by East German engineers to compete with the West's popular VW Beetle) and pick up some DDR-era jokes ("East Germany had 39 newspapers, four radio stations, two TV channels... and one opinion"). The reconstructed communist-era home lets you tour the kitchen, living room, bedrooms, and more. You'll learn about the *dacha*—the simple countryside cottages (owned by one in six East Germans) used for weekend retreats from the grimy city. (Others vacationed on the Baltic Coast, where nudism was all the rage, as a very revealing display explains.) Lounge in DDR cinema chairs as you view a subtitled propaganda film or clips from beloved-in-the-East TV shows (including the popular kids' show *Sandmännchen*—"Little Sandman"). Even the meals served in the attached restaurant are based on DDR-era recipes.

SOUTH OF UNTER DEN LINDEN

The following sights—heavy on Nazi and Wall history—are listed roughly north to south (as you reach them from Unter den Linden).

▲▲Gendarmenmarkt

This delightful, historic square is bounded by twin churches, a tasty chocolate shop, and the Berlin Symphony's concert hall (designed by Karl Friedrich Schinkel, the man who put the Neoclassical stamp on Berlin and Dresden). In summer, it hosts a few outdoor cafés, *Biergarten*s, and some-

times concerts. Wonderfully symmetrical, the square is considered by Berliners to be the finest in town (U6: Französische Strasse; U2 or U6: Stadtmitte; for eateries, see page 830).

The name of the square, which is part French and part German (after the *Gens d'Armes*, Frederick the Great's royal guard, who were headquartered here), reminds us that in the 17th century, a fifth of all Berliners were French émigrés—Protestant Huguenots fleeing Catholic France. Back then, Frederick the Great's tolerant Prussia was a magnet for the persecuted (and their money). These émigrés vitalized Berlin with new ideas and know-how...and their substantial wealth.

Of the two matching churches on Gendarmenmarkt, the one to the south (bottom end of square) is the **German Cathedral** (Deutscher Dom). This cathedral (not to be confused with the Berlin Cathedral on Museum Island) was bombed flat in the war and rebuilt only in the 1980s. It houses the thought-provoking Milestones, Setbacks, Sidetracks *(Wege, Irrwege, Umwege)* exhibit, which traces the history of the German parliamentary system— worth ▲. The parliament-funded exhibit—while light on actual historical artifacts—is well done and more interesting than it sounds. It takes you quickly from the revolutionary days of 1848 to the 1920s, and then more deeply through the tumultuous 20th century. As the exhibit is designed for Germans rather than foreign tourists, there are no English descriptions—but you can follow the essential, excellent, and free 1.5-hour English audioguide. If you think this museum is an attempt by the German government to develop a more sophisticated and educated electorate in the interest of stronger democracy, you're exactly right. Germany knows (from its own troubled history) that a dumbed-down electorate, manipulated by clever spin-meisters and sound-bite media blitzes, is a dangerous thing (free, Tue-Sun 10:00-19:00, Oct-April until 18:00, closed Mon year-round, tel. 030/2273-0431).

The **French Cathedral** (Französischer Dom), at the north end of the square, offers a humble museum on the Huguenots (€2, Tue-Sun 12:00-17:00, closed Mon, enter around the right side) and a viewpoint in the dome up top (€3, daily April-Oct 10:00-19:00, Nov-March 10:00-18:00, last entry one hour before closing, 244 steps, enter through door facing square, tel. 030/2067-4690, www.franzoesischer-dom.de).

Fun fact: Neither of these churches is a true cathedral, as they never contained a bishop's throne; their German title of *Dom* (cathedral) is actually a mistranslation from the French word *dôme* (cupola).

Fassbender & Rausch, on the corner near the German Cathedral, claims to be Europe's biggest chocolate store. After 150 years of chocolate-making, this family-owned business proudly

displays its sweet delights—250 different kinds—on a 55-foot-long buffet. Truffles are sold for about €0.75 each; it's fun to compose a fancy little eight-piece box of your own for about €6. Upstairs is an elegant hot chocolate café with fine views.

The window displays feature giant chocolate models of Berlin landmarks—Reichstag, Brandenburg Gate, Kaiser Wilhelm Memorial Church, and so on. If all this isn't enough to entice you, I have three words: erupting chocolate volcano (Mon-Sat 10:00-20:00, Sun 11:00-20:00, corner of Mohrenstrasse at Charlottenstrasse 60, tel. 030/757-882-440).

Gendarmenmarkt is buried in what has recently emerged as Berlin's "Fifth Avenue" shopping district. For the ultimate in top-end shops, find the corner of Jägerstrasse and Friedrichstrasse and wander through the **Quartier 206** (Mon-Fri 10:30-19:30, Sat 10:00-18:00, closed Sun, www.quartier206. com). The adjacent, middlebrow **Quartier 205** has more affordable prices.

Nazi and Cold War Sites

A variety of fascinating sites relating to Germany's tumultuous 20th century cluster south of Unter den Linden. While you can see your choice of the following places in any order, I've linked them by way of a short walk from Potsdamer Platz to Checkpoint Charlie.

• *From Potsdamer Platz, take a few steps down Stresemannstrasse and detour left down Erna-Berger-Strasse to find a lonely concrete watchtower.*

DDR Watchtower

This was one of many such towers built in 1966 for panoramic surveillance and shooting (note the rifle windows, allowing shots to be fired in 360 degrees). It was constantly manned by two guards who were forbidden to get to know each other (no casual chatting)—so they could effectively guard each other from escaping. This is one of only a few such towers still standing.

Cost and Hours: €3.50, open only sporadically, though officially daily 11:00-15:00.

• *Return to Stresemannstrasse, and continue south (away from Potsdamer Platz). As you round the corner turning left, you'll begin to see some...*

Fragments of the Wall

Surviving stretches of the Wall are rare in downtown Berlin, but you'll find a few in this area. On the left as you turn from Erna-Berger-Strasse onto Strese-mannstrasse, look carefully at the modern Ministry of the Environment (Bundesministe-rium für Umwelt) building; notice the nicely painted stretch of **inner wall** (inside the modern building constructed around it). The Wall was actually two

walls, with a death strip in the middle (where Stresemannstrasse is today). Across the street, embedded in the sidewalk, you can see cobblestones marking the former path of the outer wall.

At the corner with Niederkirchnerstrasse, turn left and follow the cobbles in the sidewalk. After about a block (just beyond the Martin-Gropius-Bau museum), where the street becomes cobbled, an **original fragment** of the Berlin Wall stretches alongside the right side of the street.

• *Follow the Wall until it ends, at the intersection of Niederkirchner-strasse and Wilhelmstrasse. Hook right around the end of the Wall to reach the...*

▲▲Topography of Terror (Topographie des Terrors)

Coincidentally, the patch of land behind the surviving stretch of Wall was closely associated with an even more deplorable regime:

It was once the nerve center for the most despicable elements of the Nazi government, the Gestapo and the SS. This stark-gray, boxy building is one of the few memorial sites that focuses on the perpetrators rather than the victims of the Nazis. It's chilling but thought-provoking to see just how seamlessly and bureaucratically the Nazi institutions and state structures merged to become a well-oiled terror machine. There are few actual artifacts; it's mostly written explanations and photos, like reading a good textbook standing up. And, while you could read this story anywhere, to take this in atop the Gestapo headquarters is a powerful experience. The exhibit is a bit dense, but WWII historians (even armchair ones) will find it fascinating.

Cost and Hours: Free, includes audioguide for outdoor exhibit, daily 10:00-20:00, outdoor exhibit closes at dusk, Niederkirchnerstrasse 8, tel. 030/254-5090, www.topographie.de.

Background: This location marks what was once the most feared address in Berlin: the headquarters of the Reich Main Security Office *(Reichssicherheitshauptamt)*. These offices served as the engine room of the Nazi dictatorship, as well as the command center of the SS (*Schutzstaffel*, whose members began as Hitler's personal bodyguards), the Gestapo (*Geheime Staatspolizei*, secret state police), and the SD (*Sicherheitsdienst*, the Nazi intelligence agency). This trio (and others) were ultimately consolidated under Heinrich Himmler to become a state-within-a-state, with talons in every corner of German society. This elite militarized branch of the Nazi machine was also tasked with the "racial purification" of German-held lands, especially Eastern Europe—the Holocaust. It was from these headquarters that the Nazis administered concentration camps, firmed up plans for the "Final Solution to the Jewish Question," and organized the domestic surveillance of anyone opposed to the regime. The building was also equipped with dungeons, where the Gestapo detained and tortured thousands of prisoners.

The Gestapo and SS employed intimidation techniques to coerce cooperation from the German people. The general public knew that the Gestapo was to be feared: It was considered omnipotent, omnipresent, and omniscient. Some political prisoners underwent "enhanced interrogation" right here in this building. The threat of *Schutzhaft* ("protective custody," usually at a concentration camp) was used to terrify any civilians who stepped out of line—or who might make a good example. But Hitler and his cronies also won people's loyalties through propaganda. They hammered home the idealistic notion of the *Volksgemeinschaft* ("people's community") of a purely Germanic culture and race, which empowered Hitler to create a pervasive illusion that "We're all in this together." Anyone who was not an Aryan was *Untermensch*—subhuman—and must be treated as such.

Visiting the Museum: The complex has two parts: indoors, in the modern boxy building; and outdoors, in the trench that runs along the surviving stretch of Wall. Visit the indoor exhibit first.

Inside, you'll find a visitors center with an information desk and an extensive **Topography of Terror** exhibit about the SS and Gestapo, and the atrocities they committed in Berlin and across Europe. A model of the government quarter, circa 1939, sets the stage of Nazi domination in this area. A timeline of events and old photographs, documents, and newspaper clippings illustrates how Hitler and his team expertly manipulated the German people to build a broadly supported "dictatorship of consent."

The exhibit walks you through the evolution of Hitler's regime: the Nazi takeover; institutions of terror (Himmler's "SS State"); terror, persecution, and extermination; atrocities in Nazi-

occupied countries; and the war's end and postwar. Some images here are indelible, such as photos of SS soldiers stationed at Auschwitz, gleefully yukking it up on a retreat in the countryside (as their helpless prisoners were being gassed and burned a few miles away). The exhibit profiles specific members of the various reprehensible SS branches, as well as the groups they targeted: Jews; Roma and Sinti (Gypsies); the unemployed or homeless; homosexuals; and the physically and mentally ill (considered "useless eaters" who consumed resources without contributing work).

Downstairs is a WC and a library with research books on these topics. Before heading outside, ask at the information desk for the free audioguide that describes the outdoor exhibits.

Outside, in the trench along the Wall, you'll find the exhibit **Berlin 1933-1945: Between Propaganda and Terror** (occasionally replaced by temporary exhibits), which overlaps slightly with the indoor exhibit but focuses on Berlin. The chronological survey begins with the post-WWI Weimar Republic and continues through the ragged days just after World War II.

One display explains how Nazis invented holidays (or injected new Aryan meaning into existing ones) as a means of winning over the public. Other exhibits cover the "Aryanization" of Jewish businesses (they were simply taken over by the state and handed over to new Aryan owners); Hitler's plans for converting Berlin into a gigantic "Welthauptstadt (World Capital) Germania"; and the postwar Berlin Airlift, which brought provisions to some 2.2 million West Berliners whose supply lines were cut off by East Berlin.

With more time, explore the grounds around the blocky building on a **"Site Tour."** Posted signs (and the audioguide) explain 15 different locations, including the scant remains of the prison cellars.

• *Backtrack to Niederkirchnerstrasse. Opposite the Wall remnant is one end of a huge building...*

German Finance Ministry (Bundesministerium der Finanzen)

The only major Hitler-era government building that survived the war's bombs, this once housed the headquarters of the Nazi Luftwaffe (Air Force). Notice how the whole building gives off a monumental feel, making the average person feel small and powerless. After the war, this was the headquarters for the Soviet occupation. Later the DDR was founded here, and the communists used the building to house their—no joke—Ministry of Ministries.

Walk up Wilhelmstrasse (to the north) to see an entry gate (on your left) that looks much like it did when Germany occupied nearly all of Europe. This courtyard is often used by movie producers needing a Nazi set.

On the north side of the building (farther up Wilhelmstrasse, under the portico at the corner with Leipziger Strasse) is a wonderful example of communist art.  The mural, Max Lingner's *Aufbau der Republik* (*Building the Republic,* 1953), is classic Socialist Realism, showing the entire society—industrial laborers, farm workers, women, and children—all happily singing the same patriotic song. Its subtitle: "The importance of peace for the cultural development of humanity and the necessity of struggle to achieve this goal." This was the communist ideal. For the reality, look at the ground in the courtyard in front of the mural to see an enlarged photograph from a 1953 uprising here against the communists...quite a contrast. Placards explain the events of 1953 in English.

• *Retrace your steps to the Niederkirchnerstrasse intersection and hook left onto Zimmerstrasse to the...*

Stasi Museum

This modest exhibit tells the story of how the communist-era Ministry for State Security (*Staatssicherheit,* a.k.a. Stasi) infiltrated all aspects of German life. Soon after the Wall fell, DDR authorities scrambled to destroy the copious illicit information their agents and informants had collected about the people of East Germany. But the government mandated that these records be preserved as evidence of DDR crimes, and the documents are now managed by the Federal Commissioner for Stasi Records. A timeline traces the history of the archives, and wraparound kiosks profile individual "subversive elements" who were targeted by the Stasi. There are a few actual artifacts, but the exhibit is mostly dryly written texts and reproduced photographs that don't do much to personalize the victims—making this museum worth a visit only for those with a special interest in this period. Temporary exhibits are upstairs.

Cost and Hours: Free, daily 10:00-18:00, Zimmerstrasse 90-91, tel. 030/232-450, www.bstu.bund.de.

Other Stasi Sites: If you're interested in this chapter of East German history, you may find it more satisfying (but time-consuming) to visit two other sites affiliated with the Stasi: a different **Stasi Museum,** in the former State Security headquarters (€5, Mon-Fri 10:00-18:00, Sat-Sun 12:00-18:00, Ruscherstrasse 103, U5: Magdalenenstrasse, tel. 030/553-6854, www.stasimuseum. de); and the **Stasi Prison,** where "enemies of the state" served time (€5, visits possible only with a tour; English tours daily at 14:30—call to confirm before making the trip; German tours March-Oct hourly Mon-Fri 11:00-15:00, Sat-Sun 10:00-16:00, less frequently in winter; Genslerstrasse 66, reachable on various trams from downtown—see website for specifics, tel. 030/9860-8230, www. stiftung-hsh.de). There's also a good Stasi Museum in the former State Security branch in Leipzig (see the Leipzig chapter).

• *On the final stretch of Zimmerstrasse, leading to Checkpoint Charlie, you'll pass several "Ost-algic" business ventures: vendors of DDR soft ice-cream, Trabi World (renting rides in iconic DDR tin-can cars), and the Wall Panorama Exhibition (not worth €10, as it's just huge photos). You'll wind up at...*

▲Checkpoint Charlie

This famous Cold War checkpoint was not named for a person, but for its checkpoint number—as in Alpha (#1, at the East-West German border, a hundred miles west of here), Bravo (#2, as you enter Berlin proper), and Charlie (#3, the best known because most foreigners passed through here). While the actual checkpoint has long since been dismantled, its former location is home to a fine museum and a mock-up of the original border

crossing. The area has become a Cold War freak show and—as if celebrating the final victory of crass capitalism—is one of Berlin's worst tourist-trap zones. A McDonald's stands defiantly overlooking the former haunt of East German border guards. (For a more sober and intellectually redeeming look at the Wall's history, head for the Berlin Wall Memorial at Bernauer Strasse, described on page 794.)

The rebuilt **guard station** now hosts two actors playing American guards who pose for photos. Notice the larger-than-life **posters** of a young American soldier facing east and a young Soviet soldier facing west. (Look carefully at the "Soviet" soldier. He was photographed in 1999, a decade after there were Soviet soldiers stationed here. He's a Dutch model. His uniform is a nonsensical pile of pins and ribbons with a Russian flag on his shoulder.)

A **photo exhibit** stretches up and down Zimmerstrasse, with great English descriptions telling the story of the Wall. While you could get this information from a book, it's certainly a different experience to stand here in person and ponder the gripping history of this place.

A few yards away (on Zimmerstrasse), a **glass panel** describes the former checkpoint. From there, another double row of **cobbles** in Zimmerstrasse shows the former path of the Wall.

Warning: Here and in other places, hustlers charge an exorbitant €10 for a full set of Cold War-era stamps in your passport. Don't be tempted. Technically, this invalidates your passport—which has caused some tourists big problems.

• *Overlooking the chaos of the street scene is the...*

▲▲Museum of the Wall at Checkpoint Charlie (Mauermuseum Haus am Checkpoint Charlie)

While the famous border checkpoint between the American and Soviet sectors is long gone, its memory is preserved by one of Europe's most cluttered museums. During the Cold War, the House at Checkpoint Charlie stood defiantly—spitting distance from the border guards—showing off all the clever escapes over, under, and through the Wall. Today, while the drama is over and hunks of the Wall stand like trophies at its door, the museum survives as a living artifact of the Cold War days. The yellowed descriptions, which have scarcely changed since that time, tinge the museum with nostalgia. It's dusty, disorganized, and overpriced, with lots of reading involved, but all that just adds to this museum's borderline-kitschy charm. If you're pressed for time, visit after dinner, when most other museums are closed.

Cost and Hours: €12.50, assemble 20 tourists and get in for €8.50 each, €3.50 audioguide, daily 9:00-22:00, U6 to Kochstrasse or—better from Zoo—U2 to Stadtmitte, Friedrichstrasse 43-45, tel. 030/253-7250, www.mauermuseum.de.

Visiting the Museum: Exhibits narrate a gripping history of the Wall, with a focus on the many ingenious **escape attempts** (the early years—

with a cruder wall—saw more escapes). You'll see the actual items used to smuggle would-be Wessies: a VW bug whose trunk hid a man, two side-by-side suitcases into which a woman squeezed, a makeshift zip line for crossing over (rather than through) the border, a hot-air balloon in which two families floated to safety (immortalized in the Disney film *Night Crossing*), an inflatable boat that puttered across the dangerous Baltic Sea, primitive homemade aircraft, two surfboards hollowed out to create just enough space for a refugee, and more. One chilling exhibit lists some 43,000 people who died in "Internal Affairs" internment camps during the transition to communism (1945-1950). Profiles personalize various escapees and their helpers, including John P. Ireland, an American who posed as an eccentric antiques collector so he could transport 10 refugees to safety in his modified Cadillac.

You'll also see **artwork** inspired by the Wall and its fall, and a memorial to Rainer Hildebrandt, who founded this museum shortly after the Wall went up in 1961 (he died in 2004, but the museum lives on as a shrine to his vision). On the **top floor** (easy to miss), that vision broadens to the larger themes of freedom and persecution, including exhibits on Eastern European rebellions (the 1956 uprising in Hungary, 1968's Prague Spring, and the Solidarity movement in 1980s Poland) and Gandhi's protests in India—plus a hodgepodge of displays on world religions and Picasso's *Guernica*. Fans of the "Gipper" appreciate the room honoring President Ronald Reagan, displaying his actual cowboy hat and boots. The small movie theater shows various Wall-related films (a schedule is posted), and the displays include video coverage of those heady days when people-power tore down the Wall.

▲▲Jewish Museum Berlin (Jüdisches Museum Berlin)

This museum is one of Europe's best Jewish sights. The highly conceptual building is a sight in itself, and the museum inside—

an overview of the rich culture and history of Europe's Jewish community—is excellent, particularly if you take advantage of the informative and engaging audioguide. Rather than just reading dry texts, you'll feel this museum as fresh and alive—an exuberant celebration of the Jewish experience that's accessible to all. Even though the museum is in a nondescript residential neighborhood, it's well worth the trip.

Cost and Hours: €8, daily 10:00-20:00, Mon until 22:00, last entry one hour before closing, closed on Jewish holidays. Tight security includes bag check and metal detectors. The excellent €3 audioguide—with four

The Berlin Wall (and Its Fall)

The 96-mile-long "Anti-Fascist Protective Rampart," as it was called by the East German government, was erected almost overnight in 1961 to stop the outward flow of people from East to West (3 million had leaked out between 1949 and 1961). The Wall *(Mauer)* was actually two walls; the outer was a 12-foot-high concrete barrier whose rounded, pipe-like top (to discourage grappling hooks) was adorned with plenty of barbed wire. Sandwiched between the walls was a no-man's-land "death strip" between 30 and 160 feet wide. More than 100 sentry towers kept a close eye on the Wall. On their way into the death strip, would-be escapees tripped a silent alarm, which alerted sharpshooters.

During the Wall's 28 years, border guards fired 1,693 times and made 3,221 arrests, and there were 5,043 documented successful escapes (565 of these were East German guards). At least 138 people died or were killed at the Wall while trying to flee.

As a tangible, almost too-apt symbol for the Cold War, the Berlin Wall got a lot of attention from politicians both East and West. Two of the 20th century's most repeated presidential quotes were uttered within earshot of the death strip. In 1963, US President John F. Kennedy professed American solidarity with the struggling people of Berlin: *"Ich bin ein Berliner."* A generation later in 1987, with the stiff winds of change already blowing westward from Moscow,  President Ronald Reagan issued an ultimatum to his Soviet counterpart: "Mr. Gorbachev, tear down this wall."

The actual fall of the Wall had less to do with presidential proclamations than with the obvious failings of the Soviet system, a general thawing in Moscow (where Gorbachev introduced *perestroika* and *glasnost*, and declared that he would no longer employ force to keep Eastern European satellite states under Soviet rule), the brave civil-disobedience actions of many ordinary citizens behind the Wall—and a bureaucratic snafu.

By November of 1989, it was clear that change was in the air. Hungary had already opened its borders to the West that summer, making it next to impossible for East German authorities to keep people in. A series of anti-regime protests had swept nearby Leipzig a few weeks earlier, attracting hundreds of thousands of supporters (see page 655). On October 7, 1989—on the 40th anniversary of the official creation of the DDR—East German premier Erich Honecker said, "The Wall will be standing in 50 and even in 100 years." He was only off by 99 years and 11 months. A similar rally in East Berlin's Alexanderplatz on November 4—with a half-million protesters chanting, *"Wir wollen raus!"* (We want out!)—persuaded the East German politburo to begin a gradual process of relaxing travel restrictions.

The DDR's intention was to slightly crack the door to the West, but an inarticulate spokesman's confusion inadvertently threw it wide open. The decision was made on Thursday, November 9, to tentatively allow a few more Easterners to cross into the West—a largely symbolic reform that was intended to take place gradually, over many weeks. Licking their wounds, politburo members left town early for a long weekend. The announcement about travel restrictions was left to a spokesman, Günter Schabowski, who knew only what was on a piece of paper handed to him moments before he went on television for a routine press conference. At 18:54, Schabowski read the statement dutifully, with little emotion, seemingly oblivious to the massive impact of his own words: "exit via border crossings...possible for every citizen." Reporters, unable to believe what they were hearing, began to prod him about when the borders would open. Schabowski looked with puzzlement at the brief statement, shrugged, and offered his best guess: *"Ab sofort, unverzüglich."* ("Immediately, without delay.")

Schabowski's words spread like wildfire through the streets of both Berlins, its flames fanned by West German TV broadcasts (and Tom Brokaw, who had rushed to Berlin when alerted by NBC's bureau chief). East Berliners began to show up at Wall checkpoints, demanding that border guards let them pass. As the crowds grew, the border guards could not reach anyone who could issue official orders. (The politburo members were effectively hiding out.) Finally, around 23:30, a border guard named Harald Jäger at the Bornholmer Strasse crossing decided to simply open the gates. Easterners flooded into the West, embracing their long-separated cousins, unable to believe their good fortune. Once open, the Wall could never be closed again.

The carnival atmosphere of those first years after the Wall fell is gone, but hawkers still sell "authentic" pieces of the Wall, DDR flags, and military paraphernalia to gawking tourists. When it fell, the Wall was literally carried away by the euphoria. What managed to survive has been nearly devoured by decades of persistent "Wall-peckers."

Americans—the Cold War victors—have the biggest appetite for Wall-related sights, and a few bits and pieces remain for us to seek out. Berlin's best Wall-related sights are the Berlin Wall Memorial along Bernauer Strasse, with a long stretch of surviving Wall (near S-Bahn: Nordbahnhof; page 794), and the Museum of the Wall at Checkpoint Charlie (see page 784). Other stretches of the Wall still standing include the short section at Niederkirchnerstrasse/Wilhelmstrasse (near the Topography of Terror exhibit; page 779) and the longer East Side Gallery (near the Ostbahnhof; page 790).

hours of commentary—is essential to fully appreciate the exhibits. Tel. 030/2599-3300, www.jmberlin.de.

Getting There: Take the U-Bahn to Hallesches Tor, find the exit marked *Jüdisches Museum,* exit straight ahead, then turn right on Franz-Klühs-Strasse. The museum is a five-minute walk ahead on your left, at Lindenstrasse 9.

Eating: The museum's restaurant, Café Schmus, offers good Jewish-style meals, albeit not kosher (daily 10:00-20:00, Mon until 22:00).

Visiting the Museum: Designed by American architect Daniel Libeskind (the master planner for the redeveloped World Trade Center in New York), the zinc-walled building has a zigzag shape pierced by voids symbolic of the irreplaceable cultural loss caused by the Holocaust. Enter the 18th-century Baroque building next door, then go through an underground tunnel to reach the museum interior.

Before you reach the exhibit, your visit starts with three **memorial spaces.** Follow the Axis of Exile to a disorienting slanted garden with 49 pillars (evocative of the Memorial to the Murdered Jews of Europe, across town). Next, the Axis of Holocaust, lined with artifacts from Jews imprisoned and murdered by the Nazis, leads to an eerily empty tower shut off from the outside world. The Axis of Continuity takes you to stairs and the main exhibit. A detour partway up the long stairway

leads to the Memory Void, a compelling space of "fallen leaves": heavy metal faces that you walk on, making unhuman noises with each step.

Finish climbing the stairs to the top of the museum, and stroll chronologically through the 2,000-year **story of Judaism** in Germany. The exhibit, on two floors, is engaging, with lots of actual artifacts. Interactive bits (you can, for example, spell your name in Hebrew, or write a prayer and hang it from a tree) make it lively for kids. English explanations interpret both the exhibits and the design of the very symbolic building.

The top floor focuses on everyday life in Ashkenaz (medieval German-Jewish lands). The nine-minute movie "A Thousand Years Ago" sets the stage for your journey through Jewish history. You'll learn what garlic had to do with early Jews in Germany (hint: It's not just about cooking). The Middle Ages were a positive time for Jewish culture, which flourished then in many areas of Europe. But around 1500, many Jews were expelled from the countryside and moved into cities. Viewing stations let you watch nine short, lively videos that pose provocative questions about faith. Moses Mendelssohn's role in the late-18th-century Jewish Enlightenment, which gave rise to Reform Judaism, is highlighted. The Tradition and Change exhibit analyzes how various subgroups of the Jewish faith modified and relaxed their rules to adapt to a changing world.

Downstairs, on the middle floor, exhibits detail the rising tide of anti-Semitism in Germany through the 19th century—at a time when many Jews were so secularized that they celebrated Christmas right along with Hanukkah. Berlin's glory days (1890-1933) were a boom time for many Jews, though it was at times challenging to reconcile the reformed ways of the more assimilated western (German) Jews with the more traditional Eastern European Jews. The exhibit segues into the **dark days** of Hitler—the collapse of the relatively tolerant Weimar Republic, the rise of the Nazis, and the horrific night of November 9-10, 1938, when, throughout Germany, hateful mobs destroyed Jewish-owned businesses, homes, synagogues, and even entire villages—called "Crystal Night" (Kristallnacht) for the broken glass that glittered in the streets.

The thought-provoking conclusion brings us to the present day, with the question: How do you keep going after six million of your people have been murdered? You'll see how German society has reacted to the Holocaust blood on its hands (one fascinating exhibit has footage of a 1975 sit-in of German Jews to protest a controversial play with a stereotypical Jewish villain), and listen to headphone commentary of Jewish people describing their experiences growing up in postwar Germany, Austria, and Switzerland.

Karl-Marx-Allee

The buildings along Karl-Marx-Allee in East Berlin (just beyond Alexanderplatz) were completely leveled by the Red Army in 1945. As an expression of their adoration to the "great Socialist Father" (Stalin), the DDR government decided to rebuild the street better than ever (the USSR provided generous subsidies). They intentionally made it one meter wider than the Champs-Elysées, named it Stalinallee, and lined it with "workers' palaces" built in the bold "Stalin Gothic" style so common in Moscow in the 1950s. Now renamed after Karl Marx, the street and its restored buildings provide a rare look at Berlin's communist days. Distances are a bit long for convenient walking, but you can cruise Karl-Marx-Allee by taxi, or ride the U-Bahn to Strausberger Platz (which was built to resemble an Italian promenade) and walk to Frankfurter Tor, reading the good information posts along the way. Notice the Social Realist reliefs on the buildings and the lampposts, which incorporate the wings of a phoenix (rising from the ashes) in their design. Once a "workers' paradise," the street now hosts a two-mile-long capitalist beer festival the first weekend in August.

The **Café Sibylle,** just beyond the Strausberger Platz U-Bahn station, is a fun spot for a coffee, traditional DDR ice-cream treats, and a look at its free informal museum that tells the story of the most destroyed street in Berlin. While the humble exhibit is nearly all in German, it's fun to see the ear (or buy a €10 plaster replica) and half a moustache from what was the largest statue of Stalin in Germany (the centerpiece of the street until 1961). It also provides a few intimate insights into apartment life in a DDR flat. The café is known for its good coffee and *Schwedeneisbecher mit Eierlikor*— an ice-cream sundae with a shot of egg liqueur, popular among those nostalgic for communism (Mon-Fri 10:00-20:00, Thu-Fri until 22:00, Sat-Sun 12:00-22:00, Karl-Marx-Allee 72, at intersection with Koppenstrasse, a block from U-Bahn: Strausberger Platz, tel. 030/2935-2203).

Heading out to Karl-Marx-Allee (just beyond the TV Tower), you're likely to notice a giant colorful **mural** decorating a blocky communist-era skyscraper. This was the Ministry of Education, and the mural is a tile mosaic trumpeting the accomplishments of the DDR's version of "No Child Left Behind."

More Sights South of Unter den Linden
East Side Gallery
The biggest remaining stretch of the Wall is now the "world's longest outdoor art gallery." It stretches for nearly a mile and is covered with murals painted by artists from around the world. The murals (classified as protected monuments) got a facelift in 2009, when the city invited the original artists back to re-create their work for the 20th anniversary of the fall of the Wall. This segment of the Wall makes a poignant walk. For a quick look, take the S-Bahn to the Ostbahnhof station (follow signs to Stralauerplatz exit; once outside, TV Tower will be to your right; go left and at next corner look to your right—the Wall is across the busy street). The gallery is slowly being consumed by developers. If you walk the entire length of the East Side Gallery, you'll find a small Wall souvenir shop at the end and a bridge crossing the river to a subway station at Schlesisches Tor (in Kreuzberg). The bridge, a fine example of Brandenburg Neo-Gothic brickwork, has a fun neon "rock, paper, scissors" installment poking fun at the futility of the Cold War (visible only after dark).

Kreuzberg
This district—once abutting the dreary Wall and inhabited mostly by poor Turkish guest laborers and their families—is still run-down, with graffiti-riddled buildings and plenty of student and Turkish street life. It offers a gritty look at melting-pot Berlin, in a city where original Berliners are as rare as old buildings. Berlin is

the largest Turkish city outside of Turkey itself, and Kreuzberg is its "downtown." But to call it a "little Istanbul" insults the big one. You'll see *Döner Kebab* stands, shops decorated with spray paint, and mothers wrapped in colorful scarves. But lately, an influx of immigrants from many other countries has diluted the Turkishness of Kreuzberg. For the most colorful experience, visit on Tuesday or Friday between 11:00 and 18:30, when the **Turkish Market** sprawls along Maybachufer street beside the Landwehr Canal. Take the U-Bahn to Kottbusser Tor and wander down Kottbusser Strasse, cross the canal, and turn left down Maybachufer.

NORTH OF UNTER DEN LINDEN

There are few major sights north of Unter den Linden, but this area has some of Berlin's trendiest, most interesting neighborhoods. I've listed these roughly from south to north, as you'd approach them from the city center and Unter den Linden. On a sunny day, a stroll (or tram ride) through these bursting-with-life areas can be as engaging as any museum in town.

Hackescher Markt

This area, in front of the S-Bahn station of the same name, is a great people scene day and night. The brick trestle supporting the train track is a classic example of the city's Brandenburg Neo-Gothic brickwork. Most of the brick archways are now filled with hip shops, which have official—and newly trendy—addresses such as "S-Bahn Arch #9, Hackescher Markt." Within 100 yards of the S-Bahn station, you'll find recommended Turkish and Bavarian restaurants, walking-tour and pub-crawl departure points, and tram #M1 to Prenzlauer Berg. Also nearby are two fascinating examples of Berlin's traditional courtyards *(Höfe)*—one trendy and modern, the other retro-cool, with two fascinating museums.

Hackesche Höfe (a block in front of the Hackescher Markt S-Bahn station, at Rosenthaler Strasse 40) is a series of eight courtyards bunny-hopping through a wonderfully restored 1907 *Jugendstil* (German Art Nouveau) building. Berlin's apartments are organized like this—courtyard after courtyard leading off the main roads. This complex is full of trendy restaurants (including the recommended Turkish eatery, Hasir), theaters, and cinemas (playing movies in their original languages). Courtyard #5 is particularly charming, with a children's park, and an Ampelmann store (see page 728). This courtyard system is a wonderful example of how to make huge city blocks livable. Two decades after the Cold War, this area has reached the final evolution of East Berlin's urban restoration: total gentrification. These courtyards also offer a useful lesson for visitors: Much of Berlin's charm hides off the street front.

Haus Schwarzenberg, next door (at Rosenthaler Strasse 39),

BERLIN

BERLIN

has a totally different feel. This rare surviving bit of East Berlin is owned by an artists' collective, with a bar, cinema (showing art films in their original language), an open-air art space (reminiscent of mid-1990s eastern Berlin), and the basement-level "Dead Chickens" gallery (with far-out hydro-powered art). Its Café Cinema is one of the last remaining '90s bohemian-chic bars. And within this amazing little zone you'll find two inspirational museums. **Museum of Otto Weidt's Workshop for the Blind** (Museum Blindenwerkstatt Otto Weidt) vividly tells the amazing story of a Berliner heroically protecting blind and deaf Jews during World War II (free, daily 10:00-20:00). Otto Weidt employed them to produce brooms and brushes, and because that was useful for the Nazi war machine, he managed to finagle a special status for his workers. You can see the actual brushmaking factory with pedal-powered machines still lined up. The exhibits are described well (in English and Braille), and there's a good intro video and free audioguide. **Silent Heroes Memorial Center** (Gedenkstätte Stille Helden) is a well-presented exhibit celebrating the quietly courageous individuals who resisted the persecution of the Jews from 1933 to 1945 (free, daily 10:00-20:00).

Oranienburger Strasse and Nearby

Oranienburger Strasse, a few blocks west of Hackescher Markt, is anchored by an important and somber sight, the New Synagogue (S-Bahn: Oranienburger Strasse). But the rest of this zone (roughly between the synagogue and Torstrasse) is colorful and quirky—especially after dark. The streets behind Grosse Hamburger Strasse flicker with atmospheric cafés, *Kneipen* (pubs), and art galleries. At night (from about 20:00), techno-prostitutes line Oranienburger Strasse. Prostitution is legal throughout Germany. Prostitutes pay taxes and receive health care insurance like anyone else. On this street, they hire security guards (lingering nearby) for safety. The sex workers all seem to buy their Barbarella wardrobes—notice the uniforms complete with matching fanny packs—at the same place.

▲New Synagogue (Neue Synagogue)

A shiny gilded dome marks the New Synagogue, now a museum and cultural center. Consecrated in 1866, this was once the biggest and finest synagogue in Germany, with seating for 3,200 worshippers and a sumptuous Moorish-style interior modeled after the Alhambra in Granada, Spain. It was desecrated by  Nazis on Crystal Night (Kristallnacht) in 1938, bombed in 1943, and partially rebuilt in 1990. Only the dome and facade have been restored—a window overlooks the vacant field marking what used to be the synagogue. On its facade, a small plaque—added by East Berlin Jews in 1966—reads "Never forget" *(Vergesst es nie)*. At that time East Berlin had only a few hundred Jews, but now that the city is reunited, the Jewish community numbers about 12,000.

Inside, past tight security, the small but moving permanent exhibit called Open Ye the Gates describes the Berlin Jewish community through the centuries (filling three big rooms on the ground floor and first floor, with some good English descriptions). Examine the cutaway model showing the entire synagogue (pre-destruction) and an exhibit of religious items. Stairs lead up (past temporary exhibits, with a separate entry fee) to the dome, where there's not much to see except the unimpressive-from-the-inside dome itself and ho-hum views—not worth the entry price or the climb.

Cost and Hours: Main exhibit-€3.50, dome-€2, temporary exhibits-€3, €7 combo-ticket covers everything, audioguide-€3; March-Oct Sun-Mon 10:00-20:00, Tue-Thu 10:00-18:00, Fri 10:00-17:00—until 14:00 in March and Oct; Nov-Feb Sun-Thu 10:00-18:00, Fri 10:00-14:00, closed Sat year-round; Oranien-burger Strasse 28/30, enter through the low-profile door in the modern building just right of the domed synagogue facade, S-Bahn: Oranienburger Strasse, tel. 030/8802-8300 and press 1, www.cjudaicum.de.

Eating: Next door to the New Synagogue (to the left as you face it) is every local kid's favorite traditional candy shop, **Bonbon-macherei,** where you can see candy being made the old-fashioned way (Wed-Sat 12:00-20:00, closed Sun-Tue, at Oranienburger Strasse 32, in the Heckmann Höfe—another classic Berlin court-yard). And just around the corner and down the street from the synagogue, you'll find the fully kosher **Beth Café** (closed Sat, Tucholskystrasse 40).

Nearby: A block from the synagogue (to the right as you face it), walk 50 yards down **Grosse Hamburger Strasse** to a little park. This street was known for 200 years as the "street of tolerance" because the Jewish community donated land to Protestants so they could build a church. Hitler turned it into the "street of death" *(Todesstrasse),* bulldozing 12,000 graves of the city's oldest Jewish cemetery and turning a Jewish nursing home into a deportation center. Because of the small but growing radical Islamic element in Berlin, and a smattering of persistent neo-Nazis, several police officers and an Israeli secret agent keep watch over the Jewish high school nearby.

▲The Kennedys Museum

This crisp, private enterprise (in a former Jewish girls' school build-ing that survived the war) delightfully recalls John F. Kennedy's 1963 Germany trip with great photos and video clips as well as a photographic shrine to the Kennedy clan in America. Among the interesting mementos are old campaign buttons and posters, and JFK's notes with the phonetic pronunciation "Ish bin ein Bear-leener." Jacqueline Kennedy commented on how strange it was that this—not even in his native language—was her husband's most quotable quote. The highlight: a theater where you can watch a newsreel of Kennedy's historic speech (20 minutes, plays continu-ously).

Cost and Hours: €5, Tue-Sun 11:00-19:00, closed Mon, from Oranienburger Strasse go a block up Tucholskystrasse and turn right to Auguststrasse 13, tel. 030/2065-3570, www.thekennedys.de.

Cold War Sights in the North
▲▲Berlin Wall Memorial (Gedenkstätte Berliner Mauer)

While tourists flock to Checkpoint Charlie, this memorial is Ber-lin's most substantial attraction relating to its gone-but-not-for-

gotten Wall. Exhibits line up along four blocks of Bernauer Strasse, stretching northeast from the Nordbahnhof S-Bahn station. You can enter two dif-ferent museums plus various open-air exhibits and memori-als, see several fragments of the Wall, and peer from an obser-vation tower down into a preserved, complete stretch of the Wall system (as it was during the Cold War). To prepare for a visit here, read "The Berlin Wall (and Its Fall)" sidebar on page 786.

Over the next few years, the Memorial plans to gradually add more open-air exhibitions farther along Bernauer Strasse. Even-tually the chain of sights will stretch all the way to Eberswalder Strasse and Oderberger Strasse, near the heart of Prenzlauer Berg.

Cost and Hours: Free; Visitor Center and Documentation Center open April-Oct Tue-Sun 9:30-19:00, Nov-March until 18:00, closed Mon year-round; outdoor areas accessible 24 hours daily; last English movie starts at 18:00, memorial chapel closes at 17:00; Bernauer Strasse 111, tel. 030/4679-86666, www.berliner-mauer-gedenkstaette.de.

Getting There: Take the S-Bahn (line S-1, S-2, or S-25—all handy from Potsdamer Platz, Brandenburger Tor, or Friedrich-strasse) to the Nordbahnhof. The Nordbahnhof's underground

Stolpersteine (Stumbling Stones)

As you wander through the Hackesche Höfe and Oranienburger Strasse neighborhoods—and throughout Europe—you might stumble over small brass plaques in the sidewalk called *Stolpersteine*. *Stolpern* means "to stumble," which is what you are meant to do. These plaques are placed in front of the homes of residents who were killed during World War II. The *Stolpersteine* serve not only to honor the victims, but also to stimulate thought and discussion on a daily basis (rather than only during visits to memorial sites) and to put an individual's name on the mass horror. They're also a clever rebuke to a common prewar German slur: When Gentiles tripped on a protruding rock or cobble, it was common to joke that "a Jew must be buried here." More than 44,000 of these plaques have been installed across Europe, mostly in Germany. They're made of brass so they stay polished as you walk over them, instead of fading into the sidewalk. On each plaque is the name of the victim who lived in that spot, and how and where that person died. While some Holocaust memorials formerly used neutral terminology like "perished," now they use words like "murdered" *(ermordet)*—part of the very honest way in which today's Germans are dealing with their country's past. The city of Munich, however, has banned *Stolpersteine*, saying that the plaques were insulting and degrading to victims of persecution, who would continue to be trod on by "Nazi boots." Installation of a *Stolperstein* can be sponsored for €120 and has become popular in schools, where students research the memorialized person's life as a class project.

hallways have history exhibits in English (explained later). Exit by following signs for *Bernauer Strasse,* and you'll pop out across the street from a long chunk of Wall and kitty-corner from the Visitor Center.

The Berlin Wall, which was erected virtually overnight in 1961, ran right along Bernauer Strasse. People were suddenly separated from their neighbors across the street. This stretch was particularly notorious because existing apartment buildings were incorporated into the structure of the Wall itself. Film footage and photographs from the era show Berliners worriedly watching workmen seal off these buildings from the West, brick by brick. Some people attempted to leap to freedom from upper-story windows, with mixed results. One of the unfortunate ones was Ida Siekmann,

who fell to her death from her third-floor apartment on August 22, 1961, and is considered the first casualty of the Berlin Wall.

Visiting the Memorial: From the Nordbahnhof station (which has some interesting Wall history in itself), head first to the Visitor Center to get your bearings, then explore the assorted Wall fragments and other sights in the park across the street. Work your way up Bernauer Strasse to the Documentation Center, Wall System, memorial chapel, and remaining signposts (the last of which focus on various escape attempts—see the tunnel paths marked in the grass), until you reach the Bernauer Strasse U-Bahn station.

Nordbahnhof

This S-Bahn station was one of the "ghost stations" of Cold War Berlin. It was built in 1926, closed in 1961, and opened again in 1989. As it was a dogleg of the East mostly surrounded by the West, Western subway trains had permission to use the underground tracks to zip through this station (without stopping, of course) en route between stops in the West. Posted information boards show photos comparing 1989 with 2009, and explain that East German border guards, who were stationed here to ensure that nobody got on or off those trains, were locked into their surveillance rooms to prevent them from escaping. (But one subway employee and his family used the tunnels to walk to the West and freedom.)

Follow signs down a long yellow hall to Bernauer Strasse. Climbing the stairs up to the Bernauer Strasse exit, ponder that the doorway at the top of these stairs (marked by the *Sperrmauer 1961-1989* plaque) was a bricked-off no-man's-land just 26 years ago. Stepping outside, you'll see the Wall park (directly across the street) and the Visitor Center (in a low rust-colored building kitty-corner across the street).

Visitor Center (Bezucherzentrum)

This small complex has a helpful information desk, a bookstore, and two good movies that provide context for a visit (they run in English at the top of each hour, about 30 minutes for the whole spiel): *History of the Wall* offers a great 12-minute overview of why the Wall was built and how it fell. That's followed by *Walled In!*, an animated 12-minute film illustrating the Wall as it functioned here at Bernauer Strasse (Wall wonks will find it fascinating). Before leaving, pick up the brochure explaining the outdoor exhibits.

Wall Fragments and Other Sights

Across the street from the Visitor Center is a long stretch of Wall. The park behind it is scattered with a few more Wall chunks as well as monuments and memorials honoring its victims, with clumps of info-posts offering brief personal stories and bits of background information (most of it available in English). To get your bearings, find the small model of the entire area when the Wall still stood (just across the street from the Nordbahnhof). While most items are accompanied by English explanations, the brochure from the Visitor Center helps you better appreciate what you're seeing. The rusty "Window of Remembrance" monument honors slain would-be escapees with their names, dates of death, and transparent photos that are viewable from both sides. Before it was the no-man's-land between the walls, this area was the parish graveyard for a nearby church; ironically, DDR officials had to move a thousand graves from here to create a "death strip."

Berlin Wall Documentation Center (Dokumentationszentrum Berliner Mauer)

This "Doku-Center" has two movies, a small exhibit, and a view-point tower overlooking the preserved Wall section. The two **films** shown on the ground floor are different from those screened at the Visitor Center: *The View*, dating from 1965, tells the story of an elderly West Berlin woman who lived near the Wall, and could look into the death strip and the East from her window (in German only). *Mauerflug* features aerial photography of Berlin from the spring of 1990—after the Wall had opened, but while most of the 96-mile-long barricade still stood, offering an illuminating look at a divided city (English subtitles).

Upstairs is an **exhibit** with photos and videos detailing the construction of the Wall, which began August 13, 1961. At the model of the Wall along Bernauer Strasse, notice how existing buildings were incorporated into the structure. Headphones let you listen to propagandistic, high-spirited oompah music from East Germany that celebrated the construction of the Wall: "It was high time!" There's also a list of people who died attempting to cross the Wall. From the top-floor **viewpoint,** look down at the Wall itself (described next).

Wall System

This is the last surviving in-tact bit of the complete "Wall system" (with both sides of its Wall—capped by the round pipe that made it tougher for escapees to get a grip—and its no-man's-land death strip). The guard tower came from a dif-ferent part of the Wall; it was  actually purchased on that great capitalist invention, eBay (some-where, Stalin spins in his grave). A strip of photos and descriptions explains what you're seeing. Plaques along the sidewalk below you mark the locations of escapes or deaths.

BERLIN

Just beyond the Wall section (to the left), and also viewable from the tower, is a modern, cagelike church (described next).

Chapel of Reconciliation (Kapelle der Versöhnung)

This chapel marks the spot of the late-19th-century Church of Reconciliation, which survived WWII bombs—but did not survive the communists. Notice the larger footprint of the original church in the field around the chapel. When the Wall was built, the church wound up, unusable, right in the middle of the death strip. It was torn down in 1985, supposedly because it got in the way of the border guards' sight lines. (This coincided with a pe-

riod in which anti-DDR opposition movements were percolating in Christian churches, prompting the atheistic regime to destroy several houses of worship.) If you're interested, walk around the chapel for a closer look (closes at 17:00). The carved wooden altarpiece was saved from the original structure. The chapel hosts daily prayer services for the victims of the Wall.

▲▲Prenzlauer Berg

Young, in-the-know locals agree that Prenzlauer Berg is one of Berlin's most colorful neighborhoods. The heart of this area, with a dense array of hip cafés, restaurants, boutiques, and street life, is roughly between Helmholtzplatz and Kollwitzplatz and along Kastanienallee (U2: Senefelderplatz and Eberswalder Strasse; or take the S-Bahn to Hackescher Markt and catch tram #M1 north). Similar outposts to the south—closer to Museum Island and Unter den Linden—cluster near the Hackescher Markt S-Bahn station; Rosenthaler Platz U-Bahn station; and Oranienburger Strasse (near the New Synagogue).

"Prenzl'berg," as Berliners call it, was largely untouched during World War II, but its buildings slowly rotted away under the communists. Then, after the Wall fell, it was overrun first with artists and anarchists, then with laid-back hipsters, energetic young families, and clever entrepreneurs who breathed life back into its classic old apartment blocks, deserted factories, and long-forgotten breweries.

Years of rent control kept things affordable for its bohemian residents. But now landlords are free to charge what the market will bear, and the vibe is changing. This is ground zero for Berlin's baby boom: Tattooed and pierced young moms and dads, who've joined the modern rat race without giving up their alternative flair, push their youngsters in designer strollers past trendy boutiques and restaurants.

There are no real sights—just a lively, laid-back neighborhood ignoring its wonderful late-19th-century architecture high overhead. The intersection of Oderberger Strasse and Kastanienallee is a typically convivial bit of Prenzlauer Berg to explore.

If you walk west to the end of Oderberger Strasse, you'll hit the **Wall Park** (Mauerpark). Once part of the Wall's death strip, today it's a Prenzlauer Berg green space—an alternative promenade. The park is particularly entertaining on Sundays, when it hosts a flea market and a giant karaoke party. Along the bluff runs a bit of the Wall covered in graffiti art. Just beyond that is the Friedrich-Lud-

wig-Jahn-Sportpark stadium from DDR times, built to host the World Youth Festival in 1951 and still marked by its original bombastic light towers (even light towers were designed to stir young communist souls).

Berliners have a strong sense of community. They manage in a big city by enjoying a strong neighborhood identity in areas like Prenzlauer Berg. But there is some tension these days, as locals complain about cafés and bars catering to yuppies sipping prosecco, while working-class and artistic types are being priced out.

While it has changed plenty, I find Prenzlauer Berg a celebration of life and a joy to stroll through. It's a fun area to explore and have a meal (see page 834) or spend the night (see page 818).

More Sights North of Unter den Linden
Palace of Tears (Tränenpalast) at Friedrichstrasse Station
The border station attached to Friedrichstrasse train station was where Westerners visiting loved ones in the East would be checked before crossing back into the free world. The scene of so many sad farewells, it earned the nickname Tränenpalast, or "palace of tears." It finally closed in 1990, but the 1962 building survives. An exhibit shows everyday life in a divided Germany, with a fascinating peek into the paranoid border-control world of the DDR.

Cost and Hours: Free, includes audioguide, Tue-Fri 9:00-19:00, Sat-Sun 10:00-18:00, closed Mon, on the river side of the Friedrichstrasse station, Reichstagufer 17, www.hdg.de/berlin.

Natural History Museum (Museum für Naturkunde)
This museum is worth a visit just to see the largest dinosaur skeleton ever assembled. While you're there, meet "Bobby" the stuffed

ape, and tour the Wet Collections, displaying shelf after shelf of animals preserved in ethanol (about a million all together). The museum is a magnet for the city's children, who love the interactive displays, the "History of the Universe in 120 Seconds" exhibit, and the cool virtual-reality "Jurascope" glasses that put meat and skin on all the dinosaur skeletons.

Cost and Hours: €5, €3 for kids, Tue-Fri 9:30-18:00, Sat-Sun 10:00-18:00, closed Mon, Invalidenstrasse 43, U6: Naturkundemuseum, tel. 030/2093-8591, www.naturkundemuseum-berlin.de.

Sights in Central Berlin

TIERGARTEN PARK AND NEARBY
Berlin's "Central Park" stretches two miles from Bahnhof Zoo to the Brandenburg Gate.

Victory Column (Siegessäule)
The Tiergarten's newly restored centerpiece, the Victory Column, was built to commemorate the Prussian defeat of Denmark in 1864...then reinterpreted after the defeat of France in 1870. The pointy-helmeted Germans rubbed it in, decorating the tower with French cannons and paying for it all with francs received as war reparations. The three lower rings commemorate Bismarck's victories. I imagine the statues of Moltke and other German military greats—which lurk among the trees nearby—goose-stepping around the floodlit angel at night.

Originally standing at the Reichstag, in 1938 the tower was moved to this position and given a 25-foot lengthening by Hitler's architect, Albert Speer, in anticipation of the planned re-envisioning of Berlin as "Welthauptstadt Germania"—the capital of a worldwide Nazi empire. Streets leading to the circle are flanked by surviving Nazi guardhouses, built in the stern style that fascists loved. At the memorial's first level, notice how WWII bullets chipped the fine marble columns. From 1989 to 2003, the column was the epicenter of the Love Parade (Berlin's city-wide techno-hedonist street party), and it was the backdrop for Barack Obama's summer 2008 visit to Germany as a presidential candidate.

Climbing its 270 steps earns you a breathtaking Berlin-wide view and a close-up of the gilded bronze statue of the goddess Victoria. You might recognize Victoria from Wim Wenders' 1987 arthouse classic *Wings of Desire*, or the *Stay (Faraway, So Close!)* video he directed for the rock band U2.

Cost and Hours: €3, daily April-Oct 9:30-18:30, until 19:00 Sat-Sun, Nov-March 10:00-17:00, closes in the rain, no elevator, bus #100, tel. 030/391-2961.

BERLIN

Flea Market

A colorful flea market thrives weekends on Strasse des 17 Juni, with great antiques, more than 200 stalls, collector-savvy merchants, and fun German fast-food stands (Sat-Sun 6:00-16:00, right next to S-Bahn: Tiergarten).

German Resistance Memorial
(Gedenkstätte Deutscher Widerstand)

This memorial and museum, located in the former Bendlerblock military headquarters just south of the Tiergarten, tells the story of several organized German resistance movements and the more than 42 separate assassination attempts against Hitler. While the exhibit has no real artifacts, the building itself is important: One of the most thoroughly planned schemes to kill Hitler was plotted here (the actual attempt occurred in Rastenburg, eastern Prussia; the event was dramatized in the 2009 Tom Cruise film *Valkyrie*). That attempt failed and several leaders of the conspiracy, including Claus Schenk Graf von Stauffenberg, were shot here in the courtyard.

Cost and Hours: Free, Mon-Fri 9:00-18:00, Thu until 20:00, Sat-Sun 10:00-18:00, free and good English audioguide, €4 printed English translation, no crowds, near Kulturforum at Stauffenbergstrasse 13, enter in courtyard, door on left, main exhibit on second floor up, bus #M29, tel. 030/2699-5000, www.gdw-berlin.de.

POTSDAMER PLATZ AND NEARBY

The "Times Square of Berlin," and possibly the busiest square in Europe before World War II, Potsdamer Platz was cut in two by the Wall and left a deserted no-man's-land for 40 years. Today, this immense commercial/residential/entertainment center, sitting on a

BERLIN

futuristic transportation hub, is home to the European headquarters of several big-league companies.

▲Potsdamer Platz

The new Potsdamer Platz was a vision begun in 1991, the year that Germany's parliament voted to relocate the seat of government to Berlin. Since then, Sony, Daimler, and other major corporations have turned the square once again into a city center. Like great Christian churches built upon pagan holy grounds, Potsdamer Platz—with its corporate logos flying high and shiny above what was the Wall—trumpets the triumph of capitalism.

While Potsdamer Platz tries to give Berlin a common center, the city has always been—and remains—a collection of towns. Locals recognize 28 distinct neighborhoods that may have grown together but still maintain their historic orientation. While Munich has the single dominant Marienplatz, Berlin will always have Charlottenburg, Savignyplatz, Kreuzberg, Prenzlauer Berg, and so on. In general, Berliners prefer these characteristic neighborhoods to an official city center. They're unimpressed by the grandeur of Potsdamer Platz, simply considering it a good place to go to the movies, with overpriced, touristy restaurants.

While most of the complex just feels big (the arcade is like any huge, modern, American mall), the entrance to the complex and Sony Center are worth a visit, and German-film buffs will enjoy the Deutsche Kinemathek museum (described later).

For an overview of the new construction, and a scenic route to the Sony Center, start at the Bahnhof Potsdamer Platz (east end of Potsdamer Strasse, S-Bahn and U-Bahn: Potsdamer Platz, exit following *Leipziger Platz* signs to see the best view of skyscrapers as you emerge). Find the green hexagonal **clock tower** with the traffic lights on top. This is a replica of the first electronic traffic light in Europe, which once stood at the six-street intersection of Potsdamer Platz. (The traffic cops who stood with flag and trumpet in the middle of the intersection were getting hit by cars too routinely, so this perch was built for them.)

On either side of Potsdamer Strasse, you'll see enormous cubical entrances to the underground Potsdamer Platz train station. Near these entrances, notice the slanted **glass cylinders** sticking out of the ground. The mirrors on the tops of the tubes move with the sun to collect light and send it underground (saving piles of euros in energy costs). Two lines in the pavement indicate where each layer of the **Berlin Wall** once stood (they trace about 25 miles of the wall through the city; for a string of interesting Wall and Nazi-era sites between here and Checkpoint Charlie, see page 778). On the right side of the street, notice the re-erected slabs of the Wall. Imagine when the first piece was cut out (see photo and history on nearby panel). These hang like scalps at the gate of Fort Capitalism...look up at the towering corporate headquarters: Market forces have won a clear victory. Now descend into one of the train station entrances and follow *Sony Center* signs. As you walk through the passage, notice the wall panels with historical information.

You'll come up the escalator into the **Sony Center** under a grand canopy (designed to evoke Mount Fuji). At night, multi-

colored floodlights play on the underside of this tent. Office workers and tourists eat here by the fountain, enjoying the parade of people. The modern Bavarian Lindenbräu beer hall—the Sony boss wanted a *Brauhaus*—serves traditional food (€11-20, daily 11:00-24:00, big €12 salads, three-foot-long taster boards of eight different beers, tel. 030/2575-1280).

Across the plaza, Josty Bar is built around a surviving bit of a venerable hotel that was a meeting place for Berlin's rich and famous before the bombs (€12-20 meals, daily 8:00-24:00, tel. 030/2575-9702). CineStar is a rare cinema that plays mainstream movies in their original language (www.cinestar.de).

A huge **screen** above the Deutsche Kinemathek museum (left of Starbucks) shows big sporting events on special occasions. Otherwise it runs historic video clips of Potsdamer Platz through the decades.

▲Deutsche Kinemathek Film and TV Museum

This exhibit is the most interesting place to visit in the Sony Center. The early pioneers in filmmaking were German (including Fritz Lang, F. W. Murnau, Ernst Lubitsch, and the Austrian-born Billy Wilder), and many of them also became influential in Hollywood—making this a fun visit for cinephiles. Your admission ticket gets you into several floors of exhibits (including temporary exhibits on floors 1 and 4) made meaningful by the included, essential English audioguide.

Cost and Hours: €7, free Thu 16:00-20:00, includes 1.5-hour audioguide, Tue-Sun 10:00-18:00, Thu until 20:00, closed Mon, tel. 030/300-9030, www.deutsche-kinemathek.de.

Nearby: The Kino Arsenal theater downstairs shows offbeat art-house films in their original language.

Visiting the Museum: From the ticket desk, ride the elevator up to the third floor, where you can turn left (into the film section, floors 3 and 2) or right (into the TV section, floors 3 and 4).

In the **film section,** you'll walk back in time through a fun mirrored entryway. The exhibit starts with the German film industry's beginnings, with an emphasis on the Weimar Republic period in the 1920s, when Berlin rivaled Hollywood. Influential films included the early German Expressionist masterpiece *The Cabinet of Dr. Caligari* (1920) and Fritz Lang's seminal *Metropolis* (1927). Three rooms are dedicated to Marlene Dietrich, who was a huge star both in Germany and, later, in Hollywood. (Dietrich, who performed at USO shows to entertain Allied troops fighting against her former homeland, once said, "I don't hate the Germans, I hate the Nazis.") Another section examines Nazi use of film as propaganda, including Leni Riefenstahl's masterful documentary of the 1936 Berlin Olympics and her earlier, chillingly propagandistic *Triumph des Willens (Triumph of the Will,* 1935). The postwar period was defined by two separate East and West German film industries. The exhibit's finale reminds us that German filmmakers are still highly influential and successful—including Wolfgang Petersen *(Das Boot, Air Force One, The Perfect Storm)* and Werner Herzog (documentaries such as *Grizzly Man,* and the drama *Rescue Dawn*). If this visit gets you curious about German cinema, see the recommendations in the Appendix.

The **TV section** tells the story of *das Idioten Box* from its infancy (when it was primarily used as a Nazi propaganda tool) to today. The 30-minute kaleidoscopic review—kind of a frantic fast-forward montage of greatest hits in German TV history, both East and West—is great fun even if you don't understand a word of it (it plays all day long, with 10-minute breaks). Otherwise, the TV section is a little more challenging for non-German speakers to appreciate. Upstairs (on the fourth floor) is a TV archive where you can dial through a wide range of new and classic German TV standards.

Panoramapunkt

Across Potsdamer Strasse from the Film and TV Museum, you can ride what's billed as the "fastest elevator in Europe" to skyscraping rooftop views. You'll travel at nearly 30 feet per second to the top of the 300-foot-tall Kollhoff

Tower. Its sheltered but open-air view deck provides a fun opportunity to survey Berlin's ongoing construction from above.

Cost and Hours: €6.50, €10.50 VIP ticket lets you skip the line, daily 10:00-20:00, until 21:00 in summer, last elevator 30 minutes before closing, in red-brick building at Potsdamer Platz 1, tel. 030/2593-7080, www.panoramapunkt.de.

KULTURFORUM

Just west of Potsdamer Platz, Kulturforum rivals Museum Island as the city's cultural heart, with several top museums and Berlin's concert hall—home of the world-famous Berlin Philharmonic orchestra. Of its sprawling museums, only the Gemäldegalerie is a must (and its New National Gallery is closed through at least 2017).

Combo-Tickets: All Kulturforum sights are covered by a single €12 Bereichskarte Kulturforum combo-ticket—a.k.a. Quartier-Karte, www.kulturforum-berlin.de.

Getting There: Ride the S-Bahn or U-Bahn to Potsdamer Platz, then walk along Potsdamer Platz; or from Bahnhof Zoo, take bus #200 to Philharmonie.

▲▲Gemäldegalerie

Literally the "Painting Gallery," Germany's top collection of 13th-through 18th-century European paintings (more than 1,400 canvases) is beautifully displayed in a building that's a work of art in itself. The North Wing starts with German paintings of the 13th to 16th century, including eight by Albrecht Dürer. Then come the Dutch and Flemish—Jan van Eyck, Pieter Brueghel, Peter Paul Rubens, Anthony van Dyck, Frans Hals, and Jan Vermeer. The wing finishes with German, English, and French 18th-century artists, such as Thomas Gainsborough and Antoine Watteau. An octagonal hall at the end features an impressive stash of Rembrandts. The South Wing is saved for the Italians—Giotto, Botticelli, Titian, Raphael, and Caravaggio.

Cost and Hours: €10, covered by Kulturforum combo-ticket, Tue-Fri 10:00-18:00, Thu until 20:00, Sat-Sun 11:00-18:00, closed Mon, audioguide included with entry, clever little loaner stools, great salad bar in cafeteria upstairs, Matthäikirchplatz 4, tel. 030/266-424-242, www.smb.museum.

◑ Self-Guided Tour: I'll point out a few highlights, focusing on Northern European artists (German, Dutch, and Flemish), with a few Spaniards and Italians thrown in. To go beyond my selections, make ample use of the excellent audioguide.

The collection spreads out on one vast floor surrounding a central hall. Inner rooms have Roman numerals (I, II, III), while adjacent outer rooms are numbered (1, 2, 3). After showing your ticket, turn right into room I and work your way counterclockwise (and roughly chronologically) through the collection.

Rooms I-III/1-4 kick things off with early German paintings (13th-16th century). In Room 1, look for the 1532 portrait of wealthy Hanseatic cloth merchant Georg Gisze by **Hans Holbein the Younger** (1497-1543). Gisze's name appears on several of the notes stuck to the wall behind him. And, typical of detail-rich Northern European art, the canvas is bursting with highly symbolic tidbits. Items scattered on the tabletop and on the shelves behind the merchant represent his lofty status and aspects of his life story. In the vase, the carnation represents his recent engagement, and the herbs symbolize his virtue.

And yet, the celebratory flowers have already begun to fade and the scales behind him are unbalanced, reminders of the fleetingness of happiness and wealth.

In Room 2 are fine portraits by the remarkably talented **Albrecht Dürer** (1471-1528), who traveled to Italy during the burgeoning days of the early Renaissance and melded the artistic harmony and classical grandeur he discovered there with a Northern European attention to detail. In his *Portrait of Hieronymus Holzschuher* (1526), Dürer skillfully captured the personality of a friend from Nürnberg, right down to the sly twinkle in his sidelong glance. Technically the portrait is perfection: Look closely and see each individual hair of the man's beard and fur coat, and even the reflection of the studio's windows in his eyes. Also notice Dürer's little pyramid-shaped, D-inside-A signature. Signing one's work was a revolutionary assertion of Dürer's renown at a time when German artists were considered anonymous craftsmen.

Lucas Cranach the Elder (1472-1553), whose works are in Room III, was a court painter for the prince electors of Saxony

and a close friend of Martin Luther (and his unofficial portraitist). But *The Fountain of Youth* (1546) is a far cry from Cranach's solemn portrayals of the Reformer. Old women helped to the fountain (on the left) emerge as young ladies on the right. Newly nubile, the women go into a tent to dress up, snog with noblemen in the bushes (right foreground), dance merrily beneath the trees, and dine grandly beneath a landscape of phallic mountains and towers. This work is flanked by Cranach's Venus nudes. I sense a pattern here.

Dutch painters (Rooms IV-VI/4-7) were early adopters of oil paint (as opposed to older egg tempera)—its relative ease of han-

dling allowed them to brush the super-fine details for which they became famous. **Rogier van der Weyden** (Room IV) was a virtuoso of the new medium. In *Portrait of a Young Woman* (c. 1400-1464), the subject wears a typical winged bonnet, addressing the viewer directly with her fetching blue eyes. The subjects (especially women) of most portraits of the time look off to one side; some art historians guess that the confident woman shown here is Van der Weyden's wife. In the same room is a remarkable, rare trio of three-panel altarpieces by Van der Weyden: The *Marienaltar* shows the life of the Virgin Mary; the *Johannesaltar* narrates the life of John the Baptist—his birth, baptizing Christ (with God and the Holy Spirit hovering overhead), and his gruesome death by decapitation; and the *Middelburger Altar* tells the story of the Nativity. Savor the fine details in each panel of these altarpieces.

Flash forward a few hundred years to the 17th century and Flemish (Belgian) painting (Rooms VII-VIII/9-10), and it's ap-

parent how much the Protestant Reformation—and resulting Counter-Reformation—changed the tenor of Northern European art. In works by **Peter Paul Rubens** (1577-1640)—including *Jesus Giving Peter the Keys to Heaven*—calm, carefully studied, detail-oriented seriousness gives way to an exuberant Baroque trumpeting of the greatness of the Catholic Church. In the Counter-Reformation world, the Catholic Church had serious competition for the hearts and minds of its congregants. Exciting art like this became a way to keep people in the pews. Notice the quivering brush-

strokes and almost too-bright colors. (In the same room are portraits by Rubens' student, Anthony van Dyck, as well as some hunting still lifes from Frans Snyders and others.) In the next rooms (VIII and 9) are more Rubens, including the mythological *Perseus Freeing Andromeda* and *The Martyrdom of St. Sebastian by Arrows* (loosely based on a more famous rendition by Andrea Mantegna).

Dutch painting from the 17th century (Rooms IX-XI/10-19) is dominated by the convivial portraits by **Frans Hals** (c. 1582-1666). His 1620 portrait of Catharina Hooft (far corner, Room 13) presents a startlingly self-possessed baby (the newest member of a wealthy merchant family) dressed with all the finery of a queen, adorned with lace and jewels, and clutching a golden rattle. The smiling nurse supporting the tyke offers her a piece of fruit, whose blush of red perfectly matches the nanny's apple-fresh cheeks.

But the ultimate Dutch master is **Rembrandt van Rijn** (1606-1669), whose powers of perception and invention propelled him to fame in his lifetime. Displayed here are several storytelling scenes (Room 16), mostly from classical mythology or biblical stories, all employing Rembrandt's trademark chiaroscu-

ro technique (with a strong contrast between light and dark). In *The Rape of Persephone*, Pluto grabs Persephone from his chariot and races toward the underworld, while other goddesses cling to her robe, trying to save her. Cast against a nearly black background, the almost overexposed, action-packed scene is shockingly emotional. In the nearby *Samson and Delilah* (1628), Delilah cradles Samson's head in her lap while silently signaling to a goon to shear Samson's hair, the secret to his strength. A self-portrait (Room X) of a 28-year-old Rembrandt wearing a beret is paired with the come-hither 1637 *Portrait of Hendrickje Stoffels* (the two were romantically linked). *Samson Threatens His Father-in-Law* (1635) captures the moment just after the mighty Samson (with his flowing hair, elegant robes, and shaking fist) has been told by his wife's father to take a hike. I wouldn't want to cross this guy.

Although **Johannes Vermeer** (1632-1675) is today just as admired as Rembrandt, he was little known in his day, probably

because he painted relatively few works for a small circle of Delft collectors. Vermeer was a master at conveying a complicated story through a deceptively simple scene with a few poignant details—whether it's a woman reading a letter at a window, a milkmaid pouring milk from a pitcher into a bowl, or (as in *The Glass of Wine*, Room 18) a young man offering a drink to a young lady. The young man had been playing her some music on his lute (which now sits, discarded, on a chair) and is hoping to seal the deal with some alcohol. The woman is finishing one glass of wine, and her would-be suitor stands ready—almost *too* ready—to pour her another. His sly, somewhat smarmy smirk drives home his high hopes for what will come next. Vermeer has perfectly captured the exact moment of "Will she or won't she?" The painter offers some clues—the coat of arms in the window depicts a woman holding onto the reigns of a horse, staying in control—but ultimately, only he (and the couple) know how this scene will end.

Shift south to Italian, French, and Spanish painting of the 17th and 18th centuries (Rooms XII-XIV/23-28). Venetian cityscapes

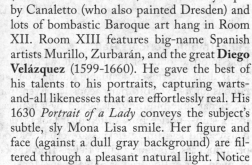

by Canaletto (who also painted Dresden) and lots of bombastic Baroque art hang in Room XII. Room XIII features big-name Spanish artists Murillo, Zurbarán, and the great **Diego Velázquez** (1599-1660). He gave the best of his talents to his portraits, capturing warts-and-all likenesses that are effortlessly real. His 1630 *Portrait of a Lady* conveys the subject's subtle, sly Mona Lisa smile. Her figure and face (against a dull gray background) are filtered through a pleasant natural light. Notice that if you stand too close, the brushstrokes get muddy—but when you back up, the scene snaps into perfectly sharp relief.

From here, the collection itself takes a step backwards—into Italian paintings of the 13th-16th century (Rooms XV-XVIII/29-41). This section includes some lesser-known works by great Italian Renaissance painters, including Raphael (Rooms XVII and 29, including five different Madonnas, among them the *Terranuova Madonna*, in a round frame) and Sandro Botticelli (Room VIII).

Museum of Decorative Arts (Kunstgewerbemuseum)

This newly renovated museum is scheduled to reopen by the spring of 2015. Wander through a thousand years of applied arts—porcelain, fine *Jugendstil* (German Art Nouveau) furniture, Art Deco, and reliquaries.

Cost and Hours: Covered by Kulturforum combo-ticket, Tue-Fri 10:00-18:00, Sat-Sun 11:00-18:00, closed Mon, Herbert-von-Karajan-Strasse 10, tel. 030/266-424-242, www.smb.museum/kgm.

▲Musical Instruments Museum (Musikinstrumenten Museum)

This impressive hall is filled with 600 exhibits spanning the 16th century to modern times. Wander among old keyboard instruments and funny-looking tubas. Pick up the included audioguide and free English brochure at the entry. In addition to the English commentary, the audioguide has clips of various instruments being played (just punch in the number next to the instrument you want to hear). This place is fascinating if you're into pianos.

Cost and Hours: €6, covered by Kulturforum combo-ticket, Tue-Fri 9:00-17:00, Thu until 20:00, Sat-Sun 10:00-17:00, closed Mon, low-profile white building east of the big yellow Philharmonic Concert Hall, tel. 030/2548-1178, www.sim.spk-berlin.de.

Philharmonic Concert Hall

Poke into the lobby of Berlin's yellow Philharmonic building and see if there are tickets available during your stay. The interior is famous for its extraordinary acoustics. Even from the outside, this is a remarkable building, designed by a nautical engineer to look like a ship—notice how different it looks from each angle. Inexpensive and legitimate tickets are often sold on the street before performances. Or you can buy tickets from the box office in person, by phone, or online (ticket office open Mon-Fri 15:00-18:00, Sat-Sun 11:00-14:00 except closed July-Aug, tel. 030/2548-8999—answered daily 9:00-18:00, July-Aug until 16:00, www.berliner-philharmoniker.de). For guest performances, you must buy tickets through the organizer (see website for details).

Sights in Western Berlin

Throughout the Cold War, Western travelers—and most West Berliners—got used to thinking of western Berlin's Kurfürstendamm boulevard as the heart of the city. But those days have gone the way of the Wall. With the huge changes the city has undergone since 1989, the real "city center" is now, once again, Berlin's historic center (the Mitte district, around Unter den Linden and Friedrichstrasse). While western Berlin still works well as a home base, it's no longer the obvious place from which to explore the city. After the new Hauptbahnhof essentially put Bahnhof Zoo out of business in 2006, the area was left with an identity crisis. Now, more than 20 years after reunification, the west side is back and has fully embraced its historical role as a chic, classy suburb.

IN THE HEART OF WESTERN BERLIN

A few interesting sights sit within walking distance of Bahnhof Zoo and the Savignyplatz hotels. For a detailed map of this area, see page 826.

▲Kurfürstendamm

Western Berlin's main drag, Kurfürstendamm boulevard (nick-named "Ku'damm"), starts at Kaiser Wilhelm Memorial Church and does a commercial cancan for two miles. In the 1850s, when Berlin became a wealthy and important capital, her "new rich" chose Kurfürstendamm as their street. Bismarck made it Berlin's Champs-Elysées. In the 1920s, it became a stylish and fashionable drag of cafés and boutiques. During the Third Reich, as home to an international community of diplomats and journalists, it enjoyed more freedom than the rest of Berlin. Throughout the Cold War, economic subsidies from the West made sure that capitalism thrived on Ku'damm. And today, while much of the old charm has been hamburgerized, Ku'damm is still a fine place to enjoy elegant shops (around Fasanenstrasse), department stores, and people-watching.

▲Kaiser Wilhelm Memorial Church (Gedächtniskirche)

This church was originally dedicated to the first emperor of Germany. Reliefs and mosaics show great events in the life of Germany's favorite *Kaiser*, from his corona-tion in 1871 to his death in 1888. The church's bombed-out ruins have been left standing as a poignant memorial to the destruction of Berlin in World War II.

Cost and Hours: Church—free, daily 9:00-19:00; Memorial Hall—free, Mon-Fri 10:00-18:00, Sat 10:00-17:30, Sun 12:00-17:30. Located on Breitscheidplatz, U2/U9 and S-Bahn: Zoologischer Garten or U1/U9: Kurfürstendamm, www.gedaechtniskirche.com.

Visiting the Church: The church is actually an ensemble of buildings: a new church, the matching bell tower, a meeting hall, and the bombed-out ruins of the old church, with its Memorial Hall. The current renovation project will strengthen the foundations of all four buildings and make it possible for visitors to get to the top of the church for the first time in 60 years.

Under a Neo-Romanesque mosaic ceiling, the **Memorial Hall** features a small exhibit of interesting photos about the bombing and before-and-after models of the church. After the war, some Berliners wanted to tear down the ruins and build it anew. Instead, it was decided to keep what was left of the old church as a memorial and stage a competition to design a contemporary, add-on section. The winning entry—the short, modern church (1961) next to the Memorial Hall—offers a meditative world of 11,000 little blue windows. The blue glass was given to the church by the French as a reconciliation gift. For more information on both churches, pick up the English flier (€0.50).

As you enter the **church,** a peaceful blue oasis in the middle of the busy city, turn immediately right to find a simple charcoal sketch of the Virgin Mary wrapped in a shawl. During the Battle of Stalingrad, German combat surgeon Kurt Reuber rendered the Virgin on the back of a stolen Soviet map to comfort the men in his care. On the right are the words "Light, Life, Love" from the gospel of John; on the left, "Christmas in the cauldron 1942"; and at the bottom, "Fortress Stalingrad." Though Reuber died in captivity a year later, his sketch was flown out of Stalingrad on the last medical evacuation flight, and postwar Germany embraced it as a symbol of the wish for peace. Copies of the drawing, now known as the *Stalingrad Madonna,* hang in the Berlin Cathedral, in England's Coventry, and in Russia's Volgograd (formerly Stalingrad) as a sign of peaceful understanding among nations. As another act of reconciliation, every Friday at 13:00 a "Prayers for Peace" service is held simultaneously with the cathedral in Coventry.

Nearby: The lively square between the churches and the Europa Center (a once-impressive, shiny high-rise shopping center built as a showcase of Western capitalism during the Cold War) usually attracts street musicians and performers—especially in the summer. Berliners call the funky fountain the "wet meatball."

The Story of Berlin

Filling most of what seems like a department store space right on Ku'damm (at #207), this sprawling history exhibit tells the stormy 800-year story of Berlin in a creative way. While there are almost no real historic artifacts, the exhibit does a good job of cobbling together many dimensions of the life and tumultuous times of this great city (and almost everything's in English). It's particularly strong on the story of the city from World War I through the Cold War. However, for similar information, and more artifacts, the German History Museum on Unter den Linden is a far better use of your time and money (see page 774).

Cost and Hours: €12, daily 10:00-20:00, last entry 2 hours before closing, tel. 030/8872-0100, www.story-of-berlin.de. Times for the 30-minute bunker tour are posted at the entry.

▲Käthe Kollwitz Museum

This local artist (1867-1945), who experienced much of Berlin's stormiest century, conveys some powerful, deeply felt emotions about motherhood, war, and suffering through the stark faces of her art. This small yet fine collection (the only one in town of Kollwitz's work) consists of three floors of charcoal drawings and woodcuts, topped by an attic with a handful of sculptures.

Cost and Hours: €6, daily 11:00-18:00, no photos, a block off Ku'damm at Fasanenstrasse 24, U-Bahn: Uhlandstrasse, tel. 030/882-5210, www.kaethe-kollwitz.de.

▲Kaufhaus des Westens (KaDeWe)

The "Department Store of the West" has been a Berlin tradition for more than a century. With a staff of 2,100 to help you sort through its vast selection of 380,000 items, KaDeWe claims to be the biggest department store on the Continent. You can get everything from a haircut and train ticket (third floor) to souvenirs (fourth floor). The theater and concert box office on the sixth floor charges an 18 percent booking fee, but they know all your options (cash only). The sixth floor is a world of gourmet taste treats. The biggest selection of deli and exotic food in Germany offers plenty of classy opportunities to sit down and eat. Ride the glass elevator to the seventh floor's glass-domed Winter Garden, a self-service cafeteria—fun but pricey.

Hours: Mon-Thu 10:00-20:00, Fri 10:00-21:00, Sat 9:30-20:00, closed Sun, S-Bahn: Zoologischer Garten or U-Bahn: Wittenbergplatz, tel. 030/21210, www.kadewe.de.

Nearby: The Wittenbergplatz U-Bahn station (in front of KaDeWe) is a unique opportunity to see an old-time station. Enjoy its interior with classic advertisements still decorating its venerable walls.

Berlin Zoo and Aquarium (Zoologischer Garten Berlin)

More than 1,500 different kinds of animals call Berlin's famous zoo home...or so the zookeepers like to think. The big hit here is the lonely panda bear (straight in from the entrance). The adjacent aquarium is world-class.

Cost and Hours: Zoo-€13, aquarium-€13, €20 for both, kids half-price, daily 9:00-18:00, aquarium closes 30 minutes earlier; feeding times—*Fütterungszeiten*—posted just inside entrance, the best feeding show is the sea lions—generally at 15:15; enter near Europa Center in front of Hotel Palace or opposite Bahnhof Zoo on Hardenbergplatz, Budapester Strasse 34, tel. 030/254-010, www.zoo-berlin.de.

Erotic Art Museum (Erotikmuseum)

This offers two floors of graphic art (especially East Asian), old-time sex-toy knickknacks, and a special exhibit on the queen of German pornography, the late Beate Uhse. This amazing woman, a former test pilot for the Third Reich and groundbreaking purveyor of condoms and sex ed in the 1950s, was the female Hugh Hefner of Germany and CEO of a huge chain of porn shops. She is famously credited with bringing sex out of the bedroom...and onto the kitchen table ("where it belongs," adds my Berliner friend).

FYI: You'll see much more sex for half the price in a private video booth next door.

Cost and Hours: €9, Mon-Sat 10:00-22:00, Sun 11:00-22:00, last entry at 21:00, hard-to-beat gift shop, at corner of Kantstrasse and Joachimstalerstrasse, a block from Bahnhof Zoo, tel. 030/886-0666, erotikmuseum.beate-uhse.com.

CHARLOTTENBURG PALACE AREA

The Charlottenburg district—with a cluster of museums across the street from a grand palace—is an easy side-trip from downtown. The palace isn't much to see, but if the surrounding museums appeal to you, consider making the trip.

Getting There: Ride U2 to Sophie-Charlotte Platz and walk 10 minutes up the tree-lined boulevard Schlossstrasse (following signs to *Schloss*), or—much faster—catch bus #M45 (direction Spandau) direct from Bahnhof Zoo.

Eating near Charlottenburg Palace: For lunch, try the traditional German grub at **Brauhaus Lemke** brewpub or sample Russian specialties at **Samowar** (see map page 815).

▲Charlottenburg Palace (Schloss Charlottenburg)

If you've seen the great palaces of Europe, this Baroque palace, also known as the Altes Schloss, comes in at about number 10 (behind Potsdam, too). It's the largest former residence of the royal Hohenzollern family in Berlin and contains the biggest collection of 17th-century French fresco painting outside France. The **Neue Flügel** (a.k.a. the Knobelsdorff Wing) has a separate entry fee and features a few royal apartments. Go upstairs and take a substantial hike through restored-since-the-war gold-crusted white rooms.

Cost and Hours: Palace-€12, includes audioguide, Tue-Sun 10:00-18:00, until 17:00 Nov-March, closed Mon, last entry 30 minutes before closing, tel. 030/320-911; Neue Flügel-€6, more during special exhibitions, includes audioguide, April-Oct Wed-Mon 10:00-18:00, Nov-March Wed-Mon 10:00-17:00, closed Tue year-round, last entry at 16:30, when facing the palace walk toward the right wing, tel. 0331/969-4200, www.spsg.de. The only WC is within the castle, mid-tour.

▲Museum Berggruen

This tidy little museum is a pleasant surprise. Climb three floors through a fun and substantial collection of Picassos. Along the way, you'll see plenty of notable works by Henri Matisse, Paul Klee, and Alberto Giacometti.

Cost and Hours: €10 combo-ticket includes the Scharf-Gerstenberg Collection—described later, open Tue-Fri 10:00-18:00, Sat-Sun 11:00-18:00, closed Mon, Schlossstrasse 1, tel. 030/326-95815, www.smb.museum.

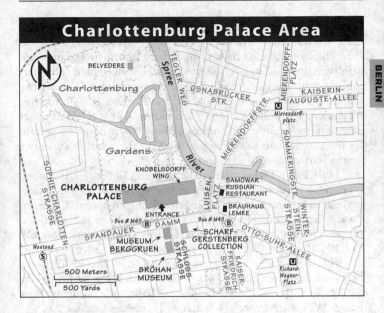

Charlottenburg Palace Area

BERLIN

▲Bröhan Museum

Wander through a dozen beautifully furnished *Jugendstil* and Art Deco living rooms, a curvy organic world of lamps, glass, silver, and posters. English descriptions are posted on the wall of each room on the main floor. While you're there, look for the fine collection of Impressionist paintings by Karl Hagemeister.

Cost and Hours: €8, Tue-Sun 10:00-18:00, closed Mon, Schlossstrasse 1A, tel. 030/3269-0600, www.broehan-museum.de.

▲Scharf-Gersternberg Collection

This small museum houses a collection of more than 250 works of Surrealist and pre-Surrealist art. The *Surreal Worlds* exhibit shows just how freaky the world looked to artists like Salvador Dalí, Paul Klee, and Francisco de Goya. Be sure to check out Dalí's film of his birth from an egg on the beach.

Cost and Hours: €10 combo-ticket includes Museum Berggruen—described earlier, open Tue-Fri 10:00-18:00, Sat-Sun 11:00-18:00, closed Mon, Schlossstrasse 70, tel. 030/266-424-242, www.smb.museum.

Nightlife in Berlin

Berlin is a happening place for nightlife—whether it's clubs, pubs, jazz music, cabaret, hokey-but-fun German variety shows, theater, or concerts.

Entertainment Info: *Berlin Programm* lists a nonstop parade of concerts, plays, exhibits, and cultural events (€2.20, in German, www.berlinprogramm.de); *Exberliner Magazine* (€3, www. exberliner.com) doesn't have as much hard information, but is colorfully written in English (sold at kiosks). For the young and determined sophisticate, *Zitty* and *Tip* are the top guides to alternative culture (mostly in German, sold at kiosks). Also pick up the free schedules *Flyer* and *030* in bars and clubs. Visit KaDeWe's ticket office for your music and theater options (sixth floor, 18 percent fee but access to all tickets; see page 813). Ask about "competitive improvisation" and variety shows.

Half-Price Tickets: Hekticket, Berlin's ticket clearinghouse, is good for whatever's happening in town. They offer regular tickets in advance and same-day half-price tickets to concerts, cabaret, theater, and so on. Drop by or call after 14:00 to see what's on the push list for this evening—ticket prices usually range from €10 to €30 (Mon-Sat 13:00-20:00, closed Sun, half-price sales start at 14:00, Karl-Liebknecht-Strasse 13, tel. 030/230-9930, www. hekticket.de). They also have a branch in western Berlin (Mon-Sat 12:00-20:00, Sun 14:00-18:00, near Bahnhof Zoo, across from Kaiser Wilhelm Memorial Church, at Hardenbergstrasse 29).

Berlin Jazz
To enjoy live music near my recommended Savignyplatz hotels in western Berlin, consider **A Trane Jazz Club** (all jazz, great stage and intimate seating, €10-25 cover depending on act, opens at 20:00, live music nightly 21:00-1:00 in the morning, Bleibtreustrasse 1— see map on page 826, tel. 030/313-2550, www.a-trane.de). **B-Flat Acoustic Music and Jazz Club,** in the heart of eastern Berlin, also has live music nightly—and shares a courtyard with a tranquil tea house (shows vary from free to €10-13 cover, open Sun-Thu from 20:00 with shows starting at 21:00, Fri-Sat from 21:00 with shows at 22:00, a block from Rosenthaler Platz U-Bahn stop at Rosenthaler Strasse 13—see map on page 832, tel. 030/283-3123, www.b-flat-berlin.de).

Berliner Rock and Roll
Berlin has a vibrant rock and pop scene, with popular venues at the Spandau Citadel, Olympic Stadium, and the outdoor Waldbühne ("Forest Stage"). Check out what's playing on posters in the U-Bahn, in *Zitty,* or at any ticket agency.

Cabaret
Bar Jeder Vernunft offers modern-day cabaret a short walk from my recommended hotels in western Berlin. This variety show— under a classic old tent perched atop the modern parking lot of the Berliner Festspiele theater—is a hit with German speakers, and can be worthwhile for those who don't speak the language (as some

of the music shows are in a sort of *Deutsch*-English hybrid). Some Americans even perform here periodically. Tickets run about €22-30, and shows change regularly (performances generally start Tue-Sat at 20:00, Sun at 19:00, seating can be a bit cramped, south of Ku'damm at Schaperstrasse 24—see map on page 826, U3 or U9: Spichernstrasse, tel. 030/883-1582, www.bar-jeder-vernunft.de).

German Variety Show

To spend an evening enjoying Europe's largest revue theater, consider the long-running "Show Me" at the **FriedrichstadtPalast.** It's a lavish visual spectacle, alternating between gentle, poetic interludes and vivid dance numbers (€20-105, no shows Mon or alternating Wed/Thu, also no shows mid-July-Sept, Friedrichstrasse 107—see map on page 832, U6: Oranienburger Tor, tel. 030/2326-2327, www.show-palace.eu).

Nightclubs and Pubs

Oranienburger Strasse is a trendy scene (page 792), with bars and restaurants spilling out onto sidewalks filled with people strolling. To the north, you'll find the hip Prenzlauer Berg neighborhood, packed with everything from smoky pubs to small art bars and dance clubs (best scene is around Helmholtzplatz, U2: Eberswalder Strasse; see page 798).

These days, the most happening scene is generally a few more tram stops or U-Bahn stops out from the center, in the neighborhoods of Friedrichshain (just east of Prenzlauer Berg) and Neukölln (immediately south of Kreuzberg). One particularly inviting venue is **Radialsystem,** a building right by the water and near the East Side Gallery, hosting a variety of events and concerts—everything from classical to electronic (and good €5 meals to boot, Holzmarktstrasse 33, take S-Bahn to Ostbahnhof station, www.radialsystem.de). The edgier **RAW-Tempel,** just north of the Warschauerstrasse S-Bahn station, is a huge complex of industrial buildings that have been renovated by a community group dedicated to hosting low-cost arts events, including club nights, concerts, a bar, and even a circus (www.raw-tempel.de).

Dancing

Dance up a storm at **Clärchens Ballhaus,** an old ballroom that's been a Berlin institution since 1913. At some point everyone in Berlin comes through here, as the dance hall attracts an eclectic Berlin-in-a-nutshell crowd of grannies, elegant women in evening dresses, yuppies, scenesters, and hippies. The music (swing, waltz, tango, or cha-cha) changes every day, with live music on Friday and Saturday (from 23:15, €5 cover; dance hall open daily from 11:00—12:00 in winter—until the last person goes home, in the heart of the Auguststrasse gallery district at Auguststrasse 24—see map on page 832, S-Bahn: Oranienburger Strasse, tel. 030/282-9295, www.ballhaus.de). Dancing lessons are also available (€9, beginners' lessons Mon at 18:30, Thu at 19:30, 1.5 hours). The Gipsy Restaurant, which fills a huge courtyard out front, serves inexpensive German and Italian food.

Berlin boasts the largest **tango** scene outside Buenos Aires, and in summer it's on display on any balmy night in Monbijou Park, the pleasant riverside green space between Museum Island and Hackescher Markt. Most nights also include sessions with one or two other dance styles (€6 beginners' classes often available; www.monbijou-theater.de).

Art Galleries

Berlin, a magnet for new artists, is a great city for gallery visits. Galleries—many of which stay open late—welcome visitors who are "just looking." The most famous gallery district is in eastern Berlin's Mitte neighborhood, along **Auguststrasse** (branches off from Oranienburger Strasse). Check out the Berlin outpost of the edgy-yet-accessible art of the New Leipzig movement at **Galerie Eigen+Art** (Tue-Sat 11:00-18:00, closed Sun-Mon, Auguststrasse 26, tel. 030/280-6605, www.eigen-art.com). The other gallery area is in western Berlin, along **Fasanenstrasse.**

Pub Crawls

The "free" tour companies that cater to students offer wildly popular pub crawls, promising "four cool bars and one hot club" for about €12. Just imagine what kind of bar lets in a tour of 70 college kids. It can be fun...if you want to get drunk with a bunch of American students in a foreign country.

Sleeping in Berlin

When in Berlin, I used to sleep in the former West, on or near Savignyplatz—and I still list good options there. But these days, the focus of Berlin is in the East, and I've recommended places in the colorful Prenzlauer Berg district.

Berlin is packed and hotel prices go up on holidays, including Green Week in mid-January, Easter weekend, the first weekend in May, Ascension weekend in May, German Unity Day (Oct 3), Christmas, and New Year's.

IN EASTERN BERLIN
Prenzlauer Berg

If you want to sleep in the former East Berlin, set your sights on the colorful and gritty Prenzlauer Berg district. After decades of neglect, this corner of eastern Berlin has quickly come back to life. Gentrification has brought Prenzlauer Berg great hotels, tasty eth-

BERLIN

Sleep Code

Abbreviations **(€1 = about $1.40, country code: 49)**
S = Single, **D** = Double/Twin, **T** = Triple, **Q** = Quad, **b** = bathroom, **s** = shower only.
Price Rankings
  $$$ Higher Priced—Most rooms €125 or more.
  $$ Moderately Priced—Most rooms between €85-125.
  $ Lower Priced—Most rooms €85 or less.
Unless otherwise noted, credit cards are accepted, English is spoken, breakfast is included, and Wi-Fi is generally free. Prices can change without notice; verify the hotel's current rates online or by email. For the best prices, always book directly with the hotel.

nic and German eateries (see "Eating in Berlin," later), and a happening nightlife scene. Think of all the graffiti as just some people's way of saying they care. The huge and impersonal concrete buildings are enlivened with a street fair of fun little shops and eateries.

This loosely defined area is about 1.5 miles north of Alexanderplatz, roughly between Kollwitzplatz and Helmholtzplatz, and to the west, along Kastanienallee (known affectionately as "Casting Alley" for its generous share of beautiful people). The closest U-Bahn stops are U2: Senefelderplatz at the south end of the neighborhood, U8: Rosenthaler Platz in the middle, or U2: Eberswalder Strasse at the north end. Or, for less walking, take the S-Bahn to Hackescher Markt, then catch tram #M1 north.

$$$ Precise Hotel Myer's Berlin rents 65 simple, small rooms. The gorgeous public spaces include a patio and garden. This peaceful hub—off a quiet garden courtyard and tree-lined street, just a five-minute walk from Kollwitzplatz or the nearest U-Bahn stop (Senefelderplatz)—makes it hard to believe you're in a capital city. Their five classes of rooms range from three to five stars, hence the wide price range (Sb-€80-195, Db-€108-235, price also depends on season—check rates online for your dates, air-con in some rooms, elevator, free guest computer, Wi-Fi, Metzer Strasse 26, tel. 030/440-140, www.myershotel.de, info@myershotel.de).

$$$ Hotel Jurine (zhoo-REEN—the family name) is a pleasant 53-room business-style hotel whose friendly staff aims to please. In good weather, you can enjoy the breakfast buffet on the peaceful backyard patio and garden (Sb-€90-110, Db-€130-160, extra bed-€35, rates vary by season, check their website for discounts July-Aug, mention this book and book direct to get courtyard-facing room at no extra charge if one's available, air-con only on upper floor, elevator, Wi-Fi or cable Internet, parking garage-€13.50—reserve ahead, Schwedter Strasse 15, 10-minute walk to U2: Sene-

BERLIN

Eastern Berlin Hotels

1. Precise Hotel Myer's Berlin
2. Hotel Jurine
3. Hotel Kastanienhof
4. The Circus Hotel
5. Karlito Apartmenthaus
6. easyHotel Berlin Hackescher Markt
7. Hotel Augustinenhof
8. The Circus Hostel
9. Meininger Hotels (3)
10. EastSeven Hostel
11. Hotel Transit Loft
12. To Ostel
13. Motel One (3)
14. Bike Rentals (2)

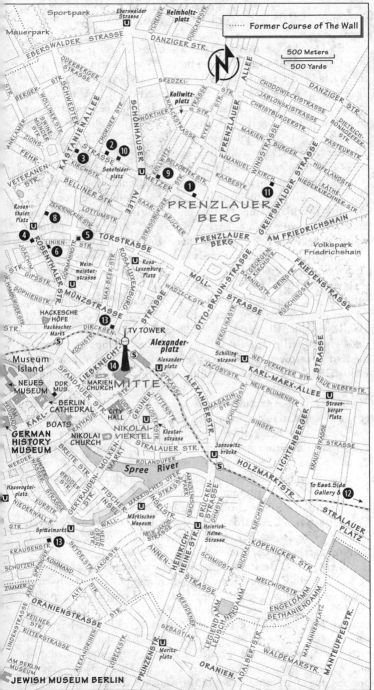

BERLIN

felderplatz, tel. 030/443-2990, www.hotel-jurine.de, mail@hotel-jurine.de).

$$ Hotel Kastanienhof feels less urban-classy and more like a traditional small-town German hotel. It's wonderfully located on the Kastanienallee #M1 tram line, with easy access to the Prenzlauer Berg bustle (but since trams run all night, you may want to ask for a room on the back). Its 44 slightly overpriced rooms come with helpful service (Sb-€74-94, Db-€105-140, extra bed-€20, wheelchair-accessible room, elevator, Wi-Fi, parking-€9/day, 20 yards from #M1 Zionskirche tram stop at Kastanienallee 65, tel. 030/443-050, www.kastanienhof.biz, info@kastanienhof.biz).

$$ The Circus Hotel is both fun and entirely comfortable. Each of its 60 colorful, trendy rooms has a unique bit of decoration. It overlooks a busy intersection, so there's some nighttime noise—try asking for a quieter back room. Owing to its idealistic youth-hostel roots (it's run by the same folks who run the popular Circus Hostel listed later), it's very service-oriented, with lots of included extras, a very "green" attitude, and occasional special events for guests (Sb-€75, small standard Db-€95, larger Db-€105, junior suite Db-€120, breakfast-€9, elevator, free guest computer, Wi-Fi, mellow ground-floor restaurant, Rosenthaler Strasse 1, directly at U8: Rosenthaler Platz, tel. 030/2000-3939, www.circus-berlin.de, info@circus-berlin.de). The Circus also offers a range of spacious, modern **apartments** two blocks away on Choriner Strasse (Db-€130-€250 depending on size and furnishings, 3-night minimum stay preferred).

$ Karlito Apartmenthaus offers 12 well-located, modern, and comfortable apartments above a hip café on a tranquil side street near Hackescher Markt. All of the sleek, Ikea-esque units have miniature balconies and are fully equipped (Sb-€62-77, Db-€72-85, price depends on season, extra person-€15, up to 2 children under 8 sleep free with 2 paying adults, breakfast in Café Lois-€5, no minimum stay, elevator, Wi-Fi, bike rental-€8/day, Linienstrasse 60—check in at Café Lois around the corner on Gormannstrasse, 350 yards from S-Bahn: Hackescher Markt, even closer to U8: Rosenthaler Platz, mobile 0179-704-9041, www.karlito-apartments.de, info@karlito-apartments.de).

$ easyHotel Berlin Hackescher Markt is part of an unapologetically cheap Europe-wide chain where you pay for exactly what you use—nothing more, nothing less. Based on parent company easyJet's sales model of nickel-and-dime air travel, the hotel has inexpensive base rates (small Db-€25-65, larger Db-€35-65, prices vary by season, it's cheaper to book earlier), then charges you separately for optional extras (breakfast, Wi-Fi, using the TV, and so on). The 125 orange-and-gray rooms are very small, basic, and feel popped out of a plastic mold, but if you skip the extras, the price is right, and the location—at the Hackescher Markt end of Prenzlauer Berg—is wonderful (elevator, after booking online call to request a quieter back room, Rosenthaler Strasse 69, tel. 030/4000-6550, www.easyhotel.com).

Near Oranienburger Strasse: **$$$ Hotel Augustinenhof** is a clean hotel with 66 spacious rooms, nice woody floors, and some of the most comfortable beds in Berlin. While not exactly in Prenzlauer Berg, the hotel is on a side street near all the Oranienburger Strasse action. Rooms in front overlook the courtyard of the old Imperial Post Office, rooms in back are a bit quieter, and some rooms have older, thin windows (prices vary with demand, but you'll likely pay around Sb-€80 or Db-€100, elevator, Wi-Fi or cable Internet in rooms, Auguststrasse 82, 50 yards from S-Bahn: Oranienburger Strasse, tel. 030/3088-6710, www.hotel-augustinenhof.de, augustinenhof@albrechtshof-hotels.de).

Hostels in Eastern Berlin

Berlin is known among budget travelers for its fun, hip hostels. These range from upscale-feeling, with some hotelesque private rooms comfortable enough even for non-hostelers, to more truly backpacker-type places where comfort is secondary to socializing. These are scattered around eastern Berlin, including some (Circus, Meininger, and EastSeven) in the Prenzlauer Berg area just described.

Comfortable Hostels with Hotelesque Rooms

$$ Meininger is a Europe-wide budget-hotel chain with several locations in Berlin. With sleek, nicely decorated rooms, these can be a great-value budget option, even for non-hostelers. They have three particularly appealing branches: in Prenzlauer Berg (Schönhauser Allee 19 on Senefelderplatz), at Oranienburger Strasse 67 (next to the Aufsturz pub), and near the Hauptbahnhof, at Ella-Traebe-Strasse 9 (rates vary—quite widely—by availability, but usually about €20-30/bed in 6-bed dorms, Sb-€65-85, Db-€70-120, Tb-€85-175; pricier Fri-Sat, cheaper on Sun, rates at Hauptbahnhof location about €5-10 more; all locations: breakfast-€6, elevator, 24-hour reception, pay guest computer, Wi-Fi in lobby, tel. 030/666-36100, www.meininger-hostels.de).

$ The Circus Hostel is a brightly colored, well-run place with 230 beds, a trendy lounge with upscale ambience, and a bar downstairs. It has typical hostel dorms as well as some very hotel-like private rooms; for a few steps up in comfort, see the listing for the Circus Hotel, earlier (€23/bed in 8- to 10-bed dorms, €27/bed in 4- to 5-bed dorms, S-€50, Sb-€60, D-€66, Db-€85, Tb-€95, 2-person apartment with kitchen-€100, 4-person apartment-€160, breakfast-€4-8, no curfew, elevator, pay guest computer, Wi-

Fi, bike rental, Weinbergsweg 1A, U8: Rosenthaler Platz, tel. 030/2000-3939, www.circus-berlin.de, info@circus-berlin.de).

$ EastSeven Hostel rents the best cheap beds in Prenzlauer Berg. It's sleek and modern, with all the hostel services and more: 60 beds, inviting lounge, fully equipped guest kitchen, lockers, quiet backyard terrace, and bike rental. Children are welcome. Easygoing people of any age are comfortable here (€15-20/bed in 8-bed dorms, €17-21/bed in 4-bed dorms, S-€35, D-€54-57, T-€54-63, cheapest on Sun, priciest on Fri-Sat, private rooms have bathrooms down the hall, includes sheets, towel-€1, continental breakfast-€2, guest computer, Wi-Fi, laundry-€7, no curfew, 100 yards from U2: Senefelderplatz at Schwedter Strasse 7, tel. 030/9362-2240, www. eastseven.de, info@eastseven.de).

$ Hotel Transit Loft, actually a hostel, is located in a refurbished factory. Its 81 clean, high-ceilinged, modern rooms and wide-open lobby have an industrial touch. The reception—staffed by friendly, hip Berliners—is open 24 hours, with a bar serving drinks all night long (€22/bed in 4- to 6-bed dorms, Sb-€63, Db-€73, Tb-€94, Qb-€104, includes sheets and breakfast, elevator, free guest computer, Wi-Fi, fully wheelchair-accessible, down alley facing inner courtyard at Immanuelkirchstrasse 14A; U2/U5/U8 or S-Bahn: Alexanderplatz, then tram #M4 to Hufelandstrasse and walk 50 yards; tel. 030/4849-3773, www.transit-loft.de, loft@hotel-transit.de).

$ Ostel is a fun retro-1970s-DDR apartment building that re-creates the lifestyle and interior design of a country relegated to the dustbin of history. All the furniture and room decorations have been meticulously collected and restored to their former socialist glory—only the psychedelic wallpaper is a replica. Guests buy ration vouchers (€7.50/person) for breakfast in the attached restaurant. Kitschy, sure—but also clean and memorable (€15/bed in a 4- or 6-bed "Pioneer Camp" room or in 12-bunk dorm—includes lockers, S-€33, Sb-€40, D-€54, Db-€64, 4-person apartments-€120, includes sheets and towels, 24-hour reception, Wi-Fi in lobby, bike rental, free parking, free collective use of the people's barbeque, right behind Ostbahnhof station on the corner of Strasse der Pariser Kommune at Wriezener Karree 5, tel. 030/2576-8660, www.ostel.eu, contact@ostel.eu).

IN WESTERN BERLIN
Near Savignyplatz and Bahnhof Zoo

While Bahnhof Zoo and Ku'damm are no longer the center of the action, this western Berlin neighborhood is still a comfortable and handy home base (thanks to its easy transit connections to the rest of the city). The streets around the tree-lined Savignyplatz (a 10-minute walk behind the station) have a neighborhood charm, with an abundance of simple, small, friendly, good-value places to sleep and eat. The area has an artsy aura going back to the cabaret days in the 1920s, when it was the center of Berlin's gay scene.

The hotels and pensions I list here—which are all a 5- to 15-minute walk from Bahnhof Zoo and Savignyplatz (with S- and U-Bahn stations)—are generally located a couple of flights up in big, run-down buildings. Inside, they're clean and spacious enough so that their well-worn character is actually charming. Asking for a quieter room in back gets you away from any street noise. Of the accommodations listed here, Pension Peters offers the best value for budget travelers.

$$ Hecker's Hotel is a modern, four-star hotel with 69 big, fresh rooms and all the Euro-comforts. Their "superior" rooms cost €10 more than their "comfort" rooms, and—while the same size— have more modern furnishings and air-conditioning. Herr Kiesel promises free breakfasts (otherwise €16/person) for Rick Steves readers who book direct via the hotel's website or email, plus show a current edition of this book at check-in (Sb-€85, Db-usually €95-100—though all rooms €160 during conferences, generally €100 July-Aug, look for deals on their website—such as 3 nights for the price of 2, a few rooms with kitchenettes—ask, elevator, Wi-Fi, parking-€14-20/day, between Savignyplatz and Ku'damm at Grolmanstrasse 35, tel. 030/88900, www.heckers-hotel.com, info@heckers-hotel.com).

$$ Hotel Askanischerhof, the oldest B&B in Berlin, is posh as can be, with 16 sprawling, antique-furnished living rooms you can call home. Photos on the walls brag of famous movie-star guests. It oozes Old World service and classic Berlin atmosphere (prices depend on season, but roughly Sb-€100, Db-€120, Tb-€130, mention this book for best price, elevator, Wi-Fi, sticker for street parking-€4/day, Ku'damm 53, tel. 030/881-8033, www.askanischer-hof.de, info@askanischer-hof.de).

$$ Hotel Carmer 16, with 34 bright and airy (if a bit dated) rooms, is both business-like and homey, and has an inviting lounge and charming balconies (Sb-€80, Db-€110, Qb-€154, extra person-€30, breakfast-€10, some rooms have balconies, family suites, elevator and a few stairs, pay Wi-Fi, parking €9.50/day, Carmerstrasse 16, tel. 030/3110-0500, www.hotel-carmer16.de, info@hotel-carmer16.de).

$$ Hotel-Pension Funk, the former home of a 1920s silent-movie star, is a delightfully quirky only-in-Berlin time warp. Kind manager Herr Michael Pfundt offers 15 elegant old rooms with rich Art Nouveau furnishings and hardly any modern trappings (S-€45, Ss-€65, Sb-€75, D-€75, Ds-€89, Db-€99, extra person-€25, cash preferred, Wi-Fi in common areas and some rooms, a long

BERLIN

Western Berlin

1. Hecker's Hotel
2. Hotel Askanischerhof
3. Hotel Carmer 16
4. Hotel-Pension Funk
5. Pension Peters
6. Motel One Berlin-Ku'damm
7. Restaurant Marjellchen
8. Rest. Leibniz-Klause
9. Dicke Wirtin Pub
10. To Weyers Restaurant
11. Café Literaturhaus
12. Die Zwölf Apostel Rest.
13. Zillemarkt Restaurant
14. Ullrich Supermarkt
15. Schleusenkrug Beer Garden
16. Winter Garden Buffet
17. A Trane Jazz Club
18. Bar Jeder Vernunft
19. Fat Tire Bikes

block south of Ku'damm at Fasanenstrasse 69, tel. 030/882-7193, www.hotel-pensionfunk.de, berlin@hotel-pensionfunk.de).

$ Pension Peters, run by a German-Swedish couple, is sunny and central, with a cheery breakfast room and a super-friendly staff who go out of their way to help their guests. With its sleek Scandinavian decor and 33 renovated rooms, it's a good choice. Some of the ground-floor rooms facing the back courtyard are a bit dark— and cheaper for the inconvenience. Annika and Christoph (with help from his sister, Daisy) have been welcoming my readers for decades, and offer the following special prices with this book and cash in 2015—be sure to mention this when booking (Sb-€59, Db-€76, big Db-€82, extra bed-€15, family room-€85, breakfast-€5, up to 2 kids under 13 free with 2 paying adults, cash preferred, good organic breakfast, free guest computer, Wi-Fi, bike rental, 10 yards off Savignyplatz at Kantstrasse 146, tel. 030/312-2278, www.pension-peters-berlin.de, info@pension-peters-berlin.de).

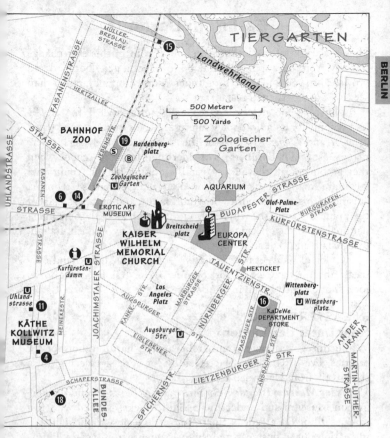

ACROSS THE CITY

$ Motel One has eight locations across Berlin; all have the same aqua-and-brown decor and posh-feeling but small rooms. The four most convenient locations in Berlin are right on Alexanderplatz (Dircksenstrasse 36, tel. 030/2005-4080, berlin-alexanderplatz@motel-one.com); near the Bahnhof Zoo (Kantstrasse 10, tel. 030/3151-7360, berlin-kudamm@motel-one.com); just behind the Hauptbahnhof (Invalidenstrasse 54, tel. 030/3641-0050, berlin-hauptbahnhof@motel-one.com); and a few blocks east of Gendarmenmarkt (Leipziger Strasse 50, U2: Spittelmarkt, tel. 030/2014-3630, berlin-spittelmarkt@motel-one.com). These four tend to charge the same prices (Sb-€69, Db-€84); you'd likely save about €10 by staying at one of the less central locations (all charge €20-50 more during events, breakfast-€7.50, air-con, guest iPad at front desk, Wi-Fi, elevator, limited parking-€10-15/day, www.motel-one.com).

Eating in Berlin

There's a world of restaurants to choose from in this ever-changing city. Your best approach may be to select a neighborhood and browse until you find something that strikes your fancy, rather than seeking out a particular restaurant.

Don't be too determined to eat "Berlin-style." The city is known only for its mildly spicy sausage and for its street food (*Currywurst* and *Döner Kebab*—see the sidebar on next page). Germans—especially Berliners—consider their food old-school; when they go out to eat, they're not usually looking for the "traditional local fare" many travelers are after. Nouveau German is California cuisine with scant memories of wurst, kraut, and pumpernickel. If the kraut is getting the wurst of you, take a break with some international or ethnic offerings—try one of the many Turkish, Italian, pan-Asian, and Balkan restaurants.

Colorful pubs—called *Kneipen*—offer light, quick, and easy meals and the fizzy local beer, *Berliner Weiss*. Ask for it *mit Schuss* for a shot of fruity syrup in your suds.

IN EASTERN BERLIN
Near Unter den Linden

While this government/commercial area is hardly a hotspot for eateries, I've listed a few places handy for your sightseeing, all a short walk from Unter den Linden.

Near Museum Island: Georgenstrasse, a block behind the Pergamon Museum and under the S-Bahn tracks, is lined with fun eateries filling the arcade of the train trestle—close to the sightseeing action but in business mainly for students from nearby Humboldt University. **Deponie3** is a reliable Berlin *Kneipe* usually filled with students. Garden seating in the back is nice if you don't mind the noise of the S-Bahn passing directly above you. The interior is a cozy, wooden wonderland of a bar with several inviting spaces. They serve basic salads, traditional Berlin dishes, and hearty daily specials (€5-8 breakfasts, €8-13 lunches and dinners, open Mon-Fri daily from 10:00, under S-Bahn arch #87-88 at Georgenstrasse 5, tel. 030/2016-5740). For Italian food, a branch of **Die Zwölf Apostel** is nearby (food served until 23:00).

Near the TV Tower: **Käse König am Alex** is a wonderfully old-school eatery that's been serving traditional sauerkraut-type dishes since 1933 to hungry locals (with Prussian forks, flat to fit better into a soldier's mess kit). It's fast, the photo menu makes ordering fun, prices are great, and the waitresses are surly (€6-10 dinner plates, daily, free Wi-Fi, Panoramastrasse 1 under the TV Tower, tel. 030/8561-5220). Nearby, **Brauhaus Mitte** is a fun, tour-group-friendly DDR-era beer hall that makes its own beer and offers a

BERLIN

Berliner Street Fare

In Berlin, it's easy to eat cheap, with a glut of *Imbiss* snack stands, bakeries (for sandwiches), and falafel/kebab counters. Train stations have grocery stores, as well as bright and modern fruit-and-sandwich bars.

Sausage stands are everywhere (I've listed a couple of local favorites). Most specialize in **Currywurst,** created in Berlin after World War II, when a fast-food cook got her hands on some curry and Worcestershire sauce from British troops stationed here. It's basically a grilled *Bockwurst*-type pork sausage smothered with curry sauce. *Currywurst* comes either *mit Darm* (with casing) or *ohne Darm* (without casing). If the casing is left on to grill, it gives the sausage a smokier flavor. (*Berliner Art*—"Berlin-style"—means that the sausage is boiled *ohne Darm,* then grilled.) Either way, the grilled sausage is then chopped into small pieces or cut in half (East Berlin style) and topped with sauce. While some places simply use ketchup and sprinkle on some curry powder, real *Currywurst* joints use tomato paste, Worcestershire sauce, and curry. With your wurst comes either a toothpick or small wooden fork; you'll usually get a plate of fries as well, but rarely a roll. You'll see *Currywurst* on the menu at some sit-down restaurants, but local purists say that misses the whole point: You'll pay triple and get a less authentic dish than you would at a street stand under elevated S-Bahn tracks.

Other good street foods to consider are *Döner Kebab* (Turkish-style skewered meat slow-roasted and served in a sandwich) and *Frikadelle* (like a hamburger patty; often called *Bulette* in Berlin).

For a quick, cheap, and tasty local hot dog, find one of the portable human hot-dog stands. Two companies, Grillrunner and Grillwalker, outfit their cooks in clever harnesses that let them grill and sell hot dogs from under an umbrella.

menu of Berliner "specialties" and Bavarian dishes. They have decent salads and serve a four-beer sampler board (daily 11:00-24:00, across from the TV Tower at Karl-Liebknecht-Strasse 13, tel. 030/3087-8989).

In the Heart of Old Berlin's Nikolai Quarter: The *Nikolaiviertel* marks the original medieval settlement of Cölln, which would eventually become Berlin. The area was destroyed during the war but was rebuilt for Berlin's 750th birthday in 1987. The whole area has a cute, cobbled, and characteristic old town feel...Middle Ages meets Socialist Realism. Today, the district is pretty soulless by day but a popular restaurant zone at night. **Brauhaus Georgbräu** is a thriving beer hall serving homemade suds on a picturesque courtyard overlooking the Spree River. Eat in the lively and woody but mod-feeling interior, or outdoors with fun riverside seating—thriving with German tourists. It's a good place to try one of the few typical Berlin dishes: *Eisbein* (boiled ham hock) with sauerkraut and mashed peas with bacon (€11 with a beer and schnapps). The statue of St. George once stood in the courtyard of Berlin's old castle—until the Nazis deemed it too decadent and not "German" enough, and removed it (€7-14 plates, daily 12:00-24:00, 2 blocks south of Berlin Cathedral and across the river at Spreeufer 4, tel. 030/242-4244).

Near Gendarmenmarkt

South of Unter den Linden, the twin churches of Gendarmenmarkt seem to be surrounded by people in love with food. The lunch and dinner scene is thriving with upscale restaurants serving good cuisine at highly competitive prices to local professionals (see map on page 832 for locations). If in need of a quick-yet-classy lunch, stroll around the square and along Charlottenstrasse. For a quick bite, head to the cheap *Currywurst* stand behind the German Cathedral.

Lutter & Wegner Restaurant is well-known for its Austrian cuisine (*Schnitzel* and *Sauerbraten*) and popular with businesspeople. It's dressy, with fun sidewalk seating or a dark and elegant interior (€9-18 starters, €16-24 main dishes, daily 11:00-24:00, Charlottenstrasse 56, tel. 030/202-9540).

Augustiner am Gendarmenmarkt, next door to Lutter & Wegner, lines its sidewalk with trademark Bavarian white-and-blue-checkerboard tablecloths; inside, you'll find a classic Bavarian beer-hall atmosphere. Less pretentious than its neighbor, it offers good beer and affordable Bavarian classics in an equally appealing location (€6-12 light meals, €10-16 bigger meals, daily 10:00-24:00, Charlottenstrasse 55, tel. 030/2045-4020).

Galeries Lafayette Food Circus is a French festival of fun eateries in the basement of the landmark department store. You'll find a good deli and prepared-food stands, dishing up cuisine that's good-quality but not cheap (most options €10-15, cheaper €8-10 sandwiches and savory crêpes, Mon-Sat 10:00-20:00, closed Sun, Friedrichstrasse 76-78, U-Bahn: Französische Strasse, tel. 030/209-480).

Between the River and Prenzlauer Berg

All of these eateries are within a 10-minute walk of the Hackescher Markt S-Bahn station, in the area butting up against Prenzlauer Berg.

Near Hackescher Markt

Hasir Turkish Restaurant is your chance to dine with candles, hardwood floors, and happy Berliners savoring meaty Anatolian specialties. As Berlin is the world's largest Turkish city outside of Asia Minor, it's no wonder you can find some good Turkish restaurants here. But while most locals think of Turkish food as fast and cheap, this is a dining experience. The restaurant, in a courtyard next to the Hackesche Höfe shopping complex (see page 791), offers indoor and outdoor tables filled with an enthusiastic local crowd. The service can be a bit questionable, so bring some patience (€6-10 starters, €14-20 main dishes, large and splittable portions, daily 12:00-24:00, in late evening the courtyard is dominated by an unpleasantly loud underground disco, a block from the Hackescher Markt S-Bahn station at Oranienburger Strasse 4, tel. 030/2804-1616).

Weihenstephaner Bavarian Restaurant serves upmarket Bavarian traditional food for around €10-15 a plate; offers an atmospheric cellar, an inner courtyard, and a busy people-watching streetside terrace; and, of course, has excellent beer (daily 11:00-23:00, Neue Promenade 5 at Hackescher Markt, tel. 030/8471-0760).

On or near Oranienburger Strasse

Oranienburger Strasse, a few blocks west of Hackescher Markt, is busy with happy eaters. Restaurants on this stretch come with happy hours and lots of cocktails. **Aufsturz,** a lively pub, has a huge selection of beers and whisky and dishes up "traditional Berliner pub grub" to a young crowd (Oranienburger Strasse 67). **Amrit Lounge** is great on a warm evening if you'd like Indian food outdoors with an umbrellas-in-your-drink Caribbean ambience (€5 cocktails, €10-14 meals, long hours daily, Oranienburger Strasse 45). Next door is **QBA,** a fun Cuban bar and restaurant.

Schwarzwaldstuben, between Oranienburger Strasse and Rosenthaler Platz, is a Black Forest-themed pub—which explains the antlers, cuckoo clocks, and painting of a thick forest on the wall. It's friendly, with good service, food, and prices. The staff chooses the music (often rock or jazz), and the ambience is warm and welcoming. If they're full, you can eat at the long bar or at one of the sidewalk tables (€6-15 meals, daily 9:00-23:00, Tucholskystrasse 48, tel. 030/2809-8084).

Gipsy Restaurant serves good, cheap German and Italian dishes, including brats, pizza, and homemade cakes, in a bohemian-chic atmosphere—especially nice on a balmy evening outdoors (daily 12:30-23:00, at Clärchens Ballhaus, Auguststrasse 24, tel. 030/282-9295).

SPEEDWAY PUBLIC LIBRARY
SPEEDWAY, INDIANA

Eastern Berlin Eateries & Nightlife

1. Deponie3 Pub
2. Die Zwölf Apostel
3. Käse König am Alex
4. Brauhaus Mitte & Hekticket Half-Price Tix
5. Brauhaus Georgbräu
6. Lutter & Wegner Rest.; Augustiner am Gendarmenmarkt
7. Galeries Lafayette Food Circus
8. Hasir Turkish Restaurant
9. Weihenstephaner Bavarian Restaurant
10. Oranienburger Strasse Eateries
11. Schwarzwaldstuben Pub
12. Gipsy Restaurant & Clärchens Ballhaus
13. Luigi Zuckermann Deli & Transit Restaurant
14. Restaurant Simon
15. Prater Biergarten
16. Zum Schusterjungen Speisegaststätte
17. La Bodeguita del Medio Cuban Bar Restaurant
18. Konnopke's Imbiss
19. Restaurant Die Schule
20. Kauf Dich Glücklich
21. Gugelhof Restaurant
22. Metzer Eck Pub
23. To Café Sibylle
24. Bonbonmacherei Candy Shop
25. Beth Café
26. Fassbender & Rausch Chocolate Shop
27. B-Flat Acoustic Music & Jazz Club
28. FriedrichstadtPalast

BERLIN

Near Rosenthaler Platz

Surrounding the U8: Rosenthaler Platz station, a short stroll or tram ride from the Hackescher Markt S-Bahn station, and an easy walk from the Oranienburger Strasse action, this busy neighborhood has a few enticing options.

Luigi Zuckermann is a trendy young deli with Israeli/New York style. It's a great spot to pick up a custom-made deli sandwich (choose your ingredients at the deli counter), hummus plate, salad, fresh-squeezed juice, or other quick, healthy lunch. Linger in the interior, grab one of the few sidewalk tables, or take your food to munch on the go (€5-8 meals, daily 8:00-24:00, Rosenthaler Strasse 67, tel. 030/2804-0644).

Transit is a stylish, innovative, affordable Thai/Indonesian/pan-Asian small-plates restaurant. Sit at one of the long shared tables and dig into a creative menu of €3 small plates and €8 big plates. Two people can make a filling meal out of three or four dishes (daily 11:00-24:00, Rosenthaler Strasse 68, tel. 030/2478-1645).

Restaurant Simon dishes up tasty Italian and German specialties—enjoy them either in the restaurant's simple yet atmospheric interior, or opt for streetside seating right on the park across the street (€8-12 main dishes, Mon-Sat 12:00-22:00, Fri-Sat until 23:00, Sun 17:00-22:00, Auguststrasse 53, at intersection with Kleine Auguststrasse, tel. 030/2789-0300).

In Prenzlauer Berg

Prenzlauer Berg is packed with fine restaurants—German, ethnic, and everything in between. Even if you're not staying in this area, it's worth venturing here for dinner. (For more on Prenzlauer Berg, see page 798; for restaurant locations, see the map on page 832.) Before making a choice, I'd spend at least a half-hour strolling and browsing through this bohemian wonderland of creative eateries.

Near Eberswalder Strasse

The area surrounding the elevated Eberswalder Strasse U-Bahn station is the epicenter of Prenzlauer Berg—a young, hip, and edgy place to eat and drink. While a bit farther north than other areas I recommend (and a 10- to 15-minute walk from most of my recommended hotels), it's worth the trip to immerse yourself in quintessential Prenzlauer Berg.

Prater Biergarten offers two great eating opportunities: a rustic indoor restaurant and a mellow, shaded, super-cheap, and family-friendly outdoor beer garden (with a playground)—each proudly pouring Prater's own microbrew. In the beer garden—Berlin's oldest—you step up to the counter and order (simple €3-5 plates and an intriguing selection of beer munchies, daily in good weather

12:00-24:00). The restaurant serves serious traditional *Biergarten* cuisine and good salads (€8-19 plates, Mon-Sat 18:00-24:00, Sun 12:00-24:00, cash only, Kastanienallee 7, tel. 030/448-5688).

Zum Schusterjungen Speisegaststätte ("The Cobbler's Apprentice") is a classic old-school, German-with-attitude eatery that retains its circa-1986 DDR decor. Famous for its filling €9-13 meals (including various types of schnitzel and Berlin classics such as pork knuckle), it's a no-frills place with quality ingredients and a strong local following. It serves the needs of those Berliners lamenting the disappearance of solid, traditional German cooking amid the flood of ethnic eateries (small 40-seat dining hall plus outdoor tables, daily 12:00-24:00, corner of Lychener Strasse and Danziger Strasse 9, tel. 030/442-7654).

La Bodeguita del Medio Cuban Bar Restaurant is purely fun-loving Cuba—graffiti-caked walls, Che Guevara posters, animated staff, and an ambience that makes you want to dance. Come early to eat or late to drink. This restaurant has been here since 1994—and in fast-changing Prenzlauer Berg, that's an eternity. The German-Cuban couple who run it take pride in their food, and the main dishes are big enough to split. You can even puff a Cuban cigar at the sidewalk tables (€4-10 tapas, €8 Cuban ribs and salad, Tue-Sun 18:00-24:00, closed Mon, cash only, a block from U2: Eberswalder Strasse at Lychener Strasse 6, tel. 030/4050-0601).

Konnopke's Imbiss, a super-cheap German-style sausage stand, has been a Berlin institution for more than 70 years—it was  family-owned even during DDR times. Berliners say Konnopke's cooks up some of the city's best *Currywurst* (€2.20). Located beneath the U2 viaduct, the stand was demolished in 2010 during roadwork. Berliners rioted, and Konnopke's was rebuilt in a slick glass-and-steel hut (Mon-Fri 9:00-20:00, Sat 12:00-20:00, closed Sun; Kastanienallee dead-ends at the elevated train tracks, and under them you'll find Konnopke's at Schönhauser Allee 44A, tel. 030/442-7765). Don't confuse this with the nearby Currystation— look for the real Konnopke's.

Restaurant Die Schule is a modern place with a no-frills style where you can sample traditional German dishes tapas-style. Assemble a collection of little €2.50 plates of old-fashioned German food you might not try otherwise (€8-18 main dishes, €26.50 three-course meal, good indoor and outdoor seating, daily 11:00-22:00, Kastanienallee 82, tel. 030/780-089-550).

After-Dinner Dessert and Drinks: Oodles of characteristic funky pubs and nightspots fill the area around Helmholtzplatz (and elsewhere in Prenzlauer Berg). Oderberger Strasse is a fun zone to explore. Along here, **Kauf Dich Glücklich** makes a great capper to a Prenzlauer Berg dinner. It serves an enticing array of sweet Belgian waffles and ice cream in a candy-sprinkled, bohemian lounge on a great Prenzlauer Berg street (daily 11:00-24:00 but opens at 10:00 on Sat-Sun, indoor and outdoor seating—or get your dessert to go, wait possible on busy nights, Oderberger Strasse 44, tel. 030/4862-3292).

Near Kollwitzplatz

This square, home of the DDR student resistance in 1980s, is now trendy and upscale, popular with hip parents who take their hip kids to the leafy playground park at its center. It's an especially good area to prowl among upmarket restaurants—walk the square and choose. Just about every option offers sidewalk seats in the summer (great on a balmy evening). It's a long block up Kollwitzstrasse from U2: Senefelderplatz.

Gugelhof, right on Kollwitzplatz, is an institution famous for its Alsatian German cuisine. You'll enjoy French quality with German proportions. It's highly regarded, with a boisterous and enthusiastic local crowd filling its minimalist yet classy interior. In good weather, outdoor seating sprawls along its sidewalk. Their fixed-price meals are fun, and they welcome swapping (€20-30 three-course meal, €5-10 starters, €13-22 main dishes, Mon-Fri 16:00-23:30, Sat-Sun 10:00-23:30, reservations smart, where Knaackstrasse meets Kollwitzplatz, tel. 030/442-9229, www.gugelhof.de).

Metzer Eck is a time-warp *Kneipe* with cozy charm and a family tradition dating to 1913. It serves cheap, basic, typical Berlin food with five beers on tap, including the Czech Budvar (€5-9 meals, Mon-Fri 16:00-24:00, Sat 18:00-24:00, closed Sun, Metzer Strasse 33, on the corner with Strassburger Strasse, tel. 030/442-7656).

IN WESTERN BERLIN
Near Savignyplatz

Many good restaurants are on or within 100 yards of Savignyplatz, near my recommended western Berlin hotels (for locations, see map on page 826). Savignyplatz is lined with attractive, relaxed, mostly Mediterranean-style places. Take a walk and survey these; continue your stroll along Bleibtreustrasse to discover many trendier, more creative little eateries.

Restaurant Marjellchen is a trip to East Prussia. Dine in a soft, jazzy elegance in one of two six-table rooms. While it doesn't have to be expensive (€12-20 main courses), plan to go the whole nine yards here, as this can be a great experience, with caring service. The menu is inviting, and the place family-run—all the recipes were brought to Berlin by the owner's mother after she was expelled from East Prussia. Reservations are smart (daily 17:00-23:30, Mommsenstrasse 9, tel. 030/883-2676, www.marjellchen-berlin.de).

Restaurant Leibniz-Klause is a good place for a dressy German meal. You'll enjoy upscale presentation on white tablecloths, hunter-sized portions, service that's both friendly and professional, and no pretense. Their *Berliner Riesen-Eisbein* ("super-pork-leg on the bone"), with sauerkraut and horseradish, will stir even the tiniest amount of Teutonic blood in your veins (€11-22 plates, good indoor and outdoor seating, daily 12:00-23:30, Leibnizstrasse near corner with Mommsenstrasse, tel. 030/323-7068).

Dicke Wirtin ("Fat Innkeeper") is a pub with traditional old-Berlin *Kneipe* atmosphere, six good beers on tap, and solid home cooking at reasonable prices—such as their famously cheap *Gulaschsuppe* (€4.60). Their interior is fun and pubby, with soccer on the TV; their streetside tables are also inviting. Pickled eggs are on the bar—ask about how these can help you avoid a hangover (€6-16 main dishes, Bavarian Andechs beer on tap, open daily from 12:00, dinner served from 18:00, just off Savignyplatz at Carmerstrasse 9, tel. 030/312-4952).

Weyers offers modern German cuisine in a simple, elegant setting, with dining tables in the summer spilling out into the idyllic neighborhood park in front (€10-16 dishes, daily 8:00-24:00, facing Ludwigkirchplatz at corner of Pariser Strasse and Pfalzburger Strasse, tel. 030/881-9378).

Café Literaturhaus is a neighborhood favorite for a light meal, sandwich, or dessert (but also serves an elegant if limited menu of full meals). It has the ambience of an Old World villa with a big garden perfect for their evening poetry readings (€5-15 small plates, €14-27 meals, daily 9:30-23:00, smart to reserve for dinner if eating inside, Fasanenstrasse 23, tel. 030/882-5414).

Die Zwölf Apostel ("The Twelve Apostles") is popular for good Italian food. Choose between indoors with candlelit ambience, outdoors on a sun-dappled patio, or overlooking the people parade on an atmospherically narrow pedestrian street. A local crowd packs this restaurant for €12 pizzas and €15-20 meals (long hours daily, cash only, immediately across from Savignyplatz S-Bahn entrance, Bleibtreustrasse 49, tel. 030/312-1433).

Zillemarkt Restaurant, which feels like an old-time Berlin *Biergarten,* serves traditional Berlin specialties in the garden or in the rustic candlelit interior. Their *Berliner Allerlei* is a fun way to sample a bit of nearly everything (cabbage, pork, sausage, potatoes, and more for a minimum of two people...but it can feed up to five).

They have their own microbrew (€10-15 meals, daily 12:00-24:00, near the S-Bahn tracks at Bleibtreustrasse 48A, tel. 030/881-7040).

Supermarket: The neighborhood grocery store is **Ullrich** (Mon-Sat 9:00-22:00, Sun 11:00-22:00, Kantstrasse 7, under the tracks near Bahnhof Zoo). There's plenty of fast food near Bahnhof Zoo and on Ku'damm.

Near Bahnhof Zoo

Schleusenkrug beer garden is hidden in the park overlooking a canal between the Bahnhof Zoo and Tiergarten stations. Choose from an ever-changing self-service menu of huge salads, pasta, and some German dishes (€8-14 plates, daily 10:00-24:00, food served 12:00-22:00, cash only; from Bahnhof Zoo, it's a 5-minute walk, following the path into the park between the zoo and train tracks; tel. 030/313-9909).

Self-Service Cafeterias: The top floor of the famous department store, **KaDeWe,** holds the Winter Garden Buffet view cafeteria, and its sixth-floor deli/food department is a picknicker's nirvana. Its arterials are clogged with more than 1,000 kinds of sausage and 1,500 types of cheese (Mon-Thu 10:00-20:00, Fri 10:00-21:00, Sat 9:30-20:00, closed Sun, U-Bahn: Wittenbergplatz).

Berlin Connections

BY TRAIN

Berlin used to have several major train stations. But now that the Hauptbahnhof has emerged as the single, massive central station, all the others have wilted into glorified subway stations. Virtually all long-distance trains pass through the Hauptbahnhof (see page 724). Before buying a ticket for any long train ride from Berlin (over 7 hours), consider taking a cheap flight instead (buy it well in advance to get a super fare). Train info: Tel. 0180-599-6633, www.bahn.com.

EurAide, an agent of Deutsche Bahn (the German railway), sells reservations for high-speed and overnight trains, with staff that can answer your travel questions in English (located in the Hauptbahnhof; see "Arrival in Berlin" on page 724).

From Berlin by Train to: Potsdam (2/hour, 30 minutes on RE1 train; or take S-Bahn from other points in Berlin, S-1 direct, S-7 with a change at Wannsee, 6/hour, 30-50 minutes—see page 845 for details), **Oranienburg** and Sachsenhausen Concentration Camp Memorial (hourly, 25 minutes; or take the S-1 line from Friedrichstrasse or other stops in town, 3/hour, 45-50 minutes), **Warnemünde** cruise-ship port (sporadic but roughly every 2 hours, 3.5 hours, most include a transfer in Rostock), **Wittenberg** (a.k.a. *Lutherstadt Wittenberg,* hourly on ICE, 45 minutes; also every 2 hours on slower regional train, 1.5 hours), **Dresden** (every 2 hours, more with a transfer in Leipzig, 2.5 hours), **Leipzig** (hourly direct, 1.5 hours), **Erfurt** (hourly, 2.5-3 hours, transfer in Leipzig or Naumburg/Saale), **Eisenach** and Wartburg Castle (hourly, 3-3.5 hours, transfer in Leipzig or Naumburg/Saale), **Hamburg** (1-2/hour direct, 2 hours), **Frankfurt** (hourly, 4 hours), **Bacharach** (hourly, 6.5-7.5 hours, 1-3 changes), **Würzburg** (hourly, 4 hours, change in Göttingen or Fulda), **Rothenburg** (hourly, 5-6 hours, 3 changes), **Nürnberg** (hourly, 4.5 hours), **Munich** (1-2/hour, 6-7 hours, every 2 hours direct, otherwise change in Göttingen), **Cologne** (hourly, 4.5 hours), **Amsterdam** (roughly hourly to Amsterdam Zuid, 6.5 hours; plus 1 night train/day to Amsterdam Centraal, 9.5 hours), **Budapest** (3/day including one overnight, 12-14.5 hours, these go via Czech Republic and Slovakia; if your rail pass doesn't cover these countries, save money by going via Vienna—but this route takes longer), **Copenhagen** (8/day, 7-8 hours, reservation required, change in Hamburg, 1/day direct departs at 11:25; also consider the direct overnight train-plus-ferry route to Malmö Central Station, Sweden, which is just 20 minutes from Copenhagen— covered by a rail pass that includes Germany or Sweden), **London** (8/day, 11-13 hours, 2-3 changes—you're better off flying cheap on easyJet or Air Berlin, even if you have a rail pass), **Paris** (11/day, 9-10 hours, change in Cologne—via Belgium—or in Mannheim), **Zürich** (1-2 hour, 8.5-9 hours, transfer in Basel; 1 direct 11-hour night train), **Prague** (6/day direct, 5-5.5 hours, 3 overnight trains, 11-13 hours), **Warsaw** (6/day, 5.5-6.5 hours, reservations required on all Warsaw-bound trains), **Kraków** (1/day direct, 10 hours; 2 more with transfer in Warsaw, 8.5 hours), **Vienna** (9/day, most with 1-2 changes, 1/day plus 1/night are direct, 10-12 hours; some via Czech Republic, but trains with a change in Nürnberg, Munich, or Würzburg avoid that country—useful if it's not covered by your rail pass). It's wise but not required to reserve in advance for trains to or from Amsterdam or Prague.

Night trains run from Berlin to these cities: Amsterdam, Vienna, Budapest, Basel, and Zürich. There are no night trains from Berlin to anywhere in Italy or Spain. A *Liegeplatz,* a.k.a. *couchette* berth (€15-36), is a great deal; inquire at EurAide at the Hauptbahnhof for details. Beds generally cost the same whether you have a first- or second-class ticket or rail pass. Trains are often full, so reserve your *couchette* a few days in advance from any travel agency or major train station in Europe.

BY BUS

The city's bus station, **ZOB** (Zentraler Omnibusbahnhof), is west of Bahnhof Zoo, in Charlottenburg (Masurenallee 4-6, U2: Kaiserdamm). **MeinFernBus, Flix, Berlin Linien**, and **Eurolines** all operate from here to locations around Germany and Europe (see page 959).

BY PLANE

Berlin is the continental European hub for budget airlines such as easyJet (lots of flights to Spain, Italy, Eastern Europe, the Baltics, and more—book long in advance to get best fares, www.easyjet. com). Ryanair (www.ryanair.com), Air Berlin (www.airberlin. com), and German Wings (www.germanwings.com) make the London-Berlin trip (and other routes) dirt-cheap, so consider this option before booking an overnight train. Consequently, British visitors to the city are now outnumbered only by Americans. For more on cheap flights, see page 968.

Berlin is trying to finish construction of its new airport, **Willy Brandt Berlin-Brandenburg International**, located about 13 miles from central Berlin (airport code: BER; next to what's now the still-busy Schönefeld Airport), but the project has been perennially delayed.

You'll most likely use **Tegel Airport,** which is four miles from the center (airport code: TXL). Bus #TXL goes between the airport, the Hauptbahnhof (stops by Washingtonplatz entrance), and Alexanderplatz in eastern Berlin. For western Berlin, take bus #X9 to Bahnhof Zoo, or slower bus #109 to Ku'damm and Bahnhof Zoo (€2.60). Bus #128 goes to northern Berlin. A taxi from Tegel Airport costs about €20 to Bahnhof Zoo, or €30 to Alexanderplatz (taxis from Tegel levy a €0.50 surcharge).

Most flights from the east and discount airlines arrive at **Schönefeld Airport** (12.5 miles from center), at least until the adjacent Willy Brandt Berlin-Brandenburg International Airport opens. From the old Schönefeld arrivals hall, it's just a three-minute walk to the train station, where you can catch a regional express train into the city (ignore the S-Bahn, as there are no direct S-Bahn trains to the city center). Airport Express RE and RB trains go directly to Ostbahnhof, Alexanderplatz, Friedrichstrasse, Hauptbahnhof, and Bahnhof Zoo (€3.20, 2/hour, take trains in the direction of Nauen or Dessau, rail pass valid). A taxi to the city center costs about €35. Similar train and taxi connections are expected at the new Willy Brandt airport when it opens.

BY CRUISE SHIP (PORT OF WARNEMÜNDE)

Many cruise lines advertise a stop in "Berlin," but the ships actually put in at the Baltic seaside town of Warnemünde—a whopping 150 miles north of downtown Berlin. By train, by tour bus, or by Porsche on the autobahn, plan on at least three hours of travel time each way between Warnemünde and Berlin. Even if you have a generous 12 to 14 hours in port (as many cruises do here), side-tripping to Berlin means you'll spend about as much time in transit as you will in Berlin itself.

This leads Warnemünde-bound cruisers to the unavoidable question: To Berlin or not to Berlin? If this is your one and only chance to see the German capital, it may well be worth the hassle. With even just five or six hours in Berlin, you can get a good feel for the city. First, follow my self-guided walk from the Reichstag through the Brandenburg Gate and up Unter den Linden. This provides a helpful orientation, and leaves you a couple of hours to grab a quick lunch and visit a museum before heading back to your ship.

Getting to Berlin: You have two good options for making the trip to the city: by train, or on a package tour (one offered by your cruise line or through a third party).

Several **train** connections run each day from Warnemünde to Berlin (typically with a transfer in Rostock). While the schedule can change, in 2014 trains departed Warnemünde at 8:04, 10:03, and 12:03 (all change in Rostock, 3.25 hours total to Berlin); return trains departed Berlin's Hauptbahnhof at 14:45 (change in Rostock, arriving Warnemünde 17:54), 17:24 (direct ICE train, arriving Warnemünde 19:43), and 18:45 (change in Rostock, arriving Warnemünde 21:54). Go online to www.bahn.com and check the times for trains between "Warnemuende" and "Berlin Hbf" on the date you'll arrive. Figure €90-106 round-trip for the train.

Warnemünde's train station is a simple 5- to 10-minute walk from the cruise docks: Exit your ship to the right and walk along the water, keeping an eye out for bull's-eye and *City* signs; about 50 yards beyond the car-ferry dock, look for *Tourist Information/Historischer Ortkern* signs on the left. Follow these through the trees and into an underpass that leads to the train station.

An easier but less flexible choice is to pay for a **package excursion.** Cruise lines run trips from Warnemünde into Berlin (typically by bus, though some charter a train). For maximum freedom, opt for a "Berlin On Your Own" excursion—a bus transfer to downtown Berlin with a few unguided hours to explore on your own (generally $150-175). All-day, fully guided bus tours typically cost double ($300-350), but may commit too much time to sights you're not interested in—before you book, carefully read the itinerary specifics. You can also book a tour directly with a local Berlin-based operator; it's worth teaming up with others on your cruise to reduce the per-person cost. For example, **Ship2shore** offers Berlin day trips tailored to your interests starting at €99 per person (based on a minimum of 12 people); smaller groups are also possible, though pricier (€799/2 people, €880/3-4 people, €949/5-6 people, €1,149/7-11 people, mention this book when you reserve, tel. 030/243-58058, info@ship2shore.de). The **Original Berlin**

Walks walking-tour company also runs excursions from Warnemünde into Berlin (€815 for up to 3 people in a minibus, €60/additional person up to a maximum of 7; see contact information on page 736).

Staying near Warnemünde: If you'd rather not make the trip to Berlin, you can stick around the port to explore the beach town of Warnemünde and the larger, adjacent city of Rostock. Both towns were part of communist East Germany, which has left them with some less-than-charming architecture. But today **Warnemünde** is a fun, borderline-tacky seafront resort, with a vast sandy beach and a pretty harbor lined with low-impact diversions. And parts of **Rostock** (a 22-minute train ride away) verge on quaint—it has a fine old church, some museums, and a pedestrian core lined with shops and eateries that cater more to locals than tourists.

For details on both towns—as well as much more detail on how to get into Berlin and spend your time once there—pick up the *Rick Steves Northern European Cruise Ports* guidebook.

NEAR BERLIN

Potsdam • Sachsenhausen Concentration Camp Memorial

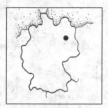

While you could spend days in Berlin and not run out of things to do, a few worthwhile side-trips are just outside the city center (within an hour of downtown Berlin). Frederick the Great's opulent palace playground at Potsdam is a hit with those who enjoy ornate interiors and pretty parks. On the opposite side of Berlin—and the sightseeing spectrum—Sachsenhausen Concentration Camp Memorial provides a somber look at the Nazis' mass production of death during the Holocaust. (A third side-trip possibility—the small town of Wittenberg, with excellent Martin Luther-related sights—is within a 45-minute train ride of Berlin, and covered in the Lutherland chapter.)

PLANNING YOUR TIME

Potsdam or Sachsenhausen can take anywhere from a half-day to a full day of your time, depending on your interests. Think twice before visiting Potsdam on a Monday (when Sanssouci Palace is closed) or a Tuesday (when the New Palace is closed); make your pilgrimage to Sachsenhausen any day but Monday (when the grounds are open but interior exhibits are closed).

Potsdam: It takes about an hour one-way from downtown Berlin to reach the palaces at Potsdam (including the train to Potsdam, then a bus to the palaces). The two main palaces—Sanssouci and the New Palace—are quite different but complementary, and connected by a long (30-minute) but pleasant stroll through a park. Visiting either takes about an hour to an hour and a half, plus a potential wait for your Sanssouci entry time (arrive at Sanssouci by 10:00 to avoid waiting in the ticket line). Give yourself five hours round-trip to do the whole shebang. On a quicker visit, you

can make a beeline from the train station to your choice of palaces (Sanssouci is closer and more intimate, but may require a wait; New Palace is grander but at the far end of the park). It's tempting to stretch your Potsdam visit into a full day so you can linger in the park and tour other royal buildings, poke around the inviting town center of Potsdam, or visit nearby attractions (such as Cecilienhof, the site of the post-WWII Potsdam Conference attended by Churchill, Stalin, and Truman).

If you're an avid cyclist, it's particularly enjoyable to combine a visit to Potsdam with a bike ride along skinny lakes and through green parklands back into the city (rent a bike in Berlin and bring it on the train; for details, see page 731).

Sachsenhausen: Two hours at the camp is just enough for a quick walk through the grounds; three hours is a minimum if you want to read the many worthwhile exhibits. Factoring in transit time, leave yourself at least six hours round-trip from central Berlin.

Both: For an exhausting day of contrasts, you could get an early start to visit Sachsenhausen (opens at 8:30), munch a picnic lunch on the train down to Potsdam (connected by the S-1 line in about 1.5 hours; several basic lunch options in Potsdam train station), and tour Frederick the Great's palaces before collapsing on an evening train back to Berlin.

Potsdam

Featuring a lush park strewn with the escapist whimsies of Frederick the Great, the sleepy town of Potsdam has long been Berlin's holiday retreat. It's your best opportunity to get a taste of Prussia's Hohenzollern royalty. While Potsdam's palaces are impressive, they don't quite crack Europe's top 10—perhaps because the audioguides don't inject the Hohenzollerns' personalities into the place (or maybe the Hohenzollerns really were that boring). But Potsdam is convenient to reach from downtown Berlin, and it makes for a great break from the city's heavy history. It's also ideal on a sunny day, thanks to its strolling- and picnic-friendly park.

GETTING TO POTSDAM

Potsdam is about 15 miles southwest of Berlin. You have two easy train options for zipping from the city to Potsdam's Hauptbahnhof (main train station; round-trip covered by €7 Berlin transit day pass with zones ABC). Direct **Regional Express/RE1 trains** depart twice hourly from Berlin's Bahnhof Zoo (20 minutes to Potsdam), Hauptbahnhof (30 minutes), and Friedrichstrasse (35 minutes; any train to Brandenburg or Magdeburg stops in Potsdam). Note: Some RE1 trains continue past the Potsdam Hauptbahnhof to a stop called Park Sanssouci, which is even closer to the palaces (check the schedule).

The **S-Bahn** is slightly slower, but more frequent and handier from some areas of Berlin. The S-1 line goes directly to Potsdam from Potsdamer Platz, Brandenburger Tor, Friedrichstrasse, and Oranienburger Strasse (6/hour, 30-45 minutes depending on starting point). The S-7 line, which requires a transfer at Wannsee, leaves from Alexanderplatz, Hackescher Markt, Friedrichstrasse, Hauptbahnhof, Bahnhof Zoo, Savignyplatz, and other city-center stations; after the line ends at Wannsee, cross the platform to an S-1 train, and ride it three more stops to Potsdam (6/hour, about 45-50 minutes total from downtown Berlin).

Orientation to Potsdam

The city center is enjoyable to explore, but most visitors head right to Frederick the Great's palaces, which surround the gigantic, sprawling Sanssouci Park at the northwest edge of town.

TOURIST INFORMATION

A handy TI is inside Potsdam's **train station** (Mon-Sat 9:30-20:00, Sun 10:00-16:00, tel. 0331/2755-8899, www.potsdamtourismus.de). Another TI branch, closer to the **town center** at Luisenplatz, is less convenient for most visitors (April-Oct Mon-Sat 9:30-18:00, Sun 9:30-16:00; Nov-March Mon-Fri 10:00-18:00, Sat 10:00-16:00, Sun 10:00-14:00; Brandenburger Strasse 3, same contact info as main branch). Get a map and ask about bus tours if you're interested (see "Tours in Potsdam," later).

The **palace information office** is very helpful, with friendly English-speaking staff. It's across the street from the windmill near the Sanssouci entrance (daily April-Oct 8:30-18:00, Nov-March 8:30-17:00, tel. 0331/969-4200—then press 1, www.spsg.de; clean WC in same building, €0.50).

To supplement the English tour handouts and audioguides at the palaces, consider picking up the blue "official guide" booklets (available individually for each of the sights, €4 apiece at palace information office and gift shops).

ARRIVAL IN POTSDAM

From Potsdam's Hauptbahnhof **(main train station),** you have several options for reaching the palaces. It's a long (but scenic) 45-minute **walk** (get directions and pick up a map at the TI), or—easier—you can take a bus or tram. To find the bus/tram stops, exit the station toward *Landtag/Friedrich-Engels-Strasse/ReiseZentrum*; this takes you out the main door, where you'll find a row of stops. Various **buses** leave the station about every 10 minutes and connect to either palace (single ride-€1.90, all-day pass-€4, buy tickets at machine on board the bus, also covered by any Berlin pass with zones ABC). The convenient but packed bus #695 cruises through the appealing town center of Potsdam, stopping first at Sanssouci, then at the New Palace (3/hour, 15-20 minutes, leaves from lane 4). Bus #606 only goes to Sanssouci, and bus #605 stops only at the New Palace (3/hour apiece, 10-15 minutes, both leave from lane 4). If you're up for a hike, another option is to take **tram** #91 to Luisenplatz (3/hour, 11 minutes, leaves from lane 1), then walk 20 minutes uphill through the park, which lets you enjoy a classic view of Sanssouci Palace.

If you arrive at Potsdam's **Park Sanssouci Station,** just walk straight out and head up the boulevard called Am Neuen Palais, with the big park on your right-hand side. In about 10 minutes, you'll reach the New Palace.

Tours in Potsdam

Local Tours
Various bus tours (including hop-on, hop-off options) conveniently connect this town's spread-out sights. Pick up brochures at the TI or check their website (www.potsdamtourismus.de).

Tours from Berlin
Original Berlin Walks, Brewer's Berlin Tours, and other companies offer inexpensive all-day tours from Berlin to Potsdam (1-3/weekly, small groups, English-language only, admissions and public transportation not included, doesn't actually go into Sanssouci Palace). **Original Berlin Walks'** tour leaves Berlin at 9:40 every Thursday and Sunday from April through October (€15, no reservations necessary, meet at taxi stand at Bahnhof Zoo, tel. 030/301-9194, www.berlinwalks.de). The guide takes you to Cecilienhof Palace, through pleasant green landscapes to the historic heart of Potsdam for lunch, and finishes outside Sanssouci Palace. **Brewer's Berlin Tours** depart Berlin at 10:10 on Wednesdays and Saturdays from May through October (€15, no reservations necessary, meet at Bandy Brooks ice cream store at Friedrichstrasse S-Bahn station, tel. 030/2248-7435, mobile 0177-388-1537, www.brewersberlintours.com).

Sights in Potsdam

FREDERICK THE GREAT'S PALACES
Frederick the Great was a dynamic 18th-century ruler who put Prussia on the map with his merciless military prowess. Yet he also had tender affection for the finer things in life: art, architecture, gardens, literature, and other distinguished pursuits (for more on Frederick, see the sidebar on page 720). During his reign, Frederick built an impressive ensemble of palaces and other grand buildings  around Sanssouci Park, with the two top palaces located at either end. Frederick's super-Rococo Sanssouci Palace is dazzling, while his equally extravagant New Palace was built to wow guests and disprove rumors that Prussia was running out of money after the costly Seven Years' War.

   Getting Between the Palaces: It's about a 30-minute walk between Sanssouci and the New Palace. To save time, you can hop on bus #695, which takes you between the palaces in either direction (covered by a cheap €1.30 *Kurzstrecke* ticket, as well as by a Berlin transit pass with zones ABC). If you do walk, you'll find the park wilder, more forested, and less carefully manicured than other big-league European palace complexes (such as Versailles or Vienna's Schönbrunn).

Combo-Ticket: The €19 combo-ticket, covering nearly all the royal buildings in the park, is only worthwhile if you're visiting Sanssouci, New Palace, and at least one other sight (though for most visitors, those two are enough). It's sold only at the Sanssouci Palace ticket office and the New Palace visitors center.

Photos: You'll pay a €3 fee for a one-day pass to take photos (without flash) at all royal buildings.

▲▲Sanssouci Palace

Sans souci means "without a care," and this was the carefree summer home of Frederick the Great (built 1745-1747). Of all the palatial

buildings scattered around Potsdam, this was his actual residence. While the palace is small and the audioguide does little to capture the personality of its former resident, it's worth seeing for its opulence.

Cost and Hours: €12, €8 Nov-March, includes audioguide; April-Oct Tue-Sun 10:00-18:00, Nov-March Tue-Sun 10:00-17:00, closed Mon year-round, last entry 30 minutes before closing; in winter (Nov-March), entrance is with a live guided German tour only (departs about every 20 minutes)—about once an hour, they let English speakers with audioguides tag along; tel. 0331/969-4200, www.spsg.de.

Crowd-Beating Tips: At this popular sight, your ticket comes with an appointed entry time. (Tickets are sold for the same day only.) For the most stress-free visit, come early: In the summer, if you arrive by 10:00 (when the ticket office opens), you'll get right in. If you arrive after 11:00, plan to stand in line to buy your ticket. You'll probably have to wait for your entry time, too—usually an hour or two later (pass this time visiting the Ladies' Wing and Palace Kitchen or exploring the sprawling gardens; if you have a very long wait, zip over to visit the New Palace, then circle back to Sanssouci).

Visiting the Palace: Your ticket covers three parts—The Ladies' Wing (to the left as you face the palace from the front/garden side); the Palace Kitchen (to the right); and the living quarters and festival halls (the main, central part). You can visit the first two sights anytime, but you must report to the main part of the palace at the time noted on your ticket (you'll receive your audioguide there).

The **Ladies' Wing (Damenflügel),** worth a visit only if you have time to kill (and maybe not even then), contains apartments for ladies-in-waiting and servants. Borrow the dull English descriptions and walk past rooms cluttered with cutesy decor. The servants' quarters upstairs have been turned into a painting gallery.

At the **Palace Kitchen (Schlossküche),** see well-preserved mid-19th-century cooking equipment (with posted English information). Hike down the tight spiral staircase to the wine cellar, which features an exhibit about the grapes that were grown on the terraced vineyards out front.

The **Main Palace** was where Frederick the Great spent his summers. The dry audioguide narrates your stroll through the classic Rococo interior, where golden grapevines climb the walls and frame the windows. First explore the Royal Apartments, containing one of Frederick's three libraries (he found it easier to buy extra copies of books rather than move them around), the "study bedroom" where he lived and worked, and the chair where he died. The domed, central Marble Hall resembles the Pantheon in Rome (on a smaller scale), with an oblong oculus, inlaid marble floors, and Corinthian columns made of Carrara marble.

Finally you'll visit the guest rooms, most of which exit straight out onto the delightful terrace. Each room is decorated differently: Chinese, Italian, all yellow, and so on; the niche at the back was for a bed. As you exit (through the servants' quarters), keep an eye out for the giant portrait of Frederick by Andy Warhol.

▲▲New Palace (Neues Palais)

This gigantic showpiece palace (with more than 200 rooms) is, in some ways, more impressive than the intimate Sanssouci. While

Frederick the Great lived primarily at Sanssouci, he built the New Palace later (1763-1769) to host guests and dazzle visiting dignitaries. And unlike at Sanssouci, there's rarely a long wait to buy tickets or enter the palace.

Cost and Hours: €8, includes audioguide, April-Oct Wed-Mon 10:00-18:00, Nov-March Wed-Mon 10:00-17:00, closed Tue year-round, last entry 30 minutes before closing. To see the king's ho-hum apartments—eight small rooms that are a watered-down

NEAR BERLIN

version of what you'll see at Sanssouci—you must take a required 45-minute tour in German (May-Oct daily at 10:00, 11:00, 14:00, and 16:00). During the off-season (Nov-March), the king's apartments are closed, and you can visit the rest of the New Palace by tagging along with a German tour (with an English audioguide; may have to wait up to 30 minutes for next tour). Tel. 0331/969-4200, www.spsg.de.

Visiting the Palace: The tour includes a pair of loaner slippers (to protect the floors) and a one-hour English audioguide that takes you through the ornate halls. From the Grotto Hall, decorated with seashells, you can peer into the lavish Marble Hall, used for fancy gatherings. Continue on through the eight suites of the Lower Princes' Apartments, which accommodated guests and royal family members. In the 19th and early 20th century, German emperors Frederick III (different from the earlier Frederick who built the place) and Wilhelm II (the last Kaiser) resided here. The Gentlemen's Bedchamber holds the red-canopy bed where Kaiser Frederick III died in 1888. The Ladies' Bedchamber is a reminder that noblemen and their wives slept separately.

Upstairs, the Upper Princes' Quarters include a small blue-tiled bathroom that was later installed for Kaiser Wilhelm II. You'll also find Wilhelm's bedroom, as well as a small painting gallery with portraits of Frederick the Great and Russia's Catherine the Great (who was actually a German princess). From up here, you also get a look into the sumptuous, 52-foot-high Marble Hall, with its ceiling painting of the Greek myth of Ganymede and the floors inlaid with Silesian marble. Through the windows, enjoy the views out into the gardens, which recede into the horizon.

Other Palaces

The two main palaces (Sanssouci and the New Palace) are just the beginning. The sprawling Sanssouci Park contains a variety of other

palaces and royal buildings, many of which you can enter. Popular options include the Italian-style **Orangerie** (the last and largest palace in the park, with five royal rooms that must be toured with a German guide, plus a view tower; closed Nov-March); the **New Chambers** (a royal guest house); the **Chinese House;** and other viewpoints, including the **Klausberg Belvedere** and the **Norman Tower.**

Cost and Hours: Each has its own entry fee (€2-4; all but Belvedere covered by €19 combo-ticket—see earlier) and hours, some are open weekends only (get a complete list from the Potsdam TI or the palace information office).

Bornstedt Royal Estate (Krongut Bornstedt)

Designed to look like an Italian village, this warehouse-like complex once provided the royal palaces with food and other supplies.

Today the estate houses the Bornstedt Buffalo brewery and distillery, which delivers fine brews and (sometimes) schnapps, as it has since 1689. The brewpub's restaurant is a good place for lunch, serving local specialties (€10-16 plates). The kid-friendly grounds also house a wood-fired bakery with fresh bread and pastries. You can watch hatmakers, candlemakers, coopers, potters, and glassmakers produce (and sell) their wares using traditional techniques.

Cost and Hours: Free except during special events, daily 11:00-19:00, restaurant serves food until 22:00, Ribbeckstrasse 6, tel. 0331/550-650, www.krongut-bornstedt.de.

Getting There: From Sanssouci, walk toward the windmill and follow the street An der Orangerie about 500 yards.

MORE SIGHTS IN POTSDAM
Potsdam Town

The easy-to-stroll town center has pedestrianized shopping streets lined with boutiques and eateries. For a small town, this was a cosmopolitan place: Frederick the Great imported some very talented people. For example, Dutch merchants and architects built the Dutch Quarter (Holländisches Viertel, at the intersection of Leiblstrasse and Benkertstrasse) with gabled red-brick buildings that feel like a little corner of Amsterdam. The city also has a good film museum and a museum of Prussian history (both near Breite Strasse). Even if you're just racing through Potsdam on your way to the palaces, you can still catch a glimpse of the town center by riding bus #695 (described earlier, under "Arrival in Potsdam"). Skip Potsdam's much-promoted Wannsee boat rides, which are exceedingly dull.

Cecilienhof

This former residence of Crown Prince William was the site of the historic Potsdam Conference in the summer of 1945. During these meetings, Harry Truman, Winston Churchill, and Joseph Stalin negotiated how best to punish Germany for dragging Europe through another devastating war. It was here that the postwar map of Europe was officially drawn, setting the stage for a protracted Cold War that would drag on for four-and-a-half decades.

Designed to appear smaller and more modest than it actually is, Cecilienhof pales in comparison to the grand palaces concentrated around Sanssouci Park; it's only worth visiting if you're a WWII or Cold War history buff (or would like to visit the nearby Meierei brewpub).

Cost and Hours: €6, April-Oct Tue-Sun 10:00-18:00, Nov-March Tue-Sun 10:00-17:00, closed Mon year-round, last entry 30 minutes before closing, tel. 0331/969-4200, www.spsg.de.

Eating: Try the brewery called **Meierei** ("Creamery") at Cecilienhof. Its nice beer garden offers spectacular views of the lake, solid German food, and great homemade beer. When you walk down the hill into the restaurant, note the big open field to the right—it used to be part of the Berlin Wall (€6-15 meals, Tue-Sun 11:00-22:00, closed Mon, follow *Meierei* signs to Im Neuen Garten 10, tel. 0331/704-3211).

Getting There: Ride the bus to the Reiterweg stop, at the northern end of Potsdam (from Sanssouci Palace, take bus #695; from the train station, ride tram #92 or #96). At Reiterweg, transfer to bus #603 (toward Höhenstrasse), and get off at the Schloss Cecilienhof stop.

Babelsberg

Movie buffs might already know that the nearby suburb of Babelsberg (just east of Potsdam) hosts the biggest film studio in Germany, where classics such as *The Blue Angel* and *Metropolis*, as well as recent hits *The Reader* and *Inglourious Basterds*, were filmed (for information about visiting, see www.filmpark-babelsberg.de).

Sachsenhausen Concentration Camp Memorial

About 20 miles north of downtown Berlin, the small town of Oranienburg was the site of one of the most notorious Nazi concentration camps. Sachsenhausen's proximity to the capital gave it special status as the place to train camp guards and test new procedures. It was also the site of the Third Reich's massive counterfeiting operation, depicted in the Oscar-winning 2007 movie *The Counterfeiters*. Today Sachsenhausen, worth ▲▲, is open to visitors as a memorial and a museum (Gedenkstätte und Museum Sachsenhausen), honoring the victims

and survivors, and teaching visitors about the atrocities that took place here.

GETTING THERE
Take a train to the town of Oranienburg (20-50 minutes); from there, it's a quick trip by bus or taxi to the camp, or a 20-minute walk. The whole journey takes just over an hour each way.

From downtown Berlin, a regional **train** speeds from the Hauptbahnhof to Oranienburg (hourly, 25 minutes). Or you can take the S-Bahn (S-1) line from various stops downtown, including Potsdamer Platz, Brandenburger Tor, Friedrichstrasse, and Oranienburger Strasse (3/hour, 45-50 minutes depending on starting point). Note that the slower S-Bahn may not necessarily take longer if you factor in the time it takes to get to the Hauptbahnhof, find the correct platform, and wait for your connecting train. The S-1 line also goes southward to Potsdam—making it possible to connect Sachsenhausen and Potsdam's palaces in one extremely busy day.

Once at the Oranienburg train station, the **bus** to the memorial departs from lane 4, right in front of the station (on weekdays the hourly #804 is timed to meet most regional trains but runs only every 2 hours on weekends, direction: Malz; bus #821 also possible but only 5/day, direction: Tiergarten; €1.30, covered by Berlin transit day pass for zones ABC, get off at Gedenkstätte stop). You can also take a **taxi** (€6, ask for the *Gedenkstätte*—geh-DENK-steh-teh).

Otherwise, it's a 20-minute **walk** to the memorial: Turn right out of the train station and head up Stralsunder Strasse for about two blocks. Turn right under the railroad trestle onto Bernauer Strasse, following signs for *Gedenkstätte Sachsenhausen*. At the traffic light, turn left onto André-Pican-Strasse, which becomes Strasse der Einheit. After two blocks, turn right on Strasse der Nationen, where you'll pass a memorial stone commemorating the death march (see page 855). This leads right to the camp, where you enter the grounds through the gaps in the wall.

ORIENTATION
Cost and Hours: Free, mid-March-mid-Oct Tue-Sun 8:30-18:00, mid-Oct-mid-March Tue-Sun 8:30-16:30; avoid visiting on Mon, when the grounds and visitors center are open but the exhibits inside the buildings are closed; Strasse der Nationen 22.

Information: The visitors center has WCs, a bookshop, and a helpful information desk. The map in this book is sufficient to navigate the camp, but the €0.50 map sold at the visitors center is probably worth getting for the extra background informa-

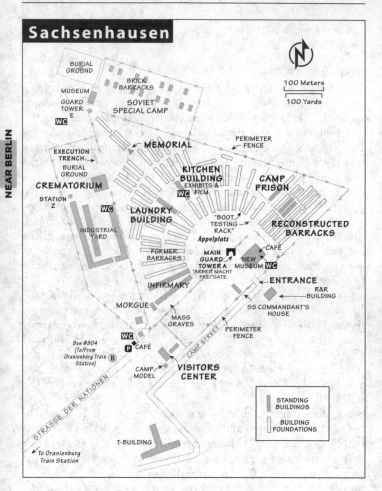

Sachsenhausen

BURIAL GROUND

BRICK BARRACKS

MUSEUM

GUARD TOWER E

SOVIET SPECIAL CAMP

WC

100 Meters

100 Yards

MEMORIAL

PERIMETER FENCE

EXECUTION TRENCH

BURIAL GROUND

KITCHEN BUILDING

EXHIBITS & FILM

CAMP PRISON

CREMATORIUM

STATION Z

WC

WC

LAUNDRY BUILDING

"BOOT TESTING RACK"

Appelplatz

RECONSTRUCTED BARRACKS

INDUSTRIAL YARD

FORMER BARRACKS

MAIN GUARD TOWER A

"ARBEIT MACHT FREI" GATE

NEW MUSEUM

CAFÉ

WC

INFIRMARY

ENTRANCE

R&R BUILDING

MORGUE

MASS GRAVES

SS COMMANDANT'S HOUSE

Bus #804 (To/From Oranienburg Train Station)

WC

CAFÉ

P

B

PERIMETER FENCE

CAMP STREET

CAMP MODEL

VISITORS CENTER

STANDING BUILDINGS

BUILDING FOUNDATIONS

S (STRASSE DER NATIONEN)

T-BUILDING

To Oranienburg Train Station

tion it includes. I'd skip the €3 audioguide (which includes the map) even if it were free: Its five hours of slow commentary are unnecessary, given the ample English information posted within the camp. Tel. 03301/2000, www.gedenkstaette-sachsenhausen.de.

Tours from Berlin: While you can visit Sachsenhausen on your own, a tour helps you understand the camp's complicated and important story. Virtually all walking-tour companies in Berlin offer side-trips to Sachsenhausen. You'll meet in the city, then ride together by train to Oranienburg, and walk to the camp. The round-trip takes about six hours, much of which is spent in transit—but the time that you spend at the camp is made very meaningful by your guide's commentary.

Check the walking-tour companies' websites (see page

733), or compare brochures to find an itinerary that fits your schedule. Options include **Original Berlin Walks** (€15, April-Oct Tue-Fri and Sun at 10:00, runs less frequently off-season) and **Insider Tour** (€15, Tue-Sun at 10:00). Warning: A few unscrupulous tour companies run trips to Sachsenhausen even on Mondays, when the grounds are technically "open," but all of the museum exhibits are closed.

Eating: Pack a lunch or buy lunch en route, as dining choices at the camp are minimal. The little "Info Café" inside the camp offers small snacks, and Bistro To Go, just outside the visitors center, serves basic fare (wurst, soup).

BACKGROUND

Completed in July of 1936, Sachsenhausen was the first concentration camp built under SS chief Heinrich Himmler. It was custom-designed in the panopticon ("all-seeing") model popular in British prisons. The grounds were triangular so they could be observed from a single point, the main guard tower. The design was intended to be a model for other camps, but they soon discovered a critical flaw that prevented its widespread adoption: It was very difficult to expand without interfering with sight lines.

Sachsenhausen was not, strictly speaking, a "death camp" for the mass production of murder (like Birkenau); it was a labor camp, intended to wring hard work out of the prisoners. Many toiled in a brickworks, producing materials that were to be used in architect Albert Speer's grandiose plans for erecting new buildings all over Berlin.

Between 1936 and 1945, about 200,000 prisoners did time at Sachsenhausen; about 50,000 died here, while numerous others were transported elsewhere to be killed (in 1942, many of Sachsenhausen's Jews were taken to Auschwitz). Though it was designed to hold 10,000 prisoners, by the end of its functional life the camp had up to 38,000 people. In the spring of 1945, knowing that the Red Army was approaching, guards took 35,000 able-bodied prisoners on a death march, leading them into the forest for seven days and nights with no rations. Rather than "wasting" bullets to kill them, SS troops hoped that the prisoners would expire from exhaustion. On the eighth day, after 6,000 had already died, the guards abandoned the group in the wilderness, leaving them free. When Soviet troops liberated Sachsenhausen on April 22, 1945, they discovered an additional 3,000 prisoners who had been too weak to walk and were left there to die (all but 300 ended up surviving).

Just three months after the war, Sachsenhausen was converted into a Soviet Special Camp No. 7 for the USSR's own prisoners. It was a notorious "silent camp," where prisoners would disappear—allowed no contact with the outside world and their imprisonment officially unacknowledged. The prisoners were Nazis as well as anti-Stalin Russians. By the time the camp closed in 1950, 12,000 more people had died here.

In 1961, Sachsenhausen became the first former concentration camp to be turned into a memorial. The East German government created the memorial mostly for propaganda purposes, to deflect attention from the controversial construction of the Berlin Wall and to exalt the USSR as the valiant anti-fascist liberators of the camp and all of Germany.

Since the end of the DDR, Sachsenhausen has been redeveloped into a true memorial, with updated museum exhibits (scattered throughout the grounds in various buildings) and an emphasis on preservation—documenting and sharing the story of what happened here.

● SELF-GUIDED TOUR

The camp's various exhibits offer a lot more information than you probably have time to take in. This outline covers the key parts of your visit.

Entrance

In the courtyard next to the visitors center, a **model** of the camp illustrates its unique triangular layout, containing the prisoners' barracks. This allowed guards stationed in tower A (at the main gate) to see everything going on inside those three walls. Along the left (east) side of the triangle is the crematorium, called Station Z. (Camp guards joked that inmates entered the camp at A and exited at Z.) The smaller buildings outside the main triangle served as workshops, factories, and extra barracks that were added when the camp ran out of room.

Walk up the dusty lane called Camp Street. On the right is the SS officers' R&R building, nicknamed the **"Green Monster,"** where prisoners were dressed in nice clothes and forced to wait on their keepers. Officials mostly chose Jehovah's Witnesses for this duty, because they had a strong pacifist code and could be trusted

not to attempt to harm their captors.

A left turn through the fence takes you into the courtyard in front of **guard tower A.** The clock on the tower is frozen at 11:07—the exact time that the Red Army liberated the camp. The building on the right—misnamed the "**New Museum**"—has an interesting DDR-era stained-glass window inside, as well as temporary exhibits and a small café.

Go through the gate cruelly marked *Arbeit Macht Frei*— "Work will set you free."

Main Grounds

Entering the triangular field, you can see that almost none of the original buildings still stand. Following the war, locals salvaged the barracks here for much-needed building materials. Tracing the perimeter, notice the electric fence and barbed wire. A few feet in front of the wall is a gravel track called the "**neutral zone**"—any prisoner setting foot here would be shot. This became a common way for prisoners to attempt suicide. Guards quickly caught on: If they sensed a suicide attempt, they'd shoot to maim instead of kill. It was typical upside-down Nazi logic: Those who wanted to live would die, and those who wanted to die would live.

Every morning, after a 4:15 wake-up call, prisoners would scramble to eat, bathe, and dress in time to assemble in the **roll-call grounds** in front of the guard tower by 5:00. Dressed in their standard-issue uniforms—thin, striped pajamas and wooden clogs—prisoners would line up while guards, in long coats and accompanied by angry dogs, barked orders and accounted for each person, including those who had died in the barracks overnight. It could take hours, in any weather. One misbehaving prisoner would bring about punishment for all others. One day, after a prisoner escaped, SS officer Rudolf Höss (who later went on to run Auschwitz-Birkenau) forced the entire population of the camp to stand here for 15 hours in a foot of snow and subzero temperatures. A thousand people died.

To the far right from the entrance, the wooden **barracks** (containing good museum displays with English descriptions) are reconstructed from original timbers. Barrack 38 focuses on the Jew-

ish experience at Sachsenhausen, as well as the general mistreatment of German Jews under the Nazis (including anti-Semitic propaganda). Barrack 39 explains everyday life, with stories following 20 individual internees. You'll see how prisoners lived: long rows of bunks, benches

NEAR BERLIN

for taking paltry meals, latrines crammed wall-to-wall with toilets, and communal fountains for washing. Inmates would jockey for access to these facilities. The strongest, meanest, most aggressive prisoners—often here because they had been convicted of a violent crime—would be named *Kapo,* the head of the barrack (to discourage camaraderie, the worst prisoners, rather than the best, were "promoted"). Like at many other camps, the camp leaders at Sachsenhausen ran a system of organized rape, whereby they brought in inmates from the women's-only Ravensbrück concentration camp and forced them to "reward good prisoners" at Sachsenhausen.

Next to the barracks is the camp prison, where political prisoners or out-of-line inmates were sent. It was run not by the SS, but by the Gestapo (secret police), who would torture captives to extract information. Other prisoners didn't know exactly what went on here, but they could hear screams from inside and knew it was no place they wanted to be. This was also where the Nazis held special hostages, including three Allied airmen who had participated in a bold escape from a Nazi prisoner-of-war camp (the basis for *The Great Escape;* they later managed to escape from Sachsenhausen as well, before being recaptured) and Joseph Stalin's son, Yakov Dzhugashvili, who had been captured during the fighting at Stalingrad. (The Nazis offered to exchange the young man for five German officers. Stalin refused, and soon after, Yakov died here under mysterious circumstances.) The cells contain exhibits about the prisoners and the methods used by their captors.

Just outside the back of the building stand three posts (out of an original 15) with iron pegs near the top. Guards would execute people by tying their hands behind their backs, then hanging them on these pegs by their wrists until they died—a medieval method called *strappado.*

Walk around the inner semicircle toward the buildings in the middle of the camp. On this **"boot-testing track,"** prisoners were forced to put on boots two sizes too small and walk in a circle on uneven ground all day, supposedly to "test" the shoes for fighting at Stalingrad.

The rectangles of stones show where each of the barrack buildings once stood. At the center, a marker represents the location of the gallows, where prisoners would be publicly executed as a deterrent to others.

Two buildings stand in the middle of the triangle. On the left is the **laundry building,** with special exhibits on topics such as Operation Bernhard, Sachsenhausen's counterfeiting ring. Nazi authorities created the world's largest counterfeiting operation by forcing inmates who were skilled forgers to create fake bills that would flood the US and British economies and devalue their currencies. The 2007 movie *The Counterfeiters* depicts the moral dilemma the prisoners faced: whether to create perfect fakes, and support the Nazi cause... or risk execution by intentionally doing bad work to sabotage the operation.

On the right is the kitchen building, with exhibits that trace the chronological history of the camp. You'll learn how Sachsenhausen was actually built by prisoners, and see original artifacts including the gallows, a bunk from the barracks, uniforms, and so on. There are also photos, quotes, and a 22-minute film. The basement walls feature some bizarre cartoons of vegetables preparing themselves to be eaten (these were drawn later by Soviets).

Memorial and Crematorium

Head back to the far end of the camp, which is dominated by the towering, 130-foot-tall, 1961 pro-communist DDR **memorial** to the victims of Sachsenhausen. The 18 triangles at the top are red, the color designated for political prisoners (to the communists, they were more worthy of honor than the other Nazi victims who died here). At the base of the monument, two prisoners are being liberated by a noble Soviet

soldier. The prisoners are unrealistically robust, healthy, and optimistic (they will survive and become part of the proud Soviet proletariat!). The **podium** in front was used by the East German army for speeches and rallies—exploiting Sachsenhausen as a backdrop for their propaganda.

From here, head left and go through the gap in the fence to find the execution trench, used for mass shootings. When this system proved too inefficient, the Nazis built "Station Z," the nearby **crematorium,** where they could execute and dispose of prisoners more systematically. Its ruins are inside the white building (prior to the camp's liberation by Soviet troops, Nazi guards destroyed the crematorium to remove evidence of their crimes).

The crematorium's ramp took prisoners down into the "infirmary," while the three steps led up to the dressing room. This is where, on five occasions, the Nazis tested Zyklon-B (the chemical later responsible for killing hundreds of thousands at Auschwitz). Most of the building's victims died in the room with the double row of bricks (for soundproofing; the Nazis also blasted classical music to mask noise). Victims would re-

port here for a "dental check," to find out if they had gold or silver teeth that could be taken. They would then stand against the wall to have their height measured—and a guard would shoot them through a small hole in the wall with a single bullet to the back of the skull. (The Nazis found it was easier for guards to carry out their duties if they didn't have to see their victims face-to-face.)

Bodies were taken to be incinerated in the ovens (which still stand). Notice the statue of the emaciated prisoner—a much more accurate depiction than the one at the DDR monument. Outside, a burial ground is filled with ashes from the crematorium.

The Rest of the Camp

Back inside the main part of the camp you can head left, up to the tip of the triangle (behind the big monument) to find a museum about the postwar era, when Sachsenhausen served as a **Soviet Special Camp**. Nearby is a burial ground for victims of that camp. At this corner of the triangle, the gate in the fence—called **tower E**—holds a small exhibit about the relationship between the camp and the town of Oranienburg.

Heading back toward the main guard tower, along the wall toward the front corner, are the long, green barracks of the **infirmary,** used for medical experiments on inmates (as explained by the exhibits inside). This was also where Soviet soldiers found the 3,000 remaining survivors when they liberated the camp. The small building in back was the morgue—Nazis used the long ramp to bring in the day's bodies via wheelbarrows. Behind that is a field with six stones, each marking 50 bodies for the 300 prisoners who died after the camp was freed.

While all of this is difficult to take in, as with all concentration camp memorials, the intention of Sachsenhausen is to share its story and lessons—and prevent this type of brutality from ever happening again.

HAMBURG

Hamburg (HAHM-boork) is Germany's second-largest city, the richest judged by per-capita income, and its most important port. Like other "second cities"—such as Chicago, Marseille, Antwerp, and St. Petersburg—it has a special pride. It's popular with German tourists, who come here to eat fish, watch soccer games, marvel at its mighty port, and experience the fabled nightlife of the Reeperbahn, the German answer to "Sin City" (and famous for launching the Beatles' career). Foreign visitors are in the minority, and American tourists are rare. Like many port towns, Hamburg can have rough edges, but a short stay can be memorable.

Hamburg lacks a quaint medieval center. Ye Olde Hamburg was flattened by a one-two punch that occurred over a 101-year span: First, a devastating 1842 fire gutted the town center, and then an equally devastating firebombing by Allied forces in 1943 wiped out whole neighborhoods (see sidebar on page 873). Today the city center is a people-friendly but charmless collection of office buildings and chain shops—not unlike the downtown cores of many American cities.

Around its edges, however, the city shows off Germany's industrial prosperity in the 19th and 20th centuries. "Hamburg" very loosely derives from "castle on wet ground"—and the city, with its 2,000 bridges, is built to accommodate a 13-foot tide. A century ago, Hamburg's port was the third largest in the world. Today, the city's fishy maritime atmosphere—with a constant breeze and the evocative cries of seagulls—gives Hamburg an almost Scandinavian, Dutch, or English feel that's worlds away from the sun-drenched, Baroque joviality of Bavaria.

If you have German ancestors, there's a good chance they left for America from here: Between 1850 and 1930, more than five million Germans emigrated to the US from Hamburg's port. After the Iron Curtain cut off trade to the east, port traffic—and the city's influence—dwindled. But since reunification, Hamburg has been growing back to its former status as one of the biggest trade centers in Central Europe, and the city is expanding rapidly as it focuses on redeveloping its old docklands. The burgeoning Hafen-City district and its spectacular Elbphilharmonie concert hall are turning Hamburg back toward its Elbe riverside. No longer content to be famous merely for its lusty sailors' quarter and as the Beatles' springboard to stardom, the new Hamburg expects to be seen as a cultural capital moving boldly into a promising future.

PLANNING YOUR TIME

If you're passing through on your way between Germany and Denmark, Hamburg is certainly worth a quick stop. At the very least, toss your bag in a train-station locker and enjoy the 1.5-hour quickie bus tour and a harbor cruise before taking an evening train out.

But with its variety of attractions, Hamburg can easily fill a rewarding day (or more) of sightseeing. While you could see the sights in any order, consider this busy all-day tour on public transit, using a day pass or Hamburg Card (leave by 9:30 if you plan to take the worthwhile noon harbor tour): Start at the Hauptbahnhof (main train station). Walk 10 minutes down Mönckebergstrasse, or take the U-3 subway two stops to the Rathaus (City Hall) and the Binnenalster lakefront. Then, take the U-3 farther on to the St. Pauli stop, and follow my self-guided Reeperbahn walk, ending by the Reeperbahn S-Bahn stop. Take the S-Bahn one stop back to Landungsbrücken. Here, get out on the water by catching the noon harbor tour or taking the public ferry #62 toward Finkenwerder. Afterward, return to the Landungsbrücken, then ride one stop on the #72 ferry to HafenCity and tour this urban-renewal quarter made of brick, home to the Elbphilharmonie concert hall and Speicherstadt's renovated warehouses. Return to the train station (or your hotel) by walking to the Baumwall station to catch the U-3 subway.

Orientation to Hamburg

Hamburg is big (1.8 million people, sprawling to five million in the surrounding metropolitan area), and its sights are too spread out to rely on walking—to reach its top sights, you'll need to use public transport. The city center, which sits between the Elbe ("ELL-beh") River to the south and a lake called the Binnenalster to the north, is surrounded by a ring road that follows the route of the old city walls. Most places of interest in Hamburg are just outside this central core: The train station and the St. Georg neighborhood (with good hotels and restaurants) are just east of the center; the harbor, old Speicherstadt warehouse district, and the new HafenCity zone are to the south along the Elbe; and the St. Pauli waterfront district and the red light/entertainment zone along the Reeperbahn lie to the west.

TOURIST INFORMATION

Hamburg's main TI is in the train station, above the north end of platforms 3-4. It has good, free maps and sells Hamburg Cards (Mon-Sat 9:00-19:00, Sun 10:00-18:00, www.hamburg-tourism. de). There are also TIs at the St. Pauli Landungsbrücken (Sun-Mon 9:00-18:00, Tue-Sat 9:00-19:00) and the airport (daily 6:00-23:00). For tourist information by phone, call 040/3005-1300 (Mon-Sat 9:00-19:00, closed Sun).

Hamburg Card: If you'll be seeing at least two or three museums, especially with a travel partner or two, this card is a sound investment. Sold at TIs and public-transit ticket machines (see "Getting Around Hamburg," later), it comes with full-day public-transit privileges plus reduced-priced entry to many sights. While these discounts are modest (10-33 percent), the card costs only a little more than a transport pass (for single travelers: €10/1 day, €23/3 days; for groups of up to 5: €15.50/1 day, €40/3 days).

ARRIVAL IN HAMBURG

By Train: Hamburg's main train station *(Hauptbahnhof)* has a handsome interior with a classic steel-arch design. The station is within walking distance of Hamburg's City Hall and recommended hotels in the St. Georg neighborhood. For other destinations, use the subway and buses—the station is a convenient hub for public transit.

From the platforms, escalators lead up to bridges that span the tracks at the north and south ends of the building; at each end of each bridge is an exit (four exits in all). The northern bridge—look for *McDonald's* and *Wandelhalle* signs—has most services, including ticket counters in the *Reisezentrum* (long hours daily). You'll also find the city-run TI (above tracks 3-4), pay WCs, a left-luggage service (next to the *Reisezentrum*, €5/day, daily 9:00-20:00), and several banks of lockers (€4-6; one is above tracks 5-6). Exit from here to reach my recommended St. Georg neighborhood hotels.

By Bus: Long-distance buses arrive at, and leave from, the large, covered bus terminal *(ZOB)* located just around the corner from the southern end of the main train station, across the street from the entrance to the Arts and Crafts Museum.

By Plane: Hamburg's airport is a simple ride from the train

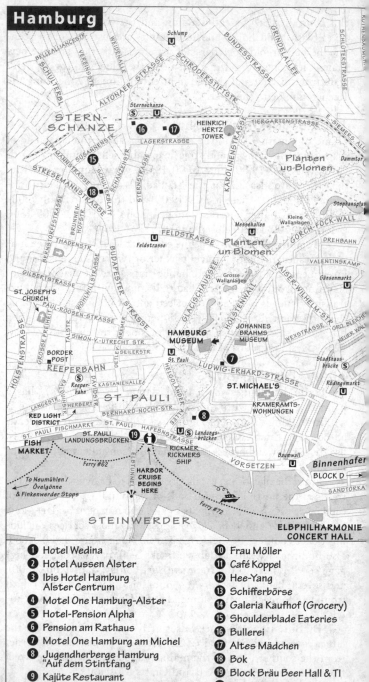

Hamburg

HAMBURG

1. Hotel Wedina
2. Hotel Aussen Alster
3. Ibis Hotel Hamburg Alster Centrum
4. Motel One Hamburg-Alster
5. Hotel-Pension Alpha
6. Pension am Rathaus
7. Motel One Hamburg am Michel
8. Jugendherberge Hamburg "Auf dem Stintfang"
9. Kajüte Restaurant
10. Frau Möller
11. Café Koppel
12. Hee-Yang
13. Schifferbörse
14. Galeria Kaufhof (Grocery)
15. Shoulderblade Eateries
16. Bullerei
17. Altes Mädchen
18. Bok
19. Block Bräu Beer Hall & TI
20. Launderette

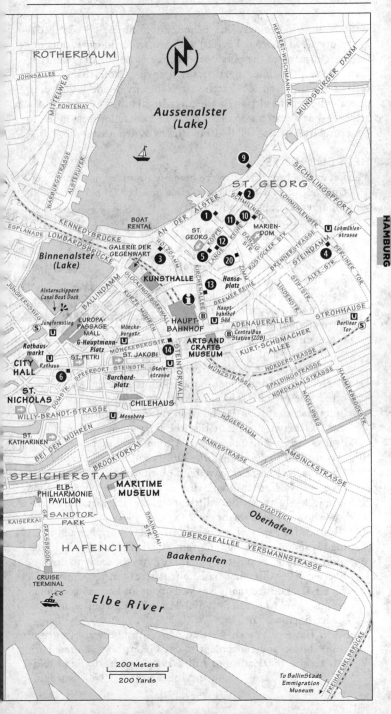

HAMBURG

station on the S-1 subway line (6/hour, 30 minutes, 4:30-24:00). A Hamburg *Grossbereich* ticket (€3) will cover your journey, but consider getting one of the public-transit day passes or the Hamburg Card if you'll be doing more travel that day. Note that if you're traveling *to* the airport, S-1 trains from the city divide at Ohlsdorf, one stop before the airport. Generally, the first three cars go to the airport—but pay attention to the signs and ask fellow passengers to be sure. Airport info: Tel. 040/50750, www.airport.de.

HELPFUL HINTS

Market at Fischmarkt: If you're here on a Sunday, it's worth getting out of bed for this venerable market (about 5:00-9:30, though the action usually lingers at least an hour later). It's a rich sensory experience: Smell the fresh flowers (and even fresher fish), wander among colorful baskets of produce, hear the stall-keepers shout out closing-time deals, enjoy the fun music-festival vibe, and marvel at the

Germans drinking beer this early in the morning (many are wrapping up a night out in St. Pauli).

To reach the market from the St. Georg neighborhood, catch bus #112 and ride it to the Fischmarkt stop (leaves from other side of train station, across the street from the end of Spitalerstrasse; runs 2-3/hour on Sunday mornings, 15 minutes). Otherwise, walk or ride the ferry from the Landungsbrücken (ferry #62, one stop to Altona/Fischmarkt).

Bike Lanes and Pedestrians: The city is a delight to explore on two wheels. Red-brick pavement on the sidewalk means it's a bike lane. Pedestrians make sure to stay on the gray part of the sidewalk—bicyclists show little tolerance or patience for tourists who stray onto the brick.

Bike Rental: Like many European cities, Hamburg has a government-run bike-sharing program. Called StadtRAD, it has more than 100 automated rental stations stocked with distinctive red bikes. The first half-hour is free, but you must pay a €5 registration fee that gives you about an hour of additional credit. To register, call 040/822-188-100 or go online at www.stadtradhamburg.de.

Laundry: Express Wasch-Center, a five-minute walk from the train station and convenient to St. Georg hotels, offers both self-service (€6/load) and full service (wash, dry, and fold-€9, generally takes 2 hours; Mon-Fri 8:00-19:00, Sat 8:00-

18:00, closed Sun, facing Hansaplatz at Zimmerpforte 6, tel. 040/280-4655).

Taxi: Call 040/211-211.

Local Guide: Consider **Tomas Kaiser** (€140/2 hours, €240/half-day, mobile 0170-232-7749, tomas_kaiser@web.de).

GETTING AROUND HAMBURG

Public transport makes sightseeing efficient in this spread-out city. Hamburg's subway system includes both the U-Bahn (with four lines, U-1 to U-4) and S-Bahn (commuter rail lines). Buses and public ferries, which are both covered by the various transit passes, round out the system.

An HVV information office is next to the TI in the train station (Mon-Fri 6:00-21:00, Sat-Sun 8:00-21:00, tel. 040/19449, www.hvv.de). Buy tickets from the machines at each U-Bahn or S-Bahn stop, marked *HVV*; these take coins and small bills. For bus tickets, you can purchase them from the driver, who makes change. Tickets bought from machines or bus drivers are already validated; you don't need to stamp them again.

Single ticket prices vary; the shortest trips cost €1.50, longer ones €2, and the longest ones (within the *Grossbereich*—greater city limits, including the airport) cost €3. Key your destination into a ticket machine, and it will tell you the price of the ticket.

Day passes pay for themselves quickly and give you the run of the whole system, including ferry rides on the Elbe River. For one person making two long trips or four short trips in a day, a *9-Uhr-Tageskarte* day pass usually saves money (€5.90, not valid Mon-Fri 6:00-9:00). Groups of up to five people can get a *9-Uhr-Gruppenkarte* for €10.80. If you need to use the system between 6:00 and 9:00 on weekday mornings, you'll have to buy the full-day pass (*Ganztageskarte*, €7.30).

Tours in Hamburg

Do-It-Yourself Orientation Tour: U-3 Subway

This circular subway line, which runs mostly above ground (often on old-style elevated tracks), is good for a quick and cheap orientation to the city, bringing you back to your starting point in 45 minutes (covered by single transit ticket, day pass, or Hamburg Card). From the train station (Hauptbahnhof Süd U-Bahn stop, at the south end of the station), take the subway in the direction of Rathaus and St. Pauli. The first two stops are underground; then, with the Rödingsmarkt stop, you'll emerge onto elevated tracks that run past downtown office buildings (at this stop, look right to see the church tower of St. Michael's Church, and left to see the memorial tower of St. Nicholas Church). At the next stop, Baumwall, you can see Speicherstadt ("Warehouse City"), Hamburg's warehouse district, and the striking new Elbphilharmonie concert hall. On the way to the next stop (Landungsbrücken), enjoy the view of the harbor, with its massive port and thriving riverfront. The train dips underground again at St. Pauli and then re-emerges above ground for the northern arc of the ring, which runs through the pleasant residential neighborhoods of the city. If you're short on time, just enjoy the short stretch between the Rathaus and Landungsbrücken stops.

▲▲Bus Tours

Because Hamburg's most interesting sights are scattered on the perimeter of the boring city center, the city lends itself particularly well to a quick orientation bus tour. Several companies run circular city bus tours with a multilingual commentary (€15-18 for 1.5 hours, generally 10 percent discount with Hamburg Card). The double-decker buses (which go topless when it's sunny) offer a smooth, high ride with a steady flow of sights and brief narration (especially the English), allowing you barely enough time to identify what you're seeing.

While you can hop on or off at points throughout the city, the most logical starting points are at the train station (the double-decker buses park along Kirchenallee) and near the Landungsbrücken pier. Before boarding, make sure that you're on a bus with English commentary (either live or via headphones), and check timetables if you plan to hop off and on. One company with frequent departures and good English guides is **Die Roten Doppeldecker;** look for red buses with white *Stadtrundfahrt* lettering (€17.50 ticket good for all day, 27 stops, departs every half-hour April-Oct 9:30-17:00, less frequently Nov-March—generally hourly 10:00-16:00 or a bit more on weekends, tel. 040/792-8979, www.die-roten-doppeldecker.de). Their €30 combo-ticket covers a city bus tour as well as the recommended Rainer Abicht harbor boat tour (described on page 882), saving you about €6.

Boat Tours

You have two main options for getting out on the river: a **tour** that runs just once a day in English, or one of the less interesting (but cheaper and more frequent) public **ferries;** see page 882 for details on both. Within the city center, **canal boats** leisurely circle the Binnenalster lake, with a few routes also swinging through the Speicherstadt/HafenCity development (described on page 884).

Sights in Hamburg

IN THE CITY CENTER
City Hall
Hamburg's impressive Rathaus, a mix of Historicist styles (but actually from 1897), was designed to showcase the wealth and gran-

deur of turn-of-the-20th-century imperial Germany. While the building is called a "City Hall," Hamburg actually forms its own *Land* (state) within the Federal Republic of Germany, and the council that meets in the City Hall chambers is also like a state legislature.

Cost and Hours: Free to enter the entrance hall and inner courtyard, Mon-Fri 7:00-19:00, Sat-Sun 10:00-17:00; daily €4 English tours run hourly 10:15-15:15, plus Sat-Sun at 16:15 and Sat at 17:15 (45 minutes, can be canceled because of special events, more frequent German-language tours); tel. 040/428-312-470, www.hamburgische-buergerschaft.de.

Getting There: The City Hall has its own stop on the U-3 subway line (Rathaus); it's also very near the Jungfernstieg stop on the U-1, U-2, and U-4 lines. Enter the building through the archway and go into the lobby, where you'll find a desk selling tickets for tours.

Hamburg's Lakes
Hamburg's delightful lakes started as one big lake that formed when townsfolk built a mill that dammed the Alster River. During the Thirty Years' War, however, the city fortified itself behind a defensive wall that split the millpond in two.

To reach the first of these lakes from City Hall, simply walk to the canal and turn right. From anywhere else in the city, ride the S-Bahn or U-Bahn to the Jungfernstieg stop.

Binnenalster: The smaller and (as its name suggests) inner of the two lakes, the Binnenalster lies just a few steps from the plaza in front of City Hall. For a good look at it, head out to the little viewpoint at the south corner of the lake (near the bridge, under the flags). Look left along the waterside **Jungfernstieg,** the city's most elegant promenade and home to its top-of-the-line shops. These include a huge Apple Store and the flagship showroom of Nivea (established in Hamburg in 1911). Along the shore to the right, you can see the headquarters of Hamburg's most important shipping company, Hapag-Lloyd. This area gives you a good look

HAMBURG

Hamburg at a Glance

▲▲▲**Harbor and Port Guided Boat Tour** Excellent chance to marvel at the city's mighty container port and burgeoning Hafen-City. **Hours:** One-hour English tour leaves daily at noon April-Oct; no English tours off-season. See page 882.

▲▲**Quickie City Bus Tour** Convenient way to learn about the history, and future, of this sprawling city. **Hours:** Departs from the train station every 30 minutes April-Oct 9:30-17:00, less frequently Nov-March. See page 868.

▲▲**Reeperbahn Walk** A stroll through Hamburg's famous Red Light District, sizzling with nightclubs and lots of ladies. See page 877.

▲▲**St. Pauli Landungsbrücken Harborfront** Atmospheric people zone with boardwalk ambience, ferry docks, and views of the port. See page 882.

▲▲**Elbphilharmonie Concert Hall** Unfinished, architecturally striking centerpiece of the new HafenCity development. See page 885.

▲▲**St. Nicholas Church** Bombed-out church memorializing the destruction of WWII, with excellent museum and view from its scaffolded tower. **Hours:** Ruins always viewable; museum and tower open daily May-Sept 10:00-18:00, Oct-April 10:00-17:00. See page 873.

▲▲**Hamburg Museum** Sprawling exhibit of the city's history since its founding in A.D. 800. **Hours:** Tue-Sat 10:00-17:00, Sun 10:00-18:00, closed Mon. See page 876.

▲▲**International Maritime Museum** Huge former warehouse filled with exhibits on nautical history, both military and civilian. **Hours:** Tue-Sun 10:00-18:00, closed Mon. See page 887.

▲**Harbor Tour by Public Ferry** Low-cost, do-it-yourself tour of the harbor with views of port action. See page 882.

▲**HafenCity and Speicherstadt** Exciting new urban development featuring Elbphilharmonie concert hall and repurposed warehouses with attractions. **Hours:** Always open. See page 884.

▲**Miniatur Wunderland** Tiny world with (full-sized) German families thrilling to the model trains. **Hours:** Daily at least 9:30-18:00 but can open as early as 8:00 and close as late as 22:00. See page 887.

▲**BallinStadt Emigration Museum** Germany's version of Ellis Island, now housing history exhibits instead of emigrants. **Hours:** Daily April-Oct 10:00-18:00, Nov-March 10:00-16:30. See page 888.

▲**Kunsthalle** Expansive art gallery with works by Old, New, and Modern Masters. **Hours:** Tue-Sun 10:00-18:00, Thu until 21:00, closed Mon. See page 872.

▲**Arts and Crafts Museum** Three floors filled with decorative arts. **Hours:** Tue-Sun 10:00-18:00, Thu until 21:00, closed Mon. See page 872.

Binnenalster and Aussenalster Hamburg's two lakes, with inviting waterside promenades, chic shops, and a thriving boating/biking scene. See page 869.

City Hall Hamburg's architecturally eclectic, century-old Rathaus. **Hours:** Daily English tours hourly 10:15-15:15, plus Sat-Sun at 16:15 and Sat at 17:15. See page 869.

St. **Michael's Church** Historic church with panoramic view tower. **Hours:** Daily May-Oct 9:00-19:30, Nov-April 10:00-17:30. See page 875.

"Shoulderblade" Neighborhood Colorful, artsy, and edgy district with fun eateries. See page 880.

Planten un Blomen Relaxing garden filled with flowers, ponds, cafés, and Hamburgers at rest. **Hours:** Daily 7:00-20:00, later in summer. See page 881.

St. Pauli Elbtunnel Old industrial tunnel leading beneath the Elbe River to panoramic Hamburg views from the opposite bank. **Hours**: Always open. See page 884.

SS *Rickmer Rickmers* Century-old sailing ship expertly restored by a corps of volunteers. **Hours:** Daily 10:00-18:00 See page 884.

HAMBURG

at how the city rebuilt after its fire in the mid-19th century, when it turned its back on the Elbe and instead faced this lake. Inside the huge Europa-Passage mall, the Thalia bookstore has a second-floor café with a nice view of the water.

Red-and-white Alsterschippern **canal boats** leave from the dock on Jungfernstieg for sleepy one-hour tours around the lakes (€14.50, April-Sept leaves every 30 minutes 10:00-18:00, less frequently Oct-March—canceled if icy, live German guide and headphone English commentary, tel. 040/357-4240, www.alstertouristik.de). An enticing two-hour version adds a trip through the Speicherstadt and HafenCity urban-renewal zone (€20, April-Oct 3/day, off-season 1/day).

Aussenalster: The "outer Alster" is the bigger, more park-like and residential of Hamburg's lakes. The St. Georg neighborhood, with many recommended hotels and eateries, basically runs alongside the shore of this lake. In the past, when private gardens tumbled down from mansions lining the lake, much of this lake was off-limits to most citizens. But a 1953 law guaranteed public lake access for everyone, and walking and biking paths now parallel its shore, providing Hamburg—one of Germany's greenest cities—with a sprawling parkland. On a nice day, the lake is jam-packed with sailboats. With extra time here, you could take a bike ride (see "Helpful Hints," earlier) or rent a rowboat or sailboat at the small marina. Tiny arms of the lake stretch scenically into fancy residential neighborhoods at the north end.

▲Kunsthalle

This sprawling art collection fills two buildings (just north of the train station) with Old Masters, New Masters, 19th-century artists, and Modern Masters; in a separate but connected building, the Galerie der Gegenwart (Gallery of the Present) features contemporary works. Everything is labeled in English. Though the older building is under renovation until May 2016, most of the permanent collection will remain on view. The museum also presents excellent special exhibits, which—if you're interested in the featured artist—may be reason enough to visit.

Cost and Hours: €12 includes special exhibits, €8 for just the permanent collection; Tue-Sun 10:00-18:00, Thu until 21:00, closed Mon; English audioguide-€2, café, Glockengiesserwall, tel. 040/428-131-200, www.hamburger-kunsthalle.de.

▲Arts and Crafts Museum
(Museum für Kunst und Gewerbe)

South of the train station, this museum has three floors of decorative arts: historical European items on the ground floor, Asian objects on the first floor, and modern pieces—including several Art

Operation Gomorrah: The Firebombing of Hamburg

With its port, munitions factories, and transportation links, Hamburg was a prime target for Allied bombers during World War II. After studying what the Luftwaffe did to Coventry in 1940, the British decided to use the same techniques against Hamburg on July 27, 1943. They hit targets first with explosive bombs to open roofs, break water mains, and tear up streets (making it hard for firefighters to respond), then followed up with incendiary bombs. Designed to destroy a city known for its lustful ways, the attack was given the codename Operation Gomorrah.

But it had been a hot, dry summer, and when 700 RAF bombers concentrated their attack on a relatively small area, the result was a firestorm never seen before in the annals of war. A tornado of flames raged at up to 150 miles per hour, reaching temperatures of 1,500°F. Many inhabitants were baked to death huddling inside their air-raid shelters. Some who went outside were sucked off their feet, disappearing up into the super-heated vortex. The roads and sidewalks were on fire—those who tried to run across the roadways got their shoes stuck in boiling asphalt.

In three hours, the inferno killed an estimated 35,000 people, left hundreds of thousands homeless, and reduced eight square miles of Hamburg to rubble and ashes. At the end of the eight-day bombing campaign, which included US raids, about one million survivors had fled the city. The firebombing of Dresden two years later is more famous, but far more people died in Hamburg. And while the earlier Nazi bombings of London, Rotterdam, and Coventry were deadly, some historians say the firebombing of Hamburg was World War II's first widespread destruction of a major city.

Nouveau-period rooms—on the top floor. Its temporary exhibits are often excellent—check to see what's on.

Cost and Hours: €10, reduced to €7 Thu after 17:00; Tue-Sun 10:00-18:00, Thu until 21:00, closed Mon; English audioguide may be available, café, Steintorplatz, tel. 040/428-134-880, www.mkg-hamburg.de.

▲▲St. Nicholas Church Museum, Memorial, and Tower (Mahnmal St. Nikolai)

Before the mid-20th century, downtown Hamburg's skyline had five main churches, each with a bold tower. Today there are still five towers...but only four churches. The missing one is St. Nicholas' Church. It was designed in Neo-Gothic style by British architect George Gilbert Scott, and for a brief time after its completion in 1874, it was the world's tallest church at 483 feet (its spire is still the fifth tallest in the world). The church was destroyed by the Operation Gomorrah firebombing in 1943 (see sidebar). Its tower and a few charred walls have been left as a ruin for the past seven decades, to commemorate those lost and to remind everyone of the horrors of war. As with similar ruined churches in Coventry, England, and Berlin (Kaiser Wilhelm Memorial Church), a stroll here, between the half-destroyed walls of a once-stunning church, is poignant.

Cost and Hours: It's free to explore the footprint memorials, but you'll pay €5 to go up the tower and enter the museum (covered by one combo-ticket). Ruins always viewable; museum and tower open daily May-Sept 10:00-18:00, Oct-April 10:00-17:00, Willy-Brandt-Strasse 60, tel. 040/371125, www.mahnmal-st-nikolai.de. It's a five-minute walk from the Rödingsmarkt U-Bahn station—just follow busy Willy-Brandt-Strasse toward the tower—or a 10-minute walk from Speicherstadt.

Visiting the Memorial: The **footprint** of the church has a few information posts as well as some modern memorials. Where the original altar once stood is now a simple concrete altar; behind it is a 1977 mosaic *(Ecce Homo)* by Expressionist artist Oskar Kokoschka, showing Jesus on the cross being offered a vinegar-soaked sponge. The tower's 51-bell **carillon**, funded with local donations in 1993, plays music daily at 9:00, 12:00, 15:00, and 18:00. A live carillonneur plays 30-minute concerts every Thursday at noon, and in summer also on Saturdays at 17:00.

The **tower** still stands tall above the shell of the former church—and even though it's currently under renovation, you can still ride a speedy elevator 250 feet up to its observation platform. This vantage point is higher and the views arguably better than those from St. Michael's tower (even with the panorama somewhat blocked by scaffolding). The views of City Hall and lakes in one direction, and the Speicherstadt in the other, are particularly good.

The underground **museum** has an effective exhibit that starts with a timeline of the church's history, with photos of the interior in all its pre-WWII glory along with bits salvaged after the bombing (including some original stained-glass windows). It then takes you counterclockwise through a detailed retelling of the firestorm that destroyed it and finishes with a thoughtful examination of how the city came to grips with its aftermath—logistically, culturally, and morally. Consider that Hamburg is still full of senior citizens who experienced the firebombing firsthand—and yet the museum does not paint the Allied forces as bad guys, and reminds visitors that Hitler had done much the same to other cities (see the photos of a destroyed Warsaw) long before the destruction was visited upon German soil. One display even invites visitors to imagine the fear and guilt experienced by the British bombers (many of whom hadn't been aware they'd be attacking a civilian center).

Chile-Haus
Architecture fans will enjoy this interesting red-brick, flatiron building (north of Willy-Brandt-Strasse near the Messberg U-Bahn station). The Chile-Haus is shaped like a ship, down to the railing-lined balconies that resemble decks, and comes to a razor-sharp point at the corner. Designed by Henry Sloman in 1922-1924, it's considered the single best example of the "Brick Expressionist" school of architecture. While there's no museum, you can poke around the courtyard (with unpretentious cafés and shops that seem oblivious to the site's significance) and step into the entrance lobbies, still decorated with the Art Deco-style directories of the original tenants.

BETWEEN DOWNTOWN AND THE REEPERBAHN
St. Michael's Church
While unexceptional by European standards, Hamburg's best-known church, known around here simply as *"der Michel,"* is worth a look if you have time. The interior is bright and wide; the decoration, unusually ornate for a Protestant church, recalls its Baroque origins (it was opened in 1768). A total rebuild after a 1906 fire—started by workers repairing the roof—lent the church a little of the flavor of an early 20th-century movie palace. The church has fine acoustics (a special channel brings the organ's sound through a latticed grate in the ceiling) and hosts many concerts. You can ascend its 350-foot-high, lantern-shaped tower (52 steps plus an elevator, or 452 steps if you prefer to walk all the way up or down to see the clock and bell mechanics). While the views are fine, they're

not quite spectacular—revealing how dull and modern Hamburg's urban core is.

Cost and Hours: Free but €2 donation requested, tower-€5, skippable crypt-€4, combo-ticket-€7; daily May-Oct 9:00-19:30, Nov-April 10:00-17:30; Englische Planke 1, tel. 040/376-780, www.st-michaelis.de. Several U- and S-Bahn stops are each about a 10-minute walk away, including Baumwall, Rödingsmarkt, and Stadthausbrücke.

Nearby: At Krayenkamp 10, about 50 yards behind the

church, duck through the archway for a glimpse of the **Krameramtsstuben,** a few half-timbered buildings along a narrow lane that are rare survivors from 17th-century Hamburg. Tour-bus visitors crowd the souvenir shops in the lane.

▲▲Hamburg Museum

Like the history of the city it covers, this museum is long, complex, and multilayered. Filling a giant old building with a staggering variety of artifacts and historical re-creations, the modern, thoughtfully presented exhibits work together to illuminate the full story of Hamburg (with an understandable emphasis on the evolution of its status as one of the world's biggest shipping ports). Multiple large models of the city at various points in its history help you track how the place changed over time—industrial development, devastating 1842 fire, WWII firebombing, modern sprawl—and the included English audioguide engagingly ties everything together.

The core of the exhibit is on the first floor; the ground floor has exhibits on the 20th century and a delightful *Jugendstil* (Art Nouveau) café with seating in the glassed-in courtyard; and the top floor has large exhibits on Hamburg's Jewish community and beautifully re-created Baroque-era rooms. As the museum is close to the St. Pauli U-Bahn stop, it's easy to combine with a visit to the Reeperbahn (described later) for a day of contrasts.

Cost and Hours: €9, Tue-Sat 10:00-17:00, Sun 10:00-18:00, closed Mon, ticket includes audioguide, Holstenwall 24, big building marked with its former name—*Museum für Hamburgische Geschichte,* tel. 040/428-132-100, www.hamburgmuseum.de.

Nearby: The museum sits within the very inviting park around the **Grosse Wallanlagen** rampart in the Planten un Blomen gardens (described on page 881), which curls around the route of the former moat through the heart of town to the Binnenalster and Aussenalster lakes. For a nice approach to the museum from the St. Pauli U-Bahn stop, cut through the park and around the back of the museum (see orientation maps at park entrance).

Johannes Brahms Museum

Although the composer was born in this part of Hamburg, his actual boyhood home is long gone. This museum has a modest collection that would interest only Brahms devotees.

Cost and Hours: €4, Tue-Sun 10:00-17:00, closed Mon, about a block from Hamburg Museum at Peterstrasse 39, tel. 040/4191-3086, www.brahms-hamburg.de.

REEPERBAHN NEIGHBORHOOD

Take New Orleans' Bourbon Street, the Strip in Las Vegas, and Amsterdam's Red Light District, mix them up in a cocktail shaker, and you've got a tall glass of Reeperbahn ("roper's path"—pronounced "RAY-pehr-bahn"). It's named after the legions of rope makers who once labored here to supply Hamburg's shipping industry. Now, however, it's Germany's most famous nightlife district, home to some of Hamburg's musical theaters and a thriving prostitution scene.

Many tourists are understandably put off by the area's sleaziness—but consider that by concentrating it all right here, the Reeperbahn makes the rest of the city classier. (Those who want sleaze know where to get it, and those who don't can simply avoid this district.) The Reeperbahn may be less of a big deal in the age of online porn and Internet-based prostitution, but the street remains a huge destination for Germans. While the tourists stick mostly to the main thoroughfares, clued-in deviants know which of this neighborhood's back streets to head down. Don't fear the Reeper... it's a fascinating look at a facet of German society.

▲▲Reeperbahn Walk

The 30-minute walk described here is possible at any time of day, but is much more lively after dark—the later the better. The area is generally safe (as long as you don't go looking for trouble), with a prominently located police station in the middle of the Reeperbahn.

St. Pauli U-Bahn Station to Davidstrasse

Start at the St. Pauli U-Bahn station (after hours, the stop announcement on the loudspeaker says, *"Nächste halt: St. Pauli...viel Spass!"*—Have fun!). Exit the platform following signs to *Reeperbahn*. Towering above the U-Bahn station is a landmark skyscraper nicknamed **"The Dancing Tower"** for the way one half of it leans romantically into the other. (History buffs may want to detour from here to the nearby Hamburg Museum, described earlier; as you face the Dancing Tower, it's over your left shoulder, across the park.)

Cross the street, keeping the Dancing Tower on your left, and begin walking down the busy Reeperbahn. Most of the action in the neighborhood is along this main drag, a broad avenue with heavy car traffic that runs between the St. Pauli U-Bahn stop and the Reeperbahn S-Bahn stop. The east end of the avenue, which we'll see first, is something of a construction zone, and will likely stay that way over the next decade—it's gentrifying quickly, with high-rise buildings, chain hotels, and classier clubs going up—along with real-estate prices (this is some of the most expensive land in town). The west end (which we'll reach later), however, is more run-down.

As you stroll down the street, you'll see nightclubs, casinos, restaurants, fast-food joints, glitzy brothels, erotic theaters, and sex

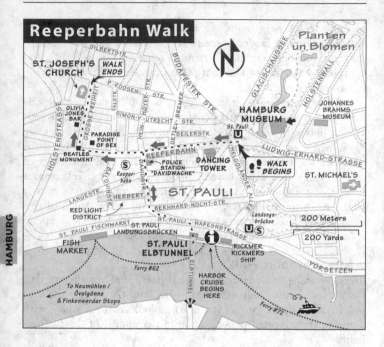

Reeperbahn Walk

Map labels: Planten un Blomen, ST. JOSEPH'S CHURCH, WALK ENDS, GILBERTSTR., T-ROOSEN-STR., BUDAPESTER STR., GLACISCHAUSSEE, HOLSTENWALL, JOHANNES BRAHMS MUSEUM, HAMBURG MUSEUM, OLIVIA JONES BAR, GROSSE FREIHEIT, TALSTR., SIMON-UTRECHT-STR., HEIN-HOYER-STR., DETLEV-BREMER-STR., St. Pauli, SEILERSTR., LUDWIG-ERHARD-STRASSE, PARADISE POINT OF SEX, HOLSTENSTRASSE, BEATLES MONUMENT, REEPERBAHN, POLICE STATION "DAVIDWACHE", DANCING TOWER, HELGOLÄNDER ALLEE, WALK BEGINS, ST. MICHAEL'S, Reeperbahn S, DAVIDSTR., ST. PAULI, KASTANIENALLEE, HERBERTSTR., BERNHARD-NOCHT-STR., Landungsbrücken, 200 Meters, 200 Yards, RED LIGHT DISTRICT, LANGESTR., ST. PAULI-HAFENSTRASSE, ST. PAULI FISCHMARKT, ST. PAULI LANDUNGSBRÜCKEN, FISH MARKET, ST. PAULI ELBTUNNEL, ELBTUNNEL, RICKMER RICKMERS SHIP, VORSETZEN, Ferry #62, To Neumühlen / Övelgönne & Finkenwerder Stops, HARBOR CRUISE BEGINS HERE, Ferry #72

shops displaying toys and gadgets for every persuasion. On weekend evenings, and into the wee hours, this place is hopping with thousands of young partiers from all over north Germany, who've converged on Hamburg to dance the weekend away. Dance clubs coordinate in a kind of throbbing relay to keep the beat going from Friday evening straight through to Monday morning.

Daylight makes the area feel seedy—the buildings look bleary-eyed and in need of makeup, and the sidewalks, littered with broken glass and puke, await cleaning. Nighttime is when it comes to life.

Red Light District

After a couple of blocks, on the left, you'll see the most famous **police station** in Germany: a cute little red-brick building that keeps

an eye on things here (it's where the Reeperbahn meets the street called Davidstrasse, to the left, and Hein-Hoyer-Strasse, to the right). Turn left here and follow Davidstrasse a couple of blocks. Streetwalkers are only allowed in a few specific places here (such as the west side of Davidstrasse), and

only after 20:00. If you walk on the left side of the street, you won't be hassled at all.

If you're a guy, expect aggressive flirtation after dark on the right side of the street. The women may be down-and-out, but they're clever at helping each other; if one figures out your language, she'll whisper it to the next prostitute down the street so she'll know how to engage you.

Except for the scraggly streetwalkers and a few brothels nearby, Hamburg's Red Light District is limited to **Herbertstrasse,** one small lane set apart by two Nazi-era metal barriers (two blocks up Davidstrasse, on the right). The fascist ideal was a Germany with no prostitution, but the Third Reich pragmatically allowed it in Hamburg to accommodate the hordes of sailors who'd come ashore here after many lonely weeks at sea. The rest of society, however, was meant to be oblivious to the city's sex trade, so up went the barricades. Any man who wants to can scoot around them and stroll down the street, which is lined with glass-doored cabins where women try to entice prospective customers. Women, however, are by custom not allowed on Herbertstrasse (except the ones working here, of course), but I've seen female tourists walk around the barriers to gaze at the scene. Don't take photos here. The prostitutes here are self-employed and run their businesses without pimps. Compared to the prostitutes on the streets and in the brothels, these are pricier and considered top-end.

From here you're a short walk to the St. Pauli Landungsbrücken harborfront (described on page 882); if you want to visit it now, follow Davidstrasse—and the sound of seagulls—downhill as it curves and empties onto St. Pauli Hafenstrasse (landing you just across from the green-domed St. Pauli Elbtunnel entrance).

To finish this walk, however, return up Davidstrasse to the Reeperbahn, cross the boulevard, and turn left. A couple of blocks along, stop at a brothel called **Paradise Point of Sex**, featuring several floors of women in windows (it's free to enter, nearly always open, and staffed with security guards). In front you'll see an old, tall, iron lamppost in the sidewalk that looks like it might be a portal to another dimension; it marks the historic border between Denmark and Germany (the long entry corridor leading to the brothel actually traces the old border). Go a few more paces to the next corner, with the round vinyl record-shaped pattern in the pavement and the cheap tin statues of a certain four English rock-n-rollers. This cross street is...

Grosse Freiheit

The street's name means "Great Freedom"—a reference not to sexual liberation, but the religious and economic freedom of this formerly Danish border zone. For most of the 17th, 18th, and 19th centuries, Denmark was particularly powerful, with borders that extended farther south than they do today (and much, much farther north). What's now the Altona district (the area just west of the Reeperbahn S-Bahn stop) was, until 1864, the Danish city of Altona. In its heyday, it was Denmark's second city, a leading port, the southern terminus of the Danish railway system, and a magnet for Germans seeking free trade (unconstrained by the regulations of guilds) and religious tolerance.

Walk down Grosse Freiheit toward a church buried in all this sex and booze. Hamburg was an officially Protestant city, and, as elsewhere in Germany, any Christian denominations other than the locally established one were strongly discouraged. Danes, though also mostly Protestant, had a more tolerant attitude, and the street of "Great Freedom" was home to **St. Joseph's Church,** the first Catholic church built in northern Europe after the Reformation (in 1660). Hamburg's Catholics could sneak over the border to worship here at Grosse Freiheit 41.

Today, Grosse Freiheit is lined with noisy teen dance clubs and table-dancing bars. While the Beatles Museum closed in 2012 (a sign of a declining Beatles fan base?), you can still visit a nearby **monument** to the now-gone Star Club, where the Beatles played a number of gigs (in a courtyard 30 yards before the church, behind the bar at #35 that features famous German transvestite Olivia Jones—go down the brick passage under the *Biergarten* sign and look left).

The Reeperbahn S-Bahn stop and the St. Pauli U-Bahn stop are nearby, and it's a quick and easy €10 taxi ride back to your hotel any time of day or night. You're also a short walk north to the youthful Shoulderblade area (described below).

NORTH OF THE REEPERBAHN
"Shoulderblade" (Schulterblatt) Neighborhood

For a colorful slice of today's Hamburg and a wonderful breath of fresh cultural air (especially if you're coming here after walking the Reeperbahn), walk or ride the U- or S-Bahn to Sternschanze and explore an up-and-coming neighborhood with so many cafés it's nicknamed "Latte Macchiato Boulevard." While the broader area is known as the Schanzenviertel (for its main drag), the liveliest subsection is at the corner of Susannenstrasse and Schulterblatt ("shoulderblade"). This trendy, youthful little area has piles of character, unique boutiques, and great places for a meal (for suggestions, see "Eating in Hamburg," later). The streets feel enlivened by the creative energy of a squatter-building-turned-arts-venue (look for the ruins covered with graffiti overlooking Schulterblatt), an edgy-yet-charming park behind it (with a WWII-era bunker-

Das Beatlemania

For music lovers, the Reeperbahn's greatest significance is the role it played as the launching pad for the Beatles, who were

unknowns when they arrived in Hamburg from Liverpool to play a season's worth of gigs in 1960. The group consisted of John, Paul, and George, plus drummer Pete Best (later replaced by Ringo Starr) and bassist Stuart Sutcliffe (who gave up music for art school in 1961, and died shortly thereafter).

Unpolished amateurs when they arrived, the band members became tight, hard-driving musicians by playing to a tough crowd night after night—they played 98 days straight at one point. While they were here, Ringo joined the band, and Sutcliffe's German girlfriend gave them their signature haircuts. By the time they left Hamburg for good in 1962, the Beatles had released several hit singles, had made their first TV appearance back in England, and were just months away from international stardom.

turned-climbing wall), and a strip of fun eateries booming with a professional clientele composed of media/software/publicity-types.

Planten un Blomen

The wide strip of parkland called Planten un Blomen stretches all the way from the harbor to the Binnenalster lake. Of the park's

varied sections, the most worthwhile is the northern stretch, near the Stephansplatz U-Bahn or Dammtor S-Bahn stops. It's an oasis of calm ponds, playful fountains, happy bunny rabbits, and colorful gardens (including a rose garden and a Japanese garden). Dotted with cafés, it's an ideal place to stroll with an ice-cream cone after a day of sightseeing—or sit back in an Adirondack chair under the shadow of the ray-gun TV tower.

Cost and Hours: Free; daily 7:00-20:00, later in summer, best before dark; S-11, S-21, or S-31 to Dammtor or U-1 to Stephansplatz; www.plantenunblomen.hamburg.de.

▲▲ST. PAULI LANDUNGSBRÜCKEN HARBORFRONT

Once Hamburg's passenger ship terminal, this long, floating dock, which parallels the waterfront, is now a thriving, touristy, borderline-tacky wharf that locals call "the Balcony of Hamburg." From here you can inhale the inviting aroma of herring and French fries while surveying the harbor and the city's vast port.

From the Landungsbrücken S- and U-Bahn stop (or from Davidstrasse, if you're walking down from the Reeperbahn), head out toward the water. As you walk down, you'll be assailed by employees of the many tour-boat companies, each pitching their trips—ignore them (most are German language-only excursions). You'll see the venerable light-brown stone former terminal building (now filled with shops), with its appropriately grandiose tower meant to evoke the ancient lighthouse in Alexandria, Egypt. The half-mile stretch of harbor beyond the terminal building has nine numbered docks, a.k.a. the Landungsbrücken ("landing bridges"). Notice how this area, like the rest of Hamburg's waterfront, is designed to accommodate the Elbe's 13-foot tides.

From this terminal you can catch a public ferry, hop the guided boat tour, hike under the river, and tour a historic ship. Consider a lunch break at the harbor's own brewery, the recommended Block Braü.

▲▲▲Harbor and Port Guided Boat Tour

Of the hundred or so big-boat harbor tours that go daily here, only a few come with English narration. The best is **Rainer Abicht**, whose excellent tour (once a day in English) gives you a skyline view from the water of all the construction in Hamburg. The industrial port is a major focus of the trip, and getting up close to all those massive container ships, cranes, and dry and wet docks is breathtaking. The live commentary (which switches between English and German) is fascinating and entertaining. You can order a drink to sip as you take it all in from the deck (bring a sandwich for a discreet picnic).

Cost and Hours: One-hour harbor tour-€18 (€30 combo-ticket with Roten Doppeldecker bus tour), English tour runs April-Oct daily at 12:00, no English tours off-season, tel. 040/317-8220, www.abicht.de. Their waterside ticket windows are by bridge 4 (look for the blue-and-white boats).

▲Harbor Tour by Public Ferry

Hamburg's ferries, which take the same tickets and passes as the S-Bahn and U-Bahn, give you a fine look at the harbor and a lot of the port action, but won't actually take you into the industrial port area—for that, you'll need to take one of the privately operated tour boats (see previous listing). There's no point in riding this ferry if you're already taking a privately operated tour. Take ferry line

#62 (4/hour 7:00-21:00, 2/hour 21:00-23:00), and use your transit-system day pass (ticket machines on the docks and on board) or Hamburg Card. The ride described below takes about one hour. Only bigger ferries have WCs and snack booths—but bringing a picnic on board is fully OK.

⊘ **Self-Guided Tour:** From the Landungsbrücken terminal building, go to bridge 3 and find the signs for ferry line #62 to Finkenwerder. With stops, it's a 28-minute trip downstream and another 28 minutes back—if you like, you can stay on the same ferry, but boats leave often enough that hopping on and off is easy.

Riding toward Finkenwerder, just after the new cruise port, you'll soon encounter the enormous **"Dockland"** office building, designed to look like a gigantic yacht. Its "stern" is actually a series of climbable terraces that lead to a viewpoint rooftop.

The first stop is **Fischmarkt,** which hosts a popular market (produce, fish, flea market) that's only open on Sunday morning (see page 866).

Soon after the second stop, watch on the right for the *Schlepper* **(tugboat) station,** with a row of tugs lined up and ready to go. Because Hamburg sits about 60 miles inland from the sea, arriving ships have to traverse a long stretch of river—and at the regulated low speeds, very large ships can't get enough momentum going to steer, forcing them to rely on this fleet of plucky tugboats. Behind them, notice the red line on the quay. This was the high-water mark of the 1962 flood, which killed more than 300 people and destroyed about 6,000 buildings within the city.

As you pull into the next stop, consider that you're cruising right over the eight lanes of autobahn traffic that speed through a newer Elbtunnel (built in 1975). You could break your journey here at **Neumühlen,** the third stop, below hillside villas in the posh neighborhood of Övelgönne. Here you can see the modest "museum harbor" (Museumshafen) of retired boats bobbing near the ferry dock, eat lunch at one of the two reasonably priced cafés nearby (Elbterrassen and Museumshafen Café), or enjoy Hamburg's beach (a short walk downstream from the ferry pier). Bus #112, which terminates at the Neumühlen pier, runs every 15 minutes and is an alternative way to get from Övelgönne back to St. Pauli and the train station (it also gives you a look at the suburb of Altona). Or, ride the boat all the way to Finkenwerder, then turn around to sail back to Landungsbrücken.

The **Finkenwerder** stop, where the ferry turns around, is on an island that's home to Airbus' test runway (closed to the public), which was used to develop the superjumbo A380.

Quickie Option: If you'd rather take a shorter ferry ride than the one I've just described, try this: At Landungsbrücken, go to bridge 1 (by the *Rickmer Rickmers* museum ship—all the way to the left, as you face the water) and catch line #72 toward the city center to HafenCity and the Elbphilharmonie concert hall (7-minute trip, 2/hour, daily 9:00-20:00, until 21:30 on weeknights; can ride one-way with a *Kurzstrecke* ticket).

St. Pauli Elbtunnel
Continental Europe's oldest underwater tunnel, built in 1911, is marked by a green-domed entry hall designed to resemble the Pantheon in Rome (at the right end of the big terminal building, as you face the water). To take a memorable look at some century-old technology, walk down the stairs or ride an elevator—ogling the big wooden industrial elevators that cars use (free entrance). At the bottom, you can look down the full quarter-mile length of the tunnel and wonder how it can safely lie just 40 feet under the surface of the Elbe (meaning big ships cannot go upstream past here). Inside, it's 15 feet high—just high enough for a coachman to hold his horse whip upright. For a little exercise, and a great view of Hamburg from across the river, walk or bike through the tunnel to the other side. Once across, ride the elevator or huff up the stairs to the surface, and follow *Aussichtsplatform* signs to a terrace with a great panoramic view of Hamburg and a helpful orientation board that identifies the major landmarks.

SS *Rickmer Rickmers*
Sailboat enthusiasts will enjoy this three-masted, steel-hulled ship (moored near bridge 1). Built in Bremerhaven in 1896, it's been restored—largely by volunteers—and is now open to the public. You can explore the ship's four decks, including the crew quarters, engine room, and a handful of exhibits.

Cost and Hours: €5, daily 10:00-18:00, last entry 30 minutes before closing, tel. 040/319-5959, www.rickmer-rickmers.de.

Nearby: In front of the ship is a café that's a little quieter than the others along the Landungsbrücken—it's a pleasant place to eat lunch while watching the ferries come and go.

▲HAFENCITY AND SPEICHERSTADT
A century ago, Hamburg's port was the world's third largest, and in Europe it's still second only to Rotterdam's. Unlike Rotterdam's port, Hamburg's was built right up next to the city center, as the small city-state of Hamburg couldn't defend a remote port. But with the advent of huge modern container ships, which demanded more space than Hamburg's industrial zone could accommodate, most business shifted to a larger and more modern port nearby (you'll see these big container ships docking under the huge cranes after their North Sea voyage)—and all this prime real estate (just half a mile from the City Hall) suddenly became available.

The result is **HafenCity,** Europe's biggest urban development project (and, they claim, the biggest ongoing project in the world for the next 20 years). When it's done, downtown Hamburg will be 40 percent bigger, and the city will again face the Elbe River. The area seems a city in itself, with a maritime touch, interesting modern architecture, and a mix of business, culture, and leisure. Planners hope that 45,000 people will eventually work here and 12,000 will call it home.

Speicherstadt ("Warehouse City"), between HafenCity and the city center, is a huge stand of red-brick riverside warehouses.

It was originally built over a 40-year span, starting in the 1880s. Half of it, however, was destroyed in World War II; it was subsequently rebuilt and officially remained part of Hamburg's port zone until 2003. But after the arrival of the modern container terminals across the river, it no longer made sense to store goods here. Nevertheless, the city decided to renovate the area and preserve the warehouses as part of the urban landscape. A few museums and theme-park-like attractions have moved into Speicherstadt's warehouses and cater mostly to German visitors. These older, restored warehouses are each labeled with a letter (see listing for Block D, later). The redevelopment is still a work in progress, and the new buildings are not yet fully occupied, but the project is a great source of pride and interest among locals and German tourists (it's the best-known waterfront revival effort in this mostly landlocked country).

Getting to HafenCity and Speicherstadt: For an atmospheric approach, go to the Landungsbrücken S- and U-Bahn stop and take public ferry #72 one stop upstream (see page 882). You'll disembark by HafenCity's striking new Elbphilharmonie concert hall.

You can also take the U-3 subway line to Baumwall, walk across either of the Niederbaumbrücke bridges, and turn left. After strolling between the canal (on your left) and a row of warehouses (on your right) for about five minutes, along the street called Kehrwieder, look for Block D (described later). The Elbphilharmonie Pavilion and International Maritime Museum are farther in.

▲▲Elbphilharmonie Concert Hall

The centerpiece of the HafenCity development, and a building that promises to become a symbol of modern Germany, is the jaw-dropping Elbphilharmonie—a combination concert hall, hotel,

apartment complex, and shopping mall, all contained in a towering and wildly beautiful piece of architecture. Though it's staggeringly behind schedule and over budget (so far costing about €800 million instead of €77 million), it's nevertheless a source of pride and excitement among Hamburg's citizens. Its daring design and huge size fit in well with the massive scale of the port around it—and when approached by water, resembles the looming prows of the steamer ships that first put Hamburg on the world map. When

it's finished, Hamburgers will ride a 90-yard-long escalator into a plaza level of shops, bars, and cafés to the entry level of this 360-foot-tall, 360-foot-long structure.

While work is still under way (it's due to wrap up in 2017... at the earliest), the cube-shaped **Elbphilharmonie Pavilion** welcomes the curious to a small, free exhibit describing the project. You'll see drawings of the final vision, look out the window to a distant view of the construction site, and climb a ladder to poke your head up into a mock-up of the main performance hall—originally built to test acoustics (tucked back between the wharfs of Kaiserkai and Sandtorkai at Magellan Terrassen, across from Sandtorpark).

Speicherstadt Block D

This warehouse in Speicherstadt contains a café with historical photos and a museum of miniatures, each worth a visit. (Less worthy is the Hamburg Dungeon attraction—a cheap knockoff of London's tackiest sight.)

The **Speicherstadt Kaffeerösterei** (coffee roasters) serves sandwiches, cakes, and desserts, and sells coffee by the bag and other small gifts (daily 10:00-19:00, tel. 040/3181-6161). You'll enter the café through a flood gate—which can be closed in high water. (Tidal bores are a real danger along the Elbe, so all new building in Hamburg is well above water level.) In the entry hall, on the wall on the right, check out the photographs of Speicherstadt when it was still lined with medieval-looking half-timbered warehouses. After 1881, when Hamburg joined the German customs union, these were torn down and the current, then-state-of-the-art buildings were constructed.

As you leave the café, look straight ahead across the canal into the city center to see a single, short row of surviving half-timbered warehouses that still stand along Deichstrasse...and mentally expand this stretch across the harbor area to imagine the industrious, salty charm of 17th-century Hamburg.

▲Miniatur Wunderland

The most fun of Block D's sights, worth its high entry fee, is Miniatur Wunderland, which claims to have the world's largest model railway, covering over 14,000 square feet with more than eight miles of track. Marvel at the tiny airport (with model planes taking off), and watch night fall every 15 minutes. Visit the Alps, Scandinavia, Italy, and the US in miniature (the latter complete with a shootout scene, and even Area 51). Little bits come to life with a press of a green-lit button—bungee jumpers leap, the drive-in plays a movie, and tiny Bavarians hoist teeny beer mugs to their mini-mouths. Hamburg's harbor is lovingly rendered—including the building you're standing in—with a model of the Elbphilharmonie that lets you peek inside.

Cost and Hours: €12, daily at least 9:30-18:00 but can flex up to 8:00-22:00 depending on demand, tel. 040/300-6800, www. miniatur-wunderland.com.

Crowd-Beating Tips: The model railway is wildly popular—there's often an hour's wait to get in—so it's a good idea to reserve online at least a day in advance (no extra charge). If you haven't reserved, arrive early (before 9:00) or late (ideally after 18:00, if it's open later). It's most crowded from midmorning through early afternoon, and totally swamped on school holidays.

Nearby: Make sure to cross one of the side bridges in Speicherstadt to experience the long, industrial-feeling loading canals and to imagine this area when it was full of barges and dockworkers. On the Pickhuben bridge, a couple of blocks down from Block D at the corner of Pickhuben and Kannengieserort, a plaque shows photographs of the warehouses after they were bombed in World War II.

▲▲International Maritime Museum

This state-of-the-art exhibit fills 10 floors of a towering brick ex-warehouse with thousands of maritime artifacts—while reminding visitors that "the sail came before the wheel" and "rowing came before the saddle." Despite its name, its perspective is more German than international, but that's part of what makes it interesting (and nearly everything is well-described in English).

Ride the lift to the ninth "deck" (floor) to start with the world's biggest collection of miniature ship models, and then work your way down—each floor has a different military or civilian maritime theme: paintings and ship models; deep-sea research; the history of merchant shipping and cruise ships; exploration, colonization, and warfare (with good exhibits on the naval warfare of World Wars I and II); uniforms, medals, and insignias from around the world; the history of shipbuilding; global seafaring history; and navigation. Between the first and second decks is an enormous model of the RMS *Queen Mary 2* (which often sails from just a few blocks away)...made entirely of Legos.

Cost and Hours: €12.50, Tue-Sun 10:00-18:00, closed Mon, English audioguide-€3.50, Kaispeicher B, tel. 040/3009-2345, www.imm-hamburg.de.

OUTSIDE THE CITY CENTER
▲BallinStadt Emigration Museum

This engaging museum, a German counterpart to Ellis Island, tells the story of emigration to America through Hamburg from the

mid-19th century up through World War II. Especially after 1890, many emigrants from the Austro-Hungarian and Russian empires—today's Eastern Europe—went first to Hamburg, by train or even on foot, before boarding a ship to cross the ocean. The museum occupies three restored dormitory buildings that were opened in 1901 to house and quarantine sick emigrants until they were healthy enough to be allowed on board. With less in the way of actual artifacts, and more in the way of big, colorful re-creations of living conditions and interactive exhibits—most with English descriptions—this is a dynamic and kid-friendly look at a powerful topic.

Cost and Hours: €12.50, daily April-Oct 10:00-18:00, Nov-March 10:00-16:30, last entry one hour before closing, tel. 040/3197-9160; www.ballinstadt.net.

Getting There: BallinStadt is right by the Veddel S-Bahn station, two stops from the train station on the S-3 or S-31 (direction: Neugraben, Stade, Buxtehude, or Harburg Rathaus; about a 7-minute ride). From the S-Bahn platforms, follow the BallinStadt signs for about 80 yards to the museum.

Visiting the Museum: Buy your ticket in Haus 1 (where you may also see special exhibits), then head into Haus 2 for the core of the museum. Here, creative exhibits give a look at the origins of the five million German emigrants who passed through here, the reasons they chose to leave (from poverty to pogroms), their experiences on the transatlantic ships, their arrival in New York City, and their challenges forging a new life in the new land. Along the way, you can pick up phones and press the English button to hear first-person accounts of people before, during, and after their journeys.

Haus 3 is mostly a cot-filled re-creation of what these buildings looked like when they held up to 1,200 immigrants waiting to cross the Atlantic. The visit ends with a room where you can search online genealogy databases (basically just Ancestry.com).

The museum complex is named after Albert Ballin, who at the time it was built was director of the Hamburg-America Line (also known as HAPAG, and now part of Hapag-Lloyd). Ballin is considered the father of the modern cruise industry. He was the son of Danish Jews who had moved to Hamburg, and he started his career working in his father's small emigration agency. Ballin committed suicide in November 1918, worried (rightly, as it turned out) that HAPAG's ships would be confiscated after Germany's impending defeat in World War I.

Eating: The museum's reasonably priced restaurant, in Haus 3, is a good place to try *Labskaus,* a Hamburg specialty similar to corned beef hash; see page 892.

Day Trips

Visitors disappointed by Hamburg's lack of a cute medieval old town should consider an outing to **Lübeck**, almost on the Baltic, 45 minutes northeast of Hamburg by train; or to **Lüneburg**, a small university town that got rich off local salt mines, 30 minutes to the south. Both have classic, well-preserved old centers with typical North German/Hanseatic brick architecture.

Sleeping in Hamburg

Hamburg has plenty of reasonably priced places to stay and only a few of the special events that send prices skyrocketing in Frankfurt or Cologne. As the city is a popular musical theater destination for Germans, Friday and Saturday nights can be more expensive than the rest of the week. Staying somewhere with good public transport links is a must in this not-very-walkable city. I've listed hotels in the St. Georg district, conveniently near the train station and the walking paths around the Aussenalster.

NEAR THE TRAIN STATION, IN ST. GEORG

The St. Georg neighborhood is a convenient place to sleep, thanks to its good midrange hotels, easy walking distance from the train station, and good restaurants and lively street life. Lange Reihe, the main thoroughfare in this area, is a delightful neighborhood to call home; it's busy with inviting eateries, cafés, and shops (reach it via the station's north exit by track 3 onto Kirchenallee). As you walk off Lange Reihe toward the water (the Aussenalster), the buildings become more and more elegant, with an upper-class, diamonds-and-poodles feel. Just a few streets in the other direction is Steindamm, St. Georg's other major avenue (reached from the station's south exit); it's a raucous immigrant boulevard and feels like Queens compared with Lange Reihe's Manhattan.

$$$ Hotel Wedina—hip, full of character, and design-

HAMBURG

Sleep Code

Abbreviations (€1 = about $1.40, country code: 49)
S = Single, **D** = Double/Twin, **T** = Triple, **Q** = Quad, **b** = bathroom, **s** = shower only.
Price Rankings
 $$$ **Higher Priced**—Most rooms €110 or more.
  $$ **Moderately Priced**—Most rooms between €75-110.
   $ **Lower Priced**—Most rooms €75 or less.
Unless otherwise noted, credit cards are accepted, breakfast is included, Wi-Fi is generally free, and English is spoken. Prices change; verify current rates online or by email. For the best prices, always book directly with the hotel.

---

conscious—has 63 rooms in five renovated townhouses in a people-friendly neighborhood that's a 10-minute walk from the station. Each building has a different theme (literature, architecture, the Mediterranean, tradition, and art). Three of the buildings are connected; the fourth, with reception, breakfast room, and a tranquil garden oasis in back, is across the street. The fifth, in a charming old half-timbered townhouse, is two blocks away, right on Lange Reihe. Every room is a little different, with its own extra touches (very small Sb-€70, Db-€125-145 depending on size, Tb-€155, more for apartments and suites with kitchen, lots of stairs, guest computer, Wi-Fi, bike rental-€8/day, parking-€18/day; Gurlittstrasse 23, tel. 040/280-8900, www.hotelwedina.de, info@hotelwedina.de). From the station, walk up Lange Reihe, then go left on Gurlittstrasse. Or catch bus #6 from the station (stop is across the street, just right of Hotel Fürst Bismark, direction: U Borgweg, leaves every 5-10 minutes) and hop off at the first stop (Gurlittstrasse).

$$$ Hotel Aussen Alster, in a handsome townhouse near the lakeside, has 27 pleasant, straightforward rooms over a polished lobby. It's a little more expensive than the other listings here. The hotel has loaner bikes for guests, as well as a sailboat that you can take out on the Aussenalster, just a block away (reserve ahead). The garden in back is a fine place to relax (Sb-€95-130, Db-€130-165, slippery rates depend on demand, elevator, Wi-Fi, parking-€15/day, Schmilinskystrasse 11, tel. 040/284-078-570, www.aussen-alster.de, info@aussen-alster.de). It's a 10-minute walk from the station up Lange Reihe, then left on Schmilinskystrasse. Or you can hop bus #6 from the station (see end of previous listing), and get off at the second stop (AK St. Georg), then backtrack a half-block to Schmilinskystrasse and turn right.

$$ The **Ibis Hotel Hamburg Alster Centrum** is entirely lacking in character, but has 170 reliable rooms right by the station.

Ask for a front-side, street-facing room—they're quieter than the back-facing ones, which overlook the train tracks (generally Sb-€80-120, Db-€90-150—but rates vary wildly with demand, check website for cheaper special rates, breakfast-€10, air-con, elevator, Wi-Fi, parking-€10/day; Holzdamm 4-12, tel. 040/248-290, www.ibishotel.com, h1395@accor.com). Exit the station at the north end of track 3 to Kirchenallee, then turn left and walk five minutes, with the tracks on your left, onto Holzdamm.

$$ Motel One Hamburg-Alster, a monstrous (460-room), inexpensive hotel with cookie-cutter but surprisingly stylish rooms, is a good-value option, especially if cozier places are booked. Though the location isn't as convenient—it's one U-Bahn stop from the station or a 10-minute walk down the seedy Steindamm—the rates are better and rooms are more comfortable and trendier than at the Ibis (Sb-€69, Db-€84, higher during infrequent special events, breakfast-€7.50, air-con, elevator, guest iPad at front desk, Wi-Fi, parking-€11/day; Steindamm 102, tel. 040/4192-4970, www.motel-one.com, hamburg-alster@motel-one.com). The hotel is right at the Lohmühlenstrasse U-Bahn stop.

$$ Hotel-Pension Alpha, a decent budget choice, has 21 rooms almost in sight of the station. The rooms are basic and some are quite tight, but they're more than adequate, and everything is well-kept by kindly Georg (Sb-€53, Db-€85, Tb-€130, 2 percent more if paying with credit card—but 3 percent less if paying with cash, breakfast-€8, Wi-Fi, Koppel 4, tel. 040/245-365, www.alphahotel.biz, info@alphahotel.biz). From the station, exit by track 3 north onto Kirchenallee and look for the red-brick church (St. Georg); the hotel is across the street that runs on the right side of the church. Georg may not be around in the evening; be sure to confirm your arrival time, and if he won't be there, he'll give you a code for the door.

ELSEWHERE IN HAMBURG

These budget options are in different neighborhoods, but still easy to reach from the train station by U-Bahn.

Near City Hall: **$ Pension am Rathaus** is—true to its name—just a block from City Hall, in an appealing downtown neighborhood. The 15 rooms are simple and bright, and many share bathrooms (S-€32, Ss-€42, D-€48, Db-€72, T-€63, family room available, all prices €5 more on weekends, no breakfast, reception open 9:00-14:00 & 15:00-20:00, pay Wi-Fi, no elevator, Rathausstrasse 14, U-Bahn: Rathaus, tel. 040/337-489, www.pension-am-rathaus.de, pension-am-rathaus@hamburg.de).

Near the Hamburg Museum: **$$ Motel One Hamburg am Michel** is a stylish and affordable chain hotel fantastically located right next to the Grosse Wallanlagen area within Planten un Blomen gardens, steps from the Hamburg Museum, St. Pauli, and St. Michael's Church (Sb-€69, Db-€84, €20-70 more during conventions and other events, breakfast-€7.50, air-con, elevator, guest iPad at front desk, Wi-Fi, limited parking-€15/day; Ludwig-Erhard-Strasse 26, tel. 040/3571-8900, www.motel-one.com, hamburg-am-michel@motel-one.com).

Near the Landungsbrücken: **$ Jugendherberge Hamburg "Auf dem Stintfang"** is a hostel with a super location and commanding view of the Elbe, atop a hill right behind the Landungsbrücken S- and U-Bahn station. It's big (356 beds), bright, colorful, modern, and well-run. As most rooms have their own bath, it's worth considering as an affordable alternative to staying in a hotel—but be aware that all doubles are bunk beds (bed in mixed 8-bed dorm with shared bath-€23, bed in 6-bed gender-segregated dorm with its own bath-€26, Db-€70, Tb-€84, Qb-€110, Quint/b-€135; €4/person extra for those 27 and over, €3.50 more if you're not a hostel member; nonrefundable "Fixdeal" discount saves €2-3/person when booked at least 3 weeks ahead, includes breakfast and sheets, towels-€4, dinner-€7.50, elevator, laundry-€5.20/load, pay guest computer, 1 hour free Wi-Fi—then pay, Alfred-Wegener-Weg 5, tel. 040/570-1590, www.jugendherberge.de/jh/hamburg-stintfang, jh-stintfang@djh.de). From the train station, take the S-1 or S-3 three stops to Landungsbrücken, then follow the signs up the steep stairway, or—if you have wheeled luggage—take the long way, circling around back.

Eating in Hamburg

Hamburg's food traditions have much in common with Scandinavia's. Fish is a fixture on local menus, even if little of it is actually caught in the nearby North Sea. Herring is common in sandwiches, as a main dish, and at breakfast (often rolled up with pickled vegetables inside and secured with a toothpick, called *Rollmops*). *Labskaus*, a traditional northern German dish, is not unlike corned beef hash; it's typically served with pickles, red beets, a fried egg, and sometimes a herring filet.

After Dinner: To walk off your dinner, stroll the Reeperbahn area after dark, following my self-guided walk (described on page 877). Home to Hamburg's Red Light District, this is one of Germany's liveliest and most famous nightlife scenes.

NEAR THE TRAIN STATION, IN ST. GEORG

The following listings are near my recommended hotels and close to the train station. The main street through the area, Lange Reihe, is lined with a great variety of places to shop and eat. During the daytime it makes good sense to pick up lunch while sightseeing; see "Sights in Hamburg" for some suggestions.

Kajüte sits on pontoons on the Aussenalster (opposite Hotel Bellevue) and is good if you're willing to pay a little more for atmosphere—come in the evening to watch sailboats and the setting sun across the water (€13-25 main courses, expensive drinks, reservations smart, indoor and outdoor seating, daily 11:00-23:00, An der Alster 10a, tel. 040/243-037, www.kajuete.de).

Frau Möller is a popular neighborhood hangout—a rollicking bar serving up very affordable, hearty Alsatian and Hamburger classics (sandwiches, huge salads, and daily specials that usually include one or two local specialties). The interior can be jammed and the service overwhelmed; try for one of the sidewalk tables, ideal for taking your time while people-watching (€5-9 meals, daily 11:30-24:00, Lange Reihe 96, tel. 040/2532-8817).

Café Koppel, a bright, inexpensive vegetarian café, occupies an art center reachable from St. Georg's main drag—Lange Reihe—by walking through an archway and across a courtyard. Choose between two indoor floors or quiet garden seating; there are a couple of main courses available every day (€6-8, chalked on the board) as well as soups and big salads (daily 10:00-23:00, Lange Reihe 75, tel. 040/249-235).

Hee-Yang, at the train-station end of Lange Reihe, is crammed with locals enjoying sushi and Thai dishes (€9-14 meals, €30 two-person meals, daily 11:30-24:00, Lange Reihe 15-17, tel. 040/2805-6227).

Schifferbörse sits right across the street from the train station (making it quite touristy), but it cooks up solid northern German food at fair prices, served in a fun dining room elaborately decked out to look and feel like a Cubist take on a ship's galley (€8-11 lunches, €13-20 main courses at dinner, daily 11:30-23:00, Kirchenallee 46 between Bremer Reihe and Ellmenreichstrasse, tel. 040/245-240).

Supermarket: The **Galeria Kaufhof** department store, by the train station, has a supermarket at basement level (Mon-Sat 10:00-20:00, closed Sun; exit the south bridge of the train station by track 14 toward Mönckebergstrasse and look for the entrance to your left). The **Edeka** supermarket inside the train station, on the upper level of the north bridge over the tracks, has longer hours, but is smaller and more expensive (daily 7:00-23:00).

IN THE "SHOULDERBLADE" NEIGHBORHOOD

Fun restaurants with good people-watching fill the streets just south and west of the Sternschanze U-Bahn stop (see listing on page 880). There's a whole world of options here: Asian, Turkish/Middle Eastern, Italian, Greek, crêpes, tapas, and more. I'd just wander and browse. The highest concentration of good eateries is along Schulterblatt, from where it forks off of Schanzenstrasse up to the Susannenstrasse intersection (many places serve tapas or pizza and have generous outdoor seating, due to the particularly wide sidewalks). If you're having a hard time deciding where to eat, here are a couple of suggestions.

Bullerei, conveniently located right next to the Sternschanze U-Bahn stop, is the most serious restaurant in this neighborhood. The brainchild of German celebrity chef Tim Mälzer, it fills a gorgeously restored red-brick meatpacking hall with a vast, vibrant dining room and a cozy bistro—both stylish and dressy—with high-energy diners. There's also outdoor seating on a tree-lined brick patio. The restaurant is pricey (€8-15 starters, €20-30 main dishes, extensive steak options), while the bistro is a bit more casual and affordable (€7-18 meals). On the menu: meat, of course. Reservations are smart (bistro open daily 11:00-24:00, restaurant daily 18:00-24:00, Lagerstrasse 34b, tel. 040/3344-2110, www.bullerei. com).

Altes Mädchen, just around the corner from Bullerei in a re-purposed brick warehouse, serves up a short-but-refined food menu alongside seemingly unlimited varieties of craft beer, much of it brewed right here at the Ratsherrn microbrewery (€6 sampler available). Dishes are made with largely locally sourced ingredients, and the bread's baked fresh in their wood oven. The expansive, retro-rustic interior houses a fireplace and lots of bare wood; the self-service tables outside are equally pleasant (€14-25 main dishes inside, €8-15 dishes outside, daily 12:00-22:00, Lagerstrasse 28, tel. 040/800-077-750).

Bok serves up well-executed pan-Asian cuisine in an airy, modern atmosphere (€10-15 Japanese, Thai, and Korean dishes; daily 12:00-24:00; Schulterblatt 3, tel. 040/4319-0070).

ON THE HARBOR
Block Bräu, a huge, modern beer hall, features local cuisine and its own beer in the Landungsbrücken terminal building. It has a thousand seats, including great rooftop terrace seating with harbor views (€8-17 meals, daily 11:00-24:00, Landungsbrücken 3, tel. 040/4440-5000).

Lining the harborfront is a long row of fast-food booths, selling big glasses of beer, paper cones of French fries, gut-bomb *Currywurst,* and more—to go, to stand up, or to sit down. If you're in a hurry to catch your boat, just grab what looks good—it's all equally marginal.

Hamburg Connections

From Hamburg by Train to: Berlin (1-2/hour direct, 2 hours), **Leipzig** (hourly, 3-3.5 hours, some direct, others transfer in Berlin), **Cologne** (hourly, 4 hours), **Frankfurt** (hourly, 4 hours), **Munich** (hourly, 6-6.5 hours), **Copenhagen,** Denmark (direct trains almost every 2 hours, 5 hours), **Amsterdam,** the Netherlands (hourly, 5.5 hours, 1 change). Train info: Tel. 0180-599-6633, www.bahn.com.

GERMAN HISTORY

A united Germany has only existed since 1871, but the cultural heritage of the German-speaking people stretches back 2,000 years.

Romans (A.D. 1-500)

German history begins in A.D. 9, when Roman troops were ambushed and driven back by the German chief Arminius. For the next 250 years, the Rhine and Danube rivers marked the border between civilized Roman Europe (to the southwest) and "barbarian" German lands (to the northeast). While the rest of Western Europe's future would be Roman, Christian, and Latin, most of Germany followed a separate, pagan path.

In A.D. 476, Rome fell to the Germanic chief Theodoric the Great (a.k.a. Dietrich of Bern). After that, Germanic Franks controlled northern Europe, ruling a mixed population of Romanized Christians and tree-worshipping pagans.

Charlemagne and the Franks (A.D. 500-1000)

For Christmas in A.D. 800, the pope gave Charlemagne the title of Holy Roman Emperor. Charlemagne, the king of the Franks, was the first of many German kings to be called *Kaiser* ("emperor," from "Caesar") over the next thousand years. Allied with the pope, Charlemagne ruled an empire that included Germany, Austria, France, the Low Countries, and northern Italy.

Charlemagne (Karl der Grosse, or Charles the Great, r. 768-814) stood a head taller than his subjects, and his foot became a standard unit of measurement. The stuff of legend, Charles the Great had five wives and four concubines, producing descendants with names like Charles the Bald, Louis the Pious, and Henry the Quarrelsome. After Charlemagne died of pneumonia (814), his

Why We Call Deutschland "Germany"

Our English name "Germany" comes from the Latin *Germania,* the Roman name for the lands north of the Alps where "barbarian" tribes lived. The French and Spanish call it *Allemagne* and *Alemania,* respectively, after the Alemanni tribe. Italians call the country *Germania,* but in Italy the German language is known as *tedesco.* Completely confused by all this, the Slavic peoples of Eastern Europe simply throw up their hands and call Germany *Německo* (Czech), *Niemcy* (Polish), or other variations of a word that basically means "people who can't speak right." The Hungarians borrowed this word from the Slavs and call anything German *német.*

To Germans, their country is *Deutschland,* their language is *Deutsch,* and they themselves are *Deutsche.* A few hundred years ago, this word was spelled *Teutsch* (later, the "t" changed to a "d"). The English word Teutonic, the Italian *tedesco,* and the Scandinavian *tysk* all come from this earlier form. *Alles klar?*

united empire did not pass directly to his oldest son but was divided into (what would become) Germany, France, and the lands in between (Treaty of Verdun, 843).

The Holy Roman Empire (1000-1500)

Chaotic medieval Germany was made up of more than 300 small, quarreling dukedoms ruled by the Holy Roman Emperor. The title was pretty bogus, implying that the German king ruled the same huge European empire as the ancient Romans. In fact, he was "Holy" because he was blessed by the Church, "Roman" to recall ancient grandeur, and the figurehead "Emperor" of what was an empire in name only.

Holy Roman Emperors had less hands-on power than other kings around Europe. Because of the custom of electing emperors by nobles and archbishops, rather than by bestowing the title through inheritance, they couldn't pass the crown from father to son. In addition, there were no empire-wide taxes and no national capital. This system gave nobles great power: Peasants huddled close to their local noble's castle for protection from attack by the noble next door.

When Emperor Henry IV (r. 1056-1106) tried to assert his power by appointing bishops, he was slapped down by the nobles, and forced to repent to the pope by standing barefoot in the alpine snow for three days at Canossa (in northern Italy, 1077; see the sidebar on page 226).

Emperor Frederick I Barbarossa (1152-1190), blue-eyed and

GERMAN HISTORY

Church Architecture

History comes to life when you visit a centuries-old church. Even if you wouldn't know your apse from a hole in the ground, learning a few simple terms will enrich your experience. Note that not every church has every feature, and a "cathedral" isn't a type of church architecture, but rather a designation for a church that's a governing center for a local bishop.

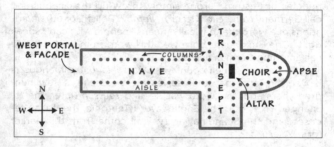

Aisles: The long, generally low-ceilinged arcades that flank the nave.

Altar: The raised area with a ceremonial table (often adorned with candles or a crucifix), where the priest prepares and serves the bread and wine for Communion.

Apse: The space beyond the altar, often bordered with small chapels.

Barrel Vault: A continuous round-arched ceiling that resembles an extended upside-down U.

Choir: A cozy area, often screened off, located within the church nave and near the high altar where services are sung in a more intimate setting.

Cloister: Covered hallways bordering a usually square-shaped, open-air courtyard, traditionally where monks and nuns got fresh air.

Facade: The exterior surface of the church's main (west) entrance, viewable from outside and generally highly decorated.

Groin Vault: An arched ceiling formed where two equal barrel vaults meet at right angles. Less common usage: term for a medieval jock strap.

Narthex: The area (portico or foyer) between the main entry and the nave.

Nave: The long, central section of the church (running west to east, from the entrance to the altar) where the congregation sits or stands through the service.

Transept: In a traditional cross-shaped floor plan, the transept is one of the two parts forming the "arms" of the cross. The transepts run north-south, perpendicularly crossing the east-west nave.

West Portal: The main entry to the church (on the west end, opposite the main altar).

red-bearded (hence *barba rossa*), gained an international reputation as a valiant knight, gentleman, bon vivant, and lover of poetry and women. Still, his great victories were away in Italy and Asia (on the Third Crusade, where he drowned in a river), while back home nobles wielded the real power.

This was the era of Germany's troubadours *(Meistersingers)*, who traveled from castle to castle singing love songs *(Minnesang)* and telling the epic tales of chivalrous knights (Tristan and Isolde, Parsifal, and the Nibelungen) that would later inspire German nationalism and Wagnerian operas.

While France, England, and Spain were centralizing power around a single ruling family to create nation-states, Germany remained a decentralized, backward, feudal battleground.

Medieval Growth

Nevertheless, Germany was strategically located at the center of Europe, and trading towns prospered. Several northern towns (especially Hamburg and Lübeck) banded together into the Hanseatic League, promoting open trade around the Baltic Sea. To curry favor at election time, emperors granted powers and privileges to certain towns, designated "free imperial cities." Some towns, such as Cologne, Mainz, Dresden, and Trier, held higher status than many nobles, as hosts of one of the seven "electors" of the emperor. To this day, every German town keeps careful track of whether it was "free" during the Middle Ages—or answered to a duke, king, archbishop, or elector in another place.

Textiles, mining, and the colonization of lands to the east made Germany an economic powerhouse with a thriving middle class. In towns, middle-class folks (burghers), not the local aristocrats, began running things. In about 1450, Johann Gutenberg of Mainz figured out how to use moveable type for printing, an innovation that would allow the export of a new commodity: ideas.

Religious Struggles and the Thirty Years' War (1500-1700)

Martin Luther—German monk, fiery orator, and religious whistle-blower—sparked a century of European wars by speaking out against the Catholic Church (see page 593).

Luther's protests ("Protestantism") threw Germany into a century of turmoil, as each local prince took sides between Catholics and Protestants. In the 1525 Peasant Revolt, peasants attacked their feudal masters with hoes and pitchforks, fighting for more food, political say-so, and respect. The revolt was brutally put down.

The Holy Roman Emperor, Charles V (r. 1519-1556), sided with the pope. Charles was the most powerful man in Europe, hav-

Typical Castle Architecture

Castles were fortified residences for medieval nobles. Castles come in all shapes and sizes, but knowing a few general terms will help you understand them.

Barbican: A fortified gatehouse, sometimes a stand-alone building located outside the main walls.

Crenellation: A gap-toothed pattern of stones atop the parapet.

Drawbridge: A bridge that could be raised or lowered, using counterweights or a chain-and-winch.

Great Hall: The largest room in the castle, serving as throne room, conference center, and dining hall.

Hoardings (or Gallery or Brattice): Wooden huts built onto the upper parts of the stone walls. They served as watch towers, living quarters, and fighting platforms.

The Keep (or Donjon): A high, strong stone tower in the center of the castle complex that was the lord's home and refuge of last resort.

Loopholes: Narrow slits in the walls (also called embrasures, arrow slits, or arrow loops) through which soldiers could shoot arrows at the enemy.

Machicolation: A stone ledge jutting out from the wall, fitted with holes in the bottom. If the enemy was scaling the walls, soldiers could drop rocks or boiling oil down through the holes and onto the attackers below.

Moat: A ditch encircling the wall, often filled with water.

Parapet: Outer railing of the wall walk.

Portcullis: A heavy iron grille that could be lowered across the entrance.

GERMAN HISTORY

ing inherited an empire that included Germany and Austria, plus the Low Countries, much of Italy, Spain, and Spain's New World possessions. But many local German nobles took the opportunity to go Protestant—some for religious reasons, but also as an excuse to seize Church assets and powers.

The 1555 Peace of Augsburg allowed each local noble to decide the religion of his realm. In general, the northern and eastern lands became Protestant, while the south (today's Bavaria, along with Austria) and west remained Catholic.

Unresolved religious and political differences eventually expanded into the Thirty Years' War (1618-1648). This Europe-wide war, fought mainly on German soil, involved Denmark, Sweden, France, and Bohemia (in today's Czech Republic), among others. It was one of history's bloodiest wars, fueled by religious extremism and political opportunism, and fought by armies of brutal mercenaries who worked on commission and were paid in loot and pillage.

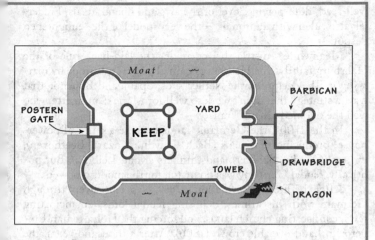

Postern Gate: A small, unfortified side or rear entrance used during peacetime. In wartime, it became a "sally-port" used to launch surprise attacks, or as an escape route.

Towers: Tall structures serving as lookouts, chapels, living quarters, or the dungeon. Towers could be square or round, with either crenellated tops or conical roofs.

Turret: A small lookout tower projecting up from the top of the wall.

Wall Walk (or Allure): A pathway atop the wall where guards could patrol and where soldiers stood to fire at the enemy.

The Yard (or Bailey or Ward): An open courtyard inside the castle walls.

By the war's end (Treaty of Westphalia, 1648), a third of all Germans had died, France was the rising European power, and the Holy Roman Empire was a medieval mess of scattered feudal states. In 1689, France's Louis XIV swept down the Rhine, gutting and leveling its once-great castles, and Germany ceased to be a major player in European politics until the modern era.

Austria and Prussia (1700s)

The German-speaking lands now consisted of three "Germanys": Austria in the south, Prussia in the north, and the rest in between.

Prussia—originally a largely Slavic region colonized by celibate ex-Crusaders called Teutonic Knights—was forged into a unified state by two strong kings. Frederick I (the "King Sergeant," r. 1701-1713) built a modern state around a highly disciplined army, a centralized government, and national pride. His grandson, Frederick II "The Great" (r. 1740-1786), added French culture and worldliness, preparing militaristic Prussia to enter the world stage. A well-read, flute-playing lover of the arts and liberal ideals, Frederick also ruled with an iron fist—the very model of the "enlightened despot."

Meanwhile, Austria thrived under the laid-back rule of the Habsburg family. The Habsburgs gained power in Europe by marrying it. They acquired the Netherlands, Spain, and Bohemia that way (a strategy that didn't work so well for Marie-Antoinette, who wed the doomed king of France).

In the 1700s, the Germanic lands became a cultural powerhouse, producing musicians (Bach, Haydn, Mozart, Beethoven), writers (Goethe, Schiller), and thinkers (Kant, Leibniz). But politically, feudal Germany was no match for the modern powers.

After the French Revolution (1789), Napoleon swept through Germany with his armies, deposing feudal lords, emancipating Jews, confiscating church lands, and forcing the Holy Roman Emperor to hand over his crown (1806). After a thousand years, the Holy Roman Empire was dead.

German Unification (1800s)

Napoleon's invasion helped unify the German-speaking peoples by rallying them against a common foreign enemy. After Napoleon's defeat, the Congress of Vienna (1815), presided over by the Austrian Prince Metternich, realigned Europe's borders. The idea of unifying the three Germanic nations—Prussia, Austria, and the German Confederation, a loose collection of small states in between—began to grow. By mid-century, most German-speaking people favored forming a modern nation-state; the only question was whether the confederation would be under Prussian or Austrian dominance.

Economically, Germany was becoming increasingly efficient and modern, with a unified trade organization (1834), railroads (1835), mechanical-engineering prowess, and booming factories benefiting from a surplus of labor.

Energetic Prussia took the lead in unifying the country. Otto von Bismarck (served 1862-1890), the strong minister of Prussia's weak king, used cunning politics to engineer a unified Germany under Prussian dominance. First, he started a war with Austria, ensuring that any united Germany would be under Prussian control. (Austria remains a separate country to this day.) Next, Bismarck provoked a war with France (Franco-Prussian War, 1870-1871), which united Prussia and the German Confederation against their common enemy, France.

Fueled by hysterical patriotism, German armies swept through France and, in the Hall of Mirrors at Versailles, crowned Prussia's Wilhelm I as Emperor *(Kaiser)* of a new German Empire, uniting Prussia and the German Confederation (but excluding Austria).

Germany in the Early 1800s

This Second Reich (1871-1918) featured elements of democracy (an elected *Reichstag*—parliament), offset by a strong military and an emperor with veto powers.

A united and resurgent Germany was suddenly flexing its muscles in European politics. With strong industry, war spoils, overseas colonies, and a large and disciplined military, it sought its rightful place in the sun. Fueled by nationalist fervor, patriotic *Volk* art flourished (Wagner's operas, Nietzsche's essays), reviving medieval German myths and Nordic gods. The rest of Europe saw Germany's rapid rise—and began arming themselves to the teeth.

World War I and Hitler's Rise (1914-1939)

When Archduke Franz Ferdinand, the heir to the Austro-Hungarian Empire, was assassinated in 1914, all of Europe took sides as the political squabble quickly escalated into World War I. Germany and Austria-Hungary attacked British and French troops in France, but were stalled at the Battle of the Marne. Both sides dug defensive trenches, then settled in for four brutal years of bloodshed, boredom, mud, machine-gun fire, disease, and mustard gas.

Finally, at 11:00 in the morning of November 11, 1918, the

Nazi Terminology

Many Nazi military terms are familiar to English speakers. "Nazi" is an abbreviation for *Nationalsozialismus* (National Socialism), Hitler's political party. Other terms you'll probably recognize are SS (short for *Schutzstaffel*, or "protective unit"), *Luftwaffe* (air force), and *Blitzkrieg* ("lightning war"). Nazis also devised the *Endlösung,* or "final solution" for doing away with Jewish people, by interning and killing them in *Konzentrationslager* (KZ, concentration camp). The *Widerstand* (resistance) stood up against the Nazis. *Vergangenheitsbewaltigung* (coming to terms with the past) continues to be a major issue in Germany. Many concentration camps and other wartime symbols have been turned into *Gedenkstätte* (memorials). You'll also see *Dokumentationzentrum* (documentation centers), where locals and visitors can learn about Nazi atrocities. The message of these sites is *Vergesst es nie*—"Never forget."

fighting ceased. Germany surrendered, signing the Treaty of Versailles in the Hall of Mirrors at Versailles. The war cost the defeated German nation 1.7 million men, precious territory, colonies, their military rights, reparations money, and national pride.

A new democratic government called the Weimar Republic (1919) dutifully abided by the Treaty of Versailles, and tried to maintain order among Germany's many divided political parties. But the country was in ruins, its economy a shambles, and the war's victors demanded heavy reparations. Communists rioted in the streets, fascists plotted coups, and inflation drove the price of a loaf of bread to a billion marks. War vets grumbled in their beer about how their leaders had sold them out. All Germans, regardless of their political affiliations, were fervently united in their apathy toward the new democracy. When the worldwide depression of 1929 hit Germany with brutal force, the nation was desperate for a strong leader with answers.

Adolf Hitler (1889-1945) was a disgruntled vet who had spent the post-World War I years homeless, wandering the streets of Vienna with sketchpad in hand, hoping to become an artist. In Munich, he joined other disaffected Germans to form the National Socialist (Nazi) Party. In stirring speeches, Hitler promised to restore Germany to its rightful glory, blaming the country's current problems on communists, foreigners, and Jews. After an unsuccessful coup attempt (the Beer Hall Putsch in Munich, 1923), Hitler was sent to jail, where he wrote an influential book of his political ideas, called *Mein Kampf (My Struggle)*.

By 1930, the Nazis—now wearing power suits and working within the system—had become a formidable political party in Germany's democracy. They won 38 percent of the seats in the Reichstag in 1932, and Hitler was appointed chancellor (1933). Two months later, the Reichstag building was mysteriously set on fire—an apparent act of terrorism with a September 11-sized impact—and a terrified Germany gave Chancellor Hitler sweeping powers to preserve national security.

Hitler wasted no time in using this Enabling Act to jail opponents, terrorize the citizenry, and organize every aspect of German life under the watchful eye of the Nazi Party. Plumbers' unions, choral societies, schoolteachers, church pastors, filmmakers, and artists all had to account to a Nazi Party official about how their work furthered the Third Reich.

For the next decade, an all-powerful Hitler proceeded to revive Germany's economy, building the autobahns and rebuilding the military. Defying the Treaty of Versailles and world opinion, Hitler occupied the Saar region (1935) and the Rhineland (1936), annexed Austria and the Sudetenland (1938), and invaded Czechoslovakia (March 1939). The rest of Europe finally reached its appeasement limit, and World War II began when Germany invaded Poland in September 1939 (see timeline on next page).

Two Germanys (1945-1990)

After World War II, the Allies divided occupied Germany into two halves, split down the middle by an 855-mile border that Winston Churchill called an "Iron Curtain." By 1949, Germany was officially two separate countries. West Germany (the Federal Republic of Germany) was democratic and capitalist, allied with the powerful United States. East Germany (the German Democratic Republic, or DDR) was a communist state under Soviet control. The former capital, Berlin, sitting in East German territory, was itself split into two parts, allowing a tiny pocket of Western life in the Soviet-controlled East. Armed guards prevented Germans from crossing the border to see their cousins on the other side.

In 1948, Soviet troops blockaded West Berlin. The Allies responded by airlifting food and supplies into the stranded city for nearly a year, forcing the Soviets to back off. In 1961, the East Germans erected a 12-foot-high concrete wall through the heart of Berlin. The Berlin Wall—built at the height of the Cold War between the United States and the USSR—was designed to prevent the westward flow of East German citizens (although officials claimed it was built to keep the West Germans out). The Berlin Wall came to symbolize a divided Germany.

In West Germany, Chancellor Konrad Adenauer (who had suffered imprisonment under the Nazis) tried to restore Germany's good name, paying war reparations and joining international organizations of nations. Thanks to US aid from the Marshall Plan,

Germany During World War II (1939-1945)

1939 Soldiers singing *"Muss ich denn, Muss ich denn zum Städtele hinaus"* ("I must leave, I must leave my happy home") march off to war. On September 1, Germany invades Poland to seize the free city of Danzig (Gdańsk), sparking World War II. Germany, Italy, and Japan (the Axis) would eventually square off against the Allies—which included Britain, France, the United States, and the USSR.

1940 The Nazi Blitzkrieg (lightning war) quickly sweeps through Denmark, Norway, the Low Countries, France, Yugoslavia, and Greece. With fellow fascists ruling Italy (Mussolini), Spain (Franco), and Portugal (Salazar), all of the Continent is now dominated by fascists, creating a "fortress Europe."

1941 Hitler invades his former ally, the USSR. Bombastic victory parades in Berlin celebrate the triumph of the Aryan race over the lesser peoples of the world.

1942 Allied bombs begin falling on German cities. That autumn and winter, German families receive death notices from the horrific Battle of Stalingrad. The German army suffers around 850,000 casualties (by comparison, the US had roughly 214,000 casualties for the entire Vietnam War). Back home, Nazi officials begin their plan for the "final solution to the Jewish problem"—systematic execution of Europe's Jews in specially built death camps.

1943 Germany fights a two-front war: against tenacious

West Germany was rebuilt, democracy was established, and its "economic miracle" quickly exceeded pre-WWII levels. Adenauer was succeeded in 1969 by the US-friendly Willy Brandt.

Meanwhile, East Germany was ruled with an iron fist by Walter Ulbricht (who had been exiled by the Nazis). In 1953, demonstrations and protests against the government were brutally put down by Soviet—not German—troops. Erich Honecker (a kinder, gentler tyrant who had endured a decade of Nazi imprisonment) succeeded Ulbricht as ruler of the East in 1971.

Throughout the 1970s and 1980s, both the US and the Soviet Union used divided Germany as a military base. West Germans debated whether US missiles aimed at the Soviets should be placed in their country. Economically, West Germany just got stronger while East Germany stagnated.

On November 9, 1989, East Germany unexpectedly opened

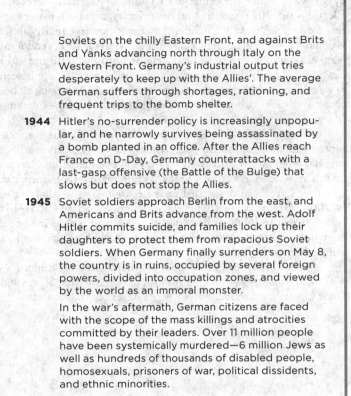

Soviets on the chilly Eastern Front, and against Brits and Yanks advancing north through Italy on the Western Front. Germany's industrial output tries desperately to keep up with the Allies'. The average German suffers through shortages, rationing, and frequent trips to the bomb shelter.

1944 Hitler's no-surrender policy is increasingly unpopular, and he narrowly survives being assassinated by a bomb planted in an office. After the Allies reach France on D-Day, Germany counterattacks with a last-gasp offensive (the Battle of the Bulge) that slows but does not stop the Allies.

1945 Soviet soldiers approach Berlin from the east, and Americans and Brits advance from the west. Adolf Hitler commits suicide, and families lock up their daughters to protect them from rapacious Soviet soldiers. When Germany finally surrenders on May 8, the country is in ruins, occupied by several foreign powers, divided into occupation zones, and viewed by the world as an immoral monster.

In the war's aftermath, German citizens are faced with the scope of the mass killings and atrocities committed by their leaders. Over 11 million people have been systemically murdered—6 million Jews as well as hundreds of thousands of disabled people, homosexuals, prisoners of war, political dissidents, and ethnic minorities.

GERMAN HISTORY

the Berlin Wall (see sidebar on page 786). Astonished Germans from both sides climbed the Wall, hugged each other, shared bottles of beer, sang songs, and chiseled off souvenirs. At first, most Germans—West and East—simply looked forward to free travel and better relations between two distinct nations. But before the month was out, negotiations and elections to reunite the two Germanys had begun. October 3, 1990, was proclaimed German Unification Day, and Berlin re-assumed its status as the German capital in 1991.

Germany Today (1990-present)

Differences between "Ossies" (rude slang for former East Germans) and "Wessies" remain, but they're diminishing as the two economies seek equilibrium. Germany remains a major economic and political force in Europe. The country spent a decade under a center-right government led by Chancellor Helmut Kohl, followed by a decade under the center-left Chancellor Gerhard Schröder. Elections in 2005 resulted in no clear victory, and both major parties formed a "Grand Coalition," sharing power equally under Germany's first female chancellor, Angela Merkel. Voters endorsed Merkel's cautious, pro-business policies in both the 2009 and 2013 elections. Though she governs with a coalition partner, she is seen as one of the world's most powerful women and is on track to become Europe's longest-serving elected female leader—breaking Margaret Thatcher's 11-year record.

Germany is fully integrated into the international community as a member of the European Union—an organization whose original chief aim was to avoid future wars by embracing Germany in the economic web of Europe. While many other European countries have been devastated by the economic crisis that began in 2008, Germany—with the largest economy in the EU—has emerged relatively unscathed. In 2014, the country's spirit got a huge boost when its soccer team won the World Cup, its first as a united nation.

If you want to read more about German history, consider *Europe 101: History and Art for the Traveler*, written by Rick Steves and Gene Openshaw (available at www.ricksteves.com).

PRACTICALITIES

Contents

This chapter covers the practical skills of European travel: how to get tourist information, pay for purchases, sightsee efficiently, find good-value accommodations, eat affordably but well, use technology wisely, and get between destinations smoothly. To study ahead and round out your knowledge, check out "Resources" for a summary of recommended books and films.

Tourist Information

Germany's national tourist office **in the US** is a wealth of information. Before your trip, scan their website (www.germany.travel) for maps and Rhine boat schedules, as well as information on festivals, castles, hiking, biking, genealogy, cities, and regions. Travel brochures can also be downloaded from their website.

In Germany, your best first stop in every town is generally the tourist information office—abbreviated **TI** in this book. Throughout Germany, you'll find TIs are usually well-organized and have

English-speaking staff. TIs are good places to get a city map and information on public transit (including bus and train schedules), walking tours, special events, and nightlife. Many TIs have information on the entire country or at least the region, so try to pick up maps for destinations you'll be visiting later in your trip. If  you're arriving in town after the TI closes, call ahead or pick up a map in a neighboring town.

A few TIs, notably in Berlin, have been privatized. This means they have become sales agents for big tours and hotels, and their "information" is unavoidably colored.

While TIs are eager to book you a room, use their room-finding service only as a last resort. They are unable to give hard opinions on the relative value of one place over another. The accommodations stakes are too high to go potluck through the TI. Even if there's no "fee," you'll save yourself and your host money by going direct with the listings in this book.

Travel Tips

PRACTICALITIES

Emergency and Medical Help: In Germany, dial 112 for police help or a medical emergency. If you get sick, do as the Germans do and go to a pharmacist for advice. Or ask at your hotel for help—they'll know the nearest medical and emergency services.

Theft or Loss: To replace a passport, you'll need to go in person to an embassy (see page 975). If your credit and debit cards disappear, cancel and replace them (see "Damage Control for Lost Cards" on page 915). File a police report, either on the spot or within a day or two; you'll need it to submit an insurance claim for lost or stolen rail passes or travel gear, and it can help with replacing your passport or credit and debit cards. For more information, see www.ricksteves.com/help. Precautionary measures can minimize the effects of loss—back up your digital photos and other files frequently.

Time Zones: Germany, like most of continental Europe, is generally six/nine hours ahead of the East/West Coasts of the US. The exceptions are the beginning and end of Daylight Saving Time: Europe "springs forward" the last Sunday in March (two weeks after most of North America) and "falls back" the last Sunday in October (one week before North America). For a handy online time converter, see www.timeanddate.com/worldclock.

Business Hours: In Germany, most shops are open from about 9:00 until 18:00-20:00 on weekdays, but close early on Saturday (generally between 12:00 and 17:00, depending on whether you're in a town or a big city). In small towns, a few shops may take a mid-afternoon break on weekdays (roughly between 12:00 and 14:00 or 15:00). Throughout Germany, most shops close entirely on Sundays. Sightseeing on Sunday has the same pros and cons as it does for travelers in the US (special events, limited hours for sights, no rush hour, less frequent public transportation). Many museums and sights close on Monday. Banks are generally open Monday-Friday from 9:00 to 15:00 (or may close later, even 19:00), and close on Saturday and Sunday.

Catholic regions, including Bavaria, shut down during religious holidays (see page 976). Turkish-owned shops are usually open later than other stores, as are shops in train stations, which often have grocery stores that are open long hours.

Watt's Up? Europe's electrical system is 220 volts, instead of North America's 110 volts. Most newer electronics (such as laptops, battery chargers, and hair dryers) convert automatically, so you won't need a converter plug, but you will need an adapter plug with two round prongs, sold inexpensively at travel stores in the US. Avoid bringing older appliances that don't automatically convert voltage; instead, buy a cheap replacement in Europe.

Discounts: Discounts are not listed in this book. However, seniors (age 60 and over), youths under 18, and students and teachers with proper identification cards (www.isic.org) can get discounts at many sights. Always ask. Some discounts are available only for citizens of the European Union (EU).

Online Translation Tip: You can use Google's Chrome browser (available free at www.google.com/chrome) to instantly translate websites. With one click, the page appears in (very rough) English translation. You can also paste the URL of the site into the translation window at www.google.com/translate.

Money

This section offers advice on how to pay for purchases on your trip (including getting cash from ATMs and paying with plastic), dealing with lost or stolen cards, VAT (sales tax) refunds, and tipping.

WHAT TO BRING

Bring both a credit card and a debit card. You'll use the debit card at cash machines (ATMs) to withdraw local cash for most purchases, and the credit card to pay for larger items. Some travelers carry a third card, in case one gets demagnetized or eaten by a temperamental machine.

For an emergency stash, bring several hundred dollars in hard cash in $20 bills. If you need to exchange the bills, go to a bank;

avoid using currency-exchange booths because of their lousy rates and/or outrageous fees.

CASH

Compared to the US, Germany is a cash-focused country. Especially in smaller cities, expect to use cash for most purchases. Small businesses (pensions, mom-and-pop cafés, shops, etc.) prefer that you pay your bills with cash. Some vendors will charge you extra for using a credit card, and some won't take credit cards at all. Cash is the best—and sometimes only—way to pay for cheap food, bus fare, taxis, and local guides.

Throughout Europe, ATMs are the standard way for travelers to get cash. To withdraw money from an ATM (known as a *Geldautomat* in Germany; *Bankomat* in Austria), you'll need a debit card (ideally with a Visa or MasterCard logo for maximum usability), plus a PIN code. Know your PIN code in numbers; there are only numbers— no letters—on European keypads. For increased security, shield the  keypad when entering your PIN code, and don't use an ATM if anything on the front of the machine looks loose or damaged (a sign that someone may have attached a "skimming" device to capture account information). Try to withdraw large sums of money to reduce the number of per-transaction bank fees you'll pay.

When possible, use ATMs located outside banks—a thief is less likely to target a cash machine near surveillance cameras, and if your card is munched by a machine, you can go inside for help. Stay away from "independent" ATMs such as Travelex, Euronet, Moneybox, Cardpoint, and Cashzone, which charge huge commissions, have terrible exchange rates, and may try to trick users with dynamic currency conversion (described at the end of "Credit and Debit Cards," next).

Although you can use a credit card for an ATM transaction, it only makes sense in an emergency, because it's considered a cash advance (borrowed at a high interest rate) rather than a withdrawal.

While traveling, if you want to monitor your accounts online to detect any unauthorized transactions, be sure to use a secure connection (see page 948).

Pickpockets target tourists. To safeguard your cash, wear a money belt—a pouch with a strap that you buckle around your waist like a belt and tuck under your clothes. Keep your cash, credit cards, and passport secure in your money belt, and carry only a day's spending money in your front pocket.

Exchange Rate

1 euro (€) = about $1.40
To convert prices in euros to dollars, add about 40 percent: €20 = about $28, €50 = about $70. (Check www.oanda.com for the latest exchange rates.) Just like the dollar, one euro (€) is broken down into 100 cents. Coins range from €0.01 to €2, and bills from €5 to €500.

CREDIT AND DEBIT CARDS

Many shops and restaurants in Germany don't accept plastic (except for the local "EC" debit cards). Larger hotels, restaurants, and shops that do take US cards more commonly accept Visa and MasterCard than American Express. I typically use my debit card to withdraw cash to pay for most purchases. I use my credit card only in a few specific situations: to book hotel reservations by phone, to cover major expenses (such as car rentals, plane tickets, and long hotel stays), to buy train tickets at the ticket counter (Deutsche Bahn ticket machines may not accept US cards without a chip), and to pay for things near the end of my trip (to avoid another visit to the ATM). While you could use a debit card to make most large purchases, using a credit card offers a greater degree of fraud protection (because debit cards draw funds directly from your account).

Ask Your Credit- or Debit-Card Company: Before your trip, contact the company that issued your debit or credit cards.

• Confirm that your **card will work overseas,** and alert them that you'll be using it in Europe; otherwise, they may deny transactions if they perceive unusual spending patterns.

• Ask for the specifics on transaction **fees.** When you use your credit or debit card—either for purchases or ATM withdrawals—you'll typically be charged additional "international transaction" fees of up to 3 percent (1 percent is normal) plus $5 per transaction. If your card's fees seem high, consider getting a different card just for your trip: Capital One (www.capitalone.com) and most credit unions have low-to-no international fees.

• If you plan to withdraw cash from ATMs, confirm your daily **withdrawal limit,** and if necessary, ask your bank to adjust it. Some travelers prefer a high limit that allows them to take out more cash at each ATM stop (saving on bank fees), while others prefer to set a lower limit in case their card is stolen. Note that foreign banks also set maximum withdrawal amounts for their ATMs. Also, remember that you're withdrawing euros, not dollars—so if your daily limit is $300, withdraw just €200. Many frustrated travelers walk away from ATMs thinking their cards have been rejected,

PRACTICALITIES

when actually they were asking for more cash in euros than their daily limit allowed.

• Get your bank's emergency **phone number** in the US (but not its 800 number, which isn't accessible from overseas) to call collect if you have a problem.

• Ask for your credit card's **PIN** in case you need to make an emergency cash withdrawal or encounter Europe's "chip-and-PIN" system; the bank won't tell you your PIN over the phone, so allow time for it to be mailed to you.

Chip and PIN: Europeans are increasingly using chip-and-PIN cards, which are embedded with an electronic security chip (in addition to the magnetic stripe on American-style cards). To make a purchase with a chip-and-PIN card, the cardholder inserts the card into a slot in the payment machine, then enters a PIN (like using a debit card in the US) while the card stays in the slot. The chip inside the card authorizes the transaction; the cardholder doesn't sign a receipt. Your American-style card might not work at payment machines using this system, such as those at train and subway stations, toll roads, parking garages, luggage lockers, bike-rental kiosks, and self-serve gas pumps.

If you have problems using your American card in a chip-and-PIN machine, here are some suggestions: For either a debit card or a credit card, try entering that card's PIN when prompted. (Note that your credit-card PIN may not be the same as your debit-card PIN; you'll need to ask your bank for your credit-card PIN.) If your cards still don't work, look for a machine that takes cash, seek out a clerk who might be able to process the transaction manually, or ask a local if you can pay them cash to run the transaction on their card.

And don't panic. Many travelers who use only magnetic-stripe cards don't run into problems. Still, it pays to carry plenty of euros; remember, you can always use an ATM to withdraw cash with your magnetic-stripe debit card.

If you're still concerned, you can apply for a chip card in the US (though I think it's overkill). One option is the no-annual-fee GlobeTrek Visa, offered by Andrews Federal Credit Union in Maryland (open to all US residents; see www.andrewsfcu.org). In the future, chip cards should become standard issue in the US: Visa and MasterCard have asked US banks and merchants to use chip-based cards by late 2015.

Dynamic Currency Conversion: If merchants offer to convert your purchase price into dollars (called dynamic currency conversion, or DCC), refuse this "service." You'll pay even more in fees for the expensive convenience of seeing your charge in dollars. "Independent" ATMs (such as Travelex and Moneybox) may try to confuse customers by presenting DCC in misleading terms. If an ATM offers to "lock in" or "guarantee" your conversion rate, choose "proceed without conversion." Other prompts might state, "You can be charged in dollars: Press YES for dollars, NO for euros." Always choose the local currency in these situations.

DAMAGE CONTROL FOR LOST CARDS

If you lose your credit, debit, or ATM card, you can stop people from using your card by reporting the loss immediately to the respective global customer-assistance centers. Call these 24-hour US numbers collect: Visa (tel. 303/967-1096), MasterCard (tel. 636/722-7111), and American Express (tel. 336/393-1111). In Germany, to make a collect call to the US, dial 0800-225-5288. Press zero or stay on the line for an English-speaking operator. European toll-free numbers (listed by country) can be found at the websites for Visa and MasterCard.

Providing the following information will allow for a quicker cancellation of your missing card: full card number, whether you are the primary or secondary cardholder, the cardholder's name exactly as printed on the card, billing address, home phone number, circumstances of the loss or theft, and identification verification (your birth date, your mother's maiden name, or your Social Security number—memorize this, don't carry a copy). If you are the secondary cardholder, you'll also need to provide the primary cardholder's identification-verification details. You can generally receive a temporary card within two or three business days in Europe (see www.ricksteves.com/help for more).

If you report your loss within two days, you typically won't be responsible for any unauthorized transactions on your account, although many banks charge a liability fee of $50.

TIPPING

Tipping in Germany isn't as automatic and generous as it is in the US. For special service, tips are appreciated, but not expected. As in the US, the proper amount depends on your resources, tipping philosophy, and the circumstances, but some general guidelines apply.

Restaurants: Tipping is an issue only at restaurants that have table service. If you order your food at a counter, don't tip. At German restaurants that have a wait staff, it's common to tip after a good meal (usually 10 percent). Rather than leaving coins, Germans usually pay with paper, saying how much they'd like the bill to be. For example, for a €10 meal, you can hand over a €20 bill and

PRACTICALITIES

say *"Elf Euro"*—"Eleven euros"—to include a €1 tip and get €9 in change.

Taxis: For a typical ride, round up your fare a bit (for instance, if your fare is €4.70, pay €5). If the cabbie hauls your bags and zips you to the airport to help you catch your flight, you might want to toss in a little more. But if you feel like you're being driven in circles or otherwise ripped off, skip the tip.

Services: In general, if someone in the service industry does a super job for you, a small tip of a euro or two is appropriate...but not required. If you're not sure whether (or how much) to tip for a service, ask your hotelier or the TI.

GETTING A VAT REFUND

Wrapped into the purchase price of your German souvenirs is a Value-Added Tax (VAT) of 19 percent. You're entitled to get most of that tax back if you purchase more than €25 (about $35) worth of goods at a store that participates in the VAT-refund scheme. Typically, you must ring up the minimum at a single retailer—you can't add up your purchases from various shops to reach the required amount.

Getting your refund is usually straightforward and, if you buy a substantial amount of souvenirs, well worth the hassle. If you're lucky, the merchant will subtract the tax when you make your purchase. (This is more likely to occur if the store ships the goods to your home.) Otherwise, you'll need to:

Get the paperwork. Have the merchant completely fill out the necessary refund document, called a "Tax-Free Shopping Cheque." You'll have to present your passport. Get the paperwork done before you leave the store to ensure you'll have everything you need (including your original sales receipt).

Get your stamp at the border or airport. Process your VAT document at your last stop in the European Union (such as at the airport) with the customs agent who deals with VAT refunds. Arrive an additional hour before you need to check in for your flight to allow time to find the local customs office—and to stand in line. It's best to keep your purchases in your carry-on. If they're too large or dangerous to carry on (such as knives), pack them in your checked bags and alert the check-in agent. You'll be sent (with your tagged bag) to a customs desk outside security, where someone will examine your bag, stamp your paperwork, and put your bag on the belt. You're not supposed to use your purchased goods before you leave. If you show up at customs wearing your new lederhosen, officials might look the other way—or deny you a refund.

Collect your refund. You'll need to return your stamped document to the retailer or its representative. Many merchants work with a service, such as Global Blue or Premier Tax Free, that has offices at major airports, ports, or border crossings (either before or after security, probably strategically located near a duty-free shop). These services, which extract a 4 percent fee, can refund your money immediately in cash or credit your card (within two billing cycles). If the retailer handles VAT refunds directly, it's up to you to contact the merchant for your refund. You can mail the documents from home, or more quickly, from your point of departure (using an envelope you've prepared in advance or one that's been provided by the merchant). You'll then have to wait—it can take months.

CUSTOMS FOR AMERICAN SHOPPERS

You are allowed to take home $800 worth of items per person duty-free, once every 30 days. You can take home many processed and packaged foods: vacuum-packed cheeses, dried herbs, jams, baked goods, candy, chocolate, oil, vinegar, mustard, and honey. Fresh fruits and vegetables and most meats are not allowed. However, canned meat is allowed if it doesn't contain any beef, veal, lamb, or mutton.

As for alcohol, you can bring in one liter duty-free (it can be packed securely in your checked luggage, along with any other liquid-containing items). To bring alcohol (or liquid-packed foods) in your carry-on bag on your flight home, buy it at a duty-free shop at the airport. You'll increase your odds of getting it onto a connecting flight if it's packaged in a "STEB"—a secure, tamper-evident bag. But stay away from liquids in opaque, ceramic, or metallic containers, which usually cannot be successfully screened (STEB or no STEB).

To check customs rules and duty rates, visit help.cbp.gov.

Sightseeing

Sightseeing can be hard work. Use these tips to make your visits to Germany's finest sights meaningful, fun, efficient, and painless.

PLAN AHEAD

Set up an itinerary that allows you to fit in all your must-see sights. For a one-stop look at opening hours, see the "At a Glance" sidebars for Munich, Salzburg, Berlin, and Hamburg. Most sights keep stable hours, but you can easily confirm the latest by checking with the TI or visiting museum websites.

Don't put off visiting a must-see sight—you never know when a place will close unexpectedly for a holiday, strike, or restoration. Many museums are closed or have reduced hours at least a few days a year, especially on holidays such as Christmas, New Year's, and Labor Day (May 1). A list of holidays is on page 976; check museum websites for possible closures during your trip. In summer, some sights stay open late. Off-season, many museums have shorter hours.

Going at the right time helps avoid crowds. This book offers tips on the best times to see specific sights. Try visiting popular sights very early or very late. Evening visits are usually peaceful, with fewer crowds.

Study up. To get the most out of the sight descriptions in this book, read them before you visit.

AT SIGHTS

Here's what you can typically expect:

Entering: Be warned that you may not be allowed to enter if you arrive 30 to 60 minutes before closing time. And guards start ushering people out well before the actual closing time, so don't save the best for last.

Some important sights have a security check, where you must open your bag or send it through a metal detector. Most museums in Germany require you to check any bag bigger than a purse, and sometimes even purses. Museum lockers are free, but be prepared to pay a €1 or €2 deposit.

Photography: If the museum's photo policy isn't clearly posted, ask a guard. Generally, taking photos without a flash or tripod is allowed. Some sights ban photos altogether.

Temporary Exhibits: Museums may show special exhibits in addition to their permanent collection. Some exhibits are included in the entry price, while others come at an extra cost (which you may have to pay even if you don't want to see the exhibit).

Expect Changes: Artwork can be on tour, on loan, out sick, or shifted at the whim of the curator. To adapt, pick up a floor plan as you enter, and ask museum staff if you can't find a particular item.

Audioguides: Many sights rent audioguides, which generally offer useful recorded descriptions in English (about $3-6; often included with admission). If you bring along your earbuds, you can enjoy better sound and avoid holding the device to your ear. To save money, bring a Y-jack and share one audioguide with your travel partner. Increasingly, sights are offering apps (often free) that you can download to your mobile device. I've produced free downloadable audio tours of Berlin, Munich, Salzburg, and the Rhine; see page 12.

Services: Some sights offer tours in English. They are most likely to be available during peak season (they can be included with your admission or cost up to $10, and range wildly in quality). If sights offer short films featuring their highlights and history, they're generally well worth your time.

Important sights often have an on-site café or cafeteria (usually a good place to rejuvenate during a long visit). The WCs at many sights are free and generally clean.

Before Leaving: At the gift shop, scan the postcard rack or thumb through a guidebook to be sure that you haven't overlooked something that you'd like to see.

Every sight or museum offers more than what is covered in this book. Use the information in this book as an introduction—not the final word.

SIGHTSEEING PASSES

In some cities, you can buy a combo-ticket for discounted entry to two or more sights. I've noted these in this book. If you'll be visiting several castles in Bavaria—including two of "Mad" King Ludwig's castles, and those in Munich, Würzburg, Nürnberg, and more—look into **Bavaria's 14-day ticket** (called *Mehrtagesticket*), which can save you a lot of money (€24/1 person, €40/2 adults plus children, valid 14 days; described on page 17).

Sleeping

Good-value accommodations in Germany are generally easy to find, comfortable, and include a hearty breakfast (typically an all-you-can-eat buffet). Choose from hotels; smaller, cheaper hotels and bed-and-breakfasts (called *Gasthof, Gasthaus,* or *Pension*); rooms in private homes (advertised as *Zimmer Frei*); self-catering apartments rented by the week *(Ferienwohnung);* and hostels *(Jugendherberge).*

I favor hotels that are handy to your sightseeing activities. Rather than list hotels scattered throughout a city, I describe two or three favorite neighborhoods and recommend the best accommodations values in each, from dorm beds to fancy doubles with all of the comforts.

A major feature of this book is its extensive and opinionated listing of good-value rooms. I like places that are clean, central, relatively quiet at night, reasonably priced, friendly, small enough to have a hands-on owner and stable staff, run with a respect for German traditions, and not listed in other guidebooks. (In Germany, for me, meeting six out of these eight criteria means it's a keeper.) I'm more impressed by a convenient location and a fun-loving philosophy than flat-screen TVs and a pricey laundry service.

Book your accommodations well in advance, especially if

Sleep Code

(€1 = about $1.40, country code: 49)

Price Rankings

To help you sort easily through my listings, I've divided the accommodations into three categories based on the highest price for a standard double room with bath during high season:

$$$ Higher Priced

$$ Moderately Priced

$ Lower Priced

I always rate hostels as $, whether or not they have double rooms, because they have the cheapest beds in town. Prices change; verify current rates online or by email. For the best prices, always book directly with the hotel.

Abbreviations

To pack maximum information into minimum space, I use the following code to describe accommodations in this book. Prices listed are per room, not per person. When a price range is given for a type of room (such as double rooms listing for €100-150), it means the price fluctuates with the season, day of week, size of room, or length of stay; expect to pay the upper end for peak-season stays.

S = Single room (or price for one person in a double).

D = Double or twin room. "Double beds" can be two twins sheeted together and are usually big enough for non-romantic couples.

T = Triple (generally a double bed with a single).

Q = Quad (usually two double beds; adding an extra child's bed to a T is usually cheaper).

b = Private bathroom with toilet and shower or tub.

s = Private shower or tub only (the toilet is down the hall).

According to this code, a couple staying at a "Db-€100" hotel would pay a total of €100 (about $140) for a double room with a private bathroom. Unless otherwise noted, breakfast is included, English is spoken, and credit cards are accepted. There's almost always Wi-Fi and/or a guest computer available, either free or for a fee.

you'll be traveling during busy times. See page 976 for a list of major holidays and festivals in Germany; for tips on making reservations, see page 924. When booking, be aware that some German towns have hotels with the same name—so double-check that you are contacting the right one.

Some people make reservations as they travel, calling hotels a few days to a week before their arrival. If you'd rather travel without any reservations at all, you'll have greater success snaring rooms if you arrive at your destination early in the day. If you anticipate crowds (weekends are worst), on the day you want to check in, call hotels at about 9:00 or 10:00, when the receptionist knows who'll be checking out and which rooms will be available. If you encounter a language barrier, ask the fluent receptionist at your current hotel to call for you.

I've noted family-friendly hotels in the listings. Families do well to send an email with the ages of all those traveling and let the staff suggest a good-value configuration. Most hotels give families with smaller children a discounted triple or quad room, and a few let children as old as 12 stay free.

Air-conditioning is rare (and rarely needed). If you're here during a heat spell, ask to borrow a fan. Learn how the windows work: You'll often find the windows tipped open from the top to air out the room, with the window handle pointing up. To close the window, push it in and rotate the handle so it points down. The third handle position is horizontal, which lets you swing the entire window open.

In Germany, as elsewhere in northern Europe, beds don't come with a top sheet or blankets, but only with a comforter. A double bed comes with two comforters—rather than one bigger one. What's more, a double bed, even one intended for married couples, frequently has two separate mattresses and sometimes two separate (but adjacent) frames. (A "real" double bed with a single mattress is called a *Französisches Bett*—a French bed.) Rooms with truly separate twin beds are less common in German hotels. When Americans request separate beds, German hotels sometimes give them normal doubles with complete sincerity—reasoning that the mattresses, though adjacent, are separate.

Because the train system in Germany is convenient and popular, both locals and foreigners have discovered that staying near the station saves hauling your luggage by foot or taxi. The concept of the train-station hotel, which went out of favor during the 20th century, is making a big comeback in Germany. Frankfurt, Würzburg, Füssen, Munich, Cologne, Dresden, Leipzig, Nürnberg, and Baden-Baden are among the destinations in this book that have good-value lodgings within steps of the train station.

RATES AND DEALS

I've described my recommended accommodations using a Sleep Code (see sidebar on page 920). Prices listed are for one-night stays in peak season, and assume you're booking directly with the hotel (not through an online hotel-booking engine or TI). Booking services extract a commission from the hotel, which logically closes the door on special deals. Book direct.

All of my recommended hotels have a website (often with a

PRACTICALITIES

built-in booking form) and an email address; you can expect a response in English within a day (and often sooner). If you're on a budget, it's smart to email several hotels to ask for their best price. Comparison-shop and make your choice. This is especially helpful when dealing with larger hotels that use "dynamic pricing," a computer-generated system that predicts the demand for particular days and sets prices accordingly: High-demand days will often be more than double the price of low-demand days. This makes it impossible for a guidebook to list anything more accurate than a wide range of prices. I regret this trend. While you can assume that hotels listed in this book are good, it's very difficult to say which ones are the better values unless you email to confirm the price.

As you look over the listings, you'll notice that some accommodations promise special prices to Rick Steves readers. To get these rates, you must book direct (that is, *not* through a booking site like TripAdvisor or Booking.com), mention this book when you reserve, and then show the book upon arrival. Rick Steves discounts apply to readers with ebooks as well as printed books. Because I trust hotels to honor this, please let me know if you don't receive a listed discount. Note, though, that discounts understandably may not be applied to promotional rates.

At some places, singles are actually double rooms used by one person—so they cost about the same as a double. Single travelers get the best value at other places (usually smaller ones) where the price of a single is only a little more than half that of a double. This includes hostels, which always charge per person. In contrast, groups of four adults can often snare a four-bed room (with its own bath) in a hotel or B&B for about the same price a hostel would charge.

Especially in vacation areas and in private homes, where the boss changes the sheets, people staying several nights are most desirable. Some hotels phrase this as a discount for longer stays, while others call it a surcharge for one-nighters.

In some resort towns such as Baden-Baden and Staufen, visitors have to pay a small spa tax (per person and per night) that's added to their bill. Some cities require hoteliers to charge a daily tourist tax (about €1-4/person per day; in Berlin, it's 5 percent of the room rate). This can either be included in the room price or can appear as an extra charge on your bill.

Most hostels and some hotels and B&Bs offer half-board *(Halbpension)*, which means that dinner is included in the room price. This is often a good deal and gets you a hassle-free, value-priced three-course meal, but limits your choices. A few hotels (including the Ibis chain) give you the option of skipping breakfast and paying less. Although German hotel breakfasts are usually excellent, you can buy breakfast easily and cheaply at a bakery or supermarket—the savings add up, especially for families.

In general, prices can soften if you do any of the following: offer to pay cash, stay at least three nights, or mention this book. You can also try asking for a cheaper room or a discount, or offer to skip breakfast.

TYPES OF ACCOMMODATIONS
Hotels

In this book, the price for a double room in a hotel ranges from €45 (very simple, toilet and shower down the hall) to €200-plus (maximum plumbing and the works). In small towns, such as Bacharach or Rothenburg, you can find a good double with a private bath for under €80; in more expensive cities like Munich or Trier, you'll usually pay €100 or more.

While I favor smaller, family-run hotels, occasionally a chain hotel can be a good value; the Europe-wide Ibis/Mercure chain has several branches in Germany (www.accorhotels.com). I'm impressed with the homegrown, Hamburg-based German chain called Motel One, which specializes in affordable style and has branches in Berlin, Munich, Nürnberg, Hamburg, Frankfurt, Cologne, Leipzig, Dresden, and other cities (www.motel-one.com).

Room prices depend on the season and the day of the week, but peak times vary from one town to the next. Low season in Rothenburg is January-March, in Füssen it's October-May, and in Nürnberg it's July and August. While weekends are cheaper in Frankfurt and Nürnberg, weekdays are cheaper in Trier, Dresden, and Füssen. Munich hotels keep the same prices all week.

Hotel lobbies, halls, and breakfast rooms are off-limits to smokers, though they can light up in their rooms. Most hotels have non-smoking rooms or floors—let them know your preference when you book. Some hotels have gone completely non-smoking.

Bigger hotels commonly have elevators. When you're inside an elevator, press "E" if you want to descend to the "ground floor" *(Erdgeschoss)*. Hotel elevators, while becoming more common, are often very small—pack light, or you may need to send your bags up separately.

If you're arriving early in the morning, your room probably won't be ready. You can drop your bag safely at the hotel and dive right into sightseeing.

Hoteliers can be a great help and source of advice. Most know their city well, and can assist you with everything from public transit and airport connections to finding a good restaurant, the nearest launderette, or a Wi-Fi hotspot.

Even at the best places, mechanical breakdowns occur: Air-conditioning malfunctions, sinks leak, hot water turns cold, and

Making Hotel Reservations

Reserve your rooms several weeks in advance—or as soon as you've pinned down your travel dates. Note that some national holidays merit your making reservations far in advance (see page 976).

Requesting a Reservation: It's easiest to book your room through the hotel's website. (For the best rates, always use the hotel's official site and not a booking agency's site.) If there's no reservation form, or for complicated requests, send an email (see below for a sample request). Most recommended hotels take reservations in English.

The hotelier wants to know:

- the number and type of rooms you need
- the number of nights you'll stay
- your date of arrival (use the European style for writing dates: day/month/year)
- your date of departure
- any special needs (such as bathroom in the room or down the hall, cheapest room, twin beds vs. double bed, and so on)

Mention any discounts—for Rick Steves readers or otherwise—when you make the reservation.

Confirming a Reservation: Most places will request a credit-card number to hold your room. If they don't have a secure online reservation form—look for the https—you can email it (I do), but it's safer to share that confidential info via a phone call or two emails (splitting your number between them).

Canceling a Reservation: If you must cancel, it's courteous—and smart—to do so with as much notice as possible, especially

toilets gurgle and smell. Report your concerns clearly and calmly at the front desk. For more complicated issues, don't expect instant results.

If you suspect night noise will be a problem (if, for instance, your room is over a nightclub), ask for a quieter room in the back or on an upper floor. To guard against theft in your room, keep valuables out of sight. Some rooms come with a safe, and other hotels have safes at the front desk. I've never bothered using one.

Checkout can pose problems if surprise charges pop up on your bill. If you settle your bill the afternoon before you leave, you'll have time to discuss and address any points of contention (before 19:00, when the night shift usually arrives).

Above all, keep a positive attitude. Remember, you're on vacation. If your hotel is a disappointment, spend more time out enjoying the city you came to see.

From:	rick@ricksteves.com
Sent:	Today
To:	info@hotelcentral.com
Subject:	Reservation request for 19-22 July

Dear Hotel Central,

I would like to reserve a room for 2 people for 3 nights, arriving 19 July and departing 22 July. If possible, I would like a quiet room with a double bed and a bathroom inside the room.

Please let me know if you have a room available and the price.

Thank you!
Rick Steves

for smaller family-run places. Be warned that cancellation policies can be strict; read the fine print or ask about these before you book. Internet deals may require prepayment, with no refunds for cancellations.

Reconfirming a Reservation: Always call to reconfirm your room reservation a few days in advance. For smaller hotels and pensions, I call again on my day of arrival to tell my host what time I expect to get there (especially important if arriving late—after 17:00).

Phoning: For tips on how to call hotels overseas, see page 939.

Smaller B&Bs

Compared to hotels, bed-and-breakfast places (*Pensions, Gasthäuser,* or *Gasthöfe*) give you double the cultural intimacy for half the price. While you may lose some of the conveniences of a hotel—such as in-room phones, frequent bed-sheet changes, and the ease of paying with a credit card—I happily make the trade-off for the lower rates and personal touches. If you have a reasonable but limited budget, skip hotels and look for smaller, family-run places.

The smallest establishments consist of private homes with rooms *(Zimmer)* rented out to travelers. Look for *Zimmer Frei* or *Privatzimmer* signs. These are inexpensive—as little as €20 per person with a hearty breakfast—and very common in areas popular with travelers (such as Germany's Rhine, the Romantic Road region, and southern Bavaria, and Austria's Tirol and Salzburg). Signs indicate whether they have available rooms (*Zimmer frei,* green) or not (*Zimmer belegt,* orange). TIs often have a list of private

The Good and Bad of Online Reviews

User-generated travel review websites—such as TripAdvisor, Booking.com, and Yelp—have quickly become a huge player in the travel industry. These sites give you access to actual reports—good and bad—from travelers who have experienced the hotel, restaurant, tour, or attraction.

My hotelier friends in Europe are in awe of these sites' influence. Small hoteliers who want to stay in business have no choice but to work with review sites—which often charge fees for good placement or photos, and tack on commissions if users book through the site instead of directly with the hotel.

While these sites work hard to weed out bogus users, my hunch is that a significant percentage of reviews are posted by friends or enemies of the business being reviewed. I've even seen hotels "bribe" guests (for example, offer a free breakfast) in exchange for a positive review. Also, review sites can become an echo chamber, with one or two flashy businesses camped out atop the ratings, while better, more affordable, and more authentic alternatives sit ignored farther down the list. (For example, I find review sites' restaurant recommendations skew to very touristy, obvious options.)

Remember that a user-generated review is based on the experience of one person. That person likely stayed at one hotel and ate at a few restaurants, and doesn't have much of a basis for comparison. A guidebook is the work of a trained researcher who has exhaustively visited many alternatives to assess their relative value. I recently checked out some top-rated TripAdvisor listings in various towns; when stacked up against their competitors, some are gems, while just as many are duds.

Both types of information have their place, and in many ways, they're complementary. If a hotel or restaurant is well-reviewed in a guidebook or two, and also gets good ratings on one of these sites, it's likely a winner.

PRACTICALITIES

rooms; use the list to book rooms yourself to avoid having the TI take a cut from you and your host.

You'll get your own key to a private room that's clean, comfortable, and simple, though usually homey. Germans, especially in the south, are enthusiastic builders who like showing off their carpentry and decorating skills. Some private rooms are like mini-guesthouses, with a separate entrance and several rooms, each with a private bath. Others are family homes with spare bedrooms (the rooms sometimes lack sinks, but you have free access to the bathroom and shower in the home).

Germans depend heavily on expensive imported fuel and are very aware of their energy use. In any smaller establishment, you'll endear yourself to your hosts if you turn off lights when you leave and avoid excessively long showers.

Hostels

You'll pay about €25 per bed to stay at a *Jugendherberge*. Travelers of any age are welcome if they don't mind dorm-style accommodations and meeting other travelers. Most hostels offer kitchen facilities, guest computers, Wi-Fi, and a self-service laundry. Nowadays, concerned about bedbugs, hostels are likely to provide all bedding, including sheets. Family and private rooms may be available on request.

Independent hostels tend to be easygoing, colorful, and informal (no membership required); www.hostelworld.com is the standard way that backpackers search and book hostels, but also try www.hostelz.com and www.hostels.com.

Official hostels are part of Hostelling International (HI) and share an online booking site (www.hihostels.com). HI hostels typically require that you either have a membership card or pay extra per night.

Other Accommodation Options

Whether you're in a city or the countryside, renting an apartment, house, or villa can be a fun and cost-effective way to delve into Europe. Hotels and B&Bs, including those in this book, often have an apartment or two (breakfast is not included). In rural areas, you can find reasonably priced vacation rentals *(Ferienwohnungen)*, ideal for families and small groups who want to explore a region. This kind of arrangement is very popular with German vacationers. You usually get a suite of two or three rooms with a kitchen. The owners discourage short stays and usually require a minimum rental period (3-5 days), and sometimes a deposit. If you'll be in one place for a while, the rate per night generally works out cheaper than in a normal hotel or guesthouse room.

Websites such as HomeAway and its sister sites VRBO and GreatRentals let you correspond directly with European property owners or managers. Airbnb and Roomorama make it reasonably easy to find a place to sleep in someone's home. Beds range from air-mattress-in-living-room basic to plush-B&B-suite posh. If you want a place to sleep that's free, Couchsurfing.com is a vagabond's alternative to Airbnb. It lists millions of outgoing members, who host fellow "surfers" in their homes.

PRACTICALITIES

Eating

Germanic cuisine is heavy, hearty, and—by European standards—inexpensive. Each region has its specialties, which are often good values. Order house specials whenever possible. Though it's tasty, German food can get monotonous unless you look beyond the schnitzel and wurst. Fortunately, German chefs are increasingly adopting international influences, picking up previously unknown spices and ingredients to jazz up "Modern German" cuisine. Be adventurous.

When restaurant hunting, choose a spot filled with locals, not the place with the big neon signs boasting, "We Speak English and Accept Credit Cards." Venturing even a block or two off the main drag leads to higher-quality food for less than half the price of the tourist-oriented places. Locals eat better at lower-rent locales.

Traditional restaurants go by many names. For basic, stick-to-the-ribs meals—and plenty of beer—look for a beer hall *(Bräuhaus)*

or beer garden *(Biergarten)*. *Gasthaus, Gasthof, Gaststätte,* and *Gaststube* all loosely describe an informal, inn-type eatery. A *Kneipe* is a bar, and a *Keller* (or *Ratskeller*) is a restaurant or tavern located in a cellar. A *Weinstube* serves wine and usually traditional food as well.

Germans are health-conscious and quite passionate about choosing organic *(Bio)* products: *Bio* fruits and vegetables, and even *Bio* bread, ice cream, and schnitzel. You'll often see footnotes on restaurant menus marking which dishes have artificial ingredients. However, despite Germans' healthy ways, many starchy, high-fat, high-calorie traditional foods remain staples of the national diet.

Most eateries have menus tacked onto their front doors, with an English menu inside. If you see a *Stammtisch* sign hanging over a table at a restaurant or pub, it means that it's reserved for regulars—don't sit here unless invited. Once you're seated, take your time—only a rude waiter will rush you. Good service is relaxed (slow to an American).

To wish others "Happy eating!" offer a cheery *"Guten Appetit!"* When you want the bill, say, *"Die Rechnung, bitte"* (dee REHKH-noong, BIT-teh). For information on tipping, see page 915.

BUDGET TIPS

It's easy to eat a meal for €10 or less in Germany. At lunchtime, locals grab a sandwich (around €2.50) and perhaps a pastry (€1-2) from one of the ubiquitous bakeries, which often have tables to sit at (but not table service). If there aren't any sandwiches on display at the bakery counter, ask to have one made for you.

Department-store cafeterias (usually on the top floor with a view) are common and handy, and they bridge the language barrier by letting you see your options. A *Schnell Imbiss* is a small fast-food takeaway stand where you can get a bratwurst or other grilled sausage (usually less than €2, including a roll). Turkish-style *Döner Kebab* (gyro-like, pita-wrapped rotisserie meat) stands and shops are also common.

Most restaurants offer inexpensive €6-9 weekday hot-lunch specials that aren't listed on the regular menu (look for the *Tageskarte* or *Tagesangebot*, or just ask—sometimes available at dinner, too). For smaller portions, order from the *kleine Hunger* (small hunger) section of the menu. Simple dishes of wurst with sauerkraut and bread tend to run €6-8. All schnitzeled out? See "Ethnic Food," on page 934.

Hang on to the half-liter mineral-water bottles (sold everywhere for about €1). Buy juice in cheap liter boxes, then drink some and store the extra in your water bottle.

BREAKFAST

Most German hotels and pensions include breakfast in the room price and pride themselves on laying out an attractive buffet spread.

Even if you're not a big breakfast eater, take advantage of the buffet to fortify yourself for a day of sightseeing. Expect sliced bread, rolls, pastries, cereal, yogurt (both plain and with strawberries), cold cuts, cheese, and fruit. You'll always find coffee, tea, and some sort of *Saft* (juice). Along with orange, apple, and grapefruit, multivitamin juice is popular. This sweet, smooth blend of various fruits is less acidic than a citrus juice. A bottle of mineral water is standing by to mix with any juice to turn it into a *Schorle* (spritzer).

Rather than eggs for breakfast, most Germans prefer a sandwich with cold cuts and/or a bowl of *Müsli* (an oat cereal like granola, but less sweet), sometimes mixed with corn flakes. Instead of pouring milk over their cereal, most Germans begin with a dollop of yogurt (or *Quark*—sweet curds that resemble yogurt), then sprinkle the cereal on top. If it's not sweet enough, drizzle on some *Honig* (honey). *Bircher Müsli* is a healthy mix of oats, nuts, yogurt, and fruit. To make a German-style sandwich for breakfast, begin with various types of sliced bread or a roll. On top, layer *Aufschnitt* (cold cuts), *Schinken* (ham), *Streichwurst* (meat spread, most often *Leberwurst*—liver spread), and *Käse* (cheese).

If there are eggs, they're most likely soft-boiled *(weichgekocht Eier)*. Set the egg upright in its little stand, gently break the shell around its perimeter, remove the top half of the shell, salt and pepper it, and eat it as if from a tiny bowl. If the eggs are hard-boiled *(hartgekocht Eier)*, just peel and slice. Occasionally a buffet will have *Rühreier* (scrambled eggs) or *Spiegeleier* (fried eggs—literally "mirror eggs"—typically sunny-side up).

In some hotels, they set a little plastic garbage can on the table for you to dispose of trash as you eat.

TRADITIONAL FARE

The classic dish is sausage—hundreds of varieties of bratwurst, *Weisswurst,* and other types of wurst are served with sauerkraut as an excuse for a vegetable.

Many traditional eateries serve some kind of meat on the bone, such as pork knuckle *(Schweinshaxe)* or shoulder, which has been roasted tender and goes down well with a big mug of beer. The fish and venison here are also good.

Another ubiquitous meat dish is schnitzel (a meat cutlet that's been pounded flat, breaded, and freshly fried). It's traditionally made with veal, but you'll more often find pork schnitzel, which is cheaper.

One word you'll often see stuck on the beginning and end of menu items is *braten* (which can mean "roasted" or "grilled" or "fried")—as in *Bratkartoffeln* (roasted potatoes), *Schweinebraten* (roasted pork), or, of course, *Bratwurst* (grilled sausage).

Here are a few other specialties—both regional and nationwide—to look for:

Dampfnudel: Steamed bread roll with various toppings (also available sweet).

Flammkuchen (or **Dünnele**): German version of white pizza, on a thin, yeastless dough.

Frikadelle (also called **Klopse;** in Berlin, **Buletten;** and in Bavaria, **Fleischpfanzerl**): Giant meatball, sometimes flattened like a hamburger.

Geschnetzeltes: Strips of veal or chicken braised in a rich sauce and served with noodles.

Kassler: Salted, slightly smoked pork.

Kohlroulade: Cabbage leaves stuffed with minced meat.

Königsberger Klopse (or **Sossklopse**): Meatball with capers and potatoes in a white sauce (a staple of eastern Germany).

Kümmelbraten: Crispy roast pork with caraway.

Labskaus: Mushy mix of salted meat, potatoes, often beets, and sometimes herring, onions, and sour cream.

Maultaschen ("mouth pockets"): Ravioli with various fillings, such as veal, cheese, and spinach.

Ratsherrentopf: Stew of roasted meat with potatoes.

(Rinder-)Roulade: Strip of beef rolled up with bacon, onion, and pickles, then braised.

Rostbrätel: Marinated and grilled pork neck.

Sauerbraten: "Sour"-marinated and roasted cut of beef (sometimes pork), typically served with red cabbage and potato dumplings.

Saure Zipfel: Bratwurst cooked in vinegar and onions.

Schäufele: Oven-roasted pork shoulder with gravy.

Schlachtplatte (or **Schlachtschüssel**): "Butcher's plate"—usually blood sausage, *Leberwurst*, and other meat over hot sauerkraut.

Schweinebraten (or **Schweinsbraten**): Roasted pork with gravy.

Spargel: Big, white asparagus in season in May and June.

Speckpfannkuchen: Large, savory crêpe with bacon.

Stolzer Heinrich: Grilled sausage in beer sauce (Berlin).

BEST OF THE WURST

Sausage (wurst) is a staple of the Germanic diet. Most restaurants offer it (often as the cheapest thing on the menu), but it's more commonly eaten at take-out fast-food stands (called *Würstchenbude* in Germany or *Würstelstand* in Austria). Sausage is fast, tasty, very local—and even a chance for culinary adventure, as your options go far beyond the hometown hot dog. Some sausages are boiled *(gekocht)*, and some are grilled *(gegrillt)*. Most are pork-based. Generally, the darker the weenie, the spicier it is.

The generic term *Bratwurst* (or *Rostbratwurst*) simply means "grilled sausage," as opposed to boiled *Brühwurst*. Regional variations of both abound. While some types of wurst can be found all over, others are unique to a particular area (as noted below).

When surveying your options at a sidewalk sausage stand, these terms may help:

Bockwurst: Thick pork-and-veal sausage with a mild, grassy flavor and a toothsome, smoky casing.

Bosna: Spicy sausage with onions and sometimes curry (Austrian).

Blutwurst (or **Blunzen**): Made from congealed blood. Variations include *Schwarzwurst, Rotwurst,* and *Beutelwurst*.

Bregenwurst: Pork sausage traditionally made with brain (though usually not anymore).

Burenwurst: Pork sausage similar to what we'd call "kielbasa"; customarily boiled rather than grilled.

Cervelat: Smoky, mild, chewy sausage that's butterflied at each end before grilling (mostly Swiss).

Currywurst: Grilled pork sausage (usually *Bockwurst*), often chopped into small pieces, with ketchup/curry sauce, served *mit* or *ohne Darm* (with or without skin—with skin tastes smokier). Though this dish originated in Berlin, it's becoming very popular everywhere.

Debreziner: Boiled, thin, and spicy, with paprika (Austrian; named for the Hungarian town of Debrezin).

Frankfurter: A skinny, pink, boiled sausage—the ancestor of our hot dog (also called *Wienerwurst, Wienerwürstchen,* or simply *Wiener*).

Käsekrainer: Boiled, with melted cheese inside (Austrian).

Knackwurst (or **Knockwurst**): Short, stubby, garlicky, beef or pork sausage with a casing that "cracks" *(knackt)* when you bite into it.

Kochwurst: Generic term for sausages made of pre-cooked ingredients; these are only lightly steamed *(gekocht)* before eating. Examples include *Beinwurst* (made of smoked pork, herbs, and wine) and *Kohlwurst* (a.k.a. *Lungwurst*—very smoky poached sausage made from, among other things, lungs).

Lyoner: Thicker, shorter Frankfurter, often chopped up with onions and vinegar in *Wurstsalat; Regensburger* and *Pfälzer* are similar but with more herbs and spices.

Mettwurst: Spicy, soft sausage made with raw (but cured) pork; it can be grilled or eaten raw (as a spread). It comes *fein* (smooth) or *grob* (chunky).

Milzwurst (or **Milzstücken**): Made of pig spleen *(Milz).*

Nürnberger: Short and spicy grilled pork sausage from Nürnberg (also available throughout Bavaria), usually eaten three or six (or more) at a time, often lined up in a bun *(Drei im Weggla* means "three in bun").

Rauchzepferl: Smoky and slightly spicy (Munich).

Saumagen: "Sow's stomach" stuffed with meat, vegetables, and spices.

Thüringer: Long, skinny, peppery, and wedged into a much shorter roll. *Thüringer Rotwurst* is a blood-sausage variation.

Waldviertler: Smoked sausage (Austrian).

Weisswurst: Boiled white sausage (peel off the casing before you eat it), served with sweet mustard and a pretzel. While traditionally from Munich, you can find this at any Bavarian-themed restaurant. If it's *frisch* (fresh), you're supposed to "eat it before the noon bell tolls."

Wollwurst: Like *Weisswurst* (see above), but peeled and grilled.

Zwiebelwurst: Liver and onion sausage.

Accompaniments: Sauces and sides include *Senf* (mustard; ask for *süss*—sweet; or *scharf*—hot), Ketchup, Curry-Ketchup, or *Currysauce* (a tasty curry-infused ketchup), *Kraut* (sauerkraut), and sometimes horseradish (called *Meerrettich* in the north, *Kren* in the south and Austria).

At sausage stands, your wurst will usually come with a roll *(Semmel*—not your typical hot-dog bun). The sausage might be inside the roll, or it may come on a plate with the roll to the side. You might be given the choice of a slice of bread *(Brot)*, a pretzel *(Brezel)*, or in restaurants, potato salad.

At the Butcher
In addition to the sausages you'll see at open-air grills, here are a few you can shop for at a *Metzgerei* (butcher):

Bündnerfleisch: Air-dried beef.

Jagdwurst: Baloney-like "hunter's sausage"—smoked pork with garlic and mustard.

Landjäger: Skinny, spicy, air-dried (almost withered) salami. *Ahle Wurst* is similar.

Leberkäse: "Liver cheese" meatloaf made of pork, beef, and sometimes liver (but, confusingly, no cheese and often no liver). *Leberkäsesemmel* is a meatloaf sandwich.

Streichwurst: Generic name for meat spread.

Teewurst: Air-dried, often smoked sausage similar to Italian prosciutto, traditionally eaten at teatime (hence the name).

Tirolerwurst: Thick, sliced smoked sausage (Austria).

In addition, the butcher may also grill up some of the sausages listed earlier, or may sell some of them to be eaten cold. Assemble a few of these items for a bang-up German picnic.

STARCHES AND SALADS
Besides bread *(Brot)* and potatoes (*Kartoffeln;* boiled, fried, or grilled), typical starches include *Spätzle* (little noodles made from egg dough scraped through a wide-holed sieve; often served with melted cheese and fried onions as a meal in itself called *Käsespätzle*); various kinds of *Knödel* (large dumplings, usually made from potatoes but also from wheat, sourdough, semolina, or even liver; baseball-size dumplings are called *Klösse*); *Schupfnudeln* (stubby, diamond-shaped potato noodles); and *Kartoffelsalat* (potato salad).

Germans make excellent salads, and most menus feature big, varied, dinner-size salad plates. For a starter, a side dish, or a tiny appetite, consider a *grüner Salat* (mostly lettuce) or—for more variety—*gemischter Salat* (a.k.a. *buntner Salat*), a mixed salad of lettuce, fresh and (often) pickled veggies, and a tasty dressing. Other salad options include *Bauernsalat* (Greek salad, sometimes with sausage), *Bohnensalat* (bean salad), *Gurkensalat* (cucumber salad—usually just cukes in vinegar), *Nudelsalat* (pasta salad), or *Oliviersalat* (Russian-style salad—potatoes, eggs, vegetables, and mayonnaise). For something meatier, it's *Fleischsalat* (chopped cold cuts mixed with pickles and mayonnaise), *Wurstsalat* (chopped sausage in onion and vinegar), or *Ochsenmaulsalat* ("ox mouth salad" with vinegar, onion, and herbs).

SNACKS

Pretzels (*Brezel* or—in Bavaria—*Brez'n*), either plain or buttered, make for an inexpensive snack. The brown crust comes from dunking them in water boiled with baking soda or lye.

Brotzeit ("bread time") is the all-purpose word for a light between-meals snack that's served cold. *Brotzeit* involves cold cuts, cheeses, breads, and other cold snacks, such as salads and some sausages. Other items you may see:

Streichwurst: Meat spread; the most popular is *Leberwurst*, made from liver.

Obatzda: Pungent Bavarian cheese spread with paprika and onions.

Krautsalat: "Coleslaw," basically cold sauerkraut.

Matjesfilet: Raw herring in yogurt.

Schmalzbrot: Bread smeared with lard.

Schnittlauchbrot: Bread with cream cheese and diced chives.

Kartoffelkäse: "Potato cheese" spread made of mashed potatoes, onion, and sour cream (but no cheese).

ETHNIC FOOD

Ethnic restaurants provide a welcome break from Germanic fare. Italian, Turkish, and Asian food are generally good values, and Asian restaurants tend to serve inexpensive lunches. An Asian rice or noodle dish, a freshly baked pizza, or a Turkish sandwich will cost you only €4-7, and can be packed up to enjoy on a park bench or in your room.

Originally from Turkey, *Döner Kebab* (sliced meat and vegetables served in pita bread) has become a classic take-out meal for Germans of all stripes (€4 at any time of day). Turkish cafés abound, even in small towns. Take a moment to study the menu; beyond the basic *Döner*, you can get a *Döner Teller* (on a plate instead of in bread), a *Döner Dürüm* (in a thin, tortilla-like flatbread wrap, also called *Dürüm Kebab* or *Yufka*), falafel (chickpea croquettes), "Turkish pizzas," and much more.

SWEETS

Make sure to visit a bakery *(Bäckerei)* or pastry shop *(Konditorei)* to browse the selection of fresh pastries and cakes. Pastries *(Feingebäck)* can include the familiar *Apfelstrudel* and *Croissant* (sometimes called *Gipfel,* "peak"), as well as *Amerikaner* (a flat, round donut with a thick layer of glaze frosting on top), *Berliner* (a jelly-filled donut; also called *Krapfen* in Bavaria, or *Pfannkuchen* in Berlin),

Rohrnudel (roll-like sweet dumpling with raisins), and *Schnecken* ("snail"-shaped pastry roll with raisins and nuts). Pastries often have a filling of jam (*Marmelade* or *Konfitüre*), apple *(Apfel)*, cherry *(Kirsche)*, raisins *(Rosinen)*, nut *(Nuss)*, almond *(Mandel)*, poppy seeds *(Mohnen)*, or the sweet cheese curds called *Quark*.

Gummi Bears are local gumdrops with a cult following (look for the Haribo brand). Ice-cream stores, often run by Italian immigrants, abound. While you can always get a cone to go (ask for *ein Kugel*, a scoop—literally "ball"), many Germans sit down to enjoy their ice cream, ordering fancy sundaes in big glass bowls.

BEVERAGES

Germany has excellent wine and beer. Sampling some helps create fond memories of your trip.

Wine

The best-known white wines are from the Rhine and Mosel, and there are some good reds, especially from the south. You can order wine by the glass or sometimes by the *Viertel* (quarter-liter, or 8 oz.). Just ask for *"Ein Viertel Weisswein* (white wine) or *Rotwein* (red wine), *bitte."* Order your *Weisswein süss* (sweet), *halbtrocken* (medium), or *trocken* (dry). Many hotels serve the inexpensive *Sekt*, or German champagne, at breakfast. *Weinschorle* is a spritzer—white wine pepped up with a little sparkling water.

A few white wines you'll likely find in Germany include *Riesling* (fruity, fragrant, elegant), *Gewürztraminer* (aromatic, intense, and "spicy"), *Silvaner* (or *Grüner Silvaner;* acidic, fruity white from Franconia, comes in jug-shaped bottle), *Müller-Thurgau* (light and flowery, best when young, smooth, and semi-sweet), *Liebfraumilch* ("beloved maiden's milk"; semi-sweet white blending Riseling with Silvaner and Müller-Thurgau), and *Grauburgunder* (German for "pinot gris"—a soft, full-bodied white). Reds include *Dornfelder* (velvety, often oaky, sometimes sweet) and *Spätburgunder* (or *Blauburgunder;* German for "pinot noir").

Also keep an eye out for *Apfelwein* ("apple wine"—hard cider, especially popular in Frankfurt), *Eiswein* (ultra-sweet dessert white made from frozen shriveled grapes), and—in winter—*Glühwein* (hot spiced wine).

Beer

The average German drinks 40 gallons of beer a year and has a tremendous variety to choose from. *Flaschenbier* is bottled, and *vom Fass* is on tap. Broadly speaking, most beers you'll see fall into four main categories:

Helles Bier: Closest to American-style beer, this is the generic name for pale lager. Light-colored (but not "lite" as in low-calorie), a *helles Bier* is similar to a *Pilsner*, but with more malt. *Helles Bier* is usually served either in a straight glass (*Stange*, meaning "rod," which its shape resembles) or a mug. Unfiltered lager (like cask ale) is *Kellerbier* or *Zwickelbier*.

Dunkles Bier: This is a general term for dark beer. Munich-style *dunkles* is sweet and malty, while farther north it's drier and hoppier. Variations include *Schwarzbier* (a "black" lager with a chocolaty flavor), *Rauchbier* (with a "smoky" flavor, from Bamberg), and *Weihnachsbier* (or *Festbier*—a seasonal Christmas beer). *Dunkles Bier*, like *helles Bier*, is typically served in a straight glass or mug.

Weissbier or **Weizenbier:** "White" or "wheat" beer (better known in North America as "Hefeweizen") is a yeasty, highly caloric beer. It is poured slowly to build a frothy head in a tall, rounded-top glass with a wedge of lemon. Unfiltered *Weissbier*, especially common in the south, is cloudy (and usually called *Hefeweizen*). *Kristallweizen* is a clear, filtered, yeast-free wheat beer. *Roggenbier* is darker colored and made with rye.

Pilsner (a.k.a. **Pilsener** or simply **Pils**): This is a barley-based, bottom-fermented, flavorful, hoppy, light-colored beer. Particularly common in the north, a *Pilsner* is usually served in a tall, slender, tapered, and sometimes stemmed glass. If it takes a while for the beer to arrive, it's because they're waiting for the head to die down.

Regional Specialties and Variations: *Kölsch* is Cologne's mild brew, served in trays of small, straight glasses. *Berliner Weisse* is Berlin's fizzy, slightly sour brew, often sweetened with a shot of syrup. The same approach helps sweeten *Leipziger Gose*, Leipzig's very sour wheat beer. And Bavaria (Munich especially) has a wide array of special beers. Most famous are *Bockbier*, a high-alcohol, high-calorie, hoppy, bittersweet amber traditionally consumed during Lent (when monks were fasting and needed liquid nourishment); and *Märzenbier*, a light, malty, and highly alcoholic lager brewed in March *(März)* to be ready for Oktoberfest.

When ordering beer in Bavaria, the standard order is *eine Mass* (a whole liter, or about a quart); for something smaller, ask for *eine Halbe* (a half-liter, not always available). *Radler* (literally "bicyclist"—designed to be refreshing and not too intoxicating for a biker on a hot day) is half lager and half lemon soda. Wheat beer and lemon soda is *Russ* (or *Russ'n*). Cola-beer mixes are also common: *Diesel* (a.k.a. *Schmutziges* or *Krefelder*) is cola and lager, and *Colaweizen* is cola and wheat beer.

Nährbier ("Near Beer") is just that—low-alcohol lager. The closest thing to our "lite" beer is *leichtes Bier*—a low-calorie, low-alcohol wheat beer.

For tips on visiting a *Biergarten*, see page 118.

Other Drinks

Teetotalers—or anyone who wants a refreshing beer at lunch without being tipsy all afternoon—find a world of enticing non-alcoholic beer options. Look for *"ohne Alkohol"* or *"alkoholfrei."* While virtually all non-alcoholic brews in the US are watery, bitter lagers, Germany produces some excellent non-alcoholic white/wheat beers *(Weisses),* which have a somewhat sweeter flavor—very smooth drinking on a hot day. Or look for the non-alcoholic drink called *Malztrunk* (or *Malzbier*)—the sweet, malted beverage (resembling dark beer) that children quaff before they start drinking the real thing.

Waiters aren't exactly eager to bring you *Leitungswasser* (tap water), preferring that you buy *Mineralwasser* (*mit/ohne Gas*, with/without carbonation). Popular soft drinks include *Apfelschorle* (half apple juice, half sparkling water) and *Spezi* (cola and orange soda). Menus list drink sizes by the tenth of a liter, or deciliter (dl): 0.2 liters is a small glass, and 0.4 or 0.5 is a larger one.

If you buy bottled drinks from a store, you'll have to pay a deposit (*Pfand,* often €0.15 or €0.25), which gets refunded if you return the bottle. The deposit amount is listed in small print on the shelf's price label. While I appreciate Germany's efforts to be green, they make it hard on the tourist, who winds up carrying around empty bottles looking for a place to reclaim their *Pfand*. While legally any place that sells *Pfand* bottles must also buy bottles of those same brands, many shops flat-out refuse to accept bottles that they didn't actually sell you. Some supermarkets have vending machine-like bottle-return stations (marked *Flaschenrückgabe* or *Flaschenannahme*); when you're done feeding bottles in, the machine issues a coupon that you can redeem when you pay for your groceries. Easier still, just give returnable bottles to your hotel.

Communicating

"How can I stay connected in Europe?"—by phone and online—may be the most common question I hear from travelers. You have three basic options:

1. "Roam" with your US mobile device. This is the easiest option, but likely the most expensive. It works best for people who won't be making very many calls, and who value the convenience of sticking with what's familiar (and their own phone number). In recent years, as data roaming fees have dropped and free Wi-Fi has become easier to find, the majority of travelers are finding this to be the best all-around option.

2. Use an unlocked mobile phone with European SIM cards. This is a much more affordable option if you'll be making lots of calls, since it gives you 24/7 access to low European rates. Although remarkably cheap, this option does require a bit of shopping around for the right phone and a prepaid SIM card. Savvy travelers who routinely buy European SIM cards swear by this tactic.

3. Use public phones, and get online with your hotel's guest computer and/or at Internet cafés. These options work particularly well for travelers who simply don't want to hassle with the technology, or want to be (mostly) untethered from their home life while on the road.

Each of these options is explained in greater detail in the following pages. Mixing and matching works well. For example, I routinely bring along my smartphone for Internet chores and Skyping on Wi-Fi, but also carry an unlocked phone and buy SIM cards for affordable calls on the go.

For an even more in-depth explanation of this complicated topic, see www.ricksteves.com/phoning.

HOW TO DIAL

Many Americans are intimidated by dialing European phone numbers. You needn't be. It's simple, once you break the code.

Dialing Within Germany

The following instructions apply whether you're dialing from a German mobile phone or a landline (such as a pay phone or your hotel-room phone). If you're roaming with a US phone number, follow the "Dialing Internationally" directions described later.

Germany, like much of the US, uses an area-code dialing system. To make domestic calls, if you're calling within the same area code, you just dial the local number to be connected; but if you're calling outside your area code, you have to dial both the area code (which starts with a 0) and the local number.

For example, Munich's area code is 089 and the number of one of my recommended Munich hotels is 545-9940. To call the hotel within Munich, you'd dial 545-9940. To call it from Frankfurt, you'd dial 089/545-9940.

Area codes are listed throughout this book, or you can get them from directory assistance (tel. 11833). Be aware that some numbers, typically those that start with 018 (including some train and airline information numbers), are premium toll calls, costing more than a regular land-line call. The per-minute charge should be listed in small print next to the phone number. Mobile phone numbers start with 015, 016, or 017, and cost much more to call than landlines. Off-hour calls are generally cheaper.

In Germany, phone numbers can have varying lengths. For

Hurdling the Language Barrier

German—like English, Dutch, Swedish, and Norwegian—is a Germanic language, making it easier on most American ears than Romance languages (such as Italian and French). These tips will help you pronounce German words: The letter *w* is always pronounced as "v" (e.g., the word for "wonderful" is *wunderbar,* pronounced VOON-der-bar). The vowel combinations *ie* and *ei* are pronounced like the name of the second letter—so *ie* sounds like a long *e* (as in *hier* and *Bier,* the German words for "here" and "beer"), while *ei* sounds like a long *i* (as in *nein* and *Stein,* the German words for "no" and "stone"). The vowel combination *au* is pronounced "ow" (as in *Frau*). The vowel combinations *eu* and *äu* are pronounced "oy" (as in *neu, Deutsch,* and *Bräu,* the words for "new," "German," and "brew"). To pronounce ö and ü, purse your lips when you say the vowel; the other vowel with an umlaut, ä, is pronounced the same as *e* in "men." (In written German, these can be depicted as the vowel followed by an *e—oe, ue,* and *ae,* respectively.) The letter Eszett (ß) represents *ss.* Written German capitalizes all nouns.

Though most young or well-educated Germans—especially those in the tourist trade and in big cities—speak at least some English, you'll get more smiles if you learn and use the German pleasantries. Study the German Survival Phrases on page 983. Give it your best shot. The locals will appreciate your efforts.

PRACTICALITIES

instance, a hotel might have a seven-digit phone number and an eight-digit fax number.

Dialing Internationally to or from Germany

Always start with the **international access code**—011 if you're calling from the US or Canada, 00 from anywhere in Europe. If you're dialing from a mobile phone, simply insert a + instead (by holding the 0 key).

• Dial the **country code** of the country you're calling (49 for Germany, or 1 for the US or Canada).

• Then dial the area code (without its initial 0) and the local number. The European calling chart lists specifics per country.

Calling from the US to Germany: To call the Munich hotel from the US, dial 011 (US access code), 49 (Germany's country code), 89 (Munich's area code without the initial 0), then 545-9940 (the hotel's number).

Calling from any European country to the US: To call my office in Edmonds, Washington, from anywhere in Europe, I dial 00 (Europe's access code), 1 (US country code), 425 (Edmonds' area code), and 771-8303.

More Dialing Tips

The chart on the next page shows how to dial per country. For online instructions, see www.countrycallingcodes.com or www. howtocallabroad.com.

Remember, if you're using a mobile phone, dial as if you're in that phone's country of origin. So, when roaming with your US phone number in Germany, dial as if you're calling from the US. But if you're using a European SIM card, dial as you would from that European country.

For tips on communicating over the phone with someone who speaks another language, see the sidebar on previous page.

USING YOUR SMARTPHONE IN EUROPE

Even in this age of email, texting, and near-universal Internet access, smart travelers still use the telephone. I call TIs to smooth out sightseeing plans, hotels to get driving directions, museums to confirm tour schedules, restaurants to check open hours or to book a table, and so on.

Most people enjoy the convenience of bringing their own smartphone. Horror stories about sky-high roaming fees are dated and exaggerated, and major service providers work hard to avoid surprising you with an exorbitant bill. With a little planning, you can use your phone—for voice calls, messaging, and Internet access—without breaking the bank.

Start by figuring out whether your phone works in Europe. Most phones purchased through AT&T and T-Mobile (which use the same technology as European providers do) work abroad, while only some phones from Verizon or Sprint do—check your operating manual (look for "tri-band," "quad-band," or "GSM"). If you're not sure, ask your service provider.

Roaming Costs

"Roaming" with your phone—that is, using it outside its home region, such as in Europe—generally comes with extra charges, whether you are making voice calls, sending texts, or reading your email. The fees listed here are for the three major American providers—Verizon, AT&T, and T-Mobile; Sprint's roaming rates tend to be much higher. But policies change fast, so get the latest details before your trip. For example, as of mid-2014, T-Mobile waived voice, texting, and data roaming fees for some plans.

Voice calls are the most expensive. Most US providers charge from $1.29 to $1.99 per minute to make or receive calls in Europe. (As you cross each border, you'll typically get a text message explaining the rates in the new country.) If you plan to make multiple calls, look into a global calling plan to lower the per-minute cost, or buy a package of minutes at a discounted price (such as 30 minutes for $30). Note that you'll be charged for incoming calls whether or not you answer them; to save money ask your friends to stay in contact by texting, and to call you only in case of an emergency.

Text messaging costs 20 to 50 cents per text. To cut that cost, you could sign up for an international messaging plan (for example, $10 for 100 texts). Or consider apps that let you text for free (iMessage for Apple, Google Hangouts for Android, or WhatsApp for any device); however, these require you to use Wi-Fi or data roaming. Be aware that Europeans use the term "SMS" ("short message service") to describe text messaging.

Data roaming means accessing data services via a cellular network other than your home carrier's. Prices have dropped dramatically in recent years, making this an affordable way for travelers to bridge gaps between Wi-Fi hotspots. You'll pay far less if you set up an international data roaming plan. Most providers charge $25-30 for 100-120 megabytes of data. That's plenty for basic Internet tasks—100 megabytes lets you view 100 websites or send/receive 1,000 text-based emails, but you'll burn through that amount quickly by streaming videos or music. If your data use exceeds your plan amount, most providers will automatically kick in an additional 100- or 120-megabyte block for the same price. (For more, see "Using Wi-Fi and Data Roaming," later.)

Setting Up (or Disabling) International Service

With most service providers, international roaming (voice, text, and data) is disabled on your account unless you activate it. Before your trip, call your provider (or navigate their website), and cover the following topics:

• Confirm that your phone will work in Europe.

• Verify global roaming rates for voice calls, text messaging, and data.

• Tell them which of those services you'd like to activate.

• Consider add-on plans to bring down the cost of international calls, texts, or data roaming.

When you get home from Europe, be sure to cancel any add-on plans that you activated for your trip.

Some people would rather use their smartphone exclusively on Wi-Fi, and not worry about either voice or data charges. If that's you, call your provider to be sure that international roaming options are deactivated on your account. To be double-sure, put your phone in "airplane mode," then turn your Wi-Fi back on.

Using Wi-Fi and Data Roaming

A good approach is to use free Wi-Fi wherever possible, and fill in the gaps with data roaming.

Wi-Fi is readily available throughout Europe. At accommo-

European Calling Chart

Just smile and dial, using this key:
AC = Area Code, LN = Local Number.

European Country	Calling long distance within ...	Calling from the US or Canada to ...	Calling from a European country to ...
Austria	AC + LN	011 + 43 + AC (without initial zero) + LN	00 + 43 + AC (without initial zero) + LN
Belgium	LN	011 + 32 + LN (without initial zero)	00 + 32 + LN (without initial zero)
Bosnia-Herzegovina	AC + LN	011 + 387 + AC (without initial zero) + LN	00 + 387 + AC (without initial zero) + LN
Croatia	AC + LN	011 + 385 + AC (without initial zero) + LN	00 + 385 + AC (without initial zero) + LN
Czech Republic	LN	011 + 420 + LN	00 + 420 + LN
Denmark	LN	011 + 45 + LN	00 + 45 + LN
Estonia	LN	011 + 372 + LN	00 + 372 + LN
Finland	AC + LN	011 + 358 + AC (without initial zero) + LN	999 (or other 900 number) + 358 + AC (without initial zero) + LN
France	LN	011 + 33 + LN (without initial zero)	00 + 33 + LN (without initial zero)
Germany	AC + LN	011 + 49 + AC (without initial zero) + LN	00 + 49 + AC (without initial zero) + LN
Gibraltar	LN	011 + 350 + LN	00 + 350 + LN
Great Britain & N. Ireland	AC + LN	011 + 44 + AC (without initial zero) + LN	00 + 44 + AC (without initial zero) + LN
Greece	LN	011 + 30 + LN	00 + 30 + LN
Hungary	06 + AC + LN	011 + 36 + AC + LN	00 + 36 + AC + LN
Ireland	AC + LN	011 + 353 + AC (without initial zero) + LN	00 + 353 + AC (without initial zero) + LN
Italy	LN	011 + 39 + LN	00 + 39 + LN

PRACTICALITIES

European Country	Calling long distance within ...	Calling from the US or Canada to ...	Calling from a European country to ...
Latvia	LN	011 + 371 + LN	00 + 371 + LN
Montenegro	AC + LN	011 + 382 + AC (without initial zero) + LN	00 + 382 + AC (without initial zero) + LN
Morocco	LN	011 + 212 + LN (without initial zero)	00 + 212 + LN (without initial zero)
Netherlands	AC + LN	011 + 31 + AC (without initial zero) + LN	00 + 31 + AC (without initial zero) + LN
Norway	LN	011 + 47 + LN	00 + 47 + LN
Poland	LN	011 + 48 + LN	00 + 48 + LN
Portugal	LN	011 + 351 + LN	00 + 351 + LN
Russia	8 + AC + LN	011 + 7 + AC + LN	00 + 7 + AC + LN
Slovakia	AC + LN	011 + 421 + AC (without initial zero) + LN	00 + 421 + AC (without initial zero) + LN
Slovenia	AC + LN	011 + 386 + AC (without initial zero) + LN	00 + 386 + AC (without initial zero) + LN
Spain	LN	011 + 34 + LN	00 + 34 + LN
Sweden	AC + LN	011 + 46 + AC (without initial zero) + LN	00 + 46 + AC (without initial zero) + LN
Switzerland	LN	011 + 41 + LN (without initial zero)	00 + 41 + LN (without initial zero)
Turkey	AC (if there's no initial zero, add one) + LN	011 + 90 + AC (without initial zero) + LN	00 + 90 + AC (without initial zero) + LN

PRACTICALITIES

- The instructions above apply whether you're calling to or from a European landline or mobile phone.

- If calling from any mobile phone, you can replace the international access code with "+" (press and hold 0 to insert it).

- The international access code is 011 if you're calling from the US or Canada.

- To call the US or Canada from Europe, dial 00, then 1 (country code for US and Canada), then the area code and number. In short, 00 + 1 + AC + LN = Hi, Mom!

dations, access is usually free, but you may have to pay a fee, especially at expensive hotels. At hotels with thick stone walls, the Wi-Fi signal from the lobby may not reach every room. If Wi-Fi is important to you, ask about it when you book—and be specific ("In the rooms?"). Get the password and network name at the front desk when you check in.

When you're out and about, your best bet for finding free Wi-Fi is often at a café. They'll usually tell you the password if you buy something. Or you can stroll down a café-lined street, smartphone in hand, checking for unsecured networks every few steps until you find one that works. Some towns have free public Wi-Fi in highly trafficked parks or piazzas. You may have to register before using it, or get a password at the TI.

Data roaming is handy when you can't find Wi-Fi. Because you'll pay by the megabyte (explained earlier), it's best to limit how much data you use. Save bandwidth-gobbling tasks like Skyping, watching videos, or downloading apps or emails with large attachments until you're on Wi-Fi. Switch your phone's email settings from "push" to "fetch." This means that you can choose to "fetch" (download) your messages when you're on Wi-Fi rather than having them continuously "pushed" to your device. And be aware of apps—such as news, weather, and sports tickers—that automatically update. Check your phone's settings to be sure that none of your apps are set to "use cellular data."

I like the safeguard of manually turning off data roaming on my phone whenever I'm not actively using it. To turn off data and voice roaming, look in your phone's settings menu—try checking under "cellular" or "network," or ask your service provider how to do it. If you need to get online but can't find Wi-Fi, simply turn on data roaming long enough for the task at hand, then turn it off again.

Figure out how to keep track of how much data you've used (in your phone's menu, look for "cellular data usage"; you may have to reset the counter at the start of your trip). Some companies automatically send you a text message warning if you approach or exceed your limit.

There's yet another option: If you're traveling with an unlocked smartphone (explained later), you can buy a SIM card that also includes data; this can be far cheaper than data roaming through your home provider.

USING EUROPEAN SIM CARDS

While using your American phone in Europe is easy, it's not always cheap. And unreliable Wi-Fi can make keeping in touch frustrating. If you're reasonably technology-savvy, and would like to have

---

Internet Calling

To make totally free voice and video calls over the Internet, all you need are a smartphone, tablet, or laptop; a strong Wi-Fi signal; and an account with one of the major Internet calling providers: Skype (www.skype.com), FaceTime (preloaded on most Apple devices), or Google+ Hangouts (www.google.com/hangouts). If the Wi-Fi signal isn't strong enough for video, try sticking with an audio-only call. Or...wait for your next hotel. Many Internet calling programs also work for making calls from your computer to telephones worldwide for a very reasonable fee—generally just a few cents per minute (you'll have to buy some credit before you make your first call).

---

the option of making lots of affordable calls, it's worth getting comfortable with European SIM cards.

Here's the basic idea: With an unlocked phone (which works with different carriers; see below), get a SIM card—the microchip that stores data about your phone—once you get to Europe. Slip in the SIM, turn on the phone, and bingo! You've got a European phone number (and access to cheaper European rates).

Getting an Unlocked Phone

Your basic options are getting your existing phone unlocked, or buying a phone (either at home or in Europe).

Some phones are electronically "locked" so that you can't switch SIM cards (keeping you loyal to your carrier). But in some circumstances it's possible to unlock your phone—allowing you to replace the original SIM card with one that will work with a European provider. Note that some US carriers are beginning to offer phones/tablets whose SIM card can't be swapped out in the US but will accept a European SIM without any unlocking process.

You may already have an old, unused mobile phone in a drawer somewhere. Call your service provider and ask if they'll send you the unlock code. Otherwise, you can buy one: Search an online shopping site for an "unlocked quad-band phone," or buy one at a mobile-phone shop in Europe. Either way, a basic model typically costs $40 or less.

Buying and Using SIM Cards

Once you have an unlocked phone, you'll need to buy a SIM card (note that a smaller variation called "micro-SIM" or "nano-SIM"—used in most iPhones—is less widely available).

SIM cards are sold at mobile-phone shops, department-store electronics counters, and newsstands for $5–10, and usually include about that much prepaid calling credit (making the card itself virtually free). Because SIM cards are prepaid, there's no contract and no commitment; I routinely buy one even if I'm in a country for only a few days.

However, an increasing number of countries—including Germany—require you to register the SIM card with your passport (an antiterrorism measure). This takes only a few minutes longer: The shop clerk will ask you to fill out a form, then submit it to the service provider. Sometimes you can register your own SIM card online. Either way, an hour or two after submitting the information, you'll get a text welcoming you to that network.

When using a SIM card in its home country, it's free to receive calls and texts, and it's cheap to make calls—domestic calls average 20 cents per minute. You can also use SIM cards to call the US—sometimes very affordably (Lebara and Lycamobile, which operate in multiple European countries, let you call a US number for less than 10 cents a minute). Rates are higher if you're roaming in another country. But if you bought the SIM card within the European Union, roaming fees are capped no matter where you travel throughout the EU (about 25 cents/minute to make calls, 7 cents/minute to receive calls, and 8 cents for a text message).

While you can buy SIM cards just about anywhere, I like to seek out a mobile-phone shop, where an English-speaking clerk can help explain my options, get my SIM card inserted and set up, and show me how to use it. When you buy your SIM card, ask about rates for domestic and international calls and texting, and about roaming fees. Also find out how to check your credit balance (usually you'll key in a few digits and hit "Send"). You can top up your credit at any newsstand, tobacco shop, mobile-phone shop, and at many other businesses (look for the SIM card's logo in the window).

To insert your SIM card into the phone, locate the slot, which is usually on the side of the phone or behind the battery. Turning on the phone, you'll be prompted to enter the "SIM PIN" (a code number that came with your card).

If you have an unlocked smartphone, you can look for a European SIM card that covers both voice and data. This is often much cheaper than paying for data roaming through your home provider.

LANDLINE TELEPHONES AND INTERNET CAFÉS

If you prefer to travel without a smartphone or tablet, you can still stay in touch using landline telephones, hotel guest computers, and Internet cafés.

Types of Telephone Cards

Europe uses two different types of telephone cards. Both types are sold at post offices, newsstands, street kiosks, tobacco shops, and train stations.

Insertable Phone Cards: These cards can only be used at pay phones. Simply take the phone off the hook, insert the card, wait for a dial tone, and dial away. The phone displays your credit ticking down as you talk. While you can use these cards to call anywhere in the world, it's only cheap for making quick local calls from a phone booth. Each European country has its own insertable phone card—so your German card won't work in an Austrian phone. Be warned that the national telecom companies in Germany levy a hefty surcharge for using any international phone card from a pay phone—which effectively eliminates any savings.

International Phone Cards: These prepaid cards can be used to make inexpensive calls—within Europe, or to the US, for pennies a minute—from nearly any phone, including the one in your hotel room. The cards come with a toll-free number and a scratch-to-reveal PIN code. If the voice prompts aren't in English, experiment: Dial your code, followed by the pound sign (#), then the phone number, then pound again, and so on, until it works.

Landline Telephones

Phones in your **hotel room** can be great for local calls and for calls using cheap international phone cards (described in the sidebar). Many hotels charge a fee for local and "toll-free" as well as long-distance or international calls—always ask for the rates before you dial. Since you'll never be charged for receiving calls, it can be more affordable to have someone from the US call you in your room. Even small hotels in Germany tend to have a direct-dial system, so callers can reach you in your room without going through reception. Ask the staff for your room's telephone number.

While **public pay phones** are on the endangered species list, you'll still see them in post offices and train stations. Pay phones generally come with multilingual instructions. Most public phones work with insertable phone cards (described in the sidebar).

You'll see many cheap **call shops** that advertise low rates to faraway lands, often in train-station neighborhoods. While these target immigrants who want to call home cheaply, tourists can use them, too. Before making your call, be completely clear on the rates.

Internet Cafés and Public Internet Terminals

Finding public Internet terminals in Europe is no problem. Many hotels have a computer in the lobby for guests to use. Otherwise, head for an Internet café, or ask the TI or your hotelier for the nearest place to access the Internet.

European computers typically use non-American keyboards. A few letters are switched around, and command keys are labeled in the local language. Many European keyboards have an "Alt Gr" key (for "Alternate Graphics") to the right of the space bar; press this to insert the extra symbol that appears on some keys. German keyboards are a little different from ours; to type an @ symbol, press the "Alt Gr" key and Q at the same time. If you can't locate a special character (such as the @ symbol), simply copy it from a Web page and paste it into your email message.

Internet Security

Whether you're accessing the Internet with your own device or at a public terminal, using a shared network or computer comes with the potential for increased security risks. Ask the hotel or café for the specific name of their Wi-Fi network, and make sure you log on to that exact one; hackers sometimes create a bogus hotspot with a similar or vague name (such as "Hotel Europa Free Wi-Fi"). It's better if a network uses a password (especially a hard-to-guess one) rather than being open to the world.

While traveling, you may want to check your online banking or credit-card statements, or to take care of other personal-finance chores, but Internet security experts advise against accessing these sites entirely while traveling. Even if you're using your own computer at a password-protected hotspot, any hacker who's logged on to the same network can see what you're up to. If you need to log on to a banking website, try to do so on a hard-wired connection (i.e., using an Ethernet cable in your hotel room), or if that's not possible, use a secure banking app on a cellular telephone connection.

If using a credit card online, make sure that the site is secure. Most browsers display a little padlock icon, and the URL begins with *https* instead of *http*. Never send a credit-card number over a website that doesn't begin with *https*.

If you're not convinced a connection is secure, avoid accessing any sites (such as your bank's) that could be vulnerable to fraud.

MAIL

You can mail one package per day to yourself worth up to $200 duty-free from Europe to the US (mark it "personal purchases"). If you're sending a gift to someone, mark it "unsolicited gift." For details, visit www.cbp.gov and search for "Know Before You Go."

Get stamps at the neighborhood post office, newsstands within fancy hotels, and some mini-marts and card shops. Avoid standing in line at the post office by using the handy yellow stamp

(*Briefmarke*) machines found just outside the building. Warning: These machines give change only in stamps, not in coins.

The German postal service works fine, but for quick transatlantic delivery (in either direction), consider services such as DHL (www.dhl.com).

Transportation

Cars are best for three or more traveling together (especially families with small kids), those packing heavy, and those scouring the countryside. Trains and buses are best for solo travelers, blitz tourists, city-to-city travelers, those with an ambitious, multi-country itinerary, and those who don't want to drive in Europe. While a car gives you more freedom, trains, buses, and boats zip you effortlessly and scenically from city to city, usually dropping you in the center, often near a TI. Cars are an expensive headache in big cities such as Munich, Berlin, and Frankfurt.

I've included a sample itinerary for drivers (with tips and tweaks for those using public transportation) to help you explore Germany smoothly; you'll find it on page 10.

TRAINS

Deutsche Bahn (DB) is the name of the German railway system. German trains are speedy, comfortable, and non-smoking. They cover cities and small towns well, but a few out-of-the-way recommendations (such as Bavaria's Wieskirche) are only reachable by bus. Though German trains are fairly punctual, very tight connections can be a gamble. Once the obvious choice for long-distance travel within Germany, trains are now facing competition from buses offering ultra-low fares (described later).

If you have a rail pass, you can hop on any train without much forethought (though for a small fee, you can reserve a seat on a fast train). Without a rail pass, you can save a lot of money by understanding the difference between fast trains and cheaper "regional" trains.

Types of Trains

There are big differences in price, speed, and comfort between Germany's three levels of trains. **ICE** trains (white with red trim and streamlined noses) are the fastest, zipping from city to city in air-conditioned comfort, and costing proportionately more. Mid-level **IC and EC** trains are white with red trim, but look older than the ICEs. The slowest are the **regional trains** (mostly red and labeled RB, RE, IRE, or S on schedules), but they cost much less. Milk-run S and RB trains stop at every station.

If you have a rail pass, take the fastest train available; rail-

German Public Transportation

North Sea

50 Kilometers
50 Miles

NETHERLANDS

Westerland
Niebüll
Husum
Heide
Tønder
Tinglev
To Copenhagen
Flensburg
Schleswig
Rendsburg
Kiel
Neumünster

Norden
Wilhelmshaven
Cuxhaven
Emden
Leer
Bremerhaven
Weener
Oldenburg
Bremen
Hamburg
Lüneburg
Uelzen
Celle
Wolfsburg

Den Helder
Groningen
Haarlem
Amsterdam
Schiphol
The Hague
Rotterdam
Utrecht
Arnhem
Hengelo
Bad Bentheim
Rheine
Osnabrück
Münster
Hannover
Braunschweig
Emmerich

Antwerp
Brussels
To Brussels
Maastricht
Namur
Liege
Duisburg
Venlo
Mönchengladbach
Essen
Dortmund
Hagen
Wuppertal
Düsseldorf
Cologne
Aachen
Bonn
Siegburg
Siegen

GERMA
Göttingen
Kassel

BELGIUM

LUX.
Luxembourg
Cochem
Moselkern
(BURG ELTZ)
Hahn
Beilstein
Trier
Koblenz
St. Goar
Mainz
Bacharach
Worms
Darmstadt
Heidelberg
Mannheim

Frankfurt
Marburg
Giessen
Fulda
Bebra
Eisenach
Meiningen
Würzburg

To Paris
Metz
Forbach
Nancy
Saarbrücken
Steinach
Rothenburg
ob der Tauber
Nürnberg
Ansbach
Crailsheim
Ellwangen
Dinkelsbühl

FRANCE
Baden-Baden
Oos
Karlsruhe
Strasbourg
Kehl
Baden-Baden
Offenburg
Stuttgart
Nordlingen
Treuchtlingen
Ingolstadt
Colmar
Triberg
Ulm
Dachau
Augsburg
Munich
Buchloe

Bad Krozingen
Titisee
Freiburg
Staufen
Mulhouse
Belfort
Basel
Singen
Konstanz
Fried.
Lindau
Kempten
Oberammergau
Murn.
Füssen
Reutte
Mitt.

SWITZERLAND
Bern
To Lausanne
To Interlaken
Luzern
Zürich
To Lugano
Bregenz
Feldkirch
LIECH.
Garmisch
To Innsbruck
To Italy

PRACTICALITIES

pass holders don't pay a supplement for the fast ICE trains (with one exception, the "ICE Sprinter"). If you're buying point-to-point tickets, taking a slower train can save a lot of money. You also save with day-pass deals valid only on slower trains.

Schedules

Schedules change by season, weekday, and weekend. Verify train times listed in this book at www.bahn.com. This website also includes public transport in cities (buses, trams, and subways).

At staffed train stations, attendants will print out a step-by-step itinerary for you, free of charge. You can also produce an itinerary yourself by using the computerized trackside machines marked *Fahrkarten* (usually silver, red, and blue). The touch-screen display gives you an English option; choose "Timetable Information," indicate your point of departure and destination, and then hit "Print" for a personalized schedule, including transfers and track numbers.

If you're changing trains en route and have a tight connection, note the numbers of the platforms (*Bahnsteig* or *Gleis*) where you will arrive and depart (listed on printed and online itineraries). This will save you precious time hunting for your connecting train.

To reach Germany's train information number from anywhere in the country, dial 0180-599-6633 and ask for an English speaker.

Rail Passes

The German Pass is a great value for rail travel within Germany if you're making several train journeys, or even just a Frankfurt-Munich round-trip. Rail passes are a better deal if you're under 26 (you qualify for a youth pass) or traveling with a companion (you save with the Twin pass). For only shorter hops, a rail pass probably isn't worth it, especially if you get discounts on point-to-point tickets and day passes (explained later).

If you're traveling in a neighboring country, two-country Eurail passes allow you to pair Germany with Austria, Switzerland, France, the Benelux region, Denmark, Poland, or the Czech Republic. The Select Pass gives you more travel in four adjacent countries (but not Poland). If you're planning a whirlwind tour of more than four countries, another possibility is the Global Pass, covering most of Europe. These passes are available in a saverpass version, which gives a 15 percent discount on rail passes for two or more companions traveling together.

For more detailed advice on figuring out the smartest rail pass options for your train trip, visit the Trains & Rail Passes section of my website at www.ricksteves.com/rail. German rail passes can also be purchased at certain locations in Germany, such as Frankfurt Airport.

PRACTICALITIES

When choosing how many travel days you need for your rail pass, note that it can be worthwhile to buy an extra day (about $15-20 per person) even to cover short trips on regional trains—for instance, from Würzburg to Rothenburg—simply for the convenience of not having to buy tickets.

Rail-pass travelers should know what extras are covered by their pass: for example, travel on any German buses marked "Deutsche Bahn" or "DB" (run by the train company), travel on city S-Bahn systems (except in Berlin, where only S-Bahn lines between major train stations are covered), and travel on K-D Line boats on the Rhine and Mosel Rivers. Rail passes get you a 20 percent discount on the Romantic Road bus, and possibly also on boats on the Danube River (ask locally). Flexipass holders should note that fully covered ("free") trips start the use of a travel day, while discounted trips do not. In other words, the flexipass day can also cover your train travel on that day (but if you're not planning to travel more that day, it makes sense to pay for, say, a short boat ride rather than start the use of a day of your pass).

Because Salzburg in Austria is so close to the German border, traveling to or from the city on the main line from Munich counts as traveling within Germany, as far as your rail pass is concerned (Salzburg is the official border station on that line).

Point-to-Point Tickets

Ticket fares are shown on the map on page 956, and for some journeys, at www.bahn.com (though not for most trains outside of Germany). Deutsche Bahn can charge a wide variety of fares for the same journey, depending on the time of day, how far ahead you purchase the ticket, and other considerations. Know your options to get the best deal.

First Class vs. Second Class: First-class tickets usually cost 50 percent more than second-class tickets. While first-class cars are always a bit more spacious and quiet than second class, the main advantage of a first-class ticket is the lower chance that the train will fill up. Riding in second class gets you there at the same time, and with the same scenery. As second-class seating is still comfortable and quiet, most of my readers find the extra cost of first class isn't worth it—Germans themselves tell me they never ride in first class unless someone else is paying for it.

Full-Fare Tickets (*Normalpreis*): The most you'll ever have to pay for a journey is the unrestricted *Normalpreis*. This full-fare ticket allows you to easily change your plans and switch to an earlier or later train, without paying a penalty. (If you buy a *Normalpreis* ticket for a slower train, though, you can't use it on a fast one without paying extra.)

Discount Fares (*Sparpreis*): If you reserve a ticket on a fast train at least three days in advance and are comfortable committing to particular departure times, you can usually save 25-75 percent over the *Normalpreis*. But these tickets are more restrictive; you have to take the train listed on the ticket. Changing one of these discounted tickets costs at least €15. Discounted fares go on sale three months before departure and remain available until three days before departure—unless all the cheap seats are sold earlier (which often happens).

Self-Service vs. Counter Service: You'll always pay €2 extra for a ticket bought at a counter rather than from a machine or online.

Savings on Slow Trains: You can always save money on point-to-point tickets if you're willing to skip Germany's high-speed trains (IC, EC, and ICE) and limit yourself to regional trains (most commonly labeled RB, RE, IRE, or S, but also TR, MRB, ALX, VIA, and OE). For example, Freiburg to Baden-Baden might cost €30 by ICE, €25 by EC, and €20 by RE train. The Deutsche Bahn website and ticket machines give you the option to limit your search to these slower, cheaper trains if you wish (by checking "only local transport").

Day Passes

You may save even more with three types of extremely popular day passes valid only on slow trains: the various Länder-Tickets, the Schönes-Wochenende-Ticket, and the Quer-durchs-Land-Ticket. They are most cost-effective for groups of two to five people traveling together, but single travelers can benefit from them, too.

With a **Länder-Ticket,** up to five people traveling together get unlimited travel in second class for one day for a very cheap price (usually €22 for the first person plus €3-4 for each additional person). The catch: A Länder-Ticket only covers travel within a certain *Land* (Germany's version of a US state, such as Bavaria, Baden-Württemberg, Saxony, or Rheinland-Pfalz). Also, these tickets don't cover travel on weekdays before 9:00. Still, Länder-Tickets offer big savings, don't require advance purchase, and are also valid on local transport. For example, a Bayern-Ticket (the Bavarian version of a Länder-Ticket) not only gets you from Munich to Füssen, but also covers the bus from Füssen to Neuschwanstein and back.

Some scenarios: From Munich to Nürnberg, ICE express trains take one hour and 10 minutes and cost €55, and RE regional trains take 35 minutes longer and cost €35. However, a Bayern-Ticket (Bavaria) lets one person ride the RE trains for only €22 (and just €38 covers five adults), as long as you leave after 9:00. Plus, if you return that day, there's no additional cost. The Baden-Ticket offers similar deals on the run from Freiburg to Baden-

Baden, and the Rhineland-Pfalz-Ticket makes sense for longer day trips around the Rhine and the Mosel (for example, from Bacharach or Trier to Burg Eltz). Sometimes several smaller *Länder* are covered by a single ticket: Thus the Sachsen-Ticket covers trips in Saxony (including Dresden and Leipzig) as well as the neighboring *Länder* of Sachsen-Anhalt (Wittenberg) and Thuringia (Erfurt and Eisenach).

The **Quer-durchs-Land-Ticket** works like a Länder-Ticket, but gives you the run of the whole country. It's valid on any regional train anywhere in Germany, but doesn't include city transport (first person–€44, each additional passenger–€8, up to a maximum of 5 travelers, only valid weekdays after 9:00). The **Schönes-Wochenende-Ticket** is a cheaper weekend version of the Quer-durchs-Land Ticket, with looser conditions: It's valid on all regional trains on a Saturday or Sunday (starting at midnight, not 9:00), it does cover local transport in some areas (buses, trams, subways—check specifics when you buy); and additional travelers pay nothing extra (the same €44 price covers 1-5 people). Two people could make the four-hour trip from Frankfurt to Trier on regional trains for €52 with a Quer-durchs-Land ticket and for €44 with a Schönes-Wochenende-Ticket. This trip would otherwise cost €80 for two people. For even larger groups, these tickets save serious money.

Kids 6-14 travel free with a parent or grandparent, but the ticket needs to list the number of children (except if purchased from a regional-train ticket machine). Kids under 6 don't need tickets.

Buying Tickets

At the Station: Major German stations have a handy *Reisezentrum* (travel center) where you can ask questions and buy tickets (with

a €2 markup for the personal service). Many smaller stations are unstaffed, so you'll have to buy tickets from machines, which come in three types.

The silver, red, and blue touch-screen machines (marked with the Deutsche Bahn logo and *Fahrkarten*, which means "tickets") are user-friendly machines that sell both short- and long-distance train tickets. They also print schedules for free (described earlier, under "Schedules"). Touch the flag to switch to English (although some screens are German-only). You can pay with bills, coins, or credit cards—but US credit cards may not work. There's one exception: Any trip that is entirely within the bounds of a regional transport network is considered

Rail Passes

Prices listed are for 2013 and are subject to change. For the latest prices, details, and train schedules (and easy online ordering), see www.ricksteves.com/rail. See Web site for more passes, including France-Germany and Germany-Czech passes.

"Saver" prices are per person for two or more people traveling together. "Youth" means under age 26.

GERMAN PASS

	Indiv. 1st Cl.	Indiv. 2nd Cl.	Twin 1st Cl.	Twin 2nd Cl.	Youth 2nd Cl.
3 days in 1 month	$339	$262	$258	$191	$206
4 days in 1 month	363	274	278	208	223
5 days in 1 month	396	305	298	222	237
6 days in 1 month	444	335	328	245	254
7 days in 1 month	488	366	360	267	268
8 days in 1 month	532	397	387	293	282
9 days in 1 month	585	428	423	316	300
10 days in 1 month	632	460	453	338	315

Twin price is per person for 2 traveling together. Odd-numbered groups must buy one individual adult, youth, or child pass. Youth passes are for travelers under 26 only. Kids 6–11 half of full adult (not Twin) fare. Kids 5 and under free. Also sold at main train stations in Germany.

Map key:
Approximate point-to-point one-way second-class rail fares in US dollars. First class costs 50 percent more. Add up the approximate ticket costs for your trip to see if a railpass will save you money.

SELECTPASS

This pass covers travel in three adjacent countries. For four- and five-country options, please visit **www.ricksteves.com/rail**.

	Individual 1st Class	Saver 1st Class	Youth 2nd Class
5 days in 2 months	$486	$414	$317
6 days in 2 months	536	457	350
8 days in 2 months	634	540	413
10 days in 2 months	735	625	479

PRACTICALITIES

GERMANY–AUSTRIA PASS

	Indiv. 1st Cl.	Indiv. 2nd Cl.	Saver 1st Cl.	Saver 2nd Cl.	Youth 2nd Cl.
5 days in 2 months	$435	$373	$373	$320	$321
6 days in 2 months	479	410	410	351	351
8 days in 2 months	571	487	487	418	419
10 days in 2 months	664	565	565	487	487

The fare for children 4–11 is half the adult individual fare or Saver fare. Kids under age 4 travel free.

GERMANY–SWITZERLAND PASS

	Individual 1st Class	Saver 1st Class	Youth 2nd Class
5 days in 2 months	$468	$400	$329
6 days in 2 months	516	440	364
8 days in 2 months	609	520	429
10 days in 2 months	704	601	495

The fare for children 4–11 is half the adult individual or Saver fare. Kids under age 4 travel free.

BENELUX–GERMANY PASS

	Indiv. 1st Cl.	Indiv. 2nd Cl.	Saver 1st Cl.	Saver 2nd Cl.	Youth 2nd Cl.
5 days in 2 months	$457	$343	$343	$279	$279
6 days in 2 months	504	381	381	304	304
8 days in 2 months	596	448	448	359	359
10 days in 2 months	694	520	520	416	416

The fare for children 4–11 is half the adult individual fare or Saver fare. Kids under age 4 travel free.

DENMARK–GERMANY PASS

	Indiv. 1st Cl.	Indiv. 2nd Cl.	Saver 1st Cl.	Saver 2nd Cl.	Youth 2nd Cl.
4 days in 2 months	$372	$304	$304	$236	$234
5 days in 2 months	418	343	343	264	264
6 days in 2 months	463	381	381	290	290
8 days in 2 months	558	457	457	332	332
10 days in 2 months	670	509	509	375	375

The fare for children 4–11 is half the adult individual fare or Saver fare. Kids under age 4 travel free.

GERMANY–POLAND PASS

	Indiv. 1st Cl.	Indiv. 2nd Cl.	Saver 1st Cl.	Saver 2nd Cl.	Youth 2nd Cl.
5 days in 2 months	$451	$386	$386	$326	$328
6 days in 2 months	493	427	427	362	362
8 days in 2 months	585	504	504	429	430
10 days in 2 months	674	583	583	492	492

The fare for children 4–11 is half the adult individual fare or Saver fare. Kids under age 4 travel free.

PRACTICALITIES

local—tickets can only be bought on the day of travel, and you must pay cash. Examples are Frankfurt-Bacharach or Nürnberg-Rothenburg.

Each German city and region also has its own style of machines which sell only same-day tickets to nearby destinations (usually including Länder-Ticket day passes). In cities, these machines also sell local public transport tickets. At some smaller stations, these machines are the only ticket-buying option. You'll see the logo of the city or regional transport network on the machine. Increasingly, these machines are multilingual, with touch screens, and some even take American credit cards with a PIN (though others take only cash and German debit cards).

Some cities and regions haven't gotten the new touch-screen terminals yet, and still have older, silver ticket machines with smaller screens and plenty of buttons. Again, these sell public transport tickets plus same-day-only train tickets to nearby destinations. To buy a train ticket from these machines, press the flag button until it gives you a screen in English. Then look for your destination on the long list of towns on the left side of the machine. If your destination isn't on the list (because it's too far away), you can buy the ticket on board (let the conductor know where you boarded, and you won't even have to pay the small markup for buying a ticket on the train). If your destination *is* on the list, note its four-digit code and enter it on the number pad. The machine will automatically issue you a ticket for a one-way *(Einfache)* second-class fare, but you can alter that with the buttons below the keypad (press *Hin- und Rückfahrt* if you want a round-trip ticket, and *1./2. Klasse* for first class; also note the buttons for Länder-Ticket day passes and children's tickets). Feed the machine cash (small bills are OK, but it won't take your credit card), then collect your ticket and change. *Gut gemacht!* (Well done!)

On the Train: If you have enough cash, you can buy a ticket on board from the conductor for a long-distance journey by paying a small markup (US credit cards won't work on board unless they have a chip). But if you're riding a local (short distance) train, you're expected to board with a valid ticket...or you can get fined. Note that ticket-checkers on local trains aren't necessarily in uniform.

Online: You can buy German train tickets online and print them out yourself or (for a small fee) have them delivered by mail; visit www.bahn.com and create a login and password. If you print out your own ticket, the conductor will also ask to see the ID that you specified in the booking (typically the credit card you paid with). You can also book seat reservations (optional) with a rail pass for trips within Germany—start to buy a regular ticket, then check the box for "reservation only."

Getting a Seat

As you board or exit a train, you'll usually have to push a button or flip a lever to open the door. Watch locals and imitate.

On the faster ICE, IC, and EC trains, it costs €4.50 extra per person to reserve a seat, which you can do at a station ticket desk, a touch-screen machine, or online. German trains generally offer ample seating, but popular routes do fill up, especially on holiday weekends. If your itinerary is set, and you don't mind the small fee, seat reservations can be worth it for the peace of mind. They're especially smart for small groups and families (€9 reservation cap for families).

On ICE trains, families with small children can book special compartments called *Kleinkindabteil,* which have room for strollers and diaper changing, for the regular seat-reservation price.

Note that a few fast trains require reservations (specified in schedule), but slower regional trains don't accept them. With rare exceptions, it doesn't make sense to go through a US agent to make a seat reservation in advance of your trip; just do it online or at a German station.

If you have a seat reservation, while waiting for your train to arrive, note the departure time and *Wagen* (car) number and look along the train platform for the diagram *(Wagenstandanzeiger)* that shows what sector of the platform the car will arrive at (usually A through F). Stand in that sector to avoid a last-minute dash to the right car or a long walk through the train to your seat. This is especially important for ICE trains, which are often divided into two unconnected parts.

If you're traveling without a reservation and are looking for a free seat, check the displays (or, in older trains, the slips of paper) that mark reserved seats. If you have a hard time finding an unreserved seat, take a closer look at the reservations—if you find a seat that's reserved for a leg of the journey that doesn't overlap with yours, you're free to take the seat. For example, if you're traveling from Frankfurt to Würzburg on a Munich-bound train, and you find a seat reserved only from Würzburg to Munich, it's all yours—you'll be getting off the train as the reservation-holder boards in Würzburg.

In stations without elevators, make sure to take advantage of the luggage belts along the stairs to each platform. They start automatically when you put your bag on the bottom or top of the belt.

Bikes on Board

Your bike can travel with you for €5 per day on regional trains or €9 per trip on fast trains. Deutsche Bahn's helpful website even has a list of bike-rental shops that are in or near train stations. Rentals usually run about €10 to €15 a day, and some rental outfits offer easy "pick up here and drop off there" plans.

LONG-DISTANCE BUSES

While most American travelers still find the train to be the better option—mainly because rail passes make German train travel affordable and no-hassle—cheap buses are worth considering.

Ever since the market was opened up to let long-distance bus companies compete with Deutsche Bahn, Germans have been snapping up ultra-low bus fares. For example, a full-fare (second-class) train ticket between Munich and Nürnberg costs about €55, while a bus ticket for this route can cost €20 or less (as low as €5 if you're willing to buy a few days ahead and aren't picky about departure times).

While buses don't offer as extensive a network as trains, they do cover the most popular cities for travelers (including nearly all of the destinations recommended in this book), quite often with a direct connection. The primary disadvantage to buses is a lack of travel flexibility: Buses are far less likely than trains to have a seat available for those who show up sans ticket (especially on either end of a weekend). And compared to trains, buses also offer fewer departures per day, though your options probably aren't too shabby on major routes served by multiple operators. Trains also beat buses in travel time and convenience, although often not by much. For the Munich-Nürnberg trip described above, bus travelers will spend about an hour longer en route than they would on the train (more if stuck in traffic—though train delays can happen, too).

Bus tickets are sold on the spot (on board and/or at kiosks at some bus terminals), but because the cheapest fares often sell out, it's best to book online as soon as you're sure of your plans (at a minimum, book a few days ahead to nab the best prices). The main bus operators to check out are MeinFernBus (with the most extensive network, http://meinfernbus. de), FlixBus (www.flixbus.de), Berlin Linien Bus (www.berlinlinienbus.de), and City2City, the German brand of Britain's National Express (www.city2city.de).

Though not as comfortable as trains, each company's brightly-colored buses are surprisingly well-outfitted and make for a more pleasant ride than your average Greyhound trip. Most offer free Wi-Fi (quality is variable) and on-board snack bars and WCs.

Bus terminals—in some cities a true depot with ticket kiosks and overhead shelter, in other cities just a stretch of street with a cluster of bus stops—are labeled across Germany as "ZOB" (for *Zentraler Omnibusbahnhof*—central bus station). While most cities' bus terminals are usually a block or two from the train station, in some bigger cities (such as Munich and Berlin), bus travelers have to go a little farther afield to catch their ride.

RENTING A CAR

To rent a car in Germany, you likely have to be 21 years old (most companies will not rent to anyone under that age), and restrictions and "underage fees" can apply if you're 21-24. There's generally not a maximum age limit, but if you are 75 or older, it's smart to ask. If you're considered too young or old, look into leasing (covered later), which has less-stringent age restrictions.

Research car rentals before you go. It's cheapest to arrange most car rentals from the US. Call several companies or look online to compare rates.

Most of the major US rental agencies (including Avis, Budget, Enterprise, Hertz, and Thrifty) have offices throughout Europe. The two major Europe-based agencies are Europcar and Sixt. It can be cheaper to use a consolidator, such as Auto Europe (www.autoeurope.com) or Europe by Car (www.ebctravel.com), which compares rates at several companies to get you the best deal—but because you're working with a middleman, it's especially important to ask in advance about add-on fees and restrictions.

Regardless of the car-rental company you choose, always read the fine print carefully for add-on charges—such as one-way drop-off fees, airport surcharges, or mandatory insurance policies—that aren't included in the "total price." You may need to query rental agents pointedly to find out your actual cost.

For the best deal, rent by the week with unlimited mileage. To save money on gas, ask for a diesel car. I normally rent the smallest, least-expensive model with a stick shift (generally much cheaper than an automatic). Almost all rentals are manual by default, so if you need an automatic, request one in advance; beware that these cars are usually larger models (not as maneuverable on narrow, winding roads).

Figure on paying roughly $200 for a one-week rental. Allow extra for supplemental insurance, fuel, tolls, and parking. For trips of three weeks or more, look into leasing; you'll save money on insurance and taxes.

Be warned that international trips—say, picking up in Munich and dropping off in Vienna—can be expensive (it depends partly on distance). As a rule, always tell your car-rental company up front exactly which countries you'll be entering. Some companies levy extra insurance fees for trips taken in certain countries with certain types of cars (such as BMWs, Mercedes, and convertibles). Double-check with your rental agent that you have all the documentation you need before you drive off (especially if you're crossing borders into non-Schengen countries, such as Croatia, where you might need to present proof of insurance).

Big companies have offices in most cities; ask whether they

can pick you up at your hotel. Small local rental companies can be cheaper but aren't as flexible.

Compare pickup costs (downtown can be less expensive than the airport) and explore drop-off options. Always check the hours of the location you choose: Many rental offices close from midday Saturday until Monday morning and, in smaller towns, at lunchtime. When selecting a location, don't trust the agency's description of "downtown" or "city center." In some cases, a "downtown" branch can be on the outskirts of the city—a long, costly taxi ride from the center. Before choosing, plug the addresses into a mapping website. You may find that the "train station" location is more central. But returning a car at a big-city train station or downtown agency can be tricky; get precise details on the car drop-off location and hours, and allow ample time to find it.

When you pick up the car, check it thoroughly and make sure any damage is noted on your rental agreement. Find out how your car's lights, turn signals, wipers, radio, and fuel cap function, and know what kind of fuel the car takes (diesel vs. unleaded). When you return the car, make sure the agent verifies its condition with you. Some drivers take pictures of the returned vehicle as proof of its condition.

Navigation Options

When renting a car in Europe, you have several alternatives for your digital navigator: Use your smartphone's online mapping app, download an offline map app, or rent a GPS device with your rental car (or bring your own GPS device from home).

Online mapping apps used to be prohibitively expensive for overseas travelers—but that was before most carriers started offering affordable international data plans. If you're already getting a data plan for your trip, this is probably the way to go (see "Using Your Smartphone in Europe," earlier).

A number of well-designed apps allow you much of the convenience of online maps without any costly demands on your data plan. City Maps 2Go is one of the most popular of these; OffMaps, Google Maps, and Navfree also all offer good, zoomable offline maps for much of Europe (some are better for driving, while others are better for navigating cities).

Some drivers prefer using a dedicated GPS unit—not only to avoid the data-roaming fees, but because a standalone GPS can be easier to operate (important if you're driving solo). The major downside: It's expensive—around $10-30 per day. Your car's GPS unit may only come loaded with maps for its home country—if you need additional maps, ask. Make sure your device's language is set to English before you drive off. If you have a portable GPS device at home, you can take that instead. Many American GPS devices come loaded with US maps only—you'll need to buy and download European maps before your trip. This option is far less expensive than renting.

Car Insurance Options

When you rent a car, you are liable for a very high deductible, sometimes equal to the entire value of the car. Limit your financial risk with one of these three options: Buy Collision Damage Waiver (CDW) coverage from the car-rental company, get coverage through your credit card (free, if your card automatically includes zero-deductible coverage), or get collision insurance as part of a larger travel-insurance policy.

CDW includes a very high deductible (typically $1,000-1,500). Though each rental company has its own variation, basic CDW costs $10-30 a day (figure roughly 30 percent extra) and reduces your liability, but does not eliminate it. When you pick up the car, you'll be offered the chance to "buy down" the basic deductible to zero (for an additional $10-30/day; this is sometimes called "super CDW" or "zero-deductible coverage").

If you opt for **credit-card coverage,** there's a catch. You'll technically have to decline all coverage offered by the car-rental company, which means they can place a hold on your card (which can be up to the full value of the car). In case of damage, it can be time-consuming to resolve the charges with your credit-card company. Before you decide on this option, quiz your credit-card company about how it works.

If you're already purchasing a **travel-insurance policy** for your trip, adding collision coverage is an option. For example, Travel Guard (www.travelguard.com) sells affordable renter's collision insurance as an add-on to its other policies; it's valid everywhere in Europe except the Republic of Ireland, and some Italian car-rental companies refuse to honor it, as it doesn't cover you in case of theft.

For more on car-rental insurance, see www.ricksteves.com/cdw.

Leasing

For trips of three weeks or more, consider leasing (which automatically includes zero-deductible collision and theft insurance). By technically buying and then selling back the car, you save lots of money on tax and insurance. Leasing provides you a new car with unlimited mileage and a 24-hour emergency assistance program. You can lease for as little as 21 days to as long as five and a half months. Car leases must be arranged from the US. One of many companies offering affordable lease packages is Europe by Car (www.europebycar.com/lease).

PRACTICALITIES

Driving

Road Rules: Be aware of German rules of the road; for example, kids under age 12 (or less than about 5 feet tall) must ride in an appropriate child-safety seat. It's illegal to use a mobile phone while driving—pull over or use a hands-free device. Seat belts are mandatory for all, and two beers under those belts are enough to land you in jail. You're required to use low-beam headlights if it's overcast, raining, or snowing. In Europe, you're not allowed to turn right on a red light, unless there's a sign or a signal that specifically authorizes it, and on expressways it's illegal to pass drivers on the right.

Ask your car-rental company about these rules, or check the US State Department website (www.travel.state.gov, search for your country in the "Learn about your destination" box, then click on "Travel & Transportation").

Fuel: Unleaded gasoline comes in "Super" (95 octane) and "Super Plus" (98 octane). Pumps marked "E10" or "Super E10" mean the gas contains 10 percent ethanol—make sure your rental can run on this mix. You don't have to worry about learning the German word for diesel. Your US credit and debit cards may not work at self-service gas pumps. Pay the attendant or be sure to carry sufficient cash in euros.

Navigation: Use good local maps and study them before each drive. Learn which exits you need to look out for, which major cities you'll travel toward, where the ruined castles lurk, and so on. Every long drive between my recommended destinations is via the autobahn (super-freeway), and nearly every scenic backcountry drive is paved and comfortable. Learn the universal road signs (explained in charts in most road atlases and at service stations). To get to the center of a city, follow signs for *Zentrum* or *Stadtmitte*. Ring roads go around a city.

The Autobahn: The shortest distance between any two points is the autobahn (no speed limit in many sections, toll-free). Blue signs direct you to the autobahn. To understand this complex but super-efficient freeway, look for the *Autobahn Service* booklet at any autobahn rest stop (free, lists all stops, services, road symbols, and more). Learn the signs: *Dreieck* ("three corners") means a Y-intersection; *Autobahnkreuz* is where two expressways cross. Exits are spaced about every 20 miles and often have a gas station, a restaurant, a mini-market, and sometimes a tourist information desk. Exits and intersections refer to the next major city or the nearest small town. Peruse the map and anticipate which town names to look out for. Know what you're looking for—miss it, and you're long autobahn-gone. When navigating, you'll see *nord, süd, ost,* and *west.* Electronic signs warning of dangerous conditions may include one of these words: *Unfall* (accident), *Nebel* (fog), or *Stau* (congestion).

Autobahns in Germany are famous for having no speed limit, but some sections actually do have a limit, particularly in urban areas and near complicated interchanges. Sometimes there are electronic signs with "dynamic" limits that change depending on traffic conditions. There are also cameras that take pictures of the speeder's license plate—so obey the law or be prepared to pay. In areas without an "official" maximum speed, you will commonly see a recommended speed posted. While no one gets a ticket for ignoring this recommendation, exceeding this speed means your car insurance no longer covers you in the event of an accident.

It's important to stay alert on the autobahn: Everything happens much more quickly, and the speed differential between lanes can be dangerous for unaccustomed drivers. Watch for potential lane changers, whether from your right or from behind—a roaring Mercedes can appear out of thin air in your rearview mirror.

Even if you're obeying posted limits, don't cruise in the passing lane; stay right. Since it's illegal to pass on the right on the autobahn, drivers will angrily flash their lights, and possibly tailgate, if you drive in a passing lane. Obstructing traffic on the autobahn is against the law—so running out of gas, or even cruising in the far-left lane—is not only dangerous, it can earn you a big ticket. In fast-driving Germany, the backed-up line caused by an insensitive slow driver is called an *Autoschlange,* or "car snake." What's the difference between a car snake and a real snake? According to locals, "On a real snake, the ass is in the back."

***Umweltplakette* for Driving in German Cities:** To drive into specially designated "environmental zones" or "green zones" *(Umweltzone)* in the centers of many German cities—including Munich, Freiburg, Frankfurt, Cologne, Dresden, Leipzig, and Berlin—you are required to display an *Umweltplakette.* Literally "environmental sticker," these already come standard with most German rental cars (ask when you pick up your car). If you're renting a car outside of Germany and plan to enter one of these cities, be sure you have one (sold cheap—around €6—at the border and at

PRACTICALITIES

PRACTICALITIES

Note: Your times may vary based on traffic, construction, and road conditions.

m = miles
h = hours
...... = ferry

North Sea

To Copenhagen
Flensburg
95m • 1.25h

Hamburg

NETHERLANDS

Amsterdam

GER

265m • 4.25h

310m • 4.5h

360m • 5.5h

165m • 2.5h

Cologne
40m • .75h

Brussels

90m • 1.5h
Aachen

230m • 3.5h

Erfur

BELGIUM

55m • .75h

Koblenz
25m • .5h

140m • 2.25h

Cochem
55m
1h
30m
.5h
Bacharach
60m • 1h

Frankfurt

LUX.

Trier
70m • 1h

125m • 2h

200m • 3.2

60m • 1h

Würzburg

175m • 2.5h

135m • 2.5h

100m • 1.5h

40m
.5h

Rothenburg

70m
1.25h

135m • 2h

Nürnberg

Strasbourg

Baden-Baden

40m
1h

150m • 2h

100m • 1.7h

200m • 3.25h

FRANCE

Colmar

260m • 4h

60m • 1.25h

Freiburg

175m • 3.75h

Munich

Füssen

95m • 2.25h

70m
1.5h

Zürich
55m • 1h

95m
1.75h

70m • 1.25h
Appenzell

70m
1.75h
(via Reutte)

Bern
SWITZERLAND
LIECH.

Innsbruck
To Brenner Pass

35m
1h

40m
1h

Driving in Germany

DENMARK

To Copenhagen · 100m · 1.75h

Rødby

Puttgarten

0m · 1.5h

Rostock

Baltic Sea

Sassnitz

180m · 3h

140m · 2.25h

200m · 3.25h

MANY

Berlin

60m · 1.25h

Frankfurt an der Oder

305m · 6h · To Warsaw

POLAND

200m · 3.25h

75m · 1.25h

120m · 2.25h

Wittenberg

45m · 1h

Leipzig

5m · 1.75h

70m · 1.5h

Dresden

70m · 1.25h

Görlitz

195m · 3h

95m · 3h

190m · 3h

Prague

CZECH REPUBLIC

105m · 2.253h

185m · 3.25h

240m · 4h

Český Krumlov

135m · 2.5h

140m · 3.25h

80m · 1.25h

Salzburg

125m · 2h

Melk

55m · 1.25h

Vienna

SLOVAKIA

15m · .5h

50m · 1.5h

110m · 2h

Berchtesgaden

Hallstatt

AUSTRIA

HUNGARY

50 Kilometers

50 Miles

PRACTICALITIES

gas stations; you'll need the registration and legal paperwork that came with your rental; see www.umwelt-plakette.de).

Parking: To park, pick up a cardboard clock (*Parkscheibe*, available free at gas stations, police stations, and *Tabak* shops). Display your arrival time on the clock and put it on the dashboard, so parking attendants can see you've been there less than the posted maximum stay. Your US credit and debit cards may not work at automated parking garages—bring cash.

Driving in Austria: If you side-trip by car into Austria, bring your US driver's license and get an International Driving Permit (for details, go to www.ricksteves.com and search for "IDP"). Austria charges drivers who use their expressways. You'll need to have a *Vignette* sticker stuck to the inside of your rental car's windshield (buy at the border crossing, big gas stations near borders, or a rental-car agency). Place it on your windshield exactly as shown on the back of the sticker, and keep the lower tear-off portion—it's your receipt. The cost is €8.50 for 10 days, or €24.80 for two months. Dipping into the country on regular roads—such as around Reutte in Tirol—requires no special payment. In Austria, green signs direct you to the autobahn, and autobahn speed limits are enforced.

FLIGHTS

The best comparison search engine for both international and intra-European flights is www.kayak.com. For inexpensive flights within Europe, try www.skyscanner.com or www.hipmunk.com; for inexpensive international flights, try www.vayama.com.

Flying to Europe: Start looking for international flights four to five months before your trip, especially for peak-season travel. Off-season tickets can be purchased a month or so in advance. Depending on your itinerary, it can be efficient to fly into one city and out of another. If your flight requires a connection in Europe, see our hints on navigating Europe's top hub airports at www.ricksteves.com/hub-airports.

Flying within Europe: If you're considering a train ride that's more than five hours long, a flight may save you both time and money. When comparing your options, factor in the time it takes to get to the airport and how early you'll need to arrive to check in.

Well-known cheapo airlines include easyJet (www.easyjet.com) and Ryanair (www.ryanair.com). Those based in Germany are Air Berlin (www.airberlin.com), Germanwings (www.germanwings.com), and TUIfly (www.tuifly.com).

Be aware of the potential drawbacks of flying on the cheap: nonrefundable and nonchangeable tickets, minimal or nonexistent customer service, treks to airports far outside town, and stingy baggage allowances with steep overage fees. If you're traveling with lots of luggage, a cheap flight can quickly become a bad deal. To avoid unpleasant surprises, read the small print before you book.

Resources

RESOURCES FROM RICK STEVES

Rick Steves Germany 2015 is one of many books in my series on European travel, which includes country guidebooks, city and regional guidebooks, Snapshot guides (excerpted chapters from my country guides), Pocket Guides (full-color little books on big cities), and my budget-travel skills handbook, *Rick Steves Europe Through the Back Door*. Most of my titles are available as ebooks. My phrase books—for German, French, Italian, Spanish, and Portuguese—are practical and budget-oriented. My other books include *Europe 101* (a crash course on art and history designed for travelers); *Mediterranean Cruise Ports* and *Northern European Cruise Ports* (how to make the most of your time in port); and *Travel as a Political Act* (a travelogue sprinkled with tips for bringing home a global perspective). A more complete list of my titles appears near the end of this book.

Video: My public television series, *Rick Steves' Europe*, covers European destinations in 100 shows, with four episodes on Germany plus one on Salzburg. To watch full episodes online for free, see www.ricksteves.com/tv. Or to raise your travel I.Q. with video versions of our popular classes, including talks on Germany and Austria, see www.ricksteves.com/travel-talks.

Audio: My weekly public radio show, *Travel with Rick Steves*, features interviews with travel experts from around the world. I've also produced free, self-guided **audio tours** of the top sights in Munich, Berlin, Salzburg, and along the Rhine River. All of this audio content is available for free at Rick Steves Audio Europe, an extensive online library organized by destination. Choose whatever interests you, and download it for free via the Rick Steves Audio Europe smartphone app, www.ricksteves.com/audioeurope, iTunes, or Google Play.

PRACTICALITIES

Begin Your Trip
at www.RickSteves.com

My **website** is *the* place to explore Europe. You'll find thousands of fun articles, videos, photos, and radio interviews on European destinations; money-saving tips for planning your dream trip; monthly travel news; my travel talks and travel blog; my latest guidebook updates (www.ricksteves.com/update); and my free Rick Steves Audio Europe app. You can also follow me on Facebook and Twitter.

Our **Travel Forum** is an immense, yet well-groomed collection of message boards, where our travel-savvy community answers questions and shares their personal travel experiences (www.ricksteves.com/forums).

Our **online Travel Store** offers travel bags and accessories that I've designed specifically to help you travel smarter and lighter. These include my popular bags (rolling carry-on and backpack versions), money belts, totes, toiletries kits, adapters, other accessories, and a wide selection of guidebooks, planning maps, and DVDs.

Choosing the right **rail pass** for your trip—amid hundreds of options—can drive you nutty. Our website will help you find the perfect fit for your itinerary and your budget: We offer easy, one-stop shopping for rail passes, seat reservations, and point-to-point tickets.

Want to travel with greater efficiency and less stress? We organize **tours** with more than three dozen itineraries and more than 800 departures reaching the best destinations in this book...and beyond. We offer a 14-day tour of Germany, Austria, and Switzerland; a 12-day tour of Berlin, Prague, and Vienna; and a 12-day "unguided" My Way tour (covering hotel and transportation) of alpine destinations in Germany, Austria, Italy, Switzerland, and France. You'll enjoy great guides, a fun bunch of travel partners (with small groups of 24 to 28 travelers), and plenty of room to spread out in a big, comfy bus when touring between towns. You'll find European adventures to fit every vacation length. For all the details, and to get our Tour Catalog and a free Rick Steves Tour Experience DVD (filmed on location during an actual tour), visit www.ricksteves.com or call the Tour Department at 425/608-4217.

MAPS

The black-and-white maps in this book are concise and simple, designed to help you locate recommended places and get to local TIs, where you can pick up more in-depth maps of cities or regions (usually free). Better maps are sold at newsstands and bookstores. Before you buy a map, look at it to be sure it has the level of detail you want.

European bookstores, especially in touristy areas, have good selections of maps. For drivers, I'd recommend a 1:200,000- or 1:300,000-scale map. Train travelers usually manage fine with the freebies they get with the train pass and from the local tourist offices.

RECOMMENDED BOOKS AND MOVIES

To learn more about Germany past and present, check out a few of these books and films.

Nonfiction

Anne Frank: The Diary of a Young Girl (Anne Frank, 1947). Frankfurt-born Anne Frank chronicles the two years her family spent hiding in the secret annex of their Amsterdam business.

Berlin Diary: The Journal of a Foreign Correspondent (William Shirer, 1941). Stationed in Berlin from 1934 until 1940, CBS radio broadcaster Shirer delivers a vivid, harrowing account of the rise of Nazi Germany.

Culture Shock! Germany (Richard Lord, 2008). Cultural insights on German customs and etiquette.

Here I Stand: A Life of Martin Luther (Roland Bainton, 1950). Authoritative biography of the man who initiated the Reformation.

In the Garden of Beasts (Erik Larson, 2011). A chronicle of 1930s Berlin, seen through the eyes of America's ambassador to Nazi Germany and his daughter.

Inside the Third Reich (Albert Speer, 1970). Based on 1,200 manuscript pages, this authoritative account of the years 1933-1945 was written by Hitler's main architect.

Martin Luther: A Life (Martin E. Marty, 2004). A short, vivid biography of the irascible German reformer who transformed Western Christianity.

Night (Elie Wiesel, 1960). Candid and horrific account of survival in a Nazi concentration camp.

Peeling the Onion (Günter Grass, 2007). Memoir of the Nobel Prize-winning author's childhood in Danzig and experiences as a drafted member of the Waffen SS.

Stasiland: Stories from Behind the Berlin Wall (Anna Funder, 2002). A powerful account about the secrets of the Stasi, the East German Ministry for State Security, and how it affected the citizens of East Germany.

When in Germany, Do as the Germans Do (Hyde Flippo, 2002). The do's and don'ts of being German.

PRACTICALITIES

Fiction

1632 (Eric Flint, 2000). This sci-fi/time travel book sends West Virginians back to 17th-century Germany.

Address Unknown (Kathrine Kressmann Taylor, 1939). Published before World War II and banished in Nazi Germany, a series of letters between a Jewish art dealer living in San Francisco and his former business partner, which warns of the terrors yet to come.

All Quiet on the Western Front (Erich Maria Remarque, 1929). Young German classmates enlist in the German Army of World War I, only to find that war is not about glory and pride.

Berlin Noir (Philip Kerr, 1993). An ex-policeman turned detective struggles with secrets and crime in 1930s and '40s Berlin.

The Book Thief (Markus Zusak, 2007). Award-winning novel about a German girl who steals books and shares them with victims of World War II.

Floating in My Mother's Palm (Ursula Hegi, 1998). This bestselling novel follows the life of a young girl growing up in 1950s Burgdorf, a small German town on the Rhine.

The Magic Mountain (Thomas Mann, 1924). One of Germany's most influential and celebrated works of the 20th century takes place in a sanatorium in the Swiss Alps before and during World War I. Other good titles by Mann include *Death in Venice* and *Buddenbrooks*.

Marrying Mozart (Stephanie Cowell, 2008). This novel reveals a more intimate side of the famous composer.

Narcissus and Goldmund (Hermann Hesse, 1930). A story about two medieval men, one choosing life in a monastery and the other traveling the world. Also by German-born Hesse is the popular *Siddhartha,* about a young man leaving his family.

The Reader (Bernhard Schlink, 1995). Told by a sympathetic narrator, this book challenges readers to ponder, "What if my loved ones had been Nazis?"

Saints and Villains (Denise Giardina, 1999). Fictionalized account of Dietrich Bonhoeffer, a Protestant theologian who protested against Hitler's rise.

The Silent Angel (Heinrich Böll, 1994). Soldier Hans Schnitzler returns from World War II unknowingly secreting a will that will change his life. Also by Böll: *Group Portrait with Lady,* about a war widow's attempt to save her Cologne apartment building from being demolished.

The Tin Drum (Günter Grass, 1959). A young boy stands defiant against the Nazis, armed with only a drum and a piercing scream.

Film and TV

The Baader Meinhof Complex (2008). The still-fragile German democracy is rocked in 1967 by acts of terrorism committed by radicalized Germans.

Backbeat (1994). Chronicles the years the Beatles played in Hamburg just before becoming famous.

Cabaret (1972). With Hitler on the rise and anti-Semitism growing, the only refuge in Berlin is in the Cabaret.

Das Boot (1981). A war film following the crew of a U-boat as they search for Allies during World War II.

Downfall (2004). The story of the Führer's final days.

Good Bye, Lenin! (2003). A funny, poignant look at a son's struggle to re-create long-gone Eastern Europe for his mother.

Hannah Arendt (2012). Film about the woman who reported on Adolf Eichmann's Nazi war crimes trial for the *New Yorker*.

The Lives of Others (2006). A member of East Germany's secret police becomes too close to the lives he surveils.

Lore (2012). With Allies swarming Germany, one girl must lead her siblings to safety.

The Marriage of Maria Braun (1979). Gritty meditation on post-WWII Germany, seen through the romantic woes of a young woman.

Mephisto (1981). Allegorical tale about one man's artistic approach to the Nazis' rise to power.

The Miracle of Bern (2008). The story of a West German soccer team's unexpected win in the 1954 World Cup in Bern.

Nowhere in Africa (2001). In this Best Foreign Language Film winner, Jewish refugees flee Germany in the 1930s and settle in Kenya.

Schindler's List (1993). A factory owner's inspirational efforts to save his Jewish employees from deportation to concentration camps, this movie won Steven Spielberg the Best Picture and Best Director Oscars.

Shoah (1985). A 9.5-hour Holocaust documentary that includes no wartime footage, only interviews with those who lived through it.

Sophie Scholl: The Final Days (2005). Beautiful, devastating account of a student who defied Hitler.

The Tin Drum (1979). Based on Günter Grass' seminal novel.

Triumph of the Will (1935). Leni Riefenstahl's infamous Nazi propaganda turned film classic.

Two Lives (2012). Bouncing between Norway and Germany, this film explores the struggle of war children through one Norwegian woman's experience.

The Wave (2008). Students at a high school quickly learn how easy

PRACTICALITIES

it is to give in to the same social forces that enabled Nazi Germany (based on a real-life classroom experiment from 1967).

The White Ribbon (2009). A black-and-white film depicting the roots of evil through the story of a family in Germany just before World War I.

The White Rose (1982). A group of Munich students questions the Nazi government.

Wings of Desire (1987). Set in Berlin, Wim Wenders' best film depicts an angel who falls in love and falls to earth.

APPENDIX

Contents

Useful Contacts

Emergency Needs
Police and Ambulance: Tel. 112

Embassies
US Embassy in Berlin: Pariser Platz 2, tel. 030/83050; consular services at Clayallee 170, open by appointment only Mon-Fri 8:30-12:00, closed Sat-Sun and last Thu of month, tel. 030/8305-1200—consular services calls answered Mon-Thu 14:00-16:00 only, germany.usembassy.gov

Canadian Embassy in Berlin: Consular services open Mon-Fri 9:00-12:00, closed Sat-Sun; Leipziger Platz 17, tel. 030/203-120, www.germany.gc.ca

Directory Assistance
Directory Assistance: Tel. 11833
International Directory Assistance: Tel. 11834

Information
Train Info: Tel. 0180-599-6633; ask for an English speaker.
German Tourist Offices: Dial the local area code, then 19433.

2015

JANUARY
S	M	T	W	T	F	S
				1	2	3
4	5	6	7	8	9	10
11	12	13	14	15	16	17
18	19	20	21	22	23	24
25	26	27	28	29	30	31

FEBRUARY
S	M	T	W	T	F	S
1	2	3	4	5	6	7
8	9	10	11	12	13	14
15	16	17	18	19	20	21
22	23	24	25	26	27	28

MARCH
S	M	T	W	T	F	S
1	2	3	4	5	6	7
8	9	10	11	12	13	14
15	16	17	18	19	20	21
22	23	24	25	26	27	28
29	30	31				

APRIL
S	M	T	W	T	F	S
			1	2	3	4
5	6	7	8	9	10	11
12	13	14	15	16	17	18
19	20	21	22	23	24	25
26	27	28	29	30		

MAY
S	M	T	W	T	F	S
					1	2
3	4	5	6	7	8	9
10	11	12	13	14	15	16
17	18	19	20	21	22	23
24/31	25	26	27	28	29	30

JUNE
S	M	T	W	T	F	S
	1	2	3	4	5	6
7	8	9	10	11	12	13
14	15	16	17	18	19	20
21	22	23	24	25	26	27
28	29	30				

JULY
S	M	T	W	T	F	S
			1	2	3	4
5	6	7	8	9	10	11
12	13	14	15	16	17	18
19	20	21	22	23	24	25
26	27	28	29	30	31	

AUGUST
S	M	T	W	T	F	S
						1
2	3	4	5	6	7	8
9	10	11	12	13	14	15
16	17	18	19	20	21	22
23/30	24/31	25	26	27	28	29

SEPTEMBER
S	M	T	W	T	F	S
		1	2	3	4	5
6	7	8	9	10	11	12
13	14	15	16	17	18	19
20	21	22	23	24	25	26
27	28	29	30			

OCTOBER
S	M	T	W	T	F	S
				1	2	3
4	5	6	7	8	9	10
11	12	13	14	15	16	17
18	19	20	21	22	23	24
25	26	27	28	29	30	31

NOVEMBER
S	M	T	W	T	F	S
1	2	3	4	5	6	7
8	9	10	11	12	13	14
15	16	17	18	19	20	21
22	23	24	25	26	27	28
29	30					

DECEMBER
S	M	T	W	T	F	S
		1	2	3	4	5
6	7	8	9	10	11	12
13	14	15	16	17	18	19
20	21	22	23	24	25	26
27	28	29	30	31		

Holidays and Festivals

This list includes selected festivals in major cities, plus national holidays observed throughout Germany. Many sights and banks close on national holidays—keep this in mind when planning your itinerary. Austria's Salzburg has music festivals nearly every month. Before planning a trip around a festival, make sure you verify the dates by checking the festival's website or the German national tourist office (www.cometogermany.com).

Jan 6	Epiphany (Heilige Drei Könige)
Early Jan	Perchtenlaufen (winter festival, parades), Tirol and Salzburg, Austria
Feb 16-18	Fasching (carnival season, balls, parades in the days leading up to Ash Wednesday), throughout Germany

April 3	Good Friday
April 5	Easter (Ostern); Easter Festival, Salzburg
April 6	Easter Monday (Ostermontag)
May 1	May Day with maypole dances, throughout Austria and Germany
May 14	Ascension
May 22-25 (Pentecost weekend)	Carnival of Cultures (www.karneval-berlin.de), Berlin; Meistertrunk Show (play and market, medieval costumes, *Biergarten* parties, www.meistertrunk.de), Rothenburg
May 24-25	Pentecost (Pfingsten) and Pentecost Monday (Pfingstmontag)
June 4	Corpus Christi (Fronleichnam), southern and western Germany
June	Fressgass' Fest (www.frankfurt-tourismus.de), Frankfurt
Late June	City Festival (www.elbhangfest.de), Dresden; Frankfurt Summertime Festival (arts); Midsummer Eve Celebrations, Austria
July 11	Lichter Festival (fireworks and music, www.koelner-lichter.de), Cologne
July 17-26	Kinderzeche Festival (www.kinderzeche.de), Dinkelsbühl
Late July-Early Aug	Klassik Open Air (fireworks and classical music, www.klassikopenair.de), Nürnberg
Late July-Early Aug	Bardentreffen Nürnberg (world music, www.bardentreffen.de/english-infos)
Late July-Aug	Salzburg Festival (music, www.salzburgerfestspiele.at)
Aug 15	Assumption (Mariä Himmelfahrt)
Aug (last weekend)	Museum Riverbank Festival (www.frankfurt-tourismus.de), Frankfurt
Late Aug-Early Sept	Rheingau Wine Festival (www.frankfurt-tourismus.de), Frankfurt
Sept	International Literature Festival (www.literaturfestival.com), Berlin
Sept 6-7	Reichsstadt Festival (fireworks), Rothenburg
Sept 19-Oct 4	Oktoberfest (www.oktoberfest.de), Munich

Oct 3	German Unity Day (Tag der Deutschen Einheit)
Oct 31	Reformation Day celebration, Wittenberg
Nov	Jazzfest Berlin (www.berlinerfestspiele.de)
Nov 1	All Saints' Day (Allerheiligen), southern and western Germany
Nov 11	St. Martin's Day (Martinstag, feasts)
Dec	Christmas markets throughout Germany, good ones in Nürnberg, Munich, Rothenburg, and Freiburg
Dec 6	St. Nikolaus Day (parades), throughout Germany
Dec 24	Christmas Eve (Heiliger Abend), when Germans celebrate Christmas
Dec 25	Christmas
Dec 31	New Year's Eve (Silvester, fireworks), throughout Germany, especially lively in Berlin

Conversions and Climate

NUMBERS AND STUMBLERS

- Europeans write a few of their numbers differently than we do. 1 = 1, 4 = 4, 7 = 7.
- In Europe, dates appear as day/month/year, so Christmas 2015 is 25/12/15.
- Commas are decimal points and decimals are commas. A dollar and a half is 1,50, one thousand is 1.000, and there are 5.280 feet in a mile.
- When counting with fingers, start with your thumb. If you hold up your first finger to request one item, you'll probably get two.
- What Americans call the second floor of a building is the first floor in Europe.
- On escalators and moving sidewalks, Europeans keep the left "lane" open for passing. Keep to the right.

METRIC CONVERSIONS

A kilogram is 2.2 pounds, and 1 liter is about a quart, or almost four to a gallon. A kilometer is six-tenths of a mile. I figure kilometers to miles by cutting them in half and adding back 10 percent of the original (120 km: 60 + 12 = 72 miles, 300 km: 150 + 30 = 180 miles).

APPENDIX

1 foot = 0.3 meter
1 yard = 0.9 meter
1 mile = 1.6 kilometers
1 centimeter = 0.4 inch
1 meter = 39.4 inches
1 kilometer = 0.62 mile

1 square yard = 0.8 square meter
1 square mile = 2.6 square kilometers
1 ounce = 28 grams
1 quart = 0.95 liter
1 kilogram = 2.2 pounds
32°F = 0°C

CLOTHING SIZES

When shopping for clothing, use these US-to-European comparisons as general guidelines (but note that no conversion is perfect).

- Women's dresses and blouses: Add 30
  (US size 10 = European size 40)
- Men's suits and jackets: Add 10
  (US size 40 regular = European size 50)
- Men's shirts: Multiply by 2 and add about 8
  (US size 15 collar = European size 38)
- Women's shoes: Add about 30
  (US size 8 = European size 38-39)
- Men's shoes: Add 32-34
  (US size 9 = European size 41; US size 11 = European size 45)

GERMANY'S CLIMATE

J	F	M	A	M	J	J	A	S	O	N	D

GERMANY • Berlin

J	F	M	A	M	J	J	A	S	O	N	D
35°	37°	46°	56°	66°	72°	75°	74°	68°	56°	45°	38°
26°	26°	31°	39°	47°	53°	57°	56°	50°	42°	36°	29°
14	13	19	17	19	17	17	17	18	17	14	16

GERMANY • Munich

J	F	M	A	M	J	J	A	S	O	N	D
35°	38°	48°	56°	64°	70°	74°	73°	67°	56°	44°	36°
23°	23°	30°	38°	45°	51°	55°	54°	48°	40°	33°	26°
15	12	18	15	16	13	15	15	17	18	15	16

APPENDIX

First line, average daily high; second line, average daily low; third line, average days without rain. For more detailed weather statistics for destinations in this book (as well as the rest of the world), check www.wunderground.com.

FAHRENHEIT AND CELSIUS CONVERSION

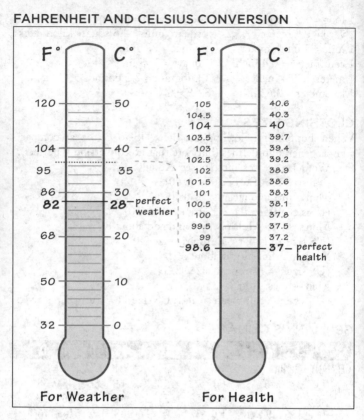

For Weather | For Health

Europe takes its temperature using the Celsius scale, while we opt for Fahrenheit. For a rough conversion from Celsius to Fahrenheit, double the number and add 30. For weather, remember that 28°C is 82°F— perfect. For health, 37°C is just right. At a launderette, 30°C is cold, 40°C is warm (usually the default setting), 60°C is hot, and 95°C is boiling.

Packing Checklist

Whether you're traveling for five days or five weeks, you won't need more than this. Pack light to enjoy the sweet freedom of true mobility.

Clothing

- ❑ 5 shirts: long- & short-sleeve
- ❑ 2 pairs pants or skirt
- ❑ 1 pair shorts or capris
- ❑ 5 pairs underwear & socks
- ❑ 1 pair walking shoes
- ❑ Sweater or fleece top
- ❑ Rainproof jacket with hood
- ❑ Tie or scarf
- ❑ Swimsuit
- ❑ Sleepwear

Money

- ❑ Debit card
- ❑ Credit card(s)
- ❑ Hard cash ($20 bills)
- ❑ Money belt or neck wallet

Documents & Travel Info

- ❑ Passport
- ❑ Airline reservations
- ❑ Rail pass/train reservations
- ❑ Car-rental voucher
- ❑ Driver's license
- ❑ Student ID, hostel card, etc.
- ❑ Photocopies of all the above
- ❑ Hotel confirmations
- ❑ Insurance details
- ❑ Guidebooks & maps
- ❑ Notepad & pen
- ❑ Journal

Toiletries Kit

- ❑ Toiletries
- ❑ Medicines & vitamins
- ❑ First-aid kit
- ❑ Glasses/contacts/sunglasses (with prescriptions)
- ❑ Earplugs
- ❑ Packet of tissues (for WC)

Miscellaneous

- ❑ Daypack
- ❑ Sealable plastic baggies
- ❑ Laundry soap
- ❑ Spot remover
- ❑ Clothesline
- ❑ Sewing kit
- ❑ Travel alarm/watch

Electronics

- ❑ Smartphone or mobile phone
- ❑ Camera & related gear
- ❑ Tablet/ereader/media player
- ❑ Laptop & flash drive
- ❑ Earbuds or headphones
- ❑ Chargers
- ❑ Plug adapters

Optional Extras

- ❑ Flipflops or slippers
- ❑ Mini-umbrella or poncho
- ❑ Travel hairdryer
- ❑ Belt
- ❑ Hat (for sun or cold)
- ❑ Picnic supplies
- ❑ Water bottle
- ❑ Fold-up tote bag
- ❑ Small flashlight
- ❑ Small binoculars
- ❑ Insect repellent
- ❑ Small towel or washcloth
- ❑ Inflatable pillow
- ❑ Some duct tape (for repairs)
- ❑ Tiny lock
- ❑ Address list (to mail postcards)
- ❑ Postcards/photos from home
- ❑ Extra passport photos
- ❑ Good book

APPENDIX

German Survival Phrases

In the phonetics, ī sounds like the long i in "light," and bolded syllables are stressed.

English	German	Pronunciation
Good day.	Guten Tag.	**goo**-tehn tahg
Do you speak English?	Sprechen Sie Englisch?	**shprehkh**-ehn zee **ehgn**-lish
Yes. / No.	Ja. / Nein.	yah / nīn
I (don't) understand.	Ich verstehe (nicht).	ikh fehr-**shtay**-heh (nikht)
Please.	Bitte.	**bit**-teh
Thank you.	Danke.	**dahng**-keh
I'm sorry.	Es tut mir leid.	ehs toot meer līt
Excuse me.	Entschuldigung.	ehnt-**shool**-dig-oong
(No) problem.	(Kein) Problem.	(kīn) proh-**blaym**
(Very) good.	(Sehr) gut.	(zehr) goot
Goodbye.	Auf Wiedersehen.	owf **vee**-der-zayn
one / two	eins / zwei	īns / tsvī
three / four	drei / vier	drī / feer
five / six	fünf / sechs	fewnf / zehkhs
seven / eight	sieben / acht	**zee**-behn / ahkht
nine / ten	neun / zehn	noyn / tsayn
How much is it?	Wieviel kostet das?	**vee**-feel **kohs**-teht dahs
Write it?	Schreiben?	**shrī**-behn
Is it free?	Ist es umsonst?	ist ehs oom-**zohnst**
Included?	Inklusive?	in-kloo-**zee**-veh
Where can I buy / find...?	Wo kann ich kaufen / finden...?	voh kahn ikh **kow**-fehn / **fin**-dehn
I'd like / We'd like...	Ich hätte gern / Wir hätten gern...	ikh **heh**-teh gehrn / veer **heh**-tehn gehrn
...a room.	...ein Zimmer.	īn **tsim**-mer
...a ticket to ____.	...eine Fahrkarte nach ____.	**ī**-neh **far**-kar-teh nahkh
Is it possible?	Ist es möglich?	ist ehs **mur**-glikh
Where is...?	Wo ist...?	voh ist
...the train station	...der Bahnhof	dehr **bahn**-hohf
...the bus station	...der Busbahnhof	dehr **boos**-bahn-hohf
...the tourist information office	...das Touristen-informations-büro	dahs too-**ris**-tehn-in-for-maht-see-**ohns**-**bew**-roh
...the toilet	...die Toilette	dee toh-**leh**-teh
men	Herren	**hehr**-rehn
women	Damen	**dah**-mehn
left / right	links / rechts	links / rehkhts
straight	geradeaus	geh-**rah**-deh-**ows**
What time does this open / close?	Um wieviel Uhr wird hier geöffnet / geschlossen?	oom **vee**-feel oor veerd heer geh-**urf**-neht / geh-**shloh**-sehn
At what time?	Um wieviel Uhr?	oom **vee**-feel oor
Just a moment.	Moment.	moh-**mehnt**
now / soon / later	jetzt / bald / später	yehtst / bahld / **shpay**-ter
today / tomorrow	heute / morgen	**hoy**-teh / **mor**-gehn

In a German Restaurant

English	German	Pronunciation
I'd like / We'd like...	Ich hätte gern / Wir hätten gern...	ikh **heh**-teh gehrn / veer **heh**-tehn gehrn
...a reservation for...	...eine Reservierung für...	ī-neh reh-zer-**feer**-oong fewr
...a table for one / two.	...einen Tisch für eine Person / zwei Personen.	ī-nehn tish fewr ī-neh pehr-zohn / tsvī pehr-**zoh**-nehn
Non-smoking.	Nichtraucher.	**nikht**-rowkh-er
Is this seat free?	Ist hier frei?	ist heer frī
Menu (in English), please.	Speisekarte (auf Englisch), bitte.	**shpī**-zeh-kar-teh (owf **ehng**-lish) **bit**-teh
service (not) included	Trinkgeld (nicht) inklusive	**trink**-gehlt (nikht) in-kloo-**zee**-veh
cover charge	Eintritt	**īn**-trit
to go	zum Mitnehmen	tsoom **mit**-nay-mehn
with / without	mit / ohne	mit / **oh**-neh
and / or	und / oder	oont / **oh**-der
menu (of the day)	(Tages-) Karte	(**tah**-gehs-) **kar**-teh
set meal for tourists	Touristenmenü	too-**ris**-tehn-meh-**new**
specialty of the house	Spezialität des Hauses	**shpayt**-see-ah-lee-**tayt** dehs **how**-zehs
appetizers	Vorspeise	**for**-shpī-zeh
bread / cheese	Brot / Käse	broht / **kay**-zeh
sandwich	Sandwich	**zahnd**-vich
soup	Suppe	**zup**-peh
salad	Salat	zah-**laht**
meat	Fleisch	flīsh
poultry	Geflügel	geh-**flew**-gehl
fish	Fisch	fish
seafood	Meeresfrüchte	**meh**-rehs-**frewkh**-teh
fruit	Obst	ohpst
vegetables	Gemüse	geh-**mew**-zeh
dessert	Nachspeise	**nahkh**-shpī-zeh
mineral water	Mineralwasser	min-eh-**rahl**-vah-ser
tap water	Leitungswasser	**lī**-toongs-vah-ser
milk	Milch	milkh
(orange) juice	(Orangen-) Saft	(oh-**rahn**-zhehn-) zahft
coffee / tea	Kaffee / Tee	kah-**fay** / tay
wine	Wein	vīn
red / white	rot / weiß	roht / vīs
glass / bottle	Glas / Flasche	glahs / **flah**-sheh
beer	Bier	beer
Cheers!	Prost!	prohst
More. / Another.	Mehr. / Noch eins.	mehr / nohkh īns
The same.	Das gleiche.	dahs **glīkh**-eh
Bill, please.	Rechnung, bitte.	**rehkh**-noong **bit**-teh
tip	Trinkgeld	**trink**-gehlt
Delicious!	Lecker!	**lehk**-er

For more user-friendly German phrases, check out *Rick Steves' German Phrase Book and Dictionary* or *Rick Steves' French, Italian & German Phrase Book*.

APPENDIX

INDEX

INDEX

MAP INDEX

Explore Europe

At ricksteves.com you can browse through thousands of articles, videos, photos and radio interviews, plus find a wealth of money-saving travel tips for planning your dream trip. And with our mobile-friendly website, you can easily access all this great travel information anywhere you go.

TV Shows

Preview the places you'll visit by watching entire half-hour episodes of Rick Steves' Europe (choose from all 100 shows) on-demand, for free.

ricksteves.com

your travel dreams into affordable reality

Radio Interviews

Enjoy ready access to Rick's vast library of radio interviews covering travel

tips and cultural insights that relate specifically to your Europe travel plans.

Travel Forums

Learn, ask, share! Our online community of savvy travelers is a great resource for first-time travelers to Europe, as well as seasoned pros. You'll find forums on each country, plus travel tips and restaurant/hotel reviews. You can even ask one of our well-traveled staff to chime in with an opinion.

Travel News

Subscribe to our free Travel News e-newsletter, and get monthly updates from Rick on what's happening in Europe.

Audio Europe™

Rick's Free Travel App

Get your FREE **Rick Steves Audio Europe**™ app to enjoy…

- Dozens of self-guided tours of Europe's top museums, sights and historic walks

- Hundreds of tracks filled with cultural insights and sightseeing tips from Rick's radio interviews

- All organized into handy geographic playlists

- For iPhone, iPad, iPod Touch, Android

With Rick whispering in your ear, Europe gets even better.

Find out more at ricksteves.com

Pack Light and Right

Gear up for your next adventure at ricksteves.com

Light Luggage

Pack light and right with Rick Steves' affordable, custom-designed rolling carry-on bags, backpacks, day packs and shoulder bags.

Accessories

From packing cubes to moneybelts and beyond, Rick has personally selected the travel goodies that will help your trip go smoother.

Shop at ricksteves.com

Rick Steves has

Experience maximum Europe

Save time and energy

This guidebook is your independent-travel toolkit. But for all it delivers, it's still up to you to devote the time and energy it takes to manage the preparation and logistics that are essential for a happy trip. If that's a hassle, there's a solution.

Rick Steves Tours

A Rick Steves tour takes you to Europe's most interesting places with great

great tours, too!

with minimum stress

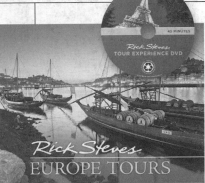

guides and small groups of 28 or less. We follow Rick's favorite itineraries, ride in comfy buses, stay in family-run hotels, and bring you intimately close to the Europe you've traveled so far to see. Most importantly, we take away the logistical headaches so you can focus on the fun.

customers—along with us on 40 different itineraries, from Ireland to Italy to Istanbul. Is a Rick Steves tour the right fit for your travel dreams? Find out at ricksteves.com, where you can also get Rick's latest tour catalog and free Tour Experience DVD.

Join the fun

This year we'll take 18,000 free-spirited travelers— nearly half of them repeat

Europe is best experienced with happy travel partners. We hope you can join us.

See our itineraries at ricksteves.com

EUROPE GUIDES

Best of Europe
Eastern Europe
Europe Through the Back Door
Mediterranean Cruise Ports
Northern European Cruise Ports

COUNTRY GUIDES

Croatia & Slovenia
England
France
Germany
Great Britain
Ireland
Italy
Portugal
Scandinavia
Spain
Switzerland

CITY & REGIONAL GUIDES

Amsterdam, Bruges & Brussels
Barcelona
Budapest
Florence & Tuscany
Greece: Athens & the Peloponnese
Istanbul
London
Paris
Prague & the Czech Republic
Provence & the French Riviera
Rome
Venice
Vienna, Salzburg & Tirol

SNAPSHOT GUIDES

Basque Country: Spain & France
Berlin
Bruges & Brussels
Copenhagen & the Best of
   Denmark
Dublin
Dubrovnik
Hill Towns of Central Italy
Italy's Cinque Terre
Krakow, Warsaw & Gdansk
Lisbon
Madrid & Toledo
Milan & the Italian Lakes District
Munich, Bavaria & Salzburg
Naples & the Amalfi Coast
Northern Ireland
Norway
Scotland
Sevilla, Granada & Southern Spain
Stockholm

POCKET GUIDES

Amsterdam
Athens
Barcelona
Florence
London
Paris
Rome
Venice

Rick Steves guidebooks are published by Avalon Travel,
a member of the Perseus Books Group.

NOW AVAILABLE:
eBOOKS, DVD & BLU-RAY

TRAVEL CULTURE

Europe 101
European Christmas
Postcards from Europe
Travel as a Political Act

eBOOKS

Nearly all Rick Steves guides are available as ebooks. Check with your favorite bookseller.

RICK STEVES' EUROPE DVDs

11 New Shows 2013–2014
Austria & the Alps
Eastern Europe
England & Wales
European Christmas
European Travel Skills & Specials
France
Germany, BeNeLux & More
Greece, Turkey & Portugal
Iran
Ireland & Scotland
Italy's Cities
Italy's Countryside
Scandinavia
Spain
Travel Extras

BLU-RAY

Celtic Charms
Eastern Europe Favorites
European Christmas
Italy Through the Back Door
Mediterranean Mosaic
Surprising Cities of Europe

PHRASE BOOKS & DICTIONARIES

French
French, Italian & German
German
Italian
Portuguese
Spanish

JOURNALS

Rick Steves Pocket Travel Journal
Rick Steves Travel Journal

PLANNING MAPS

Britain, Ireland & London
Europe
France & Paris
Germany, Austria & Switzerland
Ireland
Italy
Spain & Portugal

RickSteves.com 🅕 🅣 **@RickSteves**

Rick Steves books and DVDs are available at bookstores and through online booksellers.

Photo © Patricia Feaster

Credits

RESEARCHERS
To help update this book, Rick relied on...

Sandra Hundacker
A German immigrant herself, Sandra developed a passion for travel when her parents took her to numerous countries throughout the Continent (including Eastern Europe during the Cold War). Sandra lives in Seattle and creates maps and graphics for Rick Steves guidebooks.

Gretchen Strauch
Before Gretchen became an online editor for Rick Steves, she lived in Konstanz, Germany, for three years, where she taught English and became an expert on the *Eiscafes* of southern Germany. She still does not like sauerkraut.

Cary Walker
Cary started traveling internationally during college and never stopped. A former teacher, she believes that Europe is the best classroom for those who travel with an open mind. When not researching guidebooks or leading Rick Steves tours, she lives in Dallas planning her next adventure.

Ian Watson
Ian has worked with Rick's guidebooks since 1993, after starting out with Let's Go and Frommer's guides. Originally from upstate New York, Ian speaks several European languages, including German, and makes his home in Reykjavík, Iceland.

CONTRIBUTOR
Gene Openshaw
Gene is the co-author of a dozen Rick Steves books. For this book, he wrote material on Europe's art, history, and contemporary culture. When not traveling, Gene enjoys composing music, recovering from his 1973 trip to Europe with Rick, and living everyday life with his daughter.

ACKNOWLEDGMENTS

Thanks to Cameron Hewitt for writing the original versions of the Dresden, Nürnberg, Leipzig, and Lutherland chapters; and to Ian Watson for writing the original version of the Hamburg chapter.

Avalon Travel
a member of the Perseus Books Group
1700 Fourth Street
Berkeley, CA 94710

Text © 2014 by Rick Steves. All rights reserved.
Maps © 2014 by Rick Steves' Europe. All rights reserved.
Photos are used by permission and are the property of the original copyright owners.

Printed in Canada by Friesens. First printing December 2014.

ISBN 978-1-61238-970-7
ISSN 1553-6866

For the latest on Rick's lectures, guidebooks, tours, public radio show, and public television series, contact Rick Steves' Europe, 130 Fourth Avenue North, Edmonds, WA 98020, 425/771-8303, www.ricksteves.com, rick@ricksteves.com.

Rick Steves' Europe
Managing Editor: Risa Laib
Editorial & Production Manager: Jennifer Madison Davis
Editors: Glenn Eriksen, Tom Griffin, Cameron Hewitt, Suzanne Kotz, Cathy Lu, John Pierce, Carrie Shepherd
Editorial & Production Assistant: Jessica Shaw
Editorial Intern: Mallory Presho-Dunne
Researchers: Sandra Hundacker, Gretchen Strauch, Cary Walker, Ian Watson
Maps & Graphics: David C. Hoerlein, Sandra Hundacker, Lauren Mills, Mary Rostad

Avalon Travel
Senior Editor and Series Manager: Madhu Prasher
Editor: Jamie Andrade
Associate Editor: Maggie Ryan
Copy Editor: Patrick Collins
Proofreader: Suzie Nasol
Indexer: Claire Splan
Production & Typesetting: Tabitha Lahr and Jane Musser
Cover Design: Kimberly Glyder Design
Maps & Graphics: Kat Bennett, Mike Morgenfeld

Photo Credits
Front Cover: Berliner Dom and River Spree ©Aubrey Stoll/Getty Images
Page i: Pretzel Girl, Munich © Dominic Bonuccelli
Page xii: Burg Eltz © Dominic Bonuccelli
Chapter openers: p. 1, Füssen; p. 16, Marienplatz, Munich; p. 126, Neuschwanstein Castle; p. 194, Salzburg; p. 272, Baden-Baden; p. 332, Rothenburg; p. 383, Residenzplatz, Würzburg; p. 406, Frankfurt; p. 438, Bacharach and the Rhine; p. 489, Mosel Valley; p. 514, Trier; p. 534, Cologne Cathedral; p. 557, Market Square, Nürnberg; p. 591, Erfurt; p. 642, Leipzig; p. 671, Zwinger, Dresden; p. 718, Gendarmenmarkt, Berlin; p. 843, New Palace, Potsdam; p. 861, Hamburg; p. 896, Rheinfels Castle, St. Goar; p. 909, Main Train Station, Frankfurt
Additional Photography: Dominic Bonuccelli, Cameron Hewitt, David C. Hoerlein, Sandra Hundacker, Rick Steves, Gretchen Strauch, Ragen Van Sewell, Ian Watson, Wikimedia Commons—PD-Art/PD-US (photos are used by permission and are the property of the original copyright owners).

Although the author and publisher have made every effort to provide accurate, up-to-date information, they accept no responsibility for loss, injury, bad strudel, or inconvenience sustained by any person using this book.

ABOUT THE AUTHOR

RICK STEVES

Since 1973, Rick Steves has spent 100 days every year exploring Europe. Along with writing and researching a bestselling series of guidebooks, Rick produces a public television series *(Rick Steves' Europe)*, a public radio show *(Travel with Rick Steves)*, blog on Facebook, and an app and podcast *(Rick Steves Audio Europe)*; writes a nationally syndicated newspaper column; organizes guided tours that take over 15,000 travelers to Europe annually; and offers an information-packed website (www.ricksteves.com). With the help of his hardworking staff of 90 at Rick Steves' Europe—in Edmonds, Washington, just north of Seattle—Rick's mission is to make European travel fun, affordable, and culturally enlightening for Americans.

Connect with Rick:

facebook.com/RickSteves

twitter: @RickSteves

Foldout Color Map

The foldout map on the opposite page includes:
- **A map of Germany on one side**
- **City maps, including Berlin, Munich, Salzburg, and Vienna on the other side**